SQL Server 2000: The Complete Reference

Jeffrey R. Shapiro

Osborne/**McGraw-Hill**

Berkeley New York St. Louis San Francisco
Auckland Bogotá Hamburg London Madrid
Mexico City Milan Montreal New Delhi Panama City
Paris São Paulo Singapore Sydney
Tokyo Toronto

Osborne/**McGraw-Hill**
2600 Tenth Street
Berkeley, California 94710
U.S.A.

For information on translations or book distributors outside the U.S.A., or to arrange bulk purchase discounts for sales promotions, premiums, or fund-raisers, please contact Osborne/**McGraw-Hill** at the above address.

SQL Server 2000: The Complete Reference

1234567890 CUS CUS 01987654321

ISBN 0-07-212588-8

Publisher
Brandon A. Nordin

Vice President & Associate Publisher
Scott Rogers

Acquisitions Editor
Ann Sellers

Project Editor
Pamela Woolf

Acquisitions Coordinator
Tim Madrid

Technical Editor
Jason Beres

Copy Editor
Robert Campbell

Proofreader
Rachel Lopez

Indexer
Karin Arrigoni

Computer Designers
Lauren McCarthy
Gary Corrigan

Illustrator
Michael Mueller

Series Design
Peter F. Hancik

Series Cover Design
Amparo Del Rio

This book was composed with Corel VENTURA™ Publisher.

This book is dedicated to the following special people that I miss dearly: my mother, Elaine Shapiro, my grandparents Beno and Rose Frank, and my great aunt, Phyllis Koppel.

About the Author...

Jeffrey Shapiro has been a consulting engineer and IT specialist for more than 13 years. He has written several books on software development, technology, and telecommunications, and has written numerous articles on technology for magazines such as *Call Center* and *Network World*. A frequent speaker at software development conferences, Jeffrey has worked with hundreds of companies such as Microsoft, Novell, and IBM; a number of public institutions; and several governments. When he is not writing books, he is managing complex data, e-commerce, and telecommunications projects.

Contents

Part IV

SQL Server 2000 Analysis Services

Acknowledgments

I have often imagined what it must be like for a sailor stranded alone on a small yacht in the middle of a giant angry ocean. Besides the loneliness there is an ever present danger that something will go bump in the night, and your boat will go down with you in it, food for the sharks or some giant squid that is waiting with hungry tentacles.

This book was completed over a period of five and a half months, which included the set up and testing of the servers, and the development of a call center application using SQL Server 2000 at the data tier. During this time I felt like that desperate sailor trapped in my lab surrounded by eight SQL Server machines, which at times seemed more like the life threatening tentacles of that giant calamari lurking beneath the waves.

Fortunately just as the boat seemed to take on water, the life lines would get thrown out to me, and the one soul that gets to be promoted to admiral is my wife Kim. Without her support, I would not have made it into safe harbor.

As any seafaring person knows you can keep off the rocks if there is a beacon of light guiding the way. The lighthouse on this project is Ann Sellers, acquisitions editor, who was always there to point out the obstacles that might wreck the ship, and guide me through some rough waters, with a smile you hear from thousands of miles away, beats the fog horn any day. On Ann's team is Tim Madrid, acquisitions coordinator whom I could always trust to be in the office for what seems like 24 × 7.

Osborne has a very special editing team, and I want to extend my gratitude to Pamela Woolf, project editor, and Robert Campbell, copy editor, for their effort to make sense of my technical jibe.

The team at Osborne is led by editorial director, Wendy Rinaldi, to whom I am indebted for the opportunity to do this book and be part of Osborne's vision for excellence in technical publications.

My right-hand wizard on this project was technical editor Jason Beres (MCT, MCSD), a Microsoft trainer and guru with Microsoft CTEC, Homnick Systems in Boca Raton, Florida, who also went the extra mile for me and wrote the XML chapter, Chapter 23.

I would also like to thank my agent, David Fugate, of Waterside Productions, Inc. for all his support.

—Jeffrey Shapiro

Introduction

You don't have to read this introduction, but you should. It will save you some browsing time because it lays out the roadmap for this book, and it will allow you to best determine which parts to tackle according to your needs or discipline, your experience level, and your knowledge of SQL Server 2000.

SQL Server 2000 (or just SQL Server) is Microsoft's database management system and data analysis product. This book's aim is to provide as complete an independent reference as possible to the product and where permissible and warranted we will delve into general database and computing references to illustrate applications with or for SQL Server 2000.

We have a long road ahead so I am going to kick off with some advice on how to get the most out of this book. First, you do not need to have any database, programming, or system administration experience to use this book, but it would help—a lot. If this were a classroom setting, I would require you to take Databases 101 or Programming 101 as a prerequisite, only because you would hold up the class and it would help you get the most out of this book. But I am going to make the assumption that you know about programming, object-oriented technology, database management systems, data and computer communications, IS/IT practice, and so on. And when you come across concepts that confuse or befuddle you, you should take time out and get up to speed before continuing, because it will help you avoid costly mistakes down the road. At times I will go back to basics, just so that we all have a common point of departure.

For example, you are not going to find whole chapters devoted to normalization, object-oriented design, or programming primers. This is not a book about building database applications with SQL Server, although several chapters cover the elements of Transact-SQL, the language you use to program SQL Server. There is no material here that provides a facility for teaching you how to build database applications with Visual Basic or Java or Delphi or C++. Nor are you going to get any long-winded historical "data," such as where SQL Server 2000 came from or and where it might be heading. SQL Server 2000 is too complex and vast a product to choke a reference to it with information covered in hundreds of brilliant books devoted to these special subjects.

Book for All Teammates

This aim of this book is to be as complete a reference to SQL Server 2000 as possible. It is of benefit to database administrators, operators, developers, consultants, network administrators, marketing and communications people, financial controllers, business and enterprise analysts, decisions support staff, data owners, data stewards, business owners, and more.

What's Inside

The book is divided into four parts, each consisting of several chapters.

Part I: SQL Server 2000 System and Platform Architecture

Part I opens with an overview of both the system and platform architecture of SQL Server 2000. Gone are the days when a Microsoft product ran on just Windows 9.x or Windows NT. There are now several platforms on which you can deploy the product, albeit they are all Windows operating systems. Chapter 1 discusses all versions of SQL Server, from the Enterprise Edition that runs on mega-servers and can scale to support huge databases and serve thousands of concurrent users, to the Windows CE Edition that can run on tiny devices and appliances like the Pocket PC.

Chapter 1 is designed to get you familiar with SQL Server as quickly as possible. It also places the product at the core of Microsoft's .Net (formerly Windows DNA) initiative. Chapter 2 discusses SQL Server database architecture, while Chapters 3 and 4 go on to discuss the client/server and DBMS architecture respectively. Of particular note in Part I is the early introduction to Meta Data Services in Chapter 5. Here we delve into the world of metadata, modeling and analysis, which I believe is critical for the success of any database or application development project. Chapter 6 provides a leg up on installing SQL Server.

Part II: SQL Server 2000 Platform Administration

Part II deals exclusively with database installation and setup and platform administration. Building on the overview in Chapter 1 we discuss server and service administration, performance and availability, and the management of SQL Server databases. This part is aimed particularly at database administrators and operators (DBAs), the teammates tasked with platform administration, such as backing up and restoring databases, keeping servers healthy, keeping servers and data secure, supporting users, configuring administrations, availability, performance, and so on. Chapter 7 is the place to start if you are new to the platform and need a short overview of its administration architecture. Chapters 8 and 9, respectively, deal with the critical subjects of security and disaster recovery. In Chapter 9 we discuss the backup/restore services in some detail.

Chapter 10 provides an introduction to replication and is suitable for DBAs just starting in this area. The replication subject would fill several chapters and even a book in its own right. You will thus be able to "graduate" from this chapter to a more advance dedicated treatise on the subject, or at least make some headway with the documentation in SQL Server Books Online.

Part III: Programming SQL Server 2000

Application development is covered extensively in Part III. We kick off with a general discussion of programming SQL Server 2000. We look at language support and also discuss OLE DB, ActiveX Data Objects (ADO), development environments, and more. This part also provides extensive coverage of advanced data-processing features such as stored procedures, triggers, SQL queries, data manipulation (or modification) language, and so on.

We also investigate support for XML and English Query. English Query allows users to use natural language syntax to query databases and SQL Server ships with a comprehensive English Query development environment you can use to provide English Query support in your applications. The subject if fully explored in Chapter 22. With XML now the de facto data exchange language of the Internet, SQL Server's new support for XML is mind-blowing to say the least. Chapter 23 thus provides an excellent introduction to this essential subject and even provides you with examples and guidance to get you on the road to building Web-based XML applications.

Part IV: SQL Server 2000 Analysis Services

The final two chapters in this book provide an introduction to SQL Server Analysis Services, which includes data mining, data warehouses, and online analytical processing or OLAP. These are foundation chapters that introduce the concept of data warehouses and marts using Data Transformation Services (DTS) for loading the data warehouse, building the schema for multidimensional databases, cubes, and so on. Appendix A provides a list of Transact-SQL functions, data types, stored procedures and so on.

Feedback

It goes without saying that no book can contain every fact that needs to be known, every tip that needs to be tried, and every note that needs to be noted, especially about something as vast as SQL Server. There is a ton of information about SQL Server that cannot fit into a book of any size.I would appreciate your advice and criticisms. I can be reached at jeffrey.shapiro@mcity.org and you can pick up where many these chapters leave off at the Internet Web page I have dedicated to this book: www.mcity.org/sqlsbook. You can also e-mail Jason Beres on SQL Server and XML-related matter at jason@vbxml.net

Conventions Used in This Book

The following conventions are used in this book:

- Transact-SQL keywords, such as CREATE DATABASE, are in uppercase.
- Vertical bars are used to separate choices of items.
- Brackets signify optional syntax; braces signify required syntax.

Notes are used to raise a point or draw your attention to an important aside.

Tips are used to suggest an alternate, additional, or important option or suggestion.

Cautions are used to alert and steer you around potential pitfalls.

The Complete Reference

Part I

SQL Server 2000 System and Platform Architecture

The Complete Reference

Chapter 1

Getting to Know SQL Server 2000

SQL Server 2000 is Microsoft's relational database management system (RDBMS). It builds on a legacy of accomplishments spanning more than a decade of SQL Server development and critical success. But it is more than that. It is fast becoming the most widely used data management system in the world; currently deployed in tens of thousands of companies where it is in service day in and day out, storing the records of the digital universe that now supports our very existence.

Despite the lofty capabilities of this product, and its reputation for being complex, one of the key—and ambitious—objectives of this book is to get *all* database administrators and developers, young and old, using SQL Server 2000. If within a few chapters you don't see your way to becoming permanently hitched to this product, then my mission has failed. This chapter has thus been designed to be a warm-up for the benefit of novice users, traditional desktop RDBMS users, and gurus working on other platforms, or older versions. If you are a beginner then this chapter will get you on familiar ground with the experts.

While the material discussed here is mostly aimed at newcomers to the SQL Server 2000 platform, it also serves as a refresher for experts and users of earlier versions of SQL Server. If you eat, drink, and sleep this stuff, as I do, you may want to skim over much of this chapter. As you are going to be introduced to some exciting new features, however, I would not skim too lightly.

Note *Throughout this book I will often use "SQL Server" and "SQL Server 2000" interchangeably. When referring to an earlier version of SQL Server prior to SQL Server 2000, I will include the version being referenced.*

A DBMS for Everyone . . . and Everything

SQL Server 2000 is for old and new companies, small and large. It is equally at home with huge teams of developers and database administrators (DBA) as it is with lone rangers or the DBA++ who does it all. It does not matter whether you work for a small concern with no more than a handful of workers or for a giant multinational with tens of thousands of employees; SQL Server 2000 is for everyone.

Most database developers and administrators are introduced to databases through the likes of Microsoft's Access or FoxPro, Corel's Paradox and its infamous Borland Database Engine (BDE), or the legendary dBase. (I, for one, came up through the ranks—I still have my first dBase application that I created back in 1987. The last time I looked at it, it had more GOTO clauses than off-ramps on the Interstate between Miami and Nova Scotia.)

You have probably always connected SQL Server with big companies, a complex programming environment, geeks like me and my friends who talk in tongues few understand—and very expensive computer equipment. Those days are over, gone forever. Not only do you have a choice of several Windows platforms for SQL Server (from Windows 98 to Windows 2000), but you can carry SQL Server around with you in your back pocket on any Windows CE version 3.0 appliance.

But why would you want to move to SQL Server? There are still many situations or applications today that can be satisfactorily serviced with a relational database product like Microsoft Access or Corel Paradox. For starters, SQL Server is still expensive and complex to use . . . or is it?

How Critical Is Your Data?

There are important distinctions you need to make between SQL Server and a product like Access or Paradox, and these revolve around the following three concepts, seen or felt mainly from the data consumer's perspective:

- Concurrent access to data
- Integrity of data
- Availability of data

Each of these factors spawns collateral factors that either support or violate modern trends in computing and technology, business rules and needs, and database modeling. Let's explore these three terms and see how they justify your consideration of a product like SQL Server 2000.

Concurrent Access to Data

It is becoming rare these days for businesses to create databases for one pair of eyes only, or a single process. Concurrent access to data, the sharing of databases among many users and processes, is thus an important consideration, if not the most important, when you are designing and creating data-driven software or relational database applications.

If you start with a "tiny" concern of 1–50 people, the more people that need access to your data and the faster they need it, the sooner will concurrency support break down. Yes, products like Access and FoxPro can support dozens, even hundreds, of users, all accessing the database concurrently. However, the database engines that underpin desktop relational database products begin to fall apart when the number and frequency of "hits" on the database files escalates to levels beyond which the desktop engines can cope.

A traditional desktop database product, such as the Joint Engine Technology (Jet) database engine in Access and the Borland Database Engine (BDE) in Paradox, uses file/server functionality to share the database files. This means that every time a client requires access to data, it needs to connect to the local database engine, which opens the database files on the network server to haul data across the network. The client application must thus be capable of making calls to a database engine installed in the local machine's processing space, because all that is installed on the server is the database files (such as *data.mdb*).

Opening and working with a database in this fashion requires every client to have access to a local database engine on the local machine. Each database engine makes its connection to the database, locks tables, and excludes everyone else until the data is either abandoned at the client or updated to the database table. The lock may not be noticeable to anyone requiring casual access, but it may cause a disaster when a write becomes critical and every process hitting the database files needs service.

Having complex database engine code on every desktop or client is a cumbersome and expensive exercise. No matter the cost of the RDBMS software, there will be considerable costs at the client to continue to support the traditional file/server database solution. You will often read about total cost of ownership (TCO) in this book, directly and indirectly, but it behooves you to know that the cost of deploying file/server data engines to fat clients is greater than that of deploying client/server database engines using thin clients. Even with the initial cost of the SQL Server product (free if you just need the Desktop Engine—MSDE), client/server solutions are far cheaper. You also need to factor in the cost of hardware obsolescence and the cost of developing for and supporting fat client solutions.

When selling managed data services or managed network services to a company, I draw attention to cost of ownership by showing how going cheap on software and development invariably costs more in the long term. It can even threaten the business. Support costs add up when you have consultants trying to fix corrupt flat-file databases, or your users sit around idle with nothing to do because Access has been corrupted for the umpteenth time, or the database files were destroyed.

And when dozens of clients all access such data independently of one another, you end up with what I call "the highway hysteria" factor. You can have hundreds of drivers who all use the turnpike all day long, and there are no accidents, and everyone stays clear of each other, and everything is just "cool." But come rush hour, everyone hits the road as units of independent insanity. Not one driver can know or predict what the other is doing, or react in time to avert disaster. At every rush hour, you can be sure someone is going to get hurt.

Client/server database systems are used everyday by all of us on the Internet. While an increasing number of these servers are SQL Server solutions, your client software need never know what technology is being implemented on the back end. The local computing device or client software can be "thin," such as a Web browser—and the user interface or client process can run on any operating system, on any platform. If every machine on the Internet required a local database engine to access data on the Internet . . . the Internet would have been a bad idea.

In client/server databases, the database server's engine alone controls access to the data, performs the queries, manages the database and the requests of every client, and keeps the database server operating in the best possible way. There is no highway hysteria, because the server is in control of every read or write request for data and can take the necessary steps to avoid accidents. If the highway itself were in control of all the cars, we would not have deaths on the road. The difference between the file/server engine and the client/server engine is illustrated in Figure 1-1.

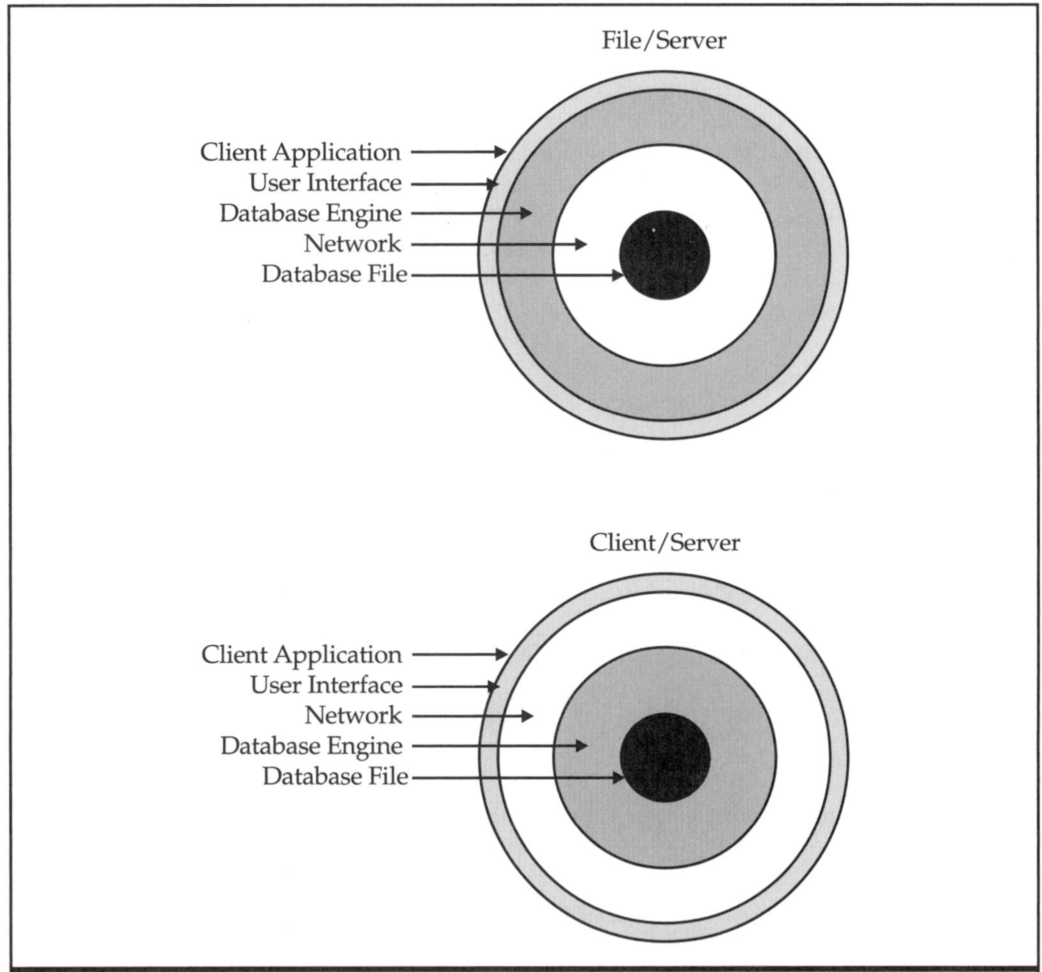

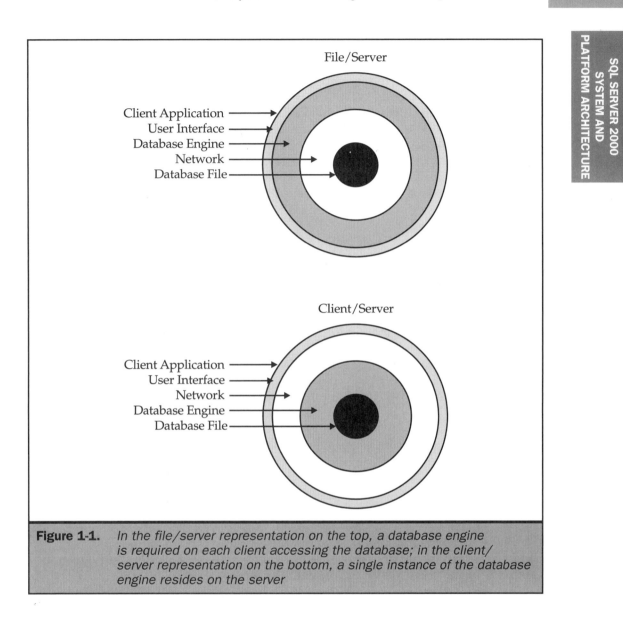

Figure 1-1. *In the file/server representation on the top, a database engine is required on each client accessing the database; in the client/server representation on the bottom, a single instance of the database engine resides on the server*

Obviously many situations, and many users, are dependent on traditional file/server database solutions. You can even argue that you are doing fine on your old dBase files. But as soon as you start sharing your data with more people and processes more often, and as soon as access to that data becomes mission critical, you have arrived at the bridge you will need to cross to come over to a client/server database solution like SQL Server. Many of the chapters ahead will help you make the transition, easily and painlessly, without having to spend a lot of money.

Not all client/server RDBMS products are cheap. Some are priced out of the range of nearly all small businesses, and buying development for them can cause you to auction off one of your kidneys. SQL Server is one of the cheapest products on the market and one of the cheapest to buy applications for. In the past it would have been a mistake not to admit that the other products were more expensive because they were so much better. That is definitely history. SQL Server 2000 is a killer package, and since it still has the best price in the industry, it's like buying an oceangoing yacht for the price of an average speed boat.

Integrity of Data

Data integrity constraints have never been high on the list of priorities on desktop databases, probably because it is not very difficult to violate them. Sure you have your validation rules. Access 2000 even supports declarative referential integrity, which means the *constraints* are defined in the database schema. But as long as your solutions rely on the client applications for validation, you expose the database to unreliable data.

It is too easy to modify a front-end application, like Access, and bypass validation rules and logic. You can secure the databases, but have you ever needed to find the password for an Access MDB file? If not, you should try it sometime. Dozens of tools on the Internet will hack the password for you in under a minute. And you thought the database was safe.

A client/server database is much more committed to ensuring the validity of data, along with ensuring that what goes into the database is as plausible as possible. The bigger the databases become, and the more complex the data model, the more vulnerable the data. It is thus vital to use technology that has been specifically designed to absolutely enforce integrity rules where needed, especially where your life and the lives of others depends on it. Only a dedicated service component like the SQL Server database engine can be trusted to enforce the constraints.

New Feature: Cascading Integrity Constraints

In addition to several well-established SQL Server integrity features inherited from the earlier versions, SQL Server 2000 introduces new integrity constraint support in what is known as a *cascading integrity constraint*. This item has been on the wish list of SQL Server fans for many years, and it's finally arrived.

It works like a dream and saves many hours of programming because you use it everywhere to ensure that no orphaned records exist in your precious normalized tables and that related values are all concurrently updated when they need to be. Here's a simple example in a delete scenario: Let's say you modularize a little more by splitting *ship-to* and *bill-to* into two separate tables, leaving you with three tables, the main one being the customer's details, such as the name of the company and the primary contact information. Now what do you do when you need to delete the customer from the database? Well, to ensure referential integrity, you have to delete the customer's record—usually linked to related tables via foreign key elements—in each table individually. If you don't, you'll either have records that can no longer be referenced or data that cannot be deleted (or updated) because of referential integrity constraints on the data. This might require you, as it has up to now, to build a manual cascade using triggers, a process that is time-consuming to code and that will derogate performance.

The new cascade feature supports the ANSI definition for supporting cascaded delete and update operations. In other words, it means that a delete or update can automatically be *cascaded* from the record in the referenced table to a record in a referred table without the need for special trigger code. In the past, your triggers would typically have included code to switch between taking no action on an UPDATE or cascading a delete operation on DELETE. I will cover this new feature in detail in Chapter 17, which is devoted to the subject of integrity.

New Feature: INSTEAD OF Triggers and AFTER Trigger Functionality

And while we are on the subject of triggers, SQL Server 2000 has new stuff here as well. SQL Server has always supported *triggers.* Triggers are a form of stored procedure. They can be used to analyze data and take necessary steps to alert an administrator or a data entry worker to a possible violation of data entry (integrity) rules, a risky change, a delete, and so on. They can also be used to alter the logic used to manipulate data, and as you will see, they can now completely suppress originally intended code upon conditions you define. This helps you catch problems with values that are very difficult to trap when there is nothing wrong with the data being entered.

Here's a good example. A few weeks after we had just moved to a new medical insurance company, my wife attempted to make an appointment with a doctor. But she was told she was not in the system. When she went to get medication, the same story ensued. I was in the system; my son was in the system; but my wife was not. This situation became stressful because my wife was actually being denied coverage because of a database error. It was a relief that she did not have an accident, because coverage would have been denied, and it could have led to a serious situation. What had actually happened is that instead of my wife's last name being entered into the field for "spouse," the last name of the primary care physician was entered instead. While it is very difficult to invalidate what is technically correct, a trigger should have been programmed to notice the difference between the primary policyholder's last name and that of the spouse. A sophisticated algorithm, making use of the full power and extent of the Transact-SQL language, external calls, and so on, could have averted the frustration. The medical insurance company was exposing itself to possible litigation because of sloppy database programming—or the lack of sufficient data integrity tools.

I can now program the previously described logic using an AFTER trigger that I can specify to be fired at the end of a collection of triggers to check the entry. The order of the AFTER trigger can be specified by a new system stored procedure, sp_settriggerorder.

But AFTER triggers are not really new; this trigger was all that was supported in earlier versions. They were named as such to accommodate a new trigger called the INSTEAD OF trigger. The INSTEAD OF trigger executes *instead of* the triggering action, the original statement. In other words, upon a certain condition the code in the INSTEAD OF trigger executes instead of the originally intended code. So if the data meets a certain validation check, or does not match a certain pattern, you can switch to the code in the INSTEAD OF trigger. As you know, you can practically code anything in a trigger, so the INSTEAD OF trigger can become a completey new course of action, a new processing "thread."

Another valuable feature of the INSTEAD OF trigger is that it can be used to update views that previously could not be updated. The INSTEAD OF trigger provides the update, where a direct update statement run against the view would return an error. I have covered triggers and the new functionality in Chapter 18. Views are covered in Chapter 19.

Availability of Data

Not a second goes by in our lives in which data is not critical to us. I once saw a bumper sticker that read "stuff happens—know about it." It is becoming more difficult to get along in our wired world without constant access to databases and accurate information.

A person is denied access to drugs because a pharmacy's database is offline; a telecommunications system drops a call because a table is corrupt; an order is placed with our competitors because a price cannot be met or a quantity cannot be fulfilled; the list could go on forever. Businesses, people, processes, life itself, all depend on the availability of data every day. While both *data access* and *data integrity* might themselves be judged components of *availability*, it has mostly to do with just being online; being there when you need it; responding in a reasonable time frame.

With SQL Server 2000, Microsoft has made great strides in this area, and I touch on the new features in a mini-discussion on availability later in this chapter. Availability is a very large and complex subject, fully tackled in Chapter 13. When you consider what would ensure that a system or a database remains available, you will be looking at many factors. These include load balancing, distribution and replication, access to large memory resources, capability to work with very large databases, symmetric multiprocessing (SMP), and so on. Let's now look at the key applications for SQL Server 2000.

Line-of-Business Applications

Client/server database technology is most widely used in line-of-business (LOB) applications . . . wherever and in whatever situation you require a data repository in which to store, retrieve, query, and analyze information. These situations might be customer relationship management (CRM), enterprise resource planning (ERP), marketing and sales support (from simple contact management to sophisticated list management), technical support (arguably a function of CRM), manufacturing, financial services, research, and so on.

Line-of-business applications also are no longer about rows of characters. Any form of data should be stored and made retrievable from a database, including large graphics files, sound and visual material, documents, and so on.

We need 360-degree views of our worlds, and especially of our customers, and sophisticated database solutions give us that. Take CRM, for example: Information about a customer needs to be made available to everyone in the enterprise. And the data should be used to better serve the customers, meet their expectations, anticipate their needs, and be responsive to their demands. This not only means that you need to be able to store data in multiple forms, such as sound and documents, but that once data is stored, it continues to provide value for the space in the database it occupies.

The Distributed Network Application

Computing today is a networked and distributed phenomenon. Enterprise networks (intranets) and the Internet support millions of clients. Client/server is the dominant model employed, and this is fast transforming into the new model of thin-client/server computing. While it seems we have come full circle, clients no longer need to be more than the weight of their user interface. Almost 100 percent of the functionality and processing resides at the server.

Our networked and highly distributed world demands that software product be built according to interoperable client/server component systems. In this regard, the relational database products of yesteryear, which dump a huge footprint of code and functionality on a user's desktop computer, are out of touch with reality; essentially obsolete. Later, you'll learn how to move your data from these bloated legacy applications to the SQL Server environment.

SQL Server 2000 is also one of the core products of the Microsoft .Net initiative, formerly known as Windows Distributed interNet Applications Architecture (Windows DNA). But .Net is not a really a new concept or a new initiative. It is a phenomenon that has matured and now has a new name. But let's explore it in general now, and see how Microsoft is presenting it.

The Net experts project business-to-business trade over the Internet to exceed $1.3 trillion by 2003. The Internet has changed the way business is transacted between individuals and enterprises. Continents and oceans no longer separate the silk or spice routes of the world. Distances between partners, buyers, and sellers are measured in hops between routers on the Internet and not by physical distance any more. Whether you call it e-business or e-commerce, the Internet brings the following key benefits:

- Faster time-to-market
- Increased revenues, decreased expenses, greater profit
- Customer satisfaction and loyalty
- Greater agility in delivery of custom-configured products and value-added services
- Competitive advantage

We are fast approaching critical mass on the Internet with respect to e-commerce. Soon everything will be online. And Microsoft defines .Net as its "comprehensive, integrated platform for building and deploying applications for the Business Internet . . . ."

Another important buzz-phrase to remember is *digital nervous system* or *Dns* (in lowercase so as not to confuse it with Domain Name System). A Dns is what you have when the convergence of technology brings businesses together, allows businesses to instantly respond to dramatic changes in supply and demand, and allows businesses to reach customers quicker and to connect people to information. The Dns has many components, and the RDBMS supplies the storage facility, access to its data, and the interpretation and analysis of that data in the Dns. Taking SQL Server 2000 out of the Microsoft Dns, or .Net, would be akin to taking the brain out of the human body (and possibly the soul too, if you believe that knowledge survives death).

.Net applications support the following tenets:

- **Support for Internet standards** The Microsoft .Net technologies support the pervasive standards for data interchange, information exchange, data presentation, and data transportation, such as HTML, XML, and XPath.
- **Software scale out and scale up** SQL Server can start out in your back pocket and scale out to incredibly powerful multiprocessor megaserver systems.
- **Reliability** Downtime is minimized when systems can be scaled out or distributed. The service level is practically guaranteed because an increasing number of single points of failure are eliminated. Physical memory in a system is no longer an issue.
- **Interoperability** The more you integrate heterogeneous systems from a collection of reliable venders, the greater will be your ease of integrating these systems, hence the .Net platform.
- **Time-to-market** Interoperation translates into direct savings of time and materials. Result: faster time-to-market. The deeper and tighter the integration and interoperation of systems, the faster and easier they will be to deliver.

- **Ease of deployment, administration, and management** The Windows 2000 platform makes it easier to deploy and administer systems. The more complex your system becomes, the more important it is to be able to easily deploy and manage it. While there is a steep learning curve in Windows 2000, especially with the new technologies such as Active Directory, you can drastically ease your administrative burden converting to the platform (see Chapter 6).
- **Full exploitation of Windows 2000** Windows 2000 comes jammed with technologies and services to meet the availability, service level, and change control demands of the most demanding multitiered, distributed applications.

So What Is SQL Server 2000?

SQL Server 2000 is not a database application development environment in the sense that Microsoft Access or Visual FoxPro is. It is a collection of components and products that holistically combine, as a client/server system, to meet the data storage, retrieval, and analysis requirements of any entity or organization. It is equally at home in environments ranging from the largest companies and commercial Web sites posting millions of transactions per day to small companies and even individuals and specialized applications that require robust data storage and persistent service.

SQL Server 2000 comes in several editions to accommodate the needs and budgets of a wide range of applications. The specific features of each edition are discussed in more detail in Chapter 6. The editions are listed as follows:

- **SQL Server 2000 Enterprise Edition** is the complete package and includes all the advanced features and components that make up the product. It is aimed at banks, large multinational conglomerates, large manufacturing concerns, medical facilities, government institutions, Internet or DNA applications, .Net functions, and e-commerce. This version is optimized for high availability and scalability support. Its SMP code can work with up to 32 processors and 64GB of random access memory (RAM). If you are deploying mission-critical applications or catering to Internet projects, or you are involved in any situation requiring unfaltering service for thousands of concurrent users, over any network, this is the edition you need.
- **SQL Server 2000 Standard Edition** is aimed at small- to medium-sized businesses, or other entities that do not have the extensive needs of large organizations or large data center applications. Besides more modest SMP support of up to four CPUs and 2GB of RAM, catering to conservative scalability requirements, it is also not as heavily armed as the Enterprise Edition on the analysis side.
- **SQL Server 2000 Personal Edition** ships with all the management tools that complement the product and contains most of the functionality of the Standard

Edition. However, it has been packaged for personal use and can service small groups, typically five or less concurrent active users. Besides being a server environment, Personal Edition is also designed to run on the desktop, from Windows 2000 Professional Edition down to Windows 98.

- **SQL Server 2000 Developer Edition** is the complete Enterprise Edition aimed at developers. It ships with a special development and test end-user license agreement (EULA) that expressly prohibits installation in production environments.
- **SQL Server 2000 Enterprise Evaluation Edition** is the complete Enterprise Edition that can only be deployed for a limited time. This edition is used solely for evaluation and should not be deployed in any production environment.
- **SQL Server 2000 Desktop Edition** now occupies the space originally intended for the Microsoft Data Engine (MSDE). It is the heart of SQL Server 2000, without all the management goodies, user interfaces, analysis services, client access licenses (CALs), and so on. It is also limited to databases of no more than 2GB in size—just as the legacy Jet engine is—and will only allow a limited user workload. It is nevertheless more powerful than the standard desktop database engines and provides an ideal starter client/server solution if you are new to SQL Server and are looking for a product to leverage existing skills in Microsoft Access or to support a small business application. It can be fully programmed against (as is further discussed in the programming chapters in Part III), and database solutions you build with it can be scaled without losing the investment in code and existing application penetration.
- **SQL Server 2000 Windows CE Edition** runs on appliances and devices powered by the Windows CE operating system (Pocket PC). Its application development architecture is compatible with all editions of SQL Server 2000, which means that existing code and applications can be ported to Windows CE with ease. This means that it is now possible to install and run a relational database store and application on any Windows CE device, which opens a world of new opportunities and possibilities for you.

Note *While all SKUs of SQL Server were tested for this book, most of R&D and deployment was done with the Enterprise Edition.*

The following overview of the key SQL Server 2000 design themes and base architectures provides a quick introduction to the product for newcomers graduating from desktop systems and users of the other SQL Server platforms eager to make the jump to hyperspace. The architectures are then fully discussed over the next few chapters in Part I and in the other parts of the book.

Central Design Themes

When Microsoft delivered SQL Server 7.0, it became very apparent that SQL Server 6.5 and earlier would become legacy products, essentially pre–Internet Age applications. A trio of tenets became the central theme in SQL Server 7.0: The product had to be *Internet enabled*, be *highly scalable* (to compete with the midrange and mainframe systems), and deliver the *fastest time-to-market*. In its quest to be the best, Microsoft's SQL Server development team has become obsessed with these themes.

But the release of SQL Server 2000 has also revealed a component model that allows SQL Server to scale down and compete in the small systems and desktop arena, even the tiny Pocket PC, running the Windows CE operating system. This capability has taken many people by surprise, but as mentioned earlier, databases are not the domain of the large enterprise alone. In review, we really have four design themes. SQL Server 2000 is designed to be

- Fully Internet-enabled
- Fastest in time-to-market
- Highly scalable
- Highly portable

So you can see that no matter your needs, SQL Server 2000 can meet them. In the past, you might have gone with a small relational database product because SQL Server was a "big-business" product that came with a big price tag. But now you can find several editions to meet the needs and budget of small business. This is why I call SQL Server 2000 a *DBMS for everyone* (later you will see why it has also become a *DBMS for everything*).

Overview of the Core Architectures

Experienced SQL Server users (with at least versions 6.5 and 7.0 under their belts) can breeze through this overview because I have written it for newcomers with two objectives in mind. First, it should be regarded as an orientation to get you to a level that will give you a better grasp of the fuller discussions of the architecture coming later. Second, during this overview you will be looking at the central design themes introduced earlier in more depth, and this overview will help you appreciate the new power you now have. I also point out several new features you can zero in on if you intend to breeze through this section.

You will also notice that I discuss several key architectures of SQL Server, but this is not the whole story. SQL Server is composed of number of collateral technologies and architectures, many of them lengthy and complex subjects in themselves, that you will learn about in later chapters. And these include the replication architecture, the I/O architecture, the query processing architecture, language support, and much more.

The Database Architecture

SQL Server's database architecture is the subject of the next chapter, so I will save the interesting (and complex) stuff until then. However, to get a good footing in SQL Server, you should understand the basic database structure as early as possible, and this is why I go direct to the database architecture in Chapter 2.

SQL Server is not a difficult product to comprehend, even though (and I agree) it is often considered the most complex server product in Microsoft's server offering. I have managed all of the Microsoft server products in busy production environments and data centers, and not one other server product presents the challenge and technological "high" that SQL Server does.

I consider this to be the case in large part due to the three levels at which an IT professional interacts with and services the product: the DBA level, the SQL Server developer level, and the client applications developer level (expanded on in Chapter 13). This is the only server product in the Microsoft server lineup in which the system administrator of a high-end, mission-critical system requires a lot more on the job than to be certified in bells and whistles. He or she needs to have a solid grounding in relational database theory and more than a smattering of programming skills. Quite frankly, if you want to be the best DBA in the company, you need to know about the server platform, such as Windows NT and Windows 2000; its hardware needs, such as storage, memory, and processing requirements; networking (for replication, linked servers, and so on); security; disaster recovery; administration; SQL and T-SQL; relational theory; object-oriented design (the basics)...and you should be proficient in at least one mainstream computer language, such as Visual Basic or Java.

The SQL Server 2000 relational database engine comprises a number of highly scalable and well-tested components for storing, manipulating, analyzing, and accessing data. With the number of systems in use in the world running into the multimillions and the number of certified DBAs fast approaching six figures, SQL Server is most certainly proven technology.

However, it is also a brilliantly elegant product. It is by no means as convoluted as it appears, which is not the case for many of its competitors. While you can deploy SQL Server in the most demanding and complex situations, it also has the lowest barrier to entry of all the database products on the market. This is due in part to its architecture, and in large part to the huge installed base, which is supported by many books such as this one, dozens of devotee Web sites, and user groups in just about every major city in the world.

SQL Server 2000 101—The Freeze-Dried Overview

The SQL Server database engine stores your data in tables. Each of the tables holds data that represents information of interest and value to your organization. This data consists of a collection of classes of information (called domains) that, when understood as a whole, represent a unique and complete record of data in the database. For example, a row holding a social security number is not itself a complete record, according to your model, without somehow being linked to the name of a person. That person's name can be in the same row of data, in a value representing the domain "last names," or in another table in the same database. The two rows taken together represent the record of your data, even though its values are spread among different tables.

Collections of tables, and there can be thousands of them, are stored in a container object known as a SQL Server database. Each database also stores objects that pertain to each database and its tables, including stored procedures, triggers, and so on.

A collection of databases can be managed as a unit by a single instance of SQL Server. Systemwide management features include functions such as backup/restore, logins and security, replication, and data transformation.

To talk to SQL Server—that is, to ask it to save data, change it, return it, process it—you need to know SQL (or more accurately, Transact-SQL; but more about this in a moment). SQL is the international standards–supported computer language of the relational database. It is represented by ANSI (the American National Standards Institute) as well as the ISO (the International Standards Organization). Its official name is the International Standard Data Base Language SQL (Structured Query Language), 1992. It is often known as SQL-92 and commonly referred to as "Sequel."

All relational database products support a flavor of SQL that is infused with support for the individual product and its extensions. Microsoft calls its version of SQL for SQL Server "Transact-SQL." SQL, the base language, is not a perfect language by any means; it has its share of inconsistencies and mistakes, and each product deals with them in certain ways that reflect the needs of the users. For example, SQL supports the concept of a Persistent Storage Module (PSM), which allows stored procedures and similar functions to be grouped together where they can share and reuse programmatic data. However, the members of the Transact-SQL development team have had so little demand for adding PSM to SQL Server that they feel their time would be better spent in other badly needed areas (user-defined functions is an example and is discussed a little later in this chapter).

T-SQL is compliant with the SQL-92 standard. It fully complies with SQL-92's Entry Level features and also supports a number of features from the Intermediate and Full Levels. T-SQL is discussed in Part III, which deals exclusively with development. The latest version of SQL is the SQL 99 (or SQL-99) specification. Already there have been a number of requests for implementation of SQL 99 features; but these will be SQL Server "futures," and we will not see them in the product until at least the next major release (around 2002/2003).

The DBMS or Administration Architecture

SQL Server also ships with a rich and powerful set of administrative tools. These are the tools that DBAs use to manage databases, user access, backups and restores, and other administrative functions. Microsoft has published the full APIs to these tools, enabling independent software developers to provide turnkey solutions that use SQL Server as their storage database. A computer telephony application is an example of a turnkey application that would typically include many automated administrative features, so that actual hands-on administrative involvement on the part of end-user database owners would be minimized or obviated. The chapters in Part II cover all the DBA tools and then some.

The Application Development Architecture

If you are a database applications developer (the client developer or SQL Server developer), you have a wide choice of APIs and technologies to use in programming SQL Server. If you are building applications that depend on SQL Server databases for their data stores, or that need to obtain the functionality of the SQL Server database engine and its other components, you can use a number of interfaces and technologies.

The oldest way is the traditional call-level interface (CLI) database API or library of functions (DLLs) that can be called from any modern programming language capable of invoking DLL functions. This is the legacy DB-Library or C API that was provided with the earlier versions of SQL Server. Although this API is still supported by SQL Server 2000, it predates many of the newer object-oriented APIs and the language of SQL Server, Transact-SQL, or T-SQL. It will probably be retired by the next version of SQL Server.

Note *I will use the more convenient T-SQL acronym most of the time.*

If you are accustomed to developing to the Open Database Connectivity (ODBC) API, you can code directly to it to work with SQL Server. However, you can also get to ODBC functionality via the object-oriented (OO) APIs, such as ActiveX Data Objects (ADO) and OLE DB. A full discussion of these object model APIs, and their relative complexity, is included in Chapter 14.

All Microsoft's modern object-oriented database APIs enable you to encapsulate or encase T-SQL statements within your code. Also, T-SQL can be used to access the ODBC extensions, even from within ADO and OLE DB methods, and from standard ODBC applications. You can also continue to program SQL Server from the object model APIs that encapsulate ODBC, such as Remote Data Objects (RDO) and Data Access Objects (DAO).

However, SQL Server application development is simplest and fastest using the ADO components, which can be used in any application development environment that supports ActiveX technology. Naturally, the easiest environment a novice can start with is Visual Basic. Others include Imprise's Delphi, Visual J++ and Visual C++ from Microsoft, PowerBuilder from Sybase, and Oracle's Oracle Designer.

OLE DB is more complex and typically used in C++ applications, but it is extremely powerful. (You will investigate it in Chapter 3, as the native interface between SQL Server's relational engine and its storage engine, and as the primary API in Chapter 14.)

New Features for Developers

For developers, both client and server, SQL Server 2000 includes several new features. I won't list them all here, as they are discussed in their respective places throughout the book. But several deserve some early accolades.

New Data Types

SQL Server 2000 introduces several new data types, which reflects the needs of the installed base especially with respect to new applications for the Internet and the .Net initiative. The new data types are the following:

- **Bigint** This integer is more than big, it's huge. It can support data from –2^63 (–9,223,372,036,854,775,808) through 2^63–1 (9,223,372,036,854,775,807). It naturally comes in a big shoe size too. It needs eight bytes for storage. What would you use such a big number for? Well, if you consider how fast the Internet is growing and how fast we are warehousing information, in a decade we might have to rename this "bigint" to "smallint."
- **Variant** Cool, we finally have a variant data type in SQL Server! Officially called the *sql_variant,* it can store values of several different data types. This data type can be used in several objects, such as columns, parameters, and variables, as well as for return values of the new user-defined functions I will discuss next. The best example for now would be to consider its use on a column. If you define the data type for the column as sql_variant, you can store characters, whole numbers, decimals, binary values, and so on. Actually, it can take all the data types except text, ntext, image, timestamp, and itself.
- **Table** This one was worth the wait. The table type is a local variable (confined to your connection) that can return a result set. To use it, you simply declare the variable of type table and insert records into it using your INSERT INTO . . . SELECT code (see Chapter 19). The big advantage of the table type is performance. It is memory resident throughout its life, and thus access to the data in a table type is very fast.

I bet you just can't wait to get your teeth into these new data types. You can chew on them in several chapters in Part III, and they are fully discussed in Chapter 16.

New Feature: User-Defined Functions

You know it is believed that if we pray hard enough as a group the collective energy can make our dreams come true. And so it has come to pass the Microsoft has given us the user-defined function (UDF).

A UDF is executed similarly to a stored procedure, but it has some marvelous applications. For example, it can accept input parameters like a stored procedure, but it can return scalar data types such as integers, decimals, and even data from the new sql_variant and the new table data type discussed earlier.

How often have you wished you could reference the result set of a stored procedure in the FROM clause of the SELECT statement (see Chapter 19)? Now you don't need to, because you can build a UDF that returns the table data type and throw the entire code segment into the FROM clause.

I see UDFs becoming one of the most popular features in T-SQL. It even makes for a much more powerful alternative to a view. For example, you can only use a single SELECT statement in a view, but a UDF is limited by the boundaries of your imagination.

New Built-in Functions

Several new built-in functions have been added to SQL Server 2000. Of special interest are the new functions that support the identity column, respectively SCOPE_IDENTITY() and IDENT_CURRENT().

The identity column uniquely identifies each row in a table, and it has similar application to the auto-increment data type in Microsoft Access.

Before I tell you how these help you, consider how you would obtain the last value inserted into a SQL Server version 7.0 identity column. Using the @@IDENTITY() function, you would be able to obtain the last value inserted into the identity column. But what if more than one table was affected by the transaction, say a trigger inserted a row into another table that also has an identity column? You could not get the value in the second insert, because it was considered outside of the scope of the originating transaction.

The scope of the transaction now encompasses all cascading or nested inserts as part of the scope. If you have a table X and a table Y and both have an identity column (there can be only one in each), and as a result of an insert in X there is also an insert in Y, then both inserts are now considered within the same scope. Now when you run @@IDENTITY(), you will get the identity column value for the last insert in the scope . . . table Y. So how do you get the value for table X?

Enter these new identity functions. The SCOPE_IDENTITY() returns the last value inserted into Table Y within the scope of stored procedure, trigger, function, or batch. In other words, the SCOPE_IDENTITY() returns the value for Table Y.

As for IDENT_CURRENT(), it ignores the scope and returns the value for the current table, Table X. If this confuses you a little, don't worry; we will examine some code examples in Chapter 20.

Another useful function that is a new addition to the family is the GetUTCDate() function. This function returns the UTC date format, the Universal Time Coordinate, better known as Greenwich Mean Time (as a teen I thought the BBC was based in Greenwich).

This means that instead of recording the local data and time with the GetDate() function, which is not very helpful when your servers are spread across multiple time zones, you can now record the UTC time, which has more meaning because you don't have the issue of time zones. No matter what time zone the server is in, this new function will return the UTC date and time. In other words, if you have a server in Los Angeles and one in London and you record the UTC date and time for both at the same time, the date and time will be the same. Both date functions can be used interchangeably.

There are more new functions than the ones I discussed here, but I deal with them in detail in Chapter 16 and in the chapters in Part III.

Extended Properties

If you think in OO design terms, the concept of extended properties on SQL Server's database objects will not be too foreign a concept. This new support for extended properties—similar to extended properties on Microsoft Access tables—lets you attach multiple, user-defined, extended properties to an object for any purpose.

For example, you can now create a caption property on a column in a table or view so that whenever the column is referenced in a SELECT, the column caption is returned for display at the client. This saves you from having to code an alias for the column field as demonstrated in Chapter 19, or settling for the "(no column name)" value that gets returned in ad hoc queries.

Another example that I find useful is the ability to set input masks for the column. The extended property can specify the format for a social security number in the United States as being xxx-xx-xxxx.

Language Collations

Prior to the advent of SQL Server 2000, all databases were locked into a single code page and language set sort order. This meant that if the server was set for French as the default code page, then everything was locked into French. That's all very well for a server that only services the French; it can sit on a rack in Paris locked away from the rest of the world. But the Internet changes everything. What if the French business wanted to makes its product available to the rest of the world? Must it then set up a different server for every country in the world accessing its database? Dedicating a server to every major language is going a bit far.

Enter the *language collation*. Collation support is not new, but in SQL Server 2000 the collation has much finer application. Instead of being limited to the server or the database, SQL Server now supports different languages at the table and column levels. This means that any number of languages can be supported within a single instance of SQL Server on one machine. In addition to supporting legacy collations, SQL Server 2000 also now supports the new Windows collations.

What is a collation? The word is simply a collective noun describing three attributes of language support in a system: It specifies the sort order for Unicode character data types, the sort order for non-Unicode character data types, and the code page that is used to store non-Unicode character data types. SQL Server can support multiple collations in each instance.

As an example of how you would use collations at the column level, remember what would happen using the default language on a database when you inserted a record in which one value only differed from the other by the diacritical accent used on a letter. Using the default without support for the accent in question, you would not be able to insert the record, because SQL Server would see it as a duplicate record. But if you used a collation on that column that supported all the diacritics of the language, such as the German umlaut, each value would be regarded as unique even if all the letters in the word were the same and just the accent were different. Collations are further discussed in Chapter 2, Chapter 6, and in the chapters of Part III.

Full-Text Search and Document Management

Full-text search was introduced in SQL Server 7.0 but was not a central facility and was not deemed part of the core product. That has all changed in SQL Server 2000. Full-text search is not only installed by default; it is also included free of charge in the Enterprise, Standard, Personal, Developer, and Evaluation Editions. But what is full-text search? The following is a brief introduction to the facility:

- It enables you to perform full-text queries on plain text stored in relational tables.
- The full-text query language or syntax is fully incorporated into the T-SQL language.
- It enables you to search across all indexed columns in a table.
- An API enables you to gain programmatic access to information about an executed query, including rank of hits, weighting of search criteria, and so on.

The document search facility on the Microsoft Web site is a good example of a full-text search implementation. It also supports searching in formatted documents, such as HTML files and Microsoft Office documents. This is achieved by use of filters, and you can build your own custom document filters to suit any document management application you can dream up. In Chapter 19, you will learn about full-text search and how to use it to build a document database management system.

Indexed Views

Views have been around since the dawn of the relational DBMS, and with each new version of SQL Server the support for views is further improved. The need for index support on views has been on the wish list for several years now, but it was not always clear how Microsoft would support the need.

A view is often thought of as a virtual table, but virtuality actually has nothing to do with a view, because there is nothing really virtual about it. The records or result set actually exists in the view, albeit only in memory, which is essentially the result of a select statement on the base table. A view may be better thought of as a temporary table created when a view definition is referenced. The view definition provides the "field of vision" (my quote) you allow for the client. A view is thus not actually stored in table form; it persists as the code segment—the select statement—waiting to be referenced.

But the SELECT statement that generates a view can be as complex as it needs to, and it often needs to do some significant calculations and sorting. So in order to index a view, the solution is to store the result set of the view in the database. Now the view is permanent. However, the view still depends on the base table for record changes. This happens automatically; if you update the base table, then the view result set also changes.

The problem comes when you need to change the base table. What if I decide to take the e-mail addresses out of the base table and link in a new table that's devoted to the e-mail addresses for the clients? When the view selects the e-mail columns, it will discover that they are no longer there and fail. Well, the workaround is a feature called *schema binding*. The catalog notes the relationship between the view and the base table and prevents the base table from being changed if an indexed view depends on it (vanilla views without indexes are not affected, because their result sets are created on the fly).

The SCHEMABINDING option prevents the table from being altered until the view with the bind is dropped. After the table has been altered, you can easily reestablish an indexed view on it. We'll get back to this subject in Chapter 19.

SQL Server and the Internet

SQL Server has to date been one of the most widely used database products on the Internet. However, its earlier Internet deployment was mostly indirect; it was merely an RDBMS on a wide area network. SQL Server 2000 is very different. It now comes with support specifically intended for Internet applications, especially as one of the cornerstones of the Microsoft .Net initiative.

In order to make SQL Server an Internet compliant product that supports Internet standards as opposed to workarounds and kludges, the product needed work in two areas: data exchange and connectivity. The connectivity component has been achieved by providing access to SQL Server over HTTP uniform resource locators (URLs). And the data exchange component comes in the form of native support for XML, widely considered the most important technology to emerge since the start of the Internet several decades ago, and the key enabling factor leading to the critical mass of the Internet.

Virtual Roots

While it has always been possible to access SQL Server over a TCP/IP network, doing so over the Internet has always raised the eyebrows of security-conscious DBAs. Instead of direct access, however, the HTTP access to SQL Server works through a proxy, the Internet Information Server. IIS has always had the capability, like all the popular Web and FTP servers, to create a virtual root for an FTP directory abstracted above the actual file system underpinning the server. It can now do the same for SQL Server.

To visualize how it works, consider the connection string you create for DSN or DSN-less connections to SQL Server using direct client/server implementations. The URL works on the same concept, but the database provided in the connection string is the name of the virtual root, instead of an actual server name, instance name, and network address. (In Chapter 23, I will show you how this is configured.)

You can, for example, create a URL that directly executes SQL queries. These are typically cast in the form of HTTP://server/virtualroot?SQL="xxx". This is a URL string that makes a call to a certain instance of SQL Server using a T-SQL statement. Sending the statement to the virtual root results in return of a standard rowset. If the FORXML clause is passed, an XML document is returned instead of the rowset.

The new Web support allows direct access to SQL Server objects, such as tables that can return graphics or documents to the calling applications. SQL Server also includes support for Web-based analysis services.

SQL Server functionality can also be accessed from functions in an ISAPI DLL which can be accessed from Internet Information Server (IIS) applications (HTML documents, ActiveX components, Java applets, scripts, and so on). You can thus build URLs that connect front-end applications to SQL Server data sources. URLs can also be used to specify IIS virtual roots that reference instances of SQL Server.

In addition to the sophisticated XML support, SQL Server 2000 has extended the HTML support that was introduced with SQL Server 7.0. The previous edition allowed you to generate HTML pages infused with SQL Server data and post or install them to HTTP and FTP locations, but now with the extended functionality in the ISAPI DLL discussed here, these pages can be stored in SQL Server and directly accessed by referencing the virtual roots.

Native XML Support

As for XML data, Microsoft has provided native support for XML in all the components traditionally used to transport and work with relational data. For starters, it has built XML support directly into the OLE DB provider, which allows XML documents to be represented as command text and XML data to be returned from the database as a text stream.

SQL Server also supports a subset of the XPath language that is defined and supported by the World Wide Web Consortium (W3C). XPath is a graph navigation language that can be used to select nodes from within XML documents that can then be used in queries to retrieve the data from SQL Server.

XML functionality is designed to eliminate the complexities of building database applications for the World Wide Web. Using XML and technologies such as XPath, URL queries, and XML updategrams (see Chapter 23), Web developers are essentially shielded from having to apply traditional OO development practices to the Web-centric database applications.

XML is fast becoming the *lingua franca* of e-commerce on the Internet; it enables Web developers to gain access to SQL Server data using XML constructs such as the FOR XML clause that returns XML data from a T-SQL SELECT statement instead of tabulated data, using the OPENXML keyword (see Chapters 16, 19, and 23).

SQL Server 2000 includes a robust XML parser, which translates XML in your queries to retrieve data. Conversely, SQL Server is able to return the data to the requesting client applications as XML data, as opposed to the rowset or recordset typical of traditional database applications. This has applications on both intranets and the Internet.

But SQL Server does not only understand how to read an XML-based query; it is also able to store data as XML. It can provide a relational view of the data as well as map XML data into tables. In other words, XML views enable tables to be accessed as if they were XML documents. OPENXML is a T-SQL keyword that returns an updatable rowset over in-memory XML documents. Chapter 23 fully explores the new XML updategrams that let you insert, update, and delete data in SQL Server tables from the Web. You will also explore the XML bulk load facility that lets you process bulk loads of XML-packaged data.

The Client/Server Architecture

As explained earlier, SQL Server is a client/server database system. At home in both two-tier and multitier environments, it is capable of servicing very small databases in limited storage areas, or very large databases, also known as VLDBs, in huge storage silos. A huge number of users can be connected to SQL Server at the same time, all sending queries and instructions to the server, performing inserts, updates, deletes, queries, and just about anything you can imagine doing with a database. But you can also install and operate multiple instances of SQL Server on the same computer, or your users can be querying a database under the control of instance x on one server while inserting data into a database under the control of instance *y* on another server. But before we get carried away, let's also look at more modest implementations.

SQL Server, as a client/server system, can be easily implemented as a two-tiered system on a single machine. Both the SQL Server engine and the user interface are installed on the same computer, much as you would install and use Access or FoxPro applications. Front-end or user-interface database applications communicate with SQL Server via the Windows Interprocess Communications (IPC) facilities (explained in Chapter 2) and not over a network.

This capability makes SQL Server 2000 ideal for single-user needs; but it is also ideal for thin-client/server environments in which all users operate in terminal sessions on the same server-class machine hosting SQL Server. When the product is installed on Windows 2000 in Application Server mode, your users would have access to applications that send requests to the database server engine via IPC facilities. This is a much more elegant, safer, and cheaper solution than giving every user a copy of

Access (which must be licensed), or a custom application, and having every user tax the system with application-side processing overhead.

But what if you need to implement a high-end or demanding application on the local machine? A good example that does not involve human users at all, but that is one I am intimately familiar with, is computer telephony.

Computer telephony systems are not small or trivial applications. A computer telephony application often requires access to a locally installed database, mainly because network latency, even measured in milliseconds, is not an option when you have hundreds of callers on telephone lines all waiting for service. Using file/server system architecture for a high-end application can lead to disaster.

A computer telephony system has several telephony cards in it that can answer calls on a number of channels (in some systems the number of calls all appearing at the same time can be as high as several hundred per server). A file/server database engine like Jet or the BDE (child of the old Paradox engine) cannot handle such a dramatic burst of read or write requests during peak hours, often sustained for long periods. Each request for data or write to the database is essentially a user connection to the database, the user being a process thread spun out of the computer telephony application to the database server. Some of the requests for data services can be as simple as checking an extension number, or the number of rings to wait before forwarding the call, whereas others can be very complex, for instance, recording a voice message, or accepting an incoming stream of fax data.

Internet applications are not unlike computer telephony applications from a load perspective. You might have one stock exchange server chugging along servicing a modest number of buys and sells over the Web. Then suddenly an issue goes "gold" and ten servers are not enough.

This is where SQL Server's capabilities as a key role player in a multitier or *n*-tier client/server system come to the foreground. In high-traffic Internet environments, you have situations in which zero data processing can be performed at the client, which does nothing but present data in a browser. In such situations numerous "client" processes might come into play to connect to more than one instance of SQL Server for a variety of reasons. Transactions can be handed to services like the COM+ Component Services (formerly known as Microsoft Transaction Server, or MTS) and Microsoft Message Queuing Services (MMQS) for a variety of reasons. Such technology is key, for example, in banking applications over the Internet. Take funds transfer: First you need assurance from the server that money debited from *account A* gets credited to *account B*, and that the execution and result (success/failure) of the transaction is properly communicated to the user even over an unreliable connection like the Internet.

SQL Server's client/server architecture does not support traditional mainframe-type load balancing for extremely high volume. Instead the work is shared between servers that hold data partitions. The servers cooperate to share the load as a server "federation," which is a SQL Server term that means, essentially, the same thing as a server farm that allows a client to connect to any of a number of servers for the same service. You will learn about database federations again in Chapter 13, but they and the other new features aimed at availability deserve some introduction here.

New Features Supporting High Availability

SQL Server 2000 benefits from the host of new scalability and reliability features of the truly mission-critical facilities of the Windows 2000 server platform, and the client/server architecture.

SQL Server can scale up and scale out. On the scale up side, one Datacenter Server can address up to 64GB of RAM and can take advantage of the 32-way SMP support built into its Windows 2000 host architecture. And for advanced fail-over in the scale-up model, SQL Server 2000 now includes enhanced fail-over clustering, between two nodes on Windows 2000 Advanced Server and among four nodes on Windows 2000 Datacenter Server, for the most critical of applications.

While SQL Server 2000 can be deployed as a cluster of servers, it cannot be load-balanced in a similar fashion to mainframe or midrange system clustering, in which clustering typically revolves around shared resources such as storage arrays or controllers but all systems are active. The SQL Server cluster is an *active-passive* solution (which is typically how the Microsoft Cluster Service works in Windows NT, Windows 2000 Advanced Server, and Datacenter Server high-availability deployments), which means that only one server, a virtual server, services clients. The others sit by in passive mode waiting in case the active server, which supports the virtual server, takes a stray bullet. Then one of the passive members in the cluster (warm and ready) springs to life (fail-over) to take over the load (technically the fail-over continues to support the virtual server). The system does skip a few heartbeats when the new server becomes active, but the wait is measured in seconds. Currently, there can only be four nodes in a cluster, as opposed to *n*-nodes on several midrange products that are all active. (Check out the clustering information in Chapter 13.)

But SQL Server also does software scale-out. It operates on a high-availability model known as *shared nothing federations.* A federation of servers share load by distributing hits across all available SQL Servers that are members of the federation. Instead of sharing physical resources, the servers share nothing. This is also known as the shared-nothing approach to clustering. Instead of servers sharing physical resources, identical, distributed, and updatable copies of the databases reside on each server, in an architecture made possible by a technique known as Distributed Partitioned Views. All SQL Server servers are active in a federation, while only one is active on the virtual server of a cluster.

New Feature: Distributed Updatable Partitioned Views

Shared-nothing clustering is proving to be a sound alternative to clustering that shares physical components, because it eliminates single point-of-failure scenarios, such as an array of hard disks that, should the array go belly up, takes out all servers relying on it.

This is made possible by the capability to partition data horizontally across a group (federation) of servers. The servers all participate in the management of the partitioned data, but their underlying operating systems, the SQL Server engines, and hardware operate autonomously and independently of the other servers in the federation. This is not really new stuff. What is new is that SQL Server now supports the concept of an updatable UNION view, which, distributed over several servers, is called a *distributed partitioned view.*

The servers cooperate to provide a single view of the partitioned data, and this can achieve almost infinite scale-out capability. This is basically how it works (the subject catches fire with the advanced how-to stuff in Chapter 13):

1. First you would link your servers (see "Linking Servers" in Chapter 10) to form a SQL Server federation.
2. Next you would place a copy of the database on each server, which is easy as pie using several methods of making a copy of the target database (see Chapter 11).
3. Then you would define the member tables that are destined to be horizontally partitioned across the servers. You also need to consider factors like integrity checks and constraints, and updates, but we'll discuss that in Chapter 13.
4. Finally you would partition the database tables in each server as updatable UNION views of the data to the clients.

With the introduction of fully updatable UNION views (partitioned views), data updated in a view on server a is likewise updated—through the UNION with the other servers—to the base database tables on all the servers.

New Feature: Log Shipping

SQL Server transaction logs are the key elements of database recovery that allow you to restore databases almost immediately after a system crash, and they are practically corruption proof. Being able to recover the transaction logs is a critical requirement of SQL Server recovery. So important is it that many administrators agree that backing up the transaction logs is more important that backing up the actual databases. What if, as a result of a terrible system crash (say a train runs over your server), you cannot recover the transaction logs? This is where *log shipping* comes into play.

An item on the wish lists of many DBAs, log shipping is new to SQL Server. The shipping technique is simple: The transaction logs are continuously fed to a warm standby server, which can be safely tucked away in another location if necessary. Should your primary server vanish, you can simply promote your warm standby to active server status, because it has a fresh copy of the transaction logs.

Microsoft claims that SQL Server 2000 can support the growth requirements of any Web site and can accommodate the most demanding of enterprise data and information systems. A full discussion of SQL Server's scalability and availability architecture is discussed in Chapter 13 and in numerous places throughout this book. We could devote this entire chapter to all the new features and enhancements in SQL Server 2000 availability, but there are so many that the impact would be lost.

While the new technology and features will be flagged in the various chapters throughout the book, one deserves a quick mention here because of its application in the availability discussion, multi-instance support.

New Feature: Multi-Instance

This feature is so simple, it's a wonder it was never implemented before SQL Server 2000. In the past you would install SQL Server on a machine and that was that. The SQL Server copy was named after the name of the server, and you could only run one instance of SQL Server on the machine. Now with multi-instance support, you can install additional instances on the same host and each instance can operate concurrently and independently of any other instance of SQL Server.

This feature is chiefly aimed at the application service provider market. I welcome it as a component of managed data services (a remote database hosting solution) in which I install several instances on a server (limited only by the processing power, memory, and hard disk space) and devote each one to a different account or client. Well, SQL Server is secure enough to allow you to do that even on one instance, in which each client and its users get one database. But for security reasons and other logistical considerations, there will be times when the application will demand its own instance, and not just its own database.

Multiple instances also play a key role in service level and availability in the busy data center. You can install more than one instance on a mission-critical server and keep it running as a warm standby instance. As a worst-case scenario, if you lose the primary, you attach the primary's databases to the secondary and keep going, leaving the primary down until it is safe to restart the server. Find out how to do this in Chapter 11.

The first instance of SQL Server, which is also known as the default instance, goes by the machine name. Any new instances installed have to be explicitly given their own names. You can also run multiples instances on a server that has SQL Server version 6.5 or version 7.0 running as the default instance.

The Analysis Services

SQL Server was originally conceived as an online transaction processing (OLTP) system or DBMS, built around the need to store large amounts of records, operational data, or transaction data culled from the concurrent transactions of a larger number of human users and computer processes. It has excelled at this capability, and this is what makes it ideal not only for the data storage needs of large enterprises and public institutions but for those of small- to medium-sized businesses as well. (See Chapter 22 on concurrency and transactions.)

However, operational data and the storage and retrieval thereof are only a part of what companies need in a DBMS. The ability to query data is one of the cornerstones of a relational database application, hence the invention of a query language like SQL.

The ubiquitous SELECT statement allows us to obtain information from our data and allows us to drill into the data to obtain information that could assist with decisions, and with business rules and direction.

An example: The statement SELECT * FROM CUSTOMERS WHERE CREDIT EQUALS GREEN lets a marketing team safely derive a new list from the customer base list to which additional product offerings can be made. Marketing people will have a measure of sales confidence using the list because they know that any new customers garnered from their marketing efforts will be able to pay for the goods and thus generate cash flow.

This example is very simple because SQL SELECT statements can be vastly more sophisticated, complex, and deep. The more advanced and sophisticated the query, the more demanding it is to make it against a huge database holding thousands, millions, even billions of items. Aggregate queries, for example, are extremely taxing on huge databases. Reports might typically take days to generate. For the most part, therefore, relational data and relational (normalized) tables do not make effective analytical data storage facilities, but the specialized warehousing facilities offered by the Analysis Services do.

Apart from the strain, a more scientific analysis of data is needed to support the decision-making processes of enterprises, fields of research and endeavor, and even the whims of individuals. Humans have the uncanny habit of going around in circles, always making the same mistakes, never breaking out of the cycle. And they do this with their companies. It takes a lot of effort to make changes . . . and we need to be convinced by hard facts.

SQL Server's analysis services were introduced to the product back in version 6.5. Known as online analytical processing (OLAP), these features are used to support decision support systems (DSSs) that can, for example, help a company to position itself in new and emerging markets, and to use data to detect shifts in market perception, buying trends, consumer habits, opinion, corporate health, and much more.

OLAP data is organized into multidimensional structures known as CUBES, and the analysis data is stored in data structures known as data warehouses and data marts. OLAP services are supported by a number of SQL Server components that form the Analysis Services.

Analysis Services and the transformation of data for analysis make up a highly complex subject that is obviously beyond the scope of this "warm-up" chapter. Analysis Services are comprehensively covered in Part IV. The Analysis Services are now a major and critical component of SQL Server, which is why it is described as a Relational Database Management and Analysis System, and why I call it the "DBMS for everyone and everything."

Some of the new stuff I have discussed here is not all that's new in SQL Server 2000; there are improvements in all areas, including the graphical tools, such as Enterprise

Manager and Query Analyzer, which now sports an object browser; English Query, which is now fully supported in Visual Studio; the Replication and Data Transformation Services; and Meta Data Services. These are all discussed at length in their respective chapters.

I hope you are ready to tackle the complex material that lies in the chapters ahead. I also know that you are keen to see SQL Server 2000 in action and to get a feel for what it is capable of. You will be seeing a ton of code in this book, most of it in Part III. The chapters remaining in Part I will help you understand how SQL Server works, how to assess your needs, and how to install and deploy the product.

The Complete Reference

Chapter 2

Database Architecture

At the conceptual level, the facility for data storage in SQL Server 2000 is the *database.* SQL Server's databases are fully compliant with the ANSI SQL-92 definition of a database…with some remarkable extensions you will learn about in this chapter.

The databases do not themselves store data. Rather, the data is stored in *tabulated* structures (hereafter called *tables*), and these tables are stored within the confines of the database file, in a number of sophisticated file structures we will investigate later in this chapter.

Contrary to the terminology used in many circles, the term *database* will not be used to refer to the system as a whole. A SQL Server database is just the barn where the grain stores or silos are kept. It encompasses the mechanisms of management and functionality. Instead I will refer to the "system" as the *database management system* or *DBMS.* The client/server architecture and the DBMS will be the central subjects of Chapter 3 and Chapter 4, respectively.

This chapter will thus explore the database architecture of SQL Server on various levels, often in very abstract terms. We will dig deeper in other parts of the book where we need to clarify both development and administration techniques.

From a conceptual level, the database is the container for all tables, indexes, constraints, and other objects and properties used by the DBMS to manage the data. SQL Server databases are viewed from both the logical perspective—by developers, clients and users, and server components—and the physical perspective—by database administrators, system administrators, and server "machinery."

The logical perspective is essentially the external view of the *database,* seen by users and software developers alike. The physical perspective encompasses the internal view of the database. The internal view is primarily the view of the database administrator or DBA. Figure 2-1 illustrates the three abstract SQL Server database levels and the "entities" that "appreciate" these perspectives.

Besides the physical parts of the database, such as its file groups, this chapter kicks off with an overview of the logical components of a SQL Server database, such as tables and indexes.

Introducing Enterprise Manager

There is no better place in this book than this chapter to introduce you to the *SQL Server Enterprise Manager,* because it provides a graphical user interface to manage SQL Server databases and their objects. SQL Server Enterprise Manager (Enterprise Manager from here on) was first introduced to SQL Server back in Version 6.0, in 1995. In Version 7.0, Enterprise Manager was moved to the Microsoft Management Console. In SQL Server 2000, it is a highly sophisticated MMC snap-in that can be used to graphically administer SQL Server databases and their objects, as well as the DBMS itself, handling security, schedules, backups, performance, replication, and more.

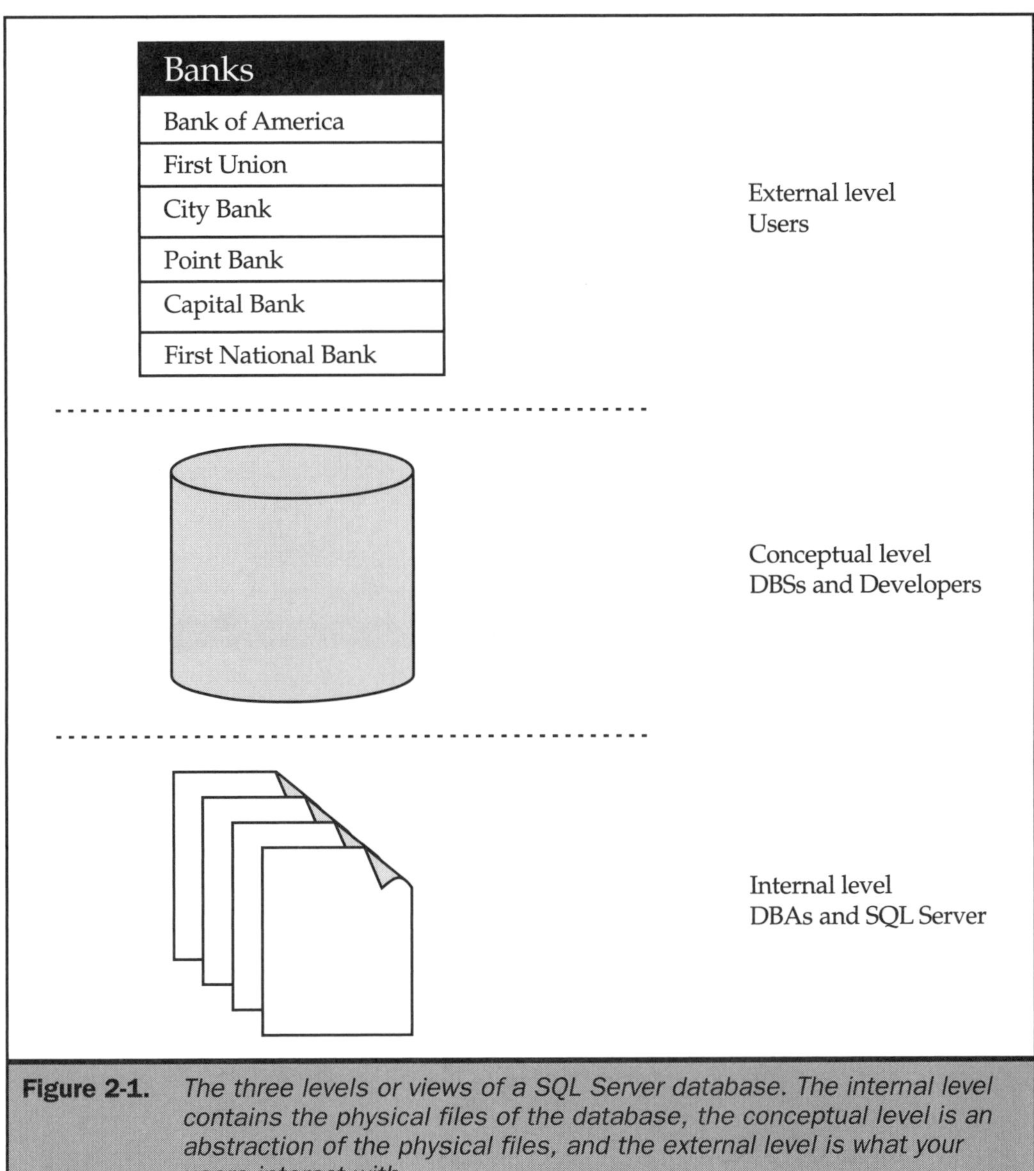

Figure 2-1. *The three levels or views of a SQL Server database. The internal level contains the physical files of the database, the conceptual level is an abstraction of the physical files, and the external level is what your users interact with.*

If you are new to SQL Server, you do not need to install the product and run Enterprise Manager, or any other application, for this chapter. Several areas of Enterprise Manager are illustrated in this chapter only to provide a visual connection with much of what we discuss. However, poking around in Enterprise Manager will not hurt at this early stage of the book, and it can only enhance your understanding of the complex database architecture discussion that begins with this chapter. If you want to install SQL Server, jump to Chapter 6 before continuing.

Once you have installed SQL Server, the Enterprise Manager can be launched from your menus by choosing Start | Programs | Microsoft SQL Server | Enterprise Manager. You can also create a link to the Enterprise Manager MSC file *(SQL Server Enterprise Manager.MSC)* and place this link on your desktop or wherever you need it. Figure 2-2 illustrates Enterprise Manager in action.

Introduction to SQL Server Databases

The databases are split into two groups, *system* databases and *user* databases. The conceptual view of the databases is illustrated in Figure 2-3. The system databases include master, model, tempdb, and msdb. Two additional databases installed at setup are pubs and northwind. These are demo databases, and you can safely delete them if you need space.

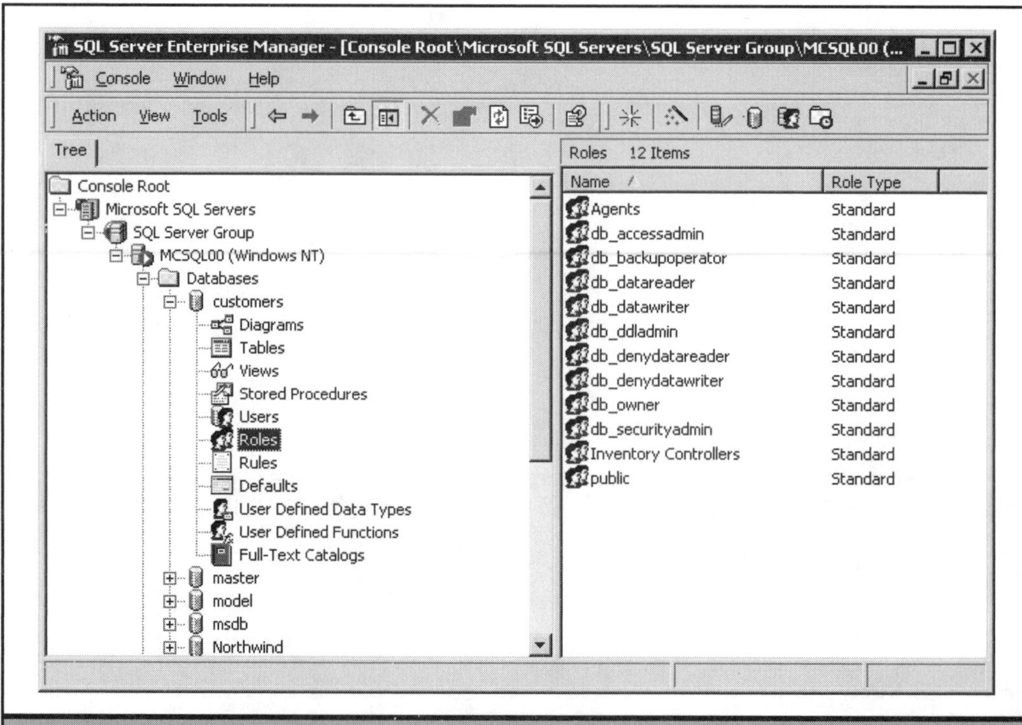

Figure 2-2. *Enterprise Manager is a graphical tool for configuring and maintaining SQL Server databases and their objects, and for managing the DBMS*

Note *If you plan to follow the administration guidelines in Part II and the code examples in Part III, you should keep pubs and northwind around because I use them extensively in examples, especially northwind. I could have drawn on examples from my own field, but I felt it better to use the databases that ship with the product so that you can work with the same data that I did for this book.*

The master database is used by SQL Server to keep an eye on the state of the system. It also records information about other databases in the system, disk space, usage, DBMS configuration, object information and source code, and so on. Master represents the database schema; it is also often referred to as the *catalog*, which is database parlance, and not really a SQL Server term.

The model database is a database template. When you create a new database, the new database is a copy of model . . . actually it is derived from it. If you need to create databases that are preconfigured with certain settings, you would create the settings in model, and all new databases would inherit the settings. The model database does not need to be installed in turnkey environments.

Note *You will learn about model and its application in later chapters, especially Chapter 11. It should be used to "bequeath" only, and most positively, the base properties that will form the foundation of all your databases, and not as a means of automatically configuring applications.*

Also derived from model is the tempdb database. This database stores all the temporary data that is needed by SQL Server during the lifetime of the SQL Server instance; in other words, until it is stopped and restarted. The data in tempdb is not saved, and the database and its tables are recreated when SQL Server is started.

Last in the system group is the MSDB database, which is used by the SQL Server Agent service, discussed in Chapter 12. SQL Server Agent is used for performing scheduled tasks such as database backup and data transformation.

The user databases are the databases created for and used by your applications. You can have one database in the system with a certain number of tables, or you can have many databases. Most small line-of-business (LOB) applications needed by a small company would suffice with one database, serving many needs and users. For the larger entities, you might have many databases, used by a number of departments and key management entities (KMEs). Only one instance of SQL Server is needed to manage all the databases. Thousands of users can connect to and be serviced on any number of databases, all under the auspices of one instance of the SQL Server engine. (You will learn much more about the role of the server in Chapters 3.)

The physical database files are nothing more than your typical file system files. In that the database can contain objects and properties—and the objects also contain properties—you might prefer to refer to the database file as, itself, an object. And you would be correct. SQL Server regards all the elements of and in its databases as objects; this goes for tables and indexes as well.

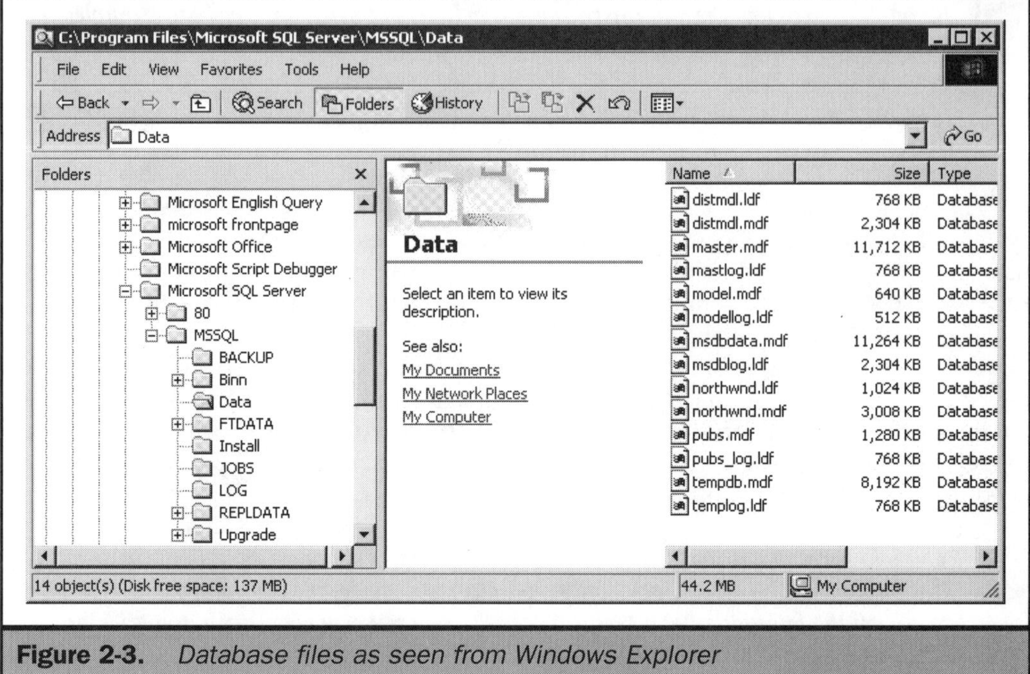

Figure 2-3. *Database files as seen from Windows Explorer*

A database is split into two or more files as follows:

- **The Primary data files,** which are named with the MDF extension, keep tabs on the rest of the *user* files in the database. They are also used for data storage.
- **The Secondary data files** are also used for storage and are given the extension *.ndf.* There can be more than one *.ndf* file.
- **The Log files** are where all the transaction log entries are stored. These transaction logs account for SQL Server's recoverability prowess, which I introduced in the previous chapter. These log files are identified by the *.ldf* extension.

The files and their location can be viewed, in their physical abstraction, in Windows Explorer, as illustrated in Figure 2-3.

The database and log files are shown living together in one folder, which is not a good idea, especially if the disks are not redundant. Better to put the log files on their own hard disk.

Figure 2-4 illustrates the conceptual view of the internal environment from the Enterprise Manager snap-in.

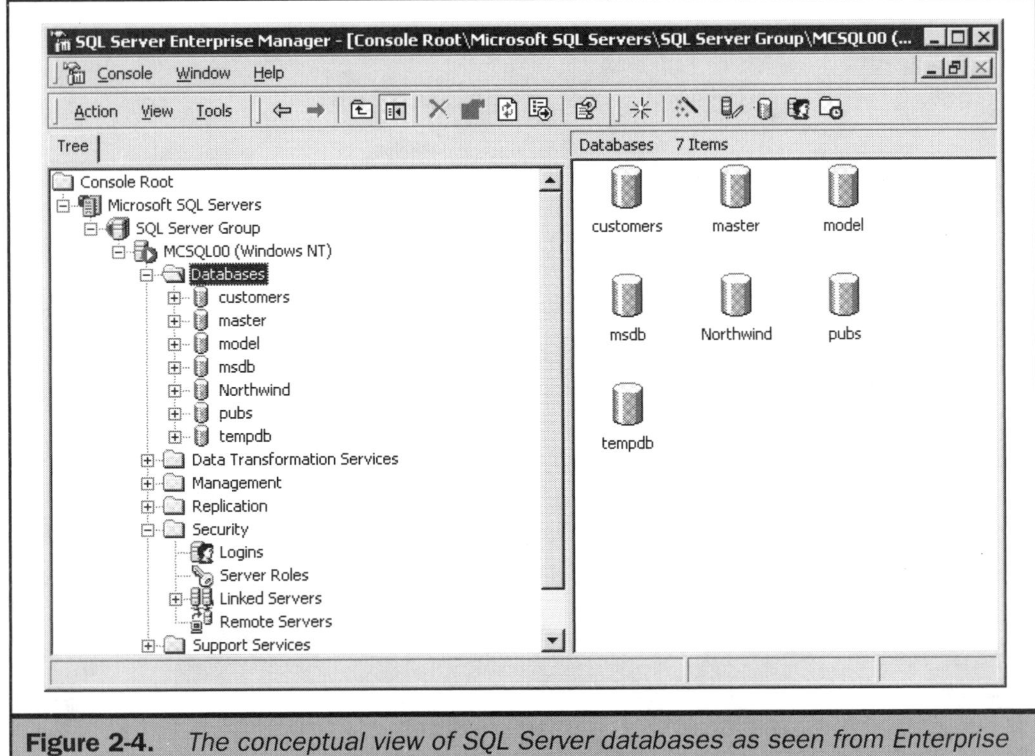

Figure 2-4. *The conceptual view of SQL Server databases as seen from Enterprise Manager*

Any number of instances of SQL Server 2000 can attach to a specific collection of databases. You can also detach from a collection of databases and reattach from another instance . . . even from another server. SQL Server can attach version 7.5 and earlier databases. Earlier versions of the server cannot, however, attach SQL Server 2000 databases. Attaching and detaching are demonstrated in Chapter 11.

The Logical Database Architecture

The window into the logical abstraction, the external level, of SQL Server 2000's database world uncovers an assortment of components. These objects and their properties are what you or your users work with, directly and indirectly, for the storage, manipulation, and retrieval requirements of your various applications. These components can also be managed from the Enterprise Manager as illustrated in Figure 2-5.

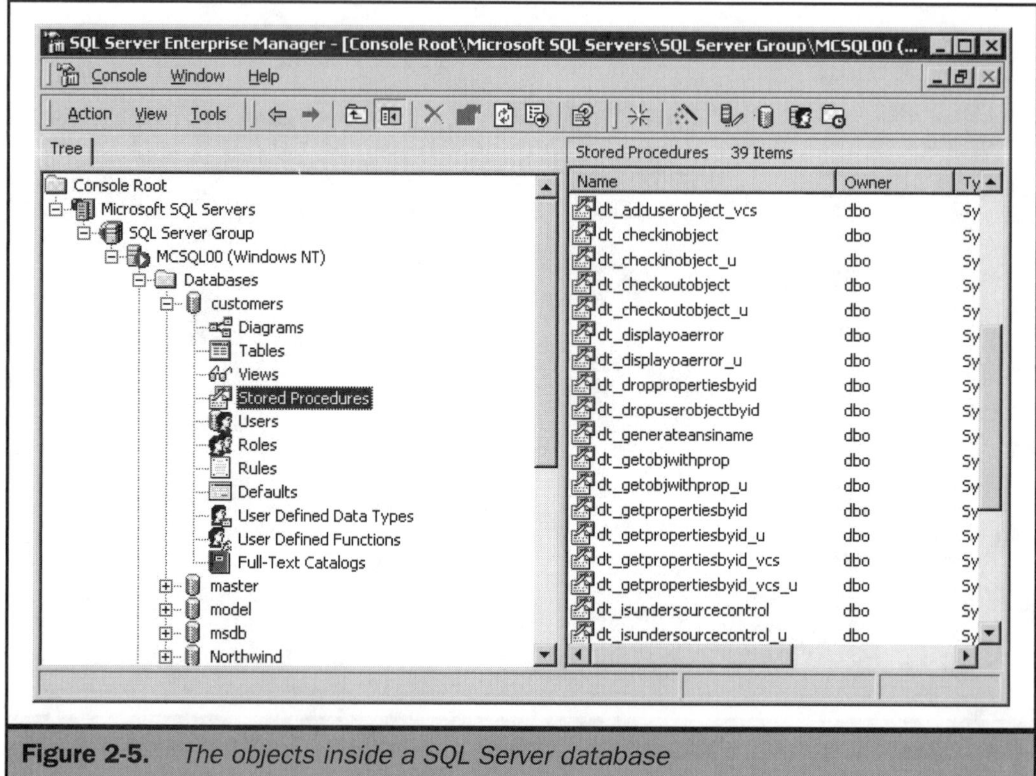

Figure 2-5. *The objects inside a SQL Server database*

Introduction to SQL Server Tables: The Conceptual Level

The unit or object of data storage in a SQL Server database is the *table,* which is the same thing as a *relation* in relational systems parlance. Each table contains data that relates to entities known, again, as objects. For example, a table in the accounts receivable database might contain debtors and their attributes such as the names of the debtors, their account balances, terms, and credit periods.

Tables are similar to spreadsheets; they contain columns and rows. The comparison to a spreadsheet, however, is a dangerous one because it can lead you down the wrong road to understanding how SQL Server works. Each column represents one attribute of the object, such as *name* or *customer number.* The rows represent the instances or quantity of the objects in the table.

In the previous chapter I described how each row can be thought of as a record if it is not related to rows in any other table. For example, if you have 10 rows in the *debtors* table, you actually have 10 instances of debtors, or 10 "records" of type debtor. (The instances can also be identical if there is no *unique* rule, primary key, or similar constraint in effect over the table . . . but more about that shortly.) The similarity to the spreadsheet's *page* or *worksheet* ends here, however, because the individual *"cells"* of the table are not accessed in the same way as cells of a spreadsheet.

The term *record* is correct database terminology, but you should take care not to confuse *records* and *rows,* because they are different things. The concept of a record extends beyond a single row in a table. In fact, a record is a combination of all the related rows of all tables in the entire database, which are linked by keys (discussed a little later in this chapter).

If you only have one table in the database, then of course each row can represent a complete and unique record. But if you break out the data into several tables, then your record spans to the other tables as well. I will refer to rows when our operations affect or act upon the individual rows in a table, such as the sorting of rows, a physical operation. But I will refer to records when referring to the actual data, such as when updating the value in a column. As you will also learn, deleting a row and deleting a record are two different things. Understanding the difference between a record and a row is a precondition to grasping the concept of referential integrity, which is covered in Chapter 17.

Creating Tables

There are two means of creating tables in SQL Server databases: interactively (through GUI tools such as Enterprise Manager) or directly with ANSI-compliant T-SQL syntax. The T-SQL code is a Data Definition Language (DDL), and no matter which method you use, DDL is what gets sent to the server to create or alter the table. The following code is a simple clause that creates the "inventory" table:

```
CREATE TABLE inventory (item char(120))
```

The code creates the table *inventory* and inserts one column called *item* of data type *char,* which is 120 characters in length. This example is illustrated in the Enterprise Manager in Figure 2-6.

Naming Convention

Tables are named in code using dot notation representing a hierarchy comprising the database name, the owner of the table, and the table name. This is represented as follows: *databasename.ownername.tablename.* The owner of the database, which is defaulted to *dbo* if it is not specified, or a *user* with ownership rights and permission to create an object, is the only entity allowed to create or edit the objects within a database or a table.

Owners, users, groups, and roles are discussed in depth in the next chapter and in Chapter 8. You should not overly concern yourself with ownership at this point.

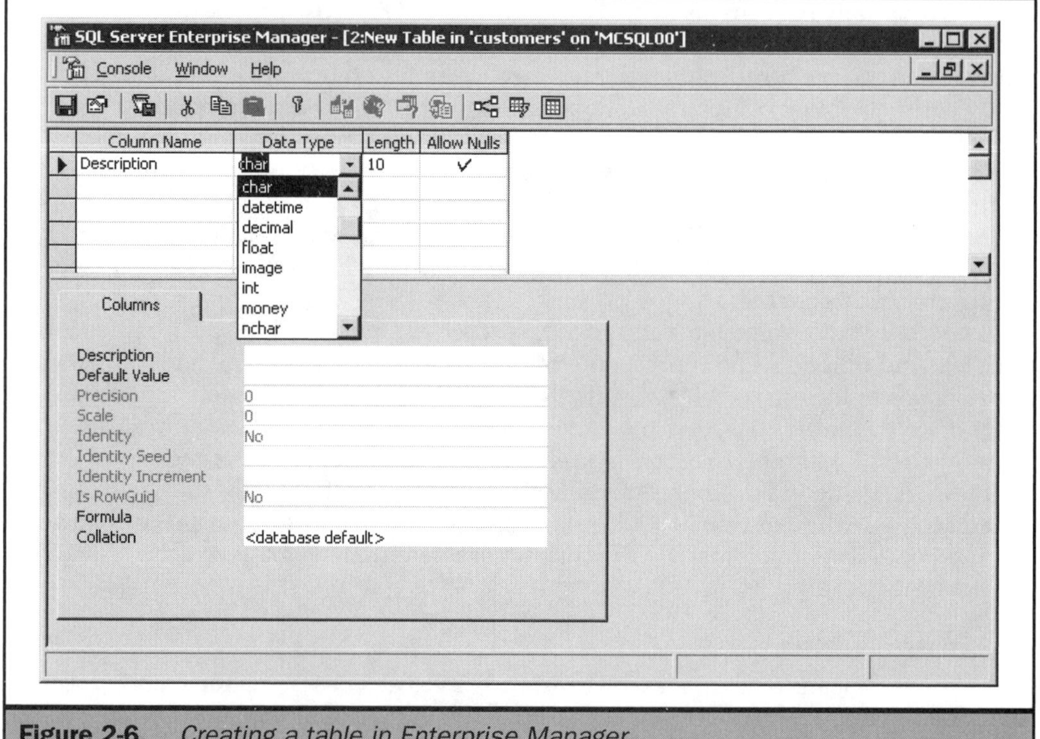

Figure 2-6. *Creating a table in Enterprise Manager*

Naming columns requires nothing more than common sense and conformance to the SQL Server convention, which specifies that the column must be no more than 128 characters long. It can consist of letters, digits, or the symbols #, @, $, and _ (underscore). See Chapter 16 for more specific information about naming and usage in T-SQL code.

You also need to be careful not to use reserved words in your column names. A good example is the word "group," which is a SQL Keyword. You could use the term "category" instead if the aim, for example, is to classify a collection of items. (See SQL Server Books Online, which lists SQL Server keywords.)

Data Types and Their Domains

As mentioned earlier, the objects in the database have properties, as do their child objects, and one of the properties of the column in the table is the data type. The data type defines the type of data that can be stored in the records of the column. In the preceding example, we specified that the *item* column supports the data type *char.*

The *domain* of a data type is an ANSI SQL term for specifying a set of allowable values in a column. In other words, it is all the allowable attributes that describe the data type, including its name and other properties, such as color and class. Domain is often thought to be synonymous with data type, but that is incorrect at the worst, confusing at the least. In a table identifying the records of used cars on a lot, one column of type varchar holds information pertaining to the color of each car. Color is not the data type, it is the domain (although you can create a custom data type called "car_color" with no problem). The domain can be used to specify a constraint on the column. For example, the inventory person is not allowed to use the term "off-white" but should rather use "cream."

Table 2-1 provides a list of the base data types supports by SQL Server tables.

Data Type	Data	Specification	Storage Size
Binary	*binary(n)*	Binary data of up to 255 bytes	Specify *n* bytes and use up to *n*
Big integer	*Bigint*	Exact numbers from –2^63 (–9223372036854775808) through 2^63–1 (9223372036854775807)	8 bytes
Bit	*Bit*	0 or 1	1 byte
Character	*char(n)*	8,000 characters; must be predefined using the value *n*	1 byte per character, even if actual length is less than *n*
Date and time	*Datetime*	The combination of date and time. 01-JAN-1753 to 31-DEC-9999	8 bytes
Decimal values	*Decimal(p,s)*	Whole numbers or fractions from -10^{38} to 10^{38}	Precision *p* holds up to 17 bytes
Floating point	*float(n)* (15 digit precision)	Approximations from $-1.79E^{38}$ through $1.79E^{38}$	8 bytes
	real(n) (real data where *n* is between 1 and 7)	Approximations from $-3.40E^{38}$ through $3.40E^{38}$	4 bytes
Image	*image*	Up to 2GB	Data is stored in 8KB pages if too large for record
Integer (see also Big integer)	*int*	Whole numbers from –2,147,483,648 through 2,147,483,647	4 bytes

Table 2-1. *SQL Server 2000 Data Types*

Data Type	Data	Specification	Storage Size
Money (see also Small money)	*money*	-922,337,203,685,477.5808 through 922,337,203,685,477.5807	8 bytes
Nchar (unicode data)	*nchar(n)*	1 to 4,000 characters	2 bytes per character declared
Ntext (Variable-length Unicode data)	*ntext*	Length is 230 – 1 (1,073,741,823) characters	2 bytes per character declared
Nvarchar	*nvarchar(n)*	1 to 4,000 characters	2 bytes per character declared
Numeric (see Decimal)	*numeric*	Numeric is the SQL server synonym for *decimal*	
Real (see Float)	*real*		
Smalldatetime (see Datetime)	*smalldatetime*	01-JAN-1900 to 06-JUN-2079	4 bytes
Smallint (see Integer)	*smallint*	Whole numbers from –32,768 to 32,767	2 bytes
Smallmoney (See Money)	*smallmoney*	For values that need accuracy to four decimal places	8 bytes
Sql_variant	*sql_variant*	For values of various SQL Server-supported data types. Cannot be used for values of text, ntext, timestamp, and sql_variant.	<= 900 bytes
Sysname	*sysname(n)*	Used for storing system object names	2 bytes per character
Text (See Image)			
Timestamp (used to monitor row activity)		A database value obtained from the @@DBTS function	
Tinyint	*tinyint*	Numbers from 0 to 255	1 byte
Varbinary (See Binary)	*varbinary(n)*	Bit patterns up to 255 bytes	What you use
Varchar (See character)	*varchar(n)*	up to 8,000 characters	1 byte per character actually used
Uniqueidentifier	*uniqueidentifier*	The 16-byte hexadecimal number indicating a globally unique identifier (GUID)	16 bytes

Table 2-1. *SQL Server 2000 Data Types* (continued)

Null

Data types can also hold the value NULL, which might seem confusing to you. While *null* is understood to be "nil" or "zero" or "no value" in some programming environments, SQL Server interprets the NULL value in a record to mean "unknown" or "missing." Also a blank space and zero are legal values in database records, so you need to be very careful about passing these as parameters.

Using NULL requires special discussion, and it will be covered in Chapters 19 and 20. Also, in Chapters 11 and 16, I discuss NULL along with instructions on how to create tables and data types that either take or refuse NULL values. For now, when you create a table interactively, keep this option checked. In other words, allow NULL values in your records until you fully understand the implications of NULL usage and have properly modeled your database. You can always alter the table at a later date, but allowing a NULL is a convenient way to "play" with records that have missing values.

There are many circumstances where it seems impossible to accept anything other than NULL. On the well-known online auction site eBay, for example, the registration asks for several items that could be unknown or missing, such as gender. In many sections they use the item "unknown" as a possible value.

System Tables

You will notice when you create a new *user* database that a collection of system tables is also created by SQL Server which is associated with the user database. These tables are used by SQL Server to store configuration and various system data, such as indexes, relating to the user databases and applications (do not confuse these with the master database tables, but they can be considered as extensions to the catalog). You will have little need to work with the system tables in your database; however, SQL Server does not preclude you from referencing them in your applications, especially through stored procedures, or using the data in them for some special reason. System tables are further discussed in Chapter 11.

I mentioned earlier that you might also notice tables that are prefixed with the pound or number sign, such as *#temptable.* These are SQL Server temporary tables, which are stored in the tempdb database. They are used for storing temporary information. The server usually drops them when a user disconnects or they are no longer needed.

There are two types of temporary tables, *local* and *global.* The local temporary tables are application or user specific, and they are thus only visible to the connecting user. Global temporary tables, prefixed with two number signs, *##temptable,* are visible to all connections and are usually referenced by SQL Server and system-wide tasks.

The Table Data Type

SQL Server 2000 supports a new special data type that represents a table. Such a data type is similar to a temporary table that can be used to hold a result set for later application. Indexes and constraints (discussed shortly) can be applied to this *table* data type, but they have to be declared in the CREATE TABLE statement. The table data type is also discussed in Chapters 16 and 19.

Views

Views are essentially virtual tables created with SQL code that can perform relational algebra on the data in a table or collection of tables.

The term virtual *is an ANSI SQL-92 term, but it is not a description I like (and I say so again later in this book). "Virtual" implies something that appears to be real but is not, such as virtual reality. "Views," on the other hand, are actual result sets, derived from base tables, and created using the SELECT statement, as demonstrated in Chapter 19.*

Views are very similar to Microsoft Access queries in that they are created using the query language and return data in tabular format. What makes a *view* a *view,* and not a *table,* is that the view's tabular structure is not stored in any database, nor is it persistent. Instead, a SELECT statement that retrieves the data for the view is stored in the database. In other words, *views* are for *viewing* only. Views are useful for a number of tasks:

- They can be used to hide rows in a table. In other words, a view might return only the collection of rows that pertain to a particular user or process.
- They can be used to hide columns in a table. A user, for example, can be restricted from viewing confidential information in the *customer* table, such as credit card information or credit status.
- They can be used in join constructions to collect columns from a number of tables into one object representing a single table.
- They can be used to perform operations on the data in tables, such as presenting the sum of all values in a specific column.

Creating a view is straightforward, although the SELECT statement of the entire view object can be as complex as a SELECT statement needs to be. Performance of views can also be enhanced using indexes on the views. The following code is an example of a simple view, and a simple SELECT statement. SELECT statements inside views can run to hundreds of lines of code.

```
CREATE VIEW inventory_view AS
SELECT item, quantity, value
FROM inventory_base
```

Views can also reference other views. In other words, you might return view "A" from the first CREATE statement and then create view "B" from the "A" view. The following code is such an example:

```
CREATE VIEW user_view AS
SELECT item, quantity
FROM inventory_view
```

Views are also a key feature used in SQL Server 2000's high availability initiative. Using UNION views, data is partitioned across a number of SQL Server databases or instances of SQL Server running on separate servers. Partitioned views are the key component of SQL Server's scalability (scale out) architecture. In terms of availability they provide a similar benefit, to the clustering of servers, without the possibility of shared hardware, such as the hard disk array, becoming the point of failure that crashes everything. The difference between clustering SQL Server and partitioned views is that all servers participating in the view are active. A cluster of SQL Servers allows only one server to be active. You will learn about data partitioning and partitioned views in Chapter 13.

Data in views can also be manipulated using INSERT, UPDATE, and DELETE statements. Updates are "cascaded" down to the base tables, including all member tables that are referenced by the view.

Later, in Chapter 19, I look into the finer points of handling views, especially with respect to performance, joins, unions, and so on. I will also discuss indexed views, which, as I told you in the previous chapter, force a view result set to be stored in the database until the base table has to be altered.

Indexes and Keys

SQL Server indexes can be associated with tables and views to speed up the retrieval of rows, and to speed up updates and deletes. Indexes are very important in SQL Server, especially for complex databases. That's because, like all relational engines, SQL Server must first find a row in a table before the data can be presented or manipulated. By referencing an index, you are thus helping SQL Server find the row quicker. Indexes arrange the rows in the internal structures of the table, according to a peculiar logic or sorting algorithm.

A *key*, on the other hand, does not directly influence sorting, searching, and retrieval. A key ensures that a row in a table is unique. The debate on uniqueness has been raging since mankind emerged from a hole in the ground in the middle of nowhere. You cannot be lax about uniqueness in your database. Ask yourself how confused you would feel if you woke one day to find an identical person living in the same world as you. The same reasoning applies to the rows in a table. It might not seem a problem at first to add a duplicate row to a table, but what do you do when you need to delete one of those cloned rows? Exactly which row do you delete? How sure are you that you are deleting the right one?

You can create a key in a table on one or more columns. When you create a key on more than one column, you are allowing a value in a column to be unique by combining it with a value in another column. In other words, the key protects the uniqueness of the row if the combination of values in the unique one combines to give a unique key. An example: red + spanner and red + hammer gives you two unique tools that have identical values for the color column. If the unique key were specified on color alone, you would have more than a slight glitch.

The recognized name for the unique key on your primary table (you could call it a root table) is known as the *primary key*. You can also call it the candidate key, especially when it involves more than one column.

If you break out or modularize your tables into several related tables, you will need to connect them (so as to preserve the record) by creating a key in the foreign tables. This "table-hopping" key is called the foreign key, which is essentially the tie that binds the rows in the foreign table to the rows in the primary table, thus making them one record. The primary key/foreign key relationship is illustrated in Figure 2-7.

You can only have one primary key in a table, signified with the little key icon in the table designer. When you create the key, SQL Server automatically creates a clustered index in association with it. In Chapter 19, I have included examples of how searching on the primary key index helps speed up location of records.

Tables without indexes make SQL Server work harder. My son's room is like a database table without an index (and certainly without a key). Everything is lying around in no particular stack or order. He can never find what he is looking for. If the room were sorted, he would be able to locate the things he needs (although he swears he can find things faster in the chaos). I often call his room a garbage *heap*. When you create a table or a view and do not impose any index on it, the rows are not stored according to any logic or system. Such a structure is also called a *heap* in SQL Server lingo.

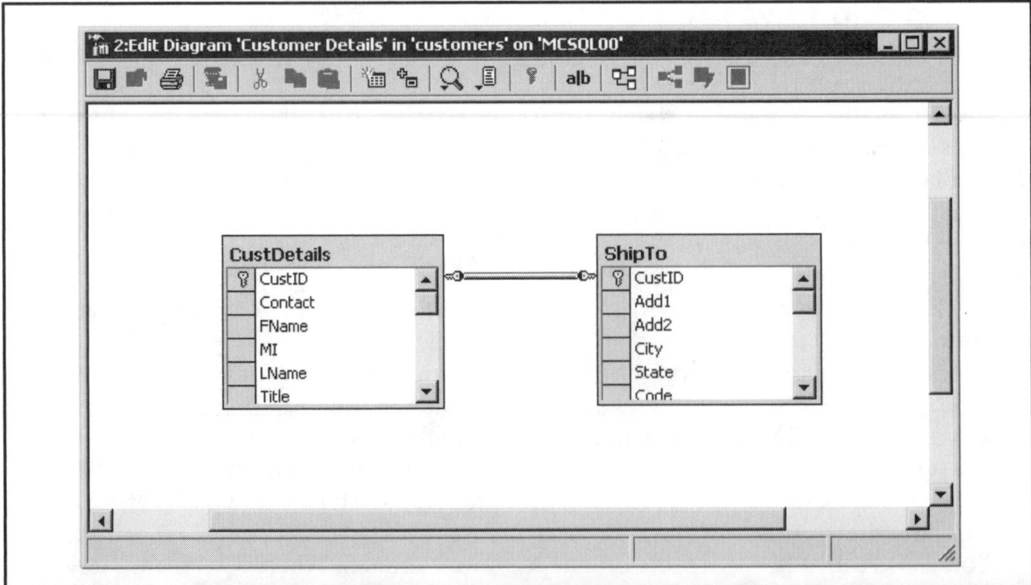

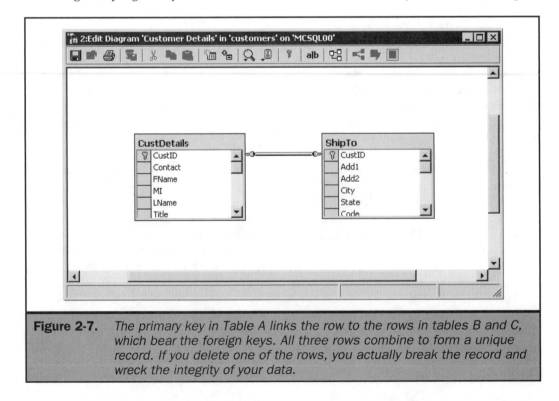

Figure 2-7. *The primary key in Table A links the row to the rows in tables B and C, which bear the foreign keys. All three rows combine to form a unique record. If you delete one of the rows, you actually break the record and wreck the integrity of your data.*

Indexed keys can also be created when you define an index from the combinations of one or more columns in a table or view. Indexes and keys are persistent; that is, they are also objects and properties that are stored in a database. SQL Server thus maintains the sort order of rows—even when they are not being accessed. When you create an index, you can also specify that the data be stored in ascending or descending order.

Note *SQL Server 2000 keys have a 900-byte limit that caps the maximum size on an index key. SQL Server will permit the creation of an index key larger than the limit, but it will process the key with a warning or failure notice. Programmatic handling of indexes and key attributes is discussed at length in Chapter 11.*

Indexes can be created interactively using Enterprise Manager, as illustrated in Figure 2-8, or in T-SQL code using the CREATE INDEX statement (see Chapter 11 for creating indexes interactively).

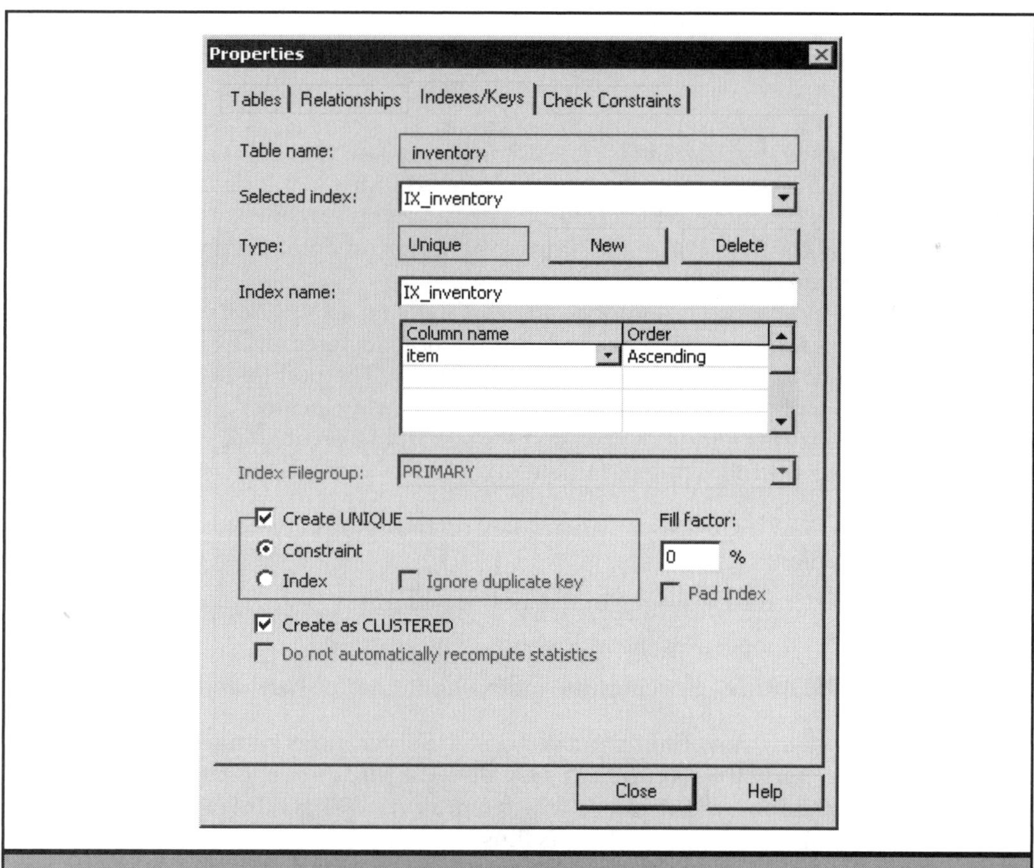

Figure 2-8. *Creating an index using Enterprise Manager*

The creation and management of indexes is usually the responsibility of the DBA, so it will pay big dividends to become fully conversant in this subject.

An index can also be created, as a substatement, inside the CREATE TABLE statement. (This is further discussed in Chapter 11, which discusses Data Definition Language.) The CREATE TABLE statement is illustrated as follows:

```
CREATE TABLE inventory
(item_id int PRIMARY KEY CLUSTERED)
```

You can create additional indexes for a table, targeted at certain columns. Multiple indexes require more resources, however, so you need to be conservative and limit new indexes to columns you know are frequently searched on. In other words, no two rows can have identical values for the index key. You can also specify a nonunique index, and that means you can have duplicate values for a particular indexed column in your table.

Another important attribute of the indexing architecture is that SQL Server indexes can be either *clustered* or *nonclustered.* The application of the two types of index is described as follows:

Clustered indexes store data in a table according to key values. The rows in the table are sorted in the order specified by the clustered index key. You can only create one clustered index per table, which is logical because you can only sort the rows according to one algorithm. When you impose an index on data, the data is *sorted,* which is the opposite of a *heap.*

Nonclustered indexes do not impose any sort logic on a collection of rows in a table, and the rows are essentially heaped. But the nonclustered index does maintain a pointer to rows in the table, which is in essence the key. The pointer starts out with the lowest row in the table. This pointer is also known as a row locator.

So, when you create an index you can specify that it be created according to certain requirements using the following parameters:

- PRIMARY KEY   Creates a primary key on the column or columns in the primary table
- UNIQUE   Creates a unique index, not necessarily a key
- CLUSTERED   Specifies the index should be clustered
- NONCLUSTERED   Specifies the index should not be clustered

You can also control how tightly packed a SQL Server index should be when you create one. The property that controls this is called the *fill factor,* and the higher the fill factor, the smaller the size of the index, which conserves disk reading energy. The *fill factor* default is usually 0 percent, which is illustrated in Figure 2-8. The more active a table (for instance, the more aggressive delete and insert activity it has), the lower should be the fill factor you set. This leaves space in the index for future keys.

Often complex queries that return a large number of rows in a view would benefit from indexing. Examples are views that are returned from complex aggregation routines and complex joins. Performance is greatly improved by defining indexes on such views. All indexes on views are dropped as soon as the views are dropped. For more information on placing indexes on views, see Chapter 19.

Large and complex databases and applications will require you to spend more effort designing adequate indexed solutions. An Index Tuning Wizard is included with Enterprise Manager and SQL Query Analyzer. This wizard is discussed in detail in Chapter 11.

Data Integrity Mechanisms

There are two classes of data integrity definitions that can ensure the "plausibility" of the data entered into SQL Server 2000 tables. (For a blow-by-blow account of Integrity in SQL Server, see Chapter 17.)

First you have data integrity definitions, which act upon the data values that are placed in the records stored within each column. These integrity definitions ensure that the data is of the right type, that they follow the value declarations encompassed in the domains of each data type, and that the data conforms to your own business or database rules and constraints. Data integrity definitions are thus local to an individual table and its records.

Second you have referential integrity definitions that ensure that the relationships between tables are sound. *Referential integrity* ensures that data in a table refers only to data that actually exists in other tables. In other words, if you are going to refer to rows in other tables, you need to be certain that those rows exist. Referential integrity, and data integrity, is discussed at length in Chapter 17.

SQL Server provides four formal types of integrity machinery as follows:

- Constraints
- Rules
- Defaults
- Triggers

Constraints Constraints are the mechanism of choice for ensuring data integrity. Constraints are essentially a system of rules that are applied to values that are inserted into a column. A constraint can be defined over the table or the column, or both. The column constraint applies only to the column, while the table constraint is declared independently of the column constraint and can encompass more than one column. This subject is further described in Chapter 17.

SQL Server 2000 supports five classes of constraints:

- NOT NULL
- CHECK

- UNIQUE
- PRIMARY KEY
- FOREIGN KEY

NOT NULL is the simplest constraint to implement; it prevents a column from accepting a NULL value. (As discussed earlier, NULL means that the record is deemed to be unknown or missing.)

A *CHECK* constraint enforces domain integrity by limiting what values can be inserted into the record. The CHECK evaluates a Boolean value; it determines if the value you are trying to insert meets the constraint (TRUE) or does not meet the constraint (FALSE). If a value "checks" out to be TRUE, it is rejected and cannot be applied to the row. Each column in a table can be protected with multiple CHECK constraints.

You can create CHECK constraints with the services of Enterprise Manager (see Chapter 7). You can also specify a CHECK constraint in your T-SQL DDL code when you create a table. The following code is an example of a CHECK constraint (quantity) created in the T-SQL CREATE TABLE statement:

```
CREATE TABLE inventory
(item char(120), quantity int PRIMARY KEY, (quantity > 100))
```

A *UNIQUE* constraint enforces the uniqueness of the values in a column or it can be used to check that no two rows are identical. As mentioned earlier, you can use a unique index to enforce uniqueness. However, the UNIQUE constraint is preferred, first; all you want to do is enforce uniqueness, because it requires a lot fewer resources than a primary key index. Indexes tax the system more than constraints do because constraints evaluate when the column value is referenced, while indexes need to be updated every time you update the table.

The *PRIMARY KEY* constraint identifies the column with the values that uniquely identify the row in a table.

The *FOREIGN KEY* constraint applies to the relationship between tables and thus supports referential integrity. The integrity rule here ensures that the *candidate key* in the primary table refers to the *foreign key* in another table. This constraint prevents the problem of a row with a foreign key that has no corresponding candidate keys in the remote table.

The foreign key rule also ensures that you cannot delete a row that is linked to a foreign key (which would break the record). When you try to delete the row, the ON DELETE or ON UPDATE actions can trigger one of two predefined events:

- NO ACTION This will specify that the delete operation fails with an error.
- CASCADE This will specify that the rows with the foreign keys that are related to the candidate keys are also deleted. This action is known as a *cascading delete.*

The ON UPDATE clause is used extensively to validate input; it is further discussed in Chapter 18.

Rules Rules are similar to constraints and are the legacy integrity features of SQL Server. They have been kept in the product for compatibility with legacy code. CHECK constraints are more powerful than rules, and you should use CHECK constraints in all new code. (When you have designed a complex database with many tables, you'll thank heaven, or the SQL Server development team, for features such as cascading deletes.)

Rules are created externally to the CREATE TABLE statement and are thus objects that are bound to the column. This means that you can only have one rule bound to a column. Multiple CHECK constraints, on the other hand, can be applied to a column.

Rules will most likely become dearly departed by the next major release of SQL Server in 2002/2003. It will pay you to end your nostalgia and change to the newer constraints as soon as possible.

Defaults Defaults are a form of "failsafe" value applied to a column so that no NULLs make it into the row. In other words, if your code creates a row and your user does not apply a certain value to a column, the default value is applied instead. Defaults can be generated out of the following constants:

- A constant value; for example, the value "0" for the column *quantity*
- A built-in or user-defined function that generates the value
- A mathematical expression that generates a value

Defaults are typically created using the DEFAULT keyword in the CREATE TABLE statement. They can also be applied using the system stored procedure sp_bindefault.

Triggers Triggers are a valuable integrity tool that can be used alone or in conjunction with the integrity features we have just discussed. Triggers fire automatically when defined over UPDATE, INSERT, and DELETE statements issued in certain areas of your code, against target tables and views. A trigger is similar in purpose and function to an event that fires in software components, such as the *OnClick* events found in all software controls. Trigger creation is demonstrated in Chapter 18.

A trigger is defined with the FOR UPDATE, FOR INSERT, and FOR DELETE clauses to point the trigger at the correct actions. Triggers can be used in many different scenarios. They can be used in a similar fashion to IF…THEN…ELSE logic in most development languages. For example, you can define a trigger when the *quantity* value of a certain item in the *inventory* table reaches a certain level. You can then execute a number of routines that request replenishment or alert users or set applicable wheels in motion.

Triggers are essentially stored procedures that also contain T-SQL statements. They can also be used to return a result set, or a dialog box when SELECT or COUNT statements are used within the trigger code. For example, let's say your order taker is about to make a sale that debits 50 units of X *items* to the *inventory* table. If there are fewer than 50 units of X, the trigger could query *inventory* and show the order taker just how many units he or she can debit from the table.

The FOR clause is used to dictate when the trigger fires. Triggers can be fired after your T-SQL code has executed or instead of the triggering action. (As mentioned in Chapter 1, the INSTEAD OF trigger is a new feature of SQL Server 2000 and was not available to earlier versions.) Both AFTER and INSTEAD OF triggers are discussed in more detail in Chapter 17.

Stored Procedures

A stored procedure is to SQL Server what a function call in a dynamic linked library (DLL) is to an application (although the new user-defined functions are more like the functions of standard programming languages). It allows you to implement a collection of routines that can be accessed by any number of applications. Stored procedures are some of the most powerful features in all client/server database systems and can be used to enforce application logic and administer business or enterprise rules to all applications. Stored procedures are compiled T-SQL statements that return data in one of four ways:

- They can provide parameters that can return data, such as an integer or a character, a cursor variable, and an error message.
- The can provide return codes (integers).
- The can provide result sets that are created from SELECT statements embedded in the stored procedure.
- They can reference external cursors (result sets) and stored procedures.

(Stored procedures are compiled into so-called execution plans, which will be covered in the next chapter.) You, the SQL Server developer, create stored procedures that can then be called from any application. You can also create stored procedures for applications written by other parties. Stored procedures do not necessarily have to return data to the user either. They are executed on the server and can thus comprise logic that performs functionality without the knowledge or intervention of the user or referencing application. SQL Server is itself maintained by a collection of system stored procedures that cannot be accessed by users. Using stored procedures exclusively in certain applications means that absolutely all processing is performed on the server.

Your applications can execute stored procedures by merely issuing EXECUTE, EXEC, or CALL (ODBC) statements in the code. This is a similar practice to linking in or loading a DLL and issuing a call to a function. The difference is that a call to a function in a DLL results in the function being processed in the processing space of the calling application. All applications that have access to the DLL can call the function or procedure in the DLL.

Stored procedures are also very useful for applications that use SQL Server as a data storehouse. You would use them, for example, with the administrative software of a computer telephony application or an Internet application to perform automated system administration, without requiring manual intervention or human input in any way.

Your applications can also build stored procedures on the fly to meet certain requirements. These stored procedures can then be saved or stored in the tempdb. If they are stored in tempdb, they are later dropped when the application terminates or the user disconnects. If, however, your application needs frequent use of the stored procedure, it would be better to create the stored procedure once and then maintain it in the system for later use. We will discuss stored procedures at length in Chapter 18.

User-Defined Data Types

User-defined data types are made possible by extending the existing SQL Server 2000 base types with custom names and formats. To create a user-defined data type, you would call the stored procedure sp_addtype. The example in the following code creates a user-defined data type, *timeofdeath,* extended from the base data type datetime.

```
EXEC sp_addtype timeofdeath, datetime, 'NULL'
```

In this emergency room database, the user-defined timeofdeath data type records the time of death of patients. It can take values of NULL in the event the time of death is not recorded or the subject arrived DOA. User-defined data types are discussed further in Chapter 16.

User-Defined Functions

SQL Server supports user-defined functions. These functions are built using T-SQL code, specifically the CREATE FUNCTION statement. The functions are used to return a value or a result code. They can return values as single scalars, such as integers, characters, and decimals. User-defined functions are useful for many application scenarios and can be used extensively in analytical and statistical applications.

SQL Server 2000 UDFs can also return the *table* data type. For example, a function can declare the internal table variable, insert rows into the table, and then return the table as the return value. You can also use a class of functions known as *in-line* functions that can perform relational algebra on your tables, using the SELECT statement, and returning the *table* variable.

User-defined functions can contain complex code comprising multiple SELECT statements. They are thus an ideal mechanism for returning tables where the complexity of the code precludes the generation of a view. Likewise, the user-defined function can also replace a stored procedure.

Properties

The concept of user-defined properties has been introduced to SQL Server 2000. These properties are known as *extended properties* and can be applied to all database objects. The architecture is thus OO in design (properties can publish information) and allows the database designer or developer to extend the collection of properties on database objects. The properties are essentially placeholders for information that can be used by applications.

The values of an extended property are of the sql_variant data type and can hold up to 7,500 bytes of data. The extended properties are created, managed, and deleted by the stored procedures sp_addextendedproperty, sp_updatextendedproperty, and sp_dropextendedproperty. The system function, fn_listextendedproperty, lets you read the value of an extended property.

Full-Text Indexes

SQL Server 2000 can create full-text indexes that are used for sophisticated searching of character string data. The full-text index stores information about certain words and their locations within their columns. This will allow you to create full-text queries and return either character string data or complete documents. You can search for instances of individual words or combinations of words.

The indexes are stored in catalogs, and each database you create can contain one or more full-text catalogs. The actual catalog and the indexes are not, however, stored in the database. They are stored externally as files and managed by the Microsoft Search service (see Chapter 12). Also, a full-text index can only be defined on a base table and not on the virtual objects, such as views and temporary tables.

The Physical Database Architecture

SQL Server 2000's physical architecture, its internal level, is highly complex. The architecture was extensively overhauled in Version 7.0, and this version builds on those foundations. Earlier versions of SQL Server were very different on the inside, so if you are here from Version 6.5, and bypassed Version 7.0 on the way over, you need to listen up.

Pages and Extents

Pages and *extents* are to SQL Server what *cells* and *combs* are to a beehive. *Pages* contain the *rows,* which contain the data. Collections of pages make up *extents.* Extent collections are essentially what makes up your database. This next section explores pages and extents in more detail.

Pages

Looking at the internal level, we find that the fundamental base data storage object is the *page*. Each page is only 8KB in size, which means that a SQL Server 2000 database can store 128 pages in a megabyte.

Pages are managed and controlled in a similar fashion to other Windows 2000 objects. First, the page is identified with a globally unique identifier or object ID. Second, each page contains a 96-byte header that is used to store pertinent information about the page, including its type, available space, and so on. Table 2-2 lists the six types of pages that are used by the SQL Server 2000 database:

Data pages store all the data in the rows except, as indicated, large amounts of data for the types text, ntext, and image. The latter types are large extents of character and binary information, which are stored in separate pages (more about the large object data types later).

Note *The capability to store small amounts of text, ntext, and image data in rows is a new feature of SQL Server 2000.*

The layout of a data page is illustrated in Figure 2-9, which illustrates that the data is laid out serially on the pages in rows. The rows start from the top of the page, immediately after the header. Each page contains a region that stores the row offsets for the data pages. These row offsets are stored at the end of the data pages. The row

Page Type	Contents
Data	Rows of data except for the large objects of data types text, ntext, and image
Index	Index entries
Index Allocation Map (IAM)	Information about the extents used by a table or index
Global Allocation Map (GAM)	Information about allocated extents
Page Free Space	Information about free space on pages
Text/Image	Storage for text, ntext, and image data

Table 2-2. *The Page Types Used by SQL Server 2000*

offsets contain one entry for each row on the page. The row offsets also indicate how far the first byte of the row is from the start of the page. The row offsets are started at the end of the page—in other words, the first row offset is the last offset, stored at the end of the page. Each row on a page can hold up to 8,060 bytes of data. And the rows cannot span to other pages.

Extents

Extents are used to allocate space to tables and indexes. Each extent contains up to eight contiguous pages, which means that each extent is 64KB in size. The database can thus maintain 16 extents per available MB of storage space.

There are two types of extents in SQL Server 2000, *uniform extents* and *mixed extents*. Uniform extents are the property or ownership of a single object. In other words, the object that owns the uniform extent also owns all eight pages in the extent. The mixed extent can be shared by up to eight objects. Each object is allocated a page. The object retains ownership of the page until its data requirement exceeds the limits of the page, after which it is assigned to a uniform extent.

Database Files and Filegroups

As discussed earlier, SQL Server databases are made up of a collection of three files: the primary data files, the secondary data files, and the log files. The data pages described

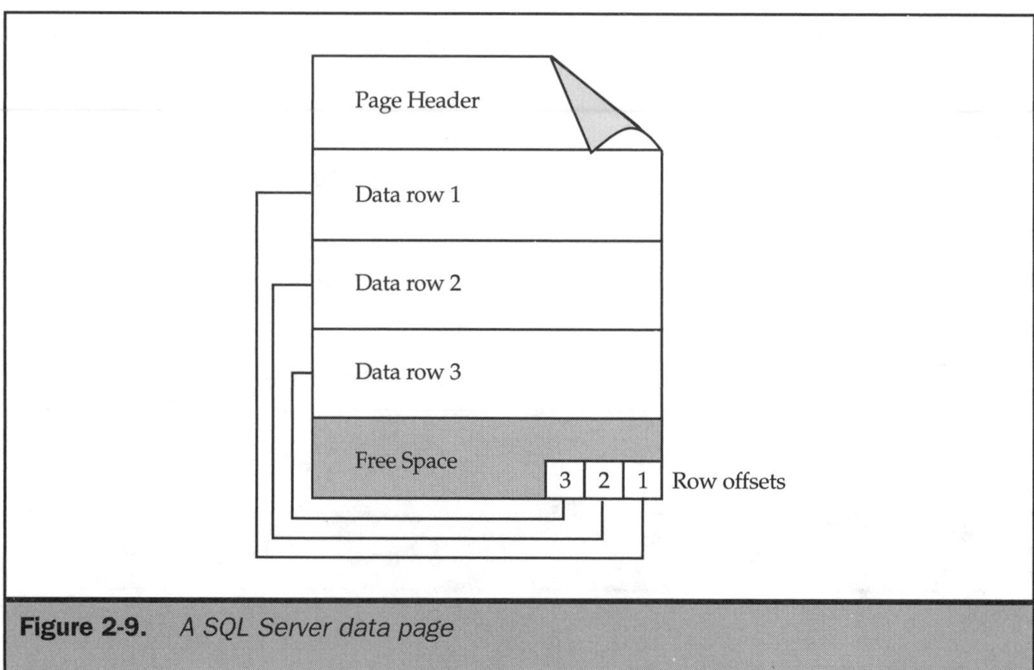

Figure 2-9. *A SQL Server data page*

previously are stored in these database files. Transaction logs are of course stored in the log files.

SQL Server gives these files the *.mdf*, *.ndf*, and *.ldf* extensions respectively but does not enforce these extensions for its own functionality. It is not recommended that you change them, however, especially if your backup mechanisms and scripts are associated with these file extensions.

When you create database files, either interactively with Enterprise Manager or in T-SQL code, you can specify that the database files grow and shrink automatically (autoshrink). You need to specify a growth increment/decrement by which the file will grow or shrink as needed. This is illustrated in Figure 2-10. The file can also be allowed to grow until it has used all the space available to it on the system. You can also specify a maximum size for a database file.

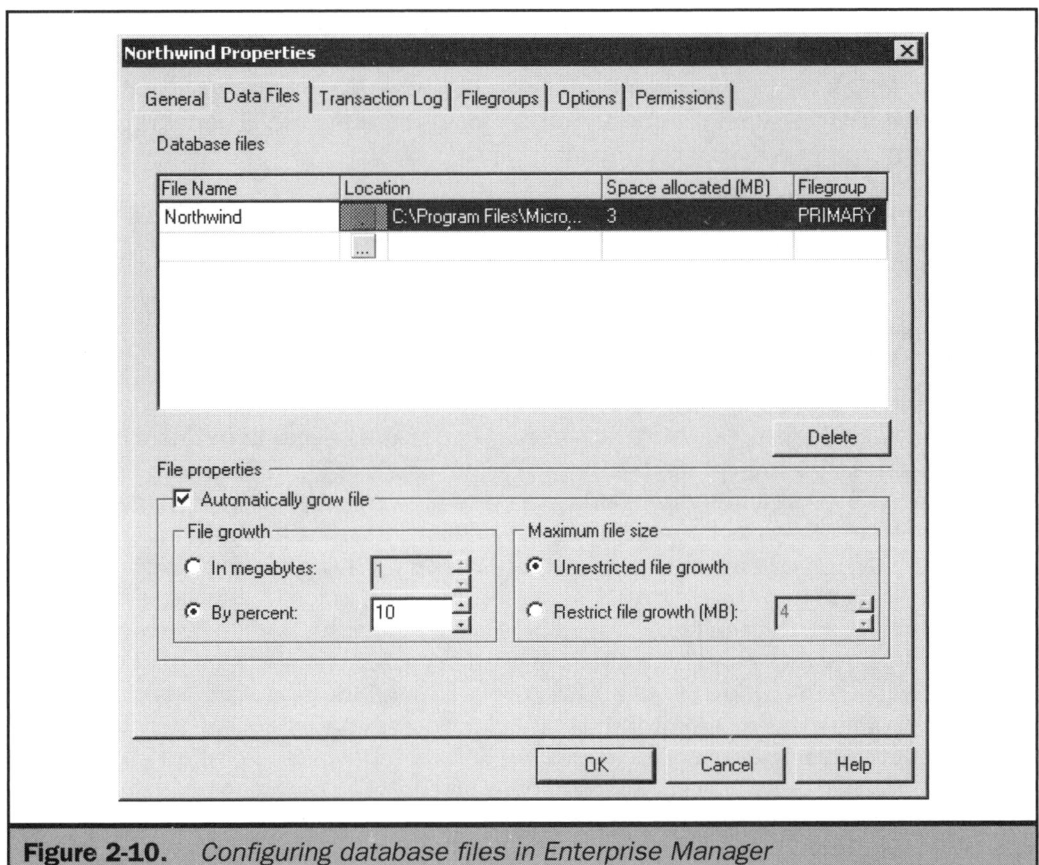

Figure 2-10. *Configuring database files in Enterprise Manager*

Filegroups *Filegroups* are a useful management feature in SQL Server that let you assign database files to a group object. You can improve system performance by collecting files into groups and placing them onto specific disk drives and storage arrays. You can create filegroups for each disk drive and then assign the tables; indexes; or text, ntext, and image data to these filegroups.

Log files cannot be part of a filegroup because they are maintained separately from data files. Also, you cannot assign files to more than one group. The following is a list of the three types of filegroups:

- **Primary** The primary filegroup contains primary data. The system or built-in files are gathered up into the primary group.
- **User-defined** The user-defined files groups can be created in T-SQL code using the FILEGROUP keyword in CREATE DATABASE and ALTER DATABASE statements.
- **Default** The default filegroup is where all the files that have not been assigned to either primary or user-defined groups are kept. If you create a database and do not specify a group for it, it will automatically be assigned to the default group. Members of the db_owner fixed database role can manually move a file between groups. If you do not define a default group, the primary group assumes the role of default.

Filegroups are not an essential element in SQL Server 2000, but they can greatly ease the administrative burden. For example, you can create a backup regimen that backs up certain files or filegroups, instead of backing up the entire database. We will return to the filegroups in Chapter 11. Figure 2-11 illustrates working with filegroups interactively using Enterprise Manager.

Space Allocation and Reuse

SQL Server's database architecture has been designed to respond to frequent changes in the size and disposition of its databases. The net result of the wizardry in its internal mechanisms is a faster and more responsive system. This is especially important when you are working with very large databases (VLDBs), critical online transaction processing (OLTP) systems, or a large number of users. What goes on at the lower levels is not something a user can see (only feel), but both database developers and DBAs alike can benefit from knowledge of the architecture and how it operates.

At work under the "hood" is a data usage and space tracking system that appears to be relatively simple, which is its beauty. Coupled with the page-extent architecture, the system is able to easily monitor database allocation and space occupancy with little overhead. On close inspection of the pages, we find that the space allocation information is confined to only a few pages, which are densely packed. This means that you need less physical memory to hold the free space information, which translates into less use of virtual memory and thus less hard disk reads.

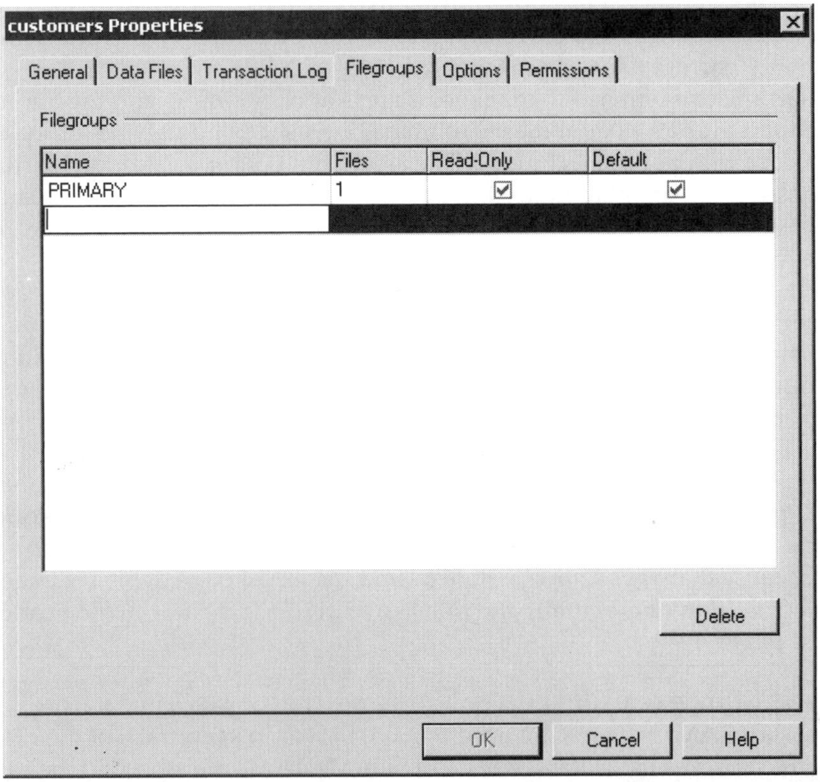

Figure 2-11. *Configuring filegroups in Enterprise Manager*

I alluded earlier to several types of allocation maps used by SQL Server to store the allocation of extents. Two are key to the recording of the extent allocations. These are the Global Allocation Maps (GAMs) and the Shared Global Allocation Maps (SGAMs), which are derived from the GAM bitmap.

The GAM records information that describes what extents have been allocated. Each GAM covers a whopping 64,000 extents, which translates into 4GB of data. The GAM, a bitmap, provides one bit for each extent it covers. If a bit in the map is set to 0, it means that the extent related to the bit is being used. If the bit is set to 1, it means the extent is free.

The SGAM bitmaps provide information about which extents are being used as mixed extents. The reverse order of the bits is applied in the SGAM bitmap. If the GAM bit is set to 1, then the SGAM bit is set to 0. If the SGAM bit is 0, it means the extent is either free or not in use as a uniform or full mixed extent. In other words, it could be a mixed extent whose pages are currently in use. Table 2-3 further illustrates the bitmap information for current use of an extent:

Microsoft's use of bitmaps to manage usage is at once simple and ingenious because it allows for an elegant means of managing usage of databases using a tried and tested bitmapping technique. The algorithm is simple, and thus virtually bulletproof. All the server is required to do is search the bitmaps for free extents and then change the state of the GAM bit and its alter ego, the SGAM bit. To free an extent, SQL Server ensures the GAM bit is set to 1 and the SGAM bit is set to 0.

Another use of bitmaps is demonstrated with the Page Free Space (PFS) pages that record whether an individual page has been allocated and how much free space is in the page. The bitmap records whether the page is empty, up to 50 percent full, up to 80 percent full, up to 95 percent full, or between 96 and 100 percent full. SQL Server uses this information when it needs to find free space for a row, or when it has to allocate a new page.

Closer inspection is required to fully appreciate the architecture at work here. Figure 2-12 provides a conceptual view of the data file and the order and sequence of pages in the data file. The sequence is not accidental. It allows SQL Server to search the data files because it always knows where to find the GAM page, which is page 2 in a zero-based collection (it is actually the third page in the data file; the file header at page 0 is the first page).

Space Used by Indexes Indexes can consume a ton of space in databases. Index Allocation Map (IAM) bitmaps are used by SQL Server to keep track of the extents in databases that indexes use. Like GAMs and SGAMs, IAMs are stored in the respective databases that contain the objects in question. These IAM pages are allocated as needed and are stored at random in the file. SQL Server uses IAM pages to allocate extents to objects in the same fashion it allocates pages and extents to table data.

State of Extent	GAM Bit State	SGAM Bit State
Free, or not in use	1	0
Uniform extent, or a full mixed extent	0	0
Mixed extent with free pages	0	1

Table 2-3. *The bit states for reporting the current state of an extent*

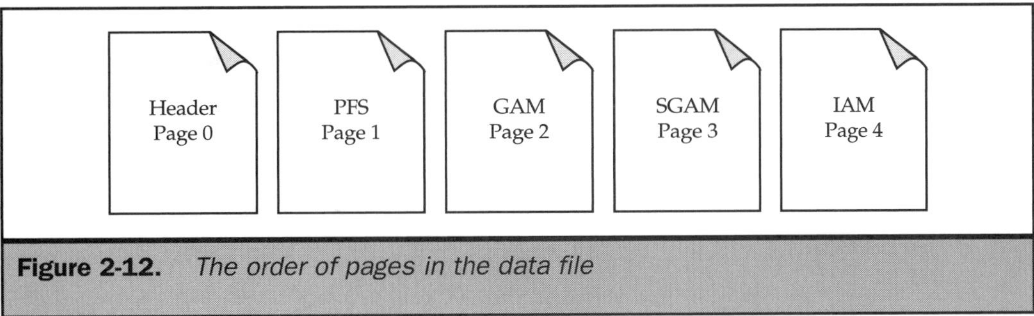

Figure 2-12. *The order of pages in the data file*

How Tables and Indexes Are Organized in SQL Server

The SQL Server table pages we described earlier are organized according to a system of linked or unlinked lists. When a clustered index is defined for a table or a view, the data rows are stored in the pages in the order based on the clustered index key. The data pages are linked by a doubly linked list, and the index is implemented as a B-tree index structure that provides a fast retrieval mechanism based on the clustered index key.

Data rows that are not stored in any order are called heaped tables, and do not require their data pages to be sorted in any order either. And the data pages are not linked in a linked list. Rows in heaped tables are found by scanning the IAM pages that manage the space allocated to a heap. SQL Server essentially scans the IAMs serially to find the extents holding pages for heap data. The table scan on a heap takes place as follows:

1. SQL Server reads the first IAM in the filegroup and scans all extents defined by the IAM.
2. SQL Server repeats the process for each IAM in the file.
3. SQL Server repeats the preceding steps for every file in the database or filegroup until the last IAM for the heap has been processed.

A single instance of SQL Server can support up to 249 nonclustered indexes on each table or indexed view. Nonclustered indexes also have a B-tree index structure similar to the one established for clustered indexes. However, nonclustered indexes have no control over the order of the data rows. In other words, the only time that data pages are sorted according to a system or order is when clustered indexes are established for the tables.

Every table, index, and indexed view is represented by a row inserted in the sysindexes table in its respective database. The row is uniquely identified by the combination of the object identifier (id) column and the index identifier (indid), which is illustrated in Figure 2-13. The allocation of the tables, indexes, and indexed views is managed by a chain of IAM pages. A FirstIAM column in sysindexes points to the first

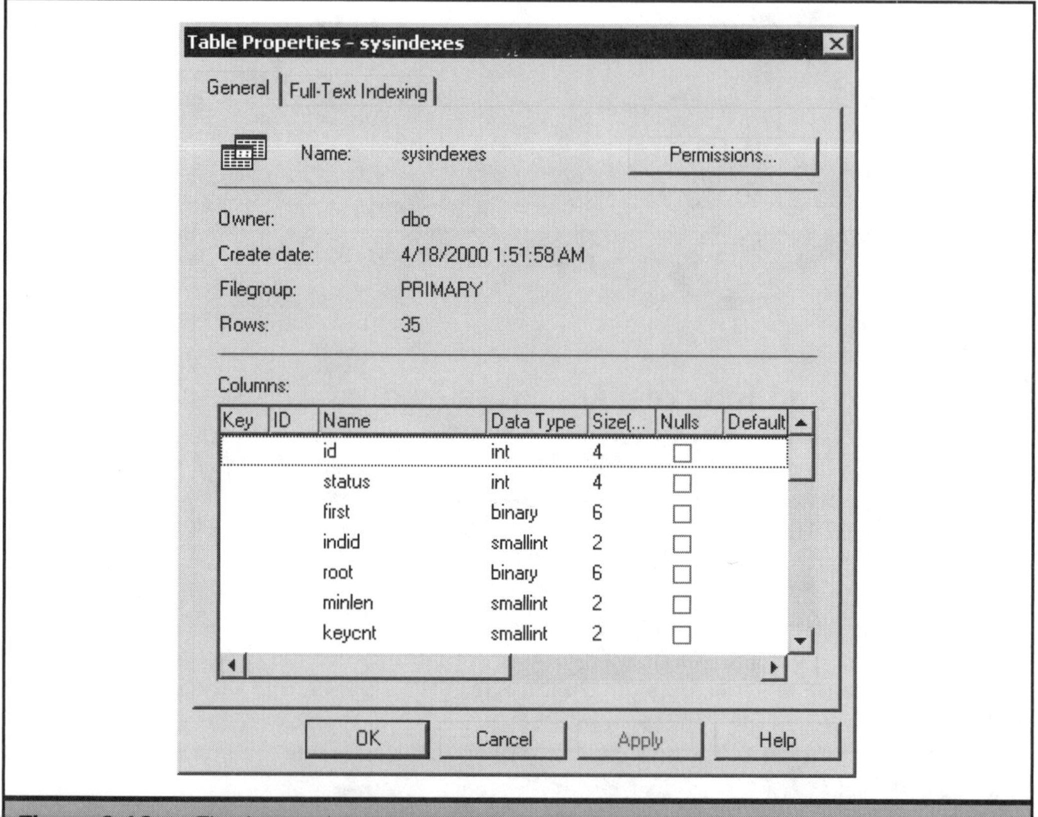

Figure 2-13. *The internal structure of the sysindexes table in Enterprise Manager*

IAM page in the chain of IAM pages managing the space allocated to the table, indexed view, or index.

Heaps are also allocated rows in the sysindexes table but have an index identifier of 0. When dealing with a heap, SQL Server uses the IAM pages to find the heap table pages in the data page collection because they are not linked.

Clustered indexes, tables, and views each have a representative row in sysindexes that has an index identifier or *indid* of 1. The *root* column points to the top of the clustered index B-tree to allow the server to use the index B-tree to locate data pages.

Nonclustered indexes, tables, and views also have rows in sysindexes. The values, however, of the indid range from 2–250. The root column thus points to the top of the nonclustered B-tree.

Tables that also have a text, ntext, or image column also have rows in sysindexes with an indid of 255. The FirstIAM column points to the chain of IAM pages that manage the text, ntext, and image pages.

Transaction Logs

Transaction logs can be studied as components at both the conceptual and internal levels of the database; from a physical perspective as well as a logical one. The subject is important enough to warrant introduction here under its own heading. Transaction logs are the footprints of SQL Server transactions. Not only can they trace transaction activity, but also they provide a near-perfect mechanism for recovery and redundancy of the data stored in tables. The transaction logs are capable of the following functions:

- They can be used to recover individual transactions. These are known as *rollbacks* in database server parlance. If a transaction's data is determined to be "questionable," the transaction that led to the insertion of the questionable data can be rolled back. The questionable data is removed from the database. The ROLLBACK statement is akin to the instant replay you see on television or in films.
- They can be used to recover incomplete transactions. Incomplete transactions may occur when SQL Server crashes in the middle of a transaction. The incomplete transaction is recovered when SQL Server restarts. When SQL Server restarts, it runs a recovery of each database. If certain transactions are found not to have completed (but they are sound in the log), they are rolled forward. At the same time, any transactions found to have caused questionable data are rolled back.
- They can be used to bring a database current from the last full or differential backup to the last transaction in the transaction log. It may, for example, happen that tables are damaged and you will need to restore a database from the last backup. The transaction log closes the "gap" between the last backup and the last transaction in the log. Any transactions that are not in the restored database are rolled forward and installed to the database.

The following list describes some of the operations stored in the transaction logs:

- The start and end of every transaction
- All INSERT, UPDATE, and DELETE transactions, including any transaction performed by system processes
- All extent allocations and deallocations
- The creation or termination of tables and indexes

Transaction Log Architecture

SQL Server transaction logs use a write-ahead log mechanism. This means that SQL Server ensures that no data updates are written to disk until they have been written to the log. The log record must in fact be written to disk before the data pages in the buffer are written to disk. In other words, SQL Server can ensure that a dirty page is not flushed before the log record associated with the dirty page is flushed (see the section "How Data Is Saved" in Chapter 4).

Bulk insert and copy operations can cause a transaction log to fill up quickly. When you need to insert huge amounts of data for which you don't need transaction logs, nonlogged operations are supported. This is discussed in Chapters 9, 11, and 12.

Transaction logs are not tables but exist as separate files or collections of files in the database. The layout or structure of the data pages has no bearing on the log files. The log cache is also managed separately from the data cache. The log cache is, however, controlled by the database engine, but the code that is executed is not related to any data page functionality.

Log files are implemented over several files as needed. Like databases, they can be configured to "autogrow" as needed by the logging engine. This prevents you from running out of space in the transaction log (although truncation plays an important part here too). However, you will still need to make sure you do not run out of hard disk space. In Chapter 11, I will show you how to work with the Windows 2000 Disk Quota functions to assist with the management of SQL Server files such as transaction logs. Chapter 11 also looks at the truncation of transaction logs, which is an important subject for DBAs, because if stale log records are not deleted from the transaction log, your log files will just keep growing until your server runs out of hard disk space.

I felt the finer points of transaction logs and their management would be better off presented in Chapter 9 on disaster recovery and Chapter 11 on database management.

Uncovering More About SQL Server

This chapter was a kick-start to SQL Server 2000's database architecture. We discussed the structure of the databases, the system tables collection, the user tables, the catalog or schema of your database, integrity mechanisms, stored procedures, and so on. We also delved, albeit very briskly, into data types; indexes and keys; and the other database objects such as triggers and stored procedures, rules, user-defined functions, and properties.

We could have continued for another few hundred pages, but you know there is a belief that the closer you look at a subject the harder it is to understand. The next two chapters will respectively delve into the client/server architecture and low-level workings of the DBMS (how data is saved and so on). However, everything introduced in this chapter will be further expanded on throughout the book, especially by example.

Chapter 3

SQL Server 2000 Client/Server Architecture

Let's take a break now from database architecture and look holistically at the roles played by the client and server components of SQL Server 2000. For the most part, we will be studying the physical implementation of a client/server (C/S) system, but we also need to learn about the SQL Server client or application perspective and the conceptual models that have been implemented by the Microsoft SQL Server 2000 development team.

Chapter 1 discusses the differences between a desktop—file/server—database application and a C/S database management system, admittedly in very broad terms. If you are new to the C/S DBMS world, the first section in this chapter builds on what you learned in Chapter 1. And if you are not a "newbie," you can skip the first part of this chapter. However, if you are visiting from other RDBMS planets, you would be doing yourself a great service by reading the first part as well. The remainder of the chapter investigates the SQL Server 2000 C/S architecture in particular.

What Is a C/S DBMS?

Imagine for a moment you are pulling up for a shake and a burger at the local roadhouse—you know, the ones that make those great chocolate malt milkshakes, grilled chicken and mayonnaise sandwiches, footlongs with mustard.... My favorite is chicken-in-a-basket with chips and a huge pickle. Every week, my mom used to take my sister and me to one, which was called the Doll House.

I remember that as cars drove into the lanes, the "waiters" would pour out from the door of the Doll House and come running to the cars to take our orders. We had to flash our lights (no horn-tooting was allowed) to get the attention of the waiter. He or she would take the order from us and then run back to the Doll House to place it. There were cars parked all around the Doll House, 360 degrees. We would pick our meals from a huge menu just above the order-placing window of the Doll House.

When the meals were ready, the waiter would bring the food to the car and balance a metal tray on the driver's side window. What a pleasure: drive up with your car and get the ultimate in service. I'll take a 1960s-style roadhouse over a junk food drive-through any day.

I was not thinking about C/S technology in those days . . . a boy of seven was thinking about his hamster, his friends, and looking for frogs in the lake. But my mother's 1960s Doll House is the best metaphor I can concoct to describe SQL Server's C/S architecture almost 35 years later. No matter how many cars pulled up at the Doll House, they always seemed to have enough waiters, order takers, chefs, food, and cashiers to keep the Doll House serving clients all the time. The Doll House was a 24 × 7 operation.

SQL Server 2000 works according to the same service principles the Doll House did in the 1960s (and still does); that is, almost all the data processing required by the client is performed on the server (at least that's how you need to model your application). SQL Server has been built to international standards and specifications for a C/S database server. There is nothing more complex in its operational philosophy than the business model that has kept the Doll House in business for half a century.

On close inspection of SQL Server, you expect to find highly sophisticated mechanisms at work that require scores of operator manuals to decipher, but all that's there is a straightforward C/S architecture, and this is what makes it both simple and yet sophisticated and powerful at the same time. But don't get me wrong on this; I am not saying that SQL Server is a simple product, I am saying that its C/S processes have been implemented according to standard software development practices and developed against an open and robust operating system architecture and its respective APIs.

You will also find, the more you get to know the product, that all of its architecture has been built to integrate or interface with operating system services that are also used by other Microsoft products. For example, it hooks into the very same Win32 API services that products like Exchange 2000, WINS 2000, and IIS use. If you "understand" Windows, you are already one-third of the way to becoming a fine SQL Server DBA; if you understand databases and have software development experience on the Windows platform, the sky's the limit. Let's find out more.

SQL Server in a Basket

Clients send "orders" to the "waiters" of SQL Server for processing and "cooking." A query engine then optimizes these orders, or queries, sent as T-SQL statements to the database engine, for processing. The result sets (the meals) are then sent back to the clients and balanced on the "metal" trays of their "windows."

If you've been around the C/S block a few times, it will not take much for you to think about all the C/S processes at work in the "Doll House," which I am sure is in your neck of the woods. However, in case you have never eaten at a roadhouse, Figure 3-1 illustrates my metaphor, from a robin's viewpoint.

Key Principles of the C/S DBMS

Before we look at the C/S processes and components that make up Microsoft's SQL Server, you should familiarize yourself with the key principles of the C/S database management system (DBMS) model, which are as follows:

- **Centralization and concurrency** The database is stored in a centralized location and made available to a number of users or processes. This is probably the most important tenet of the C/S DBMS. The DBMS server is endowed with sophisticated mechanisms that monitor transactions, ensure that the transactions are adequately isolated from one another, manage conflicts, and guarantee the consistency, atomicity, and durability of the data. No DBMS components, such as databases, tables, indexes, storage, or relational engine components, are installed on the client computer *whatsoever.* The only exception to this is if the client computer is also the host for the servers, a configuration that is explored in Chapter 6.

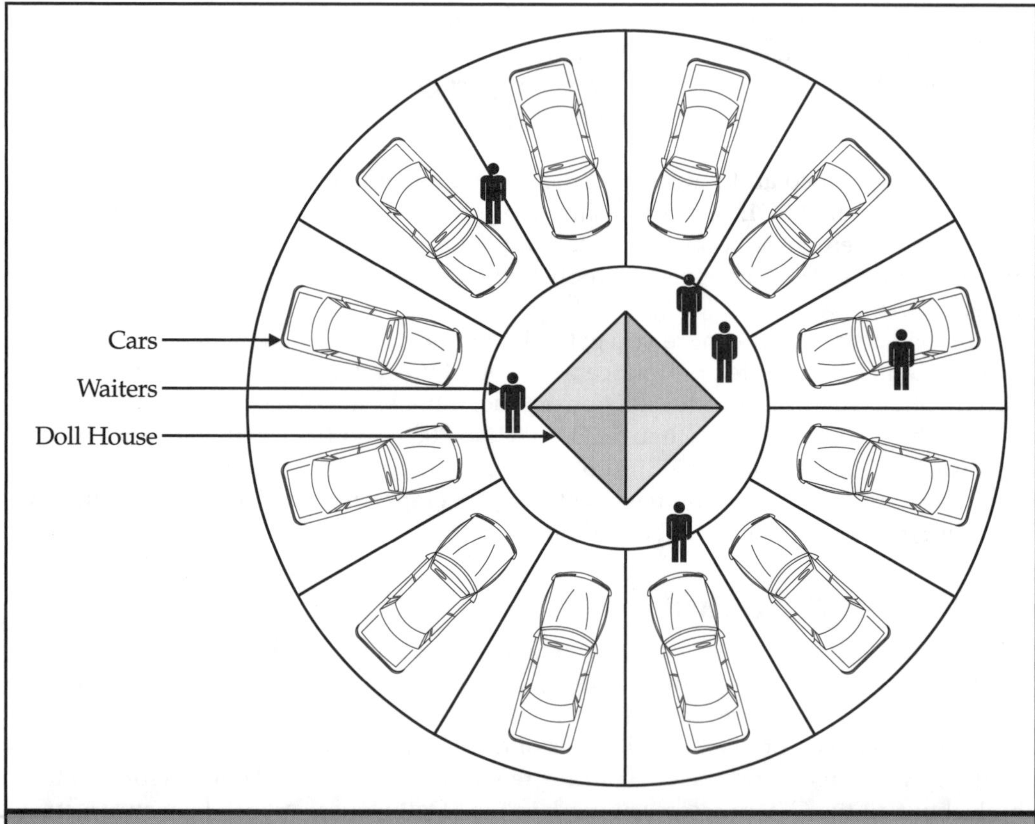

Figure 3-1. *A bird's-eye view of Doll House, a C/S system*

All users, human or computer, work with the same data, although *views* are used to partition the data so that only selected users can see the data or regions of the database they are authorized to see. A user may understand that the view he or she is seeing is the entire database, but it may only be a window opened in a remote region of the database, a coverage field. The server is thus like the Doll House kitchen: Only one kitchen serves all the cars, and the menu on the side of the building is accessed by everyone—a small database of meals and their prices.

The client workstations or devices need no complex database engine components installed on them. They can be ultra-thin, working through the services of a Web browser, or as standard executables. In the past, client network libraries needed a measure of configuration, but no matter what device now hosts the interface, access to the server and the data requires very little setup. The most you might need to configure if you are attaching through ODBC is a system or user DSN, set up in the Data Sources (ODBC) applet in the Control Panel of all 32-bit Windows operating systems.

- **Integrity—rules and constraints** Business rules are centrally defined on the server and enforced once for all users, all applications, and the business. We discussed constraints in the previous chapters, and it is precisely these rules that can be set for the database and its data, and enforced centrally. Any user or process that desires access to the data has to go by the rules of the database and its security mechanisms. In the Doll House example, anyone who honks the horn would be asked to leave, and no one is allowed to walk up to the window of the Doll House to place an order.
- **Security** Centralization and secure connectivity enforce security and the protection of the data. A C/S DBMS not only lets you to protect data from corruption, but it also ensures protection from destruction and theft. All database servers should be locked up in secure server rooms and data centers.
- **Conservation and optimization** The C/S DBMS ensures that only the data that the client requests are returned to the client. There is no need for the client to open tables or import entire databases across the network. This means that network traffic is optimized and the server can concentrate its power on performing complex computations and then send only the results to the client. In the same light, the roadhouse would go out of business if its waiters brought out raw food and asked the clients to cook the food in their cars. *Energy* is stored in the centralized location where it is wisely utilized and conserved.

  Even low-bandwidth environments, like remote access to the Internet over a dial-up modem, yield sufficient performance because the data being sent across the network is minimal. Of course, if you write or provide code that returns huge result sets (which is not recommended even for local users), a low-bandwidth connection is going to feel the squeeze. Applications that need to work with images and text would also naturally suffer from a low-bandwidth connection (see Chapter 6 for deployment considerations).
- **Total Cost of Ownership (TCO)** Hardware investment is minimized and applied to the server components. Thin-client hardware and thin-client processing allow you to "throw" hardware at the server instead of the client. The centralized administration and management of that server, from centralized backup/restore to protected and clean power supplies, reduces Total Cost of Ownership. The roadhouse also benefits from the C/S model when it comes to TCO: By not having to worry about tables, chairs, fancy cutlery, and special seating, more resources can be pumped into the kitchen and the cooking.

During the writing of this book, I outfitted a busy call center in Miami that had relocated from New York City. I gave them cheap workstations (old Compaq Deskpro machines) still outfitted with the original copies of Windows 95 they shipped with in the mid 90s, which I acquired for $30 each. I installed DCOM 95, the client binaries for Windows 95, and the call center application and advised my client to put most of the money into the servers. Running Windows 2000 and SQL Server 2000, they are now in production, processing about 2,000 telephone calls a day.

These five principles of the C/S DBMS are rarely highlighted. However, they are the principles that I have used in designing C/S database systems for more than a decade, starting with computer telephony systems, and then venturing into telecommunications systems, call centers, help desks, POS systems, Web sites, intranets, and more. You have the ACID test, Codd's relational database rules, rules of inference, and so on, but no C/S DBMS compliance rules. I don't think we need another set of rules in this business—although I was tempted to suggest the "roadhouse rules of C/S DBMS"—but you should test your DBMS design or model against the five principles discussed here. Then rate your compliance against a desirability or sanity factor of 50, just for your information. Our C/S system is thus designed much like our roadhouse, as demonstrated in Figure 3-2.

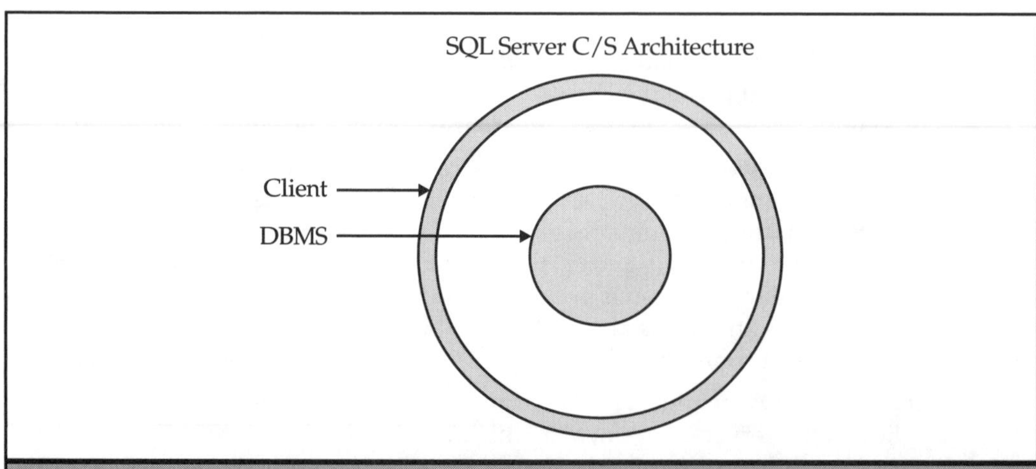

Figure 3-2. *A DBA's-eye view of SQL Server 2000, a C/S DBMS*

I see the desirability or implementation scores constructed as follows:

- **Concurrency and centralization** Score between 1 and 5 for *concurrency* and between 1 and 5 for *centralization;* then rate your system on a scale of 1 to 10 for this tenet. You will naturally score high for this if you use a client/server database management system like SQL Server, unless your client apps are still processing data on the front end.
- **Integrity** Score between 1 and 10 for *integrity.* You will score badly if your tables are not properly constrained and if your applications makes little use of triggers, stored procedures, checks, and so on.
- **Security** Score between 1 and 10 for *security.* A high score would make wise use of Windows Authentication techniques, Kerberos, roles and so on.
- **Conservation and optimization** Score between 1 and 5 for *conservation* and between 1 and 5 for *optimization;* then rate your system on a scale of 1 to 10 for this tenet. See Chapter 14 about suggested programming models for SQL Server 2000.
- **Total Cost of Ownership** Score between 1 and 10 for *TCO.* (TCO may seem difficult to score when you have no choice but to ignore the client side altogether. A DNA or .Net application [*n*-tiered systems] on the Internet is a good example of an application in which the client hardly factors into the cost of the C/S DBMS. However, you can still rate yourself according to the systems you use on the back end—software, hardware, and so forth—and we'll talk a little about service level and change management in the chapters to follow.) The less you have to worry about the client, the better, even if it means a fundamental and career-threatening change in your software development paradigm.

When you have completed scoring, multiply your score by 2 to get a compliance or desirability percentage. This is simple math as follows, where A = client/server DBMS:

```
A = CC + I + S + CO + TCO X 2
```

Now let's explore SQL Server 2000 as a C/S DBMS with the preceding five principles—and your score—as a backdrop. From time to time, I will flag the components that help us build the ideal C/S DBMS. Implementation and tools to support these aforementioned principles is left to dedicated chapters in Part II and Part III of this book, although some will be introduced here.

C/S Architecture

The client in SQL Server's C/S architecture is skinny to say the least. Every possible mechanism or routine for viewing, updating, manipulating, transforming, and analyzing data can be invoked or performed on the server.

If you are still building applications using SQL Server as the data store and transforming or processing data on the front end, you are not using SQL Server to its full potential at best, and you are using it incorrectly at worst. An example: Your application *can* query the database to determine the quantity of a certain class of items. The server's simplest action is to send back the result of the query, the number of items in the record. Your application *can* then evaluate the result and take some action, which might be to alert the store manager that he or she is running out of a certain widget.

But what you have here is a serious case of misplaced priorities because performing the calculation at the client causes all sorts of problems, of which we only have time to mention one or two. Not only do you have to implement the algorithm to evaluate the returned value on the client, which requires processing power and memory, but every client will be performing the same routine unless you take time-consuming and counterproductive steps to customize each client in some way.

Instead, a simple stored procedure alerts the store manager as soon as the quantity drops below a certain level. All this server-side functionality has nothing to do with the client in any way, because it is a business rule that is enforced by the server, where it belongs once, centrally, period.

You may be forgiven if you are in the process of shedding the last vestiges of file/server or PC desktop database architecture, or you are in the process of converting an application. Unless you can let go of the data processing code that's buried in your client application, you will not find it easy to develop robust SQL Server solutions. You will also not be able to take advantage of the coming revolution in thin–C/S database applications (browser-hosted or terminal clients), .Net applications, and *n*-tier solutions.

The following exposé into SQL Server 2000's C/S architecture is designed to help you understand not only how you connect to SQL Server, but also how to "think" server-side processing in general and how to think SQL Server processing in particular. Let's kick off by discussing how your client applications connect to the database server.

Connecting to SQL Server

Remember, in Chapter 1 I briefly discussed the client-side application development environments, APIs, and libraries you can use to write applications that connect to SQL Server. Now you will learn about the communications mechanisms and data streams that make it possible for any modern programming language to create applications that can connect to and exchange data with SQL Server.

Interprocess Communications

SQL Server 2000 communicates with its clients via interprocess communication (IPC) mechanisms. A facility of the Win32 API interprocess communications architecture, IPC allows separate or isolated processes to safely communicate with each other. IPC can be invoked between processes on the same host or between remotely placed hosts over a network, even one as large as the Internet. The process on one computer opens a connection to a process running on another computer, and data is transmitted and returned between the two processes. Such a facility makes it easy to communicate and interact with a SQL Server centrally and concurrently with many users.

SQL Server clients can connect to SQL Server, open connections, transmit data such as XML and T-SQL, and call functions and procedures (like Java's remote method invocation and other distributed processing architecture). IPC is an asynchronous facility and does not block the client from performing local duties, or even from opening up communications with other processes. If you wish to dig into IPC further, any good book that comprehensively covers the Win32 API will do. For SQL Server application development and DBA work, understanding the different protocols to use over an IPC connection is sufficient.

There are two parts to an IPC: the *API* and the *protocol*. The API is the function set used to "speak" to and "listen" to the network IPC. A good example of a network API is NetBIOS; its favorite protocol is the nonroutable NetBEUI, but NetBIOS packets can also be encapsulated in TCP/IP and IPX/SPX packets. When an IPC is between a client and server on the same host, the local *Named Pipes* or *shared memory* components are used for the IPC. If the processes are split across a network, the network IPC is used. SQL Server has facilities for a number of network IPC options. You will learn about client IPC configuration a little later in this chapter. Now, let's look into SQL Server's so-called Net-Libraries, the staging ground for SQL Server IPC communications.

The Client and Server Net-Libraries

SQL Server makes use of a collection of libraries called Net-Libraries that provide the necessary communication between the client applications and SQL Server. The stack of services in which the Net-Libraries is located is illustrated in Figure 3-3. The Net-Libraries handle the task of calling the IPC APIs to send data from client to server and vice versa. The Net-Library essentially allows the service providers to hand off this task to a separate collection of functions.

The client applications you build or support make a call to one of a number of service providers—OLE DB, ODBC, DB-Library, or the Embedded SQL API—which then exchanges data with one of the Net-Libraries supported by SQL Server 2000. Table 3-1 lists the supported Net-Libraries.

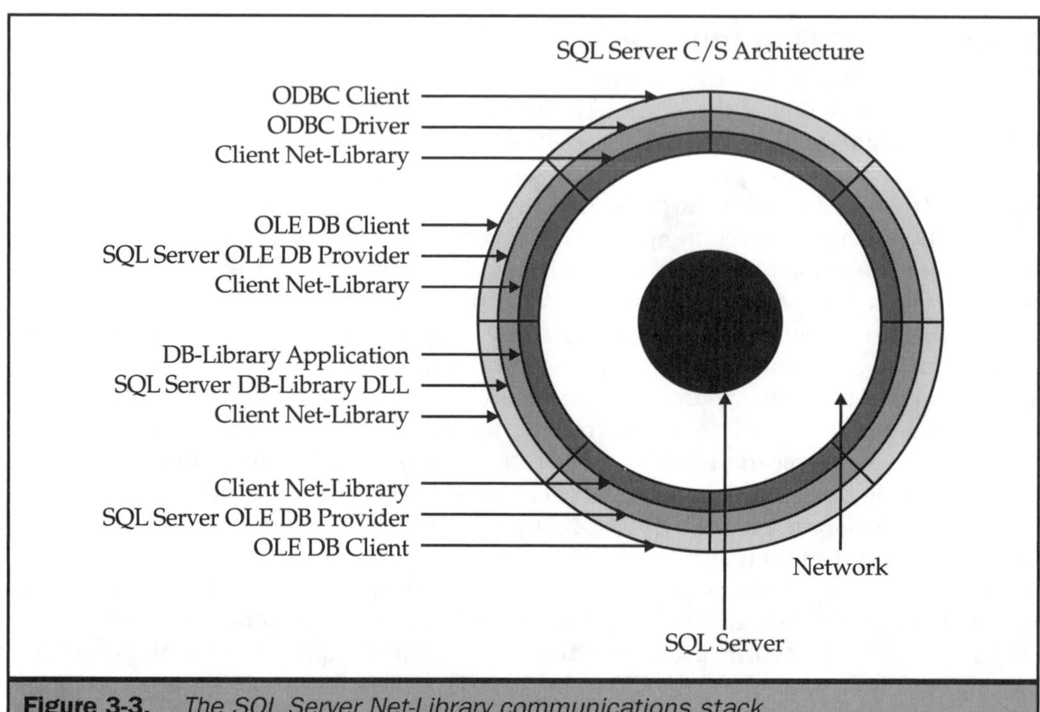

Figure 3-3. *The SQL Server Net-Library communications stack*

API Protocol Specified	Client Net-Lib	Server Net-Lib	IPC-API	Transport Protocol Supported
TCP/IP Sockets	Dbnetlib.dll (Primary)	Ssnetlib.dll (Primary)	Windows Sockets 2	TCP/IP
Named Pipes	Dbnetlib.dll routes to Dbnmpntw.dll (Secondary)	Ssnetlib.dll routes to ssnmpn70.dll on Windows NT only	Windows Named Pipes	File system (local) TCP/IP, NetBEUI, NWLink

Table 3-1. *Supported Net-Libraries on SQL Server 2000, showing IPC APIs and protocols supported*

API Protocol Specified	Client Net-Lib	Server Net-Lib	IPC-API	Transport Protocol Supported
NWLink IPX/SPX	Dbnetlib.dll	Ssnetlib.dll	Windows Sockets 2	NWLink
Multiprotocol	Dbnetlib.dll routes to Dbmsrpcn.dll	Ssnetlib.dll routes to ssmsrpc.dll (default instance only)	Windows RPC	File system (local) TCP/IP, NetBEUI, NWLink
AppleTalk	Dbnetlib.dll routes to Dbmsadsn.dll	Ssnetlib.dll routes to ssmsad70.dll on Windows NT only	AppleTalk ADSP	AppleTalk
Banyan VINES	Dbnetlib.dll routes to Dbmsvinn.dll	Ssnetlib.dll routes to ssmsvi70.dll (default instance only)	Banyan VINES SPP	Banyan VINES

Table 3-1. *Supported Net-Libraries on SQL Server 2000, showing IPC APIs and protocols supported* (continued)

If SQL Server is installed on the local host, illustrated by Figure 3-4, the client's shared memory Net-Library is used. If SQL Server is installed on a remote host, the client's network Net-Libraries are used to establish IPC communications over the network.

Figures 3-3 and 3-4 show the network communications paths between a client application and an instance of SQL Server. The clients can use any of the Net-Libraries available to them.

In order to support multiple protocols, especially the legacy ones, a primary Net-Library is positioned at the top of the network stack to filter and route data to the correct Net-Library dedicated to a protocol. This primary Net-Library is called the Super Socket Net-Library, named Primary Net-Library from here on.

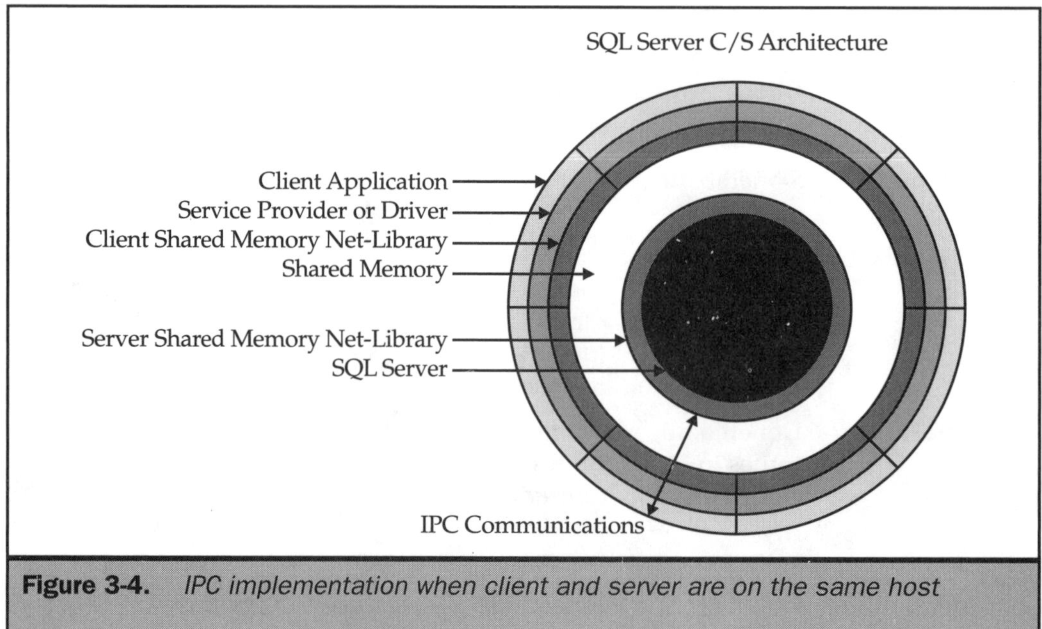

Figure 3-4. *IPC implementation when client and server are on the same host*

Figure 3-5 illustrates the Primary Net-Library at the top of the communications stack on the client side. A server-side Primary Net-Library is also required for communications from the server to the client.

The main purpose of the Primary Net-Library is to route packets over legacy networks to the secondary Net-Library routers that are required for supporting such legacy network APIs. Thus the two routes over the entire stack are as follows:

- Route one directs communications over TCP/IP Sockets or NWLINK IPX/SPX ports. In this case, the Primary Net-Library makes direct calls to the Windows Socket 2 API for TCP/IP socket transmission and to IPX/SPX ports for NWLINK (NetWare) support. In other words, no Secondary Net-Library is needed.
- Route two directs communications over Named Pipes, Multiprotocol, Banyan VINES, or AppleTalk. The Primary Net-Library invokes the services of a packet router, called the Net-Library router, to call a Secondary Net-Library for specific legacy protocol support.

Communications from SQL Server to the client take place over the same stack. Both routes are illustrated in Figure 3-5, and Table 3-1 lists which specific Net-Library is used for a specific protocol, the IPC API called, and the library implementations' filenames. You cannot use Windows 98 as a host for instances of SQL Server that are placed on a Named Pipes or Banyan VINES network, because Windows 98 does not

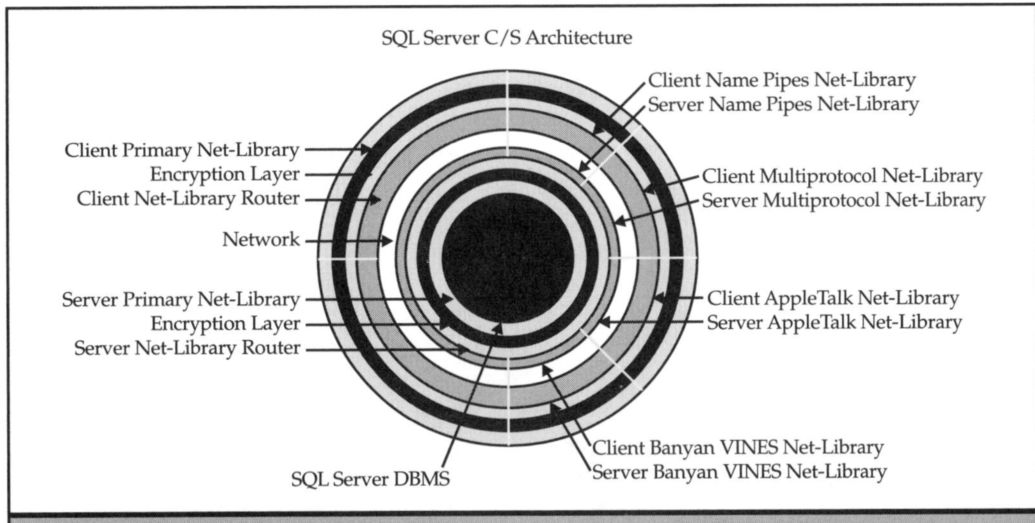

Figure 3-5. *The Primary Net-Library, known as the Super Socket Net Library, is positioned closest to either the client or the server in the call stack (note also the position of the encryption [SSL] layer)*

support the server side of these APIs. However, the client libraries are supported on Windows 98, which can be used on a SQL Server client on a Named Pipes or Banyan VINES network. You can also use Windows 95 as a client for any of these protocols, as I described earlier, but not as a server host. AppleTalk is not supported on Windows 95 or Windows 98.

Also, named instances, which you will learn about later in Chapters 6 and in the chapters in Part II, only support Named Pipes, TCP/IP Sockets, NWLink IPX/SPX, and shared memory Net-Libraries. Default server instances support all Net-Libraries, for backward compatibility. The AppleTalk Net-Library does not work with anything else but the AppleTalk protocol; however, the Named Pipes and Multiprotocol Net-Libraries can support a number of different protocol stacks.

The Net-Library–IPC communications functionality is positioned far below both the client and server processes, and you will have little to do with them. As a software developer, you need only configure your applications to support the respective service provider used by your code. ADO, for example, sits above OLE DB and ODBC. You will learn more about the service providers in Chapter 14.

As a DBA, you might have more to configure, especially if you are not using a Microsoft network. For example, the Primary Net-Library is also used to implement the Secure Sockets Layer (SSL) for encrypted communications between client and server. You will learn about this support, SQL Server in a public key infrastructure, IPSec, and so on in Chapter 8.

Each instance of SQL Server can listen in on a collection of Net-Libraries, and you might find that when you installed SQL Server, you installed the default Net-Library on a network that does not support it. For example, perhaps you installed the TCP/IP Net-Library on a NetWare network and you did not install the NWLink Net-Library. This is where the Client Network Utility comes into the picture.

Working with Net-Libraries

You can use two utilities that ship with SQL Server 2000 to set up and configure the client and server Net-Libraries. They are called the Client Network Utility and the Server Network Utility. The two utilities are illustrated in Figures 3-6 and 3-7.

When you install the server, both the client and server Net-Libraries are installed, as are the aforementioned utilities. If you're distributing client applications, you will need to ensure that the Microsoft Data Access Components you are supporting in your client are installed on the target computers. The specifics of installing components and configuring the Net-Library environment are covered in the installation and configuration chapter, Chapter 6. Chapter 6 also covers deployment plans, *n-tier* solutions and browser database access, as does Chapter 23 on SQL Server and the Internet.

SQL Server installs all the Net-Libraries, but only one or two may actually be Active. Chapter 6 demonstrates preselection of the Net-Libraries during setup. The default

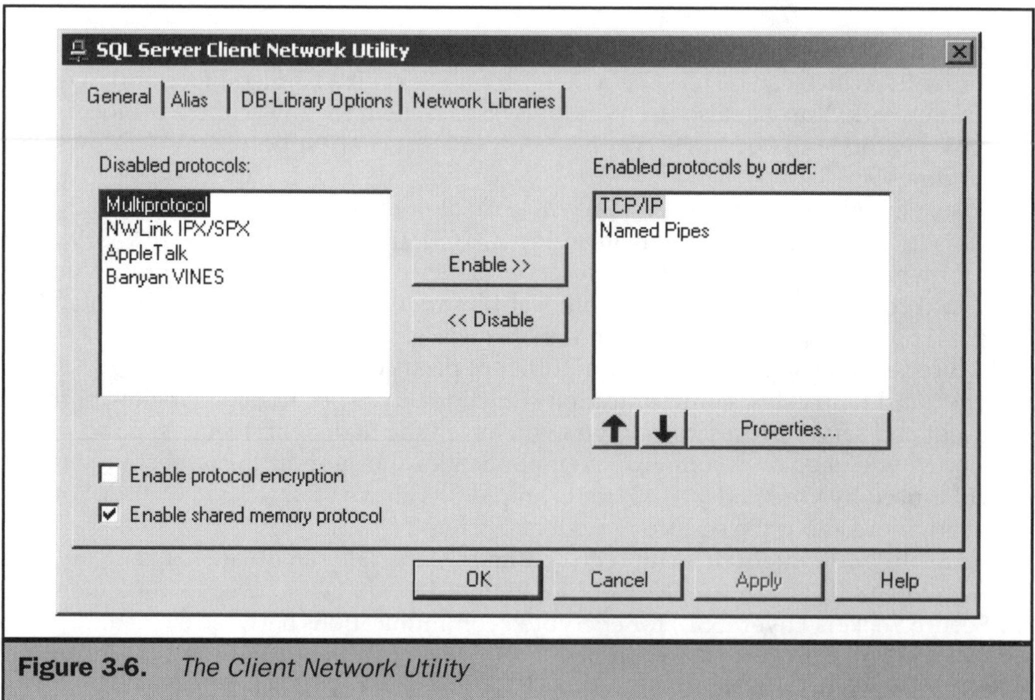

Figure 3-6. *The Client Network Utility*

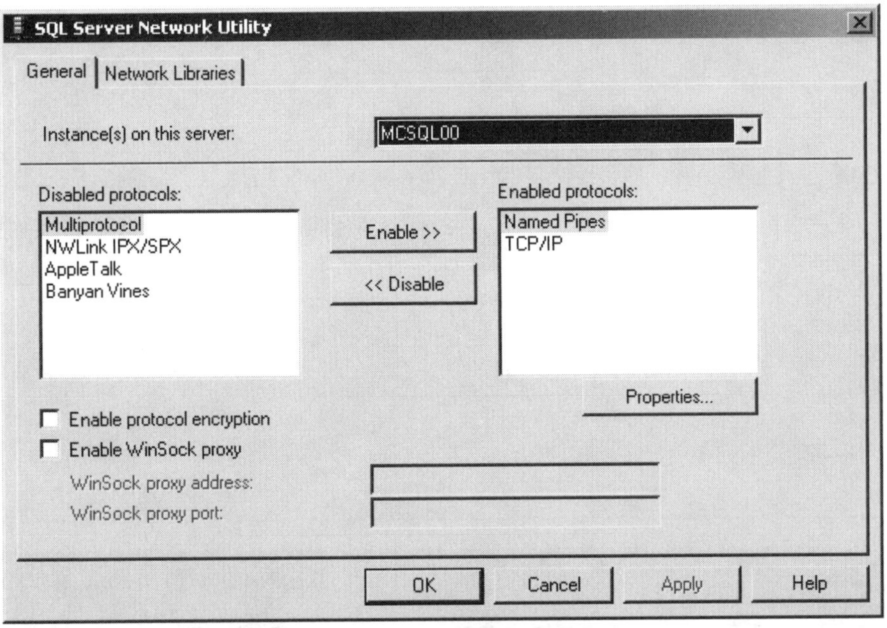

SQL Server Network Utility

General | Network Libraries

Instance(s) on this server: MCSQL00

Disabled protocols: Multiprotocol, NWLink IPX/SPX, AppleTalk, Banyan Vines

Enable >> | << Disable

Enabled protocols: Named Pipes, TCP/IP

Properties...

Enable protocol encryption

Enable WinSock proxy

WinSock proxy address:

WinSock proxy port:

OK | Cancel | Apply | Help

Figure 3-7. *The Server Network Utility*

Net-Libraries are usually TCP/IP Sockets, Shared Memory, and Named Pipes for Windows NT/2000 server and TCP/IP Sockets and Shared Memory for Windows 98.

The client and server Net-Libraries can be enabled or disabled, as you need, for each instance of SQL Server and for every client, or proxy process. When you disable a Net-Library, or deactivate it, it remains on the system for later use.

On Windows 9.*x*, Windows NT, and Windows 2000 clients, the ODBC data sources already provide the client Net-Libraries for ODBC that your applications can use. This configuration is illustrated in Figure 3-8. But, as mentioned, you will have to install the Microsoft Data Access Components suite, which includes the Client Network Utility, before you can use the other Net-Libraries, such as OLE DB and Named Pipes support.

On the client side, you will need to be involved in the following DBA work:

- Enable or Disable client Net-Libraries.
- Specify the order in which client Net-Libraries are made available for all connections (except server aliases).
- Define server aliases that define specific Net-Libraries and connection parameters to invoke when connecting to instances of SQL Server from version 7.0 and earlier.

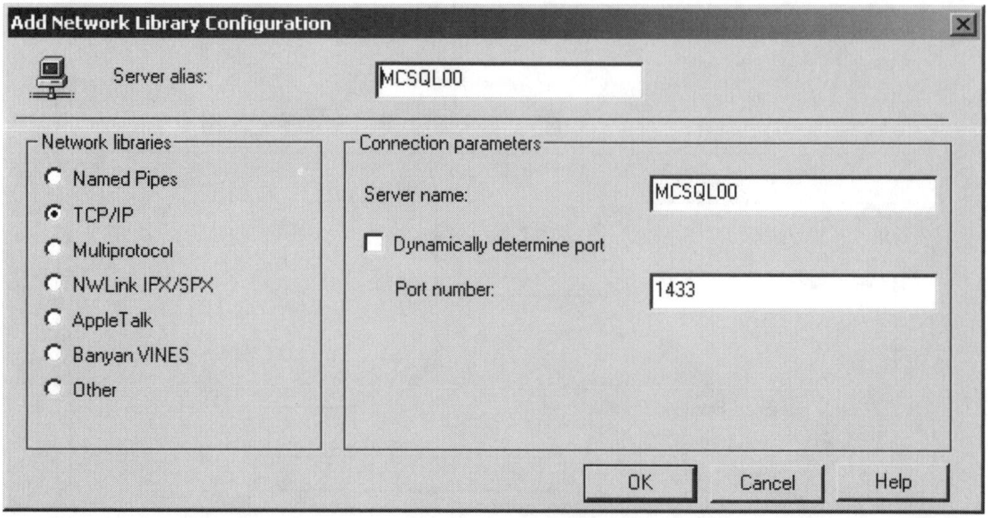

Figure 3-8. *Configuring the Net-Libraries on an ODBC data source name (DSN)*

The default instances of SQL Server listen on the same default, or preconfigured, network addresses as earlier versions of SQL Server. This allows clients that were once connected to earlier versions of the DBMS to maintain connectivity, albeit to a new version of the server. Table 3-2 shows the default network addresses that instances of SQL Server listen on.

Net-Library	Default Instance Address	Named Instance Address
TCP/IP Sockets	TCP Port 1433.	This port is chosen dynamically when the instance is started.
Named Pipes	\\computername\pipe\sql\query	\\computername\pipe\MSSQL$instancename\sql\query
NWLink IPX/SPX	IPX Port 33854.	The first available port after 33854 for each instance.

Table 3-2. *The Default Network Addresses That SQL 2000 Monitors*

What Table 3-2 also demonstrates is that when your client Net-Library connects to an instance of SQL Server 2000, it needs only the network name of the computer running the instance, and the instance name (discussed in Chapter 6). For example, when your application attempts to connect to SQL Server, *dbnetlib.dll* opens the connection to UDP port 1434 (the monitor) on the computer network name specified in the connection definition. The name need not be a UNC or NetBIOS name either, because the network name could be a TCP/IP address followed by the name of the SQL Server instance. Such hard coding is, however, not good practice or practical for software deployment. And if your network is unable to resolve the name, there is obviously a "pothole" in your network somewhere.

There are several possible causes for a connection failure related to the Net-Libraries over a network:

- The requested instance of SQL Server is not running. The host may be down, or the service may be stopped.
- The Net-Library being invoked on the client is not active on the server. (This is akin to trying to call someone who does not have telephone service.)
- The computer name cannot be resolved. (You could troubleshoot this by trying to attach to a TCP/IP address instead.)
- The SQL Server port 1433 is unavailable. This can happen if the network administrator prevents access to this port, or some other application is blocking the access. For example, over a wide area network a firewall or a router may inadvertently filter out ports 1433 and 1434.

If the client and server are on the same machine, it is relatively easy to reference the default instance. Table 3-3 lists the references you can use on Windows NT/2000 and Windows 98. You would use such a configuration on a terminal server or application server running SQL Server. Client applications are opened on the same machine through terminal service client connections.

Windows NT/2000	**Windows 9.*x*/CE 3.0**
Computer Name	Computer Name
(local)	(local)

Table 3-3. *Applications running on the same host as the server can use the naming conventions listed here (local) requires the parentheses in your application connection code; the period (.) applies only to the local instance configured in SQL Server utilities*

Inside SQL Server Data Streams

Now that you know how your clients open communications to SQL Server, the C/S communications architecture will become clearer when you find out what gets sent up and down the connection. Client and server make use of an application level formatting protocol known as the Tabular Data Stream (TDS) to format data for transmission and reception. You might think of this protocol as the pattern-storing technology in your average Star Fleet transporter. Without the pattern protocol, we would not be able to reassemble a human or an object after transportation. TDS packets are encapsulated in the packets that are built by each protocol's Net-Library. The TCP/IP Sockets Net-Library, for example, encapsulates the TDS packets inside the TCP/IP packets or the TCP/IP protocol.

With the new support for XML, the contents of the TDS packets could be either a relational result set or an XML document. If you specify the FOR XML (refer to the coverage of FOR clause in Books Online for syntax) argument in your T-SQL code, the database engine will stream an XML document back to the application (this is also supported in OLE DB). If FOR XML is not specified, the database engine will send a result set back to the client application.

Without FOR XML, the TDS packet contains the rows of the result set, with each row tabulated to show one or more columns according to what you specify in the SELECT statement. XML is packaged in the TDS packet as one long stream of data, with each packet restricted to being no more than 4KB in size.

SQL Server's packet size can also be configured. The default is the same size as TDS packets. If SQL Server packets are configured smaller than TDS packets, the packets will be disassembled on the sending computer and packaged into smaller packages. The protocols on the client computer reassemble the inbound packets.

Security and Access Control in SQL Server 2000

One of the most important data streams to travel through the IPC process just described is user account and context information for authentication by SQL Server. Clients can legally cloak themselves in the context of a domain user account, which is a validation protocol used by SQL Server. As mentioned earlier, security is an important factor in C/S architecture. The more robust and secure the environment, the safer the data.

SQL Server 2000 is a secure DBMS that requires its users to be properly authenticated by a security service before they can access the server and any databases. Two security mechanisms, the external network authentication service and the internal SQL Server authentication service, can be used to ensure this objective. SQL Server requires your authentication with at least one of these services.

Before an application can send a request for data or services to SQL Server 2000, it must first make an authorized connection to the server. To allow the connection, SQL

Server requires the user or application to appropriately log on. This identification is known as the *server login* or just *login*. The login is stored in the catalog and SQL Server associates it with a *user account* in a database. You cannot connect to a SQL Server database without the pairing of *the login and the database user information*. The login can be used to hook up with any database user, but a database user is confined to the database in which it was created.

SQL Server will terminate your connection if it cannot validate the login. This validation can come from either the Windows NT/2000 authentication or from SQL Server Authentication.

Windows Authentication

Under Windows authentication, access to SQL Server 2000 is controlled by either the NTLM authentication process under NT 4.0 and Windows 2000 on down-level clients (Windows NT 4.0 and Windows 9.*x*) or the ticket services of the Kerberos protocol and Active Directory on native Windows 2000 clients. When you attempt to establish the connection to SQL Server, the client's connection environment establishes the requirements for a trusted connection to SQL Server 2000, in much the same way as a client tries to access shares and group- or user-protected files. It goes without saying that you cannot connect to any domain resource unless you have first been authenticated to the Windows domain in which resource, or more specifically, SQL Server, is a member, or another domain that has a trust relationship with the local domain.

SQL Server 2000 Authentication

SQL Server authentication requires a user to log on with a valid internal user name and password when Windows authentication is absent or fails. The login ID is internal to SQL Server and is not derived or passed from the Windows NT/2000 domain authentication mechanisms. Login IDs and passwords are set up by a member of the *sysadmin* role (discussed shortly) by means of the dialog shown in Figure 3-9.

Mixed or Dual-Mode Authentication

You can specify during SQL Server installation and later that authentication can or should be either SQL Server authentication or both Windows authentication and SQL Server authentication. In other words, if a user attempts to connect and succeeds, he or she can bypass the SQL Server user-password login . If the user is unable to connect with Windows domain authentication, the internal login ID and password , if provided, needs to be used. Windows domain authentication is termed *trusted,* and SQL Server 2000 authentication is termed *untrusted.*

The subject of security and access control warrants much more attention and thus is the subject of Chapter 8. However, some understanding of the internal login mechanisms is useful at this point.

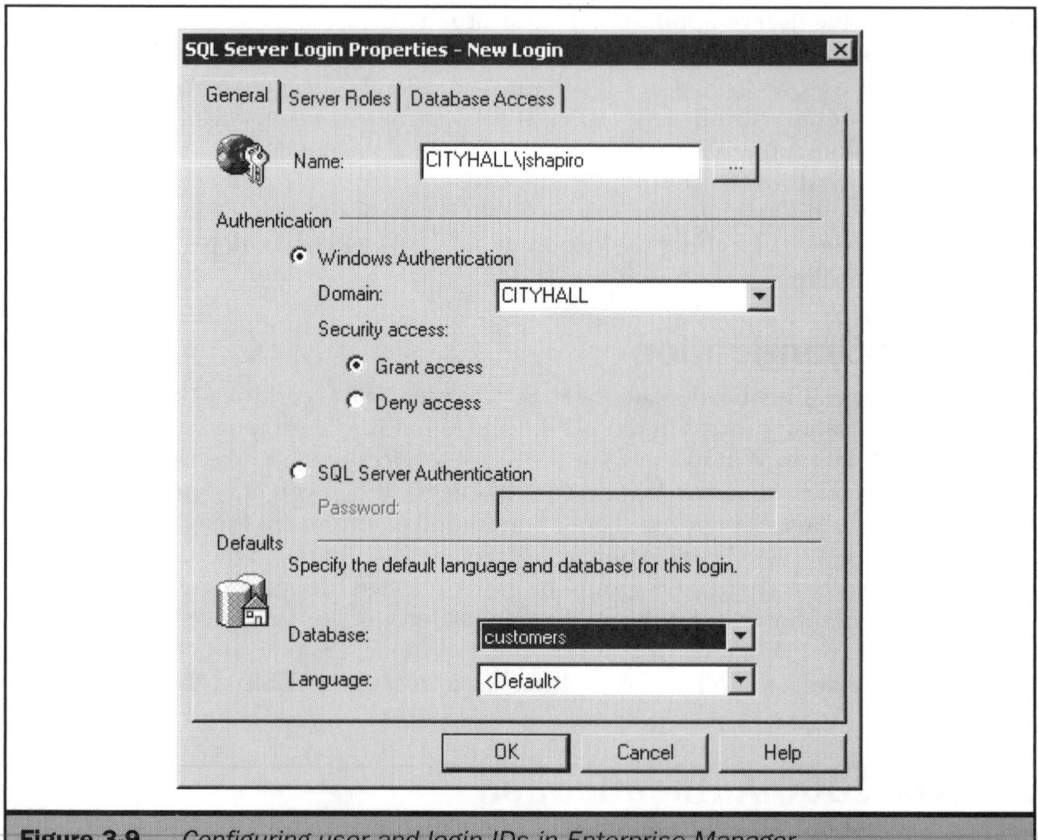

Figure 3-9. *Configuring user and login IDs in Enterprise Manager*

The SQL Server Login IDs

The login ID is essentially a moniker for an authenticated or otherwise trusted domain, realm, or external user (or group of users) that is required when he or she (and even a process) connects to SQL Server 2000. You cannot connect to SQL Server without being able to prove authority by presenting the login ID and the password that goes with it. Windows security acts as the proxy, as mentioned earlier, that "vouchsafes" the user to SQL Server; the user does not need to authenticate to SQL Server in Windows or mixed-mode authentication.

So if you are presenting credentials on a Windows authentication or mixed-mode system, how does SQL Server handle the login request? The stored procedure sp_grantlogin grants the access on the basis of a predefined "account" in SQL Server that is created when you call the sp_addlogin stored procedure, as illustrated in

Figure 3-9. In other words, the external Windows NT/2000 domain account or group has to be predefined in SQL Server before it can be used. The just-mentioned stored procedures are used by Enterprise Manager, which is used by you, the DBA, to add login IDs to SQL Server. The only time you might call the sp_addlogin stored procedure in code is in specialized applications that use SQL Server for storage of configuration data, such as a PBX. Calling the sp_grantlogin stored procedure is not unusual and is demonstrated in Chapter 8.

The SQL Server Users

The login ID, however, cannot itself willy-nilly access databases in SQL Server or attach to any objects. The login ID first has to be associated with a database *user* account inside SQL Server, associated or defined within a database, that controls access to the database and its objects. Every login ID must be associated with a user ID. When you create a login ID in SQL Server, you have to assign the user ID in the same stroke. You cannot later unhinge the two objects and reassign either to other partners. If you desire such flexibility, your database users should instead be made members of a group, which is in any event mandatory on my networks and should be the same on yours. Of course there are caveats, and we will investigate these in Chapter 8.

The SQL Server Roles

Roles are similar to Windows groups in functionality and to Active Directory organizational units (OU) in purpose, although the influence of a role member does not extend beyond the "borders" of SQL Server and relates instead to the SQL Server *user* and its database. Roles can be established to represent a class of specific database users in the organization and the level of access they have in a database. For example, *temp_users* might be a role created for temporary data input people, which prevents them from doing anything but inputting data into a certain database.

Roles are useful for broadening or narrowing the scope of functionality or authority of a user in a database. If you need a data entry person to delete old records, you can simply move that person out of the *d_entry* role and into the *d_editing* role as needed. Roles allow you to centrally manage permissions rather than having to manage the rights or privileges of individuals; however, how they work and are configured can be a little confusing and I have thus covered them extensively in Chapter 8.

There are several fixed server roles and a number of fixed database roles that are preconfigured or built in. For example, the *public* database role is the default role assigned to each SQL Server user. This role is a convenient means for conveying a set of rights and privileges to all users. Techniques and rules for role assignment are also discussed in Chapter 8. However, you need to remember that roles are assigned to SQL Server database users, while groups are a Windows NT/2000 container object. The two live in different worlds; the one world inside the other.

Object Ownership and Permissions

Before we move on with our discussion of SQL Server C/S architecture, you should know that all objects in SQL Server are owned by a user, much the same way as network objects are owned by user or computer accounts. The object's owner is the database *user*, which means that when an object is created, say a table, the owner of that table is the *user* that created it. The only way another database *user* can access the table is for the owner to grant permission. For example, the owner can grant the UPDATE, INSERT, DELETE, SELECT, EXEC, and DRI (Declarative Referential Integrity) permissions to other users or user roles.

Similarly, a stored procedure is a good example of an object to which permissions first have to be assigned or granted before a *user* can invoke or execute the stored procedure. By controlling access to some objects and restricting or denying it to others, you maintain security and rights to data, and you prevent applications and users from having access to data they do not need or that is sensitive and restricted. On the one hand, a stored procedure is sufficient to prevent direct access to a table, but by denying access to the physical table itself you would be more sure that users cannot get to the sensitive data via other means (see Chapter 8).

The Server-Side Components

A small but very powerful collection of server components makes up the so-called "back end" of SQL Server 2000. The collection consists of the following components:

- **Database Engine** Implemented in the MSSQLServer service
- **SQL Server Agent** Implemented in the SQLServerAgent service
- **Microsoft Search Service** Implemented as the Microsoft Search service
- **Microsoft Distributed Transaction Coordinator** Implemented as the MS DTC service
- **Microsoft Analysis Server** Implemented as MSSQLServerOLAPService

Besides Windows NT and Windows 2000 Server, the only other platforms that can support the server components are Windows 98 and Windows CE 3.0. The Microsoft Search service is not available on any client or workstation operating system. On Windows 98, the server services are implemented as applications because Windows 98 does not support services, nor does Windows CE. The services can, of course, be implemented as applications on their host servers, but this is not recommended.

SQL Server 2000 can also be installed in multiple instances, even on the same host Windows NT or Windows 2000 Server computers. Each instance is controlled by its own set of services; however, the Distributed Transaction Coordinator (overview coming up) is shared among all the instances on the same host. You can also run different versions of SQL Server on the same server. Working with multiple instances and different versions is fully discussed in Chapter 5.

I have included the Analysis Services service in this list because you will see it in the Service Control Manager and the SQL Server Service Manager. However, the Analysis Server service is for all intents and purposes a subproduct of SQL Server, practically a separate environment. It can and does work with non-SQL Server databases and even an Access MDB database or an Oracle database. You will learn about the Analysis Services architecture in Chapters 24 and 25.

The Server components can be started and stopped in a number of ways:

- On startup of the operating system, determined by the Service Control Manager (SCM)
- Via the services of the SQL Server Service Manager, which is available from the menus or the system tray. The SQL Server Service Manager provides the same services as the SCM, dedicated to the SQL Server services
- From the command line or command prompt using the *net* commands

Let's now look briefly at the four server components that, combined, make up the SQL Server 2000 DBMS.

The Database Engine

The Microsoft SQL Server 2000 database engine, MSSQLServer, manages the databases and all related files and mechanisms that its instance owns on the host server. It is also responsible for processing all the T-SQL statements sent to it by client applications and processes. It also controls the execution of SQL Server components (the objects) installed in the database, such as stored procedures, triggers, and the various integrity mechanisms we discussed in the previous chapters.

The SQL Server Database Engine *is* the DBMS. It is the only engine on the server that creates and manages the databases, juggles concurrent connections, enforces security, processes queries, builds and applies indexes, and so on. The database engine, which we will refer to as the DBMS from here on, is the largest and most important SQL Server entity. It is discussed in depth in the next chapter.

SQL Server Agent

SQL Server Agent has been designed to make the job of the DBA a lot easier, lowering TCO and the administrative burden. It is essentially a service that is used to schedule maintenance routines and activities on a target server. It is also used to monitor DBMS activities and alert operators, the DBAs, to potential threats and problems. The SQL Server Agent service is accessed and managed in Enterprise Manager—and fully investigated in Chapter 12.

The SQL Server Agent is divided into the following three services. This architecture has been similarly implemented in a number of Windows 2000 services, such as the Removable Storage Services:

- **Alerts** These are the actions that need to be taken when a specific event occurs on the server. Errors are good examples of alerts that a DBA or operator needs to be made aware of. For example, errors generated by incorrect logins or security problems can be sent to a DBA via e-mail, paging or beeper services, the Windows messenger service, or a telephone call. The alert mechanism can also be configured to run certain jobs.
- **Operators** The Operators service lets you define operators using their domain accounts or e-mail IDs. These people are typically members of a "database administrators group" defined in the Windows NT or Windows 2000 domain. You can send messages to all operators using a single e-mail message that gets sent to a group.
- **Jobs** The jobs are the collections of steps that get executed by the Agent service. Jobs are defined in the service and then scheduled for execution at a later time or in response to an alert or event.

In addition to the Agent services in Enterprise Manager, you can interface with SQL Server Agent from applications that use SQL Distributed Management Objects architecture (SQL-DMO), which is discussed in Chapter 7, and from any SQL Server client application that is programmed to transmit T-SQL statements to the server.

Microsoft Search

Microsoft Search extends the SQL-92 definitions for standard character-based searching, which is based on a system of comparison operators (equal to, less than, and greater than) applied to character constants and character strings stored in the database.

The engine, first, supports a powerful indexing model, which is implemented as full-text catalogs and indexes that you define for a database. These are not stored as objects in a SQL Server database but rather as independent files. Second, the engine processes full-text queries and determines which entries in the index meet the full-text selection criteria obtained from user input. The criteria can be words or phrases, words that are within a certain proximity to each other, or the inflections on verbs and nouns.

The search algorithm works as follows: For each search criterion processed by the engine, the identity of a row that meets the criterion and its ranking value is returned to the DBMS, which then builds the result set to return to the client.

The full-text catalogs and indexes are stored in separate files on the server, which are administered by the search service.

The Microsoft Distributed Transaction Coordinator

The Microsoft Distributed Transaction Coordinator (MS DTC or just DTC) is a service that lets you program applications that can work with data drawn from several different data sources in one transaction. It also coordinates the updating of data to different databases, even databases that are installed in remote servers. The DTC is a key component of Microsoft's maximum availability strategy in that it ensures that an UPDATE succeeds on all distributed servers or on none of the servers. We use the DTC when users update data in distributed partitioned views on a federation of SQL Servers.

You can easily enlist the services of DTC in your applications by calling remote stored procedures from your application that apply to all "enlisted" servers. The DTC service can be managed from Enterprise Manager and the SQL Server Services Manager. DTC services are discussed in Chapter 12, 13, and 24.

The Network Ahead

If you are new to client/server database systems, the paradigm shift from desktop applications, such as Microsoft Access and Corel Paradox, might seem steep. A number of areas will entail a learning curve. Understanding how to configure users in the database, server security and logins, roles, and so on can be a challenge. In Chapter 8, I go into the security aspect in a lot more depth. I have also included a deployment plan that offers step-by-step instructions on setting up your users for access.

As wonderful as SQL Server is, one of the drawbacks for newcomers is that it is so vast. It is not unusual to do everything right in the test or development environment, only to find users cannot connect when you roll out or deploy your production system. Chapter 8 will help you troubleshoot such situations.

In the next chapter, I will put SQL Server's entrails under the spotlight again as we discuss the DBMS architecture.

Chapter 4

DBMS Architecture

This chapter investigates the core of the SQL Server 2000—the Database Management System (DBMS). You will be learning about its storage architecture and data input/output (I/O). I might add that the architecture and processes discussed in this chapter relate mostly to the SQL Server storage engine, while the architecture and processes discussed in Chapter 2 relate mostly to the relational engine.

For the most part, all SQL-driven database management systems operate on the same principles, just as all cars run on tires, gas, and a combustion engine. Some systems, however, work better than others do, and each DBMS is unique in how it makes use of memory, CPU, hard disks, and its query processing algorithms.

In this chapter, it will seem that I am straying into general relational database theory and architecture and moving away from SQL Server 2000. But the opposite is the case. If you are new to databases, C/S RDBMS systems, SQL, and SQL Server, you will greatly benefit from a general discussion on how a DBMS works in general and how SQL Server works in particular. You also need to investigate the claims that SQL Server 2000 leads the field in many transaction processing areas and is currently the most scalable product available; this chapter helps you meet that objective.

I believe you should first understand how a DBMS works—and then learn how SQL Server works in relation to general DBMS or transaction processing theory. It is thus a good idea to combine this chapter with a good book on the principles of relational database systems. Combining knowledge of the two will enable you to appreciate SQL Server better, understand how to make it work for you, and ultimately become a better DBA and SQL Server developer as you tackle the more complex "data" in the chapters that lie ahead.

If you are an experienced SQL Server or C/S DBMS engineer, you can skim the first part of this chapter. If you are new to SQL Server, however, I strongly recommend you understand how this DBMS works. Coupled with an understanding of the collateral components and resources, this understanding will help flatten the learning curve before you.

For the most part, you will be learning conceptually about SQL Server's internal environment: how data gets into the DBMS; how it gets stored, retrieved, and sent back out to the clients. But first let's get familiar with some of the important pieces before getting into deeper water. I will launch the discussion with a subject that all vendors are making a lot of noise about: the Transaction Processing Performance Council's (TPC) transaction processing benchmarks.

The TPC Benchmarks

You should make a special effort to understand the TCP benchmark data that the important database vendors now publish. Microsoft published a number of benchmarks in 2000 indicating that SQL Server 2000 has become the leading DBMS system with the lowest cost per transaction rating on the market. What does this mean to you?

TPC benchmarks are to the DBMS what the MIPS ratings are to processors or CPUs or what horsepower is to a combustion engine. A DBMS needs to meet certain performance benchmarks before it can be considered worthwhile or competitive in both online transaction processing and decision support systems. The benchmarking is used to test algorithms, new versions of code, new hardware platforms, and so on. So DBMS vendors, including Microsoft, Informix, IBM, Oracle, Sybase, and others, use the benchmarks to test the veracity and reliability of their systems on certain platforms and in controlled testing environments. TPC benchmark tests are like Formula 1 events in motor racing. The manufacturers not only compete to prove superiority or market share, but they take what they learn at the races and incorporate the results into new products for consumers.

The nonprofit Transaction Processing Performance Council (TPC)—which can be found on the Internet at www.tpc.org—conducts the TPC benchmark tests. The TPC's purpose is to define the tests and disseminate objective performance data based on the benchmarks. The benchmarks have stringent test requirements and include a number of durability and reliability tests. The results of the tests are independently audited and published.

The two important benchmarks for SQL Server 2000 (and SQL Server version 7.0) are the TPC-C benchmarks and the TPC-H benchmarks, respectively, for Online Transaction Processing (OLTP) and decision support systems (DSS, discussed in Part IV). They are described as follows:

- **TPC-C: OLTP** TPC-C measures both performance and scalability of OLTP DBMS systems. TPC-C tests a wide range of database functionality such as selects, updates, and batch transactions. Most important, however, is that TPC-C measures *throughput* in business transactions per minute in a simulated order entry and distribution environment. The tests measure how many new orders are generated in a minute while the DBMS is executing four other transaction types, such as payments, status updates, shipping or deliveries, and inventory level updates.

  Throughput, in TPC terms, is a measure of maximum sustained system performance. The five transaction types have a certain predefined user response time requirement. The new order response time is set at five seconds. So, if your system generates a 500 tpmC number, it means that the system is generating 500 new orders per minute while fulfilling the other four requirements in the TPC-C workload. When you consider Internet applications or e-commerce solutions, you can see how the TPC-C benchmark becomes especially important. At the time of this writing, the TPC-C benchmark for SQL Server

2000 on Compaq ProLiant 8500 servers is illustrated in the following table, derived from statistics published jointly by Microsoft and Compaq:

Hardware	TpmC	Price/tpmC	Total System Cost
Compaq ProLiant 8500-700-96P (12 node)	262,243	$20.24	$5.3M
Compaq ProLiant 8500-550-96P (12 node)	229,913	$23.08	$5.3M
Compaq ProLiant 8500-700-64P (8 node)	179,658	$19.75	$3.5M
Compaq ProLiant 8500-550-64P (8 node)	161,719	$21.86	$3.5M

Microsoft and Compaq achieved these benchmarks with SQL Server 2000 Enterprise Edition on Windows 2000 Advanced Server using clusters of 8 and 12 Compaq ProLiant 8500 database servers. Each server had eight Intel Pentium III Xeon 700 MHz or 550 MHz processors and 8 GB of memory. In addition, the measured systems included 24–36 application servers (3/node) running Microsoft's Web server, Internet Information Server. Compaq's ServerNet II provided high-speed interconnect between the database servers.

- **TPC-H: DSS** This benchmark, measured as TPC-H Composite Queries per Hour (QphH), simulates a decision support system containing large volumes of data that is synchronized with online production databases. The benchmark makes use of highly complex ad hoc queries designed to answer real-world questions. These include questions concerning pricing, promotions (such as target markets), supply and demand, profit and loss, and so on. It should come as no surprise, given the preceding tmpC rating, that SQL Server 2000 also leads the field in the TPC-H benchmarks.

TPC-C and TPC-H also produce price/performance numbers, the $/tpmC and $/QphH rates, respectively. These ratings are especially useful when determining cost for transaction or analysis performance. But the rating is not about the cost of the platform or computer, because that actually represents only a small part of the costing criteria in a DBMS. The rating takes into consideration the entire computing environment, including terminals, client computers, software, operating systems, the DBMS software, three-year maintenance plans, and so forth.

An example: How do you derive the $/tpmC for an OLTP system? Take the cost of the entire system and divide it by the tpmC benchmark. In the benchmark illustrated in the previous table, we take the cost of the entire system (which is published at

$5.3 million for the first solution) and divide that by the tpmC, or 262,243, to arrive at the $/tpmC of $20.24. No doubt the highly scalable server platform (and these Compaq server clusters would fill a small data center) is even more juicy than the actual tpmC number because an IBM RS/6000 with about 24 processors would cost you four times the $/tpmC for nowhere near a comparable tpmC.

It is also key to stress an interesting finding about scalability—and we will get into this further in Chapter 13—that the TPC benchmarks prove. When it comes to SMP scalability, less often means more, especially for DBMS systems. Linear SMP scalability is a jihad among DBAs, and many seem to think that midrange or UNIX systems with OS support for hundreds of processors is the answer to achieving DBMS scalability. Many also point out a so-called flaw in Windows 2000 that it cannot support as many processors as its rival UNIX. The benchmarks thus prove SMP scalability to be a myth with respect to DBMS systems.

The TPC monitors other benchmarks as well, such as the TPC-R rating, which measures the performance of standardized report generation. The benchmarks can be researched at www.tpc.org.

An Overview of the DBMS Components

The SQL Server 2000 DBMS comprises a number of interconnected I/O architectures or modules. The following are key components you should make a special effort to understand before attempting to program SQL Server 2000:

- **The Relational Database Engine** This component comprises several modules or collateral components that interact with each other on a common code base. With the storage engine and its modules, the relational database engine makes up the DBMS. The system also includes statement parsing and processing modules (for both SQL and XML), and the query processing system. The engine receives all communications from the client, passed to it as events from the Net-Libraries. The query containing T-SQL statements are first parsed, then preprocessed, and then compiled into execution plans, which are sent up against the data store, via the storage engine, for extraction. The extracted data is then built into the tabular data formation (the TDS protocol) that is sent back to the client, through the Net-Libraries.
- **The Storage Engine** This suite of components is responsible for the management of the database files and the management of the space within the files. While we include it as part of the DBMS, it is really at the center of SQL Server's database architecture, which is discussed in Chapter 2. The storage engine is also responsible for transaction logging and database recovery.

- **The Transaction Architecture** Understanding the transaction architecture is key to understanding most of what makes up SQL Server 2000 and how you adapt the various features to your ends. There are essentially two transaction architectures that you will learn about in this book: a local transaction architecture responsible for the work that performs deletes, updates, inserts, and so on; and the distributed transactions architecture that involves or encompasses data from external sources. The latter is discussed in Chapter 21.
- **Concurrency Control and Transaction Management** Part of the transaction architecture, it deserves separate treatment. It is really a system of methods and algorithms that allow multiple users to exploit the databases under the management of an instance of the DBMS. Concurrency in SQL Server is handled by a pessimistic locking architecture built into the relational engine. The locking mechanism allows you to obtain locks on rows, pages, ranges of keys, indexes, tables, and whole databases. Besides the architecture discussed here, locking is also discussed extensively in Chapter 21.

The Relational Database Engine

You can look at the relational engine in two ways: you can study it at the core, or the relational kernel, or you can study it at a higher level with all its surrounding components that the kernel hands functionality off to. Studying the kernel at any lower level is beyond the scope of this book. A good analogy, however, is what we need to study in a steam locomotive engine, the pistons and drive shaft being the kernel, and the rest of the engine, comprising the coal burners, wheels, knobs, pulleys, levers, (not to mention the engineer and the horn) representing a higher level. Let's look at the kernel in all its functional glory.

Note *At the very core of the SQL Server relational engine, the kernel is the same code used for each version of SQL Server, from the CE Edition (which is embedded into your average CE device) to the Enterprise Edition parked on the shared or clustered disks of a TerraServer. This is the reason you can write code for the CE edition and execute it with very little modification on any other version of SQL Server 2000.*

At the kernel level, you have a highly optimized chunk of code that picks up inbound T-SQL statements from the Net-Libs and optimizes it into native code for the most effective execution plan. (In many respects, the relational engine is like a compiler that preprocesses code into object code before compiling it into machine code. It is no different from the preprocessing algorithms used in many different kernels, aside from database systems.)

Memory Architecture

Sophisticated memory management architecture ensures that SQL Server 2000 gets all the memory it needs within limitations of the platform. Its memory management is conservative: The engine obtains memory as it needs it, and releases it as resources become free. The advanced memory management facility on the Windows 2000 server platform (Address Windowing Extensions or AWE) enables SQL Server Enterprise Edition to work with a 8GB address space on Windows 2000 Advanced Server, and up 64GB on Windows 2000 Data Center.

DBAs are still able to override the default and automated memory settings and specify fixed allocations (discussed in Chapter 12) should the application or environment require it. One area where this may be required is in the management of the memory pool, which is discussed shortly. The memory pool is where SQL Server stores its buffer cache of data pages.

SQL Server tries to maintain virtual memory on the server at between 4MB and 10MB less than physical memory. And the only way SQL Server can do this is by changing the size of its memory pool. When SQL Server loads up collateral processes, such as calls to remote stored procedures and OLE DB providers, or when other applications or other instances of SQL Server start, it will have to reduce the size of the memory pool to release memory it has acquired. You can set limits on just how much the memory pool can vary by setting values for *min server memory* and *max server memory*, which are exposed in the Enterprise Manager (see Chapter 12).

Any new applications that start up on the server are instead allocated paged memory. Each instance of SQL Server 2000 is thus able to work with the memory on the system, to the mutual benefit of the other instances. (When using AWE, however, the system will require the assignment of static memory addresses.)

The Windows memory architecture consists of a memory model based on a flat, linear, 32-bit address space on Windows NT, Windows 2000 Server, and Windows 2000 Advanced Server, and a 64-bit address space on Windows 2000 Datacenter. Two types of memory are used in the Windows NT and Windows 2000 operating systems: *physical* memory and *virtual* memory. The physical memory is the memory in the RAM chips installed on the system motherboards. Then you have virtual memory, which is a combination of all memory in the system and the architecture that makes it available to the OS. An important aspect of virtual memory is that it can include hard disk platter memory.

Note *Chapter 6 discusses various memory configurations.*

Page Files and the VMM

The *virtual memory manager* (VMM) manages all system memory and ensures that applications and the operating system have access to more memory than what is provided by the RAM chips installed in the modules on the motherboard. Memory chips are faster than virtual memory, a fact that is important for SQL Server.

The VMM has another important role: It guarantees that memory addresses used by multiple instances and applications do not "trespass" on each other. In the olden days of DOS, this problem created disasters. Memory management has evolved over the years, from the first versions of the Windows operating system to Windows 2000 Datacenter, which is one of the most sophisticated operating systems in existence. With each new version of the operating system, the virtual memory management has been improved, so the algorithms used by Windows 95 differ from the algorithms used in Windows 98, and so on. The memory management of Windows NT has also been greatly improved on Windows 2000. This means that for SQL Server 2000 to support instances on all 32-bit and 64-bit operating systems (except for Windows 95, which SQL Server 2000 does not support), the DMBS must use different caching algorithms.

The VMM has two major functions:

- The VMM manages a memory-mapped table that keeps track of the list of virtual addresses assigned to each process. An analogy might be a hotel in which all the guests are assigned to rooms and the concierge can consult a table to manage the guests, their check-in times, check-out times, dirty laundry, and so on. The VMM coordinates exactly where in the system the actual data mapped to the addresses resides. In other words, it acts as a translator service, mapping virtual memory to physical memory. This function is transparent to the applications, and they operate oblivious to the process that is providing them the illusion that they have access to physical memory.
- When processes use up all available RAM, the VMM moves the memory contents least accessed out to the hard disk. This is called *paging*.

Windows 2000 thus basically has access to a 4GB address space, although the space is virtual and can be made up of both RAM and hard disk space. Getting back to our hotel analogy, this is like having some important or high-rate guests residing in the main hotel building overlooking the ocean, while longer-term or low-rate guests occupy the annex overlooking the street. The total room count, however, is a sum of all the rooms in both buildings.

Although we talk about a 4GB address space, this space is actually relative to how the system uses memory. In actual fact, on Windows 2000 Server, the address space available to applications is only 2GB; in fact, it is even less than that, because the 2GB assignment is shared by all processes running in user mode. The other 2GB is reserved for kernel-mode execution.

So if you study Windows NT or Windows 2000 memory architecture, you see that the 4GB space is divided into an upper and a lower segment, both containing 2GB address spaces. The kernel mode threads and processes are allocated the upper portion, while the lower space is reserved for both user mode and kernel mode processes. The upper portion also reserves certain lower regions of total address space, which is used for hardware mapping.

The lower portion is also maintained in paging pools comprising 4KB pages. There are a nonpaged pool and a paged pool. The pages in the paged pool are the pages that can get swapped out to disk. It is usually reserved for applications, which are the processes most likely to become idle. The nonpaged pool remains in physical RAM and supports the operating system functions and critical services. The size of each page is 4KB.

More About Paging

Paging is the process of moving data in and out of physical memory, a.k.a. RAM. When the RAM-based memory pool becomes full and the operating system is called on to deliver more memory, the VMM will kick idle data out of physical memory and relocate it to the hard disk in a structure called a *page file.*

The VMM manages the memory pool by assigning space in the pages that are identified as either *valid* or *invalid* pages. The valid pages are located in physical memory and become immediately available to an application when it needs it. You can think of them as being "online" to the application, like a line of credit. Invalid pages are "offline" and not available to any demanding application. The invalid pages are stored on disk.

Although idle applications and data are stored in the offline pages, the VMM maintains pointers to the addresses so that it can recover the data when it needs to. For example, when an application or data in the page file is referenced, the operating system needs to get it back to RAM as quickly as possible. At this point, a page fault is triggered, spawning a new thread to access the data in the page file. But for the recalled data to fit back into the active memory pool, idle data that has been hanging around gets bumped and sent offline to disk. Now you know why fast and reliable hard disks are recommended in data- and memory-intensive applications.

The VMM performs a series of housekeeping chores as part of the paging routines:

- It manages the data in the offline page file on a first-in, first-out basis. Data that has been on disk the longest is the first to make it back to physical memory when RAM frees up, unless something on the disk is explicitly needed. In other words, the VMM does not simply recall data idle on the hard disk to be idle in RAM. But the VMM continues to move data back and forth from RAM as long as RAM keeps freeing up and idle data needs to be paged out to the hard disk. The "hot" data the VMM keeps an eye on is known as the *working set.*
- The VMM performs what is known as *fetching* when it brings back data from the page file. In addition, the VMM also performs what is known as *page file clustering.* Page file clustering means that when the VMM fetches, it also brings back some of the surrounding data in the page file, on the premise that data immediately before and after the required data might be needed in the next

instant as well. This technique thus tends to speed up data I/O from the page file.

- The VMM is smart enough to conclude that if there is no space in RAM to place returning data from the hard disk, the least needed data in RAM must be displaced and banished to the hard disk.

You can manage and control the parameters in which the VMM operates and factors such as the size of the page file; it is very important to understand.

Address Windowing Extensions

To support very large address spaces, such as 8GB on Windows 2000 Advanced Server and as much as 64GB on Datacenter, the Address Windowing Extensions (AWE) have to be invoked. The AWE is to Windows 2000 what the old DOS extenders and EMS libraries were to the legacy PC-based operating systems and the early 16-bit versions of Windows (remember Pharlap). The AWE is included in the 32- and 64-bit APIs that allow applications to address more than the 4GB that is addressable through the standard 32-bit API.

AWE lets applications acquire physical memory as nonpaged memory. It then dynamically maps the views of nonpaged memory to the 32-bit address space . . . you could call this *conjoined memory addressing*. A comprehensive, bit-by-bit investigation of AWE is beyond the scope of this book, because as a DBA or application developer, you can let Windows 2000 and SQL Server 2000 handle the additional addressing for you. All you have to do is enable the use of AWE.

Note *You can unravel AWE in the MSDN library.*

AWE is enabled for SQL Server 2000 applications using the system stored procedure sp_configure, which can take an *on* or *off* bit for enabling or disabling AWE respectively.

The SQL Server Address Space

Each instance of SQL Server started up on your computer consumes an address space that is divided into a number of areas that hold the various modules of code that make up the DBMS. Each address space, for each instance, holds the following components:

- **The Executable Code** This area of the address space includes the Open Data Services (ODS), the SQL Server engine code, and the SQL Server Net-Libraries. In addition, distributed queries can also independently load an OLE DB provider DLL into the address space, as will extended stored procedures and OLE Automation objects.

- **The Memory Pool** This area of the address space is used for the data structures that use memory in an instance of SQL Server. The typical objects using the memory pool comprise the following:
  - **System-level data structures** These are structures that hold global data for the instance, such as database descriptors and the lock table.
  - **The buffer cache** This is the cache that holds the buffer pages into which data pages are read (discussed shortly).
  - **The procedure cache** This is the cache that holds the execution plans for T-SQL queries that have been executed, or are in the process of being executed, in the instance. (See the section "SQL, Query Optimization, and Query Processing" later in this chapter.)
  - **The log caches** These are the caches of buffer pages used to read and write the log pages. As discussed in Chapter 2, the log buffers and the associated log files are managed separately from the data buffers and the actual data files.
  - **The connection contexts** The connection contexts maintain data representing each connection in the instance. The data includes state information and the parameter values for queries and stored procedures, cursor positions, and tables under reference.
- **The Stack Space** The stack space is allocated by the operating system for threads that are started in SQL Server. The default stack size is 512KB.

The memory pool is a fluid structure, and SQL Server constantly adjusts the amounts of memory being allocated to various components to optimize performance. Every time a client connects, for example, SQL Server has to allocate memory to the new connection. And then it has to release it when the client disconnects. New and altered databases and all their objects are also constantly changing the allocation and usage of memory. The buffer cache, the procedure cache, and the log caches are also factors that influence how memory is used and released.

Tip *The applications you create and how you code your queries can have a direct bearing on SQL Server performance. You want to keep the number of one-way and round-trips to the server as low as possible, but conversely you also have to keep the amount of data sent up and down as low as possible. I discuss this consideration in more detail in Chapters 14 and 19.*

SQL Server, like all DBMS systems, strives to minimize disk thrashing by using the services of a buffer cache in memory. This buffer cache holds pages read from the database. According to the SQL Server development team, they have spent a lot of time making sure that SQL Server 2000 makes maximum use of the buffer cache and minimizes the disk I/O of database files. When the buffer runs out of memory, the operating system will start swapping pages out to the page file, using the processes described earlier. Naturally, the system will slow down, so it is important on mission-critical systems to add more "real" memory when the VMM goes into overtime. The bigger the buffer cache, the better SQL Server will respond.

SQL Server I/O Architecture

The I/O architecture, which defines how data is read from and written to the databases, is the architecture underpinning all database management systems. It is also one of the key components of these products and one of the key architectures that sets them apart from one other. The system that has the fastest, leanest, and most innovative I/O architecture wins the transaction-load war and ultimately market share, as discussed earlier on the subject of TPC benchmarks.

SQL Server 2000 has lofty goals set for it. On the one hand, it must meet the needs of small businesses, while on the other, it must compete with the heavyweights of the world. I believe Microsoft met the challenge, because SQL Server can scale from a single-user solution to an Internet deployment supporting thousands of users. Let's take a closer look at the I/O architecture that achieves this feat.

There are two locations from which an instance of SQL Server can read (and write) data: from memory and from the physical hard disk. It does not take much effort to imagine what would become of a hard disk if all the data required by clients was constantly read from the database—a barrage of continuous transactions might, literally, set the server on fire. So SQL Server, like all DBMS systems, stores a virtual copy of its most accessed data, and most recently accessed data, in memory. In other words, the read or write does not require the movement of physical parts.

When SQL Server starts and data is requested, it is loaded into virtual memory and occupies spaces allocated for it in the so-called buffer cache we discussed earlier. As you learned in Chapter 2, the data is stored in 8KB data pages on disk. The pages are made contiguous to form 64KB extents. Accordingly, the virtual data pages in the buffer cache are also 8KB in size.

Now, a *virtual read* (sometimes referred to as a "logical read," a term I have a problem with) occurs every time a client requests data that is stored in the buffer cache. If the data required is not in the buffer cache, SQL Server has to get the data from the hard disk, a *physical read.* Conversely, a *virtual write* takes places when data is updated or changed in memory. By *virtual write,* we mean that the data is updated in the cache as opposed to being updated on the disk. However, the data is not persistent, and if the electrical power that provides life to the cache is terminated, data loss ensues. From time to time, data must then be *physically written* to disk. But performance takes precedence over persistence, and the DBMS pushes the virtual management envelope by reading and writing to data more than once before it is saved to the disks.

The DBMS thus has to maintain a suitable buffer so that performance is maintained and the server is not forced to write and read excessively to and from the hard disk.

However, the larger the buffer cache used by SQL Server, the less memory resources are made available to other applications. A point of diminishing returns arrives when the server saves on physical I/O but loses through the excessive paging that occurs to support other applications.

SQL Server pushes the so-called I/O envelope by using two Windows NT I/O features: *Scatter-Gather I/O* and *Asynchronous I/O.* Scatter-Gather I/O has often been cited as a new feature in Windows 2000, but it was introduced to the operating system with Windows NT 4.0 SP2 several years ago. No doubt it was a target for enhancement in Windows 2000, and it is now built into the operating system. Essentially, this technology is responsible for moving data from disconnected areas of RAM to contiguous blocks of data on a hard disk. While you, the DBA or system administrator, do not have any control over the operating system's use of this technology, systems and software have to be specifically written to take advantage of it. SQL Server 2000 is one such system—actually, Scatter-Gather I/O was originally created for SQL Server.

Note *This is not exactly the same thing that the VMM does, because the shunting around of data by the VMM occurs without the cognizance of the application.*

The performance boost for SQL Server is more obvious when the DBMS reads data from the hard disk. For example: If SQL Server reads in a 64KB extent, it does not have to reserve a 64KB area in the buffer cache for the data. It can scatter the eight buffer pages directly into the buffer cache and later gather the eight pages by maintaining the cache addresses of the eight buffer pages.

Another I/O feature SQL Server makes heavy use of is *Asynchronous I/O.* If I/O were synchronous, every time SQL Server spawned a thread to read or write data, the entire system would have to wait for the I/O operation to complete before regaining control and moving on with the next process. But under *Asynchronous I/O,* SQL Server can carry on with other tasks while checking back periodically on the status of the I/O thread.

Using Asynchronous I/O functionality, SQL Server can spawn multiple concurrent I/O operations against files. You can throttle the maximum number of I/O operations by setting the *max async io* configuration option. The default is 32 threads of I/O execution. Only the most demanding of applications will require you to set more than the default. This is now a good point to launch into the subject of SQL Server's thread and task architecture.

SQL Server's Thread and Task Architecture

All DBMS products, like all major applications, are built on solid multithreading systems architecture. We don't need to discuss threading technology here at any deep level save to say that threading technology allows complex processes to make more effective use of the central processing unit (CPU). If you are new to software engineering practice or new to the concept of threading, you can find many books on the subject, and the subject is well covered in the MSDN library and in the Microsoft online knowledge base.

In the not-too-distant past, the only way we could execute processes in a system concurrently was to have multiple instances of applications running on the operating system. A multitasking kernel (the OS) was responsible for deciding which applications got preferential use of the CPU and when. This was how the early Windows operating systems worked. Later it became possible for an application to obtain a level of concurrent processor use within the application's address space by executing multiple process threads. Multithreading led to more reliable software because the operating system could properly manage the order and priority of thread execution.

It is important to understand that you cannot execute threads at exactly the same time on a single CPU, because threading is a synchronous technology. The operating system can, however, determine when to kill a thread or allow one thread to execute ahead of others (priority). On multiple-CPU systems, threads can run in a true concurrent state by being executed on parallel processors. In other words, if a computer has eight processes, it can concurrently execute eight threads.

An allied technology to threads is *fibers*. Fibers are similar to threads, but the application rather than the operating system gets to control them. Fiber technology does not require the operating system's overhead of threading, which requires resources in both the user mode and kernel mode of the OS. That said, fibers are not exactly separate from threads. They are derived from threads. A thread can spawn multiple fibers.

Fiber execution is an advanced technology, and only the Enterprise Edition of SQL Server 2000 supports it. Many different activities go on in SQL Server at the same time, and all these processes compete for CPU time. At the core of the DBMS we find what appears to be functionality that is very similar to the part of the operating system that works with threads. This SQL Server kernel thus allows the system to work with both threads and fibers without having to engage the kernel and user mode resources of the OS. And each instance of SQL Server maintains a pool of threads and fibers that are executed in this thread-fiber layer.

This is just one of the features that makes SQL Server as powerful as it is. You control the configuration of the pool via the *max worker threads* configuration option (see Chapter 12). You can also determine if your Enterprise Edition of SQL Server makes use only of threads or of threads and fibers. If you choose threads and fibers, the server is then placed into *fiber mode*. In fiber mode, SQL Server establishes one thread per CPU and then establishes one fiber per concurrent client connection. The number of fibers issued is based on what you set in the *max worker threads* configuration option (the default is 255).

When SQL Server receives a T-SQL statement over the wire, it issues a free thread or fiber (depending on the mode) from the thread stack to the inbound connection. If there are no free threads or fibers and the max worker threads value has not been reached, SQL Server will allocate a new thread or fiber. If the thread ceiling has been reached, SQL Server will have to find threads or fibers that are not being used and free them up.

While you may be tempted to set the *max worker threads* configuration higher than the default, you should note that a point will be reached at which SQL Server performance will begin to deteriorate. The reason is simple: Thread and fiber management and creation themselves consume resources, and a runaway thread scenario can bring an application to a standstill. In any event, most of the threads created spend a lot of time waiting around doing nothing, and they can safely be freed and reused without reallocation of resources—so you should never have a need to set the *max worker threads* value higher than the 255 default.

SQL Server Transaction Architecture

Every DBMS system needs to be a good online transaction processing system (OLTP). This means that the integrity of the data must be ensured by the transactions that take place in the database whenever data is read, written, removed, or updated.

A *transaction* is a complete unit of work from the start of a query to the end of a query. A transaction cannot be broken or suspended, or resumed at some later date, without risking the integrity of the data, because it cannot lock up or command the exclusive service of the entire DBMS. Other transactions also need to do work in the DBMS (concurrency); that's the purpose of a DBMS or an OLTP system. A transaction cannot own the DBMS, exclusively holding or locking it until its work completes sometime in the unknown future.

Integrity is ensured by an "all or nothing" philosophy (atomicity). In other words, a transaction must complete without errors or not at all. A typical transaction is represented by the following code:

```
BEGIN TRANSACTION
      INSERT INTO CustDetails (CustID) VALUES ('15')
COMMIT TRANSACTION
```

A database table is assumed to be in a consistent or plausible state at the beginning of a transaction. The client signals the start of a transaction; this can be done explicitly by enclosing the transaction steps between, typically, the BEGIN TRANSACTION—COMMIT TRANSACTION statements. Transactions can also be started implicitly in SQL Server without BEGIN…COMMIT by merely sending a T-SQL query to the server, which places it into autocommit mode.

During the transaction, the DBMS takes whatever steps it needs to take in the execution of a query to maintain the integrity of the data under control of the transaction. At this point, the transaction "owns" the data it is currently working with, but at any point in the transaction the data may be in an inconsistent state. If multiple tables are being referenced or updated in the transaction, they naturally cannot all be updated at exactly the same time. During the course of the transaction, some rows may be updated and others not.

If an error thus occurs during the transaction, tables that have not yet been touched by the transaction will be left out of the loop. In the case of an error, a ROLLBACK TRANSACTION is required to restore all data affected in the transaction to its previous state. If no error occurs and the transaction completes successfully, the COMMIT TRANSACTION can be issued. After the issuance of a commit, all modifications become part of the database.

As discussed in Chapter 2, the transaction log provides us with the ability to roll back the database to a former state, even if the transactions were successful. The transaction logs record the sequence of events in a transaction from start to finish. The log contains sufficient information to either redo a transaction, in what is known as *roll forward,* or undo a transaction, in what is known as *roll back.* The subject of recovery and the work performed by transaction logs is fully covered in Chapters 9 and 21.

Isolation, Concurrency, and Locking Architecture

Isolation and concurrency management is part and parcel of transaction management. All DBMS systems implement a system of isolation and concurrency mechanisms to ensure that multiple transactions, representing at least two and perhaps many thousands of users all working on the same database at the same time, are able to access the same data at—almost—the same time without crashing into each other. The isolation algorithms implemented by a DBMS, SQL Server included, also ensure that the transactions being instantiated by concurrent sessions in the DBMS do not interfere with one another.

Two concurrency specifications underpin the methods for ensuring concurrency: *pessimistic concurrency control* and *optimistic concurrency control.* They are defined as follows:

- **Pessimistic concurrency control** consists of a system of locking mechanisms that prevents more than one application from accessing the same data at the same time. The reason it is called *pessimistic concurrency control* is that it is deployed, usually, in high-transaction situations in which it is highly likely that many connections are going to contend for the same data in an uncontrolled state. Most transaction applications fall into this category. Shopping carts on the Web are a good example of a high-transaction environment in which the middle tier is required to open a huge number of connections to the same database and access the same rows of data for all the connections.

- **Optimistic concurrency control** involves situations in which connections or client applications do not lock the data they are accessing. The system simply checks the data, and if a contention arises, someone has to stand down from his or her transaction and start over. Optimistic control is possible in low-traffic or highly controlled environments.

Your applications or solutions will have to take into account the cost of locking database objects during transactions. Many high-stakes or mission-critical applications are controlled by a single scheduler that is perfectly aware of all the transaction threads it is establishing to a database server, such as a PBX system. Locking and unlocking are resource intensive, and the milliseconds that add up might cause serious problems for the application. A single scheduler needs to be aware of how and when contentions arise and deal with them using optimistic concurrency control algorithms.

On the other hand, most transaction processing DBMS environments will use locking mechanisms, especially when all sessions or connections are established by independent applications on the client, most likely initiated by human users who have no idea who else is in the databases they are working in.

Locks and Latches

SQL Server 2000 makes use of a sophisticated locking architecture to implement pessimistic concurrency control. Locking is essential in a system that can potentially have tens of thousands of users all working with the same pool of data. Locking is a means of enforcing or ensuring data integrity. It is a system of assurances that allow a process to safely work with data and to be assured that data is not going to be changed "behind its back," so to speak.

Locks are managed on a connection basis. In other words, a connection *AA* that requires a lock cannot use the lock created by connection *AB*, even if both connections were initiated by the same client application. Each connection must establish a lock created exclusively within the context of its connection. An exception can be found in the concept of bound connections, but I leave that subject for discussion in Chapter 21.

SQL Server also supports several types of locking modes. The modes include *shared, update, exclusive, intent,* and *schema.* Lock modes indicate the level of dependency the connection obtains on the locked object. SQL Server also controls how the lock modes relate to one another. You cannot, for example, obtain an exclusive lock on an object if shared locks are already acquired on the same object.

SQL Server threads or fibers place locks on databases, tables, rows, indexes, keys, key ranges, and pages. This approach is known as *locking granularity.* The locking granularity is dynamically determined by SQL Server (during formulation of the query plan discussed later) and needs no overt action on the part of the application or you; although this does not preclude the application from requesting a specific lock and lock mode. SQL Server determines exactly what locking level is needed for each T-SQL query it receives. One query may generate a row-level lock, while another may generate a lock that smacks down the entire database. The connections also respect the locks no matter what the levels. In other words, if connection *AA* has a table lock on data, connection *AB* is prevented from establishing a row lock on the same table.

From time to time, SQL Server may decide to escalate a lock. For example, if a row-level lock consumes most of a table, the relational engine may escalate the lock to the whole table. The query processor usually determines the correct lock required by the query.

Locks are maintained only for the length of time needed to protect data at the level request by the client. For example, share locks in SQL Server are held for a duration that depends on the transaction isolation level. The default transaction isolation level is READ COMMITTED, which corresponds to a share lock that persists as long as it takes to read the data. Scans also result in locks, but the duration of the lock in a scan is much shorter—essentially as long as it takes to scan the page and place a lock on the next page. Other locks are held for the duration of transactions, such as when a transaction isolation level is set to REPEATABLE READ or SERIALIZABLE READ (which are "clean" reads requiring noninterference by any other process).

Cursors are also protected from concurrency operations. A cursor may acquire a share-mode scroll lock to protect a fetch. Scroll locks are typically held until the end of a transaction. And updates also require locks on data, for the duration of the update transaction.

Like all modern DBMS systems, SQL Server includes mechanisms to prevent lock conflicts. If a connection attempts to acquire a lock on data that is already locked, the late connection is blocked from obtaining the lock and essentially waits until the first connection has completed the transaction. You will have to write your own "lock wait" handler in the client or stored procedure to decide how long your application's thread will wait for the opportunity to lock data. Applications obtain their locks on a first-come, first-served basis.

SQL Server also supports deadlock detection. The detection is proactive. In other words, an algorithm is employed to go out and ensure that threads are not frozen in a *lock deadlock,* which is a condition in a DBMS when two or more connections (mostly two) have blocked each other in a deathly embrace. If SQL Server detects such a condition, it will terminate one of the transaction threads, which will allow the remaining thread to continue (see "Deadlocking" in Chapter 21).

Latching and the Storage Engine

The storage engine manages another concurrency mechanism known as a *latch.* Latches occur when the relational engine asks the storage engine to return a row during the processing of a query. The storage engine latches the data page to ensure that no other process modifies the page during a transaction. For example, a latch will ensure that the page offset table entry pointing to the row does not get changed until the transaction has completed.

Reading and Writing the Data Pages

In previous versions of SQL Server, versions 6.5 and earlier, and other legacy DBMS products, the storage functionality and the relational functionality were part and parcel of a single unit. Today the two areas of functionality are encapsulated in separate engines: the storage engine and the relational engine. Both engines include a number of submodules responsible for the reading and writing of data. For the most part, you do not need to concern yourself with the core architecture; however, an understanding of how SQL Server accesses data will help you decide if you need to improve performance with additional or fewer indexes, or if you need to rewrite queries and so forth.

The role played by the storage engine was described in Chapter 2, but it works closely with the relational engine, across the OLE DB "bridge" that is the means by which the two components interface. This is illustrated in Figure 4-1. All read requests are generated by the relational engine, which makes use of specialized access algorithms (encapsulated in access objects) to read data in tables, with or without indexes or other objects.

Access methods are not part of any standard, such as SQL. The language is too abstract for that (although I will discuss Data Definition Language and the syntax for creating and working with indexes in Chapter 11). And access methods are proprietary; each vendor is free to do something special.

The relational engine determines the access method it needs to use to obtain data. These methods might involve local table scans, remote table scans, foreign tables scans, native files reads, index scans, keyed reads, and so on. The combination of these

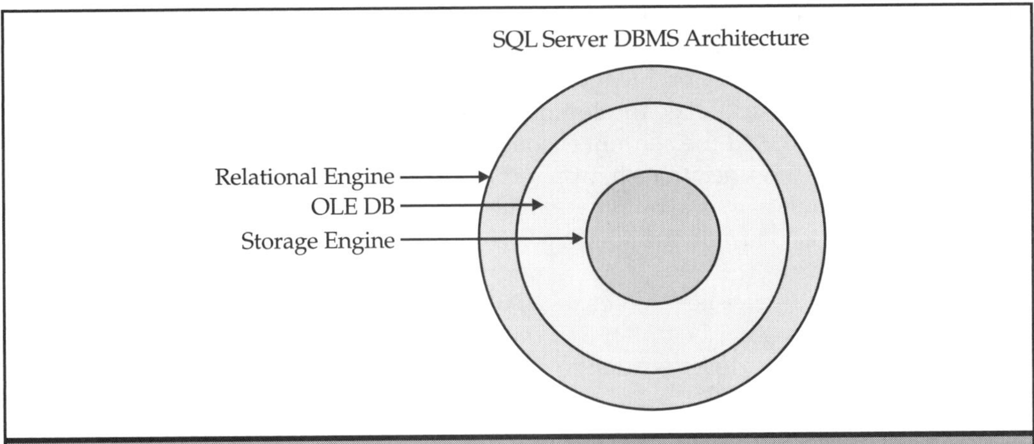

Figure 4-1. *The relational engine and the storage engine are separate components that communicate via OLE DB*

methods determines the general pattern of reads used by SQL Server. SQL Server can make use of a number of different access methods, including the Indexed Sequential Access Method (ISAM), which is used by desktop database systems such as Microsoft Access and Microsoft FoxPro. The database architecture discussed in Chapter 2 makes the reading of data as fast and efficient as possible.

How Data Is Saved

SQL Server works with a singly linked list that contains the addresses of free buffer pages. As soon as a data-reading thread requires a buffer page, it uses the first page in the free buffer list. We say that data pages are *dirty* when they contain data that has not been written to disk. Each buffer page contains a reference counter and an indicator that specifies whether the data page contains dirty data. Every time a query references a buffer page, the reference counter is incremented.

Each instance of SQL Server maintains a lazywriter thread that has the honor of scanning through the buffer cache. Its first job upon system startup is checking the size of the free buffer list. If the free buffer list is below a certain preset point, which depends on the size of the cache, more free pages are added. The buffer pages are scanned frequently by the lazywriter thread, and at each scan the reference counter in the buffer page header is divided by 4. The remainder of the division is discarded. Finally when the reference counter is reduced to 0, the dirty page indicator is checked. If the indicator specifies that the page is dirty, the lazywriter schedules an event to save the data to disk. The writer event coincides with a predetermined free buffer page value internally determined.

The log files come into the picture because data in the buffer cache is first written to the transaction log as the transaction progresses. The purpose of writing to the log first is to allow SQL Server to roll back or roll forward the data before it is committed to the table. Then, in the event of a problem that causes suspect or no data to be written to the table on the physical disk, the commit or bad data can be rolled back. After the data is written to disk and the commit is sound, or if the data page did not contain dirty data, it is freed. Associations between the buffer pages and the physical data pages are removed. Finally the buffer page is returned to the free list. The size of the free buffer list is internally decided by SQL Server and cannot be configured by the DBA.

The writing of the transaction logs takes place outside of the regimen scheduled by the threads working on the buffer and data pages. The *commit* directive forces all pending log transactions to be written to disk.

SQL, Query Optimization, and Query Processing

It might seem a bit patronizing to call attention to the *query* word in Structured Query Language (SQL). It is crucial, though, that you as a PC database developer or administrator understand the special significance of the word in SQL Server, even in

SQL Server Desktop Engine, which will replace Jet as the default Access database. Most Microsoft Access users, for example, never really construct or work with more than the most basic SQL statements because most of the time they are working at a very high, often visual, level above the database and doing little else than storing data and navigating a grid. But for C/S databases in general and SQL Server in particular, everything you do starts and ends with the SQL Query.

On the face of it, a *query* is a question or an enquiry into the data in the DBMS, but a SQL query goes a lot further than being just a question. A SQL query can be combined with Data Definition Language (DDL) and Data Manipulation Language (DML) to create and manipulate storage objects within a database; to add, delete, and transform data in the data storage objects; and to inquire into and analyze that data. And database management systems are managed and driven by humans using SQL.

Each database manufacturer supports the SQL standard. And to support custom and proprietary extensions in their products, they have each extended SQL in certain ways. To extend the SQL language to suite proprietary extensions in SQL Server, Microsoft invented the Transact-SQL extensions to the language. And now Transact-SQL, or rather T-SQL, is the de facto language you use to talk to SQL Server. If you have a background in standard SQL, adopting T-SQL will be easy. T-SQL is covered in Part III.

A good database client application should never place the burden of constructing SQL query statements on application users. I have been developing database applications for many years, and every client eventually requests features that enable users to sort, group, and interpret data. Even the smallest companies I have dealt with, three to four computers max, would tell me they need to know why they are doing better or worse this year than last, and that they need data that can shed light on the health of their businesses. And yet we experienced DBAs tend to think that data analysis is only for the Fortune 500.

How we allow our users to query and analyze data without having to learn SQL is a challenge. And if you think you can get away with giving them simple SQL to use for queries, then you can forget about the language of OLAP cubes. When I first stumbled onto the multidimensional expression (MDX), I tripled my health insurance.

We tackle this tricky subject in later chapters, especially Chapter 23, which covers the English Query. A good start on this road to user empowerment is to appreciate that SQL is really a very high-level language. It is the language that developers and administrators use to "talk" to a DBMS in a language and syntax that have been widely adopted; but at the developer or administrator level, and not the general user level. We will return to this thread in later chapters.

No DBMS, SQL Server included, uses (or can use) SQL as a procedural or instructional language. It is used to convey to the DBMS what a client requires; the server goes off and makes use of any optimal computer language it has been programmed to use to satisfy the request, after the SQL code has been translated.

At a lower level than SQL, the methods used to manipulate and analyze data are both algebraic and calculus in nature. In other words, the procedures to satisfy a query or directive on data are based on mathematical formulations. If we were required to study "raw" relational algebra or relational calculus, there would not be many of us DBAs and SQL developers around, but SQL Server is precisely programmed to deal with that. Consider the following expression:

```
TX WHERE EXISTS CREDITX
    (CREDITX < 5 AND
    T ( T#:TX, CREDIT:CREDITX, STATE:'NEW YORK'))
```

This is relational calculus, and the SQL version is

```
SELECT * FROM CUSTOMERS WHERE CreditRating < 5 AND State = 'NEW YORK'
```

For most of us, talking to a computer in such mathematical terms is difficult to say the least. SQL, on the other hand, lets us talk to the computer in more comfortable terms. Hebrew is one of the best comparisons as a communications language. The old Hebrew comprises certain vowels and variations adopted by the ancient Rabbis who used the language to talk to God (whether God replied is another matter). Today, however, Hebrew is also available in a form without the vowels and variations of the Biblical code, which makes it a better lingua franca for the Jewish people of Israel, and yet a third variation of Hebrew, very different from the former, is used for handwriting.

The view from SQL on the underlying data is no different from the view from VB on machine code. You would only need to go down to assembler if you were writing code for the low levels of the operating system and talking directly to hardware. In the same way, a developer would not use the internal language of the database server unless he or she was programming logic into the engine, or creating a new engine.

To sum up, then, SQL offers a wide range of developers, administrators, and advanced analysts a means of conversing with a database management system. SQL is not ideal or enabled in any way to work directly on the data structures, storage systems, and mechanisms of a database.

But the computer still needs to translate our requirements into its own language, which is better optimized and suited to perform relational algebra and relational calculus at the lower level to carry out the queries. This field of study in databases is known as *query optimization.*

What Is Query Optimization?

If SQL's SELECT statement imposed constant procedures on the database engine, they would all operate in an identical fashion to obtain a result set. The net result would be inflexible architecture and the inability of the engine to take advantage of new technology, new processing power, and zillions of variables.

In the study of analytical problem solving, you learn that there is always more than one solution to a problem, and millions of possible outcomes, palatable or not. The methods used to query data address problems that can be solved in a variety of different ways.

The cliché "there are many ways to skin a cat" describes the problem that query optimization was obviously created to address. A result set can be derived through many different steps, and the optimizer's job is to evaluate each query to determine the quickest means of solving the query problem for the least cost. Cost analysis, performed by most database servers, and especially SQL server, is applied mainly in terms of file I/O (as opposed to I/O on rowsets), with memory and other resources being taken into account. The cost analysis is then combined with each step in the query, and an optimum *execution plan* is the result.

Of course, it is possible for a genius to knock out a theorem that proposes a solution an optimizer might deduce . . . after all, humans are responsible for the logic used by a computer to make such deductions in the first place. But a computer is able to solve such puzzles far quicker than humans, no matter their IQs. The computer, or its optimizer module, is suitably equipped to perform that optimization with a benefit of addressable memory that can tell it about the form that data is in (such as data types and structure), the number of records in a table, the number of distinct values, and so on. The optimizer is capable of taking into account all this data while it determines how best to carry out the whims of its users, expressed as SQL.

Optimization is thus a fundamental database server function that is required to empower a database server product to achieve acceptable performance and to continue to better this performance as it evolves. It is also needed because instructions received from humans in the form of SQL (and now XML) are too high above its native processing architecture to serve any performance function. And the more widely adopted SQL becomes, the more opportunity a database server has of becoming better at what it does at the low level. Humans don't care about how optimal a SQL statement is for a server, but they will notice if a query takes a few milliseconds longer to produce results, which can easily turn into seconds or minutes or hours the more complex the query and the fewer the resources available. In other words SQL Server has to care about optimization. Its life depends on it.

The Optimization Process

Every database server, every version of SQL Server, and every other DBMS system, such as those produced by Sybase and Oracle, are required to take the standard SQL request and convert it into the procedural language each product uniquely understands. How each product converts the SQL statement and what it then does with it are what make it unique. Algorithms, techniques, and guile are what are used to acquire market share and set the products apart from each other.

An UPDATE may cause triggers, functions, stored procedures, and integrity constraints to fire. These events thus kick off a chain reaction resulting in the opening of other result set comparisons, and complex evaluations of collateral or linked data. A simple UPDATE could actually result in a hefty execution plan . . . a query domino effect in a manner of speaking.

Although the optimizer is cost-based, it cannot be accurate all the time. What's more, a point of diminishing returns must come when the optimizer must realize that it cannot optimize any further, and that performance may even suffer on all further optimizations. So a certain amount of heuristic logic has to be built into a DBMS engine to allow it to determine when to draw the line . . . or decide when more is becoming less. SQL Server is no exception.

SQL Server invokes a number of essential steps that are required to optimize a query, but it is worthwhile to mention the three most important ones here:

- It must first transform the query into the low-level language of the engine. And it can do this by first parsing the SQL statement.
- It must then identify the possible procedures it can use to satisfy the query. Remember, the query can be manipulative, resultant, or both. This is essentially the optimization process.
- It must then generate query plans and choose the one that costs the least.

Let's look at the first steps taken by the SQL Server optimizer code:

The SELECT or any other SQL statement is a standard request format and does not influence procedures or invoke or define the functionality of the engine and its capability to extract or update data. It is merely a means of requesting and updating data and presenting it in a certain way. It does not tell the server how to go about getting that data, but the server understands what is required of it from the syntax and keywords of the SELECT statement. In other words, the SELECT statement is a "desire" or an end—not a means to obtain the end.

Note *I mentioned XML earlier, and it is important to see XML as both an extension to T-SQL and as a new definition language for SQL Server. A powerful XML parser is now built into this product. I discuss XML in a number of chapters in Part III, especially Chapter 23.*

For the record, the SELECT statement is used to define only the following things:

- The format of the result set returned to the client. Usually the default format is sufficient for the client because it follows the schematic layout of the columns, but often "qualifiers" such as GROUP BY and ORDER BY clauses instruct the engine to present the data in alternative formats.
- The objects, mostly tables, that contain the data, or a part of the data, required by the client. The FROM clause is the subordinate component in a SELECT statement that identifies the source of the data. The FROM clause can specify more than one source.

- How tables and other source objects are connected for a combined result set. The JOIN clause is another subordinate clause that specifies the logical connection of the two or more data sources.
- Conditions or criteria that row data must meet to be included in the selection process. The subordinate clauses include the WHERE and HAVING statements.

Before the SQL statement—or the services requested by it—is passed to the query optimizer, it must first be validated by the statement parser, which is part of the greater relational engine, as opposed to the kernel we talked about earlier. The parser ensures that the SQL statement is syntactically correct; and that it will be fully understood and productive. If the SQL code you sent is flawed, the parser will "throw" an exception and return a syntax error to the client application. (The error is sent out-of-band to the client; in other words, it is sent via a separate channel and not via the connection established by the client. SQL Server's error reporting mechanisms are explained more fully in Chapter 16).

If the syntax "flies," the parser will break the statement into logical units. Such units include keywords, parameters or arguments, operators, and identifiers. The parser scans the text, inspecting delimiters, and determines what represents actual objects and what represents row values or variables. You can specify how SQL Server should evaluate what you send it. For example, you can change the character that represents a delimiter in a SQL Server statement. This can be done interactively through settings in the Enterprise Manager or in T-SQL code (in similar fashion to *define* statements in C or C++ code). We will deal with such advanced subjects in the programming chapters in Part III.

Tip *Many a SQL Server expert will come to a situation that might require (or tempt) him or her to second-guess the optimizer and suggest a "hint" for consideration. While you might not be so bold, it is important to understand the factors that can influence performance.*

When all parsing is complete, the parser performs a grouping function, breaking down complex statements into smaller logical collections of routines and operations. In this fashion, using typical problem-solving techniques, the best query execution plan can be determined. In other words, the last function of the parser is to help the optimizer, which kicks in next, to see the "wood" for the "trees" in a complex request, thus contributing to the best execution plan. It is thus fitting that the format into which the original T-SQL statement is translated is called the *query tree.*

Note *A query tree is also known as a syntax tree or a sequence tree.*

The kernel finally compiles the query tree into a series of operations to perform against native rowsets stored in the databases. The kernel gains access to the databases via the services of the storage engine. The relational kernel and the storage kernel communicate via the OLE DB API using standard SQL SELECT statements that OLE DB can pass to the storage engine (as you are aware, OLE DB is complex to code against—hence ADO—but it is highly efficient and ideal for the interlocution of two kernels). The following code represents a simple SELECT query issued by the relational engine to the storage engine:

```
SELECT CustID FROM CustDetails
```

Obviously, the execution plan here is a no-brainer for the kernel because the SELECT statement is of the simplest form. The plan here would thus consist of a simple SELECT statement. This is represented in the simple flow diagram illustrated in Figure 4-2.

The operations are defined against table or index objects or are both stored in the database. If no index objects are defined against the data, the execution plan is constructed only to perform the necessary table scan.

But what takes place when a SELECT statement rivaling Fermat's Last Theorem arrives over the wire? Here is something a little more complex, but still relatively simple:

```
USE PUBS
SELECT OD.OrderID, OD.CustomerID, CUST.ContactName
 FROM dbo.Orders OD INNER JOIN
 dbo.Customers CUST ON OD.CustomerID = CUST.CustomerID
```

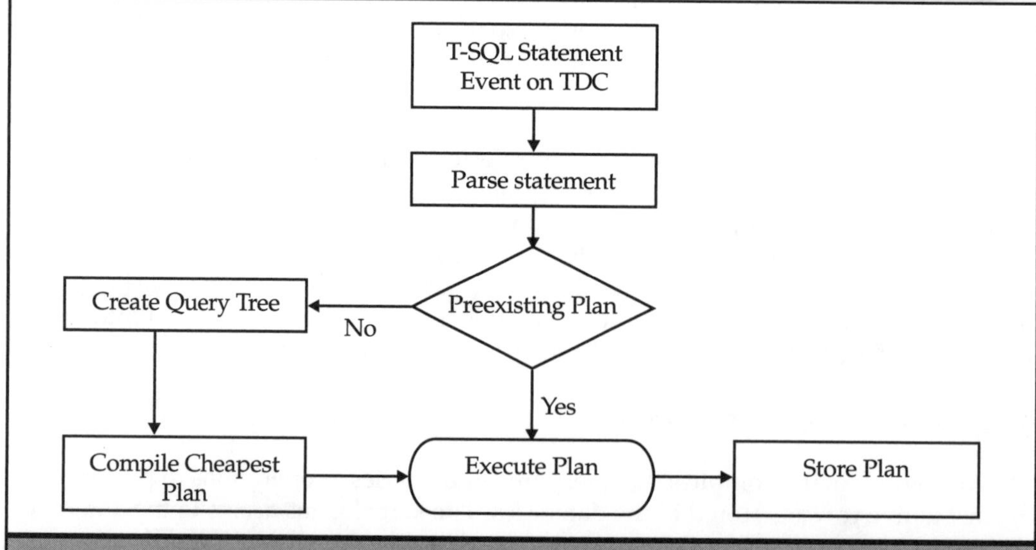

Figure 4-2. *The steps taken by SQL Server to parse and optimize a T-SQL statement and create an execution plan*

What you have here is a request for the return of two result sets from two tables that are joined to form a third result set. Although it is still not the most complex SELECT, the kernel breaks the statement into two execution steps, one for each table. It will call the OLE DB OPENROWSET method once for each table and then finally perform the necessary join of each rowset returned. When the relational kernel has finished working with the storage engine, it will format the result set to be sent to the client into the necessary tabular format and place that back onto the wire.

So what intervention, insight, or control do you have on the process I have just described? The good news for DBAs and developers is that SQL Server 2000 comes equipped with some marvelous tools to play with. Besides query hints, a tool called the SQL Query Analyzer (illustrated in Figure 4-3) will let you test a query for syntax, check out the execution plan, estimate execution plans, and so forth. It even lets you inspect the metrics derived in the optimization process, in calculations, and in steps taken to carry out the execution plan. I don't want to go into much detail about the SQL Query Analyzer here, because we use it a lot in the chapters in Part III. You will also later investigate and learn about the Index Tuning Wizard introduced in Chapter 2.

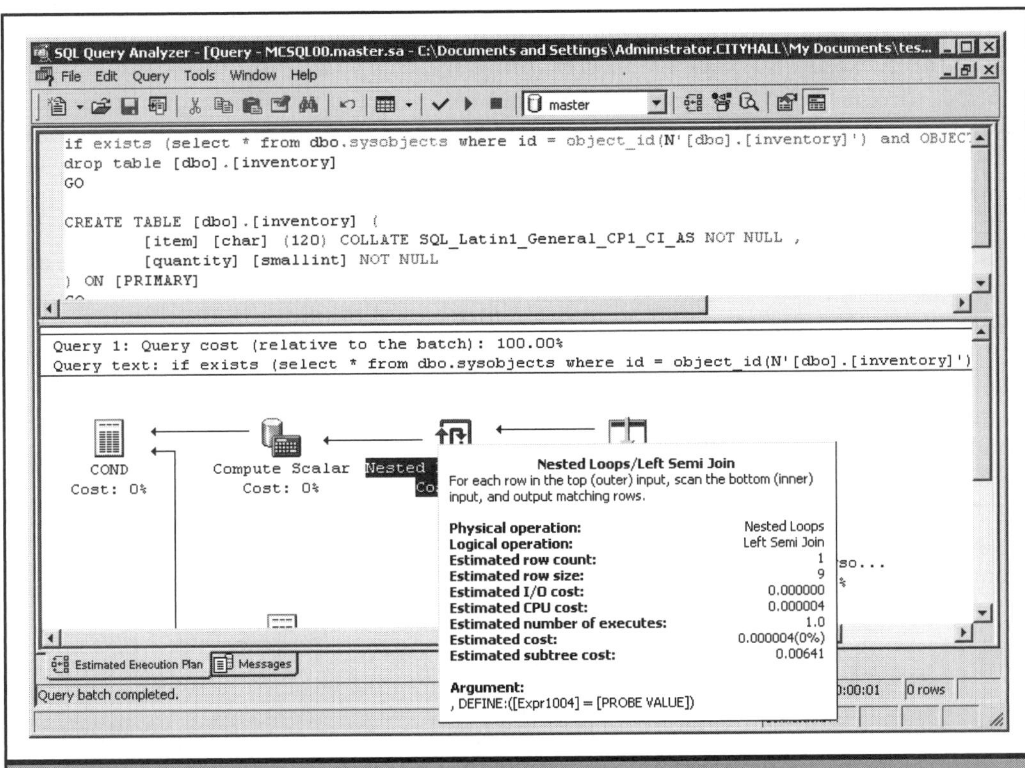

Figure 4-3. *The Query Analyzer in action, preparing an execution plan for a complex query*

DML, DDL, and so on have specialized processing requirements, which I discuss in Chapters 15, 16, 19, and 20.

How the SQL Server query processor resolves indexes, views, partitioned views, stored procedures, and so on is discussed in the chapters that focus on these areas.

Caching and Reusing Execution Plans

Most SELECT statements are identical or may differ only in the values specified in the search expression. Consider the following SELECT statements:

```
SELECT * FROM CustOrds WHERE OrdValue < '400'
SELECT * FROM CustOrds WHERE OrdValue < '1000'
SELECT * FROM CustOrds WHERE OrdValue < ?
```

It is no doubt obvious that an intelligent optimizer will deduce that the preceding SELECT statements are likely to result in the same or very similar execution plans. It therefore would make no sense for SQL Server to recompile an execution plan if one has already been compiled for a previous user not too long ago.

SQL Server thus maintains a pool of memory, called the *procedure cache,* that it uses to store both execution plans and data buffers. I might add that the preceding examples are very simple, and if SQL Server determines that it would cost more to store such a plan than to recompile it, the plan will not be stored. The memory pool size varies and is different from system to system. It also changes according to state of the system. Any number of users can reuse SQL Server execution plans.

To further support a reuse policy, SQL Server also maintains a parameter data structure that is used to store the parameters sent in by each user. These structures are known as *execution contexts.* SQL Server places each user—actually each connection—executing a query into an execution context.

An execution plan that matches a user's query can be used instead of compiling a new execution plan. SQL Server needs only to obtain the parameter or variable value in the SQL statement and combine that with the already compiled execution plan. The result represents significant savings in time and resources, which translates into better response time by the end user.

At any time a statement is sent to the server, the server will first inspect the procedure cache to see if there is an existing execution plan that can satisfy the SQL statement.

A number of factors can cause SQL Server to drop a plan. A change of data type is such a factor. I explore this issue further in Chapter 21.

The saving comes by obviating the need to build a new execution plan. It should thus be obvious that you can do a lot in your code to ensure that your SQL statements have a higher probability of being matched. Your goal as a DBA and systems programmer is to increase the chance that SQL Server will reuse complex plans that have already been compiled. The use of parameters in stored procedures and parameter markers in ADO, OLE DB, and ODBC applications goes a long way to ensuring this. No doubt this becomes more difficult when we start dealing with NULL values and three- and four-dimensional values, which will be discussed in Chapter 16.

The execution plan and context-matching algorithms have been enhanced in SQL Server 7.0 and SQL Server 2000, and this greatly improves performance over versions 6.5 and earlier. SQL Server 2000 keeps the execution plan in the procedure cache until it is needed. Only old and unused plans are purged from the cache when space is needed, and, obviously, when the system is restarted.

Note *The DBCC FREEPROCCACHE is a directive you can use to purge the procedure cache and force SQL Server to recompile the procedure.*

The algorithm maintains an age counter that contains a replica of the query cost factor. This replica is incremented by the cost value in the age field each time the object is referenced by a connection. For example, let's say a query plan is given a cost factor of eight. Each time it is referenced, the value in the age counter doubles, becoming 16, 32, 64, and so forth. The lazywriter process, discussed earlier in this chapter, periodically scans the procedure cache and decrements each number in the age field by 1. Eventually, if the query plan is not being used, it is devalued to zero (0) and thereafter ignored. The plan will be kept in the cache until SQL Server needs memory, and any plans at zero will be flushed.

There are other reasons to destroy the execution plans. They include the following:

- The schema is altered or objects, such as tables, are dropped or changed (the ALTER TABLE or ALTER VIEW statement is an example of such a change that will flush the cache).
- An index used by a plan is dropped.
- You explicitly issue a request to recompile (this is done by calling the sp_compile stored procedure).
- Keys are being significantly changed. This could result from excessive transaction processing that fundamentally alters the table referenced by a query.
- Triggers, stored procedures, functions, and so forth are placed on tables referenced by your plan.
- Any function that causes the table to grow considerably will render an execution plan obsolete.

The subject of optimization and execution plans is exhaustive but essential when it comes to fine-tuning and optimization of both systems and applications, for DBMS systems in general and SQL Server in particular. In later chapters, you will build on the foundation you have gained in this chapter.

Inside Data Streams, Again

In the preceding chapter—in the section "Inside SQL Server Data Streams"—we discussed the tabular data streams (TDS), packet-moving mechanisms, that encapsulate data in a special transmission format that is sent to and from the server. TDS, however, is a constantly evolving protocol, and as SQL Server matures like the finest sauvignon, so will you have to deal with ensuring that legacy clients configured or developed for down-level TDS access can send and receive data to the server.

For the most part, down-level support requires no special intervention or labor on your part because SQL Server 2000, which is version 8.0 TDS, talks to TDS version 7.0 and TDS version 4.2. However, there are a few points that can trip you up.

The advanced data type support in TDS 8.0 can choke a TDS 4.2 client. TDS 4.2 was originally built for SQL Server 4.2, and the protocol was inherited by versions 6.0 and 6.5. It became obsolete with the great rewrite "event" of SQL Server in 1997 and 1998, which begot SQL Server 7.0 with its TDS 7.0 protocol. The TDS changed again with the advent of SQL Server 2000.

Specifically, TDS 4.2 clients do not support Unicode data types. When it happens that a TDS 4.2 client pulls Unicode data out of a version 8.0 table, the relational engine will have to convert the data to legacy character data before it can be sent onward to the client. What will happen is that Unicode data that has no ASCII equivalent, and there are more than 65,000 such characters, will draw a blank, literally, when it sends the data back. The result set data will then be full of holes back at the client.

Note *Unicode, or the Unicode Character System (UCS), is a two-byte (16-bit) system that represents all the languages of the world in a collection of 65,536 characters. ASCII is a 7- or 8-bit (1-byte) system that can only support 256 characters. Comparing TDS 4.2 and 8.0 is like comparing the vocabulary of a two-year-old with the vocabulary of an adult.*

TDS 4.2 clients do not support the version 7.0 and version 8.0 char, varchar, binary, and varbinary data types that are larger than 255 bytes, and SQL Server will thus truncate any values it needs to return to the client through TDS 4.2. As mentioned in Chapter 2, the preceding data types can now hold data up to 8,000 bytes.

TDS 7.0 clients also come up a little short against SQL Server 2000 and TDS 8.0. The sql_variant data type (discussed at length in Chapter 16) is new to SQL Server 2000 and is essentially "Greek" to TDS 7.0. The relational engine will need to convert any data type of sql_variant to Unicode before transmission. TDS 4.2 clients need not apply.

What then is your strategy for ensuring that your clients can interpret and correctly present TDS 8.0 data? If you are new to SQL Server support and administration and are taking over a DBA function, you will need to know this.

First, as I will often repeat in this book, "thinner is better." The thinner the client, the less work you have to do later—as both a developer and a DBA—when new versions of SQL Server ship (roughly every two years). There is nothing worse for a DBA than to have to upgrade hundreds or thousands of fat clients that have more components than an early twentieth-century chronometer. And we'll debate client versus server processing again in Chapter 14, as well as *n*-tier deployment strategies in Chapter 23.

Second, when a client connects to SQL Server, its TDS packets are built according to the logic programmed into the data provider it is using. The data provider could be either the Microsoft OLE DB provider for SQL Server, or the ODBC driver, or the DB-Library DLL (which is currently in the sunset years of its life). So you need to ensure that your clients are calling the correct versions of these drivers or providers on their computers; otherwise, the TDS packets they will be sending will be targeted to earlier versions of SQL Server. This does not cause as many problems for data on the way in, because the server-side libraries will be able to understand the inbound packets. The problems arise, as discussed, when the packets are sent back to the client and data get transformed beyond recognition. A blob of thousands of bytes will just not make it to the other side, because SQL Server will see that you connected on TDS 4.2 and make the necessary adjustments.

Pulling the Relational Train

What I describe in this chapter is very sparse in comparison to what SQL Server does to execute the fastest queries and return data quickly to impatient clients. There are a number of collateral processes that take place, and I describe them in later chapters as necessary. You will also be introduced to techniques that can produce more efficient queries that result in faster responses from SQL Server 2000.

The Complete Reference

Chapter 5

Meta Data Services

Every enterprise, no matter the size, thrives or dies on access to information and the management of information. We put information into Access Databases, Oracle, SQL Server, Microsoft Exchange, Active Directory, DB2, databases on the Internet, and so on. We get information back from all these repositories and more. We use this information to manage our businesses, to carry out invoicing, order entry, stock and asset management, and decision support. Our very lives depend on the creation, manipulation, storage, and analysis of all this data.

The knowledge is managed and manipulated in our enterprise information systems, on the enterprise information network, and in decision support systems. The tools and applications we use are either custom built or are turnkey systems provided by independent software vendors (ISVs) and companies specializing in niche markets. Whoever or whatever creates the tools and applications spends a large portion of development time brainstorming, planning, and then building to specifications. They generate huge quantities of metadata to describe what is required to sew the fabric of our creations.

Despite the significant advancements in software development and computer science and in the collateral fields of processor design, networking, and so on, the very logic that creates these systems remains largely unharnessed and out of control. Software projects continue to cost 10 times their budgets and blow deadlines by factors of four or more. Absolutely everything we do in the fields of information technology requires modeling for design, tracking, reuse, documentation, and so on. It is essential not only for sanity checking, but for stop loss, milestone management, versioning, and so on.

When I first started out in software development more than a decade ago, I was struck by two quotes from college professors and gurus in the know: First, software engineering could be compared to structural engineering; a complex application of million of lines of code, as complex as designing and building the San Francisco Bay Bridge. Second, you can never rid an application of all its bugs; for every million lines of code, it would take 30 million years to perfect it (in other words, one never could). What you can do is properly plan or architect a software application to minimize the introduction of bugs as far as possible. Most bugs are caused by poor design and lack of forethought in the first place.

In that software engineering is as complex as structural engineering, a complex application or database program has to be built from blueprints, just like a bridge, so that everyone has access to a planned, systematic order of execution and strategy. The cliché, "so that we are all reading from the same sheet of music" did not become a cliché for nothing. This is the essentially what a data model provides—a means for an entire team of developers or architects to read from the same model or plan. Many database applications cannot and should not be built without these essential blueprints; in some cases—such as a data warehouse project—it is impossible to proceed without a data model.

While modeling and design tools have been around for decades, they have never been able to store, share, reuse, and track the information or models they generate or acquire as efficiently as they could have, and this has mostly been due to the inability to manage and store metadata. In client/server database management systems, the ability to store metadata has only emerged within the last couple of years. Without a metadata repository and a unified modeling language to allow for information exchange and interchange, we will not be able to advance as much as we would like to, and as fast as we need to.

Metadata is not new; in fact, it's been around since the big bang. If you think about it, the universe appears (on the face of it) to be a well-organized system that somehow is able to generate, store, and reuse its metadata. There is an uncanny but obviously well-designed system that uses the metadata being generated every instant to adapt and evolve life, to produce new species and retire old and tired ones.

And in our software or computer engineering worlds, it is this metadata that describes the applications we build and the solutions we derive. When you look at SQL Server, you see a lot of services that are extremely complex and not for the faint of heart. Building OLTP applications using transactions monitors, message queues, and more is so daunting that architects and project managers are hard to come by. Building analytical applications with OLAP objects or natural language query solutions with English Query is certainly not for the faint of heart either. Take a peek at Appendix A and you see hundreds of functions, procedures, and more that we use to build vast and extremely powerful systems, at the beck and call of millions of users.

It is in this light that I felt it critical to provide an introduction, albeit it very sparse, to SQL Server's Meta Data Services because modeling is critical to everything you do in SQL Server 2000, especially when you sit down to create database applications and solutions with it. Also, if you look at the job definitions for SQL Server developers and administrators on the hot career Web sites like Monster, Dice, and Brainbuzz, you'll notice that many of the top positions require you to have modeling acumen. If you want that extra edge, you need to bring an understanding of Meta Data Services to the table as well. The Meta Data Services and the metadata repository are critical to your modeling needs, and to your success in SQL Server development and administration.

Meta Data Services comprise many different components that ship with all versions of SQL Server 2000. Besides the repository engine, Meta Data Services includes tools, APIs, standard information models, a browser, and the Meta Data Software Development Kit (MDK).

Before you can provide a metadata management service to a product, a development environment, or an information system, however, you need to know what metadata is and how it is used. This chapter will introduce metadata and serve to start you on the road to getting familiar with Meta Data Services; however, it will be most useful if you already have a good grasp of metadata concepts, modeling and modeling languages, and so on.

We will also delve into the concept of the Information Model in general and the Open Information Model (OIM) in particular. The OIM is a set of metadata specifications that will allow you to facilitate the sharing and reuse of metadata in the database application development and data warehousing and analysis disciplines. The OIM is supported by the Meta Data Coalition, which supports the OIM (but more about that later).

What Is Metadata?

Take the job of the psychoanalyst. He or she breaks down a patient's illness into metadata. The first task is to identify the malady at the highest level, such as manic depression, schizophrenia, attention deficit, desire to write huge database books, and so on. The psychoanalyst makes her assessment by processing the metadata at the root of the illness, such as observing how the patient reacts to certain stimuli, relates to past events, handles relationships, answers questions, and so on.

All the data that leads to this analysis or conclusion is metadata: data that describes a phenomenon or a thing in some way. So it is with database design; the architect sets out to describe database structures at the higher level, underpinned by metadata at the lower level.

If you think about how SQL Server has evolved, you can imagine the metadata available on its architecture. Looking back at the earlier chapters, especially Chapter 2, we talk about a table being an object, but the table is made of certain elements that comprise metadata which describes the table, rows and columns, indexes, and so on. When you go into the index itself, a whole new world of metadata can be found.

Digging for metadata is like peeling back the layers on an onion. You can describe something, such as by saying "the database has 10 tables," and then peel back another layer and proclaim "each table has one identity column." Now peel back another layer and proclaim "each identity column obtains its value by . . . ." You could keep peeling layers and describe metadata until the metadata arrives at a limit where it is no longer of practical use to the architect.

In most cases, going lower than how the identity value is arrived at is not of importance to the database architect; but it is to the architects at Microsoft who use that metadata to describe the algorithms that create the value. The software engineers will talk about the process that creates the value in terms of classes, methods and properties, and so on.

Metadata Has Context

To understand what metadata is requires you to understand the distinction between a data type and a data instance. Making this distinction will also help you understand data integrity a lot better and will make the constraint concepts discussed in Chapter 17 a lot easier to grasp. If you are a model architect or designer, you typically formulate or construct object or instance types. These could be classes or relationships, for instance. On the other hand, a software developer creates and manipulates objects and their properties.

Part of the difficulty in working with metadata is knowing the difference between metadata and data. To do that you have to put the data into a context. Think about the SQL Server catalog (master). On the one hand, it holds the schema for your database and all the definitions for all the objects that operate on your data. So as a schema catalog, master or msdb has metadata describing your database and its components—data about data.

And then when you in fact try to delete an object from your database, you first ask the catalog if such an object exists and, if so, to delete it first so that it can be replaced. You are no longer relating to master as a system that describes your system, but as a database from which to obtain and modify data.

But there is more to metadata than its obtuse definition, data describing data. As discussed, you can work with metadata type and instance information just as you would with any kind of application or data design elements. When you express design information in metadata terms, you allow it to be reused and shared. Describing a T-SQL stored procedure provides an excellent example of using metadata to document an application or system. The definition of the proc is then made available to other developers for use in their client applications or elsewhere.

By creating new relationships among existing metadata types, you can extend existing applications or spawn new applications or processors. You all know how complex application development can be, and metadata allows you to expand exponentially but orderly and in a way that you can retrace or make sense of the tracks you are laying and the paths you are taking.

Metadata and how it is managed and articulated is what now drives the Internet. Consider HTML and XML: One is a language that describes to a browser how a document or an image is supposed to look or be displayed, hence the name *metatag.* XML, on the other hand, is a metadata language that describes data, also using metatags. When an XML document is parsed by SQL Server, the metadata information it gleans tells it how to store the data and where (see Chapter 23).

Meta Data Services in SQL Server

Part of the problem in processing and working with metadata over the years has been that no open repository has been available for the storage of metadata, accessing it, and managing it. That's where SQL Server 2000's Meta Data Services comes into play.

Meta Data Services is a service that provides a way to holistically store and manage a metadata repository. This repository, housed in a standard SQL Server database, provides access to an extensive "hub" of data and component definitions, development and deployment models, application specifics, algorithms, blueprints, software components, data warehousing and decision support specifications, and so on.

In the Meta Data Services architecture, tools and applications connect to the core engine and storage components through open standards. Information models define type information that determines the structure and behavior of metadata that is exposed by tools and applications at the top layer.

A number of Microsoft technologies use Meta Data Services as a native store for object definitions or as a platform for deploying metadata. One of the ways in which SQL Server 2000 uses Meta Data Services is to store versioned Data Transformation

Services (DTS) packages. In Microsoft Visual Studio, Meta Data Services supports the exchange of model data with other development tools. The English Query services are also underpinned by metadata services. And metadata drives data mining applications, OLAP and data warehouses.

You can use Meta Data Services for your own purposes: as a component of an integrated information system, as a native store for custom applications that process metadata, or as a storage and management service for sharing reusable models. You can also extend Meta Data Services to provide support for new tools for resale or customize it to satisfy internal tool requirements.

The Meta Data Coalition and the OMG

In the same way that psychologists and psychiatrists draw from a central institution that allows these professionals to share information and agree on definitions, remedies, and platforms, metadata too has such a central institution; in fact it has two of them. One is called the Meta Data Coalition (MDC) and the other is called the Object Management Group (OMG)

The MDC is an independent organization that comprises several hundred vendors and users who make it their business to further the development of standards surrounding metadata, its use, access and storage methods, and so on—especially with respect to data warehousing.

The MDC is also hard at work supporting a standard metadata creation language, a modeling language (UML) that everyone can use to store, access, and interpret metadata no matter where it is stored and what tools work with it.

The standard is known as the Open Information Model (OIM), which we will investigate shortly, save to say that the OIM is a generic set of information models that describe object modeling, database modeling, and component reuse. The OIM and its evolution is managed by the MDC in the same fashion as the World Wide Web is managed by the World Wide Web or W3 Consortium. You can tap into the MDC at its Web site at www.mdcindfo.com.

The OMG on the other hand supports the Common Warehouse Metamodel (CWM) which builds on various standards, including OMG's UML (Unified Modeling Language), XMI (XML Metadata Interchange) and MOF (Meta Object Facility), and on the MDC's OIM. The CWM was developed by a number of companies, including IBM, Oracle, Unisys, Hyperion, Genesis, NCR, UBS, and Dimension EDI, and is an adopted OMG standard.

Note *Microsoft has been in the MDC's camp and not the OMG and has been the chief protagonist of the OIM for some time. At the time of this writing, however, the MDC decided to merge with the OMG and the OIM will now continue live in the OMG along with the other standards. Both the OMG and the MDC supported UML so the merger was a giant step forward in merging the modeling standards into one . . . a move Microsoft and the SQL Server management supported. No doubt the single standard, underpinned by UML, will be supported in the next version of SQL Server. Despite the merger we will focus on the OIM in this chapter because that's what SQL Server Meta Data Services supports.*

Information Model Fundamentals

What is an information model? An *information model* is a collection of *metadata* types that combine to provide a description of an object—in our case, a database or some information system; in other cases, applications or tools, and so on.

For some years now I have been developing an information model that can be used to describe a business. In modeling a business, or creating a new business plan, my information model includes elements called key management entities (KMEs) that describe the business processes. Once these business processes have been described, the model can be used to build the business by identifying and managing the KMEs and monitor their various elements.

In the same way that an information model can describe a business, an information model for a database management system describes tables, indexes, keys, integrity constraints, stored procedures, triggers, and so on. But it is important to understand that the model does not store the actual data that these objects or elements store and manipulate.

In my enterprise analysis models, the model describes a key management entity, such as the processing of accounts payable, but it does not hold or manage information about accounts payable, only what it does. In this regard, the information model connects the dots to provide the big picture, which is always out of view and far away removed from the end user and even the code writer to a large extent.

So where does SQL Server Meta Data Services come into the picture? Essentially, as a member of the MDC, Microsoft uses SQL Server as the means of distributing an implementation of the MDC's Open Object Model. At the same time, it provides standard metadata types and tools that you can use to build a repository for metadata, based on the OIM.

The OIM is extensible, and the tools that ship with Meta Data Services allow you to add various custom elements. As you use the base OIM and find that you need certain elements that are not included in the OIM, you can easily add those elements to complete your model.

At the same time, you should know that going the way of the OIM is not a requirement; you can model and work with metadata in several environments, some of them legacy. However, going the way of OIM can provide you with integration possibilities that might not otherwise be achievable. Think of it another way: There are many ways to move data around the Internet, and you might even decide to trash TCP/IP and come up with your own protocol. You would be able to create your own Internet and you would probably be the only person using it.

Meta Data Services actually supports three open standards: the MDC's Open Information Model, the Component Object Model (COM) interfaces, and Extensible Markup Language (XML) encoding. We will talk a little more about OIM in general; but further broad discussion of COM and XML fundamentals are beyond the scope of this book.

While the MDC's OIM provides significant advantages in terms of tool and programming support, you are not required to use it in general and with Meta Data Services in particular. You can create your own information models using the Unified Modeling Language (UML) that bear no relation to the OIM, but which are supported by modeling tools aligned with the OMG. One such tool is Rational Software Corporation's Rational Rose, which I use extensively to model OLTP systems, warehouses, software applications and Web sites. Figure 5-1 illustrates the modeling of a table underway in Rational Rose.

To accommodate tool-specific metadata, Microsoft has extended the version of the OIM that it distributes to support its metadata requirements. The Meta Data Services SDK includes a version of the OIM, modeling documentation, and several resources to help you use and deploy the OIM right away. OIM resources include definition files for Visual C++ and Visual Basic, Extensible Markup Language (XML) files, Interface Definition Language (IDL) files, and installation scripts for OIM models.

Information Models and Meta Data Services

The information models you create and use with SQL Server 2000 Meta Data Services must be described using Unified Modeling Language (UML). SQL Server 2000 as installed already includes (in the msdb database) the standard OIM subject areas that describe Data Transformation Services (DTS) packages, data warehousing definitions, and online analytical processing (OLAP) cubes. You do not have to modify these OIMs in any way to ensure they perform the functions for which they are intended.

Although you can create information models programmatically, most information models are created in modeling tools like Rational Rose, ERwin, and Visio 2000 (Enterprise Edition). Custom information models must conform to the repository API. The repository API includes abstract classes that formally describe the elements you can

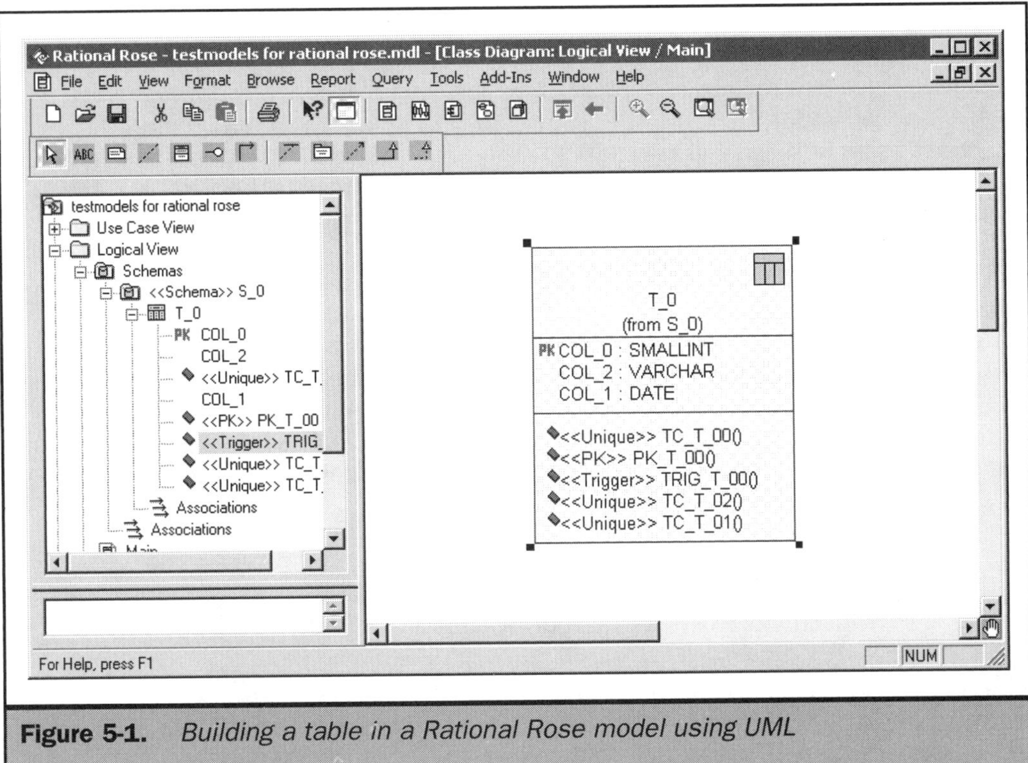

Figure 5-1. *Building a table in a Rational Rose model using UML*

include in a model. If you are creating a custom model, you may want to review the repository API for more information about the type information objects that the repository engine supports.

Overview of Meta Data Services

Your usage of Meta Data Services depends on your requirements. These could be any one of the following roles:

- **Design (modeling) and architecture** In this role you are actually designing metadata, putting in place what will be used by the programmers and engineers.
- **Programming with metadata** As an engineer or software developer, you will access metadata in the repository with which to build databases, interfaces, tools, and applications.
- **Accessing metadata at run time** Many processes require metadata at run time.

In the designer or architect role, you use modeling tools and the Meta Data Services SDK to create the metadata that will be installed into the repository database. The entire model needs to be completed and installed in the database before any development begins. You can update the OIM from your modeling tools, or you can use the API to program against it. When you are ready to move metadata to other repositories or to update other repositories, you can use XML encoding to exchange the metadata. The Meta Data Services API and SDK documentation can give you the heads up on that information.

The current version of Meta Data Services extends the metadata services that shipped with SQL Server 7.0. The old version was known as Microsoft Repository. The name is still valid, but the new one more accurately describes how Microsoft is providing an end-to-end metadata service in SQL Server 2000, and not just a repository. However, the Meta Data Services extends the repository technology initially put in motion at the development of SQL Server 7.0. In SQL Server 2000, Microsoft has introduced a new browser for viewing data in a repository database, new Extensible Markup Language (XML) interchange support, and a host of new repository engine features.

The following list describes some of the new features to be found in the Meta Data Services:

- **A new metadata browser** The browser is a tool that you can use to survey a repository database and "scroll" through the metadata.
- **XML encoding** XML Encoding has been included to support a new implementation of metadata interchange brought about by the MDC's OIM.
- **Miscellaneous repository programming enhancements** The API and SDK provide new and enhanced support and better ways to program against an information model, and to extend it.

The Browser

You can run Meta Data Browser when you select Meta Data Services. Meta Data Services is available for each copy of SQL Server you install. Before you can use the browser, you first have to register a database in Meta Data Services. I will show you how to do that later in this chapter.

XML Encoding Enhancements

The Meta Data Services now promotes XML encoding in native mode. This means that you can import, export, and publish repository metadata in a format that more closely matches your information model. (The new supports for XML encoding supersedes the XML Interchange Format—XIF—which was supported in the previous version.)

Meta Data Services can also encode, exchange, and decode XML documents for you. This functionality is provided through dual interfaces so that you can manage these operations from code.

The MDC's OIM XML encoding format defines rules for generating XML that is based on an information model. In this case the XML is describing the metadata for you (metadata describing metadata). The aforementioned rules enable Meta Data Services to generate XML that corresponds to your information model; and these same rules are what are used to convert an XML document back into the repository instance data.

Repository Engine

Meta Data Services is driven by a specialized repository engine. The repository engine has similar functionality to the database engine; however, it has been built to provide the basic functions for storing and retrieving objects and maintaining the relationships among them.

The repository engine perform its retrieval, manipulation, and storage functions within the context of an information model. In other words, it is a model-driven interpreter. The engine processes user-defined model information to determine how to store and support the objects, the objects' relationships, and actions between them.

Despite the power in the repository engine to manipulate instances of information models, it can only manipulate objects to the extent that the model structure allows. In other words, the engine cannot willy-nilly establish relationships between objects if the underlying model does not support such relationships.

Access to the repository engine is similar to accessing any database engine. It comes equipped with an API that responds to calls issued by through Component Object Model (COM) and COM Automation interfaces. The repository engine also hides the storage layer for you, only exposing the necessary functions that determine when and how transactions occur. The engine itself works with SQL to execute repository-specific activities. How to program against the repository API is fully covered in the Meta Data Services documentation and SDK that ship with SQL Server 2000.

Repository Databases

The databases that underpin SQL Server 2000 Meta Data Services can be provided through SQL Server's databases, the SQL Server Runtime Engine, or Microsoft Jet. At a minimum, a repository database must include the standard tables that are present in every repository database. You can create additional tables for custom interface definitions. See BOL for more information about the Repository SQL Schema.

As mentioned earlier, SQL Server metadata for DTS packages and OLAP cubes uses the msdb database. You can also add your custom metadata to msdb and then register it in the Meta Data Browser, as I will demonstrate later. By keeping all your metadata in one database, you can combine existing definitions in new ways by creating relationships.

Meta Data Services SDK

The SQL Server 2000 Meta Data Services SDK provides a host of development resources for both model designers and programmers. In it you will find the Modeling

Development Kit (MDK), modeling documentation, sample modeling code, and sundry add-on tools. The SDK and MDK together provide all you need to extend models, customize models, build new models, and program against models.

Specifications and Limits

SQL Server does not impose any practical limit on the size of a repository database. If you are using msdb, or if you are creating a new repository using SQL Server 2000, you can simply increase the database size when you need to.

The repository engine works with RAM available to it to process transactions and instantiate model information. The more RAM you have available, the better the repository engine performs; but it makes sense to keep your metadata repositories off production machines and any sizeable OLTP server.

The Open Information Model Formats

OIM 1.0 and the Meta Data Coalition (MDC) OIM are the two alternative modeling formats of the OIM. MDC OIM is an enhanced version of OIM 1.0 that provides support for the Unified Modeling Language (UML 1.3). OIM 1.0 and the MDC OIM in fact use the same repository tables and thus cannot be installed into the same repository database. If you want to use the MDC OIM, you must copy your OIM 1.0 metadata to the new information model. Here are a few specifics about OIM formats to consider:

- OIM 1.0 is supported by repository engine 2.0 and repository engine 3.0. A version of OIM 1.0 is distributed with SQL Server.
- MDC OIM is supported by repository engine 3.0, and it is the newer of the two formats. A version of MDC OIM is distributed with the SQL Server 2000 Meta Data Services Software Development Kit (SDK).

You can exchange and migrate metadata between these two model formats using either XML interchange format. The following section discusses backward compatibility in more detail.

Using the Meta Data Browser

You can use Meta Data Browser in the following ways:

- From within SQL Server 2000, using SQL Server Enterprise Manager
- As a standalone snap-in that you add through Microsoft Management Console (MMC) and run separately from SQL Server Enterprise Manager

The way you use the browser determines the set of features and functionality that you can work with.

In SQL Server Enterprise Manager, Meta Data Browser enables you to view metadata that you create and store in msdb. You can view this data in the Contents folder. When you use Meta Data Browser in SQL Server Enterprise Manager, you are actually accessing the repository in the context of an end user. The End User Mode provides only read-only access to the repository database, which is why it is called a browser. But you can still view information about any metadata that you store in the repository.

The idea behind End User Mode is to protect the metadata from accidental or willful destruction. If metadata is modified or deleted accidentally, that will corrupt the installation.

Meta Data Services can be run separately from SQL Server Enterprise Manager as a standalone MMC snap-in. You can also add Meta Data Services to the MMC console to work with other SQL Server repository databases.

After you add Meta Data Services to the MMC, you can run the Meta Data Browser to register the repository databases you want to work with. The browser in the MMC lets you work with any SQL Server repository database created in SQL Server version 6.5, 7.0, or 2000. However, browsing and manipulation require you use version 3.0 of the repository engine, which is what ships with SQL Server 2000.

Viewing Meta Data in Meta Data Browser

Meta Data Browser presents content in different ways, depending on whether you run the browser from within SQL Server Enterprise Manager or in standalone mode in the MMC.

Viewing Meta Data in SQL Server Enterprise Manager

When you first try to browse data in Enterprise Manager, you will find that there is nothing to view. At first, the msdb database does not contain any metadata that you own and can thus view. You first have to add content to the repository, and then you can view it by expanding the Contents folder in Meta Data Services node.

Adding content to a repository occurs when you choose to save to SQL Server 2000 Meta Data Services (for example, when saving Data Transformation Services (DTS) packages). To see a DTS package defined in the repository, do as follows:

1. Start Data Transformation Services (this is described in Chapter 12) and after configuring the DTS package choose to save the definition in the repository.
2. Next give the DTS package a name, as illustrated in Figure 5-2. Continue to save and execute the DTS package. As the package is created, its definition is stored in the msdb database as an OIM.
3. The model can now be browsed in the Meta Data Browser. It becomes immediately apparent in the Contents folder, as demonstrated in Figure 5-3.

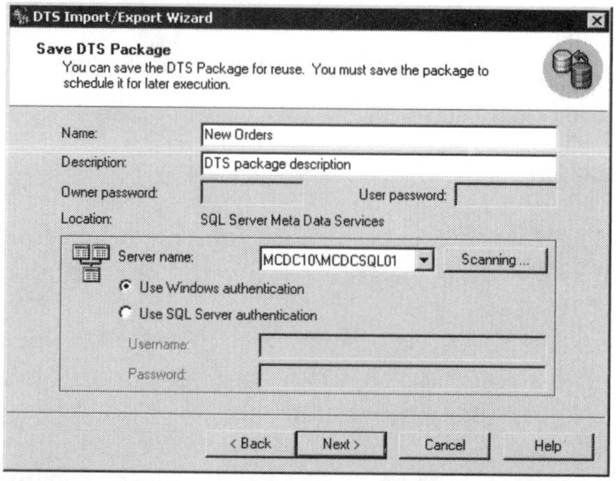

Figure 5-2. *Saving a DTS package definition to the metadata repository*

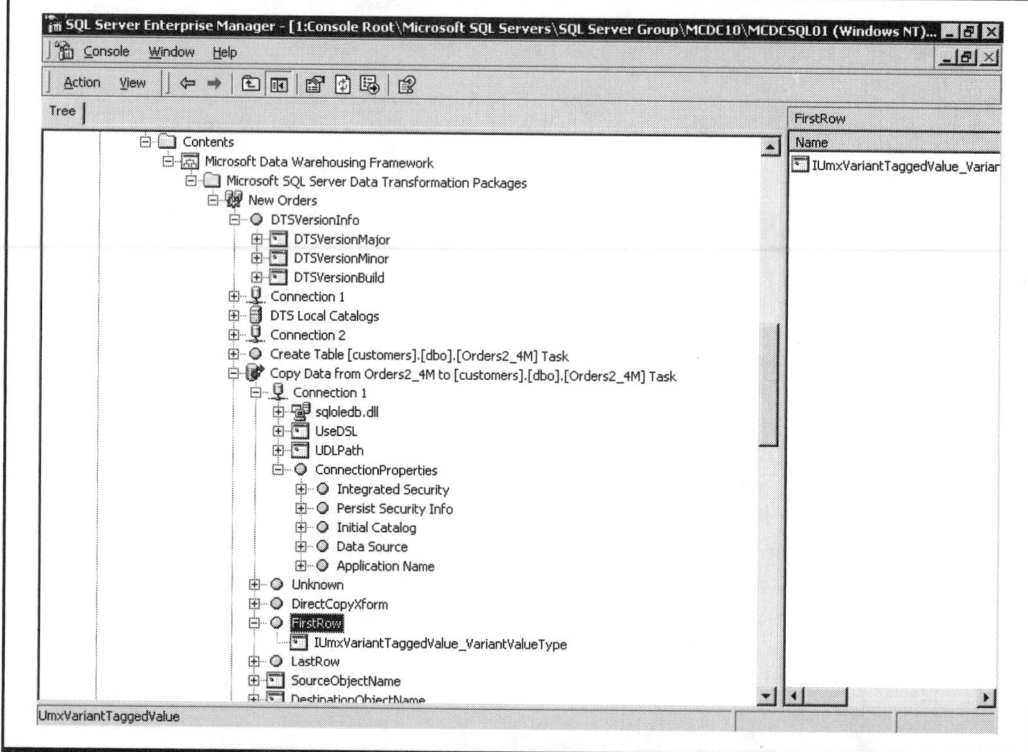

Figure 5-3. *The Meta Data Browser showing a saved DTS package definition*

Working with Meta Data Browser as a Standalone Snap-in

When you run Meta Data Browser as a separate, standalone Management Console (MMC) snap-in, you can work with more than one repository database, and you can view content and perform tasks that are not available to you from the nodes in Enterprise Manager.

Meta Data Browser organizes content by repository database. Depending on the browse mode you select for your database, the content is further organized into folders named Contents and Information Models. Within each folder, objects and collections are arranged according to a hierarchy that facilitates browsing.

When you run Meta Data Browser as a standalone snap-in, you can register any SQL Server database that contains repository tables, such as the msdb database. The registered repository databases will be automatically listed in the Meta Data Services folder, and all registered repository databases are grouped together on the same level.

When you run Meta Data Browser as a standalone snap-in, you can register only repository databases that you created in SQL Server 6.5 or 7.0, SQL Server 2000, or the SQL Server Runtime Engine. You can unregister a repository database at any time by deleting the registration information.

To register a repository database, you provide the necessary connection information similar to registering a SQL Server 2000 database. SQL Server 2000 Meta Data Services does not create repository databases, so the database must already exist before you try to register it. After you successfully register a database, you can upgrade it to use the newest features of the repository engine.

To register a repository database, do as follows:

1. Open the MMC with Meta Data Services (you install the Meta Data Console as you do any MMC console).
2. Select the root Meta Data Services folder, right-click, and select Register Database. The Database Registration dialog box, as illustrated in Figure 5-4, loads.
3. Provide the relevant connection information, choose the mode, and then click OK. Figure 5-5 illustrates the new server and database registration, showing the DTS package we earlier saved in it, in the msdb database.

You can edit, delete, rename, and do various things with the database from the same context menu.

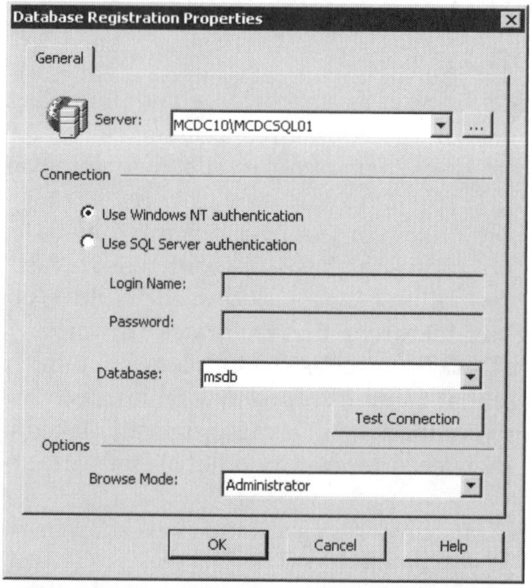

Figure 5-4. *Database Registration dialog box*

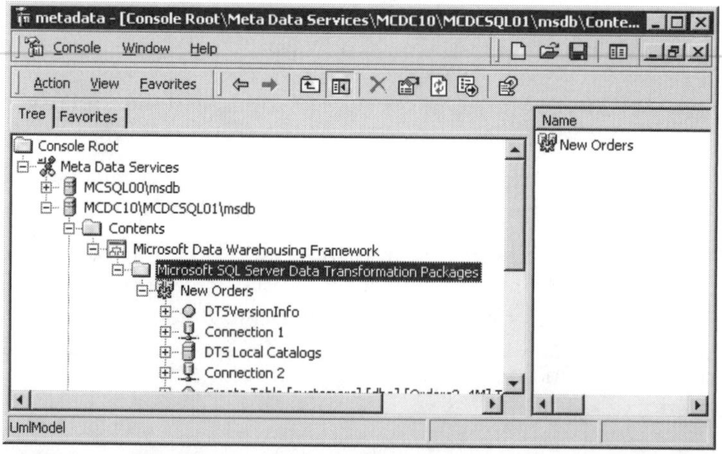

Figure 5-5. *The new server and database registration, with DTS package installed*

Changing the Browse Mode in Meta Data Browser

When you run Meta Data Browser as a standalone snap-in, you are allowed to determine the scope of actions that are available to you from the browser. Browse modes include End User, Power User, and Administrator, and you can set different browse modes for each database, to be registered in the browser.

The scope of actions for each browse mode includes the following:

- **All modes** Create, edit, view, and delete registration information.
- **Power User and Administrator browse mode** Create, edit, and delete objects and object properties. Only Administrators can view repository identifiers.

By the way, the browse modes apply exclusively to repository databases and have no impact or bearing on SQL Server 2000 user modes, Windows NT 4.0 Windows 2000 user modes, or anything else. In other words, being a repository Administrator does not give you the keys to any kingdom.

The browse mode is set during database registration; it is part of the registration information. If you need to change the browse mode, you must edit the registration properties.

Setting Display Options in Meta Data Browser

To set display options, do the following:

1. Drill down to the registered repository database or an object within the database. Right-click, and then click Browse Options.
2. This Meta Data Services Browser Display Options dialog box, illustrated in Figure 5-6, loads. You can then provide the required information to complete your browse option selections.

Working with Contents in Meta Data Browser

You can use Meta Data Browser to "stroll" through the objects that have been designed for or by an application. If you are an application developer, browsing the contents of a repository can help you identify the best object to choose when building a new application. You can also browse the contents to view details about a DTS package or application component.

Inside the Contents Folder

The Contents folder shows object instance data in a repository database, allowing you to view objects, object properties, collections, and relationships. Your browse mode selection determines how you interact with the Contents folder, and the display

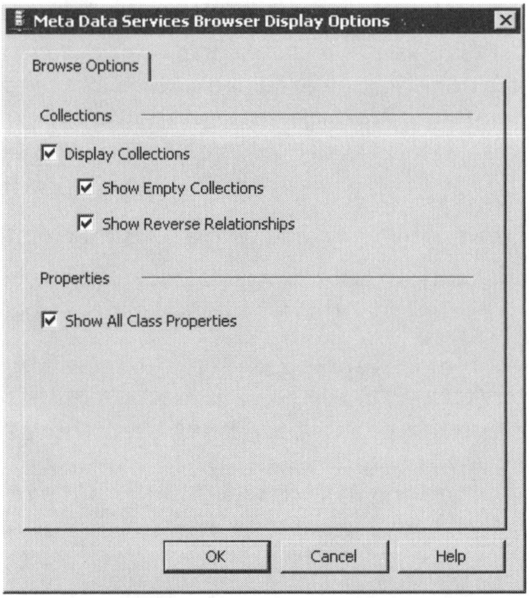

Meta Data Services Browser Display Options

Browse Options

Collections

☑ Display Collections

☑ Show Empty Collections

☑ Show Reverse Relationships

Properties

☑ Show All Class Properties

OK Cancel Help

Figure 5-4. *The Meta Data Services Browser Display Options dialog box*

option selections determine what is visible to your browse mode context. Every repository database has a Contents Folder, so if you do not see one, it is unlikely that you registered a repository database.

Objects

The objects in the database can contain collections and other objects. Before you become an expert with the browser or the Meta Data services, it will help you to choose not to display collections. This way, you limit the information explosion that results, and you can more easily view object relationships.

The object relationships are rendered hierarchically, so expanding an object exposes all the related objects into view. If, for example, you have a database object, expanding it can show the tables, columns, and so on. If you have an object for a human, expanding it can show limbs, organs, nervous system, and so on. Expanding "eye," for example, might show lenses, retina, optical nerve . . . you get the idea. The properties are listed in alphabetical order.

Collections

The collections can contain objects or they can be empty. By displaying collections, you can see how the objects are grouped. A look at the human body collection, for example, reveals that limbs, organs, and so on belong to that collection.

Working with Object and Properties in Meta Data Browser

At any time, you can display the properties of an object and view their characteristics. To do this, right-click an object and then click Properties. The Repository Object Properties dialog box loads, as illustrated in Figure 5-7.

Understanding Property Information

At this point, if you understand information models you will be able to determine what the class reveals about objects. The A–Z of the object models, however, is the domain of

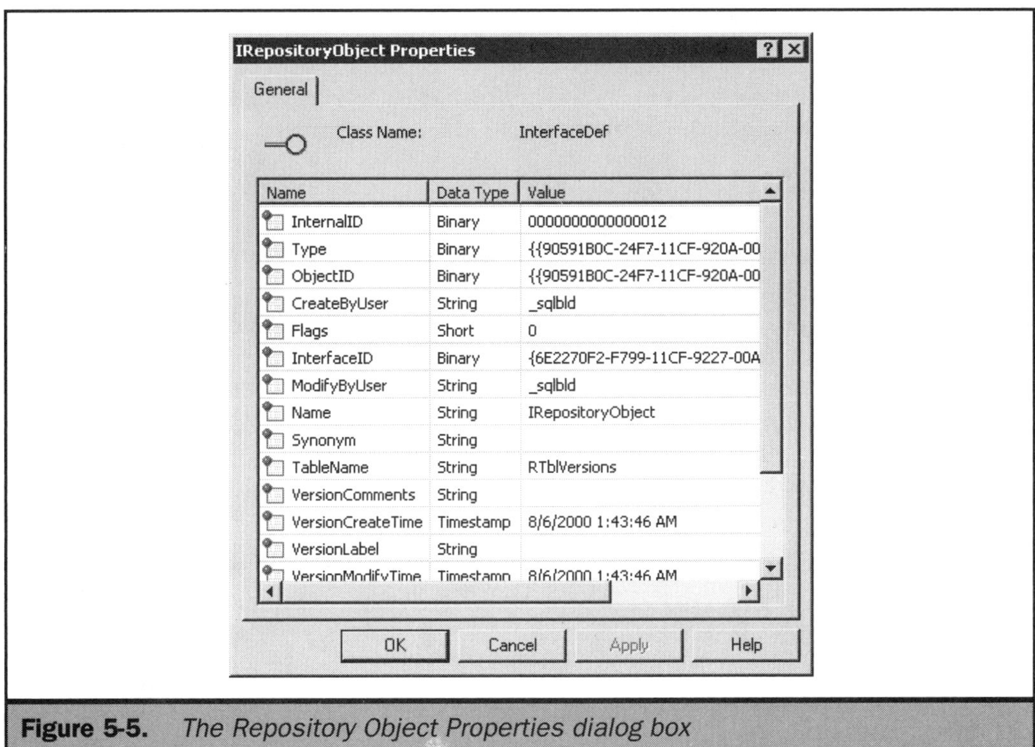

IRepositoryObject Properties
General
Class Name: InterfaceDef
Name | Data Type | Value
InternalID | Binary | 0000000000000012
Type | Binary | {{90591B0C-24F7-11CF-920A-00
ObjectID | Binary | {{90591B0C-24F7-11CF-920A-00
CreateByUser | String | _sqlbld
Flags | Short | 0
InterfaceID | Binary | {6E2270F2-F799-11CF-9227-00A
ModifyByUser | String | _sqlbld
Name | String | IRepositoryObject
Synonym | String
TableName | String | RTblVersions
VersionComments | String
VersionCreateTime | Timestamp | 8/6/2000 1:43:46 AM
VersionLabel | String
OK
Cancel
Apply
Help

Figure 5-5. *The Repository Object Properties dialog box*

a dedicated book. You might want to start with a general text on UML before getting into the specifics of what you can see and do with Meta Data Services.

You can search Books Online for more information about repository API definitions and properties.

Creating Objects

You can populate a repository with new object instance data that you create. The objects you create must be compatible with the definitions of an installed information model. For example, to create a new table object, the underlying information model must support a table object definition.

To create objects, right-click the parent object under which the new object is to reside, and then click Create Object. You cannot create objects from within Enterprise Manager. You also cannot create objects without connecting as a power user or administrator. Creating an object requires choosing a collection, choosing a class, and defining a name. Your choices determine the characteristics assumed by the object.

Collections that you can choose from belong to the parent element. For example, if the parent object is a Table object, you can choose from the collections that belong to the Table object (in this case, the Columns collection). You cannot create collections. You can only choose from collections that are provided for the parent object by way of the information model. Class selections are derived from the collection. If a collection supports multiple classes, you must choose which class to use. Names are object names that you define. The name you define must be under 255 characters in length. Names can include spaces.

After you create the object, you can edit its properties.

Deleting, Renaming, and Removing Objects from Collections

When you run Meta Data Browser as a standalone snap-in, you can delete, rename, or remove object instance data from collections. You must be a repository Administrator to perform these actions. You can only perform these actions on object instance data that appears in the Contents folder.

When you delete, rename, or remove an object from a collection, your changes are immediately saved in the repository database. Except for renaming, you cannot reverse these changes using the Meta Data Browser.

To perform these actions, right-click an object in the Contents folder, and then click Delete, Rename, or Remove.

- **Delete** This action permanently deletes the object instance data from the repository database.
- **Rename** This action activates an in-place editor so that you can type over the existing name. If you are naming an object in a collection that requires unique names, Meta Data Services does not allow you to duplicate a name in that collection. Otherwise, duplicate names are supported.
- **Remove** This deletes reference information that associates an object with a collection. The object instance data is not deleted.

Working with Information Models in Meta Data Browser

The Information Models folder exposes the information models that are installed in a repository database. The Information Models folder is visible only to repository Administrators, and it is available only when you run the browser as a standalone snap-in. Except for sequenced relationship collections, the order in which information model objects appear is undefined.

Information models are the blueprints of items you see in the Contents folder. In its native format, an information model is typically a network of related objects. In Meta Data Browser, information models are depicted hierarchically. When you expand an object, the child nodes that appear are the objects related to the expanded object. Depicting a network structure in a hierarchical format means that some objects appear multiple times. For example, in a relationship, each object will appear as a child node of the other object.

You can install ready-to-use information models (stored as *.rdm* files) using Meta Data Browser or a separate installation tool that comes with the Meta Data Services SDK. Installing an information model extracts information from a model and places it into tables in the repository database. How an information model is used from that point forward can vary considerably across tools, users, and environments.

Inside the Information Models Folder

In the browser, you can expand an installed information model to view the objects and collections it contains. You cannot create, modify, or delete an information model, its objects, or its properties. To perform those tasks, you must use modeling tools.

You can expand an information model to view objects, collections, interfaces, and members. View the inheritance tree for each interface. View read-only object properties to see how an object is defined.

Installing Information Models in Meta Data Browser

When you run Meta Data Browser as a standalone snap-in, you can install ready-to-use information models to the repository database, making them available to applications, application developers, and model designers. You must be a repository Administrator to install an information model. After you install an information model, it remains in the repository database. You cannot currently delete an information model in Meta Data Services.

To install an information model, right-click the Information Models folder of the database in which you want the model to reside, and then click Install Information Model. This opens the Install Information Model dialog box so that you can choose a Repository Distributable Model (RDM) file to install. RDM files are compiled information model files. They are generated from a modeling tool in the Meta Data Services SDK.

It is also possible to install information models programmatically or by command line, without using Meta Data Browser.

Where to Next

This chapter introduces you to Meta Data Services, and the metadata support that comes standard with SQL Server 2000. Further exploration of OIMs and modeling is beyond the scope of this book, but essential if you want to design database applications that meet project specifications and deadlines. Also, as you progress into the advanced applications of SQL Server, such as English Query, Data Transformation, Data Warehousing, and OLAP, so will you begin to see how and where Meta Data Services plays its part.

Chapter 6

Installing SQL Server 2000

I have often read that installing SQL Server 2000 is so easy that it's laughable. In more than a decade supporting Microsoft's or any other vendor's products, the only time I laugh is when I see the message "...installation successful" pop up on my screen. Actually, I usually do the Ali shuffle around the server room as well.

Take nothing for granted. During the writing of this book, a client of a client called me up to say they had tried to install RAS and blew the whole company up (which meant they wrecked the server and now no one could log in). It took five days to restore the mess, and RAS (on NT 4.0) is usually only a five-minute install. If you read anywhere that installing SQL Server is dead-easy and you believe that, circle the word "dead"; it will become a new word in your DBA vocab.

General Prerequisites

Before you run setup, you have a number of items to check off the list first. Your list may in fact have more or less items than mine. The one presented here comprises a number of important items that specifically relate to actual installation time:

- Establish user accounts for SQL Server 2000 on a Windows NT or Windows 2000 domain. This allows your target SQL Server to communicate with other servers, services, and clients on the network. If you are new to SQL Server in general and SQL Server 2000 in particular, then first read Chapters 8 and 9 before configuring users and logins. My advice is to first set up SQL Server before worrying about users. They can be created or connected to SQL Server any time after you have settled on where the servers are going to be placed—the environment (intranet, extranet, Internet, intra-domain, UNIX realm, and so on).
- You should be logged in as a local administrator or as a user account that has local administrative privileges to install SQL Server. The installation will need access to local resources that a nonadministrative account will not have access to. You can log into the domain as the domain administrator (not recommended, see Chapter 8), but that does not guarantee you'll have the proper access. On member servers, the Domain Administrators global group is usually given administrative rights on the local machine. You can check which group has these rights as follows:
  - On a Windows NT member server, open User Manager (not User Manager for Domains) and check for the presence of a domain administrators global group. The path to the local User Manager is Start | Programs | Administrative Tools. If the group is not present, add it.
  - On a Windows 2000 member server, open the Local User and Groups, which is in the Systems Tools tree of the Computer Management MMC

snap-in. The easiest way to get to the snap-in is via the Run facility, running *compmgmt.msc* (which can also be run from the command prompt); otherwise, you can click Start | Programs | Administrative Tools | Computer Management. (Remember that there is no local user on a domain controller on either Windows NT domains or Windows 2000 domains. If you are installing into a standalone server, you will need to be logged in as local administrator.)

- Shut down any services and applications that may be affected by the SQL Server installation. Any service using or dependent on ODBC is the first place to start. This would include any local applications that use data source names (DSN). Internet Information Services also hooks in ODBC (through the IDC).
- Microsoft also recommends you shut down the Event Viewer, but I do not see how keeping it running affects installation as long as you do not open it and fiddle with event logs at the same time an installation is running.
- Also, do not tinker around in the Registry during installation. It is heavily used during the SQL Server installation process. SQL Server does not use Active Directory (Windows 2000 DC) for storing instance information (like instance names and paths to binaries, databases, and log files). The Registry is its chief storehouse for all configuration and settings.
- I have also found that installing while antivirus scans are running is not a good idea. You should ensure your virus scan is not going after binaries, or better still, stop the virus scan service altogether during installation. The same deal goes for any kind of file inspection services that hook in the file system at the stack level, such as Open File Manager from St. Bernard Software, and similar agents used with backup software.
- If you are going to tackle a version upgrade, do not forget to back up the version. Also do not forget to perform a full disaster recover image backup or tape backup of the server, even if you are just adding a SQL Server 2000 instance to the machine and you are not upgrading.
- Go over your installation or upgrade plan and make sure you can perform the required steps. This usually means that you have acquired all the necessary information.
- Keep your CD key at the ready. The SQL Server 2000 installation cannot be completed without it.

SQL Server Components

The SQL Server 2000 setup program installs the following components (see "Setup Types and Options" later in this chapter for more details on installing the components). The installation installs the following objects:

- **SQL Server** Setup installs the relational database engine (DBMS). Core tools are also installed, such as BCP, ISQL, OSQL, OCBC, OLE DB, and the DB Library.
- **Upgrade tools** Setup installs the Upgrade Wizard. This wizard upgrades SQL Server 6.5.
- **Replication** Setup installs all script and binary files used by the replication service.
- **Full-Text Search** Setup installs the MS Full-Text Search Engine.
- **Debug symbols** Setup installs the debug symbols for each installation.
- **Performance counters** Setup installs the performance counters for service level (see Chapter 12).
- **Books Online** Setup installs the full documentation set. You can choose to install it on a location on the hard disk—stick with the default unless you are short of space—or you can choose to access the SQL Server Books Online from the CD. (If you install SQL Server 2000 as the default instance, you will overwrite any previous version's Books Online.)

File Particulars

SQL Server installs itself over two disks on a multidisk installation, in which you have two or more drive letters. The actual program files, referred to as the "binaries," are installed on your root hard disk, usually the C drive. No data files whatsoever are stored in the folder hierarchy supporting the binaries. Thus, apart from service packs and in-version upgrades, the disk space will not increase during the lifetime of the installation.

Some application servers implement a higher letter as the root or system drive, so be sure you are installing to the correct drive letter. A Citrix Metaframe server on Windows NT TSE or Windows 2000 will often assign the C and D drives to client mappings; a mid-alphabet letter like M or N usually ends up as the server's root or system drive letter.

The binaries are installed to the *\Program Files\Microsoft SQL Server\Mssql\Binn* folder; but you do have an option to change this default, so make sure you have a preferred path noted. I do find that the default path makes sense, so stick with it unless you have some unearthly reason not to go with the default.

You can find the path of an instance of SQL Server 2000 using the Registry editor, which has a query function. The editor, reg.exe, is included in the Windows 2000 Resource Kit. Just run the following command at the command prompt, replacing InstanceName with the instance name you want to query:

```
C:\>REG QUERY "HKLM\Software\Microsoft\Microsoft SQL
Server\InstanceName\Setup\SQLPath"
```

SQL Server will use the instance name in addition to any location you specify in order to support multiple instances. Later, we'll discuss some advanced options used in multiinstance management.

The data files are located on a second disk, if present, and also in the *\Program Files\Microsoft SQL Server\Mssql\Data* folder. This is the location where all database and log files are stored (see Chapter 2 for information on the system and demo databases). The hierarchy also contains the folders for the SQL Server system logs, backup information, and replication data. During installation, the setup program creates the system and demo databases and stores them in the *data* folder hierarchy.

"Mssql" is the default instance name used for in the folder path of both binaries and data. This name would be different for each instance installed. For example, C:\Program Files\MSSQL$GargantuanServer\Binn.

While the drive space occupied by the binaries will not change much, it should go without saying that the "data drives" will grow. It is probably the most important part of your data center operations plan.

The file systems used on the data drives should be your standard FAT32 or NTFS, so make sure you are not using compression or encryption or the advanced features of NTSF 5.0.

Tools and other "accessories" you can install are not dependent on any particular location or folder path. As discussed in the preceding chapter, tools and applications shared among instances are installed on the root drive.

Each instance of SQL Server installed on the machine contains a full set of binaries and databases (only the tools and utilities are shared). Accordingly, you will need a lot of hard disk space on a machine supporting multiple instances.

The Code Samples

Setup installs the following code samples to your server or workstation. These code samples are useful for reference from a development workstation. The default installation on a workstation is to *\Program Files\Microsoft SQL Server\80\Tools\DevTools\Samples,* which is also the shared tools location. The following table lists the code samples available; you can choose which of the samples you need installed:

Code Samples	Description
DBLIB	DB-Library
DTS	Data Transformation Services
ESQLC	Embedded SQL for the C language
MS DTC	Microsoft Distributed Transaction Coordinator
ODBC	Open Database Connectivity
ODS	Open Data Services
OLEAut	OLE Automation
Repl	Replication
SQL-DMO	SQL Distributed Management Objects
SQL-NS	SQL Namespace
ADO	Microsoft ActiveX Data Objects
SQL-DTS	SQL Data Transformation Services

Setup Types and Options

As you know, there are several editions or "skus" of SQL Server 2000. With each edition, you also have several ways to install the binaries, databases, and tools. I also feel it best to break down the installations along service lines (DMBS, English Query, Analysis Services, Desktop Engine, and so on). This chapter deals with the standard DMBS installations. The latter services are not installed along with base install. And the cluster install will be covered in Chapter 13.

Common to all DBMS installation are the following options, which are presented to you by the Installation Wizard:

- Create a new or additional installation. If you are installing a new instance, you will have the option of providing setup with your choice of installation name.
- Upgrade, remove, or add components to an existing installation.
- Install SQL Server on cluster nodes.
- Unattended or scripted installations.
- Registry rebuild.

Besides the preceding options, you also have several additional suboptions to the ones just listed. For starters, you can install SQL Server on the local host or on a remote host. Remote installation, for obvious reasons, presents you with limited options. For example, you cannot perform the Registry rebuild or a virtual server installation on the remote machine. The options available to a full local install are as follows:

- Install client tools only. You cannot install more than one copy of the client tools (such as SQL Server Enterprise Manager) to a machine. If you are installing tools to a new machine, setup will naturally bypass all server screens and proceed directly to the tools installation.
- Install server and client tools. This option installs both the tools and the DBMS. If the installation installs a new instance of SQL Server, the tools do not get reinstalled.
- Install connectivity options only.

Setup gives you the option to choose *Typical, Minimum,* and *Custom* installs. The *Typical* install installs everything according to Microsoft. However, I noticed that the so-called typical install does not give you all the tools. The code samples are also not installed, and you only get the debugger. The *Minimum* installation installs only what is required to run the server. The *Minimum* option is the best choice if you are installing to disk drives that short on free space. I recommend the *Custom* install if you know what you are doing or you are building a setup file for a remote or unattended installation. And you also get only one copy of the upgrade tools on the first instance or default instance of SQL Server 2000.

Table 6-1 lists the types of installations and the components installed with each installation.

Naming the Server

The first installation of SQL Server can be named by default instance install, but this might not suit you or tally with the Data Center Operations Plan. Using (local) is insufficient because you can have more than one (local) instance; in other words, if you specify "(local)" in your applications, the connection attempt will be made to the default or first installation. The default installation, by the way, can also be a version 6.5 or version 7.0 installation.

During installation, you will thus be afforded the opportunity to name the server. Do not worry if you get the instance name wrong, because you can always change the name using T-SQL (discussed shortly).

The default name for this instance is usually first drawn from the computer name. The naming rules for remote installations also apply. Each additional instance will require an instance name.

SQL Server Component	Typical	Minimum	Custom
DBMS (server)	Yes	Yes	User options
Upgrade tools	Yes	No	User options
Replication	Yes	Yes	User options
Full-Text	Yes	Yes	User options
Client tools	All	No	User options
Client connectivity	Yes	Yes	No option
Books Online	Yes	No	User options
Development tools	Debugger	No	User options
Code samples	No	No	User options
Collations	Yes	Yes	User options
Net-Libraries	User options	User options	User options

Table 6-1. *Installation Components*

Naming Instances of SQL Server 2000

Have your instance names handy. The SQL Server installation provides a number of options for naming your new instance installation. If you check the Default option check box, the installation will attempt to install a default instance. The check box is disabled if a default instance already exists. The default instance might already be a version 6.5 or version 7.0 installation. If the check box is left clear, you can install a named instance. The following rules apply to named instances:

- The instance name is not case sensitive; however, the field case is left unchanged.
- Reserved words are *Default* and *MSSQLServer*.
- The instance name cannot be longer than 16 characters.
- The first letter of an instance can be most of Unicode Standard 2.0 characters a–z and A–Z. You cannot use a number for the first letter; nor dashes, the asterisk, or your typical punctuation marks; ampersand, slashes, or spaces. You can use numbers in the name after the first letter. If you get an error from a named instance, you can check if it is supported in the current code page.

New Local Install

Have Name (not an account name or user principal name) and Company handy. The SQL Server installation mandates this information. You will also need to specify the lead DBA responsible for the server after installation.

Choose Authentication Mode

This dialog box, as illustrated in Figure 6-1, brings you to the Authentication Mode options (see Chapter 9, SQL Server Security). You now have to supply and confirm a System Administrator (SA) password, even if you choose to make it a blank password. This option comes after years of leaving SQL Server more exposed after initial installation than a peeled banana.

As mentioned in Chapter 3, you have two authentication modes SQL Server will accept: Windows authentication mode and mixed mode. Mixed mode can use either SQL Server built-in security information or Windows authentication information.

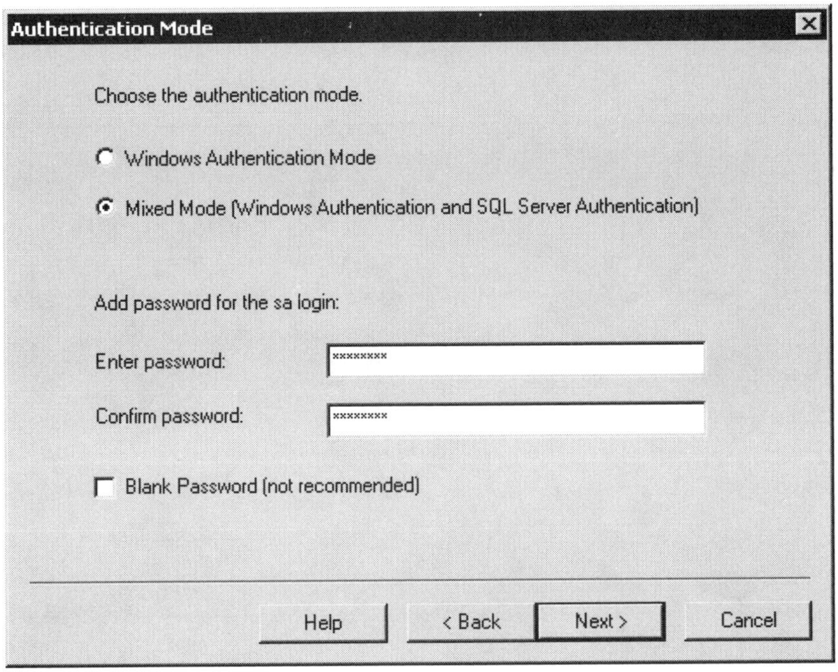

Authentication Mode

Choose the authentication mode.

Windows Authentication Mode

Mixed Mode (Windows Authentication and SQL Server Authentication)

Add password for the sa login:

Enter password: xxxxxxxx

Confirm password: xxxxxxxx

Blank Password (not recommended)

Help | < Back | Next > | Cancel

Figure 6-1. *Choosing the authentication mode*

Chapter 8 investigates these options in more detail, especially the many options you now have under Windows 2000 authentication, such as Kerberos tickets, smart cards, and so forth.

Essentially, if you try to attach to SQL Server sans a user ID or password, mixed mode will get you in by virtue of the trust the server has of the authentication of a security principal (you). In mixed mode, any SQL Server user ID is ignored for access validation, unless for some reason the domain security identifier mechanisms are not getting through to the server.

Service Accounts

Service accounts are the accounts the SQL Server services use to operate in the context of a user account (a security principal) on a Windows NT or Windows 2000 domain (do not confuse these with login IDs discussed in Chapter 8). This information is entered into the dialog box illustrated in Figure 6-2. If SQL Server is to operate as a member of domain to access services and communicate with other services and clients, it must log in as a security principal and not in the context of the system account.

You can specify the same account for all services, and the default will be the user account you used when you signed onto the machine to install SQL Server. Earlier I recommended you create a SQL Server Installer account and make it a member of the

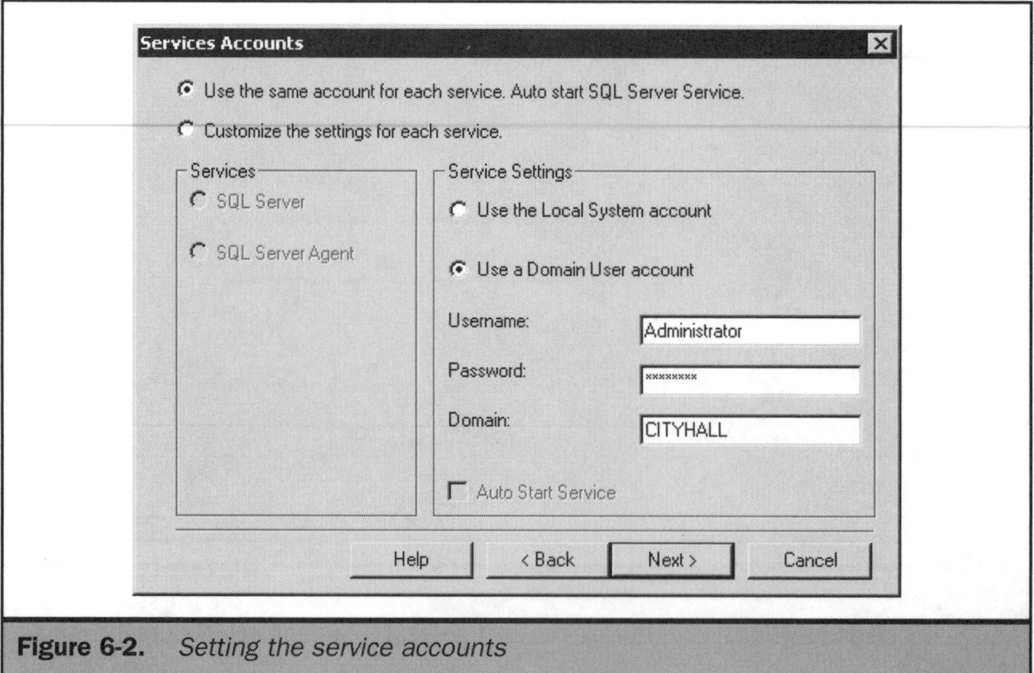

Figure 6-2. *Setting the service accounts*

Domain Administrators group. You could use this account; however, it would make for a tighter ship to create a special SQL Server user account for the SQL Server services. I created an account called SQL Server Services and gave it membership in the Domain Administrators group. The account can be monitored for any misuse using auditing and some other techniques I will discuss in Chapter 8.

The default for all services is the system account. If you specify alternate security principals and then go back (by clicking Back) to this dialog box, all settings revert to the default system account.

If you have not created the logon account for the services, follow the steps described in the preceding chapter, "Creating and Configuring SQL Server Service User Accounts."

Advanced Installation Options

The next dialog box brings up the SQL Server Advanced Installations options. From here you can record an Unattended Installation ISS file, rebuild a Registry (useful if you wreck installation), and install SQL Server on a cluster node. The clustering options (fail-over and virtual server definitions) are dealt with in Chapter 13.

Unattended Installation

The unattended installation procedure combined with a powerful information collecting process enables you to carry out unattended installation of SQL Server. This is useful for both deployment and rollout of SQL Server in a production environment (such as when you have 40 remote data centers to install) or when you are installing to commercial sites or clients that are your customers and not part of your organization (which is what I do a lot of).

The unattended installation is built with a setup initialization file, which is driven by the InstallShield engine. The *.iss* (InstallShield Silent) file is an initialization file using the standard Windows *.ini* format and runs through about 14 dialog boxes. You can modify the file with a simple text editor.

There are a number of different ways to create the *setup.iss* file, but the easiest for noncommercial installations is with the services of the setup-installation program that is included on the CD for the attended installations. This option is the "Record Unattended .ISS" option, which I will describe shortly. The *setup.iss* file is created in the system root directory (represented by the %windir% variable).

Before you begin recording an unattended installation, you should investigate the sample files included on the CD. These files represent unattended installations of a number of different types. The installations are executed using a DOS-based batch file (**.bat*). These files include the basic installations of the various editions of SQL Server 2000, custom installations, and version 7.0 upgrades. The scripts are listed in Table 6-2.

If you plan to assign domain accounts to SQL Server services (see the section "Service Accounts" earlier in this chapter), which is a likely scenario, your unattended installation will not be as straightforward, as you'll discover in one of the scripts.

Installation Type	Batch File	ISS File
Typical installation	*sqlins.bat*	sqlins.iss
Client installation of client tools, management tools, etc. (no server)	*sqlcli.bat*	sqlcli.iss
Custom installation (all components)	*sqlcst.bat*	sqlcst.iss
Upgrade (SQL Server version 7.0 to SQL Server 2000)	*sqlupg.bat*	sqlupg.iss
Edition upgrade (SKU) of SQL Server 2000 (Standard Edition to Enterprise Edition)	*sqlupg.bat* (in the folder of the respective edition)	sqlupsku.iss
Remove script	*sqlrem.bat*	*ssqlrem.iss*

Table 6-2. *Installation Scripts*

Specifying special user accounts obviously requires you to determine first if an account exists, and if not, who will create it and what name and group will be defined. You might have to spawn a script that creates the user account (easier to do into Active Directory than into the Windows NT Security Accounts Manager [SAM]); but more about this later.

The stock ISS files can be run from the command prompt. Open to the DOS command line (or run CMD for Windows NT and Windows 2000, and Command on Windows 98). Change to root folders of the edition (SKU) you plan to install and locate one of the batch files listed in Table 6-2. You can edit the file or leave it as is. To run the script, simply execute the corresponding batch files in the usual fashion.

You can also run the ISS files without the batch file by executing the setup program directory in the command console. Run *setupsql.exe* with one of the following arguments:

- –f1 <initialization file path> (for example –f1 e:\sqlcst.iss).
- start /wait command (with the –sms option). Launches setup and returns to the command prompt when the entire installation is complete.
- –s to force setup to run in silent mode or with the GUI.

Let's now record a standard ISS file using the SQL Server setup program. Start the SQL Server 2000 setup program as described earlier and perform the following steps:

1. Select the edition of SQL Serve 2000 you wish to install and click Next until you get to the Computer Name dialog box. Add the information and continue.
2. The Installation Selection dialog box loads. Click Advanced options to load the Advanced Options dialog box. Now click Record Unattended .ISS file and click Next.
3. From here on, you add the information you need to create the file for your unattended installation. When you arrive at the Setup Complete dialog box, click Finish.

At the end of the process, you will see the message "Setup has collected the information needed to create an unattended installation file *(.iss)* for use with later unattended installations of SQL Server." You can now run this file from the command line as described earlier.

SQL Server Books Online has a complete breakdown of the *.iss* file that explains each section and the values required.

Rebuild a Registry

The Registry Builder is a very useful tool, and it is essential in the management of multiple instances. It was created to repair corrupt installations (corrupt Registry settings). Each instance occupies its own namespace in the Registry. If you change or remove an instance, you may need to repair the corresponding namespace. If the namespace gets deleted and the instance is "orphaned," the Registry Builder will rebuild the namespace and anchor the instance to the Registry.

In the preceding chapter, you read that one of the chief objectives of the Installation Plan is to record the information you will use in your setup or installation process. The recollection of that information you maintained now comes into play. You cannot rebuild a Registry namespace using new information, because your installation will not correspond to the Registry settings. For example: If you installed to *Q:\MyBadInstallation\Microsoft SQL Server\Mssql\Data,* you cannot now rebuild the Registry using the C drive as the path to the binaries. However, if you change the location of the binaries, it is possible to rebuild the namespace for it as long as you supply the Registry Builder with the new path. (On the other hand, as mentioned in the preceding chapter, you also have the option to start with a fresh install and just restore your databases to the new instance.)

To rebuild a mangled SQL Server Registry namespace, you need to perform the following tasks:

1. Insert the SQL Server 2000 installation CD and execute *autorun.exe* if it does not fire on its own.
2. When the Installation Wizard launches, click Install SQL Server 2000 Components from the dialog box and click Next until you arrive at the Installation Selection dialog box illustrated in Figure 6-3. Click Advanced options. The Advanced Options dialog box now loads, as illustrated in Figure 6-4.
3. Click the Registry Rebuild button and click Next. A dialog box appears informing you that you need information handy that pertains to the installation (the actual location) of the binaries and data files.
4. Next enter the information required by the Registry Builder. When you are done entering the information, the rebuild will take place.

If you are not able to supply the correct information, or if the Registry rebuild process fails, you will have to uninstall SQL Server and start from scratch. If you have begun working with the databases, you'll need to follow disaster recover procedures explained in Chapter 10.

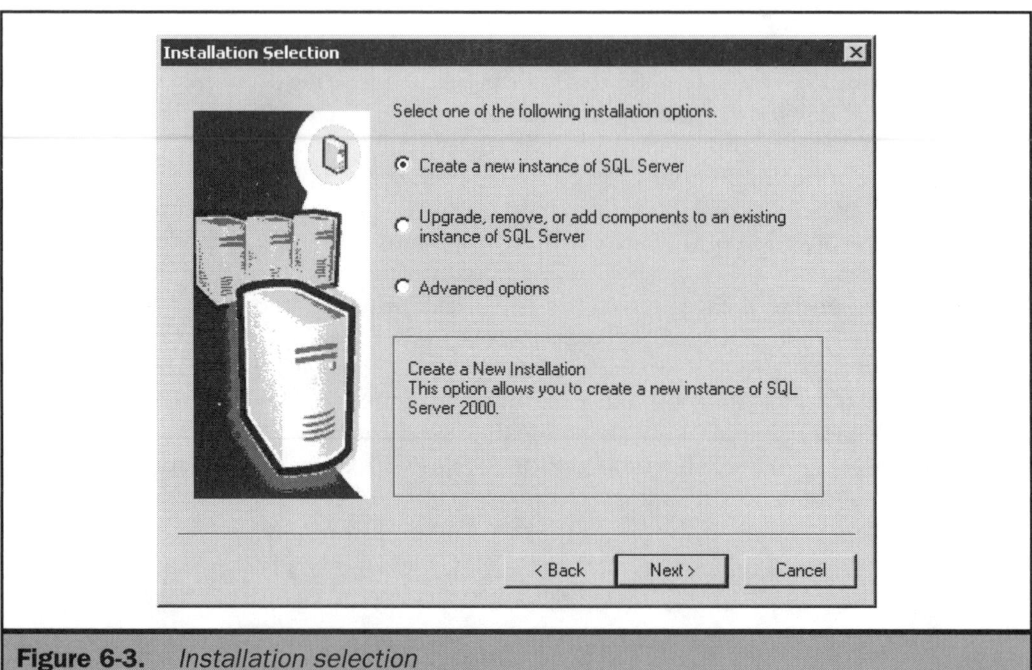

Figure 6-3. *Installation selection*

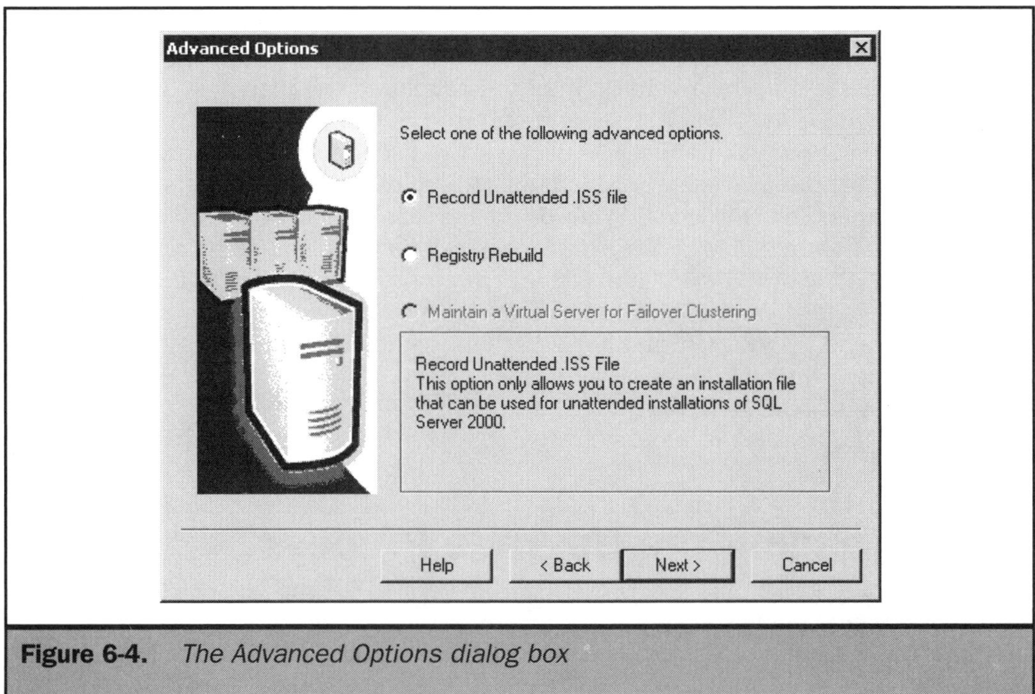

Figure 6-4. *The Advanced Options dialog box*

New Remote Install

The following are prerequisites for remote installation:

- The local and remote machines must be running Windows NT or Windows 2000. You can install from a Windows NT machine to a Windows 2000 machine and vice versa.
- The existing installations (target to be upgraded), no matter the past version, must be at their latest builds and service packs.
- The local and remote machines must be running Intel or Intel-compatible processors. The Alpha platform is no longer supported.
- You must be logged into the local machine as an administrator that has administrative rights on the remote machine as well. Thus you should log in as a domain administrator that has privileges on both machines. As discussed earlier, the user account would satisfy the requirements if it was an unencumbered security principal that is a member of domain admins.

The remote installation proceeds as follows: The setup process gathers information that you specify in the wizard and builds a *Setup.iss* file for the remote computer.

The remote computer's ISS file is built on the local computer. It is then transferred to the remote computer, where a service is started to continue with the remote installation. The remote installation is thus an unattended installation.

During a remote installation, you are asked to supply a Username, Password, and Domain. These variables refer to a user who, as previously discussed, has administrative (install) privileges on both the local and remote computers—typically a domain principal. This user should thus be logged into the local computer. Your installation plan should provide the account name, password, and domain information. As suggested in the preceding chapter, this account could be named SQL Server Installer and made a member of the Domain Administrators group. You can use the same account and domain information in both the local and remote machines.

You will need the remote computer's name handy. This should have been collected and noted in the installation plan. You should also prevalidate the path you want to install into in the remote machine.

Understanding the Upgrade Process

You can upgrade direct to SQL Server 2000 from version 6.5 and version 7.0 without having to upgrade to interim versions. Earlier versions (below 6.5) require you to upgrade first to version 6.5 before going to SQL Server 2000. You can also upgrade replication servers directly from 6.5 to 2000 without having to first "pond pebble" upgrade your way to version 7.0.

Before you decide what to do, realize that you should fully understand the upgrade process before you decide to upgrade to SQL Server 2000 or attempt to go first to SQL Server version 7.0.

If you need to upgrade to version 6.5 or 7.0 first and if you do not have SQL Server 6.5 or 7.0, you can download a trial version from Microsoft (if it is still around in the weeks and months following the general release of SQL Server 2000). If you can't find it and you need to upgrade first to SQL Server 7.0, I suggest you go out and buy a SQL Server 6.0, 6.5, or 7.0 book that has the trial CD attached to the inside cover.

If you plan to also upgrade to Windows 2000, your options of upgrading existing SQL Server 6.5 are very limited.

When you first start up the installation process, the choice to upgrade an existing installation is one of the basic choices offered. The setup program is smart enough to determine exactly what version of SQL Server you are running and also what service pack it has been maintained to. If you are running 6.5, there is a strong likelihood that you will already be at the correct service pack (5a) because you would have needed this service pack to make your SQL Server 6.5 system Y2K compliant.

During the startup of the upgrade setup, the installation process will offer the following options:

- An installation upgrade of an existing instance of SQL Server 6.5, performed using the SQL Server Upgrade Wizard. This option does not replace the version 6.5 instance.
- A complete installation upgrade of an existing instance of SQL Server 7.0. This option destroys the version 7.0 instance.
- An online database upgrade of SQL Server 7.0 databases. This is performed using the Copy Database Wizard.
- A feature set upgrade of an existing installation of SQL Server 2000. The option is deployed when, for example, you decide to upgrade from the Standard Edition to the Enterprise Edition.
- The capability to add components to an existing instance of SQL Server 2000.

If you are upgrading either version 6.5 or 7.0 on Windows NT servers, you may also need to install the latest version of the Microsoft Management Console. You can choose to leave the OS as Windows NT 4.0, and just prepare the operating system by installing the latest service pack to it. SQL Server 2000 can be installed on Windows NT 4.0 Server, as discussed in the preceding chapter. There are, however, major advantages to moving to Windows 2000, as discussed in the preceding chapter.

Replication Issues

Upgrading replication servers requires some forethought and much advanced planning, because you will typically upgrade servers synchronously. The good news is that SQL Server 2000 is smart enough to continue replication services even though the other servers in the replication environment are on the older versions (6.5 and 7.0).

However, you need to make sure you first upgrade the Distributor, then the Publisher, and finally the Subscribers. You can also create new publications and subscriptions with the servers running the older versions. See Chapter 10, which discusses replication.

You also need to make sure that any version 7.0 databases on replications servers are running in version 7.0 compatibility mode. You cannot upgrade a version 7.0 database in replication that is running in compatibility mode 65 or earlier. This compatibility change is temporary and should only be needed during the upgrade process (see also Chapter 11).

If you are using transactional replication, you can upgrade subscribers before the publisher; however, some significant changes were made to the replication architecture of SQL Server. The rows in immediate updating articles now make use of a uniqueidentifier column to identify the row versions. SQL Server 7.0 used a timestamp method that has been replaced. Also, the triggers generated for immediate updating have been changed. The trigger generation code has been modified to accommodate queued updating (see Chapter 10).

If you use immediate updating, you need to ensure the following:

1. Upgrade both publishers and subscribers before replicating data.
2. Drop the publication and all subscriptions.
3. Drop the timestamp columns that allow subscriber updates from the tables on the publisher and from the tables on the subscriber.
4. Recreate the publication and the subscriptions after installation.

Upgrading and FTP

SQL Server 2000 now stores FTP parameters as publication properties; you no longer need to manage them at the subscriber for each subscription. When you upgrade, however, the FTP option in the publication properties is turned off and you will need to reset it after installation (see Chapter 10). Also, upgraded subscribers will not be able to obtain FTP information from the Distributors still running on earlier versions of SQL Server.

Upgrading the Host

Your host server must meet the following hardware and software requirements before you can begin upgrading:

- **Operating system** All versions of Windows NT 4.0 must be maintained to at least service pack 5 (SP5). You also need at least Internet Explorer 5.0. IE 5.0 is required for Books Online, but the installation process asks you for IE 5.0 (if you don't have it) before you can opt out of installing BOL.
- **Network** Named Pipes is required for all forms of upgrade. All versions of SQL Server (6.5, 7.0, and 2000) must be listening on Named Pipes. In particular, the servers need to be listening to the default pipe at \\.\pip\sql\query.
- **Hard-disk space** To go from version 7.0 to version 2000 does not require additional hard-disk space (remember, you are doing an upgrade of an existing installation and not a new instance). To go from 6.5 to 2000 does require you to provide 1.5 times more space than the size of the 6.5 databases.

Upgrading SQL Server 7.0

The upgrade process replaces all of SQL Server 7.0's binaries and converts the existing databases to SQL Server 2000 databases. All data in the databases is preserved. However, you should not have to be told that you need to make a full backup of your databases and all transactions logs, just in case something goes wrong and your upgrade and databases go the same way as the Mars Polar Lander.

Tip *Large systems with large database can take a long time to convert or upgrade. There are a number of collateral operations to perform, post installation, that could keep your server offline for some time after installation. It would thus be a good idea to plan the upgrade to take place over the weekend or late afternoon, because you may be offline for some time.*

If something goes wrong, even after you have installed SQL Server 2000, and for some reason you need to return to the previous version, you will first have to uninstall SQL Server 2000 and then reinstall a fresh version of SQL Server 7.0. Then you'll need to restore your backed-up databases.

If you have a lot of data that you absolutely cannot afford to lose, I would consider attempting a restore on another test machine to make sure your backups are OK. SQL Server 2000 completely replaces the 7.0 binaries, so after installation there is no longer any trace of 7.0, which is why you will need to reinstall it. Uninstalling SQL Server 2000 does not restore 7.0, not one byte.

You also do not need to install to the same level as version 7.0. If you are installing to a higher level or sku of SQL Server 2000 (say Standard to Enterprise), SQL Server 2000 will do the upgrade and install to the new level during the one and the same installation process.

To perform your upgrade, do as follows:

1. Insert your SQL Server CD. If the autorun does not fire, double-click the autorun executable, which is in the root directory of the CD.
2. Select Install SQL Server 2000, select the edition to install, and then click Next at the welcome screen.
3. The next option requires the name of the computer to install on. You will stick with the default name if installing to the local host. After confirming the computer name, click Next.
4. The next dialog box presents the Installation Selection. Click Upgrade, Remove, or Add components to an existing installation of SQL Server. Then click Next. The Instance Name dialog box loads.
5. Click Next at this dialog box because an upgrade becomes the first instance of SQL Server. The Existing Installation dialog box now loads. Click Upgrade your existing installation, and then click Next. The Upgrade dialog box now loads.
6. The Upgrade dialog box will prompt you for a final decision to proceed with the upgrade. So this dialog box is actually your last chance to opt out of the installation. At this point, all version 7.0 binaries and configuration are still intact. To move forward, click Yes, upgrade my . . . and then click Next. The upgrade process now continues, and there is no turning back.

Before SQL Server comes to life, you are prompted for an authentication mode. In the Connect to Server dialog box, select the authentication mode and then click next (see Figure 6-1). The default mode is Windows NT authentication. If you are not sure which mode to use, choose the default. I suggest, however, you read Chapter 8 on the differences between the two modes. The default option is "The Windows NT account information I use to log on to my computer with (Windows NT)."

After installation is completed, you will have to restart the operating system.

Post-Installation

You should repopulate full-text catalogs and update your statistics. During installation, all full-text catalogs are disabled and undergo certain format changes. Database statistics are also no longer valid in the new server, and performance will be affected.

These procedures may take some time but will enhance the performance of SQL Server 2000. The catalog repopulation of a large system does not have to be done right away after installation. You can schedule it to run later, possibly overnight on a big system.

Updating statistics is another matter if you plan to go right to production as soon as possible after installation. However, on large databases this may take a long time because you need to update all statistics. For this reason, plan to perform the statistics update after hours.

Upgrading Databases

Despite the earlier discussion, a significant improvement over earlier version upgrades of SQL Server is the capability to perform online upgrades of databases and their associated metadata. This is made possible by the capability to install SQL Server 2000 on the same machine as the earlier version (version 7.0) without having to replace the existing server and then copy or move the databases from the old version to the new instance. The move from the old to the new upgrades the databases to version 8.0 (SQL Server 2000) compatibility. This is all made possible by the Copy Database Wizard, which shipped as a standard tool on SQL Server 2000 (see Chapter 11).

You can upgrade to either named instance of SQL Server on the local machine, that is, the same machine you have SQL Server 7.0 on, or you can upgrade the database to a remote default or named instance of SQL Server running on another machine. You can also perform this process across clustered servers. Unfortunately, SQL Server 6.5 databases are out of luck; the feature does not support them.

There are obviously significant advantages to upgrading just the database, and if you have the resources, this is the preferred method to get your databases from version 7.0 into an instance of SQL Server 2000. There are several advantages to doing this:

- There is no significant down time during the installation for either server. You only have to restart the operating system after the installation of SQL Server 2000.

- The upgrade of your databases can be performed on a phased implementation basis. In other words, you can move your databases to SQL Server 2000 when you are ready.
- You can keep SQL Server 7.0 going with a selection of databases, thus allowing users to connect to either server, where the databases they need are to be found.
- The upgrade database process keeps the version 7.0 login information and all other database objects. If you choose to upgrade a version 7.0 system database, the conversion or upgrade process will maintain your prior system configurations. For example, all jobs and login information are preserved or converted.

Upgrading databases is achieved using the Database Copy Wizard, which makes use of SQL Server 2000's capability to attach and detach to databases. This feature, built into the Data Transformation Services (DTS), lets you move a database from one server to another with ease. I was able to upgrade a number of my clients to SQL Server 2000 using this technique with minimal disruption.

After modeling the new databases and configuring the servers, I simply used DTS to cut the databases and reattached them to the new instances out in the field; it made upgrading a pleasure. There were a few snags along the way, like the need for more hard-disk space here and there and some network security issues, but on the whole if you have the hardware, this is by far the best way to get from SQL Server 7.0 to SQL Server 2000.

Obviously, replication issues can get in the way and replication partners have to be upgraded in the usual fashion. Also, if your regular source and destination servers are named the same, default or otherwise, you will get the error message "Already exists."

How to Do the Copy Upgrade

Make sure the steps you need to take are properly scripted. In order to perform the upgrade, you must have both source and target servers off limits to users. If you plan to do this during normal working hours, or there is some risk that users will attempt to reattach during the upgrade process, you need to make sure the servers are locked down—read-only condition will suffice on the source version 7.0 server. You must ensure that there is no chance that any other user can access any file or object on either server and that nothing gets changed during the process. It should go without saying that you need to back up your databases, but I will say it anyway.

At least one administrator, in the sysadmin role, must have exclusive use of all files to prevent any changes to the file set during the process. The DBA performing the operation will need both sysadmin privileges and network privileges on both servers and on both networks (if you are going across domain boundaries).

You can choose to "transform" more than one database in a single session; however, the DTS only moves or copies the databases one at a time. The process is as follows: The database is detached, and the files are copied or moved and then reattached on the target server, sort of like sending objects through a star gate, and just as risky. You can check the error logs for any messages that indicate a problem; however, routine messages, such as attaching and detaching, are also written to the error logs.

To perform the database copy upgrade, you need to attach to the version 7.0 server from Enterprise Manager.

Upgrading SQL Server 6.5

The upgrade method for SQL Server 6.5 is very different to the methods discussed for version 7.0. First you install SQL Server 2000 as discussed earlier in this chapter. Then you run the Upgrade Wizard, which is installed during the SQL Server 2000 installation.

Before the upgrade begins, you should first gather up all your 6.5 databases into one consolidated server and then run the wizard to upgrade the consolidated server.

The Upgrade Wizard does not replace or remove the version 6.5 binaries, as is the case with the version 7.0 upgrade. When you are done with the installation, you will have two separate instances of SQL Server, one on version 6.5 and one on SQL Server 2000. The SQL Server 2000 instance will be a named instance if version 6.5 occupies the default instance namespace in the Registry.

There is quite a bit to prepare for a version 6.5 upgrade; the list is as follows.

Hard-Disk Space You will need to accommodate a second and much larger installation of SQL Server when you are done on the same host. You thus need to make sure you have enough hard-disk space. You can destroy version 6.5 on the server or maintain it until you are certain you no longer need it. Be aware, however, that you also end up with two copies of data because the databases on version 6.5 are left intact. The upgrade process just copies the data over to the new instance.

Back Up Databases Back up all your SQL Server 6.5 and 2000 databases before you start the Upgrade Wizard.

Lock Out Servers Make sure the servers are off limits to users; you cannot afford to have any data or objects toyed and tampered with during the upgrade process.

Client Installation

Client installation requires you to install the client connectivity libraries (see Chapter 3). To install client binaries using the SQL Server installations CD, you can choose the "Connectivity only" option in the initial setup phase. You choose this option to install the Microsoft Data Access Components (MDAC) and the Net-Libraries for the OLE DB, ODBC, and DB-Library service providers.

To install client connectivity only, do the following:

1. Insert the SQL Server 2000 installation CD. If autorun does execute, you can open to the folder on the CD and double-click *autorun.exe.*
2. Select the Install SQL Server 2000 Components from the screens. (If you are installing to Windows 95, you will need to install the Winsock 2 Update for Windows 95 package as well as the Common Controls Library Update. These libraries came after the advent of Windows 95.)
3. Continue as you would for a complete installation of all server components. When you get to the Installation Definition dialog box, illustrated in Figure 6-5, click Connectivity Only and then click Next.
4. The Start Copying Files dialog box appears, and you can click Next to run through the installation.

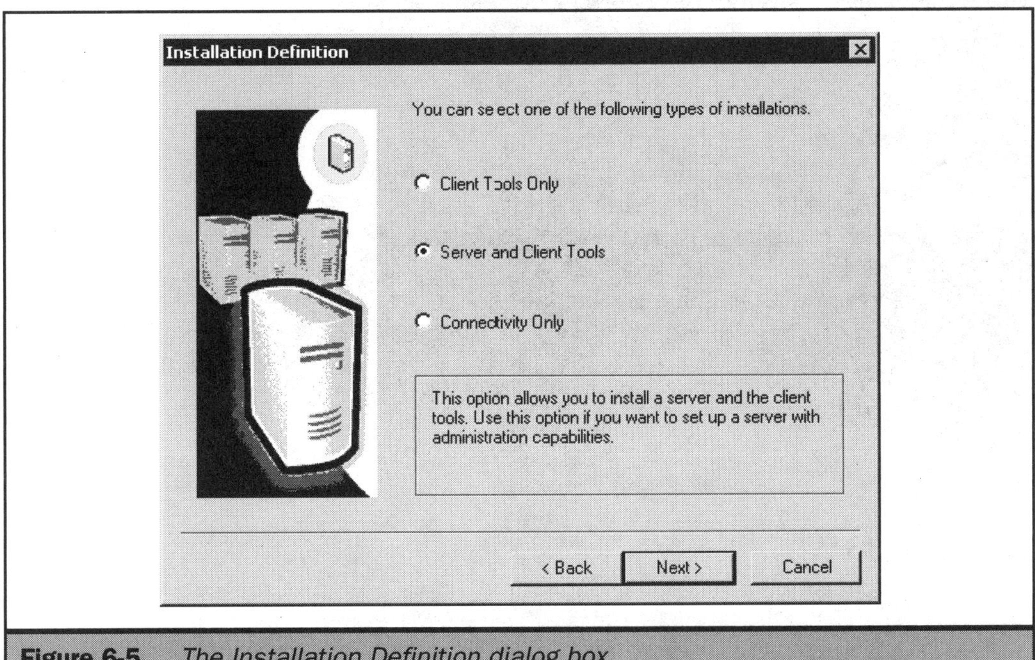

Figure 6-5. *The Installation Definition dialog box*

Language and Internationalization

Let's talk about language and internationalization issues. SQL Server 2000 now fully enables you to program or interactively manage how character strings are managed in the database, with the concept of collations. A *collation* essentially controls the physical storage of character strings in the database as opposed to how they are presented. The collation specifies bit patterns, and the rules used to sort and compare characters.

The new architecture now takes language support down to lowest objects in the database, columns (version 7.0 and earlier only supported one collation per server). In other words each column in a table can be assigned a different collation. This means that two columns in a table can be configured to support different languages or different character string representations.

This new architecture is essential for widely distributed applications or installations that cover multiple regions of the world and in situations where at any given time the databases will have to service many different languages, all at the same time. Such support is essential for Internet applications, which means that you no longer have to dedicate a single instance of SQL Server to a language. As SQL Server supports thousands of databases for a single server, and thousands of tables and columns in a database, one server is likely all you need to service many different languages and cultures.

What is the difference between a collation and a code page? As you know SQL Server supports a number of code pages. To recap what we touched on in Chapter 4, a code page is a collection of characters that are made available to a computer for representation on the screen, for sending characters from keyboards and other input devices and for rendering on output devices such as plotters and printers and so on. In this regard the code page dictates what you or your client can produce and see on the respective machines.

While the capability to change code pages on a locale per locale basis, per machine, suffices for most computing needs, it is very difficult take code pages into databases, tables, and columns, because we are dealing with a different dimension of character management—the storage of the data.

Take a mailing list management database. If the database is holding addresses for all North America, it needs to be capable of working with Spanish names used in the Latin or Hispanic communities and French names used in Canada. So it becomes a challenge to select a code page representative of all three needs—French, Spanish, and English.

The problem is further compounded when people from all over the world enter data into your Web pages that get transmitted to SQL Server. It is one thing accepting any kind of data in the data entry field of a Web form, but SQL Server needs to be capable of dealing with all the nuances of international languages being thrown at it, so that the data can be stored correctly. In the preceding mailing list example we only have to deal with three languages that have similar characteristics, but a throw Chinese or Sanskrit into the mix and you have a major problem on your hands.

Unicode makes it easier to manage the problem as long as all clients and SQL Servers are supporting Unicode, and you store characters in nchar, nvarchar and ntext data types. But you then have the overhead of managing the sort order and you still need to have the same code pages running on both client and server.

Sort orders specify the rules used by SQL Server to manage character data. For example, the sort order determines whether the character "ã" is the same thing as "a" or whether "a" is the same thing as "A".

SQL Server collations, however, define how the database engine stores and manages Unicode data. For example, if a column with a primary key receives two values identical except for an umlaut, does that mean a unique violation has occurred? No, because one name could be spelled correctly as "Shone" and another could be spelled correctly as "Shöne" and if SQL Server does not understand the difference, it will prevent of the values from being stored. So one of the first considerations in installing SQL Server and building the solution is the collations to be used for a certain object, such as a database, table, or column.

There are two groups of collations used by SQL Server: Unicode collations and SQL collations. The Windows collations are defined for SQL Server to support Windows locales. In other words, if you specify a Windows locale collation SQL Server uses the same code page as the client. This ensures that what the client "sees" or can "input" on its end can be "stored" as such be SQL Server. When the client needs to access the data it can be sure that what it receives can be rendered on its screen. An application supported by a business in the United States will have a different Windows collation to a company supporting an application in Great Britain.

SQL collations are used to match the attributes of code pages used in earlier versions of SQL Server. You may then have to use the SQL collations in a mixed version environment, which is something to consider before you begin upgrades. For the most part you will only need to use the Windows collations.

Where to Next

So you are going to tell me you know all there is to know about SQL Server so "I'll just go ahead and install the new server on a production machine or just upgrade the old machine over the weekend." And I am going to tell you that when Monday comes around the staff is going to find you hanging from the company rafters.

Bottom line is that all new servers, services, machines, and so on need to be put into test or development trials before they are rolled into production or the old servers are upgraded. Unfortunately, we don't have the time and space, nor is it within the scope of this book, to discuss an elaborate planning regimen for SQL Server 2000. A good place to start, however, is the Microsoft Knowledgebase and the SQL Server "department" on the Microsoft Web site.

Part II

SQL Server 2000 Platform Administration

Chapter 7

Administration Architecture

The responsibilities of the SQL Server database administrator (DBA) have changed a lot in recent years. As popular as this DBMS is now, its DBA of the not-too-distant past was not your typical data center resident guru. After all, it was not too long ago that a gig of memory in a Windows NT server was as wild an idea as growing asparagus on Mars.

Prior to version 7.0, SQL Server was outclassed in many high-end services, such as mission-critical support for huge numbers of concurrent users, very large databases (VLDBs), and a service level supporting tens of thousands of transactions per minute. The mainframe and midrange DBAs had it all—and nothing could challenge their eminence. Or so they thought. Now we are going to see some big changes.

The old and bold DBAs might have been pioneers, but they spent more time fiddling with settings and host platform configuration issues, like trying to optimize Windows NT 3.51, than with database design issues, data access, and mission-critical application requirements. Now we have a system that costs far less than your cheapest mainframe or midrange solutions, and that is able to push the TPC benchmarks beyond what was thought possible on the PC-Server platform. SQL Server 2000 can also support terabytes of data and attain 99.99 percent availability. SQL Server DBAs, your day has arrived!

This chapter highlights the applications that ship with SQL Server 2000 as well as the APIs and architectures that provide all the necessary hooks that can be used to directly program its maintenance and administrative services. But first, let's take a look in the mirror.

The Evolution of the SQL Server DBA

Before you go off and cheer, there are a number of caveats hanging off the coattails of SQL Server 2000. The new power features also demand new skills on your part (how many of you have worked in 64-bit environments?). You need to know a lot more about the critical issues of mainstream data centers, such as disaster recovery, service level, change management, and more. You'll need to know everything there is to know about high-end storage, how to configure and support cluster disk arrays, cluster servers, server farms, and so on. You also have a scale out burden that midrange (UNIX) DBAs might not encounter (a single UNIX system can scale to more than a hundred CPUs). A typical SQL Server data center might require many more servers than your average UNIX or mainframe data center. There are good and bad things about that, and I will cover them in Chapter 13.

So Microsoft has had to make SQL Server more "knob and button" free to allow the server to self-administer as far as possible. SQL Server 2000 has made significant advancements in this area, and it will no doubt get even better in subsequent versions. The automatic- or self-administration architecture is especially evident in the Windows CE and Desktop Editions that do not include the tool suite that ships with the cruisers in the fleet. But at the high end, there is still a ton of stuff the DBA needs to have a grip on.

The self-administration features are just as important, if not more, in the less ambitious versions. For example, SQL Server Desktop Engine can be freely distributed, and if it is to take over from the critical success of its predecessor on the desktop, Jet, the last thing it needs to be saddled with is complex setup and administrative routines. Data stores for commercial applications do not usually expose administration front ends, GUIs, and dizzy icons that turn off customers. Most users of the Desktop Edition should not even be aware that SQL Server is the data store lurking in the basement of a new service or application.

As a client/server database product, SQL Server 2000 is remarkably self-configurable and self-maintainable; however, as a DBMS product that can scale to service the most demanding of transaction or analysis systems, it makes the services of a well-trained and well-versed DBA more than essential; it makes them unavoidable. Many applications will always require a DBA (guys, we're not going anywhere). So a rich array of equipment is provided you, the DBA, for tasks like optimization and performance assurance; change management and change control; service level assurance; application support such as query analysis, index creation, and integrity management; and the administration of databases, database objects, security, access, and much more.

When I first started working with SQL Server back in the early 1990s, it was a shade of the product it now is. My job was to support the network and to set up the client applications, to ensure that our applications installed the right libraries and that we had the correct protocols to use for named pipes support, and to set up the first versions of TCP/IP and the Windows sockets library.

When I started doing DBA work, I was tasked with backup and restore, managing the transaction logs, and so on. I read many books and tried many things. I also learned the hard way . . . I thought "dumping" the database meant I should delete it or that dropping the table meant we had too much furniture. Things started to change from Version 6.5.

Today, the successful DBA needs to have many skill sets . . . at least if you are looking to pay off a Carrera, feed an Akita, or take long vacations at the Algarve. Your job might entail building schemas and converting applications. You must be able to manage the storage engine both interactively and programmatically (that means you have to learn to write code, if you don't already know how).

If you work in a large enterprise and you have a lot of Access databases lying around, expect to start moving the data out of them into SQL Server. Some of my clients in recent years put so much into Access databases that they would swell to two, three, and even four gigs, beyond what the technology was built to handle. Importing data from the likes of DB2 and Oracle is not out of the ordinary, and Microsoft hopes it will become commonplace. So you will need to be fully conversant with data import and export, the Data Transformation Services, the various service providers, bulk copy, bulk insert, and so on.

You'll be asked to manage system performance, security, and access, so you need to be able to configure and manage file groups, users, objects permissions, and so on.

You'll need to know how security is configured inside SQL Server, as well as how both Windows NT or Windows 2000 security and authentication relate to your DBMS.

If you work for a small company, do not think data warehousing and OLAP knowledge is unimportant. I may have mentioned this earlier, but the ability to analyze data and search for answers is something that every company wants and needs. I have many clients that cry out for DSS or analysis support. They may not be in a position to shell out for the Enterprise Edition, but with high bandwidth pipes to the Internet becoming commonplace, many small companies will opt to "lease" warehouse space from data management companies (at least that is what I am banking on because I have an investment in this industry).

You'll need competency in developing English Query solutions and importing data from operational databases into cubes, and you'll need to know how to develop conceptual data models, data flow charts, and so forth.

Windows NT and Windows 2000 administration, along with Windows networking, especially TCP/IP, are also essential foundations for the SQL Server DBA. While Windows system administration is beyond the scope of this book, you will not be able to avoid getting your hands dirty with Windows security principles, Active Directory objects, group policy, Performance Monitor, Event Logs, NTFS, hardware configuration, and so on.

I know you are keen to learn about tools like the SQL Server Enterprise Manager, but understanding SQL Server's Administrative Framework should be a prerequisite.

SQL Server 2000 Administrative Architecture

Several chapters in Part I provided an insight into the various database and database server architectures on which SQL Server is built. You learned that SQL Server is able to dynamically acquire and free resources as needed. In Chapter 4 we discussed its ability to automatically manage and self-administer the procedure cache, the buffer cache, the data pages, and so on. You also learned how it processes queries, parses SQL statements, compiles procedure plans, and more. However, with large OLTP or data mining environments, you may still need to monitor the system, institute change control rules, and ensure that your deployment meets the service level requirements you or your customers have set for the system.

SQL Server thus provides a collection of services that allow you to schedule the automatic execution of repetitive tasks, such as backing up data, replication, and running reports. These services also include the SQL Server Agent, which provides you with a graphical or interactive environment you can use to configure schedules and tasks to run at regular intervals or upon events that occur in SQL Server and in the operating system (see Chapter 12). You can also program SQL Server to automatically respond to errors and exception conditions, and to send e-mail or pages to operators and on-duty administrators.

Microsoft has also published the administration APIs it used to build the graphical tools that ship with the Personal, Standard, and Enterprise Editions. These APIs support all the administrative services of the server. You can thus code your own applications for end users, or include administrative routines in your data-dependent applications. The APIs and programming models have been encapsulated into a management framework, which I will introduce next. How to program them is discussed in Chapter 14.

The SQL Distributed Management Framework

SQL Distributed Management Framework (SQL-DMF) is a framework of integrated and distributed objects, services, and tools that form a holistic SQL Server management environment. The SQL-DMF is illustrated in Figure 7-1.

The services in the framework interact directly with the DBMS and allow you to define the following:

- All SQL Server 2000 objects, the distributed management objects (DMO), and the permissions that control access to them
- All repetitive administrative actions that you can schedule to run at certain intervals or times
- The actions to take when certain conditions or events detected by the objects are raised

The SQL-DMF exposes four main classes of applications and routines that access or use the objects in the SQL-DMF as follows:

- **SQL Server tools** The tools installed when you first install SQL Server 2000 make use of the SQL-DMF objects. These include the SQL Server Enterprise Administrator and the SQL Query Analyzer. Remember, you can only have one set of these tools for every instance of SQL Server 2000. If one server is host to several instances, only one set of tools is maintained on the server.
- **COM+ and Active Server Pages** The objects can be used by COM+ or transaction-based applications and Active Server Pages (ASP).
- **Third-party tools** You can use the objects to create your own tools, or embed management functionality into your own DBMS solutions. You can program administrative routines that your end users need never know about or be burdened to operate.
- **Windows Management Instrumentation** The DMF object model is also exposed to the *Windows Management Instrumentation (WMI)*. You can thus administer SQL Server 2000 from the Web, along with the Windows 2000 operating system and other services, such as IIS and Active Directory.
- **Scripting** You can also access the objects from your favorite scripting tool, such as VBScript, JScript, JavaScript, CGI, and so on.

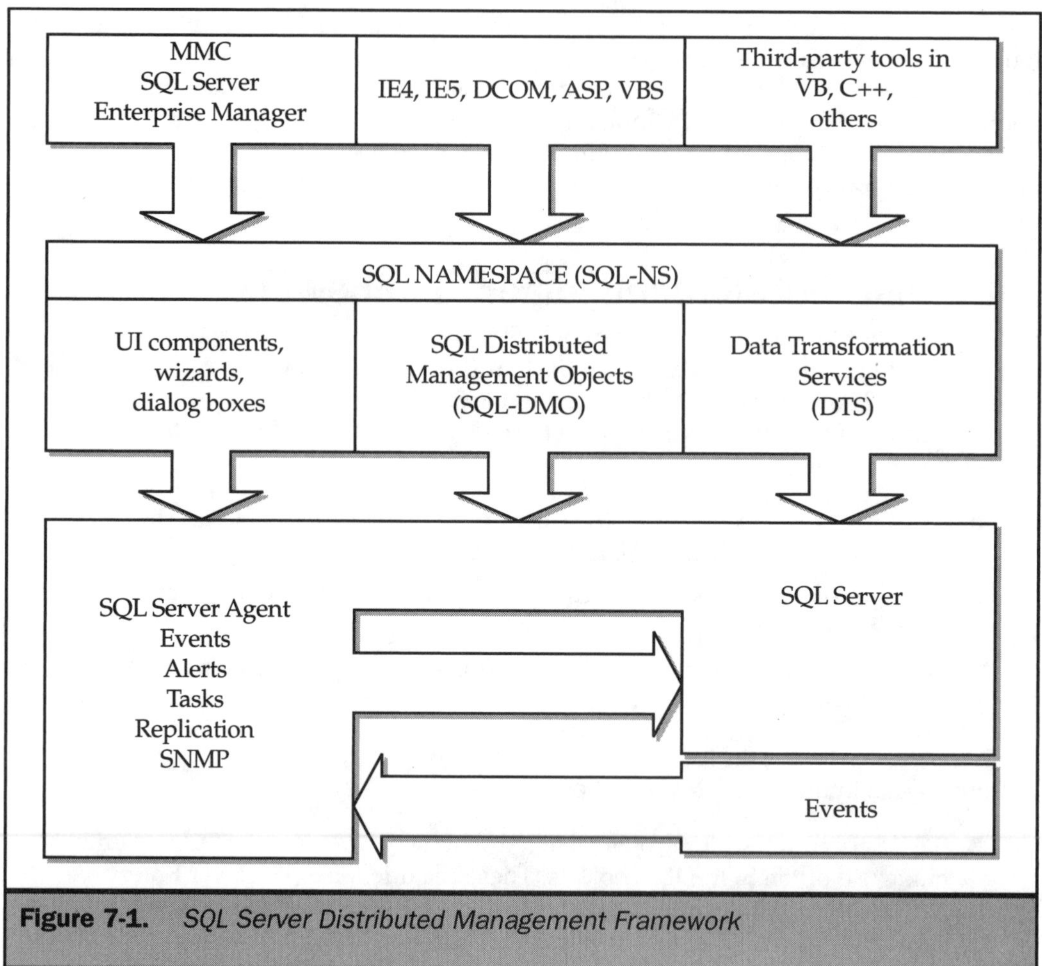

Figure 7-1. *SQL Server Distributed Management Framework*

An Introduction to the SQL-DMF APIs

Three COM component APIs make up the core interfaces of SQL-DMF. These are the *SQL Namespace (SQL-NS)*, the *SQL Distributed Management Objects (SQL-DMO)*, and the *Data Transformation Services (DTS)*.

The *SQL Namespace* exposes the user interface components or UI objects also used by the Enterprise Manager. You can use this API to create your own Enterprise Manager UI components such as wizards, dialog boxes, property sheets, and configuration and administrative commands. The components can thus be included in your own applications, adding administrative functionality for managing the SQL Server components that support your applications.

Working with the SQL-NS object model is similar to working with ADO. The following VB code sample demonstrates instantiating the SQL-NS object, which encapsulates the various SQL Server management components:

```
Dim Primary_SQLNS As SQLNamespace
  Set Primary_SQLNS = New SQLNamespace
```


Sample applications in Visual Basic (VB) and C++ using the SQL-NS API are included with SQL Server. All the code for a custom namespace browser, resembling Enterprise Manager, has been included. You can access these libraries at %drive%:\ Program Files\Microsoft SQL Server\80\Devtools\Samples\Sqlns\Vb\Browse.

The *SQL Distributed Management Objects* API is also a COM component API that sits underneath the SQL Namespace API. This API exposes a bunch of objects that encapsulate the administrative properties of SQL Server 2000 database objects, such as tables, users, and views. SQL-DMO hides some of the complexity of using Data Definition Language (DDL) and the administrative stored procedures. However, you do not lose any power programming against it but have full access to all administration and configuration tasks in SQL Server 2000. SQL-DMO also exposes Registry settings and operating system resources.

SQL-DMO is implemented as a dual-interface COM component library (DLL). You can access the objects from any IDE or language capable of instantiating COM objects, such as C++ or VB. You can also use OLE Automation controller clients to access the DMO objects.

The DMO objects are useful for automating repetitive administrative tasks in SQL Server, forcing query plan recompiles and so on. You can also use SQL-DMO to create databases; to create and drop objects in databases, such as tables and views; and to make installations. You can also use the API to program a powerful replication hierarchy. The DMO replication object, for example, encapsulates the entire replication system of an instance of SQL Server. Replication is further discussed in the next chapter.

The last of the three APIs is the *Data Transformation Services (DTS)*. DTS is really a framework unto itself, which specializes in moving data in and out of databases. Powerful DTS tools have already been provided by Microsoft and can be accessed from Enterprise Manager, and you will be learning about them in Chapter 14 and in many other places in this book. However, as with the other members of the management framework, the DTS API has been exposed to allow you to build your own data extraction, data transformation and data moving applications and routines.

A good example of a DTS API application is one that converts Microsoft Access Jet databases (those corruptible MDB files) to SQL Server databases. If you plan to convert from Jet to the Microsoft Database Engine (MSDE)—and you have a substantial installed base that uses MDB files—your upgrade software can use the DTS to move data from the legacy applications to your new version's data stores.

Another application, one of the drivers behind the creation of DTS, is the ability to move data from OLTP databases into OLAP warehouses. In other words, you use DTS to move or copy data from operational database to your temporal databases, which are used for analysis and business decision support and so on. DTS data sources can be accessed from both OLE DB and ODBC providers.

SQL Server and Windows Management Instrumentation

The Windows Management Instrumentation (WMI) API sits atop the aforementioned SQL-DMF APIs to support the administration of any instance of SQL Server 2000 via standard Web-based interfaces and standard Win 32 applications. The WMI is available for all Windows 32-bit platforms on which a version or edition of SQL Server can be run.

The WMI model is elegant and extremely useful. It comprises a three-layered model consisting of providers, which in our case is derived from the SQL-DMO API, the Common Information Model (CIM) which has been adopted by the Distributed Management Task Force (DMTF), and WMI consumers. The WMI consumers are client applications that contain management objects invoking the services of WMI on a target system.

Note *The Distributed Management Task Force (DMTF) is an open standard–neutral forum established to ease the burden of enterprise networks and computers. A key goal of its Distributed Management Interface (DMI) is to ease the cost of administration, and through a lowering of indirect costs, ease the total cost of ownership (TCO) of our PC and enterprise systems.*

Figure 7-2 illustrates the WMI with respect to SQL Server. At the lowest level is an instance of SQL Server. It could also be the operating system or one of your own applications or services. The next level exposes the provider, or the SQL-DMO API, which is the intermediary between the service at the fist level and the CIM object manager (or CIMOM). At the highest level are the applications that gain management control and information from the CIM objects in the hierarchy.

The provider is used to extract management information from an underlying data source exposed by the service being managed. The management information and any management interfaces are then mapped into the CIM object classes, via a COM interface, that can be presented to a WMI client.

The CIM object manager is implemented as a system service called WinMgmt. It has its own data store and acts as a broker for object requests coming from WMI clients. The flow of information is as follows: When a WMI client requests information,

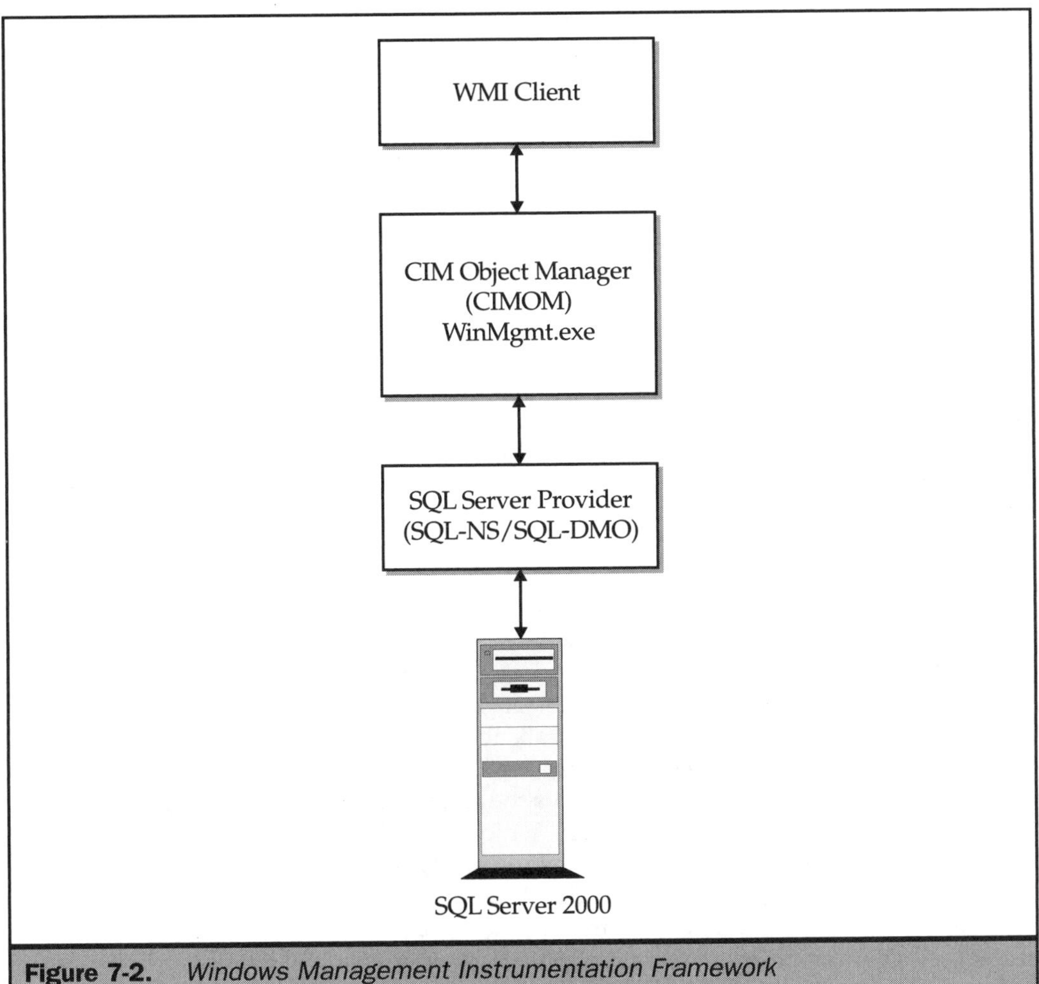

Figure 7-2. *Windows Management Instrumentation Framework*

the CIMOM evaluates the request, maps it to a provider, and requests the information. Upon reception of the data, WMI sends the data to the client. The client never needs to know what services were invoked on the systems to obtain the information. In other words, the process is entirely hidden in the host system.

The client applications of WMI can be Web browsers, in which case an intermediate engine will need to format the data as HTML or XML, MMC snap-ins, enterprise management solutions, such as Systems Management Server (SMS), and third-party applications and scripts.

WMI providers can supply several types of information and functionality to the client applications. The WMI classes can define *properties, methods, events,* and *associations.* So you not only obtain information from the underlying provider, you can also access methods that can alter application behavior or direct system execution and operations. *Associations* allow you to obtain information not only about the target components but the information about associated components as well. For example: It would be useful while looking at an event in the relational engine to also observe any associations in the storage engine. You can pursue WMI further on MSDN.

Transact-SQL and Stored Procedures for DBAs

In the past chapters, I talked a little bit about Transaction-SQL or T-SQL. If you are new to SQL Server administration, you should prepare yourself do get your hands dirty with some SQL programming. T-SQL is the language used for all commands sent to SQL Server; however, the language also supports statements that direct administrative functions and work orders in SQL Server. SQL supports several language subdivisions, the most important being Data Definition Language (DDL), which is sometimes called schema definition language, and Data Manipulation Language (DML).

DDL covers the commands that create, alter, and drop database objects, such as tables, indexes, and views. DML is the subdivision of the language that returns the values that are to be found in the tables at any given time, and that provides the directives for altering or deleting those values. Statements such as SELECT, INSERT, and UPDATE are typical DML directives. T-SQL has extended these subdivisions with directives that SQL Server will understand. A good example is the DENY statement. There are other subdivisions, but we can talk about those in the chapters in Part II.

Stored procedures are also extensively used to manage the internals of SQL Server. A good example is *sp_compile,* which forces the relational engine to recompile a query plan, or the *sp_configure* stored procedure, which is used to configure SQL Server.

Higher-level components or management objects, such as the SQL-DMO library we discussed earlier, typically call the T-SQL DDL commands and stored procedures. In other words, the methods used in the high-level objects do not provide any native manipulation or definition code but rather call across town to a DDL definition or some system-level stored procedure.

Introducing SQL Server Tools

It goes without saying that you do not need to program a line of code to effectively administer SQL Server 2000; although you open yourself up to a lot more opportunity if you do. As one Microsoft SQL Server developer put it, "ya gotta do what ya gotta do to keep your job." My assessment of where SQL Server is going as a product tells me you don't have much to worry about as long as you stay on top of things. Let's now turn to the install and go to tools you can use to administer SQL Server 2000.

SQL Server's GUI and command line tools and utilities are listed as follows:

- **SQL Server Enterprise Manager** This is the principal administration suite used to administer SQL Server 2000. It is a Microsoft Management Console (MMC) snap-in that allows you to carry out a number of administrative tasks such as adding servers and server groups; managing users and their rights and permissions; and managing databases, tables, indexes and so on.
- **SQL Query Analyzer** This tool is the DBA's and developer's test bench for designing and testing T-SQL queries, batches, scripts, and so on. You will notice that it can be started from the menus in the SQL Server program group as well as from within SQL Server Enterprise Manager.
- **Import/Export Wizard** This tool, which fires up the Data Transformation Wizard, can be started from the SQL Server program group and from the context menus of the Databases and Tables nodes in Enterprise Manager. This tool is actually a wizard that will take you through the steps required to import and export data from OLE DB and ODBC databases.
- **SQL Profiler** If you need to capture Microsoft SQL Server events from a server, this is the tool to accomplish that task. You can also use the profiler to audit SQL Server 2000. The profiler and monitoring is covered extensively in Chapter 12.
- **SQL Service Manager** The SQL Server Service Manager is used to start, stop, or pause the SQL Server services on the server. (We covered this utility in Chapters 3 and 6.)
- **Server and client network utilities** The server and client network utilities are used to manage the Net-Libraries that connect to SQL Server clients and servers. This subject is covered in Chapters 3 and 6, where we explore SQL Server networking.
- **Administrative wizards** A healthy dose of administrative wizards can be accessed from the Enterprise Manager. These include wizards to create backup jobs, indexes, stored procedures, and so on. We will be talking about them a little later in this chapter.
- **Command line utilities** A number of command line utilities ship with SQL Server 2000. These are installed by default into the *%drive%:\Program Files\Microsoft SQL Server\MSSQL\Binn* folder and the *%drive%:\Program Files\Microsoft SQL Server\80\Tools\Binn* folder. Among these utilities are the BCP, ISQL, and OSQL executables. BCP is a tool used for bulk copying of data, while ISQL and OSQL are used to send T-SQL statements to the server from the command line. ISQL works with the OLE DB provider, and OSQL works with the ODBC provider.

Let's now turn to an overview of the SQL Server Enterprise Manager. The other graphical and command line utilities are beyond the scope of this chapter, and I cover them in later chapters. After Enterprise Manager, however, we will talk about the command-line utilities.

Getting Started with SQL Server Enterprise Manager

At first glance, SQL Server Enterprise Manager (often called EM) might seem intimidating. So it helps to get an overview of it before you start using it. This section covers getting started with Enterprise Manager. If you have used Enterprise Manager for SQL Server version 7.0 or for the Beta or early adopter versions of SQL Server 2000, I suggest you go through this section because there are many new properties to configure, especially with respect to the Windows 2000 operating system.

Our work with Enterprise Manager here is going to be limited to registering and exposing servers and exploring the various nodes and options. This will help you become familiar with this exhaustive suite of tools so that you know what to grab for when working on SQL Server concurrently with the tough discussions that lie in wait. We will cover starting up, connecting to servers, navigating the environment, and some basic configuration.

SQL Server Enterprise Manager can be started from the Microsoft SQL Server menu under Programs. When its MMC snap-in first appears and when you start it for the first time, you need to configure a server group and tell it about the servers you need to manage.

The first configuration steps you might want to take would be to configure several communications options in Enterprise Manager properties. This can be done as follows:

1. Select the SQL Server Group node. Go the Tools menu on the console and click Options. The SQL Server Enterprise Manager Properties dialog box, illustrated in Figure 7-3, loads.

You can change the name of the group at any time by right-clicking and selecting Rename for the context menu.

2. Select the option to poll the server at regular intervals and view its status using the stoplight icon. The Service check box lets you specify the time, in seconds, between server polls.
3. Next set the options to read the registration information for local and remote servers.

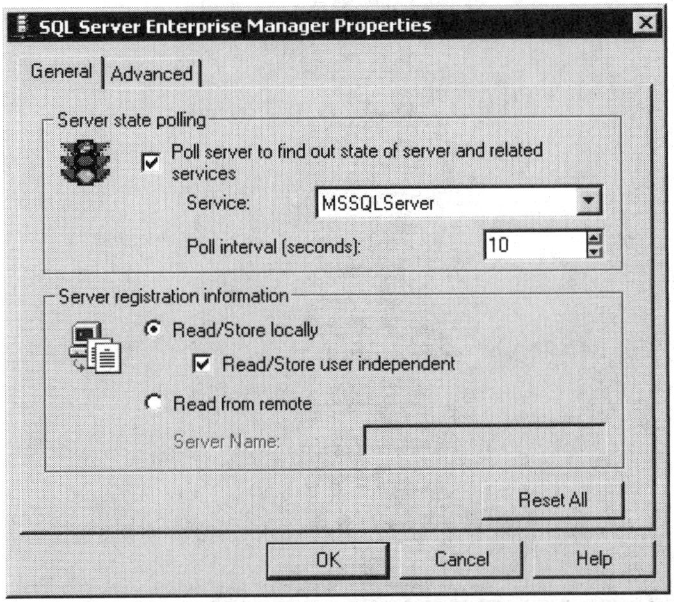

Figure 7-3. *SQL Server Enterprise Manager Properties, General tab*

4. On the Advanced tab, illustrated in Figure 7-4, select the Login time-out to specify the number of seconds to wait before an instance returns from a failed remote login.
5. Use the Query time-out option to set the number of seconds to wait for a remote query to succeed or fail. The default setting is 0, which means the remote query will not time out.
6. You can set the packet size for the Tabular Data Stream (TDS) packets. The default is 4KB.
7. You can choose to have the instance of SQL Server perform translation of the character data between different client and server code pages (see Chapter 6). This option affects the data stored in char, varchar, and text columns.
8. Finally, you can choose to have Enterprise Manager return to the last open node you were at before you closed it. This might not be so valuable for one server, but when you have several hundred in EM it's a God send.

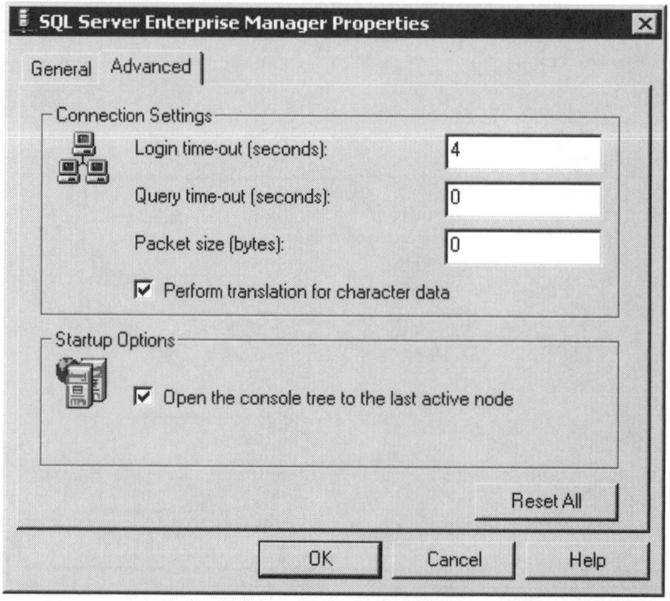

Figure 7-4. *SQL Server Enterprise Manager Properties, Advanced tab*

Server Groups and Connecting to Servers

Enterprise Manager manages the components and modules of each server as a hierarchy of services. In turn, each server is part of a collection of servers known as a SQL Server Group. Servers can be added to and removed from the server collection as needed.

The idea behind managing a collection of servers or registering them with Enterprise Manager is that you can simply attach to an instance of SQL Server from a single copy of Enterprise Manager. This means you can manage hundreds of servers or instances from a single copy of Enterprise Manager.

If you are working on a high-bandwidth network, you can hook up each server remotely from a local copy of Enterprise Manager. However, if you are working on a low-bandwidth network, it might make more sense to log in to the server and run a local copy of the Enterprise Administrator on the remote server. Remote access is best via a terminal session under Windows 2000 Server or Windows NT Terminal Server

Edition, or via the services of a remote administration tool like Carbon Copy or pcAnywhere on Windows NT or Windows 98. I dislike the latter solutions.

You can also administer servers as a group, rather than on a per server basis. For example, you can specify jobs to run on a server group, as opposed to configuring the jobs on a per server basis. Backup jobs, for example, can be targeted to a group of servers. This means that the backup job scripts and schedules will execute on all servers in the group at the same time.

To create a new server group, do the following:

1. Right-click the Microsoft SQL Servers node in the console tree and select the context menus option New SQL Server Group. The dialog box illustrated in Figure 7-5 loads.
2. Enter a group name and choose to make a new root group or to save the new group as a subgroup of an existing group.

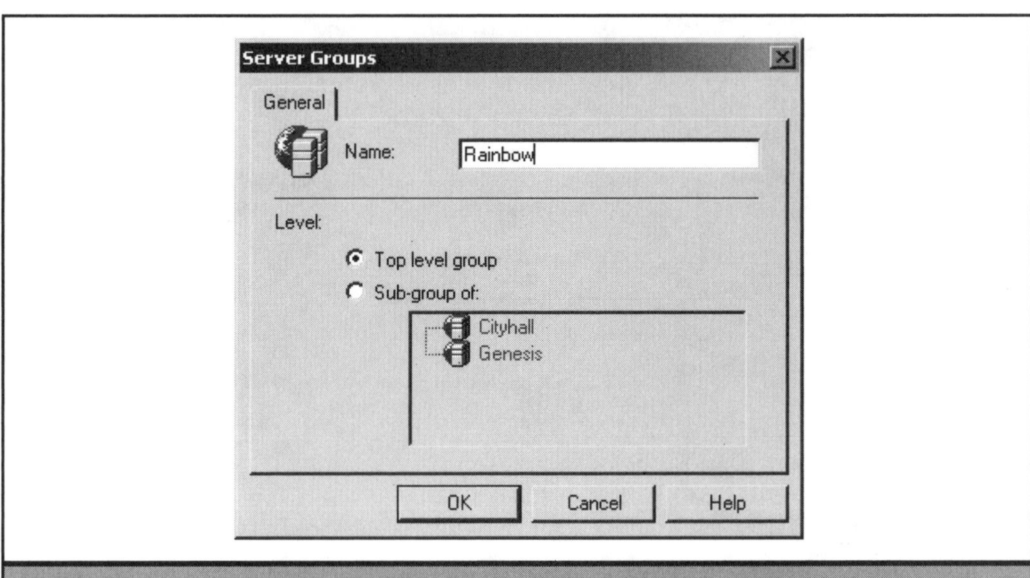

Figure 7-5. *Creating a new SQL Server group*

Server Registration and Preliminary Configuration

To install a server into a group, you must register the server. Follow these steps to register a new server (typically a new installation):

1. Select the group in the tree and right-click the node. Select the New SQL Server Registration menu option. The Register SQL Server Wizard appears as illustrated in Figure 7-6. As indicated, the Registration Wizard will allow you to select an instance of SQL Server—on a remote machine or a local ((local) or named)—machine. Remember, a single period (.) can be substituted for the name of a local default instance.
2. You will also be asked to select the authentication mode and to confirm the target group for the server. If you prefer to register servers without the use of the wizard, you can check the option on the start page of the wizard to forgo future use of it. Click Next.

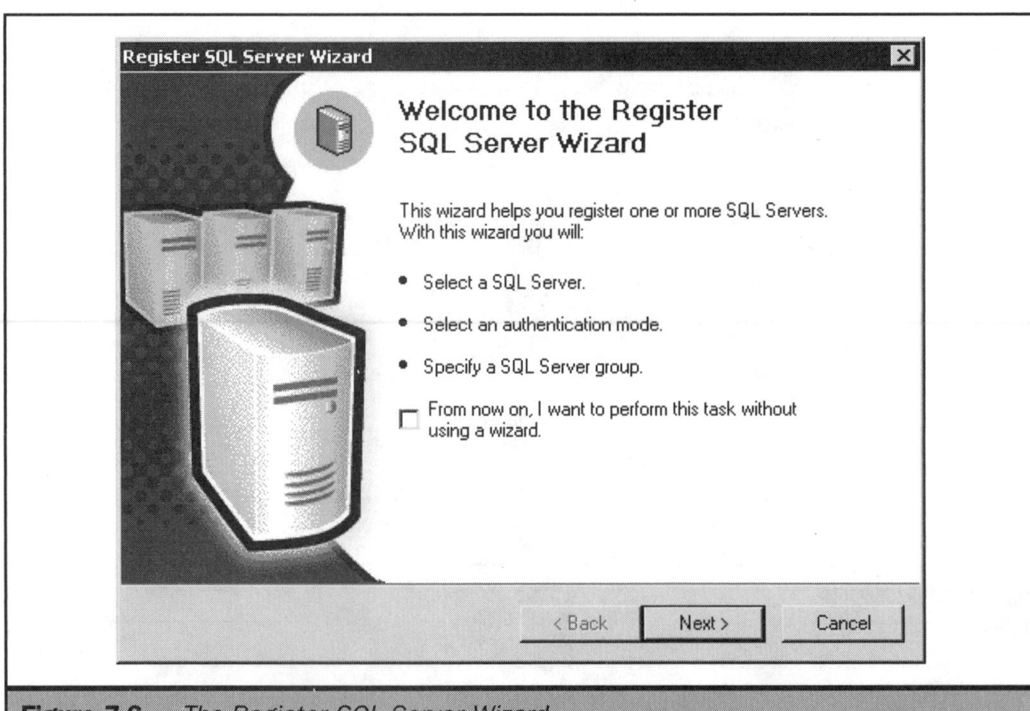

Figure 7-6. *The Register SQL Server Wizard*

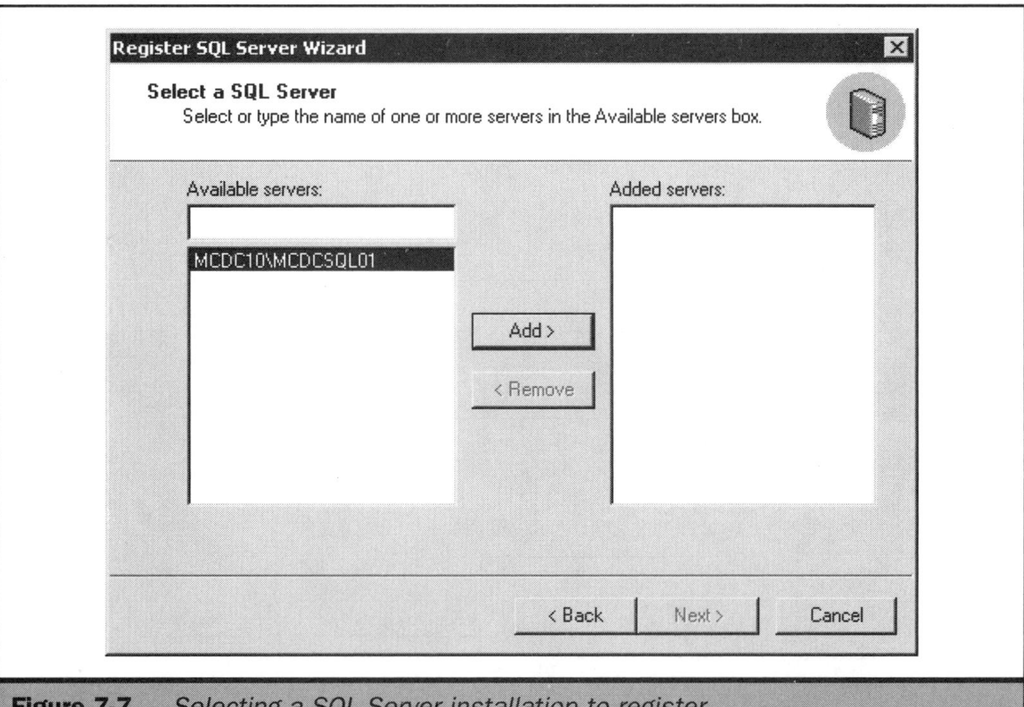

Figure 7-7. *Selecting a SQL Server installation to register*

3. The Select a SQL Server dialog box appears, as illustrated in Figure 7-7. You can enter the name of the server to register, if the dialog box does not list your server, or you can select the server in the list on the left and add it to the list of servers to be registered. To add the server, select the server name from the list on the left and click the Add button to move it to the list on the right. If you do not see your server in the list on the left, this means that Enterprise Manager was not able to find the instance of the server on the network. When you have made all your selections, click Next.
4. Now you can choose the authentication mode for your server. Choose either Windows Authentication or SQL Server Authentication, demonstrated in Figure 7-8. If you are unsure how you need to set up your server's security, choose Windows NT security for now. You can return to this step later, and it is fully covered in Chapter 8. Click Next to continue.

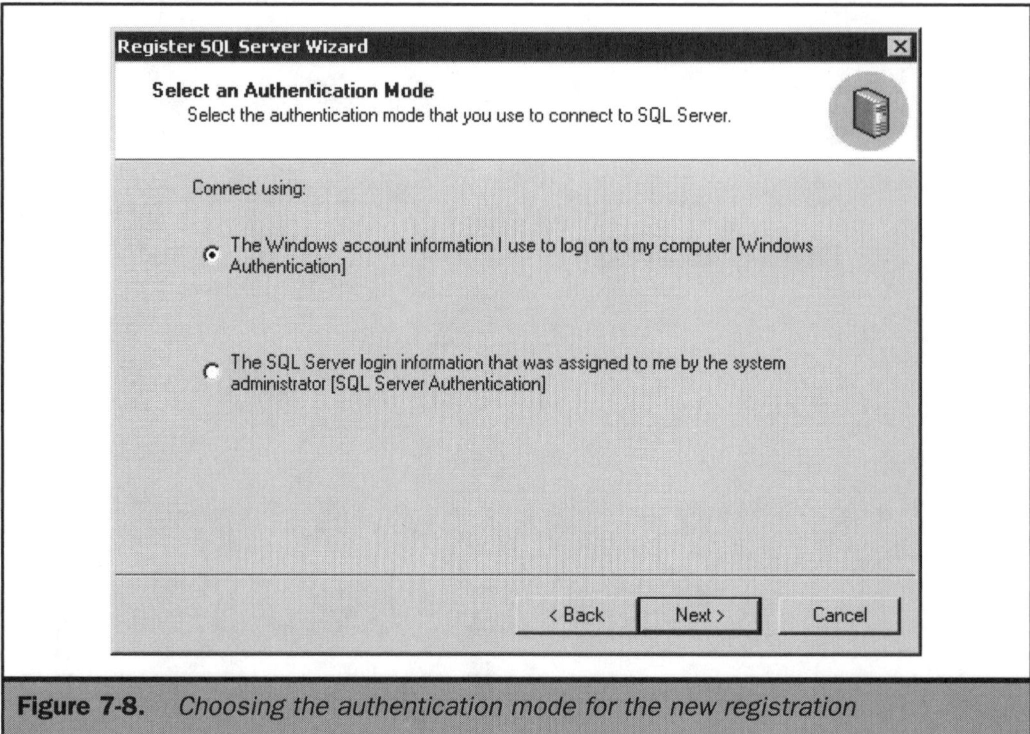

Figure 7-8. *Choosing the authentication mode for the new registration*

5. The Select SQL Server Group dialog box illustrated in Figure 7-9 loads. Now you can choose a group you created earlier on, or check the option to create a new top-level or root group. Make your choice and click Next to continue.
6. You have a final chance to review the registration, and if everything checks out, click Finish. The last dialog box in the registration process, illustrated in Figure 7-10, will update you with the success or failure status of your registration.

That's all there is to registering an instance of SQL Server in Enterprise Manager. To connect to a server, you need only drill down into the node. If you connect okay, the little server startup icon under the server icon turns from white to green. This icon was once the thin red squiggly line that appeared next to the server icon to indicate that you connected (in case you saw it in the earlier versions or the beta and were wondering what it represented). That little piece of artwork created more commentary than *Saturday Night Live.*

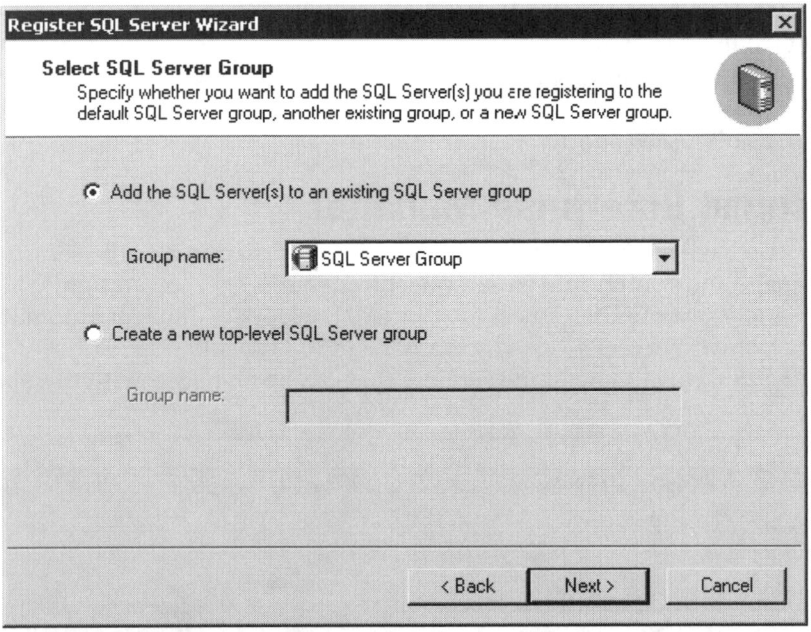

Figure 7-9. *Creating a new SQL Server group*

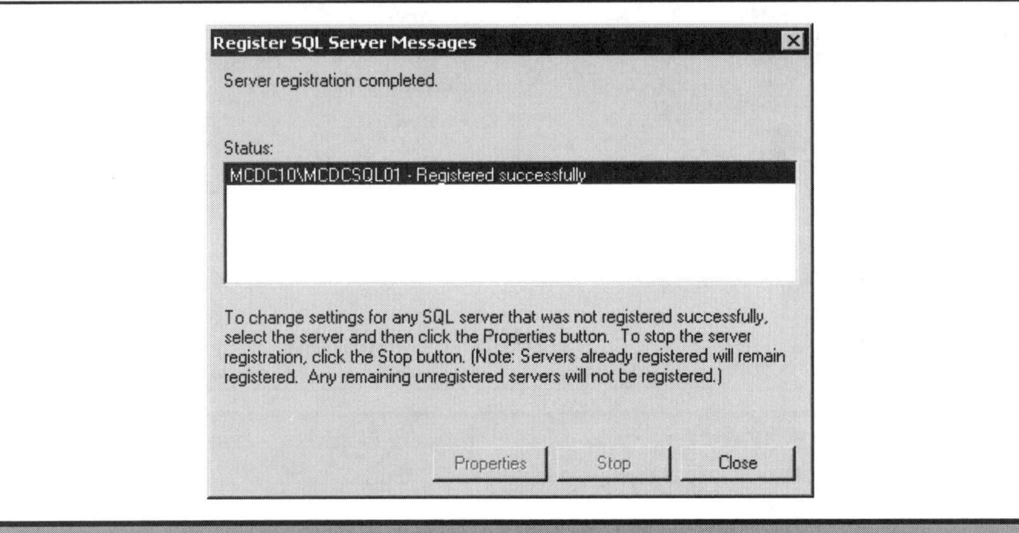

Figure 7-10. *The registration process messages dialog box*

Revisiting the Registered Server Properties

You can revisit the Registered SQL Server properties at any time after registration by right-clicking the instance of the server and selecting the option "Edit SQL Server Registration properties." This dialog box can also be accessed from the Taskpad's General tab, as discussed shortly.

Getting Around Enterprise Manager

As soon as you have connected to the server, you can drill down to the services you need to manage and configure. To disconnect from a server, you can right-click the connection and select the Disconnect menu item. Enterprise Manager automatically disconnects from all servers when you close the MMC console.

Figure 7-11 displays some of the services that can be managed with this snap-in.

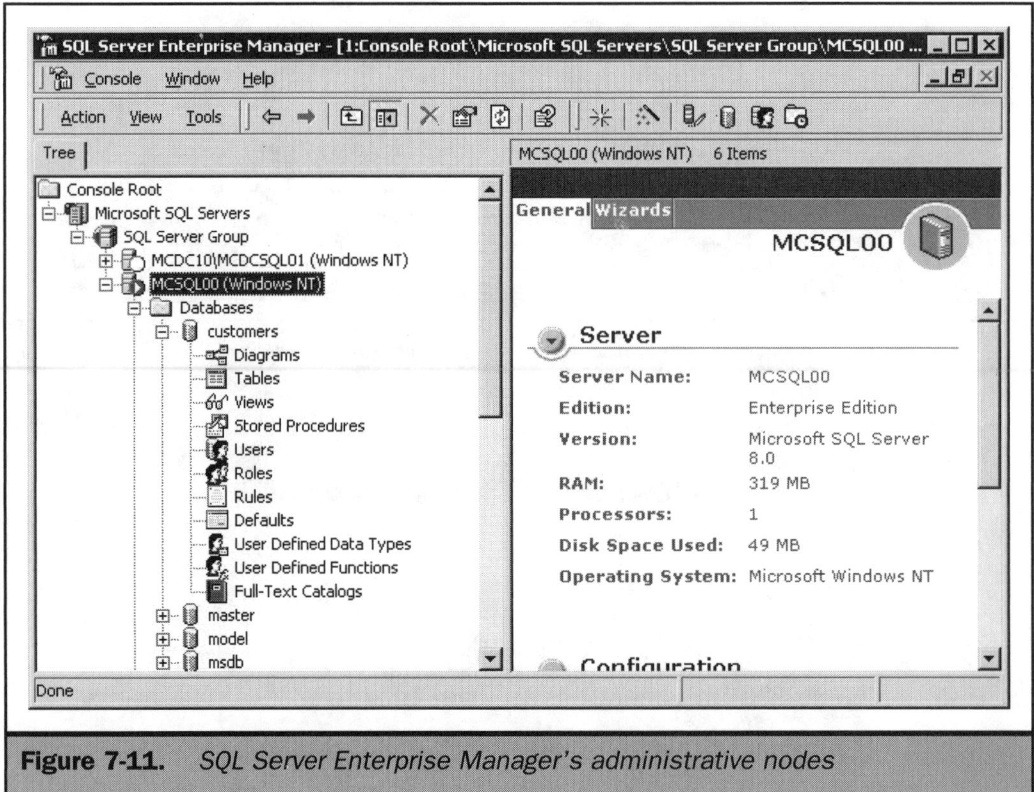

Figure 7-11. *SQL Server Enterprise Manager's administrative nodes*

A thorough understanding of how to set up and customize the Microsoft Management Console is well worth acquiring. This book is not the forum for that, but there are several works on the market that cover MMC, and the Windows 2000 MMC Help is a good place to start.

The snap-in is divided into the following hierarchy of administrative sections:

- Servers
- Server Groups
- Databases
- Data Transformation Services
- Management
- Replication
- Security
- Support Services
- Meta Data Services

The View from Above

The Enterprise Manager is home to a substantial number of Wizards. They can be easily accessed from the Task view, which can be opened as follows:

1. Click View from the console menu and select Taskpad, or select the root server node, right-click, select View, and then select Taskpad from the list of view options. The General tab is shown in Figure 7-12.
2. On the Taskpad, you can alternate between General, Table Info and Wizards. Click the Wizards tab to access the list of wizards, as demonstrated in Figure 7-13.

You can also access the Wizards from the Tools menu and in context menus as you drill down into the various folders representing your server's services. The Table Info tab presents a useful summary of table information, as demonstrated in Figure 7-14.

The Taskpad becomes available as a view option when you have a database in focus; that is, when a database node is selected.

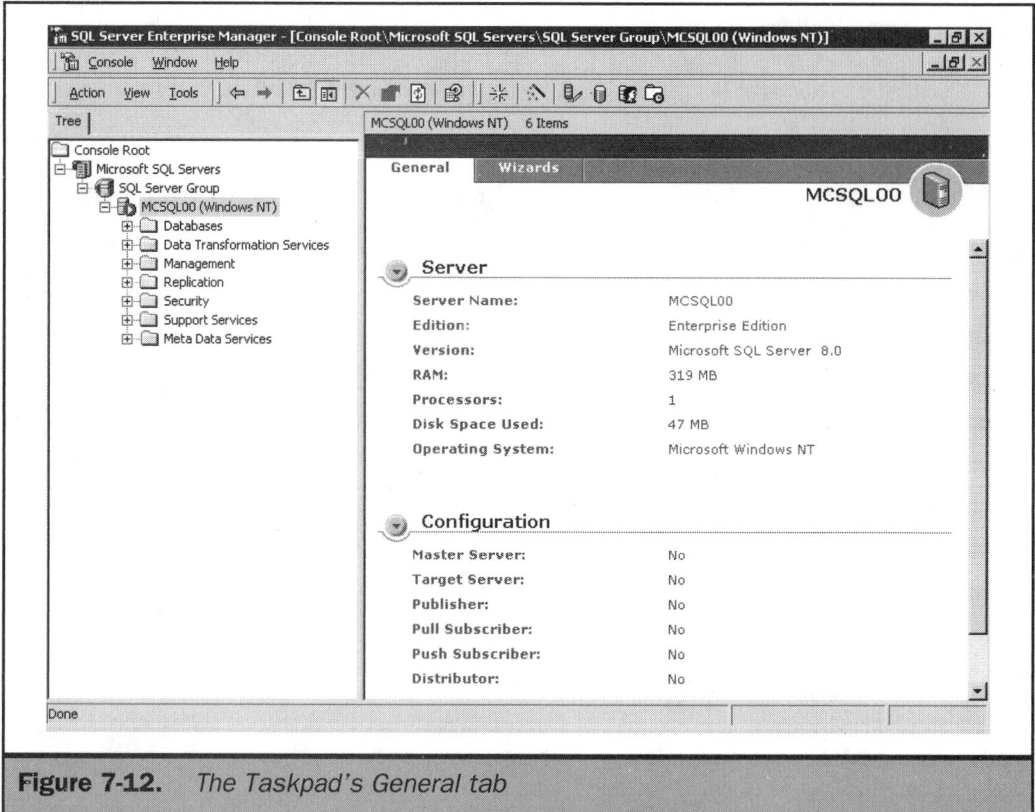

Figure 7-12. *The Taskpad's General tab*

Configuring the Server Instance

Each instance of SQL Server 2000 can be specifically configured, interactively, in the SQL Server Properties dialog box. None of the properties is set in stone, and you can return to them after this initial walkthrough as needed. Rather than offer a full explanation in this chapter, we will return to each tab as it relates to a chapter subject in the rest of Part II. To access the properties dialog box, you need to perform the following steps:

1. Select the server in the tree, right-click and select Properties, or go to the Tools menu and select SQL Server Configuration Properties. Either way, the Registered SQL Server Properties dialog box loads to the General tab as illustrated in Figure 7-15.

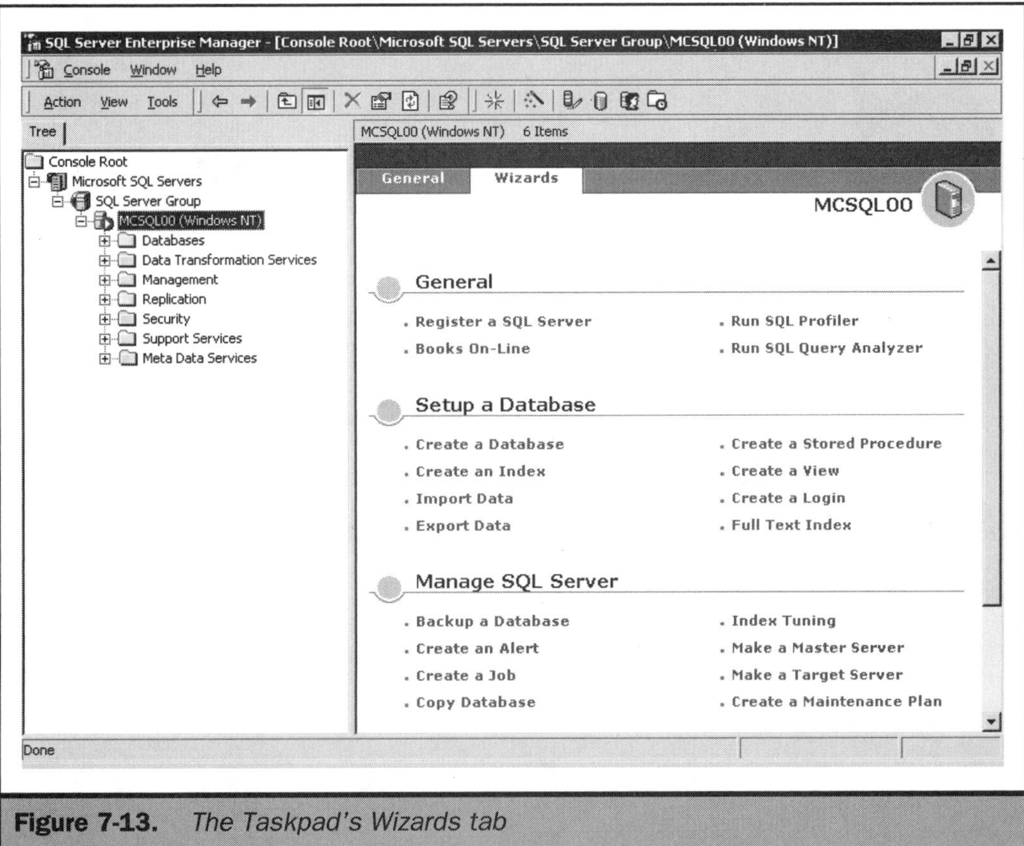

Figure 7-13. *The Taskpad's Wizards tab*

2. On the General tab, enter the general server options such as the authentication mode and general security settings.
3. The Memory tab is used for configuring the instance's management of memory. These options will vary depending on the server's role, environment, number of connections, and so forth.
4. The Processor tab lets you configure threads, fibers, the number of processors, and so forth. It also lets you manage the query plan threshold for parallel queries.
5. The Security tab, the subject of Chapter 8, lets you manage security. Of special importance is the capability to change the system account.

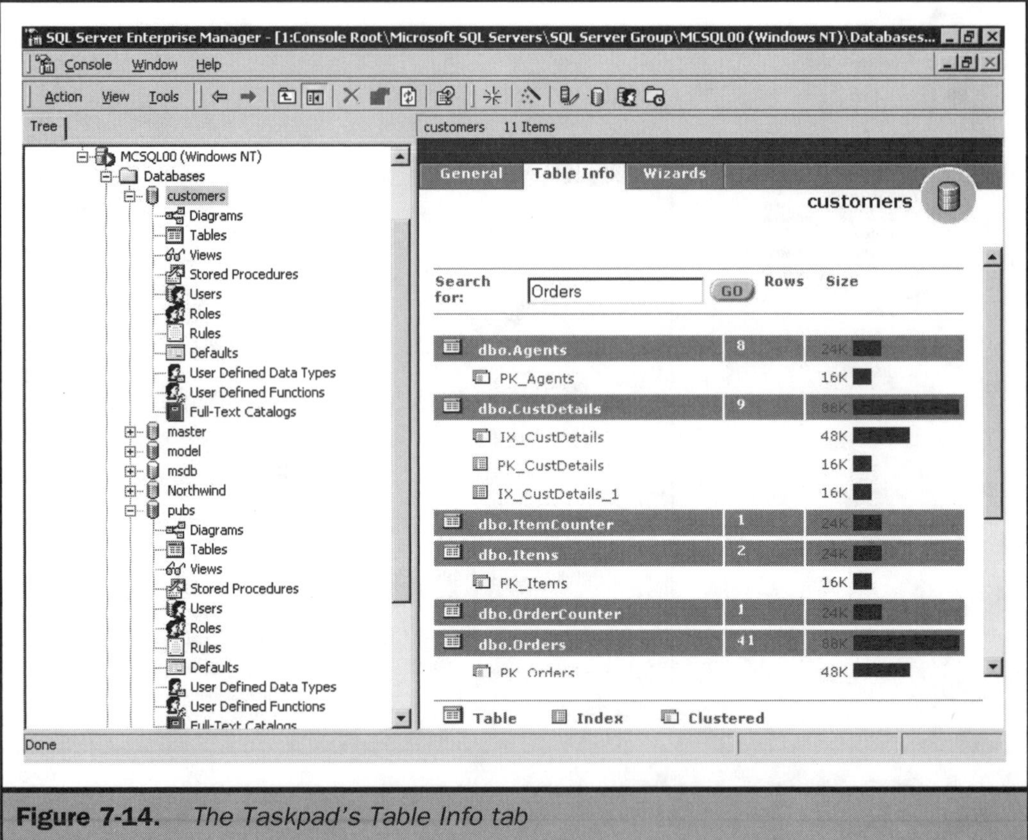

Figure 7-14. *The Taskpad's Table Info tab*

6. The Connections tab lets you change the number of concurrent connections. I have covered this in further detail in Chapter 6, with respect to licensing.
7. The Server Settings tab (which should have been named Miscellaneous Settings) lets you manage several DBMS-oriented options, such as triggers, data interpretation, and so on. The mail login name of the mail client can also be set from this tab.
8. The Database Settings tab provides the facility to interactively set a number of default database settings. These include settings for the recovery intervals, the default log directory, and the default index fill factor.
9. The Replication option launches the Replication Wizard, the main subject (and a hefty one at that) of Chapter 10.

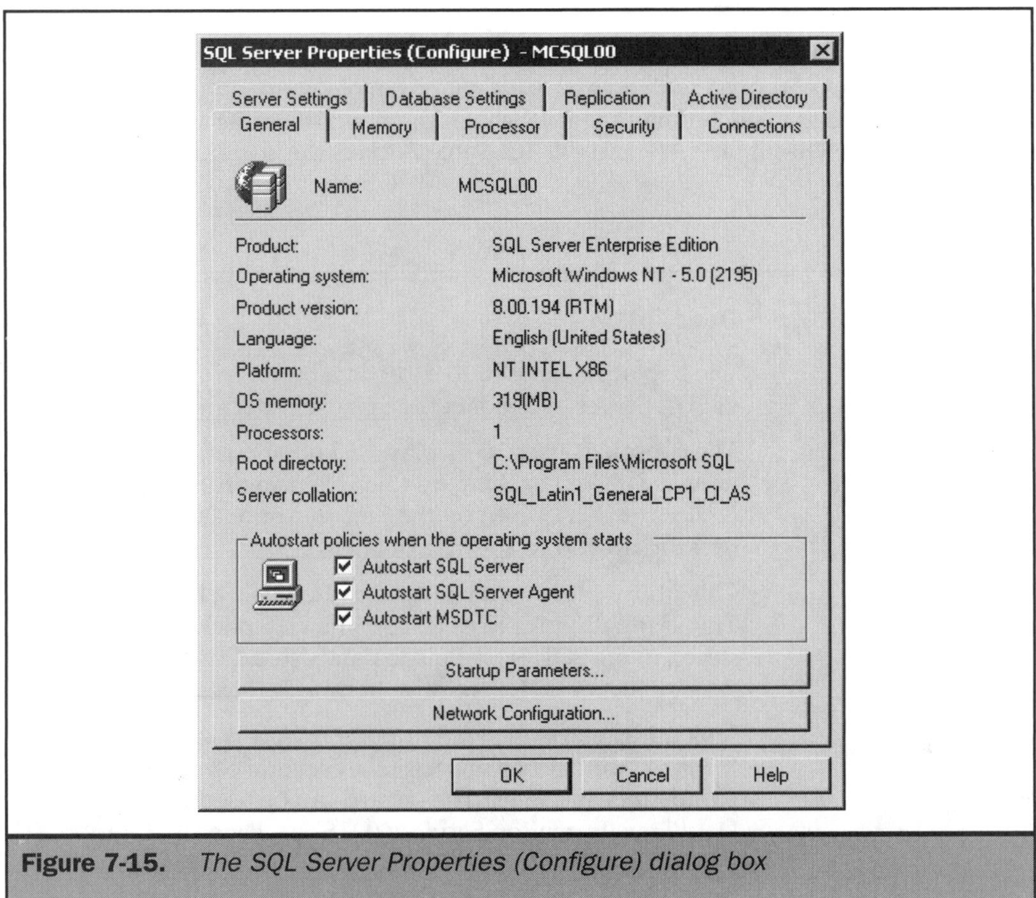

Figure 7-15. *The SQL Server Properties (Configure) dialog box*

10. The Active Directory tab is extremely important for Windows 2000 domains, especially where the domain is in Native mode and the client applications are able to query the directory service.

Many of the variables or properties that drive each instance of SQL Server can be accessed via system-stored procedures and a number of system functions. And, as discussed earlier, you can tune and lube your server via the management object models. Most experienced DBAs find it easier to work with SQL Server with tried and proven scripts they have developed over the years. Several command line utilities are another option, especially if the command prompt is more familiar turf for you than "clicky" Windows icons.

The Command Prompt Utilities

SQL Server comes equipped with an extensive collection of command prompt utilities. Many of these are not new but have come through the ranks of earlier versions supported by the DB-Library API and ODBC. Table 7-1 lists these utilities and describes their usage.

Utility	Description
Bcp	The bcp utility is used to copy data between an instance of SQL Server and a data file in a user-specified format.
Console	The console is used to display backup and restore messages when backing up to or restoring from tape devices; it is also used by the person responsible for backing up and restoring a database.
Dtsrun	This utility executes a package created using Data Transformation Services (DTS). The DTS package can be stored in the SQL Server msdb database, a COM-structured storage file, or SQL Server Meta Data Services.
Dtswiz	This utility starts the DTS Import/Export Wizard from the the command prompt. It takes several command-line parameters and flags. The wizard can be used to create Data Transformation Services (DTS) packages that import, export, and transform data between data sources. You can use it, for example, to transfer data from one instance of SQL Server 2000 to another or to a Microsoft Access database, an ASCII text file, or any ODBC data source.
Isql	This utility allows you to enter Transact-SQL statements, system procedures, and script files and then transmits them to SQL Server; it uses the legacy DB-Library to communicate with SQL Server 2000.

Table 7-1. *The Command Prompt Utilities*

Utility	Description
Isqlw	This utility starts the SQL Query Analyzer, which allows you to write and edit T-SQL statements, system stored procedures (and debug them), and script files. You can set up shortcuts or create batch files to launch a pre-configured SQL Query Analyzer with your custom options.
Itwiz	This utility allows the Index Tuning Wizard to be executed from the command prompt. The Index Tuning Wizard can also be started from SQL Server Enterprise Manager, SQL Query Analyzer, and SQL Profiler.
Makepipe	Makepipe tests the integrity of the network Named Pipe services, in conjunction with readpipe.
Odbccmpt	The odbccmpt utility enables or disables the compatibility option for an ODBC application executable file.
odbcping	The odbcping utility tests the integrity of an ODBC data source and the ability of the client to connect to a server. Use this tool for troubleshooting ODBC connections from ODBC applications that use data source names (DSN).
Osql	Osql is a utility that allows you to enter Transact-SQL statements, system procedures, and script files and send them to the server. It uses ODBC to communicate with the server and is almost identical to the Isql utility that used the DB-Library as its API to SQL Server.
Rebuild master	The Rebuild master (rebuildm) utility is used to fix a corrupt or damaged master database (the catalog). It can also be used to change the collation settings for an instance of SQL Server 2000.
Readpipe	The readpipe utility tests the integrity of the network Named Pipe services. It is used in conjunction with makepipe.

Table 7-1. *The Command Prompt Utilities* (continued)

Utility	Description
Replication Distribution Agent Utility	The Replication Distribution Agent configures and starts the Distribution Agent, which moves the snapshot (for snapshot replication and transactional replication) held in the distribution database tables (for transactional replication) to the destination tables at the Subscribers.
Replication Log Reader Agent Utility	The Replication Log Reader Agent utility configures and starts the Log Reader Agent. The agent monitors the transaction log of each database configured for replication, and copies the transactions marked for replication from the transaction log into the distribution database.
Replication Merge Agent Utility	The Replication Merge Agent utility configures and starts the Merge Agent, which applies the initial snapshot held in the database tables to the Subscribers. It also merges incremental data changes that occurred at the Publisher after the initial snapshot was created, and reconciles conflicts either according to the rules you configure or using a custom resolver you create. (See Chapter 10.)
Replication Queue Reader Agent Utility	The Replication Queue Reader Agent utility configures and starts the Queue Reader Agent, which reads messages stored in a SQL Server queue or a Microsoft Message Queue and then applies those messages to the Publisher. Queue Reader Agent is used with snapshot and transactional publications that allow queued updating.
Replication Snapshot Agent	The Replication Snapshot Agent utility configures and starts the Snapshot Agent, which prepares snapshot files containing schemas and data of published tables and database objects, stores the files in the snapshot folder, and records synchronization jobs in the distribution database.
Scm	The scm utility (the Service Control Manager) creates, modifies, starts, stops, or pauses any of the SQL Server 2000 services that run under Microsoft Windows NT and Microsoft Windows 2000. Under Microsoft Windows 98, the scm utility starts, stops, or pauses the equivalent SQL Server applications.

Table 7-1. *The Command Prompt Utilities* (continued)

Utility	Description
Sqlagent	The sqlagent application starts SQL Server Agent from the command prompt. It is not common to run SQL Server Agent from SQL Server Service Manager and Microsoft advises against this. And you can also access it from the SQL-DMO object methods in an application.
Sqldiag	The sqldiag utility gathers and stores diagnostic information and the contents of the query history trace (if running). The output file includes error logs, output from sp_configure, and additional version information. If the query history trace was running when the utility was invoked, the trace file will contain the last 100 SQL events and exceptions. Sqldiag is used primarily by Microsoft Product Support Services for gathering information (see also TechNet).
Sqlmaint	The sqlmaint is a useful command-line utility that performs a specified set of maintenance operations on one or more databases. Use sqlmaint to run DBCC checks, back up a database and its transaction log, update statistics, and rebuild indexes. All database maintenance activities generate a report that can be sent to a designated text file, HTML file, or e-mail account.
Sqlservr	The sqlservr application starts, stops, pauses, and continues an instance of SQL Server 2000 from a command prompt.
Sqlftwiz	The sqlftwiz utility allows the Full-Text Indexing Wizard to be executed from the command prompt. The Full-Text Indexing Wizard can also be started from SQL Server Enterprise Manager, which is probably the easier method. (See Chapter 12.)
Vswitch	This utility is used to switch between SQL Server 2000, SQL Server version 6.5, and SQL Server version 6.0 as the active version of SQL Server.

Table 7-1. *The Command Prompt Utilities* (continued)

The Complete Reference

Chapter 8

SQL Server Security and Access Control

I have good reason to place security this early into Part II. I have met many DBAs and developers who do not fully appreciate the security environment required in the implementation of SQL Server. There have been many horror stories: users running amok, unauthorized use of tools, external processes corrupting data, untrained administrators dropping databases and tables, theft, acts of God, self-mutating viruses, and so on. Here are two stories of many I have encountered in network and database administration:

In early 1995, I took over the administration of a database (SQL Server version 6.0) for a direct marketer. Now this person had been making millions selling mailing lists for almost 25 years and was not pleased with his "DBA." During the needs or requirements analysis I was taking before providing a quote for my services, I discovered a table called CCN. Lo and behold, what I stumbled on was a gold mine of about 75,000 credit card numbers, linked of course to the customers who had been buying the database owner's mailing lists.

I did a sort on the data and pulled about 25,000 current and active credit cards, so the database was valuable to a person of malevolent intent to say the least. To the credit (no pun intended) of my moral virtue, I deleted the view, advised the owner of the risk, did a backup of the database and the system, and then locked down the machine. The table had been completely exposed; there was no domain or network security of any sort protecting the server, nor was a system administrator password protecting the DBMS. I told the owners that by the end of the week I would give them my proposal and a quote to take over administration of the asset.

The next day I was called; the current DBA had vanished and the database server with all the credit card information had vanished with him. I had never been hired faster in my life. The server incidentally was never recovered, but the credit cards were never compromised.

The second story was more recent. In 1999 a client I was consulting for (a Fortune 500 company, and one of the world's largest food distributors) suspended credit of one of its yogurt ice-cream outlets; which threatened closure of the store because he was in a cash-flow crunch. But that did not deter the desperate ice-cream seller. He hired someone to hack into the company's databases and managed to keep himself supplied for several weeks until the credit manager found out.

My guess was that the storeowner hired someone to do the hacking; but security was so lax that breaking into the database was easier than selling frozen yogurt on a hot day in Miami. I was called in to look for evidence, but not before the hacker managed to feed several thousand hungry yogurt lovers. The hacker got away clean, having also deleted the delivery information; we had no evidence that the deliveries had actually been made to his location.

I can tell you many more stories, but you don't need a book to tell you that data security is one of the most important subjects in database administration. I find it odd it is not given more attention; and I seldom see worthwhile database security coverage at Microsoft TechEd or other SQL Server educational powwows.

Many DBAs and developers are more concerned about data integrity than data security. I don't see why the validity or plausibility of data should be deemed more important than avoiding compromise of it. After all, how valid is valid data when you don't have it any longer or it has been seriously compromised? I am not underplaying data integrity, and you'll find the chapter that deals with it (see Chapter 17) just as vociferous. I just know many DBAs out there that will tell you about the mother of all triggers or stored procedures they wrote, and yet they still manage a system with no system administrator password. So rife is this problem that Microsoft made special effort in SQL Server 2000 to force us to use a password for the system administrator (SA).

This chapter looks at data security in general and how SQL Server 2000 presents itself as a bastion of the data it keeps, and of the services it provides. It is a complex chapter for a complex subject, and you should read it before creating any facilities for logging in and using the database. And DBAs who have been baptized by fire will find discussions of new security services, especially with respect to Window 2000, refreshing.

If you need to configure SQL Server 2000 for secure access as quickly as possible, go directly to the section "Creating and Configuring Database Roles" and thereafter "Creating and Configuring Users."

Data Security Primer

I find it necessary to actually define the difference between data integrity and data security. No one defines the difference better than database guru C.J. Date does: "Security means protecting the data against unauthorized users; integrity means protecting it against authorized users." With the data integrity definition out of the way, we can deal with the subject of data security unencumbered by misconceptions.

Objects and Ownership

The meaning of *data security* comes into focus when you explore the concept and philosophy of ownership. If you have a background in network or general computer security, the concept of data ownership will be a lot clearer because objects and ownership are at the root of network and information technology security—especially on Windows operating systems and the NT file system (NTFS).

It also helps that your data "Gestalt" is formed around the concept of objects. In other words, everything that makes up your data environment comprises objects. As long as a user (human or otherwise) possesses a data object, the attributes of the objects fall under certain laws of ownership, and ownership is what makes us human (and a good reason why Communism has essentially failed).

Everything in a database management system is an object—from the service providers; to the Network-Libraries; to collections of stored procedures, functions, and more. The database is also an object. It has attributes, such as tables, that are objects.

A table is also an object that contains attributes. The attributes of a table are the rows, or tuples, which are themselves objects with attributes.

If you keep going down the "object hierarchy," you will keep discovering objects, until you get down to the world of subatomic matter, which is also understood in terms of objects and ownership. We can think of the hierarchy as an object chain, an important concept in SQL Server security we will later discuss.

Data objects, as a collection, become information at a point when the combined objects and their collections, seen as the sum of their parts, yield facts. And information, suggesting a substance of value, is also an object of ownership. Ownership, no doubt, was the reason "databases" were created hundreds of years ago, when people needed a system determining ownership. They may have used caves, or clay pots, or holes in a tree as repositories, but databases they were, no more and no less.

Trust

Adopting the view that objects have owners, software engineers can enforce rules of ownership on objects much as banks protect money. You are not the owner of the object until you can prove you are, via identity. Sure, if you deposit money in a bank account, you are the de facto owner of it because you created the account and placed the money in it. You created the credit balance with the bank. But you do not get access to the money once it is placed in the custody of the bank unless you can prove to the bank clerk that you are the owner. Like the bank teller, the database needs to know that you are who you say you are.

This brings us to the concept of *trust*. If a system, such as a database or a network, is able to validate your identity (you are who you say you are), you are allowed to interoperate or interact with the system under a certain level of trust. Each system rates its level of trust differently. Some systems, even people, trust a person fully (which you may argue is foolish). Other systems delegate levels of trust. The higher the trust relationship, the more rights of access you have.

Rights and Permissions

The more you are trusted, the more access you will get to objects and information (such as by being trusted with the delete permission). For example: If you can be fully trusted, you are given access to information and functionality, both on a network and in a DBMS. The access is a *permission,* which is not a finite quantity; the rule is the need-to-know. You can be assigned certain *levels of permission* on a need-to-know basis. In a database, you might be *permitted* to read some data but not delete it. On a file system, you might have *permission* to read some files but not to delete them. The permissions model is illustrated in Figure 8-1.

Permissions are not the same thing as *rights.* We all have rights—given to us by God and country and our systems administrators. Often those rights (even the God-given ones) are withheld from us. If you have ever had cause, as I have, to argue for or claim your human rights, you will know that the difference between *rights* and *permissions* is as profound as night is from day.

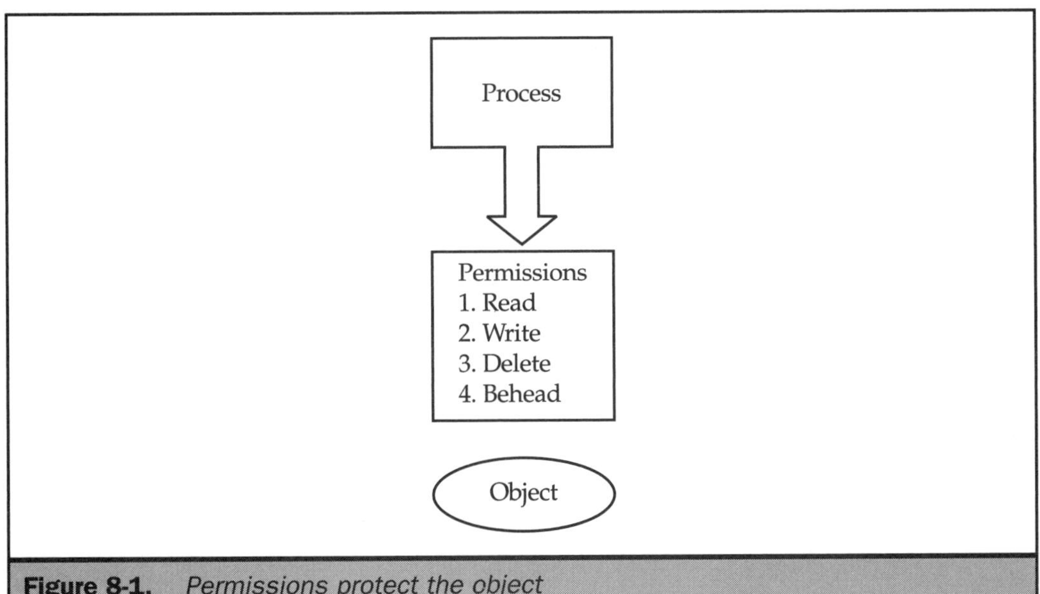

Figure 8-1. *Permissions protect the object*

The Windows NT and Windows 2000 security systems distinguish *rights* from *permissions.* The "right to log on locally" may be assigned to you. But having permission to log on locally is another matter altogether because permission to do so overrides the right. It is important as a DBA to distinguish between the two; it will make your life a lot easier when dealing with people who like to show muscle.

What kind of security soup does this all boil down to? To sum up, everything in a database, including the database, is an *object.* Objects have *owners,* and owners are usually allowed to do whatever they want to the objects. But just because you think you have the *right* to do whatever you want, with what you own, that doesn't mean you can. Society in general, and database administrators in particular, have the final word on what's *permitted.* The rules of society do not permit you to beat up your children, just because you "own" them. And business and database rules might forbid you from deleting databases and data, whether you own them or not.

Change of Ownership

Change or transfer of object ownership is perfectly feasible in computer and software engineering. Transferring ownership of databases objects is not as simple as transferring the ownership of a file. However, keep in mind that ownership can usually only be *given* or *transferred.* It can only be *taken* in most cases by a system or database administrator, or a security principal (a user or computer account) with the highest level of trust and permission of a security system, such as a file system or DBMS.

Authentication

You cannot just walk in off the street and lay claim to property that is in the *trust* of an authority, be it a bank, a network folder, or a database. You first have to prove you are the owner—not the same thing as proving identity.

Ownership can only be contested, however, after identity is verified—and this is called *authentication.* The simplest mechanism for proving identity to a network, proving that you are who you say you are, is by providing a user identification (user ID) and the password that goes with it. This combination of elements is often called the "ID-password pair." Once your identity can be proved, you are assigned a level of trust with which to go about your business, in the bank, on the network, in the database. But you are still prevented from accessing objects you have no permission to access.

Note *Windows 2000 provides several new mechanisms beyond the simple ID-password pair for proving identity. The operating system now has support for smart card readers, as well as for biometric devices that scan retinas, fingerprints, and voiceprints, and can verify signatures, hand geometry, and so on. These devices are now so sophisticated you're liable to get your horoscope when you sign in.*

Checking that the security principal has ownership of a certain object confirms or rejects ownership. Usually, if you create an object, you have full rights to it. But this rule cannot be stretched too far; just because you created an object on the network, such as an important document or database information, that does not give you the right to delete it. In fact, some employee manuals go so far as to state that anything you create automatically belongs to the corporation, and that you have to comply with policy with respect to deleting or altering what you created.

I was involved in a case recently when an employee managed to encrypt a database and refused to hand over the password when her employment was terminated. It took us a morning to crack the password, and the company had the employee arrested for attempted destruction of property.

To better understand the technical issues of ownership and access control, it helps to discuss the business (and philosophical) aspects first.

Access Control

Understanding access control is paramount if you strive to be an effective system administrator, especially a DBA who is mandated to protect information assets of the company. For many enterprises today, information is all they own; it's certainly more valuable than what can be carried off on the back of a truck.

For the most part, the system administrator implements access control as directed by senior management, such as change control boards and security councils. For example, you'll get a request to allow an accounts payable clerk named Sally to access a certain database, and to give her certain abilities in that database, such as the ability to update information. However, the levels of access control and access control management are the domain of the system administrator. In other words, you are expected to know how to implement the controls, and screwing up could cost you your job.

At all change control meetings I have attended over the years, I have seldom been told to "provide access to Sally and make sure she cannot write checks to herself." You are expected to make sure that Sally cannot write checks to herself, but you also need to ensure that she can manage accounts payable without hindrance. Remember, you are being held in the highest of trust and being paid well in return (I have heard more about CPAs embezzling from the company than about system administrators or DBAs doing so).

There's a lot of power in the hands of the DBA—a good reason why effective (and secure) security plans should be implemented and followed to the letter. But don't go anywhere; you will be getting a heads-up on that in this chapter whether you like it or not.

Access is not a technical requirement; rather, it derives from business policy and rules. So you need to put aside your technical cravings and consider some basic database access control management. (In a large company, though, you'll probably not need to make or manage access policy, just implement it.)

Levels of Security

You can divide access control policy into several classifications. I like to use what I learned in military intelligence, which classifies data according to its levels of sensitivity, using the labels *confidential*, *restricted*, *secret*, and *top secret*. Data that is sensitive, but not damaging, can be classified as *confidential*. Everyone in the enterprise is given access to this level. You are required to consider everything you learn about the business and its affairs as *confidential*. The drug testing procedures of a company could be considered confidential information.

The next level is *restricted*, which means that a subset of the members of the organization have access to information that could cause problems if the information became widely known. *Restricted* information could include short-term information, or information a company feels should be disseminated to a larger collection of its employees, such as the percentage increases for annual bonuses or product launch plans.

The definition of a *secret* has long caused aggressive debate. In a company, a secret is information shared by a very small number of employees (can you really share a secret with yourself?). For example, the discovery of a new formula might be considered secret, known perhaps only by the most senior executives and immediate product staff. Secret information is provided on a need-to-know basis. You are not given secret information unless you need it to perform your duties. And you need to be proven trustworthy first.

And finally we deal with the stuff of which spy novels are made, *top secret*. Information classified as *top secret* could be disastrous for a company if it were revealed. Such information could be corporate credit cards, bank accounts, digital signatures, cash assets, patent plans, blueprints, algorithms, information that could be used in the public trading of a corporation's shares, and so on.

I consider the passwords of employees as *top secret* information. If an employee becomes loose with his or her password, he or she should be disciplined under rules that deal with the unauthorized divulgence of *top secret* information. This is especially important when SQL Server is providing access on the basis of Windows NT authentication *alone.* Figured 8-2 provides a different "view" on the restriction levels—a pyramid whose pinnacle represents the smallest segment of people that have access to the information and whose base represent the largest segment of people that have access to the information.

How do you translate the level discussed here to databases? I consider any access to the data in the databases to be confidential, which means that everyone and anything that has access to the DBMS must meet requirements for access to confidential information. They need to be authenticated to the DBMS in some way that enforces the policy of the enterprise. This is achieved by having a user ID and a password, or some recognized means of obtaining trusted authentication and thus the trust of the DBMS.

While all data in the DBMS is considered *confidential,* certain areas of it could be considered more sensitive, upgraded to *restricted, confidential, secret,* and *top secret.* Looking at the table in Figure 8-3, we can easily identify certain columns as *restricted,* such as job descriptions (JobDesc); certain columns as *secret,* such as annual bonuses (AnnBon); and certain columns as *top secret,* such as drug tests (DrugTest).

The safest means of protecting the top secret information would be to make DrugTest a standalone table in the database and restrict access to it accordingly, but SQL Server 2000 provides sufficient mechanisms (such as views discussed in Chapters 19 and 21) to ensure that the drug test results are adequately protected. You might balk at the idea of labeling your information like a CIA or KGB agent, but you need to think along these lines if you don't want to end your career by "acts of omission." We'll get back to this later when we discuss the data security plan.

This brings us to another level in our discussion of access control: distinguishing between the protection of *information* by users or employees, and the protection of *data* by users or employees. I agree it borders on the integrity versus security issue; however, you will need to protect data used by members of trusted groups from accidental or even intentional damage. And often the lines of functionality will be

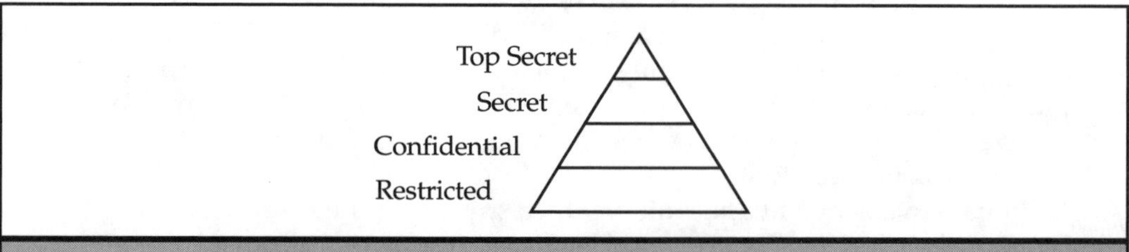

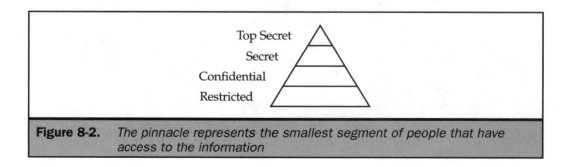

Figure 8-2. *The pinnacle represents the smallest segment of people that have access to the information*

JobDesc (Restricted)	AnnBon (Secret)	DrugTest (Top Secret)

Figure 8-3. *Columns classified according to sensitivity of the data*

blurred, because you will use the same constraints and restrictions to enforce both security policy and data integrity.

Pop Quiz: A breakdown in what at Los Alamos led to the risk of losing nuclear secrets, when two hard disks containing the data were found missing from the vault? Choose one of the following:

A. Data integrity?

B. Data security?

C. Both of the above?

Point taken?

Windows Security 101

The NT File System (NTFS) protects objects by verifying that a security principal has access to an object. The file system also verifies what level of access has been granted to a security principal, such as *read, write, delete,* and *execute. Deny* is also an access level, although it prevents access to the object. So how does the file system know who you are without having to reauthenticate you every time you need access to an object? And how does it know what level of access your authentication carries? On Windows domains, this is achieved using *access tokens, security identifiers* (SIDs), and *access control lists* (ACLs).

Access Tokens and the Security Identifier

An *access token* is a "badge of trust," which acts as a proxy, assigned to you after you successfully authenticate to a Windows NT or Windows 2000 domain. The token is the means by which the security system grants you right of passage on the network or in and across the domain, although the passage and access to resources is carried out by the system on your behalf, by the token. A token's right of passage is not open-ended or unlimited. It can be revoked by a security system, or the administrator, and is revoked when you log off.

You can compare the token to an access badge for passage in a protected area. The holder of the badge or token is given the right of free passage around the offices of the enterprise. On a Windows domain, it gives you the right of passage around the network or to connect to the database management system, SQL Server no doubt.

The access token is the "token" by which your continued trust is measured and monitored while you are connected to the network. It is not a guarantee of access to systems and services, but it is used to verify access or that a trust authority, such as the domain administrator, trusts you. As you know, it is not a guarantee that you have access to SQL Server. It is the means you have to assert your right to access.

Every access token holds the SID for a security principal, which is assigned to the access token after you log in successfully. The SID is a unique value of variable length that is used to identify a security principal to the security subsystem, and ultimately to a resource such as SQL Server. The security principal or user account is also known as a *trustee* to the Windows NT kernel. When referencing a user or a group for security purposes, Windows refers to the SID rather than the user or group name.

Every object has an associated ACL that stores the SID and the level of access a security principal might have on an object. Whenever you or the network administrator provides or denies access to an object, the SID's corresponding access level in the object's ACL is also updated. The access token-SID-ACL model is illustrated in Figure 8-4.

The permission list controls exactly what level of access you have to the file system object. The database management system, especially SQL Server 2000, operates in a similar fashion; however, there are some differences we will discuss later in this chapter.

Note *Do not confuse the SID with the object identifier or OID. The OID is a means of enumerating objects and identifying objects with a globally unique identifier (GUID); thus guaranteeing their uniqueness.*

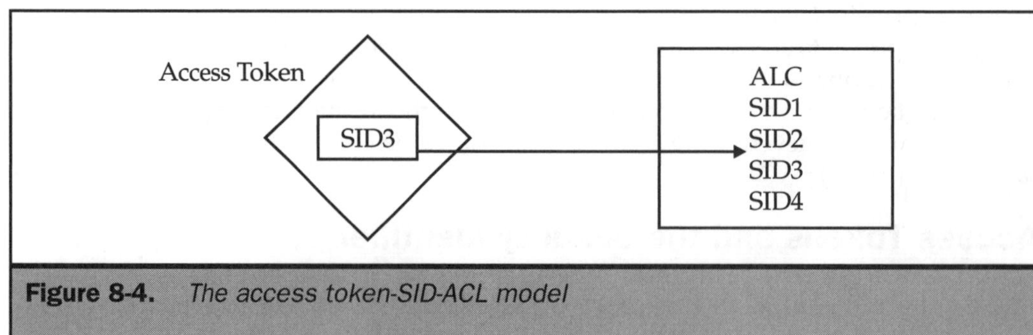

Figure 8-4. *The access token-SID-ACL model*

SIDs guarantee that an account—a security principal—and all its associated rights and permissions are unique. If you delete an account and then recreate it under the same name, you will find that all rights and permissions of the deleted account are removed. The old SID gets deleted with the original account. In this respect, if you delete an account, the login created in SQL Server will have to similarly be deleted because it will hold data related to the old SID. The old login will not work if you recreate the user account in Active Directory or User Manager for Domains on NT 4.0, because the SIDs will be different.

When you create an account, the system also creates the SID and stores it in the security structures of Active Directory or the Security Accounts Manager or SAM (depending on whether you are running a Windows 2000 Active Directory domain or a Windows NT domain). The first part of the SID identifies the domain in which the SID was created. The second part is called the *relative ID* or RID and refers to actual object created. The RID is thus relative to the domain.

When a user logs into the computer or domain, the SID is retrieved from the SAM database or Active Directory and placed in the user's access token. From the moment of login, the SID is used in the access token, a form of user impersonation, to identify the user in all security-related actions and interactions.

Windows NT Server, Windows 2000 Server, and services such as SQL Server or Exchange use the SID for the following purposes:

- To identify the object's owner
- To identify the object owner's group
- To identify the account in access-related activity

Special, well-known SIDs get created by the system during installation to identify built-in users and groups, such as the Administrator account and the Administrators security group. When a user logs into the system as *guest*, the access token for that user will include the well-known SID for the guest group, which will restrict the user from doing damage or accessing objects that a user is not entitled to.

Trusted Access

Once a security principal, or an imposter, has gained access to a system, it becomes very difficult to get them out short of shutting down the system, denying access, or terminating their network connection. Authentication is thus a very critical area for operating system manufacturers, and they rightly invest a lot of money building software to adequately validate authentic users as quickly as possible, and to block access to villains.

No matter how clever are the authentication schemes used, if a person is able to obtain a valid user ID and password, and that person obtain an unfettered connection to the network login point, he or she will gain access to your system. (Biometrics prevents this, but more about that later.) It is then up to the security mechanisms on the network, access control, to keep the "perp" in check. Tools like auditing software and alerts can help, but often they raise the alarms too late.

The answer lies with Kerberos. Microsoft made a considerable investment, for Windows 2000, in the Kerberos protocol, which is an open standard that works on a system of tickets, based on the concept of shared secrets, and implemented using secret key cryptography. Sounds like spy novel stuff for us DBAs, but it is essential in the new world of digital nervous systems and distributed computing and data services. Here is a brief introduction to shared secrets.

Shared Secrets

The Kerberos protocol operates on the concept of a *shared secret.* The term "shared secret" refers to a secret known by a few entities (two or more). Take a gang of bank robbers about to rob a bank. You know the drill. One of the robbers is disguised as a guard, and all the other robbers are hiding in plain sight, as the bank's customers. They are all sharing a secret; they know the guard is not for real, and that they are about to hold up the tellers. No one else knows this. In other words the secret is known only by the people about to rob the bank; the tellers have no idea their day is about to be ruined. But if all the gang members are disguised so well that they look like regular customers, how do they tell each other apart from the real customers? In this regard, each member of the gang can identify another member by confirming that the other person knows the secret. I can't tell you what the secret is, because I am not a member of the gang . . . it could be a triple wink means "we have three seconds to get out" or something. Likewise, the shared secret in Kerberos is between Kerberos and the *security principal* (the human user or a device). The protocol guarantees that no other entity is able to learn the secret.

Here's another analogy from the Digital Age: Two people engage in a steamy cyberspace love affair and engage each other in a private chat room every night. They need to be sure that their communications can be trusted, that they are truly from the other party, and not a spy or an investigator masquerading as the other party, lurking in the chat room. So in order to be sure that the partners are genuine, they both agree, offline, that something in the messages between them will confirm that the message can be trusted.

However if someone is analyzing the correspondence and looking for repeating word arrangements, it will not take them long to discover the secret key. For example, you cannot comment on the weather, or grandma's cat, indefinitely before someone else catches on. On a network, using inspection software, it would take seconds to intercept a message and fool an authentication service into thinking that it is engaged in trusted communications.

So how do the two cyber-lovers devise a plan to be certain that their engagement is secure? The answer is to use secret key cryptography and encrypt the communications.

They would both hold keys that can decrypt their messages. And the spy would not be able to read their steamy words. The key itself must naturally be kept secret.

For the plan to work, the secret key must be symmetric. This means that it must be capable of both encryption and decryption. In other words, as long as the two corespondents share a private secret key, they can encrypt their love letters at will and be sure that the other partner, and only the other partner, is able to decrypt it.

The practice of secret key cryptography is not new but goes back to before the Cold War days when insurgents perfected secret key techniques and cipher science. In fact, it is said that had not the allies seized the Enigma key from the Nazis and cracked the secret communications about their war plans, the Swastika would be flying over a Germany that spans the world.

The implementation of Kerberos in Windows 2000 is fully compliant with the Internet Engineering Task Force's (IETF) Kerberos v5. This standard, which was originally developed by MIT, is supported by many operating systems, which means that the authentication services in the Windows 2000 domain can be trusted in other Kerberos networks (known as realms), such as networks running Mac OS, Novell NetWare, UNIX, AIX, IRIX, and so forth.

Kerberos makes it no more difficult to access a Windows 2000 realm than a Windows NT domain; however, access becomes a lot more controlled. I have written a lot about the Kerberos protocol in Windows 2000; and I consider it largely beyond the scope of this book to explore it in actual deployment detail. However, there is one exception that has to do with the *Single Sign-on Initiative* (delegation) and the Kerberos ticket granting service; I will return to that point later in this chapter.

At this juncture, you need to grasp that the widespread security philosophy used in most IT environments is that once a security principal has gained access to the network or a system, it becomes a *trusted principal.* This means that it is granted a certain level of *trusted access.*

But trusted access, like the levels of security earlier discussed, can be controlled. If you manage a system that is very difficult to break into, or that employs highly sophisticated authentication technology, such as scanning the retina in your eye or the rings of your teeth, would it make sense to control access in the same fashion at every door within the enterprise? It all depends on the *secrets* you are holding and the respect you have for the information and data that belong to the enterprise and its shareholders.

So now we have another security pyramid, illustrated in Figure 8-5, that we can use to illustrate the issue. At the pinnacle is the highest level of trusted access, requiring the system to demand the utmost in trust from the user. And at the base is the lowest level of trusted access. At the pinnacle, you will use all the security tools in the book to make sure that trusted access stays trusted, not compromised.

Some systems, however, need facilities to allow even nontrusted access. SQL Server 2000 is one such system, and this brings us to an investigation of the *trusted-nontrusted access* mechanisms it deploys.

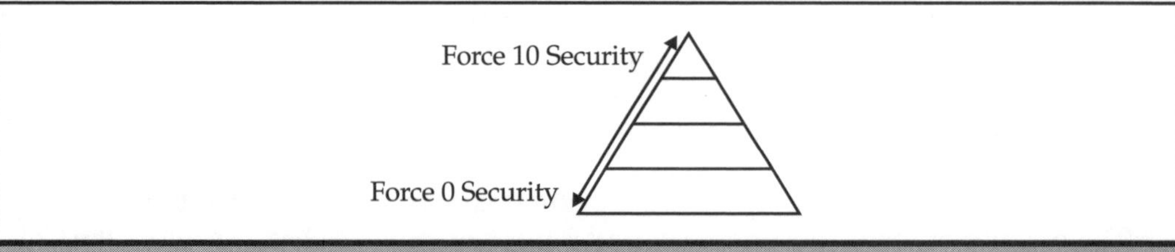

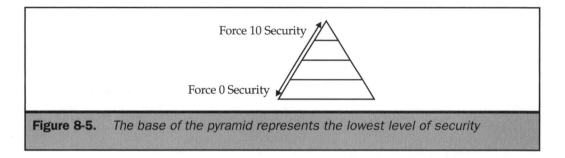

Figure 8-5. *The base of the pyramid represents the lowest level of security*

SQL Server Access

There are two ways into a SQL Server 2000 party. If you have "connections," you can enter by special invitation. This special invitation requires that you know someone on the inside, usually the Boss, a.k.a. the SA. To gain access, you need to go to the back door, where you will be asked for your login name and password. If you can match both, you can get in. This mechanism was once the primary way into SQL Server (at least for people who carried some firepower).

This first access mechanism was once known as standard mode (version 6.5 and earlier). It is nontrusted access. In other words, anyone that comes to the door is suspect and has to be authenticated on the spot; they do not have a referral but need to match a login name with a password. In SQL Server 7.0 and SQL Server 2000, this access mechanism was downgraded to the least-preferred method of gaining access.

The second way to get into SQL Server is through a referral network, a system that supports the tenet that a friend of my friend is also my friend. To gain access via the referral system, you need to go to the front door and present a vouchsafe to secure your access. The "bouncer" will recognize the vouchsafe and let you in, or toss you out onto the street.

The vouchsafe in question is the access token assigned to you when you successfully logged into the network. And advanced notice of it, using the security identifier, is stored in the SQL Server trusted login information. This second access mechanism is known as Windows Authentication (formerly Windows NT Authentication). If SQL Server does not recognize the vouchsafe, it has no (or incorrect) SID information, and you do not have a SQL Server login and password to offer as an alternative, you are politely declined entry.

There are more advanced or secure means of implementing trusted access that can be achieved by SQL Server, but for now you should understand the basics. (I touched on this in Chapter 3.)

There are thus only two ways to configure SQL Server 2000 access. The preferred method is via *Windows Authentication* (no back doors). The other, for nontrusted access, is called *Mixed Mode Authentication.* The latter lets you in via Windows Authentication or via SQL Server Authentication. Both methods are illustrated in Figure 8-6.

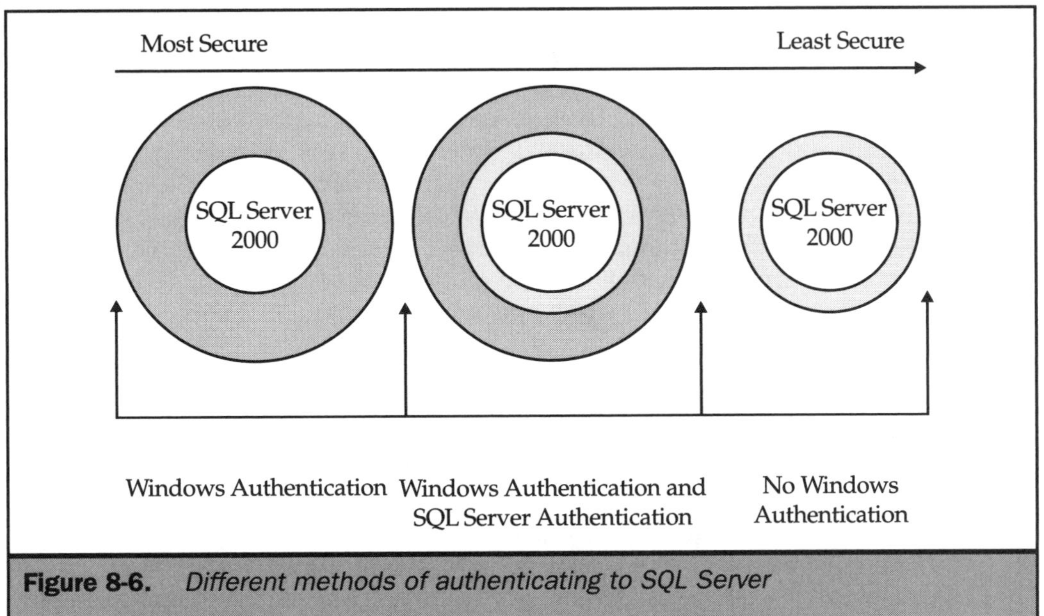

Figure 8-6. *Different methods of authenticating to SQL Server*

In the past there has been some debate concerning which method is more secure. Many DBAs felt that Windows Authentication, although defined as trusted access, was less secure. The weaknesses in Windows NT 4.0 security, via the services of NTLM, a challenge-response mechanism, were primarily responsible for this perception. There is good reason: Once you are authenticated to the network or domain, there is very little, aside from auditing, to retry or retest your trustworthiness. To many, the ability to just "slide" into SQL Server by virtue of being logged into the network using a login known by SQL Server is scary. And many NT networks are as secure as a child's shoelaces. The network administrator might have groups and permissions out the wazoo, only every ACL has the *Everyone* group with full access embedded in it for posterity.

On the other hand, how secure is SQL Server security? How secure is a lock if you have its key or the combination number . . . ? The subject of Windows 2000 domains, or rather realms, is different story, however. Thanks to Kerberos and its system of tickets, the debate of trusted versus nontrusted security can finally rest in peace. To understand how it secures SQL Server 2000, you need to understand a little about Kerberos tickets.

Kerberos Tickets: The Keys to Trusted Access

With Kerberos, authentication is a done deal as long as the information between the parties can be decrypted, or as long as one party can prove that it is the real thing by being in possession of the decrypting key in the first place, like our cyber-lovers discussed earlier. Now, what if someone on the network steals the key, or manages to bug previous authentication sessions and somehow builds a key? Kerberos takes care of this problem because it assumes that someone will be nasty enough to try and hack in.

The Kerberos authentication process kicks into gear as soon as a user or service tries to gain access to a domain (or Keberos realm to be more precise). At this stage of the authentication, Keberos assumes that the network is not secure and that it is possible for anybody to infiltrate the communication between the client and the server.

When Kerberos receives an authentication request from the Windows security services, it performs the following steps before any access to the network is permitted:

1. It looks the user up in a directory, in our case Active Directory, and retrieves the encryption/decryption key it shares with the user to decrypt the user's authentication message.
2. Next it looks at the information in the message. The first item it checks is the time field, which is the time on the clock of the user's workstation or machine from which the user attempted to log in. If the time on the sender's clock is out of sync by five minutes, Kerberos will reject the message (Kerberos can compensate for the different time zones, and daylight saving time). However, if the time is within the allowable offset of five minutes, Kerberos accepts the message. But wait, there is more.
3. Kerberos now checks to see if the time is identical or older than previous authenticators received from the partner. If the time stamp is not later than and not the same as previous authenticators, Kerberos allows the user to authenticate to the domain.

However, it is also important to know that the authentication is *mutual.* Kerberos will send back a message demonstrating that it was able to decrypt the user's message. This means that the partner server or device is able to verify that it, too, is not masquerading. This is something that NTLM, the legacy Windows authentication service, could never do. Kerberos sends back only select information, the most important being the time stamp that it obtained from the original authentication from the client. If that time stamp matches the client's information, then the client is sure that Kerberos and not some imposter decrypted the message.

Key Distribution

So authenticating to Kerberos works well for authentication to the domain, but what about accessing resources once the client has logged in? After all, the whole idea of logging in is to connect to SQL Server and to start working. So how is the connection to SQL Server trusted in the way described earlier? Remember, NTLM and Windows NT 4.0's security services cannot vouch to SQL Server that, just because the client logged in okay, he or she is touched by an angel. To put it differently, "How trusted is trusted access?" On a Windows NT network, I would balk at the idea of "trusted access" because NT is as outmoded in a digital nervous system as a Model-T on Mars. SQL Server trusting a user on an NT network is like you or me trusting a used car sales person, just because he or she is dressed well. If you really want to implement trusted access and be sure of the trust, then you need Windows 2000 and Active Directory in the picture because you need to be able to distribute keys.

Essentially, Kerberos has the capability to forward a "letter of credit" for every client it can vouch for to the server. This letter of credit is a session key, which tells SQL Server "this guy's for real." In other words, it acts as a broker. This in fact is where the name Kerberos, the protocol, comes from. You may recall from Greek mythology that Kerberos (or Cerberos) was a three-headed dog that stood guard over the gates of Hades. Kerberos, the protocol, also has three heads: the client, the server, and a mediator or proxy. The proxy is known as the *Key Distribution Center (KDC)*—it doles out session keys that it fabricates when the client authenticates. In Windows 2000, the Key Distribution Center is installed on the Active Directory Domain Controller.

If you have not studied Kerberos extensively, the authentication process just described might sound too complex and bandwidth-intensive to be of use on a modern network. If decrypting the messages and checking time stamps has to be repeated between clients and servers all the time, and if the KDC has to keep sending all the network resources copies of every user's session key all the time, it would seem to be a tremendous drain on resources. Every server would have to store sessions keys from thousands of users. But, this is not the case, what in fact takes place is ingenious, simple, and has no impact on the network.

Session Tickets

Instead of following the logical option and sending the "letter of credit" to every server and every client at one time, the KDC sends two copies of the session key (one belonging to the server) to the client and then attends to other connections. The client thus holds the SQL Server host's copy of the key until it is ready to contact the server, usually within a few milliseconds. This process is illustrated in Figure 8-7.

The KDC invents a session key whenever the client contacts it to access a SQL Server host (A). The KDC sends the session key to the client, and embedded in the session key is the session ticket (B). Embedded in the session ticket, which really belongs to the SQL Server host, is the host server's session key for the client.

As soon as the client receives the session communication from the KDC, it opens the ticket and extracts its copy of the session key. Both items are then stored in volatile memory. When the client is ready to contact SQL Server (C), it will send the server a packet that contains the ticket still encrypted with the server's secret key and the time authenticator encrypted with the session key.

If everything checks out, the SQL Server host grants access to the client (D) because the server knows that a trusted authority, the KDC, issued the credentials. After the connection is allowed, the Net-Libraries can do their thing and begin login to SQL Server; Credentials can then be passed into the instance and teamed up with the SQL

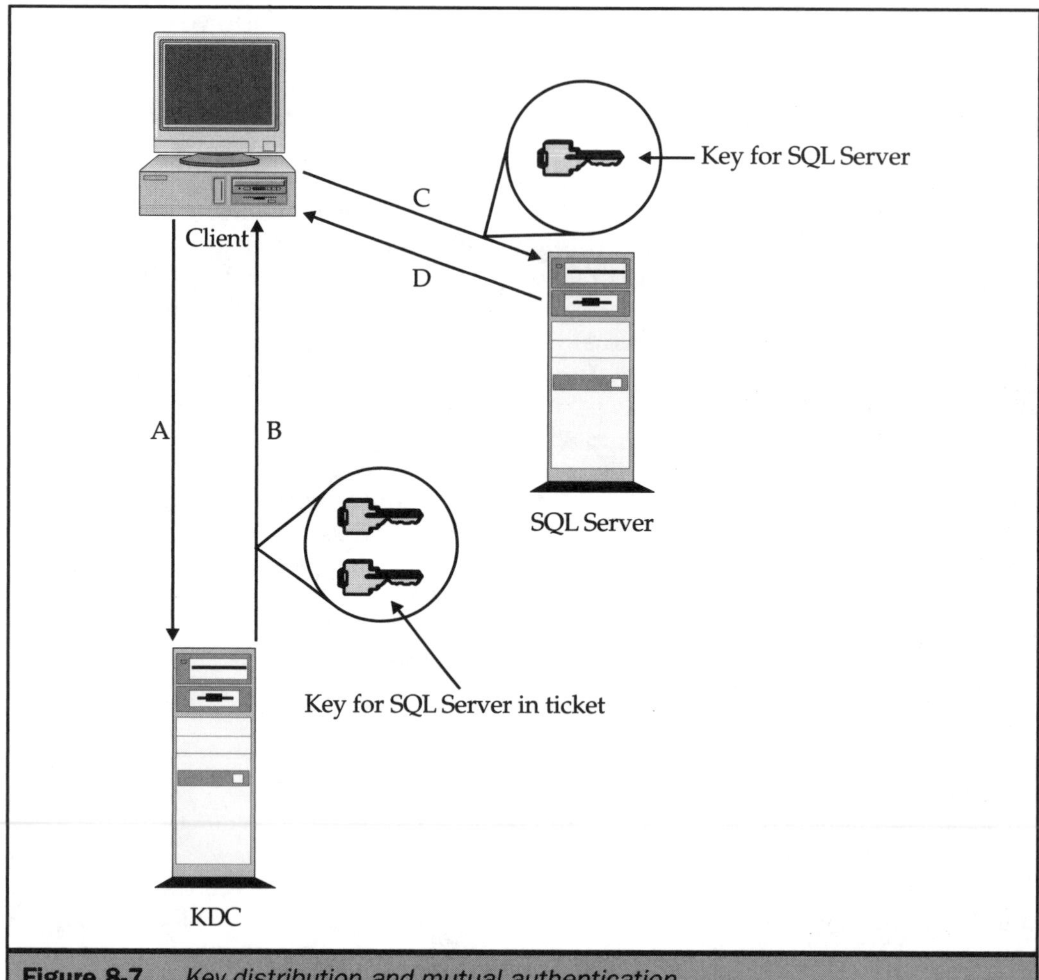

Figure 8-7. *Key distribution and mutual authentication*

Server login. As soon as the client is done using the server, the server can get rid of the session key that the client was using to communicate with the server. The client will instead hold the session key and represent it to the server each time it needs to access it. But no other client can try to connect to SQL Server under the guise of a user that just disconnected or might still be using the system.

Session tickets can also be reused, and as a safeguard against ticket theft, the tickets come with expiration times. The time-to-live for a ticket is specified in the domain security policy, which is discussed later in this chapter in the "SQL Server Security Plan" section. Typical ticket life is usually about eight hours, the average login time. When the user logs off, the ticket cache is flushed and all session tickets and keys are discarded.

Kerberos, Trusts, and Login Delegation

Kerberos provides the technology that allows Windows 2000 domains to interoperate as bidirectional, transitive trusts, as long as the domains are part of a contiguous namespace (such as an Active Directory tree). Domains in separate domain trees or in separate forests can, however, share an *interdomain key,* and one KDC becomes the proxy for the other and vice versa. This makes for a secure environment that can safely allow a user in a foreign domain to connect to SQL Server.

Once an interdomain key has been established, the ticket granting service in each domain is registered as a security principal with the other domain's KDC, allowing it to issue ticket referrals. Clients in their own domains still need to contact their local KDCs for access to foreign resource. The process is as follows:

1. The local KDC checks to see if the resource needed by the client resides in another domain.
2. If it does, it sends the client a referral ticket for the resource in the other domain.
3. The client then contacts the other domain's KDC and sends it the referral ticket. The remote KDC authenticates the user or begins a session ticket exchange to allow the client to connect to resources in the remote domain. The domain-to-domain trust model is illustrated in Figure 8-8.

My earlier remark about NT not being suitable for trusted access in a digital nervous system or .Net, multitiered environment is upheld when a connection is refused access to a remote stored procedure or cannot participate in a distributed query or transaction (see Chapters 19 and 21 respectively). Such a situation requires a scenario in which a client connects to a server that must also connect to another server. The login server must then be able to vouch for the connection to the second server. In other words, the first server needs to be able to *delegate* authentication. To do this, it must have a ticket to the second server, and thus it is clear that an NT environment precludes such advanced applications.

What takes place on a Windows 2000 network is as follows: The client delegates authentication to a server by telling the KDC that the server is authorized to represent the client. In lay terms, that is like telling the KDC that the SQL Server machine you are authenticated to has power of attorney to deal with the second SQL Server machine. This is similar in process to the concept of the access token, another form of attorney, agency, proxy, or what Microsoft calls "impersonation"—an unfortunate word.

Delegation can be done as follows:

1. The client can obtain a ticket from the KDC for the referred server. Upon connection to the login server, the client must hand this ticket to the server. Such a ticket is called a *proxy ticket.* Difficulty arises in this scenario because the

client needs advance knowledge of the other server, which becomes a management cost in both the client and server tiers.

2. The better option is to allow the client to issue the login server a ticket granting ticket (TGT), which can be set up upon initial presentation to the SQL Server login server, which can then use this TGT to obtain a ticket for the referred server as needed. Such a ticket is also known as a *forwarded TGT*.

The forwarded tickets are managed in Kerberos policy in Active Directory. Kerberos policy is managed in the Default Domain Group Policy object and is something you need to set up outside of SQL Server at your domain controller. You or your network administrator will need to manage the policy object in Active Directory, by a process you'll find described in Window 2000 Server help or a good book on Windows 2000 security.

You will notice when you set up delegation that each ticket has a timeout period that can be defined in Active Directory. If a connection remains idle for too long, the ticket will expire and all subsequent attempts to execute a distributed query or a

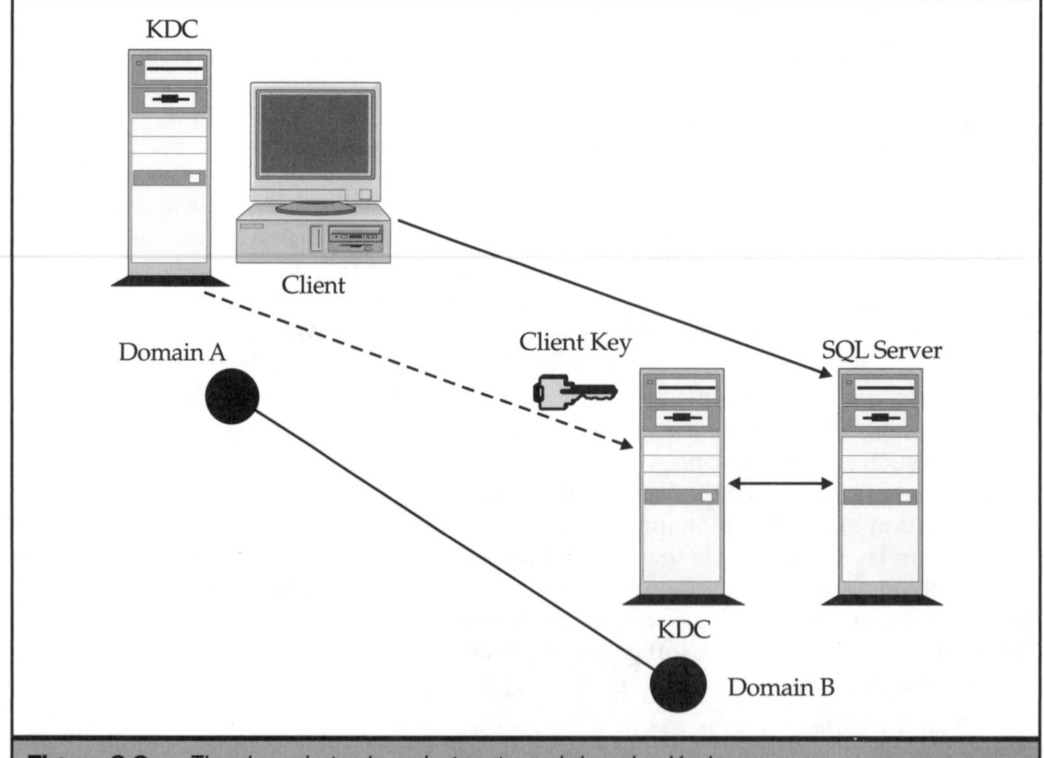

Figure 8-8. *The domain-to-domain trust model under Kerberos*

remote stored procedure will fail. The user will have to disconnect from the login server and reestablish the connection if your application keeps the connection open. This is an added security benefit, because most well-written applications should not keep connections open indefinitely. In distributed or *n*-tier scenarios, it is unlikely your client will be maintaining open-ended connectivity to the server.

Looking at the connection from the viewpoint of the secondary server, when SQL Server instance A connects to SQL Server instance B and executes a distributed query that references tables on instance B, then instance B has access to your login credentials. Instance B can then validate your individual permissions to access the data from the tables referenced.

On a Windows NT network, you have to specifically define a login on A to connect to B. The login is global and is used regardless of which user executes the distributed query on A. Instance B will not have any knowledge of the actual user executing the query, and you cannot define permissions specific to individual users connecting from A. You will have to define a global set of permissions for the login account used by A. The solution on Windows NT is also less secure. For example, you cannot audit what the specific users are doing in B.

Configuring Delegation

There are a number of things to consider before you can support delegation. The following checklist highlights the necessary components to manage or configure:

- **DNS** You need to install a DNS server as the locator service for Kerberos. The DNS service that ships as part of Windows 2000 Server is the best DNS to use because it is tightly integrated with Active Directory and supports dynamic updates. If you already use another brand of DNS, note that the governing RFC (1510) specifies how DNS should resolve KDC hosts to IP addresses. In a Windows 2000 domain, the KDC is usually installed on the Active Directory server, the domain controller. They are not connected in terms of application process space and run as separate services. However, since the KDC is always installed on the DC, it is possible to resolve a KDC by looking up the host address of a domain controller. Client computers in a Kerberos realm need to send their messages to the IP address, and if the IP address of the KDC cannot be resolved, it generates an error message to the client indicating that the domain cannot be located.
- **Active Directory** You will need to install Active Directory if your primary network is not a Windows 2000 network. It is also possible to install Windows 2000 servers in non–Windows 2000 domains or networks (such as NT 4.0, NetWare 4.*x* and earlier, or Linux), and they can still participate in Kerberos authentication. You will need to ensure that they resolve to the correct host addresses, which might not be Active Directory domain controllers. The utility called *ksetup.exe* (in the Windows 2000 Resource Kit) is used to configure clients and servers to participate in Kerberos realms that are not Windows 2000 domains.

- **TCP/IP** All computers participating in SQL Server delegation will need to be running TCP/IP, and you will need to ensure that TCP/IP is the Net-Library being used by all clients and servers.
- **Computer Account** Your SQL Server computer should have an account in Active Directory. Find or create the account, open to the General Tab of the server Properties dialog box, and ensure that the option "Computer is trusted for delegation" is checked. This is illustrated in Figure 8-9.
- **Service Principal Name (SPN)** A *service principal name* (SPN) identifies an instance of SQL Server as a security principal. The SPN is defined or set using the *setspn* utility, which can be found in the Windows 2000 Resource Kit. The SPN is typically created by a Windows 2000 domain administrator. The syntax to create the SPN is as follows:

  ```
  setspn -A MSSQLSvc/Host:port serviceaccount
  ```

  The SPN is assigned to the service account of the SQL Server instance on your primary server so that the instance, or rather the service account representing it, is attested as being authenticated, at the particular socket address. For example,

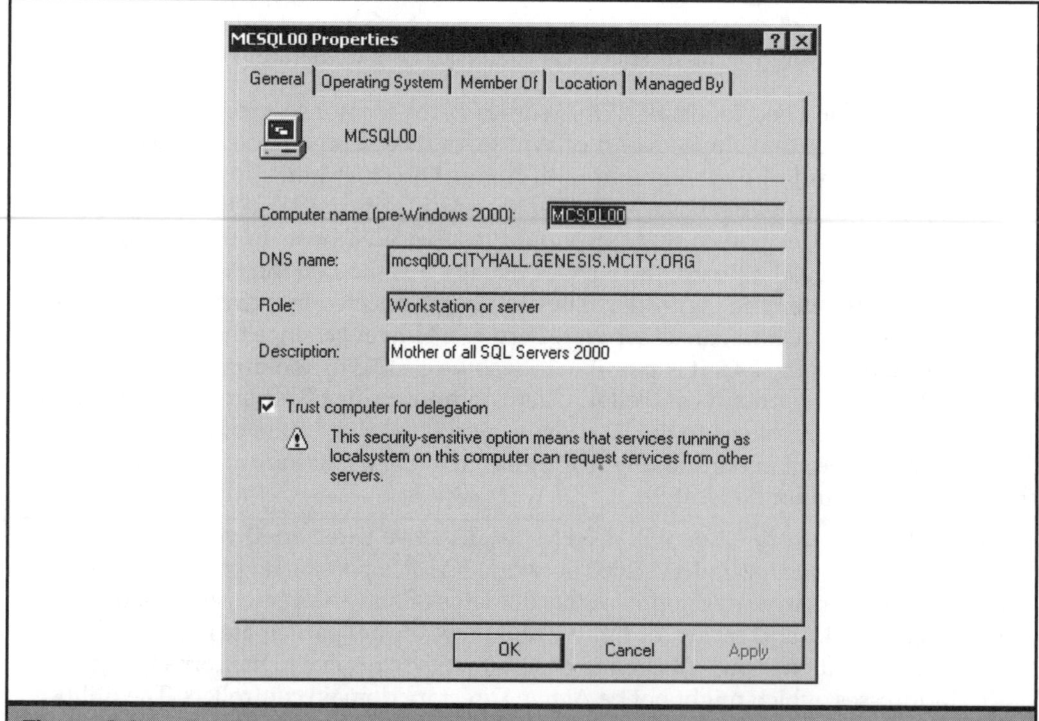

Figure 8-9. *Configuring the computer account for delegation*

to create an SPN for SQL Server, you need to run the following code at a command prompt:

```
setspn -A MSSQLSvc/mcsql00.cityhall.genesis.mcity.org:1433 micsql
```

- **User Account** The account of the user (login) must be set up for delegation. Open to the Account tab on the user's Properties dialog box in Active Directory. Make sure the option "Account is sensitive and cannot be delegated" is not checked and that the option "Account is trusted for delegation" is checked. This is illustrated in Figure 8-10.

The preceding steps are all that is needed to enlist delegation, but there is obviously a lot more to Kerberos and delegation than what we discussed here, and it exceeds the scope of this book. Numerous books have been written that deal exclusively with Kerberos. However, Kerberos security is the de facto pervasive security mechanism that protects Windows 2000 domains and their server products, such as SQL Server 2000.

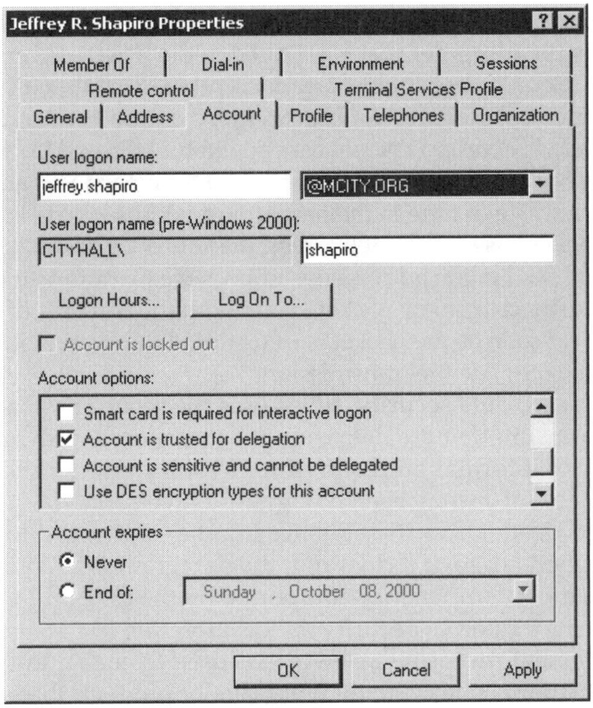

Figure 8-10. *Configuring the user account for delegation*

So given that Kerberos security provides a much higher level of trusted access than earlier, it actually makes sense to configure a server for Windows Authentication mode only.

IPSec

IPSec is a contraction of "IP" and "security." It is an Internet Protocol (IP) security solution, developed jointly by Microsoft and Cisco and employed in Windows 2000 for maximum protection of network traffic, especially over insecure networks like the Internet.

The protection, strong encryption, is applied at the IP layer, across the stack, and takes place between two computers, the client and the DBMS server. The encrypted packets are not filtered in any way by firewalls or routers in between but simply pass through the gateways. IPSec is thus transparent to the users and applications deployed on either side of the network.

IPSec is divided into four processes: encryption and encapsulation, authentication and replay tolerance, key management, and digital signing and digital certificates. All communications sent and received under IPSec are encryptedis *end-to-end*, which means that the packets remain encrypted while en route to the other computer. The packet can only be decrypted by the computer that is engaged in the IPSec conversation with the sending computer. IPSec also uses public key encryption. The shared key is generated at both ends of the encryption and is not transmitted over the network.

The IP Encapsulated Security Protocol uses 40/56-bit DES or 112/168 DES to encrypt the IP address of the sender along with a datagram. This means that any network sniffing or tapping becomes a waste of time to the perpetrator because the header information is unreadable. The attacker has no way of learning the source or destination address, and without the source or destination address it is impossible to mount an attack. The original packet is also encapsulated in a new packet, along with the contents of the packet and the header information. As soon as the packet is transmitted the destination IP address it is no longer required to complete the transmission.

In order to guarantee data security, IPSec uses the secure hash algorithm (SHA-1 or MD-5 of RSA) to ensure that the data cannot be tampered with en route to or from its partner and that no information required for a replay attack can be obtained. IPSec anti-replay mechanisms tag each datagram with a sequence number. When the datagram reaches its destination, its sequence number is checked to verify if it falls within a predetermined range. If it does not, the datagram is abandoned.

The key management component is supported by the ISAKMP protocol—a mouthful that stands for Internet Security Association Key Management Protocol/ (Oakley key management protocol v8)—which is used to enable the use of a single architecture to secure transactions with different vendor products that are IPSec-compliant. DSS and RSA technology is used to provide the proof of authorship for signatures in digital certificates.

IPSec also supports the ability to import your company's unique x.509 v.3 digital certificate into IPSec-compliant hardware and software. You are thus essentially integrating IPSec into your public key infrastructure (PKI), which I touch upon later in this chapter. The integration between IPSec and PKI provides even stronger network security and SQL Server login or delegation security and an absolutely secure passage for data between database client and SQL Server on an insecure network, never before possible in the client/server database environment.

IPSec works as follows:

1. Computer A gets ready to send data to computer B across an IP network. But before the transmission can begin, A checks to see if the security policy established on A requires that the data be secured under IPSec. The security policy contains several rules that determine the sensitivity of the communication, and the security required.
2. If security policy so dicates, computer A must first begin a security-based negotiation with B via a protocol called the *Internet Key Exchange* (IKE). The two computers then exchange credentials according to an authentication method specified in the security rule. The authentication method for this initial conversation can be Kerberos, public key certificates, or a predefined key value.
3. Once the negotiations are underway, two types of negotiation agreements called *security associations* are set up between the two computers. The first type, called *Phase I IKE SA,* specifies how the two computers are going to trust each other. The second type is an agreement on how the two computers are going to protect the data that is to be exchanged between them. This is known as *Phase II IPSec Sec Sas,* and specifies the security methods and keys for each direction of the communication. IKE automatically creates and refreshes a shared secret key for each SA. As mentioned earlier the secret key is created independently at both ends without being transmitted across the network.
4. Computer A signs the outbound packets for security and integrity and also encrypts the packets according to the methods agreed upon in the earlier negotiation. Depending on the level of security, it may decide not to encrypt the packets. The packets are then transmitted to B.
5. Computer B checks the packets to see that security and integrity is still sound and decrypts them if necessary. The data is then transferred up the IP stack to the services or application in the usual fashion.

While IPSec was designed to protect data on insecure networks, it can also be deployed on the intranet, especially in light of the widespread implementation of TCP/IP in a Windows 2000 network and the advent of the .Net initiative. and other distributed network application (DNA) architectures. It has obvious application to protect against an attack on SQL Server. The processes just described are illustrated in Figure 8-11.

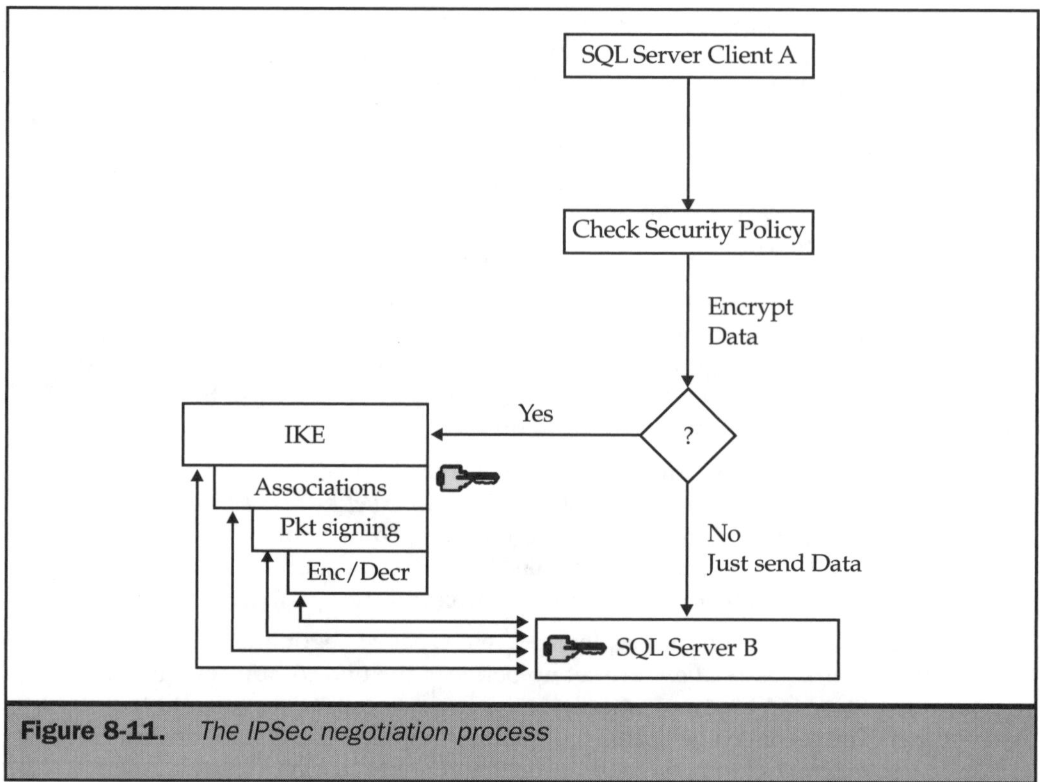

Figure 8-11. *The IPSec negotiation process*

Encryption is a processor-intensive operation and if excessively used it can impact a database server. You can, however, use an IPSec-compliant Network Interface Card (NIC) that uses the Windows 2000 IPSec driver to significantly reduce the impact on the CPU. One such company that already ships a cost-effective, CPU-driven IPSec NIC is 3Com. It's like having a hardware-based RAID controller that employs a CPU on the interface card to perform striping, as opposed to giving that burden to the main system CPU, which is how software-based RAID works.

Like Kerberos, IPSec is managed under group policy, which I touch upon at the end of this chapter. You define it per domain or per Active Directory organizational unit (OU). And it can also be defined for computers that are not affected by domain or OU security policy. Specifically, IPSec can be configured to provide variations of the following services:

- You can specify the extent of authentication and confidentiality that will be negotiated between the client and SQL Server. For example, you can specify the minimum acceptable level of security allowed between clients, which is to send clear text over the network but hide both sender and receiver information.

- You can set policy stating that communication over certain insecure networks takes place using IPSec, or not at all. This will require you specify the network routes deemed to initiate insecure information.

Secure Sockets Layer

We touched upon the SSL TLS (Secure Sockets Layer/Transport Layer Security) layer in Chapter 3, in our discussion of the SQL Server Net-Libraries. You will likely need to implement it, especially with respect to .Net rollout, and *n-tier* database applications architecture. *SSL/TLS* has been around in several Windows NT or BackOffice products for a while. It is a widely supported protocol both on corporate networks and on the Internet. SSL/TLS is also supported in Internet Information Server and Microsoft Exchange.

Windows 2000 uses SSL/TLS and X.509 certificates to authenticate smart card users for network and DBMS access and for data protection. SSL/TLS is used to secure a wide range of communications such as network traffic, IIS traffic (Web and FTP), e-mail, and client-DBMS transactions created in browsers or standard applications.

Microsoft Certificate Services

Two levels of public key cryptography from which SQL Server security can benefit are at work inside Windows 2000. One level is implicit and expressly built into the operating system. It is at work in Kerberos and IPSec described earlier, and does not require attention from you, other than some minor configuration management. (Microsoft Certificate Services also provides certificates to the Windows 2000 Encrypting File System [EFS].) The second level is explicit. It requires you to build a public key infrastructure to accommodate a pervasive use of public key cryptography to access highly sensitive data in SQL Server.

Public Key Infrastructure

A *public key infrastructure* (PKI) is a collection of services and components that work together to a common end, a secure computing environment. Such an environment will allow you to secure all database transactions, both on an intranet and over the Internet, to secure your Web sites and your company's Web-based online transactions, to deploy smart cards and biometrics for authentication, and more.

A PKI gives you the ability to support the following public key services:

- **Key Management** The PKI issues new keys, reviews or revokes existing keys, and manages the trust levels between other vendors' key issuers.
- **Key Publishing** The PKI provides a systematic means of publishing both valid and invalid keys. Keys can also be revoked if their security is compromised.

PKI handles the revocation lists so that applications can determine if a key is no longer to be trusted (this is similar in practice to the bad credit card lists published by the banks for the benefit of merchants).

- **Key Usage** The PKI provides an easy mechanism for applications and users to use keys. Key usage provides the best possible security for the enterprise.

Digital Certificates

As discussed earlier in this chapter, public keys are encapsulated in digital certificates. I can think of no better example of a digital certificate than your driver's license. The license number is the key. It is what gives you the right to get into a motor vehicle and use a public road. The driver's license is issued by the Department of Motor Vehicles (DMV). It is laminated so that it cannot be tampered with and is an object of trust that proves that you received the "key" from a trusted authority, which in this case is the DMV.

How do you validate a digital certificate? A *certificate authority* (CA), which issues the key, is the equivalent of the DMV in the preceding analogy. The CA signs the certificate with its digital signature. You can validate the digital signature with the CA's public key. But who vouches for the CA? A *certificate hierarchy,* a system of vouchsafes that extends all the way up to the root certificate authorities that have formed an association of authorities. Microsoft is a CA that can directly issue public keys which are handled by the Microsoft Certificate Services.

A PKI is a collection of services and components that collectively create the infrastructure. A Microsoft PKI depends on Active Directory for the publishing of key information, and all certificates, revocation lists, and policy information is stored in the directory.

Managing a Microsoft PKI is not difficult and is even less time-consuming than managing logins, roles and users, databases, and database access. If you are managing SQL Server 2000 on a Windows 2000 network, many of your day-to-day activities already encompass the facilities of a PKI.

Trusted Access Versus Nontrusted Access

As you can see, you can lock down access to SQL Server to the "nth" degree. Why then does the support for Mixed Mode linger? For starters, backward compatibility with earlier versions of SQL Server is a good reason. Second, if you install SQL Server on Windows 98, you cannot use Windows Authentication because Windows 98 does not support NTLM or Kerberos authenticated access. And both require you to be running NTFS, which is also not supported by Windows 98.

There is another, more important, reason. If you have a remote SQL Server 2000 system, on a secure WAN segment, or anywhere for that matter, and it sits in a nontrusted domain, or as a standalone server on a non-Windows network, there is no means of presenting client authentication in the network communication. In other words, the connection cannot raise a Security Support Provider Interface (SSPI) to the SQL Server. This means that the only way to gain access is to transmit the internal user ID and password pair to SQL Server for access.

SQL Server Security: The Internal Environment

Let's now put aside the access control story and work within the DBMS. Once users are inside SQL Server, their objectives are to access the databases, and your objectives are to ensure that they access only the data they are allowed to access. You also have to ensure that users do not destroy data, through either mala fide or bona fide actions. The mechanisms you have to secure data, at the object level, are very similar to the security mechanisms out on the file system or in the operating system.

As mentioned earlier, a database is an object that itself consists of objects . . . in much the same way a cell contains protoplasm and cytoplasm. We refer to this hierarchy of objects as an object chain, as illustrated by Figure 8-12. All objects in the chain inherit ownership from the parent object when they are created on the connection that first created the parent. Subsequent connections that can create objects become the owners of the new objects.

Permissions

Microsoft introduced a new permissions system to SQL Server starting with version 7.0, its landmark product revision of the century and precursor to what we are now trying to drive. This system has been extended and further enhanced with SQL Server 2000. It is based on the security model and the Windows NTFS permissions architecture, which we discussed earlier in this chapter. An "access control list" for a database object contains the names of users or groups of users that are granted access to an object, and the level of that access. A special "permission"—DENY—blocks a user or group (security principal) from accessing the object in a certain way.

Like its counterpart at the OS and NTFS levels, the user in SQL Server 2000 obtains the sum of permissions assigned to it at the individual and role levels (roles are discussed in a moment). In other words, if the user gets permission to select records in one role and in another role gets permission to insert and select records, the combined permissions are INSERT and SELECT. However, if another group on the same object denies SELECT, guess what, the user is denied permission to SELECT, no matter that it is granted elsewhere. In Windows NT/2000 security, the object permissions work the same way. DENY is the most restrictive permission and overrides everything.

Inside the SQL Server DBMS, not all objects have permissions. Some objects by their nature or purpose cannot be shared or accessed, yet they all have some function to perform on data that is usually only called by its owner or an internal process. An example of such an object is an index on one end of the chain and the database at the other. No other users are allowed to access the objects until the owners authorize their access and set the access level.

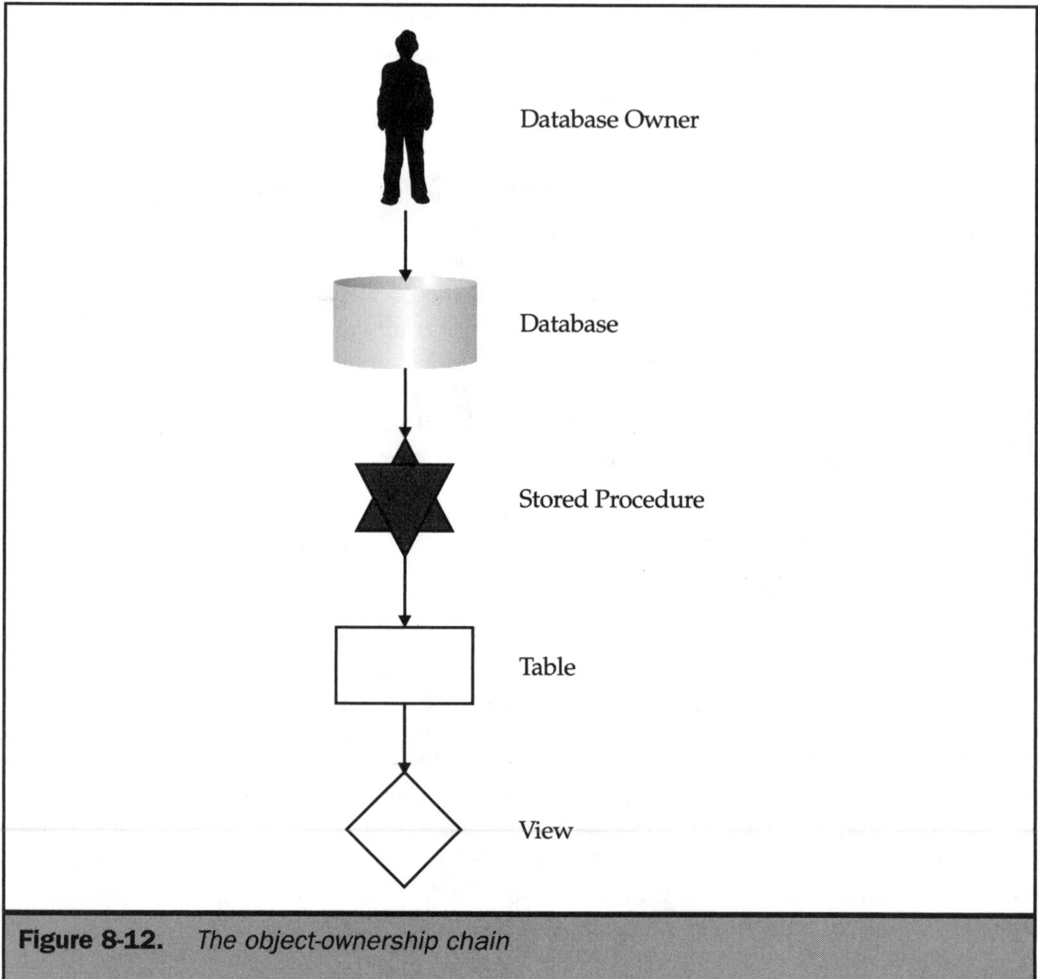

Figure 8-12. *The object-ownership chain*

A database object's access is provided through a system of permissions. At the very top of the object chain, the database itself does not immediately make itself available to users. Before users can access a database, the database owner must first explicitly grant access. This is achieved by allowing groups of users to have access to the database, and permissions can be configured interactively through Enterprise Manager or via several programmatic options. Three types of permissions can be applied to SQL Server objects. These are as follows:

- Object permissions
- Statement permissions
- Implied permissions

Object Permissions

The following table provides a list of objects that have permissions. If a user can access an object, it means that access to the object must have a system of permissions that govern its access. Table 8-1 lists the objects that fall into this access-permissions category:

Statement Permissions

Statement permissions control access to the T-SQL statements that create database objects or that cause SQL Server to perform specific database-centric activities. While a database is an object, SQL Server 2000 classifies the permissions that apply to it as statement permissions. Statement permissions also apply to stored procedures, functions, tables, views, rules and so on. The following list lists the statements that require permissions. These permissions are accessible in the database object dialog boxes in Enterprise Manager:

- BACKUP DATABASE
- BACKUP LOG
- CREATE DATABASE
- CREATE TABLE
- CREATE VIEW
- CREATE DEFAULT
- CREATE FUNCTION
- CREATE PROCEDURE
- CREATE RULE

Object	Permission	Purpose
Database	(See statement permissions)	(See statement permissions)
Table	SELECT, INSERT, UPDATE, DELETE	Permissions that can be applied to the entire table
Views	SELECT, INSERT, UPDATE, DELETE	Permissions that can be applied to the entire view
Rows	INSERT, DELETE	Permission to add or remove rows in a table or view
Columns	SELECT, UPDATE	Permission to SELECT or UPDATE data in columns in a view or table
Stored Procedure	EXECUTE	Permission to run the stored procedure

Table 8-1. *The Object Permissions*

You will seldom need to provide users with these statement permissions. But if your enterprise maintains a large SQL Server implementation and you have several DBAs assigned to specific tasks, they will require the appropriate permission in order to carry out their duties. You can't just give everyone access to SA anymore; that's a no-no in SQL Server 2000.

Implied Permissions

The third class of permissions is called *implied permissions.* These apply to a wide range of activities and can only be made available to, implicitly, members of the predefined roles in the DBMS, or the database owners. Such permissions allow the use, for example the ALTER TABLE statement, of an implied permission that is inherited by the database owner by virtue of ownership.

A database owner, for example, also does not require permission to delete a table, add data, create indexes, and so on, because these permissions are implied (inherited) through ownership.

The system administrator gets the full deck of implied permissions, from installation, through complete management, to the final removal of an instance.

Checking Permissions

SQL Server 2000 put its Windows Authentication trust to the test when a user attempts to log in. At the time of login, a trusted connection is established if the so-called security principal, a user or a group, arrives armed with an access token and SID information. When you create a login for a client derived from a domain security principal, the login is created and the SID for the security account is fetched from Active Directory or the NT Security Accounts Manager (SAM). You can also create a trusted account without the domain because the SID *varbinary* variable can store a NULL or a GUID (see Chapter 16).

Each time a user connects over the trusted connection, its SID is compared to the SID on file in the SQL Server sysxlogins table (visit the master database). If the SID does not compare, the connection is rejected. Do you remember what was discussed earlier in this chapter about the SID? If you know what goes on in the world of Windows security, you'll remember that when you delete a user, computer, or group account, you also delete the SID. If you then create the exact same account, a new SID is generated because the old one was discarded when you nixed the earlier account.

The idea to use SIDs was born during the development of SQL Server 7.0, which replaced the old version 6.5 trusted mechanism that still uses access over Registry keys installed in the local host's Registry, and we all know how secure that is. SQL Server would check if the user had access to the Registry key, and if access was proved, login was granted. SQL Security Manager (may it rest in peace) was used to insert the usernames into the old syslogins table. I am reminding you of this legacy because upgrading to SQL Server 2000 can be scary if your objective is to inherit extensive databases and configuration information you may have on the old platform (see Chapter 6). Before you upgrade, you must make a special effort to clean up your legacy installations, and the one area to start with is your user account and login information.

SIDs are stored along with the user login information in the sysusers and sysxlogins tables and are used to pair the logins with the associated user accounts. Each user ID is then stored in the sysobjects table to determine ownership and in the sysprotects table to apply permissions to the objects (in similar fashion to the ACLs out in the NTFS). Yet another table, systypes, is used to determine ownership of any user-defined types.

Every time a user connects to SQL Server and is given access, its connection information is recorded in a snapshot structure called the *process status structure* (PSS). The PSS is not persistent but is lost when the connection ends. However, every connection is recorded in its own PSS, so an application or user making multiple connections to SQL Server will have multiple PSS snapshots. The PSS in fact is very similar to the access token that is associated with the user every time it requires access to file system objects, as well as to the Kerberos tickets that are required to provide access to servers and services on a Windows 2000 domain.

When a user attempts to access a database, the server checks the sysusers tables for any negative credit that may have been placed there, in the form of specific access denials placed on the database objects. These are unlikely to occur, because users generally obtain access via the *public* role discussed shortly. If all checks out and the user has database access, the DBMS then scans the sysmembers table to check on the role memberships of the user. This allows the DBMS to check if the user is constrained from access or denied service by virtue of group or role membership.

Once a user's "persona" has been established by the server, object permissions are checked in the syspermissions table. Naturally the DENY permission information will be checked first; if it is present, the user will be blocked from accessing the respective resource on the level of access that has been denied. The combined access/denied scenario is cached to prevent system overhead every time the respective user attempts to access the same object.

SQL Server maintains a permissions cache that is kept up to date because permission status can change at any time. The permissions cache works like the procedure cache or the query plan cache. When permissions are changed, the DBMS increments a permissions counter that is compared against the value in the cache. If the value in the cache is lower than the counter value, the permissions are rescanned and the permissions cache is updated. There is a small overhead that is incurred at every permission rescan, but this is negligible because once a database model or design is settled, permissions are unlikely to be continually changed.

GUIDS for Nontrusted Users

SQL Server nontrusted users are assigned a 16-byte globally unique identifier in place of a SID (which will be absent when this user connects or when SQL Server is installed in an insecure environment, such as Windows 98). GUIDs are used in the same fashion as SIDs described previously are for trusted users. This allows the internal security architecture to remain the same for both trusted and nontrusted environments. In other words, all permissions-checking routines remain the same, no matter whether it is the SID or the GUID the security architecture revolves around.

User Access

What good are permissions if you don't have users to use them? Figure 8-13 examines the access "tree" that towers above the object and its permissions. At the root of the tree, we have the objects, and the connection to it is via the permissions we have discussed. Roles or users have to go through the permissions to access the objects, as you now know. User objects are split into two entities: They can be individual users derived from several sources, or they can be "roles," which are groups of individual user "accounts." Users can also be given aliases, but we'll get to that information soon.

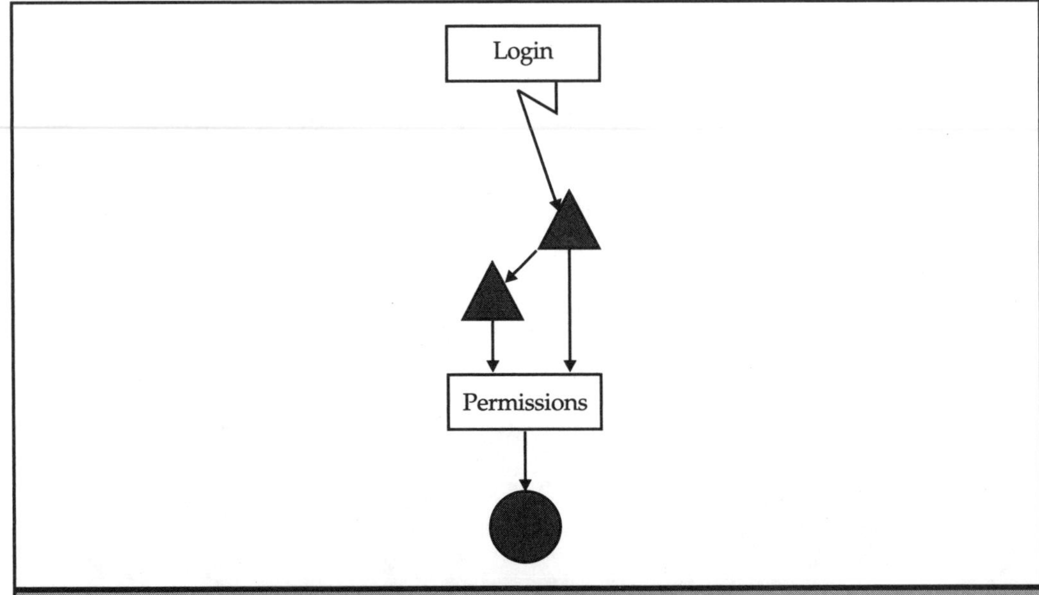

Figure 8-13. *The Access tree starts at the object and extends up through permissions, users, and roles to the login*

At the very top of the tree, you'll find an entity called the *login level*, or *logins*. The login level controls access to the system itself. Access to the database is given by connecting the user account at the lower level with the login at the "server" level. The login, as you know, is associated with either a SQL Server nontrusted login or a security principal (trusted), a domain user account given to an external trusted Windows domain account, or an external nontrusted user that is assigned an internal SQL Server user ID account and password. *Logins* are managed interactively in Enterprise Manager. They can also be managed programmatically, as is discussed in Chapter 14.

Users

SQL Server users can be described as follows:

- **Built-in users and system roles** When you first create an instance of SQL Server 2000, or install it from scratch, the first user ID created is the System Administrator, or SA. This is the first user given login access and exists for access before any form of domain or network security exists. This user is created at the big bang of SQL Server 2000, when the instance is created and it needs a "first cause," known for some time now as "SA."

  Several built-in system roles are also added (they are discussed shortly), and both domain and SQL Server users can use these roles. By the way, all members of your domain's BUILTIN\Administrators group and the server's local BUILTIN\Administrators group are members of the sysadmin system role.
- **Database users** Database users are the database "connections" your logins access. If the user is nontrusted, the login will require an ID and password pair to match what is stored in the system's user tables. Database user security is managed on the Users node of a database tree in Enterprise Manager. You can also fully manage database users programmatically, using T-SQL (and of course, triggers and stored procedures also play a part in server and database security). To be clear on the difference between logins and users: Logins allow you to connect to SQL Server per se; users allow you to connect to databases per se.
- **Guest user** The *guest* user requires special mention. The guest user is predefined in SQL Server when you first install the instance. It is automatically given access to the master database, albeit with no permissions that it could use to hang itself. The purpose of the guest user account allows any login to connect to a database, if you explicitly allow this, without having to demand "name, rank, and serial number" at every connection. The guest account is useful for casual access to the database, to look up data without risking data, and so forth.

If you add the guest account to a database, SQL Server will check a login attempt, as usual, to see if a valid user name or alias is assigned. If not, it will check to see if the guest has access to the database. If the guest has access, the nonauthenticated user will be admitted as a guest of the database owner. Allowing guests into the database is totally at the discretion of the database owner or system administrator.

Roles

To me, a security group is to a user account what a shoelace is to a shoe. If you lose the shoelace, you will either lose the shoe or lose your balance. Every domain I currently manage is put together using the building blocks of security and distribution groups. No user under my care is ever excluded from a group—even if I only have one user on the domain, that individual gets to be a member of a group.

I was thus one of many Windows sysadmin/DBAs to be delighted to discover a similar concept established in SQL Server. Roles were added to SQL Server with version 7.0; they are very important to SQL Server 2000 management and count big time toward easing the cost of administration.

If you have worked with groups, then roles will not be too difficult to grasp. Collect the users that require the same services, access, and permissions for logins on databases and objects into a role. Then apply the object's permissions to the role. The role members are then granted (or denied) access by role membership and not on an individual user basis. Whenever you have a new user that requires access, you can simply add the user to the role for it to inherit the same level of access as everyone else in the role.

When working with Windows groups, when I need to remove a security account's access from a file or folder I simply remove it from the group. Specifically denying a user access is not a common occurrence and is usually motivated by some ill intent on the part of the user. Denying access is also a costly management practice because you have to keep track of the actual account and the object that access has been denied to. And you also have to recall what level of access was denied on top of everything else.

With the exception of one role I will discuss, roles apply to database access and to the objects inside the database to which permissions must be set. Roles, like user groups in the OS, can be nested. So you can create a small role for a group of troublemakers and nest it inside a group of angels. If the troublemakers cause trouble, out they go without affecting the other kids. However, the best feature of a role, again like a user group, is that the user can be a member of more than one role, and that makes for some powerful access control and user management.

Roles are available as either predefined "house" roles or as user-defined roles. And they come in several flavors. The term "user-defined" is really a misnomer because it is the DBA that will create these roles . . . or members of the *db_owner* or *db_security* predefined database roles discussed shortly.

The following lists the roles and the primary "roles" they play in the DBMS:

- Public role (built in)
- Server roles (built in)

- Database roles (built in)
- User-defined database application roles
- User-defined standard roles

Public Role

The public role is added to every database you create and is added to the system databases when you install SQL Server 2000. The public role works like the *Everyone* group in the OS environment with one exception: The *Everyone* group can be removed from objects to fully secure the system. The Everyone group to me is like the proverbial fly buzzing around your head. The Everyone group can be a real nuisance because every time you create a resource or establish a service, the Everyone group gets added. So I go to the parent and ensure that child objects do not inherit the Everyone group from it. Simple cutting the inheritance connection from the parent object, which forces you to add exactly the groups you need to the resource, does this, but with SQL Server it is not as simple as just going the parent object and getting rid of "Everyone."

Removing Public is not so easy to do with SQL Server. For starters, access to Public is given as soon as you create the database. Second, every user that gets permission to access the database gets added to the public role. The saving grace of the public role is that it is not a weak link in the security environment of SQL Server as Everyone is to the operating system or network. Instead, it is a convenient way of providing quick default access to users of the database. If you are worried about security, you should know that while the users are added to public, they are not automatically handed the keys to the vault. You have to go into public and set access permissions for each object the role can access.

Server Roles

Server roles are fixed roles, predefined or built into SQL Server 2000. The server role is the only role that is applied outside of the database objects. The server role is a useful container that allows its members to administer the server and perform role-wide tasks. There are a number of server roles in SQL Server 2000, as defined in Table 8-2.

Database Roles

Database roles are fixed roles that apply to the databases of an instance of SQL Server. There are nine fixed administrative database roles and one fixed user role in SQL Server 2000. The fixed user role is *public,* which we have already discussed. The administrative roles permit a wide range of database administrative chores, such as backing up and restoring, running DDL against the database, and database security. Table 8-3 lists the nine roles and their functions in a database.

All databases can have the fixed database roles listed in Table 8-3, but membership is restricted to a database. For example: A member of db_ddladmin on the database

Fixed Server Role	Duties
Sysadmin	Has the run of the ship; performs everything.
Serveradmin	Configures the server; shuts down the server.
Setupadmin	Manages linked servers and startup procedures.
Securityadmin	Manages logins and can read error logs.
Processadmin	Manages processes on a SQL Server instance.
dbcreator	Creates, alters, and restores databases.
Diskadmin	Manager of the disk files.
bulkadmin	Has the right to run BULK INSERT.

Table 8-2. *Fixed Server Roles*

Fixed Database Role	Duties
Db_owner	The big Kahuna: all activity in a database. This role essentially combines all the capabilities of the other database roles.
Db_accessadmin	Adds and removes users and logins. This role allows its members to work with Windows users and groups.
Db_datareader	Power to run SELECT on any user database. However, this role does not permit access to data editing functions.
Db_datawriter	The converse of the preceding role. It has the power to run INSERT, DELETE, and UPDATE on any user database, but it does not permit the use of SELECT.
Db_denydatareader	Can deny SELECT on any user database.
Db_denydatawriter	Can prevent the change or deleting of data.

Table 8-3. *Fixed Database Roles*

Fixed Database Role	Duties
Db_ddladmin	Can run DDL statements on a user database, but has no access to GRANT, REVOKE, or DENY.
Db_securityadmin	Manages roles, membership, and permissions.
Db_backupoperator	Performs backups, restores, DBCC, CHECKPOINT.

Table 8-3. *Fixed Database Roles* (continued)

SHOES1 is not automatically a member or the same role in SHOES2. This is referred to as the *scope* of the role.

You cannot nest predefined roles, not even in a user-defined standard role. If you want to let a DBA do both backup administration and login management, the user will have to be added to both roles.

Application Roles

The first question I asked when I encountered roles for the first time was "what about applications?" Surely an application can be a "login" without having to create a special account for the operator of the client machine. For example: You are asked to create a time-entry application to track work hours. Does this mean every employee in the company must be added to a role, possibly to *public?* Which groups would you want the network administrator to create? What about change control policy, and so on? The answer lies in the application role.

This is how it works: When your application makes a connection to SQL Server, it calls the application role stored procedure *sp_setapprole* to request access. This SP takes two parameters in your statement, the name of the role and a password. The DBMS then works with the role in the context of a user on the database, and any permissions defined on objects in the database, in the application role, apply to the application. For example, if the application role only allows the application to select data, that's all the application will be allowed to do. You will not be able to write a routine that "gate crashes" a role to write data.

Application roles are user-defined and can be secured with passwords. And of course, there are a number of ways to encrypt the password, as discussed earlier. Also, no users are associated with application roles. In the time-entry example, you could create one application role that allows users to enter information, and another one for the HR managers that will allow their applications to access the information. You could also secure the application by requesting that a user provide the password required for advanced use of the application and pass the data to the SP password parameter for the application role. The application role is thus a very powerful tool, useful in a variety of client programming scenarios.

However, you should also understand that when an application makes use of application roles, any connection made to SQL Server in the context of a standard login is terminated. You have to close the connection to the application role and reconnect to the server if your require features or access in the context of a database user.

SQL Server also maintains any auditing you might have covering the *user*. So when you suspend user access and startup application access, auditing continues in the user context. In other words, SQL Server still knows who's pulling the strings.

The application role is also an excellent means of protecting data from being attacked using SQL Server tools and DBA "thorns" like Microsoft Access. Query Analyzer, for example, is extremely powerful, and in the wrong hands it can destroy a database that is not adequately protected. And Access's grids do more than just run SELECT on data: one keypress and you can be in the table.

A downside of the application role, however, is that you have to hard-code a password into the client or force the user to provide one when attempting to connect to SQL Server. We are in the business of limiting the number of passwords, and the single sign-on benefit provided by Kerberos provides that very function; and thus a second password might detract from that objective.

Standard Roles

Standard user-defined roles are containers you can create for a collection of users or groups from both trusted and nontrusted sources to provide access to a database. These roles are restricted to the database they were created in. The roles can also be used for nesting a number of roles. You can also use roles as alternative to groups from the Windows environment that you might not have access to or that may not yet exist. It will also be better to have the network administrator create the groups you need and add them to your roles.

Managing SQL Server Security

There are two directions you can come from to attack user access. First you can go directly to the database you are managing and create users, and from there set up logins for the users, or you can set up logins as part of a DBMS-wide, or data center, security plan.

I prefer—actually enforce—the latter approach. Logins are created and managed by a member of the securityadmin or sysadmin roles, according to policy and mechanisms that go through a change control or management authority. I will tackle the subject of change control at the end of this chapter. Essentially, the change control board (CCB) is approached by a department head or application manager and requests user access to databases. Change control management approves the access and forwards the request to the DBAs for execution.

The routine I just described is identical to the one required in the external environment where the CCB (or its security manager) requests the network administrator to add, change, or delete user accounts and manage group and OU membership. This practice centralizes control and prevents breakdown in security requirements outlined in your plan. If you willy-nilly added logins at every turn or allowed anyone to create user accounts and logins on the fly, very soon you would have power user logins created for one database accessing others they should not access. Remember, logins are global and exist above all databases. So a login intended for one database can be used to access any other one (associated with a user of course). I will discuss this issue further in the security plan to follow shortly.

The following sections first deal with creating *database roles,* then *logins,* and then *users.*

Creating and Configuring Database Roles

Database roles can be created programmatically or interactively using the Enterprise Manager. Roles are an internal environment security mechanism; in other words, they do not have any relationship with an external object (like a Windows NT security principal) on which their existence depends.

To create and manage a role, do the following:

1. Expand the database you are working in and select the *Roles* node. Right-click and select the New Database Role menu option. The Database Role Properties – New Role dialog loads. Choose the role type, *Standard role* or *Application role.*
2. Next click Add to add a role member. The Add Role Member dialog box, shown in Figure 8-14, loads. Note that you can nest roles here, or add user members. Click OK and your role is created.

To define permissions for the role, follow these steps:

1. Select the role from the details pane (or you can do this as part of the preceding step 2), right-click, and select Properties.
2. From the Database Role Properties dialog box, click Permissions. The Permissions dialog box for the role will load (see the section "Permissions" earlier in this chapter).

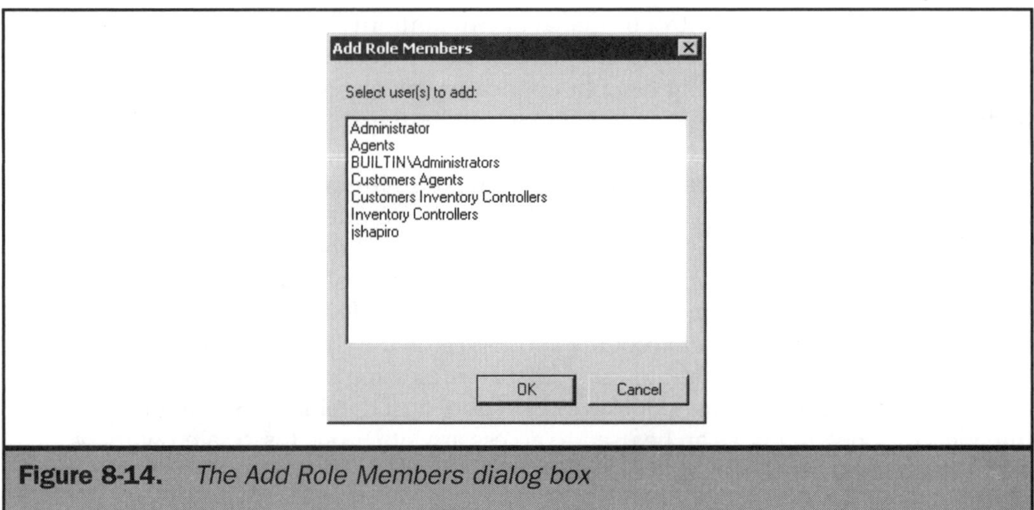

Figure 8-14. *The Add Role Members dialog box*

Creating and Configuring Logins

Logins can be created programmatically or interactively using the Enterprise Manager. Creating logins using T-SQL is discussed in Chapter 18. To create logins interactively in Enterprise Manager, do the following:

1. Go directly to the Security node in Enterprise Manager, and expand the node as illustrated in Figure 8-15. Right-click the node and select New Login from the context menu. The New Login dialog box, as shown in Figure 8-16, loads. Logins are created on the General tab of the New Login dialog box.
2. Next, either enable Windows NT Authentication or, if you are supporting nontrusted access, enable the SQL Server Authentication options. If you are going to add users from security groups in the external environment to the login, the Name field accesses user accounts from the NT SAM or Active Directory. If you are creating a nontrusted login, you need to come up with a name and password for the login.
3. The last item you need to set on this tab is the default database for the login. This default should usually be the database for which the login is being created; however, you can leave it at the default (master) or make the default database *pubs* or some other database that contains no data worth worrying about. Making *master* the default database is a risky proposition in my book, even

though the login does not get immediate access to the data because it has to go through more checkpoints before it can reach into a table.

4. Now click the Database Access tab. You will bypass the Server Roles tab because that is for DBA access, which we discussed in the earlier section on server roles. The Database Access tab will let you select the databases to permit the login to access (still no access to data). You will also be able to select the database role for the login (if it has been created), but until you save this information and connect the role to a user account in a database, you still have no direct access to data.

You can drill further into permissions at this point, by clicking the Properties button on the Database Access tab, but I recommend you manage permissions through role creation and management in the respective database first. Unless you know your way around these dialog boxes like a blind fish in a cave, navigation here can be a little stressful.

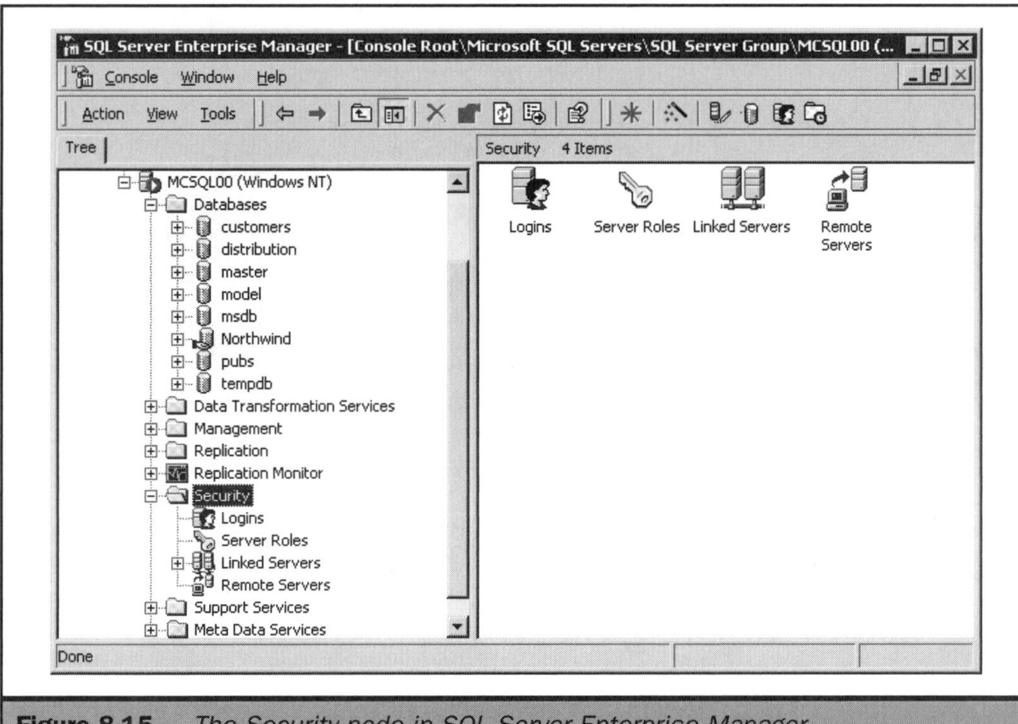

Figure 8-15. *The Security node in SQL Server Enterprise Manager*

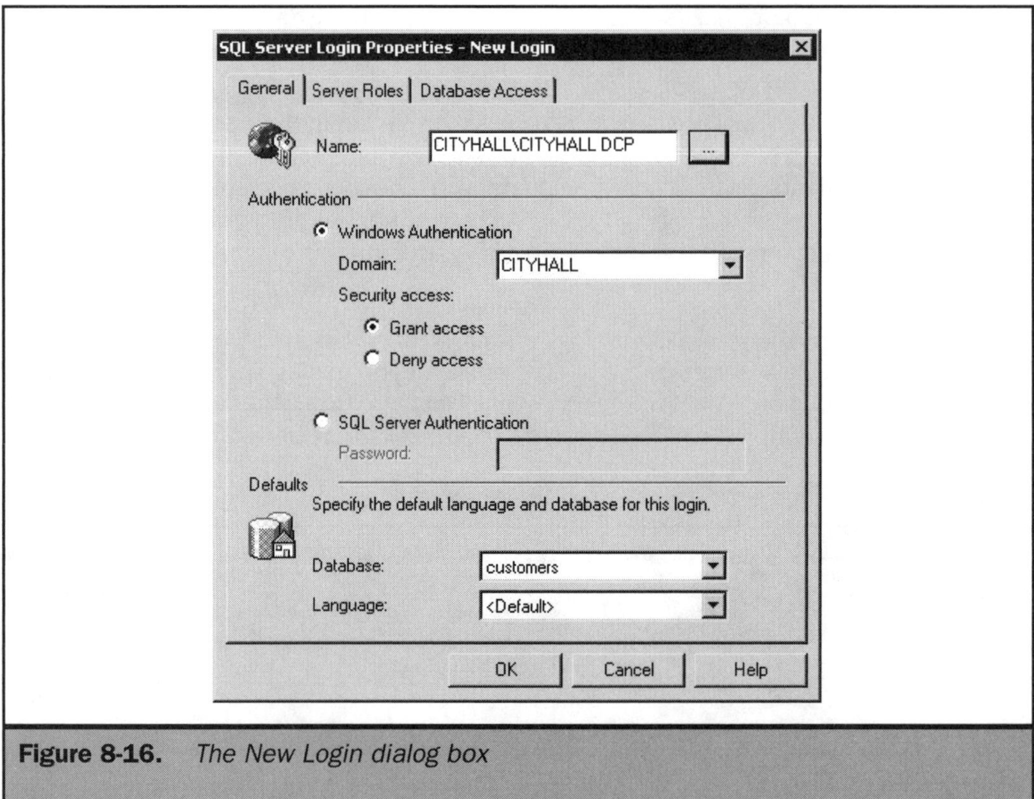

Figure 8-16. *The New Login dialog box*

Note *There are several items to notice about the logins and the Database Access tab. First you can allow a login to access more than one database. Second, the login can be in more than one database role. Third, the database role is peculiar to the database that you select in the database list, on the Database Access tab.*

If you are adding a group of users from the domain environment, make sure the Windows NT Authentication section on the General tab is checked.

Creating and Configuring Users

To create database users from Enterprise Manager, select the server in which the database resides and drill down to the database in which to create users. This is shown in Figure 8-17. To create users do the following:

1. Go to the Users node in your target database. Right-click the node and select New Database User. The New User dialog box loads, as illustrated in Figure 8-18.

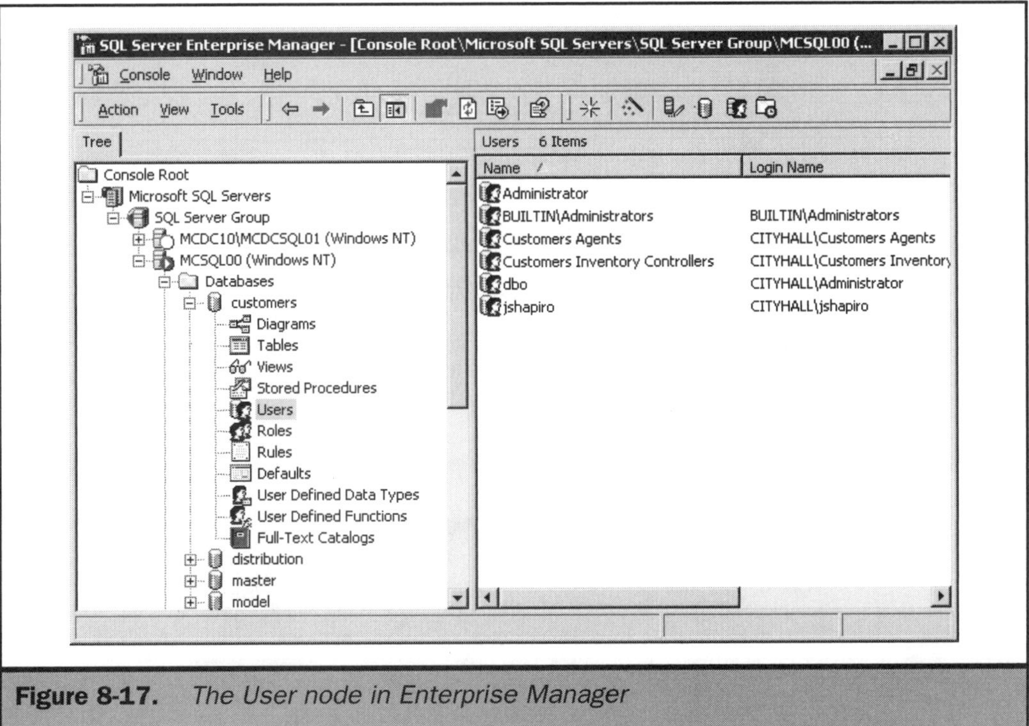

Figure 8-17. *The User node in Enterprise Manager*

2. Now select the login from the login drop-down list. Both trusted and nontrusted logins are available to be used for the new user. You can leave the Name field to the default provided, which is the same as the login, or you can provide your own name, which then becomes an alias.
3. Next, select the database role for the user. You can place the user into multiple roles (see the section "Creating and Configuring Database Roles" earlier in this chapter). You can manage roles by clicking the Properties button, but I prefer to do that while working in role management as described in the section on roles in this chapter. You can also add the user to the role at any time from either the Roles or the Users nodes.

To define permissions for the user do the following:

1. Select the user from the details pane, right-click, and select properties. The Database User Properties dialog box loads.
2. Click the Permissions button to access the object permissions dialog box (see the section "Permissions" earlier in this chapter).

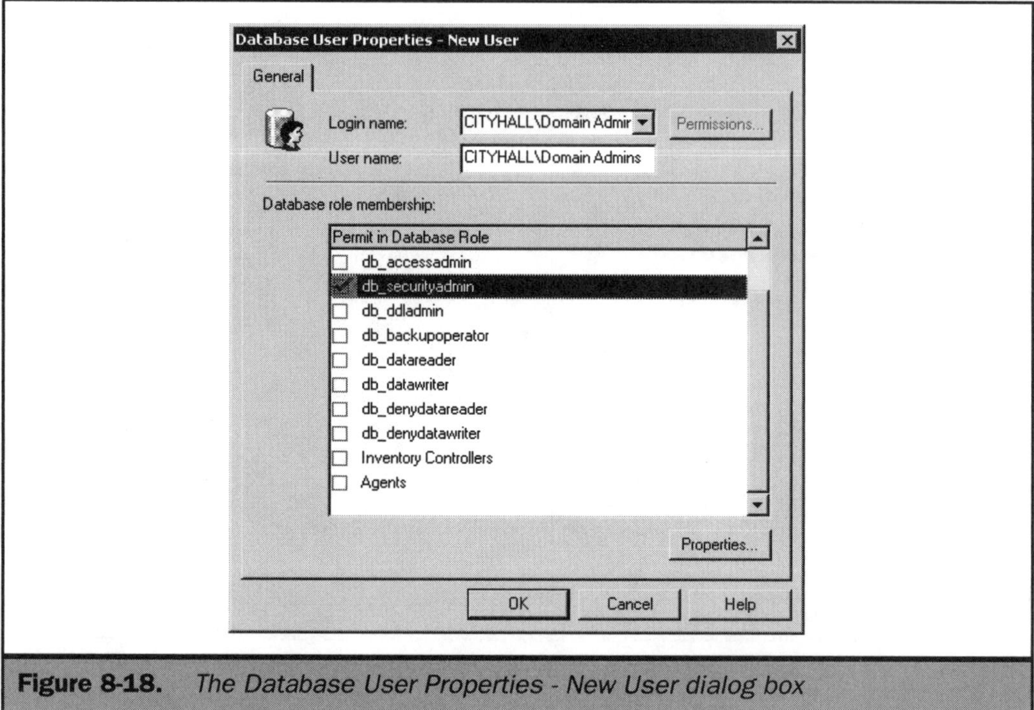

Figure 8-18. *The Database User Properties - New User dialog box*

Deleting Logins and Users

As discussed earlier, Logins and Users are not joined at the hip. Deleting a login does not cause any loose ends with respect to a database user a login was using. Deleting users does not delete a login, nor does deleting a login delete a user. To delete a login or a user, do the following:

1. To delete a login, expand the Security node under the SQL Server 2000 instance you are managing. In the details pane select the login, right-click, and then select Delete.
2. To delete a user, expand the User node in the database containing the user. Select the user in the details pane, right-click, and then select Delete.

One thing to remember concerning the deleting of users: Users can own database objects, such as tables, views, and stored procedures. If you try to delete a user that owns objects that still exist in a database, the DBMS will prevent you from deleting the user.

There are several steps you can take to rendering a user "out of service" if it still owns objects in the database:

- Remove the permissions accessible to the user. Select the user, right-click, and select the Properties menu item. The User Properties dialog box will load. Click Permissions and clear or deny any permission defined for the user.
- Or, remove the user from any roles it has been placed in. Select the Properties option as described in the preceding step and then click the Properties button. The Database Role Properties dialog box will load. Remove the user from the role and then click OK.
- Or, using the stored procedure *sp_changeobjectowner*, you can transfer the ownership of the object to another user, and then delete the user.

Auditing

SQL Server 2000 provides a highly sophisticated auditing mechanism that allows you to perform auditing on two levels depending on the security plan requirements. I refer to the two levels as auditing according to data center security requirements and C2 security requirements. Now, your data center may require less of the C2 specification and you should define your needs according to change control and data center security needs.

Note *For the record, Science Applications International Corporation's (SAIC) Center for Information Security Technology, an authorized security testing facility, upheld Microsoft's claim that the security features and assurances provided by SQL Server 2000 running on Windows NT 4.0 Service Pack 6a and C2 Upgrade meet the C2 requirements of the Department of Defense Trusted Computer System Evaluation Criteria (TCSEC) dated December 1985, as interpreted by the Trusted Database System Interpretation of the Trusted Computer System Evaluation Criteria. In other words, SQL Server 2000 on Windows NT is rated C2 by National Security Agency.*

C2, however, only applies to standalone computers, so NSA certification will really only mean something to certain parties when SQL Server 2000 and Window NT and Windows 2000 rate for the networked computer specifications (Red Book and Blue Book). Microsoft has gone above and beyond C2 with Windows 2000, which at this writing has not yet rated. So by and large the term is really meaningless on a broader security scale.

For what it's worth, C2 security is more than a just a rating because it tests things like the protection of objects and auditing. The audit trail facilities of SQL Server are highly advanced, and you can really push the event-logging envelope into outer space. I would almost go as far as saying that you can pretty much trace who passes wind in SQL Server 2000. Your auditing plans thus require careful consideration.

Auditing, like encryption, impacts performance. Every event is auditable, which means that the overhead to record the event accumulates and impacts server or DBMS performance. If you need to accommodate stringent auditing requirements, you might need to consider a second server to do nothing but audit all DBMS activity, or throw gobs of RAM and another processor or two at your base server.

SQL Server Profiler

Your auditing arsenal on SQL Server 2000 starts with the SQL Server Profiler. This is not a new tool, but it has certainly benefited from rigorous overhauling on the part of Microsoft. The SQL Server Profiler (the "profiler") lets you create a trace or a trail of all events that take place in the DBMS. The original purpose of the profiler was to provide a means of troubleshooting SQL Server.

The profiler lets you trace a series of events that lead to a problem. You can then step through the trace and attempt to pinpoint the event that causes your error. Using the profiler to troubleshoot or debug SQL Server is further discussed in Chapter 12, so let's stick to security and auditing for now.

SQL Server Profiler can be accessed from Enterprise Manager. It is also an option in the SQL Server program group. To launch the application from Enterprise Manager, select the Tools button and click the SQL Profiler menu option. The profiler is not an MMC snap-in; but it probably will be in future versions.

To set up an audit trail Profiler template, do the following:

1. Go to the File menu and click New | Trace Template. If you are not attached to a target SQL Server, the Connect to SQL Server dialog box, illustrated in Figure 8-19, loads.

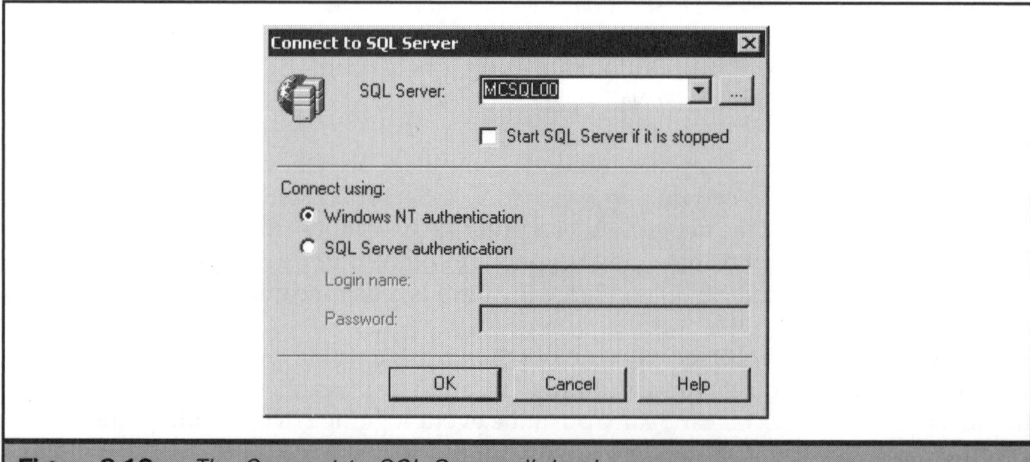

Figure 8-19. *The Connect to SQL Server dialog box*

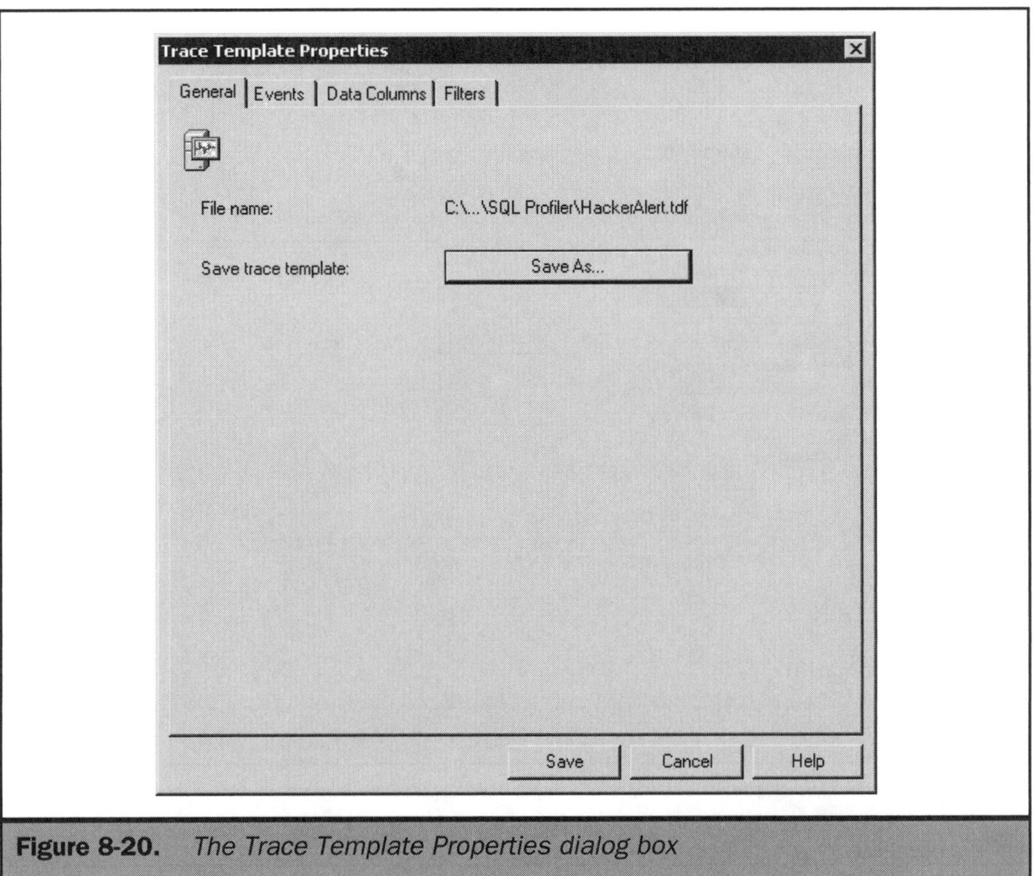

Figure 8-20. *The Trace Template Properties dialog box*

2. Select the server you are going to audit and click OK. The Trace Template Properties dialog box loads, as illustrated in Figure 8-20. (If the server is not available in the list, you can search for it against any Active Directory server on the network.)
3. On the General Tab, enter the name of the Trace Template. Save the name and move to the Events Tab as illustrated in Figure 8-21. You don't need to save at this stage, but it makes sense as you are building the template to keep saving it.
4. On the Events tab, drill down to Security Audit classes and click Add to select them (they go into the right-hand list box. You can select only the events you need by drilling down in the events list in the left-hand list box, or you can select all by double-clicking the root of the class group or by selecting the root

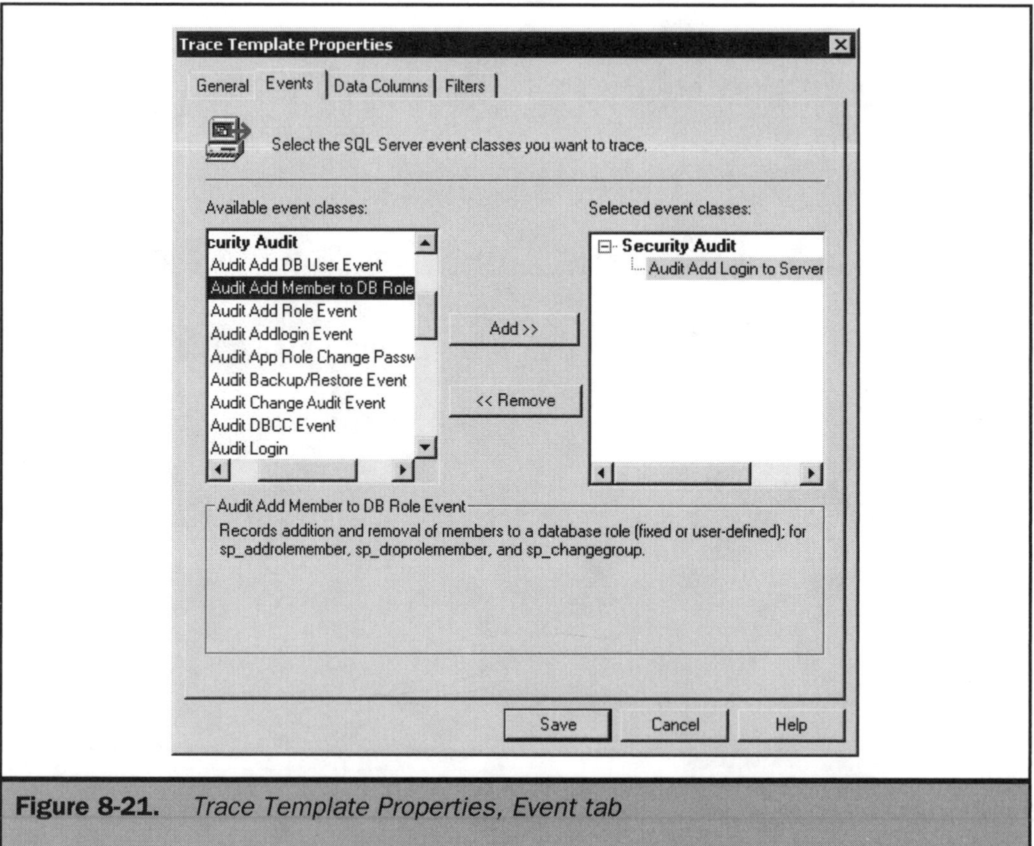

Figure 8-21. *Trace Template Properties, Event tab*

and clicking Add. In the example illustrated here we are going to spy on login events.

5. On the Data Columns tab, you will select the data that will be saved to the audit. As demonstrated in Figure 8-22, I am looking for an authorized user of a login. The data we are looking for reports which user logs into the application. It will return the user name and the account SID, which can be used to trace the user in the external environment.

6. On the Filters tab, you will select the variable information to trace. For example, filters will allow us to only pick up logins on the "Todo Para La Vida" database, as illustrated in Figure 8-23. Now save the template as described earlier.

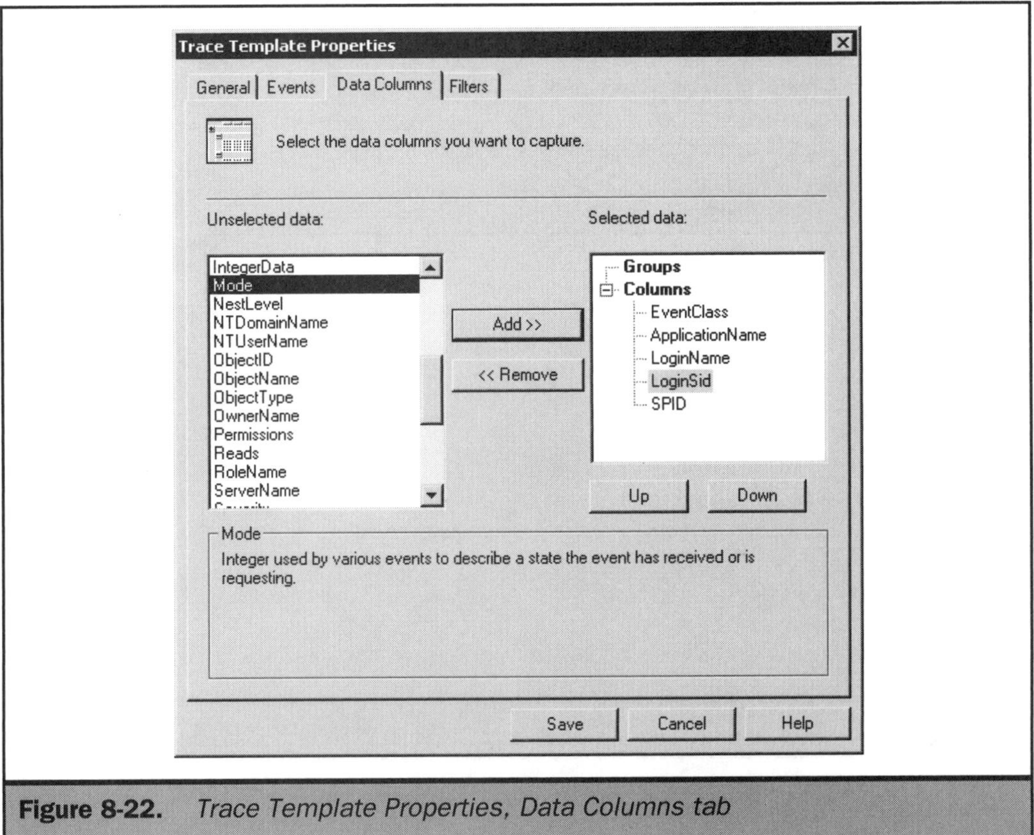

Figure 8-22. *Trace Template Properties, Data Columns tab*

Running the template is a simple process:

Go to File, New Trace. The Trace Properties dialog box, as illustrated in Figure 8-24, loads. The Events, Data Columns, and Filters tabs have already been worked into the template creation process. Notice that you can create a trace on the fly and bypass the template process as mentioned earlier. Enter a new Trace name in the provided field. Your trace files will be named to what you provide here.

Connect to a new instance of SQL Server. The button to the right of the field launches the Connect to Server dialog box. (If you connected to the wrong server when you started New Trace, or you need to change the target instance to be profiled, you can run the Connect to Server dialog box again from the General Tab, and search your Active Directory namespace for the correct instance.)

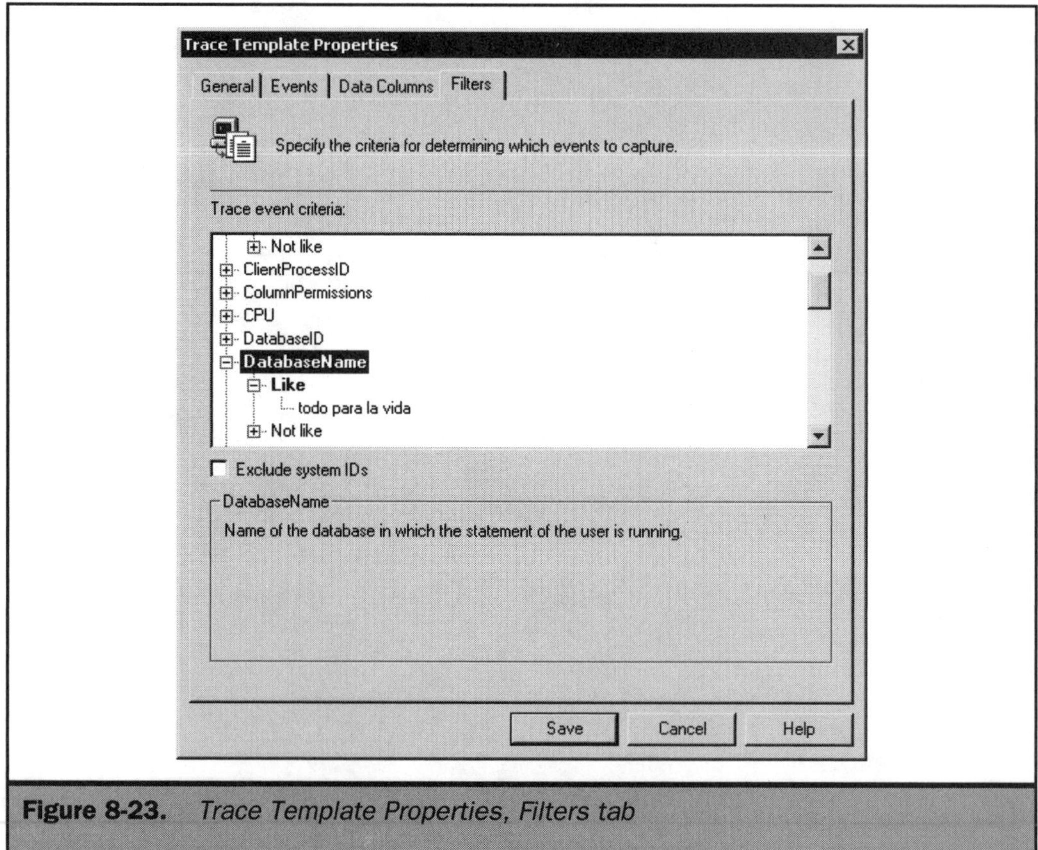

Figure 8-23. *Trace Template Properties, Filters tab*

Next select the template name. If you built a security audit template as just discussed, it will appear in the drop-down list. If you cannot find the list, the browse field below can be used to go after it.

The next options allow you to specify the output target and paths for the audit data. The Enable file rollover option means that when the first file reaches the maximum size and you are still auditing, the data will spill over into a second file, a third, a fourth, and so on. In the example shown, the first file was *HackerAlert.trc*, the second became

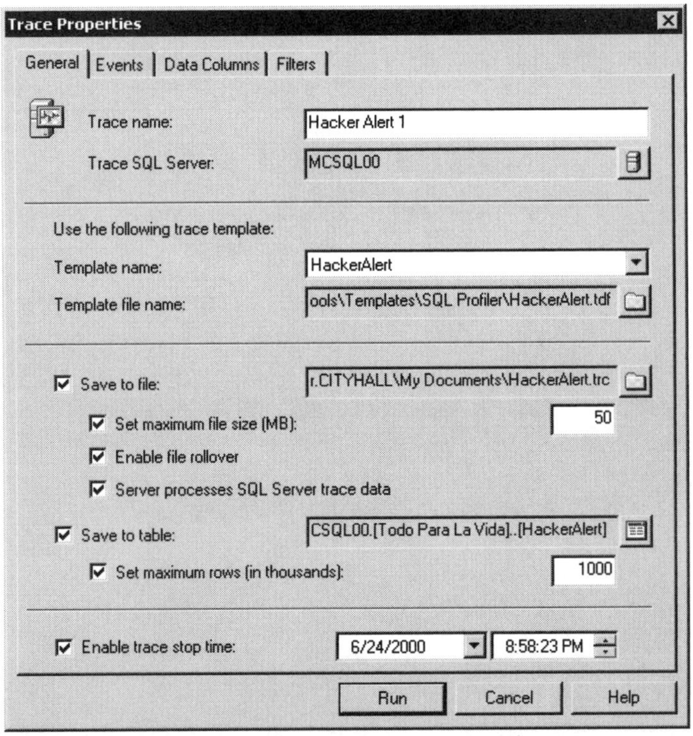

Figure 8-24. *The Trace Properties dialog box*

HackerAlert_1.trc, the third *HackerAlert_2.trc*, . . . ad nauseam. The trace begins when you click Run. The activity in the profiler is illustrated in Figure 8-25.

You can also save the data to a table, as demonstrated in Figure 8-26. I thought this was such a cool feature I ran it for a week on my Todo Para La Vida test site (a call center in Miami). When I logged in to check it out, the server was running very slowly and I noticed at once that the problem was the audit log building a mega–audit trail database like the "I Love You" virus out of control. The way around the overhead of this useful

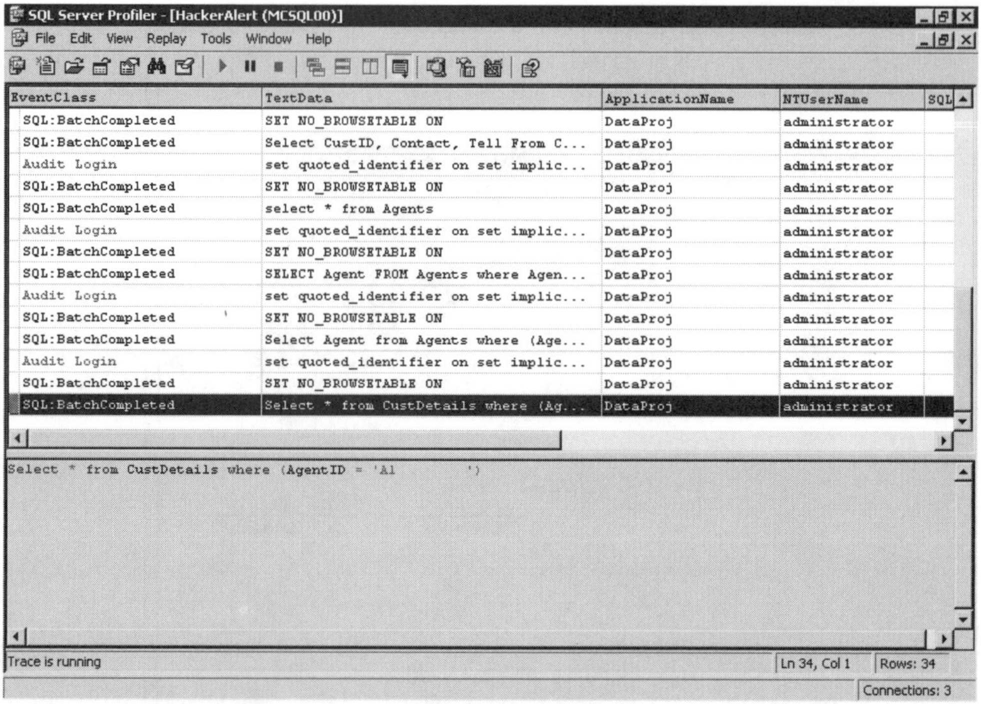

SQL Server Profiler - [HackerAlert (MCSQL00)]

File Edit View Replay Tools Window Help

EventClass	TextData	ApplicationName	NTUserName	SQL
SQL:BatchCompleted	SET NO_BROWSETABLE ON	DataProj	administrator	
SQL:BatchCompleted	Select CustID, Contact, Tell From C...	DataProj	administrator	
Audit Login	set quoted_identifier on set implic...	DataProj	administrator	
SQL:BatchCompleted	SET NO_BROWSETABLE ON	DataProj	administrator	
SQL:BatchCompleted	select * from Agents	DataProj	administrator	
Audit Login	set quoted_identifier on set implic...	DataProj	administrator	
SQL:BatchCompleted	SET NO_BROWSETABLE ON	DataProj	administrator	
SQL:BatchCompleted	SELECT Agent FROM Agents where Agen...	DataProj	administrator	
Audit Login	set quoted_identifier on set implic...	DataProj	administrator	
SQL:BatchCompleted	SET NO_BROWSETABLE ON	DataProj	administrator	
SQL:BatchCompleted	Select Agent from Agents where (Age...	DataProj	administrator	
Audit Login	set quoted_identifier on set implic...	DataProj	administrator	
SQL:BatchCompleted	SET NO_BROWSETABLE ON	DataProj	administrator	
SQL:BatchCompleted	Select * from CustDetails where (Ag...	DataProj	administrator	

```
Select * from CustDetails where (AgentID = 'A1        ')
```

Trace is running | Ln 34, Col 1 | Rows: 34 | Connections: 3

Figure 8-25. *Running a trace in Profiler*

feature (a searchable audit trail) is to either limit the number of audit counters (I captured everything) or redirect the data to another instance of SQL Server. Incidentally, a special database server, exclusively for audit trails, is not uncommon in mission-critical data center, often required by service level agreements, to maintain logs.

For more information on the security audit event counters, see SQL Server Books Online.

C2 Audit Requirements

Should your data center application require C2-level auditing (or if you want to ensure auditing occurs), you can specify that your server start auditing on all databases as a general DBMS configuration.

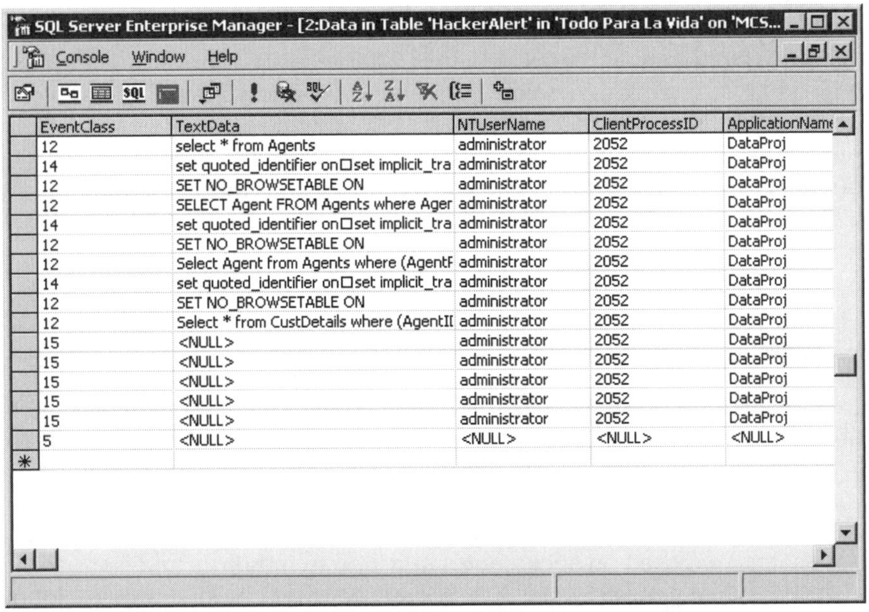

SQL Server Enterprise Manager - [2:Data in Table 'HackerAlert' in 'Todo Para La Vida' on 'MCS...

Console Window Help

EventClass	TextData	NTUserName	ClientProcessID	ApplicationName
12	select * from Agents	administrator	2052	DataProj
14	set quoted_identifier on□set implicit_tra	administrator	2052	DataProj
12	SET NO_BROWSETABLE ON	administrator	2052	DataProj
12	SELECT Agent FROM Agents where Ager	administrator	2052	DataProj
14	set quoted_identifier on□set implicit_tra	administrator	2052	DataProj
12	SET NO_BROWSETABLE ON	administrator	2052	DataProj
12	Select Agent from Agents where (AgentF	administrator	2052	DataProj
14	set quoted_identifier on□set implicit_tra	administrator	2052	DataProj
12	SET NO_BROWSETABLE ON	administrator	2052	DataProj
12	Select * from CustDetails where (AgentII	administrator	2052	DataProj
15	<NULL>	administrator	2052	DataProj
15	<NULL>	administrator	2052	DataProj
15	<NULL>	administrator	2052	DataProj
15	<NULL>	administrator	2052	DataProj
15	<NULL>	administrator	2052	DataProj
5	<NULL>	<NULL>	<NULL>	<NULL>

Figure 8-26. *Writing trace data to an SQL Server table*

There are two ways to enable this:

1. Run the SQL Server Properties dialog box from Enterprise Manager (as discussed in Chapter 7). Select the instance, then the Properties menu item, and then the Security tab.
2. Or run the stored procedure *sp_configure* to change the C2 security parameter to *C2 audit mode* (setting the value for C2 mode to 1). You need to set Show Advanced Options to 1 before you can change the audit mode.

If you need to bypass C2 Audit Mode the next time you start up, you can restart the instance with the –f flag. The flag can also be set in the SQL Server Properties dialog box as explained in Chapter 7.

If you set C2 auditing to the "All" option (see SQL Server Properties), it may have significant impact on server performance. Chapter 13 provides several advanced options you can use to minimize the impact of auditing in particular and profiling in general.

The SQL Server Security Plan

It should be clear to you now that SQL Server 2000 security is no simple matter. No matter how small or large your project might be, just blindly attacking logins, roles, permissions, users, and so on is a futile exercise that, while it seem easy enough in the beginning, can lead to certain chaos if not based on a solid security plan.

The architecture of SQL Server 2000 warrants that you divide the plan into two sections. One section deals with DBMS security, and the second section deals with data security. Splitting the plan according to the two priorities like this makes it easier to manage a complex security environment, to "divide and conquer" so to speak.

DBMS Security Plan

Locking down a DBMS is not an easy thing to do when you need to make sure that your authorized users do not have to walk the length of the Great Wall of China just to log in. Many applications typically require a user to first sign into the local area network and then again into the database. This means that you are forcing the user to remember two passwords. Such a scenario often leads to blank passwords or passwords that get exposed on sticky notes attached to monitors and so forth.

You will thus save yourself—the SQL Server security administrator—a lot of hardship by relying on the security mechanisms available to you in the external environment. The following items should be considered in the formulation of your own DBMS security strategy:

- Upgrade to Windows 2000
- Use Kerberos security and discontinue NTLM security
- Deploy IPSec and SSL in high-security environments
- Use middle tier or proxy services
- Create SQL Server login groups
- Use group policy with organizational units
- Formulate server role assignment policy

Database Security Plan

Your database security plan requires you to identify all elements in the internal environment of the DBMS that can be mustered to protect data from theft and destruction. You will also need to formulate or recognize business needs that dictate that some data, or aspects of data, need to be made available only to workers that need it to perform their jobs.

Some aspects of data security can be achieved programmatically. Other aspects can be achieved by using the tools provided by Enterprise Manager or using the administrative APIs, such as SQL-DMO, discussed in the previous chapter. The following items must be considered in devising your database security plan:

- Formulate database DBA role assignment policy.
- Create user-defined database roles to protect database objects.
- Identify columns within a database that share similar security requirements.
- Identify logins that share similar security requirements.

In Review

The DBA has his or her hands full when it comes to the question of security. There are many areas to consider as we discussed in this extensive chapter. We do not only have to focus on the internal aspects of data security, such as who has access to what database objects, tables, views. and so on, but also what takes place in the outside world.

From this discussion, it is patently obvious the DBA assigned with security will require a good background in issues including network or distributed security, encryption, security protocols such as SSL and Kerberos, Access Control and Authentication theory, and so on. In addition, I believe it essential that the DBA have a good grounding in Active Directory; in the management of users, groups, and organizational units; in trusts; in delegation; and so on.

In my book, the good DBA will have migrated from general network security, trained in all aspects, including access control, group policy, and user and group management in Active Directory. The DBA who started a career in SQL Server should thus make a concerted effort to certify or train in network security. Connectivity and a working knowledge of networking is not as critical. For example, I believe it is more important to have a good understanding of delegation than to know how to configure a router or a subnet. Chapter 10, however, deals with a number of issues requiring more networking acumen, such as configuring replication.

Chapter 9

SQL Server Disaster Recovery

Managing the disaster recovery plan for a data center is one of the most exciting roles in IT, if you like adventure, like bungee jumping or skydiving. I know this firsthand because I have been doing DR for some years now; you generally get the budget you ask for if the business's health absolutely depends on the servers you maintain (which is most of the time). In Miami, where I worked for some years, as soon as a hurricane watch goes into effect, the CEO hands the business to you. Now you're in charge and you had better have a good DR plan.

That said, disaster recovery is probably the DBA role that requires the toughest skin on an individual or a team. In businesses that can afford it, some DBAs do nothing else but manage DR and backup/restore. When disaster strikes, and it does, the future of the business, and everyone's job, is on the line. If you do things right and get the databases back online in record time, you are pretty much the darling of the company; if you fail you'll be out the door in the time it takes to spell "rollback." Over the years that I have managed DR, I have seen several SQL Server databases go to the wall, and several Exchange installations go south too, and dozens of smaller database corruption issues, and so on. You have to expect it; you have to plan for it.

While we recovered every time and saved the day (except one situation I will relate to you later), the most important piece of advice I can give is that you can never be fully prepared for your day in hell, no matter how much you practice. Many things can go wrong in the heat of disaster. I once had to ask a CEO to leave the computer room because I thought he was going to get sick all over my computers.

This chapter will introduce you to DR theory and how it applies to SQL Server 2000, especially with respect to backup and restore of SQL Server databases and their transaction logs. It will introduce you to the tools that ship with SQL Server 2000 and the recovery features inherent in the system. It will also take you step-by-step through several backup and restore procedures, and describe techniques and practices to ensure database and transaction log availability.

For the most part, this chapter assumes you are supporting a high-end data center application, and that recovery and restore will be automated and highly sophisticated. However, with this chapter you will also learn how to use the power of SQL Server's integrated visual backup/restore feature to manage smaller shops, in which you are required to perform daily backups, and to undertake manual recovery, such as by reentering lost transactions.

Establishing Baselines for Disaster Recovery

Establishing baselines is essential when it comes to assessing risk, managing disaster recovery, stopping loss, and so forth, no matter how big the database or how critical the application. When formulating a DR plan, no matter that you are starting from scratch or taking over from another DBA, it is critical to fully understand the business plan and the application's need for availability and service level. You thus need to establish the tolerance level for your enterprise or service to be without access to data and databases for a given time. In other words, how long do you have after a database goes offline, before the business begins to suffer serious harm? Many database or OLTP system clients do not understand their needs, so establishing a baseline is one of the most important exercises in a data center.

This might seem a frivolous activity, but it's not. You might think that all DR plans should aim to restore service immediately or at least very soon after failure. However, obtaining the dream of almost instant recovery requires a number of provisions. They include, in no intended order, trained DBAs, the right equipment, the right premises, the right demeanor, the right software, the right technology, and money. No doubt the last item is the most important one—a well-funded data center or contract makes life easy for everyone involved. In other words, establish the needs first and then see what you and SQL Server 2000 can do to rise to the challenge, while making sure you have the budget with which to fully implement the plan.

Baselines allow you to establish certain tolerance levels and then move out from there. For example, you might have service level agreements (SLAs) or quality of support requirements in place that will dictate requirements to you. A bank or an Internet ordering application will require a very different collection of DR ingredients than a casual order entry system.

Let's consider some base lines in terms of quality of support. First, you need to understand that no matter what technology or regimen you are using, you can only restore up to the point of your last complete backup and any available transactions that have been flushed to the transaction log file. The time from the last backup and the last duplication of the transaction log to the reception of a new transaction I refer to as *void time* or more precisely *void-backup time.* Some DBAs have called this the *transaction twilight zone*, the time just before a transaction is saved to the transaction log and saved from disaster.

I coined the term void time in the network administration realm to explain to users why the data or files they lost could not be restored to the last minute or second of their work. Void time is the useless time in which it is impossible, using conventional tape backup technology, to make a backup copy of a file. Backing up or duplicating data is a sequential process. The slowest technology, where the void time window is the widest, is tape backup. However, tape backup has the highest capacity for the least cost; the highest media safety, durability, storability, security, and so forth. The fast technology on the other end of the scale is a mirrored disk, but mirrored disks are expensive (if they are really large and fast) and have low security, storability, and safety attributes.

My aim in network administration is to narrow or close the void time window as much as possible using whatever technology is available at the time. The higher the value of the work, the easier it is to justify the cost of fast backup technology. Conversely, the lower the value of the work, the harder it is to justify the cost.

This means that unless you are backing up every millisecond of the day, it is very difficult, in the event of a disaster, to restore to the last transaction or commit point saved to the log. As you learned in Chapters 3 and 4, SQL Server can back up the databases and logs to local tape devices or remote disk files all the time. It costs the

DBMS some bandwidth—CPU and memory, but you need some powerful and expensive equipment to transfer data at terrific speeds to close the void time window as much as possible. This integrated feature of SQL Server backup is known as *active backup* in the industry, and SQL Server has demonstrated record-breaking capabilities for concurrent or active backup during highly active OLTP states, in the order of hundreds of transactions per second (TPS). So you need to understand what is possible and if it works for you and the application owner.

I established a collection of backup baseline parameters to help me determine and then establish the database owner's backup and restoration needs, and I have been refining this theory over the years. The order of the items in the list of baselines determines what can be considered adequate in terms of the age of tape or file backed-up databases and transaction logs. It helps the database owners focus on a restore level because often they are not fully informed about what is possible or what it will cost. They just tell you that losing even one transaction is a disaster without understanding what it will take to ensure zero transaction loss and 100 percent availability—neither is possible, really, because it is very possible for a system to crash when data is still in volatile memory and has not been written to the hard disk, where it can be swept up to the backup device.

Once I have established the loss-tolerance level—the baseline—with the owner, I work out how to cater to it for an individual system or application—the service level need—and the cost. First let's establish the critical nature of our backup requirement, an exercise in pigeonholing. Consider the following list:

- The backup is one month or more old. The database owner needs monthly and annual backup for archival purposes, analysis, or some legal requirement. Pretty standard stuff; probably backup of temporal data, a data warehouse and so on.
- The backup is between one and four weeks old. The database owner needs weekly backups for access to analysis data and possible rollback of the database to a certain point in time. Also pretty standard stuff . . . any inexpensive tape device will work.
- The backup is between four and seven days old. This is the same as number 2, but the rollback period is days and not weeks.
- The backup is between one and three days old. The database may have become corrupt and the database owner requires a restore of a recent backup. The lost of data can be easily or cheaply recovered. This is not standard stuff any more. You require the establishment of a rotation scheme, backup windows, and schedules.
- The backup is between 6–12 hours old. The lost data costs more to recover, but the database owner cannot afford to wait longer than a day, nor can he or she afford to return to a state older than 12 hours. The lost data of the past 12 hours can be manually recovered. We are getting onto delicate ground with this option. Backup/restore management is now a daily chore requiring operator duties and daily log reports, typical data center jobs.

- The backup is between two and five hours old. The database owner cannot afford to return to a database state older than five hours. The database must be brought current before the close of business. This involves data center operations, 24 × 7 attention of operators, access to DBAs via beepers and e-mail, and so on.
- The backup has captured all transactions saved to the transaction log files in the past sixty minutes. The database owner cannot afford to lose more than an hour's worth of data. We now need highly sophisticated backup/restore operations, hourly backups, warm standby servers with log shipping (see Chapter 13), and so on.
- The backup has captured the last transactions saved to the transaction log files. The database owner cannot afford to lose any transactions up to the point of system or database failure. There is usually little chance of manually getting back lost transactions. We now need full-blown active backup, with redundancy and fail-over architectures to ensure that all transactions can survive a disaster.

If you look at the list, you can safely say that levels 1–5 address very low transaction traffic situations and that any crash of a database or loss of the database server after the last backup will not cause the business serious harm. Such environments are typically order entry (not order taking) scenarios, and lost data can usually be recovered at low cost . . . manually reentered if need be.

Cost, of course, is relative. To lose a staff member for the day to rekey information is itself a costly exercise. Losing the day's data may mean little to one company, but a lot to another (my motto is "time lost is life lost"). If you feel you should be at a higher level, but you or the database owner can only afford a lower level, you may be dating disaster, risking a critical application on a shoestring budget—something to think about if you outsource to data centers or roll your own. If you are supporting a low transaction rate application, however, backing up databases overnight is usually not a problem, because no new data is entered to the database until the following business day. You are usually safe as long as you diligently perform backups.

From level 6 to level 8, you start to get into a gray area that requires careful attention to human and technology resources. At level 8, full or differential database backups will not capture the most recent transactions, because you'll need to be duplicating transaction logs at the same time the transactions are being flushed to the primary log. Some method of duplicating transaction logs to the last commit point is thus required. On online transaction processing systems, especially order-taking systems on the Internet, the loss of even one transaction can mean the loss of a customer. One lost customer can cause significant collateral damage.

SQL Server 2000 has the mechanisms to continue backing up data all the time it is in use, but as with any system, this can cause significant load on the server if you don't have sufficient bandwidth, both network and backup device capability. However, it is not so much the backing up or duplication or replication that takes time, but also the restoration of the lost server or the lost database, or hard disks and so on. When you get into a situation that dictates that you cannot afford to lose any transactions written to a transaction log, you might as well stop at level 6 with respect to tape backup and restore because you cannot achieve the higher levels with conventional tape backup practice (remember even a restore of the most recent backup still takes time to execute). Continuous or very aggressive conventional backups of both databases and transaction logs is not going to put you back in business seconds or minutes after meltdown.

In this regard, we might then revisit the list and classify levels 1–5 as archival or general availability backups. This means that you treat the backups as necessary only to restore a database to a certain point in time, after which time the data is not there or is bad. Levels 6–8 then require an alternative classification in terms of database access.

Levels 6–8 need to address three needs:

- **Requirement 1, Focus on availability** The system must be back online as soon as possible so as not to lose any new transactions. For example, a customer on the Internet finds he or she cannot make a transaction or place an order and goes elsewhere if the situation persists longer than a few seconds. Money lost. At this level, you are already into automatic failover systems for service level.
- **Requirement 2, Focus on transaction recovery (disaster recovery)** All transactions written to the log up to the disaster "event horizon" need to be recovered. In other words, being offline is not as critical as losing transactions.
- **Requirement 3, Equal attention to availability and transaction recovery** We need both the availability level of requirement 1 and the disaster recovery functions of requirement 2, or the application or service will not fly. The risk of transaction loss is just too high, as is being offline.

If requirement 1 is the baseline you are dealing with, then you (the DBA) and the database owner (and you could be both) need to investigate redundancy options, such as warm server standbys, mirrors, replication, and failover clusters. Your options here fall under the industry terms and practices of *high-availability*—the proactive arm of service level management.

Transaction loss due to media or data file failure is not usually an issue with requirement 1. The system goes offline, and at the point of failure no further transactions come in. You still have your database, and you still have your transaction logs. Hard-disk crashes are dealt with using RAID-level hardware, as discussed in Chapters 6 and 13, so having the most current database available when services come back up is not an issue. The issue is how quickly the actual system, the server and the hardware, returns to operational state.

If requirement 2 is the baseline you are dealing with, then you need to consider having highly available backups or duplicates of your data and transaction logs. In other words, as soon as a hard disk crashes or a database gets destroyed or a system gets destroyed, you would need to rapidly restore to the last transaction in the transaction log prior to the disaster. You would likely need both warm standbys and redundant hardware in addition to fully up-to-the-last-transaction duplicate copies of your databases and transaction logs. In requirement 2, the transaction log is the focus of your backup and duplication strategy, because only the transaction log and the safe backup or alternate duplication of it—its availability after a crash—can actually completely close the void time window for highly valuable OLTP-based systems.

Requirement 2 dictates disaster recovery procedures, but it is perfectly clear that the dividing lines between availability and disaster recovery are blurry and endure considerable overlap. To clearly see the two IT disciplines, think of DR as a reactive process, an after-the-crash reactive activity (like restoring from tape), and availability as proactive activity (making sure that, when the system does crash, the application can continue). When you need the services of both requirements 1 and 2, you are really looking at requirement 3, which will dictate what you need to meet both levels—disaster recovery and availability are in full swing.

There are many situations in which a company or a client will not need a fail-over service or a mirrored or redundant server as urgently as some data centers can provide. The database users or customers might be inconvenienced, but if they cannot go elsewhere, there is no need to go into warp drive to get the service back up. In other words, losing the service a few times a year does not constitute bad customer support.

A good example: A few years ago I won a contract from a state department to set up an online database system servicing a call center. Part of the RFP (request for proposal) was an application that allowed parents dependent on child support to phone a voice-activated system to obtain account balances and information about the status of their child support payments from the database. Agents on the back end were updating information as well as servicing callers with special needs on rotary dial phones. The RFP called for a duplicate call center to be established on the other side of the country. In my presentation, I advised that a completely redundant call center and database application would cost almost three times what a single center would, given the cost of the additional standby staff. I advised that it was a complete waste of money. It was not critical that the database never be offline for a day, because no one was losing money, a life, or sleep over not gaining access.

I cited the number of times the existing system was "downed" for service for several hours and sometimes longer than a day, without anyone complaining. In this situation, it is more critical to have up-to-the-last-transaction restorability because callers were actually updating information on every call.

What SQL Server 2000 offers in terms of system availability, as well as scalability, is covered extensively in Chapter 13, where we will look at log shipping as well. The rest of this chapter is dedicated to all DBAs that have lost their logs; it covers database and transaction recovery.

Transaction Recovery

I have been careful not to interchange disaster recovery with transaction recovery, because the latter deals mainly with SQL Server's capability to automatically recover transactions and restore the state of a database after a system crash. It has nothing to do with restoring data and backed-up, or otherwise duplicated, transaction logs.

Depending on how your backups are done and the nature of your backup technology, just starting up the disaster recovery process could take anywhere from ten minutes to several hours, spent reading the catalog, finding the right backups, and so on. In cases where backup media are off-site, you would need to take into consideration how long it takes after placing a call to the backup bank for the media to arrive at the data center. This could be anything from 30 minutes to 6 hours. And you may be charged for rush delivery.

Mission-critical disaster recovery, having backup media on-site, thus has to override the risk of data center destruction, fire, and theft. However, data center security has nothing to do with SQL Server 2000, so let's go direct to backup and restore options.

There is no question that you need a good tape backup environment with any server. For starters, you need to back up your system databases and schema catalogs as well, because that's where all system- or server-wide configurations, such as logins and maintenance plans, are stored. You also need to regularly back up your metadata repositories, data warehouses, and so on.

The most common form of backup is to a tape drive, and I will discuss the formats a little later in this chapter. The initial cost of a tape backup solution is really insignificant in relation to the benefit: the ability to back up and recover large amounts of data as quickly as possible. A good tape drive can run anywhere from $500 for good Quarter-Inch Cartridge (QIC) systems to $3,000–$4,000 for the high-speed, high-capacity Digital Linear Tape (DLT) systems. A robotic library system can cost as much as $30,000 on the low end and six and seven figures on the high end.

Let's now consider two classes of restoration. I came up with this data while managing DR for a score of data centers in the food distribution business. If Burger King were out of fries or Long John Silver out of fish, I would always call to find out if my servers were still up, so I decided to come up with a formula to help me relax while away from the data center. This data also helped get the database owners and me rowing in the same direction.

The following list defines levels of database and transaction log restoration in terms of currency (was this the last transaction written to the log, or close to it?):

- **Zero loss (0)** Transactions in the transaction log must be the last transactions taken before failure. In other words, you have zero tolerance for transaction loss (see Chapter 2 for information on transaction log management).
- **Ten minutes loss (10)** Transactions received from real time back to ten minutes can be lost. It is thus acceptable to lose 10 minute's worth of transactions. The client process or order entry person can reenter the transactions.

- **Sixty minutes loss (60)** Transactions received in the first hour can be lost. It is thus acceptable to lose one hour's worth of transactions.
- **Three hundred and sixty minutes loss (360)** Transactions received in the last six hours can be lost.

The next list assumes you are at one of the preceding levels, but it defines how quickly you need the databases and transaction logs restored.

- **Zero wait (0)** Transaction log restoration is required in real time (now). Let's call this the *critical restoration* level.
- **Ten minutes wait (10)** Restore is required within ten minutes of losing the databases and transaction logs. Let's call this *emergency restore.* (By the way, loss could mean total loss as well as bad data.)
- **Sixty minutes wait (60)** Restore is required within one hour of losing the databases and transaction logs. Let's call this *urgent restore.*
- **Three hundred and sixty minutes wait (360)** Restore is required within six hours of losing the databases and transaction logs. Let's call this *important restore.*
- All other restores that can occur later than six hours could be considered *casual restores* and are not factors for this exercise.

If we now look at both scales, we can establish a database and transaction log restoration rating in terms of an acuity index that considers the two scales: the highest level being 0/0 (zero loss for zero wait time to online status) and the lowest level being 360/360 (six hours to get back to online state, and restored data should be at the most six hours old at the time of disaster). It is no accident that the index sounds like a course in optometry. I felt it gave both the DBA and the database owner a "vision" of what was expected to be met on the service level agreement.

You can then present this index to a database owner, with the key of course, and then agree to the terms to meet the agreed-upon backup/restore acuity index. Figure 9-1 shows this in a visual hierarchy.

The pyramid in Figure 9-1 illustrates that the faster the response to a transaction log or database restore, the higher the chance of restoring poor data. Each layer of the pyramid covers the critical level of the database or transaction log backup. This does not mean that critical transaction log restores are always going to be a risk, or that the restored transaction logs are flawed. However, it shows that databases or transaction logs backed up closest to the point of failure are more likely to be at risk compared to data that was backed up hours or days before the failure. If a hard disk crashes, the data on the backup tapes is probably sound, but if the crash is due to corrupt data or bad data (which might not cause system failure), the likelihood of bad transaction log data is going to be high closest to the point in time of the crash, and you'll need to consider restoring to a safe point in time (discussed later).

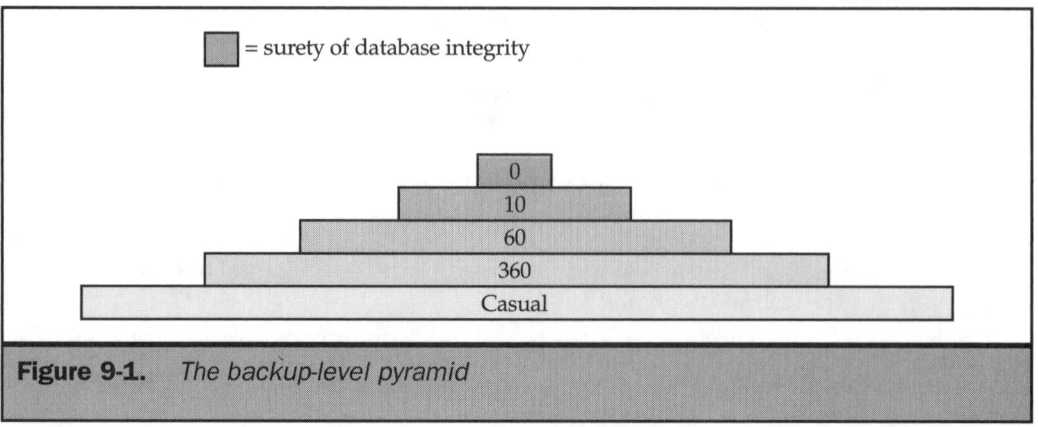

Figure 9-1. *The backup-level pyramid*

Another factor to consider is that often you'll find that the cleanest backup data is the furthest away from the point of restoration, or it is the most out-of-date. In other words, your soundest database or transaction log backup media may in fact be miles away, one hundred feet underground, in a vault.

In 1999, just prior to Y2K, I was maintaining backups of several SQL Server systems. But I was not required to check database consistency or database health. The database owner kept me out of the system except when I needed to monitor the backups or check on the schedules. One fine day the database went bad, really bad. A bunch of users somehow turned life in the easy lane upside down for the database owner. The DBA responsible for the integrity and consistency of the databases in question had me go back more than seven days to find backups that were healthy. By the time we found clean backups, the loss was running wild. The entire on-site backups for the week were corrupt (that was on a SQL Server 6.5 system, in case you were wondering). I started the restore process, and the DBA left to find a rope.

SQL Server 2000 Recovery Architecture

Before we can use the acuity index I discussed earlier and derive backup plans to meet an agreed-upon index, let's see what SQL Server 2000 is made of.

Past and present transaction log architecture in SQL Server allows the DBMS to recover to the last commit point written to the transaction log just before or at a system crash. As discussed in Chapter 2, the transaction log is a *write-ahead log*, so any committed transaction written to the transaction log (flushed from the main memory buffers of the DBMS) can be recovered upon system recovery and permanently committed to the database. Naturally this recovery process depends on the availability or consistent state of the transaction log after system recovery.

As soon as the system recovers, the DBMS rolls back all transactions that failed due to the collapse of the system, which is determined by built-in mechanisms that ensure the atomicity of the transactions. Client processes will thus be allowed to represent the transaction (I discuss how in later chapters that discuss distributed transactions, transactions in message queues, and so on). Transactions that survived the crash are committed to the database.

SQL Server 2000 introduces advanced recovery architecture to this DBMS platform in the form of recovery models. The recovery model centers on the transaction log as the object or mechanism of recovery, as mentioned earlier, that can restore to the last commit point written to the transaction log. The recovery model is really a transaction- and operation-logging mode (I am not sure why Microsoft calls it a model) that determines how much and what data is written to the transaction log and how it is used in recovery. The recovery model also determines how successful the transaction log will be in recovering the transactions between actual full and differential database file backups up to and including the last transaction written to the log.

There are three such recovery models in SQL Server 2000: *full*, *bulk-logged*, and *simple*. Table 9-1 discusses the attributes and benefits of each model.

Recovery Model	Attributes	Benefits	Transaction Loss	Recovery
Full	Logs all transactions. Optimized for high-end OLTP systems.	Can recover to any point in time after database backup.	None, if the transaction log file is available.	To any point in time up to the last written transaction in the write-ahead log.
Bulk-logged	Optimized for bulk operations (BCP, BULK INSERT, and so on). Minimal log space is used.	Permits high-performance bulk operations with a recovery safety net.	None, if log is consistent and recovered or bulk copy is not the cause of the damage.	To the end of the last database and transaction log backup.
Simple	Optimized for low-end OLTP and database operations, and high-performance bulk operations.	Keeps log footprint small in bulk copy or insert operations because log is not normally backed up.	None, if log file installs consistent data to the database.	To the end of the last database backup.

Table 9-1. *SQL Server Recovery Models*

Recovery models are set for a database as soon as the system is installed or a new database is created. The recovery model set for the *model* database is *full*. This does not mean that every time you create a database it will inherit the *full* setting installed for *model* (see Chapter 2). New databases created in Enterprise Manager are usually set for simple recovery. Changing the recovery model is done through the ALTER DATABASE statement using T-SQL as follows:

```
ALTER DATABASE <databasename>
SET RECOVERY [FULL | BULK_LOGGED | SIMPLE]
```

To determine the recovery model set for your database, you can query the setting in the `DATABASEPROPERTYEX` property of the database as follows:

```
SELECT databasepropertyex('<databasename>', 'recovery')
```

You can also change the recovery model on the Options tab of your database's Properties dialog box. But don't go looking for radio buttons marked "recovery model" on the Options tab; you will not find them. To change the recovery option on the Options tab on your database Properties dialog box (setting database options is fully discussed in Chapter 7), you need to set the following options in the "Settings" group, which is illustrated in Figure 9-2:

1. **To set the database to full recovery** uncheck the options "Select into/bulk copy" and "Truncate log on checkpoint." (In earlier versions of SQL Server, these options precluded the backup of a transaction log.)
2. **To set the database to bulk-logged recovery** check the option "Select into/bulk copy" and uncheck the option "Truncate log on checkpoint."
3. **To set the database to simple recovery** check the option "Select into/bulk copy" and check the option "Truncate log on checkpoint." You can also uncheck the "Select into/bulk copy" options if you are not using any bulk copy or SELECT INTO procedures.

Understanding the Recovery Models

Let's now examine the so-called recovery models a little closer.

The *full recovery model* provides the greatest recoverability possibility for line-of-business OLTP operations. It is thus ideally suited to meet our 0/0 acuity index as discussed earlier. In other words, we get the fastest and safest or most complete restore and recoverability of data if the database operates under full recovery. The *full recovery model* also provides you with the greatest flexibility in terms or recovering a database to any point in time after the last full or differential backup.

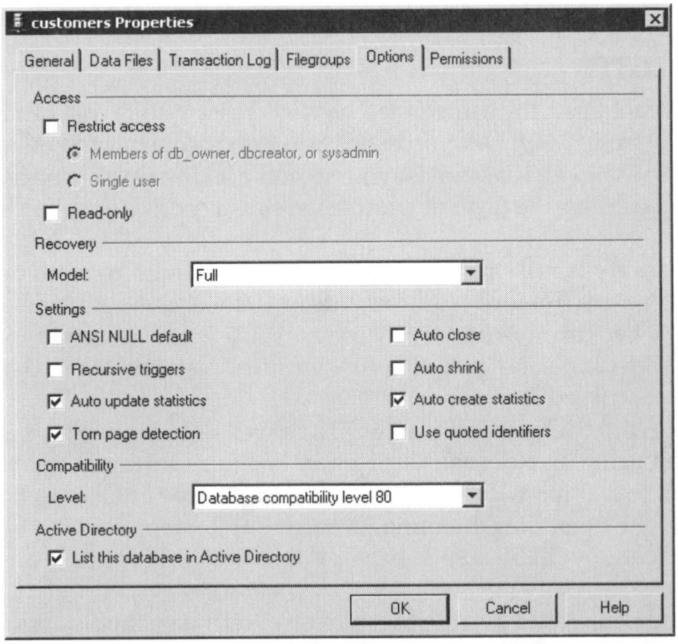

Figure 9-2. *The Database Properties, Options tab*

The *bulk-logged recover model* was engineered for recovery under bulk-copy or BULK INSERT operations. The transaction log writing algorithms have been optimized for speed and log space reduction for operations such as CREATE INDEX and BULK COPY.

The *simple recovery model* is the easiest way to back up SQL Server databases because no transaction log backups are done and the transaction log is maintained in such a manner as to ensure the simplest recovery from server failure. After log truncation, log space is no longer needed for system recovery (after the transactions have been committed to the database) and the log space is reused.

Obviously you have a higher risk of data loss if a database is damaged or lost during normal business operations. However, most LOB applications do not need the more critical recovery models because backups are usually done during the night in any event. Also, a high-level backup/restore acuity index will not apply to "simple" data entry because the business will determine that to manually recover and reenter data costs far less than the technology to close the void time backup window.

SQL Server 2000 Backup and Restore Architecture

SQL Server 2000 contains a fully integrated backup/restore suite that can also be driven programmatically from T-SQL. Microsoft has also provided a built-in interactive backup suite in Enterprise Manager that can get you up and backing up as soon as you start doing business or finish configuring (actually you never finish configuring, but you know what I mean).

The backup utility is fully functional and flexible enough to configure mission-critical backup/restore requirements or to meet the demands of an SLA demanding a 0/0 backup/restore acuity index. With the functionality you have now, you can plan an adequate and cost-effective backup/restore plan to deal with the fatalities earlier discussed.

Using the internal backup facilities of SQL Server 2000 for backups is far better and cheaper than using an external, third-party backup solution. Even the smart new Backup program that ships with Windows 2000 will not be able to do the job. The reason is simple: the open files dilemma. When a database and its log files are in use, no external application will be able to back up the files, because they are essentially in use by the DBMS.

The only time you would be able to make an external backup of the database is when everybody is out of the database and the DBMS is shut down (all services have been stopped). There are third-party products that are able to back up open database files, but they are expensive and not as integrated as SQL Server's internal backup utilities. Products like ARCserve from Computer Associates and BackUp Exec from Veritas can back up online databases. They work well for one or a few servers, but they become very expensive and clunky when dealing with many servers and hundreds of databases. In short, SQL Server Backup provides as advanced an active backup solution as you'll need, possibly the most advanced in the DBMS industry.

SQL Server's backup allows you to back up databases while they are in use. Granted, you will see a drop in system performance, which you might choose to improve with more hardware, and faster tape drives, and some other techniques I will later discuss. Naturally, SQL Server will prevent any backups from going ahead while database alterations are taking place. Such activities include the following:

- Automatic or manual database size changing
- Object creation or deletion
- Index creation or deletion
- While performing nonlogged operations

If you start a backup and one of the preceding processes takes place, the process bows out with an error. If the process starts before the backup or restore, the backup or restore process bows out with an error.

That you can back up a database while it is in use means you have a lot more flexibility in your backup schedules and a lot more possibilities of performing backups on a continuous basis as opposed to off-peak times, or some ungodly hour in the middle of the night.

Types of Database Backups for SQL Server 2000

You have several backup options to consider with SQL Server 2000, depending on your DR Plan and the baselines you have set for the data center. The following list categorizes these options:

- **Full database backup** This operation just backs up the database files, which would include all the committed transactions. Before the data gets transferred to the tape, SQL Server makes sure data in the transaction log is committed to the database.
- **Transaction log backup** This operation just backs up the transaction logs. However, the transaction log backup should be part of all database backup operations for full recovery.
- **Differential database backup** This operation just backs up the portions of the database files that have changed since the last full backup, or since the last differential backup.
- **File/filegroup backups** This operation allows you to make the target of your backup a filegroup, rather than a database or a transaction log.
- **Snapshot backups** This operation allows you to take snapshot backups, which are very high speed backups that can be accomplished with specialized hardware and software.

Table 9-2 lists the backup types in relation to the model options.

Model	Full Database	Database Differential	Log	File Differential	Snapshot
Simple	Required	Optional	Not allowed	Not allowed	N/A
Full	Required or file backups	Optional	Required	Optional	N/A
Bulk Logged	Required or file backups	Optional	Required	Optional	N/A

Table 9-2. *The Backup Models That Apply to the Different Backup Types*

Full Database Backups

A full database backup backs up the entire database. The DBMS makes copies of all database objects, users, roles, tables, and so on. You can perform a full database backup using Enterprise Manager, or you can program the backup facilities in the DBMS directory using T-SQL.

When the backup events fire, the DBMS flushes the data pages in memory to disk and then starts copying the data to the backup device assigned to the job. Any transactions that take place in the system after the backup starts are not backed up as part of the database backup. To back up the "late" transactions, you next need to back up the transaction logs.

Transaction Log Backups

The only way you can restore to the last transaction before disaster is by backing up the transaction log, and the transactions in the log might not include any transactions that come in while the log is being backed up. In many respects, you can think of the transaction log as the incremental backup of the database, because in order to restore the entire worth of data (all transactions installed to the database and all transactions still in the transaction log that have not yet been installed to the database), you would first have to restore the full database and then restore the transaction log. Transaction logs are thus only useful with full and so-called bulk-logged data.

In large systems that have a huge amount of transactions underway, the transaction log at times may take longer to back up than the database. In very large systems, the transaction has a tendency to grow to huge proportions, so you will need to balance your transaction log management requirements with your backup requirements, lest what you do for one countermands what you do for the other.

Transaction log backups are a must in the following situations:

- You cannot afford to lose any data between the last database backup and the point of failure.
- You want to return the database to a specific point in time, say 10 minutes before meltdown. It is also possible to restore to a database state a day ago or even a week ago by restoring a database from an earlier backup set (see the "Backing Up SQL Server" section later in this chapter) and then restoring the transaction log recorded soon after that time.
- If the databases are constantly changing, your database backups will become outdated very quickly. Some applications work with a database of a relatively constant size but in which the data changes frequently. A good example is an air traffic information system where for any given day the number of flights for the day remains constant but the arrival and departure information is constantly changing.

- Backing up the transaction log forces some cleanup in the process because the operation truncates the inactive portion of the transaction log for you as part of the backup process.

Transaction Log Backups in Practice

First, the transaction log backup can only work when it is part of a full or bulk-logged recovery model (see the section "SQL Server 2000 Recovery Architecture" earlier in this chapter). Second, backing up a transaction log will only serve a purpose if it is part of an unbroken sequence of transaction log backups, which are made after every full or differential backup. If you lose a transaction log backup, if you miss it, or if your backup media get destroyed, you will have to start the backup set from scratch and start backing up the transaction logs all over again.

Truncation and the Transaction Log Backups

As discussed in Chapter 2, the DBMS truncates inactive portions of the transaction log. The inactive portion of the log is already committed to the database; therefore the "dead" portions of the log are no longer needed.

Truncation is something you define in your management of the DBMS and the database, and it is something you can do manually. However, the DBMS performs truncation automatically after a transaction log has been fully backed up, so any manual truncation would cause problems with the automatic truncation that occurs after backup.

Understanding truncation log checkpoints is key to managing a backup/restore plan. Accordingly, please see Chapter 2 for both the theory and management of transaction logs.

When Not to Back Up Transaction Logs

The following rules apply to the backup of transaction logs:

- You should not back up a transaction log until a full or differential backup has successfully completed.
- If you have manually truncated the log just after performing the backup, you will have to back up the database again and then back up the transaction log.

Differential Database Backups

The SQL Server differential database backup only backs up the portions of a database file that have changed since the last database backup. It is important to understand that the meaning of the term "differential" is that the first differential backup has to compare the full backup to the database file, while subsequent differential backups are based on what has changed from the last differential backup.

You should also know that the differential backup is not a substitute for the transaction log backup. If you lost a system seconds after performing a differential backup, you will still have lost all transactions in the log that were not written to the database file on disk. Again, no matter how powerful your system, the latency between receiving the transaction and flushing it out to the transaction log on disk cannot be resolved by any backup technology (see "Establishing Baselines for Disaster Recovery" earlier in this chapter).

Differential backups should be used for backing up data in the middle of regular transaction processing time (and the full backup should take place off peak with longer intervals). On big systems receiving huge amounts of new data and data changes every day, a differential backup may seem like a full backup. In some situations a full backup might be very difficult to do on a huge database, even in the middle of the night.

Use the differential under the following circumstances:

- A small percentage of the full database changes every day.
- You need to perform more regular backups of your databases, possibly during regular hours with users logged in.

You might find that the transaction log backup is more suited to your needs for regular backups, especially during heavy or peak periods of online activity.

File/Filegroup Backups

A file or filegroup backup works just like a database backup, but your target object to be backed up is not the database, per se, but a file or collection of files that could reside anywhere on your network. (See "Filegroups" in Chapter 2.)

In this respect, backing up filegroups is similar to performing a SQL Server 2000 backup using an external backup program that has built-in open files capability. Such backup programs, such as ARCServe, also manage the backups of the transaction logs needed for the backups.

Why perform a filegroup backup? Depending on the technology used, there's one very good reason. File or filegroup backups and restores may be quicker to perform than regular backups. A very busy database, processing millions of transactions a day, may take forever to back up a database. This is not an uncommon problem in a busy data center, and database backups have often run into the next day, interfering with regular operations. If you have three filegroups, it might be quicker to back up a separate filegroup each day. In other words, you would have to back up each filegroup every third day. You would still have to back up your transaction logs on a daily basis in order to make a full restore to the point-in-time failure.

File or filegroup restores, on a piecemeal basis are also possible. For example, if you lose a drive holding a filegroup, one of many drives holding your spread of database files, you can just restore the files or filegroups that went with the disk. Backing up and restoring files and filegroups is, however, tricky. You should practice on development databases or filegroups or do pilot filegroup backups on dummy databases. You must also be fully conversant with filegroup management because it can be easy to blunder both the filegroup management and the backups (see Chapter 11 for more information on filegroups).

Snapshot Backups

The idea of a snapshot backup is a simple one. Think: "smile, say cheese, and snap" and you've got the idea. But in order to take a "photographic" image of a database, the DMBS must allow a process to come in and take the snapshot. Essentially what the snapshot means is that the entire image of the database and the log files is (almost) instantly duplicated and then placed onto tape or another disk.

SQL Server 2000 supports snapshot backup and restore, but the snapshot hardware and software are usually provided by independent hardware and software vendors, such as Computer Associates (ARCserve). SQL Server provides the necessary hooks in its backup/restore API, and it includes a virtual backup device, to allow a third party to come in and snap away, while it is fully operational.

The snapshot backups drastically reduce and practically eliminate the need for server resources to accomplish high-speed active backups. And as discussed earlier, this is very important for very large databases where availability is critical. The primary benefits of the snapshot backup are as follows:

- The snapshot backup can be created in seconds, with little or no impact on the server (depending on the hardware and software used).
- The snapshot can be restored just as fast, with little or no impact to the server (depending on the hardware and software used).
- You can back up to tape from another server without having to impact the production system.
- You can use the snapshot to very quickly create a copy of the production database for reporting, testing, or data transformation.

The snapshot backups function and provide the same features as the other type of backups discussed. And the transaction logs can be used with them just as they are with the standard full backup. Backup, restore, tracking, and cataloging takes place as if the backup were a standard backup.

Why then would you not use the snapshot backup and restore functionality all the time? The reason would be cost. The backup devices and software can be very expensive. But for very large databases or in mission-critical situations, the costs are discounted against the need to have 0/0 service level acuity, as discussed earlier.

You can also create your own snapshot backup software. SQL Server 2000 ships with example C++ source code that demonstrates the snapshot backup and how to use the virtual device interface.

Backup Devices

Three types of backup devices are defined by SQL Server 2000: disks, named pipes, and tape.

Disk Devices

The disk device is not a backup device in the same sense that a tape drive is. It is really a location, a file, on a hard disk or storage area network to place a backup file, which is the same object that gets stored on a tape cartridge. I am not sure why Microsoft called the backup file a disk device, but it is an unfortunate choice of nouns. (Windows 2000 Backup calls it a file. A file is a file in my book, so just don't go looking for any disk devices when you really need to be supplying the name of a file.) Microsoft did tell me they might drop this word by the next version.

You can back up to a file on any remote hard disk or other device (such as optical storage) on the network. All you have to do in the backup script or in Enterprise Manager is define a UNC path to the drive of your choice. Naturally, SQL Server will need permission to access the destination through share points and the appropriate permissions.

Why would you want to back up to a remote disk, and plop a huge backup file on it? For starters, you might want to back up that file to an external backup library (discussed next) because SQL Server backup only works on locally addressed devices (they have to be physically attached to the server). Naturally you need your brain scanned if you back up to the same disk on which your database filegroup resides. If you lose the disk, you're history.

Tape Devices

Tape devices are the safest and fastest means of backing up SQL Server databases; however, there are few limitations.

The tape device you are using must be physically connected to the database server. This is a limitation that I think drives a number of DBAs back out to third-party vendors for their backup solutions because data centers typically prefer a centralized backup solution, using a robotic tape library. And if you scale out to multiple servers, every server will have to have a tape device. If you are using high-end devices like DSS or DLT, you could easily throw a few thousand dollars or more at each server. In such a scenario, if you still want to use SQL Server Backup, you will have to back up to the file "device" and then sweep that file up into an external tape drive. The only limitation I see with such a solution is that to restore the database, you first have to restore the file to the location you originally backed it up to (which will cost some time).

The backup functionality does not integrate with Windows 2000 Removable Storage, so you cannot program in operator alerts and other helpful bells and whistles like media management.

Later in the chapter, I will discuss backup bandwidth and suitable backup tape formats supported on Windows NT or Windows 2000.

Named Pipes

The named pipe facility is a mechanism that will allow you to write your SQL Server database backups out to the named pipe. The data is then "piped" to a third-party application that can pick up the feed and sweep the backup into an external device, such as a database library discussed in the next section.

Using named pipes is obviously not an option in Enterprise Manager because it is a routine that you have to expressly call in your T-SQL code.

Device Names

A backup device name is the "handle" SQL Server assigns to a logical or physical backup device. The device can either be a file on the disk, an actual tape drive, or some means of storing data. The device name is an alias or nickname that you can use to reference in your backup scripts. For example, the code

```
BACKUP DATABASE Customers TO DISK =
'C:\Backups\Customers\FullBackup.Bak'
```

backs up the Customers database to the FullBackup file device, named Path\FullBackup.bak.

Backing Up SQL Server

There are several approaches to backing up SQL Server. First, you can use the Backup options in Enterprise Manager. This is SQL Server's interactive option that can get you started doing database backups from ground zero. Second, there is the noninteractive attack on the DBMS API using T-SQL. Third, you can use the SQL-DMO object model, which publishes a backup object and a restore object that access the same API as with the T-SQL approach (see Chapter 14). Fourth, you can go with a third-party vendor, but this book is not the forum to discuss the last option. If you're a whiz at T-SQL, then you may find the programmatic approach to be extremely powerful, and if you want to build your own backup application or user interface in Visual Basic or Visual C++, then go the object model. But let's first deal with Backup in Enterprise Manager because that is the easiest approach and the one most non-DBA database owners and many DBAs will use (and it is adequate in most circumstances).

Using Enterprise Manager to Back Up SQL Server

The steps to take to create local simple backups of SQL Server databases or transaction logs are as follows:

1. Create the backup device.
2. Create a backup job. The backup job is managed by SQL Server Agent, which is discussed in Chapter 12.
3. Create a schedule to run the job.

If you are new to SQL Server backup, before proceeding, you can do your initial backups using the Backup Wizard. This wizard is accessed in the Wizards dialog box under the Management Node—at Tools | Wizards in Enterprise Manager.

Create the Backup Device

The *backup device* is an object, albeit a virtual one, that maps to a physical entity the Backup program will use to save the backup to. As mentioned earlier, the device can either be something with moving parts in the local machine that the Microsoft Tape API can talk to, or it can be a file that can be written to on any addressable hard disk medium on the network. (See the section "SQL Server Backup Bandwidth" later in this chapter to determine the resources needed to write the backup files out to a network disk.)

Remember that you cannot use SQL Server Backup with a tape drive unit attached to a remote machine. You also need to leave at least 10MB free for the backup image (over and above your other needs, of course) on the hard disk where the SQL Server binaries are installed. If the DBMS cannot find free space, the backup will fail.

To create the Backup Device, perform the following steps:

1. Drill down to the Backup node under Management on the DBMS instance to which your target databases are attached (see Figure 9-3).
2. Right-click the Backup node and select New Backup Device. The dialog box in Figure 9-4 loads.
3. In the Name field, provide a name to identify the device. This is a logical name and should be easy to work with both interactively and programmatically. The example in Figure 9-4 was entered with tongue in cheek to illustrate the difference between the logical name of an actual device and the name you will give to a backup file. The name should be simple if you plan to address it in T-SQL code.
4. Now check the radio button option "Tape drive name:" for a (mechanical) tape device or the radio button option "File name:" if you are backing up to a file. If you checked the option to back up to a file, you also need to provide a path to the file location. You can use the UNC notation in this field as well.
5. Now click OK to create the device. If SQL Server is unable to find the device or the filename provided on the path, it will report that you need to cancel the

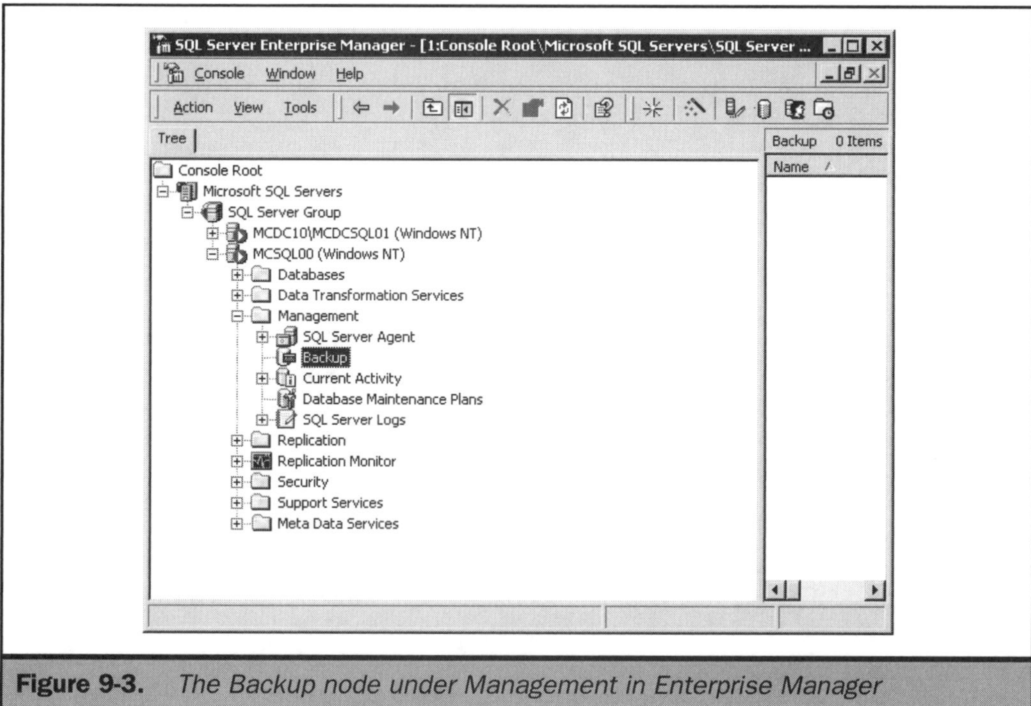

Figure 9-3. *The Backup node under Management in Enterprise Manager*

operation and reenter a valid filename. You can ignore the error and move on if you plan to create the device later, but you are better off creating it now.

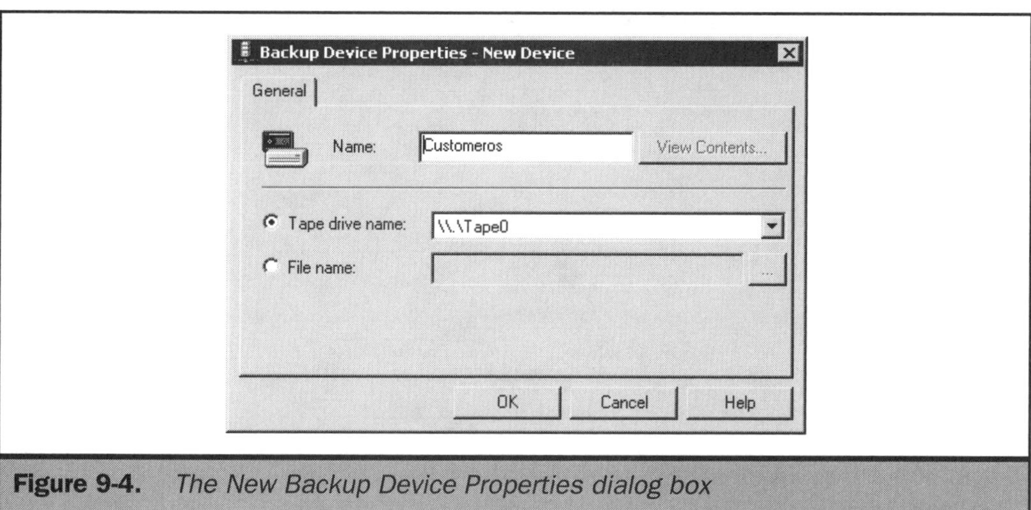

Figure 9-4. *The New Backup Device Properties dialog box*

The newly created device will appear in the details list in the Enterprise Manager console. You can change the name of the device at any time by selecting the entry in the list. If you need to change from a file device to a tape device, you will need to create a new device and recreate your backup schedule.

Create a Backup Job

Creating the backup job requires several steps. You need to determine if your backup job is going to be a full backup or a differential backup, whether to append to the media or overwrite existing media, and whether to run the job once only or schedule it to repeat at regular intervals.

If you are going to work to a full-differential rotation scheme, described later in this chapter, you'll need to create two jobs, one to run the full backup once a week, and one job to run the differential backups every day. Depending on your needs, you may have to create a third job to run transaction log and file or filegroup backups as well. You might find yourself very busy here, but the sooner you get cracking, the better.

To create a backup job, drill down to the Backup node in Enterprise Manager as described for creating a backup device. Right-click Backup and select the "Backup a database" option (this option is also available on the Tools menus as "Backup database." The SQL Server Backup dialog box loads, as illustrated in Figure 9-5.

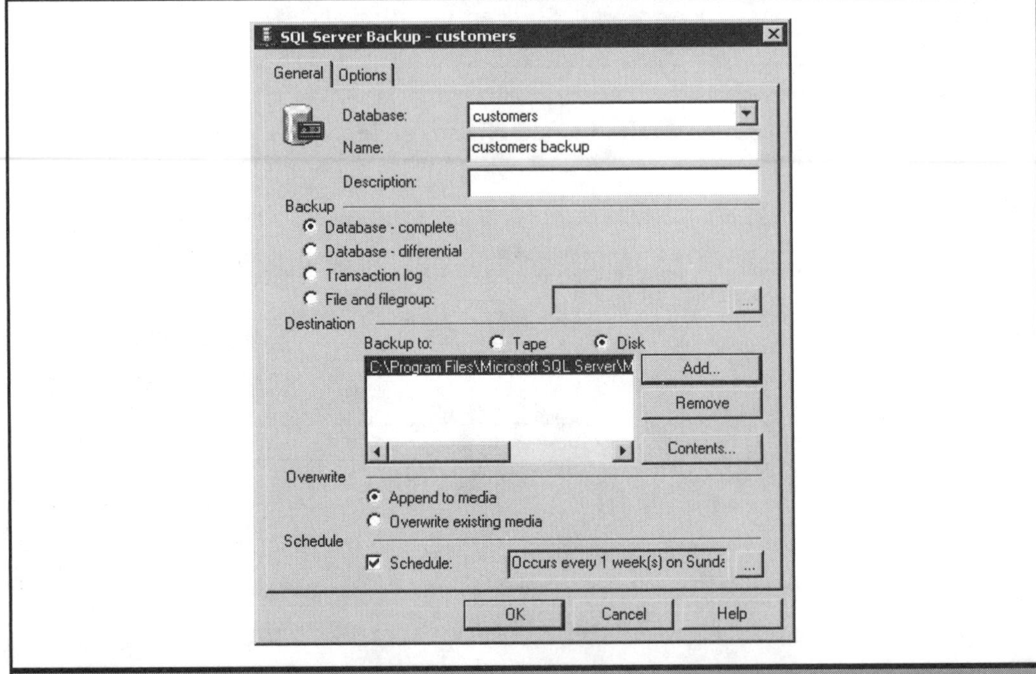

Figure 9-5. *The SQL Server Backup dialog box, General tab*

On the General tab, you need to set the following:

- **Database** Choose your database in the drop-down list.
- **Name** Provide a name for the backup; use anything you like or go with the default if that is convenient. This information gets written into the header section of the backup data. It will make it easier to find your backups in a disk or tape device when you need to restore.
- **Description** Provide a description of the backup job. This information is also written to the header of the backup data and is used to identify or manage your backups. It is not essential but makes backup life much easier.
- **Backup** Check the radio button that applies to the type of backup you need to do—complete (full), differential, transaction log, or file or filegroup. If the transaction log option is disabled, the database is probably in simple recovery mode (model), which does produce transaction log backups. The same limitation of simple recovery applies to file or filegroup backups. To obtain all four backup options, you need to set the recovery model on the target database to full (see "SQL Server 2000 Recovery Architecture" earlier in this chapter).
- **Destination** Check the radio button that applies to the destination device for your backup. You have two choices: Tape or Disk (file). To add devices to the "Backup to" list, click the Add button (or click Remove to drop devices). If you click "Add," the Select Backup Destination dialog box shown in Figure 9-6 loads.
- **Overwrite** Check the radio option to either append to the media or overwrite the media. If you choose the option to overwrite the media, then the options on the Options tab to create and manage the media set will become enabled.
- **Schedule** Check the Schedule check box to enable the schedule option. I discuss setting up schedules shortly.

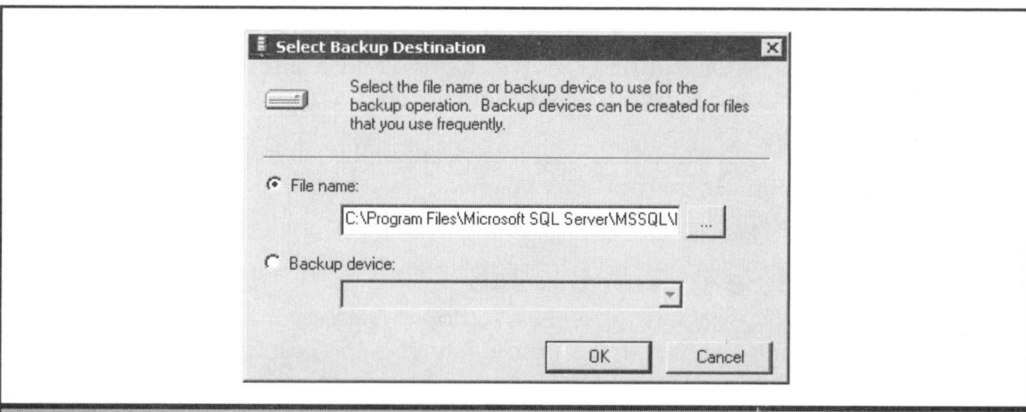

Figure 9-6. *The Select Backup Destination dialog box*

On the Options, tab you need to set the following options:

- **Verify backup upon completion** Depending on your needs, you might be better off using the appropriate DBCC command described in Chapter 12. Verification can be somewhat resource intensive and will lengthen the time it takes to complete your backups.
- **Eject tape after backup** Checking this option causes the tape to eject after the backup operation. This helps ensure that another process does not come around and overwrite the backup you just completed. The option is disabled for obvious reasons if you are backing up to a file on a disk.
- **Remove inactive entries from the transaction log** Check this option to clean up the transaction log after a backup. You can safely check this option, even after a database backup, because the DBMS will not flush any transactions that have not been installed or written to the database.
- **Check media set name and backup set expiration** This option checks a media set for a queue to use the media. The information is obtained from the header information in the backup data on file on or tape. If you check this option and the media expiration date has not passed, you will not be able to use the tape. Use this option to protect the backup rotation sets described later in this chapter. To use this option, you must supply a media set name in the enabled field.
- **Backup set will expire** Check this option to specify a day after a certain date that allows the media set to be used or overwritten by Backup. The option will be enabled if you chose the overwrite option (which is the same as initializing new media) on the General tab. You can choose to free the media up to 999 days "After" the backup, or you can free the media on a certain day entered in the "On" drop-down list, which means any suitable date in the next few millennia.
- **Media set labels** Check the Initialize and label media option to enable the fields "Media set name" and "Media set description" (see the section "SQL Server Backup by Design" later in this chapter, which discusses SQL Server 2000 media sets and families).

At this point, if you click OK you will be scheduling the job to run immediately or without a schedule. You can go back to the General tab and select the Schedule option or continue with the default.

Create a Schedule to Run the Job

If you check the Schedule option, the ellipsis button is enabled and you can create or edit a job schedule. Clicking the ellipsis button launches the Edit Schedule dialog box illustrated in Figure 9-7.

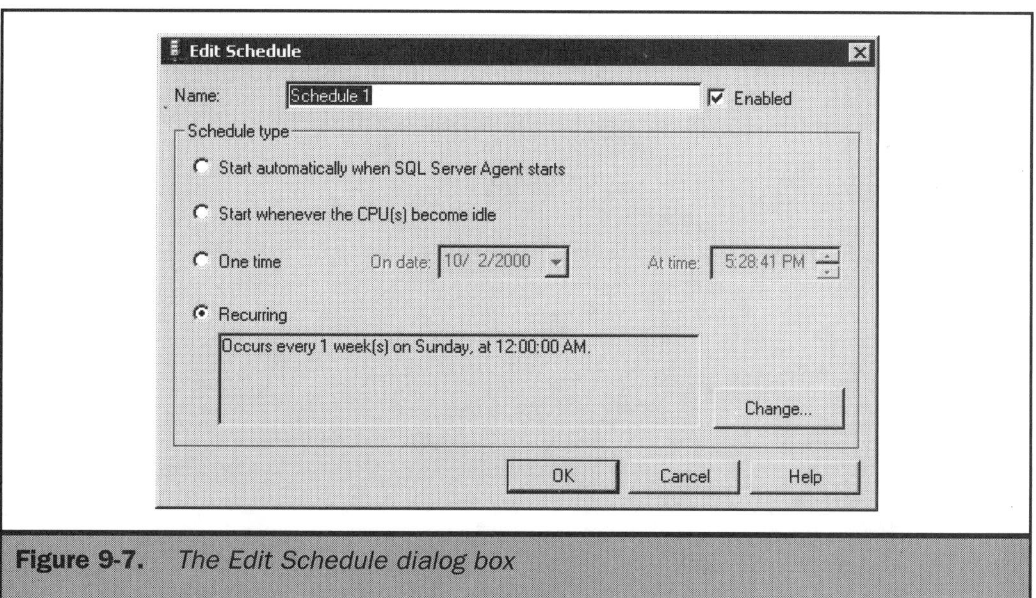

Figure 9-7. *The Edit Schedule dialog box*

To create the backup schedule, do the following:

- **Name** Enter a name for the schedule (you will have to check the Enabled button to enable the schedule).
- **Start automatically when SQL Server Agent starts** Check this radio option to start the backup when SQL Server Agent starts up.
- **Start whenever the CPU(s) become idle** Check this radio option to start the backup when the system is idle. You would check this option if you had a good reason not to start backups during system load.
- **One time** Check this option to start the backup at the time and date provided in the "On date" and "At time" fields.
- **Recurring** Check this option to start the backup according to a recurring schedule, such as a backup rotation scheme that you have set up. To create the recurring schedule, click the Change button. The Edit Recurring Job Schedule dialog box loads, as illustrated in Figure 9-8.

  Setting up a recurring job schedule is straightforward. You have the choice of choosing daily, weekly, or monthly schedules (a GFS rotation scheme can thus be set up right here. See "Rotation Schemes" later in this chapter). Depending on the radio button you choose, the option in the group box to the right lets you set up the daily, weekly, or monthly backup days. The daily frequency lets you

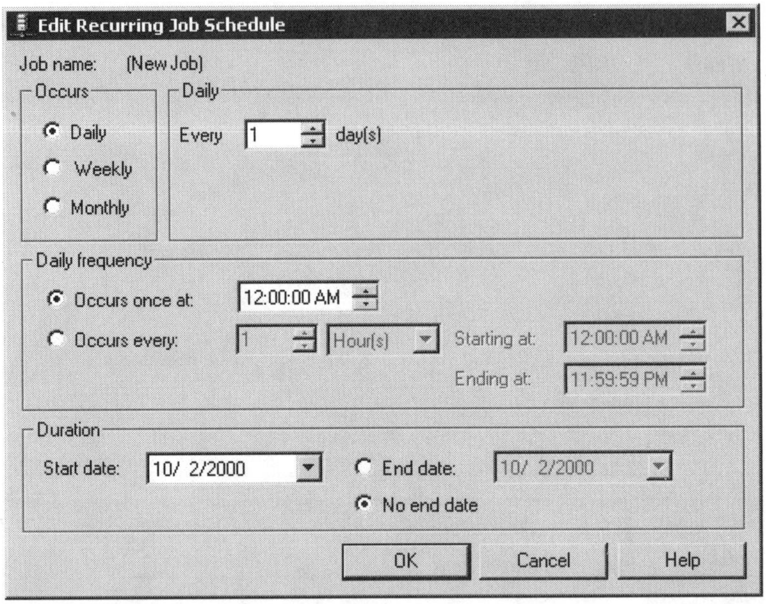

Figure 9-8. The Edit Recurring Job Schedule dialog box

specify the time of day to start the backup or regular intervals that can start and end at certain times of the day. The Duration options specify how long the recurring schedule remains in effect or if it continues indefinitely.

Using Enterprise Manager to Restore SQL Server

To restore a database, go to the Tools menu in Enterprise Manager and select the option "Restore Database." This option is not available on the Enterprise Manager tree under Management as database backup is—don't ask me why. The Restore database dialog box loads, as illustrated in Figure 9-9.

To restore a database or transaction log, you need to perform the following on the General tab:

- **Restore as database** Choose the database to restore in the drop-down list. The list can be written to, so you can provide a new name, essentially a new database, for the restore. This is a useful feature that allows you to restore a database to a new DBMS where it did not exist before.

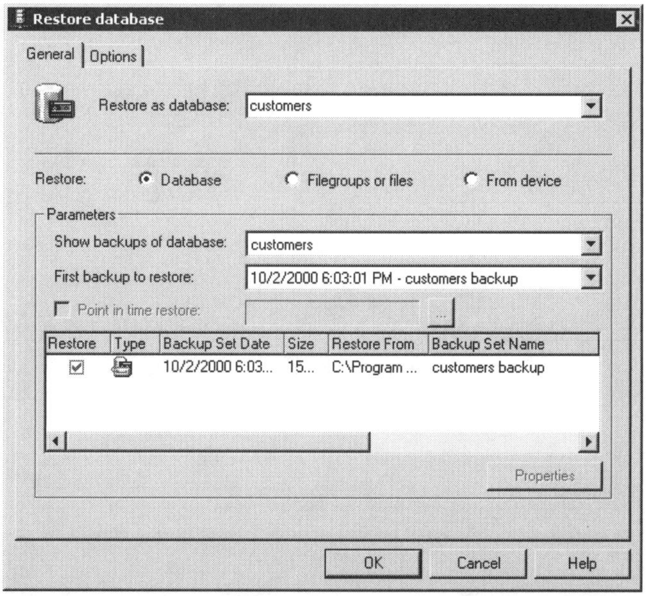

Figure 9-9. *The Restore Database dialog box*

- **Restore, Database** If you choose this radio option, the Parameters group box lets you select a database and obtain its backup history, which has been cataloged. You can then choose the backup to restore.
- **Filegroups or files** If you choose this radio option, the Parameters group box lets you select a backup of files or filegroups, which have been cataloged. This is the option you'll choose to restore your transaction logs. The "Selection criteria" loads the Filter Backup Sets dialog box as illustrated in Figure 9-10 to allow you more control over the selection of the backup sets.
- **From device** If you choose this radio option, the Parameters group box lets you select a device for the restore, and to select a backup that was made to each device. You can choose a tape device or, as discussed earlier, a file device.

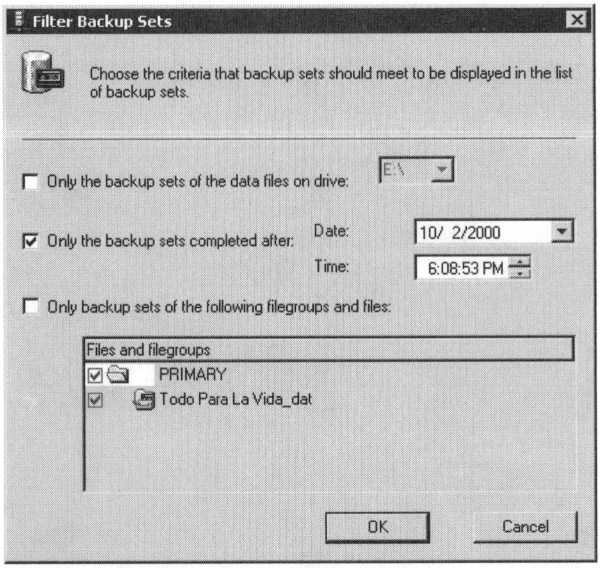

Figure 9-10. *The Filter Backup Sets dialog box*

To set additional restore options, click the Options tab on the Restore database dialog box. The contents of the tab are illustrated in Figure 9-11.

Parameters on the Options tab are as follows:

- **Eject tapes after restoring each backup** This option forces the restore process to automatically eject the tape from the tape device at the completion of the restore. This obviously does not apply to restores derived from files.
- **Prompt before restoring each backup** This option forces the restore operation to prompt you after each backup completes. You would use this option if all the restores were coming from one device or one cartridge and you wanted to cancel after the first full and the third differential restore. By having the prompt continue to pop up after each restore, you will be able to cancel before the fourth differential.
- **Force restore over existing database** This option forces the restore to automatically overwrite the existing database.
- **Restore database files as** The grid on the Options tab is related to this option, which lets you change the name and path of the restore target. You need to select the files in the left column (logical file name) and provide a new name and path in the right column (move to physical file name).

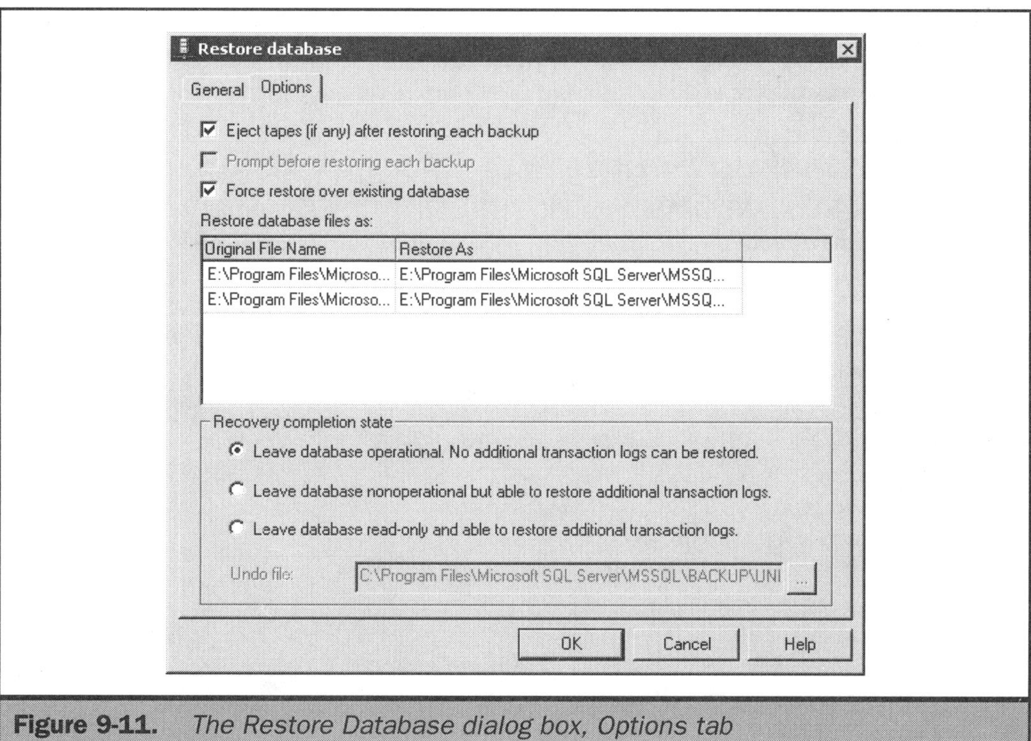

Figure 9-11. *The Restore Database dialog box, Options tab*

- **Recovery completion state, "Leave database operational"** This option completes the entire restore process and processes the transaction log as part of the restore feature. This restore will require you to restore all your databases and applicable transaction logs as part of one process. After the restore is complete, the database and transaction log state is considered final and ready for use, and no additional transaction logs can be restored.
- **Recovery completion state, "Leave database nonoperational but able to restore additional transaction logs"** This option is the opposite of the preceding one. After the restore, the database is nonoperational and you can still restore additional transaction logs.
- **Recovery completion state, "Leave database read-only and able to restore additional transaction logs"** This option allows you to restore the database, permit it to be operational but only for read-only access, and still be in a position to restore additional transaction logs. These options are important for log shipping functionality and maintaining standby servers as discussed in Chapter 13.

After you have provided all necessary parameters and you decided on the option, click OK to begin the restore. You will be notified by the DBMS whether the restore completed successfully or failed.

Using T-SQL Backup Scripts

The T-SQL BACKUP DATABASE and RESTORE DATABASE commands are very powerful and provide all the facilities you need to program extensive scripts that can completely replace the Backup/Restore facility provided by Enterprise Manager, as just discussed. The syntax for the two commands is extensive, and you should reference them in SQL Server Book Online. The following code provides an example of a simple backup script and an example of a simple restore script:

```
-- Create a backup device for customers.
USE master
EXEC sp_addumpdevice 'disk', 'CustomersD',
   'c:\Program Files\Microsoft SQL
Server\MSSQL\BACKUP\Customers.dat'
--Create a log backup device.
USE master
EXEC sp_addumpdevice 'disk', 'Customers_logD',
   'c:\Program Files\Microsoft SQL
Server\MSSQL\BACKUP\Customers_log.dat'
-- Back up the full Customers database.
BACKUP DATABASE Customers TO CustomersD
-- Back up the Customers log.
BACKUP LOG Customers_log
   TO Customers_logD

RESTORE DATABASE Customers
   FROM CustomersD
   WITH NORECOVERY
```

It is well worth your while becoming proficient in T-SQL backup scripts because once you are expert, backup and restore scripts can be easier to manage then the same process in Enterprise Manager. The scripts can also be executed automatically by SQL Agent. In many facilities or data centers, you will be required to have T-SQL capability to code backup/restore scripts. The next section, which examines point-in-time restore, includes more advanced restore scripts as well.

Restoring a Database to a Point in Time

It is possible to restore your database to a certain point in time in the transaction log or to a named mark in the transaction log. Let's say a careless programmer does a database update and updates 10,000 rows of data instead of ten (trust me, it happens). You then need to restore the database to a point in time just before your lazy hacker hit the ENTER key and all Hades imploded.

To accomplish this task, you need to recover the database to the exact point in the transaction log before disaster struck. To do this, you need to examine the transaction log header information of each transaction log backup or the information in the *backupset* table stored in *msdb*. From these sources, you can easily and quickly find the backup set that contains the time to which you recover your database. All you then need to do is apply transaction log backups up to that point.

Before you start, remember that you cannot skip any transaction logs, because this would destroy the integrity of the data in the database. You also have to consider that there might be transactions that came in after the disaster. Sometimes the errors are discovered only after a huge number of good new transactions were committed to the database. Also, the transactions that you want to undo might compromise what appear to be good transactions that were accomplished on bad data. For example, computations, aggregations, row identification, defaults, and the like may no longer be viable after you remove or alter a huge bunch of records, and you will thus have to redo them. The process is as follows:

- First restore the last database backup but do not recover the database.
- Next restore each transaction log backup in the same sequence in which they were created, recovering each database after each transaction log restore.
- Finally recover the database to the desired point in time within the final transaction log backup.

Point-in-Time Restore Using Enterprise Manager

To restore to a point in time using Enterprise Manager, do as follows:

- Drill down to the server and then drill down to the target database. Right-click the database and select All Tasks.
- Next select Restore Database (or choose Restore Database from the Tools menu). The Restore Database dialog box loads.
- Enter or select the name of the database to restore, that is, if it differs from the default in the edit field. Check the Database radio button in the Restore option.

- Now in the "First backup to restore" list, select the backup set to restore. In the Restore list that follows, select the database backup and one or more transaction logs to restore.
- Check the "Point in time restore" check box and then enter the Date and Time obtained from the catalog.
- Finally, go to the Options tab, and make sure the option "Leave database operational. No additional transaction logs can be restored" is selected.
- Click OK to run the restore.

Point in Time Restore Using a T-SQL Script

To restore to a point in time using a T-SQL script, your script needs to code the following:

1. Execute a RESTORE DATABASE statement using the NORECOVERY option.
2. Execute a RESTORE LOG statement to restore each transaction log backup. The restore needs to specify the following:
   - The name of the database against which the transaction log will be applied.
   - The backup device holding the transaction log backup.
   - The RECOVERY and STOPAT information. This information is required in the point-in-time script; if it is missing or wrong, the restore will fail.

The following is an example of a point-in-time restore script of a database to its state as of 9:00 A.M. on Oct 9, 1998; it demonstrates the restore operation involving multiple logs and multiple backup devices:

```
RESTORE DATABASE Customers
   FROM CustomersD
   WITH NORECOVERY
GO
RESTORE LOG Customers_Log
   FROM Customers_LogD
   WITH RECOVERY, STOPAT = 'Oct 9, 2000 11:19 AM'
GO
```

Hardware and Media Formats

Choosing hardware and media depends on the applications, the size of the data pool or resources, the size of the network (number of servers), the number of users, the critical nature of the data, and so on. In multiserver environments, you would be best off looking to invest in a tape library system. These sophisticated devices cost an arm and a leg (anywhere from $6,000 to $35,000), but what you will save in time and frustration, as well as speed of restore is worth it. Other choices of backup media include writable compact discs, remote storage volumes, and removable disks, such as zip disks and flopticals.

4mm Digital Audiotape (DAT)

The 4mm Digital Audiotape (DAT) is widely used in all business sizes and is one of the most popular technologies. It comes in three formats: DDS-1, DDS-2, and DDS-3—which allow you to back up 2GB, 8GB, and 12GB respectively. One DDS-3 tape can store as much as 24GB with high-end hardware compression.

A drawback of the DAT format is that the header is read every time the tape is used for backups or restores, which makes the format less sturdy than its competitors. A single tape will likely survive 300 or more runs, and that would be fine for daily backups, but you may be at risk using DAT when backing up continuously.

Another problem with DAT is that the cartridge is small and made of thin plastic. So it does not take much to break it. I have had DAT media stuck in the tape drives several times, and I have often seen an operator walk away with a tape leaving a trail of black streamer trailing behind.

DAT stores data in diagonal stripes across the medium. The data is laid down using helical scan technology, which is achieved by rotating a drum head across the media surface.

8mm Digital Audiotape (DAT)

This is an improvement over the 4mm version just discussed. The 8mm format holds up to 40GB of data, with hardware compression running at 2:1. The 8mm DAT format is fast, typically backing up 40GB of data in under five hours. Big DAT maker Sony's AME tapes are the most popular on the market. They are high-performance cartridges and very reliable.

The 8mm cartridge, however, also needs to be handled with care in a busy data center. Dropping them onto the floor and then standing on them can easily ruin the tape. The hardware can also be unkind to the media. It is not uncommon for tapes to get stuck inside the drives.

Digital Linear Tape (DLT)

DLT is by far the most popular tape format for high-end server operations and data centers. It is fast, reliable, and very hardy, and you can store a lot of data on a single high-end version of the format, upward of 70GB. DLT is a Quantum format, which was introduced in the mainframe, mid-range, and UNIX platform arena. The adoption of DLT in Windows database server environments has accelerated the success of the medium, and most high-end servers from the likes of Compaq, HP, and IBM include a DLT driver in their products.

DLT comes in several versions: DLT 2000, DLT 4000, DLT 5000, and DLT 7000. Capacity is 10GB on the low-end format (2000) to as much as 70GB compressed on the 7000 format. While DAT tends to be a faster technology, many manufacturers have introduced high-speed SCSI interface library systems capable of holding many drives and providing technology to deliver backup/restore on a continual basis.

The DLT cartridge is very tough, which make it ideal in busy data center environments where tapes are moved around in robotic library systems 24 × 7. Dropping a DLT cart or sending it flying across the data center floor will not make the slightest dent. DLT tapes can also be kept in service or storage for long periods.

DLT lays down its data horizontally along the tape in tracks, by running the tape across the stationary head, much like the recording technology in four- and eight-track audiocassettes.

DLT travels well, which is an important consideration if you manage a number of remote sites and they depend on you for supplies. I typically use retired DLT media, which might have another 50 runs of life left, to make final annual backups of a database. I then send the tape offsite into storage forever or when reference to old data is needed.

Advanced Intelligent Tape (AIT)

For extremely large quantities of data, very large databases (VLDBs), and continuous backups, the Advanced Intelligent Tape, or AIT, is the preferred format. A product of the Exabyte-Sony alliance, AIT tapes can typically stay in service for as many as 400 runs or backups per cart. Sony created a backup technology format for this medium called Advanced Metal Evaporated (AME). The material is tough and includes a carbon protective coating that keeps the tapes from melting in the high-speed drives. AIT is great, but it can be very expensive to add an AIT device to each server. The AIT medium is also very much more expensive than the tape formats discussed earlier.

AIT Tape libraries can support up to eight terabytes of data. So for speed and volume, this format is ideal for an online transaction system processing transactions in the tens of thousands per hour. An advanced version of AME consists of a small EEPROM chip that is housed in the cart. This chip holds backup information, cataloging, and backup/restore logs.

(QIC)

QIC is the acronym for Quarter-Inch Cartridge. It represents the most popular format for small business and is usually the only device carried by local mom and pop computer shops or superstores like CompUSA. The latest Travan carts (the T-series) can now back up as much as 8GB of data per cart. The casings are sturdy, usually held together by an aluminum back, making the format durable and easy to handle in situations where company servers are usually hidden in closets, pushed into office corners or onto factory floors, and so on.

QIC, however, does not scale to large systems. It is not a technology supported by magazine-loaded changers and robotic library systems typical of data center operations that use the DAT, DLT, and AIT formats. On the other hand, QIC hardware is very affordable, costing $400 or less for the top-of-the-line models, and the media are very affordable too.

I have several low-end database servers (one just prints labels) out at remote centers that each have a QIC tape in them.

SQL Server Backup Bandwidth

Bandwidth is an important consideration when backing up huge databases and extensive filegroups. For starters, forget about doing any significant backup over a WAN or Internet connection unless you have upward of a 1.5-Megabit pipe to the source; but this will still not work for critical high-end OLTP systems. Anything less, unless it is a very small filegroup, will not provide a suitable facility for backing up a SQL Server database.

I routinely back up over a 10Mbit Ethernet network. Most data centers have a 100Mbit backbone, and putting your servers directly on that is key. But even a 100Mbit backbone is only as valuable as the speed of the server bus, network links, and hard disk I/O, along with the capabilities of the backup devices and so on.

The minimum rate of backup you could expect over a 10Mbit network is between 15MB and 45MB per minute, depending on the backup device. Local tape drives on fast computers using SCSI technology and high-end hardware can even achieve levels of around 200MB per minute, and even higher rates on RAID systems and extremely high-speed disk arrays.

What you then need to do is work out how large a database file or transaction log you are going to back up and then figure out how long it is going to take you to back up the data. If the data is mission-critical, you may want to back it up more often. Remember, data changes every minute of the day. Database applications can see as much as 20 percent of the data changing on the low end and as much as 80 percent changing on the high end.

I have provided a very simple formula for you to work out how long it will take to back up your databases and log files. Let's say we want to back up X amount to a certain device in Y time. Starting with the desired unknown Y, you would want to first figure out how much data you are going to try to back up on the local machine or over the network device or named pipe. After you have calculated this, your equation will resemble:

```
Y = S / T
```

where Y = time, S = amount of data in megabytes, and T = transfer time of hardware (locally or over the network). The data transfer or backup rate of the DLT 7000 is around 300MB per minute (hauling data off the local hard drives). Thus, your equation would be

```
Y = 2000 / 300
```

and two gig would thus take just over six minutes to back up. Factor in another minute or more per 100MB for latency, cataloging, files in use, database updating, and so forth, and it would be safe to say that two gigs of data get backed up in less than ten minutes. Over the local area network, divide the transfer rate by a factor of ten, and the same two gigs takes over an hour to back up.

SQL Server Backup by Design

I included this section to help you understand management schemes and regimens that need to be built to support service level requirements . . . starting with some basic backup/restore concepts.

Practicing Scratch and Save

SQL Server 2000 does not support the concept of *scratch and save* sets directly, but it provides the facility, and you can code this logic into your T-SQL scripts. This is something you have to manually design. Remember that it is not really up to SQL Server to enforce how you manage your backup strategy. The DBMS only gives you the tools to perform a backup and to restore data, and to manage your media according to a scheme you devise. It is worth mentioning what a *scratch and save set* is because you should understand the terms for more advanced, sophisticated database backup procedures.

A *save* set is a set of media in the media pool that cannot be overwritten for a certain period of time, and a *scratch* set is a set of media that is safe to overwrite. A backup set should be stored and cataloged in a save set for any period of time during which the media do not get used for backup. You can create your own database in SQL Server that provides rotation information into and out of scratch and save sets.

The idea behind the scratch and save approach is to protect data from being overwritten for predetermined periods, according to your backup plan. For example, a monthly save set is saved for a month, while a yearly set is saved for a year. Later when the "safe" period of time has expired, you can move the save set to the scratch set and target it for overwriting.

Once a set is moved out of the save status into the scratch status, you are tacitly allowing the data on it to be overwritten, essentially destroying it. A save set becomes a scratch set when you are sure, through proper media pool management, that other media in the pool contain both full and modified current and past files of your data, and it is safe to destroy the data on the scratch media.

Save and scratch sets enable you to ensure that your media can be safely recycled. If you do not manage your media according to a scratch and save routine or schedule, you make every set a save set, which means you never recycle the tapes. This will risk tapes, because they will be constantly used and will stretch and wear out a lot sooner.

Rotation Schemes

A *rotation scheme* is a plan or system you use to rotate the media in your backup sets. At the simplest level, a rotation scheme is a daily or weekly backup using one cartridge. This is not much of a DR scheme, because you would be writing over the media every day. So in order to determine the best rotation scheme, you need to consider what you are doing with the backups: Are you just archiving, doing version control, backing up a state, or managing a disaster recovery regimen?

From this description, you can deduce that the three main reasons for backups are archives, version control, and recovery. Data in an archival state, or required for analysis, need not be located on-site and is kept for record-keeping, reporting, and decision support; data in a version control period is stored off- and on-site for access to full weekly generations of the data, and to be used to restore the databases to certain points in time. Data in the recovery period is stored both on-site and off-site and is either online or very near to the server.

Understanding Rotation Schemes

Let us now expand our rotation scheme. The first option would be to rotate the media every other day, so that you could be backing up to one tape while the alternate is in safekeeping somewhere. If the worst were to happen, a tape gets eaten by the device or something less common, you would still have a backup from the previous day. If the machine were stolen, you would be able to restore it. But rotating every other day is only useful in terms of total data loss. So you have a full backup of all your databases, every day. What about wear and tear? A tape or a platter is a delicate device. Inserting and removing it every other day and writing to it over and over can put your data at risk. Tapes do stretch, and they get stuck in tape drives. Tapes should be saved according to the scratch and save discussion earlier in this chapter.

And then what about version control? Rotating with multiple media, say a week's worth, would ensure that you could roll back to previous states of a database or to points in time. We could refer to such a concept of versioning as a "generation system" of rotation (not sufficient for critical restore, however). In fact, one such standard generation scheme is widely used by the most seasoned of backup administrators to achieve both the ideals described—versioning and protecting media from wear and tear and loss. It is known as the GFS system, or Grandfather, Father, Son system.

Let's create a GFS scheme to run under SQL Server 2000 Backup. Most high-end backup software can create and manage a rotation scheme for you, but for now you will need a legal pad. So now let's put a label on one of our tapes or disks and call it Full, or First Backup, or Normal # 1—whatever designates a complete backup of the system and collection of files and folders.

The first backup of any system is always a full backup, and the reason is simple. Backup, and you, need a catalog or history of all the files in the backup list so that you can access every file for a restore and so that Backup can perform differential analysis on the media. Do your backups according to the procedures we discussed earlier. You should have had enough practice by now. And you are ready to go from a development or trial backup to a production rotation scheme.

As soon as you have made a full backup set, label the members as discussed and then perform a second full backup (or copy the first). On the first backup set, add the following information to the label:

- Full_First: January 2001
- Retention: G (which stands for Grandfather) or one year, dd-January-2002
- Serial number: Choosing, or write some SQL code to generate it

On the second set, add the following information to your labels:

- Full_First: Week1-January 2001
- Retention: F (which stands for Father) or one month, Week1-February-2001
- Serial number: Choosing, or write some SQL code to generate it

On the next day, you need to choose a second set of media, but this time only the files that have been changed will be backed up using the differential option. Let's say we are doing differential transaction log or database backups for example's sake.

On the differential set, add the following information to the label:

- I_First (or a day of the week): Mon, or First
- Retention: Seven days or every Monday
- Serial number: Choosing, or write some SQL code to generate it

On the next day, put in a new backup set and perform the next day's differential. This time, the label information is Tues or "Second." Then retain these media in a seven-day save set and store them in a safe place. On Wednesday, perform the third differential and on Thursday, perform the fourth differential. Let's now look at what we are achieving:

We have created a Grandfather set that we store for a year. If we started this system in January 2001, we will not reuse these tapes until January 2002; the retention period is one year; these are the oldest saved versions of the databases you will have.

The second copy set is the Father set of the scheme, and this set gets reused in four weeks' time. In other words: Every four weeks, the set can be overwritten. This does not mean that we only make a full backup once a month. On the contrary: Notice that we made one full set and four differential sets, so we are making a full backup once a week and four "diffs" Monday to Thursday. We only retain the weekly set for a month, meaning that at the end of each month you will have five full backup sets, one set for each week, retained for a month, and one set for each month, retained for a year.

What about the differential sets? These sets are the grandchildren of our rotation scheme. We save them for seven days and return them for scratching on the same day the following week. So what we back up on Monday gets written over next Monday, Tuesday gets written over on Tuesday, and so on. This also means that at any given time, your people can access the previous day's data, the previous week's data, the previous month's data, and the previous year's data. What we have created here is a traditional rotation scheme for performing safe and accessible backups of SQL Server databases, for low-end OLTP systems typical of most businesses.

There are variations on this theme, and you will need more than just seven of whatever media you are using if you apply the schemes to transaction log backups. For example, for the full GFS rotation, you would need the following for a single server that used one DLT tape drive:

- Daily backups (differential, rotated weekly): 4+
- Weekly Full (rotated monthly): 4 +
- Monthly Full (rotated annually): 12+
- Total tapes: 20+

The best days for such a rotation scheme are Monday–Thursday, differential and Friday, full. Even on big systems, you're unlikely to be doing a differential into the following day. And on Friday, you have the whole day and the weekend to do the full backup, at a time when the system is most idle. You could start after the last person leaves on a Friday and you would still have about 48 hours of backup time to play with…besides, the databases in most businesses are unlikely to be used over the weekends or holidays.

Sleeping at Night

The life of a DBA is filled with surprises. I have often had the strangest requests from users and seen some really interesting stuff. One scene I will never forget is the letter opener I found jammed into one of the DSS tape drives one morning, sticking out of the server by at least a foot. It appeared that the night operator was trying to remove a jammed cartridge and had no luck dislodging it. The morning log caused a lot of chuckles because the only problem in the report was "one of the servers has been impaled by a letter opener."

But one item on your list of things a DBA has to do that should be no surprise to you is recovering a database. As sure as the sun will rise in the morning, there will come a time when frantic executives come pouring into your office like Federal agents stalking America's most wanted. If you plan well and practice disaster recovery often, you should have no problem sleeping at night.

When I say "practice," I mean that you should set up development servers, wreck them, and then recover them. Trash your databases, the server binaries, and even the operating system and then restore the whole caboodle to the last transaction. Try all forms of backup and restore, and also delete transaction logs and so on.

Only then when the bits and bytes hit the fan will you be able to calmly say to the CEO or CFO "no problem, I will have you back in a jiffy." Woe upon the DBA who sits down at his or her smoking server spewing out the last sparks of a hosed disk array and saying "uh . . . now what."

In Review

This chapter deals with backup and restore for the most common forms of installation. In the next chapter, we will look at the backup and restore of servers that are involved in replication. In Chapter 13, we will also look at log shipping scenarios and backup and restore of federated servers and cluster nodes.

Chapter 10

SQL Server Replication

SQL Servers of the world unite. I hardly think that a zillion SQL Server machines are getting ready to take over the world and crush mankind. But no SQL Server need be an island, because the system has all the necessary features that enable it to interconnect with other SQL Server instances as well as other brands of database management systems, even Microsoft Access, cousin Sybase, and (ahem) Oracle. This chapter focuses on SQL Server's powerful replication features which allow you to create a sophisticated distributed data network.

Replication is a vast subject and worthy of a book in its own right. Despite having spent several weeks testing and configuring the replication services, I found the replication subject in SQL Server Books Online to be very difficult to navigate. Facing more than 100,000 words of information, you too will find it difficult to get started with replication as quickly as you would like.

This chapter provides a quick introduction to what is an extremely complex subject. It will thus focus on what you need to know to get the skeletal replication configuration in place as soon as possible, and how to best prepare your organization for a replication topology. Once you have a basic understanding of what you are in for, and what SQL Server's replication services consist of, you will have a leg up on getting ready to build a distribution network foundation on which to build more complex distributed services. But first, let's kick off with some theory.

Distributed Databases

SQL Server's replication features make the platform one of the most powerful distributed database solutions on the planet today. Ever since the birth of data network, IT managers have striven to distribute data around their enterprises and organizations. There are many reasons to distribute data among a collection of servers. You might have some special needs; but here is a collection that almost all DBAs can identify with:

- **Availability** Making data available whenever and wherever users and data consumers need it.
- **Redundancy** Replication allows multiple sites to hold the same data. These sites may all work autonomously and access the servers closest to them on their network segments, but in mission-critical applications a redundant server holding the same information means that more than one copy of the database is accessible in the event of a disaster. This redundancy is useful when you have multiple sites spread across a wide geographical area and the users need to read the same data, especially for reporting applications. Replication is ideal for standby solutions. (Other choices in SQL Server 2000 include log shipping and fail-over clustering, which are discussed in Chapter 13.)
- **Data migration** Replications allows you to maintain multiple copies of the same data, which means that one server can cater to the OLTP read-write connections while another is configured for read-only or read-intensive

applications. These might be data transformation services pulling data into staging tables for warehouses, or performing direct, "drill"-intensive work on the data, such as in online analytical processing (OLAP).

- **Autonomy/store forward** Replication allows users, such as field agents and engineers, to work with copies of data while offline. Then when they reconnect, new data is propagated to other databases. Such a scenario could involve entering data into PDAs, Pocket PCs, portable computers, and other data entry devices. When these devices are connected to the network, replication automatically makes sure the local data is replicated to the system.
- **Scale out** Replication also allows you to scale out your data tier. In other words data can be browsed in highly distributed applications, such as when data needs to be browsed from the Web from anywhere on the planet.
- **Data mining** Replication allows you to increasingly aggregate read performance in analysis solutions.
- **Partitioning** Replication also helps reduce conflicts based on multiple user data modifications and queries because data can be distributed throughout the network, and you can partition data according to the needs of different business units, departments or users.

While availability and redundancy are your typical reasons for maintaining a distributed database network, several other factors require further discussion. Replication plays an important part in data mining and data warehousing operations. It is a useful tool that you can use to get data from point A to point B. Then when it is at point B it can be extracted, loaded into a staging database and prepared for transformation to an analysis database.

You can thus use replication to continuously update data marts and data warehouses. This is a far better solution to making periodic bulk extractions and inserts, which are resource intensive and potentially disruptive of day-to-day operations. In my book, it's better to have data replication taking place all the time than to spend evenings and weekends doing weekly extractions, loads, and scrubbing, or wasting time figuring out how to get huge amounts of batch transfers into the data warehouse before morning.

Understand that the replication services allow replicating data to be transformed. They do not enable the replication of the Analysis Services objects, such as dimensions or cubes. They are used to help you set up a uniform data distribution network moving data from OLTP (transaction) databases to data warehouses or data marts staging databases where data is transformed. These databases are used for drill- or query-intensive operations such as reporting, decision support, or analysis. Data Transformation Services (DTS) can be used with replication services for an end-to-end data transformation and migration service. (See Chapter 24 for an example of using DTS to upsize an Access data mart to SQL Server 2000.)

The data used in decision support or OLAP services is predominantly read-only (used for queries and analysis). For analysis, database loading snapshot replication or transactional replication are often the types of replication used. But the idea is not to directly get data from the live OLTP system into the database. It makes more sense to replicate to an off-limits (read-only) database and then from there extract the data into the staging area where you can treat it and scrub it before it is inserted into the data warehouse where it will remain unchanged. For example, you would want to install surrogate keys into the database (see Chapter 24) and this is not something you want to do to a OLTP system that is a replication partner with other servers. SQL Server's snapshot replication technology allows the data and database objects to be copied and distributed exactly as they appear at a specific moment in time on the source server.

Replication is also an ideal solution that caters to the problem of data accessibility while you are disconnected from the main data sources. For example, you are disconnected when you are traveling or working at remote locations, in the car or at a home office that is not connected to the corporate data center all the time. Business users often need to use laptops or handheld computers when traveling and they always need to access data, often on demand, such as in airports or hotel rooms. This is usually achieved by using a modem to dial into a corporate data center or connect to it via an intranet or the Internet connection, many of which now exist at most American airports.

When working online you can use replication to receive data from the central server in the corporate data center when you connect a wide area network or LAN, or over the Internet. Then you can make changes to data immediately, or you can modify data offline and propagate the changes to the source databases and to other locations when you reconnect to the network.

Data modifications made at remote servers are performed asynchronously at the original server and then sent to other servers. Transactional replication (using the queued updating option we will later discuss) and merge replication are the types of replication most often used for mobile or disconnected users.

For example, let's say that my company has sales representatives in various regions who need to take current customer and order information with them and update it as they travel. The corporate office decides to publish data from the CUSTOMERS, ORDERS, and ORDER DETAILS tables stored in a central online transactional processing (OLTP) database and filter the data by the region where each sales representative works. The laptop or handheld computers used by the sales representatives will be the Subscribers to the data, and the sales representatives will be able to update the data as necessary when away from the office and offline. With replication, when the sales representatives reconnect to the network, they can synchronize their data changes with changes made at other locations.

Replicating is also useful over the Internet or the Web, which allows remote, disconnected, and anonymous users to access data when they need it and wherever they need it. For example, your Web site might allows users to browse items for sale and you might have a large quantity of such hits to the main server. Using replication you can make sure that data is available for read purposes on other servers. Since the browsing can take place at any server, it allows the site, using load balancing technology, to handle more traffic.

Another use of replication and Web-based applications is to allow individual Subscribers to download or upload data changes with an application that uses an Internet browser, or by using a connection to the corporate network or share where the data resides. Obviously, you'll have collateral items on the IS list to cater to, such as integration with firewalls or with ISA Server, Microsoft Proxy Server, and IIS. You might also need to configure the File Transfer Protocol (FTP) to transfer the data over the Internet. One network solution you'll need to consider with replications services comprises the configuration of VPNs.

Establishing Replication Requirements

I found that the best way to get into replication is to investigate your enterprises needs and then formulate a requirements document—a needs synthesis. Let's suppose your company has regional offices around the world. Some regional offices will only be reading the data, while other offices are responsible for keeping up-to-date information on the customers and orders in their particular regions.

Your regional office might only need to read the data and not make any changes. If that's the case the central office can filter the data to create the appropriate partitions which would be based on region information or some other criteria and then publish that data to regional servers. The snapshot replication type or the transactional replication could be used to achieve your data distribution goals. It all depends on what you are trying to achieve.

Another example: A regional office or data center make changes to the data and needs the autonomy of the data on its site. So the data can be filtered and replicated to that region. Then the regional office can make changes to its data as needed. When the changes need to be propagated to the central or corporate data center or other regional data centers, the remote data center can synchronize with the central data center such that the changes now made in the remote data center can propagated automatically to the central data center, which in turn can synchronize with other remote data centers. If the central data centers needs to distribute the corporate data other regional sales force, it can republish the data to the necessary sites.

So you have several options for scheduling distribution of the data and modifying the data at the different remote data centers. If you maintain a continuous and reliable wide area network, multiple data centers can update the data and propagate the changes to the corporate offices immediately. The data is then propagated to other data centers within seconds (via the service of the immediate updating feature). In the case of a remote data center that is offline for a limited amount of time, data modifications can be stored in a queue until the connection is reestablished. This is called queued updating. So let's review the components of the replication service before we activate the components of our plan.

SQL Server Replication Services

SQL Server 2000's replication services are a set of technologies used for copying and distributing data and database objects from one database to another and then synchronizing between databases to ensure that the data in each database is consistent and durable.

Microsoft, obsessed with the publishing business, has built the replications services around a publishing industry metaphor to represent the components and processes in a "replication topology." The model is composed of the following components:

- **Publisher** The Publisher is a SQL Server database that makes its data available to other databases that can receive from it. The Publisher can have more than one publication, and each publication can represent a logically related set of data. The publisher servers is the source of the data to be replicated, but it is more than just a sender of data. It can also detect which data has changed during transactional replication and it keeps track of all the publications it is responsible for.
- **Distributor** The Distributor is a SQL Server database that hosts the distribution database and stores history data, and/or transactions and metadata. The role of the Distributor varies depending on which type of replication you implement. A remote Distributor is an SQL Server system that is maintained separate from the Publisher and is configured as a Distributor of replication. You can also have a local Distributor, which is a server that is configured to be both a Publisher and a Distributor of replication data.
- **Subscribers** Subscribers are database servers that receive the replicated data. Subscribers subscribe to publications, and not to individual articles within a publication. They also subscribe only to the publications that they need, not all of the publications available on a Publisher, which means they get only the data they need to have, and not data from every database on the server. The Subscriber can also propagate data changes back to the Publisher or republish the data to other Subscribers. This depends on the replication option chosen, which allows the replication to be a two-way street.
- **Publications** A publication is defined as a collection of one or more articles that originate from one database. This grouping of multiple articles makes it easier to specify a logically related set of data and database objects that you want to replicate as a unit.
- **Articles** The article is not something your read in the New York Times magazine. It is a table of data, or a partition of data, or a database object that can be designated for replication. The article can be an entire table; a collection of

columns (using the vertical filter), certain rows (using the horizontal filter), or a stored procedure or view definition; the execution of a stored procedure, a view, an indexed view, or a user-defined function.

- **Subscriptions** The subscription is a request for a copy of data or database objects to be replicated. A subscription defines what publication will be received, where it will be received and when it will be received. Synchronization or the data distribution of a subscription can be requested either by the Publisher—which is termed a push subscription—or by the Subscriber—which is termed a pull subscription. A publication can support a concoction of both push and pull subscriptions.

There are also several replication processes that are responsible for copying and moving data between the Publisher and Subscriber. These are the Snapshot Agent, Distribution Agent, Log Reader Agent, Queue Reader Agent, and Merge Agent. We'll get to those shortly.

Types of Replication

There are three types of replications available with SQL Server 2000: snapshot replication, transactional replication, and merge replication. Merge replication is relatively new to the SQL Server and made its debut in Version 7.0. Each replication option has its strengths and weaknesses; however, each is suitable only for a specific reason.

Snapshot Replication

Snapshot replication is the process of copying and distributing data and database objects in the exact state they appear in at a certain moment in time. Snapshot replication does not require continuous monitoring of changes because changes made to published data are not propagated to the Subscriber incrementally; rather they are periodically replicated in a single effort. The subscribers are thus replicated to with every complete refresh of the data set. They are not replicated to on a transaction-by-transaction basis. Snapshot replication can take longer to propagate data modifications to Subscribers than the other forms of replication because the snapshot replication replicates an entire data set at one point in time. Snapshots are typically replicated less frequently than other types of publications. Once a day in the evening is a good time to engage in snapshot replication. A data warehouse is well suited to obtain snapshot replication data because the data does not need to be propagated to the replication database on the heel of every transaction. However, the data set should be small because trying to replicate petabytes of data at one time might cause an entire city to cave in on itself as you suck up the entire neighborhood's Internet access.

Options available with snapshot replication allow you to filter published data, allow Subscribers to make modifications to replicated data and propagate those changes to the Publisher and then to other Subscribers. This filtering mechanism thus lets you transform data as it is published. Snapshot replication is useful for

- Data that is mostly static (seldom changes), such as warehouse data replicating to a data mart
- Cases in which it is acceptable to have copies of data that are out of date for a certain period of time
- Small volumes of data
- Sites that are often disconnected where high latency (the amount of time between when data is updated at one site and when it is updated at another) is acceptable

Transactional Replication

With *transactional replication,* an initial snapshot of data is propagated to Subscribers, so that the subscriber has what is called an initial load, something to start with. Then when data modifications are made at the Publisher, these individual transactions are immediately captured and replicated to the Subscriber.

Under transactional replication, SQL Server 2000 monitors INSERT, UPDATE, and DELETE statements, as well as changes to stored procedure executions and indexed views. It stores the transactions affecting replicated objects and then propagates those changes to Subscribers continuously or at scheduled intervals. Transaction boundaries are preserved. If, for example, 100 rows are updated in a transaction, either the entire transaction with all 100 rows are propagated or none of them are . When all changes are propagated, all Subscribers will have the same values as the Publisher.

Options available with transactional replication allow you to filter published data, allow users at the Subscriber to make modifications to replicated data and propagate those changes to the Publisher and to other Subscribers. You can also transform data as it is published.

Transactional replication is typically used when

- You want data modifications to be propagated to Subscribers, often within seconds of when they occur.
- You need transactions to be atomic (either all or none applied at the Subscriber).
- Subscribers are connected to the Publisher much of the time.
- Your application will not tolerate high latency for Subscribers receiving changes.

Merge Replication

Merge replication is a relatively new form of replication that allows a collection of sites to work autonomously, online or offline. The data is then merged—with updates and insertions made at multiple sites replicated into a single, uniform result at a future time. The initial snapshot is applied to Subscribers as the initial load. Then SQL Server 2000 tracks the changes to the published data at the Publisher and at the Subscribers. The data is synchronized between servers at a predetermined or scheduled time or on demand. Updates are then made independently (with no commit protocol) at more than one server. This means that the same data may be updated by the Publisher or by more than one Subscriber and thus conflicts can occur when data modifications are merged.

If merge replication can introduce conflicting data then why use it? You would use merge replication when

- Multiple subscribers need to update data at various times and the data has to be propagated to the Publisher and to other Subscribers.
- Subscribers need to receive data, make any changes offline, and then synchronize changes later with the Publisher and other Subscribers.
- The application latency requirement is either high or low.
- Site autonomy is critical.

Merge replication requires diligence on the part of the DBA. It includes default and custom choices for conflict resolution that you define when you configure a merge replication solution. So when a conflict occurs, a resolver is invoked by the Merge Agent to determine which data will be accepted and propagated to other data centers.

You have several options available to you when you configure merge replication. These include the following:

- Filtering published data horizontally and vertically (rows or columns), including join filters and dynamic filters
- The ability to use alternate synchronization partners
- The ability to optimize synchronization to improve merge performance
- The ability to validate replicated data to ensure synchronization
- The ability to use attachable subscription databases

Understanding the Replication Options

Options available with the types of replication allow you more replication solutions and greater flexibility and control in your applications. Replication options are

- Filtering published data
- Publishing database objects
- Publishing schema objects
- Updatable subscriptions
- Transforming published data
- Alternate synchronization partners

Table 10-1 presents the replication options and the replication types that support them.

Filtering Published Data

Filtering data during replication allows you to publish only the data or partitions of data that are needed by the Subscriber. You can filter data and thus create partitions that include only columns and/or only rows that you specify for replication.

With all types of replication, you can choose to copy and distribute complete tables, or you can filter your data horizontally or vertically with static filters. The merge replication is especially strong in filtering options, and you can use dynamic filters to customize the filter to correspond to a property of the Subscriber receiving the data.

Replication Option	Replication Type
Filtering Published Data	Snapshot, Transactional, Merge
Updatable Subscriptions (Immediate and Queued Updating)	Snapshot Replication, Transactional Replication
Updatable Subscriptions	Merge Replication
Transforming Published Data	Snapshot Replication, Transactional Replication
Alternate Synchronization Partners	Merge Replication
Optimizing Synchronization	Merge Replication

Table 10-1. *Replication Options and the Replication Types that Support Them*

When you filter data horizontally you have the option of publishing only the data that is needed. You can also partition data to different sites, and avoid conflicts that arise out of the situation where subscribers are viewing and updating different subsets of data. You can also manage publications in accordance with user needs or applications.

You also have the option of using user-defined functions in your static and dynamic filters and you can even make use of customized functions. Merge replication also lets you use *join filters* and *dynamic filters*. The join filters enable you to extend filters created on one table to another. Let's say you are publishing customer data according to the state where the customer resides, you may want to extend that filter to the related orders and order details of the customers in a particular state. The *Dynamic filters* on the other hand allow you to create a merge publication and then filter data from the publishing table. The filter value can be the user ID or login retrieved through a T-SQL function, such as SUSER_SNAME() or HOSTNAME().

Publishing Database Objects

You also have the option of publishing database objects, including views, indexed views, user-defined functions, stored procedure definitions, and the execution of stored procedures. You can include data and database objects in the same publication or in different publications. Publishing database objects is available with all types of replication—transactional, snapshot and merger replication.

Publishing Schema Objects

You can also specify schema objects to be published. These might include such objects as declared referential integrity, primary key constraints, reference constraints, unique constraints, clustered indexes, nonclustered indexes, user triggers, extended properties, collations and so on. You can also change destination table owner names and data formats to optimize for SQL Server 2000 or non SQL Server 2000 subscribers.

Updatable Subscriptions

An updateable subscription allows data at the Subscriber to be modified. Updateable subscriptions are possible with all three replication types, but the algorithms used differ from replication type to replication type. When using merge replication, data at the Subscriber is automatically updateable.

Specifically the updateable subscription options available with snapshot replication and transactional replication allow you to make changes to replicated data at the Subscriber and propagate those changes to the Publisher and to other Subscribers. Such updateable subscription options include the ability to force immediate updating, queued updating, and immediate updating with queued updating as a fail-over.

Immediate updating also allows Subscribers to update data only if the Publisher will accept them immediately. This is a configuration option in the Publisher. If the changes are accepted at the Publisher, they are propagated to other Subscribers. The Subscriber must be continuously and reliably connected to the Publisher to make changes at the Subscriber, and such a reliable connection would be a dedicated and high-bandwidth WAN backbone.

Queued updating lets the subscribers modify data and store the modifications in a queue. The queue builds while the subscriber remains disconnected from the Publisher. When the Subscriber reconnects to the Publisher, the changes are propagated to the Publisher. If the Publisher accepts the changes, normal replication processes occur and the changes are propagated to other Subscribers from the Publisher. You can then store data modifications in a SQL Server 2000 queue or use Microsoft Message Queuing (MSMQ).

If you use immediate updating with the queued updating option SQL Server lets you use immediate updating with the option of switching to queued updating if a connection cannot be maintained between the Publisher and Subscribers. After switching to queued updating, reconnecting to the Publisher, and emptying the queue, you can switch back to immediate updating mode.

Transforming Published Data

A huge benefit of snapshot replication or transactional replication is the feature that lets you leverage the transformation mapping and scripting capabilities of Data Transformation Services (DTS). These can come into play big time when building a replication topology for almost any situation. Replication integrated with DTS allows you to customize and distribute data according to the requirements of individual Subscribers. Your Subscriber, for example, might need to have different table names, different column names, or compatible data types.

By transforming the published data, you can filter data and simulate dynamic partitions of data so that data from one snapshot or transactional publication can be distributed to Subscribers that require different partitions of data. You also have the option of static partitions. These are created and filter separate publications for each Subscriber in accordance with the needs of each Subscriber.

Alternate Synchronization Partners

I alluded to this earlier. It allows Subscribers to merge publications to synchronize with servers other than the Publisher at which the subscription originated. This means that Subscribers can synchronize data even if the primary Publisher is unavailable; they essentially synchronize with alternate partners instead of the Publisher. This feature is also useful when mobile Subscribers connect to a faster or more reliable network connection that can give them access to an alternate Publisher, if the primary is inaccessible.

Getting Started with Replication

There are several ways to implement and monitor replication. There are many options and each replication project's configuration will depend on the type of replication and the options you choose. Replication is composed of the following stages:

1. Configure replication
2. Generate and apply the initial snapshot to the subscribers
3. Configure to modify the replicated data
4. Synchronize and propagate the data

Rather than describing each and every step in dry, excruciating steps, let's get right down to configuring a simple replication scenario in this chapter.

Configuring a Publisher

To configure a publisher, you need to take the following steps.

1. Go to Enterprise Manager and start the Configure Publishing and Distribution Wizard. The fastest route to this Wizard is to drill down to the server that is going to become a publisher and expose the Replication folder. Right-click this folder and select Configure Publishing, Subscribers, and Distribution. You can also start the Wizard from the Tools | Replication menu in Enterprise Manager. Click Next to advance past the opening dialog box.
2. The Select Distributor dialog box, as illustrated in Figure 10-1, loads. Notice here that the server you are setting up is configured as its own distributor by default. Also notice, however, that you can select another server as a distributor, but it must already be configured as such for selection here. We want to keep things this way using the default, so click Next.
3. The Specify Snapshot Folder dialog box, as illustrated in Figure 10-2, loads. Here again, accept the default and move on. You will then notice a warning about the share name used for the replication folder. By default, it is made accessible only to logins with local administrative rights. Let's not worry about that now, but remember that you may need to change this for remote services like pull agents at another time. Click OK to close the share warning, and then click Next.
4. The Customize the Configuration dialog box appears. Here you can accept the defaults chosen by the Wizard, or you can go in and "tweak" the settings. For this exercise, just choose No, and go with the defaults as shown in Figure 10-3. Later, you can work with advanced settings and go over some of this stuff in more detail. Click Next and then click Finish.

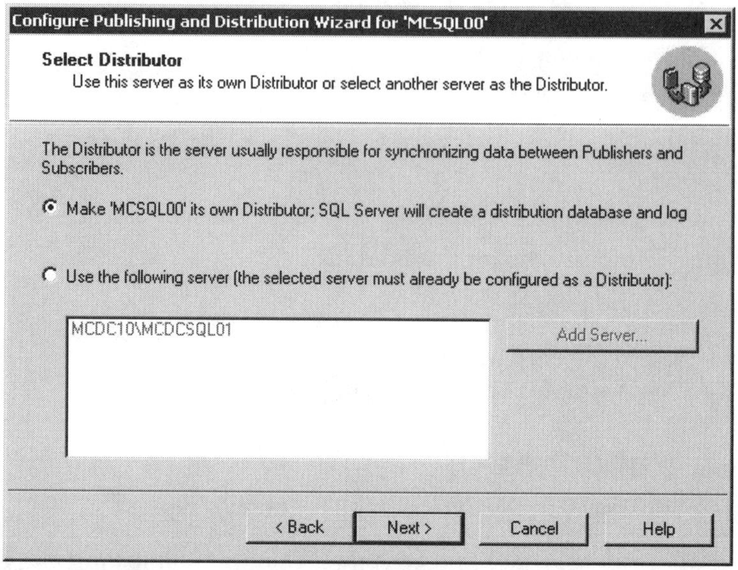

Figure 10-1. *The Select Distributor dialog box*

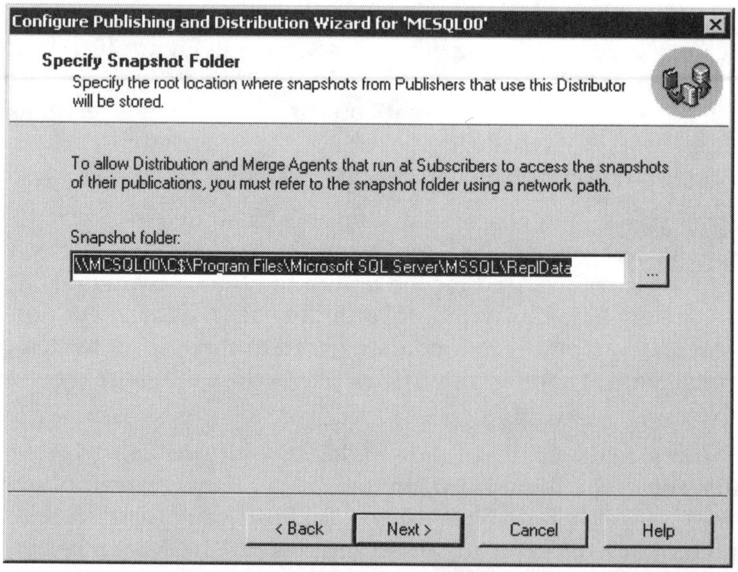

Figure 10-2. *The Specify Snapshot Folder dialog box*

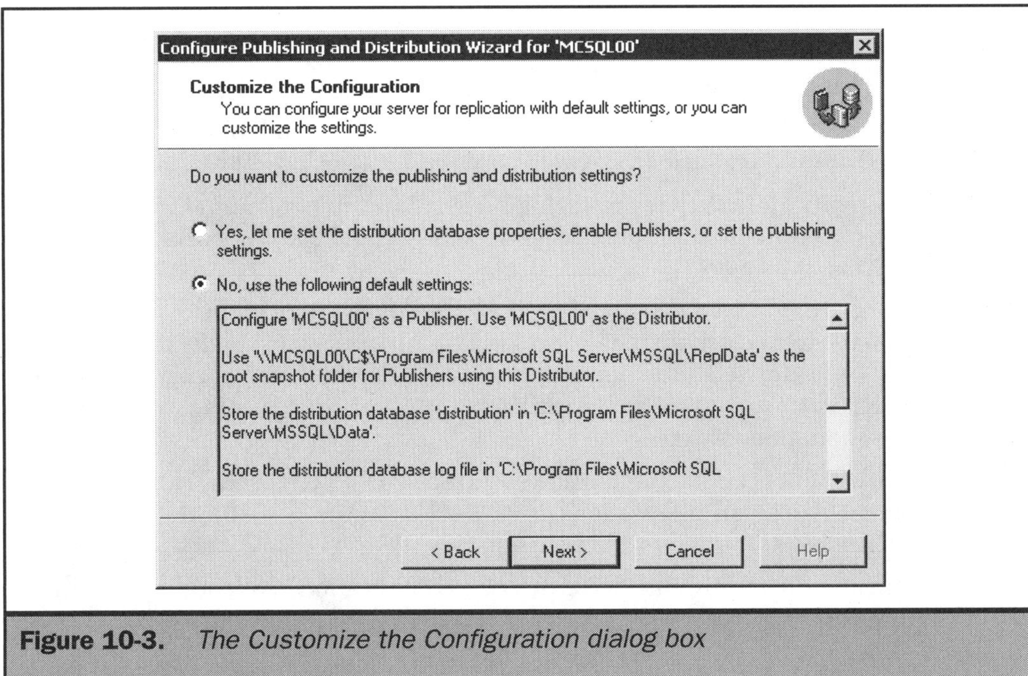

Figure 10-3. *The Customize the Configuration dialog box*

Creating a Publication

Using transactional replication, you will now be able to set up replication that lets changes made at the publisher we have just configured flow to subscribers. But before that can happen, you first need to create a publication on the publisher. The publication allows our subscribers to update their data from the publisher in almost real time. Transactions will be set to replicate as soon as they commit in the publication, or they can be propagated to the subscribers at regular intervals. In other words, the publication will be configured to allow the subscribers to update either via Immediate Updates or Queued Updates.

To do this, we need to perform a series of steps using the Create Publication Wizard as follows:

1. Connect to your server as described earlier and expose the Replication folder. Right-click on the Publications folder and select New Publication. Notice that SQL Server has now installed the Replication Monitor into the tree of our publisher, because it has been configured as a distributor.
2. The Create Publication Wizard loads. Before moving on, however, enable the Advanced Options and then click Next.
3. The Choose Publication Database loads. In my example, I also have the customer database (a call center application in development on this server), but select the Northwind database for the publication, and then click Next.

4. The Select Publication Type dialog box, as illustrated in Figure 10-4, loads. In that we are looking to replication transaction from one OLTP database to another, choose Transactional and then click Next.
5. The Updatable Subscriptions dialog box loads. Check both options to enable Immediate and Queued Updating Subscribers, then Click Next.
6. The Specify Subscriber Types dialog box loads, as illustrated in Figure 10-5. Check the option to replicate with only SQL Server 2000 databases, then click Next.
7. The Specify Articles dialog box, as illustrated in Figure 10-6, loads. In the list box on the left, select the Show and Publish All options for both tables and stored procedures. This action automatically selects all of the options in the right list box. Any tables that do not contain primary keys are ignored for publication. Click Next.
8. The Select Publication Name and Description dialog box loads. Here you need to enter a name and description for the Publication or leave the defaults as they are. Click Next.
9. Finally the Customize the Properties of the Publication box loads, as shown in Figure 10-7.

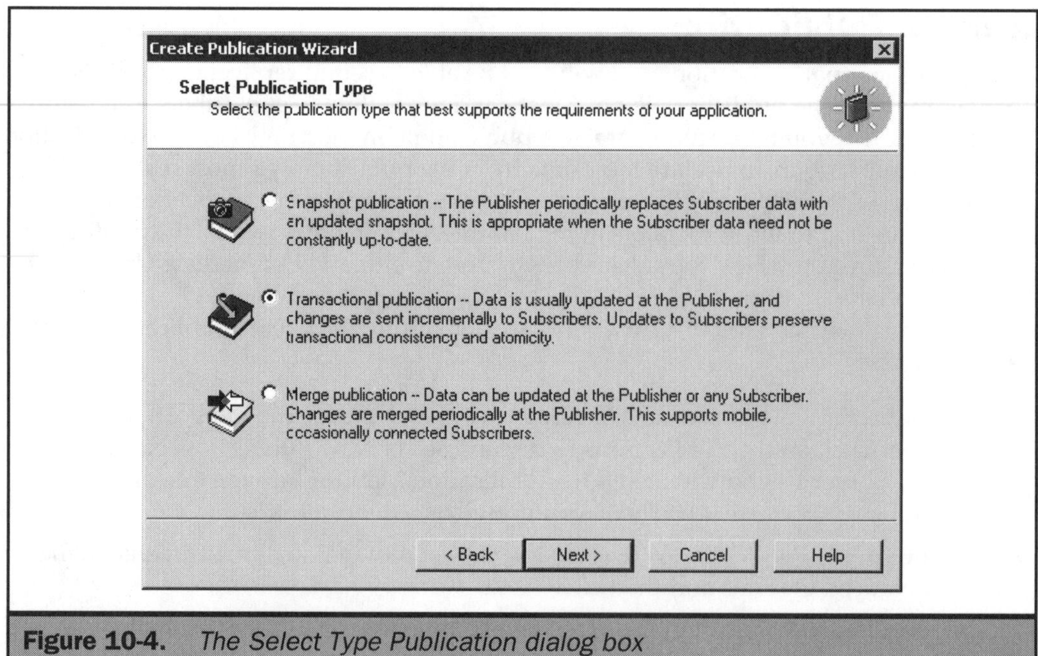

Figure 10-4. *The Select Type Publication dialog box*

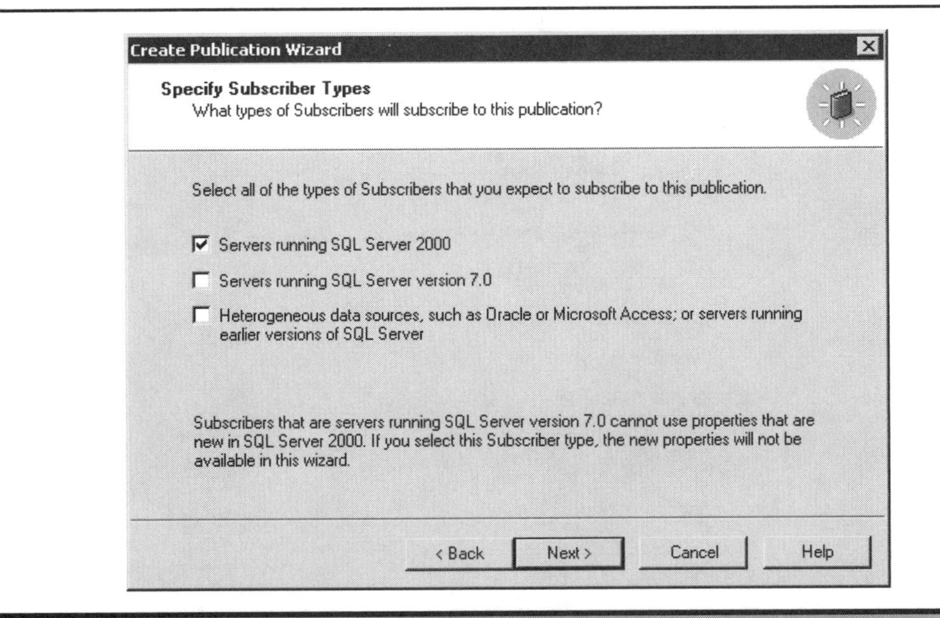

Figure 10-5. *The Specify Subscriber Types dialog box*

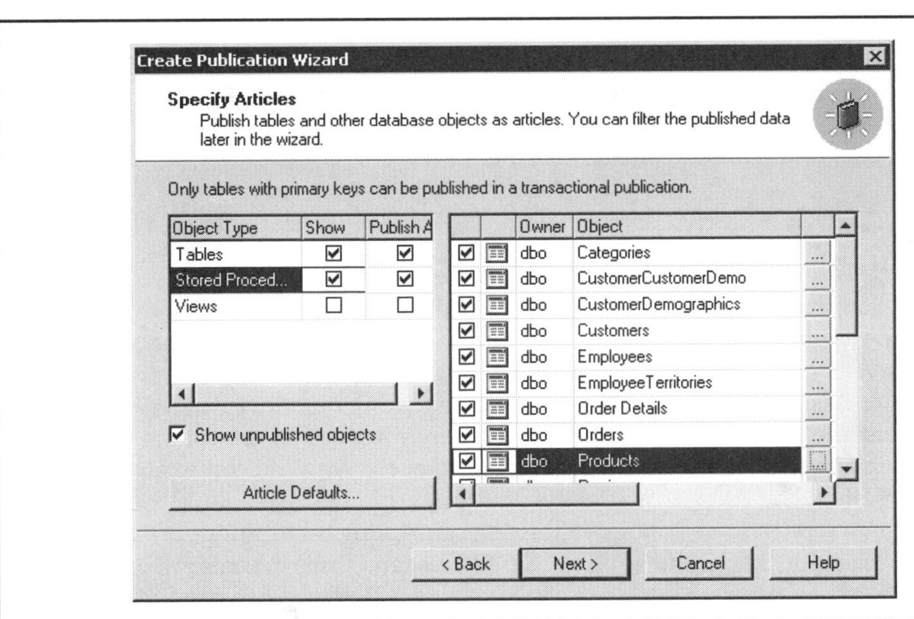

Figure 10-6. *The Specify Articles dialog box*

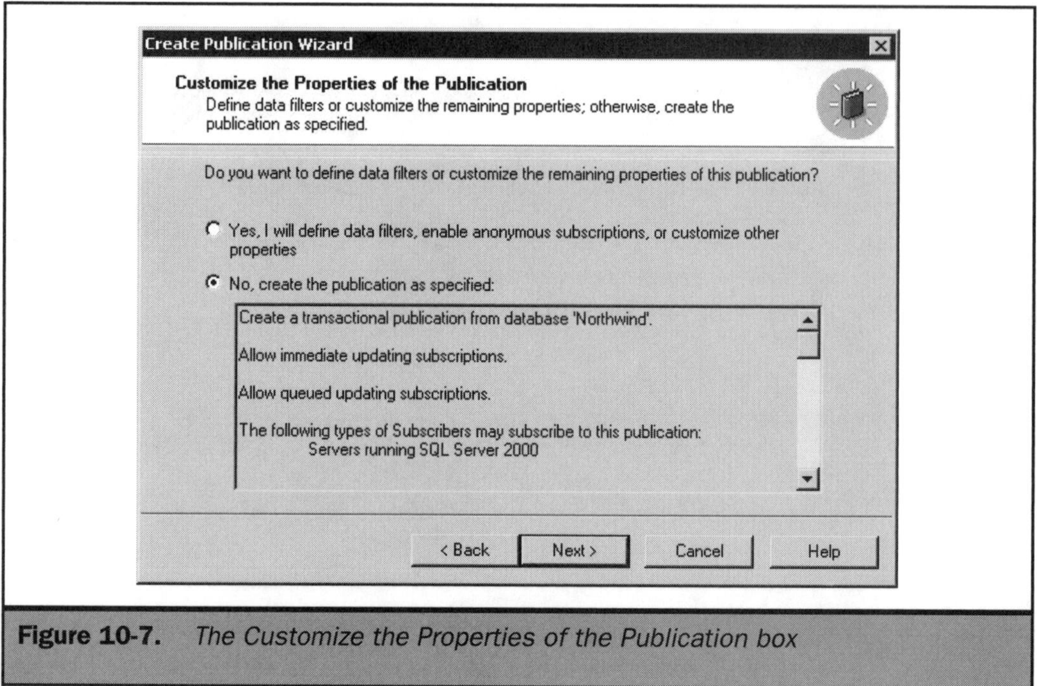

Figure 10-7. *The Customize the Properties of the Publication box*

That's pretty much all it takes to set up and configure a basic transactional replication scenario. Before you go off and replicate the world, consider the following advice on replication planning and deployment.

Designing a Replication Topology

When your databases are widely dispersed over the Internet or across an extensive corporate WAN, supporting widely dispersed data centers, and you must replicate data, you have to define a replication topology to support the interconnection of servers and replication and synchronized updating of the data that resides on them. Not only must the topology take into consideration how the servers communicate, but it must cater to the synchronization that has to occur between copies so that data remains consistent and durable across the enterprise.

Designing a replication topology will help you, among other things, determine how long it takes for changes to get from a publisher to a subscriber, how updates are propagated, and the order in which updated information arrives at a subscriber. There are several steps you must take when designing a replication topology:

- You will need to select the physical replication model. This can be any one of the following models: central publisher, central publisher with remote distributor, publishing subscriber, or a central subscriber.
- You will have to determine where to locate the snapshot files (which are used to create the first loads to the receiving databases). You will also need to determine how the publishers and subscribers will initially synchronize their data.
- You will need to decide if the distributor will be local or remote. You will also need to decide if the distribution database will be shared. More than one publisher can share a distributor, with each one using its own distribution database on the publisher. They can also share a distribution database, so you have lot to synthesize.
- There are many different types of replication options to use. You have had a tiny taste of a few in this chapter and you will need to decide what options are going to be best for your solution.
- You will also need to determine whether the replication will kick off at the publisher—which is typically called push subscription—or at the subscriber through, you guessed it, pull subscription.

On a WAN, managing many subscribers and publishers can be a complex situation and requires the dedication of DBAs devoted to the replication process. Many data paths might exist between the servers and your job will be to ensure that the data remains synchronized and the solution works to have subscribers obtain the correct versions of the data. Fortunately, replication technology has come a long way from the day data was updated in the morning and then overwritten again with yesterday's information in the afternoon.

Understanding the Physical Replication Models

The physical replication model is your blueprint for how you will allow data to be distributed across the enterprise or the Internet. Understanding the physical model means understanding how to configure the servers for replication services. If you are new to replication, and many people are, the following sections provide a point of departure, a proverbial leg up, so to speak.

The advice that you cannot be too careful about planning for replication deployment might seem like a gross understatement, but when you have a highly complex replication model I cannot stress how important it is to properly plan the whole effort. Remember you have to plan to maximize data consistency, minimize demands on network resources, and implement sound technical services that will prevent a disaster down the road. Many Internet or Web applications today consist of demanding replication needs and if there is one factor that is a business killer, it is finding out after the fact that there is a flaw in the design of your replication topology the models used, and so on. The following list of considerations should be noted before you begin to make any purchases or decisions that may prove expensive to undo later.

- Decide how and where replicated data needs to be updated, and by whom.
- Decide how your data distribution needs will be affected by issues of consistency, autonomy, and latency.
- Draw up a blueprint or architecture map illustrating your replication environment. Include your business users, technical infrastructure, network and security, and the characteristics of your data.
- Evaluate the types of replication you can use and the replication options that will work for your solution.
- Evaluate the replication topology options and the affect they will have on the types or type of replication you may be considering.

In Review

In this chapter we looked at replication in theory and introduced the three replication types available to SQL Server solutions: snapshot replication, transactional replication, and merge replication.

Microsoft has gone to great lengths to build a database management system that is ideal for distributed database solutions and wide-area deployment on networks like the Internet. While its replication architecture is not new or revolutionary it goes without saying that without replication none of the other features we discuss later in the book would be worth exploring for Internet applications. It is very unlikely today that anyone deploying SQL Server on the Internet or on a WAN would not be configuring for replication. Out of all the subjects a SQL Server DBA might have to master, none other might be as challenging and rewarding as replication.

The Complete Reference

Chapter 11

SQL Server 2000 Databases

SQL Server 2000 provides one of the most flexible database management systems around. And this flexibility does not come at a high price either. SQL Server databases can be small, large, very large, or gigantic. You can expand them, shrink them, infuse them with thousands of tables, copy them, move them, detach them, transform them, encrypt their objects, and so on. And you can have 32,767 databases for every instance of SQL Server, and, er, billions of tables.

A SQL Server database consists of numerous components and objects. I have discussed many of them in previous chapters—especially in Chapter 2—in which we studied the database architecture from several levels. This chapter guides you through creating databases and tables through several facilities provided as the data storage, data management, and data processing aspects of SQL Server databases. We will also look at table creation, working with the Design Table utility, and Database Diagrams.

Understanding Filegroups

A filegroup is another form of container in SQL Server. To refresh your memory with respect to file location flexibility, you can store your data files in various locations and use filegroups to then manage them as a unit. For example, you could locate the primary file *papazulu.mdf* in the volume it was created on and then store the secondary data files (*papazulu1.mdf, papazulu2.mdf,* and *papazulu3.mdf*), if you need them, on a number of different drives (even locating each new file on its own hard disk). Then create a filegroup (called pzulugroup1) and assign all the papazulu secondary database files to this filegroup. When it comes to backup, you can then back up the filegroups instead of the three or four separate files. (The script to back up a filegroup is covered in Chapter 9.)

One of the best features of the filegroup, however, is the flexibility you get in managing your database objects. For example, if you have a huge table that is the constant target of queries and modification, it would make sense to allocate it to a filegroup on a faster disk. Then most of the I/O for the database can be targeted to the faster disk.

Spreading database files around like this can help tremendously with performance because each file can be dedicated to its own hard disk. This might become a little expensive if you are using a RAID system for redundancy (RAID 5 will require at least three disks, as discussed in Chapter 6). On the other hand, RAID configuration aside, if you are working with really large databases, your primary and secondary files might grow to sizes that bump up against the limits of your Windows NT or Windows 2000 Server file system file size.

SQL Server fills all files in the filegroup on a proportional basis so that all files in the filegroup become full at the same time. When all the files in the filegroup are full, SQL Server will then expand all the files in the group one at a time on a round-robin scheduling basis if the database is set to grow automatically (discussed in CREATE DATABASE later).

There are four important rules to remember about filegroups; they may or may not count in your favor or figure in your database plan:

1. A filegroup cannot be used by more than one database. You cannot take *papazulu* and assign it to the filegroup for the *tangocharlie* database. Likewise, files can only be members of one filegroup. The CREATE DATABASE and ALTER DATABASE statements in Enterprise Manager have no facility for such multiallocation or designation, in any event.
2. Transaction logs are not part of filegroups, although they can be located where the database plan takes them.
3. The primary file is assigned to the primary filegroup, and the primary filegroup cannot be changed or altered.
4. If you do not specify alternative filegroups for the secondary data files, all files are then placed into the primary filegroup. The disadvantage is that if the primary filegroup is filled up, then no further data can be stored in the catalog.

The Default Filegroup

As you discovered when you created your first database, it contains a primary filegroup, which becomes the default filegroup before any new filegroups are created, including any user-defined filegroups you specify. Later you can change the default filegroup using the ALTER DATABASE statement we will be discussing shortly.

The primary filegroup can fill up if autogrow for your database is turned off and the disks holding the primary group run out of space. You can turn autogrow back on, but until you have worked out how to best reduce the size of the files, you may have no choice but to add a larger hard disk and then move the files onto this disk.

The reason for having a default filegroup is so that any object created without specifying a filegroup is assigned to the default filegroup. A problem may arise at a later date, however, where you will not be able to add to the database because you are low on hard disk space and your primary default filegroup is full. You may then have to create a new filegroup and make the new group the default. In other words, you create a new filegroup so that new user-defined objects, such as tables and views, do not compete with the system objects and tables for data space.

Setting Filegroups Read-Only

SQL Server lets you mark a filegroup as read-only. This means that you cannot modify or add to the files in the filegroup in any way. Marking a filegroup as read-only can come in handy. For example, your turnkey application can include data in the filegroup that cannot be removed, and you can store key configuration tables in the read-only file to prevent users from adding data to them.

Relational OLAP databases (ROLAP) and Hybrid OLAP (HOLAP) databases are also good candidates for read-only filegroups. By setting their filegroups read-only, you provide an additional safeguard against anyone writing to the databases. As you know, OLAP databases or warehouse data, once declared historical or temporals should not be modified in any way that could render analysis questionable. In the event you need to add data and refresh a cube, you can easily change the file to read/write.

Filegroup Tips

When creating and working with your database, consider the following recommendations for your database files and filegroups:

- When creating your filegroups, create a secondary filegroup and make it the default filegroup. This will leave the primary dedicated to the system objects, free from interference from user-defined objects.
- Place the filegroups across as many physical disks (or logical disks for RAID sets) as you can so that you can spread the work across several disks. There is nothing worse than to have one disk in an array or cluster that is doing all the work, while the others sit idle.
- Try to locate tables that are used in complex and frequently accessed joins in separate filegroups that are then located on separate disks. You will see a marked performance improvement over a single-disk implementation because two or more disks are involved in the processing of the join (in parallel) instead of one. Remember again that if you are using RAID, you will have to create several logical disks (each containing at least three disks for a RAID 5 configuration).
- Do not place transaction logs on the same physical disk as the filegroups (this was mentioned in Chapter 9), because if the disk fails, you lose not only the database but also the transaction log. Recovery will thus be slow and painful, and if you are not doing frequent online backups you could lose a lot of data.
- You can obtain a report on your filegroups at any time when you execute the system stored procedure sp_helpfilegroup. See Books Online for information about the result set returned from this proc.

Creating a SQL Server Database

Creating a database in SQL Server is as easy as cutting butter on hot corn. Many databases solutions, however, call for specialized configuration that caters to very large databases (VLDBs), replication, federations, and so on. So before you start creating away, there are a number of considerations to keep in mind with respect to the actual files:

- First, it is a good idea to make the data files as large as possible taking into account the amount of data you expect in the database.
- Second, allow the data files to grow automatically but place a ceiling on the file growth so that the files don't suck up every drop of storage juice on the server

and explode. This practice allows you to monitor the files carefully and take appropriate actions (such as installing additional storage). Alternatively, as discussed, you can add more filegroups to secondary hard disks.

- If you do not want the database to grow beyond its initial size, set the maximum growth size to zero. This parameter prevents the file from growing beyond your initial settings, which is useful in turnkey situations, like a voice mail system that gets shipped preconfigured to only store 100MB of voice messages. You can then sell additional storage quotas as needed.
- Watch for file fragmentation. Autogrowing files can become fragmented to a point where performance begins to degrade. Again, creating files on multiple disks helps keep the fragmentation in check.

There are several methods you can use to create a SQL Server database:

1. T-SQL's CREATE DATABASE statement
2. Enterprise Manager
3. The SQL-DMO object model (The SQL-DMO object model is discussed further in Chapter 14, but it is essentially beyond the scope of this book.)
4. Data Transformation Services
5. The Create Database Wizard
6. The Copy Database Wizard

No matter the option that you use to create a database, SQL Server implements the creation of databases in two steps:

1. First SQL Server initializes the new database using metadata derived from the model database to initialize the database and its metadata. To change defaults to suit the environment, you would need to alter the model database (such as by specifying collations other than the default, as mentioned in Chapter 12).
2. Next SQL Server fills the database with empty pages. The database, however, also stores the initial data that records how the space is to be used in the database.

If you created or altered objects in the model database, then these are exactly copied to all newly created databases. Whatever you add to model, such as tables, views, stored procedures, and data types, all are also included in all new databases. This is very convenient for turnkey systems or when you need to be creating new databases often, because it obviates the need to run a complex script every time you create a new database. In fact, after you've fine-tuned all the objects inside model, just executing *CREATE DATABASE database_name* would be sufficient and the database would be ready for users.

As highlighted in the CREATE DATABASE syntax coming up, the new database inherits the database option settings from the model database (unless you are using the FOR ATTACH switch that attaches an existing database).

For example, if the recovery model is set to FULL in model, the recovery model will be set to FULL in all the new databases you create. Any properties and options changed using the ALTER DATABASE statement on model are also used for new databases you create. If FOR ATTACH is specified on the CREATE DATABASE statement, the new database inherits the database option settings of the original database.

There are three types of files used to store a database:

1. First there is the primary file *(.mdf)*, which contains the startup information for the database. After the initial startup data, SQL Server uses the rest of the primary files to store user data. A SQL Server database cannot exist without its primary file.
2. When the primary fills to capacity, secondary files *(.ndf)* are used to hold the additional data. The secondary file is optional and may not be necessary if the primary is large enough or has enough hard disk accommodation to store all the data in the database. Secondary files can be installed to separate disks, or spread across multiple disks.
3. Finally, as I am sure you now know, there are the transaction log files *(.ldf)*. These files hold the transactional information used to recover the database. You cannot operate a SQL Server database without a transaction log file, but you can specify more than one. The minimum size for a transaction log file is 512KB.

Back up the master whenever a new user database is created or altered (see Chapter 9).

I decided to explore the T-SQL CREATE DATABASE statement first, before looking into the interactive procedures using the Wizards and Enterprise Manager. This will actually make it easier for you to understand what the Create Database Wizard is doing.

CREATE DATABASE

For many DBAs, the T-SQL CREATE STATEMENT is convenient because it means that you can create a T-SQL script and run the script with a new database name whenever you need. Creating such scripts is obviously ideal for large requirements and typically suits a DBA or some process that needs to create databases regularly.

You need to be a member of the sysadmin or dbcreator fixed server role or be given the appropriate permission to create and alter databases (see Chapter 8).

Setting up databases for e-commerce hosting sites is a good example of where the T-SQL script is useful. When a new client needs a database, it becomes a matter of running the script against the target server and instance from one of the command-line utilities or Query Manager.

Note *You do not need to use DISK INIT before you create a database with the CREATE DATABASE statement as was the case with SQL Server 6.5 and earlier. There is no need to go to your scripts, however, and remove this line because SQL Server 2000 honors it for backward compatibility. Check out Books Online for more information on backward compatibility, but by the next version DISK INIT will probably be history.*

The T-SQL CREATE DATABASE syntax is as follows:

```
CREATE DATABASE database_name
[ ON
[ < filespec > [ ,...n ] ]
[ , < filegroup > [ ,...n ] ]
]
[ LOG ON { < filespec > [ ,...n ] } ]
[ COLLATE collation_name ]
[ FOR LOAD | FOR ATTACH ]

< filespec > ::=

[ PRIMARY ]
( [ NAME = logical_file_name , ]
FILENAME = 'os_file_name'
[ , SIZE = size ]
[ , MAXSIZE = { max_size | UNLIMITED } ]
[ , FILEGROWTH = growth_increment ] ) [ ,...n ]

< filegroup > ::=

FILEGROUP filegroup_name < filespec > [ ,...n ]
```

Let's go through the statement parameter by parameter, argument by argument, making notes as we go along that will help us create a suitable database plan for our project.

Database Name

The database names must be unique within a server and conform to the rules for identifiers. The placeholder *database_name* can be a maximum of 128 characters. Typically SQL Server gives the log file the same name as the database name and provides the extension *.ldf.* You can specify you own log filename and path, which we will get to shortly. The following code, for example, creates a database named *papazulu* and assumes all the defaults derived from the model database:

```
CREATE DATABASE papazulu
```

In this case *papazulu.mdf* and *papazulu_log.ldf* are created in the default path and the files are entrusted with the default settings for file growth and permissions (the user that created the database is the owner). Conversely, the following code makes the databases go away as quickly as they came:

```
DROP DATABASE papazulu
```

Both the database and the log files are removed.

The user that is allowed to create the database becomes the "legal" owner of the database. There may be circumstances, however, that dictate you need to change the database owner (such as when the database is put into production). To change the database owner, you can use the sp_changedbowner system stored procedure.

ON

Now let's get a little more creative and install our database to a specific path. Naturally you need to be sure the path, server, and instance exists, or you could be trying to create into thin air. You also need to be sure you have domain permission and rights to create the remote database. *ON* is just a keyword that specifies that the disk files used to store the data portions of the database, the data files, are defined explicitly. It has nothing to do with making sure the database is switched on (which is what one newbie once asked me).

The *ON* keyword is followed by a comma-separated list represented by the *<filespec>* placeholder, which represents the items defining the data files for the primary filegroup (we will look into filegroups again later). The list of files in the primary filegroup can be followed by an optional, comma-separated list of <filegroup> items defining user filegroups and their files. The following code places the papazulu database on the C drive as follows:

```
ON
(NAME = papazulu, FILENAME = 'C:\databases\papazulu.mdf',
 SIZE = 4,
 MAXSIDE = 10,
 FILEGROWTH = 1)
```

The *n* placeholder indicates that multiple files can be specified for the database.

If an object is created with an ON *filegroup* clause specifying a user-defined filegroup, then all the pages for the object are allocated from the specified filegroup. The pages for all user objects created without an ON *filegroup* clause, or with an ON DEFAULT clause, are allocated from the default filegroup. When a database is first created, the primary filegroup is the default filegroup. You can specify a user-defined filegroup as the default filegroup using ALTER DATABASE as discussed later in this chapter.

LOG ON

This *LOG ON* argument specifies that the disk files used to store the database log (log files) are explicitly defined. If you use LOG ON, SQL Server will expect you to provide the name and path to the log file. The keyword is also followed by a comma-separated list of <filespec> items defining the log files. If you do not specify LOG ON, then a single log file is automatically created with a system-generated name (the same as the database name) and a size that is 25 percent of the sum of the sizes of all the data files for the database. The following code specifies the path for the papazulu log file:

```
LOG ON
(Name = 'papazulus_log',
  FILENAME = 'D:\data\logfiles\papazulu_log.ldf',
  SIZE = 5MB,
  MAXSIZE = 25MB,
FILEGROWTH = 5MB)
```

FOR LOAD

This clause is supported for compatibility with earlier versions of Microsoft SQL Server in which a database is created as part of a restore process. The database is created with the *dbo use only* database option turned on, and the status is set to loading. With SQL Server 7.0, this became obsolete because the RESTORE statement (see Chapter 9) recreates a database as part of the restore/backup operation.

FOR ATTACH

The FOR ATTACH is built into the CREATE DATABASE statement, but it allows you to attach a database that was detached earlier or from somewhere else. You should use the sp_attach_db system stored procedure instead of using CREATE DATABASE FOR ATTACH directly. Use CREATE DATABASE FOR ATTACH only when you must specify more than 16 <filespec> items.

Naturally, this is easier in Enterprise Manager but not always possible. You need to have the <filespec> entry to specify the first primary file. The only other <filespec> entries needed are those for any files that have a different path from when the database was first created or last attached. A <filespec> is needed for all files that need to be included in the attach process.

The statement is useful for some processes that requires you to detach and attach in code. The database you attach, however, must have been created using the same code page and sort order as the SQL Server you are trying to attach it to.

You will also need to remove any replication objects installed to the database using the sp_removedbreplication system stored procedure if you plan to attach a database to a server other than the server from which the database was detached.

Collation Name

The *collation_name* placeholder specifies the default collation for the database. The collation name can be either a Windows collation name or a SQL collation name. If none is specified, the database is assigned the default collation of the SQL Server instance that you are creating the database on. (Collations are discussed in Chapter 6.)

PRIMARY

The *PRIMARY* keyword specifies that the associated <filespec> list defines the primary file. As you know, the primary filegroup contains all of the new database's system tables. It also contains all objects not assigned to any user-defined filegroups. The first <filespec> entry in the primary filegroup becomes the primary file, which is the file containing the logical start of the database and its system tables (in other words, all other files are secondary because the database can have only one primary file). If you do not specify the PRIMARY file, the first file listed in the CREATE DATABASE statement becomes the primary file.

NAME

NAME specifies the logical name for the file defined by the <filespec>. The NAME parameter is not required when FOR ATTACH is specified. The following line from the earlier example specifies the logical filename:

```
NAME = 'papazulu',
```

The name must be unique in the database and conform to the rules for identifiers. The name can be a character or Unicode constant, or a regular or delimited identifier.

FILENAME

The FILENAME specifies the file system filename for the file defined by the <filespec>. The placeholder *os_file_name* is the path and filename used by the operating system when it creates the physical file defined by the <filespec>. The path in *os_file_name* must specify a directory on an instance of SQL Server. Also, if you try to specify the *os_file_name* on a compressed file system, the statement will fail.

You can also install a file to a raw partition, which is a hard-disk partition that has not been formatted for any file system (such as FAT or NTFS). If you create the file on a raw partition, the *os_file_name* must specify only the hard-disk letter of an existing raw partition; no path information can be used. And you can only create one file on each raw partition. Files on raw partitions do not autogrow, so the MAXSIZE and FILEGROWTH parameters are not needed when you specify the *os_file_name* for a raw partition (I will go over raw partitions a little later in this chapter).

SIZE

The SIZE keyword specifies the size of the file defined in the <filespec>. When a size parameter is not supplied in the <filespec> for a primary file, SQL Server takes the size of the primary file in the model database. When a SIZE parameter is not specified in the <filespec> for a secondary or log file, SQL Server makes the file between 512KB and 1MB.

When you specify size, you can use the kilobyte (KB), megabyte (MB), gigabyte (GB), or terabyte (TB) suffixes. If you leave out the suffix, the default is MB. The number should not be fractional or include any decimal notation, such as 5.5MB. If you must create a database and a half or some similar fraction, move down to the next measurement. For example 5.5MB would be 5632KB. The minimum value for the *size* parameter is 512KB. The size specified for the primary file must be at least as large as the primary file of the model database.

MAXSIZE

The MAXSIZE option specifies the maximum size to which the file defined in the <filespec> can grow. The *max_size* parameter is specified as explained in the *size* parameter. When you specify size, you can use the kilobyte (KB), megabyte (MB), gigabyte (GB), or terabyte (TB) suffix. If you leave out the suffix, the default is MB. The number should not be fractional or include any decimal notation, such as 5,500MB. It is important to know in advance what the *max_size* will be because if it is not specified, the file will keep growing until the disk is full.

UNLIMITED

This is the converse of the maxsize parameter and specifies that the file defined in the <filespec> grows until the disk is full.

FILEGROWTH

This argument specifies the growth increment of the file defined in the <filespec>. The FILEGROWTH setting for a file cannot exceed the MAXSIZE setting. What FILEGROWTH means is that every time space is needed, the file is expanded by the value defined here. As discussed earlier, you need to specify a whole number and no decimals. A value of zero (0) specifies no growth.

The FILEGROWTH value can be specified in MB, KB, GB, TB, or percent (%). If a number is specified without an MB, KB, or % suffix, SQL Server assumes a default in MB. When % is specified, the growth increment size is the specified percentage of the size of the file at the time the increment occurs. If FILEGROWTH is left out completely, the default value is 10 percent and the minimum value is 64KB. The size specified is rounded to the nearest 64KB.

Tip *After the database has been created, or at any time for that matter, you can display a report on a database, or on all the databases for an instance of SQL Server, by executing the system stored procedure sp_helpdb. To get information about the space used in a database, use sp_spaceused. You can also use sp_helpfile for a report of the files in a database. Books Online gives details about the results returned when you execute these system procs.*

Examples

The following script creates the papazulu database against the instance you are connected to. You do not need to specifically include USE MASTER at the start of the script, because SQL Server 2000 knows that anyway. Also, depending on the tool you are using, the use of "GO" might not be necessary (keep the code simple).

```
CREATE DATABASE papazulu
ON
(NAME = papazulu,
   FILENAME = 'c:\program files\microsoft
     sql server\mssql\data\papazulu.mdf',
   SIZE = 10,
   MAXSIZE = 50,
   FILEGROWTH = 5 )
LOG ON
( NAME = 'papazulu_log',
   FILENAME = 'c:\program files\microsoft
    sql server\mssql\data\papazulu_log.ldf',
   SIZE = 5MB,
   MAXSIZE = 25MB,
   FILEGROWTH = 5MB )
```

ALTER DATABASE

The ALTER DATABASE statement is a little more complex than its CREATE sibling. This code essentially adds or removes files and filegroups from the database. You can also use it to modify the attributes of files and filegroups, such as by changing the name or size of a file. ALTER DATABASE provides the capability to change the database name, filegroup names, and logical names of data files and log files.

Note *In previous versions of SQL Server, the options discussed here could be set with the sp_dboption system stored procedure. You can still use sp_dboption, but this proc might be discontinued. You can also use the DATABASEPROPERTYEX function to retrieve current settings for database options.*

The ALTER DATABASE syntax is as follows:

```
ALTER DATABASE database
{ ADD FILE < filespec > [ ,...n ] [ TO FILEGROUP filegroup_name ]
| ADD LOG FILE < filespec > [ ,...n ]
| REMOVE FILE logical_file_name
| ADD FILEGROUP filegroup_name
| REMOVE FILEGROUP filegroup_name
| MODIFY FILE < filespec >
| MODIFY NAME = new_dbname
| MODIFY FILEGROUP filegroup_name
{filegroup_property | NAME = new_filegroup_name }
/ SET < optionspec > [ ,...n ] [ WITH < termination > ]
| COLLATE < collation_name >
}

( NAME = logical_file_name
[ , NEWNAME = new_logical_name ]
[ , FILENAME = 'os_file_name' ]
[ , SIZE = size ]
[ , MAXSIZE = { max_size | UNLIMITED } ]
[ , FILEGROWTH = growth_increment ] )

< state_option >
| < cursor_option >
| < auto_option >
| < sql_option >
| < recovery_option >

< state_option > ::=
{ SINGLE_USER | RESTRICTED_USER | MULTI_USER }
| { OFFLINE | ONLINE }
| { READ_ONLY | READ_WRITE }

< termination > ::=
ROLLBACK AFTER integer [ SECONDS ]
| ROLLBACK IMMEDIATE
| NO_WAIT

< cursor_option > ::=
CURSOR_CLOSE_ON_COMMIT { ON | OFF }
| CURSOR_DEFAULT { LOCAL | GLOBAL }
```

```
< auto_option > ::=
AUTO_CLOSE { ON | OFF }
| AUTO_CREATE_STATISTICS { ON | OFF }
| AUTO_SHRINK { ON | OFF }
| AUTO_UPDATE_STATISTICS { ON | OFF }

< sql_option > ::=
ANSI_NULL_DEFAULT { ON | OFF }
| ANSI_NULLS { ON | OFF }
| ANSI_PADDING { ON | OFF }
| ANSI_WARNINGS { ON | OFF }
| ARITHABORT { ON | OFF }
| CONCAT_NULL_YIELDS_NULL { ON | OFF }
| NUMERIC_ROUNDABORT { ON | OFF }
| QUOTED_IDENTIFIER { ON | OFF }
| RECURSIVE_TRIGGERS { ON | OFF }

< recovery_option > ::=
RECOVERY { FULL | BULK_LOGGED | SIMPLE }
| TORN_PAGE_DETECTION { ON | OFF }
```

The arguments are explained in the text that follows.

Database

This is the name of the database (*database*) to be changed.

Add File

The ADD FILE argument specifies that a file is to be added to the database.

To Filegroup

The TO FILEGROUP argument specifies the filegroup, in the *filegroup_name*, to which to add the specified file.

Add Log File

The ADD LOG FILE argument specifies that a log file is to be added to the specified database.

Remove File

The REMOVE FILE argument removes the file description from the database system tables and deletes the physical file. The file cannot be removed unless empty.

Add Filegroup

The ADD FILEGROUP argument specifies that a filegroup is to be added. You also need to specify the name in the *filegroup_name* placeholder.

Remove Filegroup

The REMOVE FILEGROUP argument is specified to remove the filegroup from the database and delete all the files in the filegroup. The filegroup cannot be removed unless it is empty, not even from Enterprise Manager.

Modify File

The MODIFY FILE argument specifies the given file that should be modified, including the FILENAME, SIZE, FILEGROWTH, and MAXSIZE options. Only one of these properties can be changed at a time. NAME must be specified in the <filespec> to identify the file to be modified. If SIZE is specified, the new size must be larger than the current file size. FILENAME can be specified only for files in the tempdb database, and the new name does not take effect until Microsoft SQL Server is restarted.

To modify the logical name of a data file or log file, specify in NAME the logical filename to be renamed, and specify for NEWNAME the new logical name for the file.

For example, MODIFY FILE (NAME = *logical_file_name*, NEWNAME = *new_logical_name*...). For optimum performance during multiple modify-file operations, several ALTER DATABASE *database* MODIFY FILE statements can be run concurrently.

Modify Name

This argument allows you to rename the database. The new name is inserted in the = *new_dbname* placeholder.

Modify Filegroup

This argument lets you specify the filegroup to be modified. The information is required in the *filegroup_name* { *filegroup_property* | NAME = *new_filegroup_name* }. If *filegroup_name* and NAME = *new_filegroup_name* are specified, these parameters change the filegroup name. See the discussion on filegroups earlier in this chapter.

With

The WITH <termination> argument specifies when to roll back incomplete transactions when the database is transitioned from one state to another. Only one termination clause can be specified, and it follows the SET clauses. ROLLBACK AFTER *integer* [SECONDS] | ROLLBACK IMMEDIATE specifies whether to roll back after the specified number of seconds or immediately. If the termination clause is omitted, transactions are allowed to commit or roll back on their own.

No Wait

The NO_WAIT argument specifies that if the requested database state or option change cannot complete immediately without waiting for transactions to commit or roll back on their own, the request will fail.

Collate

See the section in CREATE DATABASE discussed earlier.

FILESPEC

The <filespec> section controls the file properties where the NAME argument specifies the logical name for the file.

The *logical_file_name* is the name used by SQL Server when referencing the file. The name must be unique within the database and conform to the rules for identifiers. The name can be a character or Unicode constant, a regular identifier, or a delimited identifier (see Identifiers in the Chapter on T-SQL, Chapter 16).

FILENAME

The FILENAME argument specifies an operating system filename. When used with MODIFY FILE, FILENAME can be specified only for files in the tempdb database. The new tempdb filename takes effect only after SQL Server is stopped and restarted.

The *os_file_name* refers to the path and filename used by the operating system for the file. The file must reside in the server in which SQL Server is installed. Data and log files should not be placed on compressed file systems.

If the file is on a raw partition, *os_file_name* must specify only the drive letter of an existing raw partition. Only one file can be placed on each raw partition. Files on raw partitions do not autogrow; therefore, the MAXSIZE and FILEGROWTH parameters are not needed when *os_file_name* specifies a raw partition.

SIZE

The SIZE argument specifies the file size. The placeholder *size* is the size of the file. The KB, MB, GB, and TB suffixes can be used to specify kilobytes, megabytes, gigabytes, or terabytes. The default is MB. Specify a whole number; do not include a decimal. The minimum value for *size* is 512KB, and the default if *size* is not specified is 1MB. When specified with ADD FILE, *size* is the initial size for the file. When specified with MODIFY FILE, *size* is the new size for the file and must be larger than the current file size.

MAXSIZE

The MAXSIZE parameter specifies the maximum file size, represented by the placeholder *max_size*. The KB, MB, GB, and TB suffixes can be used to specify kilobytes, megabytes, gigabytes, or terabytes. The default is MB. Specify a whole number; do not include a decimal. If *max_size* is not specified, the file size will increase until the disk is full.

UNLIMITED

This argument specifies that the file increases in size until the disk is full.

FILEGROWTH

The FILEGROWTH argument specifies a file increase increment. The placeholder *growth_increment* is the amount of space added to the file each time new space is needed. A value of 0 indicates no increase. The value can be specified in MB, KB, or %. Specify a whole number; do not include a decimal. When % is specified, the increment size is the specified percentage of the file size at the time the increment occurs. If a number is specified without an MB, KB, or % suffix, the default is MB. The default value if FILEGROWTH is not specified is 10%, and the minimum value is 64KB. The size specified is rounded to the nearest 64KB.

State_option

This <state_option> section controls user access to the database, whether the database is online, and whether writes are allowed.

- **SINGLE_USER | RESTRICTED_USER | MULTI_USER** Controls which users may access the database. When SINGLE_USER is specified, only one user at a time can access the database. When RESTRICTED_USER is specified, only members of the *db_owner*, *dbcreator*, or *sysadmin* roles can use the database. MULTI_USER returns the database to its normal operating state.
- **OFFLINE | ONLINE** Controls whether the database is offline or online.
- **READ_ONLY | READ_WRITE** Specifies whether the database is in read-only mode. In read-only mode, users can read data from the database but not modify it. The database cannot be in use when READ_ONLY is specified. The master database is the exception, and only the system administrator can use master while READ_ONLY is set. READ_WRITE returns the database to read/write operations.

Cursor_option

This section controls cursor options.

- **CURSOR_CLOSE_ON_COMMIT ON | OFF** If ON is specified, any cursors open when a transaction is committed or rolled back are closed. If OFF is specified, such cursors remain open when a transaction is committed; rolling back a transaction closes any cursors except those defined as INSENSITIVE or STATIC.
- **CURSOR_DEFAULTLOCAL | GLOBAL** Controls whether cursor scope defaults to LOCAL or GLOBAL.

Auto_option

This section controls automatic options.

- **AUTO_CLOSE ON | OFF** If ON is specified, the database is shut down cleanly and its resources are freed after the last user exits. If OFF is specified, the database remains open after the last user exits.
- **AUTO_CREATE_STATISTICS ON | OFF** If ON is specified, any missing statistics needed by a query for optimization are automatically built during optimization.
- **AUTO_SHRINK ON | OFF** If ON is specified, the database files are candidates for automatic periodic shrinking.
- **AUTO_UPDATE_STATISTICS ON | OFF** If ON is specified, any out-of-date statistics required by a query for optimization are automatically built during optimization. If OFF is specified, statistics must be updated manually.

Sql_option

The SQL_OPTION controls the ANSI compliance options.

- **ANSI_NULL_DEFAULT ON | OFF** If ON is specified, CREATE TABLE follows SQL-92 rules to determine whether a column allows null values.
- **ANSI_NULLS ON | OFF** If ON is specified, all comparisons to a null value evaluate to UNKNOWN. If OFF is specified, comparisons of non-UNICODE values to a null value evaluate to TRUE if both values are NULL.
- **ANSI_PADDING ON | OFF** If ON is specified, strings are padded to the same length before comparison or insert. If OFF is specified, strings are not padded.
- **ANSI_WARNINGS ON | OFF** If ON is specified, errors or warnings are issued when conditions such as divide-by-zero occur.
- **ARITHABORT ON | OFF** If ON is specified, a query is terminated when an overflow or divide-by-zero error occurs during query execution.
- **CONCAT_NULL_YIELDS_NULL ON | OFF** If ON is specified, the result of a concatenation operation is NULL when either operand is NULL. If OFF is specified, the null value is treated as an empty character string. The default is OFF.
- **QUOTED_IDENTIFIER ON | OFF** If ON is specified, double quotation marks can be used to enclose delimited identifiers.
- **NUMERIC_ROUNDABORT ON | OFF** If ON is specified, an error is generated when loss of precision occurs in an expression.
- **RECURSIVE_TRIGGERS ON | OFF** If ON is specified, recursive firing of triggers is allowed. RECURSIVE_TRIGGERS OFF, the default, prevents direct recursion only. To disable indirect recursion as well, set the nested triggers server option to 0 using sp_configure.

Recovery_options

This section controls database recovery options.

- **RECOVERY FULL | BULK_LOGGED | SIMPLE** If FULL is specified, complete protection against media failure is provided. If a data file is damaged, media recovery can restore all committed transactions.

If BULK_LOGGED is specified, protection against media failure is combined with the best performance and least amount of log memory usage for certain large-scale or bulk operations. These operations include SELECT INTO, bulk load operations (bcp and BULK INSERT), CREATE INDEX, and text and image operations (WRITETEXT and UPDATETEXT).

Under the bulk-logged recovery model, logging for the entire class is minimal and cannot be controlled on an operation-by-operation basis.

If SIMPLE is specified, a simple backup strategy that uses minimal log space is provided. Log space can be automatically reused when no longer needed for server failure recovery.

Note *The simple recovery model is easier to manage than the other two models but at the expense of higher data loss exposure if a data file is damaged. All changes since the most recent database or differential database backup are lost and must be reentered manually. Check out recovery models in Chapter 8.*

The default recovery model is determined by the recovery model of the model database. To change the default for new databases, use ALTER DATABASE to set the recovery option of the model database.

- **TORN_PAGE_DETECTION ON | OFF** If ON is specified, incomplete pages can be detected. The default is ON.

Creating a Database Using Enterprise Manager

If you do not need to be scripting to create a database, then using Enterprise Manager makes perfect sense. In addition to creating the database in Enterprise Manager, you can also manage or alter the database there. For example, you can manipulate the file sizes, filegroups, and so on. And you can attach and detach databases (which is a very convenient method of making copies of your database for distribution, provided you are sure the target is compatible).

To create a database interactively, do the following:

1. Expand your server group and select the specific server and instance in which you want to create a new database. Expand the server node so that the node "Databases" is accessible. Select Databases and right-click. Now select New Database. The dialog box illustrated in Figure 11-1 loads.

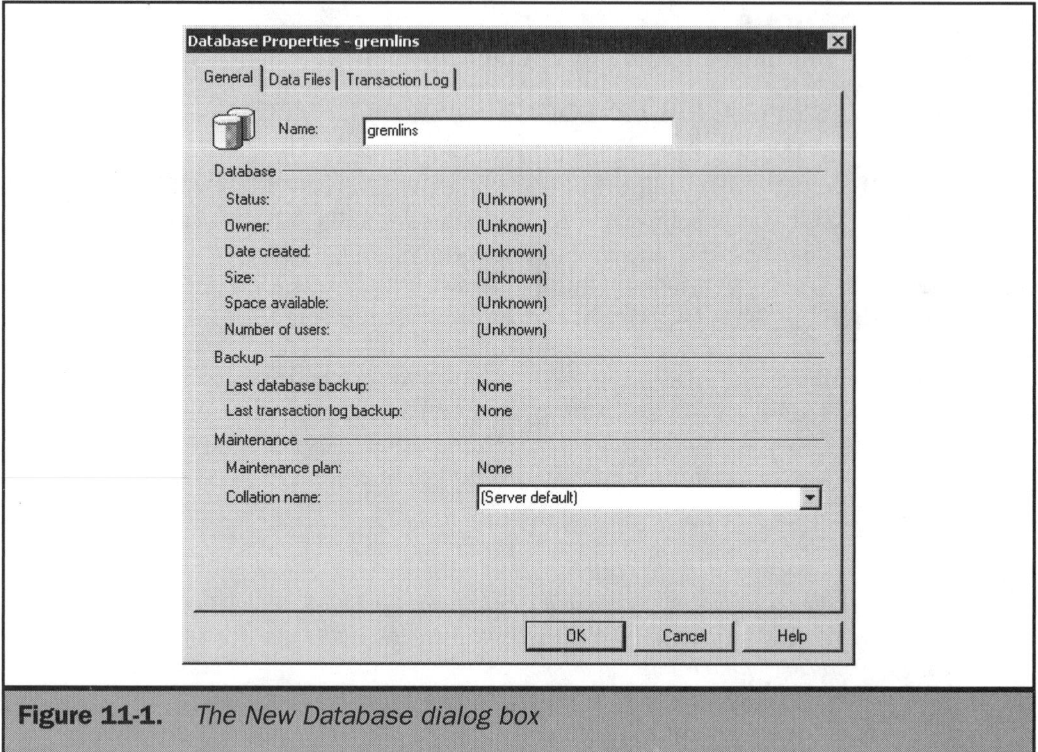

Figure 11-1. *The New Database dialog box*

2. On the General tab, enter the database name of the database and choose the collation.
3. On the Data Files tab, illustrated in Figure 11-2, enter the name of the primary data file and specify the file properties. The values for the properties follow the same recommendations I discussed in the CREATE DATABASE section earlier.
4. On the Transaction Log tab, illustrated in Figure 11-3, enter the log filename and file properties. Click OK and you're done.

After creating the new database and before you use it, you should back up *master*, which will now contain definitions and specifics related to the new database.

Creating a Database Using the Create Database Wizard

To create a database using the Create Database Wizard, you need to do the following:

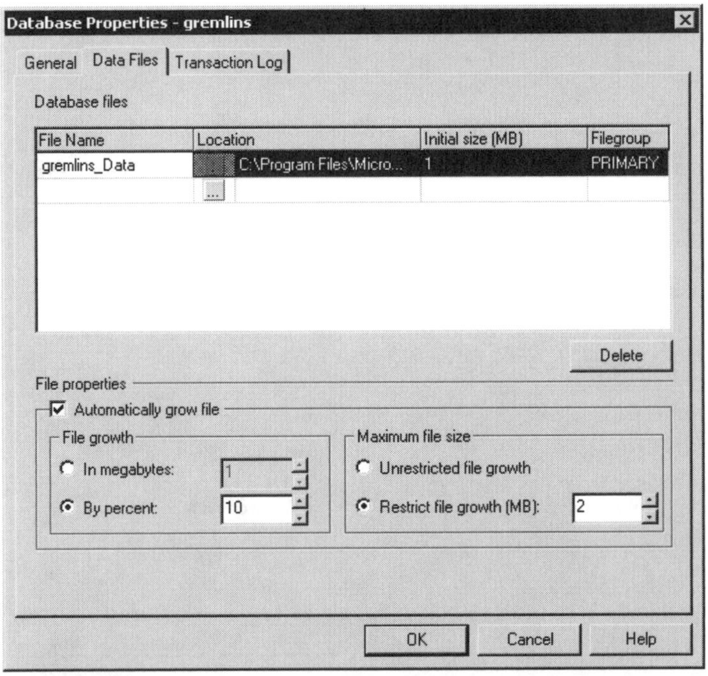

Figure 11-2. *The Data Files tab in the New Database dialog box*

1. Drill down to the target server in Enterprise Manager and then expand down to the database node. Select the database node and then select Tools | Wizards. The Select Wizard dialog box opens. This dialog box is illustrated in Figure 11-4.
2. Expand the Database node in the wizard and select the Create Database Wizard. Click Next to advance from the Welcome screen. The next dialog box will let you name the database and specify its location. This dialog box, "Name the Database and Specify Its Location," is illustrated in Figure 11-5. (As you can see, from what you have to enter, it is not much different from what we discussed earlier in creating the database from the Create Database option that can be accessed from the Database node.) Click Next to advance to the next Wizard dialog box.

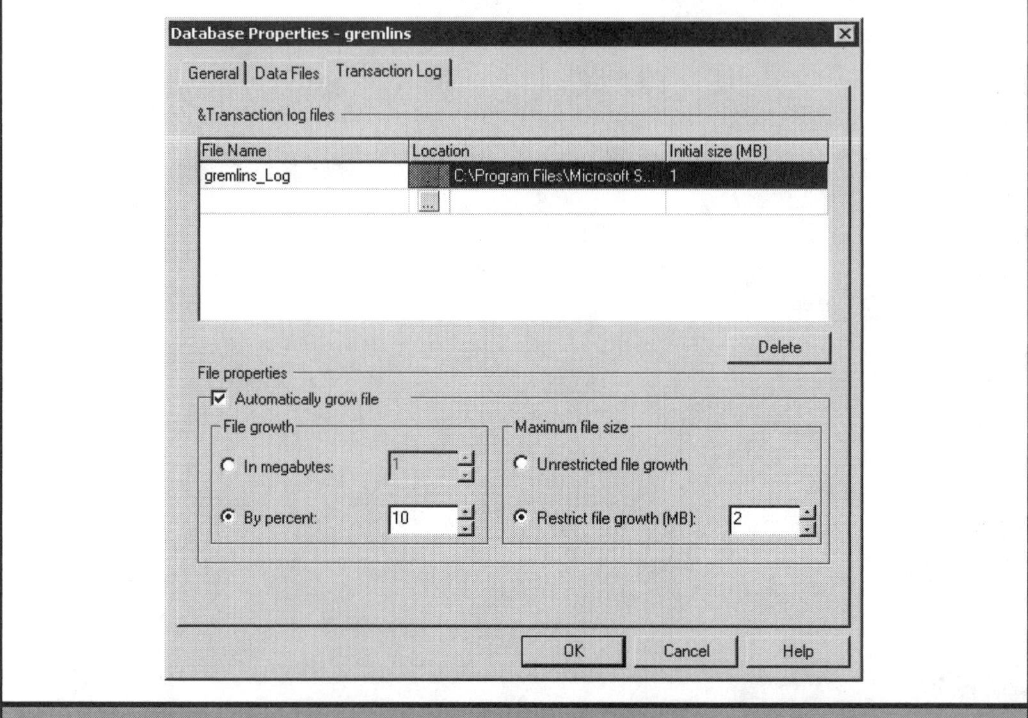

Figure 11-3. *The Transaction Log tab in the New Database dialog box*

3. The Name the Database Files dialog box loads and lets you enter the name of the database's corresponding filename (which will be assigned the *.mdf* extension, as I described earlier in "Understanding Filegroups"). Click Next.
4. The Define the Database File Growth dialog box loads, as illustrated in Figure 11-6. Here you would enter the file growth specifications, as discussed earlier. Click Next.
5. The Name the Transaction Log Files dialog box loads, as illustrated in Figure 11-7. Enter the name and initial size for the transaction log and click Next. By default, the extension of the transaction log will default to *.ldf*, as explained earlier in this chapter.
6. The Define the Transaction Log File Growth dialog box, as illustrated in Figure 11-8, loads. Here's where you enter the file growth specifications. After you are done, click Next to go to the confirmation dialog box and then click Finish. You can click Back if you need to change something. After you click Finish, there is no going back and the database is created. Later, of course, you can change growth and similar options from the Database Properties dialog box.

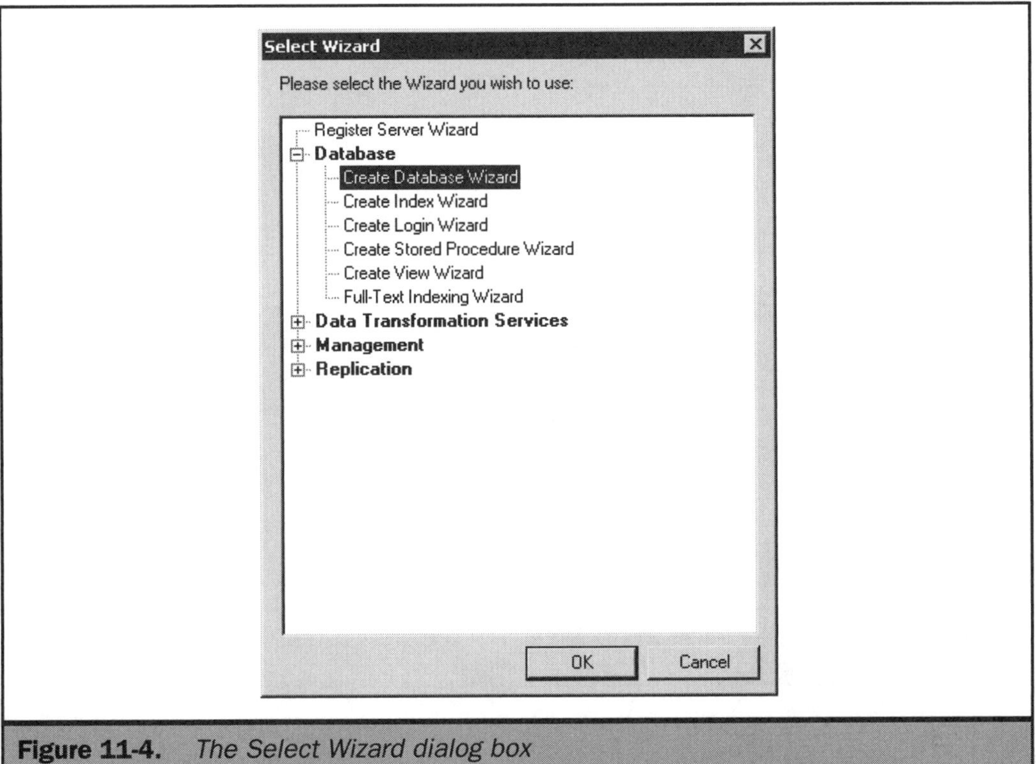

Figure 11-4. *The Select Wizard dialog box*

Tables

In the first part of this book, we discussed the architecture of SQL Server tables and how data is stored in them. Let's look at the tables in this chapter from a higher level, as objects we need to create and configure for our applications. A database can contain many tables and the tables can contain many columns designed to hold different data types.

There are several ways that you can go about creating your tables, as described in the following list:

1. Interactively in Enterprise Manager using the Design Table utility
2. Interactively in Enterprise Manager from within a Database Diagram
3. Through code, specifically the CREATE TABLE and ALTER TABLE statements
4. Through Data Transformation Services
5. Using the SQL-DMO object model

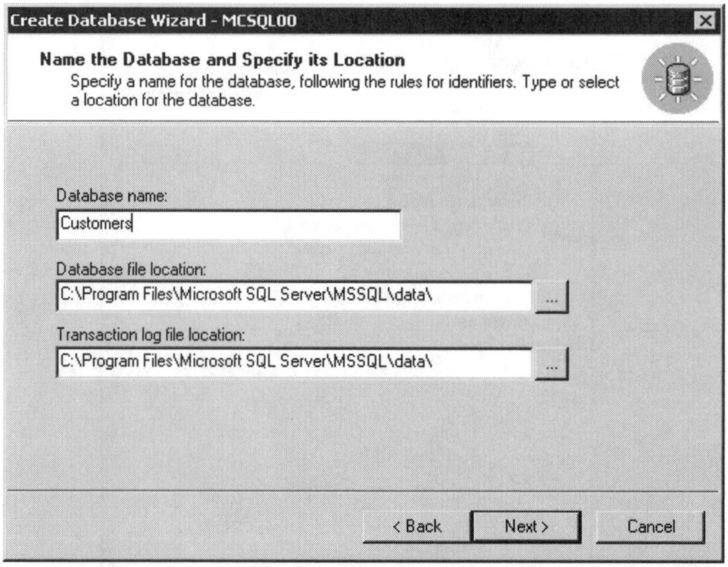

Figure 11-5. *The Name the Database and Specify Its Location dialog box*

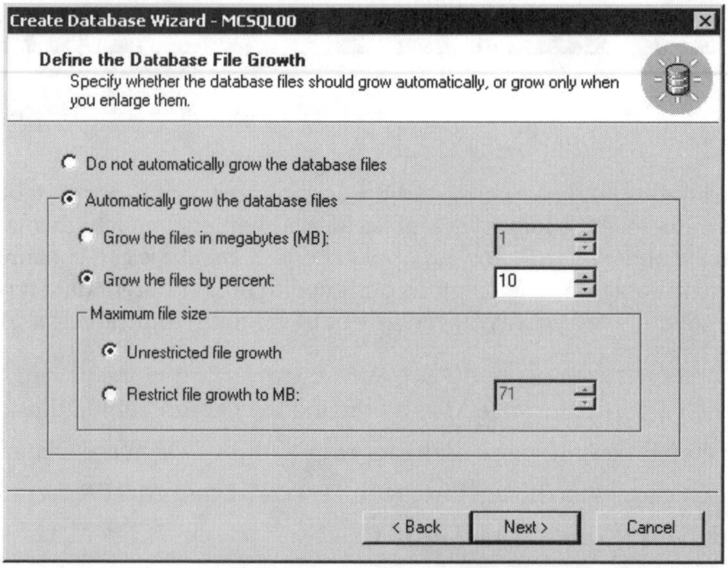

Figure 11-6. *The Define the Database File Growth dialog box*

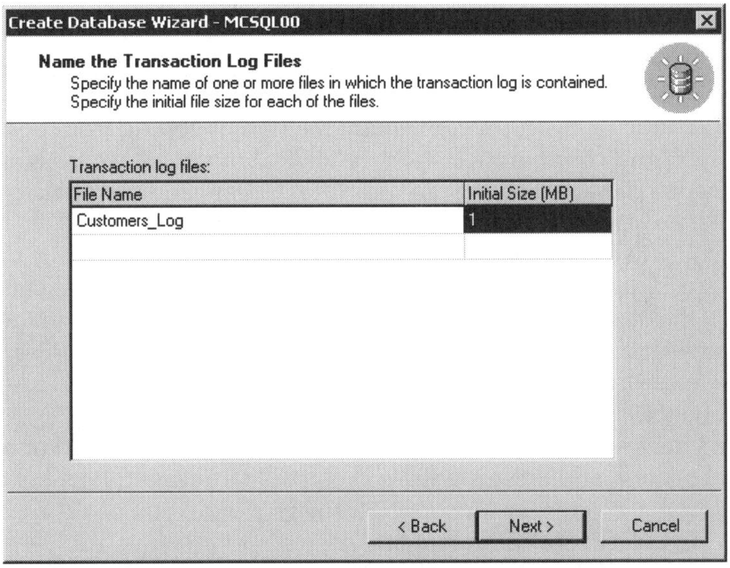

Figure 11-7. *The Name the Transaction Log Files dialog box*

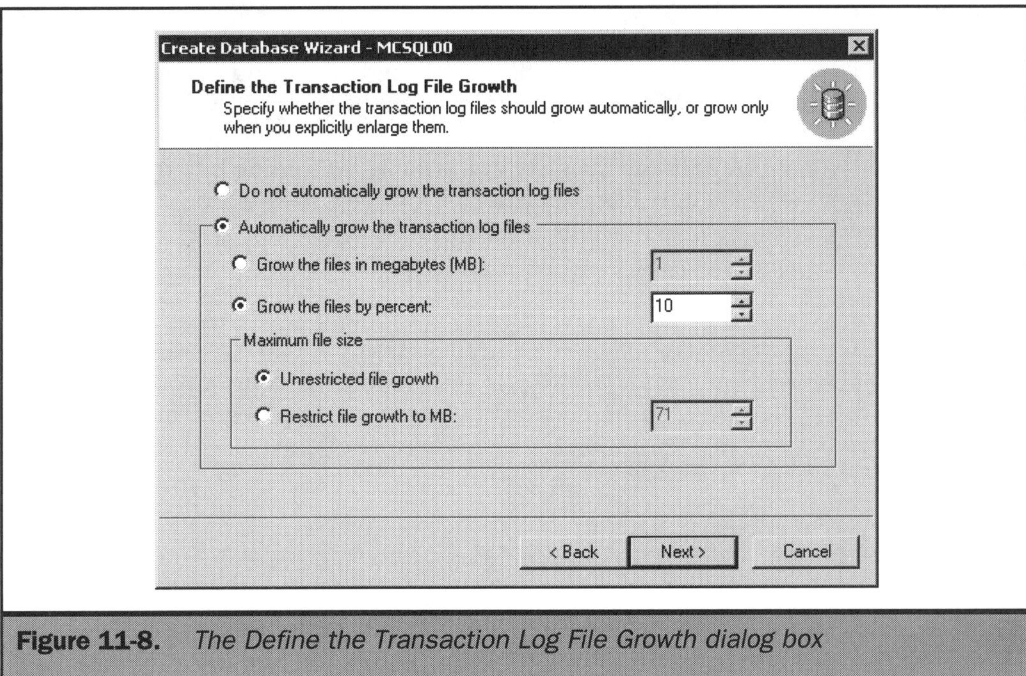

Figure 11-8. *The Define the Transaction Log File Growth dialog box*

Each route represents a different mechanism for creating a table. In this section, we'll be looking at the CREATE TABLE and ALTER TABLE statements, and the interactive design tools in Enterprise Manager. The SQL-DMO object model is beyond the scope of this book, but we'll be looking at Data Transformation Services in the next chapter.

Before you decide on the most convenient method of getting from point A to point B in table creation and configuration, let's first talk about database design. You will recall from Chapter 5 that modeling, architecture, design, and metadata creation are essential before we can build our databases and applications.

Granted, you will always be adding more tables, expanding existing ones, and changing the attributes of the tables. Initially, however, you need to sketch out the basic design of the database and its tables before creating the objects in the database. You can use sophisticated modeling tools, such as ER-Win, Rational Rose, and Visio 2000, or you can use the so-called Visual Database Tools that can be accessed from Enterprise Manager.

If you don't have any design tools handy, then a large whiteboard or a single large sheet of paper, pencils, and erasers will do. You could go from the whiteboard or paper to the Visual Database Tools, or if you are strong at T-SQL, you could create what you need using the CREATE TABLE statement.

You should design the entire database or application from the get-go, and all the tables you'll need to get the job done at version one. Working tables piecemeal can be really taxing on the overall development project and is never recommended. You really need to see the entire logical model from a much higher level, rather than working on a table-by-table basis.

You will need to understand and formulate a plan around how the tables are going to be normalized, such as to what levels—3NF, 4NF, and so on; and you need to decide on the placing of primary and foreign keys, indexes, and data types. Constraints are not that important at this stage; I believe it's more important to get the logical design in place before worrying about the integrity of the data that's going into the tables. Integrity can come with the data integrity plan.

So, on to table creation with the help of T-SQL.

CREATE TABLE

The CREATE TABLE statement may seem a little daunting if you have not seen or worked with it before. However, if working in source or script code is your thing, then you'll find CREATE TABLE (and ALTER TABLE) much more powerful and possibly a lot easier than working with the dialog boxes in Enterprise Manager.

```
CREATE TABLE
[ database_name.[ owner ] . | owner. ] table_name
( { < column_definition >
| column_name AS computed_column_expression
```

```
| < table_constraint > ::= [ CONSTRAINT constraint_name ] }

| [ { PRIMARY KEY | UNIQUE } [ ,...n ]
)

[ ON { filegroup | DEFAULT } ]
[ TEXTIMAGE_ON { filegroup | DEFAULT } ]

< column_definition > ::= { column_name data_type }
[ COLLATE < collation_name > ]
[ [ DEFAULT constant_expression ]
| [ IDENTITY [ ( seed , increment ) [ NOT FOR REPLICATION ] ] ]
]
[ ROWGUIDCOL]
[ < column_constraint > ] [ ...n ]

< column_constraint > ::= [ CONSTRAINT constraint_name ]
{ [ NULL | NOT NULL ]
| [ { PRIMARY KEY | UNIQUE }
[ CLUSTERED | NONCLUSTERED ]
[ WITH FILLFACTOR = fillfactor ]
[ON {filegroup | DEFAULT} ] ]
]
| [ [ FOREIGN KEY ]
REFERENCES ref_table [ ( ref_column ) ]
[ ON DELETE { CASCADE | NO ACTION } ]
[ ON UPDATE { CASCADE | NO ACTION } ]
[ NOT FOR REPLICATION ]
]
| CHECK [ NOT FOR REPLICATION ]
( logical_expression )
}

< table_constraint > ::= [ CONSTRAINT constraint_name ]
{ [ { PRIMARY KEY | UNIQUE }
[ CLUSTERED | NONCLUSTERED ]
{ ( column [ ASC | DESC ] [ ,...n ] ) }
[ WITH FILLFACTOR = fillfactor ]
[ ON { filegroup | DEFAULT } ]
]
| FOREIGN KEY
[ ( column [ ,...n ] ) ]
```

```
REFERENCES ref_table [ ( ref_column [ ,...n ] ) ]
[ ON DELETE { CASCADE | NO ACTION } ]
[ ON UPDATE { CASCADE | NO ACTION } ]
[ NOT FOR REPLICATION ]
| CHECK [ NOT FOR REPLICATION ]
( search_conditions )
}
```

So let's go through these arguments:

Database_name

The *database_name* argument specifies the name of the database in which the table is created. If you omit the *database_name* in the script, SQL Server will install the table to the current table by default. You will obviously need a login for the current connection and an associated user ID in the database specified here; and create table permissions are required.

Owner

The *owner* is the name of the user ID that owns the new table; this must be an existing user ID in the database. If you do not specify an *owner*, SQL Server defaults to the user ID associated with the login for the current connection in the database.

You can also transfer the ownership if you are a member of the sysadmin fixed server role or the db_dbowner or db_ddladmin fixed database roles. You can also create the table if all you have is create table rights, but you have to specify a user ID associated with the current login. If you do not specify an owner but you are a member of the sysadmin fixed server role, the owner of the table will default to the dbo user.

Table Name

The *table_name* that you provide must conform to the rules for identifiers (see Chapter 16). The identifier must also be unique and fully qualified in dot notation. An example of a qualified unique identifier is *comptroller.account_pay* or *dbo.customers.*

The *table_name* can contain a maximum of 128 characters. Temporary table names must be prefixed with a single number sign (#), and they cannot exceed 116 characters. (See Chapter 16 for a discussion on the new table data type, which might suit your purpose better than temporary tables.)

Column Name

The *column_name* represents the name of a column in the table. The column names must also conform to the rules for identifiers as discussed previously, and they must be unique in the table you are creating. The only time you do not need to specify a column name is when you create a column to hold *timestamp* data. SQL Server will just use "timestamp" for the column name if you leave it out.

Computed Column Expression

The *computed_column_expression* refers to an expression defining the value of a computed column. A computed column is not physically created and stored in the table, but is computed from an expression using other columns in the same table. You can create a computed column to hold a computing expression. For example, the expression "total AS subtotal * discount" returns a single value stored in this column.

The expression you use does not need to be a mathematical expression. It can also be another noncomputed column name, constant, function, variable, or any combination of these connected by one or more operators. The only exception is that the expression cannot be a subquery.

Computed columns can be used in select lists, WHERE clauses, ORDER BY clauses, or any other locations in which regular expressions can be used. The following exceptions, however, are important considerations:

- You cannot define a DEFAULT or a FOREIGN KEY constraint or a NOT NULL constraint definition over this so-called column. But the computed column can be used as a key column in an index or as part of any PRIMARY KEY or UNIQUE constraint. The provison is that the computed column value must be defined by a deterministic expression and the data type of the result must be compatible with index columns.

  Using the nondeterministic function GETDATE(), for example, would not fly because it changes with every invocation and thus cannot be indexed.

- You cannot reference a computed column from an INSERT or UPDATE statement.

SQL Server may insert a NULL value into the column and you can use the COLUMNPROPERTY function (AllowsNull property) to investigate the nullability of the computed columns. You can also call the ISNULL(*check_expression,* constant) function and if necessary change the value to a nonnull.

ON {*filegroup* | DEFAULT}

The ON {*filegroup* | DEFAULT} placeholder specifies a filegroup for the table (see the discussion on filegroups earlier in this chapter). If you do not specify ON, the table will be stored in the default filegroup.

The ON {*filegroup* | DEFAULT} can also be specified in a PRIMARY KEY or UNIQUE constraint. If *filegroup* is specified, however, the index is stored in the named filegroup. If DEFAULT is specified, the index is stored in the default filegroup. If you omit the filegroup from a constraint definition, then the index will be stored in the same filegroup as the table.

When you specify DEFAULT here, you must delimit it, because it not a keyword. You can delimit it with double quotes; for example ON "DEFAULT", or with square brackets; for example ON [DEFAULT].

Text Images in Filegroups

The TEXTIMAGE_ON { *filegroup* | DEFAULT } specification indicates that the text, ntext, and image columns are stored on the specified filegroup defined in the preceding argument. However, TEXTIMAGE ON is not allowed if there are no text, ntext, or image columns in the table. If you do not specify TEXTIMAGE_ON, the text, ntext, and image columns are stored in the same filegroup as the table.

Data Type

The *data_type* argument specifies the column data type. You can use any system- or user-defined data types. To add the user-defined data type, you can call the system stored procedure sp_addtype in the script, as long as you create it before trying to use it in a table definition.

The NULL/NOT NULL assignment for a user-defined data type can be overridden during the CREATE TABLE statement, but you cannot specify a length for a user-defined data type in the CREATE TABLE statement.

Default

The DEFAULT argument specifies the value that SQL Server will automatically insert in your column if you do not provide a value when using INSERT (see Chapter 17 and Chapter 20).

Constant Expression

The *constant_expression* placeholder is used to specify a constant, a NULL value, or a system function used as the default value for the column.

Identity

The IDENTITY placeholder specifies that the respective column is an identity column. (See Chapter 17 for more information on the Identity columns.) These are commonly used in conjunction with PRIMARY KEY constraints to serve as the unique row identifier for the table. The actual IDENTITY value or property can be of the data types tinyint, smallint, int, bigint, or the decimal(p,0), or numeric(p,0) columns. You must also specify both the seed and increment or you can leave them out altogether, in which case the default of (1,1) will be used (*seed, increment*).

Seed

The seed is the value SQL Server uses for the very first row loaded into the table. If the seed is "1," the first row will be "1."

Increment

The increment specifies the incremental value added to the identity value for the preceding row. For example, if the last row ID was "2785" and the increment is "5," the next row's value will be "2790."

Not for Replication

The NOT FOR REPLICATION argument specifies that the IDENTITY property should not be enforced when a replication login such as *sqlrepl* inserts data into the table. Replicated rows must retain the key values assigned in the publishing database, as demonstrated in the preceding chapter. The NOT FOR REPLICATION clause ensures that rows inserted by a replication process are not assigned new identity values. Rows inserted by other processes continue unaffected by this restriction. (You can also manage these values and values inserted by the publishers with CHECK constraints on the local table.)

Rowguidcol

This argument indicates that the new column is a row global unique identifier column. There can be only one uniqueidentifier column per table and the ROWGUIDCOL property can be assigned only to a uniqueidentifier column. (Make sure not to install a ROWGUIDCOL on a database whose compatibility level is 65 or lower (version 6.5). See Appendix A or Books Online for system stored procedure sp_dbcmptlevel.

It is important to understand that the ROWGUIDCOL property does not enforce uniqueness of the values stored in the column. It also does not behave like the identity column and automatically generate values for new rows inserted into the table. However, you can generate unique values for each column by either using the NEWID() function on INSERT statements or using the NEWID() function as the default for the column (NEWID() is discussed further in Chapter 16).

Collation Name

The *collation_name* argument specifies the language collation for the column. (Collations are introduced in Chapter 6.) The collation name can be either a Windows collation name or a SQL collation name. Collations govern the management of text strings in the database, so this argument is applicable only for columns of the char, varchar, text, nchar, nvarchar, and ntext data types. If you do not specify the collation, the column will be assigned either the collation of the user-defined data type (if the column is of a user-defined data type) or the default collation of the database. The database collation is either specifically set or inherited from msdb.

Constraint

The *constraint_name* argument is optional, but when you use it, you need to specify the constraint name, which must be unique to the database.

Null

The NULL | NOT NULL keywords are used to specify whether null values are allowed in the column. NULL is not really a constraint per se but can be specified in the same manner as NOT NULL.

Primary Key

The PRIMARY KEY argument is a constraint that enforces entity integrity for a given column or columns through a unique index.

Unique

The UNIQUE argument specifies the constraint that provides entity integrity for a given column or columns through a unique index. A table can have multiple UNIQUE constraints.

Index Clustering

Index clustering is specified through the CLUSTERED | NONCLUSTERED keywords used to indicate that a clustered or nonclustered index is created for the PRIMARY KEY or UNIQUE constraint. PRIMARY KEY constraints default to CLUSTERED, and UNIQUE constraints default to NONCLUSTERED.

You cannot specify CLUSTERED for more than one constraint in a CREATE TABLE statement, and you'll see that enforced, even by Enterprise Manager. If you specify CLUSTERED for a UNIQUE constraint and also specify a PRIMARY KEY constraint, the PRIMARY KEY defaults to NONCLUSTERED.

Fillfactor

The argument [WITH FILLFACTOR = *fillfactor*] specifies how full SQL Server should make each index page when it creates it to store the index data. You can set the *fillfactor* values from 1 through 100, with a default of 0. A lower fill factor creates the index with more space available for new index entries without having to allocate new space.

Referential Integrity

Referential integrity is specified through the FOREIGN KEY...REFERENCES arguments. The FOREIGN KEY constraints can reference only columns that are PRIMARY KEY or UNIQUE constraints in the referenced table or columns referenced in a UNIQUE INDEX on the referenced table. This is done through the following arguments:

- The *ref_table*, which specifies the name of the table referenced by the FOREIGN KEY constraint.
- The (*ref_column*[,...*n*]), which specifies a column or list of columns from the table referenced by the FOREIGN KEY constraint.

Cascading Referential Integrity

The ON DELETE {CASCADE | NO ACTION} and ON UPDATE {CASCADE | NO ACTION} arguments specify what action is taken on a row in the table created if a referential relationship with a row in a foreign table is established. The default is NO ACTION, which may not be wise (see Chapter 17). However, if CASCADE is specified and a row is deleted or updated in a parent table, then the row it references in the new table is also deleted or updated. If NO ACTION is specified, SQL Server raises an error and the delete or update actions on the rows in the parent table are rolled back. This is further discussed in Chapter 17.

Check

The CHECK argument refers to a constraint that enforces domain integrity by limiting the possible values that can be entered into a column or columns. The NOT FOR REPLICATION keywords are used to prevent the CHECK constraint from being enforced during the distribution process used by replication.

The *logical_expression* placeholder is a logical expression that returns TRUE or FALSE. The *column* placeholder is a column or list of columns, in parentheses, used in table constraints to indicate the columns used in the constraint definition.

The [ASC | DESC] placeholder specifies the order in which the column or columns participating in table constraints are sorted. The default is ASC. Finally, the *n* placeholder indicates that the preceding item can be repeated *n* number of times.

ALTER TABLE is almost identical to CREATE TABLE, so we will not go through the syntax for it, and besides, you can reference the entire syntax in Books Online.

Creating a table in Enterprise Manager is obviously a lot easier for a novice than going the T-SQL script route. As I mentioned earlier, however, by building a T-SQL script you afford yourself a thorough education on what it takes to build a database and put tables in it. In any event, most CREATE TABLE code only needs to be a few lines.

Creating a Table Using Enterprise Manager

To create a table in Enterprise Manager, you need to perform the following actions:

- Drill down to the database into which you need to add the new table. Right-click the database node and select New Table from the context menu. The Design Table dialog box, as illustrated in Figure 11-9, loads.
- Create and configure the columns as needed. Note the toolbar at the top of the designer. Four buttons (a little overkill) open the Table properties dialog box, where constraints, indexes, and so on are created and managed. The integrity constraints, checks, and so on, are fully discussed in Chapter 17.

The Design Table utility essentially does what the T-SQL scripts do.

Working with Tables in Database Diagrams

Database diagrams are not something new in Enterprise Manager, but they have been enhanced with a few features. In my opinion, the diagrams are nothing more than a redundant feature in Enterprise Manager, already catered to by the Design Table utility. At best it is useful in the beginning, and at worst it is a sorry effort on Microsoft's part to add a semblance of a modeling tool to SQL Server. You are better off working in

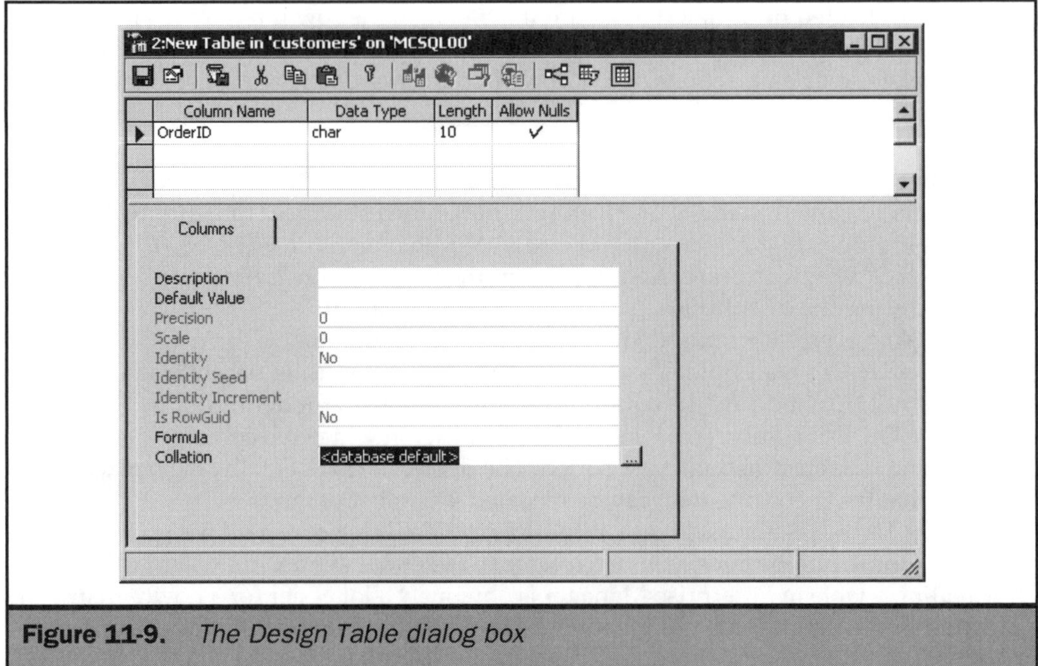

Figure 11-9. *The Design Table dialog box*

something like Rational Rose or Visio 2000, and although discussing these tools is beyond the scope of this book, they can be used to generate metadata, object information models (OIMs), and SQL code.

Nevertheless, you can start with the database diagram, as is described in the following two sections.

Creating New Tables and a New Database Diagram

To create a diagram without tables, do as follows:

- Expand the database node for the database you are working with. Right-click the Diagrams node and select New Database Diagram from the context menu. The New Database Diagram pane opens at the same time as the Create Database Diagram Wizard. Click Cancel to close the wizard.
- Right-click anywhere in the New Diagram pane and select New Table from the context menu. The Choose Name dialog box, illustrated in Figure 11-10, loads. Enter the name and click OK. The new table is inserted into the Database Diagram, as illustrated in Figure 11-11. The features you have to work with here are practically identical to what is available in the Design Table utility.

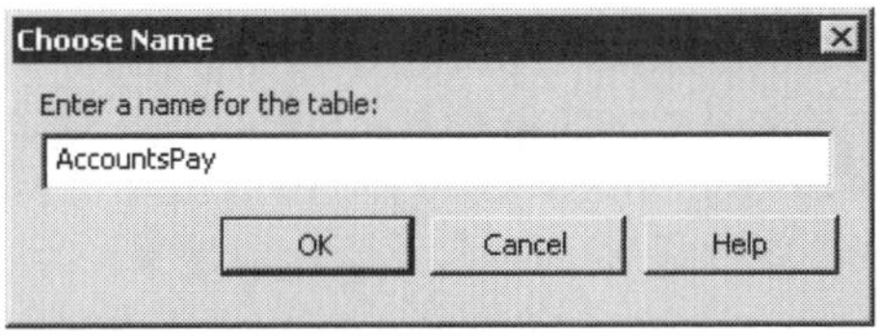

Choose Name

Enter a name for the table:

AccountsPay

OK Cancel Help

Figure 11-10. *The Choose Name dialog box*

You can now work with the tables and add or delete from the database diagram as you need.

Creating Diagrams from Existing Tables

To create a diagram using existing tables, do as follows:

- Expand the database node for the database you are working with. Right-click the Diagrams node and select New Database Diagram from the context menu. The New Database Diagram pane opens at the same time as the Create Database Diagram Wizard. Click Next to advance past the Welcome dialog box.

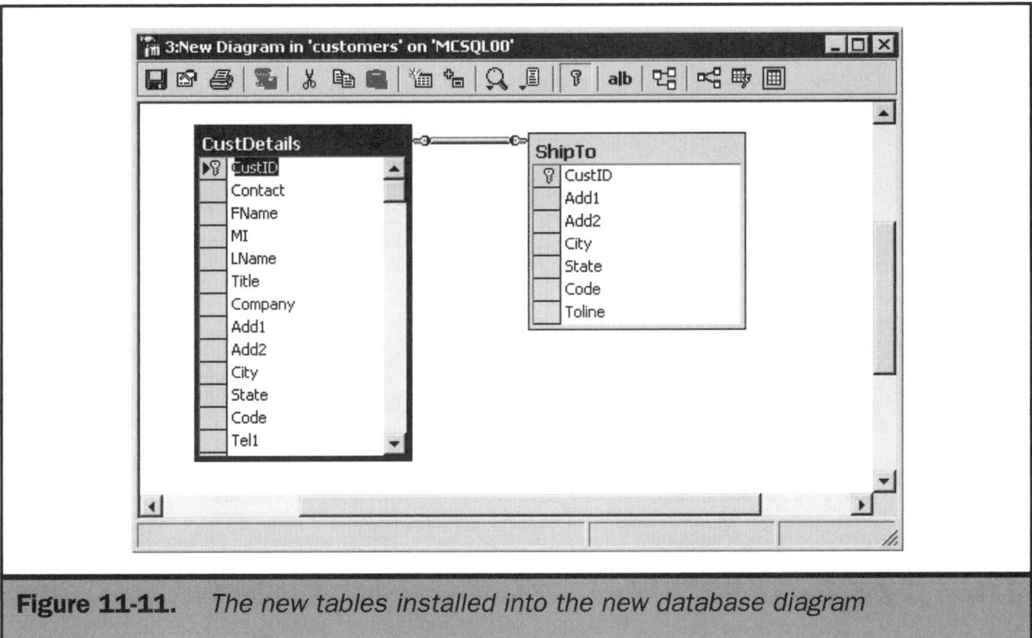

Figure 11-11. *The new tables installed into the new database diagram*

- In the Select Tables to Be Added dialog box, illustrated in Figure 11-12, transfer the tables destined for inclusion in the diagram to the right pane. Then click Next. You will get a confirmation of the tables to be included in the diagram. If you are satisfied with the choices, click Finish and the Database Diagram dialog box loads as illustrated earlier.

You can now work with the tables, and add or delete from the database diagram as discussed earlier.

Indexes

Why are indexes so important to database applications or database management systems? Well, that answer doesn't require much thought. An index helps you find data (row values) in a database quickly without the system having to step through every row in the table. Now, if you had a table with only five rows, for example, going to each row and looking at its value in a specific column, a table scan, is not a big deal. But what if the table contained a gazillion rows—not an unusual situation for the average Web site database, or my wife's contact file?

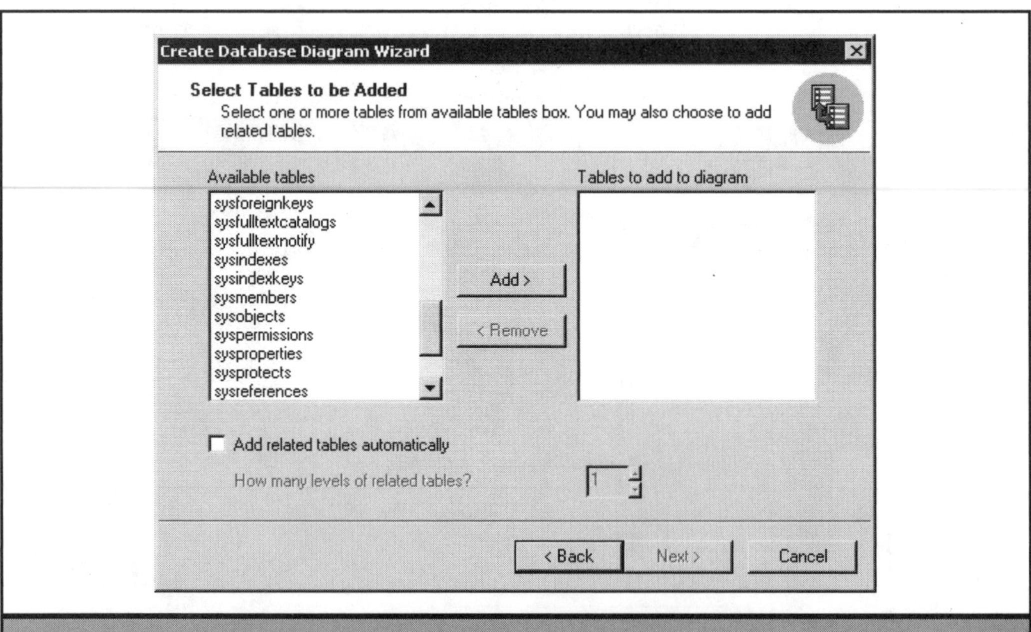

Figure 11-12. *The Select Tables to be Added dialog box*

Imagine if the books we read were only a few paragraphs on a page. Would we still need an index at the back? Not at all. But we all know that most books contain a lot of pages and without an index, it would be very difficult to find information rapidly without having to first scan through the entire book. I have indexed several books in a past life and the process is identical, from a logical or conceptual viewpoint, to the indexing of data in a table. You pinpoint exactly where in the book—the page number—a word or subject matter exists and you list that word or subject matter in the index with the page number the reader can find it on. Professional indexers who practically index in their sleep can read through the printed pages at lightening speed and quickly build an index of information on all the pages.

Indexes are critical. This book has one. When I go to a bookstore I hardly bother with the contents, or the author's bio or what he or she has to say in the preface or introduction. I go directly to the index, look up an item I want information on, and hope I find it. If the item is indexed, I go to the page and read the information to establish whether the book is imparting knowledge on the subject matter I am interested in. If not, I put the book back on the shelf and move on.

Indexing tables is absolutely essential, but there was a time in the early days of the relational engine that indexing caused such a performance hit on databases that indexes were kept to a minimum. Indexes still incur overhead, and we'll look into that aspect shortly, but without them, looking for information in a table is a very loathsome exercise for the DBMS because it has to go through every row in the table to find the information requested by your query.

Indexes are database objects. A database index is a lot like a book index; it is a list of values in a table that contains the exact storage locations of the rows in the table that contain each value. Indexes can be created for a single column of values in a table or for a combination of columns. Indexes are usually implemented as B-trees. B-trees are sorted on the search key. If we create an index on *[company name]* and *[company number]*, the B-tree index can efficiently locate a value on either column. Figure 11-13 illustrates an index and the table it was created for.

When you build queries, as discussed in the chapters in Part III, they will execute faster and return data to the client if the correct indexes have been created for the data in question. It is obviously insane to place an index on the company number when all queries are done on the company name. The index for the former value would never be used and the queries on company name would have the DBMS looking for data like a late movie-goer looking for his or her seat in the dark.

Having said that, SQL Server might at times find that an index scenario has reached a point of diminishing returns (sorry about that pun), and that the indexing process is costing more in overhead than iterating through the table row by row. This is the point at which you need to reevaluate the indexing and either drop the indexes or re-architect the table, which could mean rebuilding an index solution at the minimum or rethinking the current schema. More about this is a moment.

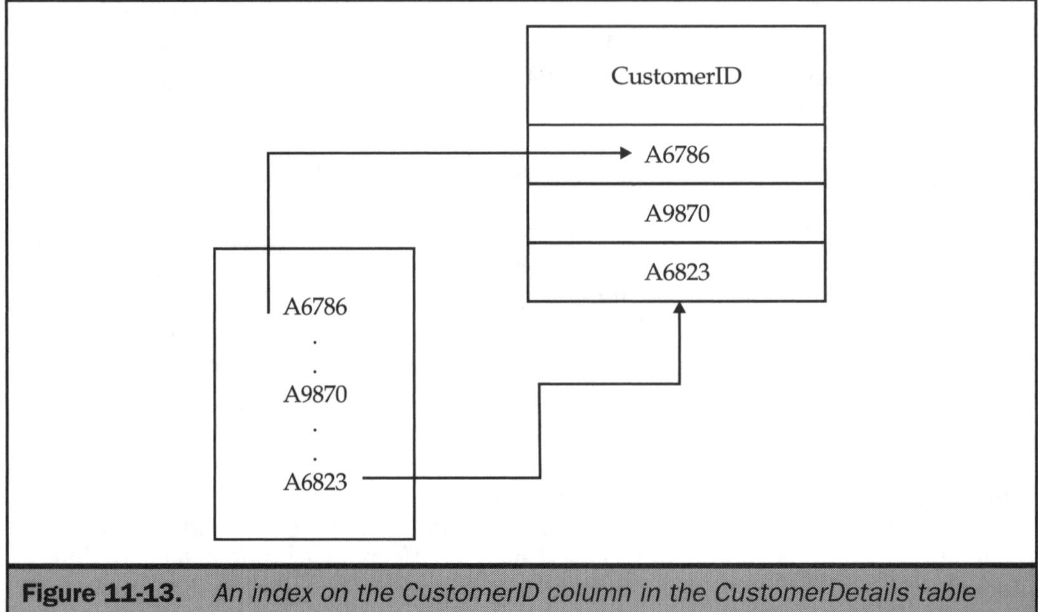

Figure 11-13. *An index on the CustomerID column in the CustomerDetails table*

Indexes on Keys and Constraints

Some indexes are created automatically by SQL Server. For example, when you create a primary key for a table, you automatically get an index thrown in, free of charge. The same applies to a unique constraint.

The Cost of Indexes

I mentioned earlier that indexes do come at a cost. They do engage additional system resources and overhead for their upkeep and operation. For starters, indexes can become rather bulky, which means they can cause the size of the database file to swell. In addition, whenever you add, change, or delete data from a table, the index has to be updated and such maintenance consumes time and resources. Imagine what would happen if after this entire book was proofread and indexed and ready for the printers that I called up the copyeditor and asked her if I could delete a chapter and replace it with new information—the people at the National Hurricane Center would have a heart attack with the storm that would ensue. SQL Server, on the other hand, understands that its data changes all the time, and so it has built-in algorithms to ensure that index regeneration happens as efficiently as possible.

The life of the DBA would not be so wonderful if SQL Server was capable of taking care of all the index details. Unfortunately, SQL Server sometimes requires your input in the creation and management of indexes. Indexes are different for every table.

The data is different and the table schemas differ from table to table. Each table might have different keys and constraints on them that impact the search and return performance. The subjects of index design and index tuning is thus not something to ignore, which is the reason we will now discuss the subject.

Index Tuning

You have to provide some thought to the index creation process. In the olden days of exposed database engin—APIs that you had to write very low level code for—index tuning was basically nothing more than creating and re-creating indexes to find solutions that provided the best rate of return on the data you were querying. Today SQL Server comes equipped with the tools to make this job a lot easier.

The system tackles index creation, management, and tuning on two fronts. Firstly, the Query Optimizer tries to do the best job it can on index creation, and for the most part it succeeds. You don't really have to second-guess the optimizer—most of the time.

Second, when you have the need or desire to take charge you can call up the Index Tuning Wizard and put it to work. We'll look at the Index Tuning Wizard in a couple of parsecs. First let's discuss what good indexing practice comprises:

- Keep the number of update queries that either change or delete rows to a minimum. In other words try and change or delete as many rows as you can in as few queries as possible. This will ensure that index recreation and maintenance overhead is kept to a minimum.
- Use non-clustered indexes on columns often queried. This practice lets you cover more columns with indexes without the cost of a clustered indexes. By the same token you need to use the Query Optimizer to see if an index on simple data is not more costly that a sequential table scan without an index, which is entirely feasible.
- Use clustered indexes on key columns. Also keep them for unique, identity, and *nonull* columns, which typically benefit from clustered indexes.
- Evaluate your disk sub-systems to help speed up data access and index creation. While SQL Server might have highly optimized index creating algorithms, the index creation and maintenance speeds depend on the hard disk technology employed. For starters, stick to hardware RAID technology, which is more efficient for database solutions than software RAID. Also use faster and more reliable hard disks in the RAID configurations.
- Get to know your data and investigate what costs and plans the query optimizer is consistently coming up with for your query and the indexes that have to live with it.
- Learn how to use the Index Tuning Wizard (which is coming up next).

Besides these tips, you should take the time to fully understand the difference between clustered and nonclustered indexes. Also, if you have not read the architecture chapters in Part I, now is the time to do so because they provide you with insight into the underlying architecture of the databases and tables and how the data pages that comprise tables are structured and maintained.

Using the Index Tuning Wizard

The Index Tuning Wizard can help you fine-tune your database engine without having to have an expert knowledge of the database structures and the underlying architecture. The Wizard performs the following functions:

- Given a workload to analyze, it can recommend the best mix of indexes for the data.
- It can analyze workload, the effects of changes, queries, index usage, and query performance.
- It allows you to specify certain advanced parameters to fine-tune the recommendations.

The Index Tuning Wizard provides recommendations in the form of T-SQL statements that you can use to create new or more effective indexes, and even drop indexes that slow operations or that no longer provide any benefit. The wizard will even make recommendations of indexed views if the solution is supporting their use.

Some exceptions to using the Index Tuning Wizard are as follows:

- It will not provide recommendations for indexes on system tables.
- It will not provide recommendations for columns with primary keys or columns with unique indexes already in place.
- It will not provide recommendations for intra-database queries.

Note *SQL Server Books Online provides a complete list of considerations to evaluate before you use the Index Tuning Wizard.*

Using the Index Tuning Wizard with QA

The Index Tuning Wizard is started from the Tools menu in Query Analyzer as follows:

1. Drill down to the server or instance that hold your data.
2. Prepare a query in Query Analyzer and ready it for execution.
3. With the server selected, choose the Query menu and click Index Tuning Wizard or select CTRL+I. The Index Tuning Wizard welcome screen appears. Move past this screen to arrive at the Select Server and Database dialog box, as illustrated in Figure 11-14.
4. Select the options that apply and click Next. The Specify Workload dialog box loads. You have a choice of selecting a Profiler trace, a workload file, or selecting a QA statement. In this case, go with third option to analyze a query. Click Next to advance. The Index Recommendation dialog box loads, as illustrated in Figure 11-15

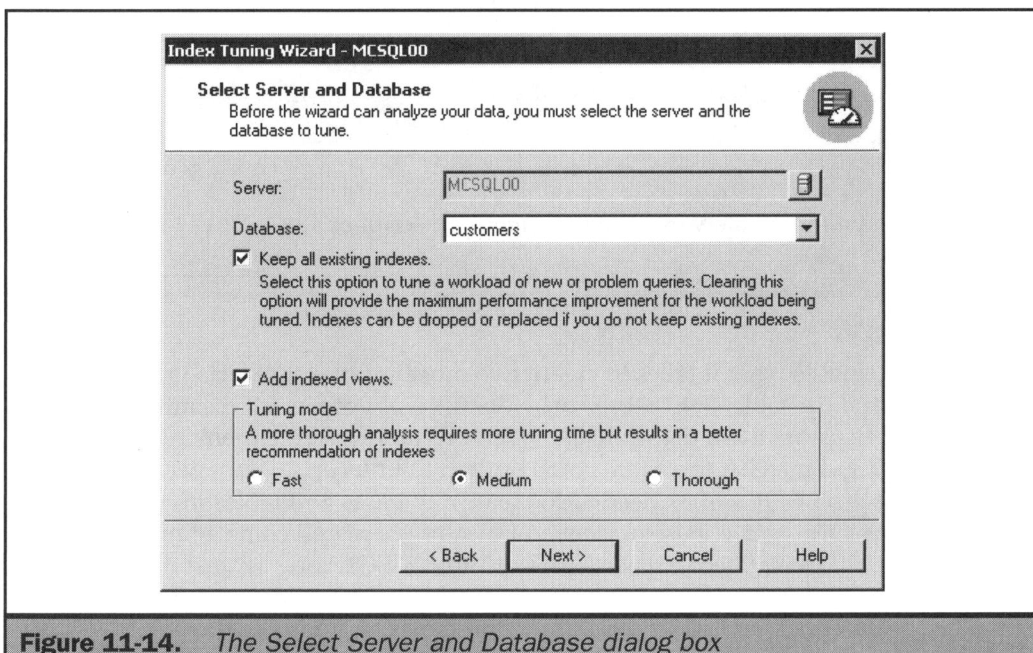

Figure 11-14. *The Select Server and Database dialog box*

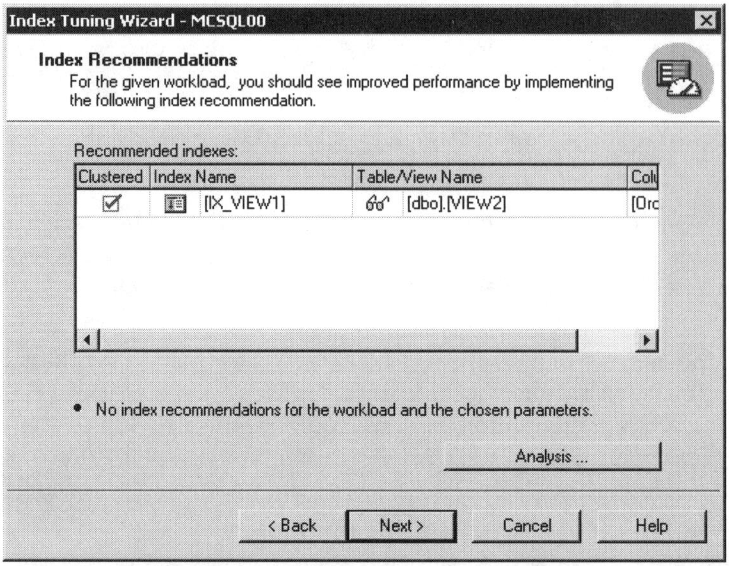

Figure 11-15. *The Index Recommendations dialog box*

You can now immediately execute the suggested script or store it away for later use.

In Review

This chapter exposes what it takes to create two most important objects in SQL Server: the database and the table. SQL Server provides several options for creating these objects. You can create them using T-SQL script or you can create them interactively, using wizards and the GUI tools that come built in to Enterprise Manager.

I explored the T-SQL syntax needed to create databases and tables in code. While it might seem easier to create these objects graphically, there will come a time when you might only be able to create the objects by executing T-SQL code against the server. Most experienced database administrators find it easier, in the long run, to create and maintain the necessary scripts to create and alter tables and databases.

The next two chapters deal with SQL Server administration: service level and availability.

Chapter 12

Administering SQL Server 2000

SQL Server 2000, like its predecessors before, comes equipped with an impressive array of management features. This chapter looks at several aspects of its administrative functionality:

- The ability to program SQL Server to perform administrative tasks automatically and to keep you, the DBA, informed
- The ability to troubleshoot SQL Server when temperatures start to rise, in the server room and under your collar
- The ability to monitor the performance of SQL Server

We will first look at the automated administrative architecture and describe how to work with SQL Agent. Then we will explore SQL Mail for automating e-mail alerts and so on. We will also look at using the DBCC commands and how to use them to get a failing SQL Server instance out of trouble, and finally we will look at the performance management and monitoring what we can do to ensure SQL Server services are used adequately.

SQL Server's Automated Administration Architecture

SQL Server 2000's administrative architecture provides a facility that allows the DBA to program the server to administer for itself the many repetitive actions and duties it needs to perform to ensure service level, availability, and optimum performance.

This is not only useful for you as the DBA, allowing you to spend more time doing things like index management, query performance optimization, and so on, but it is also an ideal mechanism for turnkey operations in which a DBA is typically not available. The ISV or integrator can install specialized scripts and upon deployment of a product can allow the SQL Server DBMS to self-administer its databases and other objects.

The automation capability is not only limited to features such as backup, index defragmentation, and so on, but you can program the server to automatically fire replication events and specialized scripts that are deployed to meet certain business rules and objectives.

SQL Server Agent

The chief component of the automated administrative capability is SQL Server Agent (named Agent for brevity in this chapter). It is a separate binary that executes your administrative jobs and alerts. The Agent runs as a service named SQLServerAgent on Windows NT or Windows 2000. You can also deploy it to the workstation or client operating systems, such as Windows Millennium Edition (ME), Windows 98, or Windows 95, where it runs as a typical application.

Jobs

A *job* is the central and definitive administrative task managed by the Agent. Each job is a collection of one or more steps. Each step can be a T-SQL statement, an operating system command, an executable program, a replication agent, or some ActiveX script. You can run the jobs once, or you can schedule them to repeat periodically. Using the many functions you have at your disposal, you can create some of the most advanced scripts that execute on SQL Server only if the server is in a specific state.

For example, using T-SQL you can assess processor activity, monitor it for a certain length of time, and then decide if the time is right to begin a backup, a defragmentation, or a distributed query, or else you can check if the boss is logged in and working so that you can go out and catch a cappuccino.

The Agent can run your jobs at the specified times, without the need for any human intervention. You can code the most complex procedures with error-checking logic and flow control and design them to allow SQL Server to address any condition it will likely encounter, at any time. The effort you put into the Agent will pay big dividends and can make the difference between working at all hours or going home early.

Events and Alerts

When SQL Server 2000 is installed on Windows NT or Windows 2000, it records all its significant events in the Windows NT or Windows 2000 application log facility. Each entry in the log is called an *event;* you can define alerts that watch the event log and trigger the Agent to start a job when such an event is encountered. The Agent compares the events in the application log against the alerts you defined; if it encounters a match, a job can be fired.

Windows ME, Windows 95 and Windows 98 do not have event logs, so installations of SQL Server Professional edition running on these "client" applications have to use a SQL Profiler–based mechanism to communicate events to SQL Server Agent. SQL Server creates events for errors with a severity of 19 or higher. These events are also raised if a RAISERROR statement is executed using the WITH LOG clause, or the *xp_logevent* system stored procedure is executed. This allows T-SQL scripts, triggers, stored procedures, and applications to raise events that can be used to fire a job.

Operators

SQL Server Agent Operators are the e-mail and page addresses you define in SQL Server for use in alerts. You can define an alert that either e-mails or pages a specific person. Instances of SQL Server running on Windows NT or Windows 2000 can also use the Windows NT or Windows 2000 net send command to send a network message to a Windows user or group. There are numerous methods for detecting an alert and making sure someone gets your message…short of sending a note in a bottle.

Triggers

Triggers are used to enforce business logic as discussed in Chapter 18; however, triggers can be integrated with automated administrative tasks by using either RAISERROR or xp_logevent to generate an event that fires an alert.

Using SQL Server Agent

To automate administration, you need to perform the following activities:

- Establish which administrative responsibilities or server events occur regularly and can be administered programmatically.
- Define a set of jobs, alerts, and operators by using SQL Server Enterprise Manager, T-SQL scripts, or SQL-DMO objects.
- Run the SQL Server Agent service.

Jobs, alerts, and operators are the three main components of SQL Server's automatic administration services.

A *job* is a specified series of operations that you must define to be performed sequentially by SQL Server Agent. You use jobs to define the administrative tasks to be executed. The jobs can be executed one or more times and they can be monitored for success or failure each time a job is executed.

You can execute jobs as follows:

- On a local server or servers; or on multiple remote servers
- According to a schedule
- On the occurrence of one or more alerts

Alerts signal the designated operator that an event has occurred. An event can be any action or process that executes on the server. For example, it can be a job starting, like a backup, or system resources reaching a certain threshold, such as CPU pegged at 100 percent for a certain amount of time, suggesting that a resource is locked or has failed. You must first define the conditions under which an alert is generated. You also need to define which of the following actions the alert will take take. For example, you can program alerts to do the following:

- Notify one or more operators.
- Forward the event to another server.
- Execute a job.

An *operator* is the individual responsible for the maintenance of one or more instances of SQL Server. In a large data center or corporation, the operator responsibilities are assigned to many individuals. A large busy data center with many servers might employ many individuals to share operator responsibilities. They watch the servers for alerts and fix small things. The operators usually escalate problems to DBAs that are usually off duty. Operators do not also have the skills necessary to fix database problems when they occur. In a small company, however, the operators might be the DBA, and possibly even the CTO. An operator is notified of alerts in one or more of the following ways:

- **E-mail** Through e-mail you can define the alias of an operator or the alias for a group of individuals. When something acts up, all the aliases are notified at the same time. With Windows 2000 you can create a distribution group and send e-mail to it. All members of the group will then be notified.
- **Pager** A message can be sent to a pager using a dial-up service. This would obviously require you to set up a modem and configure dial-up services to a host network. An e-mail can also be used to send a pager message.
- **Net send** This facility is an ideal mechanism to write net send commands to the command console.

Defining Operators

The primary attributes of an operator is its name and contact information. You need to define operators before you define alerts. To notify and operator you must set up one or more of the following in the following order:

- When sending e-mail, you must configure a MAPI-1-compliant e-mail client. SQL Server Agent demands a valid mail profile to be set up in order to send e-mail. Examples of MAPI-1 clients include Microsoft Outlook and the Microsoft Exchange client. Your mail server can be any MAPI-compliant mail server, such as MS Mail (essentially obsolete) or the modern, highly sophisticated Exchange 2000 Server. If you have a flair for programming against MAPI, often thought to be the mother of all APIs, then you can create your own MAPI mail server service that sends e-mail for you.
- When sending a page you need a third-party pager-to-e-mail software and/or hardware. Intel has such functionality in its LANDesk product, acquired from its purchase of WinBeep, a beeper/pager utility that gets activated through Windows. You need such technology in place before you can start vibration on anyone's belt.
- To use net send messages, you must be running on the Microsoft Windows NT 4.0 or Windows 2000 operating system and the Messenger Service must be running on the target computer you need to hit with a message. I find net send is the most ineffective method used to raise the attention of an operator.

You might consider configuring a TAPI service that telephones an operator upon reacting to an alert. Even a call to a mobile phone is an idea if you have to raise the alarm at all costs.

Naming an Operator

Every operator must be given a name. The operator names must be unique and they can be no longer than 128 characters. You also need to include the operator's contact information, which defines how you notify the operator. When using e-mail notification, SQL Server Agent establishes its own mail session using the mail profile information supplied in the SQL Agent Properties dialog box.

When using pager notification, paging is typically implemented using an e-mail service (using a modem to direct-dial a network can be cumbersome, yet more certain of getting a page out). To set up pager notification, you must install software somewhere that can read mail and convert it to a pager message and send it to a pager network. The software can take one of several approaches, including forwarding the mail to a remote mail server at the pager provider's site. For this to happen, the pager provider must offer this service. In many cases the software you need is part of the local mail system. If it isn't it is not hard to find, nor is it very difficult to create such a facility using Visual Basic.

A variation on the first approach is to route the mail by way of the Internet to a mail server at the pager provider's site. The mail server processes the inbound mail and then dials the network using an attached modem. The associated software is proprietary to pager service providers. The software acts as a mail client that periodically processes its inbox either by interpreting all or part of the e-mail address information as a pager number, or by matching the e-mail name to a pager number in a translation table.

If all your operators share a pager provider, you can use SQL Server Enterprise Manager to specify peculiar e-mail formatting that might be required by the pager-to-e-mail system. The special formatting can be a prefix or a suffix, as follows:

- A *Subject* line
- A *CC* line
- A *To* line

If you are using a low-end alphanumeric paging system such as a system that is limited to the transmission and reception of only 64 characters per page, you might have to shorten the text sent by excluding the error text from the pager notification.

Designating a Fail-Safe Operator

A fail-safe operator can be designated if all notifications to designated operators fail. For example, let's say you define several operators for pager notifications and not one of them receives notification. The fail-safe operator is then notified when the following takes place:

- The operator(s) responsible for the alert cannot be paged. Reasons for this include incorrect pager addresses and off-duty operators.
- SQL Server Agent cannot access system tables in the msdb database. The sysnotifications system table specifies the operator responsibilities for alerts.

The fail-safe operator is a safety feature, so you cannot delete the operator assigned to fail-safe duty without reassigning fail-safe duty to another operator or deleting the fail-safe assignment.

SQL Mail

SQL Mail is a facility that provides a mechanism for the reception of e-mail generated by SQL Server. Messages can be created that provide you with the status of a job or a warning caused by an alert. SQL Mail can even include a result set, or data obtained by a collateral query. SQL Mail lets SQL Server send and receive e-mail but must first be configured to establish and obtain a client connection with a mail server such as Microsoft Exchange.

SQL Server makes use of two services to handle e-mail. MSSQLServer processes mail for all of the mail stored procedures. SQLServerAgent, however, does not use SQL Mail to send its e-mail. The Agent has its own mail capabilities, configured and operated separately from SQL Mail.

SQL Server Book Online refers to SQL Server Agent mail features as SQLAgentMail to distinguish it from the SQL Mail features provided by MSSQLServer. SQL Mail works by first establishing an extended MAPI connection with a mail host, while SQLAgentMail establishes an extended MAPI connection on its own. Both SQL Mail and SQLAgentMail can connect with Microsoft Exchange Server, Windows NT Mail, or any Post Office Protocol 3 (POP3) server, even a UNIX POP3 server.

To get SQL Mail going you need a post office connection, a mail store (mailbox), a mail profile, and the Windows NT 4.0 or Microsoft Windows 2000 domain user account, which is used to log into an instance of SQL Server. The SQL Mail facility comprises of a number of stored procedures, which are used by SQL Server to process its e-mail messages. These are then received in the defined SQL Mail account mailbox on the mail server or to reply to e-mail messages generated by the stored procedure *xp_sendmail*.

By using SQL Mail extended stored procedures, messages can be sent from either a trigger or a stored procedure, a facility that is demonstrated in Chapter 18. SQL Mail stored procedures can also manipulate data, process queries received by e-mail, and return a result set in a reply to an e-mail.

To process e-mail automatically, you must create a regularly scheduled job that uses the stored procedure, sp_processmail, which checks your SQL Mail mail profile and then checks your mailbox for e-mail. The sp_processmail procedure uses xp_sendmail to execute query requests contained in the text of the e-mail and then returns the result set to the original sender and any additional recipients that might be included in the communication.

SQLAgentMail

SQLAgentMail can use its own domain account and mail profile that is different from the one set up for SQL Mail. With SQL Server, you can configure SQLAgentMail e-mail messages to be sent when either of the following takes place:

- **An alert is triggered** The alerts can be configured to send e-mail notification upon the occurrence of specific events. SQL Mail is not required. For example, an alert can be configured to notify an operator per e-mail of a particular database related event that needs immediate attention.
- **A scheduled task event** This fires when something like a database backup or a replication event succeeds or fails.

Your e-mail can be sent to a list of recipients, informing them of the status of scheduled jobs for possible user action. This is an ideal service if you want to make sure that a backup job is proceeding according to standard operational procedures. This facility is also useful for gathering up a regular log of events that can be later referenced. As mentioned earlier you can send a result set by e-mail to any list of recipients. That result set might be data generated from call a system stored procedure, such as *sp_who*. As demonstrated in Chapter 18 mail can be generated on firing of a trigger designed to alert and operator or administrator. An example of such a trigger is the identification of a user or users that try to access a certain database. For example, a report on an unauthorized attempt to access and inventory database could trigger an e-mail sent by SQLAgentMail to the designated operators. A result set containing connection information can also be e-mailed in the alert.

Configuring SQL Mail

SQL Mail must be configured to run in an e-mail profile created in the same domain account that is used to start an instance of SQL Server. Under the Support Services folder in SQL Server Enterprise Manager, you will find an icon representing the SQL Mail Service (a letter—what else?) and you can determine from that if the service is running (or the icon would not be there). You can also start SQL Mail automatically by clicking Autostart SQL Mail when SQL Server Starts on the General tab of the SQL Mail Configuration dialog box.

Monitoring the SQL Server Platform

A number of monitoring tools come standard with the operating system platform for SQL Server, namely Windows NT or Windows 2000. Despite the services of these operating systems, SQL Server comes equipped with its own set of tools for monitoring events in the DBMS.

Table 12-1 looks at the various options you have in monitoring SQL Server. Your choice of a monitoring tool depends on the type of events you are looking for and the activity to be monitored.

The SQL Profiler

SQL Profiler enables you to monitor server and database activity (for example, number of deadlocks, fatal errors, traces of stored procedures and Transact-SQL statements, or login activity). You can capture SQL Profiler data to a SQL Server table or a file for later analysis, and you can replay the events captured on SQL Server, step by step, to see exactly what happened. SQL Profiler tracks engine process events, such as the start of a batch or a transaction.

Event or Activity	SQL Profiler	System Monitor	Current Activity Window	Transact-SQL	Error Logs
Trend analysis	Yes	Yes			
Replaying captured events	Yes				
Ad hoc monitoring	Yes		Yes	Yes	Yes
Generating alerts		Yes			
Graphical interface	Yes	Yes	Yes		Yes
Using within custom application	Yes *			Yes	

Table 12-1. *Options for Monitoring SQL Server*
**Using SQL Profiler system stored procedures*

I introduced the Profiler in Chapter 8, which will get you started using it. It allows you to trace actions, known as events, generated within the SQL Server engine. The following list of events enables you to trace what is happening in the engine:

- Login connections, login failures, and disconnections
- SELECT, INSERT, UPDATE, and DELETE statements
- Remote procedure call (RPC) batch status
- The start or end of stored procedures
- The start or end of statements within stored procedures
- The start or end of an SQL batch
- Errors written to the SQL Server error log
- Locks acquired or released on a database object
- Opened cursors
- Security permissions checks

The data that is generated as a result of an event is displayed in the trace profiler as a single row. Each row contains columns of data that are known as event classes. These event classes describe the event in detail. The event class determines the type of data collected. Not all data columns are applicable to all event classes.

Examples of event classes include the following:

- The completion of an SQL batch
- The name of the computer on which the client is running
- The ID of the object affected by the event, such as a table name
- The SQL Server name of the user issuing the statement
- The text of the T-SQL statement or stored procedure being executed
- The time the event started and ended

The data columns in the Profiler describe the data collected for each of the event classes captured in the trace. The default data columns are populated automatically for all event classes.

System Monitor

The System Monitor lets you monitor server performance and activity using collections of predefined objects and counters—or user-defined counters—to monitor events. The System Monitor, known as Performance Monitor in Microsoft Windows NT 4.0, collects process counts as opposed to the data about the events (for example, memory usage, number of active transactions, number of blocked locks, or CPU activity). The monitor allows you to set thresholds on specific counters to generate alerts that notify operators as described earlier. System Monitor primarily tracks resource usage, such as the number of buffer manager page requests in use.

The System Monitor works only on Windows 2000. It can be used to remotely or locally monitor an instance of SQL Server installed on either Windows NT 4.0 or Windows 2000.

The Current Activity Window in SQL Server Enterprise Manager

The Current Activity window in Enterprise Manager graphically displays information about the processes running currently on an instance of SQL Server. It displays information about blocked processes, locks, and user activity. The Current Activity folder is useful for ad hoc assessment of current activity.

Error Logs

The error logs contain additional information about events in SQL Server. They contain information about errors that go beyond what is available anywhere else. You can use the information in the error log to troubleshoot SQL Server–related problems. Each error has an error ID you can use for research or to address a technical support team at Microsoft. The Windows application event log contains all the events occurring on the NT 4.0 or Windows 2000 system as a whole. However, it also picks up events generated by SQL Server, SQL Server Agent, and full-text search. As demonstrated in Chapter 16 you can code a T-SQL error handler using RAISERROR with the WITH LOG option to place an error message and other parameters into the error log.

sp_who

The sp_who stored procedure reports snapshot information about current SQL Server users and processes. It also includes the currently executing statement and whether the statement is blocked. This facility provides an alternative, through T-SQL code, to viewing user activity in the current activity window in SQL Server Enterprise Manager.

sp_lock

The sp_lock stored procedure reports snapshot information about locks, including the object ID, index ID, type of lock, and the type of resource to which the lock applies. This facility provides an alternative, through T-SQL code, to viewing user activity in the current activity window in SQL Server Enterprise Manager.

sp_spaceused

The sp_spaceused stored procedure displays an estimate of the current amount of disk space used by a table (or a whole database). This facility provides an alternative, through T-SQL code, to viewing user activity in the current activity window in SQL Server Enterprise Manager.

sp_monitor

The sp_monitor stored procedure displays statistics. It includes the CPU usage, I/O usage, and the amount of time idle since sp_monitor was last executed.

DBCC Statements

DBCC statements enable you to check performance statistics and the logical and physical consistency of a database. They also allow you to troubleshoot database problems. The DBCC statements are discussed later in this chapter.

Built-in Functions

You also have built-in functions that display snapshot statistics about SQL Server activity since the server was started. These statistics are stored in predefined SQL Server counters. You have, for example, @@CPU_BUSY, which contains the amount of time the CPU has been executing SQL Server code. Then there is @@CONNECTIONS which contains the number of SQL Server connections or attempted connections; and @@PACKET_ERRORS which contains the number of network packets occurring on SQL Server connections.

SQL Profiler Stored Procedures and Functions

The SQL Profiler uses stored procedures and functions to gather SQL Profiler statistics.

Trace Flags

Trace flags can display information about a specific activity within the server. They are also used to diagnose problems or performance issues (for example, deadlock chains).

Simple Network Management Protocol (SNMP)

The old favorite Simple Network Management Protocol (SNMP) is a member of the maintenance team offering network management services. With SNMP, you can monitor an instance of SQL Server across different platforms (for example, Windows NT 4.0, Windows 98, UNIX, and so on). With SQL Server and the Microsoft SQL Server

Management Information Base (MSSQL-MIB), an SNMP application can monitor the status of SQL Server installations. The SNMP services lets you monitor performance information, access databases, and view server and database configuration parameters.

SQL Profiler or System Monitor

The main difference between these two monitoring tools—SQL Profiler and System Monitor—is that the SQL Profiler monitors engine events, while System Monitor monitors resource usage associated with server processes. In other words, SQL Profiler can be used to monitor deadlock events, including the users and objects involved in the deadlock (see Chapter 21). System Monitor, on the hand, can be used to monitor the total number of deadlocks occurring in a database or on a specific object.

Windows NT 4.0 and Windows 2000 also provide the following monitoring tools:

- **Task Manager** This tool provides a synopsis of the processes and applications running on the system. It is useful for quick analysis, or to kill a process.
- **Network Monitor Agent** This tool helps monitor network traffic.

The Windows 2000 System Monitor, or Windows NT Performance Monitor, is a tool that can be used to monitor resource usage on a computer running Microsoft Windows NT or Microsoft Windows 2000. It lets you set up charts that present resource usage data in graphical form. The Windows System Monitor provides access to many different counters, each of which measures some resource on the computer.

The Windows System Monitor is also extensible. In other words, server applications can add their own performance counters that System Monitor can access. SQL Server 2000 adds counters to Windows System Monitor to track items such as:

- SQL Server I/O
- SQL Server memory usage
- SQL Server user connections
- SQL Server locking
- Replication activity

The monitoring and performance tools on Windows 2000 include the following:

- System Monitor
- Task Manager
- Event Viewer
- Quality of Service
- Windows Management Interface
- SNMP

Getting Ready to Monitor SQL Server

I am not going to provide an exhaustive exposé into the service-level management tools that ship with Windows 2000 or NT 4.0 or how to use each and every feature. Such an advanced level of analysis would take several hundred pages and is thus beyond the scope of this book. Performance monitoring is also one of the services and support infrastructures that ships with Windows 2000 but takes some effort to get to know and master. However, the information that follows will be sufficient to get you started.

Windows 2000 monitors or analyzes the bandwidth used by storage, memory, networks, and processing resources. The data analysis is not done on these actual devices. In other words, you do not monitor memory itself, or disk usage itself, such as how often a disk accesses data, but rather how your software components and functionality use these resources. In other words, monitoring does not present a useful service if you just report that 56MB of RAM were used between *x* time and *y* time. The investigations need to go further and uncover what processes used the RAM at a certain time and why so much was used.

Let's say a system runs out of memory. Then would it not be possible that an application is stealing the RAM somewhere. In other words, the application or process or server has a bug that is leaking memory like a ship with a hold below the water line. There was one such bug reported before SQL Server 2000 was released to manufacturing, but the SQL Server development team found it and the day was saved (as were their butts). When we refer to a memory leak, it means that a process has used the memory and has not released it after it is done processing. Software developers should watch their applications on servers and be sure they release all memory they use.

But what if you are losing memory and you do not know which application is responsible? Not too long ago, I found myself running Windows NT mail servers on the Internet supporting high-end mail applications that would simply run out of RAM. After extensive system monitoring, I found out that the leak was in the latest release of the Winsock libraries. At about the same time I discovered the leak, another company in Europe found it too. A patch was soon released by Microsoft. What transpired was that the library functions were not closing the sockets fast enough and the Winsock libraries could not cope with the traffic.

The number of software components, services, and threads of functionality in Windows 2000 are so numerous that it is very difficult, if not impossible, to monitor the tens of thousands of instances of storage, memory, network, or processor usage. But the tools you have on the platform are some of the richest in the server operating systems business.

To achieve such detailed and varied analysis, Windows 2000 comes equipped with built-in software objects that are associated with these services and applications. They are able to collect data in these critical areas. So when you collect data, you will focus your data collection on these software components. When you perform data collection, the system will collect the data from the targeted object managers in each respective monitoring location or facility.

There are two methods of data collection that are supported in Windows 2000. First you can access Registry functions for performance data, which is a legacy method that is still used. You would use function calls in your code to call performance counter DLLs in the operating system. The second is the new way introduced on the Windows 2000 platform that supports collecting data through the Windows Management Infrastructure (WMI) discussed in Chapter 7.

Under the new method using the WMI, the operating system installs a new technology for recovering data. These are known as managed object files (MOFs). These MOFs either correspond to or are associated with resources in a system. The number of objects that are the subject of performance monitoring are too numerous to list here, but they can be looked up in the Windows 2000 Performance Counters Reference. You can find the reference in the Windows 2000 Resource Kit. They also include the operating system's base services, which include the services that report on RAM, paging file functionality, physical disk usage, and so on. You can also monitor the operating system's advanced services, such as Active Directory, Active Server Pages, the FTP service, DNS, WINS and so on.

But to understand the scope and usage of these objects, it first behooves us to understand some performance data and analysis terms.

Performance Monitoring

There are three essential concepts you need to grasp before a complete understanding of performance monitoring is achieved. These concepts are *throughput*, *queues*, and *response time*. Only after you fully understand these terms can you broaden your scope of analysis and perform calculations to report transfer rate, access time, latency, tolerance, thresholds bottlenecks, and so on . . . and be sure SQL Server is performing at optimum efficiency.

What Is Rate and Throughput?

Throughput is the amount of work done in a unit of time. An example I like to use is drawn from observing my son. If he is able to construct 100 pieces of Legos or K'nex per hour, I can say that his assemblage rate is 100 pieces per hour, assessed over a period of *x* hours, as long as the rate remains constant and he gets enough chocolate milk. However, if the rate of assemblage varies, through fatigue, lack of cheese slices, lack of milk, and so forth, I can calculate the throughput.

The throughput will increase as the number of components increases, or the available resources are reduced. In a computer system, or any system for that matter, the slowest point in the system sets the throughput for the system as a whole, which is why you often hear people use the cliché "the chain is only as strong as its weakest link." We might be able to make references to millions of instruction per second, but that would be meaningless if a critical resource, such as memory, was not available to hold the instruction information, or worse, someone switched off the power.

What Is a Queue?

If I give my son too many K'nex to assemble or reduce the available time he has to perform the calculations and build the model, the number of pieces will begin to pile up. This happens too in software and IS terms, where the number of threads can back up, one behind the other, forming a *queue.* A typical scenario is the line at the bank or the supermarket that forms because there are more people waiting for service than there are tellers or cashiers. When a queue develops, we say that a bottleneck has occurred. Looking for bottlenecks in the system is the essence of monitoring for performance and troubleshooting or problem detection. If there are no bottlenecks, the system might be considered healthy; on the other hand, a bottleneck might soon start to develop.

Queues can also form if requests for resources are not evenly spread over the unit of time. If my son assembles 45 K'nex, at the rate of one K'nex per minute, he will get through every piece in 45 minutes. But if he does nothing for 30 minutes and then suddenly gets inspired, a bottleneck will occur in the final 15 minutes because there are more pieces than can be processed in the remaining time. On computer systems, when queues and bottlenecks develop, systems become unresponsive. No matter how good SQL Server 2000 may be as a DBMS if queues develop, due for example to a denial of service attached on the server, additional requests for processor or disk resources will be stalled. When requesting services are not satisfied, the system begins to break down. To be alerted of this possibility, you need to reference the response time of a system.

What Is Response Time?

When we talk about *response time* we talk about the measure of how much time is required to complete a task. Response time will increase as the load increases. A system that has insufficient memory or processing capability will process a huge database sort or a complex join a lot slower than a better-endowed system, with faster hard disks, CPUs and memory. If response time is not satisfactory, we will have to either work with less data or increase the resources . . . which can be achieved by scale-up of the server and its resources (like adding more CPUs) or scale out which means adding more servers. Scale-up and scale-out are fully discussed in the next chapter.

How do we measure response time? Easy. You just divide the queue length by the throughput. Response time, queues, and throughput are reported and calculated by the Windows 2000 reporting tools so the work is done for you.

How the Performance Objects Work

Windows 2000's performance monitoring objects are endowed with certain functionality known as *performance counters.* These so-called counters perform the actual analysis for you. For example, the hard-disk object is able to calculate transfer rate averages, while a processor-associated object is able to calculate processor time averages.

To gain access to the data or to start the data collection, you would first have to instantiate the performance object. The base performance object you need is stored in the operating system but you first need to make a copy of one to work with. This is done by calling a create function from a user interface or some other process (see Chapter 14 on the WMI interface). As soon as the object is created, its methods, or functions, are called to begin the data collection process and store the data in properties, or they stream the data out to disk, in files or RAM. You can then get at the data to assess the data and present it in some meaningful way.

The objects can be instantiated, or created, at least once. This means that, depending on the object, your analysis software can create at least one copy of the performance object and analyze the counter information it generates. There are also other performance objects that can be instantiated more than once. Windows 2000 allows you to instantiate an object for a local computer's services, or you can create an object that operates on a remote computer.

Two methods of data collection and reporting are made possible using performance objects. First, the objects can sample the data. In other words, data is collected periodically rather than when a particular event occurs. This is a good idea because all forms of data collection place a burden on resources and you don't want to be taxing a system when the number of connections it is serving begins to skyrocket. So sampled data has the advantage of being a period-driven load, but it carries the disadvantage that the values may be inaccurate when certain activity falls outside the sampling period.

The other method of data collection is called *event tracing*. Event tracing is new to the Windows 2000 platform and enables us to collect data as and when certain events occur. And as there is no sampling window, you can correlate resource usage against events. As an example you can "watch" an application consume memory when it executes a certain function and monitor when and if it releases that memory when the function completes.

But there is a downside to too much of a good thing. Event tracing can consume more resources than sampling. You would thus only want to perform event tracing for short periods where the objective of the trace is to troubleshoot, and not just to monitor per se.

Counters report their data in one of two ways: instantaneous counting or average counting. An *instantaneous counter* displays the data as it happens; you could call it a snapshot. In other words, the counter does not compute the data it receives; it just reports it. On the other hand, *average counting* computes the data for you. For example, it is able to compute bits per second, or pages per second, and so forth. There are other counters you can use that are better able to report percentages, difference, and so on.

Platform Monitoring Tools

As mentioned earlier, Windows 2000 ships with two primary monitoring tools that can be used to monitor a SQL Server platform—the Performance Console and Task Manager. Task Manager provides an instant view of systems activity such as memory usage, processor activity and process activity, and resource consumption. It is also very helpful when you need immediate detection of a system problems. On the other hand

Performance Console is used to provide performance analysis and information that can be used for troubleshooting and bottleneck analysis. Performance Console is the tool you would use to establish regular monitoring regimens and continuous server health analysis.

Performance Console comes equipped with two important tools: System Monitor and Performance Logs and Alerts. We will talk about them some more a little later in this chapter. The first tool to whip out, because of its immediacy and as a troubleshooting-cum-information utility, is Task Manager.

Task Manager

The Task Manager is useful for providing quick access to information on applications and services that are currently running on a server. This tool provides information such as processor usage in percentage terms, memory usage, task priority, response, and some statistics about memory and processor performance.

The Task Manager is thus very useful for quick system status check. It is usually started up in response to slow response times, lockups or errors, or messages pointing to lack of systems resources and so forth.

Task Manager, illustrated in Figure 12-1, is started in any of several ways:

- Right-click in the taskbar (right-bottom area where the time is usually displayed) and select Task Manager from the context menu.
- Select CTRL+SHIFT and press the ESC key.
- Select CTRL+ALT and press the DEL key. The Windows Security dialog box loads. Click Task Manager.

When the Task Manager loads, you will notice that the dialog box it comes in has three tabs: Applications, Processes, and Performance. There are a number of ways you can display the Task Manager:

- When the Task Manager is running, a CPU gauge icon displaying CPU information is placed into the taskbar on the right-bottom of the screen. If you drag your mouse cursor over this area, you will obtain a pop-up of current accurate CPU usage.
- You can also keep the Task Manager button off the taskbar if you use it a lot. This is done by selecting the Options menu and then checking the Hide When Minimized option. The CPU icon next to the system time remains in place.
- Keep the Manager visible all the time by selecting Always on Top from the Options menu.
- Press CTRL+TAB to switch between the tabs.
- Sort the columns in ascending or descending order by clicking the column heads.
- Columns can also be resized.

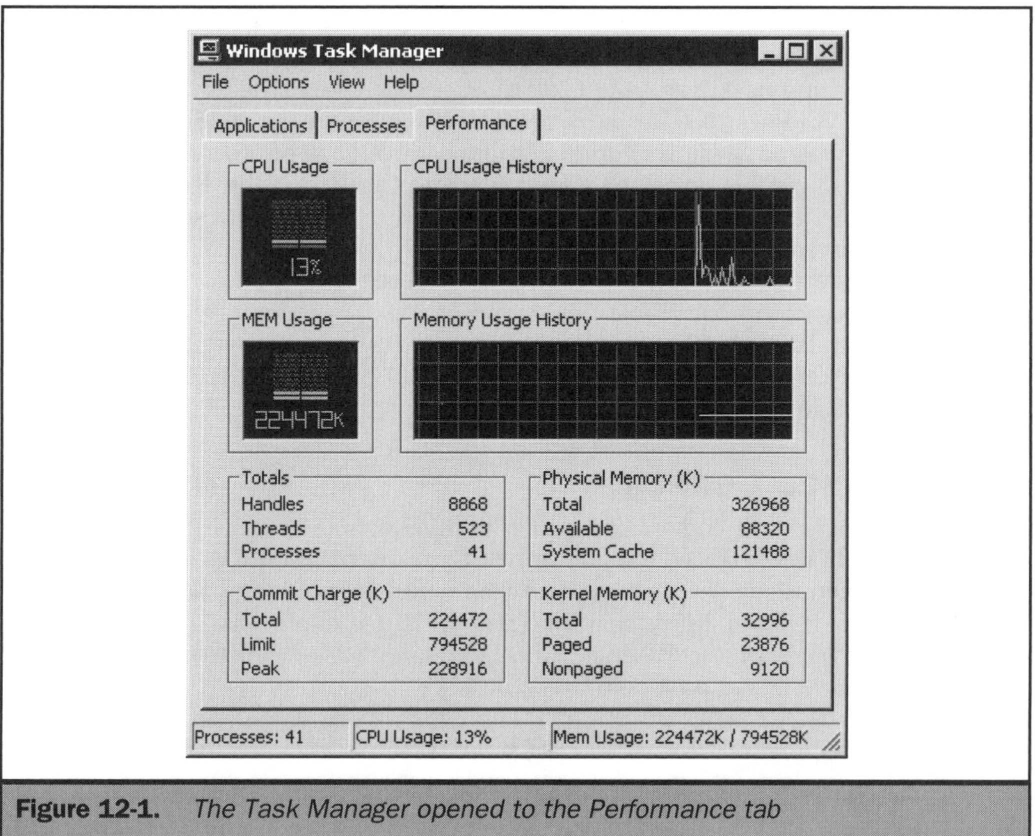

Figure 12-1. *The Task Manager opened to the Performance tab*

You can control the rate of refresh or update from the View | Update Speed menu. You can also pause the update to preserve resources and click Refresh Now to update the display at any time.

Monitoring Processes

The Processes page is the most useful on the Task Manager; it provides a list of running processes on the system and it measures their performance in simple data terms. These include CPU percent used, the CPU Time allocated to a resource, and memory usage.

A number of additional performance or process measures can be added to or removed from the list on the Processes page. Go to the View menu and click the Select Columns option. This will show the Select Columns dialog box, which will allow you to add or subtract Process measures to the Processes list. By the way, a description of each Process Counter is available in Windows 2000 Help.

You can also terminate a process by selecting the process in the list and then clicking the End Process button. Some processes, however, are protected, but you can terminate them using the kill or remote kill utilities that are included in the operating system (see the Windows 2000 Resource Kit for more information on kill and rkill.)

The Performance page allows you to graph the percentage of processor time in kernel mode. To show this, select the view menu and check the Show Kernel Times option. The Kernel Times is the measure of time that applications and services are using operating system services.

If your server sports multiple processors, you can select CPU History on the View menu and graph each processor in a single graph pane or in separate graph panes. The Application page also lists all running applications. It lets you to terminate an application that has become unresponsive. Task Manager thus makes it easy to determine what is in trouble or the cause of trouble on your server.

The Performance Console

The Performance Console comes equipped with the System Monitor, which I will discuss first, and Performance Logs and Alerts. Performance Monitor—often referred to as "perfmon"—is usually found on the Administrative Tools menu as Performance. You can also load it like all MMC snap-ins from the Run console, Task Manager, or command line as *perfmon.msc.* When perfmon starts, it loads a blank System Monitor graph into the console tree, as shown in Figure 12-2.

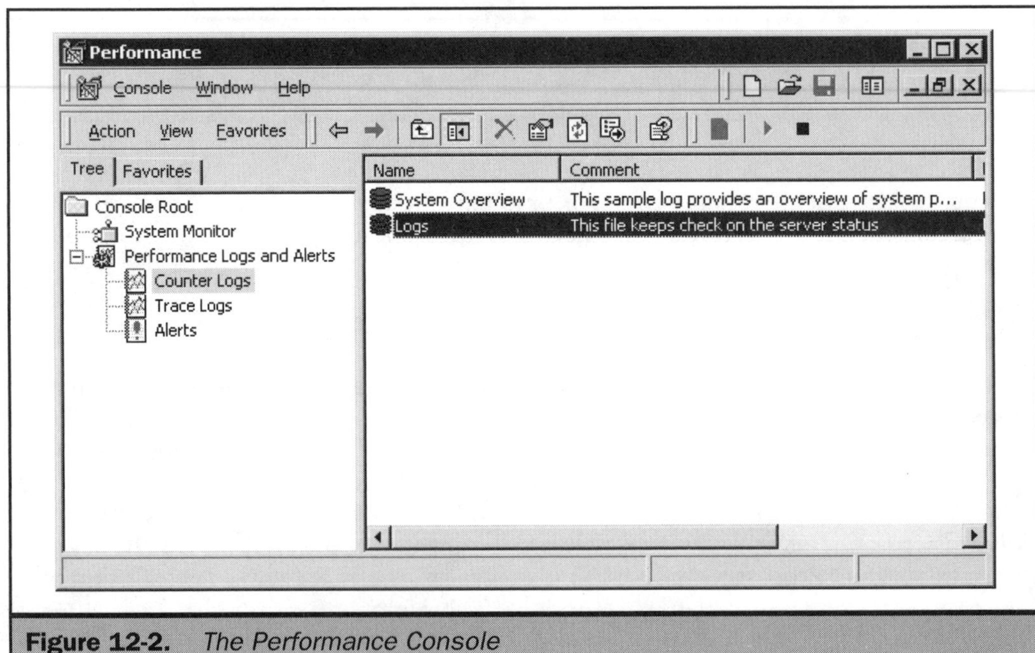

Figure 12-2. *The Performance Console*

System Monitor

The System Monitor allows you to analyze system data and research performance and bottlenecks. The utility, which is also hosted in the MMC, allows you to create graphs, histograms (bar charts), and textual reports of performance counter data. The system monitor is ideal for short-term viewing of data and for diagnostics. System Monitor is illustrated in Figure 12-3 and includes the following features:

- System Monitor is hosted in MMC, so it is portable. The snap-in can be aimed at any server and remotely monitor the processing on that computer.
- It also provides a toolbar that can be used to copy and paste counters, purge or clear counters, add counters, and so forth.
- It allows you a wide berth on how counter values are displayed. For example you can change the line style and width to suit your viewing needs. You can also change the color of the lines for clarity or to make it easier to read. You can also change the color of the chart and then manipulate the chart window as you deem fit.
- You can use the legends to indicate selected counters and associated data such as the name of the computer, the objects and object instances.

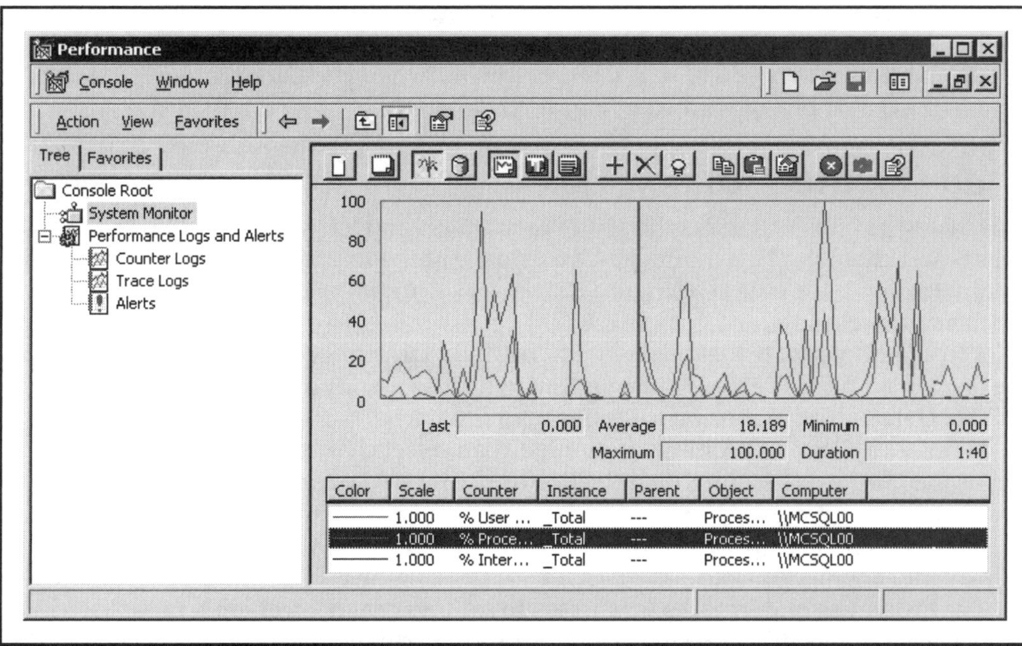

Figure 12-3. *The System Monitor*

By the way, the System Monitor is an ActiveX control named *sysmon.ocx*. This means that you can load the OCX into any OLE-compliant application, such as Microsoft Word or Visio, or even an HTML page on a Web site. The OCX is also useful in applications that can be specifically created for performance monitoring and analysis. You can load several into a browser and point them at your "stable" of SQL Server machines. This would enable you to at a glance detect a server that is in trouble.

How to Use System Monitor

First, you can configure the monitor using the toolbar or the shortcut menu. The shortcut menu is loaded by right-clicking in the blank-graph area and selecting the appropriate option. The toolbar is available by default.

With the toolbar, you can configure the type of display you want to view by clicking the View Chart, View Histogram, or View Report button. In other words, the same information can be viewed in either chart, histogram, or report format.

There are differences in the view formats which should be noted. The histograms and charts can be used to view multiple counters. However, each counter only displays a single value. You would use these to track current activity, viewing the graphs as they change. The report is better suited to multiple values.

To obtain a real-time data source click the View Current Activity button. You can also select the View Log File Data button. This option lets you to obtain data from a completed set of running logs.

You first have to select the counters. The counters buttons in the middle of the toolbar includes Add, Delete, and New Counter Set. The last button mentioned resets the display and allows you to select new counters. When you click the Add Counters button, the dialog box illustrated in Figure 12-4 loads.

The Add Counters Dialog Box

This dialog box lets you select the server to monitor, and lets you select performance objects and counters. You should also take notice of the Explain button. This is a useful feature that with the cost of a single click lets you learn more about the individual counters you select.

You can also update the display with the Clear Display option. And you can freeze the display with the Freeze Display button, which suspends data collection. Click the Update Data button to resume collection.

When you click the Highlight button you can select chart or histogram data. This serves the purpose of highlighting the line or bar for a selected counter that is positioned against a white or black background. Noticed that the display can also be exported. It is possible to save it to the Clipboard. Conversely, you can also import the display into another console.

The Properties button gives you access to settings that control fonts, colors, and so forth. Clicking it loads the System Monitor Properties dialog box loads, as shown in Figure 12-5.

Add Counters
Use local computer counters
Select counters from computer:
\\MCSQL00
Performance object:
Processor
All counters
Select counters from list
% DPC Time
% Interrupt Time
% Privileged Time
% Processor Time
% User Time
APC Bypasses/sec
DPC Bypasses/sec
All instances
Select instances from list:
_Total
0
Add
Close
Explain

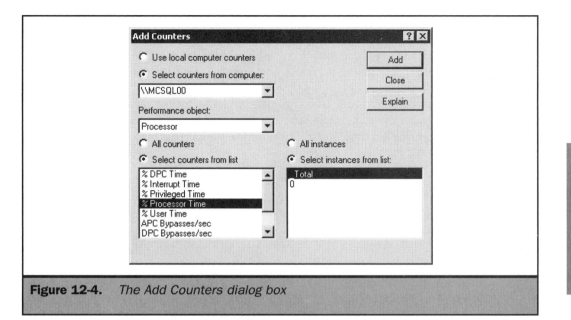

Figure 12-4. *The Add Counters dialog box*

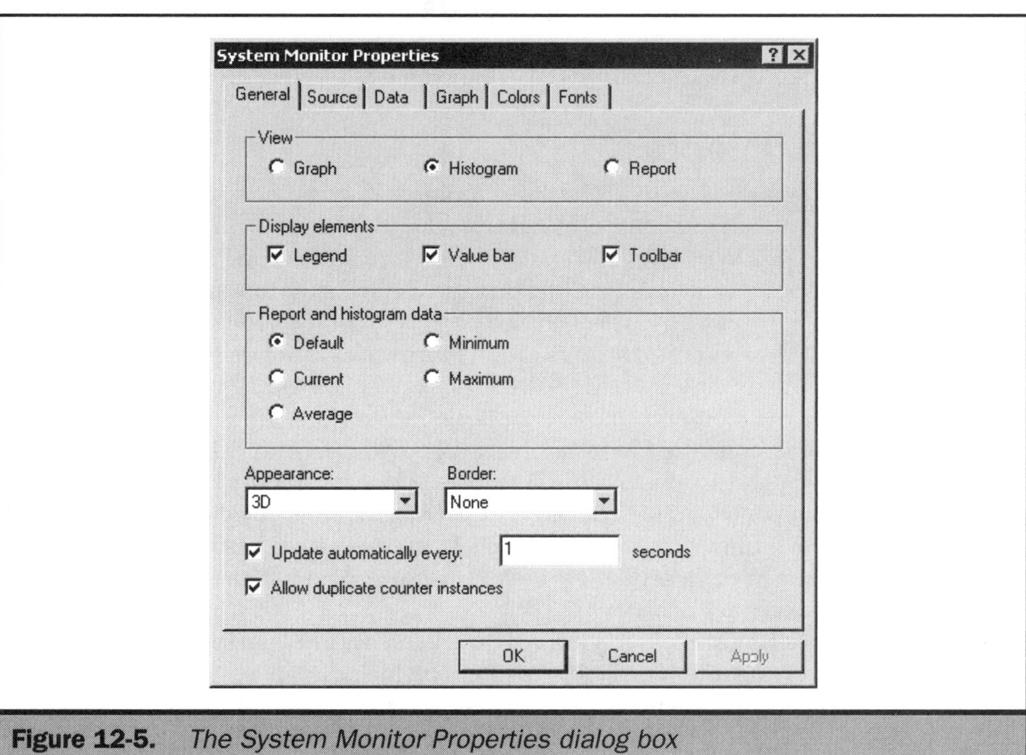

Figure 12-5. *The System Monitor Properties dialog box*

There are also several ways you can save data from the monitor. You have the option of the clipboard, and you can add the control, as discussed earlier, to a host application. You can also easily preserve the look and feel of the display by saving it as an HTML file. If you right-click in the pane you are presented the option of saving the display as an HTML file.

You can also import the log file in comma-separated (CSV) or tab-separated (TSV) format and then import the data into a spreadsheet, a SQL Server table, or in a report program such as Crystal Reports. Naturally once the data is in a SQL Server database you can report against it or use it for analysis.

The Add Counters dialog box lets you select all counters and instances to monitor, or specific counters and instances from the list. Understand, however, that the more you monitor, the more system resources you will use. If you use a large number of monitors and counters, consider redirecting the data to log files and then reading the log file data in the display. It makes more sense to work with fewer counters and instances.

It is possible to run two instances of System Monitor (in two Performance consoles). This may make it easier to compare data from different sources.

If you have a look at the Instances list box, the first value, _Total, allows you sum all the instance values and report them in the display. And the lines in the display can be matched with their respective counters. You just have to select them.

The SQL Server Objects

SQL Server comes equipped with objects and counters that can be used by System Monitor to monitor activity in computers running an instance of SQL Server. The *object* is any Windows NT 4.0, Windows 2000, or SQL Server resource, such as a SQL Server lock or Windows NT 4.0 or Windows 2000 process. Each object contains one or more counters that determine various aspects of the objects to monitor. For example, the *SQL Server Locks* object contains counters called Number of Deadlocks/sec or Lock Timeouts/sec.

Some objects have several instances if multiple resources of a given type exist on the computer. For example, the *Processor* object type will have multiple instances if a system has multiple processors. And the *Databases* object type has one instance for each database in operation on a single instance of SQL Server. Some object types, such as the *Memory Manager* object, have only one instance. If an object type has multiple instances, you can add counters to track statistics for each instance. You may also make a case for monitoring all instances at once.

The performance condition alerts are only available for the first 99 databases. Thus any databases you create after the first 99 will not be included in the sysperfinfo system table in SQL Server. If you use the *sp_add_alert* stored procedure you will get an error.

When you add counters to the chart, or remove them, and then save the chart settings, you can specify which of the SQL Server objects and counters are monitored when System Monitor is started up.

Table 12-2 provides a list of SQL Server objects and their respective counters.

You can configure System Monitor to display statistics from any SQL Server counter. You can also set a threshold value for any SQL Server counter and then generate an alert when a counter exceeds a threshold. Tie that into the Agent service and you have a system that can make your life as a DBA a lot easier to live.

The SQL Server statistics are displayed only when an instance of SQL Server is running. So if you stop the instance of SQL Server, the display of statistics stops. When you start the instance again then the statistics reporting resumes. The SQL Server objects are listed in Table 12-3.

Monitoring with Transact-SQL Statements

SQL Server 2000 provides several T-SQL statements and system stored procedures that allow you to perform ad hoc monitoring of an instance of SQL Server. You can use these resources when you need to gather, at a glance, information about server performance and activity. You can obtain information, in the form of result sets, of the following:

- Current locks
- Current user activity
- Last command batch submitted by a user
- Data space used by a table or database
- Space used by a transaction log
- Oldest active transaction (including replicated transactions) in the database
- Performance information relating to I/O, memory, and network throughput
- Procedure cache usage
- General statistics about SQL Server activity and usage, such as the amount of time the CPU has been performing SQL Server operations or the amount of time SQL Server has spent performing I/O operations.

Most of this information, however, can also be monitored in SQL Server Enterprise Manager, using the SQL-DMO, or System Monitor in Windows 2000, and Performance Monitor in Windows NT 4.0. as earlier discussed.

Performance Logs and Alerts

Windows 2000 Performance Monitor includes two types of performance-related logs: counter logs and trace logs. These logs are useful when you want to perform advanced

SQL Server Object	Counter
Buffer Manager	Buffer Cache Hit Ratio
General Statistics	User Connections
Memory Manager	Total Server Memory (KB)
SQL Statistics	SQL Compilations/sec
Buffer Manager	Page Reads/sec
Buffer Manager	Page Writes/sec

Table 12-2. *SQL Server Objects and Counters*

SQL Server Object	Description
Access Methods	This object searches through and measures allocation of SQL Server database objects. It can also handle the number of index searches or number of pages that are allocated to indexes and data.
Backup Device	This object provides information about backup devices used by backup and restore facility. With it you can monitor the throughput of the backup device, which is key to maintaining a high-end OLTP system.
Buffer Manager	This object provides information about the memory buffers used by an instance of SQL Server, such as free memory and the buffer cache hit ratio.
Cache Manager	This object provides information about the SQL Server cache which is used to store objects such as stored procedures, triggers, and query plans.
Databases	This object provides information about a SQL Server database, such as the amount of free log space available or the number of active transactions in the database. There can be multiple instances of this object, but only up to 99.
General Statistics	This object provides information about general server-wide activity, such as the number of users who are connected to an instance of SQL Server.

Table 12-3. *Objects and What They Are Used For*

Latches	This object provides information about the latches on internal resources, such as database pages, that are used by SQL Server.
Locks	This object provides information about the individual lock requests made by SQL Server, such as lock time-outs and deadlocks. There can also be multiple instances of this object.
Memory Manager	This object provides information about SQL Server memory usage, such as the total number of lock structures currently allocated.
Replication Agents	Provides information about the SQL Server replication agents currently running.
Replication Dist	This object measures the number of commands and transactions read from the distribution database and delivered to the Subscriber databases by the Distribution Agent.
Replication Logreader	This object measures the number of commands and transactions read from the published databases and delivered to the distribution database by the Log Reader Agent.
Replication Merge	This object provides information about SQL Server merge replication, such as errors generated or the number of replicated rows that are merged from the Subscriber to the Publisher (see Chapter 10).
Replication Snapshot	This object provides information about SQL Server snapshot replication, such as the number of rows that are bulk-copied from the publishing database.
SQL Statistics	This object provides information about aspects of SQL queries, such as the number of batches of T-SQL statements received by SQL Server.
User settable object	This object performs custom monitoring. Each counter can be a custom stored procedure or any T-SQL statement that returns a value to be monitored. This is a very valuable resource that can be used to monitor the resources consumed by a complex query.

Table 12-3. *Objects and What They Are Used For* (continued)

performance analysis and include record keeping that can be done over a period of time. There is also an alerting mechanism built in. The Performance Logs and Alerts tree is shown in Figure 12-6. You can find the tool in the Performance console snap-in and it is thus started as described earlier.

The *counter logs* record sampled data about hardware resources and system services based on the performance objects. They also work with counters in the same manner as does the System Monitor. The Performance Logs and Alert Service obtains the data from the operating system as soon as the update interval has elapsed.

The *trace logs* collect the event traces. Trace logs let you measure performance associated with events related to memory, storage file I/O, and so on. As soon as the event occurs, the data is transmitted to the logs. The data is measured continuously from the start of an event to the end of an event. This is different from the sampling that is performed by the system monitor.

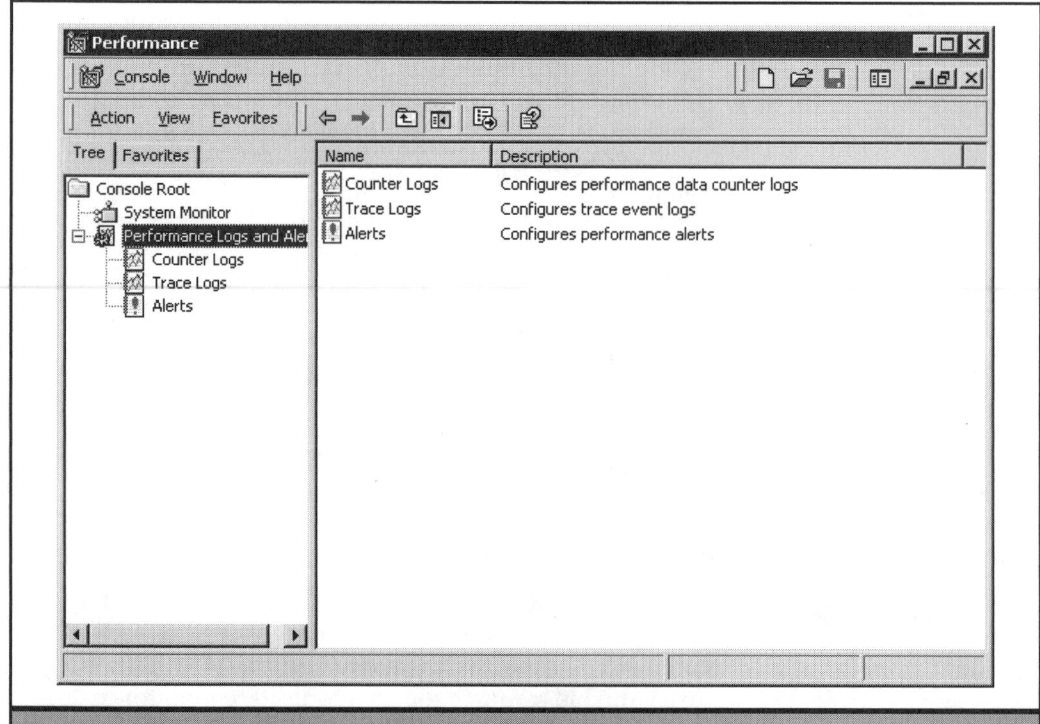

Figure 12-6. *The Performance Logs and Alerts tree*

The Performance Logs data is obtained by the default Windows 2000 kernel trace provider. You can analyze the data using a data-parsing tool, or store it in a SQL Server database for later analysis.

With the alerting function you can define a counter value that will trigger an alert that can send a network message, execute a program, or start a log. This is useful for maintaining a close watch on systems and coupled with the SQL Server Agent you can conjure up a sophisticated reporting and alerting storm. You can, for example, monitor unusual activity that does not occur consistently and define an alert to let you know when the event has been triggered. Security-related events are good candidates for the alert service. When you are trying to catch a hacker, there is no better time than when he or she is in the act, trying to break into your accounts database.

You can also configure the alert service to notify you when a particular resource drops below or exceeds certain values or thresholds or baselines that you have established. Counter logs, for example, can also be viewed in System Monitor, and the counter log data can be saved to CSV format and viewed in a spreadsheet, report software or in a special SQL Server database that can hold the data for later analysis. You can configure the logs as circular, which means that when the log file reaches a predetermined size, it will be overwritten. The logs can be linear, and you can collect data for predefined lengths of time. The logs can also be stopped and restarted according to parameters you specify.

As with the System Monitor, you can save files to various formats, such as HTML, or import the entire control OCX into an OLE container.

Using Logs and Alerts with SQL Server 2000

You can get started using Logs and Alerts by right-clicking the Details pane (the right pane, as illustrated in Figure 12-6) and select the New Log Settings option. You will first be asked to name the log or alert before you can define any of its properties.

Before you can start using Logs and Alerts, you need to check that you have Full Control access to the following subkey: HKEY_CURRENT_MACHINE\SYSTEM\CurrentControlSet\Services\SysmonLog\Log_Queries. This key provides access to administrators by default, but access can also be bestowed on a user in the usual fashion through group membership. To do this open the registry editor (Regedt32) and access the Security menu in. In addition in order to run or configure the service you will need the right to start or configure services on the server. Administrators also have this right by default. It can also be given through security group membership and group policy.

When you choose the Properties option, the Counter Log Properties or Trace Log Properties dialog box loads, as illustrated in Figure 12-7 and Figure 12-8 respectively. The Log and Alert properties are now configured as discussed here.

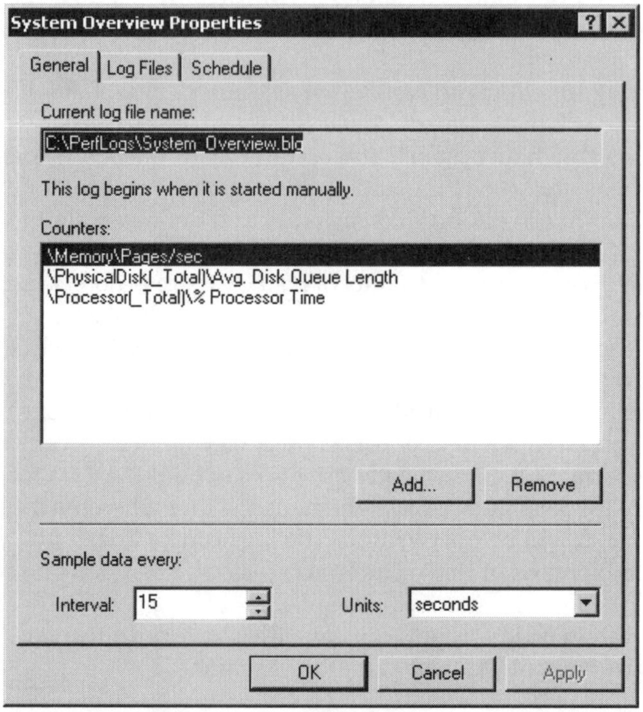

Figure 12-7. *Configuring the Counter Log properties*

To configure alerts, you first need to configure counters for the alerts, the sample interval, and the alert threshold. The next step requires you to configure an action to take when the event occurs. These can include running a program, sending a message, triggering a counter log, or writing to the event log. You can also configured Alert startup by providing the Start and Stop parameters.

In order to configure counter logs, set the counter log counters and provide a sample interval. To write to log files, provide a file type, size, and path, as well as any automatic naming parameters that might be needed. The counter logs should be defined as either CSV files or TSV files, text files, binary linear or binary circular files.

The counter logs can also be scheduled to start automatically. However, you cannot configure the service to automatically restart if a log file is configured to stop manually. This also applies to Trace Logs.

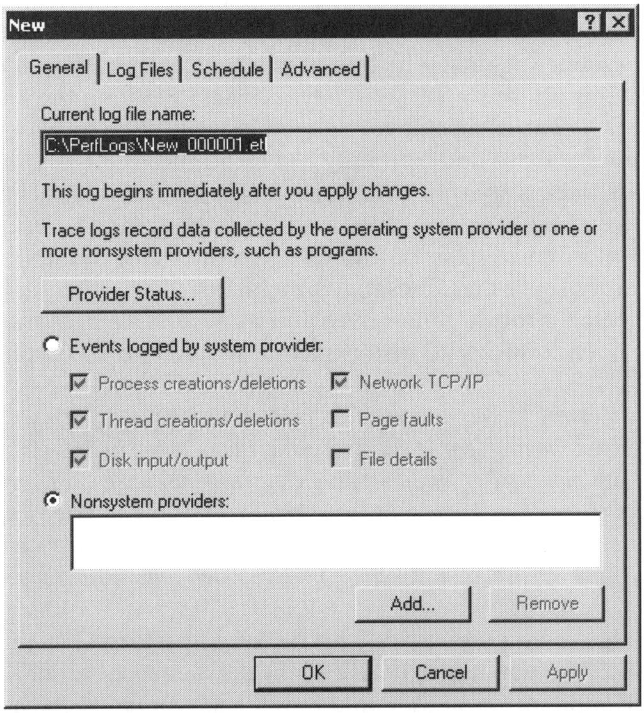

Figure 12-8. *Configuring the Trace Log properties*

Getting to Know Your Servers

It goes without saying, and any good DBA will back me up, that to maintain service level and keep servers and databases available, you need to become familiar with each server, the applications and services running on them, and the resources they need and use. I am not saying that you have to strike up an intimate relationship with a database server but it is insufficient to just maintain a subjective feel for how a server is "supposed" to operate. All the monitoring and diagnostics we have covered in this chapter will enable you to quickly reverse a bad situation, such as the shutting down of mission-critical applications, server attacks, system failures and so on. System monitoring is thus a critical job that you need to be continuously engaged in.

The first task at hand is to generate data because you basically have nothing to compare against. Only after a considerable amount of data has been collected will you have the data with which to make comparisons. Data collection should take place over several weeks, possibly even months, and then, after assessing that data, you will be able to establish baselines against which to base future observations and decision making. This is an important step for any new project involving the operation of SQL Server, especially SQL Server machines engaged in replication in widely distributed data centers. A new database underpinning a Web application is a good example of a system that needs to be gathering data from the moment it is launched. Unless you have the data for your baseline, how can you say that the system is running "normally?" You first have to determine the baseline before you can make judgement calls? What's considered normal for some machines may be aggressive for others usage. Other machines may sit idle for most of their lives and that could be because they are not getting traffic or are endowed with resources that would drive a battleship.

Tip *If a server is starting to become unstable, collecting data and setting alerts like crazy might exacerbate the problem. Your first option will be to try and stabilize the system and then set up monitoring and alerts to determine the cause of the instability in the future. In the event of an unresponsive system, you might have to run Task Manager and attempt to end the tasks, applications, and processes that are causing the problems. Fortunately, such events are unlikely to be associated with SQL Server.*

With a baseline in hand, you will quickly be alerted to performance that is out of the ordinary. For example, if you notice that at night the database server's responsiveness begins to diminish suddenly, you may find that the server has received a query that is consuming considerable processing bandwidth…the result of a bug or a trigger that has 2000 lines of cursor code in it. A memory counter would be the object that alerts you when this is taking place.

Your information should also reflect various points in system performance. You should note what constitutes "normal" on a server. For example, at a client we noticed that an OLAP server was low on RAM and had begun to page out to disk excessively. When we asked the MIS about this, he advised it was "normal" for this time of the day due to replication services that fire. So we moved the drill-downs to a later part of the day and later moved the services to a new server.

It is thus important to note periods of low use, average use, and high or peak use. Systems that provide real-time communications are a good example of servers that should be monitored continuously for this type of information.

Tip *Make baseline performance information available within an arm's reach of your server. This can be in the form of clipboards or journals into which you can paste data. This will allow other system operators to look up a server and determine what might be considered normal.*

Do not expect to obtain any instant insight into system performance either, because the baselines you develop will establish typical values to expect when your system is not experiencing problems.

Monitoring for Bottlenecks

When your system's performance deviates from the baselines you have established, as discussed earlier, bottlenecks occur. So it behooves you to have guidelines. Table 12-4 suggests thresholds for a minimum set of system counters.

The values presented in the table are recommended values for a minimum performance monitoring set. Some of these options may vary and still be satisfactory for SQL Server. The following list of notes provides some additional guidance:

1. Depending on what your server is doing (a high-end OLTP system, or an OLAP server) a threshold of 15 percent may be too low. You can also ensure that the disk quota threshold is never suddenly exceeded (you might have to manage the quota manually because most SQL Server databases are installed on standard disks (as opposed to dynamic disks) because they rely on hardware RAID technology that is not compatible with dynamic disk architecture). While not all processes can be blocked from using disk space, it is still a good idea to configure alerts to raise the alarm when this threshold is exceeded.

Resource	Object	Counter	Threshold
Disk(1)	LogicalDisk	%Free Space	15%
Disk(2)	LogicalDisk	%Disk Time	80%
Disk(3)	PhysicalDisk	Disk Reads/Sec or Disk Writes/Sec	Check manufacturer's specifications
Disk(4)	PhysicalDisk	Current Disk Queue Length	Number of spindles plus 2
Memory(5)	Memory	Available Bytes	4MB, but best not to drop below 16MB
Memory(6)	Memory	Pages/Sec	20 per second
Network(7)	Network Segment	% Net Utilization	30%
Paging File(8)	Paging File	% Usage	70% +
Processor (9)	Processor	% Processor Time	85%
Processor(10)	Processor	Interrupts/Sec	1,500 per second
Server (11)	Server	Bytes Total/Sec	N/A
Server(12)	Server	Work Item Shortages	3
Server(13)	Server work queues	Queue Length	4
Multiple Processors(14)	System	Processor Queue Length	2

Table 12-4. *Thresholds for a Minimum Set of System Counters*

2. The value given for Disk Time in the table is the length of the usage period. In other words, the disk should not be used more than 90 percent of the time. You need to check this value, however, against the advice of the manufacturer. Disks that exceed this may not last too long. I have seen disks easily overheat and crash and burn when the threshold scaled to 100 percent and pegged there for a considerable length of time. This is an important factor to watch in a high-end OLTP system.
3. The transfer rate information of your disk is usually printed on the disk or provided in a booklet that ships with the product. You should program alerts if the monitor reports that your rates are exceeding this. If the services are hammering away your disks, you should upgrade to faster technology, such as Ultra-Wide SCSI. Favor 10,000 RPM disks over the lower 7500 RPM technology. I know the former are more expensive, but it may be worth it.
4. The number of spindles is a snapshot evaluation. You should thus observe this value over several intervals. You can also use the Average Disk Queue Length for analysis.
5. If free memory drops below 4MB, the paging activity will begin to increase and system will become sluggish. If the condition continues, you get that familiar message that oten popped up on NT servers advising you that system resources are getting low.
6. If the servers memory use increases you need to keep an eye on this threshold lest the server does not exceed baselines and run out of memory.
7. This threshold varies according to the type of network you are running. In the case of your typical Ethernet network, the threshold will be around 30 percent.
8. Before you try and use this counter make sure you should fully understand how paging works. The reason I say this is that the threshold varies according to the nature of the hardware and the number of instances you have running on the server so understanding how all the factors influence paging is an important prerequisite.
9. Processor Time can be easily observed in the Task Manager and any level of processor use at the 85 percent and higher mark should make you nervous. You should first try and use Task Manager to identify the process that is using up your CPU's bandwidth. If it is a critical function in SQL Server, you might need to add another processor or upgrade to a faster CPU. When SQL Server is idle the System Idle Process uses the CPU most of the time.
10. This processor counter can be used to raise the alarm to possible hardware problems. If you notice that this counter increases dramatically without a corresponding increase in server activity, it points to a piece of hardware that is responsible for the flood in interrupts. The problem hardware might be a disk controller card or interface, a network interface card, or not as obvious.

11. You can sum the total (Bytes Total/sec) for all servers with this counter. And if the value is equal to the maximum transfer rate for the network, you may have some network topology problems to sort out.
12. Don't let this value exceed 3. If it does, you may have to change parameters in the Registry. Advanced information on WorkItems is beyond the scope of this book, but you can look up the information on WorkItems in the Microsoft Knowledge Base, which has a complete discussion of the Work Item Shortages counter.
13. The server work queue is another snapshot counter that may signal a processor bottleneck. Keep a watch on this counter over several intervals.
14. Another snapshot counter, the processor queue length, should monitored over several intervals. If you notice a value higher than 2 over several intervals, you should start an investigation.

Identifying Bottlenecks

Bottlenecks will arise as sure as the sun sets in the West when excessive demand is placed on a system's resources. Bottlenecks are present in every system, albeit to varying degrees. Even the human body can only take so much before the soul is squeezed out of it. When you monitor SQL Server for bottlenecks, you gain the ability to determine whether changes can be made to a limiting component with the objective of getting it to perform at an optimal level.

There are several reasons that bottlenecks occur:

- The server has insufficient resources. You are thus required to add additional or upgraded components.
- You have resources of the same type that do not share workloads evenly. A good example is a collection of hard disks in which one is being monopolized.
- Your have malfunctioning resources.
- Resources are incorrectly configured.

Analyzing Bottlenecks on SQL Server

When you analyze event data you will often discover that low numbers can be just as meaningful as high numbers. If you find that a number is lower than you expected, it may point to a problem in another area. For example,

- There might be another component that is preventing the load from reaching the component in question.
- Network congestion may be preventing client requests from reaching the server. It is also possible that your network connection is down and the server is still because no one is connected to it.

- A bottleneck somewhere in or on the network may be preventing client computers from accessing the server as frequently as they usually do. On the other hand the Internet might have finally shut down.
- You may also have not configured the performance monitoring tools correctly. For example, if you have not turned on the disk counters, or you are looking at the wrong instance, the wrong counters, or the wrong computer, event data numbers may appear inexplicably low and even non-existent. I guess you might need a counter for Murphy's law, all things considered.

So when a low number indicates that the system is performing better than expected you should not become nonchalant. Table 12-5 lists five key areas to monitor when tracking server performance and identifying bottlenecks.

Bottleneck Candidate	Effects on the Server
Memory usage	Insufficient memory allocated or available to SQL Server will degrade performance. Data must be read from the disk continually rather than residing in the data cache. Windows NT 4.0 and Windows 2000 perform excessive paging by swapping data to and from the disk as the pages are needed.
CPU processor utilization	A constantly high CPU rate may indicate the need for a CPU upgrade or the addition of multiple processors. You need to be sure of what the cause is. Adding another CPU might require you to fork out another $20,000 in licensing.
Disk I/O performance	A slow disk I/O (disk reads and writes) will cause transaction throughput to degrade. The higher the RPM the better the performance.
User connections	An improperly configured number of users can cause the system to run slowly. It can also limit the amount of memory that would otherwise have been made available to SQL Server.
Blocking locks	A process may be forcing another process to wait, thereby slowing down or stopping the blocking process.

Table 12-5. *Tracking SQL Server Performance*

Performance Monitoring Overhead

There are several techniques you can use to ensure that performance-monitoring overhead is kept to a minimum on any database server you are monitoring.

The System Monitor application can be demanding on resources. It may be better for you to use logs instead of displaying graphs. You can then import the data into report programs and databases for later analysis. Save the logs to storage that is not being monitored, or to a hard disk that is not the object of some form of analysis. Also make sure the logs are not growing too big. If you are restricted from setting a quota or an alert on the disk space, make sure to keep your eye on the disks.

Do not overdo it on the number of counters you are using at the same time. Some counters are costly on performance and can actually increase overhead, which will be counterproductive. It is also tough to monitor many things at once. Factor in what each counter consumes in overhead. This information is available in the Windows 2000 Resource Kit.

Tight collection intervals can also be costly and you can over-monitor if you get too eager. Microsoft recommends that you leave a ten-minute interval between data collection periods.

Keep monitoring during peak usage periods to obtain the best assessment of resource usage. And at the same time take care not to impact available resources. Naturally it makes no sense to monitor a system that is idle and that is something you should only do if you need to know what the server looks like when it is not under load.

You should also monitoring remotely. Remote monitoring allows for a centralized data collection. You can also collect data from several servers and save the data to the local machine or a local database server. However, network bandwidth increases the more data you are collecting and the more often you collect it. So consider keeping the number of servers in a monitored group to no more than between 10 and 15. To increase network bandwidth, consider saving the remote data to log files on the remote servers and then either copying the data to the local computer, database or view it remotely.

Finally, I guess there is also a case for being too cautious. As I said earlier monitoring is in itself resource intensive. As long as you frequently gather data and analyze it you'll be okay.

DBCC

T-SQL provides DBCC statements that act as Database Console Commands for SQL Server 2000. These statements check the physical and logical consistency of a database. The DBCC statements can fix detected problems. They are grouped into the categories listed in Table 12-6.

Statement Category	Process
Maintenance statements	Maintenance tasks on a database, index, or filegroup.
Miscellaneous statements	Miscellaneous tasks such as enabling row-level locking or removing a dynamic-link library (DLL) from memory.
Status statements	Status checks.
Validation statements	Validation operations on a database, table, index, catalog, filegroup, system tables, or allocation of database pages.

Table 12-6. *The DBCC Statement Categories*

The DBCC statements take input parameters and return values. All DBCC statement parameters can accept both Unicode and DBCS (double-byte character set) literals. Many DBCC commands can produce output in tabular form using the WITH TABLERESULTS option. This information can be loaded into a table for further use. The DBCC commands are fully covered in the Books Online and based on the vastness of the documentation it would be redundant to cover them in this book. As a shortcut, however, the following list provides a brief explanation of each command.

DBCC DBREINDEX

This command rebuilds one or more indexes for a table in the specified database. The syntax is as follows:

```
DBCC DBREINDEX
( [ 'database.owner.table_name'
[ , index_name
[ , fillfactor ]
]
]
) [ WITH NO_INFOMSGS ]
```

DBCC DBREPAIR

This command drops a damaged database. DBCC DBREPAIR is included for backward compatibility only. You should use DROP DATABASE to drop damaged databases. DBCC DBREPAIR may not be supported in the next release of SQL Server.

DBCC INDEXDEFRAG

This command defragments clustered and secondary indexes of the specified table or view. The syntax is as follows:

```
DBCC INDEXDEFRAG
( { database_name | database_id | 0 }
, { table_name | table_id | 'view_name' | view_id }
, { index_name | index_id }
) [ WITH NO_INFOMSGS ]
```

DBCC SHRINKDATABASE

This command shrinks the size of the data files in the specified database. The syntax is as follows:

```
DBCC SHRINKDATABASE
( database_name [ , target_percent ]
[ , { NOTRUNCATE | TRUNCATEONLY } ]
)
```

DBCC SHRINKFILE

This command shrinks the size of the specified data file or log file for the related database. The syntax is as follows:

```
DBCC SHRINKFILE
( { file_name | file_id }
{ [ , target_size ]
| [ , { EMPTYFILE | NOTRUNCATE | TRUNCATEONLY } ]
}
)
```

DBCC UPDATEUSAGE

This command reports and corrects inaccuracies in the sysindexes table, which may result in incorrect space usage reports by the sp_spaceused system stored procedure. The syntax is as follows:

```
DBCC UPDATEUSAGE
( { 'database_name' | 0 }
[ , { 'table_name' | 'view_name' }
[ , { index_id | 'index_name' } ] ]
)
[ WITH [ COUNT_ROWS ] [ , NO_INFOMSGS ]
]
```

DBCC dllname (FREE)

This command unloads the specified extended stored procedure dynamic-link library (DLL) from memory. The syntax is as follows:

```
DBCC dllname ( FREE )
```

DBCC HELP

This command returns syntax information for the specified DBCC statement. The syntax is as follows:

```
DBCC HELP ( 'dbcc_statement' | @dbcc_statement_var | '?' )
```

DBCC PINTABLE

This command marks a table to be pinned, which means SQL Server does not flush the pages for the table from memory. The syntax is as follows:

```
DBCC PINTABLE ( database_id , table_id )
```

DBCC ROWLOCK

This command is used by SQL Server version 6.5, enabling Insert Row Locking (IRL) operations on tables. Row-level locking is enabled by default in SQL Server. The locking strategy of SQL Server is row locking with possible promotion to page or table locking. DBCC ROWLOCK does not alter the locking behavior of SQL Server (it has no effect) and is included here for backward compatibility with existing scripts and procedures only. It may not be around in the next version of SQL Server.

DBCC TRACEOFF

This command disables the specified trace flags. The syntax is as follows:

```
DBCC TRACEOFF ( trace# [ ,...n ] )
```

DBCC TRACEON

This command turns on the specified trace flag. The syntax is as follows:

```
DBCC TRACEON ( trace# [ ,...n ] )
```


DBCC UNPINTABLE

This command marks a table as unpinned. After a table is marked as unpinned, the table pages in the buffer cache can be flushed. The syntax is as follows:

```
DBCC UNPINTABLE ( database_id , table_id )
```

DBCC INPUTBUFFER

This command displays the last statement sent from a client to SQL Server. The syntax is as follows:

```
DBCC INPUTBUFFER (spid)
```

DBCC OPENTRAN

This command displays information about the oldest active transaction and the oldest distributed and nondistributed replicated transactions, if any, within the specified database. Results are displayed only if there is an active transaction or if the database contains replication information. An informational message is displayed if there are no active transactions. The syntax is as follows:

```
DBCC OPENTRAN
( { 'database_name' | database_id} )
[ WITH TABLERESULTS
[ , NO_INFOMSGS ]
]
```

DBCC OUTPUTBUFFER

This command returns the current output buffer in hexadecimal and ASCII format for the specified system process ID (SPID). The syntax is as follows:

```
DBCC OUTPUTBUFFER ( spid )
```

DBCC PROCCACHE

This command displays information in a table format about the procedure cache. The syntax is as follows:

```
DBCC PROCCACHE
```

DBCC SHOWCONTIG

This command displays fragmentation information for the data and indexes of the specified table. The syntax is as follows:

```
DBCC SHOWCONTIG
[ ( { table_name | table_id | view_name | view_id }
[ , index_name | index_id ]
)
]
[ WITH { ALL_INDEXES
| FAST [ , ALL_INDEXES ]
| TABLERESULTS [ , { ALL_INDEXES } ]
[ , { FAST | ALL_LEVELS } ]
}
]
```

DBCC SHOW_STATISTICS

This command displays the current distribution statistics for the specified target on the specified table. The syntax is as follows:

```
DBCC SHOW_STATISTICS ( table , target )
```

DBCC SQLPERF

This command provides statistics about the use of transaction-log space in all databases. The syntax is as follows:

```
DBCC SQLPERF ( LOGSPACE )
```

DBCC TRACESTATUS

This command displays the status of trace flags. The syntax is as follows:

```
DBCC TRACESTATUS ( trace# [ ,...n ] )
```

DBCC USEROPTIONS

This command returns the SET options active that are set for the current connection. The syntax is as follows:

```
DBCC USEROPTIONS
```


DBCC CHECKALLOC

This command checks the consistency of disk space allocation structures for a specified database. The syntax is as follows:

```
DBCC CHECKALLOC
( 'database_name'
[ , NOINDEX
|
{ REPAIR_ALLOW_DATA_LOSS
| REPAIR_FAST
| REPAIR_REBUILD
} ]
) [ WITH { [ ALL_ERRORMSGS | NO_INFOMSGS ]
[ , [ TABLOCK ] ]
[ , [ ESTIMATEONLY ] ]
}
]
```

DBCC CHECKCATALOG

This command checks for consistency in and between system tables in the specified database. The syntax is as follows:

```
DBCC CHECKCATALOG
( 'database_name'
) [ WITH NO_INFOMSGS ]
```

DBCC CHECKCONSTRAINTS

This command checks the integrity of a specified constraint or all constraints on a specified table. The syntax is as follows:

```
DBCC CHECKCONSTRAINTS
[( 'table_name' | 'constraint_name'
)]

[ WITH { ALL_ERRORMSGS | ALL_CONSTRAINTS } ]
```

DBCC CHECKDB

This command checks the allocation and structural integrity of all the objects in the specified database. The syntax is as follows:

```
DBCC CHECKDB
( 'database_name'
[ , NOINDEX
| { REPAIR_ALLOW_DATA_LOSS
| REPAIR_FAST
| REPAIR_REBUILD
} ]
) [ WITH { [ ALL_ERRORMSGS ]
[ , [ NO_INFOMSGS ] ]
[ , [ TABLOCK ] ]
[ , [ ESTIMATEONLY ] ]
[ , [ PHYSICAL_ONLY ] ]
}
]
```

DBCC CHECKFILEGROUP

This command checks the allocation and structural integrity of all tables (in the current database) in the specified filegroup. The syntax is as follows:

```
DBCC CHECKFILEGROUP
( [ { 'filegroup' | filegroup_id } ]
[ , NOINDEX ]
) [ WITH { [ ALL_ERRORMSGS | NO_INFOMSGS ]
[ , [ TABLOCK ] ]
[ , [ ESTIMATEONLY ] ]
}
]
```

DBCC CHECKIDENT

This command checks the current identity value for the specified table and, if needed, corrects the identity value. The syntax is as follows:

```
DBCC CHECKIDENT
( 'table_name'
[ , { NORESEED
| { RESEED [ , new_reseed_value ] }
}
]
)
```


DBCC CHECKTABLE

This command checks the integrity of the data, index, text, ntext, and image pages for the specified table or indexed view. The syntax is as follows:

```
DBCC CHECKTABLE
( 'table_name' | 'view_name'
[ , NOINDEX
| index_id
| { REPAIR_ALLOW_DATA_LOSS
| REPAIR_FAST
| REPAIR_REBUILD }
]
) [ WITH { [ ALL_ERRORMSGS | NO_INFOMSGS ]
[ , [ TABLOCK ] ]
[ , [ ESTIMATEONLY ] ]
[ , [ PHYSICAL_ONLY ] ]
}
]
```

DBCC NEWALLOC

This command checks the allocation of data and index pages for each table within the page extent structures of the database. DBCC NEWALLOC is identical to DBCC CHECKALLOC and is included in SQL Server 2000 for backward compatibility only. You should use DBCC CHECKALLOC to check the allocation and use of all pages in the specified database because it is unlikely that NEWALLOC will be supported in future versions.

In Review

This chapter is devoted to the administration of SQL Server. I devoted most of this chapter to performance monitoring because it is such a critical area and not adequately covered in Books Online or in other volumes. Many a DBA forgets that the maintenance of the platform and its resources are critical to the health of any server service or DBMS.

In the next chapter we deal with high availability issues but you will no doubt see the connection between these two chapters. Often a server will be upgraded for no reason because bottlenecks were detected but not identified. Throwing in another CPU or two does not always solve the problem, and in many cases does not warrant the stress of the upgrade.

The Complete Reference

Chapter 13

SQL Server 2000 High Availability

There are a number of dimensions that you need to keep in mind when considering investment and rollout of large or very busy systems: First, every system has its point of failure (POF). In the last chapter, we examined those points. It dealt with issues affecting storage, processors, memory—as well as the bottlenecks that can materialize at those points.

Second, performance and availability come at a price. Ergo, POF has meaning in monetary terms as well . . . the point at which the budget goes supernova. There is a point at which the cost consumes available funding and consumes all generated revenue from sales or investors.

Third, linear scalability, especially of processors, is a myth. There is a point at which throwing more processors at a system no longer has any advantage and may even begin to degrade performance. This is the point at which vertical scalability tapers off and horizontal scalability takes over, becoming not only desirable but also more reliable and less risky.

Fourth, there is no such thing as 100 percent availability of any single system. If there is one thing more certain to a good DBA or system administrator than death, taxes, and a headhunter around the next corner, it is that there will come a time when your server goes up in smoke. How you plan for that event is what's important. Some people run away from fires; others run for a bag of marshmallows. This brings us to a fifth dimension—manageability.

The more complex and delicate a system is to manage, the higher the cost of management and the higher the risk of system failure or loss. We have discussed a number of graphical tools in recent chapters, so we will not tackle more here, save for the interfaces for installing onto clusters, creating federations and partitions, and so on.

In this chapter, we'll examine availability theory, service level, and availability and scalability solutions specific to SQL Server 2000. I do not intend to enter the product comparison war, but SQL Server benchmarks speak for themselves. It is also interesting to note that SQL Server scalability has been increasing on a near-linear scale since the birth of version 6.5 in the mid-1990s, and an almost 200 percent increase in scalability every year. Without contradicting what I have just said about linear scalability, it is obvious that we are only seeing the beginning of a continuous climb in terms of scalability and performance . . . as such hardware manufacturers as Intel and Hewlett-Packard continue to push the envelope.

Over the past few years, Microsoft has demonstrated impressive performance metrics for SQL Server on Windows NT and on Windows 2000. The company and its partners have adopted an "aim for the galaxy" philosophy. The belief is that if SQL Server can be scaled to levels beyond what any company or situation on Earth demands, at a still-affordable cost, it will be able to cater to *any* requirement. Recent tests have SQL Server performing excellently at levels that are an order of magnitude above the most aggressive requirements of the banking, travel, and financial industries. This means that 99.9 percent of businesses in the world will never require systems even one tenth the scale of what SQL Server can comfortably handle.

Does the fact that SQL Server can already scale to levels beyond the needs of 99.9 percent of businesses mean that it is already at its limits? Not at all. In cosmic terms, we are not even near the big bang.

High Availability Analytics

The leading Internet trends and Internet analysis companies—Gartner Group, IDC, Cap Gemini, and so on—came up with some impressive analytics in 1999, related to Internet growth, that provide an idea of what we, as SQL DBAs, IT managers, and CTOs, can expect in the coming years.

The expectations are as follows:

- By 2002, about 50 percent of the large companies will have an E-Business Intelligence Strategy in place. (I interpret this to mean that we are thus at least ten years away from a leveling off of the adoption of the Internet as the chief tool to gather business intelligence and transact with customers. Clearly SQL Server will become a key component in the gathering and housing of intelligence data, besides transactional operations with online users.)
- By 2003, about 30 percent of all consumer-oriented business will use e-business to win over customers. (This means that less than one third of the world's businesses are using the Internet competitively as I write this.)
- In the next few years, we will see about 68 percent of companies adopting the business Internet in their customer relationship management (CRM) strategy. (In other words, the demands we are experiencing now are only the tip of the iceberg.)

As I stated in a recent article I wrote for *Call Center Magazine* concerning CRM, my research indicates that most of the databases employed in the business Internet were supporting order taking systems and content storage. Most of the other CRM facilities, such as customer support, customer care, analysis, communications, and collaboration are still a long way from being catered to by large systems.

The challenges lying ahead in the near future thus include the following:

- Building systems to support very, very, very, very large databases. You need to get hands-on managing petabyte systems now. Terabyte-sized databases will be commonplace in many companies by 2003. Visualize this: In order to cater now to a large database that will be commonplace in several years, you would need to walk into a computer shop and buy every hard disk you can lay your hands on.
- Building systems to handle millions of hits (not users) per day, possibly per hour.

- Managing huge log files that will continue to expand at rates that will test your abilities in the storage management and server management area. You know the drill—if you don't set up your log files properly, the files will explode in a day of heavy trading. It will not be long before that day of heavy trading takes place in an hour.
- Backing up as much data as possible as often as possible.
- Supporting systems to analyze data. Already data explosions in the analysis arena knock out the most experienced warehouse DBAs. Multidimensional systems will easily produce exabyte-sized warehouses in the near term.

Note *One gigabyte (GB) = 1,024 megabytes (MB); one terabyte (TB) = 1,024GB; one petabyte (PB) = 1,024TB; one exabyte (EB) = 1,024PB.*

Availability in Perspective?

The demand for larger systems, the ability to support more concurrent users, and maximum uptime have been increasing at an exponential rate since the advent of e-commerce and the critical emergence of the Internet. Just a few years ago, the only way a person could interact with a bank was via an automated teller or a live teller in the bank. It somehow seemed to be frustrating, yet tolerable, to arrive at a bank and have the teller tell you that systems were offline. You might not have been able to get a bank balance, but at least you might have been able to do a manual offline deposit. The teller would only need to time-stamp your deposit offline and commit the transaction later when systems came back up. Obviously not all services were available when the system went down. On the Internet, however, if systems are offline for too long, you'll have bankruptcy on the horizon.

Take e-commerce sites like amazon.com or buy.com. These sites typically need to support tens of thousands of concurrent transactions on a daily basis, and they need to cater to peak times that can increase tenfold during periods of high demand for an item, or during peak periods, such as during Christmas shopping or during special offers, during and just after advertising campaigns or special promotions, and so on.

The possibility of receiving tens or hundreds of thousands of transactions inside of an hour is a recent phenomenon. The pre–Internet Age huge system never truly experienced system bottlenecks on the same level as today's Internet systems. For starters, companies ran out of human bandwidth (computer operators) long before they ran out of technology bandwidth. In the years of AT&T, tens of thousands of operators operated on highly distributed systems around the country. But there were few others that employed humans on the scale that Ma Bell did. For the average Fortune 500 company, a few hundred operators was about all it could employ. And thus blocking levels and ring-no-answer situations were not unexpected during peak periods.

The Internet has brought change on two fronts:

- First, the limitations of the telephone system to handle concurrent callers is no longer a factor, because Internet technology can ensure that anyone, anywhere can connect to a system.
- Second, human operators are no longer an issue, because Internet users are learning to help themselves. Many companies have in fact begun to scale back on human order takers. As users become more Net-savvy, they experience less need to connect with a live human operator to place an order.

While the pressure on human users has been reduced, the demand on systems has increased at an extraordinary rate. Hit rates on a large popular system are at numbers that were unthinkable a few years ago.

Looking at the financial industry just a few years ago, if a stock surged the ability for investors to buy it was limited to the number of stockbrokers that were sitting on it at the time the news broke. The only points of failure that factored were elbow joints—not network connections or hard-disk armateurs. Now when a stock takes off, the number of brokers available to take buys has no bearing on the ability to place an order.

SLM, DR, and Availability Management

Considering the preceding discussion, we can expect trends in the near future to be as follows:

- **User population growth** The user population growth is showing no leveling off in the short term. Network and database workload will increase exponentially in the coming years. If the unthinkable happens and an amazon.com goes belly up, the systems at sites like barnesandnoble.com and fatbrain.com could end up looking like a stilt village after a major tsunami.
- **Burgeoning databases** The explosion of database sizes will present backup, restore, and load challenges.
- **Increase in transaction complexity** Application designers will be making more complex demands on the back-end servers. Transaction complexity will become more complex and stored procedure and trigger use will skyrocket, as will the use of new features including extended stored procedures, user-defined functions, use-defined data types, and so on. The increase in the sophistication of applications will also add to the load on database servers and databases, corresponding to the demand for data storage.
- **Server clusters will be commonplace** We will be challenged to manage a large number of nodes from as few locations as possible.

It is quite easy to confuse disaster recovery with availability because both are functions of *service level* (SL). I have illustrated the three faculties of system maintenance in Figure 13-1, which shows that the parent science is service level (SL) or service level management (SLM), and its two offspring are disaster recovery and availability management.

To understand the illustration and the relationship between the nodes, let's look at service level from a higher level.

Service level is the capability of IT management or MIS to maintain a consistent, maximum level of system uptime or availability. You may also see SL as quality assurance or quality control, but it is more than that.

One of my recent extensive contracts involved a project to help a food company maintain service level in the food distribution business. In the beginning, I accompanied representatives into the field and watched how they would sit down with the clients and fill out order forms for the food the clients needed. Most of the customers were restaurant chains, and most of the orders were repeats for the food and ingredients they needed for the meals on their menus. It was, therefore, easy to migrate the application to various network ordering systems. The company I worked for needed to cater to a large number of systems, including Oracle servers, DB2, SQL Server, and so on.

To consider the legacy approach to taking orders in the food business, you would typically have a rep either fax the orders to the company (which involve many bodies to write out orders, fax orders, and receive them before the data was entered into the computer) or key the information into a digital signal transmission device that would be translated into food orders at the data center. MIS had thus to ensure that service level was maintained and that systems be available 99.9 percent of the time. If customers find systems offline, they will most certainly go to other distributors.

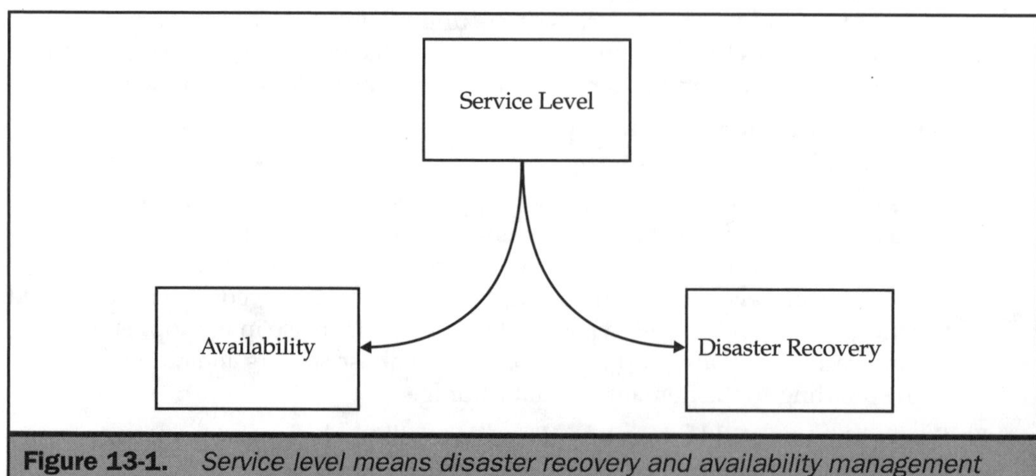

Figure 13-1. *Service level means disaster recovery and availability management*

The company I worked for maintained accounts like Burger King, Kentucky Fried Chicken, and Red Lobster, so any collapse in service level that prolonged "darkness" would have meant certain disaster for the company. We had to ensure that database crashes and other system failures were as short-lived as possible. When systems went down, it was very seldom that we were not back up within minutes, and there was never an occasion when we were offline to the customer longer than 10 or 15 minutes. On the Internet, however, in an e-commerce application, being offline for a minute or longer is an intolerable situation.

The lower two nodes, *disaster recovery* and *availability management*, support service level and are explained as follows:

- Disaster recovery is a reactive effort. A system goes down, you whip out the DR plan and take whatever steps are necessary to bring systems back online and to recover the database as quickly as possible. Disaster recovery is discussed in Chapter 9, so the remainder of this chapter will be devoted exclusively to availability and proactive management of the servers and DBMS instances. Disaster recovery efforts, however, are put in place to ensure that when service level is compromised, that damage is minimal and systems are restored and operational before the damage becomes intolerable or irreversible.
- Availability management is a proactive effort. We have to make sure that service level does not get compromised. And we do this by constantly monitoring systems for signs of pending failures and bottlenecks that can lead to system failures, and by catering to demand.

Availability is what this chapter is mostly about, but many of our IT management techniques and resources in the availability camp are shared with the disaster recovery camp, including standby servers, RAID storage, duplex components, and so on.

Availability Management

Understanding availability management is an essential requirement for IS/IT in almost all companies today. Availability management practice involves the following efforts:

- **Problem detection** This need requires IT to be constantly monitoring systems for advanced warnings of system failure. You use whatever tools you can obtain to monitor systems and focus on all the possible points of failure. For example: You will need to monitor storage, networks, memory, processors, and power.
- **Performance monitoring** The role supports SL by assuring that systems are able to service the business and keep systems operating at threshold points considered safely below bottleneck and failure levels.

- **Scaling up or out to meet demand** This level keeps the business running by guaranteeing availability of critical systems in acceptable response times; that users are serviced quickly.
- **Redundancy** Redundancy is the service-level practice of providing secondary offline and online (warm) replicas or mirrors of primary systems that can take over from a primary system (fail-over) with minimal (not longer than a few minutes) disruption of service to database users.
- **Administration** The administration role ensures 24 × 7 operations and administrative housekeeping. The administrative role manages SL budget, hires and fires, maintains and reports on service-level achievement, and reports to management or the CEO.

Problem Detection

The problem detector (or detective) is the role that is usually carried out by the DBA-analyst who knows what to look for on a high-end, busy, or mission-critical DBMS environment. You need to know everything there is about the technology, the SQL Server platform, and the SQL Server availability and performance capabilities. For example: You need to know which databases are doing what, where they are placed, use of storage services, level of maintenance, and so on. You also need to be able to collect data from SQL Server, interpret it, and forecast needs. You need to know exactly when you need to expand storage needs. There is no reason in any type of situation to have users unable to use the database because the hard disks are full, or because memory is at the max, and so on.

I know that problem detection is a lot like tornado chasing (and a data center on a bad day with poor DR models in place can make the film *Twister* look like a Winnie-the-Pooh movie). But you need to get into the mode of chasing tornadoes before they happen because you can spend all of your time listening to the earth and looking up at the sky, and then whack! It comes when you least expect it and where you least expect it. Suddenly your 100-ton IBM NetFinity is flying out the Window and there's no way to get it back. Might as well take a rope and a chair and lock your office door from the inside. According to research from the likes of Forrester, close to 40 percent of the IT management resources are spent on problem detection. With large SQL Server sites, some DBAs should be spending 110 percent of their time on problem detection and working with the tools and techniques described in the last chapter.

Note *There are several other SL-related areas that IT spends time on and that impact availability. These include change management and change control, software distribution, and systems management. Change management, or change control, is catered to by Active Directory and is beyond the scope of this book.*

The money spent on SQL Server DR gurus is money well spent. Often, a guru will restore a database that, had it stayed offline a few hours longer, would have taken the company off the Internet. So it goes without saying that you will save a lot of money and effort if you can obtain DBAs that are also qualified to monitor for performance and problems, and not just excel at recovery. Key to meeting the objective of ensuring SL and high availability is the acquisition of SL tools and technology. This is where Windows 2000 Server excels above many other platforms. While clustering and load balancing are included in Advanced Server and Datacenter Server, the performance and system monitoring tools and disaster recovery tools are available to all versions of the OS no matter where you install the DBMS.

Performance Management

Performance management aims to identify poor performance in areas such as networking, access times, transfer rates, and restore or recovery performance; it will point to problems that can be fixed before they turn into disasters. You need to be extremely diligent, and the extent of the management needs to be end-to-end because often a failure is caused by failures in another part of the system that you did notice. For example, if you get a massive flurry of transactions to a hard disk that does not let up until the hard disk crashes, is the hard disk at fault, or should you have been making plans to balance the load, or expand the disk array?

Scale-Up and Scale-Out Availability

In this area, you want to make sure that users do not find that they cannot connect to the database or that a Web page refresh takes forever because the database was choking, or that the server approaches meltdown because it is running out of memory, processor bandwidth, hard-disk space, or the like.

Availability, for the most part, is a post-operative factor. In other words, availability management covers redundancy, mirrored or duplexed systems, fail-overs, and so forth. Note that fail-over is emphasized because the term itself denotes taking over from a system that has failed.

Clustering of systems or load balancing, on the other hand, is also as much a disaster prevention measure as it is a performance-level maintenance practice. Using performance management, you would take systems to a performance point that is nearing threshold or maximum level; depending on your needs and guts, you may decide the failsafe level is 70 percent of system resources for each facility (I start topping when the gas meter shows a quarter tank).

At meltdown, your equipment should switch additional requests for service to other resources. A fail-over database server picks up the users and processes that were on a system that has just failed, and it is supposed to allow the workload to continue uninterrupted on the fail-over systems, although the users will have to reconnect.

But a fail-over is not only a server event. Other examples of fail-overs are mirrored disks, RAID-5 storage sets, and redundant controllers.

Understanding Scale-Up

How do you grow a system? The first thing that comes to the mind of most system administrators is to throw additional CPU bandwidth at the machine. In other words, if you are using a 300 Mhz CPU and need more power, then add a bigger CPU. If the hardware, the motherboard, can take additional processors or support multiple processor cards that can be inserted into slots, then by all means add additional CPUs. After all, if the machine is performing poorly at, say, 300 Mhz, bump it up another processor for an effective processor bandwidth of 600 Mhz. Right? Wrong.

Unfortunately, no system (I don't care what operating system or hardware brand) improves linearly with the processors you add to it. In other words, if you double the number of processors, you would expect the throughput to double. This is called linear scale-up. You can also look at it another way. If you double the number of processors, you would expect response time to be cut in half (linear speed-up). But continuing linear scale-up cannot be sustained in practice because we live in a world governed by the laws of gravity, friction, inertia, and so on. One such law you would do well to understand is Amdahl's Law of Scalability.

In 1967, Gene Amdahl stated that the potential speedup to be obtained by applying multiple CPUs will be bounded by the program's "inherently sequential" computations. In other words, there are always going to be some segments in the program that have no alternative but to execute serially. Examples are reading input parameters, characters entered into the system by the serial machine known as a human being, or writing output to files. The time to execute such processes cannot be eliminated, even if it is possible to execute them in an infinitely small amount of time. In that sense, the upper bound on performance improvement is independent of the number of CPUs that can be applied.

In other words, the end result of the process cannot be achieved by any parallel computation. An example from the data processing world is the standard SQL query that can only derive a result set from the result set of a subquery. Obviously the two queries cannot happen in parallel. All we can do is ensure that the inner query happens as fast as possible on one processor while the outer query waits milliseconds behind it for the inner result set to compute.

In computer science or engineering terms, we can only squeeze out every drop of performance and bandwidth from our systems by increasing the percent of the processing that can be paralleled. This can be expressed in the following equation:

$$T_N = T_1(p) \mid N + T_1(1 - p)$$

T_N is the computing time using N CPUs. T_1 is the computing time using 1 CPU, and p is the percent of the processors that can be parallelized. The linear speed-up limit as the number of processors (N) reaches infinity is 1 / 1 – p. As p will always be below 100 percent, we will never be able to achieve perfect or constant scalability.

Despite the laws of physics that come to bear on our computer system, constant scale-up linearity of a system is also an impossible objective because a computer system is not the sum of its processor cycles. Just as the human brain cannot exist without the heart and nervous system, a computer system too comprises system buses, hard disks, speed of random access memory, the I/O capabilities of the operating system, and so on. These are all elements that we identified earlier as possible sources of bottlenecks in a system.

Database operations apply pressure to all areas of a computer system: the nature of the applications; the construction of queries; the condition (such as fragmentation) of files, of indexes, of filegroups; the use of hard disks; and the list can go on. This is the reason that it makes no sense to regard MIPS as any meaningful measure of relative database system performance. To sum it all up, there is substantially more to transaction processing than just the processor. Hence the advent of TPC testing, as discussed in Chapter 4, which even takes into account cost of systems, client access, and maintenance.

Arguing that one platform or product is better than another is also an exercise in futility because no one has achieved linear processor scalability. It is thus a myth and will be for a long time to come. Vendors such as IBM and Sun might spend millions trying to achieve the ultimate, but I consider it safe to say that 99.99 percent of businesses in the world do not have the budget or access to the technology that these vendors do for their public relations exercises.

Scaling Up: The Shared Memory Model and SMP

But now let's assume that your system has more than enough memory, that your hard disks are working perfectly, that your code is highly optimized, that no significant bottleneck can be identified on the system busses, and that only the processor is the bottleneck. You still need to improve system performance by increasing the number of threads and fibers executing concurrently, in parallel, and the smartest way to cater to the need is to add additional CPUs, as many as the system can take without impacting the collateral areas such as memory and hard-disk bandwidth.

This is known as symmetric multiprocessing or SMP. You get vertical growth of the system's processing capability by adding more processors. The growth may at first continue in a straight line going up, but there will be a point that the various factors discussed earlier begin to pull the processing bandwidth or capacity down and the line starts to curve.

We call such an SMP system a shared memory system, one based on the shared memory model. Regardless of the number of CPUs in the system, there is only one contiguous memory space shared by all processors. The system runs a single copy of the operating system with the application executing oblivious to the additional processors. The DBMS software operates no differently on a single CPU; it just gets a lot more done because more tasks can be executed in parallel.

Shared memory SMP systems vary from operating system to operating system. In the server market, all vendors use the same or very similar processing architectures. We will not get into the differences between CISC and RISC and so on, because that discussion has little to offer in a book on SQL Server and the Microsoft operating systems.

Some operating systems scale better in the SMP arena than others; however, as mentioned earlier, the ability to add more processors or grow huge SMP systems, such as 96 CPUs, is not the only factor to consider, for these reasons:

- First in many cases is cost (boiled down to the $tpmC for want of a scale that has an expense factor). Once you begin to scale past eight processors, cost begins to escalate rapidly. Non-Intel platforms are known to rocket into the millions of dollars when the number of processors begins to climb into the high double-digits. A $12 million 64+ CPU system is beyond the budget of most companies. On the other hand, when compared to a legacy mid-range or mainframe system, 12 big ones might not be a lot of money.
- As SMP scales, so do the collateral systems components. A large SMP system will likely consume large amounts of memory. Storage is also another critical area. On a large SMP system, you will need huge arrays of hard disks, and the number of disks will explode as you configure for redundancy. Remember that RAID 5 requires three or more disks. Other areas that add to the costs include cooling systems, fans, duplexed controllers, redundant components, and so on.
- The parallelism achieved in multiple CPUs does not necessarily mean that all threads have equal and concurrent access to the shared resources. In fact, when you start going past the 12-CPU level, serialization in the accessing of resources can incur severe bottlenecks. In other words, you might have 32 CPUs going, but if all 32 threads operating in parallel need access to the same rows in a table, 31 of the threads have to watch their manners. All it takes is one transaction to lock the table for some time, and you have $11,999,000 of equipment standing idle for a few seconds. I am one CTO that would hate to have to explain what those seconds cost.
- Management becomes more costly. The more components you have in an SMP system, the higher the management and monitoring cost. With large arrays, multiple controllers and scores of CPUs, and miles more cabling come additional chances for bottlenecks.
- The single point of failure risk increases. Probably the most important factor detracting from a large SMP system is that the system is only as strong as its weakest link. If that breaks, whatever it might be, the system crashes and all 96 CPUs shut down . . . and a $12 million system goes south. Sure, you can fail over to another 96-CPU system; just throw another $12 million at the project.

However, probably the most unattractive aspect of the high SMP systems and the shared memory model is that you get very little more for your money and effort. If large SMP systems showed performance and processing power greater than any other system by an order of magnitude, there might be a case for them, but they don't. What model thus works best for SQL Server?

There is obviously a need to scale up a Windows 2000 and SQL Server 2000 system. Windows 2000 (and Windows NT for that matter) scale very well, far beyond the "sweet" point for a system. On a database management system, high transaction bandwidth or an extensive drill-down for analysis purposes works better when the application is able to spawn multiple concurrent threads across several CPUs. As described in Chapter 5, parallelism has been engineered not only into the operating system but also into SQL Server.

The linear curve would show how you get a significant increase in performance for a given price when you go from one CPU to four CPUs, from four to eight, and from eight onward. For the most part, most of your money is spent in adding the additional CPUs. Hard disks, memory, controllers, and PCI busses—the same components the entire industry uses—are relatively inexpensive on a quad system. Even going to eight processors is relatively easy, and companies like Compaq are routinely building such systems. Going beyond eight is when things start to go awry—prices begin to rise sharply and returns begin to diminish.

For Windows 2000 and SQL Server 2000, we thus find that practical gains for the very high-end systems cap out at eight processors. Beyond that, it starts to make more sense to scale out, as discussed later in this chapter.

Scaling Up and Availability

When planning for high availability, you cannot simply grow a single machine and then place all your money in that one vertical system. All it takes is for a single point of failure to become a failure, and no matter how much the system costs it is dead in the water. All mission-critical, 24 × 7, operations require some form of redundancy model that can ensure that, if a system goes, the enterprise does not come to a grinding halt.

There are several means of providing redundancy. The more effective the redundancy (the faster the fail-over capability), the higher the cost and the more complex the solution. On the budget scale, the cheapest fail-over system is an idle instance of SQL Server running on the same computer as the active one. The problem with this is that a hardware crash can take out the idle instance as well. Nevertheless, I will go into idle instance configuration later in this chapter.

Catering to hardware redundancy, the next cheapest fail-over is to have a warm standby server. The standby is a secondary server that will take over the connections for the primary if it fails. But there are some problems with such a scenario that make this model less than desirable in a mission-critical, 24 × 7 operation that cannot afford more than a few minutes offline.

Our next option, then, is to move to the shared-disk system model, which is catered to by the Microsoft Cluster Service that is available to the operating system as an add-on to Windows NT 4.0 or as part of Windows 2000 Advanced Server and Datacenter Server. The Cluster Service requires a single SCSI-based disk array to be shared by two servers on Windows 2000 Advanced Server platforms and four servers on Windows Datacenter Server platforms. All databases and log files that each instance of SQL Server requires are stored on the shared disk array. The array is usually a RAID-5 or RAID-10 storage unit. The two servers are connected together and communicate via a high-speed interconnect.

The Cluster Service is an active/passive cluster, which means that one server stands idle and lets the active server take all the hits, at the hardware level. The passive server waits until a fail-over event occurs from the Cluster Service and then takes over as the active server. The takeover event is known as the fail-over. The fail-over is automatic and does not require any operator intervention; however, it is not entirely seamless: clients will have to reconnect but service can be restored in under a minute in most situations. The databases are shared between the nodes on the shared storage unit, so there is no need to restore databases and transaction logs, a process that takes up considerable time.

I will not go too deeply into the Cluster Service in this book because the documentation for Windows 2000 Advanced Server and a good Windows NT Cluster Service book cover this service. Some background on how the Cluster Service works, however, is a good idea.

SQL Server 2000 Scale-Up/Scale-Out

The SQL Server database engine is a robust server that can manage terabyte-sized databases accessed by thousands of users. Additionally, when running at its default settings, SQL Server 2000 has features such as dynamic self-tuning that let it work effectively on laptops and desktops without burdening users with administrative tasks. SQL Server 2000 Windows CE Edition extends the SQL Server 2000 programming model to mobile Windows CE devices and is easily integrated into SQL Server 2000 environments.

SQL Server 2000 works with Windows NT and Windows 2000 fail-over clustering to support immediate fail-over to a backup server in continuous operation. SQL Server 2000 also introduces log shipping, which allows you to maintain a warm standby server in environments with lower availability requirements.

Multi-Platform Support

The same programming model is shared in all environments, because the SQL Server 2000 database engine runs on Windows NT Workstation, Windows NT Server, Windows 2000 Professional, Windows 2000 Server, Windows 2000 Advanced Server, Windows 2000 Datacenter Server, Windows 98, and Windows Millennium Edition.

In general, an application written for an instance of SQL Server 2000 operating in one environment works on any other instance of SQL Server 2000. The Microsoft Search service is not available on the Windows NT Workstation, Windows 2000 Professional, Windows Millennium Edition, or Windows 98 operating systems. SQL Server databases on those platforms do not support full-text catalogs and indexes. Applications running on these operating systems can, however, make use of the full-text capabilities if they connect to an instance of SQL Server 2000 on a different computer that supports them.

The differences in the behavior of SQL Server 2000 when running on the different operating systems are due mainly to features not supported by Windows Millennium Edition or Windows 98. Generally, these features, such as asynchronous I/O and scatter/gather I/O, do not affect the data or responses given to applications. They just prevent instances of SQL Server running on Windows Millennium or Windows 98 from supporting the same levels of performance as are possible for instances of SQL Server on Windows NT or Windows 2000. Instances of SQL Server on Windows Millennium Edition or Windows 98, however, do not support fail-over clustering and cannot publish transactional replications.

Federated Database Servers

SQL Server 2000 introduces support for updatable, distributed partitioned views. These views can be used to partition subsets of the rows in a table across a set of instances of SQL Server, while having each instance of SQL Server operate as if it had a full copy of the original table. These partitioned views can be used to spread the processing of one table across multiple instances of SQL Server, each on a separate server. By partitioning all or many of the tables in a database, you can use this feature to spread the database processing of a single Web site across multiple servers running SQL Server 2000. The servers do not form a cluster, because each server is administered separately from the others. Collections of such autonomous servers are called *federations of servers*. Federations of servers running SQL Server 2000 are capable of supporting the growth needs of the largest Web sites or enterprise database systems that exist today.

To improve the performance and scalability of federated servers, SQL Server 2000 supports high-speed system area networks such as GigaNet. (Distributed Partitioned Views are discussed in Chapter 19.)

The Handling of Very Large Databases

SQL Server 2000 has high-speed optimizations that support very large database environments. SQL Server version 6.5 and earlier can support databases from 200GB through 300GB. SQL Server 2000 and SQL Server version 7.0 can effectively support terabyte-sized databases.

The T-SQL BACKUP and RESTORE statements are optimized to read through a database serially and write in parallel to multiple backup devices. Sites can also reduce the amount of data to be backed up by performing differential backups that back up only the data changed after the last backup, or by backing up individual files or filegroups. In SQL Server 2000, the time required to run a differential backup has been improved, making it proportional to the amount of data modified since the last backup.

Multiple bulk copy operations can be performed concurrently against a single table to speed data entry. The database console command utility statements are implemented with reduced locking requirements and support for parallel operations on computers with multiple processors, greatly improving their speed.

Operations that create multiple indexes on a table can create them concurrently.

Intra-Query Parallelism

When running on servers with multiple multiprocessors, or CPUs, SQL Server 2000 can build parallel execution plans that split the processing of a SQL statement into several parts. Each part can be run on a different CPU, and the complete result set can be built more quickly than if the different parts were executed serially.

Understanding the Windows NT/2000 Cluster Server Models

Microsoft technology offers several cluster models which are available to support SQL Server. They are as follows:

- **Model A** High availability with static load balancing.
- **Model B** Hot spare solution with maximum availability.
- **Model C** Partial server cluster solution.
- **Model D** Virtual server only with no fail-over.
- **Model E** Hybrid solutions using the best of the previous models.

Model A: High-Availability Solution with Static Load Balancing

This model offers a high availability solution and an acceptable level of performance when only one node is online. However, you can also attain a high performance level when both nodes are kept online, meaning they are both serving clients. The model has been designed to allows for maximum utilization of hardware resources.

In this model, you can create a virtual server on each node which makes its own set of resources available to the network. The virtual servers can be detected as the usual server and accessed by clients as any other server. Capacity is configured for each node to allow the resources on each node to run at optimum performance.

You would aim, however, to configure the resources in such a way as to ensure that if one node went south, the other node would be able to temporarily take on the burden of running the resources from the other, potentially catering to a huge surge in connections and access to resources. Usually all the client services remain available during the fail-over; only performance suffers because one server is now performing the job of two.

This model is useful for the high availability needs of file-sharing and print-spooling services. For example, two file and print shares are established as separate groups, one on each server. If one goes to hell the other inherits the estate and takes on the file-sharing and print-spooling job of the deceased server. When you configure the fail-over policy you will usually ensure that the temporarily relocated group is set to prefer its original server. In other words, when the failed server rises from the grave the displaced group returns to the control of its preferred server. Operations resume again at normal performance. Client will only notice a minor interruption. This model can be summarized as follows:

- **Availability** High.
- **Suggested fail-over policies** Assign a preferred server to each group.
- **Suggested fail-back parameters** Allow fail-back for all groups to the preferred server.

Business Scenarios

Using Model A you can solve two problems that typically occur in a large computing environment:

1. First a problem will occur when a single server is running multiple large applications, which can cause a degradation in performance. To solve the problem you would cluster a second server with the first. Applications are split across the servers, both active service clients.
2. Second, the problem of availability arises when the two servers are not connected. But by placing them in a cluster, you assure greater availability of both applications for the client.

Consider a corporate intranet that relies on a database server supporting two large database applications. The databases are used by hundreds of users who repeatedly connect to the database from sunrise to sundown. During peak connect times, however, the server cannot keep up with the demand on performance.

A solution would be to install a second server and form a cluster and balance the load. We now have two servers and each one is running supports a database application. When one server goes down we would be back to our original problem, but only for as long as it takes to bring the server back online. Once the failed server is recovered we fail back, and restore the load balanced operations.

Another scenario might involve a retail business that relies on two separate servers. For example, one of them supports Internet Web services and the other provides a database for inventory, ordering information, financials and accounting. Both are critical to the business because with the Web access, customers cannot browse the catalog and place the orders. And without access to the database accounting applications, the orders cannot be completed and the staff cannot access inventory or make shipping arrangements.

One solution to ensure the availability of all services would be to join the computers into a cluster. This is a similar solution to the one formerly discussed, but with a few differences. First we would create a cluster that contains two groups, one on each node. The one group contains all resources that we need to run the Web-service applications, such as IP addresses and pooled business logic. The other group contains all of the resources for the database application, including the database itself.

In the fail-over policies of each group would specify that both groups can run on either node, thereby assuring their availability should one of the nodes fail.

Model B: The "Hot Spare"

Under this model we obtain maximum availability and performance, but we will have an investment in hardware and software that is mostly idle. The hot spare is therefor a redundant server. No load balancing is put in place here and all applications and services serve the client on the hot active server called the *primary node*. The secondary node is a dedicated "hot spare," which must always be kept ready to be used whenever a fail-over occurs. If the primary node fails, the "hot spare" node will immediately detect the failure and pick up all operations from the primary. To continue to service clients at a rate of performance that is close or equal to that of the primary node it must be configured almost identical to the primary. For all intents and purposes the two servers, primary and secondary, are like peas in a pod.

This model is ideal for critical database and web server applications and resources. We can use this model to provide a "hot spare" database node for all servers dedicated to supporting Web access to our databases, such as those servers running Internet Information Services. The expense of doubling the hardware is justified by the protection of clients' access to the data. If one of your servers fails, a secondary server takes over and allows clients to continue to obtain access to the data. Such configurations place the databases on a shared cluster. In other words the primary and secondary servers allow access to the same databases. This model provides the following benefits:

- **Availability** Very high, redundant service.
- **Suggested fail-over policies** Usually we would configure identical twin servers if the budget allowed it and we would not need a preferred server to fail back from in the event of a disaster. If money is an issue and you are forced to make one server Arnold Schwarzenegger and the other Danny DeVito then

the Arnold becomes the preferred server for any of the groups. When one node has greater capacity than the other, setting the group fail-over policies to prefer the more powerful server ensures performance remains as high as possible.

- **Suggested fail-back parameters** As discussed above, if the secondary node has identical capacity to the primary node, you can prevent fail-back for all of the groups. But if the secondary node has less capacity than the primary node, you should set the policy for immediate fail-back or for fail-back at a specified off-peak hour.

Model C: The Partial Cluster

This model caters to the applications that cannot fail over on the same servers from which resource groups are set to fail over. First we need to configure applications that will not fail over when the server goes down. The applications can be installed on the server or servers that form part of the cluster, but they cannot use the shared disk array on the shared bus. These applications have the usual availability; if the server goes down the application goes down too. Such applications would not be considered critical, otherwise they would have to be access the shared disk array and be installed on both servers.

A database application that might not be too critical to exclude from the fail-over could be the accounting database that only gets updated by a front line system once a day. Accounting staff might lose access to the application for an hour or two, which might be acceptable if they spend part of their day munching on corn chips.

When the a server failure occurs, the applications that are not configured with fail-over policies are unavailable and they will remain unavailable until the node on which they are installed is restored. They will most likely have to be restarted manually or, as services, set to automatically start them when the operating system starts. The applications you configured with fail-over policies fail over as usual, or according to those policies you set for them. This model provides the following benefits:

- **Availability** High for applications configured for fail-over; normal for others
- **Suggested fail-over policies** Variable
- **Suggested fail-back parameters** Variable

Model D: Virtual Server Only with No Fail-Over

Here we would use the virtual server concept with applications on a single-node server cluster. In other words, this cluster model makes no use of fail-over. You could also call it the cluster that wasn't. It is merely a means of organizing the resources on a server for administrative convenience and for the convenience of your clients. So what's the big deal? Well the main deal is that both administrators and clients can readily see descriptively named virtual servers on the network rather than navigating a list of actual servers to find the shares they need. There are also other advantages as follows:

- The Cluster Service automatically restarts the various groups of applications and their dependent resources after the server is restored after a crash. Applications that do not have mechanisms for automatic restart can benefit from the cluster service's automatic restart features.
- It is also possible to cluster the node with a second node at a future time, and the resource groups are already in place. All you need to do is configure fail-over policies for the groups and leave the virtual servers ready to operate. Often a full-blown fail-over cluster is reduced to a partial cluster because the primary or secondary node goes down hard and requires a few days or longer to repair.

This model lets you locate all your organization's file resources on a single server, establishing separate groups for each department. Then when clients from one department need to connect to the appropriate share-point, they can find the share as easily as they would find an actual computer.

- **Availability** Normal
- **Suggested fail-over policies** Not applicable
- **Suggested fail-back parameters** Not applicable

Model E: The Hybrid Solution

As the model name suggests, it is a hybrid of the former models just discussed. By using the hybrid solution model, you can incorporate advantages of the previous models and combine them in one cluster. By providing sufficient capacity you can configure several types of fail-over scenarios can coexist on the same two nodes. All fail-over activity occurs as normal, according to the policies you set up.

For administrative convenience, two file-and-print shares in a cluster (which do not require fail-over ability) are grouped logically by department and configured as virtual servers. The figure also illustrates that an application that cannot fail over resides on one of the clusters and operates as normal without any fail-over protection.

- **Availability** High or very high for resources set to fail-over with other resources not configured to fail-over.
- **Suggested fail-over policy** Variable

Limitations of Server Clusters

Microsoft has published the following important limitations of Windows 2000 clusters:

- **Remote Storage** These should not be installed on a shared SCSI bus used by the cluster and you should not configure remote storage devices as cluster resources.
- **Disk configuration** External disks cannot be configured as dynamic disks or spanned volumes (volume sets) if they are to be used as cluster resources. The disks to be used for cluster storage must be configured as basic disks and must be formatted using the NTFS file system. They can be configured in hardware RAID configurations in a shared cluster array cabinet or storage unit. Windows 2000 does not support the use of dynamic disks or the features of dynamic disks, such as spanned volumes (volume sets), for cluster storage. You also cannot change an existing cluster disk, such as the quorum disk, to a dynamic disk.
- **File System** The Encrypting File System, Remote Storage, mounted volumes, or parse points are not supported on cluster storage configurations.
- **RAID** You cannot enable a write cache on an internal SCSI RAID controller, nor would you want to for a database application, because the data in the cache will be lost during fail-over. An example of an internal controller is a Peripheral Component Interconnect (PCI) card inside the node. You should enable a write cache on an external RAID controller. An external RAID controller is usually inside the disk cabinet, and the data in the cache will fail over. You cannot use software RAID. You can use hardware RAID to protect the data on your cluster disk as mentioned earlier.
- **Network configuration** The Cluster Service only supports TCP/IP and a single IP address is configured in the cluster service. All network interfaces used on all nodes in a server cluster must be on the same network. The cluster nodes must have at least one subnet in common.
- **Terminal Services** You can use Terminal Services for remote administration on a server cluster node, but you cannot use Terminal Services for an application server on a server cluster node. If you require load balancing or high availability in a Terminal Service/Application Server environment you will have to acquire separate technology from Citrix Systems, Inc., the Microsoft Terminal Service partner.

SQL Server Clustering

Now that you have had a crash course in clustering, it is time to look at a SQL Server cluster that is a group of Windows NT or Windows 2000 servers—nodes—that are grouped together and appear as a single system to clients. As for the Windows 2000 operating system, the base operating system must be either Widows 2000 Advanced Server or Windows 2000 Datacenter Server. The clustering also appears to administrators as a single system, rather than separate computers, no matter what server they are actively managing.

Besides the SQL Server binaries, a server cluster runs two separate groups of software to support cluster-aware applications. There is the group that runs the cluster, called the clustering software, and the group used to administer the cluster, which is the administrative software.

Clustering Software

The clustering software allows the nodes to communicate with each other over a high-speed interconnect network that runs between the nodes, which is also known as the "heartbeat" connection. The network between the nodes is a dedicated high-speed network that is in no way connected to the local area network. It is specifically dedicated to the messages that travel between the nodes. The messages that travel across the interconnect network trigger the transfer of resources upon a fail-over event, such as the shut down of a service on one end of the disaster scale and the crash of the entire server on the other end.

The Cluster Service also includes software called the Resource Monitor. The Resource Monitor manages the communication between the Cluster Service and application resources. The Cluster Service runs under the control of the Service Control Manager on each node in the cluster. Its role is to control the activity, the intercommunications between the nodes, and the failure procedures.

The Cluster Service takes control of disaster on two fronts. First, if SQL Server on the active node fails, this signals the Cluster Service to try to restart SQL Server. If the SQL Server cannot restart or the failure is more severe, the Cluster Service will fail over to one of remaining nodes in the cluster and force the new node to become the primary server, or the active node.

The Administrative Software

As an operating system administrator, you use the cluster management software to configure, control, monitor, and maintain the cluster nodes. Windows 2000 Advanced Server and Datacenter Server include the Cluster Administrator software for cluster administration. The software is installed when you add the Cluster Server components to the node. The Cluster Service can also be administered from the command line using the cluster command.

Understanding and knowing how to work with the Cluster Service in Windows 2000 is not necessarily something the DBA needs to do. But administration of Windows 2000 Advanced Server is a prerequisite course for Microsoft Certified Database Administrator (MCDBA) certification and includes cluster administration.

When configuring clustering you cluster resources into functional units, called *groups*. The groups are then assigned to individual nodes. If a node freaks out, the Cluster Service will transfer the groups that were being hosted by the dead node to the other nodes in the cluster. This is essentially the definition of fail-over. There a reverse process known as fail-back. When fail-back takes place, the failed node becomes active again. The groups that were failed over to other nodes are then transferred back to the primary node.

SQL Server 2000 Enterprise Edition and SQL Server 2000 fail-over clustering provide high availability support. As described earlier in the discussion on fail-over or cluster models you can configure a SQL Server cluster to fail-over to a secondary node if the primary fails. This lets you minimize system downtime, and thus provide high server availability.

Before installing fail-over clustering, you must install Microsoft Windows NT 4.0, Enterprise Edition; Microsoft Windows 2000 Advanced Server; or Windows 2000 Datacenter Server; as well as the Microsoft Cluster Service (MSCS). There are specific installation steps and configurations that must be followed to use fail-over clustering:

- First you need to specify multiple IP addresses for each virtual server that you create. SQL Server 2000 lets you to use the available network IP subnets, which provides alternate ways to connect to the server if one subnet fails. This also results in increased network scalability. On a single network adapter, for example, a network failure can disrupt operations because clients will not be able to connect to their databases. But, with multiple network cards in the server, each network can be sitting on a different IP subnet. Thus, if one subnet fails, another can continue to function and provide service to the clients. Even if a router fails, MSCS can continue to function, and all IP addresses will still work. But, if the network card on the local computer fails, well then you have a problem. It is also common practice to place a redundant network card in the server and have it on standby in the event the primary card fails.
- Next you need to administer a fail-over cluster from any node in the clustered SQL Server configuration. To set up the cluster services you must be working from the node in control of the cluster disk resource. This computer is often referred to the node that owns the disk resource, a shared array of SCSI disks, usually in RAID-5 configuration.
- You must also allow one virtual server to fail over to any other node on the fail-over cluster configuration. And you must be able to add or remove nodes from the fail-over cluster configuration using the setup program.

- The setup program will allow you to reinstall or rebuild a virtual server on any node in the fail-over cluster without affecting the other nodes.
- To perform full-text queries by using Microsoft Search service with fail-over, clustering also needs to be specifically configured.

Fail-over clustering also supports multiple instances. You will find that multiple instance support makes it easier to build, install, and configure virtual servers in a fail-over cluster. Your applications can easily connect to each instance on a single server just as they connect to instances of SQL Server running on multiple computers with no fancy clustering in place.

With multiple instance support, you can isolate work environments. For example, you can isolate development systems and testing systems from production systems or volatile application environments. You can also provide a different system administrator for each instance of SQL Server residing on the same server.

Fail-Over Clustering Support

When you are running SQL Server 2000 Enterprise Edition, the number of nodes supported in SQL Server 2000 fail-over clustering depends on the operating system you are running:

- Microsoft Windows NT 4.0, Enterprise Edition; Microsoft Windows 2000 Advanced Server; and Microsoft Windows 2000 Datacenter Server support two-node fail-over clustering.
- Windows 2000 Datacenter Server supports up to four-node fail-over clustering, including a fail-over clustering configuration in which all nodes are active.

Fail-over clusters support the following tools, features, and components:

- Microsoft Search Service
- Multiple instances
- SQL Server Enterprise Manager
- Service Control Manager
- Replication
- SQL Profiler
- SQL Query Analyzer
- SQL Mail

The Analysis Services, however, are not yet supported for fail-over clustering. Data Access Components (MDAC) 2.6 is not supported for SQL Server version 6.5 or SQL Server 7.0 which are deployed in a fail-over cluster configuration.

Before using fail-over clustering you should consider the following:

- The fail-over clustering resources, including the IP addresses and network names, must be used only when you are running an instance of SQL Server 2000. You must not use the services for other purposes, such as file sharing (which should be done on a separate file server cluster).
- SQL Server 2000 supports Windows NT 4.0, Enterprise Edition on a fail-over cluster configuration, but requires that the service accounts for SQL Server services (SQL Server and SQL Server Agent) be local administrators of all nodes in the cluster.

Note *SQL Server 2000 supports both Named Pipes and TCP/IP Sockets over TCP/IP within a fail-over cluster. However, it is strongly recommended that you use TCP/IP Sockets in a clustered configuration.*

To create a SQL Server 2000 fail-over cluster, your first step is to create and configure the virtual servers on which the fail-over cluster will run. The virtual servers are created during SQL Server setup and are not provided by Microsoft Windows NT 4.0 or Microsoft Windows 2000.

You are also required to be a local administrator with rights to log in as a service and to act as part of the operating system on all computers in the fail-over cluster. The virtual server you will set up will include the following factors:

- A combination of one or more disks in a Microsoft Cluster Service (MSCS) cluster group. Each MSCS cluster group must contain at least one virtual SQL Server.
- There must be a network name for each virtual server. This network name is the virtual server name.
- There must be one or more IP addresses that are used to connect to each virtual server.
- There must be one instance of SQL Server 2000, including a SQL Server resource, a SQL Server Agent resource, and a full-text resource.

Note *If an administrator removes an the instance of SQL Server 2000 on a virtual server, then the virtual server, including all IP addresses and the network name, will also be removed from the MSCS cluster group.*

A fail-over cluster can be installed on one or more Windows 2000 Advanced Server machines or the Windows 2000 Datacenter Server servers or Windows NT 4.0, Enterprise Edition servers that are participating nodes of the cluster. A SQL Server virtual server, however, always appears on the network as a single Windows 2000 Advanced Server; Windows 2000 Datacenter Server; or Microsoft Windows NT 4.0, Enterprise Edition server.

Naming a Virtual Server

SQL Server 2000 relies on the existence of certain Registry keys and service names within the fail-over cluster to allow operations to continue correctly after a fail-over. This means that the name you provide for the instance of SQL Server 2000, which includes the default instance, must be unique across all nodes in the fail-over cluster, as well as across all virtual servers within the fail-over cluster. In other words, if all instances failed over to a single server, their service names and Registry keys would conflict. If INSTANCE1 is a named instance on virtual server VIRTSRVR1, there cannot be a named instance INSTANCE1 on any node in the fail-over cluster, either as part of a fail-over cluster configuration or as a standalone installation.

You must also use the VIRTUAL_SERVER\Instance-name string to connect to a clustered instance of SQL Server 2000 running on a virtual server. You cannot access the instance of SQL Server 2000 by using the computer name that the clustered instance happens to reside on at any given time. You should also understand that SQL Server 2000 does not listen on the IP address of the local servers. It listens only on the clustered IP addresses created during the setup of a virtual server for SQL Server 2000.

If you are using the Windows 2000 Address Windowing Extensions (AWE) API to take advantage of memory greater than 3 gigabytes (GB), then you need to make certain that the maximum available memory you configure on one instance of SQL Server will still be available after you fail over to another node. This is important because if the fail-over node has less physical memory than the original node, the new instances of SQL Server may fail to start or may start with less memory than they had on the original node. In any event, you should give each server in the cluster the same amount of physical RAM. Also ensure that the summed value of the *max server memory* settings for all instances are less than the lowest amount of physical RAM available on any of the virtual servers in the fail-over cluster.

If you need to configure or make available a cluster server configuration in a replication scenario, it is recommended that you use an MSCS cluster file share as your snapshot folder when configuring a Distributor on a fail-over cluster. When, for example, the server fails, the distribution database will be available and replication will continue to be configured at the Distributor.

Another thing: When you create publications, you need to specify the MSCS cluster file share for the additional storage of snapshot files or as the location from which Subscribers apply the snapshot. This will ensure that the snapshot files are made available to all nodes of the cluster and to all Subscribers that must access it.

If you want to use encryption with a fail-over cluster, you must install the server certificate with the fully qualified DNS name of the virtual server on all nodes in the fail-over cluster. For example, if you have a two-node cluster, with nodes named mcsql.cityhall.genesis.mcity.org and mcsq2.cityhall.genesis.mcity.org and a virtual SQL Server "Virtsql," you need to get a certificate for "virtsql.cityhall.genesis.mcity.org" and install the certificate on both nodes. You can then check the Force Protocol Encryption check box on the Server Network Utility to configure your fail-over cluster for encryption.

It is also vital that you not remove the BUILTIN/Administrators account from SQL Server. The IsAlive thread runs under the context of the Cluster Service account, and not the SQL Server service account. The Cluster Service must be part of the administrator group on each node of the cluster. If you remove the BUILTIN/Administrators account, the IsAlive thread will no longer be able to create a trusted connection, and you will lose access to the virtual server.

Creating a Fail-Over Cluster

The following steps will let you create a fail-over cluster using the SQL Server setup program:

1. Have ready all the information you need to create your virtual server. Items must include cluster disk resource, IP addresses, network name, and the nodes available for fail-over. The cluster disks that you intend to use for fail-over clustering should thus all be in a single cluster group and owned by the node from which the setup program is run. You must configure your cluster disk array before you run the setup program, and this is done through Cluster Administrator in Windows NT 4.0 or Windows 2000. You will need one MSCS group for each virtual server you want to set up.
2. Start the setup program to begin your installation as described in Chapter 6. After you have entered all the required information, the setup program will install the new instance of SQL Server on the local disk of each computer in the cluster. It then installs the system databases on the cluster disk or array. The binaries are installed in exactly the same path on each cluster node, so you must ensure that each node has a local drive letter in common with all the other nodes in the cluster.
   There are some differences is cluster deployment between the different SQL Server versions. For example SQL Server 2000, during a fail-over, only lets the databases fail over. But with SQL Server version 6.5 and SQL Server version 7.0, both the SQL Server databases and binaries fail over.

   If any resource (including SQL Server) fails for any reason, the services (SQL Server, SQL Server Agent, Full-Text Search, and all services in the fail-over cluster group) fail over to any available nodes defined in the virtual server.
3. You install one instance of SQL Server 2000, creating a new virtual server and all resources.

Before you create a SQL Server 2000 fail-over cluster, you must configure Microsoft Cluster Service (MSCS) and use Cluster Administrator in Microsoft Windows NT 4.0 or Windows 2000 to create at least one cluster disk resource. Note the location of the cluster drive in the Cluster Administrator before you run SQL Server Setup because you need this information to create a new fail-over cluster. To create the cluster, do as follows:

1. Run Setup and when you get to the Computer Name dialog box, click Virtual Server and enter a virtual server name. If Setup detects that you are running MSCS, it will default to Virtual Server. You must have configured your shared SCSI disks first. Click Next. The User Information dialog box loads.
2. On the User Information dialog box, enter the user name and company. Click Next. The Software License Agreement dialog box loads. Enter your license information. The Failover Clustering dialog box loads.
3. On the Failover Clustering dialog box, enter one IP address for each network configured for client access. That is, enter one IP address for each network on which the virtual server will be available to clients on a public (or mixed) network. Select the network for which you want to enter an IP address, and then enter the IP address. Click Add.
   The IP address and the subnet are displayed. The subnet is supplied by MSCS. Continue to enter IP addresses for each installed network until you have populated all desired networks with an IP address. Click Next. The Cluster Disk Selection dialog box loads.
4. On the Cluster Disk Selection screen, select the cluster disk group where the data files will be placed by default and click Next. The Cluster Management Dialog box loads.
5. On the Cluster Management dialog box, review the cluster definition provided by SQL Server 2000. By default, all available nodes are selected. Remove any nodes that will not be part of the cluster definition for the virtual server you are creating. Click Next. The Remote Information dialog box loads.
6. On the Remote Information dialog box, enter login credentials for the remote cluster node. The login credentials must have administrator privileges on the remote node(s) of the cluster. Click Next. The Instance Name dialog box loads.
7. On the Instance Name dialog box, choose a default instance or specify a named instance. To specify a named instance, clear the Default check box, and then enter the name for the named instance. Click Next. The Setup Type dialog box loads. (You cannot name an instance DEFAULT or MSSQLSERVER.)
8. On the Setup Type dialog box, select the type of installation to install. The Setup program automatically defaults to the first available cluster disk resource from the group you previously selected.

If you need to specify a different clustered drive resource, however, under Data Files, click Browse and then specify a path on a clustered drive resource. You will be required to select a clustered drive resource that is owned by the node on which you are running the setup program. The drive also must be a member of the cluster group you previously selected. Click Next. The Services Accounts dialog box loads.

On the Services Accounts dialog box, select the service account that you want to run in the fail-over cluster. Click Next. The Authentication Mode dialog box loads. From here on installation continues as described in Chapter 6.

Redundancy

So far we have discussed fail-over, which is generally considered an element of high availability. Let's now look at redundancy, which can provide some level of high availability without the cost of full-blown clustering.

Standby Servers

A *standby server* is a redundant server that you maintain and bring online if the main production server crashes and burns. The idle server contains a copy of the databases on the primary server, which can be used when the standby server becomes available due to scheduled maintenance or crash of the primary. The standby server is useful if the primary is power-cycled one a week, or according to some schedule that takes it offline for a few hours or longer.

The standby server will allow your users to continue working oblivious to the fact that the primary server is unavailable. When the primary server becomes available again, any changes to the standby server's copies of databases must be restored back to the primary server. If you do not restore the databases, the data will be lost. When users start using the primary server again, its databases should be backed up and restored on the standby server.

There are three phases to implementing a standby server:

- **Phase I** Creating the database and ongoing transaction log backups on the primary server
- **Phase II** Setting up and maintaining the standby server by backing up the databases on the primary server and restoring them on the standby server
- **Phase III** Bringing the standby server online if the primary server fails

All your user processes must log into the standby server and restart any tasks they were performing when the primary server became unavailable. The user processes are not switched automatically to the standby server, and transactions are not maintained between the primary server and the standby server. If the primary server is taken off the network or renamed manually, and the standby server is renamed, the standby server will have a network name and address different from the server the users were using previously.

You must also periodically apply transaction log backups from the databases on the primary server to the standby server. This will ensure that the standby remains synchronized with the primary server and that the databases are the same. The more restores you do the more in sync will be the two servers.

A standby server configuration is not the same thing as the virtual server configuration used in SQL Server 2000 fail-over clustering discussed earlier. A standby server contains a second copy of the SQL Server databases and no shared cluster array is necessary. In a virtual server/cluster setup there is only one copy of the databases, stored on the shared cluster disk, available to any node that becomes active.

Creating the Backups on the Primary Server

When you set up the secondary standby server you must create a full database backup of each database to be duplicated and then attach them to the standby servers. Frequently apply transaction log restores to the standby databases to keep them current with the main server. The frequency of transaction log backups created on the primary server will of course depend on the volume of transaction changes of the production server database and you should follow the same guidelines discussed in Chapter 9.

When restoring a copy of *master* from a production server to a standby server, you cannot back up the transaction log of *master*. Only a database backup and restore of *master* is possible.

Setting Up and Maintaining the Standby Server

To setup and maintain a standby server do as follows: Restore the database backups from the primary server onto the standby server in standby mode, specifying an undo file (one undo file per database). Standby mode is either specified in T-SQL backup/restore code or it can be set interactively using the read only/undo file option on the Options tab on the Restore Database dialog box in Enterprise Manager.

When a database or transaction log is restored in standby mode, recovery needs to roll back any uncommitted transactions so that the database can be left in a logically consistent state and used, if necessary, for read-only purposes. Pages in the database affected by the uncommitted, rolled-back transactions are modified. This will undo the changes originally performed by the uncommitted transactions. The undo file is used to save the contents of these pages before recovery modifies them to prevent the changes performed by the uncommitted transactions from being lost. Before a subsequent transaction log backup is next applied to the database, the uncommitted transactions that were previously rolled back by recovery must be reapplied first.

The saved changes in the undo file are reapplied to the database, and then the next transaction log is applied.

Be certain that there is enough disk space for the undo file to grow so that it can contain all the distinct pages from the database that were modified by rolling back uncommitted transactions. You must also apply each subsequent transaction log, created on the primary server, to the databases on the standby server. Remember to apply each transaction log in standby mode, specifying the same undo file used when previously restoring the database.

In standby mode, the database is available for read-only operations, such as database queries that do not attempt to modify the database. This allows the database to be used for decision-support queries or DBCC checks as necessary.

Bringing the Standby Server Online

When a primary server crashes all the databases on the standby server are unlikely to be in complete synchronization. Some transaction log backups created on the primary server may not have been applied to the standby server yet. Also, it is likely that some changes to the databases on the primary server will have occurred since the transaction logs on those databases were last backed up, especially in high-volume systems. Before the users try and connect to the standby copies, you should try to synchronize the primary databases with the standby copies and bring the standby server online in the following manner:

1. Apply any transaction log backups created on the primary server that have not yet been applied to the standby server in sequence, assuming you have access to the primary server.
2. Create a backup of the active transaction log on the primary server and apply the backup to the database on the standby server. The backup of the active transaction log when applied to the standby server allows users to work with an exact copy of the primary database as it was immediately prior to failure (although any noncommitted transactions will have been permanently lost [see Chapter 9]).
   If the primary server is undamaged, which is usually the case when planned maintenance or upgrades occur, you can back up the active transaction log with NORECOVERY. This will leave the database in the restoring state and allow you to update the primary server with transaction log backups from the secondary server. Then you can switch back to the primary server without creating a complete database backup of the secondary server.
3. Recover the databases on the standby server. This action recovers the databases without creating an undo file and it makes the database available for users to

modify. A standby server can contain backups of databases from several instances of SQL Server. For example, you could have a bunch of servers, each running a mission-critical database system. Rather than five separate standby servers, you could have one standby server. The database backups from the five primary systems can be loaded onto the single backup system, reducing the number of resources required and saving you money. It is unlikely that more than one primary system would fail at the same time. Additionally, the standby server can be of a higher specification than the primary servers to cover the remote chance that more than one primary system is unavailable at a given time.

Log Shipping

With Enterprise Edition, you can use the log shipping feature to transport transaction logs from one database to another on a continuous basis. This obviates the need to constantly restore transaction logs to the standby server as discussed earlier. This means that the two databases are in constant synchronization. This not only allows you to have a backup server, but it provides a way to offload query processing from the main computer (the source server) to read-only destination servers.

The Log Shipping Model

Let's say your company has five servers: They are marked server **A**, **B**, **C**, **D**, and **E**. Server **B** is the source server, the server on which log backups and restores are performed and copied. Server **C**, server **D**, and server **E** contain the destination databases on which the log backups from server **B** are restored, keeping these servers in synchronization with server **B**. Server **A** is the monitor server on which the enterprise-level monitoring of log shipping occurs. Each destination or source server is maintained by only one monitor server.

Use the Database Maintenance Plan Wizard access from Enterprise Manager to define an appropriate delay between the time server **B** backs up the log backup and the time server **C**, server **D**, and server **E** must restore the log backup. If more time elapses than defined, then server **A** generates an alert using SQL Server Agent. This alert can aid in troubleshooting the reason the destination server has failed to restore the backups.

Do not use the monitor server as the source server, because the monitor server maintains critical information regarding the log shipping system. The monitor server should be regularly backed up. Keeping the monitor server independent is also better for performance, because monitoring adds unnecessary overhead. Also, as a source server supporting a production workload, it is most likely to fail, which would disrupt the monitoring. The source and destination servers can be on the same computer. But, in this case, SQL Server 2000 fail-over clustering might be a better option, albeit one that is a tad more expensive (the shared cluster disk array).

Configuring Log Shipping with the Database Maintenance Plan Wizard

To configure log shipping you can use the Database Maintenance Plan Wizard. It will allow you to do the following:

- You can define how often the logs are generated, the time between a backup operation and a restore operation, and when a destination server is out of synchronization with a source server.
- Register any new servers whenever you need to.
- Create the source databases on all destination servers. When you add a destination database through the Database Maintenance Plan Wizard, you will have the option of creating the databases on the destination server or you can use existing databases. The existing databases must be in standby mode before you can configure them for log shipping.
- You must also specify which destination servers might assume the role of the source server.
- Set a restore delay. This delay defines how old a transaction log must be before it is restored. If something goes wrong on the source server, this delay provides an extra time before the corrupted log is restored onto the destination server.
- Create a schedule that sets the backup schedule.

Before using the Database Maintenance Plan Wizard, consider the following:

- The user configuring log shipping must be a member of the sysadmin server role in order to have permission to modify the database to log-ship.
- You can configure log shipping only on one database at a time. If you select more than one database, the log shipping option on the wizard is disabled.
- The login used to start the MSSQLServer and SQLServerAgent services must have access to the log shipping plan jobs, the source server, and the destination server.
- When you use the Database Maintenance Plan Wizard to configure log shipping, you can log-ship only to disks. The backup-to-tape option is not available.

Configuring Log Shipping Manually

SQL Server 2000 lets you perform manual log shipping from a SQL Server version 7.0 Service Pack 2 (SP2) transaction log if the pending upgrade option is enabled on the computer running SP2.

To enable this option, execute the following code:

```
EXEC sp_dboption 'database name', 'pending upgrade', 'true'
```

When you are restoring the database after log shipping, however, you can recover only with the NORECOVERY option. But when you manually configure log shipping between a computer running SP2 and a computer running an instance of SQL Server 2000, you cannot use SQL Server replication.

Configuring Log Shipping with Enterprise Manager

You can configure log shipping in Enterprise Manager, but before you do so, you must create a share on the primary database to make the transaction logs available. This is a sharepoint on the directory that the transaction logs are dumped to (backed up). For example, if you backup the logs to the directory *e:\data\tlogs*, you could create the \\logshipping\tlogs share off the directory.

In the Select Databases dialog box, select the "These Databases" check box, and then select the database to log-ship. If you select more than one database, log shipping will not work, and the log shipping option will not be available. You are not allowed to select a database that is already configured for log shipping.

Select the "Ship the transaction logs to other SQL Servers (Log Shipping)" check box. Continue through the wizard, specifying the rest of the database maintenance options, until you get to the Specify the Log Shipping Destinations dialog box. Click Add to add a destination database. In order to use this option to be available, you must have selected to use log shipping earlier in the wizard.

In Review

This chapter deals with the high availability features now available in SQL Server 2000. We discussed the various scale-up and scale-out options and investigated the myth of linear scale-up and how adding more and more processors to a system has a point of diminishing return, both in terms of price and performance.

We also investigated the various clustering models possible using the cluster services of either Windows NT with the Microsoft Cluster Service or Windows 2000 Advanced Server or Datacenter Server. Creating virtual SQL Server servers and setting up the cluster server is not as difficult as it was with SQL Server 7.0.

If you do not need a cluster solution, or have budget constraints, you can configure standby (warm) servers that can be configured to replace the primary server if it goes down. Availability is not as immediate and there will also be delays and additional work involved in backing up databases and transaction logs and applying them to the standby server. The standby server will also have to be kept in read-only or standby mode so that the data cannot be modified, rendering it out of sync with the primary server.

This chapter caps our sojourn into the life of the SQL Server database administrator and his or her typical duties. The next part deals with programming SQL Server.

The Complete Reference

Part III

Programming SQL Server 2000

Chapter 14

SQL Server 2000 Programming Concepts, Strategies, and Models

SQL Server 2000 is a client/server relational database management system. It has a number of attributes that set it apart from other database management systems, paradigms, and so on. As demonstrated in Part I, the architecture of SQL Server 2000 is such that you can be extremely flexible in what you do with it, what you require of its database management services, its relational engine, its storage engine, and so on.

It does not help to position SQL Server below or above the other products. It has a "personality" and special capabilities that set it apart from anything else being used. I have worked in colorful data centers in which SQL Server stands next to DB2, Oracle, and Informix and provides a service that no other product can, either as efficiently or as inexpensively as SQL Server. In this respect I see this "cohabitation" in the data center continuing for some time, although SQL Server 2000 has the potential to take over many services from the other products that are harder to program, more costly to program, and also harder and more expensive to acquire and deploy.

Where SQL Server 2000 shines is that as a product it is very clear what its purpose is and where it fits in the grand scheme of things at Microsoft, and in its technology offerings. Wherever the Microsoft train takes us—DNA around this bend, .Net around the next—SQL Server is the one coach that will always be along for the ride, no matter what station we stop at next. And the Microsoft Data Access Components will continue to be some of the most important technologies to come out of Microsoft since the company was founded.

Microsoft has created several other data storage products. Microsoft Exchange, for example, has a built-in data storehouse for e-mail and Web documents. Active Directory stores objects in an object database, underneath data engine architecture and numerous components you will also find in Exchange. But these storage engines serve very tightly defined functions and are for the most part only for the exclusive use of these niche server products.

SQL Server is also a storehouse for data, but the primary difference between the Exchange storage technology, Active Directory storage technology, and SQL Server is that SQL Server is a system that provides (relational) data management, data manipulation, and data analysis services . . . in addition to effective storage facilities.

While you can program SQL Server to just store data, if that's all you see in it, or that's all you plan to use it for, then you are underutilizing it and ignoring many of its capabilities and resources (which is why there are now several versions available). This chapter was thus written to provide you with an application development and programming strategy that will help you make the most of SQL Server 2000.

This chapter is not only for beginners because we discuss some new concepts in SQL Server 2000. It can also be considered the introduction to Part III, which deals exclusively with programming SQL Server, using T-SQL and XML, and providing facilities for data access clients. From time to time, I will point out which chapters deal directly with each subject.

The SQL Server Programming Environments

When evaluating how best to adopt SQL Server 2000, it helps to view or survey the entire programmatic and data access architecture holistically. First, you should understand that you build applications and software to interact with SQL Server in two environments, one external and one internal.

In the external environment, you will build data access/data consumer applications that rely on SQL Server for data, but you do not actually program directly in SQL Server for the most part. In the internal environment, you program SQL Server for configuration, management, and client access functionality. Developers in the external environment work with SQL Server from a distance, and in many cases they need to know very little, if anything, about what cooks inside the server. Those on the inside work with the internals of SQL Server; they can be either DBAs or stored procedure, trigger, and SQL API developers.

SQL Server, like many other RDBMS environments, has thus cultivated three breeds of developer: SQL Server "front-end" data access or data consumer programmers (clients), SQL Server "back-end" functionality programmers, and SQL Server configuration, management, and administration programmers. The following list highlights the responsibilities of the programmers in both the internal and external environments.

- **Front-end data access/data consumers (clients)** This developer—the client developer—works with the client access technologies in the presentation and middle tiers. Technologies include—besides user interface components and language-specific environments—data access object models like ADO and its extended models, such as the ActiveX Data Objects Extensions for Data Definition Language and Security (ADOX) and ADO MD, which includes objects specific to multidimensional data; and OLE DB, ASP, XML, HTML, JScript and VBScript, and so on.
- **Server functionality** This developer—the SQL Server developer—works primarily in Transact-SQL (T-SQL), coding server-side functionality such as stored procedures, triggers, and extended stored procedures. This developer will spend much of his or her time coding procedures, working with stored procedure debugging and testing tools, performing query analysis, server tracing, optimization, and so on.
- **Server configuration and management** This developer is your typical database administrator (DBA), who makes use of interactive tools like Enterprise Manager and Query Analyzer and T-SQL to configure and optimize SQL Server, model the databases, create and manage tables, create and manage indexes, manage integrity and constraints, write backup/restore scripts, and so on.

I believe further discussion of each "class" of developer is warranted and will lead us to fully position SQL Server in the correct context for the three classes. From there, we can move to the first logical phases in programming SQL Server and the data access clients. I am sure that you are probably at home in all three digs. After all, the smaller the shop, the less likelihood of having the resources to hire developers that work exclusively in each area. Large, busy data centers, or ISVs, do separate out the developers and manage their roles vigorously. And the busier and more involved you become in the middle and presentation tiers, or in the client realm, the less likely you are to have the time to work on the back end as either a SQL Server developer or a DBA. We get back to this subject later in the chapter.

Let's now start from the internal environment and work our way out.

Server Configuration and Management

We have just worked through a hefty part of this book that focuses on the activities in the life of the SQL Server administrator, so we will not need to repeat anything here. However, typical DBA development responsibilities are numerous.

If you thought programming was not a DBA role, you made a big mistake. I don't believe you can be a DBA without even a sniff of SQL and T-SQL programming. And I don't see how you can become an effective and highly paid DBA without experience in software development, and more than just beginner's SQL and Transact-SQL.

The good SQL Server DBA in fact now needs to be proficient in languages like Visual Basic and Visual C++, scripting languages like VBScript and Jscript (or JavaScript), XML, ASP, and so on. Many companies rely on a good DBA not only to provide the back-end services and code, but to model the databases and architecture and mentor a team of client application developers. The DBA needs to provide all the "hooks" to SQL Server, and to do that he or she needs to provide the "Velcro" . . . which means knowing what the clients need to write so that their applications properly hook up to the server. If something does not work correctly in a traditional application or a Web-based application, the DBA will often need to read the code to offer suggestions, even solutions.

Programmatic Management of the Servers

Often you will be required to undertake management of SQL Server processes for services such as replication, security, disaster recovery, data transformation, and networking. Expert knowledge of T-SQL is therefore a prerequisite to being more than your average click-and-enable DBA. This was clearly demonstrated in the administration chapters in Part II.

In the first instance, the DBA is most likely to be the person who has the highest responsibility for the servers and the data access and storage requirements. You'll be required to interface with the data analysis and data-modeling people, to provide input into database design and implementation. In some cases expect to be awarded a significant part of the modeling work as well, possibly all of it. If you are new to Meta

Data Services and modeling languages like UML and entity-relationship diagrams, then Chapter 5 provides a good place for you to ramp up.

Management of indexes, integrity and constraints, rules, and performance will often require programming directly in T-SQL. The busier the environments, and the more advanced the database requirements, the harder it will be to remain effective and responsive using just Enterprise Manager.

Setting up analysis services and data warehouses are becoming standard order of work for the SQL Server DBA. Many of the disciplines you need to manage in OLTP systems will be used in configuring and managing the OLAP systems as well.

Figure 14-1 will help you to best determine where to place your skills, what you need to learn and grasp in the development role of the SQL Server DBA. Consider the following list starting with the first segment in the figure going clockwise:

- **Using SQL-DMO and SQL-NS** These are object models that respectively let you write software to install and manage just about any service and object in SQL Server. These APIs are discussed later in this chapter. They will require you to be proficient in programming against COM objects in particular and object models in general. You'll need at least Visual Basic proficiency, or proficiency in any other environment that can adequately host COM objects or OLE automation objects.
- **Indexing** This is certainly the responsibility of the DBA. Your job here is to ensure SQL Server accesses data as efficiently and as fast as possible. You'll need to ensure that indexes are working properly and that they meet the requirements of the clients. You'll need T-SQL to create indexes on tables (see Chapters 11 and 21), drop indexes, and so on. You'll also need to become expert at analyzing SQL Server performance, especially in the area of statistics and query plan analysis (see Chapter 21). Often you'll need to resolve bottlenecks, and they might lead you to T-SQL code that you'll have to rewrite (see Chapter 15).

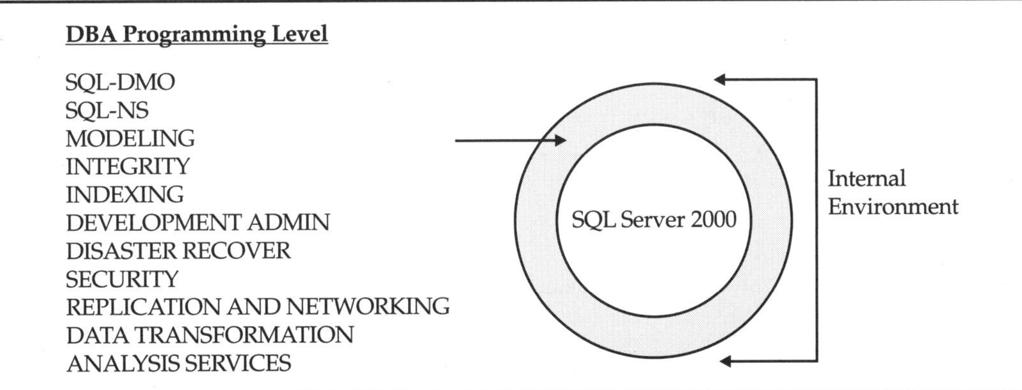

Figure 14-1. *The DBA programming level in the SQL Server internal environment*

- **Modeling and architecture** You'll need to know how best to normalize the databases, decide on the level of normalization, know when to denormalize, and so on. Some situations require under-normalization, like an OLAP database, and the right level will be your call. You'll need to know how best to lay out the tables and help choose data types (or determine which ones are to be used). In addition, all SQL Server solutions must be properly modeled and documented in a metadata repository. You can use the Meta Data Services browser to navigate and edit information in the repository, but to be effective you'll need to know how to create information models (using languages like UML) and install them into the repository.
- **Integrity** Managing database integrity is another area of DBA responsibility that will require programming skills and expert knowledge of T-SQL. Objects like triggers play an important part in maintaining the integrity of data and adhering to business rules. Integrity is extensively discussed in Chapter 17.
- **Administrative programming** In most cases Enterprise Manager will suffice, but often just knowing how to grant, revoke, and deny logins and other simple tasks in T-SQL makes the DBA's life a lot simpler. I have often stood over a new DBA who was trying to clear a table one row at a time; I had no choice but to ask him or her if they've never used T-SQL's TRUNCATE TABLE facility.
- **Disaster recovery** The integrated backup/restore facility in SQL Server 2000 has come a long way. It is one of the facilities that sets SQL Server apart from many other relational database products. In most data centers you'll be required to develop extensive, sophisticated scripts to back up databases and transaction logs and meet extensive disaster recovery requirements. Much of what we discussed in Chapter 9 will need to be expressed in T-SQL scripts, at one time or another.
- **Security** SQL Server security goes a lot further than creating logins and users and setting permissions in Enterprise Manager. You may find yourself doing security work in T-SQL, like granting and revoking access, and encrypting objects.
- **Replication** Replication between servers is not simple; requirements take on various forms and require highly complex setup and deployment. Your replication environment may go beyond what can be set up by the replication wizards, requiring extensive scripting and T-SQL code.
- **Data transformation services** The DTS is a highly sophisticated data transformation environment, consisting of collections of COM objects. Like the SQL-DMO and SQL-NS object environments, they will require you to be proficient in programming against COM objects in particular and object models in general. You'll need at least Visual Basic proficiency, or proficiency in any other environment that can adequately host COM objects or OLE automation objects.

Server Functionality

The SQL Server developer is the person or persons in charge of server-side programming and functionality. If you are not familiar with functionality development and management in SQL Server, you should be aware that the creation of programmatic objects in SQL Server is one of the most important tasks required of the SQL Server developer. It requires advanced programming skills and an expert knowledge of SQL Server that can only come from continuously working with and studying SQL Server and T-SQL.

Many data centers employ some of their top programmers to design and develop stored procedures, triggers, custom functions, and external processes that can be called from the internal procedure code.

Figure 14-2 identifies eight major programming areas that are the responsibility of the SQL Server developer. Notice that I have positioned this developer on the external ring on the server side, behind the DBA ring. This does not mean that you are necessarily coding at a higher level than the DBA, but conceptually you are positioned further away from the server than the DBA. In well-run shops, most of the access to the server will be through the DBA. Also, you'll likely only have access to the databases you are developing for under very controlled conditions.

I actually do not let any developer install code directly to a SQL Server production database. The developer first codes and tests against the development databases, and only after testing are the objects scheduled for installation against the production server. The team is required to fill out change control requests, which get e-mailed to me. The requests get approved at change control management meetings and get signed off by one of the chief executives. I schedule the updates at certain periods after backups and other system checks have been verified. Naturally, I have a strategy in place for urgent updates. If something is required to be done in the middle of the night as a matter of life and death, then I still have to be awakened to come in and do it. Then

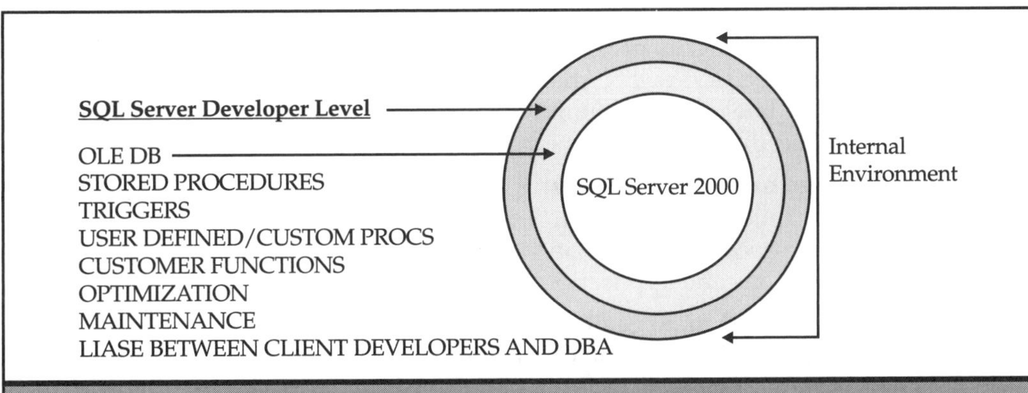

Figure 14-2. *The SQL Server developer level in the SQL Server internal environment*

I install the code to the databases . . . *not* the developer. Of course all shops work differently, and you obviously need to have rules and a regimen to adhere to.

Once I was handed the keys to a critical server, and a few days after I took over the system, a number of alterations had been made to several databases. After that, I changed access permissions and locked down the databases. I made it so that only I and my team had the ability to alter the database objects. I was confronted by the development team and their head honcho. They offered two choices: Either I or one of my team alters the databases or they can have the server back. Trust me, I have been down this road a few times, and when something goes wrong my phone goes off the hook first.

There is also a space between the two rings, suggesting that the segments on the DBA ring are not dependent on the segments of the developer ring. However, SQL Server developers will often be required to write code for the requirements (segments) on the DBA ring, from data transformation (which often makes use of stored procedures) to integrity programming and so on.

- **Stored procedures** Starting with the first segment going clockwise, this developer spends most of his or her time writing stored procedures. This person will interface and meet with the client developers to determine and propose the server-side objects required by the clients. As we will discuss shortly, properly deployed client/server applications shift the actual data query and manipulation code to the server, leaving the client developer free to concentrate on the presentation-tier requirements. (See Chapter 18 for extensive discussion on stored procedures.)
- **Triggers** Triggers are also stored procedures, but they are not called from client applications. They fire when tables are accessed and are thus an internally controlled mechanism. However, trigger writing can be as complex as stored procedure writing and triggers are often abused with huge segments of code that impact server performance. The requirements and reasons to write triggers vary from one project to another and call upon both the client developer and the DBA. Often integrity programming responsibility will shift from the DBA to this developer, or it will be shared by both. (See Chapter 17 for extensive discussion on integrity programming and Chapter 18 for extensive discussion of stored procedures and triggers.)
- **User-defined or custom procedures and constructs** SQL Server 2000 provides extensive facilities to extend SQL Server through custom data types, functions, and external procedures. You can write highly advanced facilities that access external functions and applications for just about any requirement.
- **Configuration and management** While this programming is primarily in the ambit of the DBA, you will often be required to code configuration and management routines.

The SQL Server developer is also the liaison between the client developers and SQL Server and its DBAs. In many data centers, the client developer has no access to SQL Server at all, other than through inline SQL statements. The SQL Server developer provides the client developer with the information required for data access. Together, possibly with the DBA along as an advisor, the developers will design the data tier to the business requirements at the conceptual level and the client's needs at the physical, deployment level. The client developer will then return to the client environment or presentation tier, and the SQL Server developer will get busy building the stored procedures and server-side functionality required by the specifications. I will delve into this topic again later in the chapter.

Another area you might find yourself in as a SQL Server developer is developing English Query models and applications. This is definitely a job for SQL experts who need to map natural language (English) queries to complex SQL statements and multidimensional queries for analysis. Your models can then be used by client developers for embedding in ASP pages, analysis applications, or Visual Basic or Visual C/C++ applications (or you could do the embedding yourself).

Data Access—Data Consumers (Clients)

In the external environment of SQL Server, data access development involves building software that accesses SQL Server databases, which makes use of SQL Server as the back-end data storage, data manipulation, data analysis, and data management facility. I prefer to categorize all such applications as data access and data consumer clients, or just data clients. And it makes no difference to SQL Server whether the client consumer functions are in the middle tier—where many of the business services, rules, and logic objects are being placed nowadays—or the client or presentation tier.

These applications are line-of-business applications (such as CRM and order-taking/order entry), data processing software (such as financial and accounting software), data analysis software (such as decision support and enterprise analysis software), data consumer software (such as process control, telecommunications systems, transport systems) and both business-to-consumer (B2C) software and business-to-business (B2B) software.

The tools you use on the front end operate independent of the back-end architecture, except for the T-SQL you deliver to the server. Granted, you talk to SQL Server through front-end tools or via the services of middle-tier components that can interface to providers which can in turn interface to the TDS protocol. But these facilities are merely the means by which you can package a message to SQL Server; one that is designed to solicit a response from SQL Server, run a batch of code on the server, and send data back to the client. The data returned can be in the form of result sets or individual values.

The SQL statements sent to the server from your client applications are called inline statements or inline code. It is usually the SQL code passed into the text or statement properties of the command or statement objects of your ADO, DAO, and OLE DB or ODBC Code. Embedded SQL is not the same thing as inline SQL. Embedded SQL refers to code embedded in ROM devices and other non-PC "things."

SQL Server doesn't care what you do with the data in the client application. Its purpose is to care what happens to the data you send to it. For example, if the SQL Server developer creates a new data type to store the DNA code of *velociraptor*, SQL Server's concern is how to store the new data type and work with the data it represents, and your concern is getting the data, input by your user, to send to the server.

SQL Server needs only to be a connection away from your client application or service. The back end can be in Tasmania and the front end in Chicago, with a middle tier in Cairo. As described in the architecture chapters in Part I, SQL Server can establish connections with a number of network protocols, such as TCP/IP and IPX. It can then use the connection to transmit and receive data between the client and the server. Client and server can be on the same host, or as mentioned, on opposite sides of the galaxy.

It is quite natural to expect that the client developers will often find themselves concurrently performing the roles of client developer, SQL Server developer, and DBA (which is why this book talks to all three developers). This is usually the case in small programming shops or data centers. I have often found myself hired as a network engineer, programming database clients when needed. And if you have a number of small companies that hire you for data management, as I have, you'll find yourself being the DBA, the SQL Server developer, and the client developer all at the same time . . . going from ASP and VB to T-SQL in one afternoon.

And since the desktop edition will soon replace desktop engines like Jet, which it can already do, you'll find yourself writing the back-end code required by the front-end processes. And, not to forget, you might find yourself building English Query solutions (see Chapter 22) for your client applications, and the English Query environment certainly does require knowing ANSI SQL and T-SQL, even though English Query automatically generates the query code.

But the three technical disciplines have very distinct purposes, no matter whether you are creating a standalone application in which client and server are all in the same machine, an embedded data consumer application built into the next Mars explorer, or a distributed network application accessed by 25,000 humans. The client or middle-tier developer on a large project usually has a full plate, so staying away from the SQL Server internal environment completely is probably a good idea.

Figure 14-3 shows the external environment as several layers, but completely detached from SQL Server. There are so many disciplines to master in this environment that segmenting or compartmentalizing the layers in the external environment cannot be effectively illustrated in the illustration. They are therefore listed in Tables 14-1 and 14-2. The outer ring, however, represents the client technologies, or the client and presentation tier. The inner ring represents the middle-tier technologies.

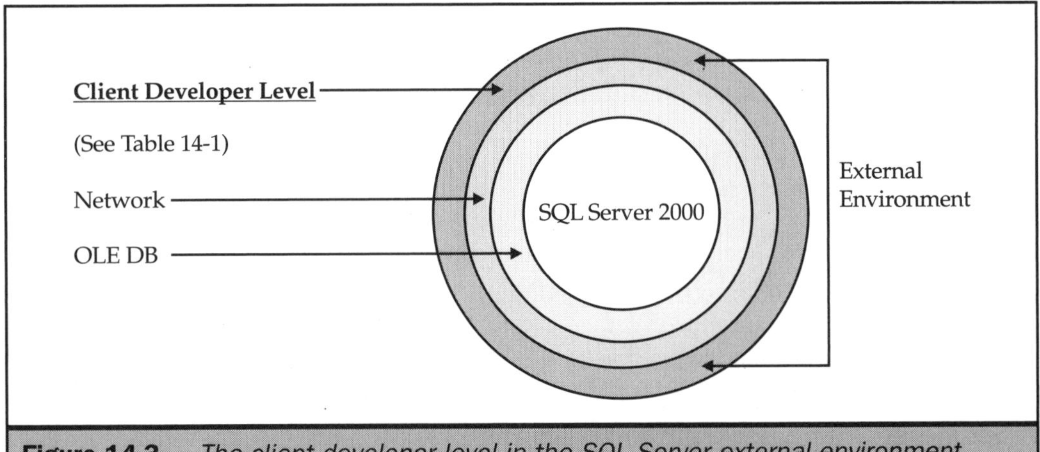

Figure 14-3. *The client developer level in the SQL Server external environment*

A lot has been written about the technologies in both tiers, and the subject matter is beyond the scope of this book (save for what we discuss in Chapter 23). If you are new to SQL Server and using it as your back-end data facility, it is important to understand that SQL Server thrives in a multitiered environment, in which the best implementation is to allow SQL Server to handle *almost* all of the data processing for you.

The client developer needs to know very little T-SQL. That said, sometimes knowing the language can be an asset and sometimes it can be a burden. A general

Client-Tier Development Technologies
Client languages (C/C++, VB, Delphi, Java, PowerBuilder, etc.)
Microsoft Data Access Components (OLE DB, ADO, ADO MD, ADOX, ODBC, JDBC, DAO, RDO, etc.)
Internet markup languages (HTML, XML, XSL, etc.)
Scripting languages (JavaScript, JScript, VBScript)
Reporting tools
Analysis tools
English Query tools

Table 14-1. *Client-Tier Development Technologies in the SQL Server External Environment*

Middle-Tier Development Technologies
Internet Information Services (IIS) and UNIX-based Web servers
Active Server Pages
Com+, Transaction Services (formerly MTS)
Message Queuing
English Query Models

Table 14-2. *Middle-Tier Development Technologies in the SQL Server External Environment*

knowledge, even expert knowledge, of ANSI SQL is major plus. For the most part, for SQL Server access, you need to know how to code simple SQL Server statements in general, and how to call a stored procedure in particular. Why? The next section uncovers the reason.

The SQL Server Programming Models

Much has been written about the multitiered (*n*-tier) environment, so we don't need to rehash the definitions here. I will, however, remark that the SQL Server tier is often called the *data tier*. The data tier can be the back end of the simple two-tiered environment (client/server) on a single computer, or it can service multiple clients on many remote machines. It supports embedded applications on the one hand and can scale out to many servers on the other.

No matter how many tiers face the data tier, SQL Server views them all as a single client tier. In these terms, as Figure 14-4 shows, there are three models that incorporate the deployment of SQL Server 2000:

- Fat client/thin server
- Thin client/fat server
- Ultra-Thin client/middle-tier functionality/fat server

Let's investigate these models further.

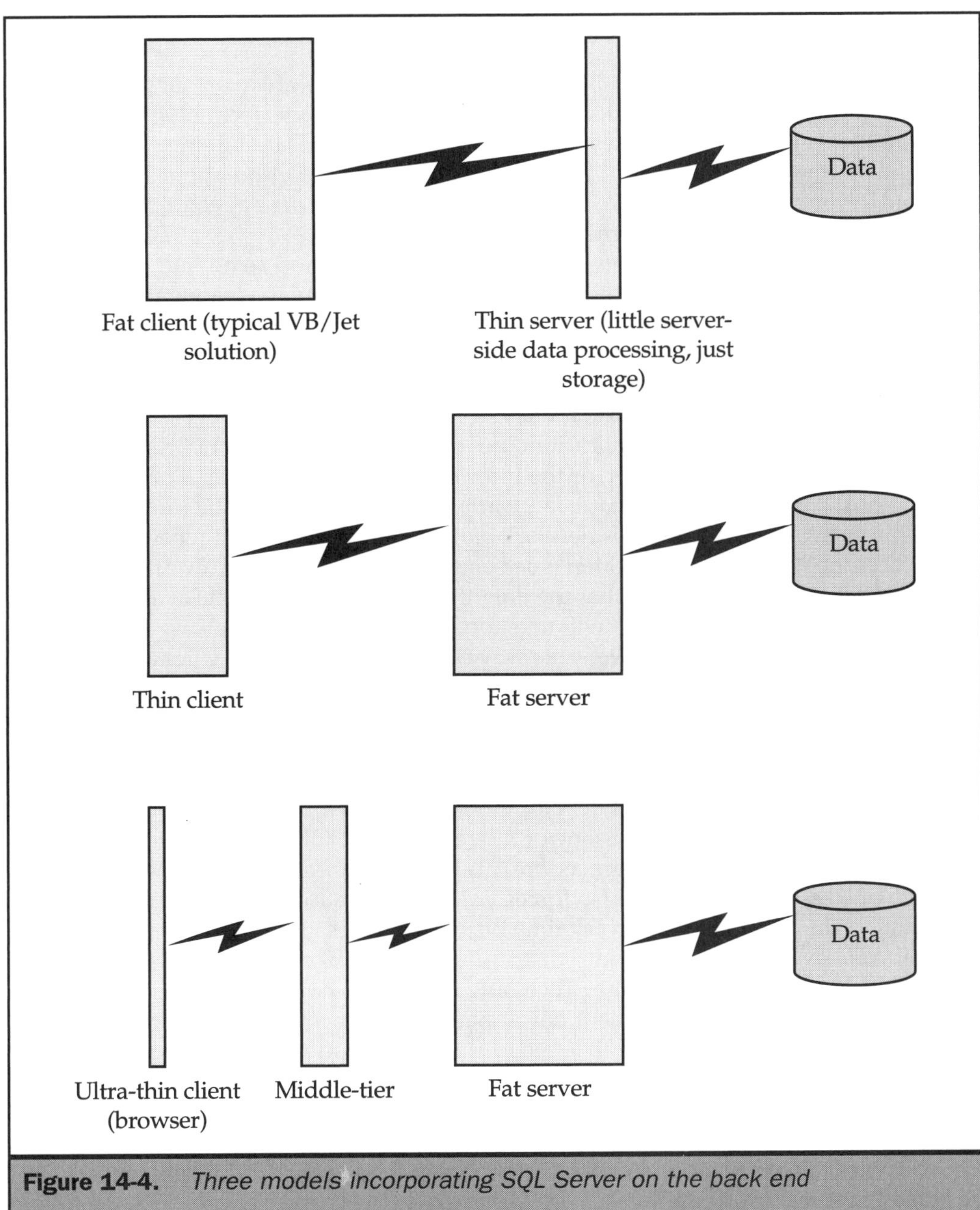

Figure 14-4. *Three models incorporating SQL Server on the back end*

Fat Client/Thin Server

In the now almost-prehistoric fat client era, the fat client was always your typical data access application infused with all manners of client data access technology. Data was typically stored in ISAM databases (like Jet and the Borland Data Engine). As discussed in Chapter 2, the client handles all the data processing and manipulation. The server, back end, or underlying data store is responsible for storing the data and providing the access. It is a thin server . . . in terms of processing.

Fat clients pull large recordsets, master and detail data, and so on into the processing space of the client application. There they manipulate, aggregate, and otherwise process the data. When the data crunching and disk grinding are done (after the office lights have dimmed), data is saved back to the database or printed in reports. Fat clients need lots of processing power, lots of hard drive space, lots of memory, and executives who know how to waste money.

The fat client/thin server application does not work well on a network, no matter if the network is a LAN, an intranet, or the Internet. As soon as more than one fat client needs to pull data from the database, large amounts of data need to be transferred across the network. Not only does network bandwidth diminish, but when network connections need to be released often (such as over the Internet) or they are unreliable, fat clients cannot be guaranteed that the data they need will always be available. Users will abandon the effort because it will take too long to present the data.

This model is outdated and went the way of Flight 19 years ago. Client developers need to concentrate on what the client does best: present and capture data . . . data I/O. Besides the performance issues in network environments, fat clients are nowadays very expensive to build and administer. If the data processing logic is compiled into the client, it means that highly complex SQL statements need to be concocted and optimized at the client. The client development environment is hardly the place for complex SQL statements, which is one of the reasons the SQL query in Access became storable in Access (like a stored procedure) and not prepared or saved at the client.

Data processing at the client also forces you to spend a lot of time and money maintaining the client, because every time businesses rules change, or data I/O needs change, you have to recompile and redistribute the fat application.

Despite the logic of moving the processing to a server-based relational database management system, many fat client developers, particularly Access and other desktop database developers, find it hard to let go of the fat client model. So widespread is this malady that millions of corruptible ISAM database applications atop Access and Xbase engines still exist today. Whenever I go to a SQL Server user's group, we always kick off with the joke : "Are there any FoxPro developers here yet?"

The reason for this is that the fat client model is well established. There are apparently more than 20 million VB programmers in the world actively programming the fat client model. Products like PowerBuilder have been around for nearly a decade, and number of lines of code written by PowerBuilder developers has more zeros than Bill Gates's net worth.

While SQL Server 2000 and Access 2000 provide you the tools to scale-up to SQL Server, most of the time you have nothing worthwhile to scale up. Most ISAM database solutions I have inspected do not scale to any DBMS solution worthy of the so-called "Scale-Up Wizard." It might make more sense to dispense with your model, trash the client applications, and start anew, modeling your new database applications along true client/server database models and methods. By all means use the data transformation services and the so-called scale-up features to move your valuable ISAM data to SQL Server (see Chapter 11). But if you want to scale up, you have to change your mindset and start thinking thin client/fat server.

Thin Client/Fat Server

The Net cannot get all the credit for the shift to thin client/fat server computing. Thin-client and network computing would have come to be without the Internet. Companies were also hard at work on this paradigm long before the advent of the Web. The thin client was also the model of the mainframe era, albeit dumb terminals only provided cryptic and cumbersome access to the user (character-based data and word processing was often the best the mainframe model could offer).

Note *It is useful to define clients as being either "rich" or "vanilla." A rich client does not necessarily have to be to fat, at least not when it comes data processing. A rich client might be packed with the latest OS and software, have a lot of memory, and have extensive storage and extensive processing power for a purpose. And there are many such clients. But many companies still deploy fat clients in businesses today for no good reason, despite the nonsensical solution it is.*

The thin client/fat database server, however, is a model that shifts the data processing to the server. The more you move to the server, the better it is for your solution. For Internet-based applications—and these are now leading the field in thin client/fat server database solutions—you have to move all the data processing to the server . . . it's the only way. With the Internet models leading the way, all your development should be based on the thin client/fat server model.

Ultra-Thin Client, Middle-Tier Functionality, and Fat Servers

This is fast becoming the most prevalent model around. It is not only being used as the primary Internet model, but many enterprises are making use of a middle-tier (multitiered or *n*-tiered) deployment across the enterprise.

Middle-tier functionality does not necessarily suggest that there is no longer a fat client out on the network. The middle tier, however, allows many concurrent connections from ultra-thin clients like Web browsers to send and receive data to and from SQL Server. Active Server Pages (ASPs) are the primary means of implementing an *n*-tier environment on the Web and on intranets.

The middle tier acts as a proxy for the client, an arrangement that offers several advantages:

- First, SQL Server should not be directly exposed to the Internet or any other nontrusted clients. The ASP model, behind Internet Information Server (which is usually contacted behind the firewall) protects SQL Server from direct access by a client.
- Second, middle-tier functionality, business objects, message queuing features, transaction monitoring, and so on, is developed and maintained on the middle-tier servers, so the thin clients never have to be updated. The only "updating" that may happen on clients is the transmission of ActiveX or Java objects that can be run in the browser, but these are usually very small extras that do not cost much in terms of bandwidth to transfer to the client. XML, discussed in Chapter 23, also provides for a highly maintainable and cost-effective thin client/middle tier solution.
- Third, the middle tier maintains connections to SQL Server and can optimize those connections, allowing a client to disconnect from the Web server without causing problems on the database server. The Web server and middle-tier technologies can also monitor resources, redirect queries to different servers, and even cache data and frequently used queries and access methods.

This model has proved entirely feasible, even in high-volume online transaction processing systems (OLTP) spread out over the Internet with all business services catered to by stored procedures.

One of the difficulties experienced by newcomers to this programming or data access paradigm is not being able to deal with the idea that a cross-process, cross-computer, and cross-network boundary exists between the data and business functionality on the back end and the presentation and data acquisition functionality on the front end.

But if you divorce yourself from the client, what the user has running on his or her computer, and concentrate on how a middle-tier environment communicates and interoperates with the back end, the model becomes easier to grasp. Technologies like the Microsoft Transaction Server (MTS, now implemented as COM+ services and discussed in Chapter 23) were specifically developed to augment or support functionality that has been typically coded to run in the processing space of the fat client. Besides transaction monitoring, MTS supports your language-independent OLE/COM in-process objects and allows them to be used by multiple thin-client connections.

It is important to understand (and keep this in mind when you embark on stored procedures, as discussed in Chapter 18) that a lot of the complexity of three or *n*-tier deployment is reduced by the implementation of functionality and business services in SQL Server.

Later in this chapter and in the chapters ahead I will offer a specific strategy to developing thin client/fat server applications with SQL Server.

SQL Server Access Facilities

Access to SQL Server facilities is provided on two levels. The first level is the API that SQL Server exposes to any API-compliant application architecture. These APIs are either call level interfaces (calls to functions) or object model interfaces (object instantiation, object method calls, and object property settings).

The second level is the language passed by the services of the API to the back-end database. The database language defines the syntax of the commands sent to the server. The server receives the language in the form of statements, and as discussed in Chapters 2 and 3, it parses the statements and translates them into an internal "DBMS-code" that the back-end server is better suited to use for internal processing.

SQL Server 2000 can receive and process two data description languages:

- **XPath** The version of XPath supported by SQL Server 2000 is a subset of the XPath pathing language as defined by the World Wide Web Consortium (W3C). XPath provides the means to navigate an XML document much as a URL is used to navigate an Internet namespace.

  XPath processing, like URL processing, is seated in the middle-tier services, such as IIS. XPath queries can be also be processed through the APIs SQL Server supports on the back end, such as ADO and OLE DB.

- **Transact-SQL** This is the principal database language of SQL Server, which can be used by general and sophisticated database applications to access SQL Server services and databases. Transact-SQL (shortened to T-SQL throughout this book) is Entry-Level SQL-92 compliant and also supports a number of features from the Intermediate and Full levels of the SQL standard.

The "Transact" in Transact-SQL represents a comprehensive extension of the language for SQL Server–specific access. T-SQL also supports the ODBC-specific extensions of the SQL language as defined in the SQL-92 standard. These extensions can also be accessed via the APIs, such as OLE DB and ADO, discussed next.

Note *While SQL Server 2000 provides rich support for XML, there is a lot of ignorance about what exactly the support is in the current version of SQL Server 2000 and where it fits, in relation to T-SQL, as a SQL Server data access language. I thus felt it necessary to stress the overriding role of T-SQL as the primary language you will use to access SQL Server by fully referencing the language before we consider XML in Chapter 23. It will later become clearer to you, as it did me when XML was born in SQL Server, where it is positioned and leveraged when building SQL Server–compliant applications and services.*

Queries are passed to SQL Server via the services of several APIs that are explained in the next section. Each API has its own facility for assembling a statement, wrapping it up as a query packet, and sending it off to the server.

In the SQL Server application world, we refer to the query text to be sent to SQL Server as the *statement*. Statements are embedded into the calling constructions that are passed into the connection interface. The following pseudocode represents all languages that can process an inline SQL statement in general and a T-SQL statement in particular:

```
\\create the connection object
MyConnection := ClientAPI.CreateConnection(NewConnection)
\\Create the statement object
MyConnection.CreateSQLStatement(NewStatement)
\\Build the statement in SQL or T-SQL
   NewStatement = "SELECT Knights FROM RoundTable WHERE
   Dragons_Slayed = 50"
\\Send the statement to the server
MyCOnnection.SendStatementToServer(NewStatement)
```

Now the preceding code is a mix of Java, Delphi, and C++ because I spent a number of years working with these fine languages. The only legitimate code in the preceding listing is the piece between the quotation marks that represents SQL that can be fully interpreted by SQL Server. No matter the language you use, if it is capable of transmitting a SQL statement, it can talk to SQL Server.

But does it talk directly to SQL Server? No. The statement can only be passed to SQL Server via the services of an API. In the pseudocode listing you just read, my code would need to have the capability to call ODBC or OLE DB directly, or use the services of an object model that interfaces to ODBC or OLE DB (or a C API). An object model is usually the easiest and fastest technology to use to send statements and data to SQL Server and receive information and data. The statement transmitted by the API is usually referred to as an *inline statement*.

The object model creates a layer, or a wrapper, around the lower-level code, like sugar on a lime, making the coding more palatable in terms of speed, time to market, reusability, learning curve, and so forth. Figure 14-5 illustrates the various object models of Microsoft's Universal Data Access (UDA) architecture that sits atop OLE DB and ODBC. It represents both the now-legacy Data Access Objects and Remote Data Objects models that sit atop ODBC and the new ADO architecture that sits atop OLE DB. All the APIs are discussed in the next section.

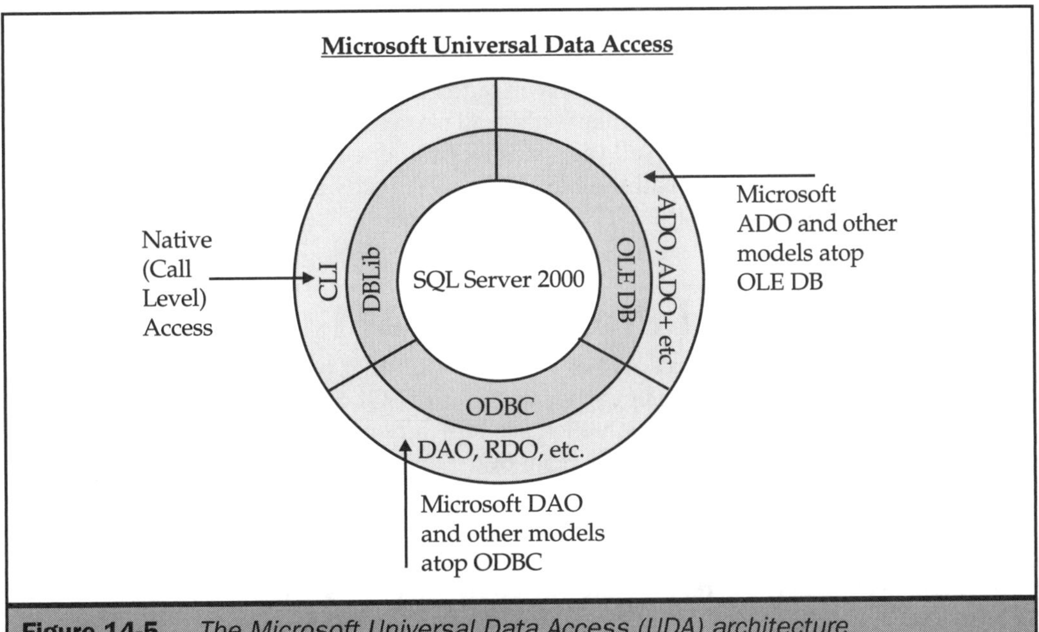

Figure 14-5. *The Microsoft Universal Data Access (UDA) architecture*

Data Transformation Services

The DTS API is a set of COM interfaces based on OLE DB that can be used for creating services that perform all manner of data transformation from one OLE DB provider to another. Using these API and OLE DB providers, you can build software (known as *DTS Packages*) that extract and transform data from one database architecture to another. The DTS API is also used to transform operational data in conventional OLTP databases to analytical data for use in data mining and analysis applications.

The DTS is essentially an object model that comprises a collection of DTS root objects, the *DTS Packages,* which expose connections to data sources, variables, transformation tasks, and so on.

MS DTC Distributed Transactions

The MS DTC component lets you create distributed transactions that can be made against a collection of SQL Server 2000 servers. Using the Distributed Transaction

Coordinator (DTC) service, you can use transaction commands in your code to implement distributed transactions (see Chapter 21). The MS DTC component distributes the transaction to multiple servers and ensures the atomicity or integrity of the transactions as a group. In other words, all servers are exposed as one server. The transaction is made either to all the servers or to none of them.

You'll have little reason to call the MS DTC API directly because SQL Server knows when to pass a transaction to the DTC service (see Chapter 21).

Extended Stored Procedures API

The Extended Stored Procedures API is a C-based API that was inherited from the Open Data Services architecture of earlier versions of SQL Server. It lets you write SQL Server extended stored procedures, which are typically packaged as dynamic-link libraries (DLLs) that can be referenced from SQL Server.

You can think of Extended Stored Procedures as a back door in SQL Server that can obtain data and execute tasks outside the system, asynchronously and synchronously. In previous versions of SQL Server, the purpose of Extended Stored Procedures was largely to create a gateway application. This is now obsolete in SQL Server 2000.

If you still need access to any gateway application you created in the past, you cannot use *opend60.dll* from SQL Server 2000. Instead, you should call the *opends60.dll* and *ums.dll* files that shipped with version 7.0.

SQL-DMO API

The SQL-DMO API is a collection of objects that can be used to access administrative and configuration properties of SQL Server 2000 (see Chapter 7). The SQL-DMO API is implemented as a dual-interface COM, in-process server packed as a DLL. The COM objects can be accessed from Visual Basic as COM components or objects from C or C++.

SQL-NS API

The SQL Namespace API is an object model created to access the visual components of SQL Server Enterprise Manager.

Replication Distributor API

The Replication Distributor API is a set of COM interfaces that can be used for programming the SQL Server replication services. While the API is optimized for defining replication between multiple SQL Server databases, it can also be used to replicate data from heterogeneous or third-party sources of data to SQL Server.

General Database Access APIs

The General Database Access (call level) APIs allow you to access and manipulate data programmatically. They include the following:

- OLE DB
- ODBC
- DB Library
- Embedded SQL for C

OLE DB

This is now Microsoft's definitive database access technology. It is a low-level COM interface API used for all manner of data access, for developing data access tools, high-performance objects, data access, and so on.

The premise of OLE DB from its inception in the dream spaces at Microsoft has been to cater to the wide array of data sources that exist in the world around us. Data is found in flat files, in indexed-sequential database files (Btrieve), in the personal or desktop database products such as Access and FoxPro, in spreadsheets, and in legacy environments on mainframe and midrange systems. OLE DB was designed to allow the database developer to get access to all these diverse data repositories.

OLE DB is built around the concept of providers, which are low-level structures—similar to drivers—that can establish a binding to a data source. You can then program against the interface of OLE DB to gain access to the underlying data. With SQL Server, for example, OLE DB binds intimately with the TDS protocol, feeding the client data receiving components with tabular data (records) sent by SQL Server and vice versa. OLE DB replaces ODBC as the primary data access API for SQL Server.

OLE DB is now a very mature technology. Providers include Active Directory, CICS, VSAM, AS/400, Exchange, and all ODBC-compliant databases. Figure 14-6 provides a birds-eye view of the OLE DB facility.

Naturally SQL Server and OLE DB have a "thing" for each other. SQL Server provides an OLE DB provider that can be used by the clients and data consumer applications to access data in SQL Server databases, and to do the other fun things we have discussed in the earlier chapters.

ODBC

ODBC is a C API that has been the primary means of accessing data in SQL Server, and many other database servers, for a number of years. Like OLE DB, mentioned earlier, ODBC binds directly to the TDS protocol. ODBC, however, is a call-level interface driven by function calls and pointer operations in what amounts to a single API. Used natively (without an object model), it relies on pointers and low-level function calls.

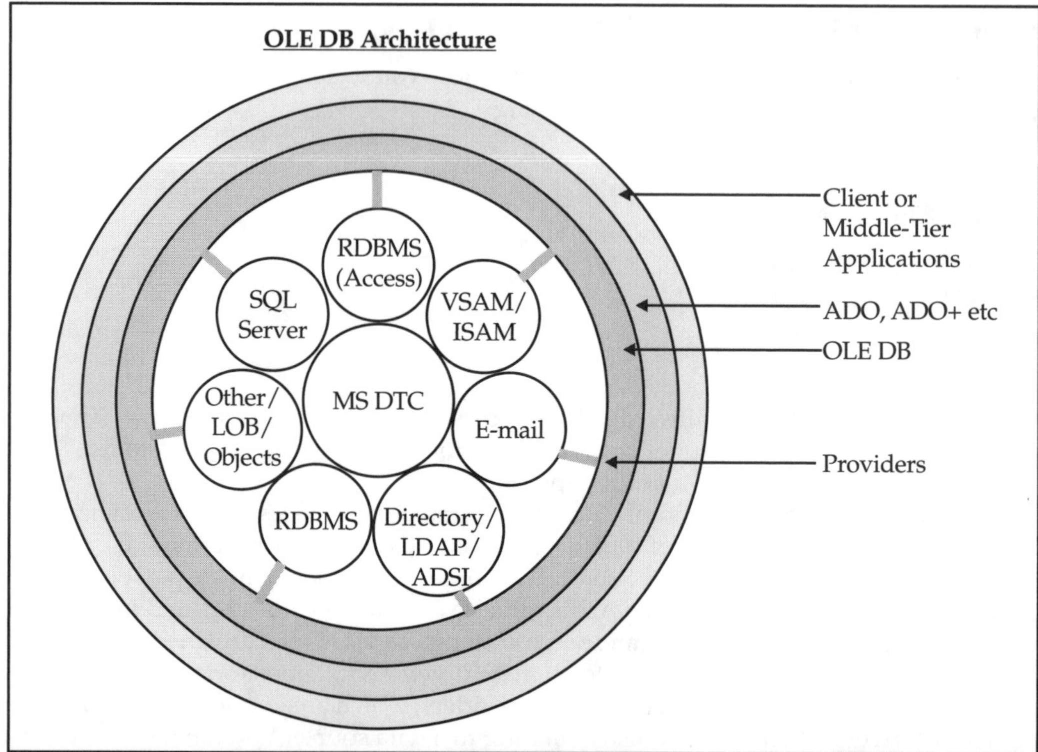

Figure 14-6. *The OLE DB data access technology comprises data providers that expose data from a variety of data sources to OLE DB data services*

DB-Library for C

This is the legacy SQL Server C API that can still be used to access SQL Server. It exists for backward compatibility, for the occasional masochistic programmer still living in the last century, or for some special purpose that precludes the use of higher-level languages. Coverage of this API is limited in this book.

Embedded SQL for C

This is also a legacy API, used for embedded applications that need access to SQL Server. It enables the creation of fast executables on small footprints from C or COBOL applications.

The Database Access Object Models

The data access object models are object interfaces that provide a high-level means of accessing and manipulating SQL Server data. The data access object model is not only a Microsoft system for high-level data access. Object models come in many different languages and vary widely in their level of abstraction, exposure to the underlying database access providers, and performance.

ADO

The ActiveX Data Objects (ADO) is a high-level object model development interface that encapsulates the functionality of OLE DB. It has been highly optimized for use in visual programming environments such as Visual Basic, Visual C++, Visual J++, Delphi, and PowerBuilder. ADO is essentially to OLE DB what the Data Access Objects API (DAO) is to ODBC. In that it encapsulates OLE DB and not SQL Server TDS, ADO allows you to access all the data sources OLE DB supports. It also supports XML processing (discussed in Chapter 23).

There is of course another layer that sits above ADO, the visual data access components. These are components that "wrap" the object model and provide visual components that can be visually programmed. Building applications with such components is extremely easy, which has led many programmers to refer to the paradigm as "programming by numbers." Data-bound controls are typically dropped onto forms and connections to the databases, tables are set via point-and-click, and virtually no code is needed.

While building applications with visual controls was a great idea, you must also expect to lose a lot of power, scalability, and reliability in your applications. The higher or more abstracted you are above the data stream, the less power and speed you have access to. In my experience, data-bound controls can cause unexpected results, and some badly designed ones can introduce data integrity problems to your application. Some years ago I built a data-aware grid using Delphi, which wrapped a DAO object one my programmers had ported to Delphi. I abandoned it on the advent of ADO, but while coding it I learned that a data-bound control has the potential to introduce undesirable matter into your data stream. Tread carefully.

This led me to abandon data-bound controls several years ago. However, even with SQL Server 2000, I have had very mixed results using the data-aware fields, list boxes, and the like that come with Visual Basic, preferring to code the data access at lower levels and handling the transmission of the data and SQL statements myself.

DAO and RDO

Object model libraries, such as the Data Access Objects (DAO) and Remote Data Objects (RDO), were built to enable the higher-level languages such as Visual Basic and

Visual C++ to access ODBC functionality. They are essentially wrapper components of ODBC functions.

The DAO object model has been replaced by the ADO object model as the primary data access object architecture. ADO also encapsulates the functionality of ODBC. Using the DAO and RDO object models is not discussed in this book. These object models have reached the end of their life at Microsoft, which will no longer add to their functionality.

Miscellaneous Services and APIs

This section describes a hodgepodge of APIs and object models that expose the various levels and services in SQL Server 2000.

URL Access

The URL, which stands for Universal Resource Locator, is an Internet standard format for a string object that is used by Internet access applications and browsers to access Internet- or intranet-addressed resources. SQL Server provides services that expose its databases and DBMS objects to the Internet as URLs. This is achieved via the services of an ISAPI function library (*isapi.dll*) supported by Internet Information Services (IIS) that supports the referencing of SQL Server resources in URLs.

I have included the URL here as a means of accessing SQL Server from the Internet because the URL is essentially a namespace path to SQL Server data, just as an OLE DB or ADO name space is. URL access is discussed in Chapter 23.

Analysis Services API and Decision Support Objects

This API lets you create OLAP, DSS, and data mining applications and services that access the facilities of SQL Server 2000 Analysis Services (see Chapters 24 and 25).

Meta Data Services API

SQL Server provides access to its metadata repositories, which are used to store metadata for a specific instance of SQL Server and its respective components. This API lets you create tools and applications that can use and manipulate the structure and data in a repository. The API essentially encapsulates the metadata engine and metadata model definitions that the engine can access. The API also enables to you add new data to the repository for specific programming objectives (see Chapter 5).

English Query API

This API lets you create a facility for querying SQL Server databases using natural language in English. Using the English Query development environment, covered extensively in Chapter 22, you can provide your users with the means of querying databases without having to learn SQL or drag, drop, and click objects in the user interface. This API will also help eliminate the cryptic user interfaces you have been building in the past to help knowledge workers build queries against SQL Server.

Getting Ready to Code

In order to help you envision your applications in this environment, single or multiuser, you should understand and observe the following rules:

- **Rule 1: Deploy fat servers** The database server model requires you to move most or all of your data processing to the server. The client processes and functions and those of the server are clearly defined. The client presents data, captures data, and can alter data. The server processes and stores the data (although it can alter and acquire as well). If you do too much processing at the client, I say that you are violating the model.
- **Rule 2: Keep network usage to a minimum** The database server model requires you to minimize network usage. The best implementation of this model makes use of one network round trip to send a command and receive data. The worst implementation makes many round trips.
- **Rule 3: Conserve network bandwidth** This requires you to "farm" your data, as in "data ecology." This may sound absurd, and you might think I have fallen out of my tree, but you need to build code in the server that can ensure that only the most valid records are selected from the cursors or result sets and sent to the clients. This results in the conservation of your network bandwidth, the resources at the client, and the patience of your users.
- **Rule 4: Keep the client thin** That universal rule, "less is more," applies here big time. You need to be stingy when sending data to the client. You must build code that only sends what is absolutely necessary to send to the client. Remember, if the client does not know which records it needs, it does not make sense to send it a result set of thousands of records. This just chews up bandwidth on the network and at the client, which results in the violation of the second and third rules. Its take some tactical code writing to come up with queries and selection mechanisms to help your users narrow their search, while at the same time making sure they don't overindulge in trips across the network. In Chapter 19, we'll look at how to code like a rifleman with a telescopic lens. Keep in mind that the client can often incorporate client-side data validation and integrity components to ensure that SQL Server accepts the data being sent to it. It makes more sense to trap bad data or clean it in the client tier than to have SQL Server smack it back over the network like the Navratilova return service. With the

preceding rules in hand, the following items make up your shopping list for proper and effective use of SQL Server 2000:

1. Learn to code in SQL and T-SQL like a pro.
2. Rewrite code to minimize network roundtrips.
3. Determine the correct database design solutions.
4. Keep transactions short and to the point.
5. Put whatever SQL code you can into stored procedures.
6. Obtain your resources *late* and release them *early*.

Time to Get Connected

This chapter introduces you to the SQL Server programming environment and paradigm. For many software developers, programming against SQL Server represents a major paradigm shift in coding database functionality. It requires you to abandon the idea of doing data processing code and functionality in the client executables because it makes more sense to allow SQL Server to handle data processing centrally and concurrently for multiple connections in an enterprise.

The server, as we have discussed in the chapters in Part I, has all the necessary components to efficiently handle all your data processing needs. The client only needs to act as a facilitator to obtain data (input) from the user, receive data back from SQL Server, and present data back to the user (output). The client access to analysis algorithms discussed in Chapter 25 is an excellent example of this paradigm at work.

What's more, database applications are going distributed big time. If you look at what's happening in the call center, support industry, and customer relationship management (CRM) spaces, you'll notice that the client applications are thinner than latex and can connect to data from anywhere on the planet. With the replication capabilities we talked about in Chapter 10, the tech support engineer or customer support representative (CSR) can take a U.S.-based call from anywhere and be able to easily update the CRM database.

Online Transaction Processing (OLTP) and Online Analytical Processing (OLAP) are now truly "online," and the online thin client/fat server model provides the departure point for the chapters that follow.

The Complete Reference

Chapter 15

Getting Started with SQL Query Analyzer

SQL Query Analyzer is the Swiss Army knife you use to develop and manage the code that drives SQL Server. But SQL Query Analyzer, or just QA from here on, is somewhat of an enigmatic name for a tool that does tons more stuff than just sit and analyze queries. The term *query* is so loosely used to describe any SQL statement, whether it queries or not, that the name probably makes no difference—at least for this version. QA is a highly specialized and sophisticated application, however, and it caters to several important functions of the DBA and developer. These are as follows:

- QA is used to write and test standard SQL and T-SQL code.
- QA is used to write, test, debug, and develop stored procedures.
- QA is used as a graphical interactive script processor-manager.
- QA is used to optimize performance, assess query plans, and manage database statistics.
- QA is used to tune indexes.

First, you use QA to develop, test, and execute DML statements, DDL statements, SELECT queries, and so on. You can execute one-liners or reams of complex scripts, from table creation to driving the backup/restore facility and so on.

Second, QA is by far the best stored procedure development tool you can use for SQL Server. It comes equipped with a sophisticated debugger that lets you quickly develop and test your procs, or you can use it to tame that "sp from Hell."

Third, you can use QA in everyday DBA or developer chores. You can search for your scripts and batches, load them up into the query panes, and execute them as needed.

Fourth, QA is essential for understanding, monitoring, and improving the performance characteristics of your queries. It shows suggestions for additional indexes and statistics on nonindexed columns that would improve the ability of the query optimizer to process a query as efficiently as possible. In particular, QA shows which statistics are missing and thus forces the optimizer to make estimates about predicate selectivity. It then permits those missing statistics to be easily created.

And QA can be used to assess and tune your indexes, giving you access to the Index Tuning Wizard, introduced in Chapter 11, right on top of your query.

There is also a lot more to QA than I will expand on in this chapter. Because of the complexity of many of the features, I have divided the discussion of QA into two chapters. This chapter introduces QA, covering its configuration and setup, its management features, and the editing and testing of your SQL queries and stored procedures.

All RDBMS platforms maintain information about their tables, columns, indexes, and so on in the system catalog. This information is used by the system as performance data for optimization and is known as database statistics.

Introducing Query Analyzer

While at first the QA might look overwhelming, as it does in Figure 15-1, it can essentially be divided into five key areas of functionality. The following discussion of its tools and capabilities expands on my earlier introduction:

- **A SQL/T-SQL editor** QA provides a free-form text editor for entering, editing, testing, and executing T-SQL statements. It is similar in purpose to standard IDEs. As powerful as it is, it still has a long way to go before it is as sophisticated as something like Visual Basic 6 (frankly, I expected it to be part of the Visual Studio product by now, but that is likely to happen by the next release).

  You can color-code your T-SQL syntax to improve the readability of complex statements and prevent errors. QA provides several tools to help you prevent and resolve errors. For example, you can use color-coding in the Editor pane to help eliminate errors. Using the default colors as examples, if you type a

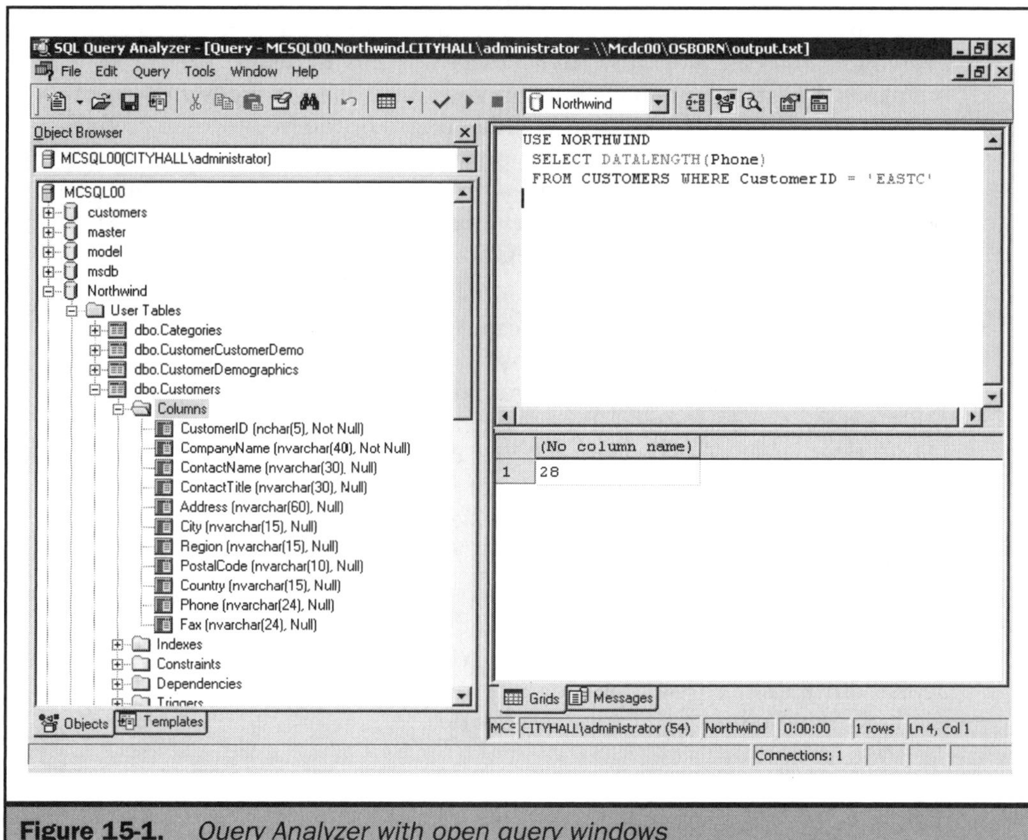

Figure 15-1. *Query Analyzer with open query windows*

keyword that does not get displayed in blue, the keyword may be misspelled. If much of your code is displayed as red, you might have omitted the closing quotation mark for a character string. If an error occurs, double-click the error message to locate the line that contains the error in your code. You can also create keyboard shortcuts for frequently used queries, create custom query shortcuts, and add commands you frequently use to the Tools menu using the Customized Tools menu feature.

- **An object browsing facility** The Object Browser allows you to manage database objects for editing and provides a search capability to easily find the objects within a database. You can search on information about the structure and properties of the objects. The Object Browser also includes query templates, which are files that include the skeletons of the T-SQL statements needed to create objects in a database. These templates are useful and can help speed development of the T-SQL statements for creating SQL Server objects. You can add your own templates, and I'll show you how later in this chapter.
- **T-SQL debugger** This is an interactive debugger that can be used for testing and analyzing your stored procedures. While other debuggers have been available in the past, you now have a place not only to debug your procs, but also to holistically manage them in your database—along with your other scripts. The results are presented in either a grid or the free-form text window. There are several T-SQL debuggers on the market, and you can debug stored procedures in Visual Studio—with Visual Basic, Visual C++, and Visual J++—as was the case with previous versions of SQL Server. The new support for debugging directly in QA, however, is a far more intelligent approach than what Microsoft had us do in the past.
- **Extensive graphical query analysis capability** This is perhaps the most significant feature in QA, and the most complex, from an optimization point of view. It provides a graphical diagram of a T-SQL statement's query plan (see Chapter 2), which can show the logical steps the query optimizer used to build the execution plan. This lets you determine what specific part of a poorly performing query is using a lot of resources. You can then investigate changing the query in ways that minimize resource use while still returning the correct data.
- **The Index Tuning Wizard** QA can be used to analyze a T-SQL statement and the tables it references to see if adding indexes or altering existing ones will improve the performance of the query. While the Index Tuning Wizard can be accessed from Enterprise Manager, it is more useful to have local access to it while working on plan statistics and queries.

QA connects to an instance of SQL Server via the SQL Server ODBC driver. It does not need to be installed on the host server itself, and it might make sense *not* to install it on the server, because a remote client installation is the environment from which your users will be executing the same queries, albeit they might not drop in via the ODBC provider. You also should not need to work on a production server with QA. As careful as you might be, it is incredibly easy to run a query or stored procedure and inadvertently turn an innocent exercise into the faux pas that costs you your job.

By default, when QA attaches it sets the following SQL-92 options to on: SET ANSI_WARNINGS, SET ANSI_PADDING, and SET ANSI_NULLS. And errors returned are formatted as ODBC errors rather than DB-Library errors, as was the case in the murky past when primary access to query plans was via the ISQL command line utility, which was built on the DB-Library API.

The SQL Server 2000 ODBC driver automatically detects the need for and sets up automatic ANSI to OEM conversion. In addition, when SQL Query Analyzer connects, automatic detection for the conversion is enabled. You should also expect changes in behavior when you use Query Analyzer with international or extended characters, or allow clients to connect to the server mainly via the OLE DB (sans DSN) provider.

Navigating and Customizing the Query Editor

QA can be started up directly from the Start menu. It can also be started up from inside SQL Server Enterprise Manager or from the command line by executing the *isqlw.exe* utility. Before you can use QA, you first have to connect to the instance of SQL Server that's holding the database and objects you need access to. This is illustrated here:

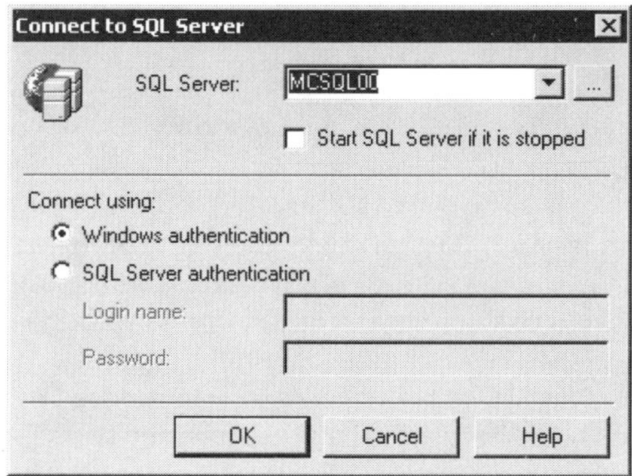

Once you have connected, the Object Browser and a blank Editor pane will load, as illustrated in Figure 15-2.

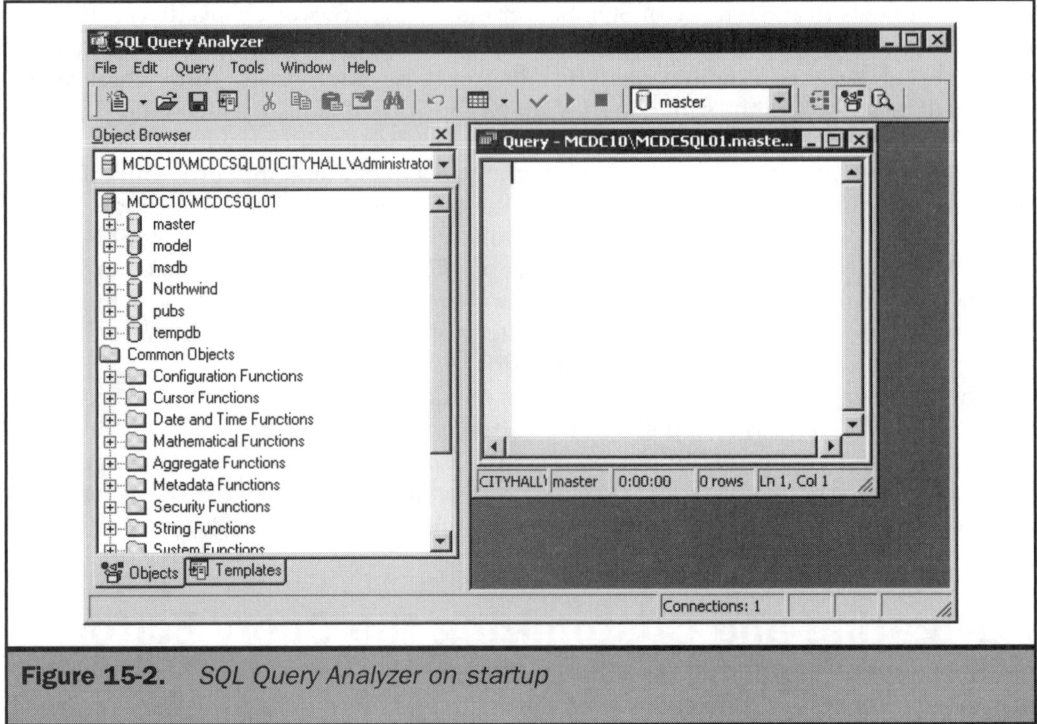

Figure 15-2. *SQL Query Analyzer on startup*

Getting Around QA

The SQL Query Analyzer provides several windows in which to work:

- A Query window
- The T-SQL Stored Procedure Debugger window
- The Open Table window

The title bar of the query window displays the name of the database server, the name of the current database, the current login name, and the query name. When in Windows 2000, the address of the server is in dot notation. If the query is saved to a file, the complete path to the file is shown.

The query window is an MDI application and is composed of multiple panes. The Editor pane is a simple text editor in which you can enter your T-SQL statements. The Results panel, which pops up underneath the Editor pane, displays the returned result sets, while the Message pane displays error messages. You can opt to send result sets to the message pane instead of the grid using the PRINT statement.

The Execution Plan pane becomes available after you run the query and displays a graphical representation of your query's execution plan. You also have a trace pane that displays the server trace information. And a statistics pane displays statistics information.

To make a pane active, you simply have to click it. You can also press SHIFT+F6 to toggle panes. QA also comes equipped with a table window, which displays a grid of your target data, Access style. The grid is fully functional and can be used to modify data, a fact that is useful if you want to tweak values to test queries. You can also insert and delete rows as needed.

Some quirks include possible query failures when you try to insert, delete, or update columns that are also referenced by a computed column. If you have an index on a computed column, you need to enable the user option ARITHABORT before you can edit the referenced column. To do this, just execute the following set of commands in an Editor pane or query window:

```
sp_configure 'user options', 64
RECONFIGURE
```

Managing SQL Query Analyzer Windows

QA allows you to extensively customize the windows and control the behavior of the Editor and Results panes. For example, you can specify certain fonts to use for certain code segments and expressions. You also have full control over size and position of the panes.

To change QA to your preferences, you'll need to work with the options you have in the Options dialog box. This box is accessible from the Tools menu. The options to customize the Editor pane are found on the Editor tab, as illustrated in Figure 15-3. The options you have are listed as follows; you can

- Set the maximum number of undo buffers and the maximum cumulative size of all undo buffers.
- Set the tab size (in spaces).
- Control whether tabs are saved as tab characters or spaces.
- Enable and disable dragging text in the Editor pane.
- Specify the default non-Unicode file open format.
- Specify whether the Results pane appears on a separate tab in the Query window (tabbed mode) or is displayed below the Editor pane (splitter mode). If you choose tabbed mode, you can also control whether the Results tab appears automatically after a query executes. You can also decide whether the Query window tabs are displayed at the top or the bottom of the window.

If you want to customize the Results pane, the Results tab options are also available in the Options dialog box. You can

- Specify the default destination for results. The options available to your are Results to Text, Results to Grids, and Results to File.

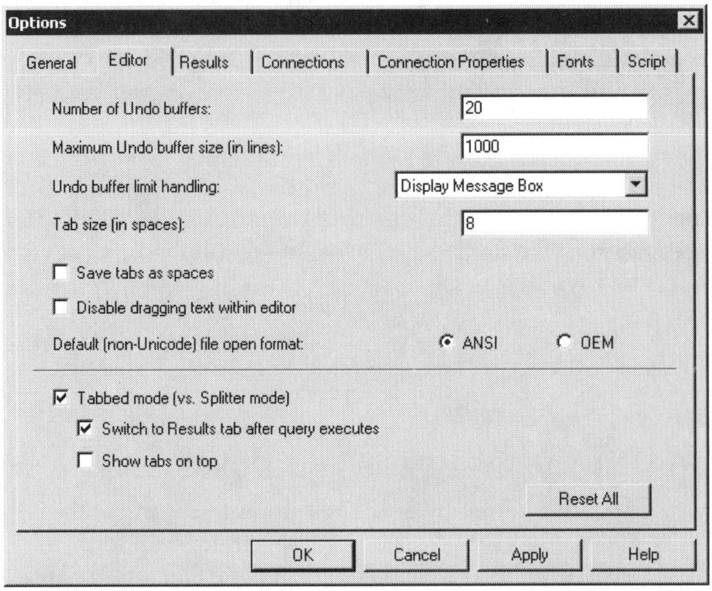

Figure 15-3. *The Editor tab in Options*

- Specify the result set format.
- Specify the maximum width for result set columns.
- Specify whether to include column headers in the output and whether numbers are right-aligned.
- Specify whether to scroll the Results pane as results are received.
- Control various actions, such as discarding results or playing a sound, when execution completes.
- Specify the fonts to be used for text in the Editor pane, the Results text pane, the Results grid pane and Open Table window, the Execution Plan pane, the Statement Profile, the Statistics pane, and the Object Browser. The Fonts tab is also available in the Options dialog box. You can also right-click the aforementioned panes and select Fonts from the pop-up context menu.

Moving the Splitter

When the Query window is split, you can change the relative size of the Editor pane and the Results pane using the mouse to drag the splitter bar up or down. The quickest way to position the pointer on the horizontal splitter bar is to press CTRL+B.

Managing Options in SQL Query Analyzer

You will learn about the myriad SET options (such as SET NOCOUNT) in the chapters to follow; you'll often need to provide these statements before the script in the Editor pane. This can become rather tedious, however, so QA allows you to control the values of SET options for the current connection and for all new connections. As mentioned earlier, you can also manage general connection options, such as timeouts, from the Options dialog box.

You can do this as follows:

- For SET options, go to the Tools menu and select Options. The Connection Properties tab will let you manage the SET options for all new connections. This is illustrated in Figure 15-4. (The options are also accessible from the Current Connection Properties on the Query menu.)
- For general connection options, such as timeouts, go to the Tools menu, select Options, and select the Connections tab. This is illustrated in Figure 15-5.

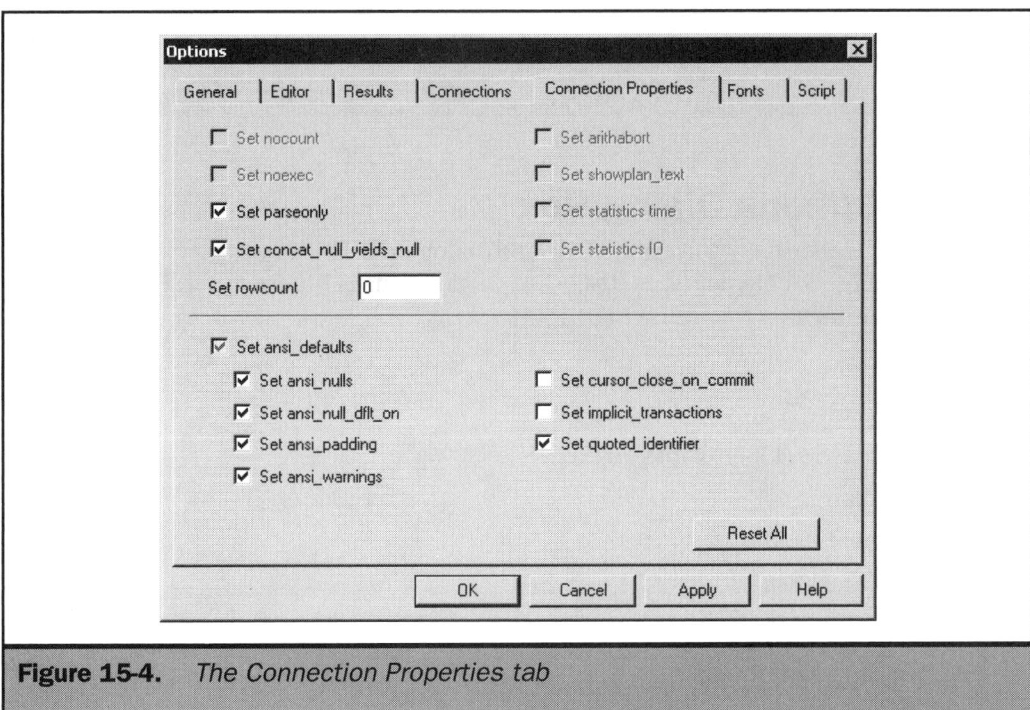

Figure 15-4. *The Connection Properties tab*

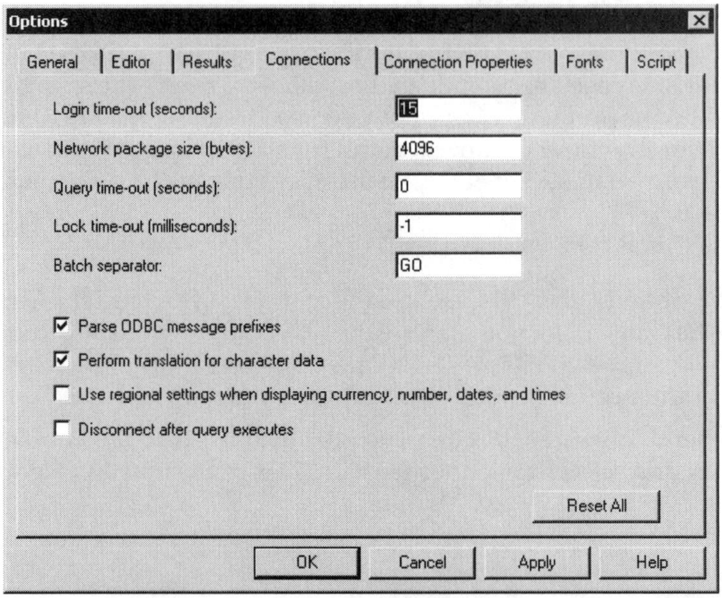

Figure 15-5. *The Connections tab*

Fonts Tab, Options Dialog Box

The Fonts tab is also available on the Options dialog box. This is where you can control the fonts used on QA elements, as discussed earlier. This is illustrated in Figure 15-6. These elements include the following:

- The Editor
- The Results Text
- Results Grid/Open Table
- Showplan
- Statement Profile
- Client Statistics
- Object Browser

The options changing the font and size to be used can visually customize the components in QA and make writing and testing your SQL stuff a lot easier and quicker. Color is also an important visual element that helps you pick up syntax errors. For example, the default for character values between quotes is red so that if you fail to

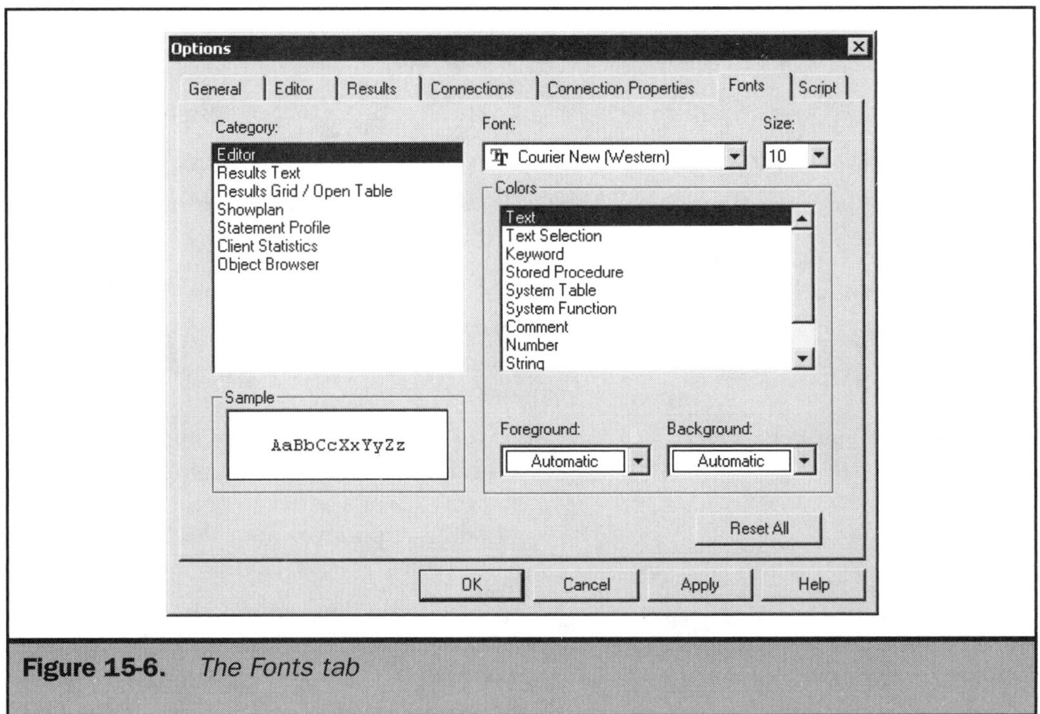

Figure 15-6. *The Fonts tab*

include the close quote, you can easily see that the statement will fail, because the remaining lines will also be in red. And you can specify different colors for the various types of text that appear in the Editor pane, brown for stored procs, blue for keywords, and so on. The options are as described in Table 15-1.

Objects	Objective
Text (Query characters)	To specify the format of alphabetic text.
Text Selection (Query characters)	To specify the format of query text when it is selected.
Keyword (Query characters)	To specify the format of Transact-SQL keywords.
Stored Procedure (Query characters)	To specify the format of stored procedures.

Table 15-1. *Font Size Options*

Objects	Objective
System table (Query characters)	To specify the format of system tables.
Global variable (Query characters)	To specify the format of global variables.
Comment (Query characters)	To specify the format of comments within a Transact-SQL script.
Number (Query characters)	To specify the format of numeric text.
String (Query characters)	To specify the format of alphanumeric text contained within single quotation marks.
Operator (Query characters)	To specify the format of symbols used to perform mathematical computations or comparisons between columns or variables. Operators are classified as Arithmetic, Bitwise, Comparison, or Join.
Foreground	To specify the foreground character color for the content type selected in the Color box.
Background	To specify the background color for the content type selected in the Color box.
Font	To specify the font for the content type selected in the Color box.
Size	To specify the point size of the content type selected in the Color box.
Sample	To display the query characters in the selected format.
Reset All	To reset all options to their original default values.

Table 15-1. *Font Size Options* (continued)

Window Selector Dialog Box

QA comes equipped with a Window Select dialog box that you can use to toggle between the windows and panes. This dialog box is opened from the Window menu and is illustrated in Figure 15-7. It also provides information about each window. The options are as follows:

- **Select Window(s)** This lists the windows that are currently open in the Query Analyzer. The active window is in blue so that you easily see it.
- **Window Type** This lists the type of window, such as Query Window, T-SQL Debugger, or Object Search.
- **Server** Database server.
- **Database** The database context for the window.
- **User** This is the login (not user) that opened the window. If the login is on a trusted connection, you can also see which domain and security principal (such as GENESIS\DCP USERS) opened the Window. (See Chapter 8 on logins and trusted connections.)
- **Description** This item provides information about the window and its contents, such as the name of an unsaved window, the name and path of a saved window, and the name of a stored procedure in the T-SQL Debugger.
- **Activate** Selecting this forces the select item to become the focus of the applications. The dialog box also closes when you select Activate.
- **Close Window(s)** Closes the selected windows.
- **Save** Saves the contents of the selected window to a filename that you specify, in several formats and coding schemes.

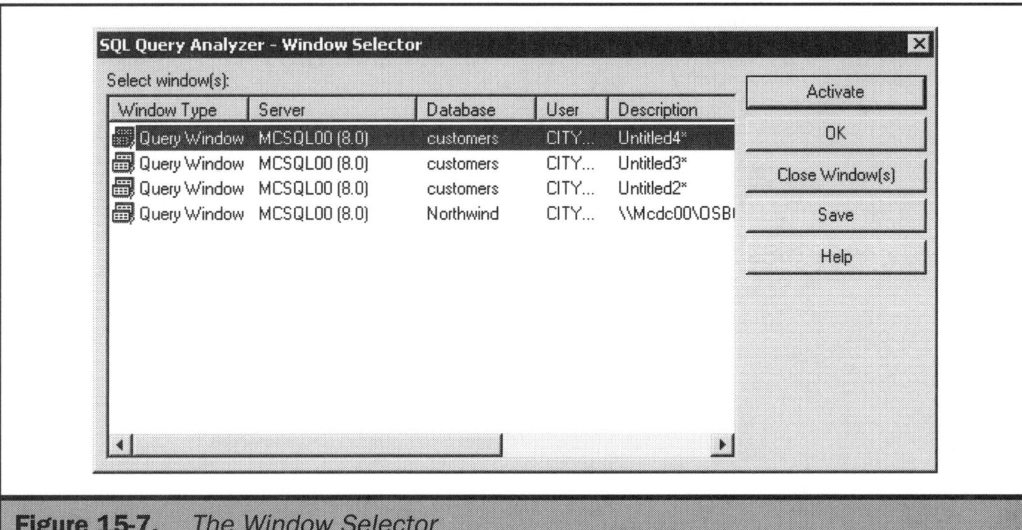

Figure 15-7. *The Window Selector*

Using Shortcuts

QA provides various shortcuts for obtaining information, customizing your development environment, and generally moving around and getting code done quickly and easily. You can quickly retrieve information about objects in the current database, and you can create custom shortcuts for any queries or stored procedures that you run frequently such as the CREATE DATABASE and the CREATE TABLE scripts we covered in Chapter 11. You can then add any frequently used commands and shortcuts to the Tools menu.

Defining Custom Shortcuts

Defining QA customizable keyboard shortcuts is easy, and you can create as many as you need. There are a few exceptions, however, some of them more limiting than others. For example, the ALT+F1 (sp_help), CTRL+1 (sp_who), and CTRL+2 (sp_lock) shortcuts are built in and cannot be modified, and your shortcut's statement cannot exceed 1,024 characters in length.

To add query shortcuts, you need to perform the following steps:

1. Go to the Tools menu and click Customize. The Customize dialog box, shown in Figure 15-8, loads.
2. Click the Custom tab.

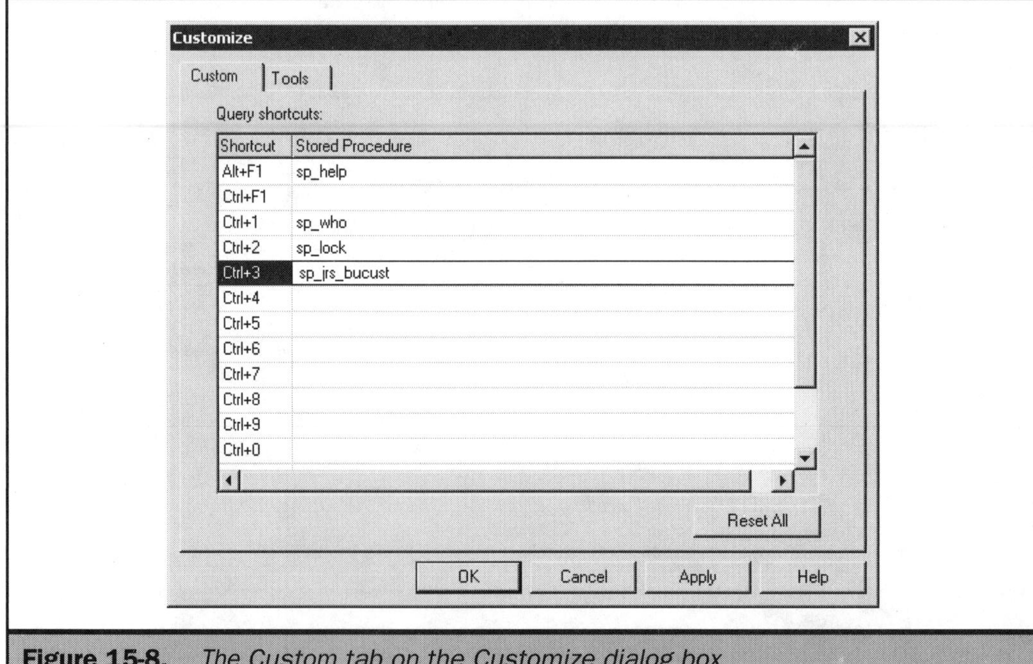

Figure 15-8. *The Custom tab on the Customize dialog box*

3. Now type the T-SQL statement to be executed in the column next to a key combination.

Customizing the Tools Menu

The Tools menu can also be customized; you can add commands to it. For example, you can add executables such as Notepad or OSQL, or provide paths to special documents and applications. I have already done a bit of work on my Tools menu, calling an interface to my SQL version control software that allows me to cut and paste scripts into QA.

To add commands to the Tools menu, do as follows:

1. Go to the Tools menu and click Customize. The Customize dialog box loads. Click the Tools tab as illustrated in Figure 15-9.
2. Click the Add button. In the Menu contents list, type the name to appear on the Tools menu. This might be the name of an executable or the name of a document to be opened. Use the up and down arrows to position the name in the menu.
3. In the Command box, enter the name and location of the file to be executed. You can use the Browse (...) button to find the directory in which it resides. You can also enter any command line parameters that might be needed, including any files that you might want to open and so on.

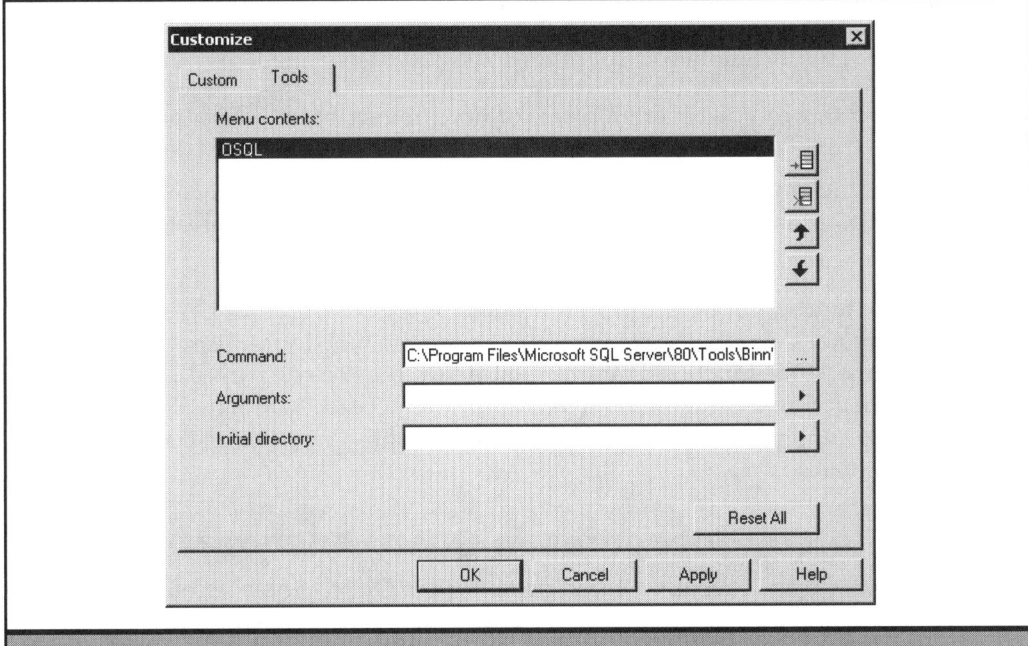

Figure 15-9. *The Tools tab on the Customize dialog box*

Using the Editor Pane

The Editor pane in Query Analyzer is a developer's text editor. You can use it to enter code, edit code, and execute SQL statements. To get code into the pane, do as follows:

- Type SQL statements directly in the Editor pane; or
- Open a saved SQL script as you open a word processing document. The contents are displayed in the Editor pane without further ado.
- You can also open a template file. The contents are also displayed in the Editor pane without further ado.
- Finally, you can use the scripting features in the Object Browser to script out the SQL statement for a selected object directly into the Editor pane.

The Editor pane works like any other text editor and development tool. You can Undo (CTRL-Z), Cut, Copy, Paste, and Select All text. You can also find and replace text, move the input cursor to a particular line, insert and remove indentation, force case, and insert and remove comment marks. Any T-SQL example code in SQL Server Books Online can be copied into the Editor pane.

Running Queries in Query Analyzer

There are several ways to run queries in Query Analyzer. You can execute SQL statements entered or loaded into the Editor pane, or you can use the various methods available for executing stored procedures.

You can execute a complete script or only selected SQL statements as follows:

- To execute a complete script, create or open the script in the Editor pane and press F5, or click the Execute Query button on the toolbar.
- To execute only selected SQL statements, highlight the lines of code in the Editor pane and press F5 or click the Execute button on the toolbar.

You can also easily execute a SELECT statement containing a built-in function. Right-click the function in Object Browser, select Script Object to New Window As, and select Execute. A SELECT statement containing the function is displayed in a new Editor pane. If the function contains arguments, they are displayed in template parameter format. Press CTRL+SHIFT+M to display the Replace Template Parameters dialog box and supply values for the function arguments. Press F5 to execute the SELECT statement.

Executing Stored Procedures in Query Analyzer

There are more ways to execute a stored procedure in Query Analyzer than there are ways to put ketchup on a hot dog. For example, as with any batch of T-SQL code, you can just select the statement to execute and press F5. QA will parse it, and if it looks like a proc and not Italian for some veal dish, then it will fly. If the statement that executes the procedure is the first in the batch, you can omit the EXECUTE (or EXEC) statement; otherwise, EXECUTE is required.

Note *I discuss executing stored procedures in Chapter 18.*

You can also right-click a stored procedure in the Object Browser or Object Search dialog box and select Open to launch the Execute Procedure dialog box. For stored procedures that take variable parameters, the dialog box lets you enter the variables in corresponding edit fields. The values are then passed to the procedure. The Execute Procedure dialog box is illustrated in Figure 15-10.

To run the proc, follow these steps:

1. Drill down to the database in which the stored procedure lives.
2. Expand the Stored Procedures folder, right-click the stored procedure, and then click Open to display the Execute Procedure dialog box.
3. Click a parameter in the Parameters list, and then type a value in the Value box. Do this for each parameter you want to use.
4. Click Execute.

The EXECUTE statement for the stored procedure is displayed in the Editor pane and the result is displayed in the Results pane.

Note *If the stored procedure is encrypted, Query Analyzer will just produce garbage, which changes every time you try to look at the stored procedure code, a feature of the encryption algorithm.*

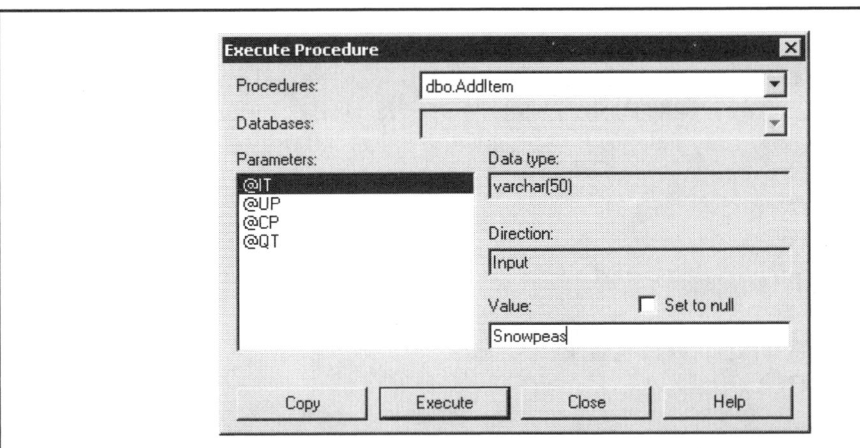

Figure 15-10. *The Execute Procedure dialog box*

Canceling a Query

Often you might want to cancel a query that is taking a long time (which might be abnormal) or that has entered an infinite loop. The best and only way out of that query short of blowing away QA is to select Cancel Executing Query in the Query menu, to click the Cancel Query button on the toolbar, or to press ALT+BREAK.

Notification of the cancellation appears in the Messages pane and in the status bar. The query might not stop for some time; I tested one with an infinite loop that I cancelled after a minute of running. But if you get notification of the cancel attempt, it means QA has received your message and you have no choice but to wait it out or kill the QA process (which is unwise). I have had to cancel a query that went up a tree on several occasions, and I used the time it took to end the query's misery to get a cuppa coffee.

Entering Data in SQL Query Analyzer

To enter data into a table directly from QA, the program provides the Open Table window, which is a graphical interface for viewing or modifying data. From either the Object Browser or the Object Search dialog box, simply right-click the table that contains the data to be updated and select Open from the context menu.

Inserting a Row

To insert a row, you need to do the following:

1. Right-click in the Open Table window and select Add from the context menu. (An empty row is inserted at the bottom of the window.)
2. Fill in the data in the columns of the new row.

Updating a Row

To update a row, you need to first locate the row to be modified and enter the changes and then select the text to be updated. If you right-click in the cell you're editing, you have access to Undo, Cut, Copy, Paste, Delete, and Select All commands on the context menu that pops up. You may have to first enable the Select All option before the update commands become available.

Deleting a Row

Right-click the row to be deleted and select Delete from the context menu.

Saving SQL Statements to a File

To save contents of the Editor pane to a file, do as follows:

1. Make the Editor pane the active pane.
2. Click Save on the toolbar.

3. If the file has never been saved, the Save Query dialog box is displayed. Specify a location, filename, file extension, and file format.

You can also save result sets to a file by making the Results pane the active pane before saving, or by selecting Results to File from the Query menu before executing the query. This is useful for simple data transformation chores. For example, I often must save the data in a table I need to drop from the database, and this choice allows me to simply dump the data to a file for later importing.

Working with Saved SQL Files

To open a SQL script and display code in the Editor pane, do as follows:

1. Open a blank Query window.
2. Click the Load SQL Script button on the toolbar.
3. In the Open Query File dialog box, specify the location and name of the file to be opened.
4. If necessary, specify a file format. If you specify Auto, the appropriate file format is used automatically.
5. You can save query definitions and other SQL scripts for reuse. The default extension for these files is *.sql.*

The Object Browser

This tool provides a graphical object tree that contains nodes representing all the objects in the DBMS you are attached to. You can navigate or traverse the tree; obtain information; and perform actions and maintenance on objects such as tables, views, and stored procedures. The Object Browser also includes templates that can be used as the starting points for creating objects such as databases, tables, views, and stored procedures.

The tree lets you generate scripts to either execute or create objects. Other enhancements include server tracing and client statistics that show information about the server-side and client-side impacts of a given query. The following section provides some useful techniques for getting the most out of the object browser.

Navigating Object Browser

You can use Object Browser to navigate the database objects of the selected database server. Object Browser is accessible through a button on the toolbar and through the Object Browser command on the Tools menu.

Tuck the Object Browser away—click the X to close it—when you are working on a statement or in the stored procedure debugger.

The Objects tab contains a tree list that displays the databases in the selected database server. For each database, Object Browser lists these folders:

- User tables
- System tables
- Views
- Stored procedures
- Extended stored procedures
- Functions

In addition to databases, the tree list displays a folder named Common Objects, which contains T-SQL built-in functions and base data types.

The Templates tab displays the templates stored in the Query Analyzer Templates directory.

Getting Database Object Information

To view information about a specific object in the current database, do the following:

1. Open a blank query window or use a current window.
2. Type in the name of the object (if you know it) and then highlight the object name in the query pane. On the Help menu, click Database Object Information.
3. The information is displayed in the Results pane.

Using Object Search

Use the object search feature to find objects in the current database server (the instance you are attached to). Object search is accessible through a button on the toolbar, and through the Object Search command on the Tools menu. To find an object, you need to do as follows:

1. Click the Object Search button. The Object Search dialog box as illustrated in Figure 15-11 loads.
2. In the Object name box, type the name of the object to be found, or use ALL to find all objects of the specified object types. For a case-sensitive search, select the Case-Sensitive check box. Case-sensitive searches are valid only if the database server is case sensitive.
3. In the Database list, click the name of a particular database or click ALL.
4. In the Hit Limit dialog box, enter the maximum number of search hits.
5. In the Object Type check boxes, select one or more types of objects to be located.

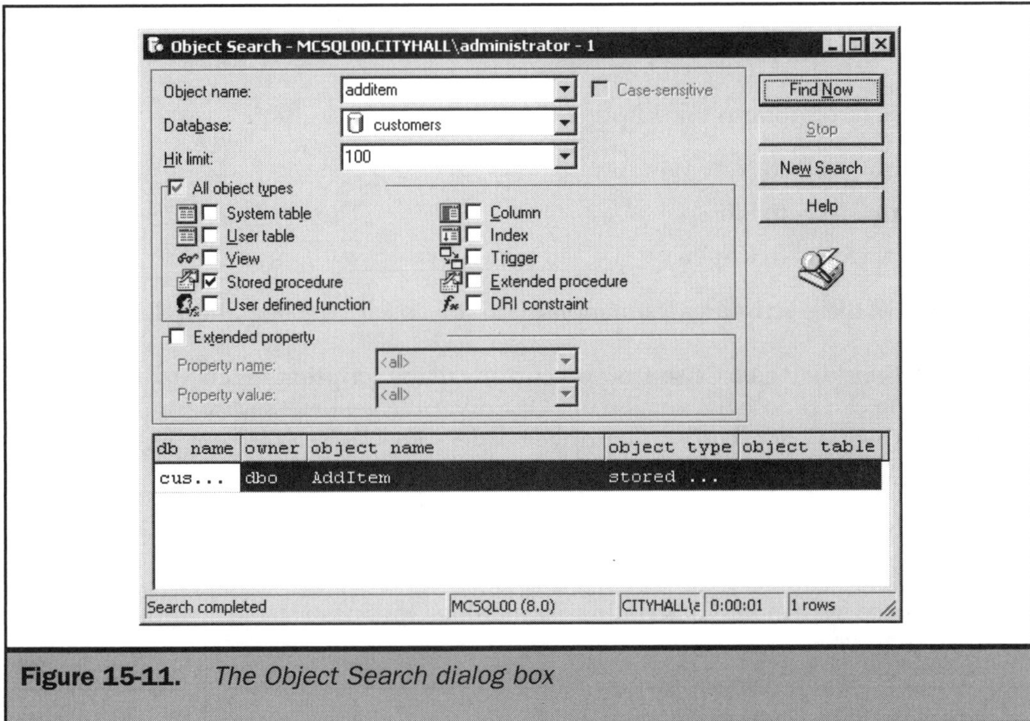

Figure 15-11. *The Object Search dialog box*

6. To locate extended properties associated with the selected object types, select Extended Property. You can search for all property names or a specific name, and you can search for all property values or a specific value.
7. Click Find Now to execute the search.
8. The results are displayed in the lower portion of the dialog box.

You can drag one or more objects in the results to the Query window. You can also right-click in the results to display the context menu, which enables you to open the selected object in the Open Table window, or perform various editing and scripting activities.

The object search feature is not available when connected to SQL Server 6.5.

Using the Scripting Feature in Object Browser

Object Browser lets you script out many of the objects in the database. The scripting support, however, varies from object type to object type. For example, using the table objects you can generate end-to-end scripts that contain SELECT statements, data definition statements (such as CREATE), or data manipulation statements (such as INSERT). View objects can only generate SELECT statements or data definition statements.

You have three options for scripting destinations:

- Script Object to New Window
- Script Object to File As
- Script Object to Clipboard

For any of these scripting destinations, you can specify the operations listed in Table 15-2.

The Options dialog box also lets you customize the scripting functionality. For example, you can choose the version of SQL Server the generated script must support, choosing to include or exclude descriptive headers, checks for object preexistence, and so on. To set your options for scripting, do as follows:

1. Go to the Tools menu again and select Options. The Options dialog box loads.
2. Select the last tab, Script, which is illustrated in Figure 15-12.
3. Choose from either of Scripting Formatting Options or Table Scripting Options.

Action	Purpose
Create	Generates a CREATE statement for the object.
Alter	Generates an ALTER statement.
Drop	Generates a DROP statement.
Select	Generates a SELECT statement containing all of the table columns in the select list.
Insert	Generates an INSERT statement and provides placeholders for the values to be inserted.
Update	Generates an UPDATE statement and provides placeholders for values and the search condition.
Delete	Generates a DELETE statement and provides a placeholder for the search condition.
Execute	Generates an EXECUTE statement for a stored procedure.

Table 15-2. *Scripting Options*

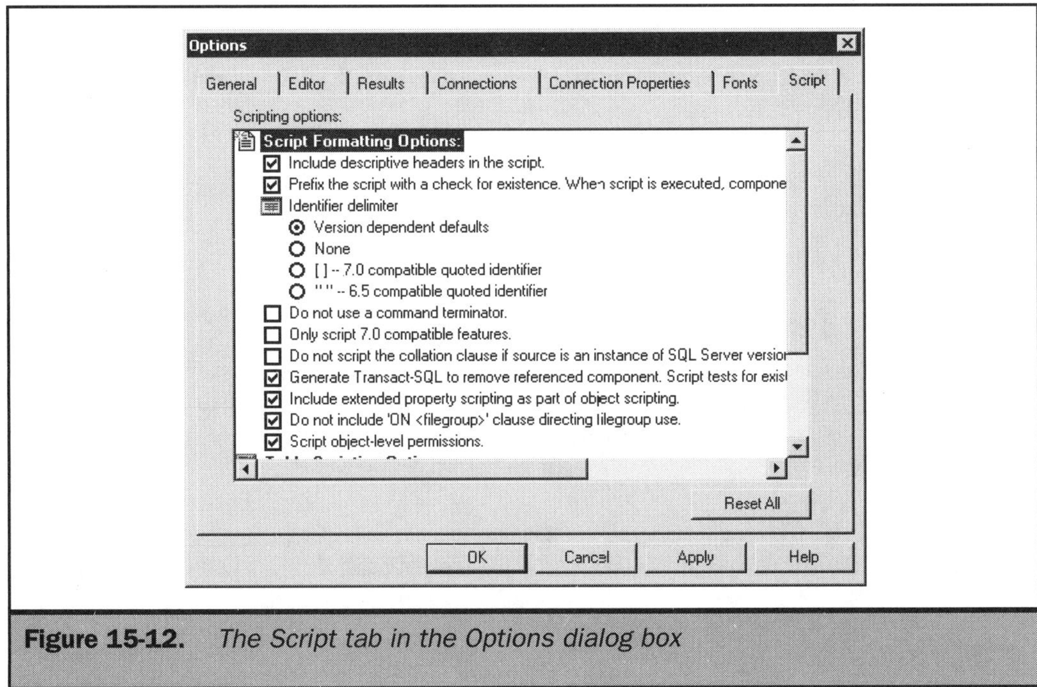

Figure 15-12. *The Script tab in the Options dialog box*

Altering Objects from the Browser

You can also use the Object Browser to alter objects in the database. To edit an object from the Object Browser, do the following:

1. Drill down to the target database that contains the objects you want to alter.
2. Right-click the object and click Edit.
3. An ALTER statement for the selected object is inserted in the Editor pane. For example, if the selected object is a stored procedure, an ALTER PROCEDURE statement is provided.
4. Use the ALTER statement to specify the changes (see Chapter 18). Execute the ALTER statement.

To Delete Objects from the Object Browser

If altering an object is not enough, you can blow it away with two clicks . . . simply right-click the object and click Delete. But don't worry about being too hasty—there is a safeguard. You are first asked to verify that you want to delete the object. If you click OK, the object is deleted.

SELECT * from Object Browser

You can use the Object Browser to interactively execute SELECT * queries. To execute a query from the Object Browser, do as follows:

1. Drill down to the target in the Object Browser.
2. Expand a folder, right-click the table, and then click Open.
3. The query results are displayed in a separate results window.

Working with Templates

The templates you see on the Object Browser's template tree, illustrated in Figure 15-13, are canned SQL or T-SQL files that contain various scripts you can use to create or alter objects in the database or perform other work. These templates are stored in the *Templates\SQL Query Analyzer* directory for easy native file access.

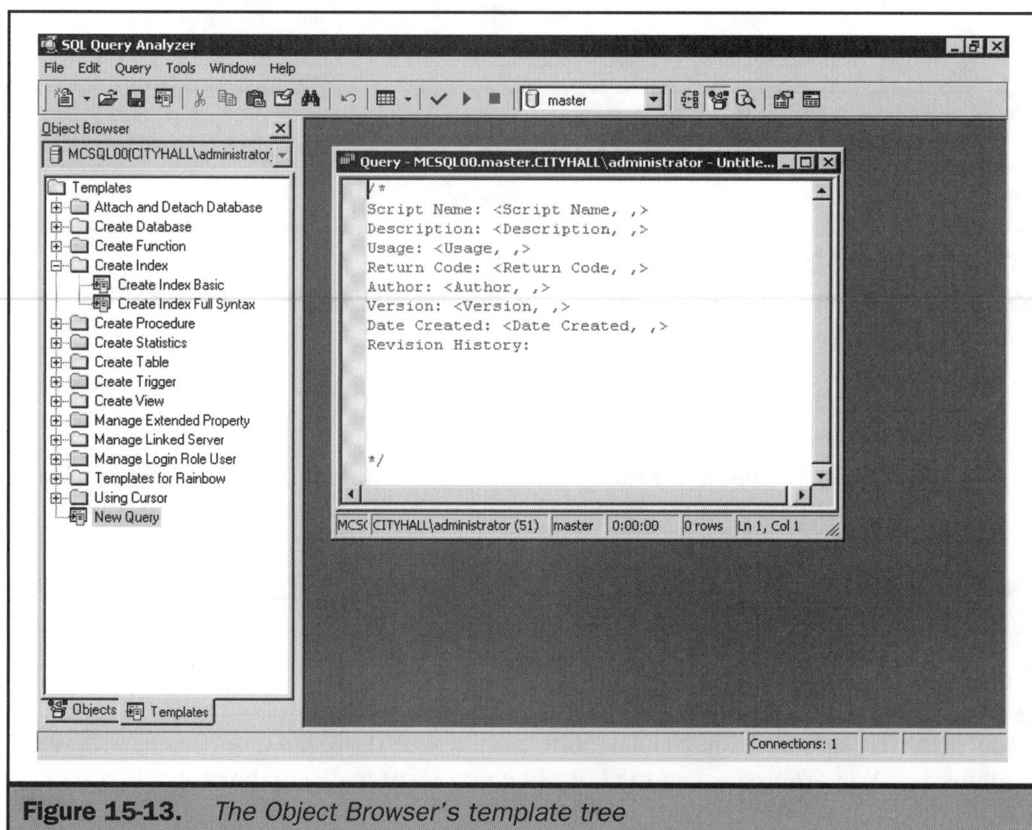

Figure 15-13. *The Object Browser's template tree*

QA provides a bunch of templates you can use to create databases, tables, views, indexes, stored procedures, triggers, statistics, and functions. The template tree also comes chock full of templates that help you to manage extended properties, linked servers, logins, roles, and users, and to declare and use cursors. There is also a template node for managing statistics.

The templates also contain various parameters that help you customize the code. The parameter definitions are saved in the template files using the following format:

```
<parameter_name, data_type, value>
```

Parameter_name is the name of the parameter in the script, *data_type* is the data type of the parameter, and *value* is the value that you use to replace every occurrence of the parameter in the script.

Using a Template

The following section describes the steps you take to use a template:

1. Go to File and select New to open a new query pane.
2. Next click the Insert Template button on the toolbar and the Insert Template dialog box appears, as shown here.

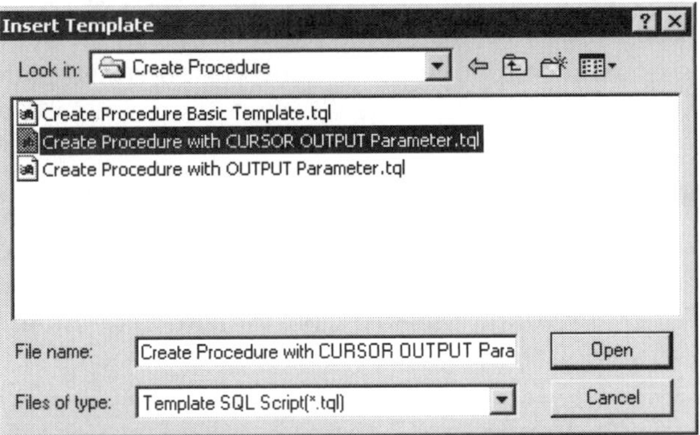

3. In the Insert Template dialog box, your standard file opener, drill down into the folders and select the template to open. All template files, by default, have the extension *.tql.* The template files are then opened into the Editor pane, as shown in Figure 15-16. (Now if you don't want to dance around the menus and dialog boxes, simply double-click a template in the Object Browser.)

4. Go to the Edit menu and select Replace Template Parameters. The Replace Template Parameters box appears, as shown here:

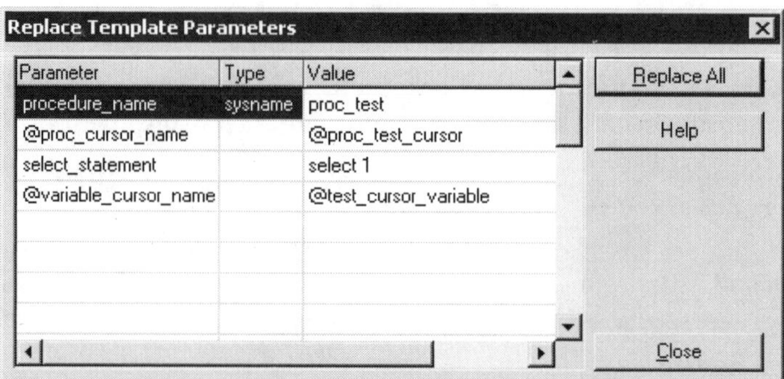

5. Use the Replace Template Parameters dialog box to specify values for the parameters. You can also do this manually; however, going through the script line by line is cumbersome, especially if the script is huge.
6. When you are done inserting all the parameters, click Replace All.
7. You can then save the new query to a new filename.

The Replace Template Parameters dialog box can be used to specify values any time a parameter definition is used in code. It parses the *<parameter_name, data_type, value>* sequence, so setting up your script or even creating your own templates that can be parsed by the Replace Template Parameters is easy, as I demonstrate in the next section.

Adding Your Own Templates

When I first started tinkering around with QA, I found an irritating quirk in the beta versions that I thought would be fixed by the time SQL Server 2000 was a *fait accompli*. If you close out all query or editor panes, the New menu item under File is disabled and no doubt the connection to the server is released. There is no way to open a new pane short of reestablishing the connection, which is silly because keeping the New button alive takes up no resources.

But I figured that you can still open a template from the Object Browser. So I decided to add my own template and infuse it with header and author template information at the same time. Each time I start a new script, I populate the header comments using the Replace Template Parameters dialog box.

If you have no query or editor windows open and you close the Object Browser, all the menu items go off and the only way to bring QA back to life is to reconnect to the server.

Adding your own template is easy: You need to create a file and save it in one of the folders under *Templates\SQL Query Analyzer.*

The T-SQL Debugger

In the past, QA seriously lacked debugger support. Now it comes equipped with a T-SQL debugger that lets you properly debug the stored procedures and monitor the execution steps against the database. The debugger also works against versions 6.5 and 7.0 servers. It has now become the tool I use to debug procs against all the versions I work with.

To use the debugger against SQL Server 6.5 or 7.0, you'll need to install the debugger binary on the server sqldbg.dll, and then register it. Check out Books Online under the topic "Troubleshooting the Transact-SQL Debugger."

The debugger is no different from your traditional developer debugger. It lets you set breakpoints, define watch expressions, and step through the procedure (step-into, step-over, and so on).

You should not use the T-SQL debugger on a production server. If you are stepping through an execution (step execution mode), the debugger can lock certain system resources that are needed by other processes.

The T-SQL Debugger window is composed of multiple, yet fused, panes, as illustrated in Figure 15-14. The Code pane displays the debugged SQL statements. In addition, the T-SQL debugger presents separate output windows for local and global variables, and for the output (result set) of the query.

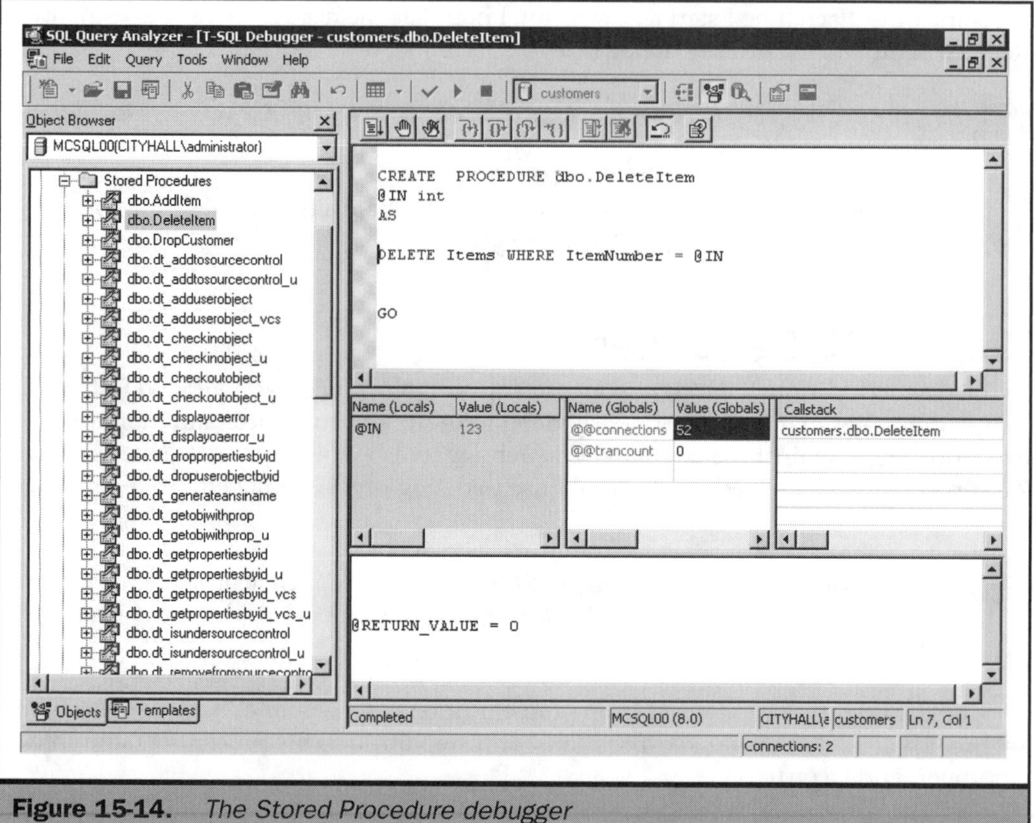

Figure 15-14. *The Stored Procedure debugger*

Navigating the T-SQL Debugger

The T-SQL Debugger window displays the text of the stored procedure to be debugged and provides the debugging options listed in Table 15-3.

Option	Function
Go	Runs the stored procedure in debugging mode.
Toggle Breakpoint	Sets or removes a breakpoint at the current line. You cannot set a breakpoint on lines not containing executable code such as comments, declaration statements, or blank lines.

Table 15-3. *Debug Options*

Option	Function
Remove All Breakpoints	Clears all breakpoints in your code.
Step Into	Executes one code statement at a time. Step Into executes the statement at the current execution point. If the statement is a call to a procedure, the next statement displayed is the first statement in the procedure.
Step Over	Executes one code statement at a time. If the current statement contains a call to a procedure, Step Over executes the procedure as a unit and then steps to the next statement in the current procedure. Therefore, the next statement displayed is the next statement in the current procedure regardless of whether or not the current statement is a call to another procedure.
Step Out	Executes the remaining lines of a function in which the current execution point lies. The next statement displayed is the statement following the procedure call. All of the code is executed between the current and final execution points.
Run to Cursor	Specifies a statement farther down in your code where you want execution to stop. Use this option to avoid stepping through large loops.
Restart	Restarts execution from the beginning of the stored procedure.
Stop Debugging	Halts debugging.
Watch	Displays the current watch expressions.
Callstack	Lists the procedure calls that have started but are not completed.
Auto Rollback	Automatically rolls back all work performed during execution of the procedure.

Table 15-3. *Debug Options* (continued)

The code pane displays the SQL statement you are debugging. Separate output panes are provided for local and global variables, for the result set of the query (and return codes), and for the call stack.

Starting the Debugger

The T-SQL debugger is run from within SQL Query Analyzer and occupies an Editor pane with the QA interface. The debugger can be started from the Object Browser or the Object Search tool.

Starting the debugger from Object Browser is the easiest method. To debug, do as follows:

1. Go to the Tools menu and click Object Browser if it is not open.
2. Click the Objects tab.
3. Drill down to the database where your stored procedure lives.
4. Expand the Stored Procedures folder in your target database.
5. Select the stored procedure to debug and right-click it.
6. Select Debug from the context menu that pops up.

Alternatively, start the debugger from Object Search as follows:

1. Go to the Tools menu and click Object Search.
2. In the Object Search window, illustrated in Figure 15-15, enter the search expression to locate the procedure you need to debug. Click the Find Now button to return matches.
3. If the search turns up your stored procedure it will be presented in the results pane of the Object Search window. Now simply right-click the name of the stored procedure you wish to debug and the same context menu just described pops up.
4. Select Debug and start debugging away.

When the T-SQL Debugger starts, the Execute Procedure dialog box loads. If you have parameters to pass to the proc, these are then stored for as long as you need them. (The dialog box has Debug Procedure as its title, but it is the same one illustrated in Figure 15-10 earlier). If you want to change the values of any parameters, you can restart the debug windows by selecting Debug from the context menu as described earlier; however, the Values (Locals) column in the first debug pane is editable. To change a value, just click in the field until the mouse pointer changes to the insert cursor.

Also, you cannot open more than one debugger window. If you try to debug a second stored procedure, you will be prompted to first cancel the currently active session. The debugger window becomes an exclusive connection to the server, so you cannot make an outside query or run some statement over to the server while the debug has the focus. If you need to make a quick call to the server, you need to toggle out of the debug window or close it.

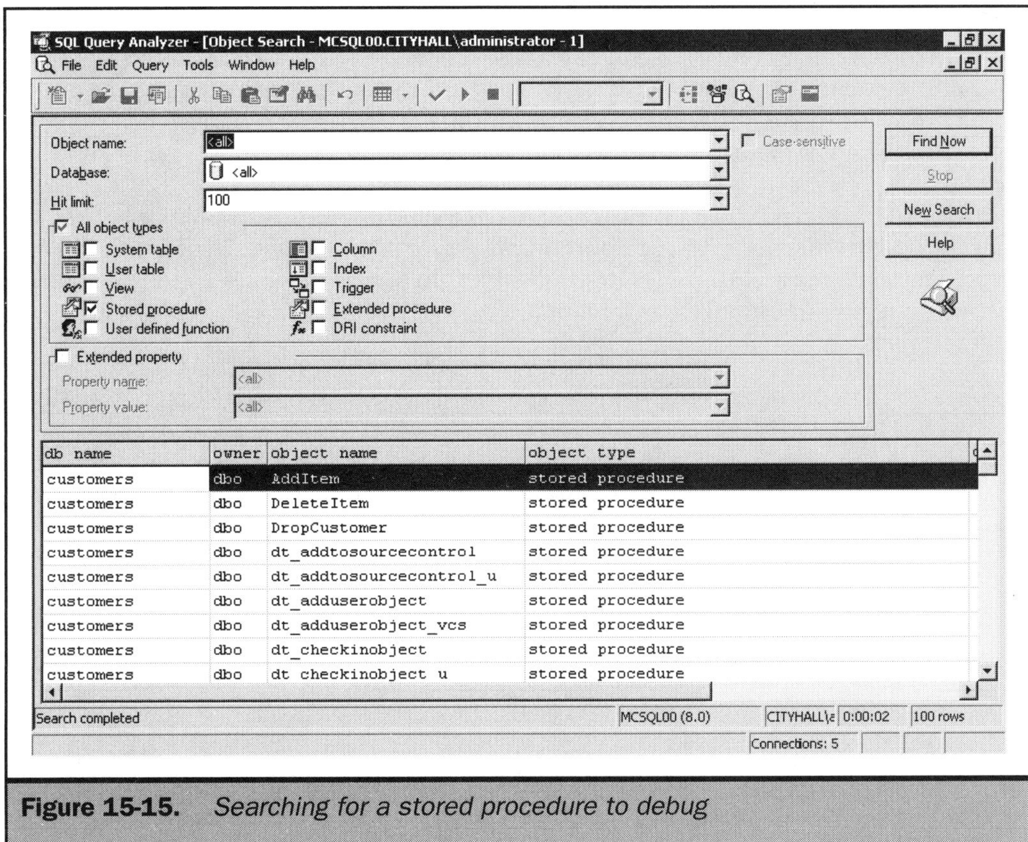

Figure 15-15. *Searching for a stored procedure to debug*

Debugging in QA is awesome compared to the grunge work we were forced to do using Visual Basic 6. The example illustrated in Figure 15-14 sets up a simple proc for testing. After you first enter the variable parameters to pass to the stored procedure, the debugger comes alive and enables the various debugging features. The debugger also shows you the return codes, which means you can force errors and test flow control around the error codes.

In Review and Looking Ahead

This chapter covers the basics of SQL Query Analyzer, encouraging you to adopt it as your primary SQL Server development tool. We examined how to navigate the application and how to configure and customize it to your preferences. I also indicated how easy it is to set up QA as the center of your T-SQL development life, much like the workbench of a carpenter, or the operating table of a surgeon.

I introduced the T-SQL stored procedure debugger, although we did not look at any stored procedure code in detail. Later, in Chapter 18—which deals with stored procedures extensively—I demonstrate using QA for some extensive trigger and stored procedure code. We will also examine how the debugger is used to test stored procedures, evaluate return codes, and step into and out of flow control segments and the like.

We also touched a little on the capability of QA to "debug" performance issues. In Chapter 21, after tacking several important programming chapters, we'll get our hands covered in SQL grease and use QA to probe the SQL Server database engine to manage statistics, query plans, indexes, and so on.

Chapter 16

Transact-SQL Primer

No pocketful of chapters makes a treatise on Transact-SQL or T-SQL, the SQLese of the SQL Server 2000 DBMS. The subject is so extensive it can easily fill a 1,000-page book, and there are several such tomes available, not to mention the venerable SQL Server Books Online. But you have to start somewhere. This chapter is both a primer to the language and an introduction to the new T-SQL features and enhancements supported by SQL Server 2000.

This chapter is a concise overview of T-SQL's building blocks. It was tackled with newcomers to SQL Server in mind, as well as battleaxes needing either a refresher or a leg up on the new elements of the language. Also, this chapter should be considered as a "briefing" or, better, an introduction to the extensive reference to T-SQL in SQL Server Books Online and the advanced features discussed in later chapters.

No matter what API or environment you use, communication between client and server is via T-SQL. Knowing and using T-SQL is independent of the type of software you are running on the clients, be they fat, thin, thick, or rich. T-SQL is also the language you use to manage the DBMS, which is discussed in later chapters.

General office applications—line-of-business applications, report generators, SQL Server Enterprise Manager, and so on—do not require a deep knowledge of T-SQL, because the code is usually embedded in the application. However, some applications need to support end-user ability to query SQL Server databases, for instance, to find all accounts 30 days past due. This usually requires a user to know some menial T-SQL query syntax, but you usually allow your end user to visually construct a SQL query, which creates a statement under-the-hood and on-the-fly so to speak.

SQL Server tools such as the SQL Server Query Analyzer and the OSQL tool require a deep knowledge of T-SQL because they accept direct T-SQL syntax for transmission to the server. The server returns results direct to these tools, usually in the form of a result set or as tabulated data displayed in a grid or text window. As you learned in the previous chapter, SQL Query Analyzer is the essential tool for building T-SQL statements.

Application developers programming access to SQL Server data need a thorough understanding of T-SQL. They need to know as much as possible about the language, which requires comprehensive study and a lot of practice (beyond the scope of this book). This chapter covers the basics, such as syntax style, operators, and data types. Later chapters cover the more complex subject matter: stored procedure programming, triggers, user-defined functions, and so on.

T-SQL knowledge is essential in Internet applications or services. Even if you are going to latch onto XML, T-SQL is essentially still the facilitator for XML, especially when it comes to returning result set data as XML documents or inserting XML data to SQL Server databases as XML documents. T-SQL statements or queries can also be transmitted to SQL Server using URLs. However, most of the discussion in the next seven chapters relates to native use of T-SQL. XML support in SQL Server is discussed in depth in Chapter 23.

T-SQL: Basic Concepts

T-SQL is a procedural language with all the gravy and relish you might be accustomed to having in a language. Architecturally speaking, it can be compared to database programming languages like Clipper and DBase because it comes with all the basic elements of a programming language, variables, flow-control structures, logic evaluation, function and procedure call capability, and so on. (Yes, even GOTO lives on here.) That's the "Transact" or "T" part of the language. However, T-SQL is neither compiled like C nor interpreted like a p-code language. Rather, it is parsed like a just-in-time script language, and its intent and logic is converted into a native "sublanguage" that stokes the SQL Server engines.

The SQL in T-SQL supports SQL-92 DDL and DML that allow a wide range of database programmers who are up to speed on SQL to obtain a broad range of database server functionality, and then some. If you have never studied T-SQL before reading this book, but you know SQL, then you are certainly not a long way from being able to create applications that access SQL Server. Many database programmers coming over from the Access, FoxPro, Delphi, PowerBuilder, and JDBC worlds, for instance, are usually very up to the max with SQL and so getting up to speed with SQL Server is very easy. And because SQL is so widely used, I have left the SQL-native facilities like SELECT, UPDATE, INSERT, and JOIN for discussion in later chapters, where it is assumed you already know to program in SQL.

T-SQL also provides access to DBMS mechanisms such as stored procedures and triggers. These are not defined by the SQL-92 standard (which is the base language for all SQL extended DBMS interfaces), although some attempt at adding stored-procedure–like facilities in SQL has been proposed in recent years. But hold your horses, we'll be getting the extended stuff like stored procedures in later chapters.

T-SQL Constants

T-SQL constants are literal or scalar values that represent a data type. The following constants are supported by the language (the data types are discussed later in this chapter, and they are also introduced in Chapter 2):

- Character strings
- Unicode strings
- Binary constants
- Bit constants
- Datetime constants
- Integer constants
- Decimal constants

- Float and real constants
- Money constants
- Unique identifier constants

Character String Constants

Character string constants are surrounded by single quotation marks and can include alphanumeric characters (a–z, A–Z, and 0–9) and the additional characters, such as exclamation point (!), at ampersand sign (@), and pound sign (#). The bounding quotation marks are the default delimiter recognized by SQL Server. Setting the QUOTED_IDENTIFIER option for a connection to OFF can, however, change this, if using single quotation marks causes problems in your development environment, where strings are usually bounded by single quote marks, as in VB, or by double quotes, as in Java.

The OLE DB and ODBC drivers automatically set the QUOTED_IDENTIFIER to ON upon connection, and often an apostrophe can trash an application because SQL Server raises hell when it sees the apostrophe and thinks it's an identifier. In this case, the "official" solution is to add an extra quote so that you send something like 'St. Elmo's Fire' to the server as "St. Elmo"'s Fire.

Asking your end users to do that, however, is a cockamamie solution to say the least because it is unacceptable for your data entry people to have to remember to type an apostrophe twice. If you have this problem, and you most likely do, you can use a function like REPLACE(), which is a VB function (and there are equivalent functions in all languages), to add the second quote mark under the "sheets." You could also use a databound ADO "text" control (which I am not fond of) to make the necessary adjustments automatically.

Also, if the QUOTED_IDENTIFIER option has been set OFF for a connection, character strings can also be enclosed in double quotation marks, but the OLE DB provider and ODBC driver automatically use SET QUOTED_IDENTIFIER ON when they connect to SQL Server. The use of single quotation marks is, however, recommended.

If a character string enclosed in single quotation marks contains an embedded quotation mark, represent the embedded single quotation mark with two single quotation marks. This is not necessary in strings embedded in double quotation marks.

Collations and code pages are also important considerations when it comes to strings. The character string constants are assigned the default collation of the current database attached to in the connection. However, you can use the COLLATE clause (discussed a little later in this chapter) to specify a different collation. The character strings you enter at the client usually conform to the code page of the computer. They are translated to the database code page, if necessary, upon transmission to the server (see also "Language and Internationalization" in Chapter 6).

Empty strings are represented as two single quotation marks with nothing in between. However, if you are working in database compatibility mode 6.*x*, an empty string is treated as a single space. The SQL Server Unicode strings support the concept of enhanced collations discussed in Chapter 5.

Unicode String Constants

The Unicode strings have a format very similar to character strings, but they are preceded by what we call the N identifier. The N stands for National Language in the SQL-92 standard. Usage requires that the N prefix be uppercase. In the following example, "Jeffrey" is the character constant, but in order to provide a Unicode constant, I would have to provide N'Jeffrey'.

Unicode constants are interpreted as Unicode data. They are not evaluated using a code page, but they do have a collation, which primarily controls comparisons and case sensitivity. When you use the Unicode constant, you are assigned the default collation of the database you are connected to. But you can change this with the COLLATE clause to specify a collation. (See "Nchar and Nvarchar" later in this chapter.) The SQL Server Unicode strings support the concept of enhanced collations discussed in Chapter 6.

Consider replacing all char, varchar and text data type with their Unicode equivalents. This will help you avoid code page conversions issues.

Binary Constants

The binary constants are identified with the suffix 0x (an empty binary string) and are strings composed of hexadecimal numbers. They are not enclosed in quotation marks.

Bit Constants

The number zero or one represents a bit constant. These do not get enclosed in quotation marks. If you use a number larger than 1, SQL Server converts it to 1.

Datetime Constants

You can use the datetime constants as character date values, in specific formats. They are enclosed in single quotation marks as follows:

```
'October 9, 1959'
'9 October, 1959'
'591009'
'10/09/59'
```

I discuss the formats for the datetime constants later in this chapter.

Integer Constants

The integer constants are represented by strings of numbers and must be whole numbers. They do not get enclosed in quotation marks like strings and cannot contain decimal points. The integer constant is illustrated as follows:

```
2001
1
```

Decimal Constants

The decimal constants are represented by strings of numbers that are not enclosed in quotation marks but that can contain a decimal point. The following examples represent decimal constants:

```
1456.987
5.1
```

Float and Real Constants

The float and real constants are represented using scientific notation (see "SQL Server Data Types" later in this chapter). They are not enclosed in single quotes as follows:

```
101.5E5
2E+100
```

Money Constants

The money constants are represented as strings of numbers. They can be whole numbers, or they can include the optional decimal point. You can also use a currency symbol as a prefix. They are not enclosed in quotation marks. Examples of money constants are as follows:

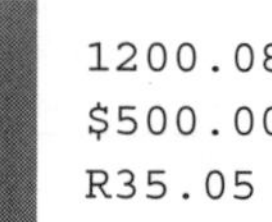

```
1200.08
$500.00
R35.05
```

Uniqueidentifier Constants

The uniqueidentifier is a string that represents the globally unique identifier (GUID), pronounced "gwid" or often as "goo ID." These constants can be specified in either character or binary string notation. The following example represents the same GUID:

```
'82B7A80F-0BD5-4343-879D-C6DDDCF4CF16'
0xFE4B4D38D5539C45852DD4FB4C687E47
```

You can use either notation, but the character string requires single quotes, as demonstrated here.

Signing Constants

To sign a numeric constant, merely apply the + or – unary operators to it. The default sign is positive if the operator is not applied. The following examples are signed:

```
+$500.00
-2001
```

T-SQL Expressions

An expression is a syntactical element or clause composed of identifiers, operators, and values that can evaluate to obtain a result. Like a sentence consisting of subject, verb, object to convey an action, the expression must be logically complete before it can compute. In other words, the elements of an expression must "add up." In the general programming environments, an expression will always evaluate to a single result. However, Transact-SQL expressions are evaluated individually for each row in the result set. In other words, a single expression may have a different value in each row of the result set, but each row has only one value for the expression.

The following T-SQL elements are expressions:

- A function, such as DB_ID() is an expression because it computes to return a value that represents a database ID.
- A constant is an expression because it alone represents a value.
- A variable is an expression for the same reason a constant is.
- A column name is an expression because it too represents or evaluates a value.
- A subquery is an expression because it computes or evaluates a result.
- Mathematical operations are expressions; for example, 1 + 1 = 2 or total * 6 / 100.
- CASE, NULLIF, and COALESCE are expressions (discussed a little later in this chapter).

The preceding list items are known as *simple expressions.* When you combine two or more simple expressions with operators, you get a *complex expression.* A good example of complex expression is your average SELECT statement. For example, SELECT * FROM CITY is a complex or compound expression because the statement can return the name of a city for each row in the table.

It is possible to combine expressions using an operator, but only if the expressions have data types that are supported by the operator. In addition, the following rules also apply:

- A data type that has a lower precedence can be implicitly converted to the data type with the higher data type precedence.
- Using the CAST function, you are able to explicitly convert the data type with the lower precedence to the data type with the higher precedence. Alternatively, you should be able to use CAST to convert the source data type to an intermediate data type, and then convert the intermediate data type to the data type with the higher precedence.

If you are unable to perform either an implicit or explicit conversion, then you cannot combine the two expressions to form a compound expression.

Expression Results

In addition to the preceding rules, the following also applies to SQL Server expressions:

- When you create a simple expression comprising a single variable, a constant, a scalar function, or a column name, the data type, the collation, the precision and scale, and the value of the expression are the data type, collation, precision, scale, and value of the referenced element.
- When you combine two expressions with comparison or logical operators, the resulting data type is Boolean and the value is one of TRUE, FALSE, or UNKNOWN. (See "Comparison Operators" in the next section).
- When you combine two expressions with arithmetic, bitwise, or string operators, the operator determines the resulting data type.
- When you create compound expressions, comprising many operators, the data type, collation, precision, and value of the resulting expression are determined by combining the component expressions, two at a time, until a final result is reached. The sequence in which the expressions are combined is defined by the precedence of the operators in the expression.

T-SQL Operators

T-SQL supports several operators that can be used to specify actions that are performed on one or more expressions. The following is a list of the operators that are supported in SQL Server 2000:

- Arithmetic operators
- Assignment operators

- Bitwise operators
- Comparison operators
- Logical operators
- String concatenation operator
- Unary operators

The Arithmetic Operators

These operators are used to perform mathematical operations on two expressions of any numeric data type. Table 16-1 lists the arithmetic operators. As indicated in the table, the + and – operators can also be used with the date data types discussed later in this chapter.

The Assignment Operator

As in most programming languages, there is a single assignment operator. In T-SQL it is the equal sign. (This is unfortunate for experts in other languages where the equal sign is used to equate one expression [comparison] with another, as it is in Java which uses the colon-equal [:=] for assignment). In the following example, a simple use of the T-SQL demonstrates assigning a numeric value to a variable:

```
DECLARE @RecordCounter INT
SET @RecordCounter = 1
```

You can also use the assignment operator to assign a string to provide a name for a column heading when you display a result set (see Chapter 17 for a demonstration of this feature). The equal sign is also a T-SQL comparison operator.

Operator	Purpose
Add (+)	Used to add two numbers. Also adds a number of days to a date.
Subtract (–)	Used to subtract two numbers. Also subtracts days from a date.
Multiply (*)	Used to multiply two numbers.
Divide (/)	Used to divide one number by another number.
Modulo (%)	Used to obtain the remainder of one number divided by another.

Table 16-1. *Arithmetic Operators*

Bitwise Operators

T-SQL provides bitwise operators that you can use within T-SQL statements to manipulate the bits between two expressions of any integer or binary string–based data types (except *image*). Also, operands cannot both be of the binary string data type. Table 16-2 lists the bitwise operators and their purposes. It also lists the Bitwise NOT (~) operator, which applies to one operand. (See also the Unary operators discussed later in this section.)

Table 16-3 lists the supported operand data types.

Comparison Operators

The comparison operators test equality between two expressions and are often used in WHERE clauses to test for a column value. They can be used on all expressions except expressions of the text, ntext, or image data types. Table 16-4 lists the comparison operators in SQL Server and their functions.

The result of a comparison expression is that the data type of the return value is a Boolean of *true, false,* or *unknown.* It is also important to take into consideration that when SET ANSI_NULLS is ON, an operator between two NULL expressions returns UNKNOWN. If you switch SET ANSI_NULLS to OFF, the equal operator will return TRUE if it is between two NULLS.

You can also use the AND keyword to combine multiple comparison expressions like the following:

```
WHEN UnitsInStock >= 5 AND UnitsInStock <= 15 THEN 'Average Mover'
```

You should also be aware that comparisons may be affected by the collations you are using.

Operator	Description	Purpose
&	Bitwise AND	Bitwise logical AND operation between two integers
|	Bitwise OR	Bitwise logical OR between two integers as translated to binary expressions
^	Bitwise Exclusive OR	Bitwise exclusive OR between two integers as translated to binary expressions

Table 16-2. *Bitwise Operators*

Left Operand	Right Operand
Binary	Int, smallint, or tinyint
Bit	Int, smallint, tinyint, or bit
Int	Int, smallint, tinyint, binary, or varbinary
Smallint	Int, smallint, tinyint, binary, or varbinary
Tinyint	Int, smallint, tinyint, binary, or varbinary
Varbinary	Int, smallint, or tinyint

Table 16-3. *Operand Data Types*

Comparison Operator	Description	Purpose
=	Equal	Used to test for equality
>	Greater	Used to test if one expression is greater than another
<	Less	Used to test if one expression is less than another
>=	Greater or equal	Used to test if one expression is greater than or equal to another
<=	Less or equal	Used to test if one expression is less than or equal to another
<>	Not equal	Used to test if one expression is *not* equal to another
!=	Not equal	Used to test if one expression is *not* equal to another (non-SQL-92)
!<	Not less	Used to test if one expression is *not* less than another (non-SQL-92)
!>	Not greater	Used to test if one expression is *not* greater than another (non-SQL-92)

Table 16-4. *Comparison Operators*

Logical Operators

The logical operators test for the truth of some expression. Like comparison operators, they also return a Boolean data type with a value of TRUE or FALSE. These operators, listed in Table 16-5, are used extensively in queries and are most common in WHERE clauses. For example, the statement

```
SELECT * FROM Customers WHERE LastName LIKE 'Shapiro%'
```

returns rows where the entire value (the operator tests the whole value) looks like "Shapiro."

String Concatenation Operator

The string concatenation operator is the addition sign (+), which is used to concatenate one substring to another to create a third derivative string. In other words, the expression 'the small bro' + 'wn fox' stores the value "the small brown fox." However, be aware that concatenation behavior can vary from database level to database level. A version 6.5 (the database versions are referenced as 65, 70, or 80) database treats an empty constant as a single blank character. For example, if you run 'the small bro' + '' + 'wn fox' on a 65 database, you'll end up with the following being stored: "the small

Operator	Purpose
ALL	TRUE if all of a set of comparisons are TRUE
AND	TRUE if both Boolean expressions are TRUE
ANY	TRUE if any one of a set of comparisons are TRUE
BETWEEN	TRUE if the operand is within a range
EXISTS	TRUE if a subquery contains any rows
IN	TRUE if the operand is equal to one of a list of expressions
LIKE	TRUE if the operand matches a pattern
NOT	Reverses the value of any other Boolean operator
OR	TRUE if either Boolean expression is TRUE
SOME	TRUE if some of a set of comparisons are TRUE

Table 16-5. *Logical Operators*

bro wn fox." (See also the string manipulation functions discussed later in this chapter and also the discussion of collation precedence).

Unary Operators

The unary operators perform an operation on only one expression of any numeric data type. Table 16-6 lists the unary operators (see the bitwise operators discussed earlier in this section).

Operator Precedence

As in all modern programming languages, T-SQL operators are governed according to rules of precedence. An operator of a higher level is evaluated before an operator of a lower level. In compound expressions, the operator precedence determines the order of operations. The order of execution or computation can significantly influence the result. The following list is in order of precedence, from highest (+) to lowest (=).

- + (Positive), – (Negative), ~ (Bitwise NOT)
- (Multiply), / (Divide), % (Modulo)
- + (Add), (+ Concatenate), – (Subtract)
- =, >, <, >=, <=, <>, !=, !>, !< (Comparison operators)
- ^ (Bitwise Exclusive OR), & (Bitwise AND), | (Bitwise OR)
- NOT
- AND
- ALL, ANY, BETWEEN, IN, LIKE, OR, SOME
- = (Assignment)

Operator	Description	Purpose
+	Positive	The numeric value is positive.
–	Negative	The numeric value is negative.
~	Bitwise NOT	Bitwise logical NOT for one integer as translated to binary expressions. Can be also be used on data types of type integer.

Table 16-6. *Unary Operators*

Operators used in an expression that have the same operator precedence level are evaluated according to their position in the expression from left to right. For example, in the expression used in the SET statement of this example, the subtraction operator is evaluated before the addition operator.

```
SET @TheNumber = 3 - 3 + 9
```

You can also use parentheses to override the defined precedence of the operators in an expression. The expression within the parenthesis is evaluated first to obtain a single value. You can then use the value outside of the parentheses.

```
5 * (3 + 2)
```

is the same as

```
5 * 5
```

In expressions that contain expressions in parentheses (nesting), the deepest expression is evaluated first.

Data Type Precedence

Often it becomes necessary to convert a constant or variable of one data type to another, and you would use the CONVERT() function described later in this chapter to do this. However, when you combine two data types with an operator, a *data type precedence rule* decides which data type gets converted to the data type of the other.

The data type precedence rule dictates that if an implicit conversion is supported (you do not require the use of the conversion function), the data type that has the lower precedence is converted to the data type with the higher precedence. Table 16-7 lists the base data types in order of precedence; the first entry in the table has the highest order, and the last entry has the lowest order. Naturally, when both data types combined by the operator are of the same precedence, no precedence ruling is required.

SQL Server Data Types

The following section explains the data types. This discussion is not in any order of preference or precedence, as discussed previously.

Data Type Order of Precedence	Type of Data
sql_variant (highest)	sql_variant
Datetime	Datetime
Smalldatetime	Datetime
Float	Approximation
Real	Approximation
Decimal	exact number
Money	exact number
Smallmoney	exact number
Bigint	exact number
Int	exact number
Smallint	exact number
Tinyint	exact number
Bit	exact number
Nvarchar	Unicode
Nchar	Unicode
Varchar	Unicode
Char	Unicode
Varbinary	Binary
Binary	Binary
Uniqueidentifier (lowest)	Uniqueidentifier

Table 16-7. *Base Data Types in Order of Preference*

Integer Types

The following list presents integers in order of precedence:

- **bigint** Integer, a whole number, data from –2^63 (–9223372036854775808) through 2^63–1 (9223372036854775807). The storage size is 8 bytes. Use bigint for large numbers that exceed the range of int. This integer costs more in terms of storage footprint. Your functions will return this data type only if the argument passed is a bigint data type. The smaller integer types are not automatically converted to bigint.
- **int** Integer, a whole number, data from –2^31 (–2,147,483,648) through 2^31 – 1 (2,147,483,647). The storage size is 4 bytes. This integer should suffice for most needs and remains the primary integer type in use on SQL Server.
- **smallint** Integer data from –2^15 (–32,768) through 2^15 – 1 (32,767). The storage size is 2 bytes.
- **tinyint** Integer data from 0–255. The storage size is 1 byte.
- **bit** This is an integer data type that takes 1, 0, or NULL. You can create columns of type bit, but they cannot be indexed. Also, if there are 8 or less bit columns in a table, the columns are stored as 1 byte by SQL Server, and if there are from 9 through 16 bit columns, they are stored as 2 bytes, and so on. This is a SQL Server conservation feature at work.

Decimal and Numeric Types

The *decimal[(p[, s])]* and *numeric[(p[, s])]* types are data types with fixed precision and scale (p = precision and s = scale). When maximum precision is used, the valid values are from –10^38 –1 through 10^38–1.

The precision (p) specifies the maximum total number of decimal digits that can be stored, both to the left and to the right of the decimal point. The precision must be a value from 1 through the maximum precision. The maximum precision is 38. The scale (s) specifies the maximum number of decimal digits that can be stored to the right of the decimal point. Scale must be a value from 0 through p. The default scale is 0; therefore, $0 <= s <= p$. The maximum storage sizes vary according to the precision.

Money and Smallmoney

The monetary data types are used for representing monetary or currency values as follows:

- **Money** Values from –2^63 (–922,337,203,685,477.5808) through 2^63 – 1 (+922,337,203,685,477.5807). This type has accuracy to one ten-thousandth of a monetary unit. The storage footprint is 8 bytes.
- **Smallmoney** Values from –214,748.3648 through +214,748.3647. This type has accuracy to one ten-thousandth of a monetary unit. The storage footprint is 4 bytes.

Precision	Storage Footprint in Bytes
1–9	5
10–19	9
20–28	13
29–38	17

Table 16-8. *Decimal and Numeric Types*

float and real

These data types are the approximate number data types you use with floating-point numeric data. Floating-point data is approximate and not all values in the data type range can be precisely represented.

The *float [(n)]:* This is for floating-point number data from –1.79E + 308 through 1.79E + 308. The *n* parameter is the number of bits used to store the mantissa of the *float* number in scientific notation. This dictates the precision and storage size. The *n* parameter must be a value from 1–53. The float[(*n*)] data type conforms to the SQL-92 standard for all values of *n* from 1–53. Table 16-9 represents values for *n* and the corresponding precision and memory costs.

The *real* is a floating-point number data type that ranges from –3.40E + 38 through 3.40E + 38. The footprint of *real* is 4 bytes.

datetime and smalldatetime

The date and time data types represent dates and times from January 1, 1753, through December 31, 9999, to an accuracy of one three-hundredth of a second (equivalent to 3.33 milliseconds or 0.00333 seconds). These values are rounded to increments of .000, .003, or .007 seconds. The footprint for *datetime* is two 4-byte integers. The first four bytes store the number of days before or after the *base date,* January 1, 1900. The base

Value for *n*	Precision	Footprint in Bytes
1–24	7 digits	4 bytes
25–53	15 digits	8 bytes

Table 16-9. *Float and Real*

date is the system reference date (values for *datetime* earlier than January 1, 1753, are not permitted). The remaining four bytes store the time of day represented as the number of milliseconds after midnight.

The *smalldatetime* type from January 1, 1900, through June 6, 2079, has accuracy to the minute. With *smalldatetime,* values with 29.998 seconds or lower are rounded down to the nearest minute. Values with 29.999 seconds or higher are rounded up to the nearest minute.

The *smalldatetime* data type stores dates and times of day with less precision than *datetime.* SQL Server stores *smalldatetime* values as two 2-byte integers, as opposed to two 4-byte values in *datetime.* The first 2 bytes store the number of days after January 1, 1900. The remaining 2 bytes store the number of minutes since midnight. Dates range from January 1, 1900, through June 6, 2079, and are accurate to the minute.

char and varchar

These are fixed-length (char) or variable-length (varchar) character data types.

- **char[(*n*)]** Fixed-length non-Unicode character data with a length of *n* bytes, where *n* must be a value from 1 through 8,000. Storage size is *n* bytes. The SQL-92 synonym for "char" is "character."
- **varchar[(*n*)]** Variable-length non-Unicode character data with a length of *n* bytes, where *n* must be a value from 1 through 8,000. Storage size is the actual length in bytes of the data entered, not *n* bytes. The data entered can be 0 characters in length. The SQL-92 synonyms for varchar are char varying or character varying.

When *n* is not specified in a data definition or variable declaration statement, the default length is 1. When *n* is not specified with the CAST function, the default length is 30. Objects using char or varchar are assigned the default collation of the database, unless a specific collation is assigned using the COLLATE clause. The collation controls the code page used to store the character data.

Sites supporting multiple languages should consider using the Unicode nchar or nvarchar data types to minimize character conversion issues. If you use char or varchar

- Use char when the data values in a column are expected to be consistently close to the same size.
- Use varchar when the data values in a column are expected to vary considerably in size.

Variable Usage Variables of these types are used to store non-Unicode characters. The first data type is a fixed char variable that is padded with spaces to the length specified in *n.* The second data type stores data of variable length and is not padded. You can use either variable for storing strings that do not exceed 8,000 characters. These structures will also truncate the strings if they exceed the number of characters declared in *n.*

If you use SET ANSI_PADDING OFF in the CREATE TABLE or ALTER TABLE statement, then a char column defined as NULL will be handled as a varchar. If the collation code page uses double-byte characters, the storage size will still be *n* bytes. Depending on the character string, the actual or final storage size of *n* bytes can still be less than *n* characters.

Nchar and Nvarchar

Nchar and Nvarchar represent Unicode character data types that are either fixed-length (nchar) or variable-length (nvarchar). They make use of the UNICODE UCS-2 character set.

- **Nchar(*N*)** This is a fixed-length unicode character data type comprising *n* characters. The characters in *n* must be a value from 1–4,000. The storage size of the string is two times *n* bytes. Sql-92 has synonyms for these types; nchar is national char or national character. Best practice suggests using nchar when the data entries in a column are expected to be constantly in the same size range.
- **nvarchar(*n*)** This is a variable-length Unicode character data type comprising *n* characters. The string represented by *n* must be a value from 1–4,000. The storage size of the string, in bytes, is two times the number of characters entered, and you are not required to actually enter characters. The SQL-92 synonyms for nvarchar are national char varying and national character varying. Best practice suggests using the nvarchar type when the sizes of the data entries in a column are expected to vary considerably.

If you do not specify *n* in a data definition or a variable declaration statement, then the length defaults to 1. It defaults to 30 when you use *n* but do not use the CAST function. When you use nchar or nvarchar without specifying a collation in the COLLATE clause, the default database collation is used. Also the SET ANSI_PADDING OFF has no effect on these data types; SET ANSI_PADDING is always ON.

Binary and Varbinary

These are binary data types that can be either fixed-length, which is a binary value, or variable-length, which is represented by the varbinary data type.

- **binary [(*n*)]** A fixed-length binary data type of *n* bytes. The value for *n* must be from 1 through 8,000. The storage size is *n* + 4 bytes. You would use binary when column data size remains constant.
- **varbinary [(*n*)]** This is the variable-length binary data type consisting of *n* bytes. The value for *n* must be a value from 1 through 8,000; however, the storage size is the actual length of the data entered + 4 bytes, not the value for *n* bytes. The varbinary type can cater to a 0-byte length. The SQL-92 synonym for varbinary is binary varying; you use this data type to hold values that vary in size.

If you do not specify n in a data definition or variable declaration statement, the default length is 1. When n is not specified with the CAST function, however, the default length of the data type is 30.

Cursor

The *cursor* is a data type for variables or stored procedure OUTPUT parameters that contain a reference to a cursor. Any variables created with the cursor data type are nullable. You should also take note that the cursor data type cannot be used for a column in a CREATE TABLE statement.

The operations that can reference variables and parameters having a cursor data type are

- DECLARE @*local_variable* and SET @*local_variable*
- OPEN, FETCH, CLOSE, and DEALLOCATE
- Stored procedure output parameters
- The CURSOR_STATUS() function
- The sp_cursor_list, sp_describe_cursor, sp_describe_cursor_tables, and sp_describe_cursor_columns system stored procedures

sql_variant

The sql_variant is a new SQL Server data type that stores the values of all standard SQL Server data types, except the data types containing large objects (LOBs) such as text, ntext, and image; and the data types timestamp and sql_variant (itself). This type may be used in columns, parameters, and variables, as well as in return values of user-defined functions. The following rules apply to this data type:

- A column of type sql_variant may contain the values of several different data types. For example, a column defined as sql_variant can hold int, binary, and char values.
- A sql_variant data type must first be cast to its base data type value before participating in operations such as addition and subtraction. You may also assign it a default value. This data may also hold NULL as its underlying value. NULL values, however, will not have an associated base type, but that will change when you replace the NULL with data.
- You can use the sql_variant in columns that have been defined as UNIQUE, primary, or foreign keys. However, the total length of the data values composing the key of a given row should not be greater than the maximum length of an index, which is currently 900 bytes.
- Your table can have as many sql_variant columns as it needs.
- You cannot use it in the CONTAINSTABLE and FREETEXTTABLE statements.

- ODBC does not support sql_variant because it has no facility to cater to the notion of a variant data type. You should check out the specifics of the limitations in the SQL Server documentation. For example, queries of sql_variant columns are returned as binary data when using the Microsoft OLE DB Provider for ODBC (MSDASQL).
- Precedence of sql_variant values goes according to the rules of precedence for the base data types they represent. For example, when you compare two values of sql_variant and the base data types are in different data type families (say int and bigint), the value whose data type family is higher in the precedence hierarchy is considered the higher of the two values.
- The precedence rule discussed previously applies to conversion as well. In other words, when sql_variant values of different base data types are compared, the value of the base data type that is lower in the hierarchy chart is implicitly converted to the other data type before comparison is made.

Table

The table data type (introduced in SQL Server 2000) can be used to store a result set for later processing. Its primary use is for temporary storage of a set of. Use DECLARE *@local_variable* to declare variables of type table. The syntax for the table type is as follows:


```
TABLE ({ column_definition | table_constraint} [ ,...n ] )
column_definition:
column_name scalar_data_type
[ COLLATE collation_definition ]
[ [ DEFAULT constant_expression ] | IDENTITY [ ( seed , increment ) ] ]
[ ROWGUIDCOL ]
[ column_constraint ] [ ...n ]
    { [ NULL | NOT NULL ]
    | [ PRIMARY KEY | UNIQUE ]
    | CHECK ( logical_expression )
    }
table_constraint:
{ { PRIMARY KEY | UNIQUE } ( column_name [ ,...n ] )
| CHECK ( search_condition )
}
```

The parameters being passed to create a variable of type table make up the same subset of information used to create a persistent table object in CREATE TABLE. The table declaration includes column definitions, names, data types, and constraints. Note that the only constraint types allowed are PRIMARY KEY, UNIQUE KEY, and NULL.

Functions and variables can be declared to be of type table, and the variables can be used in functions, stored procedures, and batches. A table variable also behaves like a local variable. It has a well-defined scope, which is the function, stored procedure, or batch in which it is declared.

Within its scope, a table variable may be used like a regular table. It may be applied anywhere a table or table-expression is used in SELECT, INSERT, UPDATE, and DELETE statements.

Collations also need to be taken into consideration when creating this variable. See Chapters 6 and 11. The type is also not suitable for use with INSERT INTO and SELECT INTO, and you cannot assign one table variable to another. Bear in mind that because the table type is not a persistent table in the database per se, it is unaffected by any transaction rollbacks. (Use of the table data type data is demonstrated in Chapter 20 with the INSERT statement.)

Timestamp

This data type exposes automatically generated binary numbers that are guaranteed to be unique within a database. Timestamp is used typically as a mechanism for version-stamping table rows. The storage footprint is eight bytes.

The Transact-SQL timestamp data type is not the same as the timestamp data type defined in the SQL-92 standard. The SQL-92 timestamp data type is equivalent to the Transact-SQL datetime data type.

SQL Server 2000 introduces a rowversion synonym for the timestamp data type. Use rowversion instead of timestamp wherever possible in DDL statements. This practice will ease the migration to a future release of SQL Server in which rowversion is expected to be introduced as a new data type.

In a CREATE TABLE or ALTER TABLE statement, you do not have to supply a column name for the timestamp data type. For example, the statement

```
CREATE TABLE MyTable (PriKey int PRIMARY KEY, timestamp)
```

is devoid of a column name, so SQL Server will generate a column name of timestamp. The rowversion data type synonym does not follow this behavior. You must supply a column name when you use the rowversion synonym.

Naturally a table can have only one timestamp column. The value in the timestamp column is updated every time a row containing a timestamp column is inserted or updated. This property makes a timestamp column a poor candidate for keys, especially primary keys. Any update made to the row changes the timestamp value, thereby changing the key value. If the column is in a primary key, the old key value is no longer valid, and foreign keys referencing the old value are no longer valid. If the table is referenced in a dynamic cursor, all updates change the positions of the rows in the cursor. If the column is in an index key, all updates to the data row also generate updates of the index.

A nonnullable timestamp column is semantically equivalent to a binary(8) column. A nullable timestamp column is semantically equivalent to a varbinary(8) column.

Uniqueidentifier

This data type represents the globally unique identifier (GUID). A column or local variable of uniqueidentifier data type can be initialized to a value in two ways:

- Using the NEWID function.
- Converting from a string constant in the following form (*xxxxxxxx-xxxx-xxxx-xxxx-xxxxxxxxxxxx*, in which each *x* is a hexadecimal digit in the range 0–9 or a–f). For example, 6F9619FF-8B86-D011-B42D-00C04FC964FF is a valid uniqueidentifier value.

The comparison operators can be used with uniqueidentifier values. However, ordering is not implemented by comparing the bit patterns of the two values. The only operations that are allowed against a uniqueidentifier value are comparisons (=, <>, <, >, <=, >=) and checking for NULL (IS NULL and IS NOT NULL). No other arithmetic operators are allowed. All column constraints and properties except IDENTITY are allowed on the uniqueidentifier data type.

Collation Precedence

The character string data types, char, varchar, text, nchar, and nvarchar, are also governed by collation precedence rules. These rules determine the following:

- The collation of the final result, the returned character string expression.
- The collation used by collation-sensitive operators that use character string arguments that do not return character strings. Operators such as LIKE and IN are examples.

Data Type Synonyms

SQL Server 2000 provides data type synonym support for SQL-92 compatibility. Table 16-10 lists the SQL-92 types and the SQL Server 2000 synonyms.

These data type synonyms can be used in place of the corresponding base data type names in data definition language (DDL) statements, such as CREATE TABLE, CREATE PROCEDURE, or DECLARE @variable. The synonym has no use after the object is created because SQL Server references the base data type and has no notion of the high-level label.

This behavior also applies to metadata operations, such as sp_help and other system stored procedures, the information schema views, or the various data access API metadata operations that report the data types of table or result set columns.

SQL-92	SQL Server 2000
Binary varying	Varbinary
char varying	Varchar
Character	Char
Character	char(1)
Character(*n*)	char(*n*)
Character varying(*n*)	varchar(*n*)
Dec	Decimal
Double precision	Float
float[(*n*)] for *n* = 1–7	Real
float[(*n*)] for *n* = 8–15	Float
Integer	Int
National character(*n*)	nchar(*n*)
National char(*n*)	nchar(*n*)
National character varying(*n*)	nvarchar(*n*)
National char varying(*n*)	nvarchar(*n*)
National text	Ntext
Rowversion	Timestamp

Table 16-10. *Data Type Synonyms*

The data type synonyms are expressed only in T-SQL statements. There is no support for them in the graphical administration utilities, such as SQL Server Enterprise Manager. The following code demonstrates the creation of a table specifying national character varying:

```
CREATE TABLE CustDetails (PKey int PRIMARY KEY, A_Varcharcolumn
national character varying(10))
```

The column A_Varcharcolumn is actually assigned an nvarchar(10) data type. It is referenced in the catalog as an nvarchar(10) column, not according to the synonym supplied on creation of the object. In other words, metadata does not represent it as a national character varying(10) column.

T-SQL Variables

One of the first big surprises to befall an experienced Visual Basic programmer is that T-SQL variables must be explicitly declared in a T-SQL module before they can be used. This is a requirement of T-SQL that makes it similar to Delphi (actually Pascal) and Java when dealing with private or local variables that are not exposed to the other modules.

T-SQL variables are declared using the DECLARE statement. T-SQL identifies the actual variable with the ampersand (@) character as follows:

```
DECLARE @VariableName VariableType
```

Note in this syntax that you cannot declare and use the variable without declaring the variable data type. For example:

```
DECLARE @aString char(10)
DECLARE @bString varchar(20)
```

This code declares two variables, the first a char string 10 characters long and the second a varchar 20 characters long. In Chapter 2, I listed the built-in data types. See the earlier section on data types.

T-SQL Functions

Past versions of SQL Server included numerous constructions and elements that were provided to obtain certain programming results and values, process the various data types, and implement various operations and conditions in the DBMS. These were persistent and were created to obviate the need to repeatedly recode such constructions. These elements, and many new ones, have now been brought together in a unified function collection in SQL Server 2000.

Note *Several Administration functions are included in the SQL Server function arsenal; see Chapter 12.*

Although they are built into SQL Server, they can be referenced from the outside—in T-SQL statements passed through the APIs and using profilers and query tools, like SQL Server Query Analyzer and the OSQL utility. Functions in SQL Server 2000 also replace the so-called "global variables" that were preceded by the double ampersand (like @@CONNECTION).

SQL Server functions are true to the definition of "function" in that they can take a number of input values and return scalar values or result sets to the calling process. They can also take a blank value to return a specific predefined or predetermined value. For example, used with the SELECT statement, the function DB_NAME() returns a value that represents the current database you are connected to. And the function GETDATE() returns the current date and time. And NEWID() takes "nothing" as an argument and returns a system generated GUID.

SQL Server 2000 also lets you create your own user-defined functions. But before we get to the user-defined functions, let's first investigate the myriad built-in functions, many of which you will want to start using the moment you put this book down.

Determinism of Functions

SQL Server functions can be *deterministic* or *nondeterministic.* This means that either they always return the same result any time they are called with a specific set of input values, which means the function is deterministic, or they return different results each time they are called with a specific set of input values, which means they are nondeterministic. This is known as the *determinism* of the function.

For example, a function like DATEADD is deterministic because it always returns the same result for any given set of argument values for the parameters passed to it. GETDATE, on the other hand, is not deterministic. It is always invoked with the same argument, but the return value, the current date and time, changes with each call of the function.

Function determinism in SQL Server 2000 is a new concept, and thus nondeterministic functions are constrained by the following usage rules:

- You cannot create an index on a computed column if the *computed_column_expression* references any nondeterministic functions.
- You cannot create a clustered index on a view if the view also references nondeterministic functions.

Built-in Function Determinism

SQL Server's built-in functions are either deterministic or nondeterministic according to how the function is implemented. You have no access to change the determinism. The aggregate and string built-in functions are deterministic; however, charindex and patindex are not, as are all of the configuration, cursor, metadata, security, and system statistical functions. See BOL for a list of functions that are always deterministic.

String Manipulation Functions

T-SQL provides a rich collection of string manipulation and sting management functions. Many of these functions have equivalent functionality in generic programming languages such as VB, C++, and Delphi.

ASCII(*character*)

The ASCII(*character*) function returns the ASCII code value of type int of the leftmost character of the character expression evaluated. For example, the expression

```
SELECT ASCII('d')
```

returns "100." The expression can be of type char or varchar.

CHAR(*integer*)

The CHAR(*integer*) function is used to return the ASCII character of its integer code assignment. For example, the expression

```
SELECT CHAR(100)
```

returns "d," which is the converse of the ASCII() function. Remember, the ASCII codes run from 0 to 255 and thus a null value is returned if you are outside this range. You will obviously not be able to return a code for noninteger values. For example, CHAR(13) is the carriage return code and has no displayable value. On the other hand, you can use the CHAR() function to insert control characters into character strings. For example, the expression

```
SELECT CHAR(100)+CHAR(9)+CHAR(68)
```

returns the values d and D separated by a tab. The most common control characters used are Tab (CHAR(9)), line feed (CHAR(10)), and carriage return (CHAR(13)).

CHARINDEX(*expression1*, *expression2*, *startlocation*)

This function can be used to determine the starting position of the specified phrase in the character string. It is useful for searching textual data. The syntax for this function is CHARINDEX(*expression1*, *expression2*, *startlocation*). The arguments taken are as follows:

- **expression1** Represents the expression that contains the sequence of characters to be found.
- **expression2** Represents the actual string of characters to be evaluated.

- **startlocation** Represents the starting position in ex2 from which to begin searching for ex1. If the start location is a negative number or zero, then the search begins at the beginning of ex2. In my testing of this function, omitting the start location after a comma delimiter causes an error. If you exclude the delimiter, the function computes.

For example, the expression

```
SELECT CHARINDEX('small', 'the very small brown fox', 0)
```

returns the value 10. Using this function, you can easily search for the starting point of a string in a particular record in your table. For example, the expression

```
USE NORTHWIND
SELECT CHARINDEX('Connection', CompanyName)
  FROM Customers WHERE CustomerID = 'EASTC'
```

returns the value 9. This type of expression is valuable when you need to get into a value and extract a subexpression. For example, in my record numbers for call centers systems I tag an agent ID onto an order number and save the entire record as a record number. If a manager needs to check which agent worked the record, the system can extract the agent ID by first locating the starting point in the record where the agent ID begins and then run the getchar() function on the rest of the record. This saves having to create another table or column that references the record number entity with the agent ID entity.

It should be noted that if either expression1 or expression2 is of a Unicode data type, the nvarchar and nchar types respectively, and the other is not, the other is converted to Unicode. In other words, if ex1 is Unicode and ex2 is not, then ex2 is converted to Unicode.

Also, if either expression1 or expression2 is NULL, the CHARINDEX() function returns NULL if the database compatibility level you have set is 70. If the database compatibility level is 65 or earlier, the CHARINDEX() function returns NULL only when both expression1 and expression2 are NULL.

DATALENGTH(*variable expression*)

This "function" is documented as a data type in Books Online, but it deserves a place in a list of string manipulation functions. It is similar to LEN() referenced later in this section but returns the declared length of a variable or field. For example, the expression

```
USE NORTHWIND
 SELECT DATALENGTH(Phone)
 FROM CUSTOMERS WHERE CustomerID = 'EASTC'
```

returns the integer value of "28," while LEN() returns "14," the actual length of the string in the variable or field (see also DATALENGTH()).

DIFFERENCE(*expression1, expression2*)

This function is used to determine the difference between the SOUNDEX algorithm values of two char or varchar strings represented in expression1 and expression2 (see SOUNDEX() later in this section). The return value is an integer on a scale of 0 to 4. The lowest value of "0" indicates the highest difference between the two strings. The highest value of "4" indicates that the two strings "sound" very similar. For example, the expression

```
PRINT DIFFERENCE ('foo', 'bar')
```

returns a value of "2" indicating the two strings do not sound the same but are similar in construction. Upon changing "bar" to "boo," the difference value increases to 3.

LEFT(*string, startindex*)

This function returns a character string that starts at a specified number of characters from the left of the varchar variable. In can be used in conjunction with the CHARINDEX() function to return the value of a string at the specified index. For example, the expression

```
USE NORTHWIND
SELECT LEFT(CompanyName, 5)
 FROM CUSTOMERS WHERE CustomerID = 'EASTC'
```

returns the varchar value "Easte." If you need to simply evaluate the string, just substitute the column name used in "expression" for a string; for example, LEFT('codered,' 4) returns "code."

The expression can be of character or binary data, a constant, a variable, or a column. It must also be of a data type that can be implicitly convertible to varchar. Use the CAST function to explicitly convert the string to varchar before you evaluate it.

LEN(*string*)

This function returns the number of characters, not the number of bytes, of the given string expression, excluding trailing blanks. For example, the expression

```
USE NORTHWIND
 SELECT LEN(Phone)
 FROM CUSTOMERS WHERE CustomerID = 'EASTC'
```

returns the integer value of "14," which will help us clean up the telephone number column in the Customer table of the Northwind database (see also DATALENGTH()).

LOWER(*string*)

This function converts all uppercase characters of character or binary data in the expression argument to lowercase and then returns the new expression. For example, the expression

```
USE NORTHWIND
SELECT LOWER(CompanyName)
 FROM CUSTOMERS WHERE CustomerID = 'EASTC'
```

returns the value "eastern connection." The string in *expression* can be a constant, a variable, or a column as shown in the example. The expression string must also be of a type that can be implicitly converted to varchar. Use CAST to explicitly convert the character. See also UPPER() later in this section.

LTRIM(*string*)

This function returns a character expression after first removing leading blanks. For example, the expression

```
PRINT('                              my bunny lies over the hillside')
```

returns the value "   my bunny lies over the hillside", with spaces, but the expression

```
PRINT LTRIM('                              so bring back my bunny to me')
```

returns the value "so bring back my bunny to me," sans the spaces. The expression must be an expression of character or binary data. It can be a constant, a variable, or a column, but it must of a data type that is implicitly convertible to varchar. Otherwise, use CAST to convert the expression to varchar.

NCHAR(*integer*)

This function returns the Unicode character with the given integer code, as defined by the Unicode standard. For example, the statement

```
PRINT NCHAR(167)
```

returns the character "§". The value must be a positive number in the range 0–65535. If you specify a value outside this range, NULL is returned.

QUOTENAME(*string, quote character*)

This function returns a Unicode string with the delimiters surrounding the string. For example, the statement

```
SELECT QUOTENAME('PHONES','"')
```

returns the value "PHONES." And the statement

```
PRINT QUOTENAME('PHONES','[')
```

returns the value [PHONES]. The ', ", [,], {, and } are valid quote characters.

REPLACE('*expression1*', '*expression2*', '*expression3*')

This function finds all occurrences of the second string in the first string and then replaces it with the string in the third expression. For example, the statement

```
PRINT REPLACE('fog', 'g', 'o')
```

results in "fog" being changed to "foo."

This function can be used with both character and binary data.

REPLICATE(*character, integer*)

This function repeats a character expression for a specified number of times. It is useful for padding if you replicate a space instead of a character. For example, the statement

```
PRINT REPLICATE('0', 2)
```

returns the value '00'. The int expression must be a positive whole number. If it is negative, a null string is returned.

REVERSE(*string*)

This function returns the reverse of a character expression. For example, the statement

```
SELECT REVERSE('evol')
```

returns the value "love".

RIGHT(*string, integer*)

This function returns the part of a character string starting a specified number of characters from the right. For example, the statement

```
SELECT RIGHT('evol', 1 )
```

returns the value "love".

RTRIM(*string expression*)

This function is the converse of LTRIM. It snips all trailing blanks from the expression passed in the argument placeholder. For example, the statement

```
SELECT RTRIM('LOVE                                    ')
```

returns the value 'LOVE'.

SOUNDEX(*string expression*)

This function returns the four-character code of the SOUNDEX algorithm that is used evaluate the similarity of two strings (see the DIFFERENCE() function discussed earlier). For example, the statement

```
SELECT SOUNDEX('WASH')
```

returns the value "W200".

The SOUNDEX() function converts an alpha string to a four-character code to find similar-sounding words or names. You can then use this value and compare it to another SOUNDEX() using the DIFFERENCE() function. The first character of the SOUNDEX code is the first character of the argument, and the second through fourth characters of the code are numbers. Vowels in the argument are ignored unless they are the first letter of the string. String functions can be nested.

SPACE(*value*)

This function returns a string of repeated spaces *x* number of times as indicated by the integer passed in the argument. For example, the statement

```
SELECT 'Y' + SPACE(1)+ '=' + SPACE(1) + '1'
```

returns the expression "Y = 1". If you are adding spaces to Unicode data, use the REPLICATE() function instead of SPACE().

STR(*float expression, length, decimal*)

This function returns character data converted from numeric data. For example, the statement

```
SELECT STR(42393.78, 8, 1)
```

returns the value "42393.8". The float expression must be an expression of an approximate numeric (float) data type with a decimal point. The length argument is the total length of the returned value including the decimal point, sign, digits, and spaces. The default is 10. The decimal argument is the number is the number of places to the right of the decimal point, rounded off as in the preceding example.

If you supply the values for *length* and *decimal* parameters to the STR() function, they must be positive. The specified length you provide should be greater than or equal to the part of the number before the decimal point plus any number sign you provide. A short float expression is right-aligned in the specified length, while the long float expression is truncated to the specified number of decimal places. For example, STR(12, 10) yields the result of 12, which is right-aligned in the result set. However, STR(1223, 2) truncates the result set to **.

STUFF(*string expression, start, length, ch expression*)

This function deletes a specified length of characters in a string and "stuffs" another set of characters at a specified starting point. You can use it to delete the characters in the middle of a string and replace them with new characters. For example, the statement

```
SELECT STUFF(PHONE,10, 1, '-')
  FROM CUSTOMERS
```

returns all telephone numbers from the PHONE column in the CUSTOMERS table with the space removed at the tenth character and the dash inserted instead. The value is returned from "(800) 555.1212" is "(800) 555-1212".

SUBSTRING(*string expression, start, length*)

This function returns part of a character, binary, text, or image expression. For example, the statement

```
SELECT SUBSTRING('(33428-5857)',2,5)
```

returns the value "33428" representing the first five digits of the nine-digit ZIP code.

The argument in the *string expression* can be a character string, a binary string, text, an image, a column, or an expression that includes a column (but not an expression that includes aggregate functions). The *start* parameter is an integer that specifies where the substring begins, while the *length* parameter takes an integer that specifies the length of the substring (the number of characters or bytes to return). (See Books Online for more information on using this function with the other data types.)

UNICODE(*unicode expression*)

This function returns the integer value, as defined by the Unicode standard, for the first character of the input expression. For example, the statement

```
SELECT UNICODE('§')
```

returns the value "167" as integer (see also NCHAR()).

UPPER(*character expression*)

This function returns a character expression with the lowercase characters converted to uppercase. For example, the statement

```
SELECT UPPER('noodle')
```

returns the value "NOODLE" (see also LOWER()) earlier in this chapter.

Mathematical Functions

The T-SQL mathematical functions are scalar functions that compute the values passed as arguments and then return a numeric value. All the functions are deterministic—in other words, they always return the same value for any given value passed as an argument—with the exception of the RAND() function, which returns a random value. The RAND() function, however, becomes deterministic when you use the same seed value as an argument.

In addition (no pun intended), the trigonometric functions, such as LOG, LOG10, EXP, SQUARE, and SQRT, cast the input value to a float before computing and then return the value as a float. Table 16-11 lists the mathematical functions and provides brief explanations of how to use them. For a complete reference to these functions consult SQL Server Books Online.

Aggregate Functions

The aggregate functions are used to perform a calculation on a set of values and then return a single value to the caller. Typically these values ignore NULL, but COUNT does not because technically NULL is a value. Aggregate functions are often used with the GROUP BY clause in a SELECT statement.

Function	Result Returned
ABS(numeric)	The absolute, positive value of the argument.
ACOS(float)	The angle, in radians, whose cosine is the given argument.
ASIN(float)	The angle, in radians, whose sine is the given float expression (also called arcsine).
ATAN(float)	The angle in radians whose tangent is the given float expression. (It is also called the arctangent.)
ATN2(float, float)	The angle, in radians, whose tangent is between the two given float expressions between the brackets. (It is also called the arctangent.)
CEILING(numeric)	The smallest integer greater than, or equal to, the given numeric expression.
COS(float)	The trigonometric cosine of the given angle (in radians) in the given expression.
COT(float)	The trigonometric cotangent of the specified angle (in radians) in the given float expression.
DEGREES(numeric)	The corresponding angle (given in radians) as degrees.
EXP(float)	The exponential value of the given expression.
FLOOR(numeric)	The largest integer less than or equal to the given numeric expression.
LOG(float)	The natural logarithm of the given float expression.
LOG10(float)	The base-10 logarithm of the given float expression.
PI()	The constant value of PI.
POWER(numeric)	The value of the given expression to the specified power.
RADIANS(numeric)	The radians when a numeric expression, in degrees, is entered.
RAND([seed])	A random float value from 0–1.

Table 16-11. *Mathematical Functions*

Function	Result Returned
ROUND(numeric, len)	A numeric expression, rounded to the specified length or precision.
SIGN(numeric)	A positive (+1), zero (0), or negative (–1) sign of the given expression.
SIN(float)	The trigonometric sine of the given angle (in radians) in an approximate numeric (float) expression.
SQRT(float)	The square root of the given expression.
SQUARE(float)	The square of the given expression.
TAN(float)	The tangent of the input expression.

Table 16-11. *Mathematical Functions* (continued)

The aggregate functions are deterministic and thus return the same value when they are called with a given set of input values. These functions can only be used in the following situations:

- The select list of a SELECT statement—in a subquery or an outer query
- In a COMPUTE or COMPUTE BY clause
- In a HAVING clause

The Transact-SQL programming language provides these aggregate functions, listed in Table 16-12.

Function	Returns
AVG	The average of the values in a group; null values are ignored.
BINARY_CHECKSUM	The binary checksum value computed over a row of a table or over a list of expressions. You can use BINARY_CHECKSUM to detect changes to a row of a table.

Table 16-12. *Aggregate Functions*

CHECKSUM	The checksum value computed over a row of a table, or over a list of expressions. CHECKSUM is used in building hash indices.
CHECKSUM_AGG	The checksum of the values in a group; ignores null values.
COUNT	The number of items in a group; returns an int.
COUNT_BIG	The number of items in a group. Like COUNT, but the difference between them is their return values. The COUNT_BIG always returns a data type of bigint.
GROUPING	An additional column is returned with a value of 1 when the row is added by either the CUBE or ROLLUP operator, or 0 when the row is not the result of CUBE or ROLLUP.
MAX	The maximum value in the expression.
MIN	The minimum value in the expression.
SUM	The sum of all the values, or only the DISTINCT values, in the expression. Null values are ignored, and you can only use it on numeric columns.
STDEV	The statistical standard deviation of all values in the given expression.
STDEVP	The statistical standard deviation for the population for all values in the given expression.
VAR	The statistical variance of all values in the given expression.
VARP	The statistical variance for the population for all values in the given expression.

Table 16-12. *Aggregate Functions* (continued)

Date and Time Functions

These scalar functions perform an operation on a date and time input value and return a string, numeric, or date and time value. Table 16-13 lists the date and time functions and the information they return.

Function	Returns
DATEADD()	The new datetime value based on adding an interval to the specified date.
DATEDIFF()	The number of date and time boundaries crossed between two specified dates.
DATENAME((*datepart* , *date*)	A character string representing the specified datepart of the specified date.
DATEPART((*datepart* , *date*)	The integer representing the specified datepart of the specified date.
DAY((*date*)	The integer representing the day datepart of the specified date.
GETDATE()	Returns the current system date and time in the standard internal format for datetime values.
GETUTCDATE()	The datetime value representing the current UTC time (Universal Time Coordinate or Greenwich Mean Time). The current UTC time is derived from the current local time and the time zone setting in the operating system of the computer on which SQL Server is running.
MONTH()	The integer that represents the month part of a specified date.
YEAR()	The integer that represents the year part of a specified date.

Table 16-13. *Date and Time Functions*

Text and Image Functions

These are scalar, nondeterministic functions that can perform an operation on a text or image argument. The following functions are supported in T-SQL:

- PATINDEX()
- TEXTPRT()
- TEXTVALID()

Interval	Value	Range
Year	Yy, yy	1753–9999
Quarter	Qq, q	1–4
Month	Mm, m	1–12
Dayofyear	Dd, y	1–366
Day	Dd, d	1–31
Week	Wk, ww	1–53
Weekday	Dw	1–7
Hour	Hh	0–23
Minute	Mi, n	0–59
Second	Ss	0–59
Millisecond	Ms	0–999

Table 16-14. *Date and Time Formats*

PATINDEX(*%pattern%*, *expression*)

This function returns the starting position of the first occurrence of a pattern in the specified expression. It returns zeros if the pattern is not found. The function works on all valid text and character data types. For example, the expression

```
USE NORTHWIND
SELECT PATINDEX('%.%', Phone)
 FROM CUSTOMERS
```

returns 11 records that contain a period in the string. Nine of these are reported to be in position three, which indicates that an IP address has been inserted into the Phone column. Records that do not qualify are returned as a zero value on the returned result set. In the preceding example, I used a single character as an example, but your pattern could be any combination of characters and spaces that form the pattern. In other words, the pattern is a literal string.

You can also use wildcard characters, but you must remember to insert the % character at the beginning and end of the pattern to be evaluated (except when searching for first or last characters). You can also use PATINDEX() in a WHERE clause. For example, the following statement

```
SELECT PATINDEX('%Shapiro%', LastName)
  FROM CUSTOMERS
```

returns all customers with a last name of Shapiro in the CUSTOMERS table.

TEXTPTR(*column*)

This function returns the text-pointer value that corresponds to a text, ntext, or image column in varbinary format. The retrieved text pointer value can then be used in READTEXT, WRITETEXT, and UPDATE statements. For example, the statement

```
SELECT @pointer = TEXTPTR(image)
 FROM
```

returns the image data you can then use in the client application.

For tables with in-row text, TEXTPTR returns a handle for the text to be processed. You can obtain a valid text pointer even if the text value is null. If the table does not have in-row text, and if a text, ntext, or image column has not been initialized by an UPDATE statement, TEXTPTR returns a null pointer.

TEXTVALID()

The TEXTVALID() function is used to check whether a text pointer exists. You cannot use UPDATETEXT, WRITETEXT, or READTEXT without a valid text pointer. Chapter 21 provides an example of the TEXTVALID() function.

Conversion Functions

SQL Server 2000 supports two conversion functions, CONVERT() and CAST(), that let you convert a variable or column of one type to another. Use of these functions is called *explicit casting* or *conversion* because SQL Server 2000 supports automatic conversion on several data types. In other words, the conversion functions can be used if you have no choice but to manually convert, or your application demands it for some reason.

CAST() does not do anything more than CONVERT(), but it is provided for compatibility with the SQL-92 standard. This discussion thus focuses on CONVERT(), and I will make mention of features that CAST() does not support. The syntax for this function is CONVERT(*data_type*, *variable*, *style*). The arguments are required as follows:

- ***Data_type*** This is the target of the conversion, for example to convert a money value to a character value data type for use in the construction of a financial report, perhaps an invoice.

- ***Variable*** This is the variable to convert to or the object of the conversion.
- ***Style*** This is the optional variable when the target data type can take one or more style changes.

You can use either of the functions in SELECT statements, and in the WHERE clause, and anywhere else you provide an expression. The following example converts a column from 40 to 25 characters:

```
SELECT CONVERT(nchar(30), StockName)
```

The data type argument you use in CONVERT() can be any valid data type supported by SQL Server. If you use a data type that takes a length argument (nchar, nvarchar, char, varchar, binary, or varbinary), then you can pass its length in the parentheses that enclose the data type length.

You can also use the CONVERT() function to obtain a variety of special data formats. For example, the style argument (not supported by CAST())is used to specify a particular date format required when you convert datetime and smalldatetime variables to character types. Table 16-15 lists the style values and the date formats returned.

The following example illustrates the differences between CAST() in the first SELECT statement and CONVERT() in the second SELECT statement. The result set is the same for both queries:

CAST():

```
USE NORTHWIND
 SELECT CAST(regiondescription AS char(2)), regionid
 FROM region
```

CONVERT():

```
SELECT CONVERT(char(2), regiondescription), regionid
FROM region
```

The result set is the same for both queries:

```
Ea          1
We          2
No          3
So          4
```

In the preceding example, we converted the region description column from 50 to 2 characters. A better example would be to convert a first name column to one character and compile a report listing of first name initials and full last names. CONVERT() is also useful when using LIKE in the WHERE clause.

As mentioned earlier, SQL Server automatically converts certain data types. If, for example, you compare a char expression and a datetime expression, or a smallint expression and an int expression, or char expressions of different lengths, SQL Server will convert them automatically. This is called an implicit conversion.

Expect the following behavior from the conversion functions:

- SQL Server reports an error when you attempt a conversion that is not possible. For example, trying to converting a char with letters to an integer will create an exception.
- If you do not specify a length when converting, SQL Server will supply a length of 30 characters by default.
- SQL Server will reject all values it cannot recognize as dates (including dates earlier than January 1, 1753) when you try to convert from datetime or smalldatetime. You can only convert datetime to smalldatetime when the date is in the proper date range (from January 1, 1900, through June 6, 2079). The time value will be rounded to the nearest minute.
- Converting to a bit will change any nonzero value to 1.
- When you convert to money or smallmoney, any integers in the conversion expression are assumed to be monetary units. For example, let's say you pass an integer value of 5 in the expression; SQL Server will convert it to the money equivalent of five dollars—expressed as U.S. dollars if us_english is the default language.

  All money value numbers to the right of the decimal in floating-point values are rounded to four decimal places by default. Expressions of data types char or varchar that are being converted to an integer data type must consist only of digits and an optional plus or minus sign (+ or –). The leading blanks are ignored. Any expressions of data types char or varchar converted to money can also include an optional decimal point and leading currency sign.
- You can include optional exponential notation (e or E, followed by an optional + or – sign, and then a number) in data types char or varchar that are being converted to float or real.
- When you pass character strings for conversion to a data type of a different size, any values too long for the new data type are truncated, and SQL Server displays an asterisk (*). This is the default display in both the OSQL utility and Query Analyzer. Any numeric expression that is too long for the new data type to display is truncated.

- You can also explicitly convert any text data to char or varchar, and image data to binary or varbinary. As discussed earlier, these data types are limited to 8,000 characters, and so you are limited to the maximum length of the character and binary data types; that is, 8,000 characters. When you explicitly convert ntext data to nchar or nvarchar, the output is confined to the maximum length of 4,000 characters. Remember that when you do not specify the length, the converted value has a default length of 30 characters. Implicit conversion is not supported with these functions.
- When you convert between data types in which the target data type has fewer decimal places than the source data type, the resulting value is truncated. For example, the result of CAST(10.3496 AS money) is $10.35.

Style

The number you supply as the *style* argument is used to determine how the datetime data will be displayed. For starters, the year can be displayed in either two or four digits. By default, SQL Server supplies a two-digit year, which may be a problem in certain transactions. For example, the statement

```
SELECT CONVERT(char(50), GETDATE(), 101)
```

returns the date 07/06/2000, while the statement

```
SELECT CONVERT(char(50), GETDATE(), 1)
```

returns the date 07/06/00. Table 16-15 provides the values for the style argument.

T-SQL Flow-Control

The T-SQL language supports basic flow-control logic that will allow you to perform program flow and branching according to certain conditions you provide the switching routines. The routines allow you to test one thing or another in simple either/or constructions, or test for multiple values in an easy-to-use CASE facility. The T-SQL flow-control options are as follows:

- If...Else
- CASE
- While
- Continue/Break
- GOTO/Return

Value sans Century	Value con Century	Date Format
1	101	mm/dd/yy
2	102	yy.mm.dd
3	103	dd/mm/yy
4	104	dd.mm.yy
5	105	dd-mm-yy
6	106	Dd mon yy
7	107	Mon dd, yy
8	108	Hh:mm:ss
9	109	Mon dd yyyy hh:mi:ss:mmmAM or PM
10	110	mm-dd-yy
11	111	Yy/mm/dd
12	112	Yymmdd
13	113	Dd mm yyy hh:mm:ss:mmm(24)
14	114	Hh:mi:ss:mmm(24)
20	120	Yyyy-mm-dd hh:mm:ss(24)
21	121	Yyy-mm-dd hh:mi:ss:mmm(24)

Table 16-15. *Style Values for Datetime*

If...Else

This branching or condition-switching statement will execute an isolated block of code in a routine according to a qualifying condition. If the condition qualifies, the code in the *If* block is executed. If it does not qualify, the program moves to the block of code in the *Else* section of the routine. The block of code in the *Else* section can contain something of substance or very little.

The syntax of this statement is as follows:

```
IF condition
 Begin
   {do something here}
 End
Else
 Begin
   {do something here}
 End
```

This syntax is a little like Pascal; however, notice that there are no "end ifs" required, but you should enclose your code in the Begin…End blocks. I say "should" because you can get away with omitting the Begin…End blocks in simple code segments. However, the Begin…End is essential when you need to make sure that all lines in the code segment are processed.

CASE

The CASE statement works the same as the CASE statements you find in all modern programming languages such as Visual Basic, or Delphi or Java. The T-SQL CASE statement can compare a variable or a field against several variables or fields. You could technically do this with multiple If…Else blocks, but that would be ugly to say the least, and you have no way to escape such a construction after a condition finds a match or tests true.

T-SQL CASE statements test a variable to be true by using the WHEN…THEN clause. For example, "WHEN the banana is yellow" THEN "eat it." After the WHEN tests true, the THEN condition is applied and execution flow continues through the CASE block. For example, the statement

```
USE NORTHWIND
SELECT ProductName AS 'Products', 'Popularity'=
CASE
  WHEN UnitsInStock <= 5 THEN 'Fast Mover'
  WHEN UnitsInStock > 5 AND UnitsInStock <= 15 THEN 'Average Mover'
  WHEN UnitsInStock > 15 AND UnitsInStock <= 1000 THEN 'Slow Mover'
END
FROM Products
```

returns the following table:

```
Chai                             Slow Mover
Chang                            Slow Mover
Aniseed Syrup                    Average Mover
Chef Anton's Cajun Seasoning     Slow Mover
Chef Anton's Gumbo Mix           Fast Mover
Grandma's Boysenberry Spread     Slow Mover
Uncle Bob's Organic Dried P..    Average Mover
Northwoods Cranberry Sauce       Average Mover
Mishi Kobe Niku                  Slow Mover
...
```

Obviously the preceding statement might make more sense if the query also checked restock dates and other factors because an item could be considered a slow mover an hour after a new shipment arrived. However, it adequately illustrates a simple CASE usage.

You can do a lot with CASE, such as assign the obtained value in a case statement and then pass that out to a stored procedure or another construction. For example, consider the following statement:

```
USE NORTHWIND
DECLARE @Discount real
DECLARE @CouponCode char(5)
SET @CouponCode = 'CDKIG'
SET @Discount =
CASE @CouponCode
  WHEN 'CXDFR' THEN 10
  WHEN 'CDKIG' THEN 7.5
  WHEN 'CKIDK' THEN 8
END
PRINT @Discount
```

I use the discount variable obtained at the end of the CASE and apply it to an item for which the customer has a discount coupon I can identify with a coupon code. In this case, the discount is 7.5%. The variable @CouponCode could change from item to item. This can be wrapped up in a trigger, as demonstrated in the next chapter, allowing the server to appropriately apply the discount.

WHILE

The WHILE loop is a flow-control statement that executes a single statement or block of code between BEGIN and END keywords. For example, the following is a simple WHILE statement that increments a value:

```
DECLARE @Count smallint
SET @Count = 0
WHILE @Count < 10
  SET @Count = @Count + 1
```

To repeatedly execute more than just a single line of code, enclose the code between the BEGIN and END blocks, as demonstrated in If…Else. We will revisit WHILE in later chapters to demonstrate some advanced T-SQL features, such as triggers, cursors, and stored procedures.

Continue or Break

Use CONTINUE and BREAK to change or stop the execution of the WHILE loop. The CONTINUE keyword restarts a WHILE loop, and the BREAK terminates the innermost loop it is in.

GOTO and RETURN

These two flow-control statements let you jump out of your current segment and move to another location in the procedure, similar to the GOTO in VB or DBase. GOTO moves to a line identified by a label followed by a colon (*ArrivedHere:*). RETURN ends a procedure unconditionally and can optionally returns a result.

The GOTO command is confined to a control-of-flow statement, statement blocks, or procedures, but it cannot go to a label outside of the current process. However, the GOTO branch can alter the flow and reroute it to a label defined before or after GOTO. The following example emulates a WHILE loop, and the RETURN is used to break out of the loop when a certain value is reached:

```
DECLARE @Counter int
SET @Counter = 0
Counter:
    SET @Counter = @Counter + 1
      GOTO CheckResult
```

```
CheckResult:
 IF @Counter = 10
  BEGIN
   PRINT 'You have reached '+ CAST(@Counter AS CHAR)
   RETURN
  END
 Else
  Goto Counter
```

WAITFOR

The WAITFOR statement suspends procedure execution until a certain time or time interval has passed. The following example prints the time exactly as prescribed in the argument, but notice the conversion and trimming that is needed to return the system time in a simple time format of 00:00 hours:

```
BEGIN
WAITFOR TIME '18:20'
  PRINT 'THE TIME IS '+ LEFT(CONVERT(CHAR(20), GETDATE(), 14), 5)
END

THE TIME IS 18:20
```

RAISEERROR

RAISERROR is a facility supported by SQL Server 2000 as a flow-control feature, which is why I tacked it onto this section. However, you will use this facility in many places, such as triggers, stored procedures, transaction processing, and so on.

The syntax for RAISERROR is as follows:

```
RAISERROR ( { msg_id | msg_str } { , severity , state }
[ , argument [ ,...n ] ] )
[ WITH option [ ,...n ] ]
```

However, the simplest syntax to observe at this point for client information is simply RAISERROR(*Message*, *Severity*, *State*). Thus the syntax for a simple message to the user would be RAISERROR('This is a non-severe error' , 1, 1). More about RAISERROR later.

Identifiers

The names that you give to databases and database objects when you create them are called *identifiers*. You don't have to supply an identifier with the same fanfare and excitement that you went through when your parents named you, but identifiers and how you use them are important.

Most of the time you need to supply an identifier at the instant you create, or define, an object. In some cases SQL Server does this for you. A good example of an object that automatically gets its own identifier from SQL Server is the *default* constraint object. In the next chapter I talk about referencing this identifier in your code.

The following code

```
CREATE TABLE CoffeeTable (KeyCol INT PRIMARY KEY, Wood NVARCHAR(8))
SELECT Wood FROM CoffeeTable . . . .
```

is an example of naming the table and then referencing it by the identifier in the same stroke.

Often it becomes necessary to delimit identifiers with open/close square brackets ([]) when the identifiers do not conform to the rules for well-formed identifiers in T-SQL. For example the table ImportedCoffee is fine but [Imported Coffee] needs to be delimited.

It also makes good business sense as a T-SQL programmer to help the optimizer reuse execution plans and connecting identifiers as a SQL Server database namespace is important. In the following code examples both styles are accepted by SQL Server, but the latter is preferred:

```
--one way
USE Northwind
SELECT CustomerID FROM Customers
--better way
SELECT CustomerID FROM Northwind.dbo.Customers
```

As discussed earlier, the ampersand (@)sign at the beginning of an expression is an identifier reserved for SQL Server use, as is the pound (#)sign, dollar ($), and the underscore (_). You cannot use pound as a subsequent character, but @, $ and underscore will fly.

Moving On

This chapter covers much of the "bits and pieces" you need to code in T-SQL. With what we discussed you'll be able to get cracking and, within a few chapters, come up with some smart queries. You might not be ready to code the query that calculates the age of the universe, so a good "complete reference" to T-SQL or SQL is a good idea.

While we dealt with a lot of the basic ingredients, we also touched on some new data type and functions, which I will refer to in the chapters ahead. So, let's move on to stored procedures and triggers and put some the stuff we learned in this chapter to work.

Chapter 17

SQL Server Integrity Programming and Management

Perhaps no other topic of discussion in database development, modeling and management circles draws more attention, and often heated debate, than that of data integrity. It is astonishing that, despite the distance we have come in understanding, practice, and technology, so many database gurus (Celko, Codd, Date, Riordan, et al.) vary so widely in their respective philosophies. As a result, administrators and developers often handle integrity modeling and thus integrity programming by the seat of their pants. Even SQL Server Books Online defines data integrity in its glossary in a way more confused than a bat in broad daylight.

This book is certainly not the forum for a discussion of data integrity and this is about as far as I want to venture in discussing relational database theory. But without exploring some concepts and accepting the only feasible definition of data integrity, you will not benefit from all the tools and new features that SQL Server 2000 supports with respect to data integrity modeling and programming.

Data integrity *definitely* is not a practice, a discipline, that ensures that data stored in a database is correct, *only that is it believable or plausible.* There is no way between this life and the hereafter that SQL Server 2000, or any other RDBMS, can guarantee that data in a database is correct. Get *correct* out of your vocab now. SQL Server 2000 has no way of knowing and thus ensuring that my area code is not 209 but rather 299, or that my last name is Shapiro and not Schapiro. I have even heard of a girl named Jeffrey. You need to start thinking, modeling, and programming SQL Server in terms of data plausibility, not in terms of being right or wrong.

Only if you accept this definition will you be able to use the tools and techniques supported by SQL Server 2000 to ensure the integrity of your data, and thus its value as an asset to your enterprise. And after you start focusing on *integrity* in scalar terms and not *correctness* in absolute terms, you will have a lot more faith in the data in your database, and you will be able to afford it the trust and respect it deserves. After all, data that is not plausible or believable is a liability.

As I discussed in Chapter 1, human error caused my wife extreme grief when, after changing medical insurance companies, she was denied coverage for some time because the last name of her doctor, instead of Shapiro, was entered in the spouse's last name field. To my wife, the data integrity issue thus became a life-threatening one. To the medical insurance company, the issue almost exploded into a liability problem.

What would or could cause a last name, or surname, to be incorrect?

1. The wife goes by her maiden name.
2. A spouse mistakenly provides a pseudonym.
3. The couple just got divorced but agreed to maintain the coverage.
4. A child is covered by a stepfather but still goes by the last name of his or her biological father.
5. The first name is entered into the last name field.

6. The last name is typed incorrectly (Shapiro becomes Ahaoeuei with just few slips of the finger).
7. The handwriting on the application form is poor, or the last name is omitted and the data entry person makes a wrong assumption.

This list could go on and on. And I am sure you could come up with dozens of scenarios that would also create questionable data, not only in last name values but also in many other places. Numbers, for example, present incredible opportunities to enter problematic data in a database.

But is this a question of *integrity?* If we accept that we program the DBMS to ensure that the data is as believable as possible, then it is. If we try to ensure that the data is correct, then it is not. Any value may in fact be correct when it is assumed to be wrong, and it may in fact be wrong when it is assumed to be correct. The only thing you can do to *help* ensure that data is believable is to help ensure that it was believable when it was entered into the database.

The best I can think of doing at the data tier to help ensure that a value, such as the spouse's last name, is believable is to force the client to go back and check the data before it can be entered, or to compare the data against known values. It is possible to even refer the record back to the client and request it to be entered by another user, possibly a supervisor who would take the fact checking to the next level. Asking Web surfers to fill in application forms over the Internet is a good idea because it cuts out the middle data entry person, the paper trail, and delay. And it puts the onus of ensuring the data plausibility on the client, who is more likely to ensure that his or her information can be relied upon.

I recently watched a horrifying story on CNN about an American pharmacist who gave a child a fatal overdose of a drug contrary to what had been correctly prescribed by the pediatrician. The excuse was human error, failure of the supervisor to double-check prescriptions, filling hundreds of prescriptions a day. Why, in heaven's name, in this day and age, are pharmacists still using typewriters and word processors to provide instructions about dosage and administration of dangerous drugs? A database should have been used to check that the dosage did not exceed safely levels for the drug prescribed. No computer program checked the dosage, and so a mother sent her child to bed and he never woke up. Now, whenever we buy drugs, we check the label and wonder "can we trust our lives to this data?"

Obviously, the subject of human error is beyond the scope of this book, other than to discuss what possible means we might have of preventing humans from entering questionable data into a database. Joe Celko touched on the subject in his marvelous book, *Joe Celko's Data & Databases: Concepts in Practice* (New York: Morgan Kaufmann, 1999). In a section titled "Models versus Reality," he talks about *errors in models,* describing Type I and Type II error levels. A Type I error is accepting as false something that is true, and a Type II error is accepting as true something that it false.

I agree without equivocation that the subject of errors in models is very important for database people to understand. Generations of people have been wiped out because of this problem. Sub-Saharan Africa, where I spent my childhood, is going to be wiped out because of AIDS. This could have been prevented, but the population there still believes, by and large, that AIDS is not sexually transmitted and that the publicity is just "Western propaganda." The fraud is in fact self-perpetuating or self-fulfilling, because millions of Africans still have unprotected sex.

Yes, we can use fancy programming tricks and system features such as triggers and stored procedures to lessen the likelihood of implausible data; we can even build more advanced *human* integrity checking into the client applications. How can we avoid problems like the one just described and still program SQL Server 2000 as wisely as possible, according to the data ecology principles discussed in Chapter 14? To arrive at a possible solution, let's first explore the integrity assurance features and functions of SQL Server 2000. After this discussion, we can redress the last name integrity issue and offer my medical insurance company some ideas before they get sued.

Understanding SQL Server Data Integrity

When it comes to the subject of data integrity, we are dealing with a whole new barrel of pickles, one that SQL Server 2000 can adequately tackle under the guidance of the SQL Server developer and DBA . . . who now fully understands that he or she is modeling to ensure that data is plausible, not that it is correct. But there is still one more subject to discuss here before you can model your SQL Server 2000 database: *business rules.*

Data Integrity and Business Rules

A check constraint or trigger can easily be used to prevent a customer from spending more than $500 on credit. You might agree that any number above $500 is considered risky, but another customer might not. To apply this reasoning to the real world, for example, an airline booking system may be programmed to resist assigning seats to frequent-flier passengers who try to redeem miles toward a ticket, because the *rules* dictate that a seat should first be assigned to a *cash* customer, as opposed to a *liability* customer. All airlines maintain seat assignment rules when it comes to frequent fliers; although they vary widely in their rules.

Another rule, at a lower level than the one just described, would be that all rows for a given table must be unique. This rule is one of the core tenets of the Date relational model (C.J. Date). According to Chris Date, one of the world's foremost database experts, the relational model should not allow for any NULLs or duplicates whatsoever. In fact, Date is outspokenly against NULLs and declares that they should never have been introduced into relational theory.

The Date rule declares that entity values (column values in a row) should never be NULL (unknown or missing). SQL Server 2000 lets you decide whether to abide by the

Date rule or code to your own business rules, which may in certain circumstances allow both duplicate rows in a table and even NULL values.

Ensuring integrity is very much part of the relational database modeling, whether it is expressed in terms akin to calculus and algebra or according to Boolean logic or some other form of analysis. But data integrity or the extent to which you manage it, as alluded to earlier, is also up to you. And this brings to us the subject of rules, specifically business rules.

Business rules are a hot topic in the new millennium. Yet they are really the abstract declaration of the data integrity requirements demanded by business owners and enterprise and data analysts. The "frequent fliers get last choice" rule discussed earlier is exactly the type of business rule about which we are talking.

We can look at this another way. We can say that the data integrity constraint logic is the formal definition of a business rule applied to corporate data. After all, you can scream about business rules and data integrity until the cows come home, but that will do nothing to a database that knows only unfettered character-based data, has more duplicates than bottle tops, and can do little about enforcing integrity (see Chapter 3). You will find, as we move from operational data support to analytical and temporal data support (discussed in Part IV) in SQL Server 2000, that the formulation of business rules becomes more of a requirement than a luxury. Analytical data comes from operational data, so the more lax your integrity control in the OLTP system, the more effort you will have to expend when you need to get analysis data scrubbed before it can be copied to the data warehouse. Values like N/A, TBA, or "unknown" lessen the value in the data mine and the information extraction becomes extremely time-consuming and expensive.

Figure 17-1 represents this discussion in conceptual terms. At the highest level—that is, the conceptual level—the enterprise and data analysts formulate rules with the business owners. This is also the requirements formulating level. In the middle is the modeling level that translates the business rules into database integrity requirements by database analysts and even DBAs. And at the lowest level is the development model that implements the integrity requirement as constraints, checks, and procedures in SQL Server 2000, implemented by DBAs and SQL Server developers.

Now that our philosophical (and emotional) banks are charged, we can look at the level you are probably most interested in: implementing the integrity requirements. To do so, we must classify integrity into several governing sections as follows:

- Database and table integrity
- Referential integrity
- Entity integrity
- Type integrity
- Domain integrity
- Transition integrity
- Transaction integrity

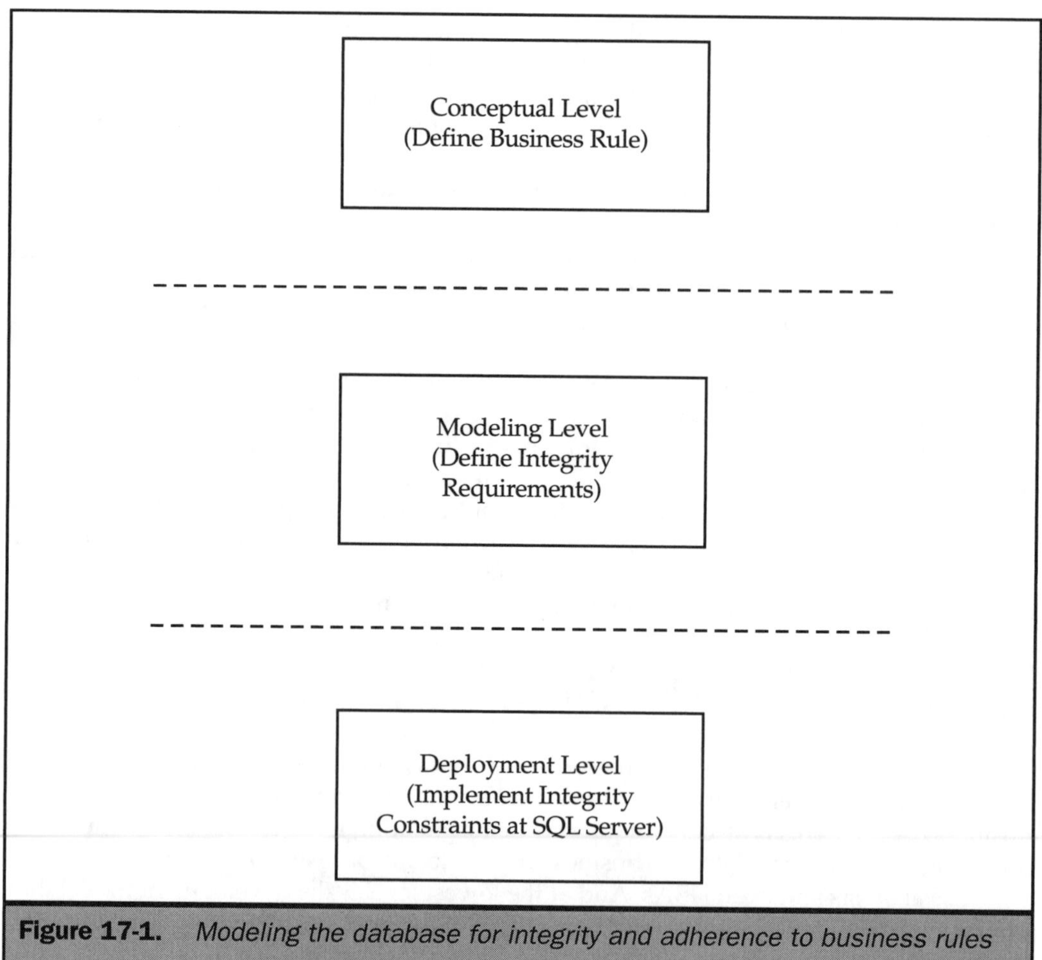

Figure 17-1. *Modeling the database for integrity and adherence to business rules*

Database and Table Integrity

Database and table constraint mechanisms are the broadest form of integrity control because they relate to the relationships between entities, multiple columns in a table, and multiple tables in a database. A good example of a database integrity violation is allowing a customer with bad credit to buy more goods and to put the order on account, or even allowing payment to be made by anything other than cash, letter of credit, or a credit card. The following pseudocode would thus enforce the rules of database integrity for the given example:

```
FOR Customers.Orders
IF Customer_Credit.Credit < 10
BEGIN
  RAISERROR 1.Message ('Customer must pay with cash or credit card')
  GOTO Cash
END
ELSE
BEGIN
  RAISERROR 2.Message('Customer is cleared for credit')
  GOTO Account
END
```

Another table-level constraint against integrity violation is the case of the orphaned row. If we delete an entity related to one or more entities through primary-foreign key relationships, we are deemed (to use a legal expression) to have violated rules of *referential integrity.* Referential integrity rules should be adhered to in every database deployment, which is why we devote a separate section to this topic.

Referential Integrity

By deleting a member row that is referenced by other entities or rows, we in fact leave the remaining undeleted entities orphaned and the record in tatters. In fact, the database is now in a poor state because no easy means now exists of identifying or finding the orphaned entities and removing the entire record. And if you have data in a database that can never be accessed or relied upon, the entire database becomes questionable.

I liken referential integrity violations to the habit some people have of not finishing an apple. If you cut the apple, take out a wedge, or only eat half of it, the remaining fruit darkens and quickly goes bad. So is it when you delete a row and violate referential integrity: over time the database goes bad also. As mentioned in the chapters in Part I, if you regard all the rows in linked tables as combining to represent a complete record, deleting a row in one table and leaving the related rows intact is akin to taking a bite out of an apple and then leaving it to go brown and rot.

On the other hand, referential integrity violation can also be said to have occurred when an entity references a nonexistent entity in the database. Referential integrity requires that there be no references to nonexistent values and that if a key value changes, all references to it change consistently throughout the database.

In the past, referential integrity would be maintained using triggers and many lines of code; we called this approach *procedural referential integrity* (PRI). Most modern

DBMS products now support *declarative referential integrity* (DRI), which is essentially the opposite of procedural referential integrity. DRI makes use of built-in mechanisms to ensure or maintain referential integrity while PRI is the responsibility of the database modeler or developer.

The declarative referential integrity constraints are enforced as follows:

- The integrity criteria are defined in the various database objects' definitions, such as foreign key existence.
- Checks, defaults, and rules trap the violations.
- SQL Server automatically enforces the integrity rules.

Procedural referential integrity constraints are enforced as follows:

- The integrity criteria are defined and enforced in your T-SQL code.
- The constraints are implemented in triggers and stored procedures (see Chapter 18), or the T-SQL code in other manual constraints.

Entity Integrity

Entity constraints, also known as *relational constraints,* define rules that govern rows and columns in tables and the tables as units. Uniqueness is one of the primary entity integrity rules to ensure. Of course, you can maintain a database that enforces no uniqueness whatsoever, but that would certainly render a table devoid of any integrity. For example, you can create and populate a table of orders and insert duplicate orders into the table willy-nilly. Your reasoning might be that, since customers can make duplicate orders, these duplicate orders should be stored without any constraints.

But is there such a thing as a duplicate order? Only in error, I believe, and a constraint should be designed to catch such an error. Each order is placed at a certain time and date. No order can be entered twice at exactly the same time. The description, quantity, price, and discount of an item might be duplicated, but the time the entry was made cannot. Besides, each order is a new transaction that differs from another transaction only in the time it was entered and the order number assigned to it. It is in fact unique.

Although highly unlikely, it is possible for two users to enter the same record or data at exactly the same time. An identity column and table locks would prevent the two rows from competing on the question of their uniqueness.

The tools we use to constrain entities are the primary keys (on identified columns), which can impose primary indexes, UNIQUE constraints, IDENTITY properties, and so forth. Table constraints are checked before any data can be allowed into the table. If the data violates the constraint rule—for instance, if it contains a duplicate row or a duplicate value on which we have installed a primary index—it is rejected.

Entity integrity is enforced using primary keys and unique indexes.

Type Integrity

Type constraint discussions generally cover domains, although data types and data domains are two separate concepts, and that is gospel. I have thus added domain constraints to the list, and we discuss domain integrity next. A type constraint enforces rules that govern correct use of the data type of a given value. Ensuring the consistent use of a date data type, for example, is a form of type constraint. Dates, decimals, currency, and the like are data types recorded in several formats that govern precision, but the data will become impossible to work with if such scalar values are not constrained to just one of the several formats required by your rules.

Assigning NULL values is another form of type constraint, even though we talk about NULL with respect to database and entity constraints. By allowing NULL values in a tuple (field), you are explicitly allowing the storage of *missing* or *unknown* values. If you disavow NULL values, you must either supply a value through some formula or supply a default value for the variable.

A NULL value, for that matter, is an oxymoron in a manner of speaking. You might ask yourself how a NULL value can be a *value* and replace something that is missing or unknown. It is, however, a convenient means of allowing a row to be inserted into the database even if it contains missing or unknown values. If your rules allow NULLs to be a temporary expedient, in they go. If not, out they go.

The rules of integrity should guide your use of the NULL. Ask yourself if your data is reliable if it is made up of missing or unknown values. If not knowing middle initials will not break your data, then the NULL represents a convenient placeholder until the initial becomes available. Inserting a default value would not be feasible, because you would be inserting a Type II error that could spell disaster: accepting as true something that may be false.

In this regard, you might consider NULL values to be a violation of database integrity as well. My rule allows NULL if it does not violate the integrity of my data or adversely affect the analytical value of the data . If it does, I must install a default value and code the logic, based on the business rule, that obtains the default. If you do not have the data for a value for a given row, you should instead assign a default value, or obtain a value through an alternate formula. There is a lot of debate surrounding NULL. Nevertheless, SQL Server 2000 permits you the flexibility of either allowing or disallowing NULL values according to your needs . . . or ignorance.

Type constraints are defined in code and in the definitions of the data types, such as specifying NULL (allowed) or NOT NULL (disavowed). Integrity is ensured with automatic checks and procedural code.

Note *A type constraint is a column-level constraint.*

Domain Integrity

Data domains are the logical grouping of values. For example, in my items table I have a color column that can only take one of five *colors.* Notice the emphasis on *only* because that is the focus of my domain constraints. The domain rule for the item dictates that it can only be red, blue, mustard, lime, or black. You might argue that mustard and lime belong to the domain *flavors*, and if you do, you have grasped the concept of a data domain, and you have joined the debate.

I tend not to agree that domain constraints govern data types; that is the work of type constraints. However, the check and constraint mechanisms might be the same for both and many domain constraints have been cast along data type lines. For example, it is very convenient to constrain a numeric value by the type of integer. Domains can represent collections of data types, which is what leads to the incorrect definition that domains are data types, period. While domains are in fact data types, the definition of a domain should refer to a logical collection or grouping of data values and entities, not data types. As long as you understand the difference, you'll be okay.

Besides checks, you can use stored procedures and triggers to ensure domain integrity. For example, a stored procedure can populate a list or table at the client with allowable values from which to choose.

Note *A domain constraint is also a column-level constraint.*

Transition Integrity

One of my clients has a simple rule that was more important to the IS managers than anything in the database. "Call center agents are only allowed to take an order and receive payment." The agent is not allowed access to any functions in the client application that debits items from inventory or causes a picker in the warehouse to go pack the items to send to shipping. Only a second-level stock manager is allowed to do that. My client manages its stock levels like a squirrel manages its acorns. Only stock managers can produce the pick and shipping data that will translate the order into a shippable collection of items. That was the business rule; I did not question it, I only implemented it.

Rules such as these are translated into what we call *transition constraints*. These constraints ensure that the status of records changes according to predetermined rules. Inventory levels and accounting databases need to adhere to strict transition constraints. For example, you should never credit to one table without debiting from another. Inventory cannot be debited if shipping is not credited.

There are several levels on which you can define or specify transition states. In most order-taking databases, these can be defined as follows:

1. Order entered.
2. Order taken, money taken, or credit approved.
3. Item back-ordered.
4. Items picked and packed.
5. Order cancelled or paused.
6. Items shipped.
7. Obligation completed.

This list relates to the various transitions in a database. For example, an order changes from entered to taken only when either credit is approved or the items have been paid for. In other words, if transition integrity is maintained or enforced on the database, then an order entered can only be considered a de facto liability (the company owes the client the items) if money has changed hands or the customer is in good credit standing. A check on cash or credit will allow the order to go from a state of *entered* to a state of *taken.* Some companies do not consider an obligation completed until the order is on the road to the client. Only then do they actually debit the credit card.

Items also move through various states. For example, an *AllowBackorders* constraint can enforce a rule that either allows or disallows part of an order from being back-ordered. For example, a customer might request that the order should not ship until a part in the shipment is available for immediate delivery.

The aforementioned client also has another very important business rule. The items cannot be shipped and the software cannot produce the shipping label unless the shipping department has called the client and obtained a verbal agreement to accept the order. If the client agrees, only at that instant will the credit card be run or a debit applied to the account.

My client advised me the main reason for this rule is that about 95 percent of the shipments rejected by customers come from customers paying on credit accounts or credit cards. The customer changes his or her mind after placing the order and then refuses the delivery. My client then has to eat the loss on the shipping costs (often UPS Red or FedEx delivery) because the shipper has fulfilled.

Transaction Integrity

A *transaction* in the sense described here is a collection of operations on data that must be completed according to business rules as a unit, or the transaction is completely cancelled. In this regard the transaction constraint is similar to the formal transaction monitoring that SQL Server engages automatically and thus displays elements of atomicity (see Chapter 21). Transaction integrity in the preceding discussion is more a procedural integrity mechanism (something you usually have to code a solution for) that ensures that all of the components that are required for a complete transaction are entered and satisfy all of the preceding integrity rules before the transaction is committed.

Such transactions can, however, be applied over long periods, depending on the business needs and rules. Transactions can also happen over a short period, and several states can make up several transactions. For example, an order might be broken up into several transactions, one for each state an order is in.

Planning Integrity

In two previous chapters—Chapters 11 and 16—we tackled DML and the CREATE TABLE statement, but the primary objective of the methods discussed and the code demonstrated was to create tables, not to demonstrate the installing of integrity mechanisms. In this chapter, we go a step further and code the formal or declarative integrity constraint definitions into the CREATE TABLE and ALTER TABLE statements.

SQL Server provides the following built-in integrity or constraint mechanisms:

- The capability to provide default values, and thereby avoid NULL
- The capability to code check constraint expressions that evaluate the values in the SQL statement to determine if they are allowed to be saved to the column
- The capability to code referential integrity constraints (cross-referencing foreign key columns)
- The capability to declare primary and unique keys that ensure uniqueness in a column or through the combination of columns
- The capability to use triggers as a form of constraint, which can also provide a trans- or intra-database integrity checking facility. Triggers are covered in the next chapter

When you first create a table, you are in fact laying down the first integrity constraints in your database because you create columns that have different data types for different data. For example, you would not store a data value in a character data type, and you would not try to store a character in an integer data type.

When you design a database, one of the basic rules to follow is to use common sense. If you are storing integer data, then store it in integer columns; date-to-date columns; character-to-character columns; and so forth. Naturally you will come to situations that will require you to decide between variations of a data type (small integers, integers, or big integers), or to make decisions that rely on the precision and scale of data, such as values of type real or float, currency, and so on. Other times, your choice of data type will be related to storage requirements, system resources, and so forth. An example would be deciding to switch to the bigint data type because of the need to store very large numbers. But you would not incur the storage overhead of a big integer (bigint) if you were storing nothing larger than 99.

The format of the data being stored is also a consideration, because modern database systems do not store only characters and numerals any more. They also store binary information, images, objects, bitmaps, large amounts of text, and so forth. And SQL Server 2000 also allows us to build our own *user-defined* data types, which are discussed in Chapter 16.

The Integrity Plan

The integrity plan is one of the most important sections of your overall database definition, model, or architecture. You can use the flow diagram in Figure 17-2 to build your integrity plan:

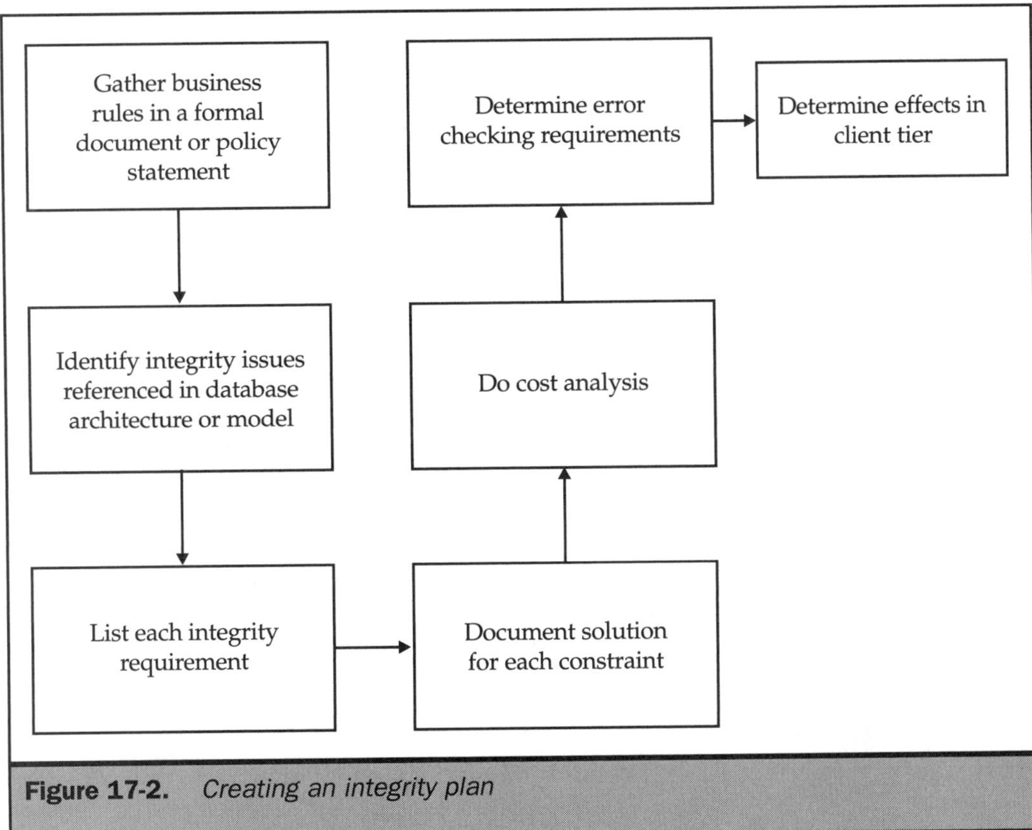

Figure 17-2. *Creating an integrity plan*

Gather Business Rules

This section of the integrity plan identifies business rules that will impact the database model and architecture. These rules, as discussed earlier, differ from the integrity issues that are built in to the relational model from the get-go, such as referential integrity.

Sit down with the people responsible for establishing the business rules, or provide the facilities in your model and code for later easy incorporation of constraints to cater to the business rules.

Identify Key Integrity Issues to Cover

These issues will be referenced in the architecture or will become patently part of it. For example, you might want to list attributes of the data that have legal implications if they render the data questionable. It is also important to plan for the prospect of warehousing the data, and constraining data in the operational databases with analysis in mind will make it easier to transform the data at a later stage.

List Each Integrity Requirement

This step is closely related to the preceding step, and they can be combined. Here you should list the precise integrity needs of the databases and tables right down to the values required.

You could list each table and link it to a list of integrity constraints required on its internals. For example, you will specify referential integrity requirements with linked tables, the primary key column, type constraints, and so on.

Document the Solution for Each Constraint

This section covers how you propose to deal with each integrity requirement. For example, do you plan to create unique constraints directly in T-SQL code or interactively in Enterprise Manager (or possibly through the DMO object library). Here you would also determine which integrity mechanism would be most suited for the task. For example, would a check constraint work or would you have to code a trigger?

Also document and establish procedures for maintaining and revising the constraints. If constraints are implemented in code, then you need to maintain source, version control, and so forth. You will also need to manage access, permissions to the constraint objects, and so on.

Do Cost Analysis

There is a cost attached to every constraint. The costs are both direct, in terms of their consumption of SQL Server resources and usefulness, and indirect, in terms of the costs of programming, maintenance, documentation, and so on. For example, using a stored procedure to check integrity is more expensive in all terms than using a trigger (besides, there are situations that only a trigger caters to). Using a trigger, on the other hand, is more expensive than using a built-in cascade. And, defaults or constraint objects are more expensive than check constraints and so on.

When performing cost analysis of constraints, you should also consider adherence to standards as a factor. For example, you should use built-in constraints because they are based on ANSI compliance and also conform to relational database rules.

Triggers, on the other hand, can be used to meet ANSI recommendations, but since triggers are entirely procedural, they cannot be considered ANSI compliant. SQL Server can check code for errors, but it is not able to check trigger code for standards compliance. In fact, even if trigger code is syntactically correct, it might still nuke your data beyond recovery.

Determine Error Checking Requirements

When integrity is violated or a constraint traps problem data, SQL Server will report errors. You need to determine how best to check these errors and establish procedure for using the error logs to trap faults in design and development, data entry, or business rule integration. In short, error checking and tracking can be used to reduce errors down the road.

Determine Effects and Requirements in the Client Tier

As discussed in Chapter 14, we don't want to build a client tier that collapses every time we make changes in the data tier, which is why we move the data processing to the data tier and code just about everything in triggers, UDFs, stored procedures, and extended stored procedures.

If you plan well and manage the database model and architecture properly, the constraints in the data tier should have little impact on the clients. However, you will have a lot to think about if you need to maintain legacy client code that still maintains a lot of client-side data processing and logic.

It is also possible to code constraint or integrity checking in the client tier without adversely affecting development costs and management. For example, it is more useful in terms of server resource conservation to check for format or type and domain integrity violations before the data gets transmitted to the server. A mask over the telephone number in a client application, even a Web browser, will obviate the need for SQL Server to bounce back with an integrity violation that incurs an additional round trip (see the section "Check Constraints" later in this chapter).

Configuring and Programming Integrity

If we examine the T-SQL CREATE TABLE or ALTER TABLE statement in the previous chapters or in Books Online, we can see that these statements accept several arguments for setting up built-in or system (declarative) integrity constraints using default values, check constraints, foreign keys, primary keys, unique keys, and so on.

Default Values

The default value is used in a column that may or may not forbid NULL values. For example, a column of type integer might take a 0 as the default, while a character-based column might take "unknown" as a default value—or even something like "pending."

A default value is not really a constraint per se because it does not restrict you from entering a certain value; it only kicks in when you do not provide a value.

Default values do not just happen automatically when you insert new rows in a table. As demonstrated in the Chapter 20, you must explicitly tell SQL Server to apply the default value when performing a row insert. SQL Server can also create the row in the INSERT statement and apply all the default values for the row (in which case you would not specify columns in the INSERT statement). This is achieved using the DEFAULT VALUES clause in your INSERT statement.

The following code demonstrates the provisioning of a default value in the CREATE TABLE statement:

```
CREATE TABLE Items
(Amount int DEFAULT 0, Description varchar(50), Notes text NULL)
```

You are not limited in terms of T-SQL code as to how you can concoct a default value, as long as the default value does not violate the data type. For example, you can use system-supplied values, such as those that are returned from built-in functions, to provide a default value. The following code automatically provides information on the user that inserted the row:

```
CREATE TABLE NewOrders
(custID INT NOT NULL PRIMARY KEY,
 custName VARCHAR(30) NOT NULL DEFAULT 'new customer',
 createdBy varchar(50) DEFAULT User)
```

However, changing the default value is another matter altogether when you need to do things in T-SQL code, because you can't easily reference the default name, at least not according to SQL-92 or Microsoft specifications. The CREATE TABLE statement also provides no facility for providing a custom name that would be easy to reference in a script. SQL Server, on the other hand, provides a name for the default property, but it too cannot be referenced easily from front-end applications or T-SQL scripts.

So you cannot willy-nilly change the default when the MIS walks in and asks you to do so. You have to first delete it and then recreate it. Deleting the default can be achieved using the following ALTER TABLE statement:

```
ALTER TABLE [dbo].[NewOrders]
  DROP CONSTRAINT [DF__defs__Items__48CFD27E]
```

The constraint name in the preceding code was provided automatically by SQL Server, so you can see how difficult it is to reference it. This code works, but I had to go to Enterprise Manager or Query Analyzer to look it up and then script it out to a new query window. This is a real pain. A better method is to look up the default name in the system tables. After looking for the information in the system tables and tinkering around with QA for an hour, I arrived at the following code to delete the default programmatically:

```
USE MASTER
DECLARE @dfltname varchar(100), @cmd varchar(1000)
SET @dfltname =
```

```
  (SELECT name FROM sysobjects sysobs
   JOIN sysconstraints scons ON sysobs.id = scons.constid
      WHERE object_name(sysobs.parent_obj)= 'NewOrders'
      AND sysobs.xtype = 'D' AND scons.colid =
  (SELECT colid FROM syscolumns where ID = object_id('dbo.defs')
    AND name = 'custName'))

SET @cmd = 'ALTER TABLE NewOrders DROP CONSTRAINT ' + @dfltname
EXEC(@cmd)
```

This is by no means an easy statement to comprehend if you are new to T-SQL, so you might want to come back to it after you have gone through the next couple of chapters, which discuss SELECT, JOIN, aliases, EXEC, and stored procedures. In the next chapter, I put the code in a stored procedure so that it's two parameters away from me when I need it.

As an alternative, you can create a default object (or several objects), install a default value as the object's property, and then bind and unbind the object to the column as needed. There are, however, a number of problems associated with default objects:

- They are not ANSI compliant. The default objects have been dragged up through the ages from the romance between Microsoft and Sybase.
- The code to create the default object (CREATE DEFAULT) and the ensuing execution of system stored procedures sp_bindefault and sp_unbindefault is tedious.
- They are not true SQL DDL and as such are not as efficient as ANSI default constraints.
- You will be limited in the expression you use to provide a default value. As demonstrated earlier, a T-SQL ANSI default value can be derived from a sophisticated query/calculation providing a unique value each time the default in invoked. The makes the ANSI default more powerful by an order of magnitude.
- Managing defaults can drive you nuts. If you need to drop a column that has a default object fused to it, you first need to unbind the default from the column. You cannot simply delete the default either, because it might be bound to other columns.

As I am sure you are aware, you can create and manage tables from Enterprise Manager, which essentially provides you with an interactive and visual "hookup" to integrity application on databases and tables.

Rules are a legacy mechanism for enforcing integrity and are supported in SQL Server 2000 for backward compatibility (see Chapter 7). I don't expect rules to survive to the next version of SQL Server, so start porting them over to triggers or formal constraints now.

You can create the default in Enterprise Manager by opening the table in the Design Table console and entering a default value in the default value for the column selected. You can easily change the defaults in this manner. Adding or changing a default value in the console is illustrated in Figure 17-3. To add or change a default using Enterprise Manager, take the following steps:

1. Drill down to the database in question and expand the tree to access the table node. Expand the table node.
2. Select the table, right-click, and choose Design Table. The Design Table dialog box loads (see Figure 17-3) and gives you access to the columns.
3. Select the column to take the default value and enter the value in Default Value list (under Description). Click the Save button on the toolbar (the first one), and close the dialog box.

The DMO object model provides similar access to the default property, but you will encounter the same difficulty in accessing the default objects in code.

The following points about default constraints should be taken into account:

- The default mechanism is only activated on the INSERT statement (see Chapter 20).
- You can obviously only have one default to a column; there is no way of specifying a member of a default collection.
- The default cannot be used on identity columns or on timestamp columns.

Check Constraints

The *check* constraint is useful because a single constraint definition can be applied to more than one column. You can also define as many check constraints as you need. For example, if you want to ensure that data for a telephone number is inserted or updated as (XXX) XXX-XXX, you can create a check to prevent a value of any other form from being committed to the database.

The first action to take in defining checks is to list the check requirements and definitions in your integrity plan as described earlier. A check constraints list might contain the following items:

- Telephone and fax numbers must be formatted (XXX) XXX-XXX
- Social Security numbers must be formatted XXX-XX-XXXX
- Invalid states for UPS ground are Hawaii and Alaska

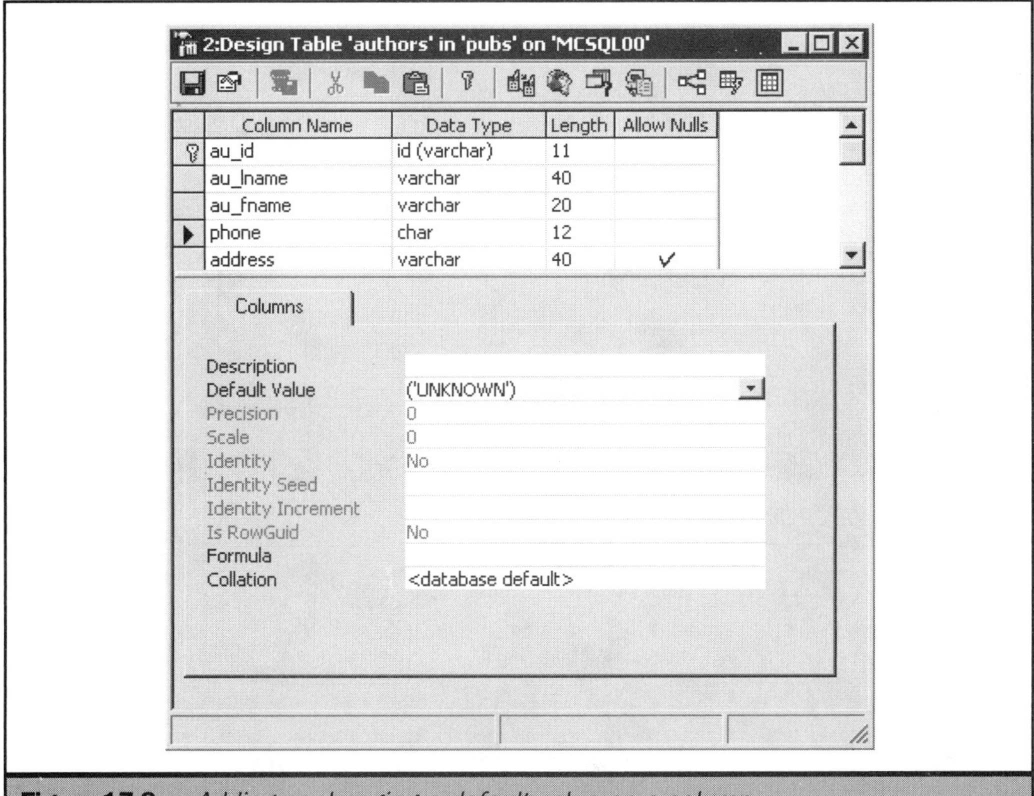

Figure 17-3. *Adding or changing a default value on a column.*

You can attach a check constraint in a database diagram (see Chapters 7 and 11) or the table designer as follows:

1. Open the Design Table dialog box as described earlier and select the table for the check described in your plan.
2. Go to the toolbar and select the Manage Constraints button (the last one). Note the three buttons at the far right of the toolbox on this console: These relate to the application of indexing, integrity, and constraints. Each button represents a different tab in this dialog box. When you click one of these three buttons, the Properties dialog box loads, as illustrated in Figure 17-3.
3. The Properties dialog box loads with the Check Constraints tab open, as illustrated in Figure 17-4.

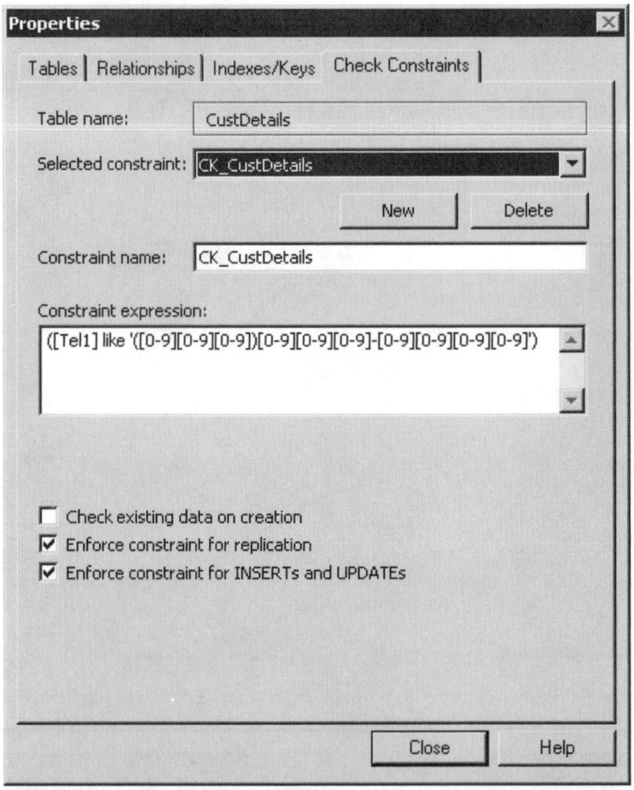

Figure 17-4. *Adding a check constraint using Design Table in Enterprise Manager*

4. Click New to create a new check constraint. Enter the check code in the constraint expression window. (You cannot check the expression syntax in this dialog box and you will not be able to close the dialog, and thus save the check expression, if the code is incorrect. You might consider building the code in QA first and testing it as T-SQL script, which for many architects, including me, is much slicker than fiddling in this dialog box.) If the expression works, click the Save button on the toolbar and close the table designer.

The following code applies the preceding check constraints:

```
ALTER TABLE Customers
ADD CONSTRAINT phones CHECK (phone_no
LIKE '(XXX) XXX-XXX'
```

and

```
ALTER TABLE Users
ADD CONSTRAINT socials CHECK (SSN
LIKE 'XXX-XX-XXXX'
```

and

```
ALTER TABLE Orders
ADD CONSTRAINT CK_states CHECK
(State <> 'Hawaii'
```

If you were just setting out to create the preceding Orders table you might script in the constraint at the same time. The following creates the Orders table and then applies the constraint at the table level:

```
CREATE TABLE Orders
    (State varchar(40) NOT NULL,
     Shipper varchar(40) NOT NULL,
     CONSTRAINT CK_states CHECK (State NOT IN ('Hawaii', 'Alaska')))
```

The T-SQL syntax is rich and so you can code for sophisticated expressions for the preceding checks and the other constraint objects. The preceding code added another U.S. state to check for in the constraint CK_states demonstrated earlier. The code obviates the need to add a second check for Alaska to keep it out of the UPS ground column in my table. Instead I used a comma-separated list and the expression tells SQL Server that *either* Hawaii *or* Alaska are *not* allowed in the column. I repeated the list technique in the ALTER TABLE statement as follows:

```
ALTER TABLE Orders
ADD CONSTRAINT CK_states CHECK
  (State NOT IN ('Hawaii', 'Alaska'))
```

The following rules governing check constraints should be kept in mind:

- They only fire on INSERT and UPDATE actions.
- They can reference more than one column in a table, in the check expression.
- They cannot be used on identity columns, timestamp columns, and unique identifier columns.
- The check expressions cannot contain subqueries.
- You can attach as many constraints as you like to a column or collection of columns.
- You do not necessarily have to include the keyword CONSTRAINT in your code, but I would do so for clarity.

- You do not need to provide a name for the constraint. Knowing SQL Server's affinity for inventing names that look and sound like ancient Greek, however, I prefer to use a naming convention that makes it easier to read the code and document our team's solutions.

Otherwise, enjoy them.

Note *Check constraints enforce domain integrity and I recommend you install them whenever necessary to keep garbage out of the database and ensure the integrity of the database. Using check constraints without regard for the client environment is a bad idea, especially in Internet applications where people connect through their Web browsers because all manner of badly formatted strings, formats, and contradictory values will come flying at SQL Server, causing it to balk and flame the client, which causes network roundtrips and a degradation of resources. You should use client or middle-tier constraint mechanisms to avoid this, such as masked edit fields, allowable values lists, and so on wherever you can, leaving SQL Server as the last line of defense.*

Foreign Keys

If you examine the T-SQL CREATE TABLE and ALTER TABLE syntax, you will see that you can create the foreign key (FK) constraints to enforce and ensure referential integrity and cascading updates when you create the table. Also note that they can be created and managed when you alter tables and their columns.

When you create the keys remember the following rules:

- The foreign key must reference a primary key or a unique key in the partner tables.
- Foreign keys do not automatically create indexes.
- Permissions apply, so you need to ensure that users have SELECT and DRI permissions enabled on the tables (this is discussed in detail in Chapter 7 and Chapter 11, and code examples working with permission are provided in Chapter 21).

The following code adds a foreign key constraint to the ShipTo table in my Customers database, which I called "FK_ShipTo_CustDetails," and the constraint references the CustDetails table:

```
ALTER TABLE [dbo].[ShipTo] ADD CONSTRAINT [FK_ShipTo_CustDetails]
FOREIGN KEY
        ([CustID]) REFERENCES [CustDetails] ([CustID])
         ON DELETE CASCADE  ON UPDATE CASCADE
```

In this code, when I update or delete the row in the CustDetails table, the constraint ensures the ShipTo table's corresponding row is likewise deleted (referential integrity) or updated.

To create the constraint in Enterprise Manager, do the following:

1. Open the table designer and click the Manage Relationships button on the toolbar. The Properties dialog box loads to the Relationships tab, as shown in Figure 17-5.
2. Select the corresponding columns that represent the primary and foreign keys.
3. Select the options such as the cascades, deletes, and updates.
4. Change the name of the constraint, if you need to, and then close the dialog box.
5. Click the Save button on the toolbar to commit the changes to the table.

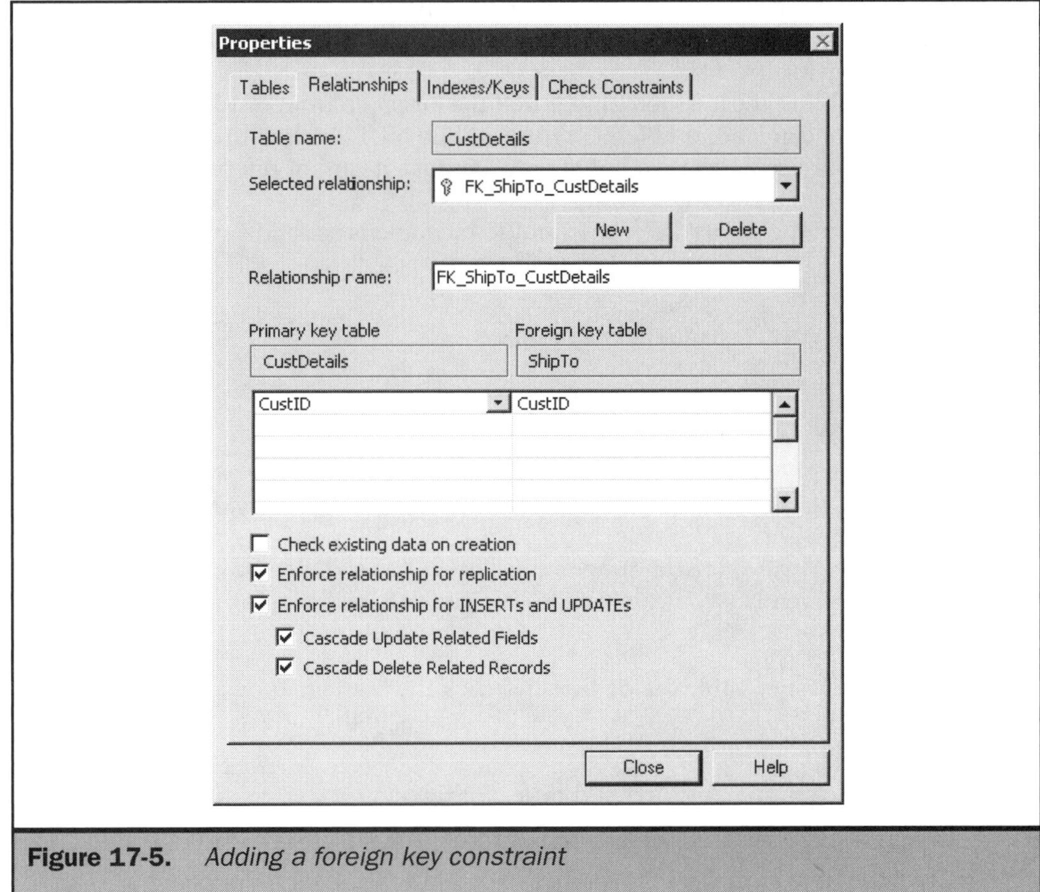

Figure 17-5. *Adding a foreign key constraint*

Primary and Foreign Keys

As discussed earlier, entity integrity ensures that rows in a table are unique. The tools to use to enforce uniqueness are the Primary Key constraints (PK), the Unique Key constraints (FK), and the identity property (discussed in Chapters 11 and 16). The primary and unique keys are also referenced in referential integrity constraints.

The primary key was discussed in depth in Chapter 3 and again in Chapter 11, so I will not go over it again here.

If you examine the CREATE TABLE and ALTER TABLE syntax, you will see that you can create the primary key when you create the table and that they can be created and managed when you alter the table and its columns.

When working with the ALTER TABLE statement, you need to remember that you can only have one primary key in a table. In other words, there can only be one column that is the beneficiary of a primary key.

While you can modify the primary key interactively with the graphical tools, such as Enterprise Manager, you have to delete the key and then recreate it in T-SQL. The ALTER TABLE statement can only be used to drop or add a primary key to the table, not to alter the key itself.

Also, when adding the key, remember that the target column must have no duplicate data, nor can it accept NULL values. While NULL values are hardly duplicates, SQL Server doesn't see it that way, because it cannot reference a unique value if the value is technically missing.

The code to add a primary key constraint to the table is as follows:

```
ALTER TABLE [dbo].[CustDetails]
  ADD CONSTRAINT [PK_CustDetails]
  PRIMARY KEY NONCLUSTERED
    ([CustID])
```

Chapter 11 also looks at the CREATE TABLE statement in more depth and highlights the differences between table-level definitions and column-level definitions.

To add a primary key constraint open the Design Table dialog box and take the following steps (remember you can also do this in a database diagram as discussed in Chapter 11):

1. Open the Design Table dialog box and click the Manage Indexes/Keys button on the toolbar. The Properties dialog box opens to the Indexes/Keys tab as illustrated in Figure 17-6.
2. Select the column name and sort order for the key.
3. Select the options to be used by SQL Server on the primary key clustering.
4. Click the Save button on the toolbar to commit the changes to the table.

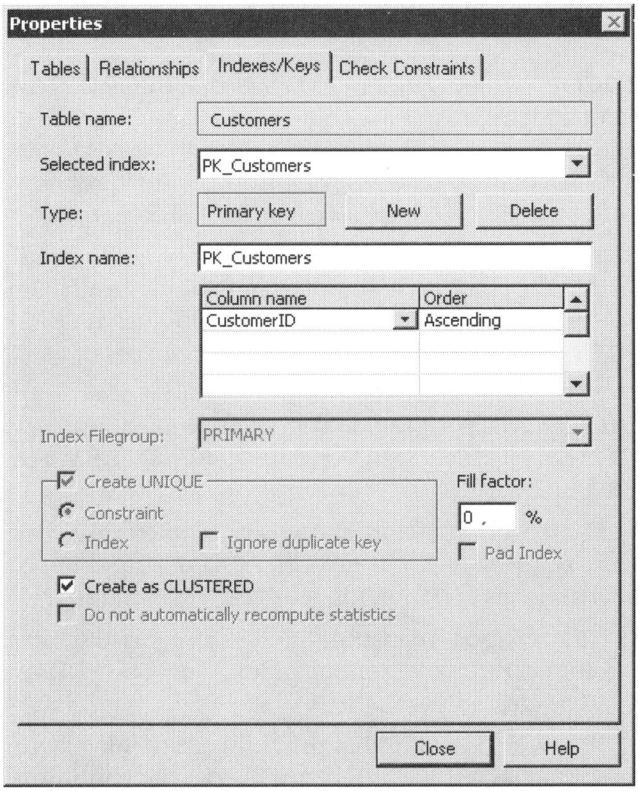

Figure 17-6. *Adding primary key constraints*

Unique keys, or unique key constraints, are very similar in function to primary keys; but the difference is that the unique key can be used to generate a non-clustered index and can live in a table that already has a primary key installed on another column. The unique key can be created in T-SQL and Enterprise Manager (or the DMO object model).

The Constraints Syntax

This section has been provided to help you better understanding the CONSTRAINTS section in the CREATE TABLE or ALTER TABLE statements and explains all the constraint options. The constraints as documented for CREATE TABLE or ALTER TABLE are as follows:

- **ROWGUIDCOL** This argument indicates that the new column can hold globally unique identifiers. It is a constraint because only one such *uniqueidentifier* column (set as such) per table can be designated as the ROWGUIDCOL column. (The ROWGUIDCOL keyword, however, is not applicable if you are using databases from SQL Server 6.5 or earlier).

  The ROWGUIDCOL property, however, does not enforce uniqueness of the values stored in the column. It also does not automatically generate values for new rows inserted into the table. To generate unique values for each column, either use the NEWID function on INSERT statements or use the NEWID function as the default for the column.
- **CONSTRAINT** This is an optional keyword indicating the beginning of a PRIMARY KEY, NOT NULL, UNIQUE, FOREIGN KEY, or CHECK constraint definition.
- **NULL | NOT NULL** These are keywords that determine if null values are allowed in the column. NULL is not strictly a constraint but can be specified in the same manner as NOT NULL, which is a constraint.
- **PRIMARY KEY** This is a constraint that enforces entity integrity for a given column or columns through a unique index. Only one PRIMARY KEY constraint can be created per table.
- **UNIQUE** This is a constraint that provides entity integrity for a given column or columns through a unique index. A table can have multiple UNIQUE constraints.
- **CLUSTERED | NONCLUSTERED** These are keywords to indicate that a clustered or nonclustered index is created for the PRIMARY KEY or UNIQUE constraint. PRIMARY KEY constraints default to CLUSTERED, and UNIQUE constraints default to NONCLUSTERED.

  You can specify CLUSTERED for only one constraint in a CREATE TABLE statement. If you specify CLUSTERED for a UNIQUE constraint and also specify a PRIMARY KEY constraint, the PRIMARY KEY defaults to NONCLUSTERED.
- **FOREIGN KEY...REFERENCES** These are constraints that provide referential integrity for the data in the column or columns. FOREIGN KEY constraints require that each value in the column exists in the corresponding referenced column(s) in the referenced table. FOREIGN KEY constraints can reference only columns that are PRIMARY KEY or UNIQUE constraints in the referenced table.

- **ON DELETE {CASCADE | NO ACTION}** These arguments specify what action takes place in a row in the table created, if that row has a referential relationship and the referenced row is deleted from the parent table. The default is NO ACTION.

  If CASCADE is specified, a row is deleted from the referencing table if that row is deleted from the parent table. If NO ACTION is specified, SQL Server raises an error and the delete action on the row in the parent table is rolled back (see Chapter 21, where this constraint is further discussed).

  On the other hand, if NO ACTION is specified, SQL Server raises an error and rolls back the delete action on the Customers row if there is at least one row in the Orders table that references it.
- **ON UPDATE {CASCADE | NO ACTION}** This argument specifies what action takes place in a row in the table created, if that row has a referential relationship and the referenced row is updated in the parent table. The default is NO ACTION.

  If CASCADE is specified, the row is updated in the referencing table if that row is updated in the parent table. If NO ACTION is specified, SQL Server raises an error and the update action on the row in the parent table is rolled back.

  If NO ACTION is specified, SQL Server raises an error and rolls back the update action on the Customers row if there is at least one row in the Orders table that references it.
- **CHECK** This is a constraint that enforces domain integrity by limiting the possible values that can be entered into a column or columns.
- **NOT FOR REPLICATION** This is not really a constraint but an "anti-constraint" that is important for integrity consideration. The argument is used to prevent the CHECK constraint from being enforced during the distribution process used by replication. When tables are subscribers to a replication publication, do not update the subscription table directly; instead update the publishing table and let replication distribute the data back to the subscribing table.

  A CHECK constraint can be defined on the subscription table to prevent users from modifying it. Unless the NOT FOR REPLICATION clause is added, however, the CHECK constraint also prevents the replication process from distributing modifications from the publishing table to the subscribing table. The NOT FOR REPLICATION clause means the constraint is enforced on user modifications but not on the replication process.

The NOT FOR REPLICATION CHECK constraint is applied to both the before and after images of an updated record to prevent records from being added to or deleted from the replicated range. All deletes and inserts are checked; if they fall within the replicated range, they are rejected.

When this constraint is used with an identity column, SQL Server allows the table not to have its identity column values reseeded when a replication user updates the identity column. See also Chapter 10 for more specifics regarding replication between SQL Server instances.

In Review

Data integrity is probably the most important subject discussed in this book, which is the reason I devoted this chapter entirely to integrity. Configuring and managing the integrity can also consume a lot of your time and can be stressful. I recommend you fully document your integrity issues and requirements in a document akin to the integrity plan I provide in this chapter. The document can then be circulated among the business's managers for input, and it will become your working document detailing all data integrity efforts.

The subject of data integrity has also been covered in the following chapters: Chapter 7 describes working with constraints, albeit superficially, in Enterprise Manager; Chapter 11 discusses integrity and the constraints in managing databases and working with the table designer and database diagrams; Chapter 15 demonstrates how to script the constraint code from the object browser; and Chapter 21 provides some advanced programming instruction related to integrity.

The Complete Reference

Chapter 18

Stored Procedures and Triggers

The next quest in meeting the optimum performance data processing requirements discussed in Chapter 14 and the integrity and business rule compliance requirements discussed in the preceding chapter is to master the art of creating and managing stored procedures and triggers. I say it is an art because both objects in SQL Server 2000 require some creative juices on your part and quite a bit of that brain power.

Stored procedures and triggers are very closely related. They are programmed T-SQL, and both are objects that are attached to your databases. When it boils down to what you can do with either object, it pays to rather list what you cannot do, and then the rest is up to your imagination.

Note *The SQL-DMO object model provides objects for creation, editing and management of triggers and stored procedures. It is, however, more important for you to master these elements in T-SQL, using Query Analyzer.*

While the code in a trigger can be identical in function to the code of a stored procedure, the major difference between the two is that the trigger is connected to a table or view object, while a stored procedure is exposed as a database object and has to be explicitly called, like a function, and be passed parameters. If you think of your table or view as an object, which you should be doing, then think of the trigger as an event (like OnClick) that fires when an inbound DML statement "triggers" the table or the view.

Triggers are central to ensuring integrity and business rule adherence procedurally, while stored procedures are central to providing functionality and business services and functions on a broad scale. How each object is used and created will now be covered in its respective section. Because triggers are the easier of the two constructs to grasp, and because they follow up our treatise on integrity in the previous chapter, let's start with them first. By the way, we'll also discuss some of the new features of triggers in SQL Server 2000, and I'll point these out as we progress. I am also going to demonstrate more code in the QA debugger, and point out some cool features that will make your hair stand up.

Triggers

The SQL Server 2000 trigger is secondary to the primary built-in mechanisms for enforcing business rules and data integrity of any application or enterprise requirement, as we discussed in the previous chapter. A trigger, however, is a lot more than a constraint check or a rule; it packs a lot more punch.

A trigger can do a lot. For all intents and purposes, it is a stored procedure that in itself is a full-blown SQL statement or batch that can query tables, calculate, evaluate, communicate and provide complex functionality. SQL Server relates to a trigger in the same way it relates to an in-line SQL statement that comes down the TDS wire. Triggers are treated as single transactions, which means that if they create an undesirable result, they can be rolled back (see Chapter 21).

Triggers are used in the following situations:

As cascades: Triggers can be used to cascade events and changes through related tables in a database. A good example is the manual cascade deletes or updates we would program in triggers on earlier versions of SQL Server before these wishes became de facto features in SQL Server 2000. In many cases, cascading triggers can be used in data integrity or business rule requirements. You should, however, only consider this if the built-in cascade features and declarative integrity functions do not supply the desired end result or don't exist. Naturally the built-in stuff is more efficient (referential integrity is a good example of a constraint effort that would be wasted in a trigger).

As checks (and then some): Triggers can do the work of the check constraints we discussed in Chapter 17, but when you need more bang for your buck, triggers come to take the lead. A trigger, created as a super-constraint, is essentially a check constraint on steroids. You can reference columns in other tables (which you can't do on a check definition). You can conjure up a result set out of a trigger and then run through the result check to analyze inserted or modified data. Triggers can also talk to your users, fire off e-mail, or wake the DBA in the middle of the night. However, while constraints are proactive "filters" so to speak, triggers are reactive processes. Even the INSTEAD OF trigger fires in reaction to the DML statement sent to SQL Server.

As rule enforcers: Like badgers to honey, the existence of a database will *invariably* tempt users to attempt contradictory data access procedures on your data. Some users may just do things that the developer or DBA did not expect, while others may attempt to access the database in ways contrary to corporate or organization rules . . . and in many cases with criminal intent. A trigger can be used to ensure that a certain action cannot be attempted on a table. For example, an attempt to retrieve all credit card numbers from a table can be blocked in a trigger. The trigger can also send out alerts and even capture connection information and perform certain auditing functions. (Auditing, of course, even C2 level, is now fully built in, as we discussed in the chapter on security, Chapter 8.) And because you can install multiple triggers on a table, you can pretty much take care of any situation that is contrary to both business rules and change control procedures.

As an evaluation mechanism: You can use a trigger to evaluate the state of your data before and after a DML statement does its work on a table or view. If the state is not up to par or compliance, then a trigger can be used to fill in the "missing links" or take some corrective action, such as rolling back, without requiring additional user input. Here's a drastic, but entirely possible, sequence of events a trigger can initiate:

```
CREATE TRIGGER Self_Destruct
  ON SwissCashAccounts
    FOR UPDATE
    AS
      IF Update(IntentToSteal)
        EXEC master..xp_sendmail 'Users,' 'This server will self-destruct
        in five seconds'
     WAITFOR DELAY '00:00:05'
     EXEC vaporize_server
```

An important attribute of triggers is that they have a long reach. While checks and rules are limited to tables in the current database, a trigger can reference beyond its parent table to other tables and other databases. But all good things have their limitations.

The Nuances of Triggers

DML statements, as opposed to row or column events, fire triggers. Rows and columns are the level on which integrity constraints operate, and integrity constraints *usually* fire before triggers on actual manipulation of the data. This means you have a general rule of thumb to follow, as alluded to in the previous chapter, that when you need a broader scope of integrity-checking, triggers are the way to go. At a more granular level, the built-in integrity constraints are what you use. The two constructs have very clearly defined "fields of coverage" so to speak. *Usually* was put in italics because there is a new trigger that fires before constraints, even before the DRI constraints.

The T-SQL statements listed here are not allowed in trigger code:

- ALTER DATABASE
- CREATE DATABASE
- DROP DATABASE
- LOAD DATABASE
- RESTORE DATABASE
- DISK INIT
- DISK RESIZE
- RECONFIGURE
- LOAD LOG
- RESTORE LOG

While you can use SELECT statements in a trigger and generate result set returns, the client connections that fire the trigger usually have no means of interpreting or working with the returned data. You should accordingly avoid returning results by avoiding open SELECT statements in trigger code. By "open" I mean that the result set is not assigned to an internal structure. In addition, you should use SET NOCOUNT at the beginning of the trigger to obviate the return of any data to the client connection. You should also refrain from using cursors in triggers, because overuse can be a drain on server resources. In any event, you should be working with rowset functionality if you need to work with multiple rows in trigger code (see the discussion of cursors in Chapter 19).

Also, keep in mind that during a TRUNCATE TABLE operation (which is a delete en masse that empties a table by deallocating the table's data pages), trigger firing is suppressed. This applies to the database owner and should not be a concern of users. And the WRITETEXT statement does not activate a trigger.

Trigger Execution Types

A new feature in SQL Server 2000 is the capability to determine when a trigger executes. In addition to the FOR clause (FOR INSERT, FOR UPDATE, or FOR DELETE), you can define two execution types for a trigger as follows:

AFTER: This trigger is fired only after the statement that fired it completes. This is the default for SQL Server 2000 (it was not called an AFTER trigger in SQL Server 7.0 or earlier). On an UPDATE statement, for example, the trigger will be activated only *after* the UPDATE statement has completed (and the data has been modified). If the DML statement fails, the AFTER trigger is never fired. You can have multiple AFTER triggers on a table (views are not supported, by the way) and list the triggers in an order of execution (see "Managing Triggers" later in this chapter). (By-the-by, AFTER triggers are never executed if a constraint violation arises.)

INSTEAD OF: This trigger is fired instead of the actual triggering action. For example, if an UPDATE arrives on the wire and an INSTEAD OF trigger is defined, the UPDATE is never executed but the trigger statement is executed instead. By contrast with its AFTER sibling, you can define an INSTEAD OF trigger for either a table or a view. INSTEAD OF triggers have much application, but one of the fanciest features is the capability to update view data, which are not normally updatable. As explained in the next chapter, it is not a simple matter to just obtain a fresh view of data using a view that has been around for a while.

Although the INSTEAD OF triggers are fired *instead* of the DML statement sent to the server, they fire before anything else, including any constraints that may have been defined (which is a big difference between the INSTEAD OF trigger and the AFTER trigger). The triggers are also not recalled, because SQL Server checks for recursion that might develop as the result of the actions the trigger itself takes on the table. In other words, it is certainly possible to create a trigger that practically replaces exactly what the original DML had intended to do to the table or view. It thus seems logical that the trigger would cause itself to be refired; but this unintended recursion is dampened.

Tip *While trigger overhead is very low, a time may come that you need to squeeze every drop of bandwidth out of your application. It thus makes sense to write trigger code within a trigger, such as flow-control logic (IF, CASE), that checks if the trigger really needs to run its course. For example, an INSTEAD OF trigger might check the underlying table state before it performs anything, and exit out if it determines the entire statement is not required. Also, if the constraint can be catered to using the check constraints described in Chapter 17, go with those because they incur much less overhead than triggers for simple integrity constraints.*

The Trigger Plan

Like the integrity plan described in the previous chapter, a *trigger plan* is another important section of your overall database definition, model, or architecture. A trigger plan should also reflect the stages of trigger deployment and provide a checklist to ensure that all factors affecting triggers and affected by triggers have been taken into consideration. You can use the flow diagram in Figure 18-1 to build your trigger plan.

Gather Business Rules and Motivation for Triggers

Identify the business rules that can be best addressed by triggers. This section of database plan identifies business rules that will impact the database model and architecture. Sit down with the people responsible for establishing the business rules and determine how best to cater to their needs using triggers.

Identify Key Trigger Issues to Cover

Issues to be catered to by triggers must be referenced or become part of the database architecture. If you are the DBA but do not write triggers, or if you are assigning the trigger writing to SQL Server developers or third parties, then it is important to list key issues that will impact the development plan. For example, note how you plan to maintain triggers. While most trigger code is straight up and down, a need may arise for the creation of a complex trigger, and the code needs to be documented and maintained and protected like all source code. Trigger code can also be dangerous if it falls into the wrong hands. And if you decide that encrypting the code is an option, then you need to be sure the source code is stored in a backup system, in documentation, or in source files that are secured.

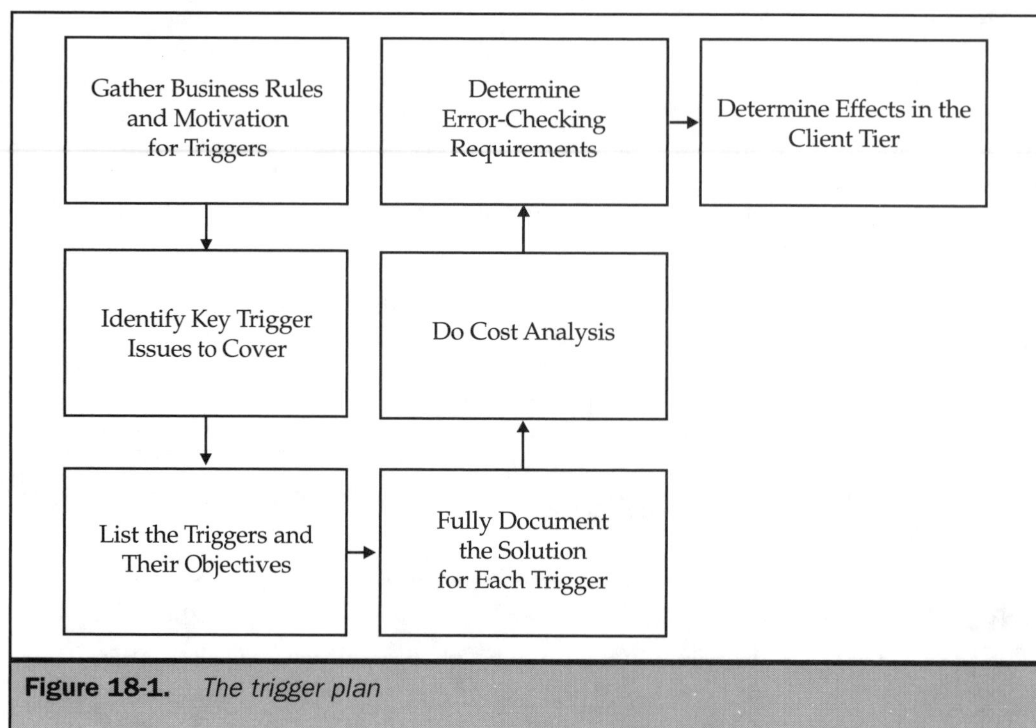

Figure 18-1. *The trigger plan*

List the Triggers and Their Objectives

In this section, list the precise objective of each trigger you need to create. As with constraints and stored procedures, an extensive system of triggers can hold a lot of trigger objects, and it will not take long for you lose track of what triggers are installed where and for what reason. This problem is further compounded by an order of magnitude when more than one trigger is installed or defined for a table, or when you create a trigger cascade or nest.

Fully Document the Solution for Each Trigger

Once you have written a trigger or a collection of triggers, then each trigger, including the actual trigger code and the trigger's relation to other triggers, constraints, checks, and stored procs, should be fully documented. This should not only help you see the trigger trees for the trigger forest but help you pinpoint areas that could use improvement.

Most important, trigger documentation—both externally in supporting documents and internally using inline comments—can help other parties read your code. The documentation will also help you debug problems. Remember that triggers are regarded as transactions, so documenting them as such will allow you to debug and recover from problems created by rogue triggers. It is not normal to have a trigger go nuts on you and do substantial damage, but when I started out writing triggers, I once created a cascading delete that cascaded my entire database down the drain. To this day I am not sure how it happened, but it did.

In addition to documenting the solution arrived at for the trigger, it is also imperative to fully document the progress being made on the trigger or triggers under assignment. Some triggers may be extensive, and many may require the trigger writer to be supervised over several weeks or even on a permanent basis. To put it in more direct terms, you should not regard the management of a trigger or T-SQL project, in terms of managing the software creation process, as any different from a C++ or VB project.

Do Cost Analysis

There are also costs attached to every trigger. As in the case of constraints, the costs are both direct, in terms of their consumption of SQL Server resources and usefulness, and indirect, in terms of the costs of programming, maintenance, documentation, and so on.

As mentioned in connection with the integrity plan, triggers are procedural and their code cannot be guaranteed by SQL Server to be ANSI compliant or even safe. SQL Server can check code for errors, but it is not able to check trigger code for standards compliance on behalf of the trigger author or warn you that you are about to take unpaid permanent leave from your very fine DBA job.

Cost analysis of triggers should also cater to resource costs, and you should thus thoroughly test trigger code in the Query Analyzer (execution plans) and in the profiler (see Chapters 12 and 15).

Determine Error Checking Requirements

Determine a system for checking errors that materialize from trigger code. Errors can be directly caused by triggers, or they can result from the correct trigger execution with unpredictable or unintended results. Investigate the feasibility of deploying an error database, something like a bug recording system, that records error messages that derive from both triggers and stored procedures. If you follow the advice dispensed in Chapter 14 and move either all or a substantial part of the processing to SQL Server, this is an essential practice.

You can also set up logging in the profiler and enable C2 security to track who does what and when they did it. But the profiler does not cater to errors that occur in T-SQL code and that create problems with the database or the data.

Determine Effects in the Client Tier

Understanding the effects in the client tier or what reporting and alerting is required at the client is important. What we do in the data tier can affect the client tier, especially if the client processes have been implemented in a middle tier. If you still need to maintain legacy client code, which means client-side data processing and logic, trigger implementation and especially stored procedure implementation can have unpredictable results, and these need to be considered.

Creating Triggers

Triggers, like most SQL Server objects, are created using T-SQL code, Enterprise Manager, and the SQL-DMO triggers collection. Depending on your needs, the SQL-DMO object model provides an alternative to T-SQL, and a very useful one at that. For the most part, however, the typical path to trigger creation and management is via T-SQL, so whip out your Query Analyzer, or whatever tool you use to write and test T-SQL code, and get cracking.

Trigger Deployment

Deploying a trigger requires more than just writing the code and assigning the trigger to a table or view and then crossing your fingers that your landing gear is down. This is engineering, so you need to approach this as an engineer. The following steps, illustrated in the flow chart in Figure 18-2, document the process of trigger creation and deployment from beginning to end. Create your own deployment plan, which can act as a checklist that will take you from concept to deployment in a logical, well-controlled manner. I do trigger work for a number of clients, and thus each one has a file and trigger deployment plan for one or more triggers (and the overall trigger plan).

Step 1: Obtain trigger requirements The requirement specs are obtained from the trigger plan. Your system may be large enough to warrant formal trigger assignment, as would large OLTP or e-commerce systems that will require several developers working on the project.

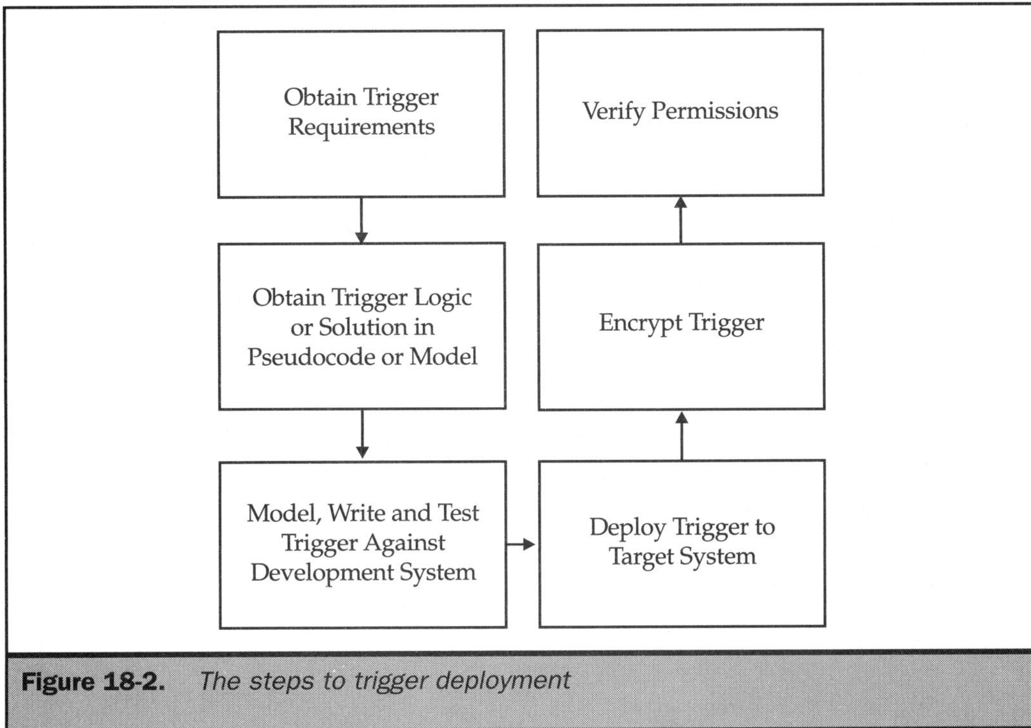

Figure 18-2. *The steps to trigger deployment*

The following specification is an example of a trigger requirement on a call center application that logs the date and time and agent connects to SQL Server on a number of tables. I could use the logging capability of the profiler, but the output is difficult to work with from the viewpoint of the call center equipment, such as the ACD scheduler that needs to have information about the CSR's open case load, and from the call center analyst who needs to export the data to decision support systems.

- **CSR Shift Log AFTER Trigger** Record the date and time the agent initially logs on to SQL Server and runs Open-Shift. The Open-Shift session gets the agent oriented, reviews shift objectives, considers past shift performance, and so on. The trigger also records the Close-Shift data . . . the date and time when the agent has concluded Close-Shift and logs off the system. The trigger can only be fired when the OpenCloseShift table is accessed, so the information records when the CSR logged into the CRM application and when the agent logged off the CRM application. The data allows the call center manager to monitor shift duration and (not shown here) check how long agents are spending in Open-Shift and Close-Shift sessions.

- **Check Credit INSTEAD OF Trigger** Check the credit rating of the client. If the credit rating is green, allow the CSR to take the order on account. If the credit rating is red, the CSR must advise the caller that only money order or credit card can be accepted. The trigger can then return call center scripting (by calling a procedure) that the CSR can read back to the caller.

Step 2: Craft trigger logic or solution in pseudocode This may be done in any custom or preferred pseudocode. The idea is to outline the trigger and sketch the scope and flow of the trigger.

In the CSR shift log specification above, the pseudocode could be as follows:

```
Get CSR name from Windows security
Function get datetime
Strip datetime into two values representing a date and the time
Write CSR name, date, and time to record
```

The check credit INSTEAD OF pseudocode could be as follows:

```
On open customer record
Query customer credit rating color
If red then restrict to cash
If green then allow to account
```

Step 3: Model, write and test trigger against development system Once all pseudocode is written and you have cross-checked it with IS managers, supervisors, or yourself, the stage is set for modeling and writing the trigger in T-SQL, testing against the development system, checking the performance of the trigger (especially under load), and so on. The next section goes into the actual trigger code.

Step 4: Deploy trigger to target system This step entails installing the trigger (the job of a DBA) to the target system if your processes have been approved by quality assurance and your trigger testing program. You can copy objects to the production system or script out the code for execution against the target system from Query Analyzer as discussed in Chapter 15.

Step 5: Encrypt Trigger Encrypt your trigger in the development system. This is obviously not essential, but it is advisable if the systems might come under attack or cannot be secured. One of my projects entails installing SQL Server in a number of data centers spread throughout the United States where I cannot guarantee that the servers are off-limits or that they are safe from access by unauthorized use of Enterprise Manager or the Query Analyzer.

Step 6: Verify Permissions You do not install permissions on triggers per se, but you need to verify that users on the connections that fire the triggers have permission either to query the table or to insert, update, or delete from it. This also applies to permissions on a view on which INSTEAD OF triggers are installed. This stage of your trigger deployment plan is critical. When I first started out installing triggers, I was so concerned with the actual trigger and how impressed my clients would be that, after testing it with my super-DBA/Developer rights, I forgot to make sure the users would be able to access the tables on the production system.

Creating a Trigger Using T-SQL and Query Analyzer

The principal T-SQL statement is CREATE TRIGGER, as follows (the full explanation and usage of the arguments are documented in SQL Server Books Online):

```
CREATE TRIGGER trigger_name
ON { table | view }
[ WITH ENCRYPTION ]
{
    { { FOR | AFTER | INSTEAD OF }
        { [ DELETE ] [ , ] [ INSERT ] [ , ] [ UPDATE ] }
        [ WITH APPEND ]
        [ NOT FOR REPLICATION ]
        AS
        T-SQL statement code
    }
    |
    { ( FOR | AFTER | INSTEAD OF ) { [ INSERT ] [ , ] [ UPDATE ] }
        [ WITH APPEND ]
        [ NOT FOR REPLICATION ]
        AS
        { IF UPDATE ( column )
            [ { AND | OR } UPDATE ( column ) ]
                [ ...n ]
        | IF ( COLUMNS_UPDATED ( ) { bitwise_operator }
updated_bitmask )
                { comparison_operator } column_bitmask [ ...n ]
        }
        T-SQL statement code
    }
}
```

You need to provide each trigger with a name and define it for a particular table or view in a database. You also have the option of encrypting the trigger so that no one (not even you, ever) can look at the original code. Triggers are secured with permissions (see Chapter 8) so that only you, the trigger creator, can alter or drop the trigger.

After you have specified which table or view is to be the "beneficiary" of the trigger , you need to define the trigger as an AFTER or INSTEAD OF trigger. This specification may seem a little late in the syntax because you cannot define an AFTER trigger for a view.

Another important argument, NOT FOR REPLICATION, has serious implications in distributed database scenarios. This argument specifies that the trigger should not be executed when replication is the cause of table manipulation (see the chapter that covers replication, Chapter 10).

Following the AFTER or INSTEAD OF argument, you must specify the DML event the trigger fires on. This can be either DELETE, INSERT, and UPDATE. Finally, following the AS keyword, you enter the segment of T-SQL code to be executed every time the DML statement lands on the table or view. So your basic create trigger statement will look something like the following:

```
CREATE TRIGGER myTrigger
  ON Employees
    FOR AFTER, INSERT, UPDATE
AS RAISERROR (500289, 16, 10)
```

This same trigger code specified as an AFTER or INSTEAD OF trigger would look like this in its most basic form:

```
CREATE TRIGGER myTrigger
  ON Employees
    INSTEAD OF INSERT, UPDATE, DELETE
AS . . .
```

Creating and Testing the Trigger in Query Analyzer

To create a trigger in Query Analyzer, click the Templates tab in the Objects Browser and right-click. Select Open as illustrated in Figure 18-3. The CREATE TRIGGER template opens into an editing window. (If you want to add header and revision information you can edit the template and install new template parameters, as discussed in Chapter 15.)

Write and test your trigger here to a development system or table. When you are ready to install the trigger to a table, all you need to do is execute the query.

To alter the trigger at any time, you can drill down to the trigger object in Query Analyzer as follows:

1. Find the database and table on the instance of SQL Server. Expand the Tables node and select the table on which the trigger is installed.
2. Expand that Table node and then expand the Triggers node to expose the trigger. This is demonstrated in Figure 18-4 (triggers are stored under the table node).
3. Right-click the trigger to alter and choose Edit from the context menu. You can also select the option Script Object to New Window As depending on what action you want to take on the trigger. The Script Object to New Window As Alter option does the same thing as Edit.

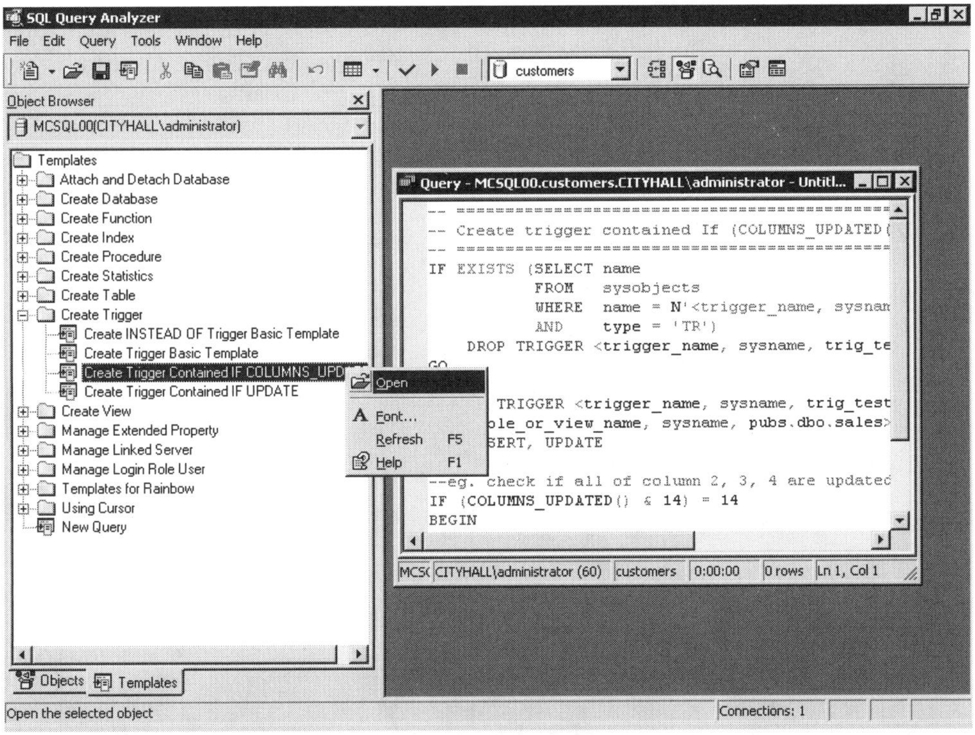

Figure 18-3. *The Create Trigger templates in Query Analyzer*

4. The trigger code under and ALTER TRIGGER statement opens to an editing window. Notice from the illustration that QA inserts a version comment into the script.

To replace the old trigger with the new one simply execute the query.

You can step through trigger code in the stored procedure debugger, which I discuss later in this chapter.

Creating a Trigger Using Enterprise Manager

To create a trigger using Enterprise Manager, do as follows:

1. Drill down to the database in which your table or view resides.

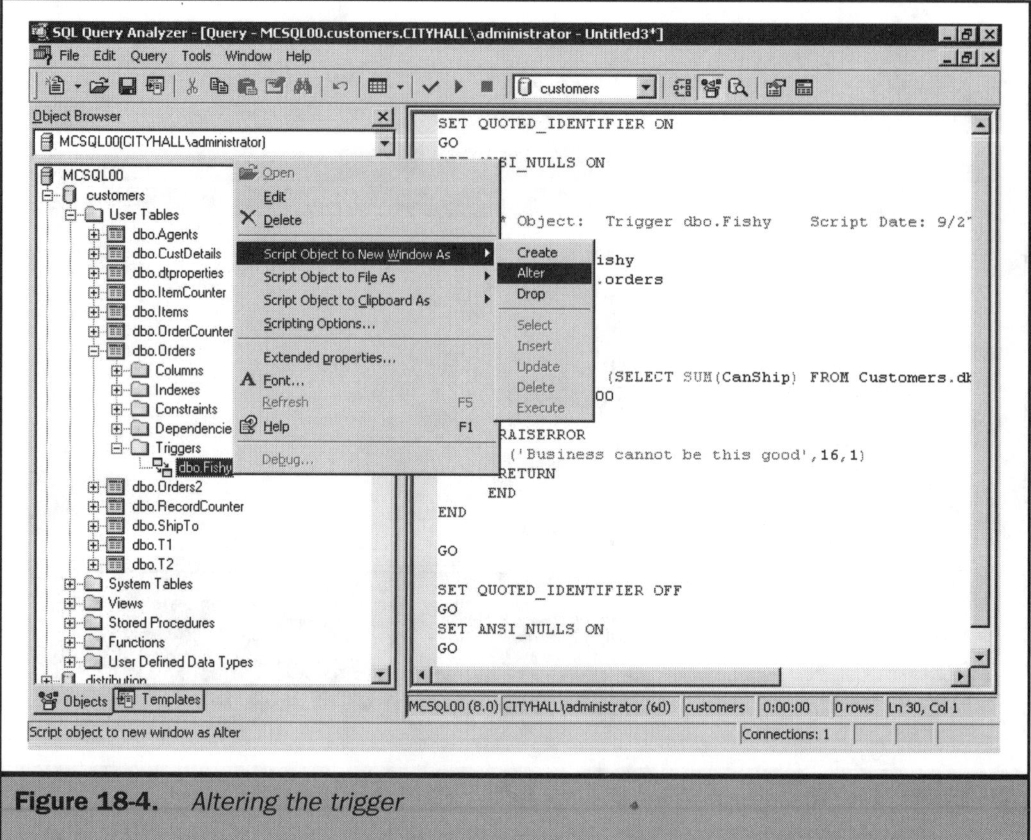

Figure 18-4. *Altering the trigger*

2. Expand the database node and click on the Tables node. The list of tables appears in the details pane to the right of the database tree. Click a table, right-click, and select All Tasks (you do not need to select any specific table). Then select the option Manage Triggers. The dialog box as illustrated in Figure 18-5 loads.
3. In the Name drop-down list box, click <new> to create a new trigger. If this is the first trigger, <new> will be the only item in the list.
4. Enter the trigger code in the Text box. You can use TAB to indent the code.
5. Check the syntax of the trigger by clicking the Check Syntax button.
6. Click Apply to save the trigger. The trigger can now be referenced by name in the Name drop-down list box.

To create and manage triggers on views, simply select the Manager Trigger menu option in the Views pane.

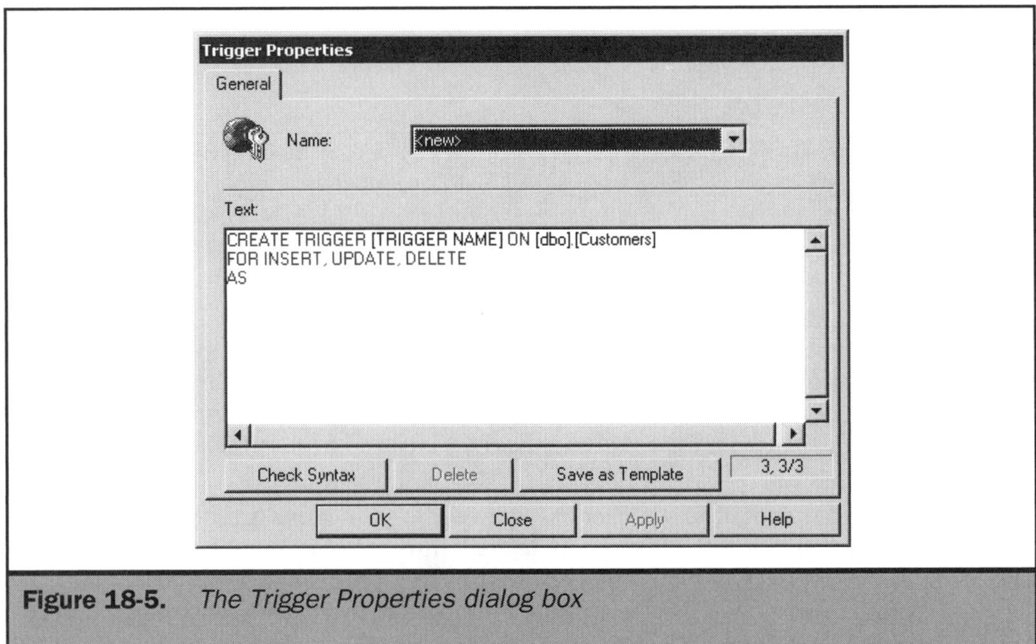

Figure 18-5. *The Trigger Properties dialog box*

Creating a trigger in Enterprise Manager has limited value because you still have to enter the code and check its syntax. You might as well work in Query Analyzer, coming up next, and after making sure your trigger code works, run the query to install the trigger.

Programming the Trigger

It is a good idea, as mentioned earlier, to apply conditional or evaluation logic to your trigger, and if necessary prevent certain operations from being run by the trigger if there is no longer a need for the trigger to complete. For example, there might not be a need to complete a trigger statement after an update, if nothing was updated.

You can use the UPDATE(*column_name*) and COLUMNS_UPDATED() statements respectively to check for the completion of updates that apply to certain columns.

You can use the IF UPDATE(*column_name*) clause in your trigger code to determine if the DML (INSERT or UPDATE) statement that fired the trigger, or an earlier one, actually made any changes to write home about. This function will return true if indeed the column was assigned a value. The IF UPDATE() trigger will look like this:

```
CREATE TRIGGER myTrigger
 ON myTable
 FOR INSERT
```

```
   AS IF UPDATE(x)
   EXEC master..xp_sendmail 'Jshapiro,' 'Column x updated'
```

Or you can use the IF COLUMNS_UPDATED() clause to check which columns in a table were updated by an INSERT or UPDATE statement. This clause makes use of an integer bitmask to specify the columns to test. And the COLUMN_UPDATED() trigger looks like this:

```
CREATE TRIGGER myTrigger
 ON myTable
 FOR INSERT
  AS IF (COLUMN_UPDATED() & 1 = 1)
  EXEC master..xp_sendmail 'Jshapiro,' 'Column x updated'
```

Unfortunately, a limitation of either of the preceding functions is that it cannot test to see if a specific value in a field has been deleted; thus neither function will return any result on a delete statement. However, you can check for row deletion using the @@ROWCOUNT function, which returns the number or rows affected by the last query.

The function @@ROWCOUNT returns the number or rows that were deleted as @@ROWCOUNT = X. Thus you can test for rows and make flow choices based on the results (see the stored procedure example in the next section). If, for example, the row count returns 0, you could exit the trigger or take some other action. If the row count is greater than 0, you could switch to a different code segment or even use a GOTO and code in a series of GOTO labels.

The Examples

Let's now look at a trigger from an actual deployment plan in which the business owner required being alerted to unusual sales activity:

```
/*
Script Name: Something Fishy
Description: Trigger to report unusually high sales
Usage: Placed on customers.dbo.orders for canship
Return Code: N/A
Author: Jeffrey R. Shapiro
Version: 1.00
Date Created: 9/25/2000
Revision History:
*/

IF EXISTS (SELECT name FROM sysobjects
```

```
   WHERE  name = N'Fishy'
   AND type = 'TR')
         DROP TRIGGER Fishy
GO

CREATE TRIGGER Fishy
ON customers.dbo.orders
FOR UPDATE
AS
BEGIN
  DECLARE @Qty int
   SELECT @Qty = (SELECT SUM(CanShip) FROM Customers.dbo.Orders)
   IF @Qty > 10000
     BEGIN
        EXEC master..xp_sendmail 'JeffreyS',
        'Business cannot be this good,
        there is something fishy going on'
      RETURN
     END
END
GO
```


As a second example, make use of the RAISERROR message function. As discussed in Chapter 16 the RAISERROR is similar to the message dialog facility in the Win32 API, which has been exposed (or wrapped) by every major language capable of producing Windows applications. If you look at RAISERROR in Chapter 16 or Books Online you will see that it can take first a message string or a message ID which can get returned to the client. You can also add as parameters severity levels and replacement parameters. The replacement parameter placeholder in the function is that old familiar %d visiting T-SQL from the C language, as demonstrated next.

In the following example the trigger code tests for the number of items scheduled for shipping and if it is over 10,000 units an error message or alert is committed to the Windows NT/2000 application log by using the WITH LOG option. In addition I have also added the SET NOCOUNT line, which will ensure that the trigger does not return the "n rows affected" message to the user. The trigger code will not modify any rows, but SET NOCOUNT will suppress anything that might slip in when later versions of this trigger are installed.

```
ALTER TRIGGER Fishy
ON customers.dbo.orders
FOR UPDATE
AS
BEGIN
```

```
SET NOCOUNT ON
DECLARE @Qty int
   SELECT @Qty = (SELECT SUM(CanShip) FROM Customers.dbo.Orders)
   IF @Qty > 10000
     BEGIN
       RAISERROR('Total CanShip items has exceeded %d.',18,1,@Qty)
        WITH LOG
       RETURN
     END
END

GO
SET QUOTED_IDENTIFIER OFF
GO
SET ANSI_NULLS ON
GO
```

Deferred Name Resolution

You can create triggers at design time, and you are not forced to specify a table or view that already exists. (Obviously, the trigger will not fire, because the table or view object does not yet exist.) This is called *deferred name resolution.* If you are working at a database compatibility level of 6.*x* (referenced as 60 or 65), a warning will be issued when you attempt create the trigger.

First and Last Triggers

If you deploy a large collection of AFTER triggers on a specific table, you can specify which of the triggers is the first AFTER trigger and which is last AFTER trigger. This essentially allows you to create a "list" of triggers with a start and an end, and all other AFTER triggers will fall in between.

You should clearly understand, however, that the feature allows you to define a first or last attribute on a trigger *after* each DML event that fires triggers. In other words, you can specify for *TableX* that trigger *triggerA* is *first after* the FOR INSERT event, that *triggerB* is *first after* the FOR UPDATE event, and that *triggerC* is *last after* the FOR DELETE event.

There are some nuances to the application of the first/last attributes you should be aware of the following:

- The first AFTER trigger cannot be the last AFTER trigger as well.
- The triggers between first and last are not executed according to any order.
- The first and last triggers must be fired by DML statements (INSERT, UPDATE, and DELETE).
- INSTEAD OF triggers are not supported by the first/last feature.

- If you alter a first or last trigger, its status as first or last is dropped.
- Replicated tables will define a first trigger automatically for any table that is an immediate or queued update subscriber. In other words, the replication trigger will be positioned as the first trigger, regardless of any other trigger attributed as a first trigger, and if you try to reassign the first manually, after configuring for update subscription, SQL Server will generate an error.
- If you use an INSTEAD OF trigger on a table, it will fire before any updates on the base table fire the AFTER triggers.
- Also, if you define an INSTEAD OF trigger on a view, and that trigger updates a base table that has AFTER triggers defined, these triggers will fire before any manipulation on the base table takes place as a result of the INSTEAD OF trigger fired at the view level.

You use the sp_settriggerorder stored procedure to specify the first and last attributes for an AFTER trigger. The options that are available are as follows:

- **First** This makes an AFTER trigger the first trigger fired *after* a fire event.
- **Last** This makes an AFTER trigger the last trigger fired *after* a fire event.
- **None** This cancels the first or last attribute on a trigger. Use *None* to reset the trigger to fire in any order.

The following example demonstrates the use of the trigger positioning stored proc:

```
sp_settriggerorder @triggername = 'myTrigger', @order = 'first'
```

Trigger Recursion

SQL Server 2000 provides a feature known as *recursive invocation*. Recursion can thus be invoked on two levels, *indirect recursion* and *direct recursion*. The two types permit the following behaviors:

- **Indirect** A statement triggers *TableA, Trigger1*, which causes an event that fires *TableB, Trigger1. TableB, Trigger1* then causes *TableA, Trigger1* to fire again.
- **Direct** A statement triggers *TableA, Trigger1*, which causes an event that fires *TableA, Trigger2. TableA, Trigger2* then causes *TableA, Trigger1* to fire again.

The recursion types can work for or against you and can break your code. You can set direct recursion off using the sp_dboption stored procedure, but that will leave indirect recursion enabled, which you may want. To disable both recursion types, you need to use sp_configure.

Trigger Nesting

Triggers can be nested (in an arrangement also described as a trigger cascade). In other words, a trigger on *tableA* can update *tableB* that fires a trigger on *TableC* that fires a trigger on TableD that . . . . SQL Server will prevent a chain of triggers from forming an infinite loop, and you cannot nest to more than 32 levels.

You can also disable nested trigger execution, on a server-wide basis, using the sp_configure stored procedure. The default is that trigger nesting is allowed. Nesting and recursion are controlled by the same argument in sp_configure, so if you turn off nesting, recursion goes as well, and vice versa; this is regardless of the setting you have used in the recursion attribute set by sp_dboption, discussed in the section on recursion. Trigger nesting also terminates if any trigger executes a ROLLBACK TRANSACTION statement.

You can also manage the nesting behavior of triggers from Enterprise Manager or from the SQL-DMO object model. To manage trigger nesting in EM, do as follows:

- Expand a server in the server group to manage, right-click, and then choose Properties. The SQL Server Properties (Configure) dialog box loads.
- Click the Server Setting tab shown in Figure 18-6 and select or clear the long-winded option "Allow triggers to be fired which fire other triggers (nested triggers)" check box.

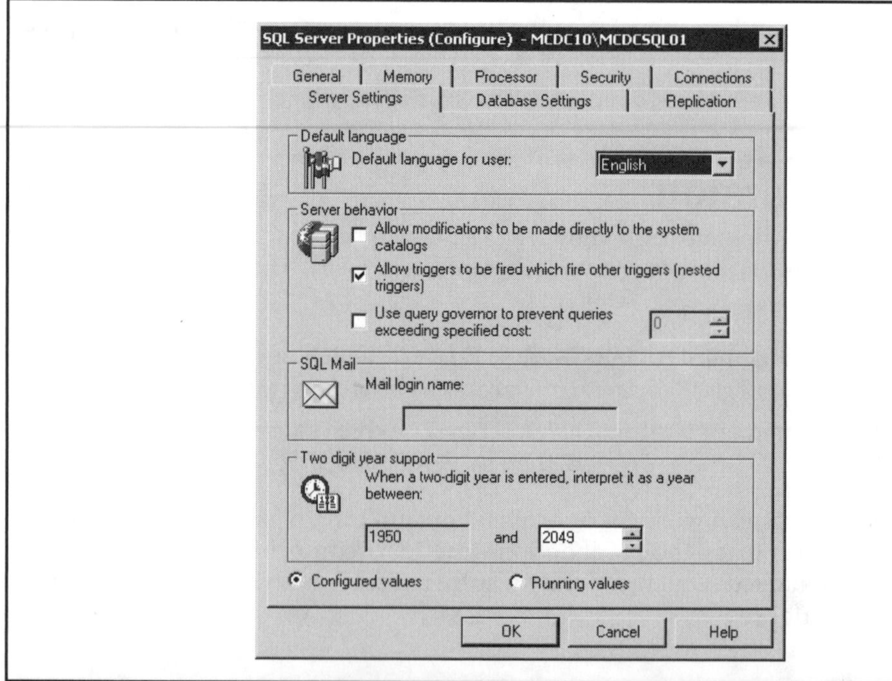

Figure 18-6. *SQL server properties*

Rolling Back Trigger Transactions

You will recall that earlier in this chapter I advised that SQL Server treats the code in a trigger as a transaction. This means that you can undo the statements that are enclosed in the trigger transaction code. It is important to understand that when you issue a ROLLBACK TRANSACTION, as demonstrated in the following code, the entire batch in the trigger is reversed out. Also, you do not necessarily need to call ROLLBACK TRANSACTION if you are relying only on SQL Server to trap an error. SQL Server automatically reverses any transaction it determines to be fatal.

```
CREATE TRIGGER VoiceMessageDelete ON Messages
FOR DELETE
 AS IF EXISTS
   (SELECT delete FROM Messages m INNER JOIN conference c
      ON m.message_no = c.message_no )
 BEGIN      RAISERROR ('Message cannot be deleted until heard by
      all conference members', 10, 1)
      ROLLBACK TRANSACTION
 END
```


Managing Triggers

Triggers are a powerful and essential attribute of any DBMS, but they can be a headache to manage, especially when you have a lot of them. For this reason you will want to architect triggers in a modeling system and provide access to trigger metadata (see Chapter 5). The following sections explain how to alter and drop triggers using either T-SQL or Enterprise Manager.

Altering Triggers

To alter a trigger in T-SQL, you need to use the ALTER TRIGGER statement. The basic statement is as follows:

```
ALTER TRIGGER trigger_name
ON . . . .
```

Query Analyzer adds the alter trigger code automatically the first time you open the trigger code for editing.

The code to apply after the ON line takes the same syntax and choice of arguments as the CREATE TRIGGER statement described earlier (see the SQL Server 2000 Books Online for the full explanation and usage of the arguments).

To alter a trigger in Enterprise Manager, follow the steps described earlier for creating a trigger in Enterprise Manager and edit your trigger accordingly.

Dropping Triggers

Dropping a trigger in T-SQL requires the DROP TRIGGER statement followed by the trigger name. Consider, for example, the following code:

```
USE MYDB
IF EXISTS (SELECT name FROM sysobjects
   WHERE name = 'SecurityViolation' AND type = 'TR')
DROP TRIGGER SecurityViolation
```

It drops the trigger SecurityViolation from MYDB.

You can specify multiple triggers in a DROP TRIGGER statement by separating trigger names with commas and enclosing the list in square brackets, as here:

```
DROP TRIGGER [x, y, z].
```

You should make sure to check for trigger dependencies with the sp_depends stored procedure before dropping a trigger.

To drop a trigger interactively in Enterprise Manager, simply drill down to the tables in your database and launch the Manage Triggers dialog box as described in the earlier section on creating triggers in Enterprise Manager. From this dialog box, you can select the trigger from the drop-down list and click the Delete button.

Getting Information about Triggers

To obtain information from SQL Server about the triggers installed on a table, you should execute the system stored procedure sp_helptrigger as follows:

```
--to check triggers installed on the table Items
EXEC sp_helptrigger Items
```

The sp_helptrigger procedurereturns information about the triggers on the table, the trigger owners, and the DML statements they are defined for. The full syntax of this stored procedure is as follows:

```
sp_helptrigger [ @tabname = ] 'table'
[ , [ @triggertype = ] 'type' ]
```

where the @triggertype option specifies the type of triggers you require information on. The result set returned from the procedure is listed is as follows:

trigger_name	Trigger_owner	isupdate	isdelete	Isinsert	isafter	Isinsteadof
MyTrigger	Dbo	1	1	1	0	1

Final Words on Triggers

The following is a short list of recommendations when using triggers:

1. Use triggers when necessary to enforce business rules and integrity not adequately handled by the built-in constraints.
2. Keep trigger code simple. If there is a lot you need to accomplish in a trigger, then consider breaking your code into more than one trigger, which is akin to how you write code in traditional programming environments such as VB, Delphi, and Java.
3. Be sure to check for excessive recursion.
4. Use NOCOUNT to suppress the "n rows affected" message returned to the connection. And don't leave result sets open or unassigned. Use them only for the benefit of the trigger, such as by using SELECT to find values or to compare values in multiple tables.
5. Minimize the use of ROLLBACK TRANSACTION.
6. If your triggers begin to look like general procedural code, requiring the return of result sets to clients, and functionality beyond integrity and enforcement of business rules, then you need to switch to a stored procedure.
7. Query Analyzer is the best place to create, edit and debug trigger code.

Stored Procedures

Stored procedures are the most important objects of a RDBMS, outside of the engines and the database tables. Stored procedures, and how a product like SQL Server 2000 supports them, are what make the product. How stored procedures are stored, compiled, optimized, and executed by a DBMS is what sets a DBMS apart from its competitors. Stored procedures help us meet the rules of deployment we discussed in Chapter 14.

If you are unfamiliar with the concept of a stored procedure, you will find that the following list sheds some light on these critical SQL Server features:

- Stored procedures are collections of Transact-SQL statements that can be referenced and executed by name from a client connection. They consist of functionality that executes remotely from the calling connection—the client—that is interested in exploiting the result of the remote execution.

- Stored procedures encapsulate repetitive tasks. Often in client applications a large number of SQL statements all do the same thing. One stored procedure that accepts variables from the client can satisfy more than one query at the client, executed concurrently or at different times. More than one client can call the same stored procedure. Variable parameters that identify columns and values can replace almost all query code at the client.
- Stored procedures share application logic and code. In this respect they have a *reuse* benefit similar to that of classes in object-oriented software.
- Stored procedures hide database schema and catalog details. When you query a database using client-side SQL code, you need to know specifics of the tables and columns you are querying. This exposes the schema to the client connection and the user, especially in Internet applications. The stored procedure does not allow the client to have the proverbial foot in the door. The only information the client or connection has is the procedure name to call. In this regard, stored procedures provide a layer of security because the client also needs appropriate permissions to execute the procedure.
- Stored procedures conserve network bandwidth and allow you to concentrate processing needs at the data tier, which can be appropriately scaled up or out as needed (see Chapter 13).
- Like functions, stored procedures return values and error messages. But they can also return result sets from server-side queries that can be further processed on the server before being sent to the client. The return values can be used to indicate success or failure of stored procedure functionality, and the status can be returned to the client or used to control the flow and scope of the procedure logic.
- Stored procedures are created using the CREATE PROCEDURE statement, edited or updated using the ALTER PROCEDURE statement, and executed by the client connections; they return the result to the clients. The flow chart in Figure 18-7 illustrates the life-cycle (abridged) of the stored procedure.

Database developers need intimate knowledge of the workings of stored procedures. For all intents and purposes, they are to the DBMS and its databases what classes are to languages like Java and C++. Stored procedures are not inherited, derived, or cloned, nor do they sport inherited properties, methods, and the like, but they share many other valuable attributes of object-based programming such as code isolation, reuse, and sharing (by both developers and users). You cannot build any form of effective application that relies on SQL Server, nor can you be an effective DBA, without having an intimate knowledge of how to code and manage stored procedures.

Types of Stored Procedures

The several types of stored procedure supported by SQL Server are as follows:

1. **System** The system stored procedures are built into SQL Server and cannot be altered or tampered with short of destroying the catalog. They provide information about the database schema, object names, constraints, data types, permissions, and so on. There are several collections of system stored procedures: the catalog stored procedures, SQL Server Agent stored procedures, replication stored procedures, and so on. The system stored procedures are discussed in their respective chapters and in Appendix A.
2. **Local** The local stored procedures, written by the DBA and SQL Server developer, are the focus of this chapter.
3. **Temporary** These provide the same or similar functionality as the local stored procedures discussed in this chapter, but as explained further a little later in this chapter, they only exist for the life of the connection.
4. **Remote** These stored procedures exist in remote servers and can be referenced by an originating server. These stored procedures are used in distributed applications.
5. **Extended** The extended stored procedures are similar in function to the local stored procedures but can reference functionality external to SQL Server, such as calling routines and functions in remote libraries and processes compiled, for example, in DLLs or object storehouses.

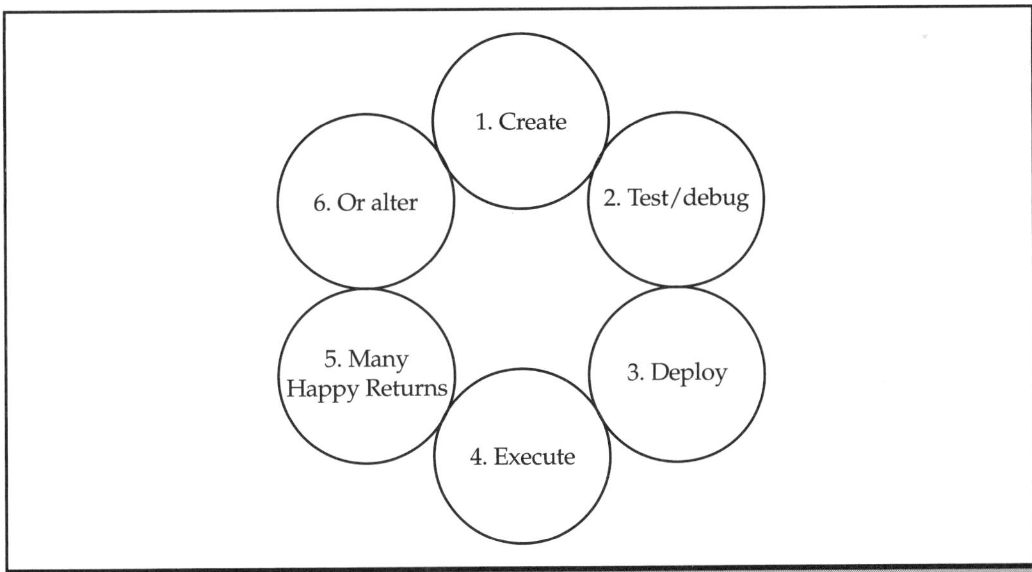

Figure 18-7. *The life cycle of a stored procedure*

How Stored Procedures Are Processed by SQL Server

Stored procedures are processed in two stages. In the first stage the procedure is first parsed by the SQL Server database engine (see Chapter 2) upon creation, after which two things happen. SQL Server stores the definition of the procedure, name and code, in the catalog. It also pushes the code through the Query Optimizer, as discussed in Chapters 4 and 21, and determines the best execution plan for the code.

Next the code is compiled and placed in the procedure cache. The only time the plan is flushed from the cache is when an explicit recompile is called by the client connection or the plan no longer exists in the cache, which means it had aged and had to be expelled. The cache can also be flushed via the DBCC freeproccache command discussed in Chapter 12.

In the second stage the query plan is retrieved when the stored procedure's name is referenced in code. The procedure code is then executed in the context of each connection that called the procedure. Any result sets or return values are returned to each connection.

The Nuances of Stored Procedures

Stored procedure code can vary from the most simple of DML statements to the most complex queries using flow-control, joins, calculations, and so on. However, the following nuances are important to keep in mind:

- Stored procedure names, like triggers, are stored in *sysobjects* and the code is stored in *syscomments.* To inspect the stored procedure code, execute sp_helptext in the parent database of the stored procedure. More on sp_helptext later.
- To check which objects are referenced by a stored procedure, execute sp_depends.
- The words PROCEDURE and PROC can be used interchangeably, and SQL Server recognizes both. The statement CREATE PROC, DROP PROC, and ALTER PROC are thus also valid.
- The following create statements cannot be used in a stored procedure: CREATE DEFAULT, CREATE PROCEDURE, CREATE TRIGGER, CREATE RULE, CREATE VIEW.
- You can create any other database object from a stored procedure and even reference it in the stored procedure, as long as you create it before you reference it. You can even reference temporary tables in a stored procedure.
- The maximum size of a stored procedure is 128 megabytes.
- The number of local variables in a stored procedure is limited by available memory.
- The maximum number of parameters in a stored procedure is 1,024.

- You cannot use remote stored procedures in remote transaction scenarios. If you execute a remote stored procedure, the transaction on the remote instance cannot be rolled back.
- Stored procedures can spawn stored procedures that can access any object created by the parent stored procedure. However, if you create a local temporary table, it only exists for the stored procedure that created it. If you exit the stored procedure, the temporary table is lost.

The Stored Procedure Plan

Your stored procedure plan is almost identical in objective and scope to the trigger plan discussed earlier. It should play as big a part, if not bigger, in the overall database architecture and modeling. If you have not gone over the trigger plan suggestions made earlier, or if you do not use a formal plan for the production of stored procedures, now is the time to adopt this practice. You can use the flow diagram in Figure 18-8 as a starting point to build your stored procedure plan. The steps in the plan are explained in the next sections.

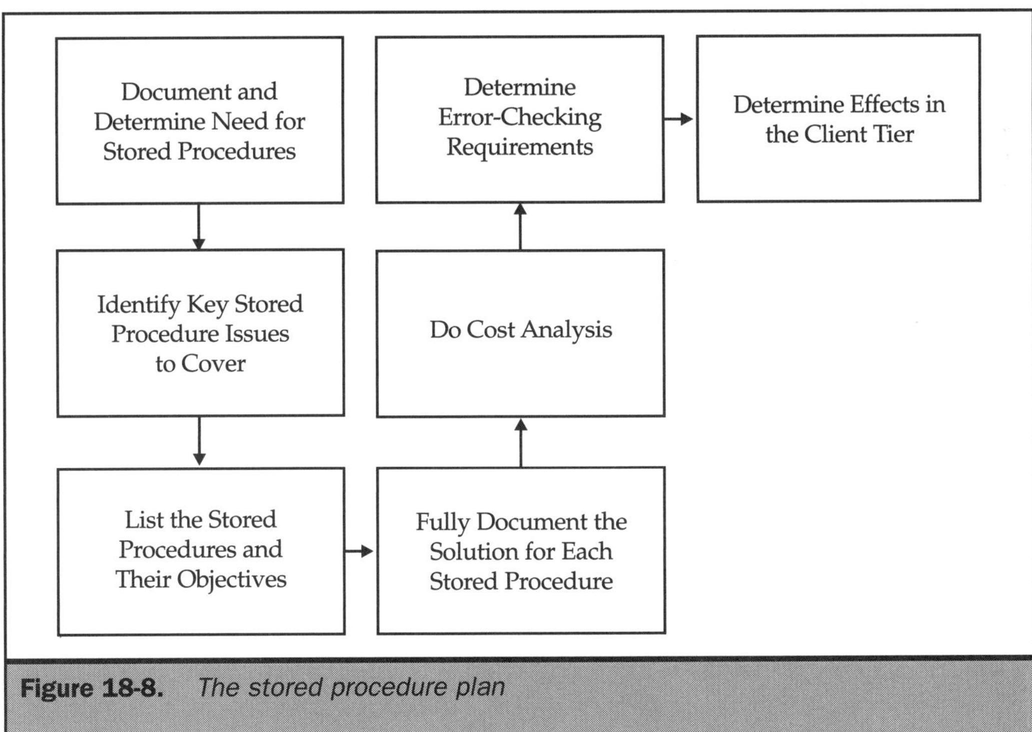

Figure 18-8. *The stored procedure plan*

Document and Determine Need for Stored Procedures

We have looked at some of the reasons to use stored procedures earlier and at length in Chapter 14. This is the section of your plan (especially if you are motivated to move away from a desktop solution like Microsoft Access) to list and discuss the needs and reasons.

Identify Key Stored Procedure Issues to Cover

The issues to be catered to by stored procedures, or the solutions to be obtained using stored procedures, must be referenced or become part of the database architecture. (In the trigger plan, I also listed a number of issues you should cover here, so go back and apply the points there to the stored procedure plan.)

One important area to address is the development tools you use to create and debug stored procedures. You can use Query Analyzer, which you probably will do to write, edit, debug and performance-test your code as described in Chapter 15 and later in this chapter. Query Analyzer for SQL Server 2000, however, still lacks some items on my wish list for a complete SQL Server developer environment, but I won't go into them here. A few third-party SQL Integrated Development Environments (IDEs) on the market are specifically suited to SQL Server. They are worthy tools for the DBA or SQL Server developer who writes a lot of stored procedures, and perhaps some very complex ones as well.

The following list provides an example of some stored procedure issues to consider in the stored procedure plan:

- Who will develop and maintain the code?
- Will we use encryption?
- What factors determine recompilation?
- How do we handle error messages and track bugs raised by the code?
- How will we monitor and assess performance and service level?
- When would we need to use an extended stored procedure, and who will create it?
- What development tools and debugging environment should we use?

List the Stored Procedures and Their Objectives

In this section, list the precise objective of each procedure you need to create. If you are converting legacy in-line SQL statements still buried in your client apps, a good way to start is to go through all the client procedures and copy the SQL statements from them. Paste each statement into a document, noting exactly where in the client code the statement is buried, and mark the statement for replacement by the stored procedure. Doing it this way can help you identify SQL statements in your code that are the same or similar and could thus make use of one stored procedure, or a variation of one or more.

In many cases, you will find that one stored procedure just needs new parameters and can be used to satisfy a number of areas in the client code. This exercise is rewarding because the code in the client application can drop dramatically. For example, a few dozen one-line EXEC PROC statements can reduce the number of code lines by several thousand.

Fully Document the Solution for Each Stored Procedure

This section is as important for stored procedures as triggers. If you have not read the trigger plan earlier and you intend to prepare a stored procedure plan, you should read the trigger plan first.

Do Cost Analysis

Stored procedures assume all the data processing overhead that was once dispersed among the clients, so a complex procedure that consumes a certain amount of processing overhead compounds the overhead for every connection associated with a procedure currently executing in the server. If you have not yet mastered the art of profiling your stored procedures and analyzing your queries, you should spend some time in Chapter 11 and Chapter 21 before embarking on an extensive stored procedure development effort.

Another cost of stored procedures is the indirect cost of adopting a new style and philosophy of programming. To obtain the data from your client that you send to the stored procedure, you will likely have to change the way your client does business with the user. Bound controls, for example, are history in many cases (you don't have them on the 'Net), and so you might have to add code in some places where data-bound controls have been excised. The following line of Java code is a good example of how you would code the assignment of data in place of a data-bound control, especially in middle-tier solutions.

```
String ProcParam1 = "Jeffrey"
String ProcParam2 = "Shapiro"
-or
String ProcParam1 = FNText.Text
String ProcParam2 = LNText.Text
```

Note *I cannot think of a better word than excise to describe getting rid of data-bound controls in a client application. Honestly, they were good in the early days of Delphi and VB, when the database engine squatted on your local PC like a warthog trapped in mud. With SQL Server solutions, they truly are a thing of the past. Since I have been working exclusively with SQL Server, I have removed all of my data-bound controls from my applications.*

Determine Error Checking Requirements

See the trigger plan discussed earlier for this section of the stored procedure plan. Error handling in stored procedures is also a lot more involved due to the code's inclination to say something to the client. I have thus discussed error handling in stored procedures in more detail later in this chapter.

Determine Effects in the Client Tier

One of the positive effects of getting rid of SQL code in the client tier is that you'll end up with clients that look a lot thinner than usual. Your code will also be cleaner and easier to document in the client. However, the downside is that the process of converting to a client/server system and adopting stored procedures can be long and involved. For example, you might make extensive use of ADO visual controls that need to have their recordset statements changed from SQL to stored procedure calls, and so on. I have simply dumped data-bound grids and the like and chosen to work only at the object level in ADO, pulling back a result set from a stored procedure and then looping the data up into a Microsoft FlexGrid or something similar.

To me, creating a stored procedure to replace a data-bound ADO grid is like guzzling a Bud on a hot August afternoon on Miami Beach. You'll likely have to spend a morning to code a complex procedure that returns the same data as the data-bound grid. But once you have tested the procedure in QA or whatever tool you use, seeing the data appear in a simple grid in the client is a wonderful feeling, knowing that all the client had to do was issue a single line of code to call the proc.

Creating Stored Procedures

Many companies employ SQL Server developers full time or as consultants to do nothing else but code stored procedures. No matter whether you are the IT Manager or a DBA in charge of a mob of "proc-programmers" or a one-person show responsible for everything, the stored procedure deployment plan is one of the most important plans discussed in this book.

Stored Procedure Deployment

The following steps, illustrated in the flow chart in Figure 18-9, document the process of stored procedure creation and deployment from beginning to end. Create your own deployment plan, which will be your checklist that will take you from concept to deployment in a logical, well-controlled manner.

Step 1: Obtain the stored procedure requirements The requirement specs are obtained from the stored procedure plan as discussed earlier. (Also see the section on trigger deployment plans discussed earlier in this chapter.)

The following specification is an example of a stored procedure requirement on an order taking system that debits stock items from the inventory or warehouse table and credits them to the customer's account.

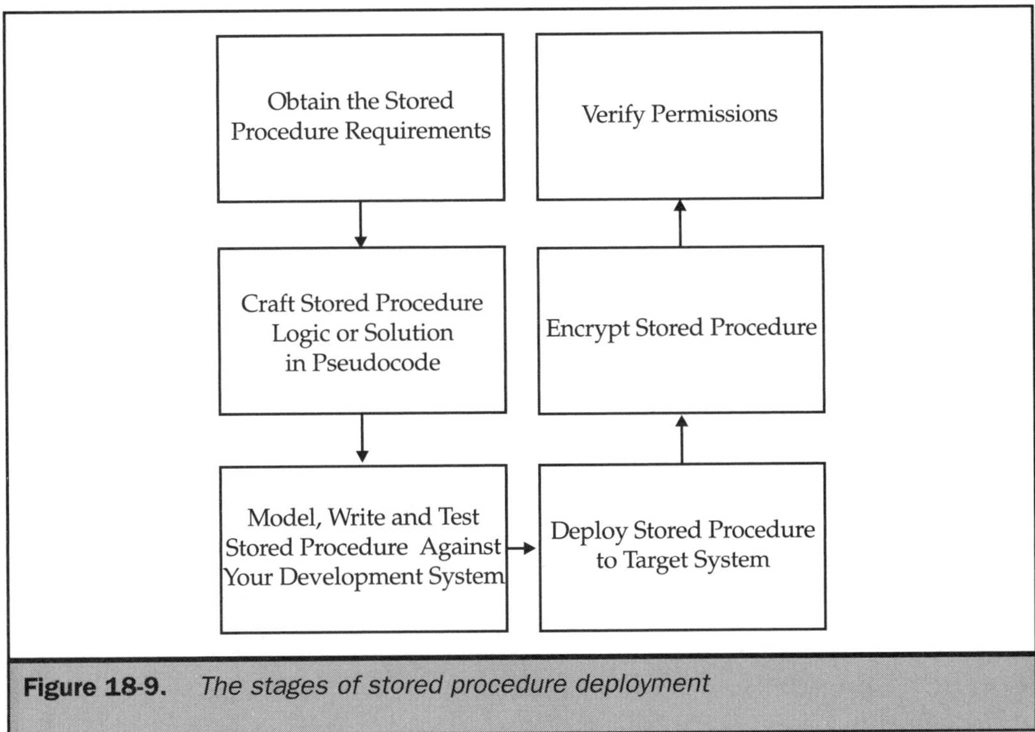

Figure 18-9. *The stages of stored procedure deployment*

Step 2: Craft stored procedure logic or solution in pseudocode You should work this section in the same fashion as described in the trigger section earlier. The idea is to sketch the scope, functionality, and final result of the procedure.

In the preceding example, the pseudocode could be as follows:

```
To follow
```

Step 3: Model, write, and test the stored procedure against your development system This work is done in Query Analyzer or the IDE of your choice (see Chapter 15). Before you begin code, however, stored procedures should be defined in a modeling language, which would aim to capture procedure-related meta data.

Step 4: Deploy the stored procedure to the target system Deployment of the stored procedure entails executing the CREATE PROCEDURE statement against the target system. You can also copy objects to the production system, as demonstrated in Chapter 7 and Chapter 11, or script out the code for execution against the target system from QA, as discussed in Chapter 15.

Step 5: Encrypt Stored Procedure The same motivation used to justify trigger encryption applies here. Just as with triggers, this step is done inside the CREATE PROCEDURE statement. You must not encrypt your trigger in the development system unless you have a separate and secure version of the source code elsewhere. The WITH ENCRYPTION clause in the CREATE PROCEDURE statement is like a loaded Uzi with the safety off. One slip and off goes your foot. Be sure that you are connected to the target product system to install and encrypt the procedure. More on encryption later in this chapter.

Step 6: Verify Permissions Permission verification is the last step you take before allowing users to obtain service from your stored procedure. Unlike with triggers, users must have direct permission to execute a stored procedure. This can be done in T-SQL code as explained in Chapter 16. It can also be done interactively in Enterprise Manager as discussed in Chapter 8.

However, the permissions issue does not stop with the right to call EXEC. You also need to verify that users on the connection that call the proc—either to query the table or to insert, update, or delete from it—have these DML permissions as well.

Creating a Store Procedure using T-SQL and Query Analyzer

You can use any of several methods to create stored procedures, and SQL Server 2000 also includes a stored procedure wizard. The principal method, of course, is to use the T-SQL statements CREATE PROC or CREATE PROCEDURE. You can also use the SQL-DMO object model to create, alter, and manage stored procedures.

To code and test stored procedures in T-SQL, you will use the Query Analyzer. The stored procedure's CREATE and ALTER templates are useful and will save you some coding time. The following syntax represents the CREATE PROC statement (the full explanation and usage of the arguments are documented in SQL Server Books Online):

```
CREATE PROC [ EDURE ] procedure_name [ ; number ]
[ { @parameter data_type }
[ VARYING ] [ = default ] [ OUTPUT ]
] [ ,...n ]

[ WITH
{ RECOMPILE | ENCRYPTION | RECOMPILE , ENCRYPTION } ]
[ FOR REPLICATION ]
AS T-SQL statements [ ...n ]
```

A stored procedure must be named. It is a good idea to name a stored procedure with the initials of the author, as in jrs_storedproc. However, you should not name your stored procedures using the sp_ prefix, because those are typically reserved for system, built-in, and user-defined stored procedures (see "Identifiers" in Chapter 16).

You can create one or more parameters in a stored procedure. The client in the execution statement that calls the stored procedure must supply the values for the parameters. If a stored procedure expecting a parameter value does not receive it, the stored procedure will fail and return an error. It is thus especially important when you code stored procedures that you handle all parameter errors properly. You can code flow-control statements, return codes, and the like, as long as errors raised in the stored procedure are properly handled.

Ownership Referencing Inside Stored Procedures

Object names get resolved when a stored procedure is executed. If you reference object names inside a stored procedure and do not reference the object by ownership (name qualification), the ownership defaults to the owner of the stored procedure, and the stored procedure is thus restricted to the stored procedure owner. In other words, only the owner gets to execute the procedure.

Also, objects referenced by DBCC, ALTER TABLE, CREATE TABLE, DROP TABLE, TRUNCATE TABLE, CREATE INDEX, DROP INDEX, and UPDATE STATISTICS must also be qualified with the object owner's name so that users can execute the stored procedure. If you create a stored procedure and do not reference any table objects in the stored procedure with qualified names, then access to the tables, during execution of the stored procedure, is restricted to the owner of the stored procedure (see how permissions affect this in Chapters 8, 11, and 12).

Encryption

As discussed in the trigger section and in the stored procedure deployment plan, you can hide the code of your stored procedure using encryption (by using the WITH ENCRYPTION clause) as you do when you create triggers. However, once the procedure is encrypted, there is no way to decrypt it; not even the SA account or an Administrator can do so. Encrypting the code is a good idea if the code you have defined in the stored procedure exposes highly sensitive data, as long as you keep a copy of the unencrypted code that only you can access. Although it has never happened to me, I did hear of someone who spent a month writing the mother of all procedures, then encrypted the code on the development system by mistake and before he made a copy of the final source.

Encryption is also useful for a turnkey product that ships with the SQL Server engine as the data store. Your product will then be in the hands of third parties, and you'll have no means of preventing them from checking out, tampering with, and even stealing the data store code. Encryption prevents all that. In fact if the product, such as a voice mail system, cannot operate without the data store, an encrypted stored procedure might obviate the need for one of those clumsy "dongles" you shove onto the parallel port to control access to the system, or prevent it from being pirated.

Grouping

You can create a group of stored procedures, each one having the same name to identify them as part of a group, by assigning each stored procedure in the group an identification number. Grouping the procedures like this allows you to maintain collections of stored procedures that pertain to a particular function or purpose. For example, I have a group of stored procedures that are all part of the accounts payable database as follows:

```
accpay;1
accpay;2
accpay;3
accpay;4…
```

Creating each member in the group is easy: Just specify the number of the individual procedure in your CREATE PROC code. Caveat? You cannot delete an individual. When you are done with the group, the statement DROP PROCEDURE destroys the whole group.

Creating, Testing, and Debugging a Stored Procedure in Query Analyzer

The steps you take to opening a CREATE PROCEDURE template or an ALTER PROCEDURE template are almost identical to what I described for triggers earlier, so forgive me if I don't repeat those steps here. Let's instead go directly to debugging the stored procedure in Query Analyzer.

Once the proc has been written and your syntax is clear of errors, the procedure code is ready to be observed in the debugger. As you step through the code you can see parameters change and statements executed without affecting underlying table data.

1. After right-clicking the procedure and selecting Debug from the context menu, the Debug Procedure dialog box loads to allow you to enter parameter values to test with. This is demonstrated in Figure 18-10. (Notice the checkbox Auto Roll Back; enable this to roll back all changes made to the data while debugging a stored procedure).
2. Close the Object Browser to expand the debugger to full screen. Notice the parameter values is the local values list in the left pane of the debugger. This is illustrated in Figure 18-11 which show the values that have been set before stepping into the code.
3. Step into the code and watch the execution of each statement in the transaction. Two tables are operated on in this procedure and both operations must complete or nothing must complete. So the code I am stepping through is enclosed in a transaction that I can rollback if I detect a failure anywhere in the transaction. (The full code of this stored procedure is listed later in this chapter in the section

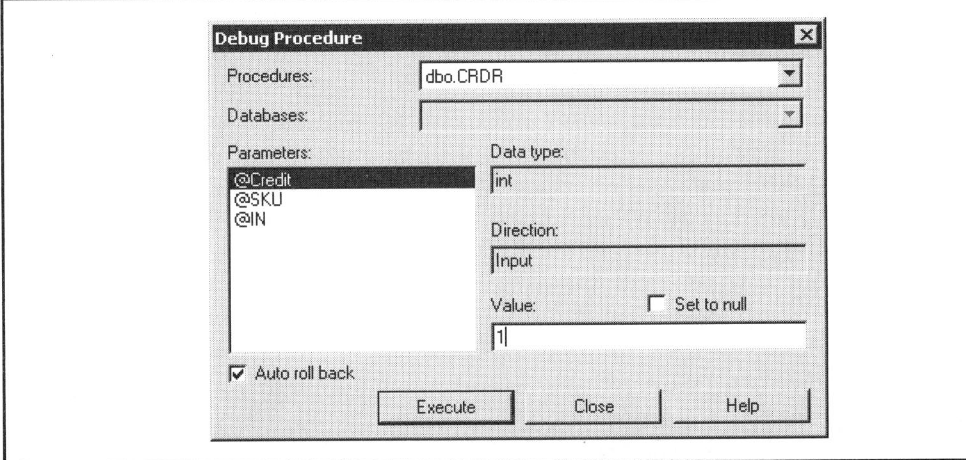

Figure 18-10. *The Debug Procedure dialog box*

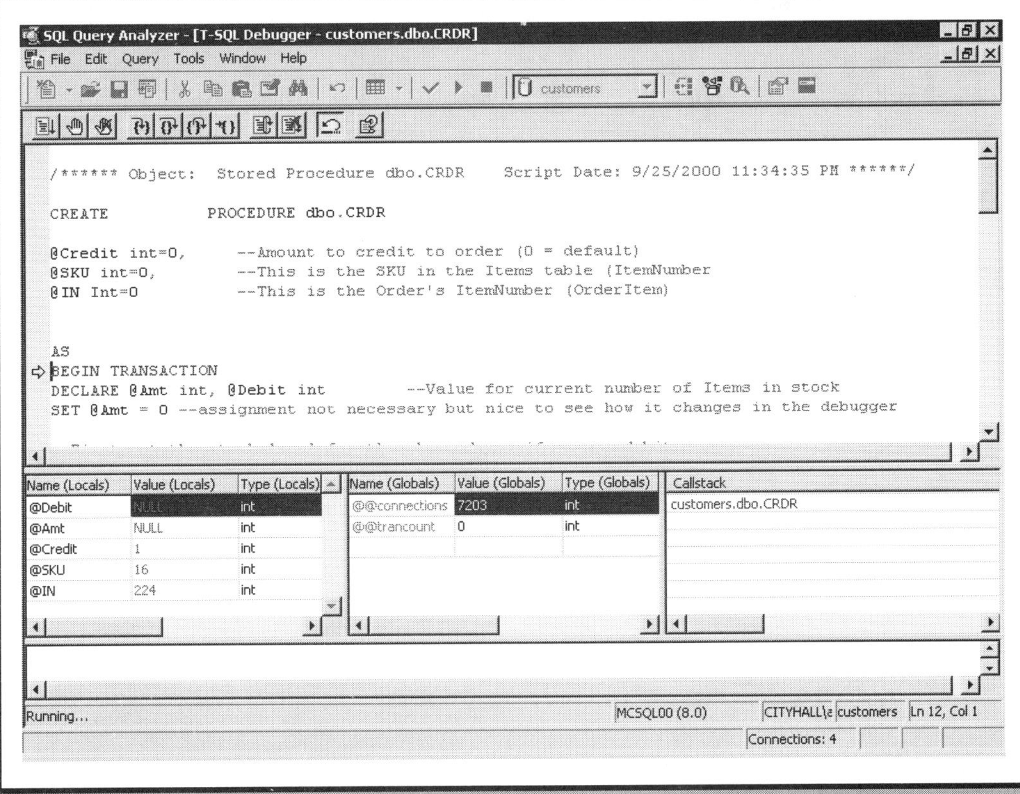

Figure 18-11. *The stored procedure debugger*

"The Example.") Figure 18-12 illustrates that the initial queries have run and the local variables (see the parameters now for @Amt and @Debit) have been changed accordingly.

4. If I keep stepping through the code, as soon as I update either of the tables in this procedure the appropriate triggers will fire. Figure 18-13 now shows that we have left the procedure and entered the trigger code after the DML statement has been executed in the transaction. I can now step into the trigger. Notice the trigger (fishy) is now in the call stack. Depending on what the trigger is looking for or to do it might or might not cause the remainder of the procedure to execute in the debugger. Naturally, if you want to step through the proc without the intervention of the trigger, just drop the trigger from the table and reinstall it later.

If you change stored procedure (or trigger) code, you must execute the ALTER query to install the latest version of the procedure to the database. You are not editing the installed procedure when you run Edit or script out the procedure code, so failing

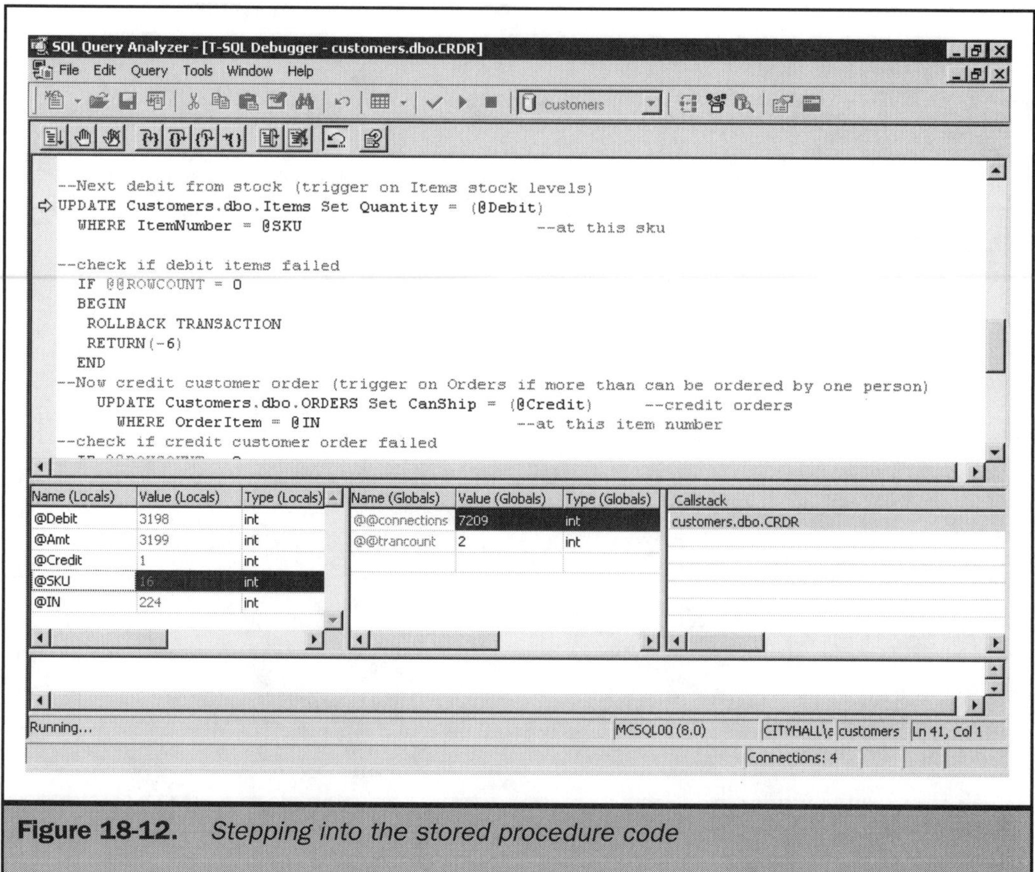

Figure 18-12. *Stepping into the stored procedure code*

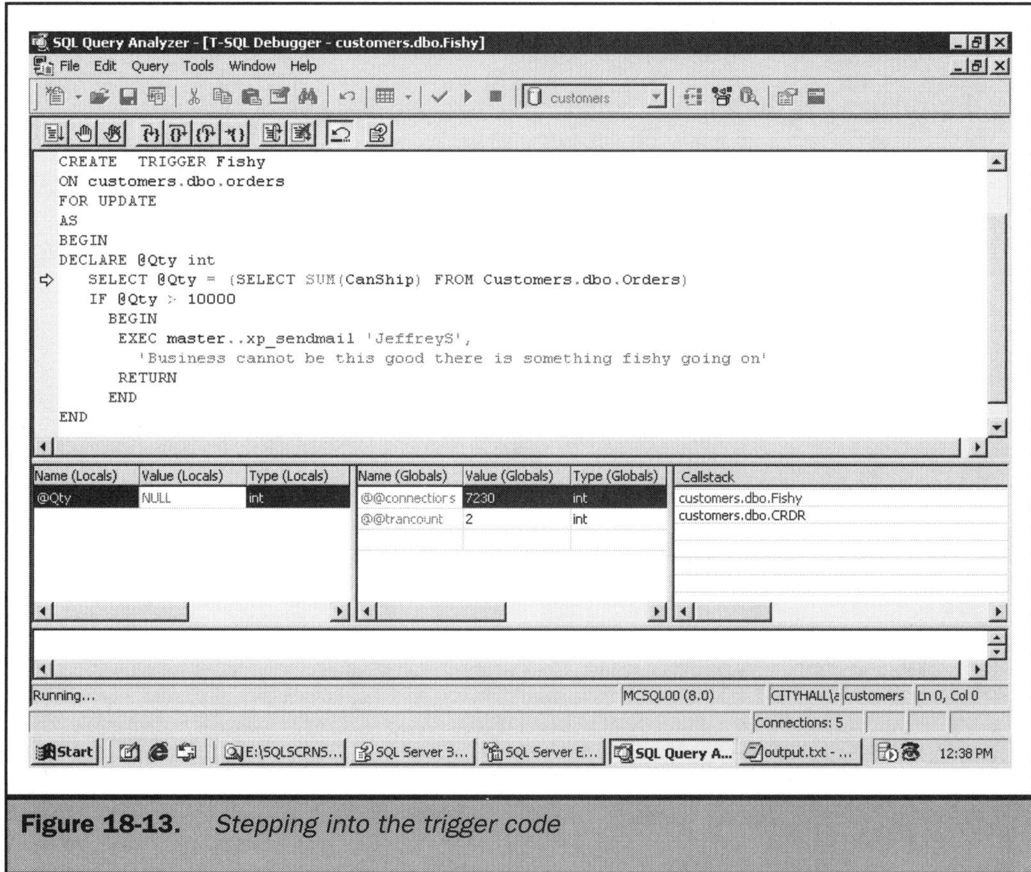

Figure 18-13. *Stepping into the trigger code*

to re-execute after changing the code will not help you , and you'll be as confused as an apple in a peach tree when the bug you just squished returns to the debugger. Think of the Execute Query as the build or compile button on your traditional IDE.

It is also a good idea to save the query out to a text file or version control system as often as possible, because if you lose power or your system crashes before you have a chance to re-execute, the ALTER query the source code will be lost.

Creating a Stored Procedure in Enterprise Manager

Coding complex stored procedures in not an easy task in Enterprise Manager. This is something you must do in Query Analyzer or Visual Studio so that you can adequately debug and test the code, as demonstrated after the next coffee break. The editor pane you use in EM is woefully inadequate and is used just to check out the text that you have already tested as working. The most useful feature of this facility in Enterprise

Manager is the ability to manage permissions visually and interactively. The following instructions describe using Enterprise Manager to create a stored procedure:

1. Drill down to the server group in which the target database resides.
2. Expand the Databases node and then drill down to the target database where you want to create the stored procedure. Expand the target down to the Stored Procedures node. This is illustrated in Figure 18-14.
3. Right-click the node and select New Stored Procedure. The Stored Procedures Properties - New Stored Procedure dialog box illustrated in Figure 18-15 loads.
4. Enter the code into the editor pane and check syntax if you need to by clicking the Check Syntax button.
5. Click the Permissions button to set permissions for the stored procedure.

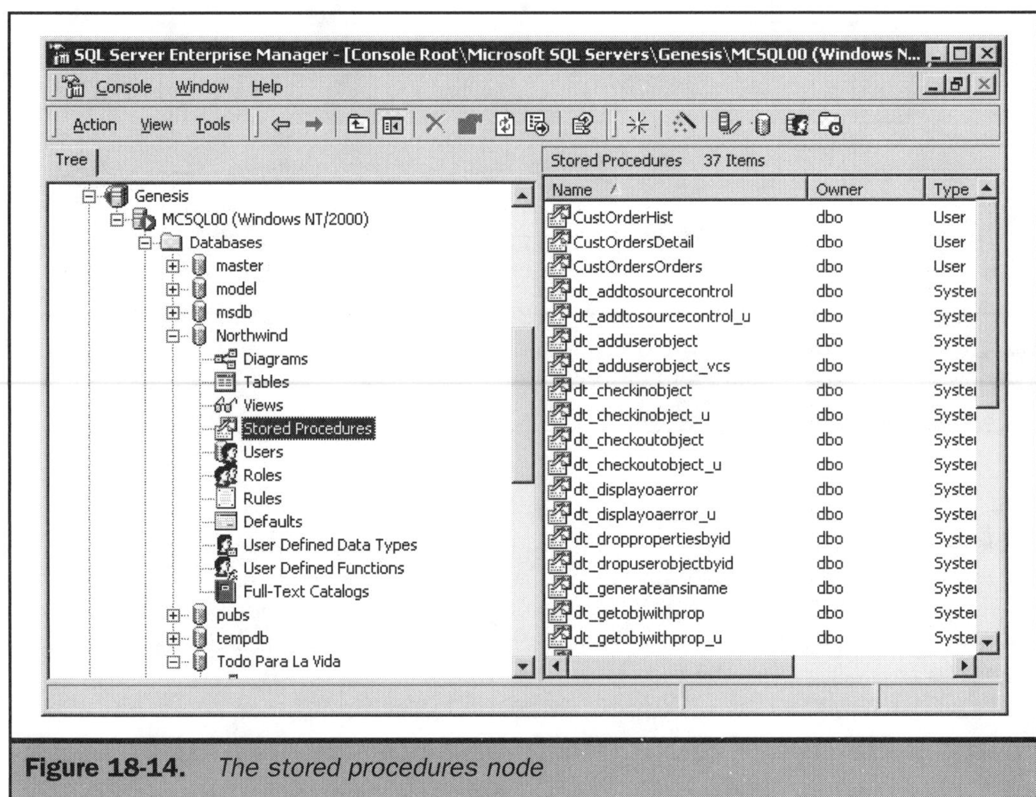

Figure 18-14. *The stored procedures node*

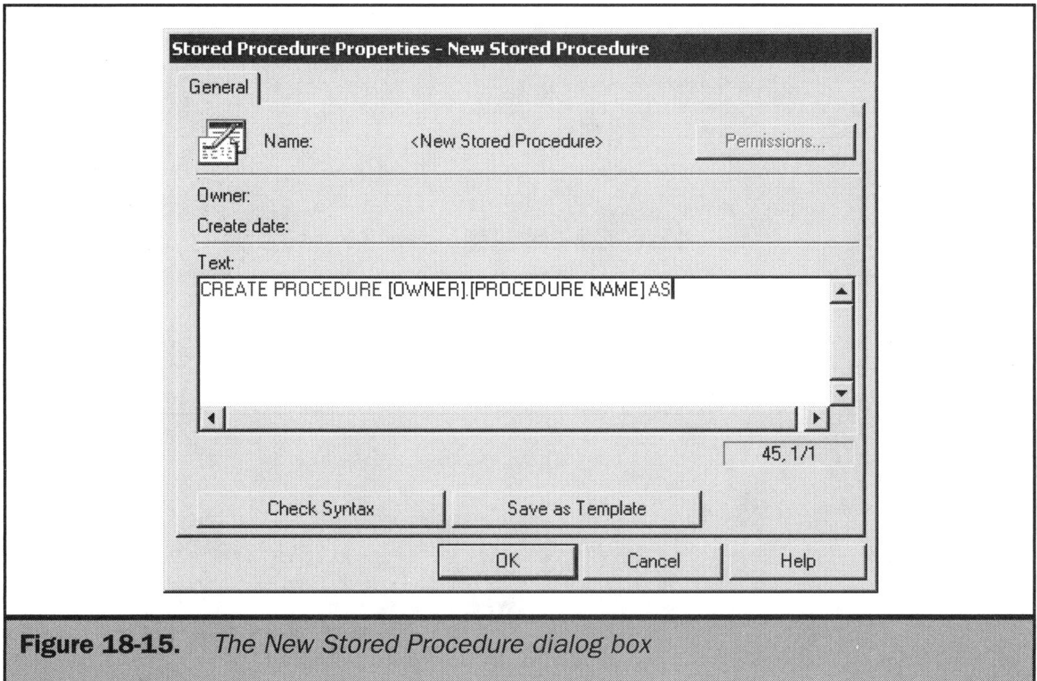

Figure 18-15. *The New Stored Procedure dialog box*

Using the Stored Procedure Wizard

SQL Server 2000 provides a wizard that is useful for stored procedure beginners. The wizard initially hides the code needed to create the stored procedure. To create a stored procedure using the Stored Procedure Wizard, do as follows:

Drill down to and expand the database in which to create the stored procedure (this is not a requirement, because the wizard ignores the selection and presents you with a drop-down list that you use to select your database; however, you must make sure you are using a wizard in the correct instance of SQL Server. The wizard does not let you select a server, only a nonsystem database).

Now go to the Tools menu and click Wizards. The Select Wizard dialog box shown in Figure 18-16 loads.

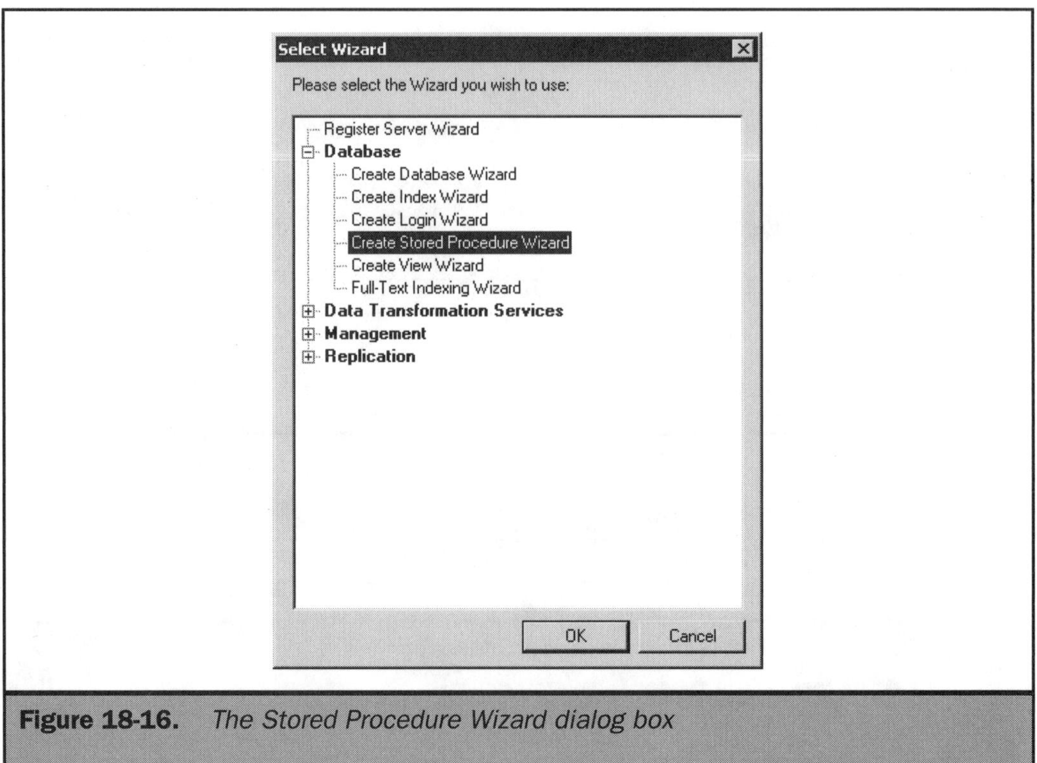

Figure 18-16. *The Stored Procedure Wizard dialog box*

Expand Database in the Wizard and double-click Create Stored Procedure Wizard.

The wizard now takes over the process but does not allow you to create anything in the system databases.

Using the wizard, you can create simple INSERT, DELETE, and UPDATE procs (as illustrated in Figure 18-17), parse the code that the wizard generated, and (even) edit it. The wizard is ideal for beginners who need to get started with stored procedures with some guidance. You should be able to graduate from the wizard after the first day of using it. Apart from being able to generate simple code, this wizard is actually quite clueless.

Calling Stored Procedures

One of the major differences between a trigger and a stored procedure is that a stored procedure needs to be explicitly called. You cannot call a trigger. A stored procedure can be called from a number of places, such as client applications, autoexecution, other stored procedures and triggers, and tools like QA and EM. A stored procedure is executed using one of the following methods.

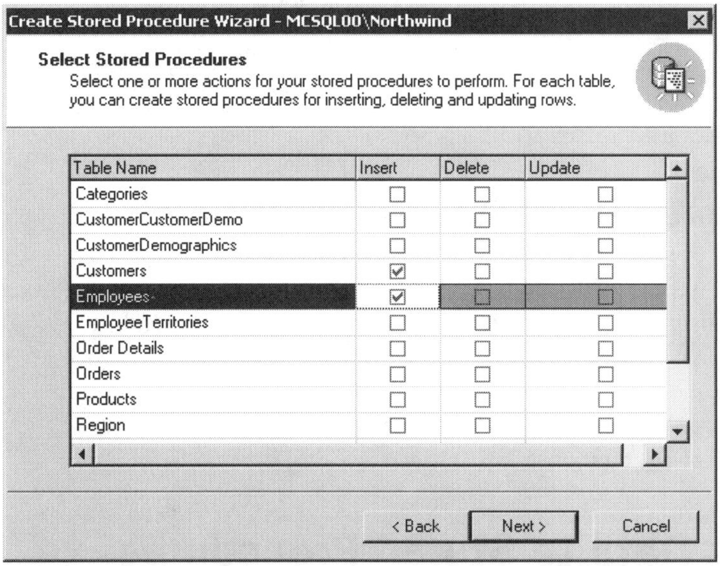

Figure 18-17. *Creating simple DML statements in the Stored Procedure Wizard*

Specifying the Name of the Stored Procedure in the Statement

For example, the code `sp_who` and nothing else in the statement will execute the stored procedure by that name. There is one caveat to just naming the procedure in the procedure. The name must be the first line of code in your statement or batch . . . even if a billion lines of code follow it. If you stick a statement above the procedure name, the code will break.

Using the Clause Exec or Execute in Front of the Stored Procedure Name

The name is then followed by the rest of the stored procedure code. As long as you prefix the procedure with Exec or Execute, the code will execute.

The following statement is thus the preferred method:

```
EXEC | EXECUTE sp_who
```

You can execute a stored procedure, as described here, that is grouped with a collection of stored procedures by specifying the procedure number assigned to the member procedure as follows:

```
EXECUTE accpay_proc;4
```

Calling a Stored Procedure Within INSERT

You can call a stored procedure in an INSERT statement, a topic that is further discussed in Chapter 20. What happens is that the result set returned from the stored procedure is inserted into the reference table. The following code provides an example of an INSERT...EXEC.

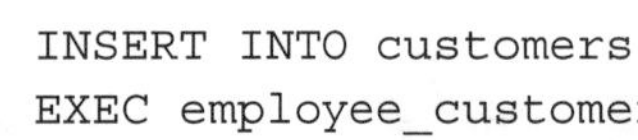

```
INSERT INTO customers
EXEC employee_customer
```

Sending Data to Stored Procedures

As an application developer or a DBA proficient in T-SQL, you need to know how to write software that can pass data (parameters) to stored procedures. Stored procedure writers, on the other hand (see Chapter 14), have to know how to code stored procedures to efficiently receive and process the data received from the clients. The architecture is very similar to that of functions, procedures, and methods that receive and return values. Stored procedures can also return values, and we will discuss how and what in the next section.

When a client calls a stored procedure (using one of the methods described in the earlier section), it can pass values to the procedure through parameters. These values are then used in the stored procedure to achieve the desired result. I mentioned earlier that you can write stored procedures that can contain as many as 1,024 parameters. To expand further, each parameter can be named, associated with a data type, given a direction, and even assigned a default value (even NULL).

You can pass parameters by name and by position. The following example demonstrates passing parameters by name:

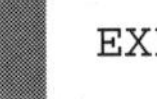

```
EXEC js_newid @id1='A-1A', @id2='A-1B'
```

This is the more robust form of coding stored procedures because it means you can use the named parameters in a stored procedure without defining the order in which the parameters were received. The following code will get hairy if you start going wild on parameters:

```
EXEC js_newid 'A-1A', 'A-1B', 'A-1C', 'A-1D'
```

Default Values in Stored Procedures

When you execute stored procedures that are expecting parameters, SQL Server will report an error if none is received in your connection. If your connection might not transmit a parameter, you could code default values in the stored procedure, or even use NULL. SQL Server will then make use of the default values or place NULL into the statement's parameter placeholder instead of returning an error.

In keeping with our discussion of NULL values in the last chapter, your first choice should be to provide a default value in the parameter that makes the most sense and will enhance rather than break your code. For example, the following procedure will use your parameter values, or a default parameter:

```
EXEC js_getdiscount @discount=0, @coupon=1
```

The following example takes NULL when and if the circumstances can live with it:

```
EXEC js_getdiscount @discount=0, @coupon=NULL
```

The following code is a simple order-adding stored procedure demonstrating the use of parameters:

```
USE rainbow
  DECLARE @returncode int
  DECLARE @CustID char(8)
  DECLARE @AgentID char(6)
  DECLARE @Item char(50)
  DECLARE @Price money, @Discount real, @Quantity int
INSERT [Orders] (CustID, AgentID, Item, Quantity, Price, Discount)
  VALUES (@CustID, @AgentID,  @Item, @Quantity, @Price, @Discount)
```

This stored procedure is kept simple to demonstrate the use of parameters. Notice that you can also group parameter declarations behind one DECLARE. The following list provides some parameter tips:

- Use default values in your parameters in preference to NULL. Use the NULL value when it makes sense.
- Write code that checks for inconsistent or missing values early in your stored procedure code.
- Use easy-to-remember names that make it easier to pass the value by name rather than position.

Receiving Data from Stored Procedures

A stored procedure would not be as marvelous a tool if it were unable to return data to you. SQL Server can return data to you in any supported data type, such as characters, strings, dates, images, user-defined data types, and even tabular data and cursors from SELECT statements.

You need to identify data intended for output with the OUTPUT keyword, which also has a short form OUT. This specifies the data intended for return to the client. The following stored procedure code returns a single integer value:

```
CREATE PROC js_getatotal
  @OrderNum
  @atotal int OUTPUT
AS
 SELECT @atotal = total
 FROM items
WHERE OrderNum = @OrderNum
```

Returning Result Sets

Returning result sets to clients from stored procedures is simply a matter of coding a SELECT statement into the stored procedure. The tabulated or multirow data is returned automatically. If you need to perform complex SELECT routines (such as SELECT INTO) in your stored procedure, you can also enclose the SELECT statement into conditional or flow-control logic to prevent any result set from being returned to the client. The following code demonstrates a simple stored procedure that returns a result set to the client:

```
CREATE PROCEDURE getcustomers_pastdue @past int=14
AS
  SELECT CustID, CustName, Tel1
  FROM Customers WHERE pastdue = @past
```

Stored Procedure Nesting

You can also nest stored procedures like triggers. SQL Server 2000 supports up to 32 levels of stored procedures. If you exceed this level in a nest, the entire procedure cascade might collapse, depending on your code. You can check the nest level in any stored procedure by calling the @@NESTLEVEL function. This function returns the current nest level of the stored procedure the function was called from.

Despite the nest limit of 32, you can also spawn as many stored procedures as you want from within the nest chain or cascade. The called procedure does not increment the nest level counter as long as it completes without spawning another stored procedure.

Rolling Back Stored Procedures

You can execute a ROLLBACK command in a stored procedure; however, the rollback works differently from the ROLLBACK discussed in the trigger section earlier on. In the case of a stored procedure rollback, if the rollback is in a member of a stored procedure chain or nest, only the outermost transaction will be rolled back. The execution of the remaining stored procedures in the nest continues.

Temporary Stored Procedures

You can also set stored procedures to be temporary, which means that once a client disconnects the stored procedure is dropped. Temporary stored procedures are stored in the tempdb database. However, heavy use of temporary stored procedures is not a recommended practice on SQL Server 2000 databases. The support exists for backward compatibility with version 6.5 databases. The older architecture had a more primitive prepare-compile-execute architecture.

Warming Up SQL Server

As discussed in Chapter 2, stored procedures are compiled and cached only at their first call by an application. You can help increase performance and ready a server for certain forms of access and functions when a server starts up, before users access it, by automatically executing certain stored procedures. This means that when users connect and use a stored procedure, it will already be in the stored procedure cache.

Automatically executing stored procedures on startup is also highly useful for certain management applications or functionality that a server needs to have soon after startup. I call this warming up SQL Server. You should take note of a few nuances and rules before you consider using this "warm-up" capability. These nuances are as follows:

- The creator or owner of an autoexecuted stored procedure can only be the system administrator or a member of the sysadmin fixed server role.
- The stored procedure must be a background process and cannot take any input parameters.

Each autoexecuted, or startup, stored procedure makes a connection to the DBMS. You can have as many autoexecuted stored procedures as you like, but if each one consumes a connection, this could be a significant drain on resources. If the stored procedures do not need to be executed concurrently, you can nest them. Thus, you could create a single stored procedure that calls a list of stored procedures synchronously. The cascade of stored procedures only consumes one connection, the one incurred by the autoexecuting stored procedure.

By cascading or nesting stored procedures, you could thus call user-defined stored procedures and even pass parameters into them. This can be useful for an application that requires certain information and objects to be available to users when the databases come back on line.

In one of my call centers if I need to restart or "IPL" a server for any reason, or we suffer a server or host crash, an autoexecuted stored procedure sends a message to database users when the server is ready and they can reconnect. This saves the help desk from having to call or e-mail users that the server is back up and can be accessed again.

If you have a problem and you ever need to delay the autoexecuting of stored procedures, you can start the instance of SQL Server 2000 with the –f flag. This will start the server in a minimal configuration (like Safe mode on Windows 2000 servers and Windows 9.*x*) and allow you to debug the problem. You can also specify trace flag 4022 as a startup parameter, which forces the startup to bypass autoexecution.

To create a startup or autoexecuted stored procedure, you need to be logged in as a member of the sysadmin role and you must create the procedure in the master database. You can also use sp_procoption to designate an existing stored procedure as a startup stored procedure, to reset the startup option on a stored procedure, or to view a list of all stored procedures that execute on startup.

Managing Stored Procedures

Stored procedure code and objects are the most complex to manage in SQL Server. On a large system, it does not take long to lose count of the number of stored procedures written and deployed on the system. The following sections explain how to alter and drop stored procedures using either T-SQL or Enterprise Manager.

Altering Stored Procedures

To alter a stored procedure in T-SQL, you need to use the ALTER PROCEDURE statement. The basic statement is as follows:

```
ALTER PROCEDURE proc_name
ON . . .
```

The code to apply after the ON line takes the same syntax and choice of arguments as the CREATE PROC statement described earlier (see the SQL Server 2000 Books Online for the full explanation and usage of the arguments).

To alter a stored procedure in Enterprise Manager, follow the steps described earlier for creating a stored procedure in Enterprise Manager and edit the stored procedure accordingly. Altering a stored procedure in Query Analyzer is demonstrated shortly.

Dropping Stored Procedures

Dropping a stored procedure in T-SQL requires the DROP PROCEDURE statement followed by the procedure name. For example, the code

```
USE Stores
IF EXISTS (SELECT name FROM sysobjects
   WHERE name = 'DebitStores')
DROP PROCEDURE DebitStores
```

drops the stored procedure DebitStores from the Stores database.

You should make sure to check for stored procedure dependencies with the sp_depends stored procedure before dropping the stored procedure.

To drop a stored procedure interactively in Enterprise Manager, simply drill down to the database and select the Stored Procedures node from the console tree. Select the stored procedure in the details pane, right-click, and select Delete.

Getting Information About Stored Procedures

To obtain information from SQL Server about the stored procedures attached to the database, you should execute the system stored procedure sp_helptext. This system stored procedure returns the code for database objects like stored procedures, rules, and defaults. It queries the code in *syscomments* as mentioned earlier. Call sp_helptext as follows:

```
sp_helptext [ @objname = ] 'name'
```

and the example would look like this:

```
--to check the code of a stored procedure
EXEC sp_helptext @objname = storedprocname
```

This obviously will not work on encrypted stored procedures.

The Example

Let's now look at the debit/credit example we documented in the stored procedure deployment plan discussed earlier.

```
CREATE PROC

/*
```

```
Script Name: jrs_CRDR
Description: Credit/Debit for Items/Orders
Usage: For stock picking
Return Code: -1 to -10
Author: Jeffrey R. Shapiro
Version: 1.1
Date Created: 9/25/2000
Revision History:

*/
SET QUOTED_IDENTIFIER ON
GO
SET ANSI_NULLS ON
GO

/****** Object:  Stored Procedure dbo.jrs_CRDR  Script Date: 9/25/2000
11:34:35 PM ******/

ALTER PROCEDURE dbo.jrs_CRDR

@Credit int=0, --Amount to credit to order (3)
@SKU int=0,    --This is the SKU in the Items table (ItemNumber)
@IN Int=0      --This is the Order's ItemNumber (OrderItem)

AS
BEGIN TRANSACTION
  DECLARE @Amt int, @Debit int        --Value for current number of
  Items in stock
  SET @Amt = 0 /*assignment not necessary but nice to see how it changes
  in the debugger*/

--First get the stock level for the sku and see if we can debit
SELECT @Amt = (SELECT Quantity FROM Customers.dbo.Items
    WHERE ItemNumber = @SKU)
  IF @Amt IS NULL
  BEGIN
   ROLLBACK TRANSACTION
   RAISERROR
     ('Bad SKU. Please call stock controller about %d', 16, 1, @SKU)
   RETURN(-4)
  END

  IF @Amt < @Credit
```

```
  BEGIN
    ROLLBACK TRANSACTION
    RAISERROR
      ('Low stock level, %d. Please call stock controller', 16, 1, @Amt)
    RETURN(-5)
    END

 --Get values for debit/credit
SELECT  @Debit = (@Amt - @Credit)
--Next debit from stock (trigger on Items stock levels)
UPDATE Customers.dbo.Items Set Quantity = (@Debit)
  WHERE ItemNumber = @SKU                         --at this sku

 --check if debit items failed
  IF @@ROWCOUNT = 0
  BEGIN
   ROLLBACK TRANSACTION
   RETURN(-6)
  END

--Now credit customer order
    UPDATE Customers.dbo.ORDERS Set CanShip = (@Credit)      --credit
    orders
      WHERE OrderItem = @IN                         --at this item number

--check if credit customer order failed
  IF @@ROWCOUNT = 0
  BEGIN
   ROLLBACK TRANSACTION
   RETURN(-7)
  END

--check if any errors from

  IF @@ERROR <> 0
  BEGIN
   ROLLBACK TRANSACTION
   RETURN(-8)
  END

COMMIT
  PRINT 'Item posted'
```

```
GO
SET QUOTED_IDENTIFIER OFF
GO
SET ANSI_NULLS ON
GO
```

In the preceding code I used PRINT to report that the item posted okay (thanks to the commit that only gets called if the transaction is kosher). But I coded in various return codes that would get returned on an error. These could be suppressed and confined to the stored procedure or returned as an output value to the client. In other words you can loop through return codes in the procedure and send a related message to the user, or just send the return code to the client and let logic on the client decide how to proceed. I prefer to keep the error codes local to the procedure, which means I can change, at any time, what I tell the client about the errors or what course of action to take.

To Recap

We covered a lot of ground together in this chapter dealing with triggers and stored procedures. As you can see, trigger and stored procedure writing and management can consume substantial resources, and without proper planning, documentation, change control, archiving, source code maintenance, modeling, and so on, you can create a lot of problems for yourself or the team.

If you are new to trigger and stored procedure writing, the change in development style and philosophy can put a lot of strain on mental and physical resources. And the conversion of client-side, in-line SQL code to server-side triggers and stored procedures can be expensive in terms of both time and materials.

In the chapters to follow in Part III, we will discuss the DML statements and some advanced programming concepts, including extended stored procedures and the new user defined functions.

If you have not already done so, you should read Chapter 8 carefully, or read it again, because trigger and stored procedure deployment require you to manage permissions and security so that your users can exploit the code you have written. Also check out Appendix A for more information on the system or built-in stored procedures, and Chapter 16 for your T-SQL building blocks. Also, query plans are discussed in Chapter 15, and understanding them is an essential prerequisite to writing and testing stored procedures and triggers.

Chapter 19

Query Fundamentals and Strategy

I begin this chapter with an abstract discussion of the SQL Server table, its attributes and elements, and then move onto dissecting the SELECT statement, before hitting view and other query facilities. The coverage of the SQL Server SELECT statement is exhaustive here, covering the new features, such as support for XML data. Our discussion of the SELECT will first focus on fundamentals and the structure of its syntax, before delving into techniques and strategies, with advanced features like its COMPUTE BY clause, ROLLUPs, and CUBEs.

I also discuss the concept of *data conservation* in a client/server relational database management system (RDBMS). Notice again the phrase *data conservation.* I use this term to stress "wise use of data" and further elaborate on the concepts I discussed in Chapter 14.

"Conservation" is an interesting term. A discipline of ecology, it means the wise use of a resource and not "protectionism" or "exploitation." I would like to apply this concept of wise use to data and retrieval methods appropriate for the fat server model—the primary paradigm of data management using SQL Server (and other DBMS server systems).

But before we can explore this further and test the validity of the concepts, let's discuss the basics.

The SQL Server Table

Let me start with some recap: By now you certainly know that the table in SQL Server is the primary unit of storage. SQL Server tables are created and maintained in databases, and we described how both databases and tables get created back in Chapter 11. The database, thus, is nothing more than a container, albeit a container with numerous features that allow us to manage the data in the table and control access to it.

Note *A database is a SQL Server object; it has no reference in relational theory, or in the SQL ANSI standard.*

A SQL Server table is made up of columns and rows. Rows, known as *tuples* in a table, represent the complete "record" of data *within the table.* The relational model, however, allows the record to spread over several tables, but taken collectively all the interrelated rows of data combine to make the record. Often, it makes sense for us to break large tables into many smaller ones, to infuse some modularity in the structure of our data, which makes it easier to work with. For example, in a simple order-entry and order management database we would typically create a table for the customer's details and a table for the customer orders and so on.

Out of a collection of customers and each customer's orders we are able to manipulate and farm our data (conservation again) to produce documents representing orders, statements, invoices, picklists, packing labels, mailing labels, and so forth.

And with analysis services and functions, we can "milk" the data for information to assist us in business decision–making. For each document or assemblage of data, however, we still need only work two or three primary tables of operational data at the minimum. We would create a table for customer details (company name, telephone number, contact, and so on), one for shipping information (physical addresses as opposed to billing addresses), and one for order details.

It is quite possible and often desirable to add columns to the general customer details table. My rules for this are to first investigate the attributes and the domains of the data you are storing. If new data you are adding to the table only represented one column, it would not make any sense to create a separate table for it. For example, if your business rules require payment only through credit cards and you need no more than a few columns to store credit card numbers, expiration, and name on the card, by all means attach a few more columns to the customer details table.

SQL Server tables can hold thousands of columns. Your model might work well with a few large tables with many columns, and it might work better (or worse) if the model called for many smaller tables. For example, if the business decided to accept several forms of payments, from cash to credit (charge and account), then it would make sense to provide tables that specialize in the storage of this information. For the most part your database lets you know when its tables should be split up.

The tables, data, and query strategies discussed in this chapter revolve around operational data (OLTP), and not analytical data (OLAP), the latter being the subject of Part IV.

The more tables you have, the more complex the model. There is also more of a chance of redundant data occurring in the database. Whether this is a poor, bad, or unconscionable thing depends on which relational guru you worship. We have guidelines for this dilemma thanks to Codd, known as *normalization*. Called the Rules of Normalization, I prefer to see them as guidelines; others treat them like the Talmud. In fact, the nature of the RDBMS is such that unless you are flexible and adopt relational theory as a guideline, as opposed to gospel, you are destined to founder. SQL Server solutions may in fact contain undernormalized data, overnormalized data, and what at times may even appear to be denormalized data. It all depends on your application, and what you are trying to achieve. A customer order-entry system, an accounts payable/accounts receivable system, and a database supporting the switching matrix of an automatic call distributor may bear no resemblance to one another.

However, the SQL Server database model requires us to be data conservationists. We need to thus strive to prevent, as far as possible, the repetition of data in our database. Otherwise, we will have to deal with unnecessary bottlenecks, slow queries, misleading query results, and so forth. On the other hand, we should not be so limiting that the database becomes impossible to access easily.

Table Concepts

It is often difficult to change our concept of a table, the abstract impression of it, as being something that looks like a spreadsheet. This is obviously due in large part to the GUI presentation of data in grid-like structures. For ISAM databases, data is almost always presented to the user in grids. What's worse, users are allowed to edit and update data within the grid, which doesn't sit well with SQL Server solutions (and we'll deal with why shortly).

While it is permissible in some cases to let this go with users, often the so-called data-bound grid does more harm than good for the database designers and modeling people. In fact, I have even met people who cannot see beyond the grid, and so severe is their habit, they prefer to store their data in spreadsheets and never go near relational databases. When you cannot see your data for the cells, you are severely hampering your ability to model and build effective SQL Server solutions. In other words, you are unable to see the entire *record* in the database, only seeing part of it in a cell.

For example, some years ago when I made the transition from Paradox and Access databases to SQL Server, one of the first habits I found hard to kick was the auto-increment feature, and I believe this is true for a lot of Access users still today. While auto-increment, which added a new number automatically to each new "row" of data, helped ensure unique records, it also perpetuated the fixation on cells, which had to exist in a precise range where no row numbers could be missing. The identity property of a column in a SQL Server table offers the same functionality; you should use it with care and avoid fixation on an exact sequence of numbers that remind you of a spreadsheet.

In the late 1990s, I experimented with several of my database contracts, dropping grids from the entire client application and only working with hierarchical data trees, lists, and a variety of string objects. I refused (and still do as far as possible) to "bind" a grid to a SQL Server table. Not only did I find it far easier to create super-thin clients, but also I found my users beginning to work with data far more sophisticatedly. I had gotten them to see beyond the grid, to the data on a much broader scale, as part of a system with depth and perspective.

While it is impossible to dismiss columns and column names as being the fabric of SQL Server tables, you should strive to view your data in terms of the domains that make up a complete record in the database. Each row or tuple is made up of one or more (seldom one) domains, and for each of the record's domains you need to provide a value. In some cases, you might not know the value (the NULL issue again), but we will delve into that little problem later. (Domains are discussed in depth in Chapter 17.)

A customer record, for example, is made up of several domains: first names, last names, street numbers, street addresses, cities, postal codes, and so on. If one row's collection of domain values is repeated in another row in the same table, we violate the rules of uniqueness. And if the row is repeated in the same table, or another table, but is unique only by virtue of a row identifier, or an identity value, then we violate rules of data redundancy (and our wise use mission goes out the window).

We strive to ensure that no two records can be identical (at least one domain value in the record makes the record unique); there are several means to ensure this. We might get away with a "clone" of a record by giving the record an instance or column identifier. You could create a record number, a customer number, a part number, and so on.

In other words, our records are nothing more than collections of domains, or, in OO terms, objects with collections of properties. In order for us to search for single records or a group of records in a table, the table needs to be ordered according to a sequence of domains. In other words, we would say that a customer number would be domain 1, called CustomerNumbers, and that CustomerName could be called domain 2. It does not matter where in the table the domains are positioned, 1 or 76, or what they are labeled, as long as each record maintains the domain order—and the data type each domain stores. In other words, the *city* domain (in the fourth column) for record A cannot also be the *state* domain (also column 4), because that would make our data impossible and nonsensical to work with.

Note *In pure object systems, this situation can be very different; in some cases, the domains may not be stored in columns. Similar to the contents of the living cell, the records as objects do not maintain properties in any order, and the property needs only be referenced in some way.*

Thus our queries are built according to the following language: "Find me records in which the customer's *city* domain is Miami, or the customer's *order number* domain contains the values of '12-08-45-A1.'" By concentrating on the value of the data in the domain as opposed to a collection of cells, you'll have a better feel for your data when it comes to modeling and building queries.

Data-bound controls in the client tier create many problems for SQL Server solutions. To begin with, they have the habit of establishing connections to the server and maintaining them with no rhythm or reason. But mostly the controls tend to perpetuate the cellular habit, encouraging you to fixate on the cells as opposed to the values. If you are moving from Access (with MDB files) to SQL Server, you should try to kick the data-bound control habit. In today's highly distributed data processing environment, the buzz word is "scalability," and nothing can trash scalability more than binding client controls to database objects.

By referencing columns according to their position in a table (thinking left to right), we can ensure that SQL Server places our values in the correct domains. Domain integrity and type constraints can of course be used to ensure that correct values get stored in the domains. But knowing the position of a column is not essential (but is outdated) because we reference the column by name, no matter where it is in the table. In other words, our insert languages would sound like "place this value into the column for the cities domain, whose record number is X."

In this regard, it is quite clear that the table is a server-side object, not something that can be instantiated or recreated in the client. In other words, it exists only within a database schema and has no foundation anywhere other than in the database.

Perhaps one of the most dangerous operators in the SQL language is the * (star, or asterisk), which means all or any. So if we say "get * from the customers table," we are asking SQL Server to send us all the rows and all domain values (every column). This really does wonders for the network and the health of our client and user. But what is worse is that it leads to the notion that the table is being reproduced outside the database, and this is a dangerous perception.

When we query SQL Server, no matter what object the data is drawn from in the database (table, view, or cursor), we are served with a replica of the data in the database, which we display at the client in grids, trees, lists, or individual text fields. Our queries thus need to be highly efficient so that only the most valid data the client needs is sent across the network, not as a table, but in tabulated form nonetheless (represented by TDS or XML), so that the client can present the data in the correct fields or containers. Can you imagine what it would be like if we sat down for dinner in a crowded restaurant and asked the kitchen to send us every meal, just because we were not sure what we felt like eating?

The query at the worst should return no more than twenty rows if the client does not know the exact row it needs, but the query should always strive to send as few rows as possible. Figure 19-1 illustrates what I consider a safety zone for sending a collection of rows to the client.

Figure 19-1 demonstrates what I earlier called data ecology or data farming, which means querying only for just enough records to satisfy the client and balance the number of round trips to the server. The best scenario, as indicated in the figure, is one row, and possibly even one value. The less known about a value being searched on, the more rows get returned to the client. And conversely, the more you know about the row, the fewer the number of rows that need to be returned. If you know the exact value that makes the rows unique, SQL Server will send you that row and no other.

The row or rows of data returned by SQL server is known as a result set. You can call it anything you like in the client development or external environment (recordset, rowset, dataset and so on), but from SQL Server it is the result of a query, no matter how simple or how complex. Your queries should also be written in such a way that the result returned contains not only as few records as possible, but only the exact columns needed. If you need to display all the values of a row, so be it.

Sometimes you need just a domain value at the client for some reason that the client does not need to know about. Understand, however, that you are not being much of a conservationist if you write software that updates 20 fields in a record when only one needed to be updated. In other words, why send packets containing 20 values back to SQL Server when you need only send a packet to update one value. Not only do you consume more network bandwidth, but you also consume more processing bandwidth on the server.

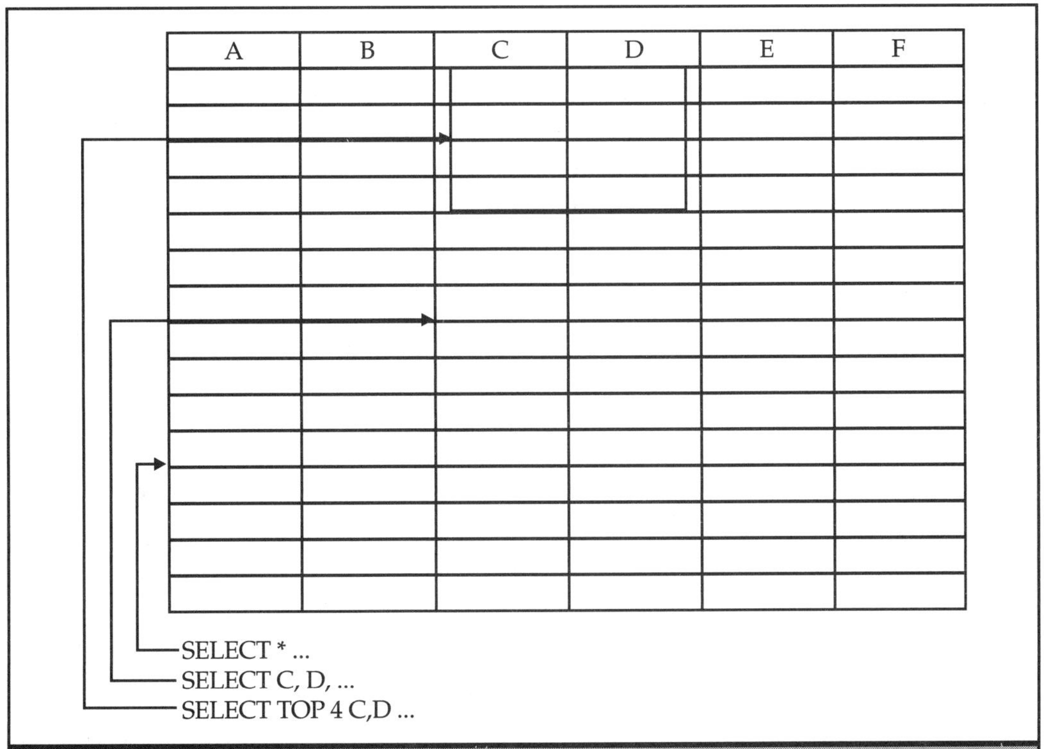

Figure 19-1. *Narrowing down the SELECT to conserve network, server, and client resources*

If you ask SQL Server for the customer 100 row so that you can update the postal code, does it not make more sense to only receive the customer number, optionally the name to keep the software user sure he or she has the right record, and the postal code? You can then transmit only this field back to the server instead of directly inserting numerous values into the table using an inline SQL statement, or better still just pass a single value to a stored procedure's parameter. You could pass the values to a stored procedure to determine the most efficient means of updating the code field, leaving everything else intact, without having to transmit the search logic to find the record. We'll get back to this later.

Let's recap before we move on:

- A table is a unit of storage, maintained in a SQL Server database.
- A table has no reference outside the database: The table exists as a database object; it cannot be transferred out of SQL Server; only its data can, but as a copy in a result set.

- The data is transmitted (copied) from a table as a tabulated datagram, which is called a result set. The result set is transmitted to the client; it is formatted by the TDS protocol or within an XML text stream.
- Client components (such as OLE DB and ADO) know how to read the tabulated data from the protocol stack and how to present it in the client.
- Data that is not changed is discarded; data that must be changed is returned to the server as an update.

Table Derivatives

The table object is not the only tabulated data structure you can query in SQL Server. It is quite possible, desirable, and often essential to query the subsets and other derivatives of the base tables for various operations. We already discussed how it makes sense to divvy up a database into several tables, and as such it is possible to draw data from multiple tables and also query the subsets of the base tables. These subsets are still, however, stored and maintained on the server. Some may be temporary, others permanent.

We can query the following subsets and derivative tables from the SQL Server base tables:

- On-the-fly result sets (the results of queries and subqueries, unions, intersections, joins, and so on)
- Views
- Partitions
- Cursors

On-the-Fly Result Sets

These are results sets, the results of SELECT statements and subqueries, that return volatile subsets of data derived from base tables. I call them "on-the-fly" because the result set, unless specifically stored in a new table or view, is not persistent. It is created within the workings of a complete SELECT statement. In other words, as soon as it is derived from the base table, it is transmitted to the client or used in a subquery and then discarded.

The only vestige of the cause of the result set remains in the form of the SELECT statement stored in the query plan cache. But no subset resulting from the query remains after it has been returned to the client. I will call these "result sets" from here on.

It is possible, however, within a stored procedure, to draw a result set from a base table and prevent the data from being returned to the client automatically, which is the opposite of what SQL Server is inclined to do. Using flow control programming and assignment, you can then derive additional result sets from the earlier result sets (nested results sets) and control exactly which data gets returned to the client, if anything. Still, upon termination of the procedure and achievement of the objective or termination through error, the result set is discarded.

Despite the volatility of the result set, a result set can explicitly be saved to a new table, in the midst of SELECT execution, by using SELECT INTO, which creates a table on the fly. I talk about SELECT INTO later in this chapter.

These nonpersistent result sets are created with the T-SQL SELECT statement and its support for ANSI or SQL-92 style structure, as well as some legacy SELECT syntax, which has been kept around for old time's sake.

Views and cursors can be queried in exactly the same fashion as tables, table derivatives, subsets, and result sets. There are several methods of catching fish; the most popular is the fishing pole (or rod). The SELECT is our fishing pole, and we first have to learn how to fish with it, before we can cast in the ponds of tables, views, cursors, and so on.

SELECT

The SELECT statement is the Swiss Army fishing pole of the SQL language. You will use it all the time in T-SQL and to build solid SQL Server solutions. The neat thing about this pole is that the entire fishing tackle tool box is wrapped up in its reel. With it you can strip, pare, screw, saw, hammer, combine, pick, scrape, dig, cut, and otherwise expose your data. For all intents and purposes, without the SELECT statement there is no such thing as a SQL query.

You can be as creative as a honey badger trying to expose a beehive, but you can also get stung. As with any programming language, the longer and more often you scratch and claw at it the better you will become. At first sight, a complex SELECT statement can seem impossible to decipher, but once broken down into its constituent parts, it becomes as exposed as the bones of a boiled carp.

The anatomy of the SELECT statement is bound by the order of the clauses. The optional clauses can be added or omitted to serve your purpose, but when used, they must be placed in the appropriate order. The abridged T-SQL SELECT, which is also used to infuse views, is as follows:

```
SELECT (select_list)
   INTO (new_table)
FROM (table_source)
   WHERE (search_condition)
GROUP BY (group_by_expression)
HAVING (search_condition)
ORDER BY (order_expression) [ ASC | DESC ]
```

I prefer not to kick off by expanding every section in one behemoth of a SELECT syntax. I believe that if you are new at SQL queries, it makes more sense to look at the bare-bones SELECT and move up from there. After you have mastered basic selects, you can start using the optional constructions and add fat where you need to.

If you are not familiar with the T-SQL SELECT statement, the following treatise takes you through the statement line by line, clause by clause, argument by argument. And if you are experienced, bear in mind that several new elements have been added since the version 7.0 days, such as XML support.

SELECT 101

The SELECT keyword in the preceding code listing is marked in bold because it is the only part of the T-SQL SELECT statement that is required. All other clauses and arguments are optional. SELECT does not need a FROM clause when you are only specifying constants, variables, and arithmetic expressions in the select list. As soon as you specify column names, you need FROM, which is discussed later in this chapter. The simplest T-SQL select statement might be something as follows:

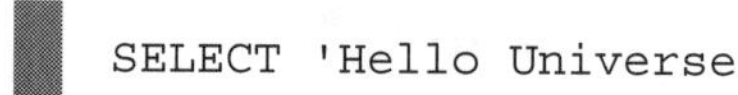

```
SELECT 'Hello Universe'
```

As I am sure you have guessed, this statement does not need any table-based data to complete successfully. It simply returns "Hello Universe" as a single value in a one-row result set. Move from characters to integers and you can perform simple arithmetic after the SELECT, which also just puts the result into a result set, albeit just one value like this:

```
SELECT 1
```

The words that come immediately after the SELECT statement in the query (in the preceding example, it's the number "1") are known as the *select list.* The select list contains the values or column names or domain names in a table you are querying. You can list as many values as you might need; but you must make sure the values are separated by the correct operators.

The rules of precedence also apply behind the SELECT statement. For example, the SELECT statements

```
SELECT 5-3/(8+9)
SELECT 5-3/8+9
```

return different results thanks to rules of precedence (which are discussed in Chapter 16).

When you use divergent data types in the SELECT, obviously type rules apply. You certainly will obtain an error if you try something like dividing "cat" by "dog." The only way this will work is if cat and dog are specifically cast as integer values.

You can have a SELECT statement that queries SQL Server as a system and is not "aimed" at any tables per se. For example, the line

```
SELECT @@SERVERNAME
```

returns the name of the server you are connected to as a result set of one record (see Appendix A for many functions and constructions that return result set data from SQL Server's system tables), But the statement

```
SELECT @@SERVERNAME+@@SERVICENAME
```

returns servernameservicename as a single value, or MCSQL00MSSQLSERVER, which is the server I am using for this little demo. In order to retrieve each value as a column, the items in the select list must be separated correctly by the comma. Thus the statement

```
SELECT @@SERVERNAME, @@SERVICENAME
```

is returned as follows:

(No column name)	(No column name)
MCSQL00	MSSQLSERVER

To add column names to the result set, the statement should look like this:

```
SELECT 'SERVER NAME' = @@SERVERNAME, 'SERVICE NAME' = @@SERVICENAME
```

which will return the following result set:

SERVER NAME	SERVICE NAME
MCSQL00	MSSQLSERVER

And you can use square brackets instead of the single quotes to designate the column names, which is often preferable if you need the single quotes for various concatenations. In other words, the statement

```
SELECT [SERVER NAME] = @@SERVERNAME, [SERVICE NAME] = @@SERVICENAME
```

returns the identical result set. The square brackets are also essential for identifying actual column names that are the combination of several words. For example, the column name *total fences jumped by the counting sheep* will cause SQL Server to blow a fuse unless it is enclosed in square brackets; thus,

```
SELECT [Total fences jumped by the counting sheep] = 196
```

you would need a psych consult if you named columns like in the preceding example, which is extreme for illustration. Column names should be easy to reference in your queries.

You can also use T-SQL functions in the select list to massage the data. For example, you can trim spaces from the left and right of character data and even manipulate the character strings. You can concatenate and do snazzy stuff like adding commas between values and so forth. Here's another take on the preceding query before we move on to the harder stuff: The statement

```
SELECT [Server and Service Name] = @@SERVERNAME + ', ' + @@SERVICENAME
```

will give you the following in return:

Server and Service Name

MCSQL00, MSSQLSERVER

Many Happy Returns

Just when you thought there was nothing between you and the select list just described, we come across three "qualifying" arguments that let you determine just how many rows of data satisfying the query should be returned in the result set. But these elements are essential tools used to fulfil those "wise use" goals we spoke about earlier. The arguments are listed in the following syntax in bold:

```
SELECT [ ALL | DISTINCT ]
[ TOP n [ PERCENT ] [ WITH TIES ] ]
. . . select_list
FROM . . . table source
```

They must also be placed immediately after the SELECT keyword and before any item in the select list, including the * (star), which specifies all columns. The rows are returned in arbitrary order, as they were entered into the table, unless you specify a particular order.

ALL

The ALL (SELECT ALL) argument is the default and can be omitted. It specifies that all rows that satisfy the query criteria must be returned in the result set, even duplicate rows (integrity rules aside) and NULLs.

DISTINCT

The DISTINCT (SELECT DISTINCT) argument specifies that only unique rows can appear in the result set. In T-SQL, the NULL values are considered equal with respect to DISTINCT (see Chapter 17 for a full discussion of NULL usage in T-SQL). As you know from the discussion of NULL in Chapter 17, NULL is never equal because an unknown or missing value can never be compared to another unknown or missing value. However, for the purposes of DISTINCT, the NULL values are returned. In other words, if you have two rows of all NULL data, only one will be returned.

TOP

This TOP argument (SELECT TOP) replaces the now passé SET ROWCOUNT command used in the days prior to version 7.0. It forces the query to return only first *n* rows that satisfy the query, in the order they were inserted into the table. The placeholder *n* must be an integer between 0 and 4294967295. For example, the query

```
SELECT TOP 2 Agent_Name FROM Agents
```

will return A1 and A2 from the table. Be careful not to forget the name of the column you are querying, or use the *, condition because it is easy to think you can just query the table as SELECT TOP 2 FROM Agents. You can also specify more than the actual number of rows in the table; SQL Server will return all available rows less than the value of *n* instead of returning an error.

If you follow the TOP argument with the PERCENT option keyword, the number represented by placeholder *n* becomes a percentage value instead of an integer. In other words, the query

```
SELECT TOP 50 PERCENT Agent_Name FROM Agents
```

will return 50 percent of the rows in the table (the TOP 50 percent, that is). As I am sure you have figured out, the PERCENT option is useful if you do not know how many records will be returned in the result set. Still, asking for the TOP 2 percent might be asking for more rows than you care to return to the client. With terabyte and exabyte databases fast becoming standard issue on the Internet, returning the TOP one percent might be enough rows to turn the network resources into something resembling mango compote. (Use the @@ROWCOUNT function to check the actual number of rows returned, and if there are too many rows you can suggest a more sensible percent value to the user).

And what about rules for PERCENT? The percent value must be between 0 and 100; anything above will error out.

The TOP can also be suffixed with the WITH TIES option. This option forces the query to return additional rows with the same value in ORDER BY columns appearing as the last of the TOP *n* (PERCENT) rows. As an essential rule, the WITH TIES qualifier can only be specified if your query specifies the ORDER BY clause. If this sounds confusing, have a look at the result set of the following SELECT TOP:

```
SELECT TOP 5 Agent_Name FROM Agents
```

The query returns the following result set:

Agent_Name
A1
A2
A3
A4
A5

Now suppose the sixth row was also "A5" and you specified WITH TIES followed by ORDER BY on Agent_NAME like this:

```
SELECT TOP 5 WITH TIES Agent_Name FROM Agents ORDER BY Agent_Name
```

The result set would now be as follows for a TOP 5 query:

Agent_Name
A1
A2
A3
A4
A5
A5

If you have reason to use TOP accompanied by WITH TIES, it is important to understand that these arguments act on the data returned in the result sets and have nothing to do with what lies below in the base table. Also, WITH TIES only works if the query is capped with the ORDER BY clause on the pertinent column and any rows that tie at the end of the result set.

If you need to, you can also tag ASC or DESC onto the end of the query to specify returning the TOP items from an ascended order or a descended order. The results will be very different because the column is sorted ASC or DESC on the base table and not on the final result of the query.

You can also specify DISTINCT with TOP to drop any duplicate rows in the result set.

Understanding the Select List

As mentioned earlier, items specified in the select list, separated by commas, represent the columns from which data is selected for the result set. If we look at the syntax of the select list, we see that it can be simple, as demonstrated previously, or complex enough to give you a hernia.

```
{ *
| { table_name | view_name | table_alias }.*
| { column_name | expression | IDENTITYCOL | ROWGUIDCOL }
[ [ AS ] column_alias ]
| column_alias = expression
} [ ,...n ]
```

The first * (star) operator forces the query to select all of the columns for extraction to the result set. The * should rarely be used, if ever, in SQL Server thin-client solutions. Large result sets do not sit well in browsers and devices where memory is scarce. Some exceptions might fly if the table, or a view above it, only holds a few rows and few columns, such as my Agents table shown earlier. The * scope can work for result sets held at the server, but make sure not to force it up against a table with many columns. And if you specify more than one table in the FROM clause, the * can end up returning more data than you care to deal with.

On the other hand, one big round trip to the server might be better than two dozen if the client can handle a thousand rows. It all depends on the solution you need. You thus need to balance "data ecology" with "network ecology."

Unless you specify an order (using GROUP BY) that you want to see in the result set, the columns are returned in the order in which they exist in the table or view. I will get back to the ORDER BY option later, but you should be aware that it applies to how the results are sorted, not how the columns are ordered in the result set.

The syntax *table_name* | *view_name* | *table_alias*.* means that you can prefix columns with the names of the tables or view, or their aliases. This practice is suggested to avoid ambiguity, especially when dealing with more than one table that has the same column names. For example, the statement SELECT Orders.CustomerID FROM Orders is the same thing as SELECT CustomerID FROM Orders. It also helps the SQL Server optimizer. (See Chapter 16 on the subject of identifiers.)

The * attached to the table name not only limits the scope of the * to the specified table or view, but it has the same result as SELECT * demonstrated earlier. The *column_name* placeholder is the name of a column to return in the result set, as mentioned earlier. However, the column name or names placeholder can also be a constant, function, or any combination of column names and functions connected by operators and subqueries, or both.

IDENTITYCOL returns the identity column values to the result set. (See Chapter 2 and Chapter 16 for more information on IDENTITY columns.) If more than one table in the FROM clause has a column with the IDENTITY property, IDENTITYCOL must be qualified with the specific table name, such as T1.IDENTITYCOL.

The ROWGUIDCOL returns the values of the global unique identifier column. As in the IDENTITY column, if more than one table in the FROM clause has a ROWGUIDCOL property, the ROWGUIDCOL must be qualified with the specific table name, such as T1.ROWGUIDCOL.

The placeholder *column_alias* refers to an alternative name that you can use in the place of the actual column name returned in the result set. The ability to alias is useful and lets you return a more suitable column name in the result set than the actual column name in the base table. Often the base table column names are not suitable for a result set and display at the client. For example, the column name Cust_Lname is hardly a visually pleasing column name. To provide an alias for this clumsy column name, you need to precede the alias with the AS directive. For example, the statement

```
SELECT Cust_Lname AS 'Last Name'
FROM Customers
```

will return the following result set:

Last Name
Smith
Smit
Smitz

You can also use the alias to specify column names returned in the result sets of expressions. For example, the statement querying the Qty column in the order details table

```
SELECT SUM(Qty) AS 'Fruit Cakes' FROM [order details] WHERE productID = 5
```

will return the following result set:

Fruit Cakes
298

You can also use the alias feature in an ORDER BY clause. Also, if the query expression is part of a DECLARE CURSOR statement, the column alias cannot be used in the FOR UPDATE clause. By the way, using the equal sign (=) as follows also works:

```
SELECT 'Fruit Cakes' = SUM(Qty) FROM [order details] WHERE productID = 5
```

However, you might find your code easier to read using AS.

SELECT . . . INTO

The INTO clause of the T-SQL SELECT statement creates a new table to hold the result set data. The syntax is as follows:

```
[ INTO new_table ]
```

The *new_table* placeholder specifies the name of a new table to be created. The new table is composed of the columns and rows in the result set. It does not contain any of the attributes of the base table. For example, if you used an alias for the names of result set columns, then these aliases carry to the new table.

The INTO functionality creates the new table based on the expressions in the select list. This alone determines the format of the new table, and each new column has the same name, data type, and value as the corresponding expression in the select list.

There are, however, some provisions. If you include a computed column in the select list, the corresponding column in the new table does not inherit the computed column attribute and the values in the new column are the values that were computed at the time SELECT...INTO was executed.

If you are moving up from earlier versions of SQL Server, you'll remember that you had to enable the *select into/bulkcopy* option. In SQL Server 2000, however, the select into/bulkcopy option has no bearing on whether you can create a table with SELECT INTO; it only has a bearing on whether you can create a permanent table. The amount of logging for certain bulk operations, including SELECT INTO, depends on the recovery model in effect for the database (see Chapters 9 and 11).

You can choose to execute the system stored procedure *sp_dboption* to turn on the select into/bulkcopy option before executing the SELECT statement; however, you should be aware of the following behavior:

- If the select into/bulkcopy option is enabled for the database in which the table is to be created, a permanent table is created. The table name must be unique in the database and must conform to the rules for identifiers as a fully qualified table name.
- If the select into/bulkcopy is not enabled for the database where the table is to be created, you will not be able to create a permanent table using SELECT … INTO. The tables you will create have to be local or global temporary tables that must begin with a number sign (#).

Permissions, of course, apply, which means you can only execute a SELECT statement with the INTO clause if you have the CREATE TABLE permission in the target database. SELECT...INTO cannot be used with the COMPUTE clause or inside an explicit transaction.

FROM

Earlier I introduced you to the FROM clause, which specifies the tables from which to retrieve the rows that satisfy the SELECT query. As discussed earlier, the FROM clause is not required when the select list contains only constants, variables, and arithmetic expressions. In other words, as soon as you specify column names, you are implicating tables, and the SELECT does not know which tables unless you list them in the FROM clause. But FROM is a lot more than a subordinate clause that specifies tables name, as we will soon discover.

The FROM clause requires a source, or more specifically a table source. The table source can be tables, views, derived tables, the results of joins, and rowset functions. The base syntax for the table source is as follows:

```
table_name [ [ AS ] table_alias ] [ WITH ( < table_hint > [ ,...n ] ) ]
| view_name [ [ AS ] table_alias ]
| rowset_function [ [ AS ] table_alias ]
| derived_table [ AS ] table_alias [ ( column_alias [ ,...n ] ) ]
| joined_table
```

The *table_name* placeholder specifies to the FROM clause the name of a table or view, or a table derived from the rowset function. Using the AS directive, you can also come up with an alias to specify as the optional alias name of the table. You can also alias the name of a view. The following example specifies an alias for the base table:

```
SELECT Customers FROM Cust AS 'Customers' . . .
```

At first sight, the alias for a table name specified in the FROM clause seems redundant. It is in fact redundant in simple expressions, but it will make sense when you need to do more with the table than just searching it, as you will soon discover.

The FROM keyword is needed whenever you are referencing tables, views, derived tables, joined tables, and table variables in a SELECT statement. (See Chapter 2 for a primer of on tables and views in SQL Server 2000. Creating them in T-SQL or interactively is covered in Chapter 11.) In this section, we will only use FROM to specify base tables as follows:

```
SELECT * FROM table_name
```

In the preceding example, the statement makes use of the * (star) operator, which instructs the query to return all rows and columns from the table. You can also specify more than one table in the query as follows:

```
SELECT * FROM table_name1, table_name2, table_name3
```

T-SQL lets you specify up to 256 source tables after the FROM clause. If a table or view exists in another database, other than the one you are attached to, or even another server, you must provide a fully qualified table name (FQTN) *database.owner.object_name* after the FROM keyword.

The fully qualified table name does not guarantee you can still connect and run the query, because permissions apply. (See Chapter 9.)

As an example, the statement

```
SELECT * FROM Agents
```

returns the following result set from a two-column table, which represents all rows and all columns:

Agent_Name	Agent_Nickname
A1	Captain
A2	Gish
A3	Kimlet
A4	Frog
A5	Lofty
A6	Hota

Using Derived Tables for the Table Source

Derived tables are virtual tables that you can construct on the fly using subqueries in the FROM clause. You can then use the derived table as a table source to query against. The following statement suggests a simple subquery that produces a derived table:

```
SELECT 'Fruit Cake Sales' = SUM(Qty) from (select Qty FROM [order
details] where productID = 5 ) Orders
```

The result is identical for this query as in the earlier statement for fruit cake sales; however, after the subquery has executed, a derived table is created called "Orders" (an alias), which becomes the de facto table source. This is a very useful feature because you can create a derived table from several different base tables or from some construction that does not use a base table at all. Derived tables can also be concocted in WHERE clauses as a means of providing keys for search conditions and other useful stuff. And speaking of searches…

The Search Is On

While you know that you can SELECT records from a table without searching for a specific record, the SELECT statement would be more than limiting without the ability to search for single rows or a small collection that meets some criteria. The search for rows in the table, or in multiple tables, is provided by a chunk of code within the SELECT statement known as the *search condition.*

The search condition makes use of comparison operators and relationship predicates to look for matching records with which to satisfy the query. The syntax looks a little arcane but is pretty simple to grasp really. The T-SQL official search condition syntax looks like this:

```
{ [ NOT ] < predicate > | ( < search_condition > ) }
[ { AND | OR } [ NOT ] { < predicate > | ( < search_condition > ) } ]
} [ ,...n ]

< predicate > ::=
{ expression { = | < > | ! = | > | > = | ! > | < | < = | ! < } expression|
string_expression [ NOT ] LIKE string_expression
[ ESCAPE 'escape_character' ]
| expression [ NOT ] BETWEEN expression AND expression
| expression IS [ NOT ] NULL
| CONTAINS
( { column | * } , '< contains_search_condition >' )
| FREETEXT ( { column | * } , 'freetext_string' )
| expression [ NOT ] IN ( subquery | expression [ ,...n ] )
| expression { = | < > | ! = | > | > = | ! > | < | < = | ! < }
{ ALL | SOME | ANY} ( subquery )
| EXISTS ( subquery )
}
```

The search condition is used in several places in the SELECT statement. It is also used in the UPDATE and DELETE statements, where it specifies the rows to be updated and the rows to be deleted, respectively. I will deal with DELETE and UPDATE in the next chapter, but let's look into the search condition here and now.

You can pretty much build a search condition that tests scores of possibilities using as many predicates and operators as you need. In addition, operators like NOT can be used to negate Boolean expressions specified by the predicate. And you can use AND to combine two conditions that must both test for TRUE to be included in the result set. OR is also here for the search posse, allowing you to combine two conditions, which will test for true if at least one of the conditions is true.

The order of precedence for the logical operators is NOT (highest), followed by AND, followed by OR. The order of evaluation at the same precedence level is from left to right. The parentheses can be used to override this order in a search condition, as discussed earlier in the chapter.

The < predicate > placeholder represents an expression that returns TRUE, FALSE, or UNKNOWN. It can test on a column name, a constant, a function, a variable, a scalar subquery, or any combination of column names, constants, and functions connected by the operators or subqueries. You can also build an expression that contains an entire CASE function. The following operators can be used in the search condition:

- The = (equal) operator tests for equality between two expressions.
- The <> (not equal) operator tests the condition of two expressions for *not* being equal to each other.
- The != is the ANSI not-equal operator that works the same as the T-SQL operator.
- The > (greater than) operator tests the condition of one expression being greater than the other.
- The >= (greater than or equal to) operator tests the condition of one expression being greater than or equal to the other expression.
- The !> (not greater than) operator tests the condition of one expression not being greater than the other expression.
- The < (less than) operator tests the condition of one expression being less than the other.
- The <= (less than or equal to) operator tests the condition of one expression being less than or equal to the other expression.
- The !< (not less than) operator tests the condition of one expression not being less than the other expression.

The [NOT] LIKE expression indicates that the subsequent character string is to be used with the pattern matching.

The ESCAPE *escape_character* expression lets you search for the exact string that also includes a wildcard character (not functioning in the capacity of a wildcard character) to be searched for.

The *escape_character* you denote replaces the usual wildcard character. To denote this, you need to place the new wildcard character in front of the old wildcard character. For example, the statement

```
select * from items where item like 'Tz_square' ESCAPE 'z'
```

lets you search for all rows that contain the column value "T_square" where "z" replaces the underscore as the wildcard. The key to remember here is that you are searching for the exact string, not a pattern match on several characters. So if you just search on "T_s" the search will fail.

The [NOT] BETWEEN lets you specify an inclusive range of values between one point and another. Use AND to separate the beginning and ending values.

IS [NOT] NULL lets you specifies a search for nulls or for values that are not null, depending on the keywords used. An expression with a bitwise or arithmetic operator evaluates to NULL if any of the operands is NULL.

The CONTAINS keyword lets you search for columns containing character-based data for precise or "fuzzy" (which means less precise) matches to single words and phrases, the proximity of words within a certain distance of one another, and weighted matches. CONTAINS can only be used with SELECT statements.

The FREETEXT keyword provides a simple form of natural language query by searching columns containing character-based data for values that match the meaning rather than the exact words in the predicate. FREETEXT can only be used with SELECT statements.

The [NOT] IN keywords let you specify the search for an expression, based on the expression's inclusion in or exclusion from a list. The search expression can be a constant or a column name, and the list can be a set of constants or a subquery, which is the usual approach. The list of values must be enclosed in parentheses.

The *subquery* clause can be considered a restricted SELECT statement and is similar to the <query_expresssion> in the SELECT statement. You cannot use the ORDER BY clause, the COMPUTE clause, or the INTO keyword in these subqueries.

The ALL keyword is used with a comparison operator and a subquery. It will return TRUE for <predicate> if all values retrieved for the subquery satisfy the comparison operation, or FALSE if not all values satisfy the comparison or if the subquery returns no rows to the outer statement.

The SOME | ANY keywords are used with a comparison operator and a subquery. They will return TRUE for the predicate if any value retrieved for the subquery satisfies the comparison operation, or FALSE if no values in the subquery satisfy the comparison or if the subquery returns no rows to the outer statement. Otherwise, the expression is unknown.

EXISTS is used with a subquery to test for the existence of rows returned by the subquery.

WHERE

The WHERE keyword specifies to the SELECT a search condition to be used to filter the rows returned in the result set. It is also used, as described earlier, to specify the legacy and outmoded outer join as indicated by the syntax as follows:

```
[ WHERE < search_condition > | < old_outer_join > ]
column_name { * = | = * } column_name
```

The < search_condition > placeholder refers to the search condition statement, which can be a simple equality check or can be a lot more complex, using a combination of one or more predicates and the logical operators AND, OR, and NOT.

Note *The search condition syntax also applies to the other DML statements, such as DELETE and UPDATE.*

The < old_outer_join > placeholder specifies an outer join using the legacy syntax and the WHERE clause. The *= operator specifies a left outer join, and the =* operator specifies a right outer join. It is possible to specify outer joins by using join operators in the FROM clause or by using the nonstandard *= and =* operators in the WHERE clause.

You can use both the old and new in your SELECT statement. The more modern syntax goes in the FROM clause, and the older one goes in the WHERE clause. The two methods, however, cannot both be used in the same statement.

GROUP BY

The GROUP BY takes the result set and chops it up into groups. Each group can thus have its own aggregate values, which is useful for ad hoc reporting, as you will soon see. The syntax of this clause is as follows:

```
 [ GROUP BY [ ALL ] group_by_expression [ ,...n ]
[ WITH { CUBE | ROLLUP } ]
]
```

Let's go over the arguments and then look at some examples.

GROUP BY Arguments

The GROUP BY ALL directive tells SQL Server to generate all possible groups and result sets. It even returns groups that do not have any rows meeting the search condition that you specified in the WHERE clause. When ALL is specified, null values are returned for the summary columns of groups that do not meet the search condition.

The *group_by_expression* placeholder offers an expression that you can use to obtain a particular grouping. It can also be used as a grouping column in which the *group_by_expression* can be a column or a nonaggregate expression that references a column. However, T-SQL does not allow you to use a column alias defined in the select list to specify a grouping column.

Note *Columns of type text, ntext, and image cannot be used in group_by_expression.*

When you have GROUP BY clauses that do not contain a CUBE or ROLLUP, the number of *group_by_expression* items is restricted to the GROUP BY column sizes, the aggregated columns, and the aggregate values involved in the query. This is an architecture limitation that originates from the storage limits on the intermediate worktables that hold the intermediate query results. In addition, you cannot use more than 10 grouping expressions when specifying CUBE or ROLLUP, which now follow.

WITH CUBE

The WITH CUBE argument lets you direct SQL Server to introduce summary rows to the result set, in addition to rows provided by the GROUP BY clause. This clause essentially results in a data explosion that returns a multidimensional cube.

ROLLUP

The ROLLUP argument also specifies that in addition to rows provided by the GROUP BY clause, summary rows must be introduced into the result set. The groups, however, are summarized in a hierarchical order, from the lowest level in the group to the highest. The group hierarchy is determined by the order in which the grouping columns are specified. Changing the order of the grouping columns can affect the number of rows produced in the result set.

Distinct aggregates such as AVG(DISTINCT *column_name*), COUNT(DISTINCT *column_name*), and SUM(DISTINCT *column_name*) are not supported as part of CUBE or ROLLUP queries.

When GROUP BY is specified in a query, either each column in any nonaggregate expression in the select list should be included in the GROUP BY list, or the GROUP BY expression must match exactly the select list expression.

If aggregate functions are included in the select list, the GROUP BY calculates a summary value for each group. However, if the ORDER BY clause is not specified, groups returned using the GROUP BY clause are not in any particular order. You should thus make it a habit to always use the ORDER BY clause to specify a particular ordering of returned data.

GROUP BY ALL is not supported in queries that access remote tables if there is also a WHERE clause in the query.

The following is a simple GROUP BY query, which you can later expand with more advanced capabilities such as joins:

```
SELECT Item, Quantity, Category FROM Items
```

returns the following result set:

Item	Quantity	Category
Cabbage	3199	Veggie
Plums	15	Fruit
Squash	98	Veggie
Apes	3434	Animals
Peaches	23423	Fruit
Monkeys	342	Animals

But if you add the GROUP BY

```
GROUP BY Category, Item, Quantity
```

the result set is grouped as follows on Category:

Item	Quantity	Category
Apes	3434	Animals
Monkeys	342	Animals
Peaches	23423	Fruit
Plums	15	Fruit
Cabbage	3199	Veggie
Squash	98	Veggie

HAVING

The HAVING keyword specifies a search condition for a particular group or aggregate. HAVING is usually used with the GROUP BY clause to limit the rows returned by the query. When GROUP BY is not used, HAVING behaves like a WHERE clause, which is why I gave it its own section. The HAVING syntax is as follows:

```
[HAVING < search_condition >]
Arguments < search_condition >
```

The search condition here specifies the search condition for the group or the aggregate to meet. When HAVING is used with GROUP BY ALL, the HAVING clause overrides ALL.

The text, image, and ntext data types cannot be used in a HAVING clause. Also, the HAVING clause in the SELECT statement does not affect the way the CUBE operator groups the result set and returns summary aggregate rows.

Getting back to our simple example, if we now add a having clause as follows:

```
SELECT Item, Quantity, Category FROM Items
  HAVING Category LIKE 'Animals'
```

the following result set is returned:

Item	Quantity	Category
Apes	3434	Animals
Monkeys	342	Animals

ORDER BY

You can use the ORDER BY clause to specify a sort order for a result set. Limitations are that you cannot use the ORDER BY clause in views, inline functions, derived tables, and subqueries, unless TOP is also specified. The ORDER BY syntax is as follows:

```
[ ORDER BY { order_by_expression [ ASC | DESC ] } [ ,...n] ]
```

The *order_by_expression* placeholder specifies the column on which to sort. The sort column can be specified as a name or column alias (which can be qualified by the table or view name), an expression, or a nonnegative integer representing the position of the name, alias, or expression in select list. Multiple sort columns can be specified. The sequence of the sort columns in the ORDER BY clause defines the organization of the sorted result set.

The ORDER BY clause can include items not appearing in the select list. However, if SELECT DISTINCT is specified, or if the SELECT statement contains a UNION operator, the sort columns must appear in the select list. Furthermore, when the SELECT statement includes a UNION operator, the column names or column aliases must be those specified in the first select list.

Note *You cannot use ntext, text, or image columns in an ORDER BY clause.*

The ASC and DESC (ascended, descend) arguments are used as follows:

- **ASC** The ASC argument directs the SELECT that the values in the specified column be sorted in ascending order, from lowest value to highest value.
- **DESC** The DESC argument directs that the values in the specified column be sorted in descending order, from highest value to lowest value. NULL values are treated as the lowest possible values, unless otherwise specified by ASC.

There is no limit to the number of items in the ORDER BY clause (...*n*). However, there is a limit of 8,060 bytes for the row size of intermediate worktables needed for sort operations. This limits the total size of columns specified in an ORDER BY clause.

In our short example, if we now add the ORDER BY as follows:

```
SELECT Item, Quantity, Category FROM Items
  HAVING Category LIKE 'Animals'
  ORDER BY Quantity
```

the following result set is returned ordered on the Quantity column with ASC as the default:

Item	Quantity	Category
Monkeys	342	Animals
Apes	3434	Animals

COMPUTE

The COMPUTE keyword directs SQL Server to generate totals that appear as additional summary columns at the end of result sets. When you use the COMPUTE with BY, the clause forces control-breaks and subtotals in the result set. You can also specify COMPUTE BY and COMPUTE in the same query. The syntax for the COMPUTE is as follows:

```
[COMPUTE
{{ AVG | COUNT | MAX | MIN | STDEV | STDEVP
|VAR | VARP | SUM }
( expression ) } [ ,...n ]
[ BY expression [ ,...n ] ]
]
```

The following list of COMPUTE arguments specifies the aggregation to be performed.

- **AVG** Average of the values in the numeric expression
- **COUNT** Number of selected rows
- **MAX** Highest value in the expression
- **MIN** Lowest value in the expression
- **STDEV** Statistical standard deviation for all values in the expression
- **STDEVP** Statistical standard deviation for the population for all values in the expression
- **SUM** Total of the values in the numeric expression
- **VAR** Statistical variance for all values in the expression
- **VARP** Statistical variance for the population for all values in the expression

Rules to consider when using the compute arguments:

- You cannot use the DISTINCT keyword with row aggregate functions when they are specified with the COMPUTE clause.
- When adding or averaging integer data, SQL Server will treat the result as an int value. This behavior persists, even if the data type of the column was set to smallint or tinyint. For more information about the return types of added or average data, see the BOL references to SUM and AVG.
- When you use a SELECT statement that includes a COMPUTE clause, the order of columns in the select list overrides the order of the aggregate functions in the COMPUTE clause. This order requirement is important for ODBC and DB-Library application programmers to remember, so that aggregate function results are placed in the correct place.
- The COMPUTE cannot be used in a SELECT INTO statement. COMPUTE statements generate tables, and their summary results do not get stored in the database. If you do use the COMPUTE in the SELECT INTO, SQL SERVER will ignore the COMPUTE results and they will not be installed in the new table.
- The COMPUTE clause cannot be used in a SELECT statement that is part of a DECLARE CURSOR statement.

The *expression* placeholder specifies a variable, such as the name of a column, on which the calculation is performed. The expression must appear in the select list and must be specified exactly the same as one of the expressions in the select list. As you can see from the syntax, you place the expression after the COMPUTE argument. A column alias specified in the select list obviously cannot be used within the COMPUTE expression.

Using BY

The BY expression is used to generate control-breaks and subtotals in the result set. Listing multiple expressions after BY breaks a group into subgroups and applies the aggregate function at each level of grouping. If you use the keywords COMPUTE BY, you must also use an ORDER BY clause. The expressions must be identical to or a subset of those listed after ORDER BY, and they must be in the same sequence. For example, if the ORDER BY clause is

```
ORDER BY s, l, t
```

then the COMPUTE clause can be any (or all) of these:

```
COMPUTE BY s, l, t
COMPUTE BY s, l
COMPUTE BY s
```

Note *The aforementioned aggregation and computer facilities of the SELECT statement are useful for ad hoc reporting and the like. If you need to present substantial statistical analysis or create extensive or repetitive financial results, these queries can be a drain on the resources of a standard OLTP database. Rather, take your reporting to the logical level and report against the data warehouse using OLAP facilities.*

FOR

The FOR clause is used to specify either the BROWSE or the unrelated XML option. The FOR syntax is as follows:

```
[ FOR { BROWSE | XML { RAW | AUTO | EXPLICIT }
[ , XMLDATA ]
[ , ELEMENTS ]
[ , BINARY BASE64 ]
}
]
```

See Chapter 23 for the complete lowdown on the XML support in SQL Server 2000.

BROWSE

The BROWSE argument specifies that updates are possible while viewing data in a DB-Library browse-mode cursor. A table can be browsed in an application if the table includes a time-stamped column (defined with the timestamp data type), the table has a unique index, and the FOR BROWSE option is at the end of the SELECT statement(s) sent to SQL Server. You also cannot use the FOR BROWSE option in SELECT statements that are joined by the UNION operator.

FOR XML

FOR XML specifies that the results of a query are to be returned as an XML document. One of these XML modes must be specified: RAW, AUTO, EXPLICIT. XML support in SQL Server 2000 is discussed in depth in Chapter 23.

RAW

The RAW mode takes the query result and transforms each row in the result set into an XML element with a generic identifier <row /> as the element tag (see Chapter 23).

AUTO

The AUTO mode returns query results in a simple, nested XML tree. Each table in the FROM clause for which at least one column is listed in the SELECT clause is represented as an XML element. The columns listed in the SELECT clause are mapped to the appropriate element attributes.

EXPLICIT

The EXPLICIT mode specifies that the shape of the resulting XML tree is defined explicitly. Using this mode, queries must be written in a particular way so that additional information about the desired nesting is specified explicitly.

XML Parameters

The following XML parameters specify the type of data returned in the XML result set:

- **XMLDATA** A parameter that returns the schema but does not add the root element to the result. If XMLDATA is specified, it is appended to the document (see Chapter 23).
- **ELEMENTS** Specifies that the columns are returned as subelements. Otherwise, they are mapped to XML attributes.
- **BINARY BASE64** Specifies that the query returns the binary data in binary base 64–encoded format. In retrieving binary data using RAW and EXPLICIT mode, this option must be specified. This is the default in AUTO mode.

JOINS

As I discussed in the opening to this chapter, it is rare, especially with SQL Server, to encase all of your columns in one table. Such a scenario certainly means denormalized data and poor performance; you would rarely escape serious data redundancy and duplication. When you have more than one table and you need to combine data from the collection into a result set, this is known as a *join*. For some reason, joins strike fear into the hearts of new converts to client/server databases and SQL Server. But we can throw this animal into the same fish stew that boiled down SELECT.

The definition of a *join* is as follows: "A join is the result set that is the product of two or more tables." A join can be a simple referencing of two or more tables as illustrated, using a copy of the Northwind database (Orders cut to 20 rows), in the following statement:

```
SELECT Customers.CompanyName AS 'Customer', Orders.OrderID AS 'Order Numbers'
FROM Customers, Orders WHERE Customers.CustomerID = Orders.CustomerID
```

The result set is as follows:

Customer	Order Numbers
Berglunds snabbköp	10278
Berglunds snabbköp	10280
Chop-suey Chinese	10254
Frankenversand	10267
Frankenversand	10791
Gourmet Lanchonetes	10790
GROSELLA-Restaurante	10268
Hanari Carnes	10250
Hanari Carnes	10253
Lehmanns Marktstand	10279
LILA-Supermercado	10283
Richter Supermarkt	10255
Romero y tomillo	10281
Romero y tomillo	10282
Suprêmes délices	10252
Toms Spezialitäten	10249
Victuailles en stock	10251
Vins et alcools Chevalier	10248
Wellington Importadora	10256
Wolski Zajazd	10792

The statement that produced the preceding result set is a legacy inner join statement, which is still supported in SQL Server 2000 (and I don't see Sequelists parting with it for some time). The ANSI/ISO SQL-92 version supported in SQL Server 2000 looks like this:

```
SELECT Customers.CompanyName AS 'Customer', Orders.OrderID AS 'Order Numbers'
FROM Customers JOIN Orders ON (Customers.CustomerID = Orders.CustomerID)
```

The result set is identical, but notice the addition of the JOIN and ON keywords and the absence of the WHERE keyword used in the legacy code. Incidentally, if you look at the query plans for both queries, you will see that they are identical in every way. The old method was more limiting because it trapped the "join" in a WHERE clause and produced ambiguities in complex operations.

The JOIN keyword specifies that the tables to the left and right of it should be joined. Additional tables can then be joined to the result set to produce an additional result set. The ON < search_condition > specifies the search condition on which the join is based. The condition can specify any predicate, although columns and comparison operators are often used as demonstrated earlier.

However, when the condition specifies columns, the columns do not have to have the same name or same data type. If the data types are not identical, they must be either compatible or types that SQL Server 2000 can implicitly convert. If the data types cannot be implicitly converted, the condition must explicitly convert the data type using the CAST or CONVERT functions.

Let's look at the syntax that uses joins as a table source in the SELECT.

```
| joined_table = < table_source > < join_type > < table_source > ON < search_condition >
| < table_source > CROSS JOIN < table_source >
| < joined_table >
```

Types of Joins

In the preceding syntax, the <join_type> placeholder (SQL-92 compliant) can represent a simple join as described earlier or a more complex left, right, or full inner or outer join. This might become more clear to you if you study the table source syntax for joins as follows:

```
[ INNER | { { LEFT | RIGHT | FULL } [ OUTER ] } ]
[ < join_hint > ]
```

The *INNER* join is the default join type if the type is NOT specified in your query. The keyword INNER specifies to the query that all rows that have matching values specified in the search condition *(Customers.CustomerID = Orders.CustomerID)* are returned. All unmatched rows from both tables are ignored (which was our first example where the orders table contained only 20 rows).

The *LEFT OUTER* join specifies to the query that all rows from the table to the left of the join type declaration that do not meet the specified condition are included in the result set in addition to all rows returned by the inner join. Output columns from the left table are set to NULL. The LEFT [OUTER] of our first INNER example now looks like this after I abridged it from 95 to 20 rows:

```
SELECT Customers.CompanyName AS 'Customer', Orders.OrderID AS 'Order Numbers'
FROM Customers LEFT OUTER JOIN Orders ON (Customers.CustomerID =
Orders.CustomerID)
```

Customers	Order Numbers
Alfreds Futterkiste	NULL
Ana Trujillo Emparedados y helados	NULL
Antonio Moreno Taquería	NULL
Around the Horn	NULL
Berglunds snabbköp	10278
Berglunds snabbköp	10280
Blauer See Delikatessen	NULL
Blondesddsl père et fils	NULL
Bólido Comidas preparadas	NULL
Bon app'	NULL
Bottom-Dollar Markets	NULL
B's Beverages	NULL
Cactus Comidas para llevar	NULL
Centro comercial Moctezuma	NULL
Chop-suey Chinese	10254
Comércio Mineiro	NULL
Consolidated Holdings	NULL
Drachenblut Delikatessen	NULL
Du monde entier	NULL
Eastern Connection	NULL

If we now tag an ORDER BY on the end of the query, we can see the 20 records returned in the default INNER join shown earlier. The following table has been abridged from 95 records for paper conservation:

```
SELECT Customers.CompanyName AS 'Customer',
  Orders.OrderID AS 'Order Numbers'
  FROM Customers LEFT OUTER JOIN Orders ON (Customers.CustomerID =
Orders.CustomerID) ORDER BY 2 DESC
```

Customers	Order Numbers
Wolski Zajazd	10792
Frankenversand	10791
Gourmet Lanchonetes	10790
LILA-Supermercado	10283
Romero y tomillo	10282
Romero y tomillo	10281
Berglunds snabbköp	10280
Lehmanns Marktstand	10279
Berglunds snabbköp	10278
GROSELLA-Restaurante	10268
Frankenversand	10267
Wellington Importadora	10256
Richter Supermarkt	10255
Chop-suey Chinese	10254
Hanari Carnes	10253
Suprêmes délices	10252
Victuailles en stock	10251
Hanari Carnes	10250
Toms Spezialitäten	10249
Vins et alcools Chevalier	10248
Die Wandernde Kuh	NULL
Wartian Herkku	NULL

Customers	Order Numbers
White Clover Markets	NULL
Wilman Kala	NULL
Tortuga Restaurante	NULL

The *RIGHT OUTER* join specifies to the query that all rows from the table to the right of the join type declaration that do not meet the specified condition are included in the result set in addition to all rows returned by the inner join. Output columns from the right table are set to NULL. The RIGHT OUTER looks like this:

```
SELECT Customers.CompanyName AS 'Customer', Orders.OrderID AS 'Order
Numbers' FROM Customers RIGHT OUTER JOIN Orders ON
(Customers.CustomerID
= Orders.CustomerID)
```

It returns the following result set, where all rows in the right table (consisting of 20 rows) were returned (in my example all 20 records met the search condition).

Customers	Order Numbers
Vins et alcools Chevalier	10248
Toms Spezialitäten	10249
Hanari Carnes	10250
Victuailles en stock	10251
Suprêmes délices	10252
Hanari Carnes	10253
Chop-suey Chinese	10254
Richter Supermarkt	10255
Wellington Importadora	10256
Frankenversand	10267
GROSELLA-Restaurante	10268
Berglunds snabbköp	10278
Lehmanns Marktstand	10279
Berglunds snabbköp	10280

Customers	Order Numbers
Romero y tomillo	10281
Romero y tomillo	10282
LILA-Supermercado	10283
Gourmet Lanchonetes	10790
Frankenversand	10791
Wolski Zajazd	10792

Your results may differ because I cut the number of rows from my Northwind tables for illustration.

The *FULL OUTER* join specifies to the query that if a row from either the left or right table does not match the selection criteria, the row be included in the result set, and any output columns that correspond to the other table be set to NULL. This is in addition to all rows usually returned by the inner join. The statement for the FULL OUTER JOIN looks like this:

```
SELECT Customers.CompanyName AS 'Customer',
  Orders.OrderID AS 'Order Numbers'
  FROM Customers FULL OUTER JOIN Orders ON (Customers.CustomerID =
Orders.CustomerID)
```

I am sure by now you can figure out what the result set looks like.

The *CROSS JOIN* specifies to the query to return the cross-product (the Cartesian product) of two tables. This join returns the same rows as if the tables to be joined were simply listed in the FROM clause and no WHERE clause was specified. For example, both of the following queries return a result set that is a cross-join of all the rows in Customers and Orders:

```
SELECT ColA, ColB FROM Customers, Orders
SELECT ColA, ColB FROM Customers CROSS JOIN Orders
```

As you can tell, joining tables can be very useful for producing test data.

Join Hint

In the preceding join syntax, the placeholder < join_hint > specifies a join hint or execution algorithm to be followed by SQL Server. If the join hint is specified, INNER, LEFT, RIGHT, or FULL must also be explicitly specified.

Union

The UNION operator is much like a marriage between two people, even two companies: The union can be consummated, but that does mean the parties are compatible. So is it with the UNION operator that can be used to combine the results of two or more queries into a single result set. The coupling results in the containment in the final result set of all the rows belonging to all the parties to the union.

While the UNION appears easy enough, it has a few sneaky rules that could scuttle the marriage:

- The number and the order of the columns in all source result sets must be identical.
- The data types in each corresponding column must be compatible. If they are different, it must be possible for SQL Server to implicitly convert them, and if not, then you will need to convert them using the CAST() or CONVERT() function (see Chapter 16) before you can attempt the UNION. If you don't, SQL Server will error out.
- If you combine columns that are assignment compatible, but of different type and thus implicitly converted by SQL Server, the resulting column is the data type of the column that was higher in the order of precedence.
- If you combine columns of fixed-length char, then the result of the UNION will produce a column that will be the length of the longer of the original columns.
- If you combine columns of fixed length binary, the result of the UNION will produce a column that will be the length of the longer of the original columns.
- If you combine columns of variable length char (varchar), then the result of the UNION will produce a column that will be the variable length of the longest character string of the original columns.
- If you combine columns of variable length binary (varbinary), the result of the UNION will produce a column that will be the variable length of the longest binary string of the original columns.
- If you combine columns of different yet convertible data types, the result of the UNION will produce a column data type equal to the maximum precision of the two columns. In other words, if the source column of table A is of type integer and the source column of table B is of type float, then the data type of the UNION result will be float because float is more precise than integer.
- If the source columns specify NOT NULL, then the result of the UNION will also be NOT NULL.
- Unless explicitly provided, column names in the final result set are inherited from the first query.

The syntax for the UNION is as follows:

```
{ < query specification > | ( < query expression > ) }
UNION [ ALL ]
< query specification | ( < query expression > )
[ UNION [ ALL ] < query specification | ( < query expression > )
[ ...n ] ]
```

UNION Arguments

According to Microsoft's documentation, the placeholder < query_specification > | (< query_expression >) represents the query specification or query expression that returns the data to be combined with the data from another query specification or query expression. As mentioned earlier, the definitions of the columns that are part of a UNION do not have to be identical, but they must be compatible through implicit conversion.

The UNION argument is the keyword that specifies that multiple result sets are to be combined and returned as a single result set.

The ALL used as in UNION ALL incorporates all rows into the results, including duplicates. If it is not specified, duplicate rows are removed. If you can deal with duplicates and your result set is large, you may think about foregoing ALL because it will force SQL Server to sort and evaluate the data in order to remove the duplicates. The UNION ALL thus costs a lot more than just UNION, as demonstrated in the two query plans.

Views, and Then Some

We have discussed views in several places in this book, starting back in Chapter 2, and it is fitting to discuss them further here on the heels of the SELECT statement and other useful SQL facilities like UNIONs and JOINs. But let's recap before we look at some of the advanced attributes of view technology in SQL Server 2000. A view is a way of looking at an underlying table through a filter. Over the years many database books, SQL Server Books Online included, have referred to a view as a virtual table. But this is simplistic, because a view is really a specialized query that computes to create the filter over the table, thereby hiding tables, schema, and thus data not specified in the query, from direct access. A view is like a pair of sunglasses. You are not seeing a copy of the world through the lenses; you are seeing the same world but with the ultraviolet and gamma rays filtered out.

A view looks like a table, feels like a table, and works like a table with a few exceptions coming up for discussion. You build a view with a SELECT query that is processed against the underlying table. The following CREATE VIEW statement creates a simple view of the Items tables, resulting in the Items2 table:

```
CREATE VIEW Items2
  AS
   Select Item, Category FROM Items
```

The view Items2 is created in the database and can now be worked just like a table. So the statement

```
SELECT * From Items2
```

returns the following view:

Item	**Category**
Cabbage	Veggie
Plums	Fruit
Squash	Veggie
Apes	Animals
Peaches	Fruit
Monkeys	Animals

The data for this table is still derived from the Items table. But the view Items2 filters out the Quantity column.

You can also think of a view as a stored query; in fact, this is probably the best explanation, and one that would be appreciated by Access converts, who no doubt still remember how to create "stored queries," built using SQL and stored in an Access database.

Views have been in use for many years. Their primary function has been to hide tables and provide a measure of security and distance from the underlying tables. You can use views to do the work of complex queries, even to prepare the data for stored procedures, by creating joins, UNION queries, select queries, and so on. Views can also contain aggregations and other complex functionality that returns precise result sets that can then be further queried against.

They continue to do all these things and more. But of late they have begun to play a much more auspicious role in SQL Server, as a partitioning facility. While it was possible to partition views across databases in a single instance and across multiple servers in version 7.0, partitioned views were not updatable, so they had limited use. That has now all changed.

Indexed Views

Indexed views are a new facility in SQL Server 2000 that allow you to store the actual view data along with the view definition in the database (as opposed to just the SELECT query). Indexed views are useful for providing faster access to view data.

We discussed indexed views, schema binding, and so on earlier, so let's go directly to creating the index on a view. For a change, let's create the view in Enterprise Manager:

1. Drill down to the database and view node into which you need to install the indexed view. Right-Click New and select New View. The New View designer loads, as illustrated in Figure 19-2.
2. Create the view using the diagram facility in the query designer as shown or create it using your own T-SQL code. Check the syntax and create the view after all checks out.
3. To create an index, right-click anywhere in the designer and select Manage Indexes from the context menu. The Indexes dialog box, illustrated in Figure 19-3, loads. Create the index and click Close. You are finished.

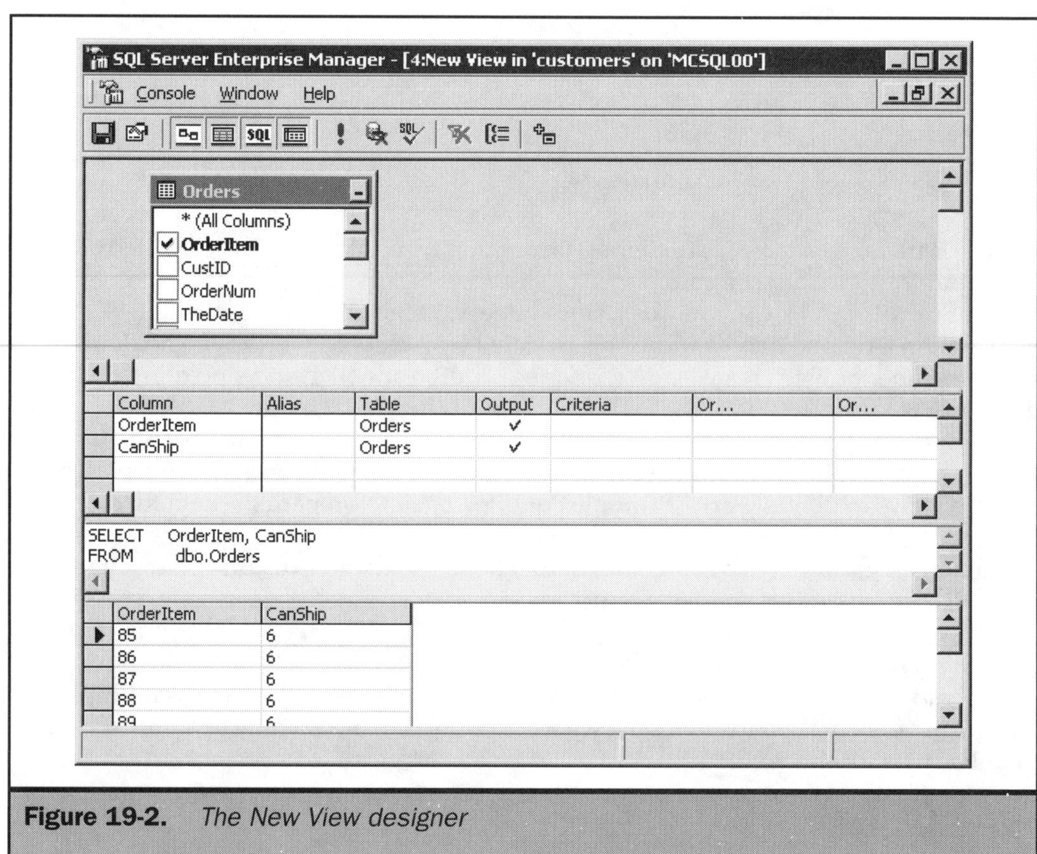

Figure 19-2. *The New View designer*

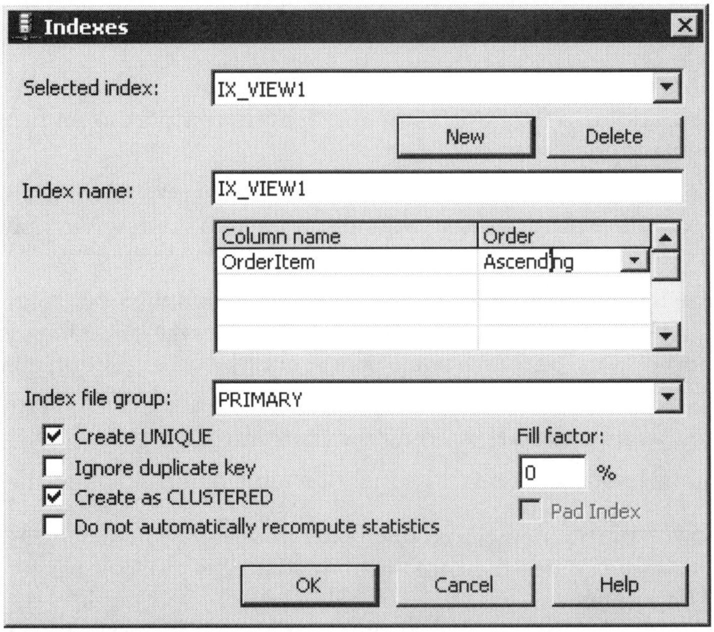

Figure 19-3. *The Indexes dialog box*

For the record, the CREATE VIEW code is as follows:

```
CREATE VIEW dbo.NOOVIEW
WITH SCHEMABINDING
AS
   SELECT OrderItem, CanShip
   FROM dbo.Orders
```

Notice that the view is created WITH SCHEMABINDING, which will prevent the source table from being altered (at the schema level). To alter the underlying table (such as by adding a column), the view and index would first have to be destroyed.

Updatable Partitioned Views

Updatable partitioned views can be used to partition data across multiple databases. They can also be used to partition data across databases on multiple servers, thus providing horizontal scalability of the highest magnitude. Partitioning tables, linking servers in federations, and building distributed partitioned views is really very easy as long as you stick to the rules and follow logic. Here's a checklist with a couple of tips:

- Build your federation in single NT domain, or across transitive Windows 2000 trusts. Intradomain federations are much more complex to set up from a security standpoint.
- Use Windows Authentication to keep the security provisioning simple. If you have a complex security setup, you might have to go down to nontrusted access using a remote login.
- Optimize the member tables so that each federation member is working as well as it can. Also balance the resources (it does not make sense to partition the tables and put one part on a small server and the other part on a large server).
- Make sure you can properly access all the linked servers from Enterprise Manager before you start building the partitions.
- Use unique identifiers and fully qualified table names to build the views.

When views are partitioned across databases in the same instance, they are known as *local partitioned views*. When they are partitioned across multiple server instances, they are called *federations*.

The route to federated partitioned views (after linking the servers) is to first divide a table into a number of smaller tables. These so-called member tables, which contain a portion of the rows from the main table, are then installed on multiple servers—each member table in a new host database on a member of the federation. The configuration looks like this for the example I am going to show here:

- Old configuration: Table 1 = 4,000,000 rows on Server1
- New configuration: Table1a on Server1 = first two million rows from Table1; Table1b on Server2 = second two million rows from Table1.

Let's say we want to partition a view across two servers using a large order table that is being constantly updated from the Internet. One server is struggling and, as discussed in Chapter 13, has reached its scale-up limit. The business is also at a point where it cannot afford the downtime to further boost the initial cluster-pair. So the answer is to add another server cluster while the primary cluster is still getting hits and then, for a small amount of downtime, partition that data across the two servers, thereby reducing the load on the primary cluster-pair. The order of business is as follows:

1. **Link the Servers** Before we can create the partitioned view over the servers, we first have to link them. To link the servers, we have to call the system stored procedure sp_addlinkedserver to add the servers to each other's respective catalogs. You can also use Enterprise Manager, but there is more clutter in the dialog boxes to distract you. If you are setting up inside a single domain, you

only need a few parameters. The details go into the sysservers table. Important: The linking is bidirectional, or two-way. Each server must configure linked servers pointing to the remote server. The code looks like this:

```
EXEC sp_addlinkedserver
     @server='FED_1',
     @srvproduct='',
     @provider='SQLOLEDB',
     @datasrc='MCDC10\MCDCSQL01'
GO
-FED_2 is the local node (default instance)
EXEC sp_addlinkedserver
     @server='FED_2',
     @srvproduct='',
     @provider='SQLOLEDB',
     @datasrc='MCSQL00'
GO
```

2. **Create member tables** The first step, after making a full backup, is to split the primary 4,000,000-row table into two smaller tables, one containing a range of rows, say 1 though 2,000,000, and the other containing the range of rows 2,000,001 through 4,000,000. There are number of ways you can do this, such as copying the database to the other server, restoring to the new server, or using DTS. The primary node is called MCSQL00, while the secondary is called MCSQL01.
3. **Create the Partitioned View** Before this step can be achieved, you must first link the servers and place the member tables on each respective member of the new federation. A primary key must be placed in each member table so that the view can be updated.

Create the Partitioned View

A view is now created that combines the two tables and makes them look like one again to the hungry Web browsers out on the shopping-mad Internet. Before the views can be created, however, there are several rules you have to follow, and these can be a bit tricky. See Books Online for the list of rules; you'll find them by searching for the topic "Creating a Partitioned View."

The T-SQL code to create the partitioned view is as follows:

```
--the view on FED_1
CREATE VIEW OrdersP
AS
```

```
    SELECT * FROM Orders1_2M
      UNION ALL
      SELECT * FROM FED_2.Customers.dbo.Orders2_4M
```

and for FED_2:

```
--the view on FED_2
CREATE VIEW OrdersP
AS
  SELECT * FROM Orders2_4M
    UNION ALL
    SELECT * FROM FED_1.Customers.dbo.Orders1_2M
```

Once the view OrdersP has been created, clients can continue to access the view without needing to know which server it resides on. In other words, the query

```
UPDATE OrdersP SET CanShip = '10' WHERE OrderItem = '246'
```

updates the table on the primary node. On the other hand, the query

```
UPDATE OrdersP SET CanShip = '53' WHERE OrderItem = '3469872'
```

updates the table on the secondary node, unbeknownst to the client. The distributed, updatable, partitioned view is now able to balance hits against the data across two server clusters. To check if the update succeeded, we can just query the partitioned view as follows:

```
SELECT OrderItem, CanShip FROM OrdersP WHERE OrderItem = '3469872'
```

and the result set will be:

OrderItem	**CanShip**
3469872	53

Remember to provide a primary key on all source tables to the view, so that the view can be updated.

Part of the effort to partition the data is discussed in terms of linking servers, in Chapter 12, with respect to data transformation, which discusses scale-out concepts in more depth. Now to an old friend…

In Review

This chapter provides an in-depth discussion of the mainstay of the SQL language, SELECT, and its Transact-SQL "additives." We looked at how SELECT queries can be used to join rows from more than one table using joins constructions and view definitions.

The new support for indexed views was also discussed, as was Microsoft's scale-out strategy for distributed partitioned views, which are built across linked servers that are combined to provide a load-balanced, single, federated access to data.

While this chapter concentrates primarily on query (returning result sets), the next chapter looks at the data manipulation language (DML).

Chapter 20

Working with Operational Data

All good things come in threes. You have the three amigos, the three stooges, the three musketeers, and so on. SQL has its famous trio too: INSERT, DELETE, and UPDATE. I often remark to my clients that you cannot expect a database management system to work for you if you do not insert data into the system. Without these three members of SQL's *data manipulation language* (a.k.a. *data modification language*), DML, there is no way to get data into your database, to modify records, or to delete them.

The SELECT statement I discussed in the previous chapter is also considered a member of the SQL's data "DMLition" team, but we were able to chew on SELECT, and its new collateral features, because we already have data to work with in the *pubs* and *northwind* demo databases. However, the three statements I will explore in this chapter often need a fourth member of the posse, in the form of SELECT, to hit on some heavyweight data crunching problems, and I will discuss this as well.

Understanding the DML three is essential before you tackle Data Transformation Services, Analysis Services, or any online transaction processing (OLTP). In this chapter, I will go over all three statements in detail, discussing the basics of their usage in T-SQL and some new and advanced features for the accomplished DBAs and developers.

Insert

The INSERT statement is straightforward. In its most basic form, it looks like this:

```
INSERT Orders VALUES (value)
```

The target table follows the INSERT keyword, and in the preceding example that table is Orders. After the table, you need to add the VALUES keyword (case doesn't matter), which is then followed by a list of values. In the preceding example, there is only one value, but if the table you were to insert into had several columns, you would need to provide a list of values separated by commas for each column you had a value for. If you didn't have values for each column, that column would have to accept default values or allow NULL values. Consider the following example and imagine only two columns to keep it simple for now:

```
INSERT Orders VALUES (5, 'Cat Food')
```

The VALUES list, which is enclosed in the parentheses (required), represents each column in the table starting with the first. Here, the value 5 of type integer is inserted into column 1 (or zero if you are looking at it from a zero-based recordset), while the second value, of a character type, is placed into the second column.

So now go back to your imagination and add a few more columns and imagine you want to install a value into the "Amount"and "Description" columns and that both columns are somewhere in the middle of a multicolumn table. Your INSERT code will now look like this:

```
INSERT Orders (column 2, column 4) VALUES (5, 'Cat Food')
```

The integer value of 5 is inserted into column 2, while the character (description) value of "Cat Food" is inserted into column 4. You can also identify the columns by name like this:

```
INSERT Orders (Amount, Description) VALUES (5, 'Cat Food')
```

Supplying the column names is essential if you specify columns that are not in order, and possibly even in the wrong sequence. The following code demonstrates switching the order of the columns in the INSERT statement:

```
INSERT Orders (Description, Amount ) VALUES ('Cat Food', 5)
```

Is this easy enough for you? Sit tight, we are still at T minus 10 and counting.... Before going further, let's look over the cryptic syntax comprising the INSERT (I have added a cut line to suggest that the hint section is optional and you will probably not use the hints for 99.9 percent of your insert operations; after all, hints are only for very accomplished developers):

```
INSERT [ INTO]
{ table_name WITH ( < table_hint_limited > [ ...n ] )
| view_name
| rowset_function_limited
}

{ [ ( column_list ) ]
{ VALUES
( { DEFAULT | NULL | expression } [ ,...n] )
| derived_table
| execute_statement
}
}
| DEFAULT VALUES
--8< ---------------------------------------------
< table_hint_limited > ::=
{ FASTFIRSTROW
| HOLDLOCK
```

```
  | PAGLOCK
  | READCOMMITTED
  | REPEATABLEREAD
  | ROWLOCK
  | SERIALIZABLE
  | TABLOCK
  | TABLOCKX
  | UPDLOCK
  }
```

So where did the INTO keyword spring from? I delayed mentioning it because the INTO is optional and belongs to the ANSI SQL specification. If you want to keep your code as standard as possible, you can include the INTO keyword, but it make no difference to the SQL parser in SQL Server.

I have already discussed the table name, but as the syntax notes, you can add the optional *with hint* directive to coerce SQL Server to optimize in a user-defined way. The *with hint* option was discussed in the previous chapter, where it was used with SELECT.

The T-SQL syntax demonstrates that you can also insert into views and the new table data type. You can also just as simply insert into temporary tables designated as temporary by the # (pound or hash) sign. For example, the following code:

```
INSERT #Orders1 (Amount, Description) VALUES (5, 'Cat Food')
```

inserts the data into a temporary table created earlier. Or your recipe might need a temporary table to be created on the fly, using DDL and DML in the middle of a stored procedure perhaps, to cause a result set to persist for the duration of the connection.

```
CREATE TABLE #Orders1
(Amount int DEFAULT 0, Description varchar(50), Notes text NULL)
INSERT #Orders1 (Amount, Description, Notes) VALUES (5, 'Cat Food',
NULL)
```

I have touched a little here on the idea that you will often need to work with default and NULL values. You will also find yourself working with identity column values and columns in which SQL Server automatically adds the value, such as columns of the timestamp data type. We will deal with default, auto, and NULL values in a moment.

The *view_name* argument implies that you can insert data into a view, and you would insert rows to a view just as you would insert rows to a table or a temporary table. The new table data type, however, presents an interesting new addition to the row receptacles now supported by T-SQL.

INSERT with NULL, Default, and System-Supplied Values

When you need to work with tables that have more columns than you are providing values with your INSERT statement, you need to either provide default values for the unspecified columns or allow the unspecified columns to accept NULL.

If your solution requires you to keep NULL out of the tables, you will have to use default values. These values must correspond to the data type accepted by the column or they must be convertible by SQL Server; or you'll need to explicitly convert them using CAST or CONVERT (see Chapter 16). You can also create default objects that have a value property and supply the object and owner name as the default's parameter.

If you do not specify the default, the insert may still succeed as long as the column accepts NULL. If the column is defined to refuse NULL, the insert will fail. In this example inserting in the temporary table we created earlier, the insert installs a default value of zero for the number of cans of cat food.

```
INSERT #Orders1 (Amount, Description, Notes) VALUES (DEFAULT, 'Cat Food',
NULL)
```

You must remember that INSERT means that you are inserting a new row into the table (actually a new row is appended), and providing data for the column values incorporated by your new row. So constraints and triggers will fire accordingly for the table, and any relationships between the target for the insert and other tables (primary and candidate keys) need to be taken into account (more about that shortly).

There are two additional circumstances in which SQL Server will automatically install values into columns. These circumstances are as follows:

- The table includes an identity column. SQL Server will automatically install the appropriate value.
- The column takes a timestamp value. SQL Server installs the timestamp automatically.

Interestingly, however, you can override the identity column value and explicitly provide a value for the identity column as long as you first invoke the IDENTITY_INSERT option. This is done using a SET statement, as follows:

```
SET IDENTITY_INSERT #Orders1 ON
INSERT #Orders1 (ItemNumber, Amount, Description, Notes) VALUES (1234,
DEFAULT, 'Cat Food', NULL)
SET IDENTITY_INSERT #Orders1 OFF
```

Don't forget to turn the IDENTITY_INSERT to OFF after the inserts complete or the next time you run the same statement, SQL Server will pop back an error telling you that IDENTITY_INSERT is already set to ON.

If you explicitly force a user-defined value into the identity column, you need to be sure that you are not going to violate integrity.

Insert and @@IDENTITY

A useful function is @@IDENTITY, which you can call after an INSERT, SELECT INTO, or BULK INSERT (discussed shortly), or after a bulk copy operation. This function returns the last identity value generated by insert operation as described earlier.

The identity value is not generated if the statement failed and tables were not affected, in which case @@IDENTITY returns NULL. The value returned is always the value supplied to the last insertion, and therefore, when you insert multiple rows, @@IDENTITY always returns the last identity value generated.

The @@IDENTITY value is generated by the system for your operation (as the identity provided to the last insert). Even if your statement causes one or more triggers to perform insert operations that generate identity values, calling @@IDENTITY immediately after the statement will return the last identity value generated by the last trigger. You can then use the value as needed by the application. In the following example, I simply select the identity value and use it as an item number:

```
INSERT ITEMS (Item)
  VALUES ('Calamari')
  SELECT @@IDENTITY AS 'New Menu Item'
```

Remember back in Chapter 1, I introduced the two new identity functions SCOPE_IDENTITY() and IDENT_CURRENT(). I am not going to repeat here what I said in Chapter 1, save to say that SCOPE_IDENTITY() returns the value only within the current scope, while @@IDENTITY is not limited to a specific scope. IDENT_CURRENT() is not connected to any scope or session; it returns the identity value of a table name that you must pass as an argument of the function. Consider the following table:

Identity Function	What Identity It Returns
@@IDENTITY	Last identity on your connection
SCOPE_IDENTITY()	Value of current scope
IDENTITY_CURRENT(T)	The last value for table T

You can quickly spot the new built-in functions that come in SQL Server, because they are no longer prefixed with the double ampersand (@@)

To see this working, knock up the following code and run it in QA against northwind or pubs:

```
CREATE TABLE T1 (ItemID Int IDENTITY)
CREATE TABLE T2 (ItemID Int IDENTITY)
GO
CREATE TRIGGER Trig1 ON T1 FOR INSERT
 AS
   BEGIN
    INSERT T2 DEFAULT VALUES
   END
GO
INSERT T1 DEFAULT VALUES
SELECT @@IDENTITY
SELECT SCOPE_IDENTITY()
SELECT IDENT_CURRENT('T1')
SELECT IDENT_CURRENT('T2')
```

These functions can be hard to grasp from code, so have a peek at the flow-diagram in Figure 20-1.

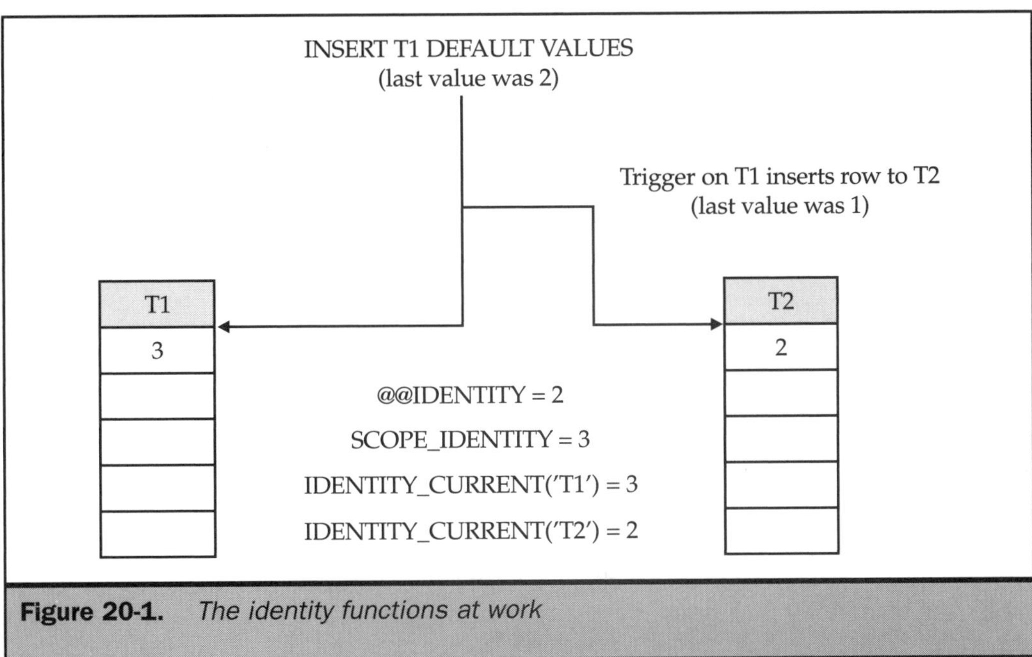

Figure 20-1. *The identity functions at work*

Using NEWID()

If you need to provide a row with an unique identifier, NEWID() will do the trick. Simply call the function and assign the returned GUID to a variable of type unique identifier as follows:

```
DECLARE @MYID uniqueidentifier
 SET @MYID = NEWID()
 SELECT @MYID
```

INSERT with SELECT

Did I not tell you that SELECT will meet up with us here? SELECT can be used in the INSERT statement for a number of useful functions. The primary reason you would toss a SELECT into the INSERT statement is to gather data from one table and insert it into another. That can be easily achieved with the following statement (I have added cut lines to emphasize the inclusion of SELECT:

```
CREATE TABLE #Orders1
 (OrderItem int, CustID varchar(20))
--8< ----add the insert/select in here ----------------
      INSERT #Orders1
      SELECT OrderItem, CustID FROM Orders
--8< -------------------------------------------
SELECT * From #Orders1
```

The INSERT…SELECT code between the cut lines specifies to SQL Server to insert into temporary table #Orders1 the result set from the ensuing SELECT statement. The SELECT statements can be as complex as you need them to be to return the desired result set for insertion into your table or table variable. It can even be the result of a JOIN from Hell.

INSERT…SELECT is very similar to SELECT INTO discussed in the previous chapter.

You can also use the SELECT in your INSERT statement to return the result set of the last insertion or a specific selection of rows. For example, on an order entry system it is useful to insert a new order to the Orders table and then pull a result set using SELECT back to the client in the same connection.

The second SELECT in the preceding code does exactly that. The result set of the first SELECT is not returned to the client, because it gets inserted into the #Orders1 table. The second SELECT returns a result set to the client. You can obviously include a sophisticated search condition described in Chapter 19 to return an updated result set that was narrowed down to the rows of interest to the client. The preceding code works for the temporary table because it persists for the connection. If you ended your session from SQL Server, you would not be able to SELECT from the same temporary table because SQL Server would have purged it from *tempdb.*

It goes without saying that you can also include the TOP optional clause in the SELECT statement:

```
CREATE TABLE #Orders1
 (OrderItem int, CustID varchar(20))
'8< ------------------------------------------
      INSERT #Orders1
      SELECT TOP 10 OrderItem, CustID FROM Orders
'8< ------------------------------------------
SELECT * From #Orders1
```

but you might need the extra garnish like ORDER BY to achieve the desired result set.

INSERT with EXECUTE

The INSERT…EXECUTE works like the INSERT…SELECT. EXECUTE fires a stored procedure, function, or SQL statement that will return a result set for insertion into the target table or table variable. In many respects, very little different is happening between the two INSERT extensions. The result set that returns for the insertion is ultimately derived from a SELECT, no matter that it is buried inside a stored procedure, an extended stored procedure, a function, or the primary code.

The syntax is also straightforward, as follows:

```
INSERT [ INTO]
{ table_name WITH ( < table_hint_limited > [ ...n ] )
| view_name
| rowset_function_limited
}
  execute_statement
```

Your EXECUTE statement can either call the procedure or provide an inline SQL statement. For example, the little statement

```
INSERT NewItems (Items)
EXEC ('SELECT * FROM OldItems')
```

copies all of the rows in OldItems and inserts them into NewItems. If you use a complete SQL statement as demonstrated earlier, remember to enclose the statement between single quotes (many of us forget that). You do not need the quotes when executing a proc or function, as follows:

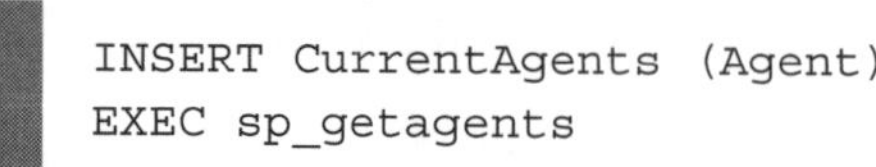

```
INSERT CurrentAgents (Agent)
EXEC sp_getagents
```

The system stored procedure sp_executesql may be used instead of EXECUTE (and temporary stored procedures) to make code easier to read and improve query performance. See "Parameterized Queries" later in this chapter.

Insert with Default Values

Inserting with default values is the easiest of the INSERT statements because you do not need to specify columns or values, relying on SQL Server to install defaults as defined for the column or as set up in the default objects. Here's the syntax:

```
INSERT [INTO]
{ table_name WITH ( < table_hint_limited > [ ...n ] )
| view_name
| rowset_function_limited
}
DEFAULT VALUES
```

Naturally, running this query against a table that does not yet have defaults established will either cause it to fail or install NULLs if the columns are set to accept them. You probably also noticed that no column list is required here. The INSERT will fail with an error even if you supply every column in the target table.

Keeping Tabs on Errors

The ability to report errors in the middle of your INSERT statements is useful, especially when you run a batch of INSERT statements. The following code checks for an error and switches out of the INSERT batch to an error handler, VB style:

```
INSERT BoundToFail (PK_Column) Values ('DuplicateValue')
IF (@@ERROR <> 0) GOTO MAKEITBETTER

MAKEITBETTER:
  EXEC DoSomethingPlease
```

As a matter of interest, a batch of several INSERTS are isolated from each other with respect to errors. When an INSERT in a batch fails, the remaining INSERT will continue unless you trap the error and stop the remainder of the batch from executing.

This error isolation between INSERT statements is useful for inserting bulk data into a table where data is drawn from several sources in which duplicate records might exist. Inserting addresses for a mailing list company or managing e-mail addresses from a Web site are good examples of where duplicate records are bound to exist. You can thus build a loop that contains an INSERT that installs data into a table without first checking for duplicate rows. A unique key constraint, even a primary key on your new table, causes the duplicate insertions to error out, which will cause the INSERT to discard the row, but the loop continues inserting until all source data is exhausted. I have done stuff like this often (even with string lists in Delphi, VB, or Java), using exceptions to achieve a tacit result.

Bulk Insert

I can guarantee that, as a SQL Server DBA or SQL Server developer, you will have your chance to insert what seems to be a bazillion records into a table. Typical scenarios I hinted at earlier include bulk inserting mailing lists, e-mail addresses culled from Web sites, moving operational data into analytical data stores and so on (the latter is becoming less of an issue thanks to SQL Server's new support for Internet applications, as discussed in Chapter 23). I also predict that bulk insert and bulk copy operations will catch fire as DBAs rush to get data out of their inferior DBMS products into SQL Server 2000. The BULK INSERT statement is a T-SQL front end to the command-line bulk copy program, *bcp.exe.*

Note *Data Transformation Services (DTS) can be used to import and export data. DTS is discussed in passing in Chapter 7 and in detail in Chapter 11; it is also accorded some mention in connection with data warehouses in Chapter 24. Also specifics of how the BCP API affects logging are discussed in Chapter 11.*

But there will be many other occasions you will need to use the BULK INSERT over a command line utility. My data center work in large Fortune 500 companies would often include receiving banking transactions from several banks the companies used. The data represented, for example, direct deposit information, and records listing which checks had cleared the bank accounts.

I would typically download each day humongous text files containing tens of thousands of lines of information from as many as ten major banks. This information comes as delimited text files, and the data has to be inserted into the database so that the financial analysts can keep tabs on the company's financial health . . . thanks to that persistent bug that plagues our existence on this earth-bound plane—affectionately known as cash flow.

The BULK INSERT is ideal for such data loading. You might run your script in Query Analyzer or Enterprise Manager, build a GUI front end, or create a service, as I did to automatically download and insert the data every day. The syntax of your T-SQL looks like this:

```
BULK INSERT [ [ 'database_name'.] [ 'owner' ].] { 'table_name' FROM '
data_file' }
[ WITH
(
[ BATCHSIZE [ = batch_size ] ]
[ [ , ] CHECK_CONSTRAINTS ]
[ [ , ] CODEPAGE [ = 'ACP' | 'OEM' | 'RAW' | 'code_page' ] ]
[ [ , ] DATAFILETYPE [ =
{ 'char' | 'native'| 'widechar' | 'widenative' } ] ]
[ [ , ] FIELDTERMINATOR [ = 'field_terminator' ] ]
[ [ , ] FIRSTROW [ = first_row ] ]
[ [ , ] FIRETRIGGERS [ = fire_triggers ] ]
[ [ , ] FORMATFILE = 'format_file_path' ]
[ [ , ] KEEPIDENTITY ]
[ [ , ] KEEPNULLS ]
[ [ , ] KILOBYTES_PER_BATCH [ = kilobytes_per_batch ] ]
[ [ , ] LASTROW [ = last_row ] ]
[ [ , ] MAXERRORS [ = max_errors ] ]
[ [ , ] ORDER ( { column [ ASC | DESC ] } [ ,...n ] ) ]
[ [ , ] ROWS_PER_BATCH [ = rows_per_batch ] ]
[ [ , ] ROWTERMINATOR [ = 'row_terminator' ] ]
[ [ , ] TABLOCK ]
)
]
```

The arguments required are all documented in Books Online, but the text is as sterile as moon rock. You will find further hands-on information here on several important arguments.

Target Databases and Tables

The first arguments before the FROM specify the *database name* and *owner* in the dot notation qualifier style of *object.owner* (also known as a fully qualified table name (FQTN). Then you need to specify the target table for the data. If you leave out the database details, the current database is assumed. You need to make sure the current database is going to accommodate the insert, or it will fail. If you do not specify the owner, and the login executing the script is not the owner, SQL Server will cancel the operation.

Source of Data

The *FROM* clause specifies the source data file. This is the text file containing the data you wish to load into the database. This file can reside anywhere on your network. Obviously if it is local to the computer on which your script will run, performance will be much better because data transfer across the bus is faster by an order of magnitude over a 10/100MBit network being shared by everyone in the company. If the files you are going to work with are huge, you might not have any choice but to source them on the local drive. Some of my bulk inserts take place across the network, however, and they are usually small files that transfer a few thousand rows every day. This should thus be a daily chore so that data does not pile up on the network and become impossible to work with.

The location of the database server is also important. Obviously you are back to square one if you locate the data on the same server as the script and the server is located out on the network. Better to run everything on one machine, or at least from separate drives (see Chapter 6). If you absolutely have no choice but to process the raw data from a network location, then the source file needs to be specified using the UNC path or a drive mapping.

Batch Size

The *BATCHSIZE* parameter is an important variable. This number specifies the number of rows inserted by each execution of the BULK INSERT statement. Well, let me tell you that the batch size you choose depends on a number of factors. For starters, the size of the data file needs to be taken into consideration. The network latency and both network and local host bandwidth discussed earlier also need to be taken into account. These factors consume resources, and if you do not work out specifically how much resources are consumed by the processing of the rows, you are likely to run out of resources and cause the bulk insert to fail, especially if server resources are already borderline.

The bad news is that when you fail in the middle of a bulk insert, the entire batch is lost because SQL Server sees the disconnection in the middle and rolls back the entire batch. So it would be crazy to try to load a bazillion rows in one iteration of the BULK INSERT statement unless you are sure your data is highly refined and you have gobs of RAM and fast hard disks. If you need to insert half a million rows, specify the batch size to be a small number that's chosen in relation to the resources and the environment. Memory is released after each batch is processed, so if you loop through the BULK INSERT script at a hundred or so rows at a time, you will be sure that, if the process crashes or fails for some reason, you have only lost the current batch. Believe me, there is nothing worse than reaching row 999,999 in the Godzilla of bulk inserts only to blow the whole caboodle away on the last record.

After each batch of rows is installed, you can test for errors and rows inserted and so forth. You should also code a routine that checks the last row that was committed to the database, and you'll need some means of identifying where in the raw data file the bulk insert should begin. If you have 900,000 rows processed and the next 1,000 rows fail, it does not make sense to reprocess the whole file all over again, and force SQL Server to manage duplicates again, and so on.

The *BATCHSIZE* argument is directly related to the *ROWS_PER_BATCH* argument that can also optionally be passed in the script. This argument applies if you do not specify the *BATCHSIZE.* But I prefer to specify the former with a parameter because *ROWS_PER_BATCH* causes SQL Server to try to eat the entire data file in one sitting (and available resources come into play again). If you do not specify either, SQL Server makes its own optimization choices, but it still has no control over disasters like a network crash, which would still cause loss of the last batch to be processed.

The Field Terminator

The *FIELDTERMINATOR* is essential to SQL Server so that it knows how to find and separate out the fields or columns in your data. If you do not specify the terminator, SQL Server will look for tabs, which are the default. As you know, there are several characters you can use to separate out the fields. The most common are commas, quotes, semicolons, and tabs. What you specify here depends on the source data file. If you have control over the process that created the source file (such as DTS or another system that outputs the data for you), then you could simply specify tabs and leave the argument to the SQL Server default. Often you have no choice, but it helps to ask the gurus in control of the output (with me it was the batch processing people at the banks) to give you the terminator of your choice, not that it makes any difference to SQL Server what you throw at it.

Important: Do not forget to enclose the terminator values between single quote marks.

```
BULK INSERT Reconciliation.dbo [First Chicago]
  FROM '\\NTS004\FTP\ACCPAY.TXT'
  WITH
  (
    FIELDTERMINATOR = ';'
    ROWTERMINATOR = ';\n'
   )
```

Firstrow/Lastrow

The *FIRSTROW* parameter is useful but only if you are keeping track of the contents of your file. You can easily create a counter in a front-end program or in T-SQL to keep track of the row number last processed by SQL Server, at the end of each successful batch, in the source data file. Then if you have to stop the process and restart it at a later time, you start the batch from the last row installed to the database.

The LASTROW argument tells SQL Server the row number to stop at. After the row number specified, the processing terminates. The default is 0 if you omit the parameter, in which case SQL Server will run until there are no more rows left in the batch.

```
BULK INSERT Reconciliation.dbo [First Chicago]
  FROM '\\NTS004\FTP\ACCPAY.TXT'
  WITH
  (
    FIRSTROW = 9875
    FIELDTERMINATOR = ';'
    ROWTERMINATOR = ';\n'
    LASTROW = 20000
   )
```

Max Errors

The *MAXERRORS* parameter is important too, especially if you use the bulk insert with unique constraints or with a primary key index on the table. If you omit the parameter, SQL Server assumes the default, which is 10 errors. After the MAXERRORS value has been reached, SQL Server terminates the processing. So if you are importing two million e-mail names and addresses and 100,000 of them are duplicates, SQL Server will continue until it has seen 100,000 errors. On the flip side of the coin, you may not be prepared to tolerate waiting around for the processing to finish if you have errors and the maximum error limit is set too high. Set it at 1 if you want the batch processing to end after the first hiccup.


```
BULK INSERT Reconciliation.dbo [First Chicago]
  FROM '\\NTS004\FTP\ACCPAY.TXT'
  WITH
   (
    FIRSTROW = 9875
    FIELDTERMINATOR = ';'
    ROWTERMINATOR = ';\n'
    LASTROW = 20000
    MAXERRORS = 100
   )
```

Order

Another important argument is *ORDER* because BULK INSERT goes easier if your data, as it is sucked out of the source file, is explicitly ordered before the inserting begins. To use it, you must have a clustered index on the target table. SQL Server ignores the order if there is no clustered index and assumes that the data in the source files is unordered on any specific column (no matter what you specify). The insert performance is greatly improved if you use a clustered index on the columns you provide in the *column_list*. The clustered index must exist in the same order as the columns listed in *column_list*. If you intend to set multiple bulk insert processes against the table, it is better to drop the indexes and use the TABLOCK argument discussed next.

Tablock

Including the *TABLOCK* argument causes a special bulk insert table-level lock to be acquired by several clients on a target table with each client holding a lock for the duration of the their respective bulk insert operations, which happen concurrently. This lock obviates lock contention, but the lock in itself greatly improves insert performance. This argument is useful only if you have no indexes installed on the table, or you would have to remove them. It would be a good idea to use it if you do not have a clustered index to take advantage of the *ORDER* clause.

As demonstrated in Chapter 3, SQL Server is able to allocate separate threads and fibers to parallel processes, which makes it one of the few products that can facilitate multiple clients without having to downgrade or share resources among the connections. This means that you can launch multiple bulk insert operations, with each BULK INSERT process performing at the same level as its peer, as close to true parallelism as you will get on one CPU. But if you omit the argument, the insert degrades to a point where you might as well run single BULK INSERT statements sequentially.

Format File

The *FORMATFILE* specifies the name and path of the format file generated with the BCP utility. A format file is used in situations in which the number of columns in the source file is different than that of the target table, the columns are in different orders, column delimiters vary, a combination of several factors. The BCP utility can also specify additional information in the format file.

Bulk Insert and Transactions

You can encase BULK INSERT operations inside transactions as discussed later in this chapter. However, using the BULK INSERT in a transaction with the BATCHSIZE argument will cause the rollback of all batches caught in a transaction that fails to commit.

Bulk Insert, Triggers, and Constraints

The foundation of BULK INSERT and BCP, the bulk copy API, can be commanded to force SQL Server to either fire or suppress triggers on your target table. By default, bulk copy or bulk insert operations ignore triggers. Pass the FIRETRIGGERS argument, *fire_triggers*, if your solution calls for you to fire the triggers.

If you fired triggers, the insert operations will be fully logged. The triggers are also fired once for each batch in the operation instead of once for each row insert (the trigger fires for each BULK INSERT statement that references the table).

```
BULK INSERT Reconciliation.dbo [First Chicago]
  FROM '\\NTS004\FTP\ACCPAY.TXT'
  WITH
  (
    FIRSTROW = 9875
    FIELDTERMINATOR = ';'
    ROWTERMINATOR = ';\n'
    LASTROW = 20000
    FIRE_TRIGGERS
   )
```

Remember to change the recovery model of the database to Bulk-Logged Recovery. This recovery model (discussed in depth in Chapter 9) offers protection against media failure with the best performance and minimal log space usage for bulk insert or bulk copy operations. The actual inserts are minimally logged.

Insert and the Table Variable

I introduced the new table data type in Chapter 16 but think it a good idea to show it in action here with the INSERT statement. The variable is created just as you create any variable, with the *DECLARE @variable* statement. You do not create the table variable as you do a regular or temporary table using the CREATE TABLE statement discussed in Chapter 11. The code

```
DECLARE @MyTableVar table (column1 varchar(30))
  INSERT Into @MyTable SELECT Item From Items
  Select * FROM @MyTable
```

creates the table variable named MyTableVar and gives it a column named column1 of type varchar(30). Next the INSERT comes along and inserts all the rows from the Items tables, restricted to the Item column, grabbed by the subordinate SELECT statement. You can then do as you want with the table type, using it as if it were a regular table.

The table is faster than a temporary table, and it makes more sense to use it instead of one when you need to store intermediate results. Often a T-SQL statement, stored procedure, or trigger requires you to store several result sets for evaluation during the process. In the past, these had to be installed as temporary tables to the tempdb, and thus their creation and maintenance were cumbersome and a drain on resources.

For example, if you used temporary tables in a stored procedure, you would have to delete the tables before or after (or both) executing the procedure.

UPDATE

The UPDATE statement can be a little more complex than INSERT or DELETE because most of the time you will use a WHERE clause and you need to specify a search condition (see Chapter 19) to find the rows that will become the target of the updates. There will also be times when you specify a FROM clause, updating data residing in more than one table. Another key clause of the UPDATE statement is the SET clause, which specifies the columns that are the target for the updates and the values to be used. A simple UPDATE statement might look like this:

```
UPDATE Orders SET ShipPostalCode = '33428' WHERE CustID = 'VINET'
```

The entire syntax for the UPDATE, however, is as follows:

```
UPDATE
{
table_name WITH ( < table_hint_limited > [ ...n ] )
| view_name
| rowset_function_limited
}
SET
{ column_name = { expression | DEFAULT | NULL }
| @variable = expression
| @variable = column = expression } [ ,...n ]

{ { [ FROM { < table_source > } [ ,...n ] ]

[ WHERE
< search_condition > ] }
|
[ WHERE CURRENT OF
{ { [ GLOBAL ] cursor_name } | cursor_variable_name }
] }
[ OPTION ( < query_hint > [ ,...n ] ) ]

< table_source > ::=
table_name [ [ AS ] table_alias ] [ WITH ( < table_hint > [ ,...n ] ) ]
| view_name [ [ AS ] table_alias ]
| rowset_function [ [ AS ] table_alias ]
| derived_table [ AS ] table_alias [ ( column_alias [ ,...n ] ) ]
| < joined_table >

< joined_table > ::=
```

```
< table_source > < join_type > < table_source > ON < search_condition >
| < table_source > CROSS JOIN < table_source >
| < joined_table >

< join_type > ::=
[ INNER | { { LEFT | RIGHT | FULL } [ OUTER ] } ]
[ < join_hint > ]
JOIN

< table_hint_limited > ::=
{ FASTFIRSTROW
| HOLDLOCK
| PAGLOCK
| READCOMMITTED
| REPEATABLEREAD
| ROWLOCK
| SERIALIZABLE
| TABLOCK
| TABLOCKX
| UPDLOCK
}

< table_hint > ::=
{ INDEX ( index_val [ ,...n ] )
| FASTFIRSTROW
| HOLDLOCK
| NOLOCK
| PAGLOCK
| READCOMMITTED
| READPAST
| READUNCOMMITTED
| REPEATABLEREAD
| ROWLOCK
| SERIALIZABLE
| TABLOCK
| TABLOCKX
| UPDLOCK
}

< query_hint > ::=
{ { HASH | ORDER } GROUP
| { CONCAT | HASH | MERGE } UNION
| {LOOP | MERGE | HASH } JOIN
| FAST number_rows
| FORCE ORDER
| MAXDOP
| ROBUST PLAN
| KEEP PLAN
}
```

The UPDATE arguments are explained in BOL in the same fashion as INSERT. But some further investigation on several clauses and arguments is warranted here.

Targets of the Update

You can update values in all base tables, derivatives, cursor result sets, and views, as well as in the table variable and the rowset functions, as long as only one target is specified in the UPDATE. The rowset functions can be either the OPENQUERY or OPENROWSET functions. You can also use the UPDATE in user-defined functions (UDFs) only if the set being updated is an instance of the table variable. And the various shades of target table types are not treated any differently by the UPDATE. Reference them as if the variable or function was nothing more than an actual base table.

Column Names

The *column_name* argument specifies the value at the column field to be updated. The column name must be in the target table specified in the UPDATE. You can qualify each column with the table name in the standard qualifying dot notation. For example, the code

```
UPDATE [Orders] SET
[Orders].CustomerID = 'VITEN' WHERE [Orders].CustomerID = 'VINET'
```

changes five rows in the northwind.orders table. The where clause specifies which rows meet the update criterion. In this case, all rows that have "VITEN" as the CustomerID qualify for the update, and VITEN is changed to VINET.

The SET Value

In the preceding example, the SET value is 'VITEN' (after the =), which can be a string, or a number, or some scalar value. However, the value to be updated by SET can also be derived from an expression that can be calculation or a value returned from a SELECT statement, or the return of a function. Consider the following code, which is valid:

```
UPDATE Orders SET ShippedDate = GetDate()
  WHERE CustomerID = 'VINET'
```

All records meeting the search criterion of CustomerID = 'VINET' are updated to reflect the ship date of the date and time the statement is executed. In this example, I have simply used a standard T-SQL function to return a value for the SET clause. The next example provides the result of a calculation as the new SET value:

```
UPDATE Products SET
UnitPrice = UnitPrice * 10/100 + UnitPrice
  WHERE ProductName = 'Chai'
```

In this code, I raised the price of Chai by 10 percent. The functions or expression you use in the SET clause can thus be a complex as you need them to be; the ultimate objective is that the expression boil down to a single value. Of course the value should be of the same type required by the column, or the value should be converted automatically or explicitly, unless the column type is of sql_variant and your value is not an image or text.

The following SET expression is a little more complex, but it illustrates what you can do to arrive at the value you need for the column data. Let's imagine that a northwind customer with two branches needed to be recorded in the Orders table under one CustomerID assigned to the phone number (503) 555-7555. We can change the CustomerID with the following code:

```
UPDATE Orders SET
 CustomerID = (SELECT TOP 1 CustomerID
 FROM Customers WHERE Phone = '(503) 555-7555')
 WHERE CustomerID = 'VINET'
```

Notice that the SELECT clause is between parenthesis—the statement fails without the brackets. Also notice how we do not need to qualify the column names in the entire statement, because the SELECT clause is unambiguous by virtue of the FROM line.

We can also provide the result of a calculation or complex search expression in the final WHERE clause of the UPDATE statement.

Conditional Updates

Using CASE expressions in UPDATE statements can result in some fancy conditional code, especially if used in stored procedures. The following code updates several prices in Northwind's Product table:

```
UPDATE Products SET
UnitPrice =
  (CASE SupplierID
    WHEN '4' THEN UnitPrice * 5/100 + UnitPrice
    WHEN '7' THEN UnitPrice * 30/100 + UnitPrice
    WHEN '23' THEN UnitPrice - UnitPrice * 10/100
   END )
```

Delete

DELETE removes rows from a table. A simple DELETE statement looks like this:

```
DELETE Products WHERE SupplierID = '7'
```

It knocks supplier 7 from our Products table because the company raised its prices by 30 percent. The full syntax of the DELETE is as follows:

```
DELETE
[ FROM ]
{ table_name WITH ( < table_hint_limited > [ ...n ] )
| view_name
| rowset_function_limited
}

[ FROM { < table_source > } [ ,...n ] ]

[ WHERE
{ < search_condition >
| { [ CURRENT OF
{ { [ GLOBAL ] cursor_name }
| cursor_variable_name
}
] }
}
]
[ OPTION ( < query_hint > [ ,...n ] ) ]

< table_source > ::=
table_name [ [ AS ] table_alias ] [ WITH ( < table_hint > [ ,...n ] ) ]
| view_name [ [ AS ] table_alias ]
| rowset_function [ [ AS ] table_alias ]
| derived_table [ AS ] table_alias [ ( column_alias [ ,...n ] ) ]
| < joined_table >

< joined_table > ::=
< table_source > < join_type > < table_source > ON < search_condition >
| < table_source > CROSS JOIN < table_source >
| < joined_table >

< join_type > ::=
[ INNER | { { LEFT | RIGHT | FULL } [OUTER] } ]
[ < join_hint > ]
JOIN

< table_hint_limited > ::=
```

```
{ FASTFIRSTROW
| HOLDLOCK
| PAGLOCK
| READCOMMITTED
| REPEATABLEREAD
| ROWLOCK
| SERIALIZABLE
| TABLOCK
| TABLOCKX
| UPDLOCK
}

< table_hint > ::=
{ INDEX ( index_val [ ,...n ] )
| FASTFIRSTROW
| HOLDLOCK
| NOLOCK
| PAGLOCK
| READCOMMITTED
| READPAST
| READUNCOMMITTED
| REPEATABLEREAD
| ROWLOCK
| SERIALIZABLE
| TABLOCK
| TABLOCKX
| UPDLOCK
}

< query_hint > ::=
{ { HASH | ORDER } GROUP
| { CONCAT | HASH | MERGE } UNION
| FAST number_rows
| FORCE ORDER
| MAXDOP
| ROBUST PLAN
| KEEP PLAN
}
```

As demonstrated by the syntax, you will always need to provide a source table or result set variable from which to delete a row or series of rows; however, the FROM is optional and represents ANSI SQL-92 standard syntax. (You use DROP if the object of the delete was the entire table.) You also do not delete columns in the DELETE statement, only rows or a range of rows that meet a certain criterion, such as where all customers are past due by five years. Of course, if you omit the WHERE clause, you could end up with an empty table, which does what TRUNCATE does (discussed shortly).

Use the system function @@ROWCOUNT in all DML statements if you need to return to the client the number of rows that were affected by any of the INSERT, UPDATE, and DELETE statements, or if it is required as a parameter in a procedure.

While the syntax says you can delete rows in a view, the delete goes down to the actual base table. But if the view is derived from two or more base tables, you would not be able to delete via the view, because there is no way to reference more than one table in the DELETE (from VIEW) statement.

TRUNCATE Table

I mentioned TRUNCATE TABLE earlier, but you should know that while both statements can be used to remove all the rows from a table, there are some important differences. TRUNCATE TABLE, for starters, is much faster than DELETE because TRUNCATE TABLE completely deallocates the data pages and any indexes attached to the table. The DELETE removes the rows one at a time and maintains the data page even at the instant it is devoid of all rows. Also, every row removal in the DELETE statement is fully logged (and thus recoverable after each row delete transaction), while TRUNCATE TABLE cannot log each row as being removed from the deallocation of the data pages, because the rows are not actually deleted; the data page is just unhinged. However, the transaction logs the TRUNCATE TABLE's resulting page removal, which also means much less log space is used.

You can recover from a TRUNCATE if it is enclosed inside transactions.

Here is an example of the TRUNCATE in action:

```
TRUNCATE TABLE Products
```

Very complex, isn't it? So complex is it that often you can forget to include the keyword "TABLE." Running "TRUNCATE Products" will not work.

While TRUNCATE TABLE provides a handy table row eradicator, there are two places you cannot take it:

- It cannot be used on tables referenced by foreign keys.
- It cannot be used on tables that are required in replication scenarios.

DML, Integrity, and Constraints

What sets the SELECT statement, covered in the previous chapter, apart from the INSERT, UPDATE, and DELETE statements is that the latter three result in changes being made to tables. Rows are inserted or appended with INSERT, values are changed with UPDATE, and rows are removed with DELETE. Each action will cause any triggers or check and integrity constraints defined on the target tables and columns to trap your code, and it is thus important to take this into account. For example, if an INSTEAD OF trigger is defined on a DELETE statement when your DELETE statement hits the table, the code in the trigger will run instead. The code might still delete the row, but based on a condition that can be checked at trigger run time, not on something the client process would know about.

The integrity constraints and how they work is adequately covered in Chapter 17, and triggers in Chapter 18; however, a number of aspects and new features must be discussed in this chapter, especially the new cascade operations.

Cascading Referential Integrity

Cascading Referential Integrity (CRI) applies to the DELETE and UPDATE statements only because they reference changes to existing rows. The CRI constraints let you define the course of action SQL Server should take when your statement hits tables on which foreign keys depend.

For example, let's say you want to delete a customer from the Customers table. What then should happen to that customer's records that still exist in the Orders table? The rows in the Orders table would then be separated from any rows in the Customers table, and thus, depending on your solution, they may no longer be accessible.

When you create a table using T-SQL DDL as discussed in Chapter 11, you can specify the action to take upon a DELETE or an UPDATE statement hitting the table. There are two courses of action that can take place for either operation:

- CASCADE or take no action on Delete ([ON DELETE { CASCADE | NO ACTION }])
- CASCADE or take no action on Update ([ON UPDATE { CASCADE | NO ACTION }])

The NO ACTION condition is the default if you incur a referential integrity condition but do not specify anything. If you do specify the cascade operation, SQL Server will cascade the DELETE or UPDATE operations to the related rows in the foreign tables. For example, a cascading delete will result in all the orders relating to the deleted customer being removed as well from the Orders table. This new feature is an incredible time saver as far as referential integrity is concerned, and I use it all the time now. It certainly saves you a ton of time having to code manual cascade operations that have you doing queries against foreign tables and then deleting the related rows.

There can also be multiple cascading actions that can take place if triggers and collateral constraints fire as a result of the cascade. For example, deleting a row from T1 can cascade to delete a row from T2. A cascading delete defined on T2 can thus cause a cascading delete on table T3, much like the domino effect.

A cascading tree or nest structure will begin to emerge, and this is okay as long as the cascade does not become circular and reference a row in a table that has already been axed or updated.

Permissions

SQL Server security will refuse permission to users to execute any of the DML statements (INSERT, DELETE, UPDATE, and SELECT) on a table or view, so you have to explicitly enable the access. Members of the sysadmin fixed server roles, the db_owner user, and the db_datawriter fixed database roles automatically have permission. Members of sysadmin, db_owner, and db_securityadmin can permit other users to run these statements (see Chapter 8).

Parameterized Queries

Use parameterized queries wherever you can. They help SQL Server reuse execution plans so that user queries execute faster after the first compile. For example, the following code suggests "legacy" and "faster" options for a simple UPDATE:

```
--legacy
UPDATE Customers.dbo.Orders SET
Orders.Customer = 'Shapiro' WHERE [Orders].CustomerID = 'A346'
--faster
UPDATE Customers.dbo.Orders SET
Orders.Customer = ? WHERE [Orders].CustomerID = ?
```

Alternatively, you can also use a special system stored procedure that lets you create and pass an entire T-SQL statement as a parameter. The system proc is sp_executesql (see Appendix A); it can be used in standard T-SQL scripts and in trigger and stored procedure code. Consider the following code:

```
DECLARE @SQL1 NVARCHAR(750)
DECLARE @P1 NVARCHAR(10)
DECLARE @P2 NVARCHAR(500)

SET @SQL1 = N' UPDATE Customers.dbo.Orders SET
Orders.Customer = @P2 WHERE [Orders].CustomerID = @P1

SET @P1 = 'A346'
SET @P2 = 'Shapiro'
EXEC sp_executesql @SQL1, @P1, @p2
```

Getting Bold

This chapter covers the legendary, yet powerful, DML statements INSERT, UPDATE, and DELETE, and it introduces some powerful new features that come with SQL Server 2000. We also investigated some advanced stuff including coding conditional logic into the DML statements, using INSERT and EXECUTE together, and so on.

Up to now, we have covered some pretty basic standard T-SQL statements. In the next chapter, we are going to get a little more bold and look at some of advanced features, including user-defined functions, transactions, cursors, updatable views, and so on. So buckle up and put that foot down.

Chapter 21

SQL Server 2000 Advanced Concepts

As powerful as SQL Server 2000 is, most applications work just fine with its default values, and often there is no need to override or assume control of its innermost data-processing functionality. But there are also many times that applications are required to have specialized and critical control over sophisticated, yet still standards-compliant, RDBMS features: locking, transactions, and so on.

No doubt many of you will require such access to functionality and control from the get-go, especially if you are supporting applications and solutions that are not run-of-the-mill. While e-commerce applications, .Net applications, transaction processing, and other distributed solutions are no longer exceptional situations (thanks to the Internet), they still represent areas in database programming that are fairly new-age stuff, especially for desktop or PC solution developers who have finally decided that they need to be liberated. This chapter uncovers what you need to know to tame SQL Server's innermost data processing services.

We will also use this chapter to talk a little about cursors.

Locking

SQL Server, like all DBMSs, supports locking and implicitly and automatically manages it for you for the most part. You can create applications that work with SQL Server and never have to worry about locking data. But in many respects, that's like driving a motor car and thinking you don't need to know what goes on in the engine—until you break down in the middle of Alligator Alley without a fan belt or a fuel line and Skeeter and his tow truck are 100 miles away.

Why Do We Need to Lock Data?

SQL Server 2000 is a multiuser database management system. Today you can have one person accessing data, and tomorrow you can have one million people all accessing the data concurrently. Some of those people may only need to read the data, and if they are allowed to, then they can all share the data or the document. But what if more than one person has a contribution to make; what if more than one person needs to modify the record? What if one user decides to modify a record you are working with and another comes along with information that requires the record to be deleted? Now you have a problem akin to two buyers fighting over an item at a garage sale, each pulling on the item until it breaks in half. When more than one person accesses a record for modification, the record or row may break—in database lingo, the data can no longer be guaranteed to be reliable. Data integrity is violated, and as discussed in Chapter 17, the data is no longer trustworthy.

I love that old saying that "there is nothing more constant than change." Change is happening all the time. But change often needs to be managed, or the transition from one state to the next may become corrupt and the outcome of the change sequence compromised. In high-end multiuser systems the concurrency problem is highly exacerbated.

My first encounter with locking in computer systems takes me back 20 years to when I was a junior reporter working for a daily newspaper. We had this huge computer system called the Atex system, and I would type my news stories into it. Once the article was finished, I would enter the send command and off it would go to the newsdesk. After that, I no longer had write access to the news story. I could read the story, and every time I accessed it I would see that it was being edited or updated and so on. If I tried to change something, the system would tell me that I no longer had write access to the file because it was being updated by the copy editor. The only way I could get write access was to be part of the copy editor group.

One day I managed to hack into the system (I made a friend in the computer room) and reprogrammed my access (so started my sojourn into computer systems and software development). I was then able to get write permission to the file in the copyediting stage, even before the chief copyeditor had finished with the file. So I would go in and change my byline from "By Daily Mail Reporter" to "By Jeffrey Shapiro." When the chief copyeditor found out, he had me "sentenced" to spend six months as a junior subeditor, and my shift started at midnight.

Today you can experience the same thing in your average word processor. It is possible to lock the document so that someone else can read it but not update it. And you can even control the access (read or write) to the file.

In SQL Server databases you cannot afford to be working with data that suddenly becomes updated under your nose. If you receive a message like "the record you are reading no longer exists in the database," then you know that the record was not locked and someone deleted it (or a serious lock or access violation has occurred). The following list explores four specific problems that occur in weak locking situations:

- **Lost update** The lost update occurs when two or more users open a record or document at the same time. One updates the record and moves on. But a second or even a third user updates the record before the original user has finished with it. When the first user finally updates the record, the update made before is lost. Getting back to my copy editing experience: I would change my byline before the copy editor was finished, only to find later that he overwrote my update with the copy still sitting in his terminal's session and my change was lost.
- **Uncommitted dependency** The uncommitted dependency occurs when you allow a record to be read or accessed while another user is still working with it. In database jargon, we say that the user or session is able to obtain a *dirty read* on the data. This means that the later session can read the data and make some decision concerning it. To speed up data processing in certain situations, it might make sense to allow a dirty read. For example, when building computer telephony systems a dirty read was a necessity on certain records because the

overhead of locking was intolerable. For example, if the user was currently setting up his or her telephone extension and locked the record, it would have been unacceptable for an inbound caller to have to wait on the phone until the user was done.

In that situation, the dirty read was acceptable, but it would not be on a financial analysis system in which a session had critical information required to be updated to a record. A lock would be required to prevent the dirty read so that no new sessions could make decisions on the data until the update was complete. If you were about to issue an urgent sell order, you would not want other sessions to keep buying the shares in the time it takes to click the Commit button that updates the record.

- **Nonrepeatable read** The nonrepeatable read is a situation a session finds itself in when it performs multiple reads on data for a specific purpose; only each time it reads the data before its processing is finished, the original variables it depends on for its analysis have changed. This is also known as an *inconsistent analysis problem.* In data centers, often reports and processing can be so complex that the analysis or processing takes hours, even the whole night or a weekend. The processor needs to lock the data from updates so that no variables can be changed before it has completed its task.
- **Expropriated data** Expropriated data, often termed *phantom data* or *phantom reads,* can cause severe integrity problems for databases, even system crashes and failure. If locking is not enforced, and access to a record is not denied for the most critical of applications, it is likely in a multiuser environment that a record you have opened in your application is moved or deleted before you or some process are done with it. Now you have data that you can no longer save because you are in edit mode and the data you need to update no longer exists or has been moved to another location. I call this "expropriated data" because you cannot update or delete a record that no longer exists. This is one of the first issues I had to deal with when developing voice mail systems. A caller would try to leave a message for a user whom the administrator had already deleted from the system.

In situations where these problems cannot be tolerated, you have to turn to locking. And if the level of automated or default locking applied by SQL Server is insufficient or does not meet the solution requirements, you need to manually manage the locking process. Let's now turn to SQL Server's locking features.

Isolation

Even though more than one transaction is executing in SQL Server at any given time, the transactions execute in complete ignorance of each other; the primary benefit being performance. This transaction "traffic" is desirable because the very purpose of a client/server database management system is to allow more than one user to have access to the database at the same time. But the isolation has a downside. It means that two or more transactions without knowledge of each other can collide when they are after the same data. A real-world analogy often amused me and my fellow New York University students in Washington Square Park. People would throw a chunk of bread into a crowd of pigeons and have a laugh on the ones that collided. When two pigeons grab the same piece of food, one of them, usually the weaker, will have to yield. If neither yields, you have a deadlock.

So data integrity is assured by the ability of the DBMS to isolate transactions from each other, and the level of that isolation, in order to prevent the collisions. This is referred to as the *transaction isolation level.* The only way to absolutely guarantee that data being used by one transaction cannot be interfered with by another transaction is to give only one transaction access to the data. Then when that transaction is done with the data, the next transaction in line gets its chance. This is known as *serialization.* However, if all transactions were simply made to wait in a long line, then a transaction that only needed to read data would have to wait unnecessarily for the transactions ahead of it to complete. This would adversely affect the concurrency of data access and result in a slow system exhibiting poor performance.

It is thus possible to relax the serialization of transactions by adjusting the isolation level of the transactions—depending on the nature of the transactions using the data. An isolation scale is thus available that permits for a lower isolation level with higher data integrity risk on the one end of the scale and a higher isolation level with lower data integrity risk on the other end.

SQL Server follows the isolation level recommendations specified by the SQL-92 standard. These are defined in Table 21-1:

What is demonstrated in the table is that a transaction given a serialized isolation level is assured that no other transaction is reading or accessing the data. Lesser isolation levels relax the serialization of the transactions; transaction performance is increased, but data integrity is at more risk.

Isolation Level	Dirty Read	Nonrepeatable Read	Phantom Read
Read uncommitted	Possible	Possible	Possible
Read committed	No	Possible	Possible
Read repeatable	No	No	Possible
Serialized	No	No	No

Table 21-1. *Isolation Levels*

SQL Server 2000 Lock Management

A *lock* is an object that obtains information about the dependency that any process might have on data. Locks are managed by the lock manager, which is responsible for setting and releasing locks, the order of priority of the locks, and so on. Working with the lock manager is discussed in Chapter 12, which deals with SQL Server 2000 administration. The lock manager controls how sessions access data that is locked. It doesn't just prevent access; it assesses how to manage access in such a way that the data is not compromised by the session that "owns" the lock.

SQL Server 2000 automatically locks data that is being accessed by multiple users. It also automatically decides when data gets locked, who gets the benefit of the lock, the duration of the lock, and so on. SQL Server employs dynamic locking architecture, which means that the DBA does not have to manage the locking thresholds of transaction, and the developer can concentrate on making good query code without having to worry about locking. We will return to dynamic locking later in this chapter.

All locks are issued to connections on a first-come, first-serve basis. The locking architecture is pessimistic by default. In terms of locking, "pessimistic" means that SQL Server assumes that the data is subject to concurrent access and could thus be compromised. The manager manages the locks on a *transaction* basis and on a *session* basis. You cannot, for example, obtain a lock in one session, even as one user, and then try and access the data from another session (connection). For example, you cannot execute a stored procedure in one connection that obtains a lock on the row and then execute another stored procedure, even another instance of the same procedure, in another session in the hope that the two sessions can access the data. This is only permitted through a bound connection, as is discussed later.

Lock Granularity

Locks can be placed at many different levels in your database. SQL Server can obtain a lock on a single row at the one end of the "granularity scale" and on the entire database at the other end of the scale. The various levels of granularity, described in Chapter 4, are, from lowest level to highest level, *row, page, key* or *key-range, index, table,* and *database.* Table 21-2 illustrates the actual objects that are protected from clashing interests.

The lock manager manages the level at which locks are acquired; the user or administrator is not required to perform any specific manual configuration unless an exceptional situation calls for it. Likewise, an application does not need to specify the granularity for a session. If a table is very small and there is only one session attached to it, the manager may place a table lock on behalf of the session. However, on a very large table that has many sessions attached to it, the manager will automatically lock rows and not tables. And, depending on the isolation level, SQL Server may resort to a key-range lock.

A key-range lock locks index rows and the ranges between the index rows. SQL Server uses a key-range lock to solve the phantom read concurrency problem. The lock also supports serialization of transactions. The lock is used to prevent phantom

Object Name	Object Description
RID	Row identifier
Key	A row lock within an index, which can protect a key or key range in serializable transactions
Page	The 8KB data or index page
Extent	The eight data or index pages that make up an extent
Table	All data pages and indexes that make up a table
Database	The entire database and all its objects

Table 21-2. *Lock Granularity*

insertions and deletes inside a range of records accessed by the transaction. If you want more detail of how the key-range lock works, consult Books Online. SQL Server pretty much handles the key-range lock for you automatically and part of its end-to-end lock management technology.

Lock Mode

The manager also ensures that sessions respect the locks, and that a lock at one level is respected by locks at other levels. The respect that locks have for each other depends on the lock mode. For example, if a session has a shared-mode lock on a row, no other session can attempt to acquire an exclusive lock on the same row. The various modes are *shared, update, exclusive, intent, schema,* and *bulk update.* Table 21-3 describes the benefit of each lock mode.

Shared Locks

A *shared lock (S)* is issued to allow transactions to read data concurrently. For example, multiple concurrent SELECT statements can all read the same data concurrently. However, the data cannot be updated by any transaction for the duration of shared locks on the object. (See "Lock Duration" later in this chapter for information peculiar to each type of lock.)

Update Locks

A common form of deadlock occurs in a database when more than one transaction has acquired a shared lock. When a transaction (T1) is ready to change data it has just read using a shared lock, it attempts to convert the shared lock to an exclusive lock. But if another transaction (T2) has a shared lock and the same idea, it must wait for T1 to

Lock Mode	Benefit
Shared	Used for operations that do not change data (read only). Can be acquired by multiple sessions.
Update	Used for operations that do change data. Can be acquired with a shared lock in place.
Exclusive	Used for operations that insert, delete, *and* update data. The lock has exclusive use of the object.
Intent (intent shared, intent exclusive, intent and shared with intent exclusive)	Used to establish a lock at one level in the hierarchy with intent to move to another level.
Schema (schema modification, schema stability)	Used for operations dependent on schema stability.
Bulk Update	Used for bulk copy with TABLOCK specified.

Table 21-3. *Lock Modes*

release its shared lock. However, T1 sees the shared lock of T2 and also has to wait for T2 to release its shared lock. The two locks wait indefinitely until a time-out or the DBA decides to throw the server out the window (if it is not SQL Server).

To avoid such a problem, SQL Server supports the concept of an *update lock (U).* Only one transaction can acquire an update lock, which means that even if another transaction tries to convert from a shared lock, it cannot. When the update lock is ready to modify the object, it converts to an exclusive lock. The update lock is akin to a shared lock with a red flag.

Exclusive Locks

Exclusive locks (X) get *exclusive* access the object and no other transaction can gain access to the same object.

Intent Lock

The best way to explain an *intent lock* is with an analogy from physical reality. When you walk into a supermarket and to the deli counter, you will often have to pull a tag with a number out of a machine. Everyone holding a number is able to maintain a serving position without having to stand in line, but it gives them the right to step forward for service when their number is called. By holding the tag and the number, they signify an intent to be served. An intent lock is similar in that instead of standing in line to place a lock on an object, a transaction can place an intent lock on an object higher up on the hierarchy when it actually needs to lock an object lower down. It is actually reserving its position for the service of a more stringent lock. Intent locks are placed on table objects. They improve performance because this is the only place the lock manager checks them.

There are three types of intent locks in SQL Server 2000:

- **Intent Shared (IS)** This lock indicates the intention to read resources lower down in the hierarchy (shared locks are placed higher up).
- **Intent Exclusive (IX)** This lock indicates the intention to lock exclusive (for updates or changes) resources lower down in the hierarchy (exclusive locks are placed higher up).
- **Shared with Intent Exclusive (SIX)** A shared lock with intent exclusive allows other intent locks to be placed on the table while one transaction is holding the option to lock exclusive an object lower down the hierarchy.

Schema Lock

A *schema lock (Sch-M)* is acquired by a transaction that issues DML statements on a table, such as column adding, changing, or dropping. This lock prevents access to the schema until the transaction has completed the schema update.

A second type of schema lock is called the *schema stability lock (Sch-S)*, which is used to prevent any operation from making changes to the schema while a query is in process. For lengthy statements that make several trips to the table or take a long time to compute, a schema lock is essential. The last thing you want to happen while executing the query of the millennium is for a DBA to make changes to the very table you are working on.

Bulk Update Lock

The *bulk update lock* (BU) is used when you need to perform a bulk copy or bulk insert and the TABLOCK is specified or the "table lock on bulk load" option is set using the *sp_tableoption* stored procedure.

Lock Duration

The manager holds locks in place for an amount of time needed to ensure the protection of the data. The duration is known as the *lock duration.* SQL Server supports several lock duration scenarios.

The transaction isolation level (discussed later in this chapter) governs shared lock duration. If the default isolation level of READ COMMITTED is specified, then the shared lock is held as long as it takes to read the page. The lock is released when the read completes. If upon opening the transaction the HOLD LOCK hint is issued or the transaction isolation level is set to REPEATABLE READ or SERIALIZABLE, the locks are persisted until the end of the transaction, or after COMMIT TRANSACTION is issued.

Cursors, which are coming up after the discussion on transactions, can fetch one row or block of rows at a time and may acquire shared-mode scroll locks to protect the fetching of additional data. Scroll locks are held until the next fetching of rows or the closing of the cursor. If HOLDLOCK is specified for the cursor, the scroll locks are held until the end of the transaction.

Locks acquired as exclusive are held until the transaction has completed.

Lock Blocks

No connection can acquire a lock if the lock it is trying to acquire conflicts with another lock already in place. This problem is known as *lock blocking*. For example, if a session attempts to acquire a table lock on a row that has an exclusive row lock established, the session attempting the lock is blocked. The block persists until either the in-place lock is released or a certain amount of time for the former connection has passed. Time-outs are not normally set for locks, but this may become necessary to prevent an indefinite wait caused by a transaction that has not completed by a certain amount of time. (See Chapter 4 for more information on the locking architecture.)

Lock Compatibility

You cannot place a lock on an object if it is not compatible with any other locks that are already in place on the objects. If a shared lock is placed on an object, only other shared locks or update locks can also be acquired. If an exclusive lock is placed on an object, then no lock of any other kind can be placed on the same object. But exclusive locks cannot acquire a lock on a resource until a transaction that owns a shared lock has been released. The matrix in Table 21-4 illustrates the compatibility of each lock type.

Note that an IX lock can be placed on the table that already has another IX lock on it. This is permitted because the IX signals intent to update one or more rows, but not all of them. However, if one IX lock wants to jump the gun, so to speak, and update the same rows as another IX lock, it is blocked.

The schema locks do not feature in the matrix illustrated in Table 21-4, because they are compatible with all the lock modes. However, the schema modification lock cannot be used on a table if a schema stability lock is in place and vice versa.

The bulk update lock is only compatible with the schema stability lock and other bulk update locks.

Lock Escalation

SQL Server automatically escalates fine-grain locks into coarse-grain locks as it needs to. This helps reduce system overhead: the finer the lock granularity, the harder SQL

RM/GM	IS	S	U	IX	SIX	X
IS	Yes	Yes	Yes	Yes	Yes	No
S	Yes	Yes	Yes	No	No	No
U	Yes	Yes	No	No	No	No
IX	Yes	No	No	Yes	No	No
SIX	Yes	No	No	No	No	No
X	No	No	No	No	No	No

Table 21-4. *Lock Compatibility Matrix*
Key: IS = Intent Shared, S = Shared, U = Update, IX = Intent Exclusive, SIX = Shared with Intent Exclusive, X = Exclusive

Server works. A key-range or row, for example, require more resources than a page lock or a table lock

SQL Server escalates row locks and page locks into table locks when a transaction exceeds an escalation threshold. In other words, when the number of locks held by the transaction exceeds its threshold, SQL Server will attempt to change the intent lock on the table to a stronger lock—an IX to an X. If it succeeds, it can release the row or key-range locks.

These lock escalation thresholds are handled automatically by SQL Server and you cannot configure their usage or reference them in T-SQL code.

Obtaining Information About Locks

You can obtain and read information about locks by executing the system stored procedure *sp_lock* in your code (see Appendix A). A result set returning a mass of information is obtained. The result set, fully documented in Books Online, returns information about lock modes, locked objects, type status, and so forth.

Examining the information about the locking activity undertaken by SQL Server can tell you a lot about your code and the optimization of queries (especially what goes into your stored procedures and triggers). SQL Server employs a dynamic locking algorithm which determines the most cost-effective locks. These decisions are made on the fly by the optimizer that considers, *inter alia,* the characteristics of the schema and the nature of the query. The *sp_lock* stored procedure will give you information about the lock activity SQL Server has been undertaking. Getting lock information can also help you troubleshoot deadlocks, as discussed shortly. The dynamic locking eases the administrative burden of SQL Server so you do not need to be adjusting lock escalation thresholds. This automation also means SQL Server works faster because it makes lock decisions on the fly and decides which locks are appropriate for the query at hand and the nature of the transaction.

Deadlocks

A deadlock occurs when a transaction cannot complete because another process has a lock on a resource it needs. The other process also cannot complete because the former process has a lock on a resource the latter needs. For example Transaction A (TA) has a lock on the credit table but requires a lock on the debit table before the transaction can complete; it is first updating the credit table and then needs update the debit table. Transaction B (TB) is working in the reverse and has a lock on the debit table, exactly where TA wants a lock. A tug of war ensues and you now have a deadlock because TA cannot complete (commit) nor can TB; each has a lock on the resource the other requires. SQL Server will have to decide which transaction yields.

While SQL Server makes use of many resources, such as threads, to prevent deadlocks, a deadlock is still entirely possible. SQL Server thus employs a sophisticated lock monitor thread which is devoted to deadlock detection and resolving. The lock monitor handles deadlocks as follows:

1. It is alerted to a thread that has been waiting for a resource for a specified amount of time. The lock monitor identifies all threads queued to the resource in the event that it needs to take further action.
2. If the scenario persists the lock monitor begins to determine where the deadlock exists and initiates what is termed and "eager deadlock search." The eager deadlock search is a process whereby the lock monitor thread traces the thread activity to the point the deadlock occurred.
3. SQL Server then chooses a deadlock victim. This is usually the thread that is the least expensive to kill (in terms of resources).

When the deadlock victim is chosen SQL Server rolls back its transaction and sends error message 1205 back to the application in the open session that led to the deadlock in the first place. The application will get the following message:

```
Your transaction (process ID #52)was deadlocked on {lock | communication
buffer | thread} resources with another process and has been chosen as
the deadlock victim. Rerun your transaction.
```

This information is also placed in the error log and thus an application does not have to store the error message, just be aware of it. You should code an error handler in the client application to deal with the error message because it means that the transaction just initiated did not complete. So you might have to ask the user to repeat the exercise or the application might have to take some special covert steps. Pushing the message up to the GUI usually serves no purpose because the user of your application will have no idea what it means. Just the words, "deadlock," "Victim," and "Rerun your transaction" are enough to cause a heart-attack.

The message is returned to the client as soon as the lock monitor "shoots" the deadlock victim so you wait about a 100 milliseconds for the deadlock mess to be cleaned up. Resubmitting immediately could end up repeating the deadlock.

You can take certain steps to minimize deadlocks because there is always a chance a deadlock will occur. Consider the following:

- **Acquire your resources late and release them early.** Don't code transactions that lock objects early, and then keep them locked while you perform the mother of all subqueries. Intelligent code should keep the object locked for the time it is needed and then immediately release it. Ensure your code accesses and releases the objects in the same order.
- **Avoid asking for user input in a transaction.** Gather up the data from the user before you start the transaction and avoid asking for data from the user in the middle of a transaction. If there is one thing you cannot control it is the user. What would happen in the middle of a transaction when you need user input and he or she has fallen asleep, switched to eBay to place a bid, or decided to leap off the roof?
- **Keep transactions short and code them in a single batch.** The longer and more complex the transaction the higher the chance of a deadlock because the resources are locked for longer. Keeping transactions short also means you can code them in a single small batch. Minimizing roundtrips means you can complete the transaction quickly and avoid deadlocks.
- **Use bound connections.** This allows two or more connections opened by the same application to cooperate and not block each other. So any locks acquired by the secondary connections are held as if they were acquired by the primary connection.
- **Use a low isolation level in your transactions.** First decide if the transaction can run at a low isolation level. For example if you use "read committed" for the isolation level the transaction is allowed to read data previously read but not modified by another transaction without waiting for the other transaction to complete. Read committed maintains the lock for less time than a higher isolation level such as serializable, which means less of a chance for lock contention. (Working with the isolation levels is discussed further in the transaction processing section of this chapter.)

Note *A block is a mechanism by which one process prevents another from obtaining access—a lock—to a resource. A block prevents a deadlock and should not be confused as one.*

Working with the Lock Time-Out Setting

SQL Server permits you to change the LOCK_TIMEOUT setting in your application. If your application is blocked from a resource and has waited longer than the LOCK_TIMEOUT setting, SQL Server will send it a message to the effect that the LOCK_TIMEOUT exceeded the time it was set for. This is message 1222 or "Lock request time-out period exceeded."

This situation needs to be explicitly handled by your application with the same diligence described in the deadlock event. Rather than automatically rolling back your transaction as SQL Server does after selecting a deadlock victim, it cancels the statement that was waiting on the resource. You need to then make a determination of what to do next, such as resubmitting the statement or rolling back the entire transaction.

To check the lock timeout execute the @@LOCK_TIMEOUT function.

Locking Hints

You can specify locking hints to SQL Server in your code within your SELECT and DML statements. Although you can use the hints to influence SQL Server, it is recommended you leave the locking process entirely to the SQL Server because they override the current transaction isolation level for the current session. Unless you know exactly what you are doing and why you are doing it hints can have a negative impact on concurrency and cause problems for you.

In the same fashion you can customize locking for an index if you have a very special reason to do so. In most cases you would be better off leaving SQL Server to make the determinations for you.

Transaction Processing

As discussed back in Part I and earlier in this chapter, the essence of a client/server DBMS is its capability to provide access to multiple users concurrently. This is achieved through establishing a session to the server and then in that session sending a series of commands to the server; possibly receiving back a result set, single values, or status information. When you connect to the server, the execution of your code at the server takes place inside a construct known in DBMS parlance as a *transaction.*

A transaction is considered a single unit of work by the DBMS. No matter what you do in the code, nested stored procedures, triggers, constraints, cascading deletes or updates, and so on, the transaction is still regarded as a single unit of work.

I know then that you would probably agree—especially if you are a DBA or a software developer—that our lives could also be considered transactions, single units of work. When you take all the activities and, logically, look at them as one unit, a life, you can see a single transaction, with each activity in it connected to the next. Life is one workload from the day we begin to the day we are committed. It is often said that when you die, time stands still and your entire life is replayed for you. We will not be able to confirm that until it happens to one of us, and we do not really know who controls our transaction logs. But DBMS transactions too have the capability to roll back. This capability to completely undo a transaction, before it too is committed, is called the *transaction rollback.*

The inherent rollback of a transaction thus makes it not only a logical unit of work, but also a logical unit of recovery, because everything that is done within the scope of the transaction is undone. The rollback ensures that, if at any point in the middle of transaction something goes wrong, the DBMS can undo the work that has preceded the processing up the point of the rollback. This makes the transaction an all-or-nothing event. Either everything in the transaction happens, or nothing happens. This is often referred to as the *atomicity* of the transaction.

If a DBMS were to allow certain statements in the transaction to carry on, and the changes they caused to persist, that would lead to suspect data, or data that cannot be considered to be in a consistent or reliable state. Even if everything that was done in the transaction up to the rollback state was copacetic, we still cannot allow only parts of a transaction to complete. It is almost impossible, and taxing on a system, to obtain up-to-the-nanosecond checks that data is "safe," because at any time in the transaction a system can fail.

The transaction management architecture in SQL Server, however, provides the next best thing to the nanosecond safety check. As long as the data persists in the write-ahead transaction log, the transaction will be committed to the database. But if the data is not in any usable form, the server will roll back the transaction to the state before the transaction began. Starting all over, so to speak, as if the transaction had not even started. This mechanism ensures the *consistency* of the data.

SQL Server employs a sophisticated transaction manager monitor that ensures an *atomicity* or "all-or-nothing" rule and a data *consistency* rule. The transaction's start is signaled by the BEGIN TRANSACTION statement, which tells the transaction processor (TP) that work has begun. Transaction failure is signaled explicitly by the ROLLBACK statement, or automatically if the TP itself detects a failure. If the transaction completes successfully, the TP is given the "thumbs-up" with the COMMIT statement and the data is committed to the database. At this point, even if the system crashes, the updates or inserts to the database survive. This is known as the *durability* rule for a DBMS.

Note *If you are wondering if the COMMIT can be undone, it can. You can use the transaction log to rebuild the database to the point of a disaster that was still logically sound according to the TP. For example, if you delete a bunch of data in a human error (like truncating the wrong table), transaction log recovery will heal that. (See Chapter 9.)*

You will recall from the discussion of locking earlier that transactions are isolated from each other (see the Isolation section earlier is this chapter). Following this, we can say that transactions have four important properties, which have become fondly known as the ACID properties or laws—*atomicity, consistency, isolation,* and *durability.* A transaction must adhere to the laws or it is considered to have failed the "ACID test."

Types of Transactions

If you are new to SQL Server development, you will probably now be wondering how in previous chapters, and any code you were writing in T-SQL or with an object model like ADO, you were able to get away with not writing transactions. Well the truth is that you have been writing transactions, or at least that's how SQL Server sees it. SQL Server considers everything executed against it a transaction. Any code you send to the server that is not part of a user-defined transaction is automatically placed into an autocommit transaction. In other words, SQL Server automatically handles the transaction management for you. If your code executes properly, SQL Server automatically commits any data changed or inserted; if not, it rolls back and you get an error.

Three types of transaction are supported by SQL Server: *explicit*, *implicit*, and *autocommit*. Let's look at the autocommit first because it is the easiest to work with. You don't have to do any transaction management.

Autocommit Transactions

The *autocommit* transaction is the default transaction mode of SQL Server. No matter what statement is issued to SQL Server, changes are committed if the transaction completes properly or rolled back if it encounters an error. The autocommit transaction is also the default of any statement transmitted to the server from ADO, OLE DB, ODBC, or the old legacy DB-Library.

However, in autocommit mode, SQL Server takes the batch of SQL statements and processes each one as a separate transaction. For example, in the following code SQL Server encounters a syntax error and is unable to formulate an execution plan for the entire batch, so the entire batch is aborted and rolled back:

```
CREATE TABLE TestTable (Col1 INT PRIMARY KEY, Col2 VARCHAR(10)
  INSERT TestTable VALUES (1, 'apples')
  INSERT TestTable BALUES (2, 'bananas')
   SELECT * FROM TestTable
```

The query at the end fails and no result is returned because the optimizer was unable to compile the batch on the second INSERT because of the syntax problem. In the next example, the first statement is committed even though there is an error in the batch. It does this because in autocommit mode every statement is considered a separate transaction:

```
CREATE TABLE TestTable (Col1 INT PRIMARY KEY, Col2 VARCHAR(10)
  INSERT TestTable VALUES (1, 'apples')
  INSERT TestTable VALUES (1, 'bananas')
   SELECT * From TestTable
```

Autocommit mode compiles the batch because the error in the primary key (1) is only trapped at the constraint check after the query has been compiled and optimized (this is known as *delayed name resolution*). There is no syntax error, and if you run the preceding code in Query Analyzer, it will tell you that the code checks out. If we run this code, perform the SELECT, and then examine the table, we see in the second batch that the first INSERT is committed but not the second.

Running this code in Query Analyzer returns the following error, which indicates that one row was committed:

```
(1 row(s) affected)
Server: Msg 2627, Level 14, State 1, Line 1
Violation of PRIMARY KEY constraint 'PK__test_table__5EBF139D'. Cannot
insert duplicate key in object 'test_table'.
The statement has been terminated.
(1 row(s) affected)
```

Now this behavior may seem contrary to what we have just learned about transactions and the atomicity rule. But if you examine the results, is it not clear that the database is still in a *durable* state, even after the error? It is; this is not the issue. What if the first statement and the second statement *are* both required by your application or code? Consider the following code for a voice message system:

```
UPDATE Extensions SET PrimaryExt = '555-1212'
INSERT NewExtension (VoiceMailExt) VALUES ('5551212')
```

If the phone extension numbers are required to be in 3 + 4 notation separated by a dash and we install a check constraint on the columns to catch the mask error, then in autocommit mode the NewExtension will never receive a call that is not answered on the primary extension. The problem with this is that only a portion of the query code will result in data being committed to the database when the entire batch should have done so. This would clearly be an error by the voice mail system because it would risk leaving an extension without message-taking capability. This is a simple example, but it illustrates the point that in autocommit mode you might have only part of your data committed to the table, leaving the application, as opposed to the data, in an inconsistent state. The way to ensure that all the values or none get installed is with an explicit transaction.

Explicit Transactions

To use an *explicit transaction,* you (and not SQL Server) explicitly define the beginning and end of the transaction. In T-SQL or with DB-Library, you use the following statements:

- **BEGIN TRANSACTION** This statement marks the starting point of your transaction.

SQL Server supports the abbreviated TRAN in place of TRANSACTION.

- **COMMIT TRANSACTION; COMMIT WORK** These statements are used to signal to the transaction manager that the transaction completed successfully and the data insertions or modifications should be committed to the database.
- **ROLLBACK TRANSACTION; ROLLBACK WORK** These statements signal to the transaction manager that the transaction failed and the work should be rolled back; completely underdone, get ready to start over.

Using our simple example demonstrated earlier, we ensure that either the entire batch is "kosher" or it all goes into the trash can. The following code rolls back everything between BEGIN TRANSACTION and ROLLBACK TRANSACTION:

```
BEGIN TRANSACTION
  INSERT Extensions (PrimaryExt) VALUES ('555-1212')
  INSERT Extensions (VoiceMailExt) VALUES ('5551212')
ROLLBACK TRANSACTION
```

SQL Server returns to autocommit mode automatically after an explicit or implicit transaction completes.

Implicit Transactions

A third mode for transactions is called *implicit mode.* To operate in implicit mode, you do not need to delineate a transaction with the BEGIN TRANSACTION statement, but you need to specifically place the session into implicit mode with the SET IMPLICIT_TRANSACTIONS ON statement. But you do need to signal the end of each transaction with the ROLLBACK TRANSACTION or COMMIT TRANSACTION statement.

Using the implicit mode allows you to issue a long batch of statements, enclosing collections of statements in implicit transactions. When you are done in the implicit mode, you need to issue the SET IMPLICIT_TRANSACTIONS OFF statement.

SQL Server also automatically starts a transaction every time it encounters one of the statements in Table 21-5 while in implicit mode.

Transactions and SQL Server Development

The database APIs, such as ODBC, ADO and OLE DB, each contain functions or methods that allow you to manage transactions from the client application. Consult each API or object model for the peculiarities of the function or method call. Naturally, you cannot mix and match the API calls; you cannot begin a transaction in ODBC and end it with a call to the ADO API.

The ACID rules no doubt extend to the client connection and the client. If a client is in the middle of an extensive transaction and then gets squashed by a steamroller, the transaction manager detects the failure and rolls back the transaction. Thus in mission-critical applications, with unreliable network connections, it makes sense not to use the default autocommit transaction mode.

An extensive update or insert to, say, a bank account, over the Internet or even filling in a form, requires you to prevent a situation in which only part of the data is committed to the database. Often it happens that as a browser fills in a form on the Internet, the user loses the connection and has to start all over. Then when the user tries to reissue the user ID that was available before, he or she gets the message that the user ID is taken—case of the partly committed form.

ALTER TABLE	REVOKE
CREATE	OPEN
DELETE	INSERT
DROP	TRUNCATE
FETCH	UPDATE
GRANT	SELECT

Table 21-5. *Statements That Require Transactions in Implicit Mode*

Distributed Transactions

In Chapter 4, I mentioned that SQL Server actually supports a form of transaction management that is not necessarily local to the server on which a session is established. This form of transaction is known as the *distributed transaction*. Instead of processing on just the local server, the transaction is able to span multiple servers that engage in the distributed processing as resource managers, while to the originating session it appears that the transaction is executing locally. The transaction manager on each server coordinates the transaction processing according to standards of operation defined by either the Microsoft Distributed Transaction Coordinator or the X/Open Specification for Distributed Transaction Processing.

Distributed transactions are mainly used to update multiple instances of SQL Server (and any other DBMS that supports either of the DT protocols just mentioned). This is how it works:

At the originating server, the session or client manages the transaction exactly as it does a regular transaction. However, when it comes time to either roll back or commit, a coordination effort is required between all the participating servers to ensure that either all or none of the servers can commit or roll back successfully. In a distributed transaction, some of the servers in the "mob" might be on the ends of unreliable network connections (like the Internet) and may be at risk of being lost in the middle of a transaction.

A coordination effort is required to ensure that all servers were able to run the transactions through to their logical conclusions. The coordination is carried out by what is known as a two-phase commit process (2PC), encompassing a prepare phase and a commit phase. The phases operate as follows:

1. **Prepare phase** When the transaction manager receives a commit request, it sends a prepare command to all the resource managers involved in the distributed transaction scenario. Each participant then goes about ensuring that it has what it takes to ensure the durability of the transaction. For example, all transaction logs are flushed to disk. As each member succeeds in the prepare phase, it updates the transaction coordinator or manager with a success or failure flag.
2. **Commit phase** If the transaction coordinator receives the okay from all servers, it sends out commit commands to the participants. The resource managers on each server complete their respective commits and notify the transaction coordinator of success or failure. If any resource manager reports a failure to prepare, or does not respond after the commit, the coordinator sends a rollback message to the other servers.

There are two options to managing distributed transactions. You can go through a database API, or you can use T-SQL, the preferred method for SQL Server developers. Going through T-SQL enlists the services of the Microsoft Distributed Transaction Coordinator (MS DTC), so there is really not much work that you have to do, and issuing a distributed transaction is not much more work than issuing a local transaction.

The transaction originates either from a stored procedure called by a client application, or a statement executed against the server, or in a script executed either from a command line application or from one of the GUI interfaces that can transmit a T-SQL batch to the server.

There are a number of ways to start a distributed transaction in T-SQL:

- **Explicit** You can start an explicit distributed transaction using the BEGIN DISTRIBUTED TRANSACTION statement.
- **Distributed Query** While in a local transaction, you can execute a distributed query against a linked server.
- **REMOTE_PROC_TRANSACTIONS** If this statement is issued ON and the local transaction calls a remote stored procedure, the local transaction is automatically promoted to a distributed transaction. If REMOTE_PROC_TRANSACTIONS is off, calls to the remote stored procedures execute outside of the scope of the local transaction. A rollback in the local transaction does not affect the remote transaction, and vice versa. Similarly, the transaction processing of the remote transaction is unaffected by the local transaction processing. They commit their work independent of each other.

Note *The REMOTE_PROC_TRANSACTIONS statement is issued if you plan to make remote stored procedure calls to the remote server defined with sp_addserver. See Chapter 18 for more information on stored procedures.*

Working with Cursors

Throughout this book I have told you that data is returned to clients as a result set—the set of rows resulting from a query. At the client the result set is looped through by a client process, which populates a grid or a collection of fields. Sharp queries allow us to return a single row of data that is used to populate the fields, but often we are not sure exactly which row is required and thus we send back as small a result set as possible and allow the user to make the final choice.

There are situations that you may find yourself in, in which it is impossible to work with a result set returned to the client. Online or Internet applications are a good example, in which a result set cannot be returned to the client for further processing. A browser has no functionality to accommodate a long stream of rows coming up the wire (although XML is beginning to make this a reality). Still, if a result set will disappear into a black hole when returned to the client you need a facility to work with the result set on the server. In other words, instead of holding the result set at the client the result set is stored on the server, where the client can work with it one row at a time. This is the essence of a cursor.

You could consider a cursor to be an extension to result set architecture because it enables the following capabilities:

- You can retrieve one row or a block of rows from the result set on the server.
- You can take aim at a specific row on the result set, a feature called row positioning.
- You can modify data at the current position in the result set.

A cursor also allows you to set different levels of visibility to changes made by other users to the underlying data of the result set. And you can access the data from scripts, stored procedures and triggers.

There are two methods for requesting a cursor on a result set:

- You can use T-SQL which is compliant with SQL-92 cursor syntax.
- You can use an API or Object Model that supports using cursors. (APIs include DB-Library, OLE DB, ODBC. And the ADO object model supports cursor functionality.)

Never mix cursor request methods in your application. If you are going native (such as ODBC) stick to the native API. If you use an ADO object then use the ADO model only.

SQL Server cursors have to be explicitly called. If you do not use a cursor call SQL Server defaults to returning the result set to the client.

Types of Cursors

SQL Server provides support for three types of cursors:

- **T-SQL Cursors** These are created using the DECLARE CURSOR syntax and are used mainly in T-SQL scripts, stored procedures, and triggers. These cursors are instantiated on the server by T-SQL statements transmitted by the client. The DECLARE CURSOR syntax is also often used in stored procedures, T-SQL batches, and triggers. Using cursors in triggers is tricky, however, and badly written for very long and involved "cursorized" triggers can bring a SQL Server instance to dead stop.
- **API Cursors** These cursors are also server-based and are instantiated by API calls from the likes of OLE DB, ODBC, and DB-Library.
- **Client Cursors** These cursors are implemented on the client though either API or Object Model features. While the result set is still supported at the server the result set rows are cached in a client facility. So the rows that are modified are the rows that are cached at the client.

You should know that many seasoned SQL Server developers eschew cursors unless they are really needed. The reason for this is simple: performance. The result set is maintained on the server and so SQL Server has to commit resources to the cursor. When a result set is sent to the client SQL Server is done with query and moves on to something else.

Cursors also have limitations that might not help you. For example, they do not support all T-SQL statements, and you cannot use statements that generate multiple results sets—so that means you are limited to one SELECT statement in a cursor-creating batch. Statements that contain the keywords COMPUTE, COMPUTE BY, FOR BROWSE or INTO are SQL *non grata* for cursors.

Why is a cursor less efficient than a default result set? The answer is this: When you query SQL Server for data, a default result set is created by a batch of code, in one connection, sent to the server from a client or from a stored procedure. But with cursors every time you need data you have to send out a FETCH statement from the client to the server, and every FETCH is parsed and compiled into an execution plan.

Getting back to the data conservation philosophy expounded in this book, you should rather code tight queries that aim to return the exact data needed by the client. If the result set is small, or you use new modern technologies such as XML (see Chapter 23) you might be able to avoid a cursor and gain not only in the performance arena, but also in the feature and complexity arenas.

If you need to use a cursor, do this: Favor server cursors and add more resources to the server if you need to because client cursors cache the entire result set on the client and that's not very efficient. Remember, think "thinner is better" for the client. On the Internet or a widely distributed application you never really know what resources the client has and asking a client to cache a cursor is like firing a torpedo that has delayed detonation technology.

Server cursors also by their nature support more features. For example, a server cursor can directly support positioned operations such as update and delete statements. Client cursors make updates and deletes a lot more difficult to manage and are more complex to code. Server cursors also allow your application to open concurrent cursor connections and support multiple active statements to those cursors.

T-SQL Cursors

I could write an entire book on using cursors, and demonstrate them in the various APIs and object models, such as ADO cursors in Visual Basic applications, but since this is a SQL Server reference let's stick to T-SQL cursors.

Where can you use a T-SQL cursor? As mentioned earlier they are best used in standard SQL script, from stored procedures, and in triggers. I am not in favor of the latter, using them in triggers. Triggers should be used for enforcing business rules and not iterating through cursors. Sure there will be times when you need to work with a collection of rows in a cursor, but most of the time you can do the job with the standard default result set held on the server, which gives you cursor benefits (server-held result sets) without the overhead. If your solution calls for a trigger-created cursor try and find a way around it, and as a last resort, keep the trigger-cursor code small.

Note *A T-SQL cursor does not support the fetching of a block of rows, and I do not see this as a big drawback.*

The following steps take you through generating a T-SQL cursor:

1. First you need to declare T-SQL variables that will hold the data returned by the cursor. You will need to declare one variable for each result set column. The variables should be large enough to hold the values. You should also use data types that can be implicitly converted from the data type of the column.
2. Next you need to associate the cursor with a SELECT statement. This is done using the DECLARE CURSOR statement. The statement also defines the characteristics of the cursor. It gives the cursor its name and properties, such as wether the cursor is read only or forward scrolling.
3. The OPEN statement is then used to run the SELECT statement into cursor.
4. FETCH INTO then gets individual rows and puts the data into the variables you created. You can also use other statements to work with variables.
5. When you are done with the cursor get rid of it using the CLOSE statement. By closing the cursor you free up resources and drop locks and the result set. But the same cursor can still be resurrected by reissuing the OPEN statement. This also means that the name you gave the cursor is still in circulation and cannot be used in another DECLARE CURSOR statement.
6. Finally you use the DEALLOCATE statement to completely destroy the cursor, its name, and properties. The name becomes available again and you cannot resurrect a deallocated cursor.

The T-SQL cursor syntax is as follows (SQL-92 and T-SQL extensions):

```
---SQL-92 Syntax

DECLARE cursor_name [ INSENSITIVE ] [ SCROLL ] CURSOR
FOR select_statement
[ FOR { READ ONLY | UPDATE [ OF column_name [ ,...n ] ] } ]

---Transact-SQL Extended Syntax

DECLARE cursor_name CURSOR
[ LOCAL | GLOBAL ]
[ FORWARD_ONLY | SCROLL ]
[ STATIC | KEYSET | DYNAMIC | FAST_FORWARD ]
[ READ_ONLY | SCROLL_LOCKS | OPTIMISTIC ]
[ TYPE_WARNING ]
FOR select_statement
[ FOR UPDATE [ OF column_name [ ,...n ] ] ]
```

Consult SQL Server Books Online for the complete explanation of the arguments. The following code is an example of a simple DECLARE CURSOR statement in action:

```
DECLARE CustomerCursor CURSOR
  FOR SELECT * FROM CustDetails
```

Next you open the cursor thus

```
OPEN CustomerCursor
```

and then fetch the first record as follows:

```
FETCH NEXT FROM CustomerCursor
```

Each time that you issue the FETCH NEXT statement you advance one row in the cursor. In the above example the FETCH NEXT is the only FETCH you can use because the SCROLL option was not specified. In other words the cursor rolls forward only (remember the DAO forward scrolling snapshot recordset). The more complex the cursor and the more options you enable on it the more resources required to operate the cursor and less efficient it will be. The complete FETCH SYNTAX is as follows:

```
FETCH
[ [ NEXT | PRIOR | FIRST | LAST
| ABSOLUTE { n | @nvar }
| RELATIVE { n | @nvar }
]
FROM
]
{ { [ GLOBAL ] cursor_name } | @cursor_variable_name }
[ INTO @variable_name [ ,...n ] ]
```

Monitoring a T-SQL Cursor

As if I needed to tell you SQL Server comes equipped with an assortment of system stored procedures and functions you can use to monitor and track cursors. (See Appendix A for the cursor stored procedures and functions.) To get a list of cursors that are visible to your connection you can execute the *sp_cursor_list* stored procedure. Then you can use the several describe cursor stored procedures to determine the characteristics of the cursor. The @@FETCH_STATUS returns the status of the last fetch.

Each fetch positions the cursor on the row whose data was just returned to you. The cursor does not advance a row after the data is returned but rather fetches the data of the row in front of it and then moves forward. The fetched row is thus called the current row and you can then execute an UPDATE or DELETE on the current row.

Of course what we have discussed on cursors is just enough to tickle your taste buds and the subject warrants a few chapters of its own. See my book's sister reference *SQL Server 2000 Developer's Guide*, by Michael Otey and Paul Conte, for more cursor "how to" stuff.

In Review

This chapter examines some of SQL Server's advanced features. We investigated its locking capability and examined how SQL Server excels for concurrent access and transaction processing. We also discussed how for the most part programming against SQL Server does not require you to explicitly manage locks, isolation levels and transactions or result sets. For advanced functionality and powerful control, however, you can take over the locking, isolation levels and transaction mechanisms from the DBMS.

We also touched on cursors. These are server maintained result sets that can be accessed by clients one row at a time. There are several types of cursors, but the SQL Server server cursor is the most convenient to work with and while the subject of cursors is still very complex, creating and working with a cursor is not rocket science.

This chapter more or less brings us to the end of a range of chapters that deal exclusively with the Transact-SQL language. The next two chapters bring us to an intersection; you can carry straight on and get your eyes into a more advanced treatise on T-SQL, or take a left turn to meet English Query in Chapter 22 or a right turn to meet XML in Chapter 23.

Chapter 22

English Query

No matter the platform, the product, the manufacturer, or the guru, the common denominator of all database applications and solutions is the user. Most of the users that work with your data do not know anything about databases. Many aren't even trained to work with your data and may even be Web surfers trying to dig up information or getting information over the telephone. Over the years, I have found the biggest challenge in delivering applications to my clients has been to provide an easy-to-use query interface that can deliver sophisticated queries that return the data the user needs.

The typical question the client asks is something like this: "How do we get a list of all our clients in, say, downtown Miami, that are past due 60 days?"

And I still remember the days when my answer would have been something like "You would need to type select CustomerID from the accounts table where status equals past 60 days and then join the result of that select on the customers table using the CustomerID values for the search parameters on the customer table." And then the room would go quiet for about what seemed like forever and then someone would say "oooohkaaaay."

While some users are trained in art of building SQL queries, most are not. Over the years, I have helped my clients by sitting down with them and making lists of the most likely queries they needed. I would then create a GUI to allow them to interactively build the query while behind the scenes their button presses, mouse clicks, and checks were being translated into SQL code.

Even for simple queries, however, trying to build a GUI that automatically generates SQL code is extremely time-consuming and not very constructive. Also, as data and databases change, the GUI solutions become outdated and have to be continuously updated. Also, many queries are just too complex to hard-code, and then there is the problem of inserting the variables, dates and numbers and IDs and so on. Last, there is the stress factor. Asking users to build queries, even with icons and graphics metaphors, signs and symbols, is not good software business. And it's impossible to implement such a solution on a Web site or a voice processing system whose user interface is a TUI (pronounced tooeee, but better known as a telephone user interface).

Large corporations can afford teams of SQL Server DBAs to work with queries and reports all day long, providing query services to analysts in constantly updated and evolving applications. Such support personnel build complex queries and reports to run checks, financials, analysis, and data processing all the time. But smaller companies do not have the luxury of big budgets and thus have to rely on their own muscle and brainpower to figure out how to query their data. Few have the time. Since databases were first ported to the computer, it has been widely acknowledged that eventually the arcane query would become the domain of the computer processor and software that would be endowed with natural language processing capability.

You don't see Star Fleet officers on Voyager coding in complex queries do you? Instead they simply ask the computer a question like ". . . list all life-preserving planets 20 light years from our position." Well, the good news is that this technology is not far-fetched or even fiction any more. It is known as natural language processing, and it's here with SQL Server 2000 and ready for you to deploy in any application or over the Web.

Microsoft's big stab at natural language processing (NLP) or queries is called English Query (MSEQ or just EQ). It allows users to use English and not SQL to query their databases. Your clients do not have to learn SQL or build queries interactively. In the preceding example, my client could be simply ask of the database server: "list all customers in North Miami past due 60 days."

EQ was introduced with SQL Server 7.0. However, the version released as part of SQL Server 2000 has been vastly improved, and it is now a lot easier to build English Query–supported applications; I did just that as part of the call center product I built to test SQL Server for this book. Thus this chapter is essential for everyone working with users and support projects for querying data. While the new version may be just what you are looking for, it has one significant downside—the initial learning curve. EQ is complex, for one reason. We have just plowed through several hundred pages of complex SQL code, which makes it very hard to think in English when building queries.

However, this chapter is designed to get you clear on what EQ can do for you, how you should go about using it, the features of EQ, its strengths and weaknesses, and so on. The one feature of this technology that I feel needs highlighting early is that EQ can be used to build support also for querying databases over the Web, and against OLAP data, in addition to supporting standard applications. In this chapter, we will work step by step to build a query-based application.

What Is English Query?

English Query comprises two components: a graphical heuristically inclined query authoring environment or workbench and a natural language processing engine that parses the English and converts the user's phrases into SQL or MDX query code. The queries are then sent to the SQL database or a data warehouse (we will look at MDX queries in Chapter 25) and returned as traditional result sets or analysis data.

You should be aware that EQ can also talk to Oracle databases. You do not need to use SQL Server data stores for your application. Now, whether you can buy English Query without SQL Server is another matter altogether.

The English Query Engine

The EQ engine is a COM object automation server. The COM server library has a small footprint and is installed on client machines or Web servers running IIS. The COM server can be called from any COM-compliant application, such as VB, Delphi, VC++, or VJ++, and your IIS ASP pages.

An extensive object model underpins the EQ engine, and the full documentation of all objects, with the collections, methods, and properties, is available in Books Online. Later I will discuss deploying the COM server to your clients or IIS.

The English Query Authoring Environment

The EQ authoring and editing tool is where you see the difference between EQ for SQL Server 2000 and the versions that shipped with SQL Server 7.0. The edition that shipped with SQL Server 7.0 was much more complex to create English Queries with, although the natural language engine was essentially in place. Now the authoring environment is built into Visual Studio 6.0 and will be familiar turf for VJ++ and Visual InterDev developers.

The official word from Microsoft is that the Visual Studio 6.0 environment that ships with SQL Server 2000 is not Windows 2000–logo compliant. However, I have worked extensively with it on Windows 2000 and have not experienced any problems.

The VS authoring environment lets you write English queries that are parsed and converted into SQL or MDX code to be used against the target database tables. The engine translates the questions into formal queries and sends the queries to the server, as a sort of query proxy. The engine then obtains the result set back from the server and loads the data up into an ADO recordset object, which can then be accessed by the client application, your compiled apps or ASP code.

Now I am going to leave further explanation of the authoring environment until a little later. First, it is a good idea to understand the elements and key definitions or components that make up your English Queries. I have also decided *not* to recommend that you start learning how to use EQ by using the EQ Wizard. If you are new to English Query (and I would say that everyone is at least new to the authoring tool and model editor), it leaves you with a "cool, so now what" impression and absolutely clueless. Later, using the Wizard will make more sense, because you will know what it does and why it does what it does. The Wizard is useful for building a framework, but it's not a learning tool.

The Elements of English Query

Before we dig deeper and explore the authoring environment, the following section lists key terminology and concepts that you will encounter when you develop EQ solutions.

Models

Models are the center of the authoring environment in Visual Studio. You can think of a model as a framework, on the one hand, and a class (like a Java or C++ class) on the other hand, that contains the logical substance of your English queries. As a framework, the model contains the questions you concoct using English sentences composed of standard linguistic elements, such as subjects (or predicates), verbs, objects, adjectives, and propositions. As a class, the model also contains the definitions of the databases and tables you are querying, connection criteria, and so on. The model is compiled and deployed to the client machines, which load it onto the engine so that it can be exposed to a querying application.

The model essentially collects all the information that is known about the objects in your EQ application. Model objects come in two flavors to separate the linguistic elements from the database elements. Database objects hold information about the specified database objects, such as tables, fields, and joins. The semantic objects hold information about the entities, the relationships between them, dictionary listings, and the global domain default options.

Some of the concepts can be confusing, and I recommend reading this section more than once so that you understand what the elements represent.

Entities

An EQ entity has nothing to do with a row in a table. You need to think in user mode now because users do not think in terms of column names, indexes, tables, keys, and other various database objects. Users think in terms of clients, customers, buyers, suppliers, days, weeks, months, who owes me money, and when I am gonna get it. You, the database application developer, think "dbo.custdetails.custorder," but your user thinks "find me the buyer's order."

So entities are your real-world objects and include anything from an alien entity in a *StarTrek* movie to anything that you can comprehend with the senses God has given you. In the preceding example, there are two entities to which the user relates. The *buyer* is an entity, and so is his or her *order,* thus

```
Entity = buyer, order
```


Entity Synonyms

Entity synonyms are not just other names for the same object—such as *customer, client,* or *buyer*—but also pronouns like first names and other descriptions that convey more meaning for the user. In a casino, for example, *gamblers* might also be referred to as *winners, losers, high-rollers, small-fry, chancers, gamers,* and so on. The entity gambler can thus be a variety of different entities, and so the synonyms convey meaning. A *high-roller* would then be a *gambler* entity that typically spends a lot of money, and a *small fry* would be a *gambler* entity that hits the casinos for comps and cheap buffets, never spending much money. Some casinos might refer to the *cheapo* gambler as an "eater," a necessary liability, but the local steak house down the road considers an "eater" as an asset, thus

```
Entity = gambler
Entity synonyms = cheapo, high-roller,
low-roller, winners, losers, eaters
```

When identifying entities, you should list plural forms as entities as well, such as *gambler, gamblers, cheapo, cheapos.*

The EQ authoring environment comes equipped with a dictionary of synonyms for you to pick from. I will show how you use it later in this chapter.

Relationships

The manner in which an entity relates to another entity is its *relationship.* Relationships are key to EQ questions. For example, the phrase *cheapos eat buffets* defines a relationship between two entities using the verb *eat.* And another phrase, *High-rollers spend money,* defines a relationship between the entities *high-rollers* and *money.*

Phrasings

The relationship sentences just described are classified as *phrasings.* We use phrasings in English to express the relationships between objects. EQ analyzes the phrasings and converts them into the SQL code that returns the results of the query we are looking for.

For example, the phrase *cheapos eat buffets* is an example of a verb phrasing. But *cheapos are fat* can be considered an adjective phrasing, because the phrase provides more information about what *cheapos* look like. You use phrasings to craft the model. Phrasings come in several forms as follows:

- **Verb** This phrasing makes use of verbs to express relationships. Example: *horses eat grass.*
- **Adjective** This phrasing make use of adjectives to express relationships. Example: *horses are big animals.*
- **Name** This phrasing makes use of names and identifiers to express relationships. Example: *gambler_number is the number of the gambler.*
- **Subset** This phrasing makes use of subset phrases to express a relationship. Example: *cheapos are non-profitable gamblers.*
- **Preposition** This phrasing makes use of prepositions to express a relationship. Example: *High-rollers are about money* or *cheapos go directly to food.*
- **Trait** A trait distinguishes one entity from another, providing information about characteristics and other qualities. Example: *High-rollers have money* or *cheapos have big tummies.*
- **Command** A command phrasing is simply a command. Example: *Credit high-rollers* or *cook food.*

We discuss phrasings in more detail later in this chapter.

Entity Roles

It makes sense when defining entities in a model to place them in *roles.* In the preceding examples, a high-roller may be defined in a role that implies money is being made (or spent if you are the gambler), and the role of the *cheapos* may be considered money lost. When you define a role for an entity, you are actually "typing" the entity. In your model, *cheapos* will be considered a role that implies money lost, while the high-roller implies money made.

Don't even look for the Roles dialog, because it's not on any menu item. Later when we go through creating the model, you "discover" the role dialog box.

English Query Modeling Primer

There are several paths you can take to get started in English Query. You can start as Books Online suggests by visiting the wizard. But as I advised, this wizard can make you more confused than a dog who suddenly finds out that he can climb a tree. I suggest you forget about the Wizard and concentrate on building the semantic objects against your database manually—from the perspective of your users. We are going to go through this step by step, constructing sentences like school kids in Grade 1.

Step 1: Create a New Project

Open the EQ authoring environment, Visual Studio, on the machine you installed it on. The Visual Studio loads with EQ as the development tool. The first dialog box that automatically pops up when EQ starts is the New Project dialog box. As in all VS environments, you get the opportunity to open existing or recent projects or to create new projects. You want to create a new project. You have the choice of three options, the two wizards and an empty project. Choose the Empty Project icon, as demonstrated in Figure 22-1. Just select it. Do not double-click or click Open.

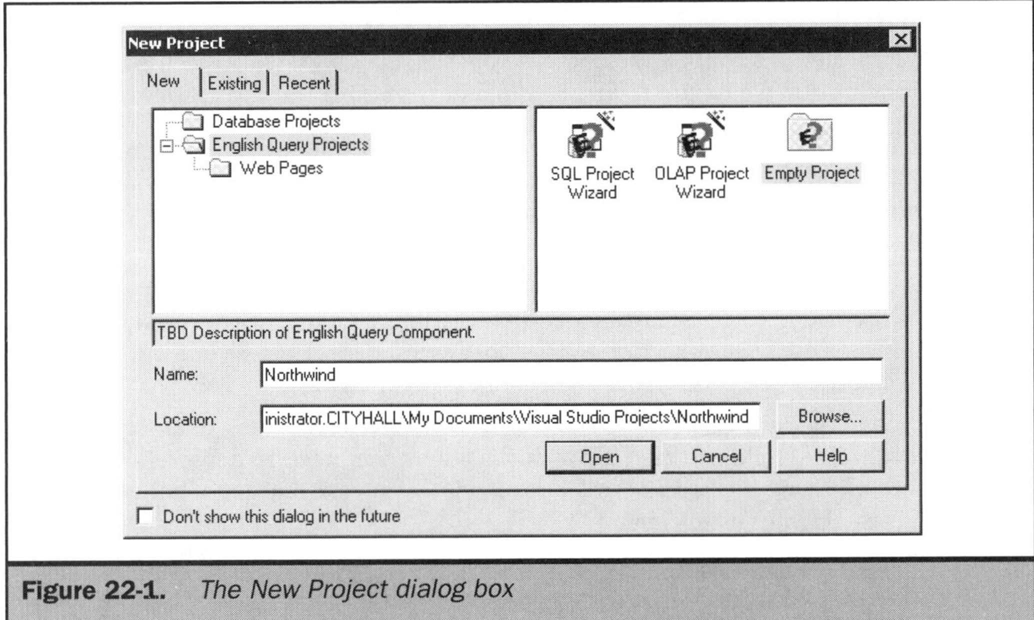

Figure 22-1. *The New Project dialog box*

In the Name field, enter the name of the project as demonstrated in Figure 22-1 and then enter the location on your computer or network for the project files. Now click Open. The empty project opens. If you look at the Project Explorer, which is usually on the right-hand side of the VS application, you will notice that it contains a project called Northwind, or whatever name you gave the project.

Now define a window layout. This can be done by selecting Full Screen from the drop-down list on the end of the toolbar or from the View menu (Define Window Layout). Full Screen is more conducive to creating your model's semantic and database objects. Later you'll change to layouts that represent your activity in the application, such as debugging or designing applications.

This might be a good time to get used to saving the module.

Step 2: Opening the Module

In the Project Explorer expand the Northwind project (er, "Solution"). Notice that you have a default module named Module1 now sitting in the project tree. This is your first default module. (Modules contain all the objects of the model; the module is the container, whereas the model is the application on the conceptual level). You can create additional modules or rename this one if you feel so inclined. But for this primer, I suggest you just keep things simple and go with the default module name.

Double-click *Module1.eqm*, and as illustrated in Figure 22-2, the model editor loads. For the moment ignore the OLAP tab in the model editor's authoring tabs.

Step 3: Defining the Database Objects

The next logical step is to define the database objects, which will become the targets of your queries. But first we have to connect to a database. This is done as follows:

1. Open the Model menu and select the Import Tables menu item. If you do not see the Model menu in the list of application menus, it means that you do not have the module opened or in focus. To gain or regain focus, double-click the module in the Project Explorer or right-click and select Open.
2. If you are not connected to a database, the Data Link Properties pages will load to allow you to establish a connection. I assume you know how to establish an ODBC or OLE DB connection to the Northwind database on your target server. You can remove or reestablish this connection at any time.
3. Establish the connection. The New Database Tables and View dialog box opens, as illustrated in Figure 22-3. Now this is where you need to pause and take a break. During the break, think about what you want to query against the database. Here is a suggestion:

   We all know Northwind like we know our own mothers. Northwind contains a table that holds a list of suppliers that sell health food and other condiments. So it only seems logical that the database users will want to know "who sells

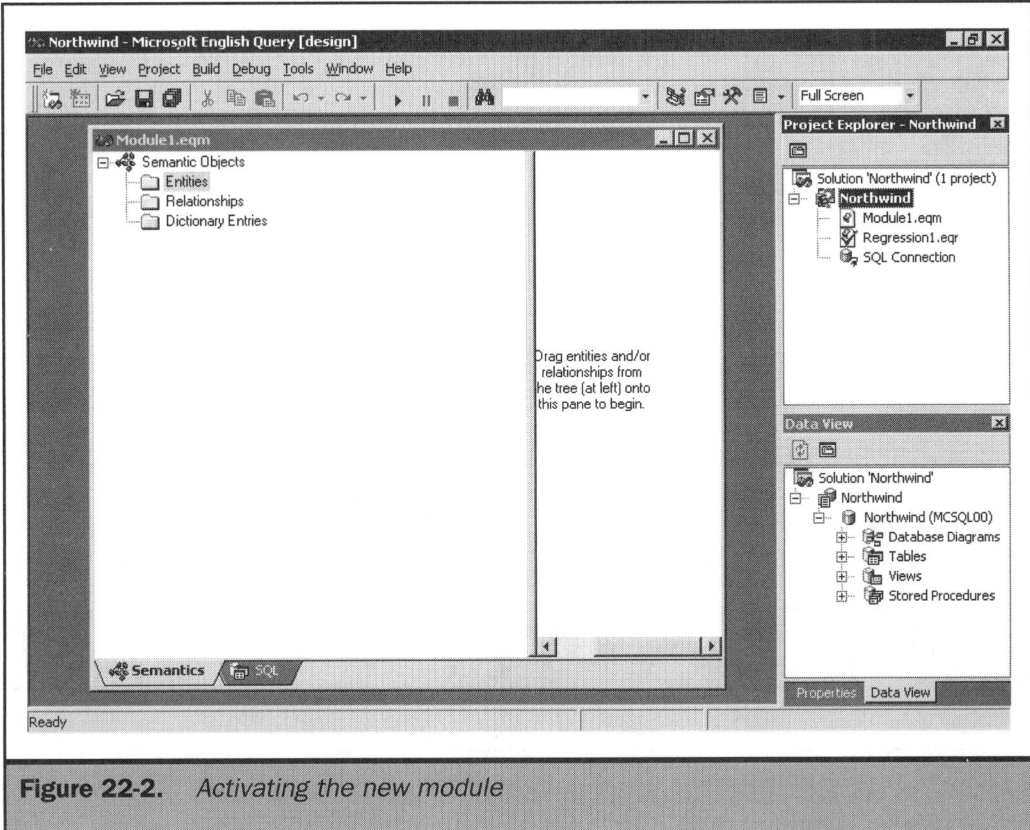

Figure 22-2. *Activating the new module*

what." In the Northwind database, "suppliers sell items." If we were to query for a list of all supplier names and the products they sell, we would need to join products with suppliers and then obtain a result set of just the supplier names and other pertinent information, such as products and cost. However, let's start with one table to keep things simple.

4. Select the products table from the Available list in the dialog box, as illustrated in Figure 22-4, and move it to the Selected list. You will notice that the table is placed on the SQL tab of the model. We have now defined a database object in the modeling tool.
5. Save the module.

Step 4: Defining the Semantic Objects, Entities

For this primer, the objective is to build English queries to obtain lists of products and their attributes. In the real world, you might put yourself in your client's shoes or sit down with the client and figure out all the likely queries that will be leveled against

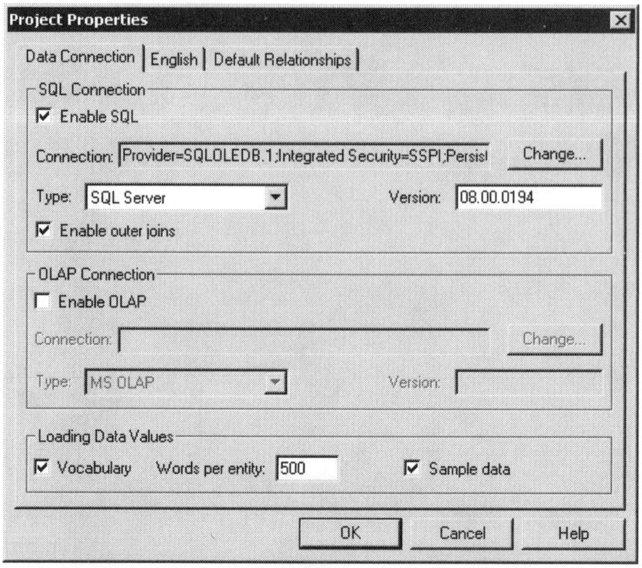

Project Properties

Data Connection | English | Default Relationships

SQL Connection
- [x] Enable SQL

Connection: Provider=SQLOLEDB.1;Integrated Security=SSPI;Persist | Change...

Type: SQL Server | Version: 08.00.0194

- [x] Enable outer joins

OLAP Connection
- [ ] Enable OLAP

Connection: | Change...

Type: MS OLAP | Version:

Loading Data Values
- [x] Vocabulary | Words per entity: 500 | [x] Sample data

OK | Cancel | Help

Figure 22-3. *Establishing the data link*

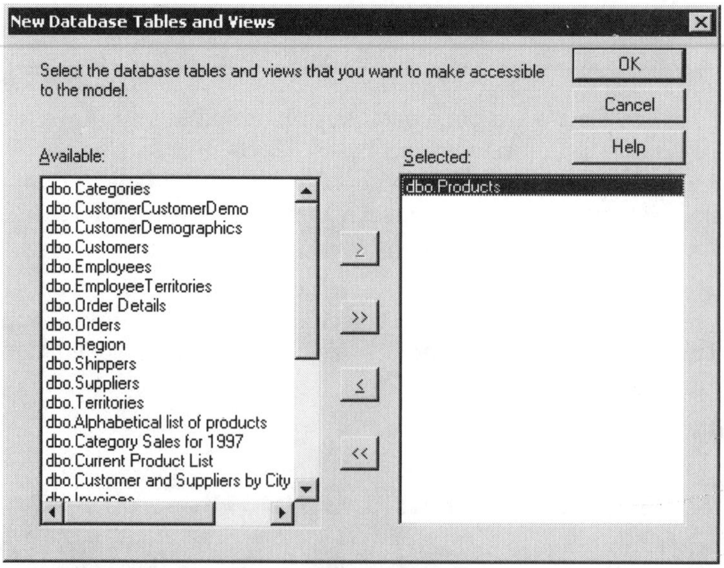

New Database Tables and Views

Select the database tables and views that you want to make accessible to the model.

OK | Cancel | Help

Available:

dbo.Categories
dbo.CustomerCustomerDemo
dbo.CustomerDemographics
dbo.Customers
dbo.Employees
dbo.EmployeeTerritories
dbo.Order Details
dbo.Orders
dbo.Region
dbo.Shippers
dbo.Suppliers
dbo.Territories
dbo.Alphabetical list of products
dbo.Category Sales for 1997
dbo.Current Product List
dbo.Customer and Suppliers by City

> | >> | < | <<

Selected:

dbo.Products

Figure 22-4. *Importing the database tables*

the products table. Here is a short list starting from what might be considered the most likely questions:

1. List, select, or show products.
2. List, select, or show goods.
3. List, select, or show skus.
4. List, select, or show produce.
5. List, select, or show stuff.

Starting with the simplest query list products, let's build the entities to query products:

1. Click the Semantics tab and expand the Semantic Objects tree. Select Entities, right-click, and then select Add Entity. The New Entity dialog box loads, as illustrated in Figure 22-5.
2. Click the Words field and enter the entity *products*. You will notice that the words may or may not have synonyms defined in the dictionary that will allow you to add as many variations on *products* as possible. See the preceding list for possible synonyms. To select the synonyms, click the ellipses button next to the Words field as shown in Figure 22-5. If there are no synonyms, add entities you think your users might consider. The icon changes to allow you to move words from one list to the other. At this stage of the primer, leave the Entity Type to none.
3. Now before you do anything else, move to the Database Properties group box and associate the words you chose with a table and fields. Click OK to save the entity. The entity is placed in the Entities folder of the Semantic Objects tree.
4. Save the module.

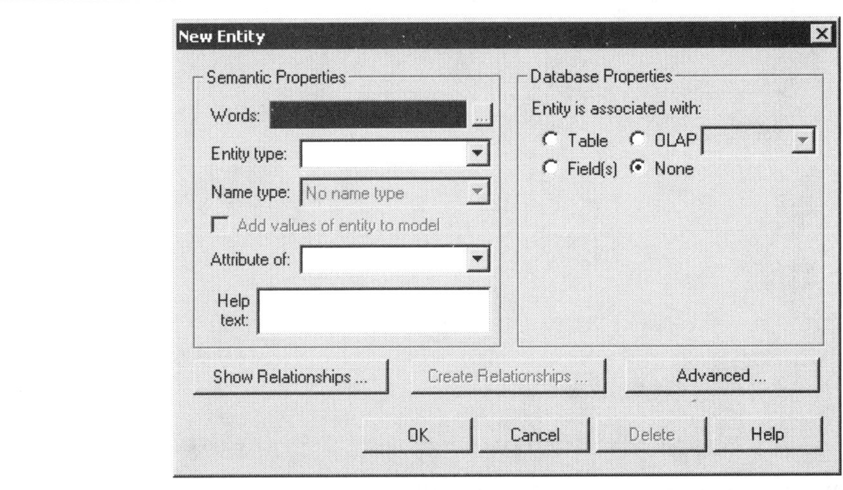

Figure 22-5. *The New Entity dialog box*

To help EQ perform better for your clients, limit them to a short list of the most popular words and have them reuse those. In a similar example for my clients, I asked them to use the word show, as in "show products."

Step 5: Defining the Semantic Objects, Relationships

Before we get too carried away (because our objective is to get a feel for EQ working as quickly as possible), let's define a relationship for the word *product* and the synonyms we selected for it. To create relationships, do as follows:

1. Select Relationships from the tree, right-click, and select Add Relationship. The New Relationship dialog box, as illustrated in Figure 22-6, loads.
2. Click Add and the Select Entities dialog box loads. Choose an entity you created earlier. In this case, choose *food* and click OK.
3. Next move to the phrasings section in the Add Relationship dialog box and click Add. The Select Phrasing dialog box, as shown in Figure 22-7, loads. (Phrasings are part and parcel of relationships, as discussed at the beginning of this chapter, so until you add phrasings you do not have a relationship.)

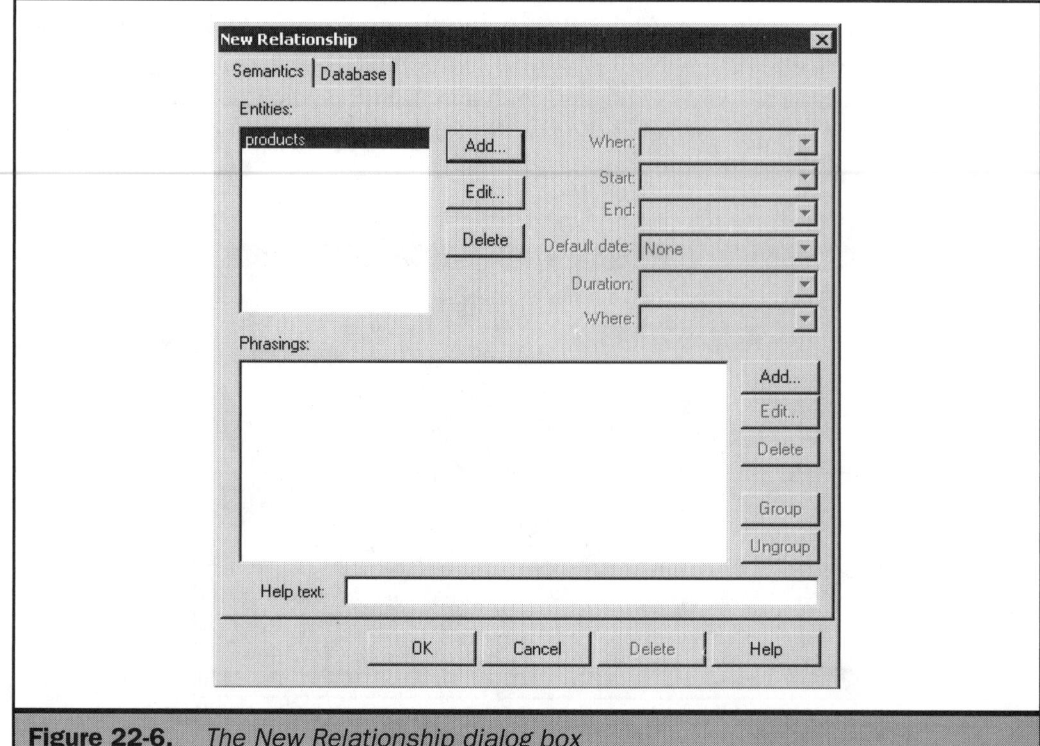

Figure 22-6. *The New Relationship dialog box*

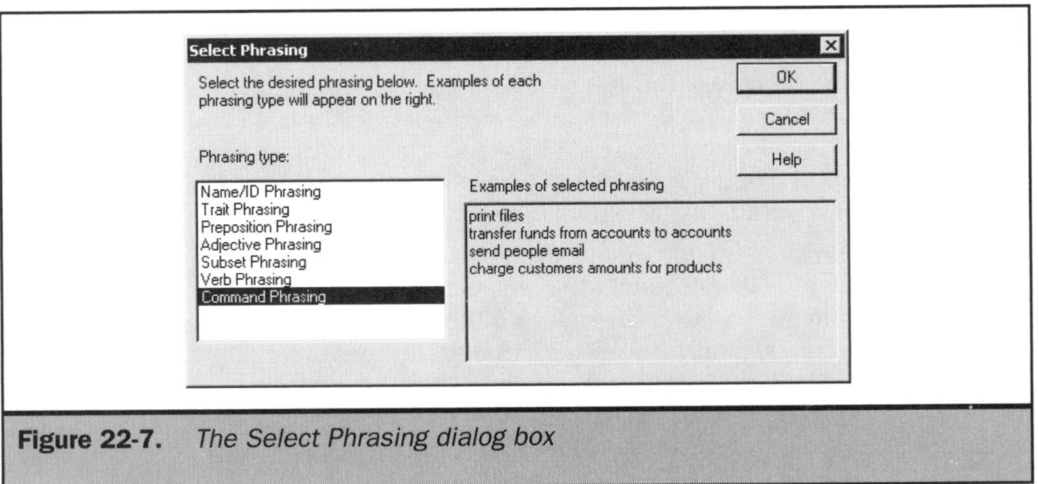

Figure 22-7. *The Select Phrasing dialog box*

We are going to create a verb phrasing for this exercise, so select Command Phrasing and then click OK. The Command Phrasing dialog box loads, as illustrated in Figure 22-8.

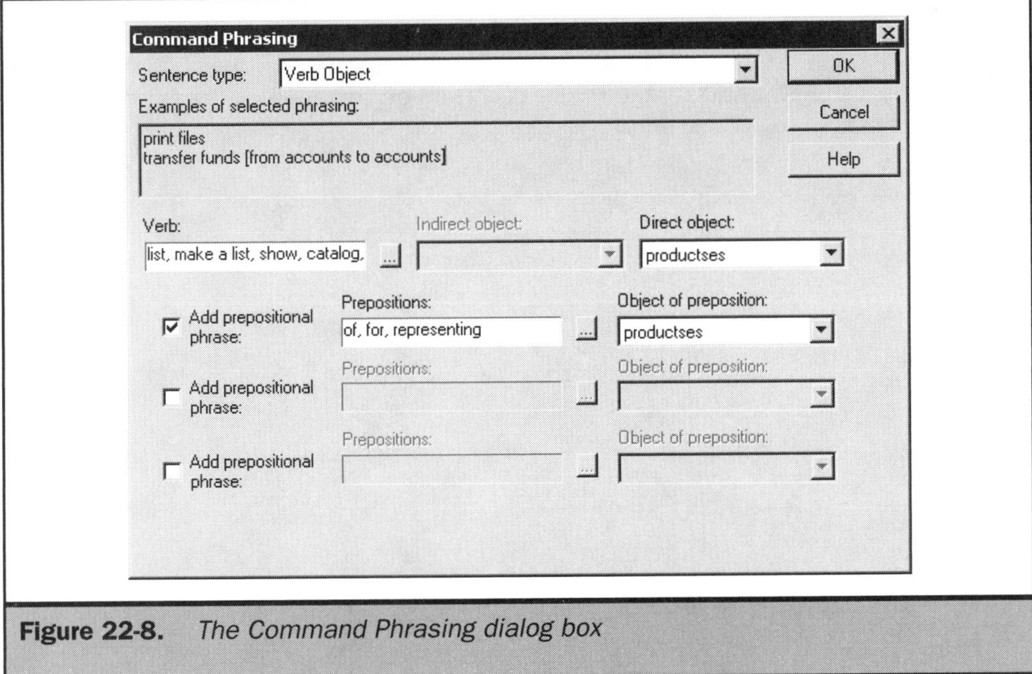

Figure 22-8. *The Command Phrasing dialog box*

4. In the Sentence type combo box, select the *Verb Object* type. Our command will allow the user to simply list all the products as we defined for the entity food. You could also choose the *verb* type, and thus your command would be either *list* or *show*. However, we need to be specific for the user, so the command *list food* is the better choice. You could use a single verb command to perform operations at the server, however, such as "backup" or "regenerate." Click OK and you are back to the New Relationship dialog box.
5. The Command phrasing requires us to install a command parameter. Click on the Command tab and provide a name that you can reference in code (not that you need to do so for this exercise or for the user). In the Parameter list, select *food*. The default parameter ID is automatically chosen for you. Click OK unless you have some changes to make on the Semantics tab.
6. Save the module.

Step 6: Testing

Okay, we are almost done. Our final step in the creation of our "list" command is to test it in the model. This is performed as follows:

1. Go to the Debug menu and click Start. You can also click the Start button on the EQ toolbar. The Model Test dialog box, as illustrated in Figure 22-9, loads.
2. Now simple type your command **list food** in the Query field and click the Submit Query button (pressing ENTER also executes the query).

The result set is returned to the Model Test grid. You can view the code that was generated by the engine and sent to the server, and you can analyze the various components that compose the query.

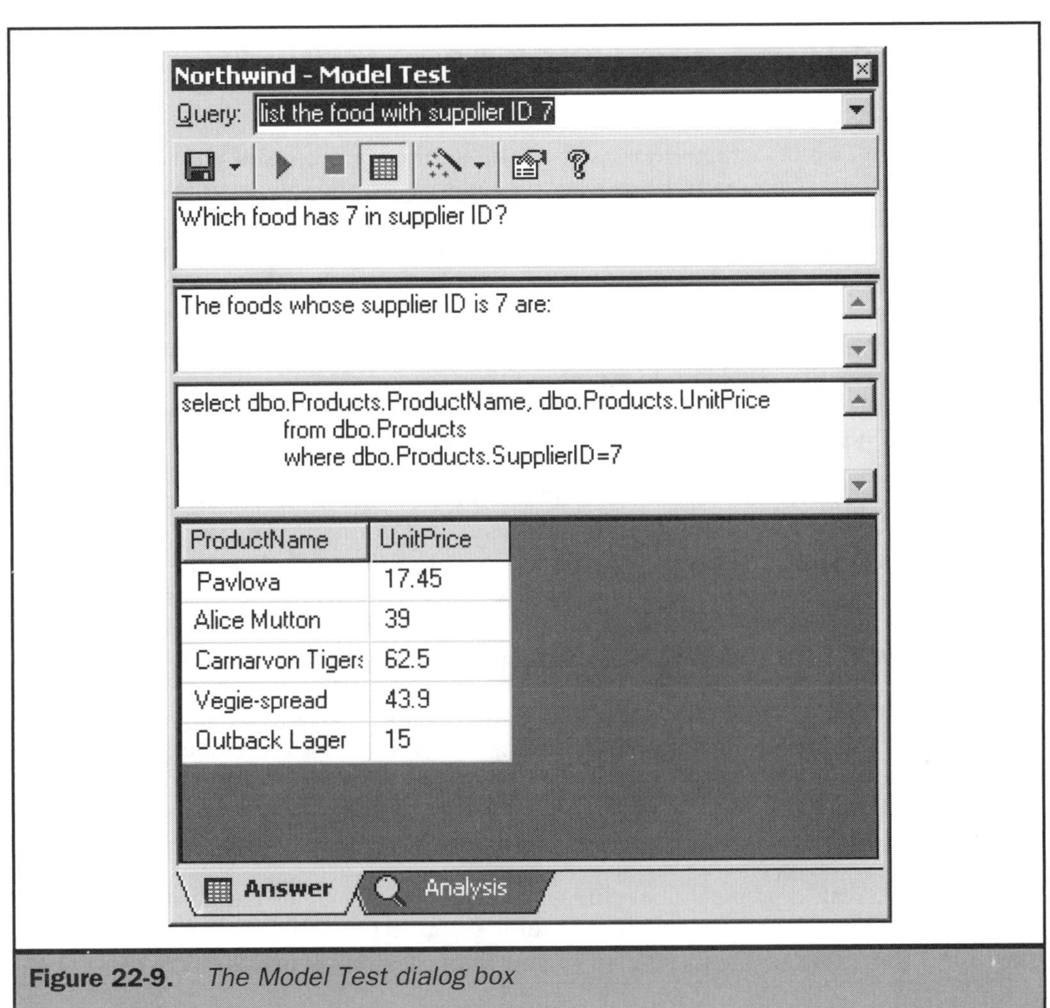
Northwind - Model Test
Query: list the food with supplier ID 7
Which food has 7 in supplier ID?
The foods whose supplier ID is 7 are:
select dbo.Products.ProductName, dbo.Products.UnitPrice
from dbo.Products
where dbo.Products.SupplierID=7
ProductName
UnitPrice
Pavlova
17.45
Alice Mutton
39
Carnarvon Tigers
62.5
Vegie-spread
43.9
Outback Lager
15
Answer
Analysis

Figure 22-9. *The Model Test dialog box*

Understanding and Using the Linguistic Phrasings

Up to this point, we have focused mostly on the Entities or objects of your queries. I also had you do the Command phrase because it is easier and gets results quickly—to kick EQ's tires so to speak. If you are new to natural language processing in general and EQ in particular, then attempting the more complex queries before you know how to move around the authoring and editing environment can be quite involved. For this reason, I have also not covered the editing canvas yet or discussed the other ways to generate relationships. This section will cover the linguistic phrasings in more detail and how each can be used to build advanced types of queries.

Preposition Phrasings

According to Webster's, a preposition is a "relation or function word, as English *in, by, for, with, to,* etc., that connects a lexical word, usually a noun or pronoun, or a syntactic construction, to another element of the sentence, as to a verb (Ex.: he went *to* the store), to a noun (Ex.: the sound *of* loud music), or to an adjective (Ex.: good *for* her)." As a guideline our EQ prepositional phrases should be constructed as *Subject Verb Object* or *SVO.* To get back to food, then, the following prepositional phrases can be constructed:

- Who is on 60 days credit?
- What accounts are at the limit?
- Which company bounced checks last month?
- What products are on order?

In order to create a prepositional phrase, you may need to create entities that relate to subjects in your databases. Customers would be your typical subjects, so you could construct a query that asks a question like "how many customers in Palm Beach County?"

Verb Phrasings

The verb phrasings describe an action relationship between a subject and an object (active voice) or the object and a subject (passive voice). An example of an active verb phrasing is *customers buy products.* The active voice is preferred over the passive voice for EQ. It would be better to write *suppliers ship food* than *food is shipped by suppliers.*

Using verb phrasings, we can ask questions like the following:

- Which customers buy chai?
- Who returned orders?
- Find customers who spend more than $50 a month.
- List suppliers that do not ship on time.

Adjective Phrasings

Adjectives describe objects. For example, *food is tasty* or *the customer is angry* or *the order is huge.* We use adjective phrasing to describe a relationship between the subject and the adjectives. We also use the adjective phrasing to describe the relationship between the adjectives and the entities that contain adjectives. With adjective phrasing, we can come up with English queries to answer questions like the following:

- Which accounts are overdue?
- Which customers are older than 65?
- What products are cheaper than $10?
- How old is the Olive Garden account?

Using the Model Editor Canvas

I remember that when I first started experimenting and building applications that use English Query, I had a couple of beers with a bunch of DBAs after a SQL Server user group meeting. One of them said: "When I opened it up, I ran the wizard, dragged an entity onto the pane thing, made a few selections, and then suddenly there were hundreds of lines everywhere. So I closed it and that was the last time I looked at it."

At first when you don't know what's going on, the canvas pane in the model editor can be daunting. However, it is nothing more than a graphical interface that helps you visualize and create relationships between entities in exactly the same fashion as we have done earlier in this chapter. It does nothing automatically; you still have to work with the dialog boxes described previously, but the picture that you can develop associating your entities with relationships helps you organize your thoughts. After a while working with EQ, you'll find using canvas pane makes building the models a lot quicker.

To advance the food example described earlier, let's go through using the pane step by step. But first, what question are we going to ask? In the earlier command phrase, we were able to get EQ to simply send the user a list of all the products in the database. But it makes more sense to group the products according to their group identification numbers and return just that group of products to the user. Looking at the Products table, we can group products by the *SupplierID* (and later join that to the table that can deliver us the supplier names), and we can also group the products by a *CategoryID*.

If we then decide to allow the user to first group by the *CategoryID*, we can construct the following question they can ask: "List or show all products in a CategoryID of X?" The question can actually be satisfied using prepositional phrasing because we are looking for the object *in* another object, the CategoryID.

First we must create a new entity representing CategoryID. You should know how to do that by now. The new entity is actually a subentity or attribute of the Product object, which we aliased as food. Let's examine the new entity in its dialog box, as illustrated in Figure 22-10.

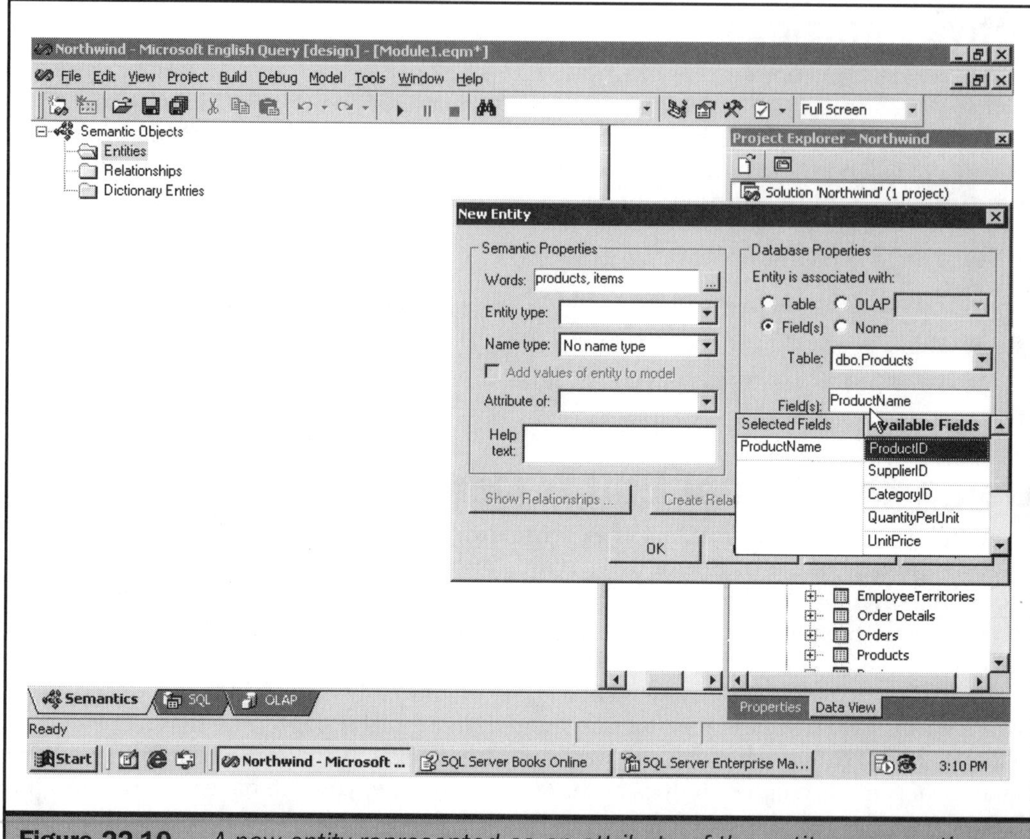

Figure 22-10. *A new entity represented as an attribute of the entity representing a table*

First, note that the new entity, *food_category_id,* is not representative of the entire table, as was the case with *food,* but rather of a column in the Products table. Second, we need to identify the entity by what it really is. This is done by setting the entity type. We cannot perform any calculations against the column, so it makes sense to set its type as a *where* type (for example, where the CategoryID is a, b, or c). We do not need to give the Entity a name type, because all we are looking to do is select the products using the search condition of CategoryID. So click OK and save the model.

So now there are two entities in the Semantic Objects tree. To create a relationship between the two entities, follow these steps:

1. Drag the food entity onto the canvas pane. This illustrated in Figure 22-11.

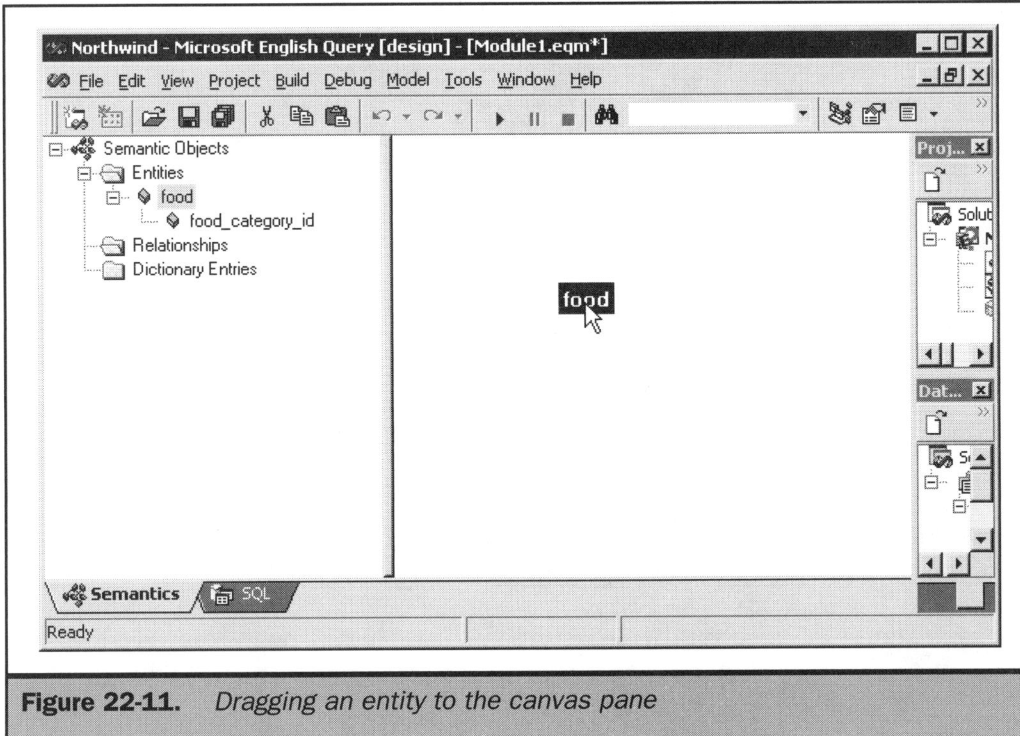

Figure 22-11. *Dragging an entity to the canvas pane*

2. Drag the categoryID entity to the canvas, but drop it onto the food entity. Boom, EQ loads the New Relationship dialog box for you and adds both entities into it. You can now proceed to create the phrasing that represents the relationship.
3. Click the Add (Phrasings) button and choose the Trait Phrasing option. The Trait Phrasing Dialog box opens, as illustrated in Figure 22-12. Notice that EQ has already constructed a trait relationship between the two entities, "foods have food_category_ids." We cannot create extra prepositional phrases at this time, because we have used up the entities for the trait phrase. So click OK and then OK again to save the new relationship. The two entities and the

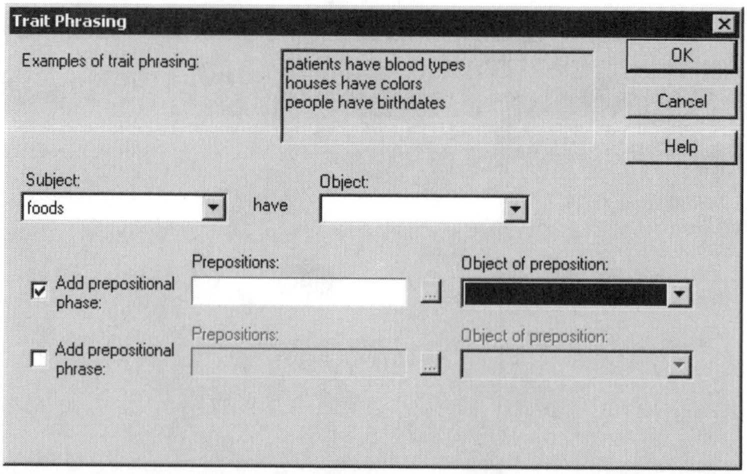

Figure 22-12. *The trait phrasing dialog box*

relationship between them are represented graphically on the canvas pane. Before we deal with the canvas pane further, we should test to see if our user can now query by categoryID.

4. Save the model.
5. Click Start to run the test and enter the question "show food in category ID 1?" Submit the query. You will likely notice that the query fails because, although we are identifying the categoryID entity, EQ only knows it as "food_entity_query." The failure is demonstrated in Figure 22-13.
6. To help EQ figure out what we are referring to in the question, click the Suggestion Wizard button on the Model Test toolbar. The Suggestion Wizard loads, as illustrated in Figure 22-14, and in it we can tell EQ what categoryID refers to. Save the suggestions and resubmit the query. The query will now succeed, as demonstrated in Figure 22-15.

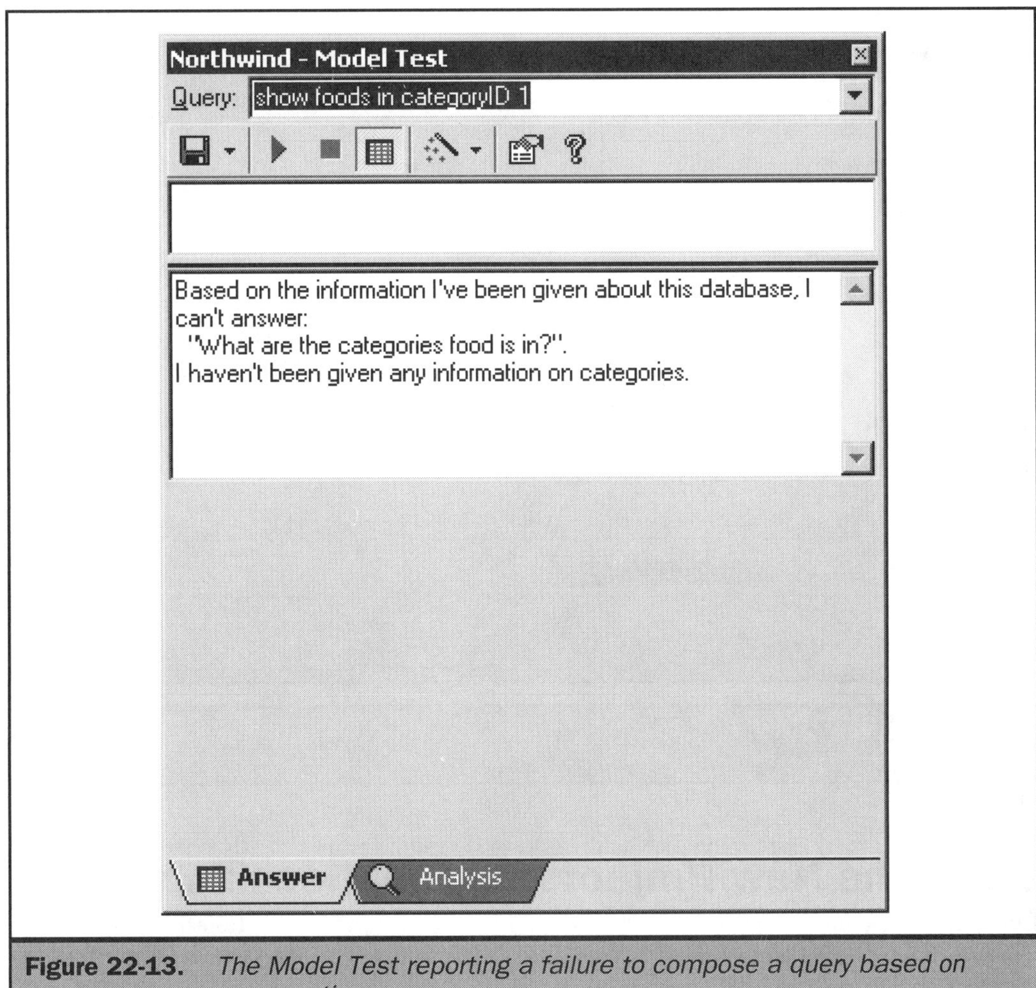

Figure 22-13. *The Model Test reporting a failure to compose a query based on our question*

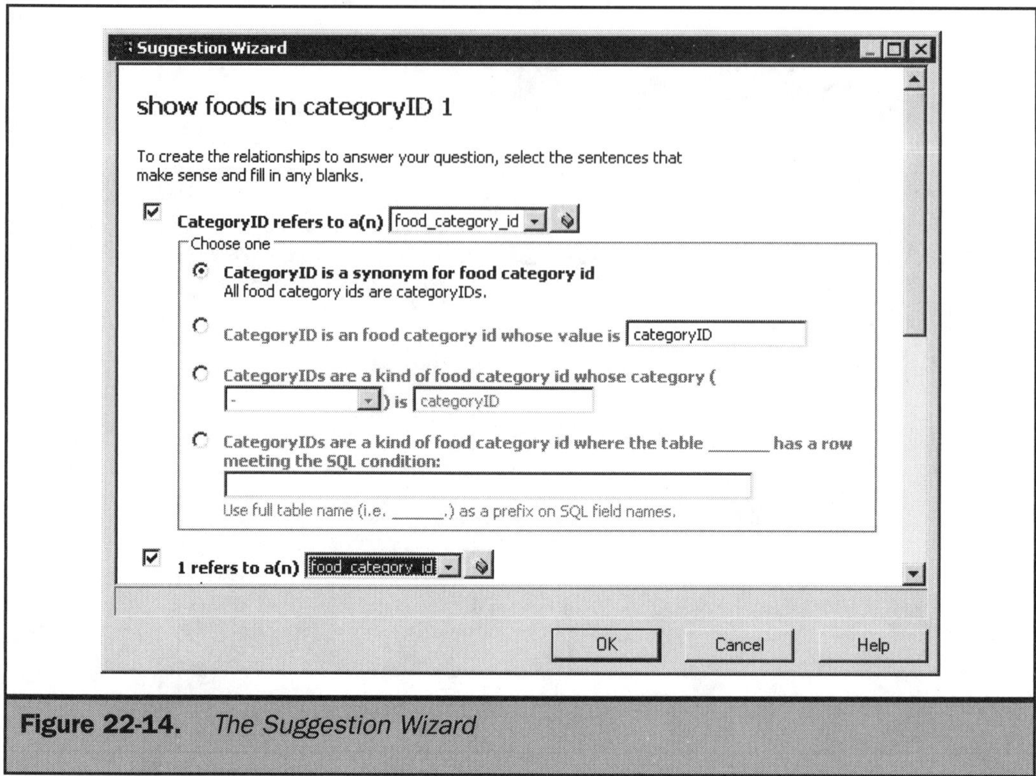

Figure 22-14. *The Suggestion Wizard*

Using the New Project and Relationship Wizard

Everything you have done in this chapter so far can be done by the Relationship Wizard. The SQL Project Wizard is available when you select New Project from the menus; it performs the following steps:

1. It first asks for a project name and location.
2. It then presents the Data Link dialog box so that you can connect to SQL Server or some other SQL data source.
3. Next you need to choose tables for the model.
4. Finally, it will create the model using the Relationship Wizard.

These wizards become especially useful when you need to rapidly create a framework for your model and already have sufficient experience with EQ and know what the relationships represent. You can then work with the automatically created relationship and the canvas pane to fine-tune or expand the model.

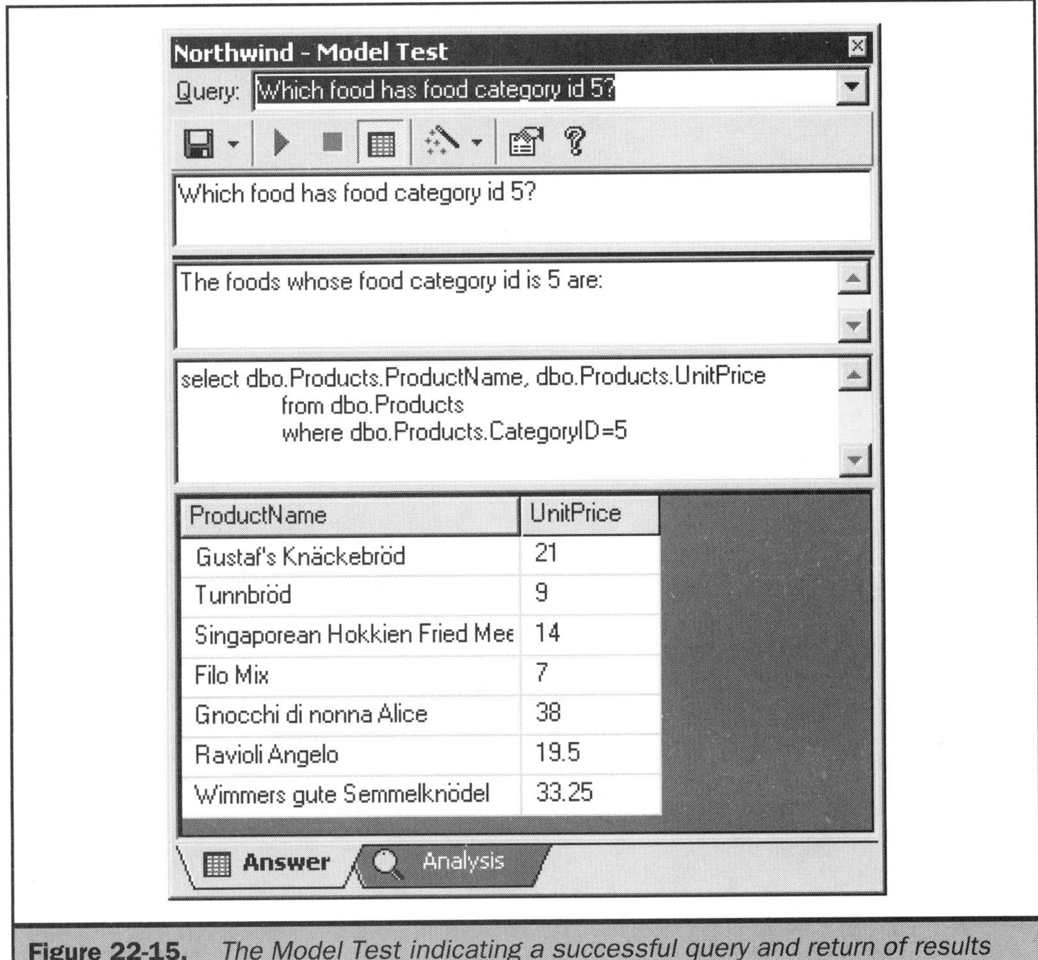

Figure 22-15. *The Model Test indicating a successful query and return of results*

To access the Relationship or Project Wizard, go to the Model menu and select Create Semantic.

In Review

Building English Query applications is a challenge and requires some dedication on your part. In this chapter I helped you "drill" into this technology; however, we only scratched the surface. You still need to build the necessary support for the model from your client applications, in browsers, servers, and client applications written with the likes of Visual Basic and so on.

Chapter 23

SQL Server and the Internet

It came out of nowhere. Suddenly there was XML, and now everyone is labeling this language as the "Lingua Franca of the World Wide Web." But there is lot more to XML than a stale cliché. While there are a lot of good books on XML and tons of material on the Net, this brief introduction investigates XML in the context of its value to SQL Server and to you, the SQL Server developer and DBA. If you are new to XML, this section will give you the heads-up, and what you need to know before you go out and grab a six-pack of XML tomes.

What Is XML and Why Do We Need It?

So what exactly is XML? Well, in short, XML is simply data formatted in a certain way. The Microsoft XML SDK defines XML as "a meta-markup language that provides a format for describing structured data." And actually, this is precisely the case. XML is simply a way of formatting data so that it is "self-describing and easy to transform."

XML has its beginnings years ago, circa 1986, as the Standardized General Markup Language (SGML) came to be a standard for marking up data in a way that would facilitate easy transformation and description of information. The goal of the SGML architects was to define a way in which any type of data could be transferred and processed by any type of application, written in any programming language, and processed automatically. This means that there would be no need to write special conversion programs, protocols, and so on, just to handle someone else's data.

The problem from the beginning was that SGML was very complex. I guess everyone was afraid of it. Anything too complex will never be totally accepted. So in comes XML, a subset of SGML. XML retains all the "good points" of SGML, and it is simpler to use. As a result of creating a simpler version of SGML, a broader developer target was reached. Along with an easier-to-use SGML, the Web is everywhere, and XML was streamlined for Web delivery, hence the XML buzz.

As of October 2000, the W3C recommendation for XML version 1.0 Second Edition was published by the XML Core Working Group. (These guys are responsible for maintaining and reporting on updates, errata, and new submissions on XML.) Currently, they are working with the XML Syntax, XML Fragment, and XML Information Set Working Groups. To be up-to-date on the latest XML recommendations and updates, keep an eye on http://www.w3.org and http://www.xml.org.

So why is XML important to me? Well, for starters, common data formats sure make life easier. In the early '90s, I worked for a large data processing firm in Michigan. The whole purpose of my existence was to write COBOL programs that converted data from one format to another. We had our defined format, but all of the companies that sent us their data had their own formats. So I would receive a magnetic tape from a bank or brokerage firm, print out a dump of the first 20 records, and start figuring out how I was going to get it into our format for printing. This was a real pain in the neck. No matter how hard we tried, we could never get all of our customers to stick to a common format. As I look back, if we had everyone sending the data in XML, my life would have been much easier. The bottom line is a common way of describing the data. If Customer X would send me their data, a schema, and some processing instructions, I could write a one-stop application that reads the XML and outputs it to my format without reinventing the wheel every time I received new data. That is the beauty of XML: data that describes itself.

SQL Server and the XML Love Affair

One of the main questions that's probably on your mind is, why do I need XML if I have T-SQL? Are they two separate languages that SQL Server supports, or are they like the doubles partners of a tennis match—where they each have their respective strengths and weaknesses that combine to make it game, set, and match? This section explains how the two languages coexist and how XML caters to the shortcomings of traditional methods of storing, manipulating, and analyzing data.

T-SQL Versus XML or T-SQL and XML

Does XML replace T-SQL, and if not, how are the two technologies used together or interchangeably? The answer to the first question is straight and easy: No, XML does not replace T-SQL. In order for us to send and receive data to and from SQL Server, we need to use T-SQL in the same manner that we use T-SQL to retrieve ADO recordsets right now. Because XML is primarily the way our data is defined, T-SQL is still the language of choice to talk to SQL Server. No two ways about it. We will explore the many ways that T-SQL and XML can be used together to produce robust SQL-XML solutions, and I think you will see that XML alone cannot really do anything all by itself. XML needs help in formatting, data retrieval, and data manipulation.

So you might ask, Why do I need to use XML if it cannot do everything all by itself? Well, in the past, we still had all of these problems with different data formats, poor data description, and the need to continuously worry about what our client was sending us. As we have stressed before, XML solves this problem by being self-describing. Self-describing data makes life easier: no more custom applications to convert every single type of data format we receive. Furthermore, XML is highly optimized for electronic transmission.

Marshalling large ADO recordsets across the wire caused poor application performance and network bottlenecks. With XML, the data is streamlined for transmission over media such as the Internet. In conjunction with the server-side processing of SQL Server, and with the combination of T-SQL, XML, and other client-side programming languages such as Visual Basic, JScript, C, and C# (C Sharp), we have all the tools for creating the most robust solution that we possible can. We are, however, leaving out a very important point: Imagine this: Oracle, DB2, and SQL Server *all* supporting XML natively. The conversion and incompatibility problems between *all* database servers will go to hog heaven. No more driver problems, or language differences between PL-SQL and T-SQL. All data can move happily from any client to any server in XML documents. What a relief that would be—no more compatibility issues. It's definitely something to look forward to.

What Is an XML Document?

Before we go any further, let's take a look at exactly what an XML document is. These details are important to understand once we start getting XML from SQL 2000. Though SQL does the formatting for us, we need to understand what we are getting out of the server before we can start manipulating it.

An XML document is made up of Tags and Elements. You might say that HTML does the same thing, and you would be correct. The difference is XML is data; HTML is how to format the data. HTML and XML work together to make our data look good. In HTML, we are given a specific number of tags we can use, which will instruct the browser how to format the output. In XML, we can generate our own tags that actually define the meaning of the data we are sending. So I may have a <company> tag that contains my company name. If I were to do this in HTML, the browser would ignore the invalid tags and continue processing.

Here, we can see how HTML describes how to display data:

```
<Table>
 <TR>
  <TD>Company</TD><TD>Microsoft</TD>
   </TR>
      <TR>
          <TD>Address</TD><TD>One Microsoft Way</TD>
    </TR>
      <TR>
      <TD>City</TD><TD>Redmond</TD>
      </TR>
      <TR>
          <TD>State</TD><TD>Washington</TD>
    </TR>
</Table>
```

Now here is XML, defining the actual meaning of data:

```
<Customer>
    <businessdetails>
      <companyname>Microsoft</companyname>
       <address>One Microsoft Way</address>
        <city>Redmond</city>
        <state>Washington</state>
      </businessdetails>
</Customer>
```

So let's go over the contents of an XML document. Understanding the contents will allow you to write well-formed XML documents. Being well-formed is very important. Remember, as with anything else, garbage in, garbage out. If we do not format our XML correctly, our processing application or browser will not know what to do with it.

Elements of an XML Document

The following are the essential elements of the XML document:

- Prolog
- Comments
- Elements
- Root
- Child element
- Empty element
- Attributes

Prolog

The Prolog contains the metadata that describes the document, such as processing instructions, telling the XML parser how to interpret the XML document, including style sheet information, encoding details or version information. The very first line of an XML document should contain the processing instruction. The tag definition for the processing instruction is "<?" for the open tag and "?>" for the close tag.

```
<?xml version="1.0"?>
```

If I wanted to include a reference to a style sheet, I would do the following:

```
<?xml-stylesheet type="text/xsl" href="URL for XSL Stylesheet"?>
```

Comments

In an XML document, *comments* can be inserted between individual elements of the documents. Comments are defined with the start tag (<.—) and the end tag (—>). In an XML document, the comments will be "grayed out" when displayed in the browser.

```
<?xml version="1.0"?>
<Customer>
    <.-- Customer details are contained below-->
```

```
        <company>
            <name>Microsoft</name>
                <businessaddress>
                        <.-- this is the address-->
                        <address>One Microsoft Way</address>
                        <city>Redmond</city>
                        <.--this is the state-->
                        <state>Washington</state>
                 </businessaddress>
      </company>
</Customer>
```

Comments can span multiple lines, so make sure you include the "-->" end tag, or else you may be excluding information that shouldn't be excluded. It is very similar to the way comments are handled in SQL Server. Without your ending the comment, everything becomes a comment (as in all programming languages).

Elements

Elements are the basis of XML documents. Without elements, there is no XML document. XML elements are made up of *start tags* and *end tags,* just like HTML. The difference is that in XML, the *start tag* and *end tag* define the data within the tags, not how to format the data, as is the case in HTML. Herein lies the power of XML. We can create our own elements as we need to; we are not boxed into a strict set of rules governing how our data gets described.

There are still some rules regarding XML elements, which is basically the definition of the "well-formed" XML document:

- The root node is a single, unique element, containing all other elements.
- Open/close tags must match.
- Elements are case sensitive.
- Correct nesting—child elements must be contained within parent elements.
- Attributes are enclosed in either single or double quotes.
- Attributes cannot be repeated within an element.

The *root node* is the very first element in your XML document. It is the single, unique element that describes the rest of the document data. In the preceding example, the root element is <customer>, and at the end of the document, we close out the document with the </customer> end tag. If we fail to include the end tag, the document errors out and is not parsed. Within the <customer> root node, we can have multiple elements and child elements.

Now that we've defined the root node, we can start describing our data. Referring to the preceding example again, the next element is <company>. The <company> element contains child elements that further describe the data. This "parent" element contains "child elements" that are actually describing the <customer> details. Since each <company> could have many addresses, such as Mailing, Shipping, or Headquarters, we can *nest* elements such as <businessaddress> to describe a particular address. That is the "X" in XML. Our document is *extensible.*

The rules still apply, though; we need to make sure that each element has the open and close portion of the element. Without these, the document becomes invalid. Notice also the nesting; the elements do not overlap. An example of poorly nested elements would be

```
<name>
      <customer>
      </name>
      </customer>
```

The <customer> element overlaps the closing </name> element. The correct nesting would look like this:

```
<name>
   <customer>
   Some Data in the middle
   </customer>
</name>
```

An empty element is an element that does *not* contain any data or child elements. Empty elements can be defined in two ways:

```
<companyname></companyname>
```

or the shorthand way:

```
<companyname/>
```

I do not like the shorthand way; it throws me for a loop when I see it. It reminds me of not declaring your variables in a Visual Basic program. So do everyone a favor and avoid them if you can, if only to make your XML easier to read.

Attributes

Attributes are another way to provide further details about an element. The only rules to follow are these:

- Attributes can be specified only once; the order is not important.
- Attributes must be defined in the start tag of an element.
- Attribute values must be enclosed in either single or double quotes.

```
<state region='Northwest'>WA</state>
```

The attribute "region" further describes the State element. In an attribute, white space is ignored, so another acceptable version of the preceding element is

```
<state
      region = 'Northwest'>
      WA
</state>
```

SQL 2000 does all the correct formatting for us, so we will always get a valid XML document back from a query. When you start to delve further into XML, you will find a couple of useful tools available on the MSDN Web site. The XML Tree Viewer and the XML Validator will both assist you in debugging your XML. They can be downloaded at http://msdn.microsoft.com/xml/demos/default.asp

Modeling the XML-SQL Server Solution

So I think that's enough talk for now about what XML is. Let's figure out what we can do with XML using all of the great new features in SQL 2000. What we are going to do is go over the many different methods of data retrieval, how IIS is involved in the foray, and what we can do with the data once we get it down to our client. In the end, we will bring it all together with a simple application that uses SQL 2000, XML, and Internet Explorer to actually see how we can use all of this functionality in a real-world solution, a Help Desk. The name for our application will be XDesk, a help desk application using XML.

XDesk: A Help Desk Application Built on XML

XDesk is a very simple example using all of the methods available to send and receive data from SQL Server 2000. The database consists of three tables: Customers, Incidents, and KnowledgeBase, as illustrated in Figure 23-1.

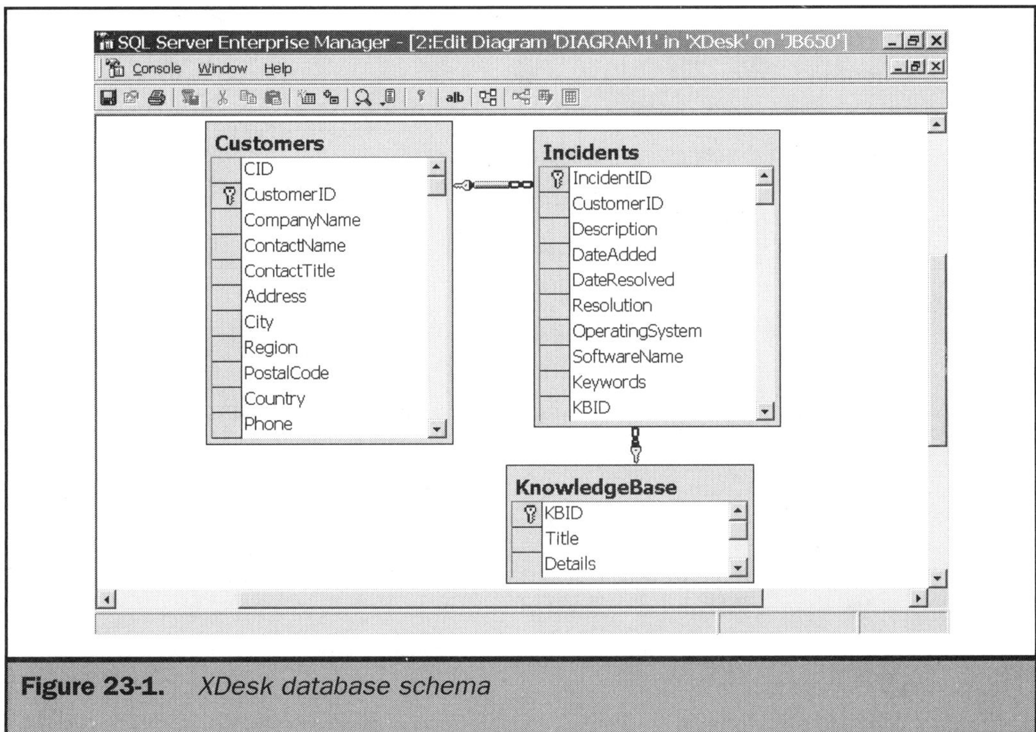

Figure 23-1. *XDesk database schema*

To make my life easier, I used the Customers table from the Northwind database and added the Incidents and KnowledgeBase tables. Since Customers has plenty of data already in it, we can start working with real data straight away.

Special Characters in HTTP and XML Queries

Before we get any further, I want to stop to mention some special characters that will come into play as we move along. This might seem a little out of place, but you might be looking at some queries later and wonder what the heck is going on.

Since we are dealing with URLs, we need to take into consideration the meaning of certain characters. If we do not, we may get errors and not know what is going on. Table 23-1 lists special characters used in URLs through HTTP, and what they mean.

XML also has special characters that are important to the success of the queries we pass. Table 23-2 lists the special characters as defined in the XML 1.0 specification as approved by the W3C. Further details can be found at www.w3.org.

Character	Meaning	Hex Value
+	Space; spaces cannot be used in a URL.	%20
/	Directory–subdirectory separator	%2f
?	Separates the URL and the parameters	%3F
%	Specifies special characters	%25
#	Bookmark indicator	%23
&	Separator between the parameters specified in the URL	%26

Table 23-1. *Special Characters used in URLs Through HTTP*

Just keep these two tables in mind as we get into writing queries. I am sure it will make more sense to you then.

Setting Up IIS

Now that we have some details on special characters, we can move on to actually getting some data. But before we begin retrieving XML data from the browser, we need to configure IIS to handle the HTTP requests from the browser. If we want to get XML output from SQL through the Query Analyzer, we do not need to set up an IIS virtual directory; to send the requests through HTTP, however, a virtual directory is necessary.

Character	Meaning	Entity Encoding
>	Begins a tag	>
<	Ends a tag	<
"	Quotation mark	"
'	Apostrophe	'
&	Ampersand	&

Table 23-2. *Special Characters Used in HTTP Queries*

By creating this new virtual directory, we are associating our application with an instance of SQL Server. In BOL, there is a great picture describing what exactly is going on between the client, IIS, and the SQL Server. Here it is in a nutshell:

1. A client (IE 4.0 and up, or a version of Netscape that supports XML) passes a request to the virtual IIS directory.
2. Once *sqlisapi.dll* receives the request, it starts communicating with the SQLOLEDB provider, which in turn connects to our SQL Server.
3. Before passing the request off to SQL Server, it routes through *sqlxml.dll.* SQLOLEDB will determine if the command is XML or non-XML, and if it is XML, it passes it to *sqlxml.dll.*

Then *sqlxml.dll* executes the command and returns the data to the SQLOLEDB provider, which in turn goes back to IIS; the end result returns to the client that made the request. So, let's get on with creating a virtual directory for the XDesk database in SQL Server.

1. Click the Configure SQL XML Support for IIS icon in the SQL Server program group. This starts up the snap-in for Virtual Directory Management for SQL Server, which is illustrated in Figure 23-2.

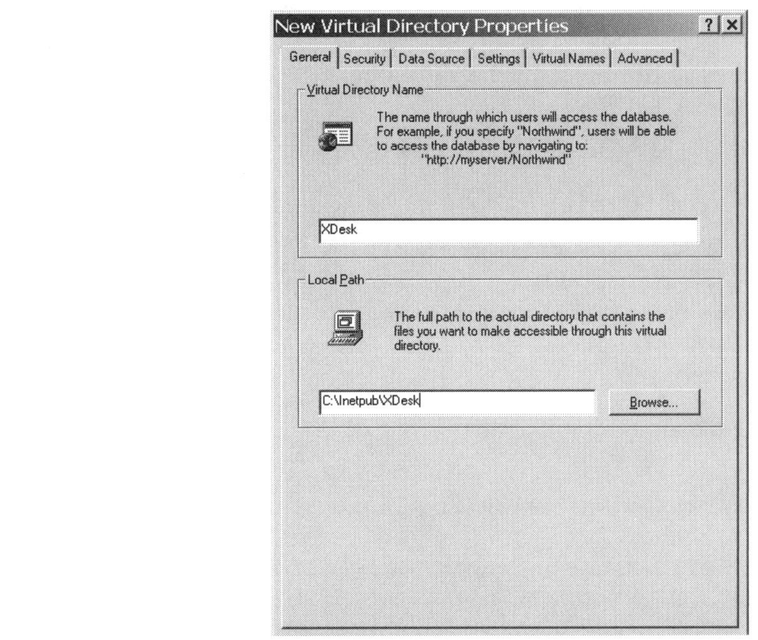

Figure 23-2. *The Configure SQL XML Support for IIS snap-in*

2. Drill down into your server name, right-click Default Web Site, click New, and select Virtual Directory.
3. On the General tab, type a name for your new Virtual Directory and select a Local Path. We are going to use *C:\Intepub\XDESK* as our directory. You need to make sure the directory exists; the wizard does not create it auto-magically for you.
4. On the Security tab, enter in your log on credential information. Since I am running a highly secure server, I will use SA with no password, of course.
5. On the Data Source tab, select your SQL Server and Database. I will choose (local) and XDESK respectively.
6. On the Settings tab, select all the Options. We will go over each data access option, URL queries, Template queries, XPATH queries, and POST queries.
7. On the Virtual Names tab, we are going to set up three virtual names, all based on the types of templates, schemas, and objects we will be referencing.
8. Click New, and type in **template** for the Virtual Name. Select template from the Type drop-down list. Browse to the Path that we created in step 3 and click OK. Click Save.
9. Click New, and type in **schema** for the Virtual Name. Select schema from the Type drop-down list. Browse to the Path that we created in step 3 and click OK. Click Save.
10. Click New, and type in **dbobject** for the Virtual Name. Select dbobject from the Type drop-down list. Click Save.
11. On the Advanced tab, leave the defaults as they are.

We are now ready to access SQL data through the browser, using HTTP. Let's run a quick test to make sure it works. If you open up Internet Explorer, type the following:

```
http://localhost/xdesk?sql=select top 2 * from customers
for XML Auto&root=MyCustomers
```

Your results should look something like this:

```
<?xml version="1.0" encoding="utf-8" ?>
- <MyCustomers>
  <customers CustomerID="ALFKI" CompanyName="Alfreds Futterkiste"
ContactName="Maria Anders" ContactTitle="Sales Representative"
Address="Obere Str.57" City="Berlin" PostalCode="12209"
Country="Germany" Phone="030-0074321" Fax="030-0076545" />
  <customers CustomerID="ANATR"
```

```
CompanyName="Ana Trujillo Emparedados y helados"
ContactName="Ana Trujillo" ContactTitle="Owner"
Address="Avda.de la Constitución 2222"
City="México D.F." PostalCode="05021"
Country="Mexico" Phone="(5) 555-4729" Fax="(5) 555-3745" />
  </MyCustomers>
```

So now we have just completed the first step in getting our application rolling. With your new understanding of the contents of an XML document, notice the following:

- <MyCustomers> is the root node.
- <customers> is an element underneath the <MyCustomers> root node.
- CustomerID, CompanyName, ContactName, and so on (the fields from the Customers table) are returned as Attributes in the XML document.

Understanding the FOR XML Clause in T-SQL

As our example shows, it is very easy to get XML from SQL Server . But we must understand the different methods of retrieving data, and what exactly the output will look like. In the preceding query, the FOR clause of the SELECT statement looked like this:

```
Query details FOR XML AUTO
```

Notice how the fields and data are returned as attributes of the XML elements. The AUTO mode of the FOR XML statement tell SQL Server that you want field names as attributes, not as elements. The syntax of a select statement is

```
Select fields from table FOR XML mode
[,XMLDATA] [,ELEMENTS] [,BINARY BASE64]
```

Mode can be any one of the following: RAW, AUTO, or EXPLICIT. RAW transforms each row from the query result into an XML element with a generic identifier row as the element tag.

```
<?xml version="1.0" encoding="utf-8" ?>
- <MyCustomers>
     <row CompanyName="Alfreds Futterkiste" ContactName="Maria Anders" />
     <row CompanyName="Ana Trujillo Emparedados y helados"
      ContactName="Ana Trujillo" />
 </MyCustomers>
```

The preceding XML document is returned from the following:

```
http://localhost/xdesk?sql=select top 2 CompanyName, ContactName
from customers for XML Raw&root=MyCustomers
```

AUTO returns the XML results as a nested XML tree. Each table in the FROM clause for which at least one column is listed in the SELECT clause is represented as an XML element. Each of the columns listed in the SELECT clause is mapped to the element's attributes.

```
  <?xml version="1.0" encoding="utf-8" ?>
- <MyCustomers>
 <customers CompanyName="Alfreds Futterkiste" ContactName="Maria
Anders" />
 <customers CompanyName="Ana Trujillo Emparedados y helados"
      ContactName="Ana Trujillo" />
 </MyCustomers>
```

The preceding XML document is returned from the following query:

```
http://localhost/xdesk?sql=select top 2 CompanyName, ContactName from
customers for XML Auto&root=MyCustomers
```

- **EXPLICIT** You can EXPLICITly define the shape of the XML tree. This requires queries to be written in a certain way, so that the additional information you wish to supply is made part of the XML document.

Optional parameters are XMLDATA, ELEMENTS, and BINARY BASE64.

- **XMLDATA** Returns the XML Schema with the result set. The root element is not added to the result set; the schema is appended to the document.
- **ELEMENTS** Columns are returned as subelements. The default is mapping columns to XML attributes.

```
  <?xml version="1.0" encoding="utf-8" ?>
- <MyCustomers>
- <customers>
 <CompanyName>Alfreds Futterkiste</CompanyName>
 <ContactName>Maria Anders</ContactName>
 </customers>
- <customers>
 <CompanyName>Ana Trujillo Emparedados y helados</CompanyName>
```

```
<ContactName>Ana Trujillo</ContactName>
</customers>
 </MyCustomers>
```

The preceding document is returned from this query (notice the [,ELEMENTS] parameter specified after the FOR XML AUTO):

```
http://localhost/xdesk?sql=select top 2 CompanyName,
ContactName from customers for XML Auto, ELEMENTS&root=MyCustomers
```

- **BINARY BASE64** Binary data from the query is returned in base64-encoded format. This must be specified when retrieving binary data using RAW and EXPLICIT mode. This is the default in AUTO mode.

Other Ways of Getting Data Through HTTP

So we have seen the basic syntax of the FOR XML clause. But there is more to retrieving XML data than just typing in a query from a URL.

Let's look at some other methods of getting XML back to the client from the browser.

First, we will look at *template files* as a means of retrieving data. A *template* is a predefined file that resides in your virtual directory. Since most queries tend to get complex, and normally we need a better format back from SQL instead of raw XML data, we can define templates that further enhance our XML experience.

With Templates, we can apply XSL formatting to our XML document (see the "XSL Primer" section later in this chapter), and we can define long queries, pass parameters easily to queries, and declare XML namespaces. Another great reason to employ templates is security. When we start putting schema information in URLs, we are opening ourselves to allowing users to see data we might not really want them to see, such as the specifics of our queries. And if we consider removing URL query processing from the virtual root, we are letting the XML SQL Server XML ISAPI process the files and return the XML document, further improving security.

So let's build a couple templates and see how they work out for us. For starters, we need to specify the template name in the IIS virtual root that we created previously. We set up these virtual directories when we configured IIS. For a refresher, review step 7 in the earlier sequence under "Setting Up IIS." It will give you a reference point as to why that was important. Without that configuration, we will not be able to execute template-based queries.

Now, open up Notepad and type in the following:

```
<ROOT xmlns:sql="urn:schemas-microsoft-com:xml-sql">
  <sql:query>
    SELECT top 2 ContactName, CompanyName
```

```
    FROM   Customers Where ContactName Like 'J%'
    FOR XML AUTO
  </sql:query>
</ROOT>
```

This is a template in its most simple form. You can isolate the T-SQL very easily. We are asking for the ContactName and CompanyName for Customers whose names begin with "J." Save this document as *xdesk1.xml* in the *C:\Inetpub\XDESK* directory. Now from the browser, type the following into the URL:

```
http://localhost/xdesk/template/xdesk1.xml
```

The result should look like this:

```
- <ROOT xmlns:sql="urn:schemas-microsoft-com:xml-sql">
  <Customers ContactName="Janine Labrune" CompanyName="Du monde entier"/>
  <Customers ContactName="José Pedro Freyre"
   CompanyName="Godos Cocina Típica" />
  </ROOT>
```

How cool is that? We define a query, save it as a file, and just reference the virtual template directory and the template name from the browser—we are off to the races. From this small sample, the power of the template should become clearer to you.

Now we need to get a little more complex. Let's run through a few scenarios that we might run into in real life. Most likely, our T-SQL resides in stored procedures on the server, and also, we normally do not do a "Select *"; we pass parameters to limit our result set to get useful data. So how can we do that? You got it: *templates.*

But let's hold on for a second and examine the syntax of a template file. Understanding the syntax of the template will ensure success as we move forward.

```
<ROOT xmlns:sql="urn:schemas-microsoft-com:xml-sql"
       sql:xsl='XSL FileName' >
  <sql:header>
    <sql:param>..</sql:param>
    <sql:param>..</sql:param>...n
  </sql:header>
  <sql:query>
    sql statement(s)
  </sql:query>
```

```
  <sql:xpath-query mapping-schema="SchemaFileName.xml">
    XPath query
  </sql:xpath-query>
</ROOT>
```

Here are the specifics:

```
<ROOT>
```

Required for a well-formed XML document. Since the template file follows the rules of a well-formed document, this is required.

```
<sql:header>
```

This tag is used to hold any header values. In the current implementation, only the <sql:param> element can be specified in this tag. The <sql:header> tag acts as a containing tag, allowing you to define multiple parameters. With all the parameter definitions in one place, processing the parameter definitions is more efficient.

```
<sql:param>
```

This element is used to define a parameter that is passed to the query inside the template. Each <param> element defines one parameter. Multiple <param> elements can be specified in the <sql:header> tag.

```
<sql:query>
```

This element is used to specify SQL queries. You can specify multiple <sql:query> elements in a template.

```
<sql:xpath-query>
```

This element is used to specify an XPath query. Because the XPath query is executed against the annotated XML-Data Reduced (XDR) schema, the schema filename must be specified using the mapping-schema attribute. We explore XPath a little later.

```
sql:xsl
```

This attribute is used to specify an XSL style sheet that will be applied to the resulting XML document. A relative or absolute path can be specified for the location of the style sheet, similar to the way you would reference a hyperlink or image in a Web page.

```
mapping-schema
```

This attribute is used to identify the annotated XDR schema. This attribute is specified only if you are executing an XPath query in the template. The XPath query is executed against the annotated XDR schema. Just as when referencing a style sheet, a relative or absolute path can be specified here.

Now that we have the details out of the way, let's do our more complex samples. Our first scenario will be to create a stored procedure that retrieves all customers who have open incidents. I have created a view that actually runs the query. We set this up by running the next two scripts in the Query Analyzer against the XDesk database:

```
CREATE VIEW vw_Open_Incidents  AS
SELECT     Customers.CompanyName, Customers.ContactName,
Incidents.IncidentID, Incidents.DateAdded, Incidents.Description,
Incidents.OperatingSystem
FROM
Customers INNER JOIN Incidents ON Customers.CustomerID =
Incidents.CustomerID
WHERE
(Incidents.DateResolved IS NULL)

CREATE PROCEDURE OpenIncidents AS
SELECT     * from vw_Open_Incidents
FOR XML AUTO, ELEMENTS
```

Open Notepad, type in the following, and save the file as *C:\Inetpub\XDesk\openincidents.xml*, which is the virtual root for template files that we created earlier.

```
<ROOT xmlns:sql="urn:schemas-microsoft-com:xml-sql">
      <sql:query>
           OpenIncidents
      </sql:query>
</ROOT>
```

Next, open the browser and type in the following URL:

```
http://localhost/xdesk/template/openincidents.xml
```

Your results should look like this:

```
- <ROOT xmlns:sql="urn:schemas-microsoft-com:xml-sql">
- <Customers>
  <CompanyName>Chop-suey Chinese</CompanyName>
  <ContactName>Yang Wang</ContactName>
- <Incidents>
  <DateAdded>2000-09-18T02:08:59.827</DateAdded>
  <Description>Cannot print</Description>
  <OperatingSystem>LINUX</OperatingSystem>
  </Incidents>
  </Customers>
- <Customers>
  <CompanyName>Island Trading</CompanyName>
  <ContactName>Helen Bennett</ContactName>
- <Incidents>
  <DateAdded>2000-09-18T02:09:55.817</DateAdded>
  <Description>Computer crashes at lunchtime</Description>
  <OperatingSystem>MAC OS8</OperatingSystem>
  </Incidents>
  </Customers>
  </ROOT>
```


And voilà: a perfectly well-formed XML document returned from SQL Server. I know this might seem exciting to you, but hold onto your shoes. Let's add a little something special to this output to make it look pretty in the browser, an XSL style sheet.

Open up Notepad and type in the following to create our style sheet. This will give our raw XML document a little flavor and class:

```
<xsl:stylesheet xmlns:xsl="http://www.w3.org/TR/WD-xsl">

      <xsl:template match="/">
            <HTML>
            <Head>
            <Style>
            </Style>
            </Head>
            <BODY>

            <.-- The heading -->
            <DIV STYLE="font-family:Tahoma;
                        font-size:18pt;
```

```
                    font-weight:bold;
                    color:Purple;
                    text-align:center">
              XDesk Open Incidents Report
        </DIV>
        <BR/>

        <.-- HTML table -->
        <TABLE WIDTH="100%" BORDER="1"
                   borderColor="blue"
                   cellPadding="1"
                   cellSpacing="2"
                   valign="top">
              <th>Company Name</th>
              <th>Contact Name Name</th>
              <th>Operating System</th>
              <th>DateAdded</th>
              <th>Description</th>
              <th>Incident ID#</th>
              <xsl:apply-templates select="//vw_Open_Incidents" />

        </TABLE>
        </BODY>
        </HTML>
</xsl:template>

<.-- Each row in the table is a separate employee -->
<xsl:template match="vw_Open_Incidents">
      <TR VALIGN="top">

      <.-- "CompanyName" -->
      <TD> <xsl:value-of select="CompanyName"/> </TD>

      <.-- "ContactName" -->
      <TD> <xsl:value-of select="ContactName"/> </TD>

      <.-- "OS"-->
      <TD> <xsl:value-of select="OperatingSystem"/> </TD>

      <.-- "Date the Incident was added"-->
      <TD> <xsl:value-of select="DateAdded"/>  </TD>

      <.-- "Problem Description"-->
```

```
            <TD> <xsl:value-of select="Description"/> </TD>

            <.-- "Incident ID# with HyperLink" -->
            <TD>
                  <A>
                  <xsl:attribute name="href">
                  IncidentDetails.xml?IncidentID=<xsl:value-of
select="IncidentID"/>
                  </xsl:attribute>
                  <xsl:value-of select="IncidentID"/>
                  </A>
            </TD>

            </TR>
      </xsl:template>

</xsl:stylesheet>
```

Save this new Notepad file into the XDesk virtual root directory as *OpenIncidents WithStyle.XSL*. Next we modify our *OpenIncidents.xml* template to point to the actual style sheet that we have created. Open up *OpenIncidents.xml* and make it look like this:

```
<?xml-stylesheet type='text/xsl' href='OpenIncidentWithStyle.xsl'?>
<ROOT xmlns:sql='urn:schemas-microsoft-com:xml-sql'>
      <sql:query>
              Exec OpenIncidents
       </sql:query>
</ROOT>
```

Notice that the only line we modified was the processing instruction at the top. It points to our *OpenIncidentsWithStyle.xsl* style sheet. Open up the browser and type the following URL:

```
http://localhost/xdesk/template/openincidents.xml
```

You should now see the following representation in Figure 23-3.

How perfect is that? With a few lines of code in a style sheet, and an XML document from SQL Server, we have created a report of all customers that have an open incident. And it was really easy.

We now have an Open Incidents page in our application all done. But how can we get the individual details of each open incident? Well, that's easy. If you notice,

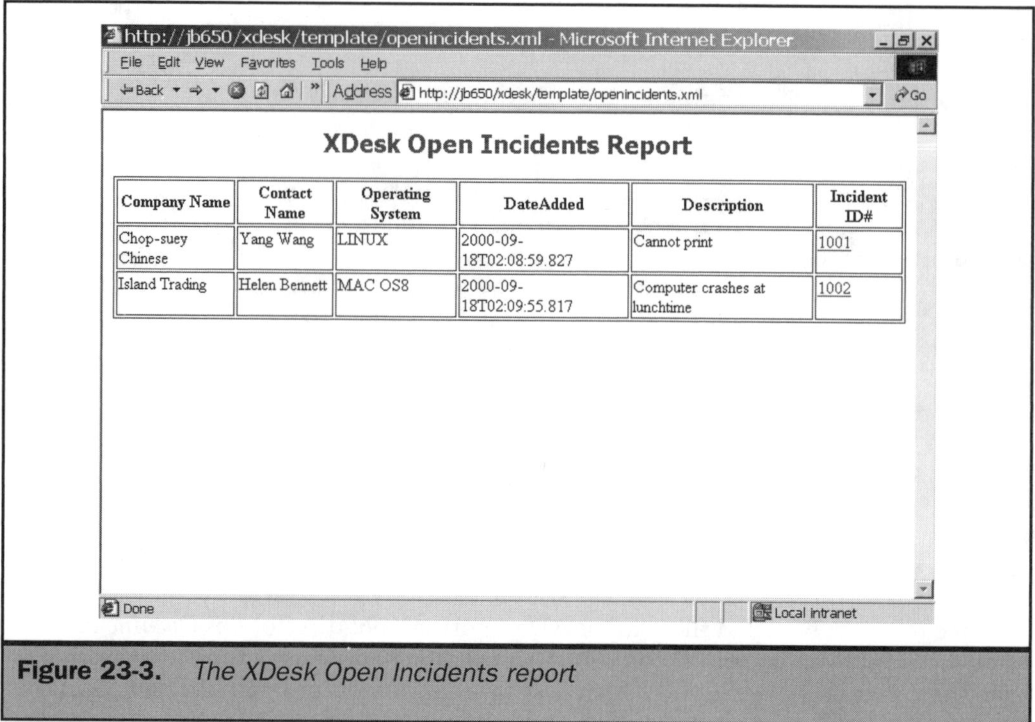

XDesk Open Incidents Report

Company Name	Contact Name	Operating System	DateAdded	Description	Incident ID#
Chop-suey Chinese	Yang Wang	LINUX	2000-09-18T02:08:59.827	Cannot print	1001
Island Trading	Helen Bennett	MAC OS8	2000-09-18T02:09:55.817	Computer crashes at lunchtime	1002

Figure 23-3. *The XDesk Open Incidents report*

there is a hyperlink defined in the XSL style sheet pointing to the *IncidentDetails.asp* page, passing the IncidentID field. All we have to do now is create another stored procedure that retrieves the incident details.

Before we get to the Incident Details page, let's go through a short primer on XSL. I believe that this will be helpful in understanding what we just did to format the XML, and how powerful XSL is in helping us format XML in an HTML page.

XSL Primer

If you recall in the first part of the chapter, we described XML as a method of formatting data, more specifically, *"a meta-markup language that provides a format for describing structured data"*. So what do we do to make this data look good? How do we format XML into tables? Add hyperlinks? Make things **bold**, *italic*, or underlined? How can I send my data to a supplier or customer, and ensure they can format the XML into the schema their applications require? Well, we do all that with Extensible Stylesheet Language, or XSL.

When we first started displaying XML from SQL Server in the browser, the browser parsed the file and displayed it into a collapsible tree hierarchy. That is all good and well, especially since in Internet Explorer the colors are so nice, but what can we really do with this data once we have it? We need a method of applying rules to the data so that we can format or transform this data, and that is where the Extensible Stylesheet Language comes into play.

XSL is a simple yet powerful syntax that offers us very robust methods of formatting data. Not only can we format raw XML into many colors, shapes, and sizes in the browser, but also we can transform one XML syntax into another XML syntax that meets our formatting needs. We will discuss the general pattern matching, filtering, and formatting syntax of XSL, and how it applies to the XML that we are retrieving from SQL Server. Since this is not a book on XSL, I am going to keep the examples very simple, and I am definitely not including everything that there is to know about XSL. For a complete XSL reference, the XML SDK has tons of detail and great examples to keep you busy for days learning everything there is to know about XSL. Also check out www.w3.org/TR/WD-xsl for details on the latest working draft; it is fascinating. Another important detail is the fact that this is still a working draft. Things may change, and as always, Microsoft has "improved" their version to work best with Internet Explorer. For all of our examples, we will be using IE 5.0.

Another reminder: XML is the data; HTML is how we format the data. We need them both to make it all work together. By separating out the data from the formatting, we are given a plethora of options on what we can actually do with the data.

XSL Document Format

An XSL document is a well-formed XML document that contains *templates* that apply *rules* to format our data. Here is the basic syntax of an XSL document:

```
<xsl:stylesheet
      xmlns:xsl=http://www.w3.org/TR/WD-xsl>
            template rule
                  output template
            template rule
                  output template
</xsl:stylesheet>
```

The <xsl:stylesheet> element is always the root element of an XSL style sheet. The xml:ns is the namespace that this style sheet conforms to. If it is not included, the style sheet does not process, and an error will occur in the browser. The individual template rules define the pattern that needs to be matched in order for the output template formatting to occur. So it's quite simple: We match to a pattern within the XML document, and then we apply a rule, or formatting, for that match.

Pattern Matching

One of the most important questions you have probably been asking yourself since you saw XML in the browser for the first time is "Cool. Blue is my favorite color. But how can I isolate individual elements within the hierarchy? What do I do next?" Well, that's where I come in. For starters, I will describe *pattern matching* in an XML document.

In an XML document, we have elements and attributes. These objects define the data in the document. In XSL, we isolate those individual elements through the *match* attribute in the <xsl:template> element. For example, in our Open Incidents XML output, how could I isolate the <companyname> element and make it a nice shade of lime? I need to match the <companyname> element and apply a rule to it.

```
<xsl:stylesheet xmlns:xsl="http://www.w3.org/TR/WD-xsl">
      <xsl:template match="/">
            <xsl:apply-templates select="//CompanyName" />
      </xsl:template>
      <xsl:template match="CompanyName">
            <FONT COLOR="lime"/>
            <B>
            <xsl:value-of/>
            </B>
            <BR/>
      </xsl:template>

</xsl:stylesheet>
```

Your output will appear as illustrated in Figure 23-4.

Is purple your favorite color? No problem, just change the HTML <font> tag and change it to whatever color you like. Remember, this is HTML and XML working hand in hand in a style sheet to produce the output. Now do me a favor, right-click in the browser window and select View Source. Notice anything strange? There is the XML data, *all* of it, and there don't seem to be any formatting directives for the company name. You do not see any <font> tags, or any formatting being applied. And why is all the XML data selected from the template query, and not just the company name? The answer to your question is that the XML and XSL are happily married together on the client. The XML document refers to an XSL file on the server, and it formats on the fly in your browser. In the template file, we execute a stored procedure that asks for all of the open incidents, not just the company name. The XSL style sheet only processes what we tell it to. By now you should be saying, "Wow, that makes XSL pretty powerful. I can take my SQL Server data, kick out some XML, match it up to an XSL style sheet, and do all kinds of processing." And we are just getting started.

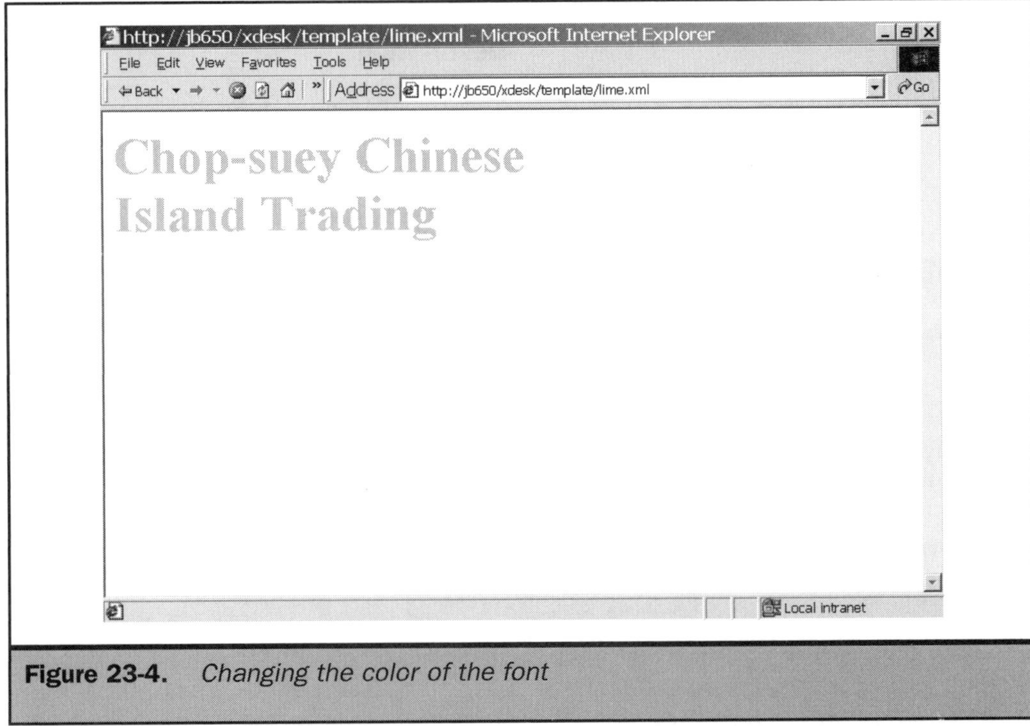

Figure 23-4. *Changing the color of the font*

Let's keep moving by introducing pattern-matching syntax, as listed in Table 23-3.

Syntax	Description
<xsl:template match="*">	Process all elements within the XML document. Unmatched elements will apply top this template.
<xsl:template match="element">	Matches children of the current node.
<xsl:template match="//element">	'//' is the recursive descendant path operator. Matches all elements at any level of the document.

Table 23-3. *XSL Pattern Matching Syntax*

Syntax	Description
<xsl:template match "element//descendant">	Recursively applies template to descendants (children) of an element.
<xsl:template match "element/descendant">	Applies template to direct descendants of a specific element.

Table 23-3. *XSL Pattern Matching Syntax* (continued)

Based on the preceding template, we can now reformat our Open Incidents page to display the XML output in a report-type format instead of a boring HTML table. We can expand the style sheet we did earlier to display the company names in green to output all of the fields we need. It should look something like the style sheet that follows. Notice that we are simply matching the fields from the XML document to rules in the template, the result of which is displayed in the browser illustrated in Figure 23-5.

```
<xsl:stylesheet xmlns:xsl="http://www.w3.org/TR/WD-xsl">
      <xsl:template match="/">
           <xsl:apply-templates select="//vw_Open_Incidents"/>
      </xsl:template>
      <xsl:template match="vw_Open_Incidents">
           <P>
           <xsl:apply-templates select="CompanyName"/>
           <xsl:apply-templates select="ContactName"/>
           <xsl:apply-templates select="IncidentID"/>
           <xsl:apply-templates select="DateAdded"/>
           </P>
      </xsl:template>

      <xsl:template match="CompanyName">
            <font style="BACKGROUND-COLOR: #6495ed"
                  color="moccasin" face="Lucida Console" size="5"/>
            <B>
            <xsl:value-of/>
            </B>
            <BR/>
      </xsl:template>
      <xsl:template match="ContactName">
             <font style="BACKGROUND-COLOR: white"
                  color="black" face="verdana" size="3"/>
```

```
            Contact: <xsl:value-of/>
            <BR/>
    </xsl:template>

    <xsl:template match="IncidentID">
          <font style="BACKGROUND-COLOR: white"
                color="black" face="verdana" size="3"/>
           IncidentID: <xsl:value-of/>
           <BR/>
    </xsl:template>

    <xsl:template match="DateAdded">
           <font style="BACKGROUND-COLOR: white"
                 color="black" face="verdana" size="3"/>
           Date/Time Entered: <xsl:value-of/>
    </xsl:template>
</xsl:stylesheet>
```


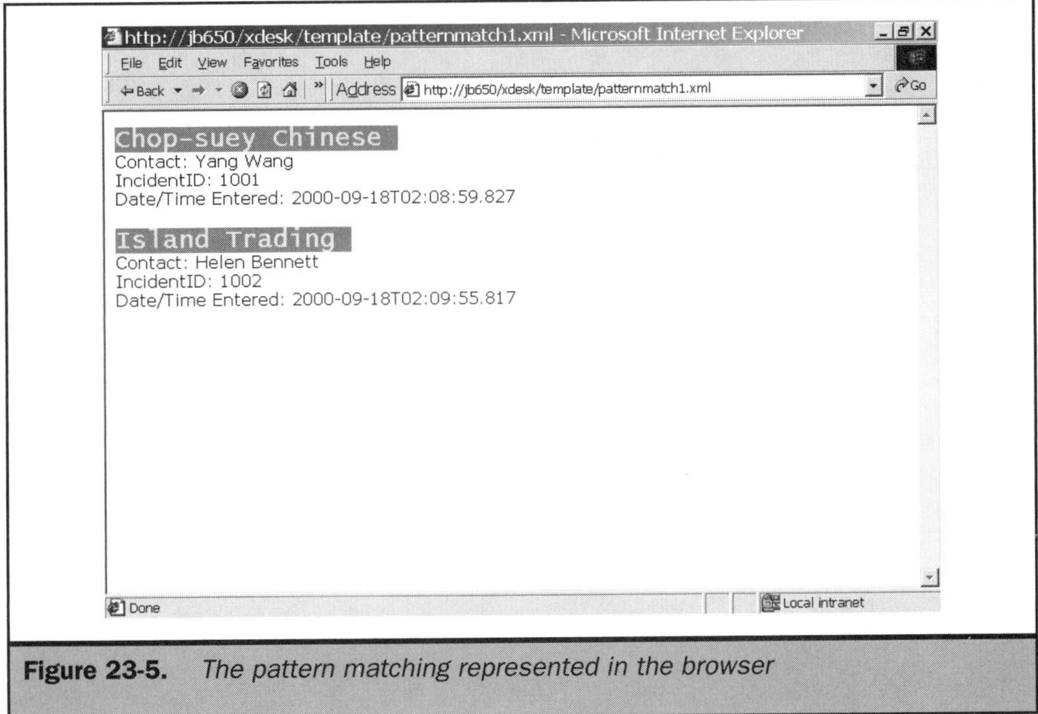

Figure 23-5. *The pattern matching represented in the browser*

What we have done is simply modify the XSL style sheet to output the XML in a different format. Sometimes tables are boring, so sprucing up our output is a nice change. And I forgot the most important line in the report, the Operating System. No problem, I'll just add another line in the style sheet matching to Operating System, as demonstrated in Figure 23-6.

So it's that easy. Informative reports with no real ASP or VB code, just XML data straight from SQL Server and a simple style sheet. Now let's assume you need a report of the entire incident from the database. Up until now, we have been creating queries based on what we actually want. For example, if I want open incidents, I create a query that only gives me records where DateResolved is null in the database. This could make for many queries. Even though SQL Server makes it very easy for me to create templates and the like, I could also accomplish the same thing with XSL. The good news is that XSL has very powerful filtering and sorting techniques built in.

XSL allows filtering nodes based on the presence of child elements, the value of child elements, or the existence of attributes with an element. This makes it very easy to isolate data criteria through the style sheet and not the actual query itself. XSL has specific grammar for filtering, defined in the next section.

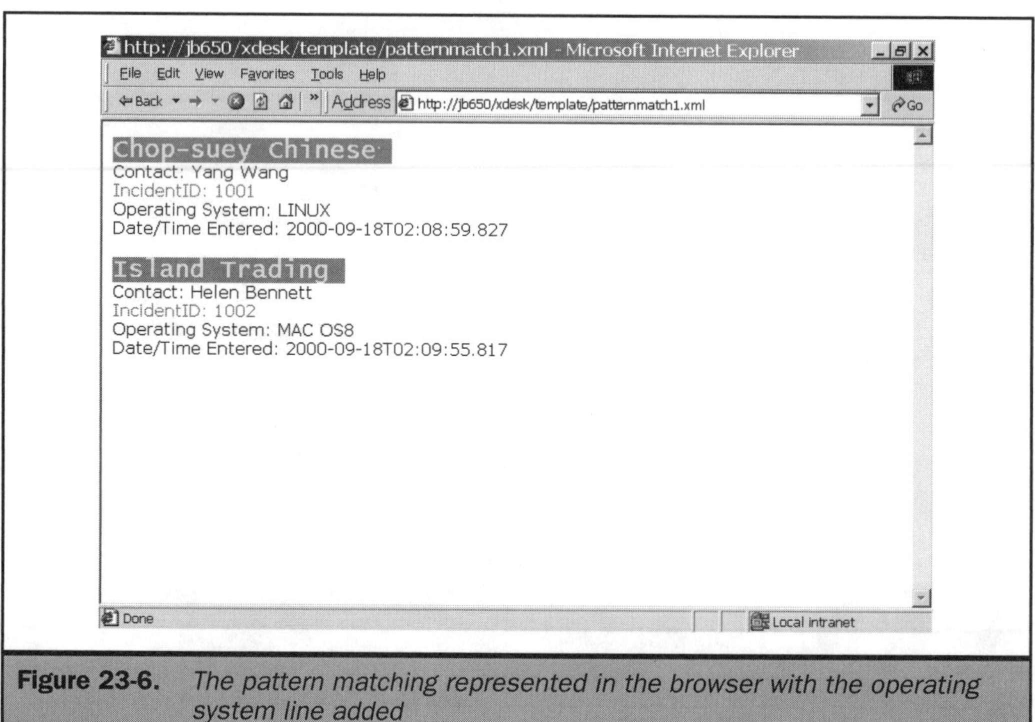

Figure 23-6. *The pattern matching represented in the browser with the operating system line added*

Comparison Operators

Table 23-4 lists comparison operators. To test an XSL style sheet that searches for incidents by Operating System in the Incidents table, try modifying the <xsl:template match="Operating System"> element in the style sheet that we created. I think you will see that it is very simple to apply filtering this way. The idea is *client side.* Remember the old days when the "fat client" was the savior of all killer apps? Well, now the killer app needs to a "rich client," or a "thin client."

Note *"Rich" and "thin" mean the same thing—in my mind anyway.*

Let's run our application through a browser, on a machine with limited resources, over a phone wire or LAN or WAN, but we need to have a whole barrel-load of functionality. XML and XSL on the client, with some VB Script or JScript mixed in the fray, and SQL Server on the back end running on Windows 2000 Server running COM+ will give us all the tools we need to create a very "thin" yet "rich" client. Why make a call back to the server to filter or search for a record? You really shouldn't have to; it is a waste of precious bandwidth. You can accomplish the same thing with XSL on the client with the pattern matching we explained, or with XSL sorting methods. So in the end we really have the ability to create applications that do things like this for us without the cost of the big client machine, or the 128MB of RAM you might need to run your old Power Builder or Access 2.0 applications.

Operator	Description
\$eq\$	Equal
\$ne\$	Not equal
\$lt\$	Less than
\$le\$	Less than / equal to
\$gt\$	Greater than
\$ge\$	Greater than / equal to
\$and\$	AND
\$or\$	OR
\$not\$	NOT
\$maybe-kind-of\$	Just kidding

Table 23-4. *XSL Comparison Operator Grammar*

Back to XDesk

We will take the same route as before, creating a view and then calling the view from the stored procedure. In the Query Analyzer, type in the following to create the views and stored procedure that we will use.

```
CREATE VIEW vw_Incident_Details AS
SELECT Customers.CompanyName, Customers.ContactName,
   Customers.EMail, Customers.Website, Incidents.*
     FROM Customers INNER JOIN
     Incidents ON Customers.CustomerID = Incidents.CustomerID

CREATE PROCEDURE IncidentDetails
  @IncidentID int AS
    SELECT * FROM vw_Incident_Details
      WHERE IncidentID = @IncidentID
         FOR XML AUTO, ELEMENTS
GO
```

This stored procedure will retrieve the Incident and Customer details for the selected IncidentID. In order for this to be successful, we will make another template file. This template file will be a little different than before, since we need to pass the IncidentID parameter to the template file. Open up your Notepad again and type in the following code to make the new template:

```
<ROOT xmlns:sql='urn:schemas-microsoft-com:x
ml-sql'>
  <sql:header>
       <sql:param name='IncidentID'>
1001</sql:param>
  </sql:header>
  <sql:query >
      exec IncidentDetails @IncidentID
  </sql:query>
</ROOT>
```

Notice the @IncidentID parameter being passed? This is where all the magic happens. Save this template as *IncidentDetails.xml.* Type the following URL in your browser:

```
http://localhost/xdesk/template/IncidentDetails.xml?IncidentID=1002
```

This results in the following well-formed XML document:

```
- <ROOT xmlns:sql="urn:schemas-microsoft-com:xml-sql">
- <vw_Incident_Details>
  <CompanyName>Island Trading</CompanyName>
  <ContactName>Helen Bennett</ContactName>
  <IncidentID>1002</IncidentID>
  <CustomerID>ISLAT</CustomerID>
  <Description>Computer crashes at lunchtime</Description>
  <DateAdded>2000-09-18T02:09:55.817</DateAdded>
  <OperatingSystem>MAC OS8</OperatingSystem>
  <SoftwareName>N/A</SoftwareName>
  <Keywords>MAC</Keywords>
  <KBID>0</KBID>
  </vw_Incident_Details>
  </ROOT>
```

Tip *You might have noticed that in our template file, we hard-coded the ID 1001 for the sql:param information. This is a "default" value. In the browser, we passed the ID 1002, which is what the results displayed. Without the default value, an error occurs, so keep that in mind when you start doing your own testing.*

We have now created another template file that generates an XML document from a template file. This will be our Incident Details page. In order to make it successful, some formatting needs to be done. So let's create a style sheet and attach it to this template. When we are done, we can open up our browser, get a list of open incidents at the help desk, and view the details in a nicely formatted report by clicking the incident ID hyperlink. This is great. We are actually creating an application, and we really haven't written much code. SQL Server seems to be doing most of the work for us. This is where you get more involved. Go ahead and take the style sheet that we created earlier, make some changes to format it how you like, and, knowing what we have discussed in the previous sections on applying style sheets to templates, add a reference to the style sheet in the template. Now rerun the following query:

```
http://localhost/xdesk/template/IncidentDetails.xml?IncidentID=1002
```

What did you get? Your browser should now display your raw XML with a little bit of style.

About-Face

Up until now we have done a complete XML, XSL, and SQL Server solution. I think that eventually this might cause you a little bit of grief with learning the new XSL syntax and understanding what all of your possibilities are. So in order to give a complete and thorough explanation of what we can do with some other tools, I want to delve into using a middle-tier approach. How about some COM+ components written in Visual Basic? How about some client-side data binding through XML Data Islands? Well, that's where we need to head to fully appreciate what SQL Server 2000 XML support has to offer us.

```
Visual Basic + Windows 2000 + SQL Server 2000 + XML = n-Tier Applications
```

If you have never written a COM component, you have definitely been missing out on a lot of good, clean fun. I am an MCT and do a lot of Visual Basic, ASP, and SQL training. When I look at my schedule and see that I am teaching a VB Enterprise Development course, or a course on ASP, I get all wound up. It means that I get another opportunity to talk about how great writing COM components really is. Taking a middle-tier approach to writing your applications, if you have not started doing it already, is the *only* way to write efficient, scalable, and available applications. This is all possible with great back-office software, like Windows 2000, COM+, and SQL Server 2000. I cannot stress enough how much more robust your applications will be if you simply put your business logic and data access code into components running in COM+, and not in Active Server Pages or fat clients written in Visual Basic. And that is why I think it is necessary to explore how we can do this exact thing with XML from SQL Server 2000.

COM+ in Brief

What exactly is COM+? Why do you want me to write components? What does it all mean? COM+, in very technical terms, is an infrastructure of run-time services that provide object pooling, loosely coupled events, transaction management, shared property management, and load balancing. There are some other things, like queued components, compensating resource managers, and very granular security in there also, but that's pretty advanced stuff. We stick to the simple here. So why write components? If you need a reason, it's reusability, maintainability, and scalability. Maybe that's two or three reasons, but we'll let it slide. And don't worry, "reusability" is really a word, even thought it's not used much in real life.

Reusability

Currently, you probably have a bevy of applications with very similar code. But in the past, the only way to use the same function from one application to another was by copying and pasting it into your new application. If you knew C++ or Delphi, maybe you wrote a DLL, but this DLL was for a specific application, with hard-coded details pertaining to that application. Wouldn't it be great to take that same exact code, stick it somewhere, and without changing a thing, use it in *all* your applications, including Web-based applications? And wouldn't it be great if your C++ apps could call methods written in COBOL, VB, or even Java? Answer: = COM+.

Maintainability

"I made a change and deployed 3,000 new EXE's through SMS last night, and, well, I screwed up a line of code and now everyone crashes." Has that ever happened to you? I have to be honest, my code always works perfectly on *my* machine, but isn't that the case with all of us? With COM+, we have a single point where all code gets executed. This means that you will not lose your job when the whole corporate office is crashing because it takes six hours to redeploy your 3,000 new EXEs. We can maintain all of our code server side. New database code? New business logic? No problem, just make a change to the component running under COM+ and the whole world has it all at once. No more maintenance issues between versions and DLLs and languages. COM+ takes care of all that for us.

Scalability

If my memory serves me correctly, a wise Vulcan once said, "The needs of the many outweigh the needs of the few or the one." What happens when 100,000 people connect to the database all at once? You guessed it, it hurts really bad. What happens when I have an Active Server Page that is 2,000 lines of server-side script? That hurts worse. In the Web world, applications need to scale. You might sign on 25,000 new customers tomorrow. What is the answer? Certainly not more hardware. It's not necessary. We need to take advantage of the features in COM+ such as object pooling, connection pooling, and just-in-time activation to ensure that our applications will scale to however many people access them. By placing database access and business logic code in components, and letting those components run under COM+, we are automatically granted scalability. We write applications with the single user in mind, and COM+ handles all of the multiuser stuff for us. It's like magic. It just works.

That is my COM+ speech. Plus I snuck in an Iron Chef reference and a *Star Trek* reference in a single sentence. I can't believe it took me that long to do that. Anyway, it is essential that you look up COM+ and start designing your applications to run under COM+. Remember, *any* language will do. We are going to now write some COM components in Visual Basic that pull XML data down from SQL Server, and then we will display that XML in an Active Server Page.

XML from Visual Basic

Up until now, we have retrieved XML from SQL Server 2000 using templates, displayed it several different ways using style sheets, and glimpsed filtering and sorting data with XSL. All along, you were probably wondering, "Where do COM+ and VB come in?" We take a journey down that road right now.

If you've never used Visual Basic before, or COM+, I think you will be amazed at how easy it is to do very powerful things with these tools. As we go along, do not stress out if you do not understand the syntax of the language, and all the little details. That takes time to learn. But I do want to stress that data access from VB to SQL Server 2000 is very easy. If you have used Java, C++, Lotus Script, or any number of other languages, you will see the similarity immediately.

We need to fire up Visual Basic and create a new ActiveX DLL project. This is the type of DLL that runs under COM+. An ActiveX DLL is an In-Process object, which means that it cannot run as a standalone object but is created in the same process as its creator. In this case, it will be created in a COM+ process.

In your project explorer, you should see a single class module called Class1. Change the name of the class module to XMLDATA in the properties dialog. And while you are there, change the name of the project to XMLDLL. Now from the Project pull-down menu, select references and scroll down the list until you see "Microsoft ActiveX Data Objects 2.6 Library." This will ensure that the ADO type library is available to us in the VB app. Little things like auto-complete make life much easier, and by referencing this type library, we get all that for free.

What we are going to do is very similar to what we did with the SQL Server 2000 templates. We are going to retrieve the incidents that are open from the database, and display the XML in a table in an Active Server Page. We are writing this code to run in the middle tier, so our application will be scalable, maintainable, and reusable.

In the XMLDATA class module, add a Public Function called Get_Open_Incidents. We need to create this as a Public Function so that we can call the method from outside of this application once it is running under COM+. The cool thing is that once it is running under COM+, any application can call this method, not just XDesk.

Here is our Visual Basic code to retrieve the XML from SQL Server:

```
Public Function Get_Open_Incidents()
    On Error GoTo erH
    ' Declare ADO variables
    Dim cn As New ADODB.Connection
    Dim rs As New ADODB.Recordset
    ' Strings for storing ADO resultset
    Dim strSQL As String
    Dim strXML As String
    ' SQL Statement
```

```
    strSQL = "Select * from vw_Open_Incidents FOR XML AUTO"
    strXML = "<root>"
    ""

Cn.provider = "SQLOLEDB"

Cn.cursorlocation = adUseClient

Cn.Open "uid=sa;pwd=;database=xdesk;initial catalog=."


rs.Open strSQL, cn, adOpenForwardOnly, adLockReadOnly
    Do While Not rs.EOF
        strXML = strXML & Trim(rs(0) & "")
        rs.MoveNext
    Loop
    strXML = strXML & vbCrLf & "</root>"
    Get_Open_Incidents = strXML
    Exit Function
erH:
    Err.Raise Err.Number, "Get_Open_Incidents", Err.Description
End Function
```


Before continuing, let's break down the masterpiece of VB code that you just wrote. The first thing that we did is to declare our variables for the connection and recordset objects. The strSQL variable is just there to hold the SQL statement that we are passing. Notice the Select statement:

```
Select * from vw_Open_Incidents FOR XML AUTO
```

This is the same FOR XML AUTO syntax that we went over in the beginning of the chapter. We are asking SQL Server to return to us an XML recordset, not your usual recordset with fields and field values. If you recall, XML data from SQL Server does not provide the ROOT node that we need to make our XML well formed. So we have to include that in the actual XML text that we are going to pass back to our Active Server Page. We then open the ADO connection to SQL Server by passing it a reference to a DSN that I created called "XDesk" that points to the XDesk database.

The "Open" method of the recordset object takes our SQL statement and the active connection as parameters, and that is what actually holds our XML recordset. Now this is very important: SQL Server returns the XML data in 2K blocks, so even though we asked for XML AUTO in the Select statement, we still need to loop through the ADODB recordset and concatenate the data into a single stream of data. The last step is appending the closing </root> element, and we simply pass the text stream to our function, which will pass it to whatever object happened to call it. In this case, we are calling the method from ASP. So now we have created a perfectly well-formed XML document from SQL Server 2000 in a Visual Basic component. Now we need to actually do something with the data.

But first we need to compile this DLL and stick it into COM+. So from the File menu select "Make XMLDLL.DLL." This will compile the code into a nice DLL for us. Make sure you remember where you have compiled the file; we will need to get to the DLL in a second.

Adding Your DLL to COM+

Now that the *xmldll.dll* is compiled, we will add it to COM+. We need to open the Component Services MMC Snap-In, which is located in the Administrative Tools folder. Once it fires up, follow these steps:

1. Drill into My Computer, and then Com+ Applications.
2. Once you see a bunch of brownish boxes on the right-hand pane, right-click Com+ Applications, select New, and then select Application.
3. The COM+ Application Install Wizard dialog box now pops up. Click Next, and on the "Install or Create Empty Application" screen illustrated in Figure 23-7, click the Create Empty Application button. For the name, type **XML_SQL**.

   The name really does not matter, since it never gets referenced. Leave the option button for Server Application selected. If you select Client Application, you automatically lose all the benefits of COM+, such as security and pooling.
4. Click Next two times, and then click Finish.

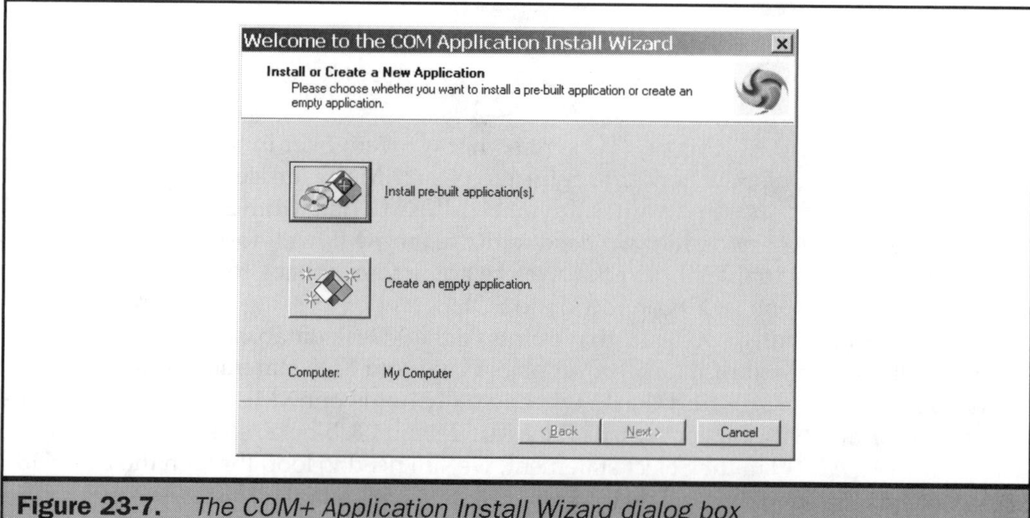

Figure 23-7. *The COM+ Application Install Wizard dialog box*

We have now completed step 1 in adding a component to COM+. In the console, you should see the XML_DLL package in the left pane. Now follow these steps to add the actual DLL to out COM+ application:

1. Drill into the package and select the Components folder.
2. Right-click the folder and select New; then select Component. The Component Installation Wizard now appears.
3. Click Next, and on the Install or Import New Component dialog box (illustrated in Figure 23-8) select Install New Component. You are now prompted with the Browse for File window. Go ahead and find *xmldll.dll* and click Open. You are returned to the COM+ Install Wizard, and you should see that COM+ found your component.
4. Click Next, and then Finish.

Congratulations! You have just created a COM component in Visual Basic and added it to COM+. On to ASP. Now we create an ASP application using Visual Interdev that will call our "Get_Open_Incidents" method running in COM+. So we need to create an empty Interdev application. Fire up Interdev, and create a new application. You can call it whatever your heart desires. Once the wizard is done creating the app, add a new Active Server Page to your project, and add in the following code:

```
<%@ Language=VBScript %>
<HTML>
<META NAME="GENERATOR" Content="Microsoft Visual Studio 6.0">
<TITLE></TITLE>
<xml id = "xmldso">
            <%
                 set x = server.CreateObject("XMLDLL.XMLDATA")
                 Response.Write x.Get_Open_Incidents
            %>
</xml>
<HEAD>
            <DIV STYLE="font-family:Tahoma;
                        font-size:18pt;
                        font-weight:bold;
                        color:Purple;
                        text-align:center">
                  XDesk Open Incidents Report
            </DIV>
</HEAD>
<BODY>
```

PROGRAMMING SQL SERVER 2000

```
<table                    WIDTH="100%" BORDER="1"
                          borderColor="blue"
                          cellPadding="1"
                          cellSpacing="2"
                          valign="top"
                          datasrc="#xmldso">
     <thead>
            <tr>
            <td>Company</td>
            <td>Customer</td>
            <td>Operating System</td>
            <td>Incident ID#</td>
            </tr>
      </thead>
      <tbody><tr>
      <td><span datafld="CompanyName"></span></td>
      <td><span datafld="ContactName"></span></td>
      <td><span datafld="OperatingSystem"></span></td>
      <td><span datafld="IncidentID"></span></td>
      </tr></tbody>
</table>
</BODY>
</HTML>
```

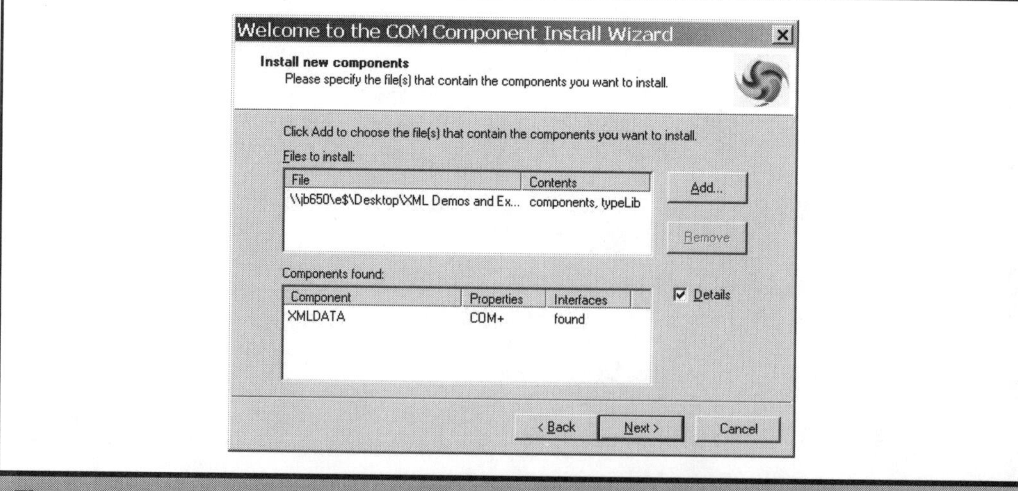

Figure 23-8. *The Install or Import New Component dialog box*

So what exactly did we just do? We created a regular old Active Server Page, but there are a few cool things here. Notice the <XML id = "xmldso> tag. This is telling the ASP that we are going to use an XML Data Island. Now the ASP can process the stream that we are passing from the component as XML, and use XML Data Binding. The next two lines, which are enclosed in server-side script, are actually creating an instance of our COM component in COM+, calling our "Get_Open_Incidents" method, and returning the XML to the ASP page through the Response object. Next we write some regular old HTML code that creates a table. The difference here from a normal table is the line of HTML in the <table> tag that says "datasrc=xmldso." Here we are instructing the HTML table to use the data island that we created in the preceding code to "bind" the XML to rows in the table. The <td> tags in the table contain a <span> with a "datafld=" instruction that corresponds to actual <elements> in our XML stream. So we are simply binding the XML stream to an HTML table.

Figure 23-9 illustrates what you should be seeing in your browser.

Look familiar? Yep, it is identical to what we did earlier with the templates. Now do something for me. Right-click in the browser and View Source. As you can see, there is our client-side code, but look between the <xml> tags. There is our XML stream that we brought down from the component, actually embedded in the Active Server Page. So still, no matter what, template, component, data binding, or style sheet; all the work of formatting is down on the client.

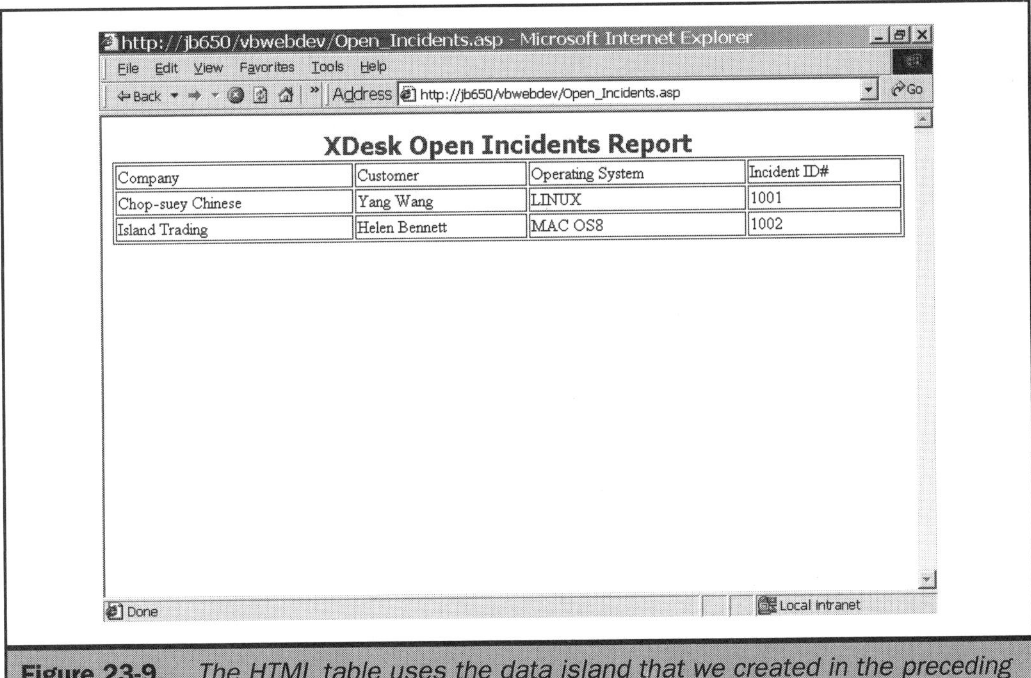

Figure 23-9. *The HTML table uses the data island that we created in the preceding code to "bind" the XML to rows in the table*

If you are familiar with Remote Data Services, you might say that XML Data-Binding is the same thing. Well you are 50 percent correct. The only difference is that this works all the time on every server you try it on. Here is a little code snippet of the "old way" of writing an Active Server Page:

```
<%@ Language=VBScript %>
<HTML>
<META NAME="GENERATOR" Content="Microsoft Visual Studio 6.0">
<TITLE></TITLE>
            <%
                  set cn = server.CreateObject("ADODB.Connection")
                  set rs = server.CreateObject("ADODB.Recordset")
                  cn.Provider = "sqloledb"
                  cn.CursorLocation = 3
                  cn.ConnectionString = "uid=sa;pwd=;database=xdesk"
                  cn.Open
                  rs.Open "Select * from vw_open_incidents", cn
            %>
<HEAD>

                  XDesk Open Incidents Report
            </DIV>
</HEAD>
<BODY>

<table      WIDTH="100%" BORDER="1" >
      <thead>
            <tr>
            <td>Company</td>
            <td>Customer</td>
            <td>Operating System</td>
            <td>Incident ID#</td>
            </tr>
      </thead>
      <tbody>
      <%while not rs.EOF%>
      <tr>
      <td><%=rs("CompanyName")%></td>
      <td><%=rs("ContactName")%></td>
      <td><%=rs("OperatingSystem")%></td>
      <td><%=rs("IncidentID")%>></td>
      <%rs.MoveNext%>
```

```
        <%wend%>
        </tr>
        </tbody>
</table>
</BODY>
</HTML>
```

It's a lot more code. Plus, look at how the Connection object is being created inside of the Active Server Page. What happens when 5,000 people access this page? You guessed it: 5,000 connections. In the COM+ way of doing things, we are pooling connections, so at any given time we might only have 200 connections for 5,000 people; maybe a little more, maybe a little less, but nowhere near 5,000. Also, in the "old way"," we are looping through the recordset to generate the table data. It is more code, and more server-side processing. The data binding is occurring on the page once it is down at the client, so the server is really only busy for the split second that COM+ gets the SQL data. And since COM+ is using just-in-time activation on the component, it is actually sitting there waiting for the next request on the method. We do not have to go through the pain of instantiating the object every time we make a request on it.

I hope so far you can see the benefits of putting code in the middle tier. It could actually be a whole book by itself (and there are many good ones). I have one book on MTS and two on COM+, and every time I am feeling a little down, I just crank open one of those books and read a few pages, and all of a sudden, everything seems better.

So now that we have successfully created our first COM+ component and actually returned data to a browser, learning a little about data binding and data islands, how much better could it possible get? Trust me, it gets even better. We now look at how to manipulate data thought XML.

XML Updategrams and OpenXML: Data Manipulation Through XML

How can we insert, update, and delete data through XML? Microsoft has released the concept of updategrams that allow us to manipulate XML on the client and pass it back to the server so that it will update the SQL Server database, in a complete XML solution. We also have the ability to insert data with the OpenXML clause. Throughout this chapter, we have covered different methods of data retrieval. But in reality, once we get data, we normally change it, and those changes must be stored in a database. Our updategrams and OpenXML give us the ability to make this a reality with SQL Server 2000.

OpenXML

OpenXML is a T-SQL keyword that provides a result set, which we can equate to a table or a view, over an XML document that is retained in memory. OpenXML allows us access to XML data as if it were a relational recordset by providing a tabular, relational view of the internal representation of an XML document.

OpenXML can be used in SELECT and SELECT INTO statements wherever a table, a view, or OPENROWSET can appear as the source of the query. The syntax for OpenXML is as follows:

```
OpenXML(idoc int [in],rowpattern nvarchar[in],[flags byte[in]])
[WITH (SchemaDeclaration | TableName)]
```

Here is a description of the syntax:

idoc

The *idoc* is the document handle of the internal representation of an XML document. Calling sp_xml_preparedocument creates this internal representation of the XML document.

rowpattern

The *rowpattern* refers to the XPath pattern used to identify the nodes to be processed as rows. These are the rows passed from the document handle received in the *idoc* parameter.

flags

The *flags* indicates the mapping that should be used between the XML data and the recordset, and how the spill-over column should be filled. *Flags* is an optional parameter.

SchemaDeclaration

The *SchemaDeclaration* is the schema definition in the form following this pattern:

```
ColName ColType [ColPattern | MetaProperty][, ColName ColType
[ColPattern | MetaProperty]...]
```

ColName *Colname* is the column name in the rowset.

ColType *ColType* represents the SQL data type of the column. If the column types differ from the underlying XML data type of the attribute, type coercion occurs. If the column is of type timestamp, the present value in the XML document is disregarded when selecting from an OpenXML recordset, and the autofill values are returned.

ColPattern The *ColPattern* is an optional XPath pattern that describes how the XML nodes should be mapped to columns. If the ColPattern is not specified, the default mapping (attribute-centric or element-centric mapping as specified by flags) takes place. The XPath pattern specified as ColPattern is used to specify the special nature of the mapping (in case of attribute-centric and element-centric mapping) that overwrites or enhances the default mapping indicated by flags. The general XPath pattern specified as *ColPattern* also supports the metaproperties.

MetaProperty *MetaProperty* is one of the metaproperties provided by OpenXML. If the metaproperty is specified, the column contains information provided by the metaproperty. The metaproperties allow you to extract information such as relative position and namespace information about XML nodes, which provides more information than is visible in the textual representation.

TableName

If a table with the desired schema already exists and no column patterns are required, the table name can be given instead of *SchemaDeclaration*.

To write queries against an XML document using OpenXML, you must first call sp_xml_preparedocument, which parses the XML document and returns a handle to the parsed document that is ready for consumption. The parsed document is a tree representation of various nodes (elements, attributes, text, comment, and so on) in the XML document. The document handle is passed to OpenXML, which then provides a recordset view of the document based on the parameters passed to it.

The internal representation of an XML document must be removed from memory by calling the sp_xml_removedocument system stored procedure to free the memory.

So those are the gory details on the specifics of OpenXML. It all looks good on paper, but what does it all mean? Here is a brief summary, and then we will do a living, breathing example of OpenXML.

Basically, OpenXML allows us to leverage our existing relational model and use that with XML. I can send XML data to the server, execute a stored procedure that inserts or selects data, and then return XML back to the client.

To read BOL is a little weird because the samples have the XML embedded within the stored procedure. It would have been nice to see an example of an XML document being passed as a parameter. So that is exactly what we will do. Up until now, we have not created a page that adds new Knowledgebase entries. We will do that with OpenXML. Here is the stored procedure that we need to create:

```
CREATE PROC sp_ins_KB @kb ntext
AS
    DECLARE @hDoc int
    EXEC sp_xml_preparedocument @hDoc OUTPUT, @kb
```

```
    INSERT INTO KnowledgeBase
      SELECT *
      FROM OpenXML(@hDoc, '/KnowledgeBase')
            WITH KnowledgeBase
     EXEC sp_xml_removedocument @hDoc
GO
```

This code is pretty simple. All we are doing is passing the XML as the @kb parameter; executing the sp_xml_preparedocument system stored procedure, which will give us a handle to the XML document; and then calling the Insert Into T-SQL against the XML document. So whatever we pass as an XML document will be inserted into the Knowledgebase table. The cool thing is that the XML document can contain multiple records to insert, so we can add many records with a single OpenXML call. An important note: Since we are creating an internal representation of the XML document, we need to run the system stored procedure sp_xml_removedocument to remove the document from memory. Just another example of good housekeeping.

Now we open up our handy Notepad and create a template called *insertKB.xml* in our XDesk virtual template directory that will accept this XML document as a parameter from an HTML page. Here is what the code should look like:

```
<root xmlns:sql='urn:schemas-microsoft-com:xml-sql'>
<sql:header>
<sql:param name="jason"><KnowledgeBase/></sql:param>
</sql:header>
<sql:query>exec sp_ins_KB @jason
</sql:query>
</root>
```

We are accepting the "Jason" parameter from the HTML form. Notice the <sql:param> elements. We used this same technique earlier to pass parameters to our template for the stored procedure. So the template syntax for accepting parameters is exactly the same here. The next element, the <sql:query> element, is also the same as we described earlier in the chapter. We are simply executing a stored procedure and passing it the parameter that we took in from the <sql:param> element.

Last, we create an HTML page that accepts some user input and then actually calls the template file. Here is a sample HTML file that will accomplish just this:

```
<html>
<META name=VI60_defaultClientScript content=JavaScript>
<body>
  <form action="http://localhost/xDesk/template/InsertKB.xml"
```

```
        method="post">
    <input type="hidden" id="kb" name="jason">
    <input type="hidden" name="contenttype" value="text/xml">
    <br>
            Q#:<input id=kbid value="Q19878" ><br>
        Title: <input id=title value="Linux-Crash" ><br>
        Description: <input id=details value="Reinstall" ><br>
        <input type=submitonclick="UpdateKB(kb,kbid,title,details)"

                   value="Update Knowledgebase"><br><br>
<script>
    function UpdateKB(kb, kbid, title, details)
     {
      kb.value = '<KnowledgeBase
      KBID="' + kbid.value +
      '" Title="' + title.value +
      '" Details="' + details.value + '"/>';
     }
</script>
</form>
</body>
</html>
```

This HTML page has a few input boxes that allow the user to enter in an Article Number, a Title, and a Description for the Knowledgebase article. On the Submit action, we execute the UpdateKB script, which builds the XML document, and then the FORM action takes over and calls our InsertKB template which inserts the XML document into the database.

Basically, we are building an XML document and passing the XML document to a template; the template in turn passes the XML document to the stored procedure, which uses OpenXML to read the XML and insert the data into the SQL Server table.

Keep in mind that in our example, we have assumed that the schema of the table (field names) is the same as the elements that we have sent over in the XML document. This works fine in a perfect world. There may be times when you need to match elements from the XML elements to field names in the database. With OpenXML, this is no problem at all. Consider the following WITH clause in the OpenXML statement:

```
SELECT *
FROM OpenXML (@idoc, '//Customers')
      WITH (CustomerID  varchar(10)   'CustomerID',
```

```
              Zipcode    datetime          'Zip',
              StateCode varchar(10)        '@STATE',
              Address    varchar(30)       '@MailAddress')
```

In the preceding example, we have elements being passed by the XML document that do not match the field names in the database. In order to correctly match up the elements to the fields, we are using a *schemadeclaration* that will map the fields correctly according to the *rowpattern* specified in the OpenXML statement. So this is another example of the great flexibility that OpenXML gives us in tailoring our inserts to the database. BOL sort of falls short in this area, so check out the samples at http://www.xmlpitstop.com for more detailed samples of OpenXML techniques. But for now, you have just completed the Add Knowledge Item page.

UpdateGrams

Updategrams consist of "blocks" of XML that describe which parts of our data we want to change. The XML data is enclosed in the < sync> element. Within this element, there are <before> and <after> elements indicating the blocks of XML that represent XML data before the changes and after the changes. SQL Server will receive this as a T-SQL update, insert, or delete query, depending on what XML the <before> and <after> blocks consist of.

Note *The Updategram technology is a Web release product, which was still in beta at the time of this writing; the version, available for download at http://msdn.microsoft.com, only works with SQL Server 2000 Beta 2. Consequently, the following code samples work on SQL Server 2000 Beta 2, and they will most likely work on the final Web release of updategrams, but they will not work on the final release product of SQL Server 2000. Nevertheless, what is discussed here should give you a head start.*

For example, the XML contained within the <before> may contain a primary key element with the actual primary key data value. The <after> element will contain XML elements that contain the updated values for the matching element/field value pairs. OLE DB, running in the middle tier through *xmlisapi.dll,* then creates the correct T-SQL update statement that will update the database with the correct data values.

The syntax for the updategram is as follows:

```
<ROOT xmlns:updg="urn:schemas-microsoft-com:xml-updategram">
 <updg:sync>
      <updg:before>
             <TABLENAME [updg:id="value"] col="value"
col="value"...../>
```

```
        </updg:before>
        <updg:after>
              <TABLENAME [updg:id="value"] [updg:at-identity="value"]
              col="value" col="value"...../>
        </updg:after>
   </updg:sync>
</ROOT>
```

Let's do a simple update, insert, and delete updategram to demonstrate how we can use this feature in real life. We will use the Customers table from the XDesk database, which if you recall is the same as the Customers table in the Northwind database, so these will work against either database.

Example 1: Update

We will use Notepad to create a template file that we will execute from a URL.

```
<ROOT xmlns:updg="urn:schemas-microsoft-com:xml-updategram">
<updg:sync >
<updg:before>
      <Incidents IncidentID="1001" />
</updg:before>
<updg:after>
      <Incidents DateResolved="7-29-2000" />
</updg:after>
</updg:sync>
</ROOT>
```

Save this file as *UpdateIncidents.xml* in the XDesk template virtual root, and type the following in the browser to execute our updategram:

```
http://localhost/XDesk/template/UpdateIncidents.xml
```

What we have done is to pass the IncidentID field as the initial element value that we are searching for in the Incidents table in the <before> block. In the <after> block, we pass the element attribute value DateResolved to instruct the updategram to update this field in the database. Even though we are passing only a single field to update, we can pass as many attributes or elements as we need in the <after> block to update fields in the database.

Example 2: Insert

In the Update updategram, we passed data in both the <before> and <after> blocks. In order to insert new values into the database, we do *not* include any elements or attributes in the <before> block. Here is an example of inserting a new record into the Incidents table:

```
<ROOT xmlns:updg="urn:schemas-microsoft-com:xml-updategram">
<updg:sync>
<updg:before>
</updg:before>
<updg:after>
      <Incidents CustomerID="ALFKI" OperatingSystem="Linux" />
</updg:after>
</updg:sync>
</ROOT>
```

How easy was that? All we do is pass attribute values and the table name, and the data is inserted into the table when we run this template from the URL. What is even more cool is that to insert multiple records, we simply add as many <Incidents> elements with attributes as we like. Here is a code snippet of an <after> block that will insert several records into the Incidents table:

```
<updg:after>
<Incidents CustomerID="ALFKI" OperatingSystem="Linux" />
<Incidents CustomerID="ISLAT" OperatingSystem="Linux"
Description="Unstable" />
<Incidents CustomerID="HSEN" OperatingSystem="Unix"
Keywords="Crash,Burn" />
</updg:after>
```

So now all of a sudden, I can insert multiple records without all the typing involved in the OpenXML statement. I think this is really cool. Another point that needs to be made is that I am using attributes instead of elements in many of the template examples. This just saves some typing on my part. Either attributes or elements will work fine in any sample.

Example 3: Delete

We have done an Insert and an Update, so Delete is next. I am so amazed at how easy this is so far. There is really nothing to it. I know that you probably can already imagine how we are going to create the Delete template, but we'll go ahead and type it in anyway:

```
<ROOT xmlns:updg="urn:schemas-microsoft-com:xml-updategram">
<updg:sync >
<updg:before>
      <Incidents IncidentID="10014" />
</updg:before>
</updg:sync>
</ROOT>
```

Notice there is no <after> block. Since we do want any after data, SQL Server looks at this as a delete. The actual T-SQL that is generated by the middle tier is

```
DELETE FROM Incidents WHERE IncidentID = 10014
```

Remember, all template processing occurs in the middle tiers, so the actual XML processing occurs in the ISAPI DLLs, which send SQL Server the T-SQL to process.

I know by now you are probably thinking that you will most likely need to pass the update, insert, or delete values as parameters. Well, the good news is you can. Since the updategrams are run though templates, we know that templates can take parameters. If you recall the <header> element, which took the <param> value in the previous templates, we were accepting parameters. We use the same syntax for passing parameters to updategram templates. So to pass, for example, an IncidentID to delete from the Incidents table, we would need to create the following template (I will save this a DeleteGram.xml in the XDesk virtual template root):

```
<ROOT xmlns:updg="urn:schemas-microsoft-com:xml-updategram">
<updg:header>
            <updg:param name="IncidentID"/>
</updg:header>
      <updg:sync >
           <updg:before>
                 <Incidents  IncidentID="$IncidentID" />
           </updg:before>
</updg:sync>
</ROOT>
```

Now from the URL, I will type the following:

```
http://localhost/XDesk/template/DeleteGram.xml?IncidentID=1043
```

Finito. So we have actually created something useful that we can use in real life. How can we pass the value from an HTML page? Just copy the same code we used to the Knowledge Base page. Modify the "Form Action=" tag to reference the *DeleteGram.xml* file, and change the OnClick code to pass the ID value that you are entering into the input box. It does not get much easier than this.

If you wish to pass the Update or Insert parameter, no problem. Simply change the parameters that the template accepts and you have a full-fledged data entry middle tier. In summation,

- If you specify only <after> data, you are doing an Insert statement.
- If you specify only <before> data, you are doing a Delete statement.
- If you specify both <before> and <after>, you are doing an Update statement.

Stuff to Chew On

I would like to make a few comments; sort of like a Jerry Springer Editorial. I really want you to understand that this is a brief overview of SQL Server 2000 XML support. There is so much to this area that there will be many articles, books, arguments, and so on written on the topic. Take, for example, the component we wrote earlier. I personally know of five different methods of returning XML from the middle tier down to the client. Which one is better than the other? Only time will tell. We are in a huge shift in data access technology that can only get better. So bear this in mind when you get out in the real world. You need to weed out the bad from the good in all of this new XML-related technology. For my part, the XDesk application and tons of other SQL Server 2000 XML–related, working, real-life samples will be posted for you to critique and use at http://www.xmlpitstop.com/sqlxml.

This is by far the most informative and groundbreaking site available for XML details, specifically those that are SQL Server 2000 related. One thing I found very frustrating was the lack of *good* samples, *good* examples, and just plain old straightforward details, in layman's terms, on the whole SQL Server 2000–XML relationship. Even as of this very moment, MSDN is very weak on anything of real substance. So be patient with all of this new stuff; I have a feeling that one day, very soon, there will be an explosion of useful information on SQL Server 2000 XML support.

Now I am off of my soap box. Wait . . . Did someone say SOAP? Okay, I guess it is a perfect opportunity for me to offer a little detail on the whole SOAP technology. This is such a great buzzword, almost as cool as XML.

Simple Object Access Protocol (SOAP) Primer

The *Star Trek* Universal Translator is not as far off as the twenty-third century after all. Since we made first contact with other species, we immediately realized the need to understand their languages. This was by no means an easy task, but thank God we first made progress in the twenty-first century with the advent of the Simple Object

Access Protocol (SOAP), which opened the way for the advances that led to the invention of a tool that will help all species understand each other. The Universal Translator. The only good thing about First Contact was that it was with the Vulcans, who just happened to speak English too. But imagine if First Contact was made with the Klingons, or even my Alyssa and Jessica, my one- and two-year-old nieces. We would be sitting across the table just looking at each other, wondering what all that gibberish was about.

This is why SOAP, or Simple Object Access Protocol, is so important. SOAP is a messaging protocol based on XML for transmitting data across the internet. The current submission of the SOAP standard to the W3C is supported by the following companies: Ariba, Inc., Commerce One, Inc., Compaq Computer Corporation, DevelopMentor, Inc., Hewlett-Packard Company, IBM, IONA Technologies, Lotus Development Corporation, Microsoft Corporation, SAP AG, and UserLand Software Inc. I would say that is a pretty impressive list, which also means that we have a support base for the future. It is not going to be a fly-by-night technology!

Currently, there are many languages: Visual Basic, C, C++, Java, CGI, COBOL, C#, and so on. Most likely, all of these languages have some pretty clever code that developers would love to use and show other developers. But we can't share, because we don't understand the other language. My Visual Basic component does not know how to process CGI instructions. With SOAP, we have an opportunity to write objects in such a way that they can be accessed from any language from any platform. How, you ask? XML—SOAP is an XML-based proposal (submitted to the W3C), which allows developers to package objects in a plain XML format so that they can be understood by any type of object that can understand XML.

So what is the deal with SOAP, and why did they really create it? Initially, the idea was to create a way for distributed applications to communicate over HTTP through corporate firewalls. This idea has grown, creating a whole new way of writing applications that are platform neutral on both the client and the server. Hence the Microsoft term "Web Service." Web Services will be everywhere from now on.

Finally, there is a platform-neutral way of accessing objects and using them in our applications. For example, DCOM is a great technology, but in order for it to work, the platform is Microsoft, or more exactly a Win32 platform. Active Server Pages are great too, but what if my component is running on a non-IIS server? How can I expose methods to other applications? Rewrite? Not anymore. With SOAP, we can *package* our components so that they can be called by anything from anywhere. Another important point is the client side. It seems nowadays everyone is writing applications that are browser based. Do we really need to rewrite our C++ or VB apps to take advantage of the new components we have written for the Web? No, because we can use SOAP from a fat client too.

When I first heard of SOAP, I thought to myself "Another way to write stuff, now I have more to learn, I need more sleep, there are not enough hours in the day to keep track of all this new technology." Well, once that thought was complete, I decided to investigate further. It really wasn't that bad. I can leverage my existing knowledge of XML with this new technology and do some pretty cool stuff.

Let's look at the basic syntax of a SOAP message:

```
<SOAP-ENV:Envelope
   xmlns:SOAP-ENV=http://schemas.xmlsoap.org/soap/envelope/
   SOAP-ENV:encodingStyle=
   "http://schemas.xmlsoap.org/soap/encoding/">
   <SOAP-ENV:Header>
      <t:XDeskTrans
        xmlns:t="some-URI"
      SOAP-ENV:mustUnderstand="1">1
      </t:XDeskTrans>
   </SOAP-ENV:Header>
   <SOAP-ENV:Body>
      <m:GetOpenIncident
         xmlns:m="Some-URI">
            <IncidentID>1001</IncidentID>
      </m:GetOpenIncident>
   </SOAP-ENV:Body>
</SOAP-ENV:Envelope>
```

SOAP Message

A SOAP consists of a SOAP envelope, SOAP header, and SOAP body.

SOAP Envelope

The SOAP envelope is a mandatory element in the SOAP message. This is the top element representing the message and optional attributes, which must be qualified by valid namespaces. In the preceding example, we include a reference to a namespace that will understand this message grammar and a namespace references the encoding of this message.

SOAP Header

The header is an optional element in the SOAP message and is always the first child element after the SOAP Envelope element. The SOAP header normally defines how a recipient of the SOAP message should process the message. Earlier, we included the "XDeskTrans" element with a "mustunderstand" value of "1", and passed the value of "1001". This really doesn't need to be here in our example, but it gives us an idea of how we can include a processing directive within the header itself.

SOAP Body

The SOAP body is actually the guts of what we need to execute our method calls and to pass any variables to the server that out method call may need. In our example, we are passing the GetOpenIncident method with the IncidentID attribute containing our variable of "1001". This will instruct the server we are executing this against to return the open incidents for the customer who has the ID of 1001.

Now that we have a brief explanation of what a SOAP message is and what all the good parts are, you are probably wondering what this means to you. Well, not much unless you have a tool that can help you use your existing COM components and start using this new SOAP way of executing methods and moving data. Here is where the SOAP Toolkit from Microsoft comes into play.

SOAP Toolkit

Microsoft realized the need to start getting developers moving in the SOAP direction, so until all the new server products come out that natively support SOAP, or Web services, we need to leverage our existing applications and knowledge to implement SOAP solutions now. The SOAP Toolkit is a download from MSDN that helps you move in the right direction. If you haven't downloaded it yet, grab it and install it on your development machine. With the SOAP Toolkit, you have a simple wizard that takes existing COM components you have written and creates all the files necessary to execute SOAP method calls—it does all the dirty work for you.

Here is how it works: Tell the SOAP Wizard which COM component you want to execute method calls against. The toolkit then creates an XML file containing the SDL, or Service Description Language, which is unique to your method calls in the component that describes the methods I am publishing. During the wizard process, a couple things happen: First, a listener file is created, either as an ASP page or an ISAPI application. This file "listens" for incoming SOAP calls on your server. The wizard also creates an Active Server Page that has is actually a wrapper function for your COM component. The cool thing about the ASP is that you can add any custom business logic that you desire, it just gives you the code needed to call the methods. Sounds easy, right? Well, there is one more thing we forgot to talk about, and that is ROPE.

Remote Object Proxy Engine (ROPE)

The ROPE.dll is a client- and server-side DLL included with the SOAP Toolkit. It allows a client to access a Web service on a server as if it were a regular COM component. The ROPE.dll is actually the COM component that receives, processes, and sends SOAP messages. For example, the listener intercepts an incoming SOAP call, and then uses the ROPE proxy to extract the information needed to call the COM component where the actual method is implemented. The ROPE proxy then uses the SDL, which the toolkit creates for you, to identify the method, verify the parameters, and create the XML that the client is requesting. It sounds a little complex, but the great thing is that the SOAP Toolkit provides all this functionality for you, so you don't get bogged down with the details. To get up and running quickly with SOAP, run the wizard and start testing.

In Review

I hope I opened up a few pathways for you to start using the XML capabilities in SQL Server 2000 out of the box. We have gone though creating a simple application using the different methods of extracting XML from SQL Server 2000. To expand on what we have accomplished here, the XDesk application and many more great SQL Server 2000 XML examples will be up on http://www.xmlpitstop.com. Keep in mind that XML is a brave new world, sort of like an undiscovered country. The amount of XML information over the next couple of years will most likely be overwhelming.

I want you to stick to the basics and understand what XML means to you right now. Start small, run some tests, show the boss, and see where it takes you. I personally am extremely impressed with the ease in which we can get a database driven Web site up and running with SQL Server 2000 templates, XML, and XSL. And it looks good. Like I always say to my customers, "No problem! Duck Soup" (and then they get a weird look on their faces). Use the OpenXML statement in your stored procedures to insert data using XML documents; keep checking the MSDN Web site for the final release of updategrams so you can use XML to insert, update, and delete SQL Server 2000 data from XML templates; and finally, use SQL Server 2000 for all your data solutions because it is hands down the most robust database server on the market, with all of the native XML support that you will ever need to create great *n*-Tier applications, which scale for eternity and hopefully make you a lot of cold hard cash.

Part IV

SQL Server 2000 Analysis Services

Chapter 24

Data Mining and Data Warehousing

We are almost at the end of a long book on SQL Server 2000, but the story continues. SQL Server provides extensive support for the management of temporal data, data mining, and enterprise or data analysis, better known as Online Analytical Processing (OLAP).

To provide as complete a reference as possible, I felt it important to cover this side of the product; especially in light of the number of companies, from teeny to gargantuan, that are beginning to aggressively analyze their data as part of day-to-day business operations. That said, this subject is extremely complex and deserves a Complete Reference dedicated to data mining and OLAP—covering theory, architecture, design, and deployment, as well as the gamut of SQL Server Analysis Services. Trust me, if we had another thousand pages, we could spend more time together in another 25 chapters.

But this chapter looks at the data warehouse, data marts, and data mining in general (with a bit of OLAP fundamentals thrown in), and Chapter 25 looks at OLAP in more detail (especially some of the new cube stuff). I am aiming Chapters 24 and 25 at both the expert and the beginner for one good reason: the offering in SQL Server 2000 is miles of that in SQL Server 7.0 and many other products. The expert will be able to zero in on support he or she was hoping for and quickly see what's new, while the beginner will at the same time get a brief overview of this part of the product and a general introduction to data warehousing and OLAP. Chapter 25 wraps up Analysis Services and OLAP in further detail and allows both the novice and the expert to become familiar with the SQL Server 2000 analysis offering.

Despite the extent of the subject, I have set out with these two chapters in mind to allow you to get cracking with SQL Server and OLAP even if you know nothing about data mining. I spent a lot of time going over the documentation on Analysis Services and felt that for novices it was just as hard to break into as the documentation that shipped with SQL Server 7.0. So, I am going to provide my own mini-tutorial here based on the FoodMart 2000 data and start from scratch in this chapter, taking you from Data Warehouse 101 to deployment of a "mini-mart" in a number of easy steps. Then we'll wrap up both chapters by browsing the cubes we created against the data.

You will also notice something really weird about the FoodMart 2000 data warehouse. It is built in Microsoft Access. No, you don't need to get your eyes tested. It is really true. You will not find the FoodMart 2000 warehouse in SQL Server. For some reason that defies logic, your highly sophisticated DBMS system schleps along its data warehouse example in a Microsoft Access (Jet) .mdb file. That's akin to the U.S. Navy demonstrating its latest ICBM on a rowboat.

I am not sure why the database was built in Access, but I decided to upsize it into SQL Server. I show you how to do this later in the chapter, which lets us learn a few things about DTS along the way.

Data Mining Components

The following components of SQL Server 2000 are used to build data warehouses and analyze the data:

- **Relational databases** The relational database is used as the foundation for the design, construction, and maintenance of a data warehouse. The services we have discussed throughout this book are used to build data warehouses and data marts and to maintain the data stored in them. (Please don't follow the FoodMart 2000 example and build your data warehouse in Microsoft Access. If you do, please go back to Part I in this book and rip out the first five chapters.)
- **Data Transformation Services (DTS)** This service is used to move data from various storehouses in SQL Server or other databases into staging areas where data can be "cleaned" (often called data scrubbing) and otherwise prepared for the insertion into the data warehouse. DTS can be used to access data from a wide variety of sources. You can also use bulk insert and the BCP utility to move data into the warehouse, but DTS provides a comprehensive data-moving environment. Later we are going to use DTS to port FoodMart 2000 to SQL Server.
- **Analysis Services** These are the tools, such as the cube editor, that you use to organize the data in the warehouse into multidimensional structures called cubes. Analysis services and the OLAP tools are able to organize huge volumes of data in such a way that client tools and applications can easily query and analyze the data as quickly as possible.
- **MDX/English Query** While operational data is queried using standard SQL, data warehouse data is queried with SQL extensions, almost another language, that have the facilities to provide analysis and aggregation of data. These extensions to SQL, called the *multidimensional extensions,* have evolved into a separate query language appropriately called Multidimensional Expressions (MDX). MDX, however, is far too complex to be used directly by the end user, as is often the case with SQL. MDX is also beyond the scope of this book. If you build English Query models that can be accessed from client applications, you afford your users the ability to query the analysis data using natural language expressions (see Chapter 22).
- **Replication** These services are used to distribute data around the enterprise. The replication services are extremely powerful (see Chapter 10), and you can use them to move data from staging or scrubbing areas to data marts and interim data warehouses and to update or maintain the main data warehouses.

- **Meta Data Services** As discussed in Chapter 5, the Meta Data Services are used to store and browse metadata. You will use the services and the Meta Data repository, a metadata database structure stored in the msdb system database, to store the information models that describe the data warehouse and analysis systems. The repository is also used to hold the metadata for English Query models, DTS packages, and any custom facilities you might build for your data warehouse. Understanding, using, and maintaining metadata is essential to warehouse architecture. For more information on modeling warehouse solutions, visit the Web site of the governing body for warehouse metadata, the Object Management Group, at www.omg.com.

Creating and Using Data Warehouses: An Overview

An enterprise collects data all the time it is in business—at least that is what it should be doing. The purpose of a data warehouse is to consolidate, store, and manage this data in such a way that it can be analyzed, interpreted, and used to support direction, analysis, interpretation, and enterprise decision making. In short, businesses accumulate a lot of data that can provide direction.

In Chapter 5, we talked a lot about metadata—data that describes data. But we also talked about the context of metadata, and that it is used to provide information and an understanding of a complicated process. Analysis data has a similar role to metadata. It is data that can provide an enterprise with information it needs to determine what business it is in, if the business is going in the right direction, or whether the enterprise should not be in the line of business it thinks it should be in. (Remember the AT&T sojourn in the PC business? It didn't last very long.)

But there is also another important reason to be analyzing data in an ongoing business every day. By analyzing data, you obtain critical information and feedback about the effects of day-to-day decision making and actions. For example, a marketing campaign produces measurable results (sales go up), but do you know if the business actually made money, or if the campaign would have been better aimed at another generation, sex, time of year, geographical region, species, or what have you? Data mining and OLAP tell you this.

A data warehouse can be viewed as a historical archive of the business, tracking it from its conception to the present. So it can tell its owners and decision-making teams where it has been and where it is going and what it might need to achieve its objectives. This information is then used in decision support, marketing, sales, and so on.

To mine for data in a data warehouse, analysts pose questions and investigate the information. Answers are given on the fly and many operations prepare extensive reports for their financial or executive officers. For example, you may query the database to obtain summarized data for the week, the month, the quarter, and so on. Or you can use the data warehouse to mine for those singularities that point to significant events that occurred during the business operations that could in turn point the way to discovering a trend or a nuance about the business. This is essentially what OLAP is all about, exploring and investigating—looking for King Solomon's Mines, the Holy Grail, the road to El Dorado.

The analysis services include the back-end Analysis server that employs OLAP technology to prepare large quantities of data and to ready it for analysis. OLAP makes use of multidimensional data storage or data containment structures called *cubes.* They are not really cubes because a cube is a square object and OLAP cubes can have as many as 15 sides, but the idea is that the OLAP server organizes data in such a way that questions can be answered without your having to actually do any querying. OLAP prepares the data so those questions can be answered as quickly as possible. Anything longer than a few seconds does not fly, because data warehouses can typically explode to contain billions of facts, and users will disconnect if they don't get their answers within a few seconds (five seconds is about as long as they should have to wait).

But before we get into OLAP in Chapter 25, let's cover the essential ground we need to get started building a data warehouse.

Data Mart Versus Data Warehouse

This is the first definition we need to address. A data warehouse can quickly grow into a huge system that quickly becomes too unwieldy to be of use to a small department in a company. Often companies will spend a lot of money preparing an enterprise data warehouse to serve the needs of the corporation. However, the warehouse grows so quickly, often into terabytes of information, that departments and individuals that need ad hoc or infrequent or even simple analysis find that access to the data becomes problematic.

Hence the advent of the *data mart.* Now the definition of the data mart depends on which expert you are reading or how they feel about their asset. What is a data mart to some is a data warehouse to others. But you can think of a data mart as being a departmental or niche data warehouse, optimized and maintained by an interested group, to serve its needs.

In a huge manufacturing concern, a single data warehouse might be maintained for all operations. The data warehouse administrators will then replicate or otherwise transfer portions of the data to departments for further manipulation, analysis, and testing. You can think of the data warehouse/mart relationship as similar to one within the typical warehouse operation. Often goods are sent to a central warehouse where they are inventoried, handled, and finally shipped to a regional warehouse that specializes in delivery to its area of responsibility.

If you want to keep things simple, think of the data mart as a departmental or niche warehouse; that is, a subset or offshoot of the main warehouse. You will likely make use of replications and DTS services to move data from warehouse to data mart and so on. You might also think of a data mart as a small data warehouse. In fact, in a large, widely dispersed enterprise that is embarking on data warehouse projects, it might be more convenient for you to first create decentralized data marts that later get consolidated (yet still remain dispersed) in one large warehouse, maintained at a central data operations center.

In one of my .com projects, huge amounts of data are warehoused from Web site transactions every day and organized for broad query and access. However, I pull data out of this main warehouse and feed it to regional data marts so that executives can have localized access to analysis data. The main warehouse is 3,000 miles away and too far to be of use to HQ; the data mart therefore provides a convenient subset of the data and brings it close to the user. The ins and outs of moving the data from the main location to the site and into the data mart, and ensuring the integrity and consistency of the data between the warehouses and the marts, is beyond the scope of this chapter.

Data Warehouse Architecture

SQL Server's relational database architecture by and large underpins your marts and warehouses. The power that has been built into the relational and storage engine, which facilitates the powerful OLTP machine that Microsoft has built, are directly applicable to data warehouse construction and management.

Designing the Data Warehouse

A data warehouse or analysis database is very different from an OLTP or operational data store. The warehouse is usually much simpler in its architecture. Rules of normalization and integrity do not always apply. In OLTP systems, you strive to prevent redundancy and to protect the integrity of data. In the warehouse, the data does not get updated, so all the effort to preserve the integrity of your data being inserted, updated, and deleted has no bearing on analysis data. For example, you will not need to concern yourself with transaction processing architecture, transaction recovery, and so on. Backup and disaster recovery processes will also be very different.

Your primary objective in designing the warehouse is to organize it so that it meets the functions required of an analysis data store. First you need to organize the data in such a way that reporting and analysis tools have rapid access to information for the analysis and reporting objectives. You will use dimensional modeling to design the warehouse databases and tables to facilitate aggregation and summarization.

Dimensional Modeling

While entity-relationship modeling is what you use to create your OLTP or operational applications and databases, dimensional modeling is what you use to create models of your peculiar business processes. OLTP models are usually single, large, and complex blueprints of the enterprise's transaction processing processes. Dimensional modeling requires you to create individual models that address niche or vertical business practices and processes.

Your business information comes in vertical slices. Sales information belongs in one model, inventory goes into another, accounts payable in a third, and so on. All the facts about the models are captured in separate tables called *fact* tables, which have a schema suited to arranging data according to multidimensional models.

Multidimensional modeling using fact tables is designed around the questions business decision-makers and analysts ask. For example: The CEO of one of my clients who runs a medical facility wants to know which parts of the United States represents the largest concentration of his provider network, which city has the largest membership, and so on. Another client wants to know where he sells more hurricane shutters and why, and at what time of the year. A third wants to know how many burgers were sold in the southeast during Q4 each year.

The tables that support multidimensional databases call for a specialized schema design. The two principal schemas of the multidimensional world are called star or snowflake schemas. If we look at the preceding hurricane shutter or burger examples, we would need to create a table that contains one record for each line item hurricane shutter or burger of each sale. The tables would also need to capture quantity sold, unit cost, sale value, store location, time and date of sale, and so on.

We would put each category of information into its own table. In other words, the customer would go in one table, the store information in another table, and the time and date information in yet another table.

The star schema gets its name from its appearance. A central fact table at the core connects to many dimensional tables, and the formation looks like a star. The snowflake schema is actually derived from the star schema; you could say it extends it. The dimension tables in the star schema connect to additional tables, and then the appearance takes on the snowflake formation. The two schemas are illustrated in Figure 24-1.

Fact Tables

Our data warehouses and data marts contain one or more *fact tables.* These are central to the star or snowflake schemas. The fact table contains numerical facts, such as sales events (burgers bought) and so on. Fact tables can be huge. On a Web site gathering single events, such as selecting an item, they can typically run into the hundreds of millions of records gathered over a period of time, such as a year or two.

Each fact table is underpinned by a multipart index that references the primary keys of related dimensional tables; the attributes of the fact records. The fact table itself does not contain any labels or descriptive data. It holds only the numerical data and the index fields that connect the facts to the corresponding records in the dimension tables.

Aggregation

Aggregation tables are now passé in data mining projects. In the past, the aggregation tables were where it all happened for SQL queries against analytical data—using SQL aggregation syntax to facilitate the queries. These tables contained the summaries of the fact table data, organized to make SQL queries against them efficient.

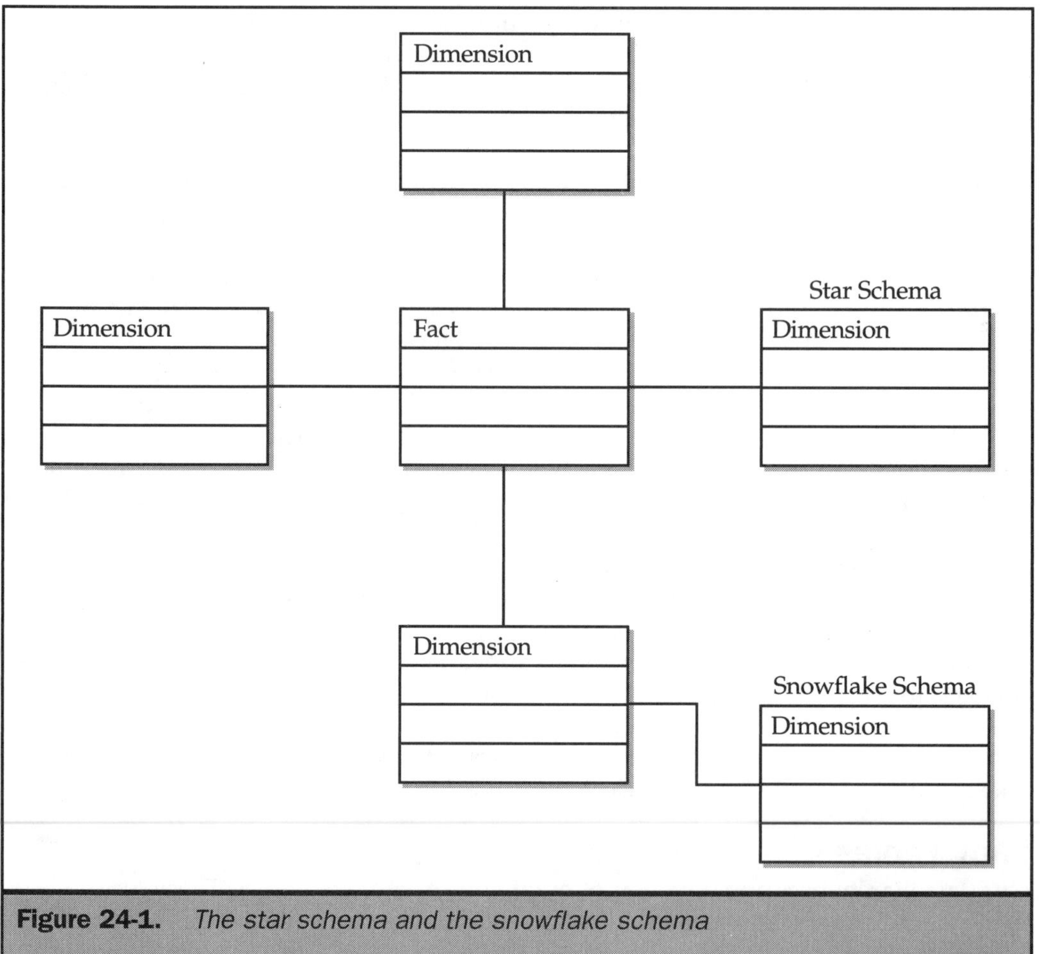

Figure 24-1. *The star schema and the snowflake schema*

However, the OLAP technology provided by Analysis Services obviates the need for aggregation tables.

You will learn in Chapter 25 how OLAP cubes work with preaggregated data to make queries highly efficient and fast. The Analysis Services component creates the aggregations and stores them in tables or in internal multidimensional structures—a.k.a. cubes.

The cubes allow queries to be answered quickly. Just what level of summarization is required to answer the questions efficiently is not a factor in modern OLAP technology. How OLAP supersedes the aggregation table solution is discussed in the next chapter.

Dimension Tables

Dimension tables store dimension data—the attributes that describe the fact records stored in the fact table. The dimension data has several uses; the two most important are as follows:

- **Descriptive information** The attributes in the table provide descriptive information about the records in the fact table. The analyst obtains information about the data he or she queries from the dimension tables.
- **Hierarchical information** The dimension data is capable of presenting hierarchies of attributes that aid in the summarization of fact table data. The analyst, for example, is capable of breaking down groceries into categories representing consumables, nonperishables, gardening, hardware, and so on. You are thus able to drill down into the hierarchy until you arrive at the base product SKU.

The data mining architect models dimension tables according to the needs of the decision makers. The architect will receive a request to provide the facility; for example, to answer the question "what were the total sales of all plywood on the day before hurricane Irene in all stores servicing Dade, Broward, and Palm Beach Counties in Southeast Florida?" The analyst can further compare the figures to other hurricanes and periods and then be able to make buying decisions so that stores do not run out of supplies the next time Mother Nature has a mood swing in the Atlantic.

While dimension tables can contain balanced hierarchies that are predefined and separated into predetermined levels, you can also construct less balanced information. A good example would be organization or departmental structures that present hierarchies as parent-child relationships.

In chapter 25, during the interactive tutorial, we'll explore the dimension data hierarchies in the FoodMart 2000 database.

Sharing Dimension Tables

Certain dimensions lend themselves to sharing, which helps maintain consistency and lessens redundancy. Shared dimensions often include customer names, geographical information, regional information, times and dates, and product information. If you enforce a rule that all cubes and marts use the same time dimensions, that ensures the consistency of information analyzed according to time.

Using Surrogate Keys

A *surrogate key* is a value (such as an object identifier) that uniquely identifies a record in a dimension table, regardless of where it came from. Considering Figure 24-2, you will see where the surrogate key comes into play. Taking the 360-degree view of the architecture, as I have done throughout this book, it is obvious that data warehouse data comes from several sources. Each source will have its own unique record identifiers. For example, the items in one database will be identified by Stock Keeping Unit (SKU) numbers, others by Uniform Product Code (UPC), others by intermediate part or inventory numbers, and so on.

A mix of unique record identification systems is often unavoidable and is not related to bad architecture or wonky database administration. Identification systems are often separated at departmental lines, company lines (from mergers and acquisitions), and so on. I remember my first encounter with the SKU back in 1973 when I would spend my afternoons helping my mother in her little "Wool Shoppe," the most popular knitting and haberdashery store in the southern hemisphere. Mom had an elaborate stockkeeping system that comprised the SKUs from many manufacturers from all over the world, but a single "surrogate" Mother's Stock Unit (MSU) allowed me to find the yarns in her store room and pack them onto the display shelves and so on.

Using her surrogate keys, my mother was able to track what sold better for the time of the year. She would also be able to create new surrogate keys for new SKUs of the same product.

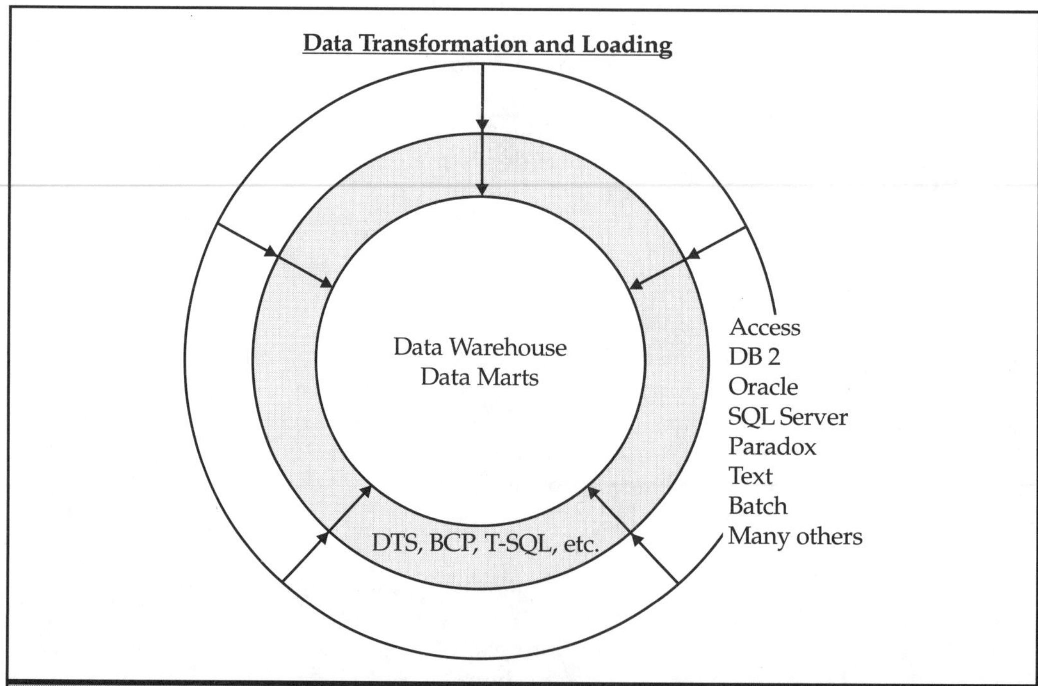

Figure 24-2. *A data warehouse receives data from a variety of sources*

It makes good sense to preserve the original keys of the source data in the marts and warehouses you are tasked with. Often you may need to question a fact, and it will be essential to have a means of tracking an item in the warehouse back to the transaction system from whence it came.

Surrogate keys also allow you to move keys in the hierarchy of the dimension tables. For example, if you transfer a salesperson from one region of the country to another and you need to track his or her performance before and after the move, you will have to create new surrogate keys for the individual after the transfer. This allows you to track the individual on two levels represented in the warehouse more than once (for each region).

Surrogate keys get created in the staging area and during transformation of the data from the OLTP systems to the warehouses and data marts.

Maintaining Referential Integrity

Referential integrity is essential in the data warehouse. Each entity in the dimension tables must uniquely refer to facts in the fact table through primary (dimension tables)–foreign key (fact tables) relationships. If referential integrity is compromised between the dimension-fact records, data analysis will be skewed and results will be inconsistent. So you see how you are responsible, through sound data management and warehousing practices, for the information being used by the decision makers. If, days after a hurricane, a hardware or home improvement store found that they were over- or under-stocked, questions will fly and fingers might point at your inconsistent data.

Indexing

Indexing is key to warehouse performance and analysis speed (the pun was not intended). You must index every dimension table by its primary key and this is not an option; it is standard practice in modeling on the star or snowflake schema. You can also index other columns, which might add more performance bandwidth.

Fact tables must also be indexed, and you should create composite keys comprising the fact tables' primary keys and the column that is referenced by the dimension tables as the foreign key.

A Star Is Born

Building a data warehouse is very different from building a relational database management system. In fact, relational modeling is far more difficult. A relational model can often involve thousands of tables and extensive Entity-Relationship (ER) modeling. The design principles underpinning the relational model support data modification and transaction atomicity and integrity. The design principles underpinning the analytical model support online analytical processing of historical data. The data is almost never modified, and no transaction monitoring is required.

The relational models are created according to the rules of normalization, essentially ensuring that data is not redundant. This is not the case in the analytical model, where data is often repeated and query performance is restricted by normalization. Often relational databases have hundreds or thousands of tables and extensive relationship references connecting them. The star schema and its snowflake sibling are usually very simple. Each dimension table maintains a direct relationship with a single fact table.

Relational models are also constantly changing to support the transaction needs of the enterprise. Analytical databases will also change, but the change will usually be in the form of new stars. Old stars need to remain in place because cubes depend on them.

Let's now begin our port of the FoodMart 2000 data warehouse to SQL Server. We are gong to do this with DTS, so open to your Enterprise Manager and do as follows:

1. Drill down to the server and database node where you need to install the FoodMart 2000 database. Right-click, select All Tasks, and then select Import Data. The DTS Import/Export Wizard loads. Click Next to advance from the welcome dialog box. The Choose a Data Source dialog box appears, as illustrated in Figure 24-3.
2. In the Data Source drop-down list, select the Microsoft Access data source provider. Then in the File Name field, drill down to the path that stores the foodmart 2000.mdb file. This is usually installed at C:\Program Files\Microsoft Analysis Services\Samples\foodmart 2000.mdb. Click Next to advance to the Choose a Destination dialog box, as illustrated in Figure 24-4.

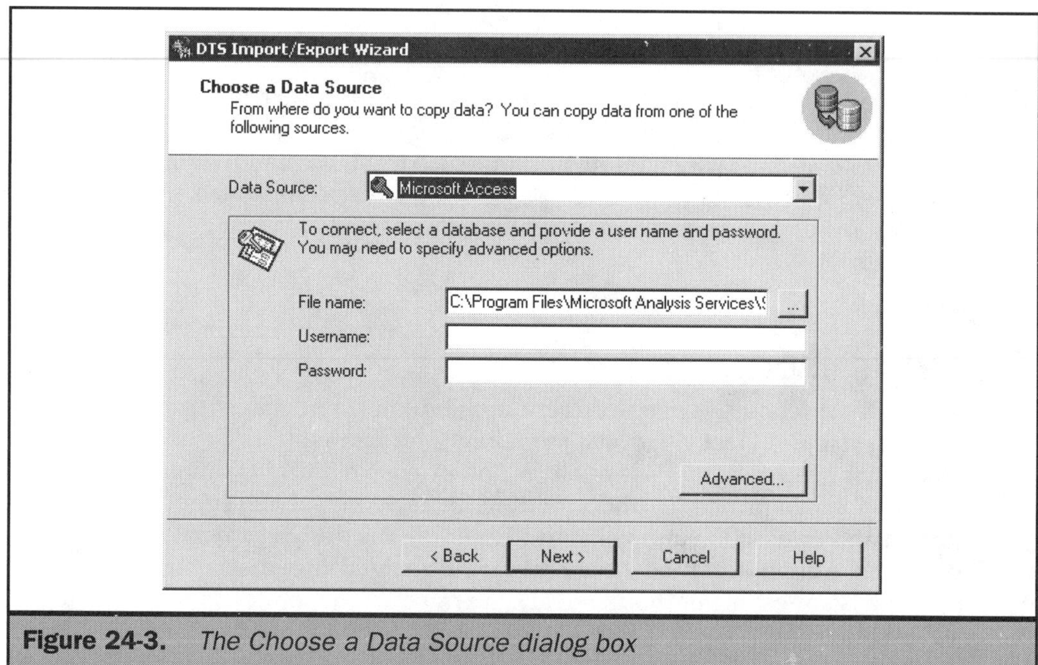

Figure 24-3. *The Choose a Data Source dialog box*

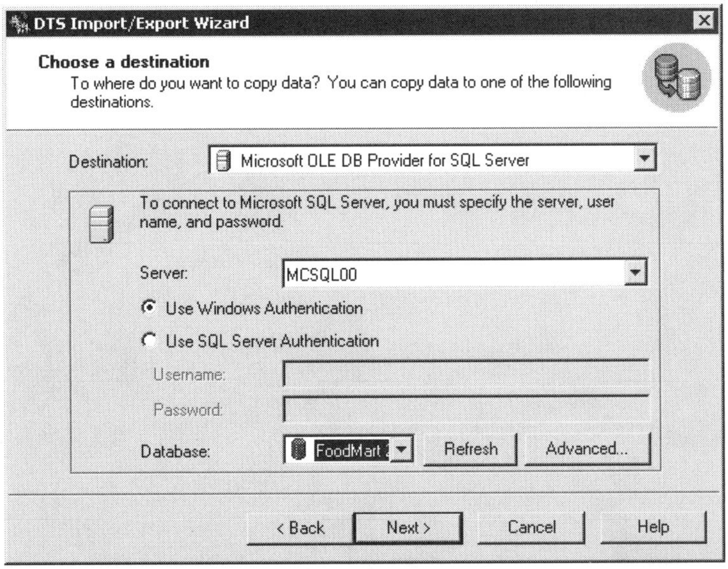

Figure 24-4. *The Choose a Destination dialog box*

3. In the Database drop-down select New to create a new database. The Create Database dialog box pops up, as illustrated in Figure 24-5. In the example, I have named the new SQL Server database FoodMart 2001. Create the database and click Next to move on.
4. The Specify Table Copy or Query dialog box loads, as illustrated in Figure 24-6. Choose to copy the Access tables to SQL Server as shown. Click Next to advance to the Select Source Tables and Views dialog box.

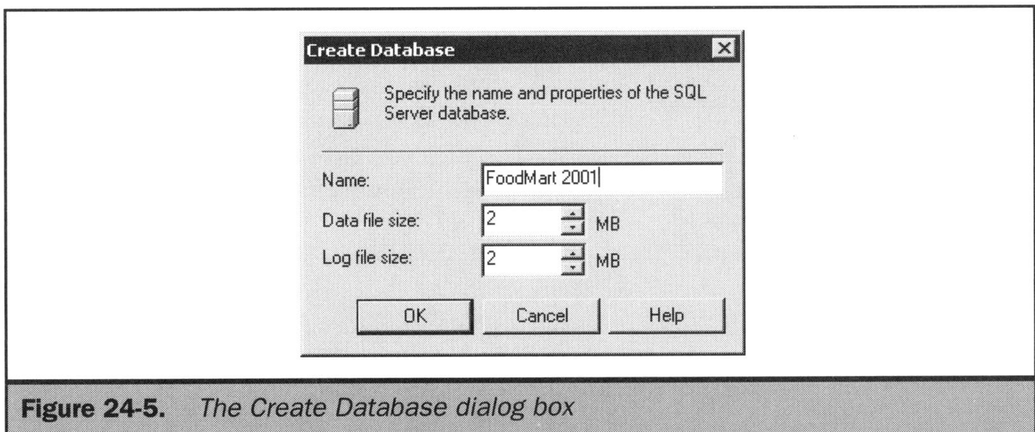

Figure 24-5. *The Create Database dialog box*

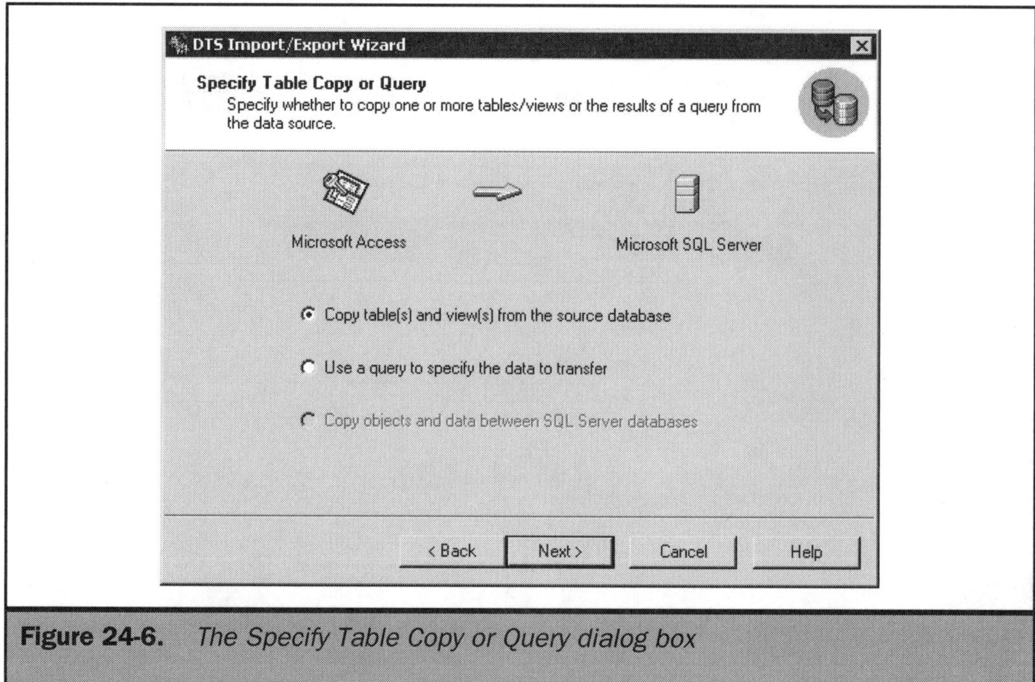

Figure 24-6. *The Specify Table Copy or Query dialog box*

5. Click the Select All button to select all the objects in the source list. Then click Next to advance to the Save, Schedule and Replicate Package dialog box. Check the Run Immediately option and click Next to advance to the next dialog box. You are now done. Click Finished and go get a cup of coffee while the Executing Package process does its thing.

After you return with your coffee, the transformation will have been done and we can now get down to creating the star. We will only create one data mart or star schema in this exercise, and I thought it a good idea to look at budgeting, specifically sales expense information.

Drill down to your databases now in Enterprise Manager and select the new FoodMart 2001 database. In the list of tables, look for the expense_fact fact table and open it up in the Table Design utility as illustrated in Figure 24-7. You will notice that we have no index and key information, so we need to create that. It is not a bad thing that the keys did not cross over in the transformation, because you need to create the

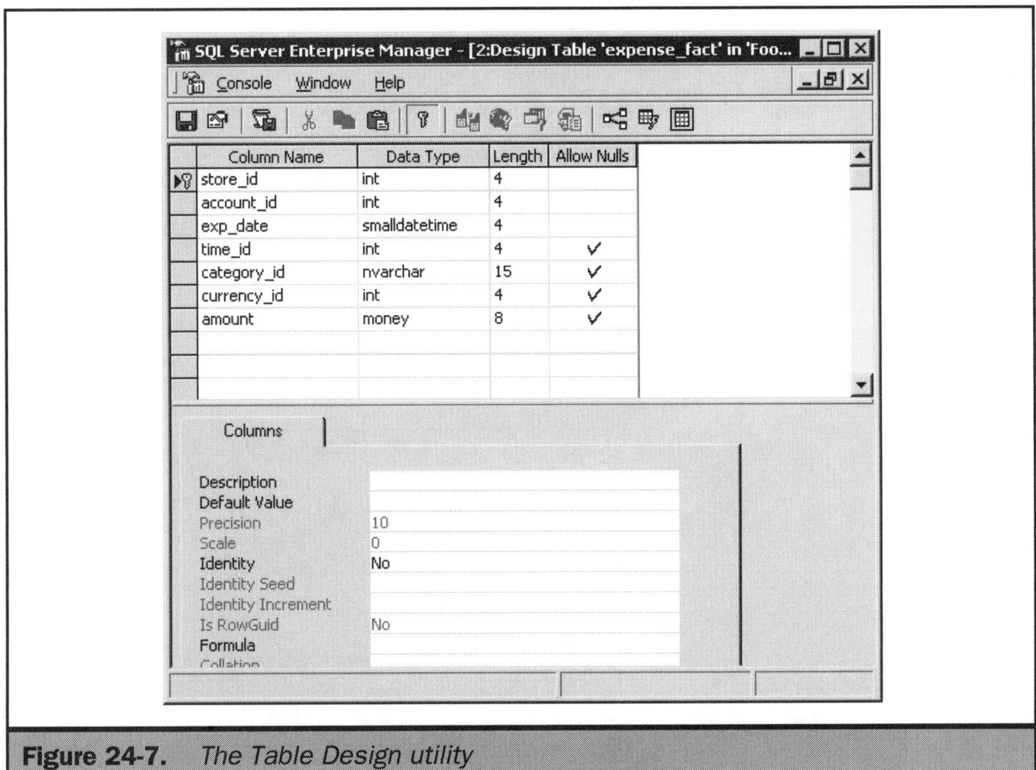

Figure 24-7. *The Table Design utility*

keys and primary-foreign key relationships when you build a new star from scratch. The following steps will let us create the expense_fact star schema:

1. On the store_id column of the fact table, expense_fact, install a unique index/key. This is illustrated in Figure 24-8 as the index (ix_expense_fact) listed in the table Properties dialog box. You will not be able to create a primary key on a single column in this table, because no column alone qualifies, so the index you create here will be a composite index, as listed in Table 24-1. Close the dialog box and then save the table information and close the Design Table utility.
2. Next we need to create primary keys and indexes for the dimension tables. For this star, the dimensions are going to be "account," "store," "time_by_day," and "category." Table 24-1 also lists the indexes you might create for this star.

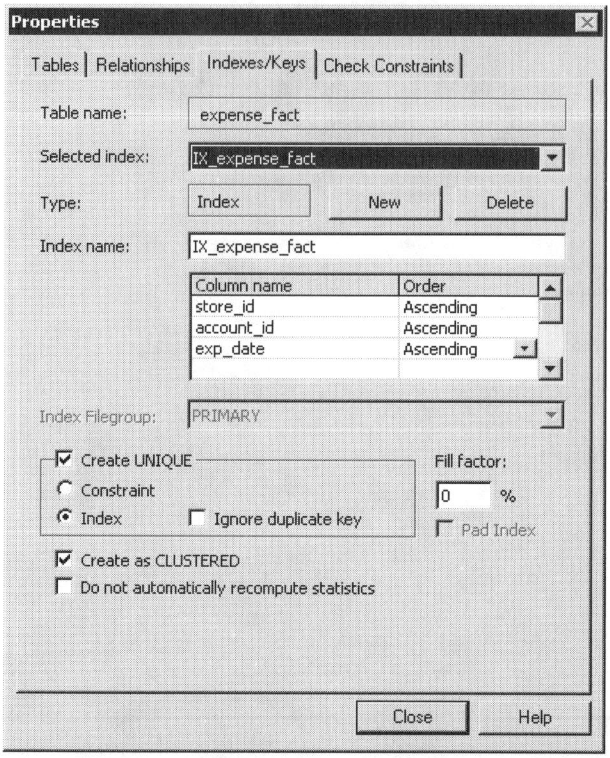

Figure 24-8. *The table Properties dialog box*

Expense_fact	Account	Store	Time_by_day	Category
ix_currency_id	pk_account_id	pk_store	pk_time_id	pk_category_id
ix_exp_date		ix_region_id		
store_id + account_id + exp_date = pk		ix_store_type		
ix_category_id		ix_store_postal_code		
ix_store_id				

Table 24-1. *Indexes and Keys for the Star Schema*

3. Next we need to provide primary-foreign key references between the fact table and the dimension tables to complete the star schema. An easy way to do this might be to use the Database Diagram utility. Drill down to the Diagrams node under the FoodMart 2001 database node. Right-click and select New Database Diagram. The New Database Diagram Wizard launches. Choose the five tables listed in Table 24-1 and click Next until the new Database Diagram is created on the Database Diagram palette.
4. Next create the primary-foreign key relationships between the fact table and the dimension tables. To do this, simply select the column in the fact table (the primary) and drag over to the dimension table (the foreign) and drop. The relationship is immediately created between the correct columns and the Create Relationship dialog box loads, as illustrated in the Figure 24-9.
5. Create the relationships between the fact table and all dimensions. You can uncheck cascade information and replication because the data is not being distributed, nor can it be updated or modified in any way. When you are done, the star schema will have taken shape. This is illustrated in Figure 24-10.

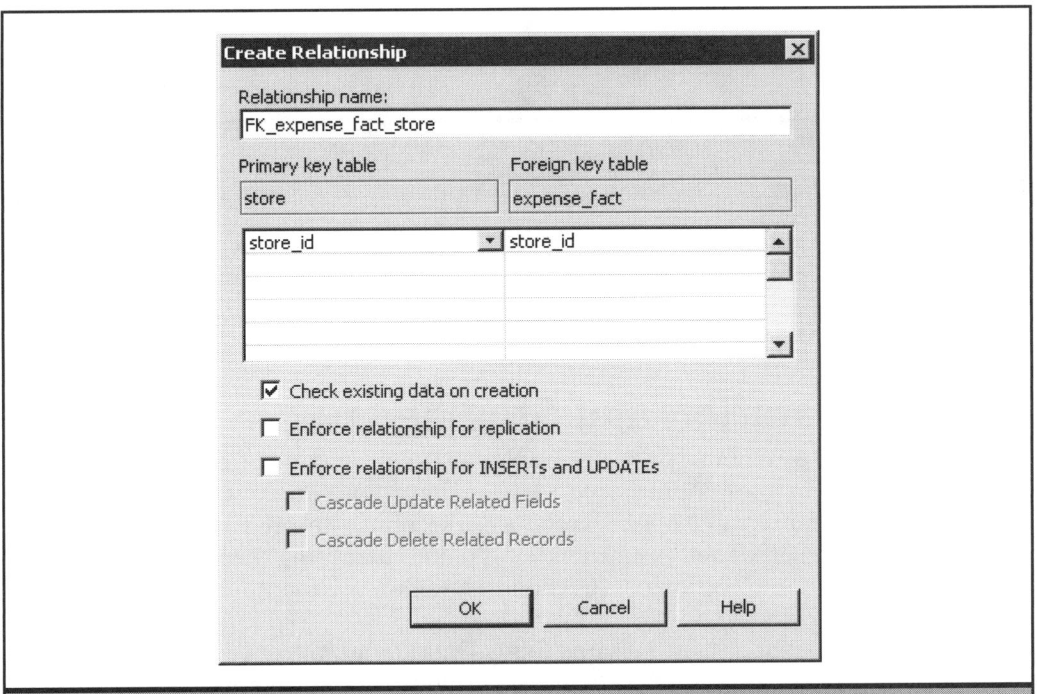

Figure 24-9. *The Create Relationship dialog box*

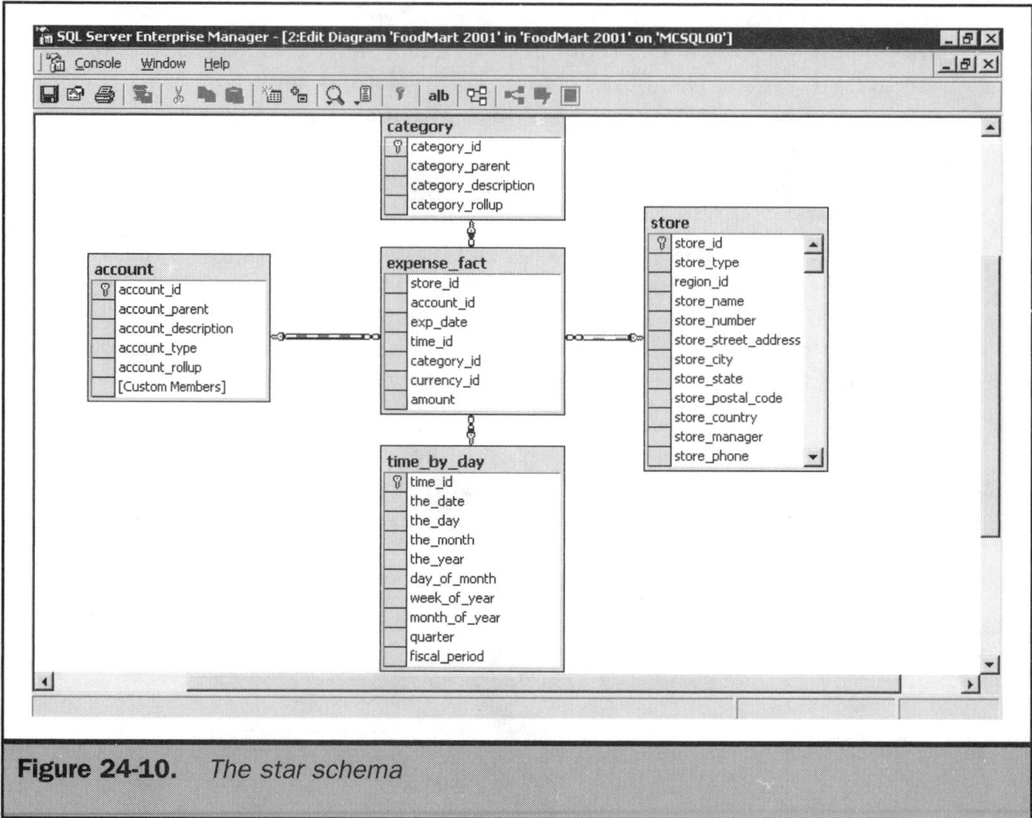

Figure 24-10. *The star schema*

That's it; our mini-data mart is now in SQL Server 2000. The next chapter will get you started on building cubes against the data mart we created here, but first, let's delve into the data warehouse subject a little further.

Data Preparation and Staging

The first item on a warehouse project shopping list is the staging or data preparation area. Getting back to the shipping warehouse analogy, you can think of the staging area as the landing, in a huge open warehouse, like a huge empty airplane hanger, where packages are offloaded from trucks and planes that bring them in from all parts of the world, sorted into sections or divisions. Here they are identified for destination, handling, shipping, and so on.

The staging area for data is the same thing. Data comes in from all over the place: OLTP systems, Web sites, PDAs, notebook computers, desktop computers, personal databases, scraps of paper (no lies), and so on. Your staging area, a server with lots of hard disk space in powerful drives, is then used to format and transform the data into a state that complies with the schema and rules of the warehouse.

For example, you might have a sales database sending you data from Texas that makes use of alphanumeric codes to uniquely identify data. The databases in New Jersey, however, might identify their data according to numeric codes. You need to establish a standard identification system for the warehouse. The staging area is thus used to "merge" and work with the data in such a way that all sources can be installed into the warehouse and still be consistently queried. You might in fact have to create a new identity column in the sources databases, reference the records back to the old identity values, and then export the data to the warehouse so that it is organized using the new system. The you need to decide if you are going to discard the old identity column in the warehouse (probably not) even though you need to be able to track the history of the records in some way.

This is what you do in the staging area. You clean up data. And when it is shiny and smells like new, ready for analysis, it can be transferred into the warehouse. Your staging area database server will need to be powerful enough to handle the processing required in transformation, manipulation, and handling of large quantities of data. You will also be using it for extensive T-SQL queries, bulk inserts, and data transformations.

Data Transfer, Extraction, and Preparation

All analytical data first resides in an OLTP system or in a number of OLTP systems. We do not want to copy transactions directly from an OLTP system, especially if it is very busy, such as an OLTP system that sits under a call center or a Web portal or Web community. Go back to Chapter 10 and investigate which of the replication options will get your OLTP data from the front line to the staging area databases. Once data is in an OLTP system in the data scrubbing area, you can then do locally what you need to do to copy data into the staging areas tables.

The data needs to be extracted and pushed into your fact tables, but before that can happen, you need to set in motion the necessary processes to ensure that all source data has been transformed into a common and consistent format before it can be loaded into the warehouse.

Scrubbing

Data scrubbing should be as automated as possible. But there are a number of steps that you might have to manually accomplish. Data scrubbing would entail the following:

- Combining multiple name fields into one field.
- Creating and applying surrogate keys, as discussed earlier.
- Mapping data from multiple representations into single representations. An example of such a scenario could be to ensure that all telephone numbers or ZIP codes are stored in a common format. Scalar representations are also important. What is good in one database might map to "fair" in another.
- Breaking down date fields into fields representing years, months, weeks, and days.

Loading Data into the Warehouse

When you create a new warehouse or mart and the data is certified clean, you will be ready for initial load into the database. This can be achieved using standard T-SQL scripts, DTS, BCP, or replication. I am fond of replication because it is so powerful and allows for ongoing, unattended data transfer. The other methods require you to choose a time, usually at night, to perform a load using the BCP utility and so on.

When loading data into the data warehouse, you also need to ensure that referential integrity is in place. You can do this in a variety of ways, including a simple SQL query that counts rows when all dimension tables are joined to the fact table using inner joins. If you extend the star schema out to a snowflake schema, you will also need to ensure that referential integrity is maintained between the dimension tables and their subordinate tables. The bottom line in all cases is that the number of rows in the primary table must match the number of rows in the foreign table.

In Review

This chapter introduces you to data mining and the basics of creating a data warehouse or data mart. Creating a data warehouse requires you to create fact tables and dimension tables in a relational database management system, like SQL Server 2000, and to populate the tables with data pulled over and transformed from your OLTP database systems. The fact tables and dimension tables will later become the foundation of your cubes, which pull data and, associated with dimensions from the dimension tables, let you access the analytical data

We also had a look at data warehouse modeling and examined the two principal schemas for a data warehouse, the star schema, and the snowflake schema, which is the star schema extended at its nodes with subordinate dimensions.

Using Data Transformation Services, we also moved (upsized) a Microsoft Access data warehouse, FoodMart 2000, into SQL Server and built a star schema data source around several fact tables and dimensions.

In the next chapter, we'll look at the OLAP services in more detail, which is essentially what SQL Server's Analysis Services is all about.

Chapter 25

Getting Started: Analysis Services and OLAP

In previous editions of SQL Server, the analytical processing functionality was known as OLAP Services. Microsoft has now renamed this to Analysis Services to reflect a much-enhanced, end-to-end data mining and OLAP environment. While the OLAP services were critically acclaimed and boosted the popularity of SQL Server 7.0, they pale in comparison to the current offering.

This chapter continues the foundational discussion we had in the previous chapter and looks specifically at the numerous enhancements provided by analysis services. Later we'll spend some time navigating the client applications and get some of that data mining and OLAP action you've been waiting for.

If you are new to the concept of multidimensional databases, analysis, and decision support systems, I suggest you use the previous chapter as a springboard. This section makes some assumptions that you are familiar with Microsoft OLAP, or OLAP and data mining in general.

Analysis Services Architecture

The SQL Server 2000 Analysis Services comprises a middle-tier server catering to online analytical processing (OLAP) and data mining. The server creates and manages multidimensional cubes of data that are used for analysis and decision support. The cubes provide fast access to cube information so that responses to queries and browsing are highly efficient. The SQL Server 2000 Analysis Services provide server functionality that creates and manages OLAP cubes and an assortment of data mining models.

The Analysis server is the server component of SQL Server 2000 Analysis Services. This server has been specifically designed to create and maintain multidimensional data structures. It is optimized to provide multidimensional data in response to client queries.

When running Setup to install the Analysis Services, you have the option of choosing to install the Analysis server component. You will notice that the name of the Analysis server matches the computer name on the network, and thus the default instance of SQL Server. In order for the client to connect to the Analysis server, he or she must specify this name in their connection string. When you install the Analysis server you also by default create the Analysis server object.

The Analysis server is the root object in the object hierarchy of the analysis services. As the root it is also the first object to be created and the object to which all other Analysis Services objects fall under. When you create an Analysis server your next task, as described in the previous chapter, is to create its databases.

The principal tool for administering the Analysis server and the objects that are subordinate to it is Analysis Manager. This utility provides an extensive user interface.

Each Analysis server also maintains a repository called the Analysis Services repository. This is where it stores the metadata, definitions, of the objects defined on the Analysis server. By default, the Analysis Services repository is actually msmdrep.mdb, which supports metadata, on the computer running the Analysis server. This was covered in Chapter 5, when we dealt with Meta Data services. If you have not already done so it is also a good idea to migrate the repository to the SQL Server database as we did with the warehouse that was built in Access.

Every Analysis server has an associated Data folder, which is used to store the multidimensional structures for the objects that are defined on the Analysis server. These structures are contained in files that are created when the objects are processed. They are are referenced to resolve the queries that are sent to the Analysis server. The Data folder also contains security files that control access to objects on the Analysis server. You should thus lock down the Data folder and protect it against unauthorized access.

Where you locate the Data folder can be decided during installation, and the location can also be changed. You can read and change the location of the Data folder in the Properties dialog box. You can also set other properties of the Analysis server in the Properties dialog box.

The service associated with the Analysis server is MSSQLServerOLAPService. By default, this service starts automatically and logs on as the system account. You can maintain the MSSQLServerOLAPService service in the Services application, which is either in Control Panel in Windows NT 4.0 or in the Administrative Tools folder in Windows 2000, as you do the services for SQL Server itself.

The analysis data can be presented to the client through the PivotTable Service. The server functionality includes the following:

- The creating and processing of cubes from relational database data warehouses.
- The storing and management of cube data in multidimensional structures, stored either in relational databases or in multidimensional storage units, or in combinations of both.
- The creating of data mining models from cubes or from relational databases.
- The storing of data for data mining models in multidimensional structures, in relational databases, or in Predictive Model Markup Language (PMML), which is a standardized XML derivative format.
- Using Meta Data Services and the repository databases in SQL Server, the metadata used to define cubes, data mining models, and other objects on the server can be stored, managed, and accessed as needed.

The PivotTable Service

The PivotTable Service is client-side functionality that communicates with the Analysis server and provides interfaces that client applications can use to access OLAP data and data mining facilities at the server. Client applications connect to the PivotTable Service using OLE DB interfaces for C++ or the ActiveX Data Objects (ADO) object model.

The PivotTable Service can also create local cube files that contain data from a cube on the server or from OLE DB relational databases. These local cubes can be stored as multidimensional cube files on the client computer and accessed offline by the PivotTable Service. This means that a connection to the Analysis server is not required. Also, connection to the local cube data sources is also not required if the local cubes have a multidimensional OLAP (MOLAP) storage mode, which is discussed shortly.

Object Architecture

The following list describes the objects used to administer SQL Server 2000 Analysis Services:

- **Analysis servers** The server component of Analysis Services is designed specifically to create and maintain multidimensional data structures and to provide multidimensional data in response to client queries.
- **Databases** The databases serve as containers for related data sources, cubes, dimensions, and data mining models and the objects they share.
- **Data sources** The data sources store the specification of the information necessary to access source data for an object such as a cube.
- **Dimensions** The dimensions serve as the structural attributes of a cube. A dimension is an organized hierarchy of categories (levels) that describe data in the fact table. These categories describe similar sets of members upon which the user wants to base an analysis.
- **Levels and members** The levels are used as elements of a dimension hierarchy. Levels describe the hierarchy from the highest (most summarized) level to the lowest (most detailed) level of data.
- **Measures** The measures are a cube's set of numeric values, which are based on a column in the cube's fact table. In a cube, measures are the central values that are analyzed.
- **Cubes** The cubes themselves contain a set of data that is usually constructed from a subset of a data warehouse and is organized and summarized into a multidimensional structure defined by a set of dimensions and measures.
- **Partitions** The partitions are the storage containers for data and aggregations of a cube.
- **Aggregations** The aggregations are defined as a table or structure containing precalculated data intended for a cube.
- **Roles** The roles are defined as groups or users in Windows NT 4.0 or Windows 2000 domains and have common access and permission to access and manipulate Analysis Services data.

- **Commands** The commands are used to hold an administrator-defined commands that are automatically executed when a client accesses a database, cube, or role. Commands include calculated members, named sets, and actions.
- **Member properties** The member properties contain information about the members of a dimension level in addition to that contained in the dimension.
- **Data mining models** The data mining models contain a virtual structure that represents the grouping and predictive analysis of relational or online analytical processing (OLAP) data.
- **Data mining columns** The data mining columns contain a structure that is used to define the content of a data mining model. A column can contain data, or it can contain further nested columns.

The Analysis Services also allows you to create data mining models from both multidimensional sources and relational data sources. Later we'll look at creating new dimensions and cubes against the FoodMart 2001 database we upsized to SQL Server 2000 in the last chapter. We will also talk about client facilitating technologies, such as the PivotTable Service, the included OLE DB–compliant provider, which is used by Excel and a host of applications to retrieve data from the server in real time, or to create local cubes to browse offline.

Analysis Services, which was known as OLAP Services in SQL Server 7.0, has been greatly improved to offer the following features:

- It has been made extremely easy to use. Cube building has never been easier.
- It comes loaded with extensive wizards that let you create objects like cubes and dimensions.
- It includes a flexible, robust data model for cube definition and storage
- It is highly scalable, having an especially robust architecture that is able to handle the data explosion syndrome of warehouse technology better than many other OLAP systems, including SQL Server 7.0.
- It is highly integratable: It come with a host of administration tools, security, data sources, and client/server caching.
- Its open and well-supported APIs allow for extensive custom applications.

The Analysis Services have been designed with ease of use in mind, supplying wizards, editors, tools, and information within Analysis Manager. This all goes a long way to lessen the learning curve that data warehousing and OLAP is infamous for. OLAP and data warehousing have often been associated with multimillion dollar budgets and have been out of reach of the small business for a number of years.

The online tutorial can be used by both beginners and experienced OLAP users alike to create a basic cube, as well as more advanced operations, such as creating partitions, virtual cubes, security roles, writable dimensions, actions, and data mining models. Other facilities include the following:

- **The Meta Data and Data View** These, accessed in the right pane of Analysis Manager, allow you to view the object properties and metadata. You can also browse data for cubes and data mining models by drilling down into the tree hierarchy.
- **Cube Wizard** This wizard lets you build the structures necessary to create an OLAP cube. Using the wizard, you can get up to speed pretty quickly on cube design and the implementation process. You use the wizard to map data sources and to create dimensions defining measures.
- **Cube Editor** This tool is a simple drag-and-drop facility you can use to edit existing cubes. You can also use it to create new cubes. The Cube Editor lets you edit or revise cubes you created with the wizard.
- **Dimension Wizard** The Dimension Wizard lets you create shared dimensions, which can be used by any cube. The wizards also lets you create private dimensions, which can be used in a single cube. You can map your database dimension table columns to dimension levels or use the built-in time dimension generator to create a variety of time dimensions based on a date-time column in your database. The Dimension Wizard can also be used to create dimensions based on star or snowflake data warehouse schemas, as discussed in Chapter 24. There is also support for parent-child, virtual, and data mining dimensions.
- **Dimension Editor** Using simple drag-and-drop operations, you can edit existing shared dimension structures and create new ones. Dimension Editor complements the Dimension Wizard, enabling you to revise dimensions you created with the wizard or to quickly create new ones. You can also preview dimension data in the editor.
- **Incremental Update Wizard** This wizard lets you incorporate new data into your cube. You use an incremental update feature to add new data to a cube without having to rebuild aggregations or reload all of the data.
- **Partition Wizard** This wizard lets you create new partitions that will contain a portion of the data in your cube. Like partitioned views, these partitions enable you to distribute and optimize a cube's data into discrete segments on a single server or across multiple servers for scalability. The partitioning services are only available for SQL Server 2000 Enterprise Edition.
- **Storage Design Wizard** This wizard lets you specify the storage mode for cube data and helps you design aggregations appropriate to the intended use of your cube (we will discuss these shortly). The wizard also lets you balance the response times with storage requirements as needed by the client application and the users.

- **Usage Analysis Wizard** This wizard displays logged query information such as date, user, query response time, and frequency in tabular and graphical format. The Usage Analysis Wizard essentially lets you know and understand how a cube is being used.
- **Usage-Based Optimization Wizard** The Usage-Based Optimization Wizard lets you tune cube performance according to your users' usage of the cube. You can also use the wizard to create aggregations to improve performance in terms of any combination of users and factors, such as the number of times a query was executed, query response time, the mode of storage, or a date range.
- **Calculated Cells Wizard** This wizard lets you create calculated cells, by allowing you to define a subsection of a cube, referred to as a subcube, whose value is determined by an MDX query. Calculated cells can affect specific cells, even a single cell, within a cube, allowing much finer control over financial and statistical calculation or analysis.
- **Action Wizard** The Action Wizard lets you create an action associated with a cube or a portion of a cube. You are thus able to trigger an operation on your selected cube or part of a cube and then automatically pass the selected item as a parameter to the operation. For example, you can select an action on a dimension member that automatically opens your browser to access a page about the member.
- **Virtual Cube Wizard** This wizard lets you join cubes and select dimensions and measures from them to create virtual cubes. The virtual cube also let you send a single query to multiple cubes, including cubes running on different servers. The virtual cube appears as a regular cube but does not require additional cube storage space. It is very similar in concept and design to a view that joins tables in a relational database.
- **Virtual Cube Editor** This editor allows simple drag-and-drop operations that you can use to edit existing virtual cube structures. It complements the Virtual Cube Wizard and lets you revise virtual cubes you created with the aforementioned wizard.
- **Mining Model Wizard** This wizard lets you create data mining models from both OLAP and relational data sources, using different data mining techniques to build the model. You will also have the option, based on OLAP data, to create dimensions and virtual cubes to analyze the mining model results.
- **Mining Model Editors** These editors, one for OLAP data mining models and the other for relational data mining models, let you edit existing mining models using drag-and-drop operations. They also let you browse the results of your mining models.
- **Data Views** The data views are used to view data for cubes, dimensions, and data mining models without leaving Analysis Manager. This means you do not have to switch to another application to check your designs.

- **OLE DB Data Source Locator Integration** This feature allows Analysis Services to select OLE DB or ODBC data sources.
- **Role Managers** The role managers are security tools that you use to create and maintain roles that control access to cubes and their components.

Understanding the Data/Storage Model Options

In the last chapter, we created a data warehouse in SQL Server by importing or upsizing the FoodMart 2000 Access database. We then created a star schema on a fact table and several dimensions. The next task in our data mining effort would be to create cubes that contain the dimensions and measures and that can be used by the OLAP features of Analysis Services. These cubes can be saved or stored using ROLAP, HOLAP, or MOLAP storage models. As in SQL Server 7.0, you are not limited to any single storage method, and you can thus choose which model is best for your database. You can even choose a combination of storage models.

SQL Server 2000 supports all data and storage models, which means you can create and maintain cubes in accordance with your analyst's needs, or the whims of your financial officers. The three storage methods for dimensions, partitions, and cubes are as follows:

Multidimensional OLAP (MOLAP) The underlying data for a cube gets stored along with the aggregation data in a high-performance multidimensional structure that makes for very fast queries and excellent response times. MOLAP storage provides excellent performance and data compression as well. MOLAP, however, pulls data out of relational storage, which means that more (a whole lot more) storage space is needed to hold the cube data. So while performance and speed are a plus, there is a heavy administrative burden in moving data into multidimensional structures and then maintaining them. For call centers and Web communities or portals, in fact any business in which point-in-time information and daily analysis are critical, MOLAP will give you the best performance. MOLAP performance also makes it conducive to Internet reporting and analysis. The MOLAP model is illustrated in Figure 25-1.

Relational OLAP (ROLAP) The underlying data for a cube is stored along with the aggregation data in a relational database, such as a SQL Server 2000 database. ROLAP storage enables you to take advantage of your investment in relational technology and enterprise data management tools. This means, however, that no multidimensional data structures are used store the data, and thus, performance for a huge volume of data might not be as good as with MOLAP storage. Analysis Services uses the ables that make up the star schema to build the cubes and aggregations. Figure 25-2 illustrates the ROLAP storage model. One important benefit of ROLAP is that you can leverage your experience in relational database administration to maintain the cube data source.

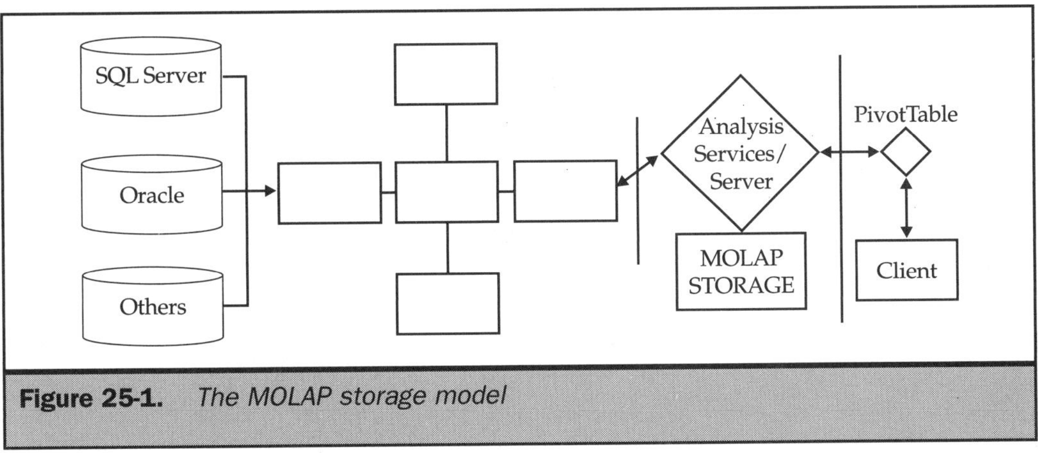

Figure 25-1. *The MOLAP storage model*

Hybrid OLAP (HOLAP) The HOLAP model takes the best of both the preceding models and combines them, hence the name Hybrid OLAP storage. In other words, the underlying data for a cube is stored in a relational database, as it is with the ROLAP model, but the aggregation data is stored in a high-performance multidimensional structure, along the lines of the MOLAP model. HOLAP storage offers the benefits of MOLAP for aggregations without necessitating duplication of the underlying detail data. The limitation, however, is that dimensions with more than 10 million members must use the ROLAP storage mode. HOLAP is available only with SQL Server 2000 Enterprise Edition. A downside is that the HOLAP drill-down is slower than MOLAP, which might not be an issue for your project. HOLAP, however, gives better performance than ROLAP. With the exception of calculated members, it is as fast and efficient as MOLAP storage. Figure 25-3 illustrates the HOLAP model.

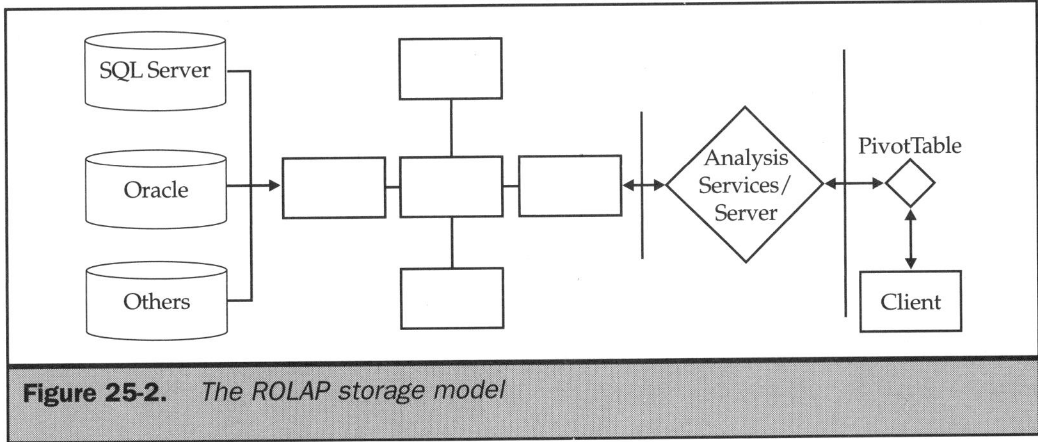

Figure 25-2. *The ROLAP storage model*

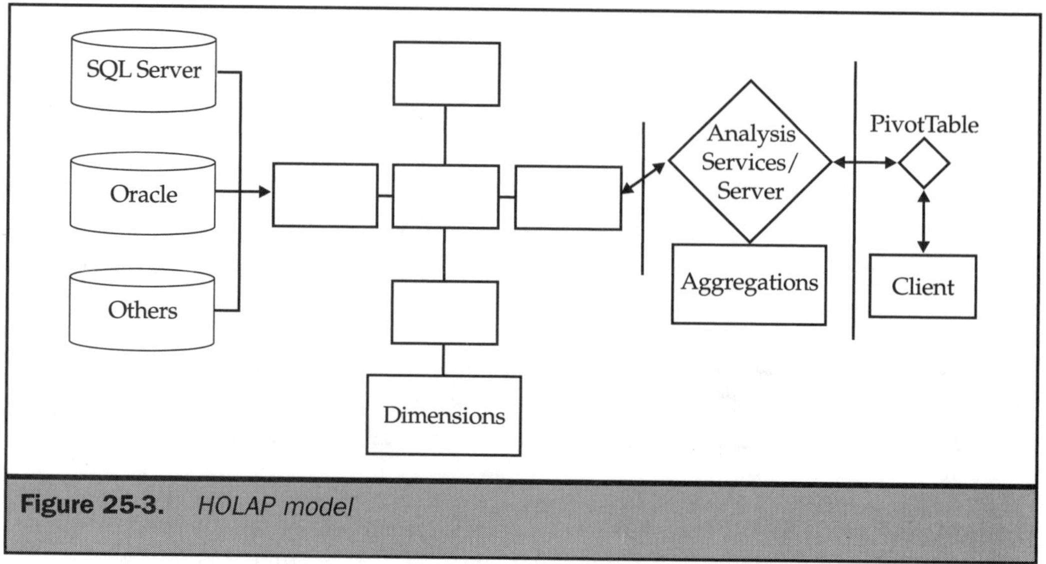

Figure 25-3. *HOLAP model*

In addition to the above storage models analysis services provides the following OLAP features:

Partitioned Cube Storage You can now partition a cube into separate physical sections such that each partition can be stored in a different storage mode, in a different physical location, and with a level of aggregations appropriate to the data in the partition. The result is that you can fine-tune the performance and data management characteristics of your system no matter what storage model or mix of models you use.

Partition Merging This features lets you combine a cube's multiple partitions back into a single physical partition. For example, you can use partition merging to merge cube data that represents fiscal quarters in annual data.

Write-Enabled Cubes This feature lets you write-enable a cube that can then be accessed by multiple concurrent users. User-initiated changes to the cube data are logged to a special, physically separated partition table associated with the cube and applied automatically as cube data is viewed.

Balanced, Unbalanced, and Ragged Hierarchies You can create dimensions with balanced or unbalanced hierarchies. The branches of dimensions with balanced hierarchies end at the same level, while the branches of unbalanced hierarchies terminate at different levels. Ragged hierarchies are also supported, which allows a dimension in which at least one member does not have its logical parent in the level immediately above the member to accommodate levels where no values exist. The logical parent of a member in a ragged hierarchy can be two levels above the member.

Parent-Child Dimensions You can create dimensions based on two-dimensional table columns that together define parent-child relationships between rows in the dimension table. Parent-child dimensions support balanced, unbalanced, and ragged hierarchies. Thus complex hierarchical relationships can be created using the parent-child dimensions.

Write-Enabled Dimensions This feature lets you enable a dimension for write access by concurrent users. Any user-initiated changes to the dimension data are then recorded in the dimension table, and your users can manipulate the dimension data to see the immediate effect on the cube data.

Virtual Cubes Cubes can be joined into virtual cubes, as earlier discussed. The virtual cube thus provides access to data in the combined cubes without necessitating the construction of a new cube. You are also still able to maintain the best design for each individual cube.

Calculated Members This features lets you create calculated measures and calculated dimension members by combining Multidimensional Expressions (MDX), mathematical formulas, and user-defined functions. You can thus define new measures and dimension members by use of a rich yet easy-to-use expression syntax. Additional libraries of user-defined functions for use in calculated member definitions can be registered.

Custom Unary Operators These unary operators use simple math operators stored in a column to determine how the value of a level member affects the value of the parent. Custom rollup operators are unique per level member.

Custom Rollup Formulas and Custom Member Formulas The custom rollup formulas and custom member formulas are MDX expressions that determine cube cell values associated with members. Custom rollup formulas apply to all members of a level, whereas custom member formulas apply to individual level members.

Calculated Cells These are similar to the custom member formulas in that they are calculated cells, defined as MDX statements, that determine cube cell values associated with a specified group of cells. Calculated cells apply only to specified cells in a cube, whereas custom member formulas must apply to all of the cells for a given member.

Member Properties These properties can be defined for dimension members that use data for these properties within a cube. Taking an SKU example, you can thus specify properties as member properties associated with the SKUs, such as size, color, and fabric.

Virtual Dimensions These dimensions can be created from member properties or levels of other dimensions. A virtual dimension can be used to evaluate the properties of a dimension's members against the members themselves. For example, measures can be evaluated for SKUs against size, color, fabric, and so on. The virtual dimensions and member properties are useful for ad hoc evaluation. Another plus is that they require no physical cube storage.

Scalability

The Analysis Services is a highly scalable architecture designed to address a variety of data warehousing scenarios:

Customized Aggregation Options Aggregation design is no longer a complex management burden of the warehouse DBA. You can now use the Storage Design Wizard to balance system performance and the disk space allocated to storing aggregations. The Analysis Services now make use of a sophisticated algorithm to determine the optimum set of aggregations from which other aggregations can be derived. This leaves you free to focus on other issues, such as application design, and leaves Analysis Services to deal with the aggregation management.

Usage-Based Optimization You can now tune the performance of a cube by directing Analysis Services, via the Usage-Based Optimization Wizard, to balance query response with optimum storage requirements. Thus, you can quickly build a system with a minimum number of aggregations and then later optimize performance according to the actual usage of the system.

Data Compression and Storage Optimization In the MOLAP and HOLAP storage modes, Analysis Services stores all or some of the cube information in multidimensional structures, as described earlier. In these structures, however, storage is not used for empty cells, so there is potential for a sophisticated data compression algorithm to be applied to the data. When you combine these features with the options for the design and optimization of precalculated aggregations, you can minimize the impact of the data explosion syndrome that plagues OLAP systems.

Distributed Calculation The PivotTable Service incorporates functionality from the server so that calculations that would normally be performed on a server can now be balanced between the client and server. Depending on the situation, this would increase the capacity of the server, help reduce network traffic, and possibly improve performance for clients. We will get into the client architectures later in this chapter.

Partitions You can spread a cube over multiple servers by dividing it into partitions. Analysis Services can then retrieve data in parallel to answer queries. Partitioning enables you to manage your storage strategy, increase scale with multiple servers, and increase performance.

Linked Cubes/Partitioned Cubes A cube can be stored on a single server and referenced as a linked cube on other servers. You can also create distributed partitioned cubes by using remote partitions to manage your storage strategy and store a cube's data across multiple servers. Users connected to any of these servers can then access these cube transparently. By linking and partitioning cubes, you avoid the more costly alternative of storing and maintaining copies of a cube on multiple servers. Linked cubes make it possible for you to create, store, and maintain a cube on one Analysis server while providing access to the cube from multiple Analysis servers. Linked cubes facilitate cube security and reduce storage and maintenance requirements. This feature is available only if you install Analysis Services for SQL Server 2000 Enterprise Edition. By partitioning cubes, you also get the added benefit of centralized administration, greater scalability, and enhanced performance through parallel processing of queries.

Incremental Updates A cube can be updated by processing only the data that has been added rather than the entire cube. This means that you can incrementally update OLAP cubes while they are in use.

LAN, WAN, Internet, and Mobile Scenarios Intelligent cache management integrates the Analysis server with the PivotTable Service client, minimizing traffic over LAN and WAN connections. The PivotTable Service contains an efficient multidimensional calculation engine to further minimize network traffic and to enable analysis of local multidimensional data when the client is not connected to the server.

You can create local cubes for storage on offline clients. These are then used without the connection to an Analysis server. HTTP or secure HTTP (HTTPS) authentication can be used in conjunction with Internet Information Services (IIS) to establish connections to an Analysis server when the user connects back to the Internet.

Integration

The Analysis Services tools and components work with other components and programs to ensure enterprise-level interoperation and integration.

- **Integrated Management Console** The Analysis Services includes Analysis Manager, which is a graphical administration tool MMC console. The Manager provides a common framework and user interface for defining, accessing, and managing Analysis servers and databases.
- **Integrated security** The cube and data mining model access is based on Windows NT 4.0 or Windows 2000 security. You can also define integration with SQL Server 2000 through trusted access at the OS level.
- **OLE DB and ODBC data sources** A variety of OLE DB and ODBC data sources can be used, such as Oracle versions 7.3 and 8.0. You can use multiple data sources concurrently.

- **Functions from Excel and Visual Basic for Applications** In Multidimensional Expressions (MDX), you can include many functions in the Excel worksheet library, which is automatically registered if installed on the computer with Analysis Services. You can also include many functions in the Visual Basic for Applications Expression Services library, which is included with Analysis Services and automatically registered.
- **Server-side cache** The Analysis Server cache allows queries, metadata, and data to be cached, enabling faster response to queries because calculations are down against cached data instead of disk.
- **Client-side cache** The client-side technologies, such as the client-based PivotTable Service component, also permit caching. If the client cache contains values required for a query, the PivotTable Service can calculate the answer from the cached data. The PivotTable Service shares much of the same functionality as the server, enabling it to bring the server's multidimensional calculation engine, caching features, and query management directly to the client computer. This client/server data management model optimizes performance and minimizes network traffic.

Open Architecture

The Analysis Services architecture is designed to meet the OLAP-specific requirements of the OLE DB 2.0 and later specifications. This means it is compatible with ActiveX Data Objects (ADO) and the extension for multidimensional objects.

You can use the server object model, the Decision Support Objects (DSO), to create applications that define and manage cubes, data mining models, and other objects. This object model can be used to extend the functionality of Analysis Manager or to automate the ongoing maintenance of your system.

The Analysis Manager is also extendable via the services of the Add-in Manager interface. Using the Analysis Services Add-in Manager interface and DSO, you can create custom extensions, dialog boxes, wizards, and other applications that integrate with Analysis Manager.

Object Architecture Overview

The SQL Server 2000 Analysis Services has been created to provide a variety of objects that can help you implement an OLAP or data mining solution with a data warehouse. In this section, we'll investigate these objects and how they are used.

The unit of analysis data storage in OLAP solutions is the *cube.* Cubes are populated with analytical data that is of interest to corporate decision makers and enterprise analysts. To support the questions that analysts ask, cubes organize data into dimensions and measures in a multidimensional structure, hence the name "cube." In other words, if you ask the question, "how many puppies did our pet store chain sell in the southeastern United States for Q1 2000," then a cube of data will be able to answer the question by articulating three dimensions and one measure as follows:

- The Animals dimension contains a puppies category.
- The Geography dimension contains the southeast region.
- The Time dimension contains the first quarter of 2000.
- The Sales measure contains quantitative numerical data that can be summarized.

There are differences between OLAP and data mining in general, but both are catered to by Analysis Services functionality. OLAP lets you perform aggregation analysis on current or past data, whereas data mining lets you perform prediction analysis to aid decision support based on current or past data. In the preceding example, data mining would allow us to ask the question, "how many puppies will we likely sell in the first quarter of 2002 in the southeast?"

The main object of data mining, the data mining model, provides a framework that lets you store the learned knowledge from your data, such as probability and distribution information, which is created from existing data to predict the behavior of new data. This, in turn, can be given new data for analysis, such as being able to predict expected values for a given case from patterns and rules discovered in past data.

Such objects are used to support OLAP and data mining and they are represented by an object hierarchy, which is used to maintain the complex relationships between the various objects, such as cubes, dimensions, and data mining models, that make up the Analysis Services.

Cube Enhancements

SQL Server cube functionality has been greatly enhanced to include the ability to distribute data across multiple servers. This means that now cubes have access to greater storage and can be linked from server to server much like the distributed partitioned views discussed in Chapter 13. Cubes can be updated in real time as the data changes, a fact that can be used to ensure that cubes are current with the underlying data source changes.

The distributed partitioned cubes make use of remote partitions that can distribute the cubes' data among multiple Analysis servers while allowing you to manage them from a single Analysis server.

SQL Server refers to the new enhancement as *real-time OLAP*. The real-time cubes make use of ROLAP storage for their partitions and dimensions, working from indexed views for aggregations and so on. Cubes are automatically updated when the base database tables are updated. This has exciting possibilities in a field of IT I have worked in for many years: call center management. No doubt it will be widely deployed in stock market analysis systems and other trading environments that need access to real-time analysis data.

You also have the ability to make use of a feature called *lazy aggregations.* What this does is allow data to be made available to analysts while aggregations are still calculating. You can also more finely manage calculation reactions to key errors, such as by deciding to stop processing on key errors after a certain number of key errors have occurred, or you can choose to ignore key errors.

You can also specify formulas that apply to individual cells or to sets of cells in a cube. These formulas can contain conditional calculations that compute a new value for a cell or set of cells from values in the cell or cells, or on values in other cells in the cube. Calculated cells use Multidimensional Expressions (MDX), and you can specify calculations to be performed in multiple passes.

The calculated cells can be used in complex financial modeling and budgeting applications; for example, you can specify a default value such as a percentage of a parent cell if the cell value is zero, or use the actual value if it is not zero.

Client applications that support drill-through can now allow end users to select a cube cell and retrieve a result set from the source data for that cell. You can use roles to control user access to the drill-through functionality.

A new DistinctCount aggregate function can be used to analyze the number of unique occurrences of events or transactions in your data, such as unique users visiting a Web site. You can hide complete cubes, dimensions, levels, measures, or member properties from analysts who browse cubes with client applications. The visibility of these objects is controlled by the Visible property.

You can also create, name, and save sets of dimension members or set expressions in a cube. Client applications can use a named set like a dimension by placing the named set on an axis.

Default measures can be specified for each cube and varied by role to control the analyst's default views of cubes. The new Virtual Cube Editor for virtual cubes, discussed earlier, provides functionality similar to that of the Cube Editor.

Dimension Enhancements

SQL Server 2000 Analysis Services has substantially updated the dimension functionality and includes a number of new dimension types, features, and improvements. A new parent-child dimension type supports hierarchies based on parent-child links between members in columns in a source table. You can use these hierarchies to represent structures such as organizational charts or part databases.

There is now also support for extremely large dimensions, which can now be accommodated using the ROLAP storage model. The dimension data remains in the relational database table and is not subject to the size limitations of MOLAP storage.

To increase the availability of cubes to analysts, you can make use of the new changing dimension type, which permits dimension members to be deleted, moved, added, or renamed without requiring the cube to be fully processed after changes.

Dependent dimensions let you improve aggregation design optimization by using knowledge of nonintersecting member combinations to reduce storage requirement estimation in the design algorithm. See SQL Server's Books Online for information covering all new dimension enhancements.

Security Enhancements

The Analysis Services now includes features that provide more flexibility in controlling access to cube data, authentication of analysts, and enhanced enforcement of analysis roles. You can use roles to control analyst access to dimensions. You can also set various read and re4ad/write permissions.

Analysis Manager now includes dialog boxes that enable you to define cell security by setting role options to control access to the actual cube cells. You can thus limit a role's access to any combination of a cube's cells. And you can now also vary the read and read/write permissions of the role.

You can now also use HTTP authentication methods for client connections to the Analysis servers. Analysis Services supports Windows 2000 negotiated protocol authentication; however, role specifications are enforced on Analysis servers installed on either file allocation table (FAT) or NTFS file systems.

Client Connectivity Enhancements in PivotTable Service

Client applications can connect to the Analysis server through the services of Internet Information Services (IIS) using either the HTTP or HTTPS protocol. Third-party security providers can also be used.

The new functionality in the PivotTable Service lets you write data to aggregation cells in a cube and, using one of four different allocation formulas, automatically distribute the data to the lowest-level members. Many of the new features for server cubes, such as new dimension types, custom rollups, and calculated members, can also be used in local cubes in an offline state. The PivotTable Service supports the advanced data mining and analysis techniques that are available in SQL Server 2000 Analysis Services, so you create and use data mining models to analyze data in server cubes or local databases.

Databases

You will notice in the Analysis Manager that you can create a database. This database is the container for related cubes and the objects they share. These objects include data sources, shared dimensions, and database roles. If these objects are to be shared among multiple cubes, the objects and cubes must be within the same database.

Databases are immediately subordinate to the Analysis server in the object hierarchy. Thus, after an Analysis server is installed, databases are the first objects to be created.

Data Sources

A *data source* defined in Analysis Services contains the information necessary to access source data for an object such as a cube. "Data source" here refers to the data source object, which is used by SQL Server 2000 Analysis Services to establish connections to the source data, our database in SQL Server.

A data source specifies an OLE DB provider and settings for the other properties in the connection string used to access the source data. The property set varies according to the selected provider. Typically, many of the properties are optional, so the creation of a data source can be accomplished quickly. You can create the data sources in the Data Link Properties dialog box.

Analysis Services supports many data sources, including SQL Server 2000 databases and databases created by other products.

To create a new source database in Analysis Manager, you need to take the following steps:

1. Drill down to the Analysis server registered in Analysis Manager. This server will usually go by the same name as the server you have registered in Enterprise Manager. Right-click and select New Database. The Database dialog box illustrated in Figure 25-4 loads. Enter the name and description and click OK.

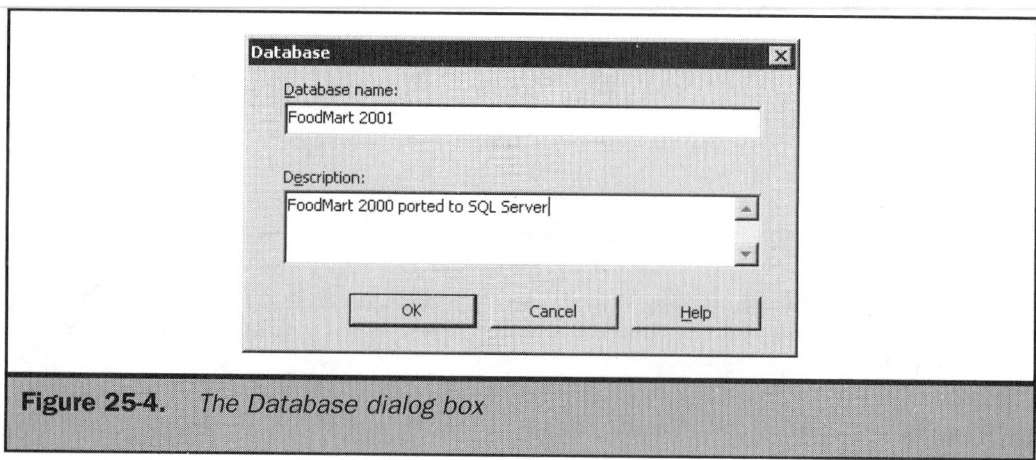

Figure 25-4. *The Database dialog box*

2. The database is created but now requires a data source. Drill down to the new database, select the Data Sources folder, and right-click to select New Data Source. The Data Link Properties dialog box loads, as illustrated in Figure 25-5. Create your connection and click OK to save the data source.

3. The data source is bound to the analysis database, and you are ready to start building cubes and dimensions. Analysis Manager with the new database we created in Chapter 24 is illustrated in Figure 25-6.

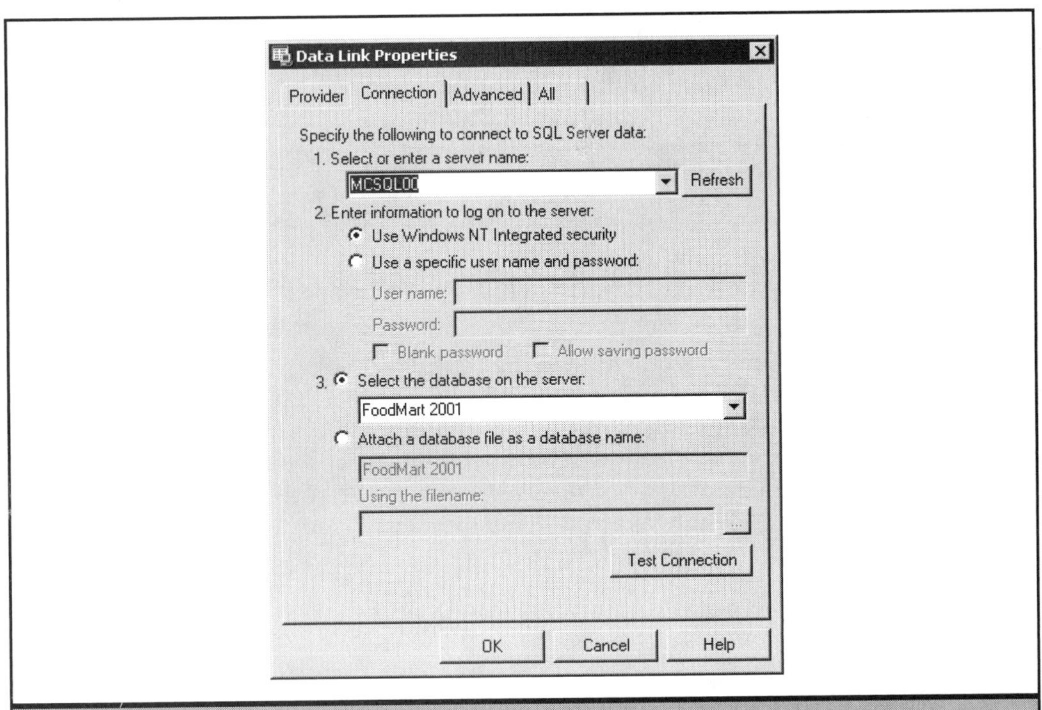

Figure 25-5. *The Data Link Properties dialog box*

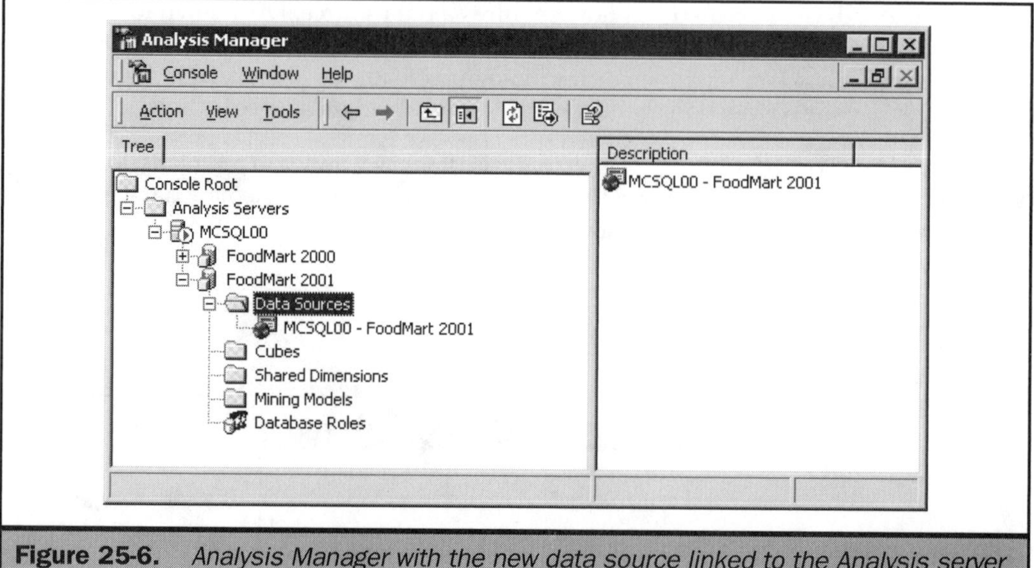

Figure 25-6. *Analysis Manager with the new data source linked to the Analysis server*

In Review

That concludes a very brief introduction to the OLAP technology, which is included in Analysis Services. As a mentioned in Chapter 24, SQL Server 2000's Analysis Services and data mining technology are a book in their own right. Working with analytical data is very different from working with transactional data, as you have seen. However, working with data warehouses and OLAP can be very rewarding. If you are new to Analysis Services, it will take you many months of study and hands on to become proficient. Good luck!

The Complete Reference

Appendix A

T-SQL Reference

This appendix provides brief explanations of the T-SQL constructions such as functions, general commands, and system stored procedures. It essentially summarizes T-SQL reference information, providing a quick look-up facility. The full text and usage code is available in Books Online. These commands can be used in your application, in Query Analyzer, Enterprise Manager, and from the command-line utilities such as ISQL and OSQL. They represent the bulk of the most frequently used facilities provided by T-SQL. Many more procedures are available, such as the extended stored procedures, but they are less frequently used and can be referenced in SQL Server Books Online. The full explanation and usage of arguments and parameters is accessible from SQL Server Books Online.

T-SQL Construct	**Usage, Usage Tips, Suggestions, and References**
+ (Add)	Adds two numbers. This addition arithmetic operator can also add a number, in days, to a date.
+ (Positive)	A unary operator that returns the positive value of a numeric expression.
+ (String Concatenation)	An operator in a string expression that concatenates two or more character or binary strings, columns, or a combination of strings and column names into one expression.
– (Negative)	A unary operator that returns the negative value of a numeric expression.
– (Subtract)	The arithmetic operator subtracts two numbers and can also subtract a number of days from a date.
* (Multiply)	The arithmetic multiplication operator multiplies two expressions.
/ (Divide)	The arithmetic division operator divides one number by another.
% (Modulo)	Provides the remainder of one number divided by another.
% (Wildcard - Character(s) to Match)	Matches any string of zero or more characters and can be used as either a prefix or a suffix.
& (Bitwise AND)	Performs the bitwise logical AND operation between two integer values.
| (Bitwise OR)	Performs the bitwise logical OR operation between two given integer values as translated to binary expressions within Transact-SQL statements.

T-SQL Construct	Usage, Usage Tips, Suggestions, and References
^ (Bitwise Exclusive OR)	Performs the bitwise exclusive OR operation between two given integer values as translated to binary expressions within Transact-SQL statements.
~ (Bitwise NOT)	Performs a bitwise logical NOT operation for one given integer value as translated to binary expressions within Transact-SQL statements.
= (Equal)	A comparison operator that compares two expressions for equality. When you compare nonnull expressions, the result is TRUE if both operands are equal; otherwise, the result is FALSE. If either or both operands are NULL and SET ANSI_NULLS is set to ON, the result is NULL. If SET ANSI_NULLS is set to OFF, the result is FALSE if one of the operands is NULL, and TRUE if both operands are NULL.
> (Greater Than)	A comparison operator that compares two expressions to determine if the left value is the *greater* value. When you compare nonnull expressions, the result is TRUE if the left operand has a higher value than the right operand; otherwise, the result is FALSE. If either or both operands are NULL and SET ANSI_NULLS is set to ON, the result is NULL. If SET ANSI_NULLS is set to OFF, the result is FALSE if one of the operands is NULL, and TRUE if both operands are NULL.
< (Less Than)	A comparison operator that compares two expressions to determine if the left value is the *lesser* value. When you compare nonnull expressions, the result is TRUE if the left operand has a lower value than the right operand; otherwise, the result is FALSE. If either or both operands are NULL and SET ANSI_NULLS is set to ON, the result is NULL. If SET ANSI_NULLS is set to OFF, the result is FALSE if one of the operands is NULL, and TRUE if both operands are NULL.
>= (Greater Than or Equal To)	A comparison operator that compares two expressions to determine if the left value is *greater than or equal to* the right value. When you compare nonnull expressions, the result is TRUE if the left operand has a higher or equal value than the right operand; otherwise, the result is FALSE. If either or both operands are NULL and SET ANSI_NULLS is set to ON, the result is NULL. If SET ANSI_NULLS is set to OFF, the result is FALSE if one of the operands is NULL, and TRUE if both operands are NULL.

T-SQL Construct	Usage, Usage Tips, Suggestions, and References
<= (Less Than or Equal To)	A comparison operator that compares two expressions to determine if the left value is *less than or equal to* the right value. When you compare nonnull expressions, the result is TRUE if the left operand has a lower or equal value than the right operand; otherwise, the result is FALSE. If either or both operands are NULL and SET ANSI_NULLS is set to ON, the result is NULL. If SET ANSI_NULLS is set to OFF, the result is FALSE if one of the operands is NULL, and TRUE if both operands are NULL.
<> (Not Equal To)	A comparison operator that compares two expressions to determine if the left value is *not equal to* the right value. When you compare nonnull expressions, the result is TRUE if the left operand is not equal to the right operand; otherwise, the result is FALSE. If either or both operands are NULL and SET ANSI_NULLS is set to ON, the result is NULL. If SET ANSI_NULLS is set to OFF, the result is FALSE if one of the operands is NULL, and TRUE if both operands are NULL.
!< (Not Less Than)	A comparison operator that compares two expressions to determine if the left value is *not less than* greater value. When you compare nonnull expressions, the result is TRUE if the left operand does not have a lower value than the right operand; otherwise, the result is FALSE. If either or both operands are NULL and SET ANSI_NULLS is set to ON, the result is NULL. If SET ANSI_NULLS is set to OFF, the result is FALSE if one of the operands is NULL, and TRUE if both operands are NULL.
!= (Not Equal To)	A comparison operator that compares two expressions to determine if the left value is *not equal to* the right value. Functions the same as the Not Equal To (<>) comparison operator.
!> (Not Greater Than)	A comparison operator that compares two expressions to determine if the left value is *not greater than* the right value. When you compare nonnull expressions, the result is TRUE if the left operand does not have a higher value than the right operand; otherwise, the result is FALSE. If either or both operands are NULL and SET ANSI_NULLS is set to ON, the result is NULL. If SET ANSI_NULLS is set to OFF, the result is FALSE if one of the operands is NULL, and TRUE if both operands are NULL.
-- (Comment)	Indicates user-provided text that is not evaluated by SQL Server. Comments can be inserted on a separate line, nested (-- only) at the end of a Transact-SQL command line, or within a Transact-SQL statement. Two hyphens (--) is the SQL-92 standard indicator for comments.

T-SQL Construct	Usage, Usage Tips, Suggestions, and References
/*...*/ (Comment)	Indicates user-provided text that is not evaluated by SQL Server. The text between the /* and */ commenting characters is ignored by SQL Server.
[ ] (Wildcard - Character(s) to Match)	The wildcard characters are used to match any single character within the specified range or set that is specified inside the square brackets.
[^] (Wildcard - Character(s) Not to Match)	The wildcard characters are used *not* to match any single character within the specified range or set that is specified inside the square brackets.
_ (Wildcard - Match One Character)	The underscore can be used to match any single character, and can be used as either a prefix or a suffix. The underscore can also be replaced by another wild card if it exists in the values you are scanning, for example jeff_shapiro@sql2ktcr.book.
@@CONNECTIONS	This function returns the number of connections, or attempted connections, that have occurred since SQL Server was last started.
@@CPU_BUSY	This function returns the time in milliseconds—based on the resolution of the system timer—that the CPU has spent working since SQL Server was last started.
@@CURSOR_ROWS	This function returns the number of qualifying rows currently in the last cursor opened on your connection. To improve performance, SQL Server can populate large keysets and static cursors asynchronously. @@CURSOR_ROWS can be called to determine that the number of the rows that qualify for a cursor are retrieved at the time @@CURSOR_ROWS is called.
@@DATEFIRST	This function returns the current value of the SET DATEFIRST parameter, which indicates the specified first day of each week: 1 for Monday, 2 for Wednesday, and so on through 7 for Sunday.
@@DBTS	This function returns the value of the current timestamp data type for the current database. This timestamp is guaranteed to be unique in the database.
@@ERROR	This function returns the error number for the last Transact-SQL statement you executed.
@@FETCH_STATUS	This function returns the status of the last cursor FETCH statement issued against any cursor currently opened by the connection.
@@IDENTITY	This function returns the last inserted identity value.

T-SQL Construct	Usage, Usage Tips, Suggestions, and References
@@IDLE	This function returns the time in milliseconds (based on the resolution of the system timer) that SQL Server has been idle since it was last started.
@@IO_BUSY	This function returns the time in milliseconds (based on the resolution of the system timer) that SQL Server has spent performing input and output operations since it was last started.
@@LANGID	This function returns the local language identifier (ID) of the language currently in use.
@@LANGUAGE	This function returns the name of the language currently in use.
@@LOCK_TIMEOUT	This function returns the current lock time-out setting, in milliseconds, for the current session.
@@MAX_CONNECTIONS	This function returns the maximum number of simultaneous user connections allowed on a SQL Server. The number returned is not necessarily the number currently configured.
@@MAX_PRECISION	This function returns the precision level used by decimal and numeric data types as currently set in the server.
@@NESTLEVEL	This function returns the nesting level of the current stored procedure execution (initially 0).
@@OPTIONS	This function returns information about current SET options.
@@PACK_RECEIVED	This function returns the number of input packets read from the network by SQL Server since last started.
@@PACK_SENT	This function returns the number of output packets written to the network by SQL Server since last started.
@@PACKET_ERRORS	This function returns the number of network packet errors that have occurred on SQL Server connections since SQL Server was last started.
@@PROCID	This function returns the stored procedure identifier (ID) of the current procedure.
@@REMSERVER	This function returns the name of the remote SQL Server database server as it appears in the login record.
@@ROWCOUNT	This function returns the number of rows affected by the last statement.
@@SERVERNAME	This function returns the name of the local server running SQL Server.

T-SQL Construct	Usage, Usage Tips, Suggestions, and References
@@SERVICENAME	This function returns the name of the Registry key under which SQL Server is running. @@SERVICENAME returns MSSQLServer if the current instance is the default instance The function also returns the instance name if the current instance is a named instance.
@@SPID	This function returns the server process identifier (ID) of the current user process.
@@TEXTSIZE	This function returns the current value of the TEXTSIZE option of the SET statement, which specifies the maximum length, in bytes, of text or image data that a SELECT statement returns.
@@TIMETICKS	This function returns the number of microseconds per tick.
@@TOTAL_ERRORS	This function returns the number of disk read/write errors encountered by SQL Server since it was last started.
@@TOTAL_READ	This function returns the number of disk reads (not cache reads) by SQL Server since it was last started.
@@TOTAL_WRITE	This function returns the number of disk writes by SQL Server since it was last started.
@@TRANCOUNT	This function returns the number of active transactions for the current connection.
@@VERSION	This function returns the date, version, and processor type for the current installation of SQL Server 2000.
ABS	This function returns the absolute, positive value of the given numeric expression.
ACOS	This function returns the angle, in radians, whose cosine is the given float expression; also called arccosine.
ALL	This compares a scalar value with a single-column set of values.
ALTER DATABASE	Adds or removes files and filegroups from a database. Can also be used to modify the attributes of files and filegroups, such as changing the name or size of a file. ALTER DATABASE provides the capability to change the database name, the filegroup names, and the logical names of data files and log files.

T-SQL Construct	Usage, Usage Tips, Suggestions, and References
ALTER FUNCTION	Alters an existing user-defined function, which was first created by executing the CREATE FUNCTION statement. It does not change permissions or any dependent functions, stored procedures, or triggers. For more information about the parameters used in the ALTER FUNCTION statement, also see the CREATE FUNCTION statement.
ALTER PROCEDURE	Alters a previously created procedure, which is created by executing the CREATE PROCEDURE statement. It does not change permissions or affect any dependent stored procedures or triggers. For more information about the parameters used in the ALTER PROCEDURE statement, see the CREATE PROCEDURE statement.
ALTER TABLE	This statement modifies a table definition by altering, adding, or dropping columns and constraints. It is also used to disable or enable constraints and triggers.
ALTER TRIGGER	This statement alters the definition of a trigger created previously by the CREATE TRIGGER statement. For more information about the parameters used in the ALTER TRIGGER statement, see also CREATE TRIGGER.
ALTER VIEW	Allows you to alter a previously created view (created by executing CREATE VIEW), including indexed views, without affecting dependent stored procedures or triggers and without changing permissions. For more information about the parameters used in the ALTER VIEW statement, see also CREATE VIEW.
AND	Used to combine two Boolean expressions and returns TRUE when both expressions are TRUE. When more than one logical operator is used in a statement, AND operators are evaluated first. You can change the order of evaluation by using parentheses.
ANY	Used to compare a scalar value with a single-column set of values. For more information, see also SOME | ANY.
APP_NAME	Used to return the application name for the current session, if set by the application.
ASCII	This command will return the ASCII code value of the leftmost character of a character expression.
ASIN	Will return the angle, in radians, whose sine is the given float expression. It is also called arcsine.
ATAN	Will return the angle in radians whose tangent is the given float expression. It is also called arctangent.

T-SQL Construct	Usage, Usage Tips, Suggestions, and References
ATN2	Will returns the angle, in radians, whose tangent is between the two given float expressions. It is also called arctangent.
AVG	Used to return the average of the values in a group. The Null values are ignored.
BACKUP	This statement backs up an entire database or transaction log, or one or more files or filegroups. For more information about database backup and restore operations see Chapter 9.
BEGIN...END	A block that encloses a series of Transact-SQL statements so that a group of Transact-SQL statements can be executed. BEGIN and END are control-of-flow language keywords, similar to standard procedures in languages like Pascal.
BEGIN DISTRIBUTED TRANSACTION	This clause specifies the start of the T-SQL distributed transaction managed by Microsoft Distributed Transaction Coordinator (MS DTC).
BEGIN TRANSACTION	This clause marks the starting point of an explicit, local transaction. BEGIN TRANSACTION increments @@TRANCOUNT by 1.
BETWEEN	This clause specifies a range to test.
binary and varbinary	Binary data types of either fixed-length (binary) or variable-length (varbinary).
BINARY_CHECKSUM	This command returns the binary checksum value computed over a row of a table or over a list of expressions. BINARY_CHECKSUM can be used to detect changes to a row of a table.
bit	Integer data type 1, 0, or NULL.
BREAK	Use this command to exit the innermost WHILE loop. Any statements following the END keyword are ignored. BREAK is often, but not always, activated by an IF test.
BULK INSERT	Used to copy data into a database table or view in a user-specified format. It is frequently used for the initial load of data warehouse tables.
CASE	Used in flow-control segments, this evaluates a list of conditions and returns one of multiple possible result expressions.
CAST and CONVERT	Explicitly converts an expression of one data type to another. CAST and CONVERT provide similar functionality.

T-SQL Construct	Usage, Usage Tips, Suggestions, and References
CEILING	This returns the smallest integer greater than, or equal to, the given numeric expression.
char and varchar	Fixed-length (char) or variable-length (varchar) character data types.
CHAR	This function converts an int ASCII code to a character.
CHARINDEX	This function returns the starting position of the specified expression in a character string.
CHECKPOINT	Forces all dirty pages for the current database to be written to disk. Dirty pages are data or log pages modified after being entered into the buffer cache, but for which the modifications have not yet been written to disk.
CHECKSUM	This function returns the checksum value computed over a row of a table, or over a list of expressions. CHECKSUM is intended for use in building hash indices.
CHECKSUM_AGG	This function returns the checksum of the values in a group. Null values are ignored.
CLOSE	Closes an open cursor by releasing the current result set and freeing any cursor locks held on the rows on which the cursor is positioned. The CLOSE leaves the data structures accessible for reopening, but fetches and positioned updates are not allowed until the cursor is reopened. CLOSE must be issued on an open cursor; it is not allowed on cursors that have only been declared or are already closed.
COALESCE	This function returns the first nonnull expression among its arguments.
COLLATE	A clause that can be applied to a database definition or a column definition to define the collation, or to a character string expression to apply a collation cast. *Windows Collation Name* specifies the Windows collation name in the COLLATE clause. The Windows collation name is composed of the collation designator and the comparison styles. *SQL Collation Name* is a single string that specifies the collation name for a SQL collation.
COLLATIONPROPERTY	This function returns the property of a given collation.
COL_LENGTH	This function returns the defined length of a column.

T-SQL Construct	Usage, Usage Tips, Suggestions, and References
COL_NAME	This function returns the name of a database column given the corresponding table identification number and column identification number.
COLUMNPROPERTY	This function returns information about a column or procedure parameter.
COMMIT TRANSACTION	Marks the end of a successful implicit or user-defined transaction. If @@TRANCOUNT is 1, COMMIT TRANSACTION makes all data modifications performed since the start of the transaction a permanent part of the database, frees the resources held by the connection, and decrements @@TRANCOUNT to 0. If @@TRANCOUNT is greater than 1, COMMIT TRANSACTION decrements @@TRANCOUNT only by 1.
COMMIT WORK	Marks the end of a transaction.
Constants	A constant, also known as a literal or a scalar value, is a symbol that represents a specific data value. The format of a constant depends on the data type of the value it represents.
CONTAINS	Is a predicate used to search columns containing character-based data types for precise or fuzzy (less precise) matches to single words and phrases, the proximity of words within a certain distance of one another, or weighted matches. CONTAINS can search for words and phrases, prefixes, words near other words, and so on.
CONTAINSTABLE	This function returns a table of zero, one, or more rows for those columns containing character-based data types for precise or fuzzy (less precise) matches to single words and phrases, matches according to the proximity of words within a certain distance of one another, or weighted matches. CONTAINSTABLE can be referenced in the FROM clause of a SELECT statement as if it were a regular table name.
CONTINUE	Restarts a WHILE loop. Any statements after the CONTINUE keyword are ignored. CONTINUE is often, but not always, activated by an IF test. For more information, see also WHILE.
COS	A mathematical function that returns the trigonometric cosine of the given angle (in radians) in the given expression.

T-SQL Construct	Usage, Usage Tips, Suggestions, and References
COT	A mathematical function that returns the trigonometric cotangent of the specified angle (in radians) in the given float expression.
COUNT	This function returns the number of items in a group.
COUNT_BIG	This function returns the number of items in a group. COUNT_BIG works like the COUNT function. The only difference between them is their return values: COUNT_BIG always returns a bigint data type value. COUNT always returns an int data type value.
CREATE DATABASE	Creates a new database and the files used to store the database, or attaches a database from the files of a previously created database.
CREATE DEFAULT	Creates an object called a *default*. When bound to a column or a user-defined data type, a default specifies a value to be inserted into the column to which the object is bound (or into all columns, in the case of a user-defined data type) when no value is explicitly supplied during an insert. Defaults, a backward compatibility feature, perform some of the same functions as default definitions created using the DEFAULT keyword of ALTER or CREATE TABLE statements. Default definitions are the preferred, standard way to restrict column data because the definition is stored with the table and automatically dropped when the table is dropped. A default is beneficial, however, when the default is used multiple times for multiple columns.
CREATE FUNCTION	Creates a user-defined function, which is a saved Transact-SQL routine that returns a value. User-defined functions cannot be used to perform a set of actions that modify the global database state. User-defined functions, like system functions, can be invoked from a query. They also can be executed through an EXECUTE statement like stored procedures.
CREATE INDEX	Creates an index on a given table or view.
CREATE PROCEDURE	Creates a stored procedure, which is a saved collection of Transact-SQL statements that can take and return user-supplied parameters.

T-SQL Construct	Usage, Usage Tips, Suggestions, and References
CREATE RULE	Creates an object called a rule. When bound to a column or a user-defined data type, a rule specifies the acceptable values that can be inserted into that column. Rules, a backward compatibility feature, perform some of the same functions as check constraints. CHECK constraints, created using the CHECK keyword of ALTER or CREATE TABLE, are the preferred, standard way to restrict the values in a column (multiple constraints can be defined on one or multiple columns). A column or user-defined data type can have only one rule bound to it. However, a column can have both a rule and one or more check constraints associated with it. When this is true, all restrictions are evaluated.
CREATE SCHEMA	Creates a schema that can be thought of as a conceptual object containing definitions of tables, views, and permissions.
CREATE STATISTICS	Creates a histogram and associated density groups (collections) over the supplied column or set of columns.
CREATE TABLE	Creates a new table.
CREATE TRIGGER	Creates a trigger, which is a special kind of stored procedure that executes automatically when a user attempts the specified data-modification statement on the specified table. SQL Server allows the creation of multiple triggers for any given INSERT, UPDATE, or DELETE statement.
CREATE VIEW	Creates a virtual table that represents the data in one or more tables in an alternative way. Views are used as security mechanisms by granting permissions for a view but not on the underlying (base) tables.
CURRENT_TIMESTAMP	This function returns the current date and time. This function is equivalent to GETDATE().
CURRENT_USER	This function returns the current user. This function is equivalent to USER_NAME().
cursor	A data type for variables or stored procedure OUTPUT parameters that contain a reference to a cursor. Any variables created with the cursor data type are nullable.
CURSOR_STATUS	A scalar function that allows the caller of a stored procedure to determine whether or not the procedure has returned a cursor and result set for a given parameter.

T-SQL Construct	Usage, Usage Tips, Suggestions, and References
Cursors	SQL Server statements produce a complete result set, but there are times when the results are best processed one row at a time. Opening a cursor on a result set allows processing the result set one row at a time. SQL Server version 7.0 also introduces assigning a cursor to a variable or parameter with a cursor data type.
DATABASEPROPERTY	This function returns the named database property value for the given database and property name.
DATABASEPROPERTYEX	This function returns the current setting of the specified database option or property for the specified database.
DATALENGTH	This function returns the number of bytes used to represent any expression.
DATEADD	This function returns a new datetime value based on adding an interval to the specified date.
DATEDIFF	This function returns the number of date and time boundaries crossed between two specified dates.
DATENAME	This function returns a character string representing the specified date part of the specified date.
DATEPART	This function returns an integer representing the specified date part of the specified date.
datetime and smalldatetime	Date and time data types for representing date and time of day.
DAY	This function returns an integer representing the day date part of the specified date.
DB_ID	This function returns the database identification (ID) number.
DB_NAME	This function returns the database name.
DBCC	The Transact-SQL programming language provides DBCC statements that act as Database Console Commands for SQL Server 2000. These statements check the physical and logical consistency of a database. Many DBCC statements can fix detected problems.
DBCC CHECKALLOC	Checks the consistency of disk space allocation structures for a specified database.
DBCC CHECKCATALOG	Checks for consistency in and between system tables in the specified database.
DBCC CHECKCONSTRAINTS	Checks the integrity of a specified constraint or all constraints on a specified table.

T-SQL Construct	Usage, Usage Tips, Suggestions, and References
DBCC CHECKDB	Checks the allocation and structural integrity of all the objects in the specified database.
DBCC CHECKFILEGROUP	Checks the allocation and structural integrity of all tables (in the current database) in the specified filegroup.
DBCC CHECKIDENT	Checks the current identity value for the specified table and, if needed, corrects the identity value.
DBCC CHECKTABLE	Checks the integrity of the data, index, text, ntext, and image pages for the specified table or indexed view.
DBCC CLEANTABLE	Reclaims space for dropped variable-length columns and text columns.
DBCC CONCURRENCYVIOLATION	Displays statistics on how many times more than five batches were executed concurrently on SQL Server 2000 Desktop Engine or SQL Server 2000 Personal Edition. Also Controls whether these statistics are also recorded in the SQL Server error log.
DBCC DBREPAIR	Drops a damaged database.
DBCC DBREINDEX	Rebuilds one or more indexes for a table in the specified database.
DBCC dllname (FREE)	Unloads the specified extended stored procedure dynamic-link library (DLL) from memory.
DBCC DROPCLEANBUFFERS	Removes all clean buffers from the buffer pool.
DBCC FREEPROCCACHE	Removes all elements from the procedure cache.
DBCC HELP	This function returns syntax information for the specified DBCC statement.
DBCC INDEXDEFRAG	Defragments clustered and secondary indexes of the specified table or view.
DBCC INDEXDEFRAG	Defragments clustered and secondary indexes of the specified table or view.
DBCC INPUTBUFFER	Displays the last statement sent from a client to SQL Server.
DBCC NEWALLOC	Checks the allocation of data and index pages for each table within the *extent* structures of the database.
DBCC OPENTRAN	Displays information about the oldest active transaction and the oldest distributed and nondistributed replicated transactions, if any, within the specified database. Results are displayed only if there is an active transaction or if the database contains replication information. An informational message is displayed if there are no active transactions.

T-SQL Construct	Usage, Usage Tips, Suggestions, and References
DBCC OUTPUTBUFFER	This function returns the current output buffer in hexadecimal and ASCII format for the specified system process ID (SPID).
DBCC PINTABLE	Marks a table to be pinned, which means SQL Server does not flush the pages for the table from memory.
DBCC PROCCACHE	Displays information in a table format about the procedure cache.
DBCC ROWLOCK	Used for SQL Server version 6.5, enabling Insert Row Locking (IRL) operations on tables.
DBCC SHOWCONTIG	Displays fragmentation information for the data and indexes of the specified table.
DBCC SHOW_STATISTICS	Displays the current distribution statistics for the specified target on the specified table.
DBCC SHRINKDATABASE	Shrinks the size of the data files in the specified database.
DBCC SHRINKFILE	Shrinks the size of the specified data file or log file for the related database.
DBCC SQLPERF	Provides statistics about the use of transaction-log space in all databases.
DBCC TRACEOFF	Disables the specified trace flag(s).
DBCC TRACEON	Turns on (enables) the specified trace flag.
DBCC TRACESTATUS	Displays the status of trace flags.
DBCC UNPINTABLE	Marks a table as unpinned. After a table is marked as unpinned, the table pages in the buffer cache can be flushed.
DBCC UPDATEUSAGE	Reports and corrects inaccuracies in the sysindexes table, which may result in incorrect space usage reports by the sp_spaceused system stored procedure.
DBCC USEROPTIONS	This function returns the SET options active (set) for the current connection.
DEALLOCATE	Removes a cursor reference. When the last cursor reference is deallocated, the data structures making up the cursor are released by SQL Server.
decimal and numeric	Numeric data types with fixed precision and scale.
DECLARE *@local_variable*	Variables are declared in the body of a batch or procedure with the DECLARE statement and are assigned values with either a SET or SELECT statement. Cursor variables can be declared with this statement and used with other cursor-related statements. After declaration, all variables are initialized as NULL.

T-SQL Construct	Usage, Usage Tips, Suggestions, and References
DECLARE CURSOR	Defines the attributes of a Transact-SQL server cursor, such as its scrolling behavior and the query used to build the result set on which the cursor operates. DECLARE CURSOR accepts both a syntax based on the SQL-92 standard and a syntax using a set of Transact-SQL extensions.
DEGREES	Given an angle in radians, returns the corresponding angle in degrees.
DELETE	Removes rows from a table.
DENY	Creates an entry in the security system that denies a permission from a security account in the current database and prevents the security account from inheriting the permission through its group or role memberships.
DIFFERENCE	This function returns the difference between the SOUNDEX values of two character expressions as an integer.
DROP DATABASE	Removes one or more databases from SQL Server. Removing a database deletes the database and the disk files used by the database.
DROP DEFAULT	Removes one or more user-defined defaults from the current database.
DROP FUNCTION	Removes one or more user-defined functions from the current database. User-defined functions are created using CREATE FUNCTION and modified using ALTER FUNCTION.
DROP INDEX	Removes one or more indexes from the current database.
DROP PROCEDURE	Removes one or more stored procedures or procedure groups from the current database.
DROP RULE	Removes one or more user-defined rules from the current database.
DROP STATISTICS	Drops statistics for multiple collections within the specified tables (in the current database).
DROP TABLE	Removes a table definition and all data, indexes, triggers, constraints, and permission specifications for that table. Any view or stored procedure that references the dropped table must be explicitly dropped by using the DROP VIEW or DROP PROCEDURE statement.
DROP TRIGGER	Removes one or more triggers from the current database.

T-SQL Construct	Usage, Usage Tips, Suggestions, and References
DROP VIEW	Removes one or more views from the current database. DROP VIEW can be executed against indexed views.
DUMP	Makes a backup copy of a database (DUMP DATABASE) or makes a copy of the transaction log (DUMP TRANSACTION) in a form that can be read into SQL Server using the BACKUP or LOAD statements.
ELSE (IF...ELSE)	Imposes conditions on the execution of a Transact-SQL statement. The Transact-SQL statement (*sql_statement*) following the *Boolean_expression* is executed if the *Boolean_expression* evaluates to TRUE. The optional ELSE keyword is an alternate Transact-SQL statement that is executed when *Boolean_expression* evaluates to FALSE or NULL.
END (BEGIN...END)	Encloses a series of Transact-SQL statements that will execute as a group. BEGIN...END blocks can be nested.
EXECUTE	Executes a scalar-valued, user-defined function, a system procedure, a user-defined stored procedure, or an extended stored procedure. Also supports the execution of a character string within a Transact-SQL batch.
EXISTS	Specifies a subquery to test for the existence of rows.
EXP	This function returns the exponential value of the given float expression.
Expressions	A combination of symbols and operators that SQL Server evaluates to obtain a single data value. Simple expressions can be a single constant, variable, column, or scalar function. Operators can be used to join two or more simple expressions into a complex expression.
FETCH	Retrieves a specific row from a Transact-SQL server cursor.
FILE_ID	This function returns the file identification (ID) number for the given logical filename in the current database.
FILE_NAME	This function returns the logical filename for the given file identification (ID) number.
FILEGROUP_ID	This function returns the filegroup identification (ID) number for the given filegroup name.
FILEGROUP_NAME	This function returns the filegroup name for the given filegroup identification (ID) number.
FILEGROUPPROPERTY	This function returns the specified filegroup property value when given a filegroup and property name.

T-SQL Construct	Usage, Usage Tips, Suggestions, and References
FILEPROPERTY	This function returns the specified filename property value when given a filename and property name.
float and real	Approximate number data types for use with floating-point numeric data. Floating-point data is approximate; not all values in the data type range can be precisely represented.
FLOOR	This function returns the largest integer less than or equal to the given numeric expression.
fn_helpcollations	This function returns a list of all the collations supported by SQL Server 2000.
fn_listextendedproperty	This function returns extended property values of database objects.
fn_servershareddrives	This function returns the names of shared drives used by the clustered server.
fn_trace_geteventinfo	This function returns information about the events traced.
fn_trace_getfilterinfo	This function returns information about the filters applied to a specified trace.
fn_trace_getinfo	This function returns information about a specified trace or existing traces.
fn_trace_gettable	This function returns trace file information in a table format.
fn_virtualfilestats	This function returns I/O statistics for database files, including log files.
fn_virtualservernodes	This function returns the list of nodes on which the virtual server can run. Such information is useful in failover clustering environments.
FORMATMESSAGE	Constructs a message from an existing message in sysmessages. The functionality of FORMATMESSAGE resembles that of the RAISERROR statement; however, RAISERROR prints the message immediately, and FORMATMESSAGE returns the edited message for further processing.
FREETEXT	Is a predicate used to search columns containing character-based data types for values that match the meaning and not the exact wording of the words in the search condition. When FREETEXT is used, the full-text query engine internally "word-breaks" the *freetext_string* into a number of search terms and assigns each term a weight and then finds the matches.

T-SQL Construct	Usage, Usage Tips, Suggestions, and References
FREETEXTTABLE	This function returns a table of zero, one, or more rows for those columns containing character-based data types for values that match the meaning, but not the exact wording, of the text in the specified *freetext_string*. FREETEXTTABLE can be referenced in the FROM clause of a SELECT statement like a regular table name.
FROM	Specifies the tables, views, derived tables, and joined tables used in DELETE, SELECT, and UPDATE statements.
FULLTEXTCATALOGPROPERTY	This function returns information about full-text catalog properties.
FULLTEXTSERVICEPROPERTY	This function returns information about full-text service-level properties.
GETANSINULL	This function returns the default nullability for the database for this session.
GETDATE	This function returns the current system date and time in the SQL Server standard internal format for datetime values.
GETUTCDATE	This function returns the datetime value representing the current UTC time (Universal Time Coordinate or Greenwich Mean Time). The current UTC time is derived from the current local time and the time zone setting in the operating system of the computer on which SQL Server is running.
GO	Signals the end of a batch of Transact-SQL statements to the SQL Server utilities.
GOTO	Alters the flow of execution to a label. The Transact-SQL statement(s) following GOTO are skipped, and processing continues at the label. GOTO statements and labels can be used anywhere within a procedure, batch, or statement block. GOTO statements can be nested.
GRANT	Creates an entry in the security system that allows a user in the current database to work with data in the current database or execute specific Transact-SQL statements.
GROUP BY	Divides a table into groups. Groups can consist of column names or results or computed columns. For more information, see SELECT.
GROUPING	Is an aggregate function that causes an additional column to be output with a value of 1 when the row is added by either the CUBE or ROLLUP operator, or 0 when the row is not the result of CUBE or ROLLUP.

T-SQL Construct	Usage, Usage Tips, Suggestions, and References
HAS_DBACCESS	This function returns information about whether the user has access to the specified database.
HAVING	Specifies a search condition for a group or an aggregate. HAVING can be used only with the SELECT statement. It is usually used in a GROUP BY clause. When GROUP BY is not used, HAVING behaves like a WHERE clause. For more information, see SELECT.
HOST_ID	This function returns the workstation identification number.
HOST_NAME	This function returns the workstation name.
IDENT_CURRENT	This function returns the last identity value generated for a specified table in any session and any scope.
IDENT_INCR	This function returns the increment value (returned as numeric(@@MAXPRECISION,0)) specified during the creation of an identity column in a table or view that has an identity column.
IDENT_SEED	This function returns the seed value (returned as numeric(@@MAXPRECISION,0)) specified during the creation of an identity column in a table or a view that has an identity column.
IDENTITY (Property)	Creates an identity column in a table. This property is used with the CREATE TABLE and ALTER TABLE Transact-SQL statements.
IDENTITY (Function)	Is used only in a SELECT statement with an INTO *table* clause to insert an identity column into a new table.
IF...ELSE	Imposes conditions on the execution of a Transact-SQL statement. The Transact-SQL statement following an IF keyword and its condition is executed if the condition is satisfied (when the Boolean expression returns TRUE). The optional ELSE keyword introduces an alternate Transact-SQL statement that is executed when the IF condition is not satisfied (when the Boolean expression returns FALSE).
IN	Determines if a given value matches any value in a subquery or a list.
INDEXKEY_PROPERTY	This function returns information about the index key.
INDEXPROPERTY	This function returns the named index property value given a table identification number, index name, and property name.
INDEX_COL	This function returns the indexed column name.
INSERT	Adds a new row to a table or a view.

T-SQL Construct	Usage, Usage Tips, Suggestions, and References
int, bigint, smallint, and tinyint	Exact number data types that use integer data.
IS_MEMBER	Indicates whether the current user is a member of the specified Windows NT group or SQL Server role.
IS_SRVROLEMEMBER	Indicates whether the current user login is a member of the specified server role.
ISDATE	Determines whether an input expression is a valid date.
IS [NOT] NULL	Determines whether or not a given expression is NULL.
ISNULL	Replaces NULL with the specified replacement value.
ISNUMERIC	Determines whether an expression is a valid numeric type.
KILL	Terminates a user process according to the system process ID (SPID) or unit of work (UOW). If the specified SPID or UOW has a lot of work to undo, the KILL command may take some time to complete, particularly when it involves rolling back a long transaction.
LEFT	This function returns the part of a character string starting at a specified number of characters from the left.
LEN	This function returns the number of characters, rather than the number of bytes, of the given string expression, excluding trailing blanks.
LIKE	Determines whether or not a given character string matches a specified pattern. A pattern can include regular characters and wildcard characters. During pattern matching, regular characters must exactly match the characters specified in the character string. Wildcard characters, however, can be matched with arbitrary fragments of the character string. Using wildcard characters makes the LIKE operator more flexible than using the = and != string comparison operators. If any of the arguments are not of the character string data type, SQL Server 2000 converts them to the character string data type, if possible.
LOAD	Loads a backup copy of one of the following: Database, Transaction Log, Load Header Only. This statement is available for backward compatibility with earlier versions of SQL Server.
LOG	This function returns the natural logarithm of the given float expression.
LOG10	This function returns the base-10 logarithm of the given float expression.

T-SQL Construct	Usage, Usage Tips, Suggestions, and References
LOWER	This function returns a character expression after converting uppercase character data to lowercase.
LTRIM	This function returns a character expression after removing leading blanks.
MAX	This function returns the maximum value in the expression.
MIN	This function returns the minimum value in the expression.
money and smallmoney	Monetary data types for representing monetary or currency values.
MONTH	This function returns an integer that represents the month part of a specified date.
NCHAR	This function returns the Unicode character with the given integer code, as defined by the Unicode standard.
nchar and nvarchar	Character data types that are either fixed-length (nchar) or variable-length (nvarchar) Unicode data and use the UNICODE UCS-2 character set.
NEWID	Creates a unique value of type uniqueidentifier.
NOT	Negates a Boolean input.
ntext, text, and image	Fixed- and variable-length data types for storing large non-Unicode and Unicode character and binary data. Unicode data uses the UNICODE UCS-2 character set.
NULLIF	This function returns a null value if the two specified expressions are equivalent.
numeric	For more information about the numeric data type, see DECIMAL and NUMERIC.
OBJECT_ID	This function returns the database object identification number.
OBJECT_NAME	This function returns the database object name.
OBJECTPROPERTY	This function returns information about objects in the current database.
OPEN	Opens a Transact-SQL server cursor and populates the cursor by executing the Transact-SQL statement specified on the DECLARE CURSOR or SET *cursor_variable* statement.
OPENDATASOURCE	Provides ad hoc connection information as part of a four-part object name without using a linked server name.

T-SQL Construct	Usage, Usage Tips, Suggestions, and References
OPENQUERY	Executes the specified pass-through query on the given linked server, which is an OLE DB data source. The OPENQUERY function can be referenced in the FROM clause of a query as though it is a table name. The OPENQUERY function can also be referenced as the target table of an INSERT, UPDATE, or DELETE statement, subject to the capabilities of the OLE DB provider. Although the query may return multiple result sets, OPENQUERY returns only the first one.
OPENXML	OPENXML provides a rowset view over an XML document. Because OPENXML is a rowset provider, OPENXML can be used in Transact-SQL statements in which rowset providers such as a table, view, or the OPENROWSET function can appear.
OPENROWSET	Includes all connection information necessary to access remote data from an OLE DB data source. This method is an alternative to accessing tables in a linked server and is a one-time, ad hoc method of connecting and accessing remote data using OLE DB. The OPENROWSET function can be referenced in the FROM clause of a query as though it is a table name. The OPENROWSET function can also be referenced as the target table of an INSERT, UPDATE, or DELETE statement, subject to the capabilities of the OLE DB provider. Although the query may return multiple result sets, OPENROWSET returns only the first one.
OR	Combines two conditions. When more than one logical operator is used in a statement, OR operators are evaluated after AND operators. However, you can change the order of evaluation by using parentheses.
ORDER BY	Specifies the sort order used on columns returned in a SELECT statement. For more information, see SELECT.
PARSENAME	This function returns the specified part of an object name. Parts of an object that can be retrieved are the object name, owner name, database name, and server name.
PATINDEX	This function returns the starting position of the first occurrence of a pattern in a specified expression, or zeros if the pattern is not found, on all valid text and character data types.
PERMISSIONS	This function returns a value containing a bitmap that indicates the statement, object, or column permissions for the current user.
PI	This function returns the constant value of PI.

T-SQL Construct	Usage, Usage Tips, Suggestions, and References
POWER	This function returns the value of the given expression to the specified power.
Predicate	Is an expression that evaluates to TRUE, FALSE, or UNKNOWN. Predicates are used in the search condition of WHERE clauses and HAVING clauses, and the join conditions of FROM clauses.
PRINT	This function returns a user-defined message to the client.
QUOTENAME	This function returns a Unicode string with the delimiters added to make the input string a valid SQL Server 2000 delimited identifier.
RADIANS	This function returns radians when a numeric expression, in degrees, is entered.
RAISERROR	This function returns a user-defined error message and sets a system flag to record that an error has occurred. Using RAISERROR, the client can either retrieve an entry from the sysmessages table or build a message dynamically with user-specified severity and state information. After the message is defined, it is sent back to the client as a server error message.
RAND	This function returns a random float value from 0 through 1.
READTEXT	Reads text, ntext, or image values from a text, ntext, or image column, starting from a specified offset and reading the specified number of bytes.
real	For more information about the real data type, see *float* and *real*.
RECONFIGURE	Updates the currently configured (the config_value column in the sp_configure result set) value of a configuration option changed with the sp_configure system stored procedure. Because some configuration options require a server stop and restart to update the currently running value, RECONFIGURE does not always update the currently running value (the run_value column in the sp_configure result set) for a changed configuration value.
REPLACE	Replaces all occurrences of the second given string expression in the first string expression with a third expression.
REPLICATE	Repeats a character expression for a specified number of times.

T-SQL Construct	Usage, Usage Tips, Suggestions, and References
RESTORE	Restores backups taken using the BACKUP command. For more information about database backup and restore operations see Chapter 9.
RESTORE FILELISTONLY	This function returns a result set with a list of the database and log files contained in the backup set.
RESTORE HEADERONLY	Retrieves all the backup header information for all backup sets on a particular backup device. The result from executing RESTORE HEADERONLY is a result set.
RESTORE LABELONLY	This function returns a result set containing information about the backup media identified by the given backup device.
RESTORE VERIFYONLY	Verifies the backup but does not restore the backup. Checks to see that the backup set is complete and that all volumes are readable. However, RESTORE VERIFYONLY does not attempt to verify the structure of the data contained in the backup volumes. If the backup is valid, SQL Server 2000 returns the message: "The backup set is valid."
RETURN	RETURN is an unconditional exit from a query or procedure that is immediate and complete and can be used at any point to exit from a procedure, batch, or statement block. Statements following RETURN are not executed.
REVERSE	This function returns the reverse of a character expression.
REVOKE	Removes a previously granted or denied permission from a user in the current database.
RIGHT	This function returns the part of a character string starting a specified number of *integer_expression* characters from the right.
ROLLBACK TRANSACTION	Rolls back an explicit or implicit transaction to the beginning of the transaction, or to a savepoint inside a transaction.
ROLLBACK WORK	Rolls back a user-specified transaction to the beginning of a transaction.
ROUND	This function returns a numeric expression, rounded to the specified length or precision.
ROWCOUNT_BIG	This function returns the number of rows affected by the last statement executed. This function operates like @@ROWCOUNT, except that the return type of ROWCOUNT_BIG is bigint.

T-SQL Construct	Usage, Usage Tips, Suggestions, and References
RTRIM	This function returns a character string after truncating all trailing blanks.
SAVE TRANSACTION	Sets a savepoint within a transaction.
SCOPE_IDENTITY	This function returns the last IDENTITY value inserted into an IDENTITY column in the same scope. A scope is a module—a stored procedure, trigger, function, or batch. Thus, two statements are in the same scope if they are in the same stored procedure, function, or batch.
Search Condition	Is a combination of one or more predicates using the logical operators AND, OR, and NOT.
SELECT *@local_variable*	Specifies that the given local variable (created using DECLARE *@local_variable*) should be set to the specified expression.
SELECT	Retrieves rows from the database and allows the selection of one or many rows or columns from one or many tables. The full syntax of the SELECT statement is complex, and is fully documented in Books Online. See Chapter 19
SERVERPROPERTY	This function returns property information about the server instance.
SESSION_USER	Is a niladic function that allows a system-supplied value for the current session's username to be inserted into a table when no default value is specified. Also allows the username to be used in queries, error messages, and so on.
SESSIONPROPERTY	This function returns the SET options settings of a session.
SET *@local_variable*	Sets the specified local variable, previously created with the DECLARE *@local_variable* statement, to the given value.
SET	The Transact-SQL programming language provides several SET statements that alter the current session handling of specific information.
SET ANSI_DEFAULTS	Controls a group of SQL Server 2000 settings that collectively specify some SQL-92 standard behaviors.
SET ANSI_NULL_DFLT_OFF	Alters the session's behavior to override default nullability of new columns when the ANSI null default option for the database is true. For more information about setting the value for ANSI null default, see also sp_dboption.

T-SQL Construct	Usage, Usage Tips, Suggestions, and References
SET ANSI_NULL_DFLT_ON	Alters the session's behavior to override default nullability of new columns when the ANSI null default option for the database is false. For more information about setting the value for ANSI null default, see also sp_dboption.
SET ANSI_NULLS	Specifies SQL-92 compliant behavior of the Equal (=) and Not Equal to (<>) comparison operators when used with null values.
SET ANSI_PADDING	Controls the way the column stores values shorter than the defined size of the column, and the way the column stores values that have trailing blanks in char, varchar, binary, and varbinary data.
SET ANSI_WARNINGS	Specifies SQL-92 standard behavior for several error conditions.
SET ARITHABORT	Terminates a query when an overflow or divide-by-zero error occurs during query execution.
SET ARITHIGNORE	Controls whether error messages are returned from overflow or divide-by-zero errors during a query.
SET CONCAT_ NULL_YIELDS_NULL	Controls whether or not concatenation results are treated as null or empty string values.
SET CONTEXT_INFO	Associates up to 128 bytes of binary information with the current session or connection.
SET CURSOR_CLOSE_ ON_COMMIT	Controls whether or not a cursor is closed when a transaction is committed.
SET DATEFIRST	Sets the first day of the week to a number from 1–7.
SET DATEFORMAT	Sets the order of the date parts (month/day/year) for entering datetime or smalldatetime data.
SET DEADLOCK_PRIORITY	Controls the way the session reacts when in a deadlock situation. Deadlock situations arise when two processes have data locked, and each process cannot release its lock until other processes have released theirs.
SET DISABLE_DEF_CNST_CHK	Specified interim deferred violation checking; was used for efficiency purposes in SQL Server version 6.*x*.
SET FIPS_FLAGGER	Specifies checking for compliance with the FIPS 127-2 standard, which is based on the SQL-92 standard.
SET FMTONLY	This function returns only metadata to the client.

T-SQL Construct	Usage, Usage Tips, Suggestions, and References
SET FORCEPLAN	Makes the SQL Server 2000 query optimizer process a join in the same order as tables appear in the FROM clause of a SELECT statement only.
SET IDENTITY_INSERT	Allows explicit values to be inserted into the identity column of a table.
SET IMPLICIT_TRANSACTIONS	Sets implicit transaction mode for the connection.
SET LANGUAGE	Specifies the language environment for the session. The session language determines the datetime formats and system messages.
SET LOCK_TIMEOUT	Specifies the number of milliseconds a statement waits for a lock to be released.
SET NOCOUNT	Stops the message indicating the number of rows affected by a Transact-SQL statement from being returned as part of the results.
SET NOEXEC	Compiles each query but does not execute it.
SET NUMERIC_ROUNDABORT	Specifies the level of error reporting generated when rounding in an expression causes a loss of precision.
SET OFFSETS	This function returns the offset (position relative to the start of a statement) of specified keywords in Transact-SQL statements to DB-Library applications.
SET PARSEONLY	Checks the syntax of each Transact-SQL statement and returns any error messages without compiling or executing the statement.
SET QUERY_GOVERNOR_COST_LIMIT	Overrides the currently configured value for the current connection.
SET QUOTED_IDENTIFIER	Causes SQL Server 2000 to follow the SQL-92 rules regarding quotation mark delimiting identifiers and literal strings. Identifiers delimited by double quotation marks either can be Transact-SQL reserved keywords or can contain characters not usually allowed by the Transact-SQL syntax rules for identifiers.
SET REMOTE_PROC_TRANSACTIONS	Specifies that when a local transaction is active, executing a remote stored procedure starts a Transact-SQL distributed transaction managed by the Microsoft Distributed Transaction Manager (MS DTC).
SET ROWCOUNT	Causes SQL Server 2000 to stop processing the query after the specified number of rows are returned.

T-SQL Construct	Usage, Usage Tips, Suggestions, and References
SET SHOWPLAN_ALL	Causes SQL Server 2000 not to execute Transact-SQL statements. Instead, SQL Server returns detailed information about how the statements are executed and provides estimates of the resource requirements for the statements.
SET SHOWPLAN_TEXT	Causes SQL Server 2000 not to execute Transact-SQL statements. Instead, SQL Server returns detailed information about how the statements are executed.
SET STATISTICS IO	Causes SQL Server 2000 to display information regarding the amount of disk activity generated by Transact-SQL statements.
SET STATISTICS PROFILE	Displays the profile information for a statement. STATISTICS PROFILE works for ad hoc queries, views, triggers, and stored procedures.
SET STATISTICS TIME	Displays the number of milliseconds required to parse, compile, and execute each statement.
SET TEXTSIZE	Specifies the size of text and ntext data returned with a SELECT statement.
SET TRANSACTION ISOLATION LEVEL	Controls the default transaction locking behavior for all SQL Server 2000 SELECT statements issued by a connection.
SET XACT_ABORT	Specifies whether SQL Server 2000 automatically rolls back the current transaction if a Transact-SQL statement raises a run-time error.
SETUSER	Allows a member of the sysadmin fixed server role or db_owner fixed database role to impersonate another user.
SHUTDOWN	Immediately stops operation of SQL Server 2000.
SIGN	This function returns the positive (+1), zero (0), or negative (–1) sign of the given expression.
SIN	This function returns the trigonometric sine of the given angle (in radians) in an approximate numeric (float) expression.
smalldatetime	For information about the smalldatetime data type, see datetime and small datetime.
smallint	For information about the smallint data type, see int.
smallmoney	For information about the smallmoney data type, see money and small money.
SOME | ANY	Compares a scalar value with a single-column set of values.

T-SQL Construct	Usage, Usage Tips, Suggestions, and References
SOUNDEX	This function returns a four-character (SOUNDEX) code to evaluate the similarity of two strings.
SPACE	This function returns a string of repeated spaces.
sql_variant	A data type that stores values of various SQL Server–supported data types, except text, ntext, image, timestamp, and sql_variant.
SQL_VARIANT_PROPERTY	This function returns the base data type and other information about a sql_variant value.
SQUARE	This function returns the square of the given expression.
SQRT	This function returns the square root of the given expression.
STATS_DATE	This function returns the date that the statistics for the specified index were last updated.
STDEV	This function returns the statistical standard deviation of all values in the given expression.
STDEVP	This function returns the statistical standard deviation for the population for all values in the given expression.
STR	This function returns character data converted from numeric data.
STUFF	Deletes a specified length of characters and inserts another set of characters at a specified starting point.
SUBSTRING	This function returns part of a character, binary, text, or image expression. For more information about the valid SQL Server 2000 data types that can be used with this function, see Books Online.
SUM	This function returns the sum of all the values, or only the DISTINCT values, in the expression. SUM can be used with numeric columns only. Null values are ignored.
SUSER_ID	This function returns the user's login identification number.
SUSER_NAME	This function returns the user's login identification name.
SUSER_SID	This function returns the security identification number (SID) for the user's login name.
SUSER_SNAME	This function returns the login identification name from a user's security identification number (SID).

System Stored Procedures	Usage, Usage Tips, Suggestions, and References
sp_add_alert	This procedure creates an alert.
sp_addalias	This procedure maps a login to a user in a database. sp_addalias is provided for backward compatibility. SQL Server version 7.0 provides roles and the ability to grant permissions to roles as an alternative to using aliases.
sp_addapprole	This procedure adds a special type of role in the current database used for application security.
sp_add_data_file_recover_suspect_db	This procedure adds a data file to a filegroup when recovery cannot complete on a database due to an insufficient space (1105) error on the filegroup. After the file is added, this stored procedure turns off the suspect setting and completes the recovery of the database. The parameters are the same as those for ALTER DATABASE ADD FILE.
sp_addextendedproc	This procedure registers the name of a new extended stored procedure to SQL Server.
sp_addextendedproperty	This procedure adds a new extended property to a database object. If the property already exists, the procedure fails.
sp_addgroup	This procedure creates a group in the current database. sp_addgroup is included for backward compatibility. SQL Server version 7.0 uses roles instead of groups. Use sp_addrole to add a role.
sp_add_category	This procedure adds the specified category of jobs, alerts, or operators to the server.
sp_add_job	This procedure adds a new job executed by the SQLServerAgent service.
sp_add_jobschedule	This procedure creates a schedule for a job.
sp_add_jobserver	This procedure targets the specified job at the specified server.
sp_add_jobstep	This procedure adds a step (operation) to a job.
sp_addlinkedserver	This procedure creates a linked server, which allows access to distributed, heterogeneous queries against OLE DB data sources. After creating a linked server with sp_addlinkedserver, this server can then execute distributed queries. If the linked server is defined as SQL Server, remote stored procedures can be executed.
sp_addlinkedsrvlogin	This procedure creates or updates a mapping between logins on the local instance of SQL Server and remote logins on the linked server.

System Stored Procedures	Usage, Usage Tips, Suggestions, and References
sp_add_log_file_recover_suspect_db	This procedure adds a log file to a filegroup when recovery cannot complete on a database due to an insufficient log space error (error number 9002). After the file is added, this stored procedure turns off the suspect setting and completes the recovery of the database. The parameters are the same as those for ALTER DATABASE ADD LOG FILE. See "Troubleshooting Recovery" in Books Online.
sp_addlogin	This procedure creates a new SQL Server login that allows a user to connect to an instance of SQL Server using SQL Server Authentication.
sp_add_log_shipping_database	This procedure specifies that a database on the primary server is being log shipped.
sp_add_log_shipping_plan	This procedure creates a new log shipping plan and inserts a row in the log_shipping_plans table.
sp_add_log_shipping_plan_database	This procedure adds a new database to an existing log shipping plan.
sp_add_log_shipping_primary	This procedure adds a new primary server to the log_shipping_primaries table.
sp_add_log_shipping_secondary	This procedure adds a secondary server to the log_shipping_secondaries table.
sp_add_maintenance_plan	This procedure adds a maintenance plan and returns the plan ID.
sp_add_maintenance_plan_db	This procedure associates a database with a maintenance plan.
sp_add_maintenance_plan_job	This procedure associates a maintenance plan with an existing job.
sp_addmessage	This procedure adds a new error message to the sysmessages table.
sp_add_notification	Sets up a notification for an alert.
sp_add_operator	This procedure creates an operator (notification recipient) for use with alerts and jobs.
sp_addremotelogin	This procedure adds a new remote login ID on the local server, allowing remote servers to connect and execute remote procedure calls.
sp_addrole	This procedure creates a new SQL Server role in the current database.

System Stored Procedures	Usage, Usage Tips, Suggestions, and References
sp_addrolemember	This procedure adds a security account as a member of an existing SQL Server database role in the current database.
sp_addserver	This procedure defines a remote server or the name of the local SQL Server. sp_addserver is provided for backward compatibility. Use sp_addlinkedserver.
sp_addsrvrolemember	This procedure adds a login as a member of a fixed server role.
sp_addtask	This procedure creates a scheduled task.
sp_addtype	This procedure creates a user-defined data type.
sp_add_targetservergroup	This procedure adds the specified server group.
sp_addumpdevice	This procedure adds a backup device to SQL Server.
sp_add_targetsvrgrp_member	This procedure adds the specified target server to the specified target server group.
sp_adduser	This procedure adds a security account for a new user in the current database. This procedure is included for backward compatibility. Use sp_grantdbaccess.
sp_altermessage	This procedure alters the state of a sysmessages error.
sp_apply_job_to_targets	This procedure applies a job to one or more target servers or to the target servers belonging to one or more target server groups.
sp_approlepassword	This procedure changes the password of an application role in the current database.
sp_attach_db	This procedure attaches a database to a server.
sp_attach_single_file_db	This procedure attaches a database having only one data file to the current server.
sp_autostats	This procedure displays or changes the automatic UPDATE STATISTICS setting for a specific index and statistics, or for all indexes and statistics for a given table or indexed view in the current database.
sp_bindefault	This procedure binds a default to a column or to a user-defined data type.
sp_bindrule	This procedure binds a rule to a column or to a user-defined data type.

System Stored Procedures	Usage, Usage Tips, Suggestions, and References
sp_bindsession	This procedure binds or unbinds a connection to other transactions in the same instance of Microsoft SQL Server 2000. A bound connection allows two or more connections to participate in the same transaction and share the transaction until a ROLLBACK TRANSACTION or COMMIT TRANSACTION is issued.
sp_can_tlog_be_applied	This procedure verifies that a transaction log can be applied to a database.
sp_catalogs	This procedure returns the list of catalogs in the specified linked server, which is equivalent to databases in SQL Server.
sp_certify_removable	This procedure berifies that a database is configured properly for distribution on removable media and reports any problems to the user.
sp_change_monitor_role	This procedure performs a role change on the log shipping monitor, setting the current secondary database to be a primary database.
sp_change_primary_role	This procedure removes the primary database from a log shipping plan.
sp_change_secondary_role	This procedure converts the secondary database of a log shipping plan into a primary database.
sp_change_users_login	This procedure changes the relationship between a SQL Server login and a SQL Server user in the current database.
sp_changedbowner	This procedure changes the owner of the current database.
sp_changegroup	This procedure changes the role membership for the security account of a user in the current database. This procedure is provided for backward compatibility. SQL Server version 7.0 uses roles instead of groups. Use sp_addrolemember instead.
sp_changeobjectowner	This procedure changes the owner of an object in the current database.
sp_column_privileges	This procedure returns column privilege information for a single table in the current environment.
sp_column_privileges_ex	This procedure returns column privileges for the specified table on the specified linked server.
sp_columns	This procedure returns column information for the specified tables or views that can be queried in the current environment.

System Stored Procedures	Usage, Usage Tips, Suggestions, and References
sp_columns_ex	This function returns the column information, one row per column, for the given linked server table(s). The sp_columns_ex returns column information only for the given column if *column* is specified.
sp_configure	This procedure displays or changes global configuration settings for the current server.
sp_create_log_shipping_monitor_account	This procedure creates the log_shipping_monitor_probe login on the monitor server, and assigns update permissions to the msdb.dbo.log_shipping_primaries and msdb.dbo.log_shipping_secondaries tables.
sp_create_removable	This procedure creates a removable media database. It essentially creates three or more files (one for the system catalog tables, one for the transaction log, and one or more for the data tables) and places the database on those files.
sp_createstats	This procedure creates single-column statistics for all eligible columns for all user tables in the current database. The new statistic has the same name as the column on which it is created. The computed columns and columns of the ntext, text, or image data types cannot be specified as statistics columns. Columns already having statistics are not touched; for example, the first column of an index or a column with explicitly created statistics. The CREATE STATISTICS statement is executed for each column that satisfies the above restrictions. The option FULLSCAN is executed if fullscan is specified.
sp_cursor_list	This procedure reports the attributes of server cursors currently open for the connection.
sp_cycle_errorlog	This procedure closes the current error log file and cycles the error log extension numbers just like a server restart. The new error log contains version and copyright information and a line indicating that the new log has been created.
sp_databases	This procedure lists databases that reside in an instance of SQL Server, or the databases that are accessible through a database gateway.
sp_datatype_info	This procedure returns information about the data types supported by the current environment.
sp_dbcmptlevel	This procedure sets certain database behaviors to be compatible with the specified earlier version of SQL Server (versions 8, 7, and so on).

System Stored Procedures	Usage, Usage Tips, Suggestions, and References
sp_dbfixedrolepermission	This procedure displays the permissions for each fixed database role.
sp_dboption	This procedure displays or changes database options. sp_dboption should not be used on either the master or tempdb databases. sp_dboption is supported for backward compatibility. You should use ALTER DATABASE to set database options.
sp_dbremove	Removes a database and all files associated with that database. This procedure is included for backward compatibility, and you should use the procedure sp_detach_db to "unhinge" a database from SQL Server.
sp_defaultdb	This procedure changes the default database for a login.
sp_defaultlanguage	This procedure changes the default language of a login.
sp_define_log_shipping_monitor	This procedure sets up the log shipping monitor account on the monitor server.
sp_delete_alert	This procedure removes an alert.
sp_delete_backuphistory	This procedure deletes the entries in the backup and restore history tables for backup sets older than *oldest_date*. Because additional rows are added to the backup and restore history tables when a backup or restore operation is performed, sp_delete_backuphistory can be used to reduce the size of the history tables in the msdb database.
sp_delete_category	This procedure removes the specified category of jobs, alerts, or operators from the current server.
sp_delete_job	This procedure deletes a job.
sp_delete_jobschedule	This procedure removes a schedule from a job.
sp_delete_jobserver	This procedure removes the specified target server.
sp_delete_jobstep	This procedure removes a job step from a job.
sp_delete_log_shipping_database	This procedure deletes a database from the log_shipping_databases table on the primary server.
sp_delete_log_shipping_plan	This procedure deletes a log shipping plan.
sp_delete_log_shipping_plan_ database	This procedure removes a database from a log shipping plan.
sp_delete_log_shipping_primary	This procedure deletes the primary server from the log_shipping_primaries table.
sp_delete_log_shipping_secondary	This procedure removes a secondary server from log_shipping_secondaries table.

System Stored Procedures	Usage, Usage Tips, Suggestions, and References
sp_delete_maintenance_plan	This procedure deletes the specified maintenance plan.
sp_delete_maintenance_plan_db	This procedure disassociates the specified maintenance plan from the specified database.
sp_delete_maintenance_plan_job	This procedure disassociates the specified maintenance plan from the specified job.
sp_delete_notification	This procedure removes all notifications sent to a particular operator in response to an alert.
sp_delete_operator	This procedure removes an operator.
sp_delete_targetserver	This procedure removes the specified server from the list of available target servers.
sp_delete_targetservergroup	This procedure deletes the specified target server group.
sp_delete_targetsvrgrp_member	This procedure removes a target server from a target server group.
sp_denylogin	This procedure prevents a Microsoft Windows NT user or group from connecting to Microsoft SQL Server.
sp_depends	This procedure displays information about database object dependencies (for example, the views and procedures that depend on a table or view, and the tables and views that are depended on by the view or procedure). It also references objects outside the current database that are not reported.
sp_describe_cursor	This procedure reports the attributes of a server cursor.
sp_describe_cursor_columns	This procedure reports the attributes of the columns in the result set of a server cursor.
sp_describe_cursor_tables	This procedure reports the base tables referenced by a server cursor.
sp_detach_dbsp_dropalias	This procedure detaches a database from a server and, optionally, runs UPDATE STATISTICS on all tables before detaching. It also removes an alias to a user in the current database from a login. The procedure sp_dropalias is provided for backward compatibility only. You should use roles and the sp_droprolemember stored procedure instead of aliases.
sp_dropapprole	This procedure removes an application role from the current database.
sp_dropdevice	This procedure drops a database device or backup device from SQL Server, deleting the entry from master.dbo.sysdevices.

System Stored Procedures	Usage, Usage Tips, Suggestions, and References
sp_dropextendedproc	This procedure drops an extended stored procedure.
sp_dropextendedproperty	This procedure drops an existing extended property.
sp_dropgroup	This procedure removes a role from the current database. The procedure sp_dropgroup is provided for backward compatibility. In SQL Server version 7.0, groups are implemented as roles.
sp_droplinkedsrvlogin	This procedure removes an existing mapping between a login on the local server running SQL Server and a login on the linked server.
sp_droplogin	This procedure removes a SQL Server login, preventing access to SQL Server using that login name.
sp_dropmessage	This procedure drops a specified error message from the sysmessages system table.
sp_dropremotelogin	This procedure removes a remote login mapped to a local login used to execute remote stored procedures against the local server running SQL Server.
sp_droprole	This procedure removes a SQL Server role from the current database.
sp_droprolemember	This procedure removes a security account from a SQL Server role in the current database.
sp_dropserver	This procedure removes a server from the list of known remote and linked servers on the local SQL Server.
sp_dropsrvrolemember	This procedure removes a SQL Server login or a Microsoft Windows NT user or group from a fixed server role.
sp_droptask	This procedure is provided for backward compatibility only. For information about the Microsoft SQL Server version 7.0 replacement procedures see Books Online.
sp_droptype	This procedure deletes a user-defined data type from systypes.
sp_dropuser	This procedure removes a SQL Server user or Microsoft Windows NT user from the current database. sp_dropuser is provided for backward compatibility. Use sp_revokedbaccess to remove a user.
sp_dropwebtask	This procedure deletes a previously defined Web task.
sp_enumcodepages	This procedure returns a list of the code pages and character sets supported by sp_makewebtask.

System Stored Procedures	Usage, Usage Tips, Suggestions, and References
sp_executesql	This procedure executes a T-SQL statement or batch that can be reused many times, or that has been built dynamically. The T-SQL statement or batch can contain embedded parameters.
sp_fkeys	This procedure returns logical foreign key information for the current environment. This procedure shows foreign key relationships including disabled foreign keys.
sp_foreignkeys	This procedure returns the foreign keys that reference primary keys on the table in the linked server.
sp_fulltext_catalog	This procedure creates and drops a full-text catalog, and starts and stops the indexing action for a catalog. Multiple full-text catalogs can be created for each database.
sp_fulltext_column	This procedure specifies whether or not a particular column of a table participates in full-text indexing.
sp_fulltext_database	This procedure initializes full-text indexing or removes all full-text catalogs from the current database.
sp_fulltext_service	This procedure changes Search Service (Full-text Search) properties.
sp_fulltext_table	This procedure marks or unmarks a table for full-text indexing.
sp_getapplock	This procedure places a lock on an application resource.
sp_getbindtoken	This procedure returns a unique identifier for the transaction. This unique identifier is referred to as a bind token. sp_getbindtoken returns a string representation to be used to share transactions between clients.
sp_get_log_shipping_monitor_info	This procedure returns status information about a "Log Shipping Pair." A log shipping pair is a set of primary server-primary database and secondary server-secondary database.
sp_grantdbaccess	This procedure adds a security account in the current database for a SQL Server login or Windows NT user or group, and enables it to be granted permissions to perform activities in the database.
sp_grantlogin	This procedure allows a Windows NT user or group account to connect to Microsoft SQL Server using Windows Authentication. See Chapter 8.
sp_help	This procedure reports information about a database object (any object listed in the sysobjects table), a user-defined data type, or a data type supplied by SQL Server.

System Stored Procedures	Usage, Usage Tips, Suggestions, and References
sp_help_alert	This procedure reports information about the alerts defined for the server.
sp_help_category	This procedure provides information about the specified classes of jobs, alerts, or operators.
sp_helpconstraint	This procedure returns a list of all constraint types, their user-defined or system-supplied name, the columns on which they have been defined, and the expression that defines the constraint (for DEFAULT and CHECK constraints only).
sp_helpdb	This procedure reports information about a specified database or all databases.
sp_helpdbfixedrole	This procedure returns a list of the fixed database roles.
sp_helpdb	This procedure reports information about a specified database or all databases.
sp_helpdbfixedrole	Returns a list of the fixed database roles.
sp_helpdevice	This procedure reports information about SQL Server database files. sp_helpdevice is used for backward compatibility with earlier versions of SQL Server that used the term "device" for a database file.
sp_help_downloadlist	This procedure lists all rows in the sysdownloadlist system table for the supplied job, or all rows if no job is specified.
sp_helpextendedproc	This procedure displays the currently defined extended stored procedures and the name of the dynamic-link library to which the procedure (or function) belongs.
sp_helpdb	This procedure reports information about a specified database or all databases.
sp_helpdbfixedrole	Returns a list of the fixed database roles.
sp_helpdevice	This procedure reports information about SQL Server database files. sp_helpdevice is used for backward compatibility with earlier versions of SQL Server that used the term "device" for a database file.
sp_help_downloadlist	This procedure lists all rows in the sysdownloadlist system table for the supplied job, or all rows if no job is specified.
sp_helpextendedproc	This procedure displays the currently defined extended stored procedures and the name of the dynamic-link library to which the procedure (function) belongs.

System Stored Procedures	Usage, Usage Tips, Suggestions, and References
sp_helpfile	This procedure returns the physical names and attributes of files associated with the current database. Use this stored procedure to determine the names of files to attach to or detach from the server.
sp_helpfilegroup	This procedure returns the names and attributes of filegroups associated with the current database.
sp_help_fulltext_catalogs	This procedure returns the ID, name, root directory, status, and number of full-text indexed tables for the specified full-text catalog.
sp_help_fulltext_catalogs_cursor	This procedure makes use of a cursor to return the ID, name, root directory, status, and number of full-text indexed tables for the specified full-text catalog.
sp_help_fulltext_columns	This procedure returns the columns designated for full-text indexing.
sp_help_fulltext_columns_cursor	This procedure makes use of a cursor to return the columns designated for full-text indexing.
sp_help_fulltext_tables	This procedure returns a list of tables that are registered for full-text indexing.
sp_help_fulltext_tables_cursor	This procedure makes use of a cursor to return a list of tables that are registered for full-text indexing.
sp_helpgroup	This procedure reports information about a role, or all roles, in the current database. This procedure is included for backward compatibility with version 7.0 and can be executed against version 7.0 database.
sp_helphistory	This procedure is provided for backward compatibility.
sp_help_job	This procedure returns information about jobs that are used by SQLServerAgent service to perform automated activities in SQL Server.
sp_help_jobhistory	This procedure provides information about the jobs for servers in the multiserver administration domain.
sp_help_jobschedule	This procedure returns information about the scheduling of jobs used by SQL Server Enterprise Manager to perform automated activities.
sp_help_jobserver	This procedure returns information about the server for a given job.
sp_help_jobstep	This procedure returns information for the steps in a job used by SQLServerAgent service to perform automated activities.

System Stored Procedures	Usage, Usage Tips, Suggestions, and References
sp_helpindex	This procedure reports information about the indexes on a table or view.
sp_helplanguage	This procedure reports information about a particular alternate language or about all languages.
sp_helplinkedsrvlogin	This procedure provides information about login mappings defined against a specific linked server used for distributed queries and remote stored procedures.
sp_helplogins	This procedure provides information about logins and the associated users in each database.
sp_help_maintenance_plan	This procedure returns information about the specified maintenance plan. If a plan is not specified, this stored procedure returns information about all maintenance plans.
sp_help_notification	This procedure reports a list of alerts for a given operator or a list of operators for a given alert.
sp_helpntgroup	This procedure reports information about Microsoft Windows NT groups with accounts in the current database.
sp_help_operator	This procedure reports information about the operators defined for the server.
sp_helpremotelogin	This procedure reports information about remote logins for a particular remote server, or for all remote servers, defined on the local server.
sp_helprole	This procedure returns information about the roles in the current database.
sp_helprolemember	This procedure returns information about the members of a role in the current database.
sp_helprotect	This procedure returns a report with information about user permissions for an object, or statement permissions, in the current database.
sp_helpserver	This procedure reports information about a particular remote or replication server, or about all servers of both types. Provides the server name; the server's network name; the server's replication status; the server's identification number; collation name; and time-out values for connecting to, or queries against, linked servers.
sp_helpsort	This procedure displays the SQL Server sort order and character set.
sp_helpsrvrole	This procedure returns a list of the SQL Server fixed server roles.

System Stored Procedures	Usage, Usage Tips, Suggestions, and References
sp_helpsrvrolemember	This procedure returns information about the members of a SQL Server fixed server role.
sp_helpstats	This procedure returns statistics information about columns and indexes on the specified table.
sp_help_targetserver	This procedure lists all target servers.
sp_help_targetservergroup	This procedure lists all target servers in the specified group. If no group is specified, SQL Server returns information about all target server groups.
sp_helptask	This procedure is provided for backward compatibility only.
sp_helptext	This procedure prints the text of a rule, a default, or an unencrypted stored procedure, trigger, or view.
sp_helptrigger	This procedure returns the type or types of triggers defined on the specified table for the current database.
sp_helpuser	This procedure reports information about SQL Server users, Windows NT users, and database roles in the current database.
sp_indexes	This procedure returns index information for the specified remote table.
sp_indexoption	This procedure sets option values for user-defined indexes.
sp_invalidate_textptr	This procedure makes the specified in-row text pointer, or all in-row text pointers, in the transaction invalid. sp_invalidate_textptr can be used only on in-row text pointers, which are from tables with the "text in row" option enabled.
sp_linkedservers	This procedure returns the list of linked servers defined in the local server.
sp_lock	This procedure reports information about locks.
sp_makewebtask	This procedure creates a task that produces an HTML document containing data returned by executed queries.
sp_manage_jobs_by_login	This procedure deletes or reassigns jobs that belong to the specified login.
sp_monitor	This procedure displays statistics about SQL Server.
sp_MShasdbaccess	This procedure lists the name and owner of all the databases to which the user has access.
sp_msx_defect	This procedure removes the current server from multiserver operations.

System Stored Procedures	Usage, Usage Tips, Suggestions, and References
sp_msx_enlist	This procedure adds the current server to the list of target servers available for multiserver operations. Only a SQL Server version 7.0 database server running on Windows NT can be enlisted.
sp_OACreate	This procedure creates an instance of the OLE object on an instance of SQL Server.
sp_OADestroy	This procedure destroys a created OLE object.
sp_OAGetErrorInfo	This procedure obtains OLE Automation error information.
sp_OAGetProperty	This procedure gets a property value of an OLE object.
sp_OAMethod	This procedure calls a method of an OLE object.
sp_OASetProperty	This procedure sets a property of an OLE object to a new value.
sp_OAStop	This procedure stops the server-wide OLE Automation stored procedure execution environment.
sp_password	This procedure adds or changes a password for a SQL Server login.
sp_pkeys	This procedure returns primary key information for a single table in the current environment.
sp_primarykeys	This procedure returns the primary key columns, one row per key column, for the specified remote table.
sp_post_msx_operation	This procedure inserts operations (rows) into the sysdownloadlist system table for target servers to download and execute.
sp_processmail	This procedure uses extended stored procedures (xp_findnextmsg, xp_readmail, and xp_deletemail) to process incoming mail messages (expected to be only a single query) from the inbox for SQL Server. It uses the xp_sendmail extended stored procedure to return the result set to the message sender.
sp_procoption	This procedure sets procedure options.
sp_purgehistory	This procedure is provided for backward compatibility only.
sp_purge_jobhistory	This procedure removes the history records for a job.
sp_reassigntask	This procedure is provided for backward compatibility only.
sp_recompile	This procedure forces stored procedures and triggers to be recompiled the next time they are run.

System Stored Procedures	Usage, Usage Tips, Suggestions, and References
sp_refreshview	This procedure refreshes the metadata for the specified view. Persistent metadata for a view can become outdated because of changes to the underlying objects upon which the view depends.
sp_releaseapplock	This procedure releases a lock on an application resource.
sp_remoteoption	This procedure displays or changes options for a remote login defined on the local server running SQL Server.
sp_remove_job_from_targets	This procedure removes the specified job from the given target servers or target server groups.
sp_remove_log_shipping_monitor	This procedure deletes the log shipping monitor information from the log_shipping_monitor table.
sp_rename	This procedure changes the name of a user-created object (for example, table, column, or user-defined data type) in the current database.
sp_renamedb	This procedure changes the name of a database.
sp_resetstatus	This procedure resets the status of a suspect database.
sp_resolve_logins	This procedure resolves logins on the new primary server against logins from the former primary server.
sp_resync_targetserver	This procedure resynchronizes all multiserver jobs in the specified target server.
sp_revokedbaccess	This procedure removes a security account from the current database.
sp_revokelogin	This procedure removes the login entries from SQL Server for a Windows NT user or group created with sp_grantlogin or sp_denylogin.
sp_runwebtask	This procedure executes a previously defined Web job and generates the HTML document. The task to run is identified by the output file name, by the procedure name, or by both parameters.
sp_server_info	This procedure returns a list of attribute names and matching values for SQL Server, the database gateway, or the underlying data source.
sp_serveroption	This procedure sets server options for remote servers and linked servers.
sp_setapprole	This procedure activates the permissions associated with an application role in the current database.

System Stored Procedures	Usage, Usage Tips, Suggestions, and References
sp_setnetname	This procedure sets the network names in sysservers to their actual network computer names for remote instances of SQL Server. This procedure can be used to enable execution of remote stored procedure calls to computers that have network names containing invalid SQL Server identifiers.
sp_settriggerorder	This procedure specifies which AFTER triggers associated with a table will be fired first or last. The AFTER triggers that will be fired between the first and last triggers will be executed in undefined order.
sp_spaceused	This procedure displays the number of rows, disk space reserved, and disk space used by a table in the current database, or displays the disk space reserved and used by the entire database.
sp_special_columns	This procedure returns the optimal set of columns that uniquely identify a row in the table. Also returns columns automatically updated when any value in the row is updated by a transaction.
sp_sproc_columns	This procedure returns column information for a single stored procedure or user-defined function in the current environment.
sp_srvrolepermission	This procedure returns the permissions applied to a fixed server role.
sp_start_job	This procedure instructs SQL Server Agent to execute a job immediately.
sp_statistics	This procedure returns a list of all indexes and statistics on a specified table or indexed view.
sp_stop_job	This procedure instructs SQLServerAgent to stop the execution of a job.
sp_stored_procedures	This procedure returns a list of stored procedures in the current environment.
sp_tableoption	This procedure sets option values for user-defined tables. sp_tableoption may be used to turn on the text in row feature on tables with text, ntext, or image columns.
sp_table_privileges	This procedure returns a list of table permissions (such as INSERT, DELETE, UPDATE, SELECT, REFERENCES) for the specified table(s).
sp_table_privileges_ex	This procedure returns privileged information about the specified table from the specified linked server.

System Stored Procedures	Usage, Usage Tips, Suggestions, and References
sp_tables	This procedure returns a list of objects that can be queried in the current environment (any object that can appear in a FROM clause).
sp_tables_ex	This procedure returns table information about the tables from the specified linked server.
sp_trace_create	This procedure creates a trace definition. The new trace will be in a stopped state.
sp_trace_generateevent	This procedure creates a user-defined event.
sp_trace_setevent	This procedure adds or removes an event or event column to a trace. sp_trace_setevent may be executed only on existing traces that are stopped (*status* is 0). SQL Server 2000 will return an error if this stored procedure is executed on a trace that does not exist or whose *status* is not 0.
sp_trace_setfilter	This procedure applies a filter to a trace. sp_trace_setfilter may be executed only on existing traces that are stopped (*status* is 0). SQL Server 2000 will return an error if this stored procedure is executed on a trace that does not exist or whose *status* is not 0.
sp_trace_setstatus	This procedure modifies the current state of the specified trace.
sp_unbindefault	This procedure unbinds (removes) a default from a column or from a user-defined data type in the current database.
sp_unbindrule	This procedure unbinds a rule from a column or a user-defined data type in the current database.
sp_update_alert	This procedure updates the settings of an existing alert.
sp_update_category	This procedure changes the name of a category.
sp_updateextendedproperty	This procedure updates the value of an existing extended property.
sp_update_job	This procedure changes the attributes of a job.
sp_update_jobschedule	This procedure changes the schedule settings for the specified job.
sp_update_jobstep	This procedure changes the setting for a step in a job that is used to perform automated activities.
sp_update_log_shipping_monitor_info	This procedure updates the monitoring information about a log shipping pair.
sp_update_log_shipping_plan	This procedure updates information about an existing log shipping plan.

System Stored Procedures	Usage, Usage Tips, Suggestions, and References
sp_update_log_shipping_plan_database	This procedure updates an existing database that is part of a log shipping plan.
sp_update_notification	This procedure updates the notification method of an alert notification.
sp_update_operator	This procedure updates information about an operator (notification recipient) for use with alerts and jobs.
sp_updatestats	This procedure runs UPDATE STATISTICS against all user-defined tables in the current database.
sp_update_targetservergroup	This procedure changes the name of the specified target server group.
sp_updatetask	This procedure is provided for backward compatibility only.
sp_validname	This procedure checks for valid SQL Server identifier names. All nonbinary and nonzero data, including Unicode data that can be stored by using the nchar, nvarchar, or ntext data types, are accepted as valid characters for identifier names.
sp_validatelogins	This procedure reports information about orphaned Windows NT users and groups that no longer exist in the Windows NT environment but still have entries in the Microsoft SQL Server system tables.
sp_who	This procedure provides information about current SQL Server users and processes. The information returned can be filtered to return only those processes that are not idle.
sp_xml_preparedocument	Reads the Extensible Markup Language (XML) text provided as input, then parses the text using the MSXML parser (*Msxml2.dll*), and provides the parsed document in a state ready for consumption. This parsed document is a tree representation of the various nodes (elements, attributes, text, comments, and so on) in the XML document.
sp_xml_removedocument	This procedure removes the internal representation of the XML document specified by the document handle and invalidates the document handle.
SYSTEM_USER	This statement allows a system-supplied value for the current system username to be inserted into a table when no default value is specified.
table	The *table* is a special data type that can be used to store a result set for later processing. Its primary use is for temporary storage of a set of rows, which are to be returned as the result set of a table-valued function.

System Stored Procedures	Usage, Usage Tips, Suggestions, and References
TAN	TAN returns the tangent of the input expression.
text	Text provides information about the text data type, see ntext, text, and image.
TEXTPTR	This function returns the text-pointer value that corresponds to a text, ntext, or image column in varbinary format. The retrieved text pointer value can be used in READTEXT, WRITETEXT, and UPDATE statements.
TEXTVALID	This is a text, ntext, or image function that checks whether a given text pointer is valid.
timestamp	This is a data type that exposes automatically generated binary numbers that are guaranteed to be unique within a database. Timestamp is used typically as a mechanism for version-stamping table rows. The storage size is 8 bytes.
tinyint	See int, bigint, small int and tinyint.
Trace Flags	The trace flags are used to temporarily set specific server characteristics or to switch off a particular behavior. For example, if trace flag 3205 is set when SQL Server starts, hardware compression for tape drivers is disabled. Trace flags are often used to diagnose performance issues or to debug stored procedures or complex computer systems.
Transactions	A transaction is a single unit of work. If a transaction is successful, all the data modifications made during the transaction are committed and become a permanent part of the database. If a transaction encounters errors and must be canceled or rolled back, all the data modifications are erased.
TRIGGER_NESTLEVEL	This function returns the number of triggers executed for the UPDATE, INSERT, or DELETE statement that fired the trigger. TRIGGER_NESTLEVEL is used in triggers to determine the current level of nesting.
TRUNCATE TABLE	This directive removes all rows from a table without logging the individual row deletes.
TYPEPROPERTY	The function returns information about a data type.
UNICODE	This function returns the integer value, as defined by the Unicode standard, for the first character of the input expression.
UNION	This clauses combines the results of two or more queries into a single result set consisting of all the rows belonging to all queries in the union. For more information, see SELECT in Chapter 19.

System Stored Procedures	Usage, Usage Tips, Suggestions, and References
uniqueidentifier	The globally unique identifier (GUID).
UPDATE	Changes existing data in a table.
UPDATE STATISTICS	This statement caused an update of information about the distribution of key values for one or more statistics groups (collections) in the specified table or indexed view. To create statistics on columns, see also CREATE STATISTICS.
UPDATETEXT	This statement updates an existing text, ntext, or image field. Use UPDATETEXT to change only a portion of a text, ntext, or image column in place. Use WRITETEXT to update and replace an entire text, ntext, or image field.
UPPER	This function returns a character expression with lowercase character data converted to uppercase.
USE	This directive changes the database context to the specified database.
USER	USER allows a system-supplied value for the current user's database username to be inserted into a table when no default value is specified.
USER_ID	This function returns a user's database identification number.
USER_NAME	This function returns a user database username from a given identification number.
VAR	VAR returns the statistical variance of all values in the given expression.
varbinary	For information about the varbinary data type, see binary and varbinary.
varchar	For information about the varchar data type, see char and varchar.
VARP	This function returns the statistical variance for the population for all values in the given expression.
WAITFOR	Specifies a time, time interval, or event that triggers the execution of a statement block, stored procedure, or transaction.
WHERE	This statement specifies the condition for the rows returned by a query.

System Stored Procedures	Usage, Usage Tips, Suggestions, and References
WHILE	This is a flow control statement that sets a condition for the repeated execution of an SQL statement or statement block. The statements are executed repeatedly as long as the specified condition is true. The execution of statements in the WHILE loop can be controlled from inside the loop with the BREAK and CONTINUE keywords.
WRITETEXT	This statement permits nonlogged, interactive updating of an existing text, ntext, or image column. This statement completely overwrites any existing data in the column it affects. WRITETEXT cannot be used on text, ntext, and image columns in views.
YEAR	This function returns an integer that represents the year part of a specified date.

Index

B

D

E

J

K

L

M

N

O

P

Q

R

S

X

Y-Z

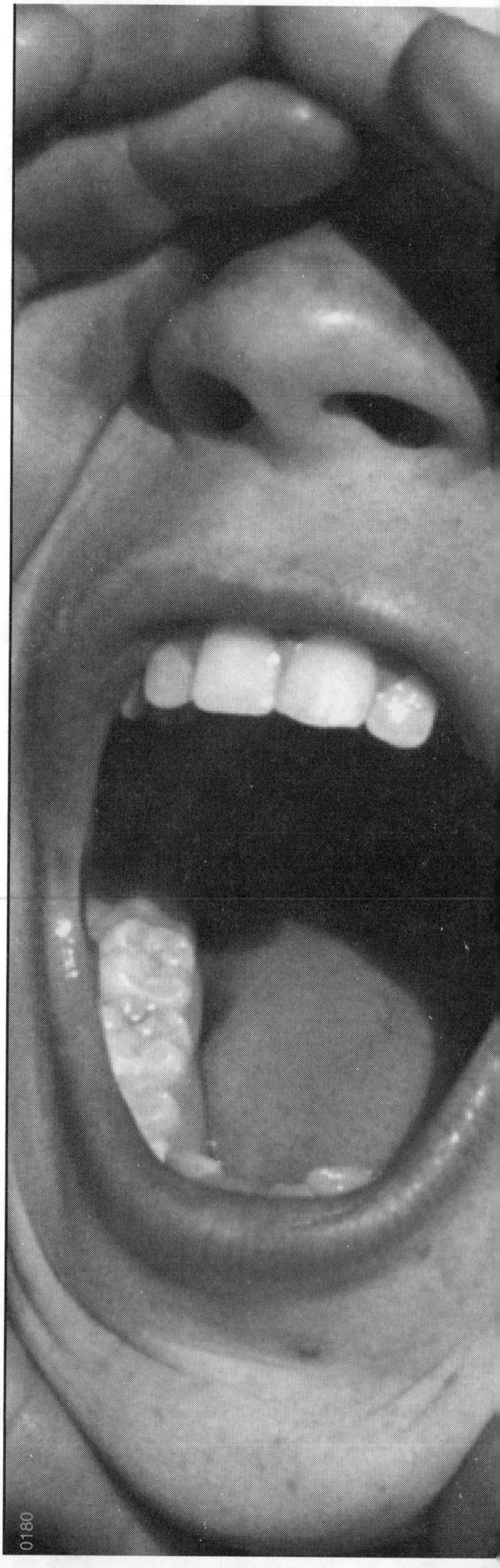